The **Rough Guide** to

Peru

written and researched by

Dilwyn Jenkins

ROUGH GUIDES

www.roughguides.com

Contents

Festivals and Celebrations colour section following p.248

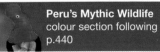

Peru's Mythic Wildlife colour section following p.440

3

◀◀ Uros Islands, Lake Titicaca ◀ Market stall, Pisac

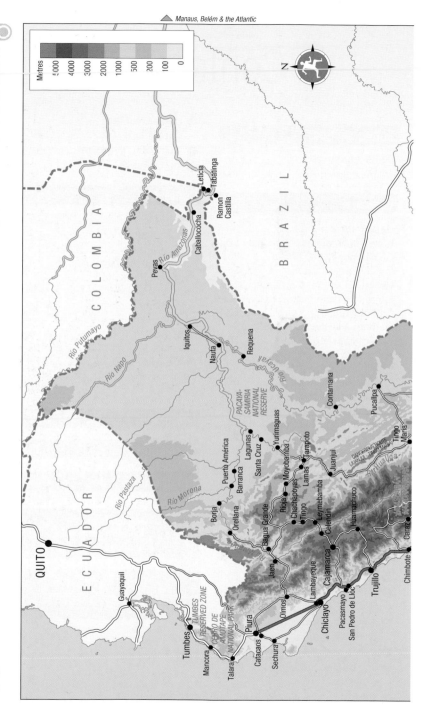

Manaus, Belém & the Atlantic

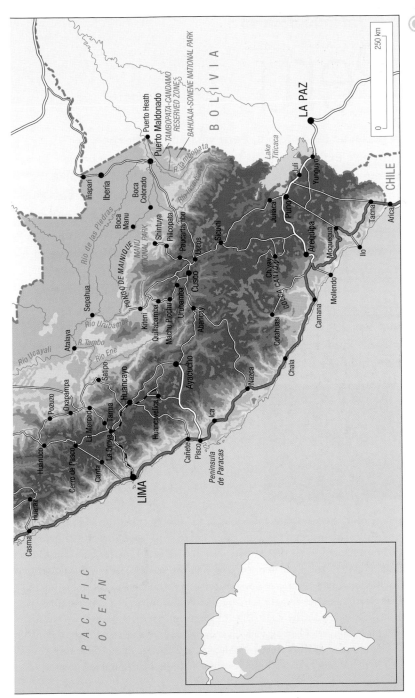

Introduction to

Peru

A fantastic land of gold, Peru was sixteenth-century Europe's major source of treasure, and once the home of the largest empire in the world – the sun-worshipping Incas. Since then, the riches of the Incas have fired the European imagination; the country was home to the world's first stone pyramids, whose genuine antiquity was only discovered in the last few years of the twentieth century. The desert coast, meanwhile, is studded with monumental adobe temples and ruins from several pre-Inca civilizations. These archeological sites generate more than enough awe and wonder to attract visitors and pilgrims from all over the globe. Equally unique and appealing, however, is the sheer beauty of the country's landscapes, the abundance of its

wildlife, and the strong character of the people – which has withstood a relatively recent, lengthy period of bloody political upheaval.

Peru is often visualized as a mountainous place, but that's not the whole story; in actual fact, it's the most varied and exciting of all the South American nations, and many visitors remain unaware of the splendour of its **desert coastline** and vast tracts of **tropical rainforest**. Dividing these contrasting environments is a range of breathtaking peaks, **the Andes**, over six thousand metres high and four hundred kilometres wide in places, rippling the entire length of the country. So distinct are these three regions that it is very difficult to generalize about the country, but one thing is for sure: Peru offers unrivalled opportunities to experience an unusually wide range of spectacular scenery, as well as a wealth of human culture. There's a rich diversity of music, dance and fiesta activity from every one of its distinctive regions, and Peruvian cuisine is some of the best in the Americas, partly because of the oceanic and tropical resources from which it draws.

Fact file

• Ancient Peru developed several very important civilizations, both coastal (Paracas, Nasca, Mochica, Sícan and Chimu) and Andean (Tiahuanaco, Chachapoyas, and, of course, the Incas). The Incas were easily and savagely defeated by the Spanish conquistadors in 1533. Peruvian independence was declared in 1821, with the remaining Spanish forces eventually defeated by the end of 1824.

• The population of Peru today is almost 28 million, with 34 percent of the population presently below the age of 16. There are two official languages – Spanish and Quechua – but there are scores of other indigenous languages spoken here, including Aymara in the Southern Andes and numerous jungle Indian tribal languages.

• The eleventh highest country in the world, Peru's mountains reach 6768m above sea level in the Cordillera Blanca range. The Andes here are the highest mountain range anywhere in the tropics.

• With 2414km of coastline, and well over half a million square kilometres of Amazon rainforest, Peru is also one of the most ecologically diverse countries in the world. Over 66 percent of Peru has forest or woodland cover, only 3 percent is arable land and around 21 percent permanent pasture. The coast is an unusually dry desert; east of the Andes the Amazon rainforest stretches thousands of miles beyond Peru, all the way to the Atlantic.

The country's natural resources were likewise motive enough for the Spanish conquistadors, whose fire-armed takeover the Incas and their native allies were unable to resist. Following the Conquest in the sixteenth century the colony developed by exploiting its Inca treasures, vast mineral deposits and the essentially slave labour which the colonists extracted from the indigenous people. After achieving independence from Spain in the early nineteenth century, Peru became a republic in traditional South American style, and although it is still very much dominated by the Spanish and *mestizo* descendants of the conquistadors' leader, Francisco Pizarro, about half the population are of pure Indian blood. In many rural parts of the country, native life has changed little in the last four centuries. However, "progress" is gradually transforming much of Peru – already most cities wear a distinctly Western aspect, and roads or tracks now connect almost

7

Peruvian food

In addition to creating great regional distinctions, Peruvian ecological diversity has helped to produce a proud **national cuisine**, and it would be a shame to spend much time at the many fast-food and Westernized places that have popped up across the country rather than in local restaurants. The national dish – **ceviche** – is made from fresh seafood marinated in lime juice and chillies, then served with sweet potato, a cob of corn and salad. Washed down on Sunday lunchtime with a cool Cusqueña beer, this is an experience not to be missed. Meanwhile, exotic local specialties like **cuy** (roast guinea pig) are also worth a try, even if the thought may at first be off-putting. **Street snacks** are quite tasty and also good value – things like grilled meats and *empanadas* are available most anywhere, alongside excellent tropical produce.

every corner of the republic with the industrial cities that dominate the few fertile valleys along the coast. Only the Amazon jungle – nearly two-thirds of Peru's landmass, but home to a mere fraction of its population – remains beyond the reach of Peru's coastal markets, and even here oil and lumber companies, cocaine producers and settlers often think of themselves as being closer to Brazil and Colombia. Over the coming decade, however, the new Transoceanic road from Brazil may begin to erode this sense of isolation, at least in the southeast corner of the jungle region.

Despite it all, mundane, unaffected pleasures remain in place. The country's prevailing attitude – despite the sometimes hectic pace that permeates the capital, Lima – is that there is always enough time for a chat, a ceviche, or

◄ Machu Picchu

▼ Alpacas, Peruvian Andes

Spiritual tourism

Spending a mosquito-ridden night with other travellers in the lively bars of downtown Iquitos, it's hard to believe that just a few miles away are hundreds of people – tourists and locals alike – communicating with plant spirits in a hallucinogen- and chant-induced trance. Increasingly, though, this jungle-locked city, reachable only by air or boat, has become a popular destination for travellers looking for sessions with traditional local shaman, who have recently begun to offer their sacred services to groups of tourists – for a fee. Many tourist lodges have their own associate shaman as an added allure to the typical ecotourist itinerary. In the sessions, shaman and participants imbibe *ayahuasca*, a bitter-tasting potion that brings on a strong hallucinatory state considered by many to be very therapeutic, physically and emotionally, though the experience is not to be entered into lightly. For more on shamans, see p.583; for details of lodges in Iquitos, see p.545.

another drink. It's a place where the resourceful and open-minded traveller can break through barriers of class, race and language far more easily than most of its inhabitants can; and also one in which the limousines and villas of the elite remain little more than a thin veneer on a nation whose roots lie firmly in its ethnic traditions and the earth itself.

INTRODUCTION | **WHERE TO GO** | WHEN TO GO

Where to go

With each region offering so many different attractions, it's hard to generalize about the places you should visit first: the specific attractions of each part of Peru are discussed in greater detail in the chapter highlights and introductions. Apart from the buzzing and at least fitfully elegant capital, **Lima**, where you are most likely to arrive, **Cusco** is perhaps the most obvious place to start. It's a beautiful and bustling colonial city, the ancient heart of the Inca Empire, surrounded by some of the most spectacular mountain landscapes and palatial ruins in Peru, and by magnificent hiking country. The world famous **Inca Trail**, which culminates

9

Transportation issues

Generally speaking, Peruvian public transport has improved significantly over the last decade. Big modern buses cruise up and down the **Pan-american Highway**, linking all the coastal cities. They also strike up into the main mountain centres, including Cusco and Lake Titicaca, and are cheap and pretty reliable. For a couple of the Andean journeys, such as from Cusco to Machu Picchu and Lake Titicaca to Cusco, the local **train service**, offering spectacular views from their high-altitude routes, can be a more enjoyable way to travel. **Air travel** around the country is relatively well developed and cheap as a result of distances in Peru being so vast, especially in jungle areas. In the jungle, **riverboats** can offer the most civilized and pleasant form of travel. For more on getting around, see Basics, p.42.

at the high, fog-shrouded Inca citadel of **Machu Picchu**, is just one of several equally scenic and challenging treks in this region of Peru alone.

Along the coast, too, there are fascinating archaeological sites – the bizarre **Nasca Lines** south of Lima, the great adobe city of **Chan Chan** and the **Valley of the Pyramids** in the north – and a rich crop of sea life, most accessible around the **Paracas National Park**. Almost all of the coastal towns come replete with superb beaches, plentiful nightlife and great food. If all that sounds too exhausting, one can always duck away to spend a day lazily sipping wine at the many **Ica Valley bodegas**.

▲ Main Plaza, Pisco

For really high mountains and long-distance treks there are the stunning glacial lakes, snowy peaks and little-known ruins of the sierra north of Lima, all located around **Huaraz** and **Cajamarca**. If it's wildlife you're interested in, there's plenty to see almost everywhere. But **the jungle** provides startling opportunities for close and exotic encounters. From the comfort of tourist lodges in **Iquitos** to exciting river excursions around **Puerto Maldonado**, the fauna and flora of the world's largest tropical forest can be experienced first-hand perhaps more easily

than in any other Amazon-rim country. Not too far from Iquitos there's the **Pacaya Samiria National Reserve**, a remote and stunningly beautiful region which is one of the least-visited parts of the Peruvian rainforest; in the south there's the newly created **Tambopata-Candamo Reserved Zone** which incorporates around 600,000 hectares of the upper Tambopata as well as the Candamo River and tributaries, and comprises some of the most exciting jungle and richest flora and fauna in the world.

When to go

Picking the **best time to visit** Peru's various regions is complicated by the country's physical characteristics. Summer along the **desert coast** more or less fits the expected image of the southern hemisphere – extremely hot and sunny between December and March (especially in the north), cooler and with a frequent hazy mist between April and November – although only in the polluted environs of **Lima** does the coastal winter ever get cold enough to necessitate a sweater. Swimming is possible all year round, though the water itself (thanks to the Humboldt Current) is cool-to-cold at the best of times. To swim or surf for any length of time you'd need to follow local custom and wear a wet suit. Apart from the occasional shower over Lima it hardly ever rains in the desert. The freak exception, every ten years or so, is when the shift in ocean currents of El Niño causes torrential downpours, devastating crops, roads and communities all down the coast. The last really heavy one was in 1983, though there have been several El Niños since then.

◀ Uros Islands

In **the Andes**, the seasons are more clearly marked, with heavy rains from December to March and a warm, relatively dry period from June to September. Inevitably, though, there are always some sunny weeks in the rainy season and wet ones in the dry. A similar pattern dominates **the jungle**, though rainfall here is heavier and more frequent, and it's hot and humid all year round. Ideally, then, the coast should be visited around January while it's hot, and the mountains and jungle are at their best after the rains, from May until September. Since this is unlikely to be possible on a single trip there's little point in worrying about it – the country's attractions are invariably enough to override the need for guarantees of good weather.

Average daily maximum and minimum temperatures, and annual rainfall

	Oct–April	May–Sept	Temp. range (approx) °C/°F	Annual rainfall mm/in
Coast				
	Sunny season	Some coastal cloud	13–30/ 55–86	0.55/ 0.02
Andes				
	Rainy season	Dry season	0–18/ 32–64	400–1000/ 16–39
Jungle				
	Rainy season	Dry season	20–35/ 68–95	2000–3900/ 79–154

29

things not to miss

It's not possible to see everything that Peru has to offer in one trip – and we don't suggest you try. What follows is a selective and subjective taste of the country's highlights: colourful neighbourhoods, awe-inspiring ruins, spectacular hikes and interesting wildlife. They're arranged in five colour-coded categories, so you can browse through to find the very best things to see, do, buy and experience. All highlights have a page reference to take you straight into the Guide, where you can find out more.

01 Llanganuco Lakes Page **376** • The deep blue colour of these lakes in the Cordillera Blanca changes with the weather.

02 **Chavín de Huantar** Page **392** • Dating back over 2500 years, this large temple has many striking stone carvings and gargoyles, both externally and within its subterranean chambers.

03 **Arequipa** Page **181** • This white stone city, beautiful and intriguing in its own right, is watched over by the awesome, ice-capped volcano of El Misti.

04 **Ceviche** Page **53** • Peru's national dish is a refreshing treat – fresh fish soaked briefly in lime juice and chillies.

05 **Trujillo** Page **397** • Though it doesn't receive the hype of Lima or Cusco, Peru's third city charms with its colonial architecture and surprisingly cosmopolitan atmosphere.

06 **Colca Canyon** Page **205** • Twice the size of the Grand Canyon, the enormous Colca, one of the deepest canyons in the world, is also one of Peru's biggest destinations.

08 Ballestas Islands Page **141** • Often called the Peruvian Galapagos, these islands located off the coast of Pisco, are teeming with bird and marine life.

07 Andean agricultural terraces Page **212** • These mountainside terraces in the magnificent Cotahuasi and Colca canyons give evidence of the impressive organization of pre-Conquest native societies.

09 Huacachina Page **153** • This sacred healing lagoon, ringed by palm trees and hidden among massive sand dunes, provides a focus for sandboarders and dune buggy riders from all over the world.

10 **Paracas National Reserve** Page **142** • Just a few hours out of Lima, Paracas is a coastal wildlife haven, boasting some fantastic beaches alongside archaeological sites and a museum.

11 **Cordillera Blanca** Page **372** • The glacial scenery of the Cordillera Blanca mountain range is among the finest and most accessible on the planet.

13 Pisac Market Page 277 • Andean markets serve as true community hubs – not to mention excellent places to sample local goods and produce – and Pisac's thriving morning market is one of the best.

12 Huaca Pucllana Page 95 • This ancient adobe pyramid, complete with recreated scenes, rises out of the desert soil in what is today a relatively affluent Lima suburb.

14 Puerto Belén Page 537 • A frenetic, floating jungle port that has been called the Venice of the Peruvian jungle.

15 Shipibo tribal arts and crafts Page **503** • Dressed in their traditional skirts and colourful seed jewellery, the women of this tribe travel all over Peru to sell their unusual and beautiful craft goods.

16 Máncora Page **471** • Peru's most popular surfer hang-out features gorgeous beaches and thriving nightlife.

17 Textiles Page **261** • Peru has been producing fine cotton textiles for over three thousand years. According to archaeologists, the Paracas culture used every known form of weaving technique, apart from those now utilised by machines.

18 Hiking the Inca Trail Page **288** • Culminating at Machu Picchu, this is one of the most popular and eye-opening trails in the world.

20 Traditional healing Page **583** • Alternative medicine, using herbs sold in markets and practised by shamans and other healers, has a long and respected history in Peru.

19 Kuelap Page **436** • The ruined citadel of Kuelap is one of the most fascinating archaeological sites in the Andes.

21 **Sacsayhuaman** Page **268** • The zigzag megalithic defensive walls of this Inca temple-fortess are home to the Inti Raymi annual sun festival.

22 **Rainforest canopy walkway** Page **546** • Peru's jungle is one of the richest in the world and can be seen at its best from the Amazon's longest tree-top canopy walkway, reaching 35m above the ground near to the Río Napo, Iquitos.

23 **Peruvian wildlife** Page **598** • Whether spotting a three-toed sloth in the Amazon tree-tops or crossing paths with a vicuña while on a hike in the Andes, Peru's sheer variety of flora and fauna never fails to amaze.

25 **Ayacucho** Page **332** • Bustling streets, an unusual quantity of churches, highly passionate religious processions and unique artesania make this Andean city a standout.

24 **Nasca Lines** Page **154** • Take a helicopter tour to get the full impact of these intricate symbols, etched into the deserts of southern Peru.

26 **Machu Picchu** Page **292** • With mysterious temples and palaces nestling among hundreds of terraces, this fabulous Inca citadel is awe-inspiring.

27 **The Archbishop's Palace** Page **89** • Restored in 1924, the palace is typical of colonial Lima, particularly the elaborate woodwork of the upper storey balconies.

28 Valley of the Pyramids
Page **453** • Over twenty adobe pyramids built by a pre-Inca civilization surround a sacred mountain at Túcume in the northern deserts.

29 Uros Islands
Page **224** • One of Lake Titicaca's many treasures, these man-and-woman-made floating villages have existed in the lake since Inca times.

Basics

Basics

Getting there

Unless you're travelling overland through South America – or are one of the hardy adventurers taking a freighter – you'll need to fly to reach Peru. Although prices vary depending on the time of year, how far in advance you buy and the type of ticket, the main airlines seem to hold fares fairly steady and tickets can easily be bought online. High season is usually mid-December to mid-January and July to mid-August; low season is mid-January to June and mid-August to mid-December.

You can sometimes cut costs by going through a **specialist flight or travel agent**, who, in addition to dealing with discounted flights, occasionally also offer special student and youth fares and a range of other travel-related services such as insurance, car rental, tours and the like.

Adventure tours or customised packages are often good value, though they can be limiting – you'll see only what's in the itinerary – but they do provide a considerable degree of comfort and peace of mind. Always check in advance about what's included – many only provide guides, planning and in-country transport costs, others may have their own vehicles and camping equipment. Other **specialist companies** organize **treks** and **overland travel**, often based around some special interest, such as the rainforest, native culture or Inca sites, usually a great opportun-ity to get to know the country in some depth. Some of the best of these operators are listed in both Basics and the relevant chapters.

Booking flights online

Websites of many airlines encourage booking online, and good deals can sometimes also be found through discount auction sites.

Online booking agents and general travel sites

ⓦ**www.ebookers.com** Good selection of main carriers' flights to Peru.

ⓦ**www.etn.nl/discount.htm** A hub of consolidator and discount agent web links with some information relevant to Peru flights, maintained by the non-profit European Travel Network.

ⓦ**www.expedia.co.uk** (in UK), ⓦ**www .expedia.com** (in US),

ⓦ**www.expedia.ca** (in Canada)

ⓦ**www.flyaow.com** Online air travel info and reservations site which includes Peru information.

ⓦ**www.hotwire.com** Bookings from the US only with links to other sites containing flight information for Peru from US and UK.

ⓦ**www.lastminute.com** (in UK)

ⓦ**www.opodo.co.uk** (in UK)

ⓦ**www.orbitz.com** (in US)

ⓦ**www.travelocity.co.uk** (in UK), ⓦ**www .travelocity.com** (in US), ⓦ**www.travelocity .ca** (in Canada) ⓦ**www.zuji.com.au** (in Australia), ⓦ**www.zuji.co.nz** (in New Zealand)

Flights from the US and Canada

With the exception of Continental's frequent non-stop service **from Newark** to Lima ($900–1500), nearly all flights to Peru from the US go **via Miami, Houston or Atlanta**. Delta, Continental and American airlines are the main carriers serving Peru from the US. Most of the airlines can book connecting flights to Miami from a range of cities throughout the US, and fares **from New York (via Miami)** cost no more than fares from Miami. A number of airlines fly Miami to Lima, including American, Taca, Lan Peru and Avianca offering similar deals with fares in the range of $480–900.

Flights from **Toronto straight to Lima** start at about Can$900 with Lan Peru; it costs around the same price when flying **from Montreal via Toronto**.

There are a huge variety of **tours and packages** on offer from the US to Peru,

Six steps to a better kind of travel

At Rough Guides we are passionately committed to travel. We feel strongly that only through travelling do we truly come to understand the world we live in and the people we share it with – plus tourism has brought a great deal of benefit to developing economies around the world over the last few decades. But the extraordinary growth in tourism has also damaged some places irreparably, and of course climate change is exacerbated by most forms of transport, especially flying. This means that now more than ever it's important to travel thoughtfully and responsibly, with respect for the cultures you're visiting – not only to derive the most benefit from your trip but also in order to preserve the best bits of the planet for everyone to enjoy. At Rough Guides we feel there are six main areas in which you can make a difference:

• Consider what you're contributing to the local economy, and indeed how much the services you use do the same, whether it's through employing local workers and guides or sourcing locally grown produce and local services.

• Consider the environment on holiday as well as at home. Water is scarce in many developing destinations, and the biodiversity of local flora and fauna can be adversely affected by tourism. Patronise businesses that take account of this rather than those that trash the local environment for short-term gain.

• Give thought to how often you fly and what you can do to redress any harm that your trips create. Reduce the amount you travel by air; avoid short hops by air and more harmful night flights.

• Consider alternatives to flying, travelling instead by bus, train, boat and even by bike or on foot where possible. Take time to enjoy the journey itself as well as your final destination.

• Think about making all the trips you take "climate neutral" via a reputable carbon offset scheme. All Rough Guide flights are offset, and every year we donate money to a variety of charities devoted to combating the effects of climate change.

• Travel with a purpose, not just to tick off experiences. Consider spending longer in a place, and really getting to know it and its people – you'll find it much more rewarding than dashing from place to place.

---

starting from around $1,500 for a two- to three-day package and ranging up to $4000–5000. You'll also find a number of packages that include Peru on their itineraries as part of a longer South American tour.

Flights from the UK

As there are no **direct flights** from the UK to Peru, getting there always involves a stopover and, more often than not, a change of planes in either Europe or America. From Heathrow you can expect the journey to take anywhere between 16 and 22 hours, depending on the routing and stopovers. The permutations are endless, but the most common routes are **via Amsterdam** on KLM, **via Madrid** on Iberia, **via Frankfurt** on Lufthansa or **via New York, Miami and Atlanta** on US airlines.

Fares vary almost as much as routings, and you'd be well advised to go to a specialist to check out what's on offer – there's also a wide range of **limitations** on the tickets (fixed-date returns within three months, yearly returns, etc), and options such as "open-jaw" flights (flying into Lima and home from Rio, for example). Having established the going rate, you can always check these prices against those on offer at discount flight outlets and other travel agents listed in the press. Flights these days start at around £650 with KLM **via Amsterdam**. Continental Airlines are usually pretty competitive too, going via **New York and Houston**. The price rapidly rises to £800 or more if you don't buy well in advance.

Some of the best **specialist operators**, like Journey Latin America, are listed here, but it's also worth checking through the classified ads in magazines and newspapers, where the cheapest of flights sometimes crop up. The best deals can usually be found advertised in the London listings magazines like *Time Out* or in any of the national papers, particularly the Sunday editions. It's best to avoid buying international air tickets in Peru, where prices are inflated by a high tax (and are not cheap to begin with). If you're uncertain of your return date, it will probably still work out cheaper to pay the extra for an open-ended return than to buy a single back from Peru.

Flights from Australia and New Zealand

Scheduled flights to Peru from this part of the world to Lima are rather limited and tend to involve changing planes, usually in the US. High season is December to February; low season is the rest of the year, but prices also vary depending on how long you stay (between a minimum of 21 days and a maximum of a year).

Aerolineas Argentinas fly **from Sydney via Auckland and Buenos Aires**, with connecting flights to Lima. Fares start at A$2000/NZ$1900 rising to around A$2800/NZ$2800 in high season. Air New Zealand fly to LA (from A$1144/NZ$1337, depending on length of stay and date of departure) from Australia and New Zealand, but have no connections to Peru. Qantas have flights from Auckland to LA via Sydney or Melbourne without connecting flights to Lima; prices start at about NZ$1200. Flights from Sydney via Melbourne or Auckland do not offer connecting flights to Peru either, and prices start at around A$1730. Lan Airlines with Delta and Air Canada also fly from Sydney to Lima via the US; their cheapest tickets are 45-day returns at A$2500/NZ$2700. Continental and American Airlines fly **regularly from Melbourne** via Sydney, Auckland and the US (stopovers available) with fares that start at A$2800/NZ$3500 and range up to A$4,000/NZ$5000 for a six-month return in high season, with connecting flights to Lima. **Round-the-world** (RTW) tickets including Peru are usually a good investment.

Airline companies are in a state of flux in Peru, although they remain dominated by Lan Peru. As new ones arrive and competition for passengers increases, air passes are likely to become available again, and it's worth checking with your travel agent or with the major airlines on arrival in Peru.

Airlines

Aerolineas Argentinas US ☎ 1-800/333-0276, Canada ☎ 1-800/688-0008, UK ☎ 0800/096 9747, New Zealand ☎ 09/379 3675, Australia ☎ 02/9234 9000, ⊛ www.aerolineas.com
Air Canada ☎ 1-888/247-2262, UK ☎ 0871/220 1111, Republic of Ireland ☎ 01/679 3958, Australia ☎ 1300/655 767, New Zealand ☎ 0508/747 767, ⊛ www.aircanada.com.
Air New Zealand ☎ 0800/737000, Australia ☎ 0800/132 476, UK ☎ 0800/028 4149, US ☎ 1800-262/1234, Canada ☎ 1800-663/5494, ⊛ www.airnz.co.nz.
American Airlines ☎ 1-800/433-7300, UK ☎ 0845/7789 789, Republic of Ireland ☎ 01/602 0550, Australia ☎ 1800/673 486, New Zealand ☎ 0800/445 442, ⊛ www.aa.com.
Continental Airlines US and Canada ☎ 1-800/523-3273, UK ☎ 0845/607 6760, Republic of Ireland ☎ 1890/925 252, Australia ☎ 02/9244 2242, New Zealand ☎ 09/308 3350, International ☎ 1800/231 0856, ⊛ www.continental.com.
Delta US and Canada ☎ 1-800/221-1212, UK ☎ 0845/600 0950, Republic of Ireland ☎ 1850/882 031 or 01/407 3165, Australia ☎ 1300/302 849, New Zealand ☎ 09/977 2232, ⊛ www.delta.com.
Iberia US ☎ 1-800/772-4642, UK ☎ 0870/609 0500, Republic of Ireland ☎ 0818/462 000, South Africa ☎ 011/884 5909, ⊛ www.iberia.com.
KLM (Royal Dutch Airlines) US and Canada ☎ 1-800/225-2525, UK ☎ 0870/507 4074, Republic of Ireland ☎ 1850/747 400, Australia ☎ 1300/392 192, New Zealand ☎ 09/921 6040, South Africa ☎ 11/961 6727, ⊛ www.klm.com.
LanChile US and Canada ☎ 1-866/435-9526, UK ☎ 0800/977 6100, Australia ☎ 1300/361 400 or 02/9244 2333, New Zealand ☎ 09/977 2233, South Africa ☎ 11/781 2111, ⊛ www.lan.com.

LanPeru US and Canada ☎1-866/435-9526, UK ☎0800/977 6100, Australia ☎1300/361 400 or 02/9244 2333, New Zealand ☎09/977 2233, South Africa ☎11/781 2111, ⊛www.lan.com.

Lufthansa US ☎1-800/3995-838, Canada ☎1-800/563-5954, UK ☎0870/837 7747, Republic of Ireland ☎01/844 5544, Australia ☎1300/655 727, New Zealand ☎0800-945 220, South Africa ☎0861/842 538, ⊛www.lufthansa .com.

Qantas Airways US and Canada ☎1-800/227-4500, UK ☎0845/774 7767, Republic of Ireland ☎01/407 3278, Australia ☎13 13 13, New Zealand ☎0800/808 767 or 09/357 8900, SA ☎11/441 8550, ⊛www.qantas.com

Taca US ☎1-800/400-TACA, Canada ☎1-800/722-TACA, UK ☎0870/2410 340, Australia ☎02/8248 0020, ⊛www.taca.com

United Airlines US ☎1-800/UNITED-1, UK ☎0845/844 4777, Australia ☎13 17 77, ⊛www .united.com

Agents and operators

Abercrombie & Kent ☎1-800/554-7016 or for direct ☎ 630-954-2944, ⊛www.abercrombiekent .com.

Adventure Associates Australia ☎02/8916 3000, ⊛www.adventureassociates.com.au. Tours and cruises to Central and South America, including Peru and the Amazon.

Adventure Center ☎1-800/228-8747 (USA toll free) or 510/654-1879, ⊛www.adventurecenter .com. Hiking and "soft adventure" specialists with some tours in Peru.

Adventure Travel Company New Zealand ☎09/355 9135, ⊛www.adventuretravel.co.nz. New Zealand agent for Peregrine Adventures (see p.31).

Adventure World Australia ☎ 02/8913 0755, ⊛www.adventureworld.com.au, New Zealand ☎09/524 5118, ⊛www.adventureworld.co.nz. Agents for a vast array of international adventure travel companies that operate trips to every continent, with several options for Peru.

Andina Tours and Travel 9805 NE 116th St, Suite 7225, Kirkland, WA 98043-4248 ☎(51)(84)251892, ⊛www.andinatravel.com. Customized tours to Peru, including airfare, transfers, accommodation, meals and excursions.

Austral Tours Level 1, 107 Puckle St, Moonee Ponds 3039 VIC, Australia ☎03 9370 6621, ⊛www.australtours.com. A Central and South American specialist, covering mainly the region from Ecuador to Easter Island and Tierra del Fuego, with special tours to Machu Picchu and the Amazon.

Australian Andean Adventures Australia ☎02/9299 9973, ⊛www.andeanadventures.com .au. Trekking specialist for Argentina, Peru, Bolivia and Chile.

Backroads ☎1-800/GO-ACTIVE or 510/527-1555, ⊛www.backroads.com. Cycling, hiking and multi-sport tour offerings, including Peru.

Classic Journeys ☎1-800/200-3887 or 858/454-5004, ⊛www.classicjourneys.com. Offer tours to Machu Picchu from Cusco by train.

Dragoman UK ☎01728 861133, ⊛www .dragoman.com. Extended overland journeys in expedition vehicles through the Americas, covering Machu Picchu, Titicaca, Arequipa, Colca, Nasca and other sites in Peru; shorter camping and hotel-based safaris, too.

ebookers UK ☎0800/082 3000, Republic of Ireland ☎01/488 3507, ⊛www.ebookers.com. ⊛www.ebookers.ie. Low fares on an extensive selection of scheduled flights and package deals.

Exodus UK ☎0870 240 5550, International ☎020 8675 5550, ⊛www.exodus.co.uk. Adventure-tour operators taking small groups on tours to South America, usually incorporating Peru's main destinations. They also have specialist programmes including walking, biking, overland, adventure and cultural trips.

Explore Worldwide UK ☎02086 755550, ⊛www.explore.co.uk. Big range of small-group tours, treks, expeditions and safaris on all continents, including the Cusco and Arequipa areas of Peru.

eXito 108 Rutgers St, Fort Collins, CO 80525, ☎1-800/655-4053, ✉info@exitotravel.com, ⊛www.exitotravel.com. Latin American specialists in cut-rate fares, student tickets, year-long tickets, land packages and tours, with savings of up to forty percent off regular fares. Good for travel advice.

Journey Latin America UK ☎020/8747 3108 or 8747 8315, ⊛www.journeylatinamerica. co.uk. Specialists in flights, packages and tailor-made trips to Latin America. Experienced tour operator using well-informed Spanish-speaking tour guides to accompany small groups, mostly on local transport. Operates a number of tours, some of which include Peru as part of a larger itinerary, and most of which have an option for doing the Inca Trail.

Mountain Travel Sobek 1266 66th Street, Suite 4, Emeryville, CA 94608 ☎1-888/MTSOBEK (687-6235) or 1-510/594-6000, ⊛www.mtsobek.com. Hiking, river rafting and trekking in Peru.

Nature Expeditions International ☎1-800/869-0639 or 954/693-8852, ⊛www.naturexp.com. Offers upscale wildlife tours and soft adventure in 25 countries around the world.

North South Travel UK ☎01245/608 291, 🌐www.northsouthtravel.co.uk. Friendly, competitive travel agency, offering discounted fares worldwide. Profits are used to support projects in the developing world, especially the promotion of sustainable tourism.

On the Go Tours UK ☎020/7371 1113, 🌐www. onthegotours.com. Runs group and tailor-made tours to Egypt, India, Sri Lanka, Africa, Jordan, Russia, China, South America and Turkey.

Overseas Adventure Travel ☎1-800/493-6824 (sales) or 1-800/221-0814 (customer service), 🌐www.oattravel.com. Offers a wide variety of adventure trips around the planet, including some South American combinations, like Machu Picchu and the Galapagos.

Peregrine Adventures Australia ☎03 8601 4444, New Zealand see Adventure Travel Company, 🌐www.peregrine.net.au. Adventure tours in South America, which aim to explore the Inca heartlands as well as Amazon rainforest.

STA Travel US ☎1-800/781-4040, UK ☎0871/2300 040, Australia ☎134 STA, New Zealand ☎0800/474 400, SA ☎0861/781 781, 🌐www.statravel.com. Worldwide specialists in independent travel; also student IDs, travel insurance, car rental, rail passes and more. Good discounts for students and under-26s.

The Surf Travel Co Australia ☎ 02/9222 9970, New Zealand ☎ 09/473 8388, 🌐www.surftravel. com.au. Packages and advice for catching the waves (or snow) in the Pacific region, including main sites on the Peruvian coastline such as Chicama and Máncora.

Trailfinders UK ☎0845/058 5858, Republic of Ireland ☎01/677 7888, Australia ☎1300/780 212, 🌐www.trailfinders.com. One of the best-informed and most efficient agents for independent travellers.

South America Travel Centre Australia ☎03/9642 5353, 🌐www.satc.com.au. Big selection of tours and city accommodation packages covering most regions of Peru. Short and long tours available.

Wilderness Travel 1102 Ninth St, Berkeley, CA 94710, ☎ 1-800/368-2794 or 510/558-2488, 🌐www.wildernesstravel.com. A variety of programmes in Peru, from nine-day hotel-based holidays to 24-day camping and trekking trips, some of which include Bolivia in the itinerary, plus Inca Trail tours culminating in the Inti Raymi festival in Cusco during the summer solstice in June.

World Expeditions UK ☎020/8545 9030, 🌐www.worldexpeditions.co.uk. Australian-owned adventure company offering more than just Antipodean expeditions, with several programmes focused on the Peruvian jungle.

Travelling overland from neighbouring countries

Although it's virtually impossible to travel overland to Peru **from North America** because of the **Darien Gap** – a section of Panamanian jungle that's uncrossed by road or rail – a few hardy souls manage to jeep, hike, sail or even cycle the swampy route. Bear in mind, though, that a few would-be explorers have met bad ends at the hands of drug smugglers in this area, and the Peruvian Consulate strongly advises against attempting the journey. There are ways, however, to avoid the dangerous Darien Gap, the shortest route being via **San Andres Island** or **Panama City** to mainland Colombia. San Andres is a useful anomaly on international air routes: it's a bit of Colombian territory in the Caribbean just east of Nicaragua, and is served by almost every national airline hereabouts at least daily. Although San Andres is quite remote from Colombian cities – 1600km from Cali, for example – the fact that the onward flight to Peru is a domestic one keeps something of a ceiling on fares. Alternatively, you can take a **ferry** or short flight directly from Panama to **Barranquilla** or Cartagena in Colombia. Allow a minimum of a week to travel the final 1800km overland from the Colombian Caribbean coast to the Peruvian frontier.

Much simpler are the obvious overland routes from other South American countries. **From Brazil**, you can take the boat ride up the Amazon, from Manaus to Iquitos – a five- to eight-day ride depending on the type of boat. Usually a memorable experience, you'll need a hammock (unless you book one of the few cabins) and plenty of reading material. From Brazil's western Amazon department of Río Acre, there is a relatively simple entry by bus and *colectivo* car along jungle roads to Puerto Maldonado in southeast Peru; from here you can go by road or fly to Cusco and the rest of Peru.

Arriving in southern Peru **from Bolivia** requires catching a bus, either direct or in stages, from La Paz across the altiplano to Copacabana on Lake Titicaca and on to Puno, or even straight to Cusco. **From Chile** it's a similarly easy bus ride, across the southern border from Arica to Tacna, which has good connections with Lima and Arequipa. **From Ecuador**, there are two routes, the most popular being a scenic coastal trip, starting by road from Huaquillas, crossing the border at Aguas Verdes and then taking a short bus or taxi ride on to Tumbes, from where there are daily buses and flights to Chiclayo, Trujillo and Lima. An alternative crossing, also by a rather scenic road, comes into Peru from Macará in Ecuador over the frontier to La Tina, from where there are daily buses to Peru's coast. An almost unused but eminently practical route also enters Peru **from Colombia** by river or air at Leticia, at the three-way frontier where Peru, Brazil and Colombia touch. From Leticia there are speedboats up the Río Amazonas more or less daily to Iquitos.

Entry requirements

Currently, EU, US, Canadian, Australian and New Zealand citizens can all stay in Peru as tourists for up to ninety days without a visa. However, the situation does change periodically, so always check with your local Peruvian embassy some weeks before departure. All nationalities need a tourist or embarkation card *(tarjeta de embarque)* to enter Peru, issued at the frontiers or on the plane before landing in Lima. Tourist cards are usually valid for between sixty or ninety days. Unless you specifically ask for ninety days when being issued a Tourist Card on arrival, you may only receive sixty.

For your own safety and freedom of movement a copy of the tourist card should be kept on you, with your passport, at all times – particularly when travelling away from the main towns.

Should you want to **extend your visa** (between thirty and sixty additional days), there are two basic options: either cross one of the borders and get a new tourist card when you come back in; or go through the bureaucratic rigmarole at a Migraciones office involving form filling, taking a photocopy of your passport and visa (or tourist card) and a visit to the Banco de la Nación to pay the required fee ($20) to the State, where you get issued an official receipt *(recibo de pago)*. This process is easiest in Lima (see p.119 for address), where it can be all done in the same building, but even there it can take a couple of hours or more, starting off at reception (for the forms), then to windows 4 to 6 in the Prórroga de Permanencia department (two floors above ground level). A further $4.5 is needed for legalising the Migraciones form

(usually issued at reception), and you may also be asked to provide evidence of a valid exit ticket from Peru. Migraciones is also the place to sort out new visas if you've **lost your passport** (having visited your embassy first) and to get passports re-stamped.

Student visas (which last twelve months) are best organized as far in advance as possible through your country's embassy in Lima, your nearest Peruvian embassy and the relevant educational institution. **Business visas** only become necessary if you are to be paid by a Peruvian organization, in which case ask your Peruvian employers to get this for you, or, if working on independent business, contact the appropriate embassy or consular services in Lima (see p.117) or your home country (see p.33). Alternatively, you can contact the related Chamber of Trade for advice (ask the embassies for details on this). Having a business visa means that you are eligible for taxation under Peruvian law and may not be allowed to leave the country until this has been accounted for, which entails obtaining a letter from SUNAT (the Peruvian State Taxation Agency) stating that all outstanding taxes have been settled. Journalist visas are obtained from the relevant Peruvian Embassy, usually for up to six months.

Peruvian embassies and consulates

An up-to-date and comprehensive list of Peruvian diplomatic missions can be accessed via ⓦ www.rree.gob.pe.

Australia
Peruvian Embassy, Canberra ☎ 02/6286 9507.
Consulate, 157 Main St, Croydon, Melbourne ☎ 03/97254655.
Consulate, Level Three, 30 Clarence St, Sydney ☎ 02/9262 6464.

Canada
Peruvian Embassy, Ottawa ☎ 613/238 1777.

New Zealand
Peruvian Embassy, Level Eight, Cigna House, 40 Mercer St, Wellington ☎ 04/499 8087.

South Africa
Peruvian Consulate, Brooklyn Gardens Building Block A, 1st Floor 235 Veale Street, Corner Middel Street, Nieuw Muckleneuk, 0181 Pretoria. ☎ 0027/1234-68744.

United Kingdom
Peruvian Embassy, 52 Sloane St, London SW1X 9SP ☎ 020/78389223.

US
Peruvian Embassy, 1625 Massachusetts Ave, NW Suite 605, Washington DC 20036 ☎ 202/ 4621081.

Costs, money and banks

Money in Peru is the nuevo sol, still simply called a "sol" on the streets, and whose symbol is S/. The sol has remained relatively steady against the US dollar for the first eight years of the twenty-first century.

Despite being closely tied to the US dollar, the value of the nuevo sol still varies slightly from day to day, so we have quoted prices throughout this book in US dollars, against which costs have so far remained relatively stable. At time of writing, the exchange rate for the nuevo sol was roughly S/3.15=$1, S/2.47=Can$1, S/4.6=£1, S/2.04=A$1, S/1.69=NZ$1 and S/0.29=ZAR1.

Costs

Peru is certainly a much cheaper place to visit than Europe or the US, but how much so will depend on where you are and when. As a general rule low-budget travellers should – with care – be able to get by on around $15–30 per day, including transport, board and lodging. If you intend on staying in mid-range hotels, eating in reasonable restaurants and taking the odd taxi, $50–70 a day should be adequate, while $100–150

a day will allow you to stay in comfort and sample some of Peru's best cuisine.

In most places in Peru, a good **meal** can still be found for under $10, **transport** is very reasonable, a comfortable double **room** costs $15–40 a night and **camping** is usually free or under $5 per person. Expect to pay a little more than usual in the larger towns and cities, and also in the jungle, as many supplies have to be imported by truck. In the villages and rural towns, on the other hand, some basic commodities are cheaper in the countryside and it's always possible to buy food pretty cheaply from local villages or markets.

In the more popular parts of Peru, costs vary considerably with the seasons. Cusco, for instance, has its best weather from June to August, when many of its hotel prices go up by around 25–50 percent. The same thing happens at fiesta times – although on such

Bargaining

You are generally expected to **bargain** in markets and with taxi drivers (before getting in). Nevertheless, it's worth bearing in mind that travellers from Europe, North America and Australasia are generally much wealthier than Peruvians, so for every penny or cent you knock them down they stand to lose plenty of nuevo soles. It's also sometimes possible to haggle over the price of hotel rooms, especially if you're travelling in a group. Food and shop prices, however, tend to be fixed.

occasions you're unlikely to resent it too much. As always, if you're travelling alone you'll end up spending considerably more than you would in a group of two or more people. It's also worth taking along an international student card, if you have one, for the occasional reduction (up to fifty percent at some museums and sites). Cards generally cost between $20 and 25; but, once obtained, youth/student ID cards soon pay for themselves in savings. Full-time students are eligible for the International Student ID Card (ISIC) or ITIC, Youth, VIP, YHA or Nomads card (see Ⓦwww.statravel.co.uk in the UK), most of which entitle the bearer to special air, rail and bus fares and discounts at museums, theatres and other attractions. For US citizens there's also a health benefit, providing emergency medical and hospital coverage, plus a 24-hour hotline to call in the event of a medical, legal or financial emergency.

You only have to be 26 or younger to qualify for the **International Youth Travel Card**, which carries the same benefits. Teachers qualify for the **International Teacher Card**, offering similar discounts. All these cards are available in the US from STA (see p.31 for contact info) and, in Canada, Hostelling International; in Australia, New Zealand and in the UK from STA.

Several other travel organizations and accommodation groups also sell their own cards, good for various discounts. A university photo ID may open some doors, but is not as easily recognizable as the ISIC card. However, the latter are often not accepted as valid proof of age, for example, in bars or clubs.

Travellers' cheques, cash and credit cards

For safety's sake the bulk of your money should be carried as **travellers' cheques**, bank or credit cards. Whether travellers'

cheques or cards, it's preferable to carry two different types, as rumoured forgeries (particularly of travellers' cheques) make individual brands difficult to exchange from time to time. American Express is a good bet since it has its own offices in Lima and Cusco, is widely recognized by casas de cambio (see p.35), hotels and travel agents, and is exchangeable in one of Peru's most efficient banks, the Banco de Credito. American Express also offers an efficient poste restante service. MasterCard travellers' cheques (such as those issued by Thomas Cook and HSBC) are exchangeable for nuevo soles in Interbanc, Banco Wiese and Banco Latino.

US dollars and euros (preferably cash) are the best foreign currency to carry in Peru – anything else, apart obviously from soles, will almost certainly prove hard to get rid of outside Lima and Cusco, and the dollar exchange rate is the one most keenly followed. US dollars are still more widely accepted beyond the major cities and tourist destinations. One thing to bear in mind, however, is that dollar notes which are in any way damaged (even the slightest tear or nick) are usually refused by shops, restaurants, hotels and even banks anywhere in Peru; so try to ensure your notes stay fresh, crisp and clean. **Pounds sterling** cash, or even as travellers' cheques, really aren't worth carrying; you often get a very poor exchange rate. **Euros** are easier to exchange than sterling in the larger cities and are rapidly growing in popularity in Peru.

Credit cards are accepted in many of the moderate and all of the more expensive restaurants and hotels throughout Peru, as well as for car rental. Peru also has nationwide coverage with ATM Global Net, so all major cities and some major towns (like Pisac and Urubamba in the Sacred Valley near Cusco) offer ATM access for most plastic, including Visa Electron and Mastercard. The better known credit cards (including MasterCard, Visa, American Express and Diners Club) can also be used with larger travel agents and tour operators, although only with a few of the major bus companies (eg Cruz del Sur). Interbanc, Banco Latino, Banco de Wiese and Banco de Credito all have ATMs and **local currency** can be withdrawn from most of them; as well as in the banks themselves, they are also found in some main public spaces, from Museums in Cusco to shopping centres in most big cities. Be careful using the machines, though: they can be a target for muggings. Banks will also advance cash on major cards (with passport as ID) for a fee – the amount varies considerably, so check beforehand.

Getting **change** from your nuevo soles is almost always a problem. Large denominations should be avoided; you'll find them more difficult to change anywhere in South America. It's particularly hard to change the larger notes in jungle towns, and even in Cusco and Lima shopkeepers and waiters are often reluctant to accept them; if they do, they'll end up running around trying to find small change, which is a time-consuming drag for both parties. It's best to break up large notes at every opportunity – in major shops, bars and post offices. If you hang on to the smaller nuevo soles notes you'll have few difficulties in even the remotest villages.

Credit card companies in Peru

American Express Pardo and Aliaga 698, San Isidro, Lima ☎01/441-4744, 372-5808 or 326-2660 (Mon–Fri 9am–5.30pm, Sat 9am–1pm); or, for travellers' cheque cancellation dial 108 (for collect calling service), then ☎001/800-8602908 or 800-221-7282.
Diners Club International Av Canaval and Moreyra 535, San Isidro, Lima ☎ 01/442-3353 or 651-1111.
MasterCard ☎ 01/442-1661 or 221-0066.
Visa ☎01/421-2195, 213-2400 or 242-2975

Banks, casas de cambio and changing money on the street

Bank opening hours vary enormously from region to region and from bank to bank, but as a general rule most are open weekdays from 8am until 5pm. In Lima, in particular, many banks close for the afternoon at about 1pm from January to March; the Banco de Credito has some branches that open on Saturday mornings, but this isn't the norm. Try to avoid going to the bank on Friday afternoons, and it's generally better to arrive first thing in the morning. Banco de Credito is the most efficient bank, with fast service, a ticket system and videos to keep you amused should there be queues. Most banks will change dollar travellers' cheques and there are often relatively shorter lines at the Banco de Credito, while Banco Continental and Interbanc usually have air-conditioned offices and shorter waits. As the rate of exchange varies daily, you're better off changing a little money at a time, although there's an enormous amount of time-consuming paperwork involved in even the simplest transactions – some places fill out several copies of each form. You'll always need to show your passport.

Peruvian **hotels** tend to offer the same rate of exchange as the banks, although they may fix their own rate, which is usually slightly worse and averages some five percent below the market rate. For convenience there's a lot to be said for the **casas de cambio**, which can be found in just about any town on the tourist circuit. They are open all day, are rarely crowded, and the rate of exchange is often better than, or the same as, the banks. Rates on the streets tend to drop during fiesta and holiday times, so change enough money beforehand to see you through.

The exchange rates found on the street are also sometimes slightly better than in the banks and usually quicker and more convenient. But in Peru the difference is never as dramatic as it is in some other South American countries. Some of these are official *cambistas* (money changers), who wear authorization badges from the local municipalities; otherwise, hotels will often change cash. Official *cambistas* can be spotted in the commercial or tourist centre of any large town, generally around the corners by the main city banks, and, rather less official ones, at all border crossings. The *cambistas* in general have become less trustworthy in recent years, so always carefully count your money before completing the transaction and avoid changing money on the street after dark when the official *cambistas* are often replaced by crooks in the larger cities. It is perfectly legal to buy nuevo soles from official street *cambistas*, but if you do exchange in the street, count your change very carefully and have someone watch your back if you're changing a large amount of money. Theft of signed or unsigned travellers' cheques, sometimes under threat of violence, is always a slight risk, particularly in Lima: when changing money on the street, play it safe – and never hand over your notes until given the cash. Going into unfamiliar buildings (with hidden back staircases) "to negotiate" is also *not* advisable. Watch out, too, for forgeries, which are generally pretty crude, but frequently good enough to pass to a tourist while street changing. Also, beware the old trick, especially used on $100 bills, where they try to give you back a forgery pretending it's the one you gave them.

Wiring money

Having money wired from home using one of the companies listed below is never cheap but can be convenient and particularly useful in emergencies. Western Union is the most ubiquitous of money-wiring companies, with offices in all major cities of Peru; their Peru

call centre number is ✆01/442-0014 or 0800-12080 (see city listings in relevant chapters of the Guide). It's also possible to have money wired directly from a bank in your home country to a bank in Peru, although this is somewhat less reliable because it involves two separate institutions and usually takes three days. If you go this route, your home bank will need the address of the branch bank where you want to pick up the money and the address and telex number of the Lima head office, which will act as the clearing house; money wired this way normally takes two to five working days to arrive, and costs around £25/$40 per transaction. The Banco Continental, Banco de Credito and Interbanc offer a relatively smooth service at the Peru end.

Money-wiring companies

Thomas Cook US ✆ 1-800/287-7362, Canada ✆1-888/823-4732, UK ✆ 01733/318 922, Republic of Ireland ✆ 01/677 1721, ✇www .us.thomascook.com.
Travelers Express Moneygram US ✆ 1-800/926-3947, Canada ✆1-800/933-3278, ✇www.moneygram.com.
Western Union US and Canada ✆ 1-800/325-6000, Australia ✆1800/501 500, New Zealand ✆09/270 0050, UK ✆0800/833 833, Republic of Ireland ✆1800/395395, ✇www.westernunion.com.

Insurance

If you fall ill, the bills can mount up rapidly, so some form of insurance – preferably including air evacuation in the event of serious emergency – is essential. Even with insurance most Peruvian clinics will insist on cash up front except in really serious hospital cases, so some emergency cash is a good idea. Keep all receipts and official papers, so that you can make a claim when you get back home.

Before paying for a new policy, however, it's worth checking whether you are already covered: some all-risks home insurance policies may cover your possessions when overseas, and many private medical

schemes include cover when abroad. In Canada, provincial health plans usually provide partial cover for medical mishaps overseas, while holders of official student/ teacher/youth cards in Canada and the US are entitled to meagre accident coverage and hospital inpatient benefits.

After exhausting the possibilities above, you might want to contact a specialist travel insurance company, or consider the travel package insurance deal we offer (see opposite). A typical travel insurance policy usually provides coverage for the loss of baggage, tickets and – up to a certain limit – cash or cheques, as well as cancellation or curtailment of your journey. Most of them exclude so-called dangerous sports unless an extra premium is paid: in Peru this can mean scuba-diving, whitewater rafting, windsurfing and trekking, though probably not kayaking or jeep safaris. Many policies can be chopped and changed to exclude cover you don't need – for example, sickness and accident benefits can often be excluded or included at will. If you do take medical cover, ascertain whether benefits will be paid as treatment proceeds or only after return home, and whether there is a 24-hour medical emergency number. When securing baggage cover, make sure that the per-article limit – typically under £500 – will cover

your most valuable possession. If you need to make a claim, you'll need to provide receipts for everything, from clothes to medicines and medical treatment, and in the event you have anything stolen, you must obtain an official statement from the tourist police (*policía de turismo*).

Rough Guides has teamed up with Columbus Direct to offer you travel insurance that can be tailored to suit your needs. Products include a low-cost backpacker option for long stays; a short-break option for city getaways; a typical holiday package option; and others. There are also annual multi-trip policies for those who travel regularly. Different sports and activities (trekking, skiing, etc) can be usually be covered if required.

See our website (ⓦwww.roughguides .com/website/shop) for eligibility and purchasing options. Alternatively, UK residents should call ☏0870/033 9988; Australians should call ☏1300/669 999 and New Zealanders should call ☏0800/55 9911. All other nationalities should call ☏+44 870/890 2843.

Health

No inoculations are currently required for Peru, but a yellow fever vaccination is sometimes needed to enter the jungle as well as being generally recommended. It's always a good idea to check with the embassy or a reliable travel agent before you go. Your doctor will probably advise you to have some anyway: typhoid, cholera, rabies and, again, yellow fever shots are all sensible precautions, and it's well worth ensuring that your polio and tetanus-diphtheria boosters are still effective. Immunization against hepatitis A is also usually recommended.

In case you don't get your shots before you leave for Peru, there is a useful 24-hour vaccination service at the International Health Department in Lima's airport ☏01/517-1845; and also a vaccination centre in the Lima suburb of Jesus Maria at C Capac Yupanqui 1400, ☏01/471-9920 (Mon–Fri 8am–1pm & 2–5pm).

Yellow fever, malaria and dengue fever

Yellow fever breaks out now and again in some of the jungle areas of Peru; it is frequently obligatory to show an inoculation

certificate when entering the Amazon region – if you can't show proof of immunization you'll be jabbed on the spot. This viral disease is transmitted by mosquitoes and can be fatal. Symptoms are headache, fever, abdominal pain and vomiting, and though victims may appear to recover, without medical help, they may suffer from bleeding, shock and kidney and liver failure. The only treatment is to keep the fever as low as possible and prevent dehydration.

Malaria is quite common in Peru these days, particularly in the Amazon regions to the east of the country, and it's very easy to catch without prophylactics. If you intend to go into the jungle regions, malaria tablets should be taken – starting a few weeks before you arrive and continuing for some time after. Make sure you get a supply of these, or whatever is recommended by your doctor (there are several commonly recommended malarial prophylactics recommended for the Peruvian jungle regions) in advance of the trip. Some are more expensive than others and some are not recommended for prolonged periods. Few people who have to spend a lot of time in the rainforest regions use prophylactics, preferring to treat the disease if they contract it, believing that the best prevention is to avoid getting bitten if at all possible, by wearing long sleeves, long trousers, socks, even mosquito-proof net hats, and sleeping under good mosquito netting or well-proofed quarters. Pills are a relatively simple option, but some do have side effects which should be investigated with your GP ideally more than a month prior to your departure for Peru. There is more information on this matter in Chapter 8 (p.486). You could also check out Ⓦwww .cdc.gov/travel/regionalmalaria.

Another illness spread by mosquito bites is **dengue fever**, the symptoms of which are similar to those of malaria, plus aching bones. Dengue-carrying mosquitoes are particularly prevalent during the rainy season, with urban jungle areas often the worst affected; they fly during the day, so wear insect repellent in the daytime if mosquitoes are around. The only treatment is complete rest, with drugs to assuage the fever – unfortunately, a second infection can be fatal.

Diarrhoea, dysentery and giardia

Diarrhoea is something everybody gets at some stage, and there's little to be done except to drink a lot of water and bide your

time. You should also replace salts either by taking oral rehydration salts or by mixing a teaspoon of salt and eight teaspoons of sugar in a litre of purified water. You can minimize the risk by being sensible about what you eat, and by **not drinking tap water anywhere**. There are several portable water filters on the market. Except in trekking-type conditions it isn't difficult to drink clean water, given the extreme cheapness and universal availability of soft drinks and bottled water, while Peruvians are great believers in herbal teas, which often help alleviate cramps.

If your diarrhoea contains blood or mucus, the cause may be dysentery (one of either two strains, see below) or giardia. Combined with a fever, these symptoms could well be caused by **bacillic dysentery** and may clear up without treatment. If you're sure you need it, a course of antibiotics such as tetracyclin or ampicillin (travel with a supply if you are going off the beaten track for a while) should sort you out, but they also destroy "gut flora" which help protect you, so should only be used if properly diagnosed or in a desperate situation. Similar symptoms without fever indicate **amoebic dysentery**, which is much more serious, and can damage your gut if untreated. The usual cure is a course of metronidazole (Flagyl), an antibiotic which may itself make you feel ill, and should not be taken with alcohol. Similar symptoms, plus rotten egg-smelling belches and gas, indicate **giardia**, for which the treatment is again metronidazole. If you suspect you have any of these, seek medical help, and only start on the metronidazole (250mg three times daily for a week for adults) if there is definitely blood in your diarrhoea and it is impossible to see a doctor.

Water and food

Water in Peru is better than it used to be, but it can still trouble non-Peruvian (and even Peruvian) stomachs, so it's a good idea to only drink **bottled water** (*agua mineral*), available in various sizes, including litre and two-litre bottles from most corner shops or food stores. Stick with known brands, even if they are more expensive, and always check that the seal on the bottle is intact, since the sale of bottles refilled with local water is not uncommon. Carbonated water is generally safer as it is more likely to be the genuine stuff. You should also clean your teeth using bottled water and avoid raw foods washed in local water.

Apart from bottled water, there are various methods of **treating water** whilst you are travelling, whether your source is tap water or natural groundwater such as a river or stream. **Boiling** is the time-honoured method, which is an effective way to sterilize water, although it will not remove any unpleasant tastes. A minimum boiling time of five minutes (longer at higher altitudes) is sufficient to kill micro-organisms. In remote jungle areas, **sterilizing tablets** are a better idea, although they leave a rather bad taste in the mouth. Pregnant women or people with thyroid problems should consult their doctor before using iodine sterilizing tablets or iodine-based purifiers. In emergencies and remote areas in particular, always check with locals to see whether the tap water is okay (*es potable?*) before drinking it.

Peruvian **food** cooked on the street has been frequently condemned as a health hazard, particularly during rare but recurrent **cholera outbreaks**. Be careful about anything bought from street stalls, particularly seafood, which may not be that fresh. Salads should be avoided, especially in small settlements where they may have been washed in river water or fertilized by local sewage waters.

The sun

The sun can be deceptively hot, particularly on the coast or when travelling in boats on jungle rivers when the hazy weather or cool breezes can put visitors off their guard; remember, **sunstroke** is a reality and can make you very sick as well as burnt. Wide-brimmed hats, sunscreen lotions (factor 60 advisable since the sun high up in the Andes is deceptively strong, especially when skin is cooled by breezes) and staying in the shade whenever possible are all good precautions. Note that **suntan lotion** and **sunblock** are more expensive in Peru than they are at home, so take a good supply with you. If you do run out, you can buy Western brands at most *farmacias*, though

you won't find a very wide choice, especially in the higher factors. Also make sure that you increase your water intake, in order to prevent dehydration.

Altitude sickness

Altitude sickness – known as *soroche* (see box, p.242) in Peru – is a common problem for visitors, especially if you are travelling quickly between the coast or jungle regions and the high Andes. The best way to prevent it is to eat light meals, drink lots of coca tea and spend as long as possible acclimatizing to high altitudes (over 2500m) before carrying out any strenuous activity. Anyone who suffers from headaches or nausea should rest; more seriously, a sudden bad cough could be a sign of **pulmonary edema** and demands an immediate descent and medical attention – altitude sickness can kill. People often suffer from altitude sickness on trains crossing high passes; if this happens, don't panic, just rest and stay on the train until it descends. Most trains are equipped with oxygen bags or cylinders that are brought around by the conductor for anyone in need. **Diamox** is used by many from the US to counter the effects of *soroche*. It's best to bring this with you from home since it's rarely available in Peruvian pharmacies.

Insects

Insects are more of an irritation than a serious problem, but on the coast, in the jungle and to a lesser extent in the mountains, the **common fly** is a definite pest. Although it can carry typhoid, there is little one can do; you might spend mealtimes swatting flies away from your plate but even in expensive restaurants it's difficult to regulate hygiene in the kitchens. A more obvious problem is the **mosquito**, which in some parts of the lowland jungle carries malaria. Repellents are of limited value – it's better to cover your arms, legs and feet with a good layer of clothing. Mosquitoes tend to emerge after dark, but the daytime holds even worse biting insects in the jungle regions, among them the **Manta Blanca** (or white blanket), so called because they swarm as a blanket of tiny flying insects. Their bites don't hurt at the time but itch like crazy for a few days after. **Antihistamine**

creams or tablets can reduce the sting or itchiness of most insect bites, but try not to scratch them, and if it gets unbearable go to the nearest *farmacia* for advice. To keep hotel rooms relatively insect-free, buy some of the spirals of incense-like **pyrethrin**, available cheaply everywhere.

HIV and AIDS

HIV and **AIDS** (known as SIDA in Latin America) are a growing problem in South America, and whilst Peru does not have as bad a reputation as neighbouring Brazil, you should still take care. Although all hospitals and clinics in Peru are supposed to use only sterilized equipment, many travellers prefer to take their own sealed hypodermic syringes in case of emergencies. It goes without saying that you should take the same kind of precautions as you would in your country when having sex (see "Contraception", below).

Contraception

Condoms (*profilacticos*) are available from street vendors and some *farmacias*. However, they tend to be expensive and often poor quality (rumour has it that some are even US rejects, which have been sold to a less discriminating market), so bring an adequate supply with you. **The pill** is also available from *farmacias*, officially on prescription only, but is frequently sold over the counter. You're unlikely to be able to match your brand, however, so it's far better to bring your own supply. It's worth remembering that if you suffer from moderately severe **diarrhoea** on your trip the pill (or any other drug) may not be in your system long enough to take effect.

Farmacias or boticas

For **minor ailments** you can buy most drugs at a *farmacia* or a *botica* without a prescription. **Antibiotics** and **malaria pills** can be bought over the counter (it is, however, important to know the correct dosage), as can antihistamines (for bite allergies) or medication for an upset stomach (try Lomotil or Streptotriad). You can also buy Western-brand **tampons** at a *farmacia*, though they are expensive, so it's better to bring a good supply. For any serious illnesses, you should go to a doctor or hospital; these are detailed throughout the Guide in the relevant town Listings, or try the local phone book.

Traditional medicines

Alternative medicines have a popular history going back at least two thousand years in Peru and the traditional practitioners – *herbaleros*, *hueseros* and *curanderos* – are still commonplace. **Herbaleros** sell curative plants, herbs and charms in the streets and markets of most towns. They lay out a selection of ground roots, liquid tree barks, flowers, leaves and creams – all with specific medicinal functions and sold at much lower prices than in the *farmacias*. If told the symptoms, a *herbalero* can select remedies for most minor (and apparently some major) ailments. **Hueseros** are consultants who treat diseases and injuries by bone manipulation, while **curanderos** claim diagnostic, divinatory and healing powers, and have existed in Peru since pre-Inca days. For further information on alternative medicine and traditional healing, see p.583.

Medical resources for travellers

US and Canada

CDC ☎1-877/394-8747, ✆ www.cdc.gov/travel. Official US government travel health site.
International Society for Travel Medicine ☎1-770/736-7060, ✆ www.istm.org. Has a full list of travel health clinics.
Canadian Society for International Health ✆ www.csih.org. Extensive list of travel health centres.

Australia, New Zealand and South Africa

Travellers' Medical and Vaccination Centre ✆ www.tmvc.com.au, ☎1300/658 844. Lists travel clinics in Australia, New Zealand and South Africa.

UK and Ireland

Hospital for Tropical Diseases Travel Clinic ☎0845/155 5000 or ☎020/7387 4411, ✆ www.thehtd.org.
MASTA (Medical Advisory Service for Travellers Abroad) ✆ www.masta.org or ☎0870/606 2782 for the nearest clinic.
Travel Medicine Services ☎028/9031 5220.
Tropical Medical Bureau Republic of Ireland ☎1850/487 674, ✆ www.tmb.ie.

Information and maps

Peru has no official tourist offices abroad, but you can get a range of information from Promperu via Peru's embassies in Britain, Europe, North America, Australia and New Zealand. Promperu has good information on ⓦwww.peru.info. However, you'll probably find that most tour companies can supply pretty up-to-date information and often in more appropriate detail.

In Peru you'll find some sort of **tourist office** in most towns, which can help with information and sometimes free local maps. Quite often, though, these are simply fronts for tour operators, and are only really worth bothering with if you have a specific question – about fiesta dates or local bus timetables, for example. A *Peru Guide* booklet is available free from hotels and travel agencies in most major cities; it has a few good city maps and gives recommendations for hotels and restaurants plus other useful information for Lima, Arequipa, Cusco, Huaraz, Chiclayo, Ica/Nasca/Paracas and Iquitos. The **South American Explorers' Club, though,** is probably your best bet for getting relevant and up-to-date information both before you leave home and when you arrive in Lima. It is a non-profit organization founded in 1977 to support scientific and adventure expeditions and to provide services to travellers. In return for membership (from $50 a year) you get four copies of the magazine *South American Explorer* a year, and you can use the club's facilities, which include an excellent library, access to the map collection, trip reports, listings, a postal address, storage space, discounts on maps, guidebooks, information on visas, doctors and dentists and a network of experts with specialist information. Some trip reports are now also available online. They have clubhouses in Lima (see p.118),

Cusco (see p.266), and their main office is in the US, at 126 Indiana Creek Road, Ithaca, NY 14850 (ⓣ607/277-0488, ⓕ277-6122, ⓦwww.samexplorers.org), plus there's a clubhouse in Ecuador at Jorge Washington 311 and Leonidas Plaza, Quito (ⓣ0593-2/225228); postal address: Apartado 21-31, Eloy Alfaro, Quito, Ecuador.

Maps

Maps of Peru fall into three basic categories. A standard **road map** should be available from good map sellers just about anywhere in the world or in Peru itself from street vendors or librerías; the Touring y Automóvil Club de Peru, Av Cesar Vallejo 699, Lince, Lima (ⓣ01/6149999; ⓦwww.touringperu. com.pe) is worth visiting for its good route maps. **Departmental maps**, covering each departemento (Peruvian state) in greater detail, albeit often very out of date, are also fairly widely available. **Topographic maps** (usually 1:100,000) cover the entire coastal area and most of the mountainous regions of Peru. In Lima, they can be bought from the Instituto Geografico Nacional (IGN Peru), and they're also available at the South American Explorers' Club (see above), along with a wide variety of hiking maps and guidebooks for all the most popular hiking zones and quite a few others.

Getting around

With the distances in Peru being so vast, many Peruvians and travellers are increasingly flying to their destinations, as all Peruvian cities are within a two-hour flight of Lima. Most Peruvians, however, still get around the country by bus, a cheap way to travel with routes to almost everywhere. In a few cases, it's possible to arrive by train – an experience in itself – despite being considerably slower than equivalent bus journeys. Approximate journey times and frequencies of all services can be found in "Travel Details" at the end of each chapter, and local peculiarities are detailed in the text of the Guide.

Driving around Peru is generally not a problem outside of Lima, and allows you to see some out-of-the-way places that you may otherwise miss. However, road traffic in Lima is abominable, both in terms of its recklessness and the sheer volume. Traffic jams are ubiquitous between 8 and 10am and again between 4 and 7pm every weekday, while air pollution from old and poorly maintained vehicles is a real health risk, particularly in Lima and Arequipa.

By bus

Peru's **buses** are run by a variety of private companies, all of which offer remarkably low **fares**, making it possible to travel from one end of the country to the other (over 2000km) for under $35. Long-distance bus journeys cost from around $1.75 per hour on the fast coastal highway, and are even cheaper on the slower mountain and jungle routes. The condition of the buses ranges from the efficient and relatively luxurious Cruz del Sur fleet that runs along the coast, to the old, battered buses used on local runs throughout the country. Some of the better bus companies, such as Cruz del Sur and

Ormeño, offer excellent onboard facilities including sandwich bars and video entertainment. The major companies generally offer two or three levels of service anyway, and many companies run the longer journeys by night with a bus-cama (comfortable deeply reclining seat) option. If you don't want to miss the scenery, you can hop relatively easily between the smaller towns, which usually works out at not much more. Cruz del Sur (ⓦwww.cruzdelsur.com.pe) now operates an excellent website with timetables and ticket purchase option (credit cards accepted).

As the only means of transport available to most of the population, buses run with surprising regularity, and the coastal Panamerican Highway and many of the main routes into the mountains have now been paved (one of ex-President Fujimori's better legacies), so on such routes services are generally punctual. On some of the rougher mountainous routes, punctures, arguments over rights of way and, during the rainy season, landslides may delay the arrival time by several hours.

At least one **bus depot** or **stopping area** can be found in the centre of any town. Peru

Addresses

Addresses are frequently written with just the street name and number: for example, Pizarro 135. Officially, though, they're usually prefixed by Calle, Jirón (street) or Avenida. The first digit of any street number (or sometimes the first two digits) represents the block number within the street as a whole. Note too that many of the major streets in Lima and also in Cusco have two names – in Lima this is a relic of the military governments of the 1970s, in Cusco it's more to do with a revival of the Inca past.

is investing in a series of **terminal terrestres**, or **terrapuertos**, centralizing the departure and arrival of the manifold operators. Lima does not have this facility and, in any case, it's always a good idea to double-check where the bus is leaving from, since in some cities, notably Arequipa, bus offices are in different locations to the bus terminal. Lima has so many buses that the major companies are constantly rationalizing their own private terminals and departure points (presently incredibly complex) while the rest still cling to depots mostly in the traffic-congested heart of Lima Centro. If you can't get to a bus depot or *terminal terrestre*, you can try to catch a bus from the exit roads or police check points on the outskirts of most Peruvian cities, though there's no guarantee of getting a ride or a seat. For intercity rides, it's best to buy **tickets** in advance direct from the bus company offices; for local trips, you can buy tickets on the bus itself. On long-distance journeys, try to avoid getting seats right over the jarring wheels, especially if the bus is tackling mountain or jungle roads.

Taxis, mototaxis and colectivos

Taxis can be found anywhere at any time in almost every town. Any car can become a taxi simply by sticking a taxi sign up in the front window; a lot of people, especially in Lima, take advantage of this to supplement their income. Whenever you get into a taxi, always fix the **price** in advance (in nuevo soles rather than in US dollars) since few of them have meters, even the professional firms. Relatively short journeys in Lima generally cost around $2 to 4, but it's cheaper elsewhere in the country. Radio taxis, minicabs and airport taxis tend to cost more. Even relatively long taxi rides in Lima are likely to cost less than $10, except perhaps to and from the airport, which ranges from $8 to 18, depending on how far across the city you're going, how bad the traffic is and how much you're prepared to pay for a stylish vehicle. Taxi drivers in Peru do not expect tips.

In many rural towns, you'll find small cars – mainly Korean Ticos and motorcycle rickshaws, known variously as *mototaxis* or *motokars* – all competing for customers. The latter are always cheaper if slightly more dangerous and not that comfortable, especially if there's more than two of you or if you've got a lot of luggage.

Colectivos (shared taxis) are a very useful way of getting around that's peculiar to Peru. They connect all the coastal towns, and many of the larger centres in the mountains. Like the buses, many are ageing imports from the US – huge old Dodge Coronets – though, increasingly, fast new Japanese and Korean minibuses are running between the cities. *Colectivos* tend to be faster than the bus, though are often as much as twice the price. Most *colectivo* **cars** manage to squeeze in about six people plus the driver (three in the front and four in the back), and can be found in the centre of a town or at major stopping places along the main roads. If more than one is ready to leave it's worth bargaining a little, as the price is often negotiable. *Colectivo* **minibuses**, also known as *combis*, can squeeze in twice as many people, or often more.

In the cities, particularly in Lima, *colectivos* (especially *combis* ie minibuses, as opposed to microbuses or cars) have an appalling reputation for **safety**. There are crashes reported in the Lima press every week, mostly caused by the highly competitive nature of the business. There are so many *combis* covering the same major arterial routes in Lima that they literally race each other to be the first to the next street corner. They frequently crash, turn over and knock down pedestrians. Equally dangerous is the fact that the driver is in such a hurry that he does not always wait for you to get in. If you're not careful he'll pull away while you've still got a foot on the pavement, putting you in serious danger of breaking a leg.

By train

Peru's spectacular **train** journeys are in themselves a major attraction, and you should aim to take at least one long-distance train ride during your trip, especially as the trains connect some of Peru's major tourist sights. At the time of writing, the **Central Railway**, which climbs and switchbacks its way up from Lima into the Andes as far as Huancayo on the world's highest standard-gauge tracks, only runs about once a month for passengers (see p.319).

The **Southern Railway** runs passenger services inland from Puno on Lake Titicaca north to Cusco, from where another line heads out down the magnificent Urubamba Valley as far as Machu Picchu. The trains move slowly, and are much bumpier than buses, depending both on the level of track maintenance (presently poor between Cusco and Puno, for instance) and, of course, the state of the comparative road the bus is taking. Trains, however, generally allow ample time to observe what's going on outside, but you do have to keep one eye on events inside, where the carriages – often extremely crowded – are notorious for **petty thefts**.

For all train journeys, it's advisable to buy **tickets** a week or two before travelling and even further in advance during high season. Information and online sales can be found at ⓦ www.perurail.com.

By plane

Some places in the jungle can only sensibly be reached by **plane** and Peru is so vast that the odd flight can save a lot of time. There are four main companies: Lan Peru, a Chilean-owned company, who fly to all of the main cities and many smaller destinations; Star Peru, a Peruvian airline which began operating in 2005; Taca Peru, which initially grew out of a military operated internal domestic service; plus the smallest operator, Aero Condor, whose flights were temporarily suspended in 2008 to allow them to improve on fleet maintenance. **Many tickets** can be booked and bought online or from travel agents or airline offices in all major towns. The most popular routes, such as Lima–Cusco, cost upwards of $80 and are generally cheaper if booked well in advance, and on all flights it's important to **confirm your booking** two days before departure. In high season some Lima–Cusco flights are fully booked months in advance. Less busy routes tend to be less expensive per air mile and can be booked the day before.

Flights are often cancelled or delayed, and sometimes they even leave earlier than scheduled – especially in the jungle where the weather can be a problem. If a passenger hasn't shown up sixty minutes before the flight, the company may give the seat to someone on the waiting list, so it's best to be on time whether you're booked or are merely hopeful. The luggage allowance on internal flights is generally 16kg, not including hand luggage.

There are also **small planes** (four- and ten-seaters) serving the jungle and certain parts of the coast. A number of small companies fly out of Jorge Chavez Airport in Lima most days (their counters are between the international check-in counters and the domestic departure area), but these have few fixed schedules as well as a reputation for being dangerous and poorly maintained. The jungle towns, such as Pucallpa, Tarapoto, Puerto Maldonado and Iquitos, also tend to have small **air colectivo** companies operating scheduled services between larger settlements in the region, at quite reasonable rates. For an *expresso* **air taxi**, which will take you to any landing strip in the country whenever you want, you'll pay over $400 an hour (shared between up to four passengers); this price is based on a half-hour flight and is calculated to include the return journey with the pilot in an empty plane (you may want to be dropped off but the plane will generally return empty, like a taxi, without new passengers for the return flight).

Airlines in Peru

Aero Condor Juan de Arona 781, San Isidro, Lima ☏01/6146000 or out of office time ☏441-8484, ⓦ www.aerocondor.com.
Lan Peru Av Los Incas 172, Eighth Floor, San Isidro, Lima ☏01/21-38200, ⓦ www.lan.com. To call collect and direct from outside Lima ring 0800-11234 for information and reservations.
Star Peru Avenida Av Comandante Espinar 331, Miraflores, Lima, ☏01/705-9000, ⓦ www.starperu .com.
Taca Peru Jose Pardo 811, Lima, ☏01/511-8222, ⓦ www.taca.com.

By car

Cars can be very handy for reaching remote rural destinations or sites, though, as stated before, not for exploring Lima.

If you bring a car into Peru that is not registered there, you will need to show (and keep with you at all times) a *libreta de pago por la aduana* (**proof of customs payment**) normally provided by the relevant automobile association of the country you are coming from. **Spare parts**, particularly tyres, will have to be carried as will a tent, emergency water and food. The chance of **theft** is quite high – the vehicle, your baggage and accessories are all vulnerable when parked.

What few **traffic signals** exist are either completely ignored or used at the drivers' "discretion". The pace is fast and roads everywhere are in bad shape: only the Panamerican Highway, running down the coast, and a few short stretches inland, are paved. **Mechanics** are generally good and always ingenious – they have to be, due to a lack of spare parts! Also, the 95-octane **petrol** is much cleaner than the 84, though both are cheap by European, North American or Australian and New Zealand standards. **International driving licences** are technically only valid for thirty days in Peru, after which a permit is required from the Touring y Automóvil Club del Peru, Cesar Vallejo 699, Lince, Lima (Mon–Fri 9am–4.45pm; ☎01/4403270, ℱ4225947, Ⓦwww.hys.com.pe/tacp); in practice, however, a US or European photo licence is generally accepted without question.

Renting a car costs much the same as in Europe and North America. The major rental firms all have offices in Lima, but outside the capital you'll generally find only local companies are represented; see the relevant Listings for details. You may find it more convenient to rent a car in advance from your own country (see below for details) – expect to pay from around $40 a day, or $200 a week for the smallest car. In jungle cities it's usually possible to **hire motorbikes** or **mopeds** by the hour or by the day: this is a good way of getting to know a town or to be able to shoot off into the jungle for a day.

Car rental agencies

Alamo US ☎1-800/462-5266, Ⓦwww.alamo.com.
Apex New Zealand ☎3/379 2647, Ⓦwww.apexrentals.co.nz.
Auto Europe US and Canada ☎1-888/223-5555, Ⓦwww.autoeurope.com.
Avis US and Canada ☎1-800/331-1212, UK ☎0870/606 0100, Republic of Ireland ☎021/428 1111, Australia ☎13 63 33 or 02/9353 9000, New Zealand ☎09/526 2847 or 0800/655 111, Ⓦwww.avis.com.
Budget US ☎1-800/527-0700, Canada ☎1-800/268-8900, UK ☎0870/156 5656, Australia ☎1300/362 848, New Zealand ☎0800/283 438, Ⓦwww.budget.com.
Dollar US ☎1-800/800-3665, Canada ☎1-800/229 0984, UK ☎0808/234 7524, Republic of Ireland ☎1800/575 800, Ⓦwww.dollar.com.
Enterprise Rent-a-Car US ☎1-800/261-7331, Ⓦwww.enterprise.com.
Europcar US & Canada ☎1-877/940 6900, UK ☎0870/607 5000, Republic of Ireland ☎01/614 2800, Australia ☎393/306 160, Ⓦwww.europcar.com.
Europe by Car US ☎1-800/223-1516, Ⓦwww.europebycar.com.
Hertz US & Canada ☎1-800/654-3131, UK ☎020/7026 0077, Republic of Ireland ☎01/870 5777, New Zealand ☎0800/654 321, Ⓦwww.hertz.com.
Holiday Autos UK ☎0870/400 4461, Republic of Ireland ☎01/872 9366, Australia ☎299/394 433, US ☎866-392/9288, South Africa ☎11/2340 597, Ⓦwww.holidayautos.co.uk. Part of the lastminute.com group.
National US ☎1-800/CAR-RENT, UK ☎0870/400 4581, Australia ☎0870/600 6666, New Zealand ☎03/366 5574, Ⓦwww.nationalcar.com.
SIXT Europe ☎1-00800/4747-4227, US ☎1-877/347-3227, Ⓦwww.irishcarrentals.ie.
Thrifty US and Canada ☎1-800/847-4389, UK ☎01494/751 500, Republic of Ireland ☎01/844 1950, Australia ☎1300/367 227, New Zealand ☎09/256 1405, Ⓦwww.thrifty.com.

By boat

There are no coastal **boat** services in Peru, but in many areas – on **Lake Titicaca** and especially in the **jungle regions** – water is the obvious means of getting around. From Puno, on Lake Titicaca, there are currently no regular services to Bolivia by ship or hydrofoil (though check with the tour agencies in Puno), but there are plenty of smaller boats that will take visitors out to the various islands in the lake. These aren't expensive and a price can usually be negotiated down at the port.

In the jungle areas **motorized canoes** come in two basic forms: those with a large outboard motor and those with a Briggs and Stratton **peque-peque** engine. The outboard is faster and more manoeuvrable, but it costs a lot more to run. Occasionally you can hitch a ride in one of these canoes for nothing, but this may involve waiting around for days or even weeks and, in the end, most people expect some form of payment. More practical is to **hire a canoe** along with its guide/driver for a few days. This means searching around in the port and negotiating, but you can often get a *peque-peque* canoe from around $50–80 per day, which will invariably work out cheaper than taking an organized tour, as well as giving you the choice of guide and companions. Obviously, the more people you can get together, the cheaper it will be per person.

On foot

Even if you've no intention of doing any serious hiking, there's a good deal of walking involved in checking out many of the most enjoyable Peruvian attractions. Climbing from Cusco up to the fortress of Sacsayhuaman, for example, or wandering around at Machu Picchu, involves more than an average Sunday afternoon stroll. Bearing in mind the rugged terrain throughout Peru, the absolute minimum **footwear** is a strong pair of running shoes. Much better is a pair of hiking boots with good ankle support.

Hiking – whether in the desert, mountains or jungle – can be an enormously rewarding experience, but you should go properly equipped and bear in mind a few of the **potential hazards**. Never stray too far without food and water, something warm and something waterproof to wear. The weather is renowned for its dramatic change-ability, especially in **the mountains**, where there is always the additional danger of *soroche* (altitude sickness – see p.242). In **the jungle** the biggest danger is getting lost (see p.491). If this happens, the best thing to do is follow a watercourse down to the main stream, and stick to this until you reach a settlement or get picked up by a passing canoe. If you get caught out in the forest at night, build a leafy shelter and make a fire or try sleeping in a tree.

In the mountains it's often a good idea to hire a **pack animal** to carry your gear. **Llamas** can only carry about 25–30kg and move slowly, a *burro* (donkey) carries around 80kg and a **mule** – the most common and best pack animal – will shift 150kg with relative ease. Mules can be hired from upwards of $5 a day, and they normally come with an *arriero*, a muleteer who'll double as a guide. It is also possible to hire mules or horses for **riding** but this costs a little more. With a guide and beast of burden it's quite simple to reach even the most remote valleys, ruins and mountain passes, travelling in much the same way as Pizarro and his men did over four hundred years ago.

Hitching

Hitching in Peru usually means catching a ride with a truck driver, who will almost always expect payment. Always agree on a price before getting in as there are stories of drivers stopping in the middle of nowhere and demanding unreasonably high amounts (from foreigners and Peruvians alike) before going any further. Hitching isn't considered dangerous in Peru, but having said that, few people, even Peruvians, actually hitch. Trucks can be flagged down anywhere but there is greater choice around markets, and at police controls or petrol stations on the outskirts of towns. Trucks tend to be the only form of public transport in some less accessible regions, travelling the roads that buses won't touch and serving remote communities, so you may end up having to sit on top of a pile of potatoes or bananas.

Hitchhiking in **private cars** is not recommended, and, in any case, it's very rare that one will stop to pick you up.

Organized tours

There are hundreds of **travel agents** and **tour operators** in Peru, and reps hunt out customers at bus terminals, train stations and in city centres. While they can be expensive, **organized excursions** can be a quick and relatively effortless way to see some of the popular attractions and the more remote sites, while a prearranged trek of something like the Inca Trail can take much of the worry out of camping preparations and ensure that you get decent campsites, a sound meal and help with carrying your equipment in what can be difficult walking conditions.

Many **adventure tour companies** offer excellent and increasingly exciting packages and itineraries – ranging from mountain biking, whitewater rafting, jungle photo-safaris, mountain trekking and climbing, to more comfortable and gentler city and countryside tours. Tours cost $45–300 a day and, in Cusco and Huaraz in particular, there's an enormous selection of operators to choose from. **Cusco** is a pretty good base for hiking, whitewater rafting, canoeing, horseback riding or going on an expedition into the Amazonian jungle with an adventure tour company (see pp.264–265); **Arequipa** and the **Colca Canyon** offer superb hiking and the surrounding area boasts two of the deepest canyons on the planet, all serviced by tour companies (see pp.196–197); **Huaraz** is a good base for trekking and mountaineering; **Iquitos**, on the Amazon river, is one of the best places for adventure trips into the jungle and has a reasonable range of tour operators (see pp.545–548). Several of these companies have branches in Lima, if you want to book a tour in advance; see Lima Listings on p.115.

 # Outdoor activities and sports

Few of the world's countries can offer anything remotely as varied, rugged, remote and stunningly beautiful as Peru when it comes to ecotourism, trekking, mountain biking and also river rafting. Ecotourism is most developed in the Amazon rainforest region of Peru, particularly around Manu, which is considered one of the most biodiverse regions on Earth; Iquitos in the northern jungle and the Tambopata region around Puerto Maldonado are similar ecotourist hotspots. These areas, and others in Peru's extensive rainforest, all offer a wide choice of operators leading tours up rivers to jungle lodges, themselves functioning as bases from which to explore the forest on foot and in smaller, quieter canoes. Naturally, the focus is on wildlife and flora; but there are often cultural elements to tours, including short visits to riverside communities, indigenous Indian villages and sometimes even mystical or healing work with jungle shaman. Prices vary and so does the level of service and accommodation quality as well as the degree of sustainability of the operation.

Trekking

Ecotourism is also very much alive in the Peruvian Andes, too, with several tour operators offering expeditions on foot or on horseback into some of the more exotic high Andes and cloud forest regions. The most popular areas for these are the same as the **trekking zones**: north and south of Cusco; the Colca Canyon; and the Cordillera Blanca. But there are many other equally biodiverse and culturally rich trekking routes in other *departamentos*: Cajamarca and Chachapoyas both possess challenging but rewarding mountain trekking, and the desert coast, too, has exceptional and unique econiches which are most easily explored from Lima, Trujillo, Chiclayo, Nasca, Pisco, Ica and Arequipa, where there is some tourism infrastructure to support visits.

The main tours and treks have been listed throughout the Guide in their appropriate geographical context. Chapter Five, which includes Huaraz and the Cordillera Blanca, contains further information on trekking in the Andes, or *Andinismo*, as it's long been known (see p.370). The Cusco and Arequipa chapters also contain extensive listings of tour and trek operators as well as camping and climbing equipment rental.

Mountaineering and winter sports information

Casa de Guias Parque Ginebra 28-G, Huaraz (Mon–Fri 9am–1pm & 4–8pm, Sat 9am–1pm; ☎044/421811, ⓦwww.casadeguias.com.pe.
Club Andino Peruano Av Dos de Mayo 1545, Oficina 216, Lima 27.
Club de Andinismo de la Universidad de Lima Av Javier Prado Este, Lima 33 ☎01/4376767, ext 30775.
Club de Montañismo Américo Tordoya Tarapacá 384, Lima ☎01/4606101 or 4311305.
Federación Peruana de Andinismo y Deportes de Invierno block 3 of Jose Diaz, Lima Centro ☎01/4240063.

Canoeing and whitewater rafting

Again, Peru is hard to beat for these adventurous activities. The rivers around Cusco and the Colca Canyon, as well as Huaraz and, nearer to Lima, at Lunahuana, can be exciting and demanding, though there are always sections also ideal for beginners. Cusco is one of the top **whitewater rafting and canoeing** centres in South America, with easy access to a whole range of river grades, from 2, 3, 4 and 5 on the Río Urubamba (shifting up grades in the rainy season) to the most dangerous whitewater on the Río Apurimac. On the Vilcanota, some 90km south of Cusco, at Chukika-huana, there's a five-kilometre section of river which, between December and April, offers a constant level 5 (see Chapter 4). One of the most amazing trips from Cusco goes right down into the **Amazon Basin** (see Chapter Eight). It should be noted that these rivers can be very wild and the best canoeing spots are often very remote, so you should only attempt running rivers with reputable companies and knowledgeable local guides.

The main companies operating in this field are listed in the relevant chapters. Trips range from half-day to several days of river adventure, sometimes encompassing both mountain and jungle terrain. Transport, food and accommodation are generally included in the price where relevant; but the costs also depend on levels of service and overnight accommodation required.

Cycling

In Peru, cycling is a major national sport, as well as one of the most ubiquitous forms of transport available to all classes in towns and rural areas virtually everywhere. Consequently, there are bike shops and bicycle repairs workshops in all major cities and larger towns. Perhaps more importantly, a number of tour companies offer guided cycling tours which can be an excellent way to see the best of Peru. Huaraz and Cusco are both popular destinations for bikers.

In Lima, cycling equipment and information is available from: Peru Bike Services, Parque Nueva Castilla, Calle A, D-7, Surco, close to the fifth block of Paseo La Castellana (☎01/449-5234 or 98724021, ⓦwww.perubike.com); Willy-Pro, Av Javier Prado Este 3339, San Borja (☎01/346-4082); Gustavo Prado, Av Tomas Marsano 2851, Higuereta, Surco (☎01/271-0247); Marcos Vasquez, Av Comandante Espinar 320 Miraflores (☎01/446-4044). Many of the above also operate excellent tours in a number of Peru's regions, as do the very professional outfit Peru Expeditions, Av Arequipa 5241 – 504, Miraflores (☎01/4472057, Ⓕ4459683, ⓦwww.peru-expeditions.com), who have some expertise in mountain biking, but also offer tours on the coast to Pisco, Ica, Nasca as well as up to Arequipa, Cusco and sometimes the Huaraz area (with 4WD support vehicle).

In Cusco, **bicycle rental** is available from Ecomontana, C Garcilaso 265, Office 3 (☎084/223216, ⓦwww.angelfire.com/pe/ecomontana, ⒺEcomontana@hotmail.com), a professionally run company operating thirty different mountain bike tour circuits; and Loreto Tours (Sr Mateo Ochoa y Margot Salas), C del Medio 111 (☎084/228264, Ⓔloretotours@planet.com.pe, ⓦwww.loreto-tours.com). Among the excellent individual guides based in Cusco who run mountain bike tours there're Russo Covarrubias Chaucca (Ⓔrussobike@hotmail.com and Omar Zarzar (☎084/96690182, Ⓔecomontana@gmail.com).

In Arequipa, mountain bike rental is available from the reputable Campamento Base, Jerusalen 401b (☎054/424223, 206217 or 9600170, ⓦcolcatrek.com.pe, Ⓔcolcatrek@gmail.com). Around Huaraz, Mountain Bike

Adventures, Jr Lucre y Torre 530, second floor, or by post Casilla Postal 111, Huaraz (℡044/424259, ⊛www.chakinaniperu.com), offer guided bike tours and rent mountain bikes and helmets. They also offer English-speaking guides for three spectacular routes that cross the Cordillera over mountain passes at a height of around 5000m, on circuits lasting from four to seven days (for cyclists with particular interests they offer a variety of alternative routes – such as Ulta–Chacas–Chavin loop).

For further information check the relevant chapter sections or contact the Federación Peruana de Ciclismo, Estadio Nacional, Lima Centro (℡01/4336646, ⊛www.fedepeci .org, ⓔfpciclo@infomodem.com.pe; Mon–Fri 9am–1pm & 2–5pm).

Surfing

People have been **surfing** the waves off the coast of Peru for thousands of years and the traditional *caballitos de totora* from the Huanchaco (p.407) and Chiclayo (p.448) beach areas of Peru are still used by fishermen who ride the surf daily. Every year around twelve thousand surfers come to Peru whose best beaches – Chicama, Cabo Blanco, Punta Rocas – rival those of Hawaii and Brazil. Good websites to find out more about the scene include: ⊛www.perusurfguides.com, ⊛www .peruecosurf.com, ⊛www.vivamancora.com /english/surf.htm and ⊛www.wavehunters .com/peru/peru.asp.

The environment and ethical tourism

Tourism's growth in Peru over the past decade has been spectacular. It has been a boon for the economy, albeit with serious and potentially disruptive effects environ-mentally, socially, culturally and economic-ally. Machu Picchu and the Inca Trail are Peru's most significant honeypots as far as tourism goes and there are already serious problems of degradation which are demanding new management measures. Local issues have been covered in their respective chapters throughout this book. If you are at all concerned about the impact of tourism or environmental matters, contact the organizations mentioned in the text, or the ones listed below. See also "Wildlife and ecology" (p.598) and "Indigenous rights and the destruction of the rainforest" (p.610), both in the Contexts section of this book.

Contacts

Partners in Responsible Tourism (PIRT) ⓔinfo@pirt.org. An organization of individuals and travel companies promoting responsible tourism to minimize harm to the environment and local cultures. Their website features a "Traveler's Code for Traveling Responsibly".

International Centre for Responsible Tourism ⊛www.icrtourism.org. This organisation plays a major role in the responsible tourism movement through research and development with industry and governments.

Tourism Concern ℡020/7133 3330, ⊛www .tourismconcern.org.uk. Campaigns for the rights of local people to be consulted in tourism developments affecting their lives, and produces a quarterly magazine of news and articles. Also publishes the *Good Alternative Travel Guide*. Their website lists tour operators that run trips to Peru which are sensitive to the concerns of local peoples.

Football

Peru's major sport is **football** and you'll find men and boys playing it in the streets of every city, town and settlement in the country down to the remotest of jungle outposts. The big teams are **Cristal**, **Alianza** and **El U** (for Universitario) in Lima and **Ciencianco** from Cusco. The "Classic" game is between Alianza, the poor man's team from the La Victoria suburb of Lima, and El U, generally supported by the middle class. In recent years the sport has taken a European turn in the unruly and violent nature of its fans. This is particularly true of Lima where, in late 1995, the "Classic" had to be stopped because of stones thrown at the players by supporters. Known as *choligans* (a mixture of the English "hooligan" and the Peruvian "cholo", which means dark-skinned Quechua-blooded Peruvian), these unruly supporters have taken to painting their faces, attacking the opposing fans and causing major riots outside the football grounds. To get a flavour for just how popular football is in Peru try a visit to the Estadio Restaurant in Lima (p.105) which has great murals, classic team shirts and life-size models of the world's top players – well worth a visit for anyone even vaguely interested in football.

Bullfighting

In many coastal and mountain haciendas (estates), **bullfights** are often held at fiesta times. In a less organized way they happen at many of the village fiestas, too – often with the bull being left to run through the village until it's eventually caught and mutilated by one of the men. This is not just a sad sight, it can also be dangerous for you, as an unsuspecting tourist, if you happen to wander into an seemingly evacuated village. The Lima bullfights in October, in contrast, are a very serious business; even Hemingway was impressed.

Accommodation

Peru has the typical range of Latin American accommodation, from top-class international hotels at prices to compare with any Western capital down to basic rooms or shared dorms in hostals, which are unaffiliated to Hostelling International. The biggest development over the last ten years has been the rise of the mid-range option, reflecting the growth of both domestic and international tourism. Camping is frequently possible, sometimes free and perfectly acceptable in most rural parts of Peru, though there are very few formal campsites.

Accommodation denominations of *hotel*, *hostal*, *residencial*, *pensión* or *hospedaje* are almost meaningless in terms of what you'll find inside. Virtually all upmarket accommodation will call itself a *hotel* or, in the countryside regions, a *posada*. In the jungle, *tambo* **lodges** can be anything from quite luxurious to an open-sided, palm-thatched hut with space for slinging a hammock. Technically speaking, somewhere that calls itself a *pensión* or *residencial* ought to specialize in longer-term accommodation, and while they may well offer discounts for stays of a week or more, they are just as geared up for short stays.

There's no standard or widely used rating system, so, apart from the information given in this book, the only way to tell whether a place is suitable or not is to walk in and take a look around – the proprietors won't mind this, and you'll soon get used to spotting places with promise.

Hotels

The **cheaper hotels** are generally old – sometimes beautifully so, converted from colonial mansions with rooms grouped around a courtyard – and tend to be within a few blocks of a town's central plaza, general market or bus or train station. At the low end of the scale, which can be fairly basic with shared rooms and a communal bathroom, you can usually find a bed for between $5 and 10 (❷), and occasionally even less. For a few dollars more you can find a good, clean single or double room with private bath in a **mid-range hotel**, generally for somewhere between $15 and 45 (❹–❻). A little haggling is often worth a try, and if you find one room

---

Accommodation price codes

Unless otherwise indicated, accommodation in this book is coded according to the categories below, based on the average price of a double room in high season.

❶ under $5	❹ $15–25	❼ $50–70
❷ $5–10	❺ $25–40	❽ over $70
❸ $10–15	❻ $40–50	

too pricey, another, perhaps identical, can often be found for less: the phrase "Tiene un cuarto más barato?" ("Do you have a cheaper room?") is useful. Savings can invariably be made, too, by sharing rooms – many have two, three, even four or five beds. A double-bedded room ("con cama matrimonial") is usually cheaper than one with two beds ("con dos camas").

Quality hotels can be found in all the larger Peruvian resorts as well as some surprisingly offbeat ones, often with swimming pools. Out of season some are relatively inexpensive (from around $15–20 (④) per person). Always check beforehand whether the quoted price includes IGV tax (as a tourist, if you register your passport and tourist card with the hotel, they don't usually charge you this tax, which is currently nineteen percent and any service extras. There are few five-star hotels in Peru and they are nearly all in Lima, Arequipa, Cusco, Trujillo and Iquitos. Even four-star accommodation offers excellent service, some fine restaurants and very comfortable rooms with well-stocked minibars. In the mid-range options, generally three-star, the service on offer is often still good, but the food and luxury levels, particularly in the bathrooms, are significantly lower (though you can still expect towels, hot water, etc).

Many of the major hotels will request a credit card number to reserve rooms in advance; be careful with this, since if you fail to turn up on the specified date (even if due to circumstances beyond your control) they may consider this a "no-show" and charge you for the room anyhow. One point of caution – it's not advisable to pay tour or travel agents in one city for accommodation required in the next town. By all means ask agents to make reservations but do not ask them to send payments; it is always simpler and safer to do that yourself.

Youth hostels

There are over forty **youth hostels** (hostals) spread throughout Peru and located in Arequipa, Cusco, Huaraz, Ica, Iquitos, Lima, Mancora and Tarma. While not the standardized institution found in Europe, they are relatively cheap and reliable; expect to pay $5–12 (①–③) for a bed (most expensive in Lima). All hostels are theoretically open 24

hours a day and most have cheap cafeterias attached. They are always great places to meet up with other young travellers and tend to have a party scene of their own. There are, of course, any number of other unaffiliated and still inexpensive "hostals" in Peru, many of these are listed in the relevant accommodation sections of this guide. Most of the hostels that are linked to Hostelling International don't bother to check that you are a member, but if you want to be on the safe side, you can join up at the Asociación Peruana de Albergues Turísticos Juveniles, Casimiro Ulloa 328, Miraflores (℡01/2423068, ℻4448187). You can get a full list of all the country's hostels from ⓦwww.trav.com/Hostels/Peru.

Camping

Camping is possible almost everywhere in Peru, and it's rarely difficult to find space for a tent; since there are only one or two organized campsites in the whole country, it's also largely free. Moreover, it's the most satisfactory way of seeing Peru, as some of the country's most fantastic places are well off the beaten track: with a tent – or a hammock – it's possible to go all over without worrying if you'll make it to a hostel.

It's usually okay to set up camp in the fields or forest beyond the outskirts of settlements, but ask **permission** and advice from the nearest farm or house first. Apart from a few restricted areas, Peru's enormous sandy coastline is open territory, the real problem not being so much where to camp as how to get there; some of the most stunning areas are very remote. The same can be said of both the mountains and the jungle – camp anywhere, but ask first, if you can find anyone to ask.

There have been reports of tourists being attacked and robbed while camping in fairly **remote areas**. Reports of robberies, particularly along such popular routes as the Inca Trail, are not uncommon; so travelling with someone else or in groups is always a good idea. But even on your own there are a few basic **precautions** that you can take: let someone know where you intend to go; be respectful, and try to communicate with any locals you may meet or be camping near; and be careful who you make friends with en route.

Camping equipment is difficult to find in Peru and relatively expensive. One or two places sell, rent or buy second-hand gear, mainly in Cusco, Arequipa and Huaraz, and there are some reasonably good, if quite expensive, shops in Lima. It's also worth checking the notice boards in the popular travellers' hotels and bars for equipment that is no longer needed or for people wanting trekking companions. Camping Gaz butane canisters are available from most of the above places and from some *ferreterías* (hardware stores) in the major resorts. A couple of essential things you'll need when camping in Peru are a mosquito net and repellent, and some sort of water treatment system (see p.39).

Eating and drinking

As with almost every activity, the style and pattern of eating and drinking varies considerably between the three main regions of Peru. The food in each area, though it varies depending on availability of different regional ingredients, is essentially a *mestizo* creation, combining indigenous Indian cooking with four hundred years of European – mostly Spanish – influence.

Guinea pig (*cuy*) is the traditional dish most associated with Peru, and you can find it in many parts of the country, especially in the mountain regions, where it is likely to be roasted in an oven and served with chips. It's likely however, that you may encounter more burgers and pizza than guinea pig – given that fast food has spread quickly in Peru over the past two decades.

Snacks and light meals

All over Peru, but particularly in the large towns and cities, you'll find a wide variety of traditional fast foods and snacks such as *salchipapas* (fries with sliced sausage covered in various sauces), *anticuchos* (a shish kebab made from marinated lamb or beef heart) and *empanadas* (meat- or cheese-filled pies). These are all sold on street corners until late at night. Even in the villages you'll find cafés and restaurants which double as bars, staying open all day and serving anything from coffee and bread to steak and fries or even lobster. The most popular sweets in Peru are made from either *manjar blanco* (sweetened condensed milk) or fresh fruits.

In general, the **market** is always a good place to head for – you can buy food ready to eat on the spot or to take away and prepare – and the range and prices are better than in any shop. Most food prices are fixed, but the vendor may throw in an orange, a bit of garlic or some coriander leaves for good measure. Markets are the best places to stock up for a trek, for a picnic, or if you just want to eat cheaply. Smoked meat, which can be sliced up and used like salami, is normally a good buy.

Restaurants

All larger towns in Peru have a fair choice of **restaurants**, most of which offer a varied menu. Among them there's usually a few *chifa* (**Chinese**) places, and nowadays a fair number of **vegetarian** restaurants too. Most establishments in the larger towns stay open seven days a week from around 11am until 11pm, though in smaller settlements they may close one day a week, usually Sunday. Often they will offer a **set menu**, from morning through to lunchtime and, often, another in the evening. Ranging in price from $1.5 to $5, these most commonly consist of three or four courses: soup or other starter, a main dish (usually hot and with rice or salad), a small sweet or fruit-based third plate, plus tea or coffee to follow. Every

Tipping

In budget or average restaurants tipping is normal, though not obligatory and you should rarely expect to give more than about ten percent. In fancier places you may well find a **service charge** of at least ten percent as well as a **tax** of nineteen percent (IGV) added to the bill. In restaurants and peñas where there's live music or performances a **cover charge** is generally also applied and can be as high as $5 a head. Even without a performance, additional cover charges of around $1 are sometimes levied in the flashier restaurants in major town centres.

town, too, seems now to have at least one restaurant that specializes in *pollos a la brasa* – spit-roasted chickens.

Along the coast, not surprisingly, **seafood** is the speciality. The Humboldt Current keeps the Pacific Ocean off Peru extremely rich in plankton and other microscopic life forms, which attract a wide variety of fish. **Ceviche** is the classic Peruvian seafood dish and has been eaten by locals for over two thousand years. It consists of fish, shrimp, scallops or squid, or a mixture of all four, marinated in lime juice and chilli peppers, then served "raw" with corn, sweet potato and onions. *Ceviche de lenguado* (soul fish) and *ceviche de corvina* (sea bass) are among the most common, but there are plenty of other fish and a wide range of seafoods utilized and on most menus. You can find it, along with fried fish and fish soups, in most restaurants along the coast for around $2. **Escabeche** is another tasty fish-based appetizer, this time incorporating peppers and finely chopped onions. The coast is also an excellent place for eating scallops – known here as *conchitas* – which grow particularly well close to the Peruvian shoreline. *Conchitas negras* (black scallops) are a delicacy in the northern tip of Peru. Excellent **salads** are also widely available, such as *huevos a la rusa* (egg salad), *palta rellena* (stuffed avocado), or a straight tomato salad, while *papas a la l luancaina* (a cold appetizer of potatoes covered in a spicy light cheese sauce) is great too.

Mountain food is more basic – a staple of potatoes and rice with the meat stretched as far as it will go. *Lomo saltado*, or diced prime beef sautéed with onions and peppers, is served anywhere at any time, accompanied by rice and a few French fries. A delicious snack from street vendors and cafés is *papa*

rellena, a potato stuffed with vegetables and fried. **Trout** is also widely available, as are cheese, ham and egg sandwiches. *Chicha*, a **corn beer** drunk throughout the *sierra* region and on the coast in rural areas, is very cheap with a pleasantly tangy taste. Another Peruvian speciality is the *Pachamanca*, a roast prepared mainly in the mountains but also on the coast by digging a large hole, filling it with stones and lighting a fire over them, then using the hot stones to cook a wide variety of tasty meats and vegetables.

In the **jungle**, the food is different to the rest of the country. **Bananas** and **plantains** figure highly, along with *yuca* (a manioc rather like a yam), rice and plenty of fish. There is **meat** as well, mostly chicken supplemented occasionally by **game** – deer, wild pig or even monkey. Every settlement big enough to get on the map has its own bar or café, but in remote areas it's a matter of eating what's available and drinking coffee or bottled drinks if you don't relish the home-made *masato* (cassava beer).

Drinking

Beer, wines and spirits are served in almost every bar, café or restaurant at any time, but there is a deposit on taking beer bottles out (canned beer is one of the worst inventions to hit Peru this century – some of the finest beaches are littered with empty cans).

Most **Peruvian beer** – except for *cerveza malta* (black malt beer) – is bottled almost exclusively brewed to five percent alcohol content, and extremely good. Traditional Peruvian beers include Cristal, Pilsen and Cusqueña (the latter, originating from Cusco, is generally preferred, and has even reached some UK supermarkets in recent years). In Trujillo on the north coast, they drink Trujillana beer, again quite similar; and in

Arequipa they tend to drink Arequipeña beer. There are several new lager beers now on the market, including the Brazilian brand Brahma. **Soft drinks** range from mineral water, through the ubiquitous Coca Cola and Fanta, to home-produced novelties like the gold-coloured Inka Cola, with rather a home-made taste, and the very sweet Cola Inglesa. **Fruit juices** (*jugos*), most commonly papaya or orange, are delicious and prepared fresh in most places (best selection and cheapest prices generally available in a town's main market), and you can get **coffee** and a wide variety of herb and leaf **teas** almost anywhere. Surprisingly, for a good coffee-growing country, the coffee in cafés outside of Lima, Cusco and Arequipa leaves much to be desired, commonly prepared from either *café pasado* (previously passed or percolated coffee mixed with hot water to serve) or simple powdered Nescafé. Increasingly it's possible to find great coffee in larger towns where certain cafés prepare good fresh espresso, cappuccino or filtered coffee. Starbucks (complete with wi-fi) has recently arrived in Lima.

Peru has been producing **wine** (*vino*) for over four hundred years, but with one or two exceptions it is not that good. Among the better ones are Vista Alegre (the Tipo Familiar label is generally OK) – not entirely reliable but only around $2 a bottle – and, much better, Tabernero or Tacama Gran Vino Reserva (white or red|) from about $10 or $15 a bottle. A good Argentinian or Chilean wine will cost from $10 upwards.

As for **spirits**, Peru's main claim to fame is **pisco**. This is a white-grape brandy with a unique, powerful and very palatable flavour – the closest equivalent elsewhere is probably tequila. Almost anything else is available as an import – Scotch whisky is cheaper here than in the UK – but beware of the really cheap whisky imitations or blends bottled outside of Scotland which can remove the roof of your mouth with ease. The jungle regions produce a sugar-cane rum, *cashassa* (basically the Peruvian equivalent of Brazilian cachaça), also called *aguardiente*, which has a distinctive taste and is occasionally mixed with different herbs, some medicinal. Whilst it goes down easily, it's incredibly strong stuff and is sure to leave you with a hangover the next morning if you drink too much.

Communications

Communictions in Peru have improved dramatically with the widespread availability of internet cafés. The phone service, too, has improved in the last seven years since it was taken over by a Spanish company. Postal services are slow but quite acceptable for normal letters and postcards.

The postal service

The Peruvian postal service – branded as Serpost – is reasonably efficient, if slightly irregular and a little expensive. Letters from Europe and the US generally take around one or two weeks – occasionally less – while outbound letters to Europe or the US seem to take between ten days and three weeks. Stamps for postcards and airmail letters to the UK, the US and to Australia and New Zealand all cost around $2.

Be aware that **parcels** take about one month to arrive and are particularly vulnerable to being opened en route – in either direction – and expensive souvenirs can't be sure of leaving the building where you mail them. Likewise, Peruvian postal workers are liable to "check" incoming parcels which contain cassettes or interesting foods. Never send money through the Peruvian post!

Poste restante

Although rapidly lapsing into obsolescence (because of the excellent internet alternatives) you can still have physical mail sent to you **poste restante** care of any main post office (Correo Central), and, on the whole, the system tends to work quite smoothly. Have letters addressed: full name (last name in capitals), Poste Restante, Lista de Correos, Correo Central, city or town, Peru. To pick up mail you'll need your passport, and you may have to get the files for the initials of all your names (including Ms, Mr, etc) checked. Rather quirkily, letters are sometimes filed separately by sex, too – in which case it's worth getting both piles checked. Some post offices let you look through the pile, others won't let you anywhere near the letters until they've found one that fits your name exactly. The **South American Explorers' Club** (see p.41) offers members a postal address service.

Fixed and mobile telephones

It's easy to make international calls from just about any town in the country. In recent years the telephone system has improved dramatically, partly due to being taken over by a Spanish telephone company and partly because of modernization and an increasing use of satellites. Mobiles are expensive to use in Peru, but almost everyone there seems to have one these days. Using your own mobile (eg brought from the UK, Australia or North America) almost always works out to be the most expensive form of telephone communication, but it may be worth checking with your particular provider before departure for Peru. It is certainly cheaper to buy a local mobile phone and SIM card (available in shops everywhere from around $25) and use this for in-Peru

Dialling codes and useful numbers

Useful telephone numbers

Directory enquiries ☏103 Operator ☏100
Emergency services ☏105 International operator ☏108

Calling home from abroad

Note that the initial zero is omitted from the area code when dialling the UK, Ireland, Australia and New Zealand from abroad.
US and Canada international access code + 1 + area code.
Australia international access code + 61 + area code.
New Zealand international access code + 64 + area code.
UK international access code + 44 + area code.
Republic of Ireland international access code + 353 + area code.
South Africa international access code + 27 + area code.

To phone Peru from abroad

Dial the international access code + 51 (country code for Peru) + area code in Peru (minus intitial zero; see below) + number.

Peruvian town and city codes

Amazonas 41	La Libertad 44
Ancash 43	Lambayeque 74
Apurimac 83	Loreto 65
Arequipa 54	Madre de Dios 82
Ayacucho 66	Moquegua 53
Cajamarca 76	Pasco 63
Cusco 84	Piura 73
Huancavelica 67	Puno 51
Huánuco 62	San Martín 42
Ica 56	Tacna 52
Junin 64	Tumbes 72
Lima and Callao 01	Ucayali 61

calls. Probably the most popular mobile company is Claró.

In April 2008, Telefónica Peru changed mobile numbers across the country, causing considerable ongoing confusion. Essentially, for everywhere except Lima and Callao, the city or area code number (less the zero at the start) has been inserted between the initial number "9" and the rest of the number. Consequently, the previous Cusco mobile number 9523475 has now become 984523475. For Lima and Callao you simply add an extra "9" before the existing initial number (usually a "9", but sometimes an "8"); consequently, the old Lima mobile number 90061787 becomes 990061787.

Phone cards (eg **Telefónica** Tarjeta 147) are the cheapest way to communciate by phone either domestically or internationally; indeed, international calls from a fixed phone often work out cheaper than ones to Peruvian mobiles or between Peruvian cities. Each card has directions for use (in Spanish) on the reverse and most are based on a scratch-card numeral basis. You can buy phone cards from corner shops, *farmacias* or on the street from cigarette stalls in the centres of most towns and cities. All Peruvian towns have at least one centrally located **Telefónica del Peru** or **Locutorio Telefónico** office, which offers an operator service; give the receptionist your destination number and they will allocate you to a numbered phone booth when your call is put through (you pay afterwards); or, just dial direct from the booth. These offices also have phones taking cards (see p.118). There are also street **telephone booths** in most towns and cities, some of which are coin operated, though these days they mostly take phone cards.

If you need to contact the **international operator**, dial ☎108. **Collect calls** are known either simply as *collect* or *al cobro revertido* and are fairly straightforward. Calls are cheaper at night. Most shops, restaurants or corner shops in Peru have a phone available for public use, which you can use for calls within Peru only.

The internet

Peru has good **internet** connections, with cyber cafés and internet cabins in the most unlikely of small towns, breaking down barriers of distance more effectively than the telephone ever did. Lima and Cusco have abundant internet facilities, closely followed by Arequipa, Huaraz, Puno, Iquitos and Trujillo; beyond that it gets a little patchy, but the odd public access office or café does exist and many hotels now offer access too. Most seem to have reasonably fast DSL or ADSL connections with Explorer, Netscape and Hotmail readily available. The general rate is 50¢ to $1 an hour, though thirty- and fifteen-minute options are often available.

The media

There are many poor-quality newspapers and magazines available on the streets of Lima and throughout the rest of Peru. Many of the newspapers stick mainly to sex and sport, while magazines tend to focus on terror, violence and the frequent deaths caused by major traffic accidents. Meanwhile, many get their news and information from television and radio, where you also have to wade through the panoply of entertainment-orientated options.

Newspapers and magazines

The two most established (and establish-ment) **daily newspapers** are *El Comercio* and *Expreso*, the latter having traditionally devoted vast amounts of space to anti-Communist propaganda. *El Comercio* (ⓦ www.elcomercio.com.pe) is much more balanced but still tends to toe the political party of the day's line. *El Comercio's* daily *Seccion C* also has the most comprehensive cultural listings of any paper – good for just about everything going on in Lima. In addition, there's the sensationalist tabloid *La Republica* (ⓦ www.larepublica.com.pe), which takes a middle-of-the-road to liberal approach to politics; and *Diario Ojo*, which provides interesting tabloid reading. One of the better weekly **magazines** is the fairly liberal *Caretas*, generally offering mildly critical support to whichever government happens to be in power. There's one environmental and travel magazine – *Rumbos* – which publishes articles in both Spanish and English and has excellent photographic features.

For serious, in-depth coverage of Peruvian and Latin American political and business news, the *Lima Post* is available online (ⓦ www.limapost.com).

International newspapers are fairly hard to come by; your best bet for **English papers** is to go to the British Embassy in Lima (see p.118), which has a selection of one- to two-week-old papers, such as *The Times* and *Independent*, for reference only. **US papers** are easier to find; the bookstalls around Plaza San Martin in Lima Centro and those along Avenida Larco and Diagonal in Miraflores sell the *Miami Herald*, the *Herald Tribune*, and *Newsweek* and *Time* magazines, but even these are likely to be four or five days old. If you're not moving around too much, consider having *The Guardian Weekly*, which has comprehensive international coverage, sent to you poste restante.

Television and radio

Peruvians watch a lot of **television** – mostly soccer and soap operas, though TV is also a main source of news. Many programmes come from Mexico, Brazil and the US (*The Flintstones* and *Bewitched* are perennial favourites), with occasional eccentric selec-tions from elsewhere and a growing presence of manga-style cartoons. There are nine main terrestrial channels, of which channels 7 and 13 show marginally better-quality programmes.

Cable and **satellite channels** are increas-ingly forming an important part of Peru's media. Partly due to the fact that it can be received in even the remotest of settlements and partly because it is beyond the control of any government or other censorship, satellite TV appears set to dominate the media scene and the worldview of the nation's youth.

If you have a **radio** you can pick up the BBC World Service at most hours of the day – frequencies shift around on the 19m, 25m and 49m short-wave bands. The Voice of America is also constantly available on short wave. The radio station Sol Armonia is dedicated to classical music on FM 89. Also, the RPP (Radio Programmes del Peru) on FM 89.7 has 24-hour news bulletins.

Alternatively, you can tune in to **Peruvian stations**, nearly all of which play music and are crammed with adverts. International pop, salsa and other Latin pop can be picked up most times of the day and night all along the FM wave band, while tradi-tional Peruvian and Andean folk music can usually be found all over the AM dial. Radio Miraflores (96 FM) is one of the best, playing mainly disco and new US/British rock, though also with a good jazz programme on Sunday evenings and an excellent news summary every morning from 7 to 9am.

Crime and personal safety

The biggest problem for travellers in Peru is, without a doubt, thieves, for which the country has one of the worst reputations in South America. Whilst pickpockets are remarkably ingenious in Peru, this country no longer deserves such a poor reputation when compared with Venezuela, Colombia and even Ecuador or Brazil. As far as violent attacks go, you're probably safer in Peru than in New York, Sydney or London; nevertheless, muggings do happen in certain parts of Lima (eg in the Centro main shopping areas and also in the parks of Miraflores), Cusco, Arequipa and to a lesser extent Trujillo. And as for terrorism – as the South American Explorers' Club once described it – "the visitor, when considering his safety, would be better off concentrating on how to avoid being run over in the crazed Lima traffic".

Theft

While the overall situation has improved, there are still real dangers of robbery and **pickpocketing**, although you don't need to be in a permanent state of paranoia and constant watchfulness in busy public situations, common sense and general alertness are still recommended. The South American Explorers' Club (see pp.41) can give you the lowdown on the latest thieving practices, some of which have developed over the years into quite elaborate and skilful techniques.

Generally speaking, **thieves** (*ladrones*) work in teams of often smartly dressed young men and women, in crowded markets, bus depots and train stations, targeting anyone who looks like they've got money. One of them will distract your attention (an old woman falling over in front of you or someone splattering an ice cream down your jacket) while another picks your pocket, cuts open your bag with a razor or simply runs off with it. Peruvians and tourists alike have even had earrings ripped out on the street. Bank **ATMs** are a target for muggers in cities, particularly after dark, so visit them with a friend or two during daylight hours or make sure there's a policeman within visual contact. **Armed mugging** is rare but does happen in Lima, and it's best not to resist. The horrific practice of "strangle mugging" has been a bit of a problem in Cusco and Arequipa, usually involving night attacks when the perpetrator tries to strangle the victim into unconsciousness. Again, be careful not to walk down badly lit streets alone in the early hours. **Theft from cars** and even more so, theft of car parts, is rife, particularly in Lima. Also, in some of the more popular hotels in the large cities, especially Lima, bandits masquerading as policemen break into rooms and steal the guests' most valuable possessions while holding the hotel staff at gunpoint. Objects left on restaurant floors in busy parts of town, or in unlocked hotel rooms, are obviously liable to take a walk.

You'd need to spend the whole time visibly guarding your luggage to be sure of keeping hold of it; even then, though, a determined team of thieves will stand a chance. However, a few simple **precautions** can make life a lot easier. The most important is to keep your ticket, passport (and tourist card), money and travellers' cheques on your person at all times (under your pillow while sleeping and on your person when washing in communal hotel bathrooms). **Money belts** are a good idea for travellers' cheques and tickets, or a holder for your passport and money can be hung either under a shirt or from a belt under trousers or skirts. A **false pocket**, secured by safety pins to the inside of trousers, skirts or shirts also makes it harder for thieves or muggers to find your cash reserve (and is easy to transfer between items of clothing). Some people go as far as lining their bags with chicken wire (called *maya* in Peru) to make them knife-proof, and wrapping wire around camera straps for the same reason (putting their necks in danger to save their cameras).

The only certain course is to **insure** your gear and cash before you go (see p.36). Take refundable travellers' cheques, register your passport at your embassy in Lima on arrival (this doesn't take long and can save days should you lose it) and keep your eyes open at all times. If you do get ripped off, report it to the **tourist police** in larger towns (see p.60), or the local police in more remote places, and ask them for a certified *denuncia* – this can take a couple of days. Many insurance companies will require a copy of the police *denuncia* in order to reimburse you, though some only require proof of your whereabouts at the time of the incident (for example a hotel bill or a tour company letter or report). Check with your insurance company before leaving for Peru as to what their requirements are.

Cities are most dangerous in the early hours of the morning and at bus or train stations where there's lots of anonymous activity. In rural areas robberies tend to be linked to the most popular towns (again, be most careful at the bus depot) and treks (the Inca Trail for instance). Beyond that, rural areas generally are, and normally feel, safe. If you're camping near a remote community, though, it's a good idea to ask permission and make friendly contact with some of the locals; and letting them know what you are up to will usually dissolve any local paranoia about tombrobbers or kidnappers.

Terrorism

You can get up-to-date information on the situation in each region from the South American Explorers' Club (see p.41), Peruvian embassies abroad (see p.33) or your embassy in Lima (see p.117). Essentially, though, **terrorism** is not the problem it was during the 1980s and 1990s when the two main **terrorist groups** active in Peru were the Sendero Luminoso (the Shining Path) and Tupac Amaru (MRTA).

The **Sendero Luminoso** sprang from rural Quechua and educated middle-class dissidents originally operating mainly in the central highlands and Lima. They had a reputation in the past for ruthless and violent tactics, sweeping away all left-wing and popular resistance to their aims and methods by the rule of the gun. When their leader Guzman was captured in 1992, the movement began to fade fast, and with the capture of their number two, Feliciano, in 1999, it appears that their activities are limited almost exclusively to narco-terrorism (cocaine producing and smuggling) in the **Alto Huallaga** and Apurimac-Ene valleys. The most dangerous area – basically the region and road between Tingo Maria and Tarapoto – should still be avoided at all costs. It's often difficult to distinguish between drug trafficking and terrorism in certain places, and much of the coca-growing area of the eastern Andes and western Amazon is beyond the law. Keep to the beaten track, keep yourself well informed, travel in the daytime, and you should be safe. For more background on this subject, see Contexts, p.616.

The police

Most of your contact with the **police** will, with any luck, be at frontiers and controls. Depending on your personal appearance and the prevailing political climate, the police at these posts (Guardia Nacional and Aduanas) may want to search your luggage. This happens rarely, but when it does, it can be very thorough. Occasionally, you may have to get off buses and register documents at the police controls which regulate the traffic of goods and people from one *departamento* of Peru to another. The controls are usually situated on the outskirts of large towns on the main roads, but you sometimes come across a control in the middle of nowhere. Always stop, and be scrupulously polite – even if it seems that they're trying to make things difficult for you.

In general the police rarely bother travellers but there are certain sore points. The possession of (let alone trafficking in) either soft or hard **drugs** (basically marijuana or cocaine) is considered an extremely serious offence in Peru – usually leading to at least a ten-year jail sentence. There are many foreigners languishing in Peruvian jails after being charged with possession, some of whom have been waiting two years for a trial – there is no bail for serious charges.

Drugs aside, the police tend to follow the media in suspecting all foreigners of being **political subversives** and even gun-runners or terrorists; it's more than a little unwise to carry any Maoist or radical litera-ture. If you find yourself in a tight spot, don't make a statement before seeing someone from your embassy, and don't say anything without the services of a reliable translator. It's not unusual to be given the opportunity to pay a **bribe** to the police (or any other official for that matter), even if you've done nothing wrong. You'll have to weigh up this situation as it arises – but remember, in South America bribery is seen as an age-old custom, very much part of the culture rather than a nasty form of corruption, and it can work to the advantage of both parties, however irritating it might seem. It's also worth noting that all police are **armed** with either a revolver or a submachine gun and will shoot at anyone who runs.

The tourist police

It's often quite hard to spot the difference between tourist police and the normal police. Both are wings of the Guardia Civil, though the tourist police sometimes wear white hats rather than the standard green. Increasingly, the tourist police have taken on the functions of informing and assisting tourists (eg in preparing a robbery report or *denuncia*) in city centres. The main Lima numbers for Tourist Police are: ☎01/428-5887 (North Lima and Northern provinces) or ☎01/460-4525 (South Lima and Southern provinces). Peru's **headquarters** for the tourist police is the Centro Policial de Servicio al Turista in Lima at Jr Tambo Belen 106, Pachitea, Lima ☎01/4242053, ✉dirpolture@hotmail.com.). In the regions you can find them through the city listings in the relevant chapter throughout the guide.

If you're unlucky enough to have anything stolen, your first port of call should be the **tourist police** (*policía de turismo*), from whom you should get a written report. Bear in mind that the police in popular tourist spots, such as Cusco, have become much stricter about investigating reported thefts, after a spate of false claims by dishonest tourists. This means that genuine victims may be grilled more severely than expected, and the police may even come and search your hotel room for the "stolen" items.

If you feel you've been ripped off or are unhappy about your treatment by a tour agent, hotel, restaurant, transport company, customs, immigration or even the police, you can call the 24-hour **Tourist Protection Service** hotline (Servicio de Protección al Turista, also known as i-peru, an arm of INDECOPI and PromPeru; ⊛www.peru.info /s_ftoiperu.asp); see below for numbers to call. Staff are trained to handle complaints in English and Spanish. If an immediate solution is not possible, the service claims to follow up disputes by filing a formal complaint with the relevant authorities.

Tourist Protection Service

Main offices
Lima

At the Airport, Sala Principal (7 days, 24hr) ✉iperu@prompreu.gob.pe.
Jorge basadre 610, San Isidro ☎01/4211627 (Mon–Fri 9am–6pm).
Malecon de La Reserva and Av Larco, Miraflores ☎01/4459400 (Mon–Sat 9am–6pm).
Municipal Tourist Information Office, Los Escribanos 145, Plaz de Armas, Lima ☎01/3151542 (Mon–Sat 9am–6pm).

Hotline numbers
National toll-free 24hr ☎01/5748000
Arequipa ☎054/221228
Ayacucho ☎066/818305
Cusco ☎/☎084/234498
Iquitos ☎065/2361443409
Lima ☎01/4211627
Puno ☎051/365088
Trujillo ☎044/294561

Living and/or working abroad

Your only real chance of earning money in Peru is teaching English in Lima, or, with luck, in Arequipa or Cusco. Given the state of the economy there's little prospect in other fields, though in the more remote parts of the country it may sometimes be possible to find board and lodging in return for a little building work or general labour.

There is a certain amount of bureaucracy involved if you want to work (or live) officially in Peru. For biology, geography or environmental science graduates there's a chance of free board and lodging and maybe a small salary if you're willing to work very hard for at least three months as a **tour guide in a jungle lodge**, under the Resident Naturalist schemes.

Several lodges along the Río Tambopata offer such schemes and other research opportunities. For more details, write to the lodges directly; for independent advice contact the Tambopata Reserve Society, PO Box 33153, London, NW3 4DR, UK. Arrangements need to be made at least six months in advance. In the same region, the Picaflor Lodge on the Río Tambopata, also has a volunteer programme (see p.519). Based in Arequipa, the relatively new Traveller Not Tourist organisation (Ⓦwww.travellernottourist.com) is not-for-profit and helps volunteers work directly to support children in poverty.

Teaching English

There are two options: find work before you go, or just wing it and see what you come up with while you're out there, particularly if you already have a degree and/or teaching experience. **Teaching English** – often abbreviated as ELT (English Language Teaching) or TEFL (Teaching English as a Foreign Language) – is the way many people finance their way around the greater part of the world; you can get a CELTA (Certificate in English Language Teaching to Adults) qualification before you leave home or even while you're abroad. Strictly speaking, you don't need a degree to do the course, but you'll certainly find it easier to get a job with the degree/certificate combination. Certified by the RSA, the course is very demanding and costs about £1000 for the month's full-time tuition; you'll be thrown in at the deep end and expected to teach right away. The British Council's website (Ⓦwww.british council.org/work/jobs.htm) has a list of English-teaching vacancies. Another pre-planning strategy for working abroad, whether teaching English or otherwise, is to get hold of *Overseas Jobs Express* (☎01273/699611, Ⓦwww.overseasjobs.com).

Study and work programs

AFS Intercultural Programs US ☎1-800/AFS-INFO, Canada ☎1-800/361-7248 or 514-288-3282, UK ☎0113/242 6136, Australia ☎1300/131 736 or ☎02/9215 0077, NZ ☎0800/600 300 or 04/494 6020, SA ☎11/447 2673, international enquiries ☎1-212-807-8686, Ⓦwww.afs.org. Intercultural exchange organization with programs in over fifty countries.
American Institute for Foreign Study US ☎1-866/906-2437, Ⓦwww.aifs.com. Language study and cultural immersion, as well as au pair and Camp America programs.
BUNAC US ☎1-800/GO-BUNAC, UK ☎020/7251 3472, Republic of Ireland ☎1/477 3027, Ⓦwww.bunac.org. Organizes working holidays in a range of destinations for students.
BTCV (British Trust for Conservation Volunteers) ☎01302/388 888, Ⓦwww.btcv.org.uk. One of the largest environmental charities in Britain, with a programme of national and international working holidays (as a paying volunteer).
Camp America UK ☎020/7581 7373, Canada ☎902/ 422 1455, Australia ☎03/9826 0111, NZ ☎9416 5337, South Africa ☎021/419 5740, Ⓦwww.campamerica.co.uk. Organizes cultural exchange programs all over the world.
Council on International Educational Exchange (CIEE) US ☎1-800/40-STUDY or ☎1-

207/533-7600, UK ☎020/8939 9057, ⓦwww
.ciee.org. Leading NGO offering study programs and
volunteer projects around the world.
Earthwatch Institute US ☎1-800/776-0188 or
978-461/0081, UK ☎01865/318 838, Australia

☎03/9682 6828, ⓦwww.earthwatch.org.
Scientific expedition project that spans over fifty
countries with environmental and archaeological
ventures worldwide.

Travellers with disabilities

Peru is not well set up in terms of access infrastructure for welcoming travellers
with disabilities (even the best buses have mostly ordinary steps), but nevertheless, in the moment many Peruvians will support and help. Airlines have facilities
and will assist in most of Peru's airports. Further information may be obtained
from the South American Explorers' Club (see p.41). Lima is the only city where
disabled access has been thought about for some of the upmarket hotels and
restaurants; elsewhere it's really a free-for-all.

While there are still few hotels or resorts
which are well designed to ensure access
for all, Peru has, since 1998, been developing accessible tourism, starting with a trial
tour held in April of that year: Lima, the
Paracas National Reserve, the city of Cusco
and the Machu Picchu ruins were all successfully visited. Moreover, the hotel chain
Posadas del Inca (ⓦwww.sonesta.com)
cater well for disabilities and have places in
Lima, Cusco, Puno and the Sacred Valley;
other pioneers in Peru include the travel

agency Apumayo Expediciones (ⓦwww
.apumayo.com), Rainforest Expeditions
(ⓦwww.perunature.com) and InkaNatura
Travel (ⓦwww.inkanatura.com). Accessible
Journeys (ⓦwww.disabilitytravel.com),
meanwhile, offer tours specifically designed
for travellers with physical disabilities, including a ten-day trip to Lima, Paracas, Cusco,
the Sacred Valley and Machu Picchu.
Additional information on access for travellers in Peru with disabilities can be found at
ⓦwww.disabilityworld.org.

Senior travellers

Senior travellers in reasonable health should have no problem in Peru. Anyone
taking medication should obviously bring enough supplies for the duration of the
trip, though most drugs are available over the counter in Lima and other cities.
The altitude is likely to be the most serious concern, so careful reading of the
section on altitude sickness (see p.242) becomes even more crucial. So does
taking great care with what food you eat (see p.52).

As far as accommodation for seniors goes,
most middle- to top-range hotels are clean
and comfortable; it's mostly a matter of
clearly asking for what you need when

booking or on arrival at the hotel. This is
particularly true if you have special requirements such as a ground-floor room.

Travelling with children

South Americans hold the family unit in high regard and children are central to this, but outlined below are some pointers to help prepare for a family visit to Peru.

Most types of nappies, creams, wetwipes and childrens' medication can be bought easily in main chemists and larger supermarkets in Lima, Arequipa and Cusco, but outside of these places it's wise to arrive ready and prepared for all eventualities. Consult your doctor before leaving home regarding **health matters**. Sunscreen is an important consideration, as are sun-hats (cheap and readily available in Peru) and even a parasol for the really small. Conversely, it can get cold at night in the Andes, so take plenty of warm clothing. In the mountains, the **altitude** doesn't seem to cause children as many problems as it does their elders, but they shouldn't walk too strenuously above 2000m without full acclimatization. In Lima, where the water is just about good enough to clean your teeth but not to drink, the issues for local children are mainly bronchial or asthmatic, with humid weather and high pollution levels causing many long-lasting chest ailments. This shouldn't be a problem for any visiting children unless they already have difficulties. The major risk around the regions is a bad stomach and **diarrhoea** from water or food. The best way to avoid and treat this is outlined on p.38; the only difference where children are concerned, particularly those under 10, is that you should be more ready to act sooner, particularly with rehydration salts. In the jungle, the same precautions for adults apply to children (see p.486).

The **food and drink** in Peru is varied enough to appeal to most kids. Pizzas are available almost everywhere, as are good fish, red meats, fried chicken, French fries, corn-on-the-cob and nutritious soups, and vitamin supplements are always a good idea. There's also a wide range of **soft drinks**, from the ubiquitous Coca Cola and Sprite to Inka Cola (now owned by Coca Cola). Some recognizable commercial **baby food** (and nappy brands) is available in all large supermarkets. **Restaurants** in Peru cater well to children and some offer smaller, cheaper portions; if they don't publicize it, it's worth asking.

Like restaurants, **hotels** are used to handling kids. They will sometimes offer discounts, especially if children share rooms or beds. The lower- to mid-range options are the most flexible in this regard, but even the expensive ones can be helpful. Many, hostels included, have collective rooms, large enough for families to share, at reasonable rates.

Prices can often be cheaper for children. Tours to attractions can occasionally be negotiated on a family-rate basis and entry to sites is often half-price or less (and always free for infants). Children under 10 generally get half-fare on local (but not inter-regional) buses, while trains and boats generally charge full fare if a seat is required. Infants who don't need a seat often travel free on all transport except planes, when you pay around ten percent of the fare.

Travelling around the country is perhaps the most difficult activity. Bus and train journeys are generally long (twelve hours or more). Crossing international borders is a potential hassle; although Peru officially accepts children under 16 on their parents' **passports**, it is a good idea for them to have their own to minimize problems. For more information, contact Travel with Your Children which publishes a regular newsletter, *Family Travel Times* (@www.familytraveltimes.com), as well as a series of books on travel with children.

Sex and gender issues

So many limitations are imposed on women's freedom to travel together or alone that any advice or warning seems merely to reinforce the situation. However, machismo is well ingrained in the Peruvian male mentality, particularly in the towns, and female foreigners are almost universally seen as liberated and therefore sexually available.

Harassment and safety

On the whole, the situations female travellers will encounter are more annoying than dangerous, with frequent comments such as *que guapa* ("how pretty"), intrusive and prolonged stares, plus whistling and hissing in the **cities**. Worse still are the occasional rude comments and groping, particularly in crowded situations such as on buses or trains. Blonde and fair-skinned women are likely to suffer much more of this behaviour than darker, Latin-looking women. Mostly these are situations you'd deal with routinely at home – as Limeña women do here in the capital – but they can, understandably and rightly, seem threatening without a clear understanding of Peruvian Spanish and slang. To avoid getting caught up in something you can't control, any provocation is best ignored. In a public situation, however, any real harassment is often best dealt with by loudly drawing attention to the miscreant.

In the predominantly Indian, **remote areas** there is less of an overt problem, though surprisingly this is where physical assaults are more likely to take place. They are not common, however – you're probably safer hiking in the Andes than walking at night in most British or North American inner cities. Two obvious, but enduring, pieces of advice are to travel with friends (being on your own makes you most vulnerable), and if you're camping, it's a good idea to get to know the locals, which can give a kind of acceptance and insurance, and it may even lead to the offer of a room – Peruvians, particularly those in rural areas, can be incredibly kind and hospitable. It's also sensible to check with the South American Explorers' Club (see p.41), particularly in Cusco, for information on the latest trouble spots.

The feminist movement

Though a growing force, **feminism** is still relatively new to Peru, and essentially urban. However, there are two major **feminist groups**: Flora Tristan, which is primarily a political organization running courses and campaigns, but a good point of contact for feminist networks:

Flora Tristan Parque Hernan Velarde 42, Lima 1
℡01/4331457, ✆postmast@flora.org.pe, ⊛www
.flora.org.pe.

Gay and lesbian travellers

Homosexuality is pretty much kept underground in what is still a very macho society, though in recent years Lima has seen a liberating advance and transvestites can walk the streets in relative freedom from abuse. However, there is little or no organized gay life. **The Peruvian Homosexual and Lesbian Movement** can be contacted at C Mariscal Miller 828, in Jesus Maria ℡01/4335519. There are few specialist gay organizations, hotel facilities, restaurants or even clubs. Where they exist they are listed in the relevant sections of the Guide. Further information can be accessed on ⊛gaylimape.tripod.com, which advises gay and lesbian travellers in Peru and lists some of the gay-friendly clubs, restaurants and accommodation. It also has a useful links page. A good website for gay information on accommodation, beaches, clubs and restaurants, plus other web links can be found at ⊛www.lima.queercity.info.

Contacts for gay and lesbian travellers

In Peru

⊛www.deambiente.com
⊛www.peruesgay.com
⊛www.gayperu.com (with chat area)

Opening hours, public holidays and festivals

Public holidays, Carnival and local fiestas are all big events in Peru, celebrated with an openness and gusto that gives them enormous appeal for visitors. The main national holidays take place over Easter, Christmas and during the month of October, in that order of importance. Be aware, though, that during public holidays, Carnival and even the many local fiestas everything shuts down: banks, post offices, information offices, tourist sites and museums. It is worth planning a little in advance to make sure that you don't get caught out.

Opening hours

Most **shops** and **services** in Peru open Monday to Saturday 9am–5pm or 6pm. Many are open on Sunday as well, if for more limited hours. Peru's more important **ancient sites** and ruins usually have opening hours that coincide with daylight – from around 7am until 5pm or 6pm daily. Smaller sites are rarely fenced off, and are nearly always accessible 24 hours a day. For larger sites, you normally pay a small admission fee to the local guardian – who may then walk around with you, pointing out features of interest. Only Machu Picchu charges more than a few dollars' entrance fee – this is one site where you may find it worth presenting an ISIC or FIYTO student card (which generally gets you in for half-price).

Of Peru's **museums**, some belong to the state, others to institutions, and a few to individuals. Most charge a small admission fee and are open Monday to Saturday 9am– noon and 3–6pm.

Churches open in the mornings for Mass (usually around 6am), after which the smaller ones close. Those which are most interesting to tourists, however, tend to stay open all day, while others open again in the afternoon from 3–6pm. Very occasionally there's an admission charge to churches, and more regularly to monasteries (*monasterios*). Try to be aware of the strength of **religious belief** in Peru, particularly in the Andes, where churches have a rather heavy, sad atmosphere. You can enter and quietly look around all churches, but in the Andes especially you should refrain from taking photographs.

Fiestas, festivals and public holidays

In addition to the major regional and national celebrations, nearly every community has its own saint or patron figure to worship at town or **village fiestas**. These celebrations often mean a great deal to local people, and can be much more fun to visit than the larger countrywide activities. Processions, music, dancing in costumes and eating and drinking form the core activities of these parties. In some cases the villagers will enact symbolic dramas with Indians dressed up as Spanish colonists, wearing hideous blue-eyed masks with long hairy beards. In the hills around towns like Huaraz and Cusco, especially, it's quite common to stumble into a village fiesta, with its explosion of human energy and noise, bright colours, and a mixture of pagan and Catholic symbolism.

However, such celebrations are very much local affairs, and while the occasional traveller will almost certainly be welcomed with great warmth, none of these remote communities would want to be invaded by tourists waving cameras and expecting to be feasted for free. The dates given below are therefore only for established events which are already on the tourist map, and for those that take place all over the country. For full details of celebrations in the Cusco region – one of the best places to catch a fiesta – see p.238.

Major festivals and public holidays

January
1 New Year's Day.

February

2 Candlemas. Folklore music and dancing throughout Peru, but especially lively in Puno at the Fiesta de la Virgen de la Candelaria, and in the mountain regions.

Date varies Carnival Wildly celebrated immediately prior to Lent, throughout the whole country.

March/April

Date varies Easter Semana Santa (Holy Week). Superb processions all over Peru (the best are in Cusco and Ayacucho), with the biggest being on Good Friday and in the evening on Easter Saturday, which is a public holiday.

May

1 Labour Day.

2–3 Fiesta de la Cruz (Festival of the Cross). Celebrated all over Peru in commemoration of ancient Peruvian agro-astronomical rituals and the Catholic annual cycle.

June

Beginning of the month Corpus Christi. This takes places exactly nine weeks after Maundy Thursday, and usually falls in the first half of June. It's much celebrated, with fascinating processions and feasting all over Peru, but is particularly lively in Cusco.

24 Inti Raymi. Cusco's main Inca festival (see p.239).

29 St Peter's Day. A public holiday all over Peru, but mainly celebrated with fiestas in all the fishing villages along the coast.

July

15–17 Virgen de Carmen. Dance and music festivals at Pisac and Paucartambo (see p.309).

28–29 National Independence Day. Public holiday with military and school processions.

August

13–19 Arequipa Week. Processions, firework displays, plenty of folklore dancing and craft markets take place throughout Peru's second city.

30 Santa Rosa de Lima. Public holiday.

September

End of the month Festival of Spring. Trujillo festival involving dancing, especially the local Marinera dance and popular Peruvian waltzes (see p.401).

October

8 Public holiday to commemorate the Battle of Angamos.

18–28 Lord of Miracles. Festival featuring large and solemn processions (the main ones take place on October 18, 19 and 28); many women wear purple for the whole month, particularly in Lima, where bullfights and other celebrations continue throughout the month.

November

1–30 International Bullfighting Competitions. These take place throughout the month, and are particularly spectacular at the Plaza de Acho in Lima.

1–7 Puno Festival. One of the mainstays of Andean culture, celebrating the founding of Puno by the Spanish conquistadores and also the founding of the Inca Empire by the legendary Manco Capac and his sister Mama Ocllo who are said to have emerged from Lake Titicaca. The fifth is marked by vigorous colourful community dancing.

1 Fiesta de Todos los Santos (All Saints Day). Public holiday.

2 Día de los Muertos (All Souls Day). A festive remembrance of dead friends and relatives taken very seriously by most Peruvians and a popular time for baptisms and roast pork meals.

12–28 Pacific Fair. One of the largest international trade fairs in South America – a huge, biennial event, which takes place on a permanent site on Avenida La Marina between Callao and Lima Centro.

December

8 Feast of the Immaculate Conception. Public holiday.

25 Christmas Day

National parks and reserves

Almost ten percent of Peru is incorporated into some form of protected area, including seven national parks, eight national reserves, seven national sanctuaries, three historical sanctuaries, five reserved zones, six buffer forests, two hunting reserves and an assortment of communal reserves and national forests.

The largest of these protected areas is the **National Reserve of Pacaya-Samiria**, an incredible tropical forest region in northern Peru covering over two million hectares. This is closely followed in size by the **Manu National Park and Biosphere Reserve**, another vast and stunning jungle area of about 1.5 million hectares, and the **Tambopata-Candamo Reserved Zone and Bahuaja-Sonene National Park**, again an Amazon area, over 1.4 million hectares in extent, with possibly the richest flora and fauna of any region on the planet. Smaller but just as fascinating to visit are the **Huascarán National Park** in the high Andes near Huaraz, a popular, 340,000-hectare trekking and climbing region, and the lesser-visited **National Reserve of Pampa Galeras**, close to Nasca, which was established mainly to protect the dwindling but precious herds of *vicuña*, the smallest and most beautiful member of the South American cameloid family.

Bear in mind that the parks and reserves are enormous zones, within which there is hardly any attempt to control or organize nature. The term "park" probably conveys the wrong impression about these huge, virtually untouched areas, which were designated by the National System for Conservation Units (SNCU), with the aim of combining conservation, research and, in some cases (such as the Inca Trail; see p.288) recreational tourism.

In December 1992, the Peruvian National Trust Fund for Parks and Protected Areas (PROFONANPE) was established as a trust fund managed by the private sector to provide funding for Peru's main protected areas. It has assistance from the Peruvian government, national and international non-governmental organizations, the World Bank Global Environment Facility and the United Nations Environment Program.

Visiting the parks

There's usually a small charge **to visit** the national parks or nature reserves. Sometimes, as at the Huascarán National Park, this is a daily rate; at others, like the Paracas Reserve on the coast south of Pisco, you pay a fixed sum to enter. If the park is in a particularly remote area, which most of them are, permission may also be needed – either from the National Institute of Culture, by the Museo de la Nación at Av Javier Prado Este 2465, San Borja (☏01/4769873), who are responsible for all matters of cultural heritage, and/or the National Institute of Natural Resources (INRENA), C 17, 355 Urb. El Palomar, San Isidro (☏01/2243298 or 2251053, ⓦwww .inrena.gob.pe), who are responsible for Peru's protected areas; you need permission from them to enter some of Peru's Natural Park areas. For more details check with the South American Explorers' Club in Lima (see p.118) or at the local tourist office.

Directory

Artesania Traditional craft goods from most regions of Peru can be found in markets and shops in Lima. Woollen and alpaca products, though, are usually cheaper and often better quality in the sierra – particularly in Cusco, Juliaca and Puno; carved gourds are imported from around Huancayo, while the best places to buy ceramic replicas are Trujillo, Huaraz, Ica and Nasca. The best jungle crafts are from Pucallpa and Iquitos.

Customs Regulations stipulate that no items of archaeological or historical value or interest may be removed from the country. Many of the jungle crafts which incorporate feathers, skins or shells of rare Amazonian animals are also banned for export – it's best not to buy these if you are in any doubt about their scarcity. If you do try to export anything of archaeological or biological value, and get caught, you'll have the goods confiscated at the very least, and may find yourself in a Peruvian court.

Diving and fishing For information on this contact the Federación Peruana de Caza Submarina y Actividades Acuaticas, Estadio Nacional, Lima Centro ☎01/4336626, ⓔdidimar@mail.cosapidata.com.pe. Also worth contacting the private company Aquasport, Av Conquistadores 645, San Isidro, Lima ☎01/2211548.

Electric current 220 volt/60 cycles AC is the standard all over Peru, except in Arequipa where it is 220 volt/50 cycles. In some of Lima's better hotels you may also find 110 volt sockets to use with standard electric shavers. Don't count on any Peruvian power supply being one hundred percent reliable and, particularly in cheap hostels and hotels, be very wary of the wiring, especially in electric shower fittings.

Insults Travellers sometimes suffer insults from Peruvians who begrudge the apparent relative wealth and freedom of tourists. Remember, however, that the terms "gringo" or "mister" are not generally meant in an offensive way in Peru.

Language lessons You can learn Peruvian Spanish all over Peru, but the best range of schools are in Lima, Cusco, Arequipa and Huancayo. Check the relevant Listings sections in the Guide.

Laundry Most basic hotels have communal washrooms where you can do your washing; failing this, labour is so cheap that it's no real expense to get your clothes washed by the hotel or in a lavandería (laundry). Things tend to disappear from public washing lines so be careful where you leave clothes drying.

Natural disasters Peru has more than its fair share of avalanches, landslides and earthquakes – and there's not a lot you can do about any of them. If you're naturally cautious you may want to register on arrival with your embassy; they like this, and it does help them in the event of a major quake (or an escalation of terrorist activity). Landslides – *huaycos* – devastate the roads and rail lines every rainy season, though alternative routes are usually found surprisingly quickly.

Photography The light in Peru is very bright, with a strong contrast between shade and sun. This can produce a nice effect and generally speaking it's easy to take good pictures. One of the more complex problems is how to take photos of people without upsetting them. You should always talk to a prospective subject first, and ask if s/he minds if you take a quick photo (*una fotito, por favor* – "a little photo please"); most people react favourably to this approach even if all the communication is in sign language. Digital photography is by far the most common format for Peruvians and travellers alike. Digital cameras, memory cards, batteries and accessories are now widely available pretty well everywhere in Peru. Most internet cafés can also help download memory cards. Slide film is expensive to buy, and not readily available outside of the main cities; colour Kodak and

Fuji films are easier to find, but black and white film is rare. If you can bear the suspense it's best to save getting films developed until you're home – you'll probably get better results. Pre-paid slide films can't be developed in Peru.

Punctuality Whilst buses, trains or planes won't wait a minute beyond their scheduled departure time, people almost expect friends to be an hour or more late for an appointment (don't arrange to meet a Peruvian on the street – make it a bar or café). Peruvians stipulate that an engagement is *a la hora inglesa* ("by English time") if they genuinely want people to arrive on time, or, more realistically, within half an hour of the time they fix.

Time Peru keeps the same hours as Eastern Standard Time, which is five hours behind GMT.

Lima and around

CHAPTER 1 # Highlights

* **A colectivo ride** Head along the Avenida Arequipa between the old Centro and downtown Miraflores, by far the most authentic experience of Lima life. See p.80

* **Museo Arqueológico Larco Herrera** One of the city's most unusual museums, and the largest private collection of Peruvian archeology, containing more than 400,000 excellently preserved ancient ceramics, including an extensive erotic section. See p.100

* **Parque de las Leyendas** Lima's traditional zoo, set in a thematic parkland representing the three main eco-zones: desert coast, Andes and Amazon; like most zoos it's sad but also fascinating to see some of this country's amazing wildlife close up. See p.101

* **Huaca Pucllana** A vast pre-Inca adobe pyramid mound in the middle of suburban Miraflores, this is a good place to get your bearings and a taste of ancient Lima. See p.95

* **Fishermen's Wharf** At the southern end of Lima's cliff-hemmed beaches, a small wooden jetty is home to the fishermen of Chorillos, whose morning catch is landed just in time for the ceviche kiosks next door to prepare inexpensive but antastically fresh fish lunches. See p.99

* **El Cordano** One of Lima's last surviving traditional bar/restaurants, bustling with locals. See p.103

▲ Erotic ceramics, Museo Arqueológico Larco Hererra

Lima and around

onsidered the most beautiful city in Spanish America during the six-teenth and seventeenth centuries and long established as Peru's seat of government, **Lima** still retains a certain elegance, particularly in the old Lima Centro, where the Colonial era has left its most visible and refined architectural mark. Though far from exotic, it is relatively clean for a Latin American city and swarms with uniformed sweepers early in the mornings. The ever-increasing traffic, as in most large cities these days, is a day-to-day problem, yet environmental awareness is rising almost as fast as Lima's *pueblos jovenes* (young towns, or shantytowns) and neon-lit, middle-class suburban neighbourhoods, and air quality has improved over the last ten years for the nine million people plus who live here: over half of them in relative poverty with little access to clean water or electricity.

Limeños, as the city's inhabitants are colloquially known, are generally very open, and their way of life is unique and compelling in its appreciation of culture and its hectic busyness. The city's nightlife, meanwhile, particularly in Barranco, is alive, distinctive and often quite hedonistic.

With its numerous facilities and firm footing as a transport and communications hub, Lima makes a good base for exploring the surrounding region or indeed the rest of Peru. The immediate area offers plenty of reasons to delay your progress on towards Arequipa or Cusco. Within an hour's bus ride south is the **coastline**, often deserted, lined by a series of attractive beaches. Above them, the imposing fortress-temple complex of **Pachacamac** sits on a sandstone cliff, near the edge of the ocean. In the neighbouring **Rimac Valley** you can visit the pre-Inca sites of **Puruchuco** and **Cajamarquilla**, and, in the foothills above Lima, intriguingly eroded rock outcrops and megalithic monuments surround the natural amphi-theatre of **Marcahuasi**. To the north, meanwhile, the oldest stone pyramids in the world sit abandoned in the desert of **Caral**.

Lima

Crowded into the mouth of the arid Rimac river valley with low sandy moun-tains closing in around its outer fringes, **LIMA** is a boisterous, macho sprawl of a city, full of beaten-up cars chasing Mercedes and 4WDs: this is a place where money rules, with an irresistible, underlying energy. Somehow, though, it still

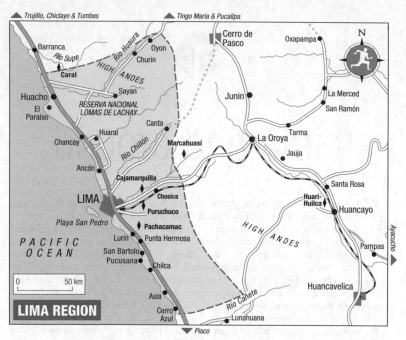

manages to appear relaxed and laid-back in the barrios and off the beaten track, and the noisy, frenetic craziness of it all is mellowed somewhat by the presence of the sea and beaches.

The old colonial heart, Lima Centro, is of both architectural and cultural interest as well as being the seat of government and religion. South of here, along and just inland from the ocean cliff top, the modern centre of Miraflores, where most tourists stay these days, buzzes with shoppers by day and revellers by night. East along the coast a few kilometres, what was once a separate seaside suburb and artists' quarter, Barranco, still boasts both tradition and a vibrant culture. Between Miraflores and Lima Centro, jammed between the Paseo de La República (also known as El Zanjón, which means "big ditch") and the Avenida Arequipa main roads which connect them, rise the skyscraping banks of San Isidro, Lima's heaving new commercial centre.

To the west, the city reaches a fine finger of low-lying land pointing into the Pacific; this is Callao, the rather down-at-heel port area, situated close to Lima's airport. The shantytowns which line the highways, meanwhile, continue to swell with new arrivals from the high Andes, responsible in large part for the dramatic surge in Lima's population over the last thirty years. Consequently, the city's main plazas, once attractive meeting places, are now thick with pickpockets, exhaust fumes and, not infrequently, riot police. The **climate** seems to set the mood: in the height of summer (December to March) Lima buzzes with energy and excitement, though during the winter months (June to September) a low mist descends over the arid valley in which the city sits, forming a solid grey blanket – what Limeños call *garua* – from the beaches almost up to Chosica in the foothills of the Andes; it's a phenomenon made worse by traffic-related air pollution, which dampens the city's spirit, if only slightly.

Lima brims with culture and history, though it's not obvious at first. There are the **museums** (the best of which are excellent and should definitely be visited before setting off for Machu Picchu or any of Peru's other great Inca ruins), the Spanish **churches** in the centre, and some distinguished **mansions** in the wealthy suburbs of Barranco and Miraflores, and many of the city centre's surviving colonial streets – set in large regular blocks – are overhung by ornate wooden balconies. The complexities of class and race run deep in Lima, a city with a burgeoning middle class which has created a huge demand for new housing on what were previously fields around the city's perimeter. Yet Lima also exudes a powerful sense of unity and striving both in the shantytowns, where Peru's landless peasants have made their homes, and on every street where there are *ambulantes* (street pedlars) or markets.

The mix of lifestyles, peoples and cultures is a fascinating world of its own: from the snappy, sassy, cocaine-influenced *criolla* style – all big, fast American cars, cruising the broad main streets – to the easy-going, happy-go-lucky attitude of the poorer citizens. This laissez-faire approach can seem a godsend when you're trying to get through some bureaucratic hassle, since in Peru anything is possible and even the most hardened paper-pushers can smile and wave an issue aside if they feel like it. Even if you choose not to spend much time seeking out the delights and agonies of Lima, it's possible to get a good sense of it all in a few days. As anyone who stays more than a week or so finds, Limeño hospitality and kindness are almost boundless once you've established an initial rapport.

Some history

When the Spanish first arrived here in 1533, the valley was dominated by three important **Inca**-controlled urban complexes: **Carabayllo**, to the north near Chillón; **Maranga**, now partly destroyed, by the Avenida La Marina, between the modern city and the Port of Callao; and **Surco**, now a suburb within the confines of greater Lima but where, until the mid-seventeenth century, the adobe houses of ancient chiefs lay empty yet painted in a variety of colourful images. Now they've faded back into the sandy desert terrain and only the larger pyramids remain sticking up here and there among the modern concrete constructions.

Francisco Pizarro founded **Spanish Lima**, nicknamed the "City of the Kings", in 1535. The name is thought to derive from a mispronunciation of Río Rimac, while others suggest that the name "Lima" is an ancient word that described the lands of Taulichusco, the chief who ruled this area when the Spanish arrived. Evidently recommended by mountain Indians as a site for a potential capital, it proved a good choice, apart perhaps from the winter coastal fog, offering a natural harbour nearby, a large well-watered river valley and relatively easy access up into the Andes. Since the very beginning, Lima was different from the more popular image of Peru in which generally Andean peasants are pictured toiling on Inca-built mountain terraces. By the 1550s, the town had developed around a large plaza with wide streets leading through a fine collection of elegant mansions and well-stocked shops run by wealthy merchants, rapidly developing into the capital of a Spanish viceroyalty which encompassed not only Peru but also Ecuador, Bolivia and Chile. The **University of San Marcos**, founded in 1551, is the oldest on the continent, and Lima housed the Western hemisphere's headquarters of the Spanish Inquisition from 1570 until 1820. It remained the most important, the richest, and – hardly believable today – the most alluring city in South America, until the early nineteenth century.

Perhaps the most prosperous era for Lima was the **seventeenth century**. By 1610 its population had reached a manageable 26,000, made up of forty percent blacks (mostly slaves); thirty-eight percent Spanish; no more than eight percent pure Indian; another eight percent (of unspecified ethnic origin) living under religious orders; and less than six percent *mestizo*, today probably the largest proportion of inhabitants.

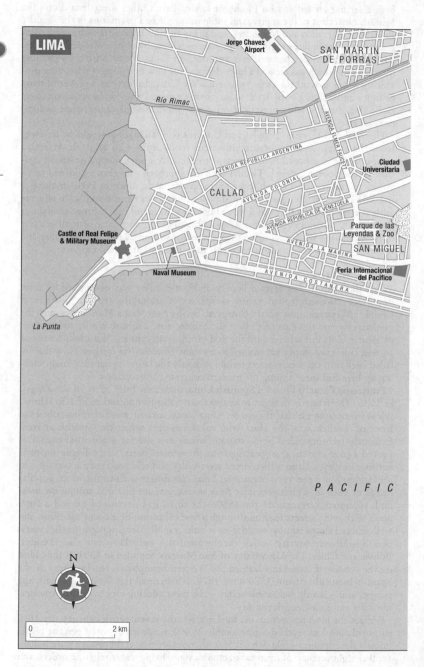

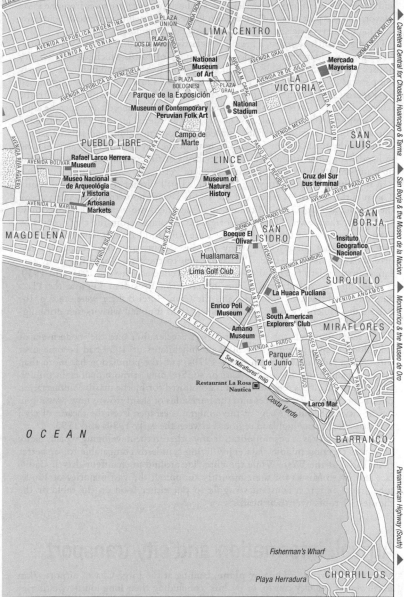

RIMAC

Río Rimac

AVENIDA PERÚ

AVENIDA REPÚBLICA ARGENTINA

AVENIDA COLONIAL

AVENIDA REPÚBLICA DE VENEZUELA

AVENIDA RIVA AGÜERO

AVENIDA BOLÍVAR

AVENIDA LA MARINA

AVENIDA MORA

See 'Lima Centro' map

Plaza de Acho (Bull Ring)

PLAZA UNION

PLAZA DOS DE MAYO

AVENIDA UGARTE

LIMA CENTRO

AVENIDA TACNA

AVENIDA M. CÁCERES

AVENIDA GRAU

AVENIDA 28 DE JULIO

National Museum of Art

PLAZA BOLOGNESI

PLAZA GRAU

LA VICTORIA

Mercado Mayorista

AVENIDA NICOLÁS AYLLÓN

AVENIDA AVIACIÓN

SAN LUIS

Parque de la Exposición

Museum of Contemporary Peruvian Folk Art

National Stadium

AVENIDA MÉXICO

Campo de Marte

LINCE

PUEBLO LIBRE

AVENIDA BRAZIL

Rafael Larco Herrera Museum

Museo Nacional de Arqueológia y Historia

Artesania Markets

Museum of Natural History

PASEO DE LA REPÚBLICA

Cruz del Sur bus terminal

AVENIDA JAVIER PRADO OESTE

SAN BORJA

Insituto Geografico Nacional

MAGDELENA

AVENIDA BRAZIL

AVENIDA SALAVERRY

AVENIDA JAVIER PRADO ESTE

Boeque El Olivar

SAN ISIDRO

Huallamarca

Lima Golf Club

COMANDANTE ESPINAR

AVENIDA AREQUIPA

AVENIDA ARAMBURU

La Huaca Pucllana

SURQUILLO

AVENIDA ANGAMOS

Enrico Poli Museum

Amano Museum

South American Explorers' Club

MIRAFLORES

AVENIDA EJERCITO

AVENIDA J. PARDO

Parque 7 de Junio

See 'Miraflores' map

Restaurant La Rosa Nautica

Costa Verde

PASEO CANJÓN REPÚBLICA

AVENIDA LARCO

AVENIDA PANAMÁ

Larco Mar

BARRANCO

O C E A N

Fisherman's Wharf

Playa Herradura

CHORRILLOS

The centre of Lima was crowded with shops and stalls selling silks and fancy furniture from as far afield as China. Even these days it's not hard to imagine what Lima must have been like, as a substantial section of the colonial city is still preserved, with elaborate Baroque facades bring some of the older churches to life, regardless of the din and hassle of modern city living. **Rimac**, a suburb just over the river from the Plaza Mayor, and the port area of **Callao**, both grew up as satellite settlements – initially catering to the very rich, though they are now fairly rundown.

The **eighteenth century**, a period of relative stagnation for Lima, was dramatically punctuated by the tremendous **earthquake of 1746**, which left only twenty houses standing in the whole city and killed some five thousand residents – nearly ten percent of the population. From 1761 to 1776 Lima and Peru were governed by **Viceroy Amat**, who, although more renowned for his relationship with the famous Peruvian actress **La Perricholi**, is also remembered for spearheading Lima's rebirth. Under his rule, the city lost its cloistered atmosphere, and opened out with broad avenues, striking gardens, Rococo mansions and palatial salons. Influenced by the Bourbons, Amat's designs for the city's architecture arrived hand in hand with other transatlantic reverberations of the Enlightenment, such as the new anti-imperialist vision of an independent Peru.

In the **nineteenth century** Lima expanded still further to the east and south. The suburbs of Barrios Altos and La Victoria were poor from the start; above the beaches at Magdalena, Miraflores and Barranco, the wealthy developed new enclaves of their own. These were originally separated from the city's centre by several kilometres of farmland, at that time still studded with fabulous pre-Inca *huacas* and other adobe ruins, many still just about surviving among the suburbs today, some (like Huaca Pucllana) open to the public or being renovated. Lima's first modern facelift and expansion was effected between **1919 and 1930**, revitalizing the central areas. Under orders from **President Leguia**, the Plaza San Martín's attractive colonnades and the Gran Hotel Bolívar were erected, the Palacio de Gobierno was rebuilt and the city was supplied with its first drinking-water and sewage systems.

This renovation was the signal for Lima's acceleration into the modern era of ridiculously rapid growth. The 300,000 inhabitants of 1930 had become over three and a half million by the **mid-1970s**, and the population has more than doubled again in the last thirty years or so. Standing at more than eight million today, most of Lima's recent growth is accounted for by the massive immigration of peasants from the provinces into the **barriadas** or shantytowns now pressing in on the city on all sides. Many of these migrants escaped from the theatre of civil war that raked many highland regions between the early **1980s and 1993**.

Today, the city is as cosmopolitan as any other in the developing world, many of whose thriving middle class enjoy living standards comparable to, or better than, those of the West. While the elite ride around in chauffeur-driven Cadillacs and fly to Miami for their monthly shopping, the vast majority of Lima's inhabitants endure a constant struggle to put either food on the table or the flimsiest of roofs over their heads.

Arrival, information and city transport

Most visitors arrive in Lima by **plane**, landing at the Jorge Chavez airport, 7km northwest of the city centre, or by **bus**, concluding their long journeys either in the older, central areas of the city, or perhaps in one of the modern terminals en route to the busy commercial suburb of San Isidro, or close to the Avenida Javier

Prado Este. **Driving** into the city for the first time is only for the truly adventurous, as the roads are highly congested and there's the general madness of fellow drivers, which will either turn you insane or into an equally skilful but unpredictable road hog. However and wherever you arrive, it can be a disorienting experience, as there are few landmarks to register the direction of the centre of town.

By air

After landing at the modern, bustling **Jorge Chavez airport** (flight enquiries ☎5116055, Ⓦwww.lap.com.pe), the quickest way into the city is by taxi, which will take around 45 minutes to Lima Centro or downtown Miraflores. The simplest way is to book an **official taxi** (to most parts of Lima for $16) from the Taxi Green (☎484-2734) kiosk inside the terminal. It is possible, if not easy without good Spanish, to negotiate with non-official taxi drivers outside the terminal building and get prices as low as $10; but there is more chance of being ripped off in other ways since the streets here are quite rough and have a bad reputation for theft. If you don't use the official service, remember it is very important to fix the price in Peruvian soles with the driver before getting in. It can be in US$, if you need, but what you want to avoid is thinking you're paying soles only to find out the driver wants the same number of notes, but in US$. Most of these taxis (which are dropping other people off) wait two road lanes away from the terminal building, but well within the airport perimeter gates. Take extra care looking for a taxi outside the perimeter at the roundabout or on the road into Lima, as there are often **thefts** in these areas. A cheaper and generally efficient alternative is to take one of the airport **express bus services** that usually leave from outside the domestic arrivals doors, some heading for Miraflores, others for Lima Centro via Tacna; tickets are $5 per person.

If you need to **change money** at the airport, there's an ATM at the top of the stairs by the internet cabins at the north end of the building. Also, there are counters (24hr; reasonably competitive rates) located in both the arrivals baggage reclaim area and close to the departure gate, but you'll get slightly better rates in the centre of Lima or Miraflores.

By bus

If you arrive in Lima **by bus**, you'll probably come in at one of the bus terminals or offices of three of the most reliable operators, Cruz del Sur, Ormeño or Tepsa, all of which are based on Avenida Javier Prado Este. Cruz del Sur has its busy depot at Javier Prado Este 1109 (☎3115050, Ⓦwww.cruzdelsur.com.pe) on the edge of La Victoria and San Isidro; Ormeño, also have a depot a couple of blocks further east. Smaller local and intercity buses serving the area north of Lima depart from the terminal Terrestre Fiori, block 15 of Avenida Alfredo Mendiola in San Martin de Porres. Some companies arrive at small depots in the district of La Victoria including those that connect with the Central Sierra and jungle regions. Some companies arrive on the Paseo de La República, opposite the Estadio Nacional, while other common arrival streets nearby include Jirón Garcia Naranjo, Calle Carlos Zavala (Cercado district of Lima) and Avenida

Luna Pizarro. However, like the three principal companies mentioned above, many operators have alternative depots out in the suburbs, in an attempt to avoid the worst of Lima Centro traffic jams. For full details of Lima bus companies and their terminals, see Listings, p.117. Whichever terminal you arrive at, your best bet, particularly if you have luggage, is to hail the first of Lima's decent-looking and inexpensive taxis you see and fix a price – about $3 to $6 pretty well anywhere in Lima.

Information and tours

Tourist **information offices** in Lima are plentiful but rather dispersed. The main public municipal office of Información Turística is hidden away in a small office behind the Palacio Municipal on the Plaza Mayor in Lima Centro at C Los Escribanos 145 (daily 9am–5pm; ℡3151505, 3151542 or 3151300 ext 1542). It provides good information on Lima and occasionally maps, though sometimes keeps the most useful brochures under the counter.

In Miraflores, there's a small municipal **tourist information** kiosk, based in the central Parque 7 de Junio (daily 9am–2pm & 2.30–7pm). Maps, leaflets and information can also be obtained from the Central de Informacion y Promoción Turística, also based in Miraflores, at Av Larco 770 (Mon–Fri 9am–1pm & 2–5pm; ℡4463959 ext 114, ⓦwww.miraflores.gob.pe and www.regionlima .gob.pe). The South American Explorers' Club (ⓦwww.saexplorers.org, see p.118) has ample good information, including maps, listings and travel reports, available to its members.

The office of Información y Asistencia al Turista, run by i-peru from Jorge Basadre 610 in San Isidro (Mon–Fri 8.30am–6pm; ℡4211627, ⓦwww.peruinfo .org), also has offices in Larcomar cliff-top mall in Miraflores (℡4459400, Eiperularcomar@promperu.gob.pe) and the airport (℡5748000); they often have a wide range of information sheets available on regions and cities of Peru, but their main function is providing assistance for tourists (see Listings, p.118). Some of the commercial **tour companies** (see p.115) are also geared up for offering good tourist information, notably Fertur Peru and Lima Vision, who both provide city tours. The *Peru Guide*, published monthly in Peru by Cominica 2 SAC, Los Negocios 219, Surquillo (℡6104242, ⓔinfo@comunica2sac.com), gives up-to-date information on most things in Lima, from scheduled tours and treks to hotels, shopping, events and practical advice; it's readily available in hotels, tour and travel agents, and information offices.

City maps can be bought from kiosks in Lima Centro or the better bookshops in Miraflores; the best is the Lima Guía "Inca" de Lima Metropolitan ($15), but there are several newer, more readily available alternatives.

City transport

It's a fairly simple matter to find your way around the rest of this huge, spreadeagled city. Almost every corner of it is linked by the ubiquitous, regular and privately owned **colectivos** that vary in appearance, but are usually either **microbuses** (basically small buses) or **combis** (minibuses); both tend to be crowded and have flat rates (from around 35¢). Quickest of all Lima transport, **combis** race from one street corner to another along all the major arterial city roads; microbuses generally follow the same routes, albeit usually in a more sedate fashion. You'll see "Todo–Arequipa" or "Tacna–Arequipa", for example, chalked up on their windscreens, which indicates that the colectivo runs the whole length of Avenida Arequipa, connecting Lima Centro with downtown

Miraflores. The Arequipa colectivos start their route at Puente Rosa in Rimac, running along Tacna and Garcilaso de La Vega (formerly Avenida Wilson) in the centre, before picking up the Arequipa all the way down to Miraflores, passing the Ovalo (a large roundabout), going down Diagonal to Calle Jose Gonzalez before starting the route back to the centre, up Larco, then via Avenida Arequipa. Some colectivos, operating 7am–11pm (till 8pm on Sundays), also run along the Paseo de La República (also known as the Via Expresa and, more familiarly, as El Zanjón), starting in Avenida Emancipacion, at the corner with Tacna, in the centre, before passing by the Centro Civico and the Sheraton, then taking the Zanjón to Barranco and Chorrillos. This route joins Lima Centro with Miraflores and continues to Barranco as well as Chorrillos. Generally speaking, buses and colectivos chalk up their destinations or routes on the windscreen and shout it out as they pull to a stop. So, for instance, the Lima Centro to Miraflores buses will have signs marked up in the front or side as "Todo Arequipa" or "Miraflores, Larco or Barranco", or else the driver will call out the destination sing-song style, competing with market-stall holders and the like for the attention of prospective passengers. Returning to the centre from Miraflores, buses will say "Todo Arequipa" or "Wilson, Tacna". Many **colectivos** dash dangerously fast, crashing frequently, and are sometimes known to speed off before their passengers have got both feet into the vehicle, so it's best to stay alert as you wave one down and step in; you can hail one from more or less any main street corner in Lima.

You can catch **buses** (but not colectivos) to most parts of the city from Avenida Abancay in the centre; for routes and destinations covered in this chapter you'll find a bus number or suburb name (written on the front of all buses) specified in the text. **Taxis** can be hailed pretty well anywhere on any street at any time, and cost $3–6 to most central parts of the city (but you should always fix the price to your destination in soles before getting in, and pay in soles only at the end of your journey). Unofficial taxis abound in the streets of Lima; they're basically ordinary cars with temporary plastic "taxi" stickers on their front windows, and are cheaper than the official taxis which are based at taxi ranks and licensed by the city authorities (most but not all their cars have taxi signs on the roof; some of the larger taxi companies are radio-controlled). It's worth reiterating that driving in Lima is incredibly anarchic – it's not so fast, but it is assertive, with drivers, especially *taxistas*, often finding gaps in traffic that don't appear to exist (one reason why there are so many damaged cars). You can find recommended reliable taxi firms on p.118. If you want to **rent a car** to take out of the city, see p.117.

Accommodation

There are three main areas of Lima in which to stay – **Lima Centro**, which boasts hotels in just about every category imaginable, **Miraflores** and **Barranco**. Even more than most Peruvian cities, modern hotels in Lima tend to be very exclusive and expensive. There are no **campsites**, official or otherwise.

Lima Centro

Most travellers on a tight budget end up in one of the traditional gringo dives around the **Plaza Mayor** or the **San Francisco** church. These are mainly old buildings and tend to be full of backpackers, but they aren't necessarily the best choices in the old centre, even in their price range, as most of them are poorly maintained. If you can spend a little bit more and opt for the mid-range hotels, you'll find some interesting old buildings bursting with atmosphere and style.

Gran Hotel Bolívar Jr de la Unión 958 ☎6197171, toll free ☎1-888-790-5264, ⓦwww.granhotelbolivarperu.com. This old, elegant and luxurious hotel is well located and full of old-fashioned charm, dominating the northwest corner of the Plaza San Martín. They often have great value online deals, and even if you don't stay here, you should check out the cocktail lounge (famous for its Pisco Sour Cathedral) and restaurant, which host live piano music most nights from 8–11pm. ❽

Hostal de los Artes Chota 1460 ☎4330031, ⒺArtes@terra.com.pe. ⓦArteswelcome.tripod.com. At the southern end of Lima Centro, one block from Plaza Bolognesi, this clean, gay-friendly place is popular with travellers, located as it is in a large attractive house. Some rooms have private bath, and there's also a dormitory with shared bath for those on a budget (though downstairs rooms are a little gloomy). English is spoken and there's a book exchange, as well as a nice patio with mosaics. ❶–❹

Hostal Granada Huancavelica 323 ☎4279033. A welcoming place with small but tidy rooms, private baths and cordial service. Breakfast is included. ❹

Hostal Residencial Don Luis Av Breña 331 ☎4239293, Ⓕ4231379. Relatively close to the city centre, by the Plaza Bolognesi, it can be noisy early in the morning, but nevertheless is a comfortable place with a colonial era feel to it; constant hot water, breakfast not included. ❺

Hostal Roma Jr Ica 326 ☎4277576 or 4277572, ⓦwww.hostalroma.8m.com. A pleasant, safe and gay-friendly place, always popular so book online in advance. It's conveniently located a few blocks from the Plaza Mayor, offers a choice of private or communal bathrooms (but only one shower for women) and a reliable luggage storage service. There's a TV room and *Café Carrara* in the entrance area. ❸

Hostal Wiracocha Jr Junin 284 ☎4271178. Run by the same owners since 1975, it's located on the second level, a couple of blocks from the Plaza Mayor. Rooms are quite spacious if simply furnished, fairly clean and with a choice of shared or private bath. ❸

Hotel España Jr Azángaro 105 ☎/Ⓕ4285546, ⓦwww.hotelespanaperu.com. A converted nineteenth-century Republican-style house very popular

with backpackers, this secure hostel has rooms available with or without private bath. There's also a dormitory with shared bath for more budget-minded travellers. Amenities include a nice courtyard and rooftop patio, internet connection, book exchange and lock-up safe. ❷–❹

Hotel Europa Jr Ancash 376 ☎4273351. One of the best-value budget pads, conveniently located opposite the San Francisco church, with a lovely courtyard. Be aware, though, that it is very popular and fills up quickly. As well as its fine location, it's a good place to meet fellow travellers. Rooms with or without private bath. ❷–❸

Hotel Kamana Jr Camana 547, Lima Centro ☎4277106 or 4267204, ⓦwww.hotelkamana.com. An adequate, small hotel in the heart of Lima Centro, with friendly staff and TVs and showers in all rooms, themselves nicely furnished. Extras include a 24hr café, room service, wi-fi internet connections and money-changing facilities. ❺–❼

Inka Path Jr de La Union 654 ☎4261919, Ⓔinformes@inlapathhotel.com. About as central as you could wish for, *Inka Path* is newly furbished and carpeted, with very comfortable rooms. Beds are queensize and baths private, with hot water 24hrs a day. Price includes breakfast and internet. ❺

Lima Sheraton Hotel Paseo de la República 170 ☎3155000, Ⓔreservas@sheraton.com.pe. A standard top-class, modern international hotel – concrete, tall and blandly elegant, though past its heyday. Also boasts casino, spa and good quality restaurant. ❽

Pensión Rodriguez Av Nicolas de Pierola 730 ☎4236465, Ⓕ4241606, Ⓔjotajot@terra.com.pe. Excellent value but often crowded, with shared rooms and baths, and prone to noise from the road outside. The pension staff will organize airport pick-up if required. ❷

La Pousada del Parque Parque Hernan Velarde 60, Santa Beatriz ☎4332412, Ⓔposada@incacountry.com, ⓦwww.incacountry.com. A truly wonderful boutique-type hotel based in a large, quiet and stylish house. Close to Lima Centro but just to the south of its' busy sectors, it's located parallel to blocks 1 and 2 of Av Petit Thouars and close to the Parque de La Exposición. All rooms are excellently kept and well furnished; service is lovely and there are good breakfasts and Internet access. ❺–❻

Miraflores, Barranco and other suburbs

Many people opt to stay further out of the city in **Miraflores**, which is still close to the seafront as well as home to most of Lima's nightlife, culture and commercial activity. However, most hostels here start at around $20 per person and quite a few hotels go above $200. As a trendy ocean-cliff-top suburb, **Barranco** is more and more the "it" place for the younger traveller. Apart from the artist's quarter vibe and the clubs and restaurants, though, the area actually has little to offer the visitor in the way of attractions and sights of historical interest. Other suburban options include **San Isidro**, a mainly residential area, but close to some of the main bus terminals; **San Antonio** which is within walking distance of Miraflores; and **Callao**, an oceanside, older part of Lima, but quite distant from most of the city's action and attractions.

Miraflores

Casa de Baraybar C Toribio Pacheco 216 ☏4412160, 🖷4219118, 🖲bnb@casadebaraybar.com. Located between blocks 5 and 6 of Av El Ejercito, this place has ten rooms available, all with private bath and hot water 24hrs a day. Beds are comfortable and the rooms are spacious and equipped with cable TV. Continental breakfast included in price, with a 10–20 percent daily discount if you stay for a few nights. ❺

Casa del Mochilero Jr Cesareo Chacaltaña 130a, second floor ☏4449089, 🖲pilaryv@hotmail.com. Located close to block 10 of José Pardo and within walking distance of central Miraflores, this place has bunk rooms with hot water, cable TV and kitchen facilities. The staff will arrange airport pick-up. ❷

Colonial Inn Av Comandante Espinar 310 ☏2417471, 🖷4457587, 🖲hotel@colonialinn.com. Great service and exceptionally clean, if slightly away from the fray of Miraflores. Has a lunchtime restaurant with surprisingly good Peruvian cuisine. ❻

Embajadores Hotel Juan Fanning 320 ☏2429127, 🖷 2429131, 🌐www.embajadoreshotel.com. Part of the Best Western chain, this is located in a quiet area of Miraflores, just a few blocks from Larco Mar and the seafront. Small but agreeable, it has comfortable rooms and access to a mini-gym, small rooftop pool, conference rooms, individual safes and a restaurant. ❽

Faraoña Grande Hotel C Manuel Bonilla 185 ☏4468218, 🖷4469403, 🌐www.faraonagranhotel.com. A plush, secure, quite modern hotel in a central part of this busy suburb; the lobby is cool and there's a rooftop pool and a pretty good restaurant with Peruvian, international and vegetarian dishes. Live piano music performed daily in the bar 7–10pm. ❽

Friends House Jr Manco Capac 368 ☏4466248, 🖲friendshouse_peru@yahoo.com.mx. Located on the second level, this is a small but well-maintained and popular hostel in a superb Miraflores location; comfortable and clean rooms, hot water, cable TV and open kitchen. ❸

🏃 **Hospedaje Flying Dog** Jr Diez Canseco 117 ☏4450940, 🖷4452376, 🌐www.flyingdogperu.com. A clean and homely back-packers bed-and-breakfast-style hostel smack dab in the middle of Miraflores; rooms are shared but the maximum size is four beds. There's an open kitchen facility and cable TV lounge and Internet access. Price includes breakfast. It has an annex over the road at Lima 457 ☏4445753. ❹

Hostal Antigua Miraflores Av Grau 350 ☏2416116, 🖷2416115, 🖲info@peru-hotels-inns.com. Within walking distance of downtown Miraflores, the Antigua is an expanding, very agreeable mock mansion with professional and helpful service, and spacious, well-appointed and very quiet rooms. There's also a small dining room with reasonable food. Good breakfast included. ❽

Hostal Buena Vista Av Grimaldo del Solar 202 ☏4473178, 🖲hostalbuenv@bonus.com.pe. Located in a distinctive twentieth century house in downtown Miraflores, the *Buena Vista* offers large rooms with private baths, and there's also outside space in the form of gardens and rooftop patios. Staff are friendly and helpful, and there's a buffet breakfast included in the price. ❻

Hostal Martinika Av Arequipa 3701, close to the boundary of Miraflores and San Isidro ☏4223094, 🖲martinika@terra.com.pe. Very reasonably priced and centrally located within the greater city area, if a little noisy in the mornings. It's also comfortable and friendly, offering fairly large rooms with private bath. Room service 24hrs; airport pick-up. ❺

Hostal El Patio Diez Canseco 341 ☏4442107, 🖷4441663, 🌐www.hostalelpatio.com. A very agreeable, gay-friendly and secure little place right in the heart of Miraflores, with comfy beds and private - albeit small - bath. More expensive mini-suites and full suites also available, and it's often fully booked, so reserve in advance. ❸–❼

Lex Luthor's House Jr Porta 550 ☏2427059, 🖲luthorshouse@hotmail.com. Located within an easy stroll from the ocean, between the first and second blocks of 28 de Julio and the eighth and ninth blocks of Larco, this hostel (named after the owner's childhood nickname) offers excellent value with hot water, kitchen facilities, cable TV in all rooms and table games; rooms are basic but clean and comfortable. ❸

🏃 **Loki Hostal** Av Larco 189 ☏2413701, 🖲lokihostel.com, 🌐www.lokihostel.com.

With a wide, grand stairway entrance including spectacular stained glass window, this converted mansion is a veritable backpackers haven and great meeting place for young travellers. It's also in a neat location, overlooking the main park in Miraflores, with dorms at the lower end of the price range costing $9 per person (more for smaller dorm), and an all-female dorm coming in at $12.50. There are also private rooms, mainly with shared bath, as well as games, free Internet, kitchen access, rooftop terrace and a good bar and café, which serves very tasty late breakfasts. ❹–❺

Marieta Bed & Breakfast Inn Malecon Cisneros 840 ⊤4449028, ⊕4466485, ⊛gato@amauta .rcp.net.pe. A spotless but small bed and breakfast in a lovely house in one of Lima's more exclusive locations overlooking the ocean, with private baths and a terrace. The family that runs the B&B also operate a number of tours in and around Lima and will pick guests up from the airport for a reasonable fee. Advance bookings only. ❻

Miraflores Colon Inn Colon 600 ⊤6100900, ⊛reservashotel@miraflorescolonhotel.com. Located near the corner of Juan Fanning. Rooms are spacious, clean and equipped with bathtubs, while Jacuzzi and hydro-massage rooms are also available. Breakfast included. ❼

🏃 **Miraflores Hotel** Av Petit Thouars 5444 ⊤2413160, ⊛reservas@hotelesmundo.com. Occupying five floors, this popular place is close to most of Miraflores' shops and nightlife. There's good service and it's hard to beat for value; all rooms have private baths and TV, and the price includes buffet breakfast. ❼

Miraflores Park Av Malecon de la Reserva 1035 ⊤2423000, ⊕2423393, ⊛mirapark @peruorientexpress.com.pe. Conspicuously modern hotel belonging to the Orient-Express Hotels World commercial chain, with a great restaurant, pub-style bar and great views over Miraflores, the city and the Pacific. In short, total luxury in terms of amenities and style. ❽

Radisson Av 28 de Julio 151 ⊤6251241, ⊛www .radisson.com/miraflores.pe. One of the latest and most modern of Lima's taller hotels. Entering the Radisson resembles boarding a space ship; lobby and bars alike have a sci-fi ambience. Rooms are excellent with all modern conveniences and luxuries. ❽

Sonesta Posada del Inca – Miraflores Alcanfores 329 ⊤2417688, ⊛reservas@sonestaperu .com. A very plush, excellently run and modern downtown hotel (part of the Sonesta Posadas del Inca chain). Offers cable TV, a/c and a decent 24hr restaurant. There's a ten percent discount and complimentary breakfast for guests who have a copy of this book; airport pick-up available. ❼–❽

Stop and Drop Backpacker Hotel and Guest House Berlin 168, 2nd floor ⊤2433101, ⊛www .stopanddrop.com. Located in the heart of the action just behind Pizza Alley and near an English pub, this is a friendly and pretty safe place. Dorms ($9 per person) and private rooms available along with TV and Internet. ❹–❺

Tinkus Hostel Av La Paz 608 ⊤2420131, ⊛www.hstinkus.com. Well located just a few blocks from Avenida Larco in central Miraflores, Tinkus is another good value option. The lobby is larger and more salubrious looking than the rooms, though the larger ones aren't too bad. Service is friendly, although the breakfast instant coffee, bread and jam is rather insubstantial. ❹–❺

El Zaguan Lodging Av Diez Canseco 736 ⊤4469356, ⊛www.elzaguanlodging.com. Located in a relatively tranquil street near the Parque Tradiciones, yet within a stone's throw of the heart of things, *El Zaguan* offers eminently accommodating rooms with or without private bath. Service is good and the breakfasts generous. ❺–❻

Barranco

Hospedaje Domeyer Domeyer 296 ⊤2471413, ⊛www. domeyerhostel.net. Close to the Municipal Plaza and nightlife of Barranco, this is a beautiful old mansion from the outside, though not particularly elegant or that well maintained internally. Shared and private rooms available, and most are small but comfortable, with private bath, hot water and cable TV; price includes breakfast. ❹–❺

The Point Hostel Malecon Junin 300 ⊤2477997, ⊛www.thepointhostels.com. A bed and breakfast backpacker hostel with twelve rooms created by two *mochilleros* (backpackers) in a colonial house with relaxing gardens; there's also a shared kitchen, billiard room and there's often music playing, sometimes live jams among travellers, sometimes rock and reggae CDs, but rarely so loud it interferes with other people's sleep. The managers are helpful and offer sensible information on travelling in Lima and Peru. ❷–❸

Other suburbs

Casa Bella Peru Las Flores 459, San Isidro ⊤4217354, ⊛www.casabellaperu.net. A modern hostel located one block from the Country Club and Golf Club in San Isidro (behind *Los Delfines Hotel*), offering exceptionally pristine rooms with state-of-the-art finishing. The service is great and includes help with tours and tickets. ❺–❼

Hi! Perú Hostel Casimiro Ulloa 328, San Antonio ⊤4465488 or 2423068, ⊛www.limahostell.com .pe. A great deal, this hostel is a base for International Youth Hostals in Peru. It's located just over the Paseo de la República highway from Miraflores in the relatively peaceful suburb of San Antonio, in a big, fairly modern and stylish house with a pool. There's also a restaurant and bar with views to the garden, and they'll pick-up from airport. ❹–❺

Hostal Mami Panchita Av Federico Gallesi 198, San Miguel ☎ 2637203, ⓦ www.mamipanchita .com. Located in the suburb of San Miguel, this is a very approachable hostel based around lovely gardens and a well-appointed, shared dining room, TV lounge and bar, with both English and Dutch spoken. They also offer an airport pick-up (just 20 min away). Price includes breakfast. ❺

Hotel Libertador Los Eucaliptos 550, San Isidro ☎ 4216666, ⓦ www.libertador.com.pe. A top-class hotel with a convenient location in a well-to-do Lima suburb. The service and room standards are excellent, and there's a laundry service available. ❽

Hotel El Marqués Chinchon 461, San Isidro ☎ 4420046, ⓕ 4420043, ⓔ reservas @hotelmarqueses.com, ⓦ www.hotelmarques. com. This is a very comfortable business hotel with small, carpeted, colonial-style rooms close to San Isidro's commercial centre. Has cable TV and meeting rooms. ❼

Malka Youth Hostal Los Lirios 165, San Isidro ☎ 4420162, ⓔ hostalmalka@terra.com.pe, ⓦ www.youthhostelperu.com. Well-located, close to block 4 of Javier Prado Este, Malka is cheerful and intimate as well as being good value for this part of the city. There are several airy rooms, one with views over the garden, but most bathrooms are shared. ❹

Pension Jose Luis Francisco de Paula de Ugarriza 727, San Antonio ☎ 4441015, ⓕ 4467177, ⓦ www .hoteljoseluis.com. Comfortable, modern house, in a good location, within walking distance of Miraflores and the ocean, and popular with English-speaking travellers. All rooms come with private baths and Internet access is available. ❹

Sonesta Posada del Inca El Olivar Pancho Fierro 194, San Isidro ☎ 7126060, ⓕ 7126080, ⓔ reservasolivar@sonestaperu.com, ⓦ www .sonesta.com. Modern but pleasant luxury retreat by the olive grove park of San Isidro and perhaps the most scenically located accommodation in the area. Very comfortable and elegant rooms, cable TV, a/c and heating. There's also room service 24hrs and large fitness centre and spa. Bookings by internet only (there's a 25 percent discount for guests who have a copy of this book). ❽

Suites del Bosque Av Paz Soldan 165 ☎ 2211108, ⓕ 2211107, ⓔ reservas @suitesdelbosque.com. Essentially a business hotel with conference rooms functioning 7am–11pm daily. Rooms themselves are smartly furnished, complete with dining/living room, cable TV, internet access, heating and a/c. There's also a restaurant and bar with salad and pasta buffet. ❼

Swissotel Lima Via Central 150, Centro Empresarial Real, San Isidro ☎ 4214400, ⓦ swissotel .com. Conveniently located near banks, bus depots and some larger department stores and supermarkets, this is luxurious accommodation with all the modern conveniences you'd expect, aimed largely at the business traveller. ❽

The City

Like most big cities, Lima looks inward and away from its rich and colourful hinterland nation of mountains, rivers and rainforests. Laid out across a wide, flat, alluvial plain, the city's buildings fan out like a concrete phoenix in long, straight avenues and roads from its heart. **Lima Centro**, the old city, sits at the base of a low-lying Andean foothill, Cerro San Cristobal, and focuses on two plazas: the colonial **Plaza Mayor** (often still called the Plaza de Armas) – itself separated from the Río Rimac by the Presidential Palace and the railway station – and the more modern **Plaza San Martín**, separated by some five blocks along the **Jirón de la Unión**, a major shopping street. At its river end, the Plaza Mayor is fronted by the Catedral and Palacio de Gobierno, while there's greater commercial activity around Plaza San Martín. The key to finding your way around the old part of town is to acquaint yourself with these two squares and the streets between.

From Lima Centro, the city's main avenues reach out into the sprawling suburbs. The two principal routes are **Avenida Venezuela**, heading west out to the harbour area around the suburb of Callao and the airport, and perpendicular to this,

Mirabus Tours of Lima

Mirabus (☎4764213, ✉reservas@mirabus.com, ⊛www.mirabus.com) operate a fleet of double-decker buses, with an open roof on the upper deck, for exploring the sites in and around Lima. The Servicio Lima Colonial starts in the Plaza San Martín (Fri–Sun 4pm & 6pm) and covers the main sites of historic Lima in an hour or so. The Servicio Miratur starts at the park in Miraflores several times daily (11am, 3.30pm & 5pm) and visits the sites and attractions of Miraflores in around 60 minutes. Both cost around $3. A three-hour tour of Lima leaves from Miraflores by the craft market at Petit Thouars 5245 (10am on Mon, Wed, Fri, Sat & Sun; $14). They also operate a tour to Pachacamac archaeological site (see p.119) some 30km south of the city centre, leaving from Av Petit Thouars 5245 (10am, Thurs & Sat; $18). Tickets can be bought from the Tourist Information kiosk in Miraflores Park.

the broad, tree-lined **Avenida Arequipa** stretching out to the coastal downtown centre of Miraflores. More or less parallel to Avenida Arequipa, the forty-year old **Paseo de La República**, more fondly known in Lima as **El Zanjón** (the Great Ditch) is a concrete, three-lane highway connecting central Lima with San Isidro, Miraflores and almost to Barranco. The suburb of **Miraflores**, the modern commercial heart of Lima, where much of the city's businesses have moved over the last thirty years, is located 7 or 8km down Avenida Arequipa and the Zanjón, by the ocean.

Lima's rapid growth means that a host of new suburbs have sprung up or been consolidated in the last twenty years, both north and south of the centre: Monterico, San Borja and Surco are modern upper-middle-class areas along the eastern edge of the city, while Magdalena, Jesus Maria and Breña are less salubrious but architecturally older areas to the west. Arguably, however, the most important other main suburban sectors include **San Isidro**, another major modern commercial centre for banks and shopping, **Barranco** and **Callao** – all have their own specific characteristics and points of interest.

Lima Centro

With all its splendid architectural attractions, **Lima Centro** might well be expected to have a more tourist-focused vibe than it does. In reality, though, the neighbourhood is very much a centre of Limeños' daily life. The main axis is formed by the parallel streets – Jr de la Unión and Jr V Carabaya – connecting the grand squares of the **Plaza San Martín** and **Plaza Mayor**. Here the roads are narrow and busy, bringing together many of the city's office and bank workers with slightly downmarket shops and street workers. There are many fine buildings from the colonial and Republican eras yet apart from a selection of the best, in terms of heritage – like the **Presidential Palace** and **Torre Tagle** – too many are in a poor state of repair. To the east of the Plaza Mayor, there are several fine colonial attractions, like the **Iglesia de San Francisco** and the **Museo de la Inquisición**. To the north you'll find the slightly run-down but fascinating **Rimac suburb**, home to the city's bullring and some fine Republican public constructions. South of the two main plazas, there are some lavish parks and galleries within walking distance.

The Plaza Mayor

Today the heart of the old town is centred around the **Plaza Mayor** – until a few years ago known as the Plaza de Armas, or "armed plaza" (Plaza Armada) as the early conquistadors called it. There are no remains of any Indian heritage in or around the square; standing on the original site of the palace of Tauri Chusko

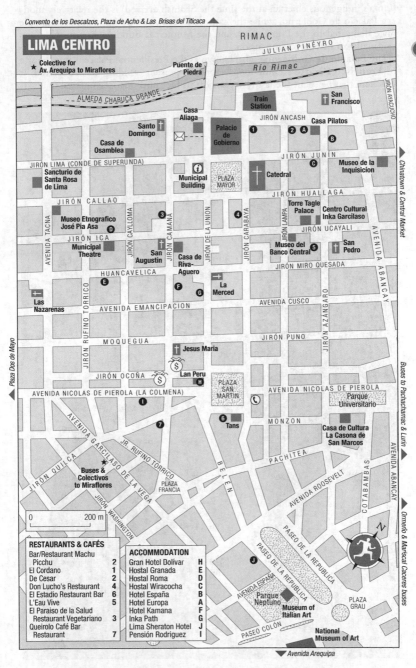

Convento de los Descalzos, Plaza de Acho & Las Brisas del Titicaca ▲

RIMAC

LIMA CENTRO

JULIAN PINÉYRO

★ Colective for
Av. Arequipa to Miraflores

Puente de
Piedra

Río Rimac

ALMEDA CHABUCA GRANDE

Train
Station

San
Francisco

Casa
Aliaga

JIRÓN ANCASH

Casa Pilatos

Santo
Domingo

Palacio
de
Gobierno

❶

❷ Ⓐ

Casa de
Osamblea

Ⓑ

JIRÓN LIMA (CONDE DE SUPERUNDA)

JIRÓN JUNIN

Chinatown & Central Market

Sancturio de
Santa Rosa
de Lima

Municipal
Building

ⓘ

PLAZA
MAYOR

Catedral

Ⓒ

Museo de la
Inquisicion

JIRÓN CALLAO

JIRÓN HUALLAGA

Museo Etnografico
José Pia Asa

Ⓓ

❸

❹

Torre Tagle
Palace

Centro Cultural
Inka Garcilaso

JIRÓN ICA

JIRÓN UCAYALI

Municipal
Theatre

San
Augustin

Casa de
Riva-
Aguero

Museo del
Banco Central

❺

San
Pedro

HUANCAVELICA

JIRÓN MIRO QUESADA

Ⓔ

❻

Ⓖ

La
Merced

Las
Nazarenas

AVENIDA EMANCIPACION

AVENIDA CUSCO

MOQUEGUA

JIRÓN PUNO

Plaza Dos de Mayo

JIRÓN OCOÑA

Jesus Maria

Ⓗ

Lan Peru

PLAZA
SAN
MARTIN

AVENIDA NICOLAS DE PIEROLA (LA COLMENA)

AVENIDA NICOLAS DE PIEROLA

❶

Parque
Universitario

Buses to Pachacamac & Lurín

❼

❻

Tans

MONZON

Casa de Cultura
La Casona de
San Marcos

Buses &
Colectivos
to Miraflores

PACHITEA

Ormeño & Mariscal Cáceres buses

PLAZA
FRANCIA

AVENIDA ROOSEVELT

0   200 m

N

PASEO DE LA REPUBLICA

Ⓙ

AVENIDA ESPAÑA

Parque
Neptuno

PLAZA
GRAU

Museum of
Italian Art

National
Museum of Art

PASEO COLÓN

▼ Avenida Arequipa

RESTAURANTS & CAFÉS

Bar/Restaurant Machu Picchu	2
El Cordano	1
De Cesar	2
Don Lucho's Restaurant	4
El Estadio Restaurant Bar	6
L'Eau Vive	5
El Paraiso de la Salud Restaurant Vegetariano	3
Queirolo Café Bar Restaurant	7

ACCOMMODATION

Gran Hotel Bolívar	H
Hostal Granada	E
Hostal Roma	D
Hostal Wiracocha	C
Hotel España	B
Hotel Europa	A
Hotel Kamana	F
Inka Path	G
Lima Sheraton Hotel	J
Pensión Rodriguez	I

(Lima's indigenous chieftan at the time the Spanish arrived) is the relatively modern Palacio de Gobierno, while the cathedral occupies the site of an Inca temple once dedicated to the Puma deity, and the Municipal Building lies on what was originally an Inca envoy's mansion.

The **Palacio de Gobierno** – also known as the Presidential Palace – was the site of **Francisco Pizarro's** house long before the present building was conceived. It was here that he spent the last few years of his life, until his assassination in 1541.

▲ Archbishop's Palace, Plaza Mayor

As he died, his jugular severed by the assassin's rapier, Pizarro fell to the floor, drew a cross, then kissed it; even today some believe the grounds to be sacred. The palace isn't much to look at apart from the facade (completed in 1938), which is sufficiently opulent. The **changing of the guard** takes place outside the palace (Mon–Sat starting at 11.45am) – it's not a particularly spectacular sight, though the soldiers look splendid in their scarlet and blue uniforms. There are free guided **tours** (daily 9.30am–noon) in English and Spanish, which include watching the changing of the guard; to go on a tour you have to register with the Departmento de Actividades, office 201, Jr de la Unión, block 2, Plaza Peru, also known as Plaza Pizarro (T 3113908 ext 378, W www.presidencia.gob.pe/index.asp), at least 24 hours prior to when you want the tour. You'll also get to see the imitation Baroque interior of the palace and its rather dull collection of colonial and reproduction furniture.

Southeast across the square, less than 50m away from the Palacio de Gobierno, the squat and austere **Catedral** (Mon–Fri 10am–4pm, Sat 10am–1pm, T 4279647), designed by Francisco Becerra, was modelled on a church from Seville, and has three aisles in a Renaissance style. When Becerra died in 1605, the cathedral was far from completion, with the towers alone taking another forty years to finish. In 1746, further frustration arrived in the guise of a devastating earthquake, which destroyed much of the building. Overall, particularly in light of the restorations over the centuries due to damage, it is eclectic in style; the current version, which is essentially a reconstruction of Becerra's design, was rebuilt throughout the eighteenth and nineteenth centuries, then again after another quake in 1940. It is primarily of interest for its **Museum of Religious Art and Treasures** (daily 10am–4pm; $1.50), which contains seventeenth- and eighteenth-century paintings and some choir stalls with fine wooden carvings by Catalan artist Pedro Noguero. Its other highlight is a collection of human remains thought to be Pizarro's body (quite fitting since he placed the first stone shortly before his death), which lie in the first chapel on the right. Although gloomy, the interior retains some of its appealing Churrigueresque (or highly elaborate Baroque) decor. The choir stalls are superb – exquisitely carved in the early seventeenth century by a Catalan artist. The **Archbishop's Palace** next door was rebuilt in 1924.

The square-set edifice directly across the square is the **Palacio Municipal** (Mon–Fri 9am–1pm; free), usually lined with heavily armed guards and the occasional armoured car, though actual civil unrest is fairly uncommon. Built on the site of the original sixteenth-century city hall and inaugurated in 1944, it's a typical example of a half-hearted twentieth-century attempt at Neocolonial architecture, designed by Alvarez C., Emilio Harth Terré and Ricardo de Jara Malachowski, and fronted by grand wooden balconies. The elegant interior is home to the **Pinacoteca Ignacio Merino Museum** (same hours), which exhibits a selection of Peruvian paintings, notably those of Ignacio Merino from the nineteenth century. For those with an interest in Peruvian constitutional history, the library has the city's **Act of Foundation and Declaration of Independence** on display.

East of the Plaza Mayor

Jirón Ancash leads away from the Palacio de Gobierno towards one of Lima's most attractive churches, **San Francisco** (daily 9.30am–5pm; $2). A large seventeenth-century construction with an engaging stone facade and towers, San Francisco's vaults and columns are elaborately decorated with Mudéjar (Moorish-style) plaster relief. It's a majestic building that has withstood the passage of time and the devastation of successive earth tremors. The Convento de San Francisco, part of the same architectural complex and a museum in its own right, also contains a superb library and a room of paintings by (or finished by) Zurbarán, Rubens, Jordaens and Van Dyck. You can take a forty-minute guided tour of the **monastery** and its **subterranean crypt** (daily 9.30am–5pm; $2), both of which are worth a visit. The museum is inside the church's vast crypts, which were only discovered in 1951 and contain the skulls and bones of some seventy thousand people.

Opposite San Francisco, at Jr Ancash 390, is **La Casa Pilatos** (Mon–Fri 11am–1.30pm; free, but you need to book in advance; ☎4275814), the home of the Tribunal Constitucional (constiutional courts). Quite a simple building, and no competition for Torre Tagle (see below), it is nevertheless a fine early-sixteenth-century mansion with an attractive courtyard and a stone staircase leading up from the middle of the patio. The fine wooden carving of the patio's balustrades adds to the general picture of opulent colonialism.

Nearby, behind a facade of Greek-style classical columns, the **Museo de la Inquisición**, Jr Junin 548 (daily 9am–5pm; free but by guided tour only, ☎3117801) contains the original tribunal room with its beautifully carved mahogany ceiling. This was the headquarters of the Inquisition for the whole of Spanish-dominated America from 1570 until 1820, and, beneath the building, you can look round the dungeons and torture chambers, which contain a few gory, life-sized human models, each being put through unbearably painful-looking antique contraptions, mainly involving stretching or mutilating.

The few blocks behind the museum and Avenida Abancay are taken over by the **Mercado Central** (central market) and **Barrio Chino** (Chinatown). Perhaps one of the most fascinating sectors of Lima Centro, Chinatown (which can be entered by an ornate Chinese **gateway**, at the crossing of Jirón Ucayali with Capon) houses Lima's best and cheapest *chifa* (Chinese) **restaurants.** Many Chinese came to Peru in the late nineteenth century to work as labourers on railway construction; many others came here in the 1930s and 40s to escape cultural persecution in their homeland.

Heading from Chinatown back towards the Plaza Mayor along Ucayali, you'll pass the **Iglesia de San Pedro** (Mon–Sat 7am–12.30pm & 5–8pm) on the corner of Jirón Azángaro. Built and occupied by the Jesuits until their expulsion in 1767, this richly decorated colonial church is home to several art treasures, including paintings and a superb main altar; definitely worth a look around. However, just over the road, you'll find the far more spectacular **Torre Tagle Palace**, at Ucayali 323 (Mon–Fri 9am–5pm; free, but you need to book two days in advance; ☎3112400), pride and joy of the old city. Now the home of Peru's Ministry for Foreign Affairs and recognizable by the security forces with machine guns on the roof and top veranda, Torre Tagle is a superb, beautifully maintained mansion built in the 1730s. It is embellished with a decorative facade and two elegant, dark wooden balconies, typical of Lima architecture in that one is larger than the other. The porch and patio are distinctly Andalucian, with their strong Spanish colonial style, although some of the intricate woodcarvings on pillars and across ceilings display a native influence; the *azulejos*, or tiles, also show a combination of Moorish and Limeño tastes. In the left-hand corner of the patio you can see a set of scales like those used to weigh merchandise during colonial times, and the house also contains a magnificent sixteenth-century carriage (complete with mobile toilet). Originally, mansions such as Torre Tagle served as refuges for outlaws, the authorities being unable to enter without written and stamped permission – now anyone can go in (afternoons are the quietest times to visit).

On the corner by Torre Tagle, you'll find the **Centro Cultural Inca Garcilaso**, Jr Ucayali 391 (Tues–Sun 11am–7pm; free; ☎3112756), built in 1685 as the Casa Aspillaga but restored during the late nineteenth century and again in 2003; it has an art gallery but is more interesting for the Neoclassical Republican-style architecture.

North of the Plaza Mayor: Rimac

Just off the main square, a block behind the Municipal Building, is the church and monastery of **Santo Domingo** (Mon–Sat 9am–12.30pm & 3–6pm, Sun & holidays 9am–1pm; $2). Completed in 1549, Santo Domingo was presented by the pope, a century or so later, with an alabaster statue of Santa Rosa de Lima. Rosa's tomb, and that of San Martín de Porres and San Juan Masias (a Spaniard who was canonized in Peru), are the building's great attractions, and much revered. Otherwise the church is not of huge interest or architectural merit, although it is one of the oldest religious structures in Lima, built on a site granted to the Dominicans by Pizarro in 1535. There's a growing concentration of **artesania shops** around Santo Domingo itself, the largest being the obviously named Santo Domingo, directly opposite the monastery. Nearby at Jr Conde de Superunda 298, you'll find the recently restored, early nineteenth-century **Casa de Osambela** (9am–5pm; free), which has five balconies on its facade and a lookout point from which boats arriving at the port of Callao could be spotted. This mansion is home to the Centro Cultural Inca Garcilaso de la Vega, which offers a **free guide service** (voluntary contribution appreciated).

Heading north from the Plaza Mayor at Jr de la Unión 224, you pass the **Casa Aliaga**, an unusual mansion, reputed to be the oldest in South America, and occupied by the same family since 1535, making it the oldest colonial house still standing in the Americas. It's also one of the most elaborate mansions in the country, with sumptuous reception rooms full of Louis XIV mirrors, furniture and doors. It was built on top of an Inca palace and is largely made of wood divided stylishly into various salons. You need to call Lima Tours in advance to arrange a visit ($3; ☎6195000 or 6196911).

Continuing up Jirón de la Unión, it's a short walk to the **Puente de Piedra**, the stone bridge that arches over the Río Rimac – usually no more than a miserable trickle – behind the Palacio de Gobierno. Initially a wooden construction, the current brick structure was built in the seventeenth century, using egg whites with the sand and lime to improve the consistency of its mortar. Its function was to provide a permanent link between the centre of town and the Barrio of San Lazaro, known these days as **Rimac**, or, more popularly, as **Bajo El Puente** ("below the bridge"). This zone was first populated in the sixteenth century by African slaves, newly imported and awaiting purchase by big plantation owners; a few years later Rimac was beleaguered by outbreaks of leprosy. Although these days its status is much improved, Rimac is still one of the most run-down areas of Lima and can be quite an aggressive place after dark. Drug addicts and thieves abound at night and it is **dangerous** to walk this area alone at any time of day. You can take taxis direct to where you want to go.

Rimac is also home to the **Plaza de Acho**, at Hualgayoc 332, Lima's most important **bullring**, which also houses the **Museo Taurino de Acho**, or Bullfight Museum (Mon–Sat 9am–6pm; $2; ☎4813433), containing some original **Goya** engravings, several related paintings and a few relics of bullfighting contests. A few blocks to the right of the bridge, you can stroll up the **Alameda de los Descalzos**, a fine tree-lined walk designed for courtship, and an afternoon meeting place for the early seventeenth- to nineteenth-century elite (the railings were added in 1853). Along the way stands the **Paseo de Aguas**, built by Viceroy Amat in the eighteenth century. It leads past the foot of a distinctive hill, the Cerro San Cristobal, and, although in desperate need of renovation, it still possesses twelve appealing marble statues brought from Italy in 1856, each one representing a different sign of the zodiac. At the far end of the Alameda there's a fine Franciscan monastery, **Convento de los Descalzos** (daily except Tuesdays 10am–1pm, 3–6pm; $2, usually including a forty-minute guided tour;

⊤4810441 or 4813433), dating from 1592 and housing a collection of colonial and Republican paintings from Peru and Ecuador; its chapel – **La Capilla El Carmen** – possesses a beautiful Baroque gold-leaf altar. The monastery was built in what was then a secluded spot beyond the town, originally a retreat from the busy heart of the city at the base of Cerro San Cristobal. Now, of course, the city runs all around it and way beyond.

West of the Plaza Mayor

Two traditional sanctuaries can be found on the western edge of old Lima, along Avenida Tacna. Completed in 1728, the **Sanctuario de Santa Rosa de Lima** (daily 9am–1pm & 3.30–6pm), on the first block of Tacna, is a fairly plain church named in honour of the first saint canonized in the Americas. The construction of Avenida Tacna destroyed a section of the already small church, but in the patio next door you can visit the saint's hermitage, a small adobe cell; there's also a 20m deep well where devotees drop written requests. A short stroll down the street takes you to the fascinating **Museo Etnográfico Jose Pia Asa** (entrance via Jr Callao 562, at the corner with Tacna; Mon–Sat 10am–5pm; $1; ⊤4310771), containing crafts, tools, jewellery and weapons from jungle tribes, plus some photographs of early missionaries.

At the junction of Avenida Tacna and Huancavelica, the church of **Las Nazarenas** (daily 8am–noon & 6–8.30pm, ⊤4235718) is small and outwardly undistinguished but it has an unusual history. After the severe 1655 earthquake, a mural of the crucifixion, painted by an Angolan slave on the wall of his hut and originally titled *Cristo de Pachacamilla*, was the only object left standing in the district. Its survival was deemed a miracle – the cause and focus of popular processions ever since – and it was on this site that the church was founded in the eighteenth century. The widespread and popular **processions for the Lord of Miracles**, to save Lima from another earthquake, take place every spring (Oct 18, 19, 28 & Nov 1), based around a silver litter, which carries the original mural. Purple is the colour of the procession and many women in Lima wear it for the entire month.

South of the Plaza Mayor

The southern stretch between the Plaza Mayor and Plaza San Martín is the largest area of Old Lima. It's here that you'll come across several important churches, as well as older offices for some of the major banks. Worth a quick look here is the church of **San Augustin** (daily 8.30am–noon & 3.30–7pm), founded in 1592 and located on the corner of Ica and Camana. Although severely damaged by earthquakes (only the small side chapel can be visited nowadays), the church retains a glorious facade, one of the most complicated examples of Churrigueresque-Mestizo architecture in Peru; it originally had a Renaissance doorway, signs of which can be seen from Calle Camana. Just across the road at Camana 459, the **Casa de Riva-Aguero** (daily 10am–1pm and 2–8pm; ⊤4279275, $1) is a typical colonial house, built in the mid-eighteenth century by a wealthy businessman and later sold to the Aguero family. Its patio has been laid out as a **Museo de Arte y Tradiciones Populares**, displaying crafts and contemporary paintings from all over Peru. The building also functions as the Riva-Aguero Institute, which looks after a library and historic archives.

Perhaps the most noted of all religious buildings in Lima is the **Iglesia de la Merced** (Mon–Sat 8am–noon & 5–8pm, Sun 7am–noon & 5–8pm; phone to arrange guided visit; ⊤4278199), just two blocks from the Plaza Mayor at Jirón de la Unión 621, by the corner with Jirón Miro Quesada. Built on the site where the first Latin Mass in Lima was celebrated, the original sixteenth-century church was demolished in 1628 to make way for the present building whose ornate granite facade, dating back to 1687, has been adapted and rebuilt several times – as have the broad columns of the nave – to protect the church against tremors. But by far the most lasting impression is made by La Cruz de Padre Urraca El Venerable (**Cross of the Venerable Padre Urraca**), whose silver staff is witness to the fervent prayers of a constantly shifting congregation, smothered by hundreds of kisses every hour. If you've just arrived in Lima, a few minutes by this cross may give you an insight into the depth of Peruvian belief in miraculous power. Be careful if you get surrounded by the ubiquitous sellers of candles and religious icons around the entrance – people have been **pick-pocketed** here. The attached **cloisters** (daily 8am–noon & 5–6pm) are less spectacular though they do have a historical curiosity: it was here that the Patriots of Independence declared the Virgin of La Merced their military marshal. A couple of minutes' walk further towards the Plaza San Martín, at the corner of Camana and Jirón Moquegua, stands the church of **Jesus María y José** (daily 7am–1pm & 3–7pm; free), home of Capuchin nuns from Madrid in the early eighteenth century; its particularly outstanding interior contains sparkling Baroque gilt altars and pulpits.

Close by, the **Museo del Banco Central de Reserva del Peru**, at the corner of Lampa and Ucayali (Tue–Fri 10am–4.30pm, Sat & Sun 10am–1pm; free; ℡6132000 ext 2655), has many antique and modern Peruvian paintings, as well as a good collection of pre-Inca artefacts, mainly from grave robberies and only recently returned to Peru.

Plaza San Martín and around

The **Plaza San Martín** is a grand, large square with fountains at its centre, virtually always busy by day, with traffic tooting its way around the perimeter. Nevertheless, it's a place where you can sit for a few minutes, at least until hassled by street sellers or shoeshine boys. **Money-changing** facilities are close by and there are some decent hotels around, not least the Gran Bolívar, right on the plaza. There are also some travel and tour agents around the plaza, but they are not necessarily the best (see p.114). The Plaza San Martín has caught most of Lima's major political rallies over the past hundred years and the sight of rioting students, teachers or workers and attendant police with water cannons and tear gas is always a strong possibility. Ideologically, the Plaza represents the sophisticated, egalitarian and European spirit of intellectual liberators like San Martín himself, while remaining well and truly within the commercial worlds. It is a place that every political march passes through. Public political meetings are still regularly held here, although the city's main rallying point for political protests is actually the nearby **Plaza Dos de Mayo**, where many of the main unions have their offices.

Built to commemorate the repulse of the Spanish fleet in 1866 (Spain's last attempt to regain a foothold in South America), the plaza is markedly busier and less visitor-friendly than Plaza San Martín, to which it is linked by the wide Avenida Nicolas de Pierola (also known as La Colmena). It sits on the site of an old gate dividing Lima from the road to Callao and hosts a great **street market** where some good bargains can be found. East of Plaza San Martín, Avenida Nicolas de Pierola runs towards the **Parque Universitario**, site of South America's first university. Located at Nicolas de Pierola 1222, right on the park itself, the **Casona de San Marcos** is home to the Centro Cultural San Marcos and the Ballet de San Marcos. Once lodgings for the Jesuit novitiate San Antonio Abad (patron saint of everything from animals to skin complaints), it's a pleasant seventeenth-century architectural complex with some fine architectural features including colonial cloisters, a baroque chapel, a small **art and archeology museum** (Mon–Sat 9am–6pm, $1.50), exhibitions and a great cafeteria for lunches. The amphitheatre in the park is sometimes used for free public performance by a range of musicians and artists.

South of Plaza San Martín

South of Plaza San Martín, Jirón Belén leads down to the Paseo de la República and the shady **Parque Neptuno**, home to the pleasant **Museo de Arte Italiano**, Paseo de la República 250 (Mon–Fri 9am–4.30pm; $1; ☎4239932). Located inside a relatively small and ornate Renaissance building unusual for Lima, the museum exhibits oils, bronze and ceramics by the Italian masters and offers a very welcome respite from the hectic modern city outside. Much larger and a couple of minutes' walk south of here at Paseo Colón 125 there's the **Museo de Arte** (daily 10am–5pm; $2; ☎4234732, ⓦwww.museodearte.org.pe), housed in the former International Exhibition Palace built in 1868 and at the city end of the extensive, leafy and very pleasant Parque de La Cultura Peruana (daily 9am–7.30pm), previously known as the **Parque de la Exposición** and originally created for the International Exhibition of Agricultural Machines in 1872. The grounds of the Museo de Arte now form the cleaned-up and remodelled version of the park after it was revamped around the Millennium.

Conspicuously green for Lima, it's where lovers meet at weekends and students often hang out amidst trees, grass, pagodas, an amphitheatre, a small lake and organised music and dance during fiesta times. In terms of size, it stretches a full couple of hundred yards down to Avenida 28 de Julio, from where it's just a few blocks to the Estadio Nacional and **Parque de La Reserva**. The art museum itself is large and commanding with interesting permanent small collections of colonial art and many fine crafts from pre-Columbian times, and also hosts frequent temporary international exhibitions of modern photography and video as well as contemporary Peruvian art. Film shows and lectures are offered on some weekday evenings (for details check website, *El Comercio* newspaper listings or posters in the museum lobby).

Not far away, at Jirón Washington 1946, is the **Casa Museo de Jose Carlos Mariategui** (Mon–Fri 9am–1pm & 2–6pm, Sat 9am–1pm; free), an early twentieth-century house – home for the last few years of his life to the famous Peruvian political figure, ideologist and writer Mariategui – which has been restored by the Instituto Nacional de Cultura. Close by, in Santa Beatriz, the Parque de la Reserva (Wed–Sun 4–10pm; $1.50), next to the Estadio Nacional, was superbly and imaginatively refurbished in 2007 to create the *circuito mágico del agua* (magical water circuit). A popular haunt, close to blocks 5–8 of the Avenida Arequipa, it has fifteen colourful and well-lit fountains, including the Fuente de Fantasia which moves to music and the Cupula Visitable which you can get drenched climbing inside. Some fountains spurt 80m into the air, there's a beautiful water pyramid and a *Tunel de Sorpresas* (Tunnel of Surprises) which you can walk through; it all makes for one of Lima's most memorable evening attractions.

The suburbs

The old centre of Lima is surrounded by a number of sprawling **suburbs**, or *distritos*, which spread across the desert between the foothills of the Andes and the coast. Just south of Lima Centro lies the lively suburb of **Miraflores**, a slick, fast-moving and very ostentatious mini-metropolis, which has become Lima's business and shopping zone and doubles up as a popular meeting place for the wealthier sector of Lima society; a relatively modern cliff top development, Larco Mar, has been built at the bottom of Miraflores' main street, adding to the appeal. Sandwiched between Lima Centro and Miraflores is the plush suburb of **San Isidro**, boasting both the city's main commercial and banking sector and a golf course surrounded by sky-scraping apartment buildings. Like many of Lima's suburbs, San Isidro is home to two modern shopping complexes, one near the Paseo de La República, the other at Camino Real. Also representative of other suburbs is San Isidro's many square kilometres of closely packed houses almost pre-Inca in style – rectangular, often flat-roofed structures gilded with subtle geometric features and symbols, even lurking within the form of metal grill gates mainly there to keep out robbers.

South of Miraflores begins the oceanside suburb of **Barranco**, one of the oldest and most attractive parts of Lima, located above the steep sandy cliffs of the **Costa Verde**, and hosting a small nightlife enclave. Southwest of Lima Centro lies the city's port area, the suburb of **Callao**, an atmospheric, if rather old and insalubrious zone and the peninsula of **La Punta**, with its air of slightly decayed grandeur. The suburb of **La Victoria**, on the other side of central Lima from Callao, does contain some once fine plazas and buildings, but is better known these days for its bus depots and pickpockets. Other than these neighbourhoods, the main reason for venturing into Lima's suburbs is if you happen to live or be staying there or to visit some of the select museums scattered about the city's sprawl, namely the comprehensive **Museo Nacional de Arqueología, Antropología y Historia del Peru**, the modern **Museo de la Nación** and the **Museo Nacional de Historia**.

Miraflores

As far as Lima's inhabitants are concerned, **Miraflores** is the major focus of the city's action and nightlife, its streets lined with cafés and the capital's flashiest shops. Although still connected to Lima Centro by the long-established Avenida Arequipa, another road – Paseo de la República (also known as the Via Expressa and El Zanjón) – now provides the suburb with an alternative approach.

A good place to make for first is the **Huaca Pucllana**, a temple, administrative centre and pre-Columbian tomb in the middle of suburban Miraflores at General Borgoño 800 (Wed–Mon 9am–4.30pm; $2.20; ✆ 4458695). This vast pre-Inca adobe mound continues to dwarf most of the houses around and has a small site museum, craft shop and very good restaurant with a nice terrace. It's just a five-minute walk from Avenida Arequipa, on the right as you come from Lima Centro at block 44, and similarly close to blocks 5 and 6 of Avenida Angamos Oeste. One of a large number of *huacas* and palaces that formerly stretched across this part of the valley, little is known about the Pucllana, though it seems likely that it was originally named after a pre-Inca chief of the area. It has a hollow core running through its cross section and is believed to have been constructed in the shape of an enormous frog, symbol of the rain god, who evidently spoke to priests through a tube connected to the cavern at its heart. This site may well have been the mysteriously unknown oracle after which the Rimac (meaning "he who speaks") Valley was named; a curious document from 1560 affirms that the "devil" spoke at this mound. From the top of the *huaca* you can see over the office buildings and across the flat roofs of multicoloured houses in the heart of Miraflores.

The suburb's central area focuses on the attractive, almost triangular **Parque 7 de Junio** (or Miraflores Central Park, often just referred to as Miraflores Park) at the end of the Avenida Arequipa. The park, neatly grassed and with some attractive flower beds, divides into four areas of activity: at the top end is the pedestrian junction where the shoeshiners hang out; further down there's a small amphitheatre, which often has mime acts or music; next you come to a raised and walled, circular, flat concrete area, which has a good craft and antiques **market** set up on stalls every evening (6–10pm); and just down from here is a small section of gardens and a children's play area. The streets around the park are lined with flashy cafés and bars and crowded with shoppers, flower-sellers and young men washing cars. In the park, particularly on Sundays, there are painters selling their artwork – some quite good, though aimed at the tourist market. **Larco Mar**, the flash new development at the bottom of Avenida Larco, has done an excellent job of integrating the park end of Miraflores with what was previously a rather desolate point. Essentially a shopping zone with patios and walkways open to the sky, sea and cliffs, Larco Mar

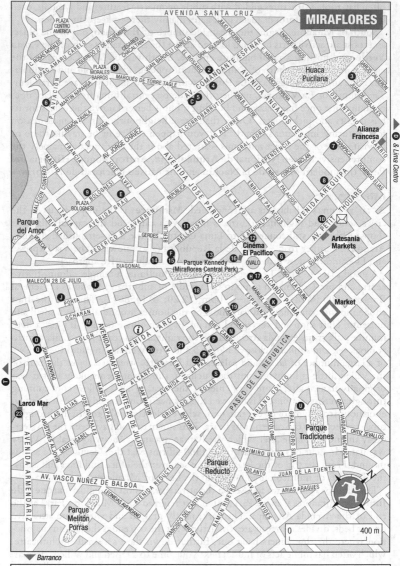

ACCOMMODATION			EATING & DRINKING			
Casa de Baraybar	A	Loki Hostal	H	Astrid y Gastón	19	Jazz Zone	22
Casa del Mochilero	B	Miraflores Colon Inn	Q	Aura	23	Madre Natura	2
Colonial Inn	C	Miraflores Hotel	G	El Bodegon	7	Mama Lola	18
Embajadores Hotel	O	Miraflores Park	T	Brenchley Arms	12	The Old Pub	15
Faraoña Grande Hotel	K	Radisson	I	Las Brujas de Cachiche	9	Patagonia Restaurant Arte y Diseno	20
Friends House	M	Sonesta Posada del		Café Café	13	Peña Sachúm	1
Hospedaje Flying Dog	L	Inca – Miraflores	P	Café Haiti	16	Restaurant Huaca Pucllana	3
Hostal Antigua Miraflores	E	Stop and Drop		Café Z	14	Restaurant NaturistaEl Paraiso	21
Hostal Buena Vista	S	and Guest House	F	Dinnos Pizza	4	Restaurant Tai-i Vegetariano	10
Hostal Martinika	D	Tinkus Hostel	U	La Divina Comida	5	Scena Restaurant Bar	11
Hostal El Patio	N	El Zaguan Lodging		Gotica	23	El Senorio de Sulco	6
Lex Luthor's House	J			La Hamaca	8	La Tiendacita Blanca	17

is also home to several bars, ice-cream parlours, reasonably good restaurants, a host of cinema screens and a couple of trendy nightclubs.

From the end of Avenida Arequipa, Avenida Larco and Diagonal both fan out along the park en route to the ocean about 1km away. Near to where Avenida Larco reaches the shore, the small but vibrant **Parque del Amor** sits on the clifftops above the Costa Verde and celebrates the fact that for decades this area has been a favourite haunt of young lovers, particularly the poorer Limeños who have no privacy in their often overcrowded homes. A huge sculpture of a loving Andean couple clasping each other rapturously is usually surrounded by pairs of real-life lovers walking hand-in-hand or cuddling on the cliff tops above the ocean, especially on Sunday afternoons. In recent years there were reports of muggings in and around here, but recently it's become relatively safe again.

Miraflores' only important mansion open to the public is the **Casa de Ricardo Palma**, at General Suarez 189 (Mon–Fri 9am–12.30pm & 2.15–5pm; $2; ☎4455836), where Palma, probably Peru's greatest historian, lived for most of his life. In terms of actual museums, there are two worth visiting in Miraflores, one of which, the **Enrico Poli Museum**, Lord Cochrane 466 (daily, hours by appointment; $15 per person for a minimum of five; ☎4222437), contains some of the finest pre-Inca archaeological treasures in Lima, including ceramics, gold and silver. The highlight of this private collection is the treasure found at Sipán in northern Peru, in particular four golden trumpets, each over a metre long and over a thousand years old. The private **Amano Museum**, on C Retiro 160, off block 11 of Angamos Oeste (Mon–Fri, hours by appointment but usually at 3 or 4pm, entry by donation; ☎4412909), also merits a visit for its fabulous exhibition of Chancay weavings (among the best of pre-Columbian textiles), as well as beautiful ceramics.

The fastest way to get to Miraflores from Lima Centro is to take at taxi ($4 should be plenty) or, alternatively, any **bus** marked "Via Expressa" from Avenida Abancay and get off, after about 25 minutes, at the Benavides Bridge. A potentially faster option than the Via Expressa bus is to take a bus or colectivo with a sign for Benavides or Chorrillos from the first few blocks of Avenida Garcilaso de la Vega (a continuation of Avenida Tacna) and get off at *El Haiti* café/bar, the stop just before Miraflores Park, usually called El Parque de Miraflores.

Barranco and the Costa Verde

Quieter than Miraflores, **Barranco**, about 3–4km from Larco Mar, overlooks the ocean and is scattered with old mansions, including fine colonial and Republican edifices, many beginning to fall apart through lack of care. This was the capital's seaside resort during the nineteenth century and is now a kind of Limeño Left Bank, with young artists, writers, musicians and intellectuals taking over some of the older properties. Only covering three square kilometres, Barranco is quite densely populated, with some 40,000 inhabitants living in its delicately coloured houses. The primary attractions of Barranco are its **bars, clubs and cafés** clustered around the small but busy and well-kept **Plaza Municipal de Barranco**, which buzz with frenetic energy after dark whilst retaining much of the area's original charm and character. There's little else to see, specifically, though you may want to take a look at the cliff-top remains of a funicular rail-line, which used to carry aristocratic families from the summer resort down to the beach.

One block inland of the funicular, the impressive **Iglesia de la Ermita** (Church of the Hermit) sits on the cliff, with gardens to its front. Local legend says that the church was built here following a miraculous vision of a glowing Christ figure on this very spot. Beside the church there's the **Puente de los Suspiros**, a pretty wooden bridge crossing a gully – the Bajada de Baños – which leads steeply down to the ocean, passing exotic dwellings lining the crumbling gully sides. A path

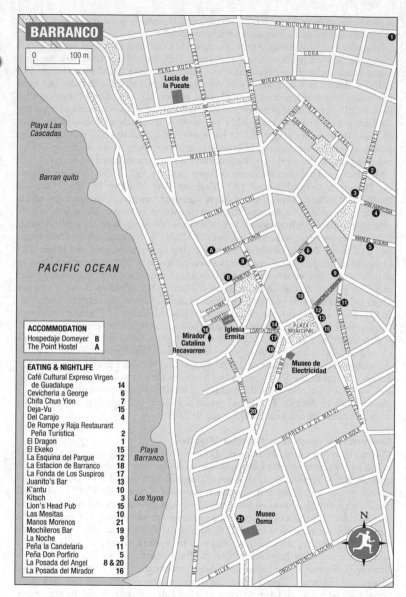

BARRANCO

0   100 m

Playa Las
Cascadas

Barran quito

PACIFIC OCEAN

Lucia de
la Pueate

PEREZ ROCA

AV. NICOLÁS DE PIEROLA

COHA

MIRAFLORES

MARTINEZ

COLINA ICOLICHI

MALECÓN JUNIN

DOMEYER

COLOMA

ARREGUI

Mirador
Catalina
Recavarren

Iglesia
Ermita

LOAYZA ZEPITA

PLAZA
MUNICIPAL

Museo de
Electricidad

ORIYA MELGAR

OSMA

HERRERA 12 DE MAYO)

Playa
Barranco

Los Yuyos

Museo
Osma

A. SILVA

INDEPENDENCIA SOLARI

SAN AMBROSIA

MANUEL SEGURA

N

ACCOMMODATION

| Hospedaje Domeyer | **B** |
| The Point Hostel | **A** |

EATING & NIGHTLIFE

Café Cultural Expreso Virgen de Guadalupe	14
Cevicheria a George	6
Chifa Chun Yion	7
Deja-Vu	15
Del Carajo	4
De Rompe y Raja Restaurant Peña Turística	2
El Dragon	1
El Ekeko	15
La Esquina del Parque	12
La Estacion de Barranco	18
La Fonda de Los Suspiros	17
Juanito's Bar	13
K'antu	10
Kitsch	3
Lion's Head Pub	15
Las Mesitas	10
Manos Morenos	21
Mochileros Bar	19
La Noche	9
Peña la Candelaria	11
Peña Don Porfirio	5
La Posada del Angel	8 & 20
La Posada del Mirador	16

leads beside the church along the top edge of the gully to the Mirador Catalina Recavarren. There's a two-storey pub, *La Posada del Mirador* at the end of the path near a seacliff, and some other pleasant cafés and bars, buzzing during weekend evenings. Also worth a browse is the **Museo de Electricidad**, Pedro de Osma 105 (daily 9am–5pm; free; phone in advance for guided visit ☎4776577), very close to the main plaza in Barranco, which displays a wide range of early electrical appliances and generating techniques. Just down the road, at Pedro de Osma

▲ Nightlife in Barranco

421, the **Museo de Arte Colonial Pedro de Osma** (Tues–Sun 10am–1.30pm & 2.30–6pm; $3.50; ℡4670141) holds a number of treasures and antiques such as oil paintings, colonial sculptures and silverware.

Down beside the pounding rollers lies the **Costa Verde beach area**, so named because of vegetation clinging to the steep sandy cliffs. A bumpy road follows the shore from an exclusive yacht club and the Chorrillos fishermen's wharf northwest past both Barranco and Miraflores, almost to the suburb of Magdalena. The sea is cold but the surfers still brave it. The Fisherman's Wharf ($0.30) is always an interesting place for a stroll, surrounded by pelicans and, early in the day, fishermen unloading their catch which is delivered immediately to the neighbouring market. Next to here there are a number of outdoor restaurants which compete vigorously for customers. They are all pretty good and, not surprisingly, have a reputation for serving the freshest ceviche in Lima.

Barranco is easily reached by picking up one of the many **buses or colectivos** (those marked Barranco or Chorrillos in their front window) travelling along Diagonal (which is one-way, from the central park towards Larco Mar and the ocean).

San Isidro and Jesus Maria

Unless you're shopping, banking or simply looking for a sauna or disco, there are few other reasons to stop off in **San Isidro**. One, though, is to take a stroll through the **Bosque El Olivar**, just 150m west from block 34 of Avenida Arequipa. A charming grove first planted in 1560, it's now rather depleted in olive trees but you can still see the old press and millstone, and there's also a stage where concerts and cultural events are often held. The grove has developed its own **ecosystem** which is home to over thirty different **bird species** including doves, flycatchers and hummingbirds. Mostly, though, El Olivar is simply one of Lima's relatively few large, open, green spaces. A few blocks northwest, just off Avenida El Rosario, is an impressive reconstructed adobe *huaca*, **Huallamarca**, Nicolas de Rivera 201 (Tues–Sun 9am–5pm; $1.80), now surrounded by wealthy suburbs. Like Pucllana, this dates from pre-Inca days and has a small museum displaying the archaeological remains of ancient Lima culture, such as funerary masks and artwork found in the *huaca* – including textiles oddly reminiscent of Scottish tartans.

The workaday suburb of **Jesus Maria**, just west of San Isidro and south of Lima Centro, has only one real attraction: the little-visited, but quite fascinating, **Museo de Historia Natural Jesus Maria**, Av Arenales 1256 (Mon–Fri 9am–3pm, Sat 9am–4.30pm, Sun 9am-12.30pm; $2.50, guided service $10 per group; ☏4710117). The museum presents a comprehensive if dusty overview of Peruvian wildlife and botany. One highlight is the largest bromeliad, a sun fish, being one of only three known examples in the world of this colourful fish that can be found in the American coastal waters. There are also great gardens with botany displays and a geology museum section.

Pueblo Libre

The less-visited, relatively quiet backstreets of **Pueblo Libre**, these days a relatively insalubrious suburb lying between San Isidro and Callao, are home to a trio of Lima's major museums. Primary among them is the **Museo Nacional de Arqueología, Antropología e Historia del Peru,** on Plaza Bolívar at the corner of San Martín and Antonio Pola (Tues–Sat 9am–5pm, Sun and fiestas 9am–4pm; $4; phone in advance for guided tours; ☏4635070; $6), which possesses a varied exhibition of pre-Inca artefacts and a number of historical exhibits relating mainly to the Republican period (1821 until the late nineteenth century). Although there's plenty to see, even more of the museum's immense collection is in storage, though some has shifted to the Museo de la Nación on the other side of town (see p.102).

Renovated displays give a detailed and accurate perspective on Peru's prehistory, a vision that comes as a surprise if you'd previously thought of Peru simply in terms of Incas and Conquistadors. The galleries are set around two colonial-style courtyards, the exhibits including stone tools some eight thousand years old, Chavin-era carved stones engraved with felines and serpents and the Manos Cruzados or Crossed Hands stone from **Kotosh**, evidence of a mysterious cult from some five thousand years ago. From the **Paracas** culture there are sumptuous weavings and many excellent examples of deformed heads and trepanned skulls: one shows post-operative growth, and a male mummy, "frozen" at the age of 30 to 35, has fingernails still visible and a creepy, sideways glance fixed on his mis-shapen head. From **Nasca** there are incredible ceramics representing marine life, agriculture, flora, sexuality, wildlife, trophy-heads and scenes from mythology and everyday life. The **Mochica** and **Chimu cultures** (see pp.558–559) are represented, too, and there are also exhibits devoted to the **Incas**. To get to the museum it's best to take a taxi, but there are **microbuses** that run along Avenida Brasil or Avenida Sucre, both only a few blocks away.

The **Museo Nacional de Historía** (National Museum of History), adjacent to the Museo Nacional de Arqueología, Antropología e Historia del Peru (same hours and ticket price) and entered by the same door, is housed in a nineteenth-century mansion. It displays dazzling antique clothing, extravagant furnishings and other period pieces, complemented by early Republican paintings. The liberators San Martín and Bolívar both lived here for a while.

A fifteen-minute walk from here – you can follow a blue line which is worn a little now but was been painted on the pavement north up Avenida Sucre then west for ten blocks to Av Bolívar 1515 – brings you to one of the city's most unusual museums, the **Museo Arqueológico Rafael Larco Herrera** (daily 9am–6pm; $9; ☏461312, ⓦwww.museolarco.org), which contains hundreds of thousands of excellently preserved ceramics, many of them Chiclin or Mochica pottery from around Trujillo. The mansion itself is noteworthy as a stylish *casa Trujillana*, from Trujillo, the northern city where this collection was originally kept. The museum houses the largest collection of Peruvian antiquities in the world and is divided into three sections: the **main museum** which contains an incredible range of household and funerary ceramics; the **warehouse museum**; and the **erotic art museum**, containing a wide selection of sexually themed pre-Inca artefacts, mainly from the explicit Mochica culture, which tend to attract the most interest.

From Lima Centro, you can get to the museum either by **bus** #23 from Avenida Abancay, by green microbus #37 from Avenida Nicolas de Pierola or on bus #41 from Avenida Emancipación or Plaza Dos de Mayo; however, it's much easier and quicker to take a taxi (about $4–5).

The Parque de las Leyendas and the Zoo

Head west from the Larco Herrera museum to the end of Avenida Bolívar, then skirt round to the southwest of the university of La Católica campus in the suburb of San Miguel, and you'll come to the **Parque de las Leyendas** and the **Zoo** (daily 9am–5pm; $3, $1.50 for students; ☎4644282). Located in a relatively deserted spot on the sacred site of the ancient Maranga culture, but close to block 24 of the Avenida La Marina, the park is laid out according to the three regions of Peru – *costa, sierra* and *selva*. The park and zoo have been much improved in recent years, though there's little attempt to create the appropriate habitats and the animals are caged. Nevertheless, it's a good place to get a glimpse of many of Peru's animal and bird species: condors, jaguars, sea lions, snakes, pumas, king vultures, bears and other exotica. It's also a fine spot for a picnic and there's an interesting **botanical garden**. Just outside there are often some good **artesania** stalls selling cases of magnificent dead insects, including colourful Amazonian butterflies and tarantulas.

Yellow **bus** #48 goes directly there from the Plaza Mayor or you can take almost any of the colectivos along Avenida La Marina or west along Avenida Javier Prado headed for Callao or La Punta; a taxi, though easier, may cost $4–5.

Callao and La Punta

Stuck out on a narrow, boot-shaped peninsula, **Callao** and **La Punta** (The Point) form a natural annex to Lima, looking out towards the ocean. Originally founded in 1537 and quite separate from the rest of the city, Callao was destined to become Peru's principal treasure-fleet port before eventually being engulfed by Lima's other suburbs during the course of the twentieth century. These days it's a crumbling but attractive and atmospheric area full of once splendid houses and restaurants. The land is very low lying and, at la Punta itself, the surf feels as though it could at any moment rise up and swallow the small rowing boat-dotted beach and nearby houses.

Still the country's main commercial harbour, and one of the most modern ports in South America, **Callao** lies about 14km west of Lima Centro. The suburb is none-too-alluring a place – its slum zones, nameless areas located in the back streets infamous for prostitution and gangland assassins, are considered virtually **no-go areas** for visitors – but if you're unworried by the potential dangers of the neighbourhood, you will find some of the best **ceviche restaurants** anywhere on the continent.

Further along, away from the rougher quarters and dominating the entire peninsula, you can see the great **Fortaleza del Real Felipe** (daily 9.30am–3.30pm; $2.5; ☎4658394), located on the first block of Avenida Saenz Peña, Plaza Independencia. Built after the devastating earthquake of 1764, which washed ships ashore and killed nearly the entire population of Callao, this is a superb example of the military architecture of its age, designed in the shape of a pentagon. Although built too late to protect the Spanish treasure fleets from European pirates like Francis Drake, it was to play a critical role in the battles for independence. Its firepower repulsed both Admiral Brown (1816) and Lord Cochrane (1818), though many Royalists (Peruvians loyal to the Spanish Crown) starved to death here when the stronghold was besieged by the Patriots (those patriotic to Peru but keen to devolve power from the Spanish colonial authorities) in 1821, just prior to the Royalist surrender.

The fort's grandeur is marred only by a number of storehouses, built during the late-nineteenth century when it was used as a customs house. Inside, the **Museo del Ejercito or Military Museum** (Mon–Fri 9.30am–4pm; free) houses a fairly complete collection of eighteenth- and nineteenth-century arms and has various rooms dedicated to Peruvian war heroes. If your interest in military matters has been piqued, try the **Museo Naval**, Av Jorge Chavez 123, off Plaza Grau (Mon–Fri 9.30am–2.30pm; $1; ⊤4294793 ext 6794), displaying the usual military paraphernalia, uniforms, paintings, photographs and replica ships. Outside is the **Canon del Pueblo,** a large gun installed in a day and a night on May 2, 1866 during a battle against a Spanish fleet; it is also claimed to have deterred the Chilean fleet from entering Lima during the War of the Pacific. From the same building as the Naval Museum, there's also access to the nearby **Museo Submarino Abtao, or Submarine Museum** (Tues–Sun 9am–5pm; $2; ⊤7956900), actually a real sub that literally opened its hatches in 2004 to allow public access for thirty-minute guided tours including a simulated attack by enemy sub. A Sierra-type vessel, this torpedo-firing battle sub was built in Connecticut, USA, between 1952 and 1954, when it first arrived in Peru. You can touch the periscope, visit the dorms, smell the kitchens and enter the engine and control rooms which were responsible for over five thousand submersions during 48 years of service.

Out at the end of the peninsula, what was once the fashionable beach resort of **La Punta** is now overshadowed by the Naval College and Yacht Club. Many of its old mansions, although slowly crumbling, still remain, some of them very elegant, others extravagant monstrosities. Right at the peninsula's tip, an open and pleasant **promenade** offers glorious views and sunsets over the Pacific and the nearby offshore islands such as Fronton (with its small, isolated prison), San Lorenzo (with evidence of human occupation, fishing and the use of both cotton and maize going back to 2,500 BC) and also Isla Palomino (with its colony of sea lions). Meanwhile at the back of the strand there are some excellent **restaurants** serving traditional local food (many of these are difficult to find – it's best to ask locally for directions).

To get to Callao and La Punta take the **bus** #25 from Plaza San Martín, which runs all the way there – and beyond to La Punta – or take a bus (marked "La Punta") from Avenida Arequipa west along either Avenida Angamos or Avenida Javier Prado.

The Museo de la Nación and the Museo de Oro

The **Museo de la Nación**, Javier Prado Este 2465, situated in the suburb of San Borja just east of San Isidro (Tues–Sun 9am–6pm; $2.20; ⊤4769878), is Lima's largest modern museum and contains permanent exhibitions covering most of the important aspects of Peruvian archeology, art and culture. Built originally as the Ministry of Agriculture, it was transformed into a national museum by the then President Alan García in the late 1980s. Exhibits are displayed mainly in vast salons and include a range of traditional, regional peasant costumes from around the country and life-sized and miniature models depicting life in pre-Conquest times.

To get to the Museo de la Nación, take a **colectivo** along Avenida Javier Prado east from Avenida Arequipa; after ten to fifteen minutes, you'll see the vast, concrete building on the left.

The Museo de Oro

Housed in a small, fortress-like building set back in the shade of tall trees and owned by the high-society Mujica family, the **Museo de Oro** is located along Javier Prado Este, in the suburb of Monterrico at Av Alonso de Molina 1100 (daily 11.30am–7pm; $11; ⊤3451292). Upstairs there are some excellent tapestry displays, while the ground level boasts a vast display of **arms and uniforms**, which bring to life some of Peru's bloodier historical episodes. The real gem, however, is the basement, crammed with original and replica pieces from **pre-Columbian** times. The pre-Inca weapons and wooden staffs and the astounding Nasca yellow-feathered poncho designed for a noble's child or child high-priest are especially fine pieces. One object which usually causes a stir is a **skull** with a full set of pink quartz teeth.

The **Casa Ecológica** in La Molina, another suburb a few kilometres directly east of Monterrico, is affiliated with the Universidad La Catolica's Group for Assistance to the Rural Sector. Located on the University campus, it has an interesting exhibit of an ecologically friendly house with wind, solar electric, solar thermal and solar cooking facilities set in an organic garden. To visit, you need to contact Sr. Urpi Vasquez in advance. (T 6262000 ext 5059)

Both places are difficult to find and quite distant from Miraflores or Lima Centro, so it's best to take a **taxi** ($4–6).

Parque Zoológico Huachipa

Much newer than the Parque de Las Leyendas zoo, if a long way out to the east of Lima where Av Las Torres meets Vitarte (take a taxi; $5–7), Huachipa (daily 9.30am–5.30pm; $3.50; T 3563666, W www.zoohuachipa.com.pe) offers a diverse, created habitat with lakes and rides, plenty of animals and a forest of birds.

Eating

Among South American capitals, Lima ranks alongside Rio and Buenos Aires for its selection of places to eat and drink, with **restaurants, bars and cafés** of every type and size crowding every corner of the city, from expensive hotel dining rooms to tiny set meal street stalls. What makes Peru's cuisine so special is a combination of diverse cultural ingredients (Andean, Spanish, Italian, African and Chinese in particular) alongside perhaps the world's greatest store of indigenously domesticated edible plants, a by-product of Peru's great biodiversity and range of ecosystems. Having the world's largest forest and source of plants for global domestication at the backdoor probably helped create a modern Lima where people take for granted fresh and varied food of great quality. Regardless of class or status, virtually all Limeños eat out regularly, and having a meal out usually ends up as an evening's entertainment in itself.

Cafés

Lima Centro

Bar/Restaurant Machu Picchu Jr Ancash 318. A busy place opposite San Francisco church, serving inexpensive snacks such as omelettes and sandwiches or even *cuy picante* (spicy guinea pig); they offer cheap set menu lunches and it's a good spot for meeting up with other travellers.

El Cordano Jr Ancash 202, T 4270181. Across the street from the Palacio de Gobierno, this is one of the city's last surviving traditional bar/restaurants with mirrored walls, racks of bottles and old-style waiters, curt but efficient, even charming in an old-fashioned way. Worth visiting if only to feel the atmosphere, eat excellent ham sandwiches and see first-hand the exquisite late-nineteenth- and early twentieth-century decor. Mon–Sat 8am–9pm.

El Paraiso de la Salud Restaurant Vegetariano Jr Camana 344 T 3475112. Offering a delivery service, this vegetarian option offers good breakfasts, as well as yoghurt, juice, salads, wholemeal breads and smoothies. It's a large space but busy at lunchtimes when it serves delicous plates like steamed broccoli and lentil tortillas.

Queirolo Café Bar Restaurant Corner of Camana 900 with Quilca. This is a classic meeting place for poets, writers and painters and worth a visit just for the splendour of its old Lima Cason-style architecture and bohemian atmosphere. They serve *comida criolla*, sandwiches, beer and pisco; great for inexpensive quality set lunches. Open 9am–2am.

▲ Café Haiti, Miraflores

Miraflores and Barranco

Café Café Martir Olaya 250 ☎4451165. Located just off Diagonal in downtown Miraflores, this is a hip, gay-friendly coffee shop that plays good rock music and serves a variety of sandwiches, salads, paellas, pastas and Peruvian dishes, as well as a selection of cocktails. Open daily 10am–midnight.

Café Haiti Diagonal 160, Miraflores ☎4463816. The most popular meeting place for middle-class Limeños, based near the Cinema El Pacifico in the heart of Miraflores. Offers excellent snacks, such as stuffed avocado or *ají de gallina*, and a decent range of soft and alcoholic drinks although it's not cheap. Open daily 8am–2am.

Café Z Corner of Jose Galvez with Diagonal, in Miraflores,☎4445579. Very pleasant ambience, with plenty of glass decor, a wooden interior balcony and two floors crowded with small round tables. Contemporary rock music is usually playing and the staff are

young and groovy; good coffee, salads and bar food are their specialities. Open daily 7am–11pm.

K'antu Av Grau 323, Barranco ☎992681419. Both a caféteria and a centre for fairly traded, handmade craft goods. It serves good organic coffee, nice cakes and is linked to the Inter-regional Centre for Artesans of Peru. Open Mon–Thurs 10am–10pm, Fri and Sat 9am–11pm.

Las Mesitas Av Grau 341, in Barranco, ☎4774199. A tasteful Lima café serving quality, delicious snacks, meals and scrumptious sweets including excellent *humitas*, *tamales*, juices and sandwiches. Open noon to 3pm & 7pm–midnight.

La Tiendacita Blanca Av Larco 111, Miraflores ☎4451412. Another popular meeting place, with a superb range of Peruvian and Swiss foods, plus cakes and pastries, though they are pricey; located right on the busiest junction in Miraflores. Live piano music Mon–Fri 7–8pm. Open daily 7am–noon.

Restaurants

Predictably, Lima boasts some of the best **restaurants** in the country, serving not only traditional Peruvian dishes, but also cuisines from all parts of the world. **Seafood** is particularly good here, with **ceviche** – raw fish or seafood marinated in lime juice and served with onions, chillis, sweet corn and sweet potatoes – being the speciality. **Chorros a la Calaca** (spicy muscles) are another speciality from Lima's port area of Callao. Traditional goat and duck feasts have made their way to Lima from the northern coast of Peru, while Argentina-style grills are commonplace and chicken broaster is everywhere. As well as a wide range of delicious meat, rice- and vegetable-based **criolla dishes**, Peru boasts a new and highly creative **novo andino cuisine**, often utilising alpaca steaks with berries or cheese sauces from lush Andean farms, and best appreciated either here in this city's best restaurants or in Cusco's finest. Many of the more upmarket restaurants fill up very quickly, so it is advisable to **reserve in advance**; where this is the case we have included the phone number. All the restaurants listed below are open roughly 10.30am–11pm daily unless otherwise indicated.

Lima Centro

Chifa Capon Ucayali 774. An excellent and traditional Limeño Chinese fusion restaurant, the best in this block of Chinatown. It offers a range of authentic, moderately priced *chifa* dishes, and stays open daily until 2 or 3am.

De Cesar Ancash 300 ☎4288740. Great little café/restaurant and bar right in the heart of old Lima, with great ambience. The spacious interior is sometimes a bit dark but the food is fine and cheap, service very friendly and the range of breakfasts and juices quite endless.

Don Lucho's Restaurant Jr Carabaya 346. Just off the Plaza Mayor, this is a busy lunchtime spot with a cool interior, popular with local office workers and offering fast service and decent set menu meals for less than $3.

El Estadio Restaurant Bar Nicolas de Pierola 926, Plaza San Martín ☎4288866, ⊛www .estadio.com.pe. A restaurant with a strong football theme and walls covered in murals and sports paraphernalia, fascinating even for those only remotely interested in the sport; you can even have your picture taken next to a life-size bust of Pele while you're here. Both the food and bar are excellent and sometimes there are disco evenings in the basement. There's also a Peruvian food festival every Fri and Sat. Open Mon & Tues noon–6pm, Wed & Thurs noon–11pm, Fri & Sat noon to 4am.

L'Eau Vive Ucayali 370, ☎4275612. Opposite the Torre Tagle Palace, this interesting restaurant serves superb French and Peruvian dishes cooked by nuns. It has a reasonable set menu for lunches and evening meals and closes after a chorus of *Ave Maria* most evenings. Open Mon–Sat 12.30–3pm & 7.30–9.30pm.

Miraflores

Astrid y Gastón Cantuarias 175, Miraflores ☎444-1496. A trendy, colonial-style signature restaurant run by the world-renowned Peruvian chef Gastón Acurio. Possibly the best in Lima, it's stylish and expensive, with a menu blending Peruvian *criolla* and Mediterranean-style cooking.

El Bodegon Tarapaca 197–199 ☎4456222. Great service in pleasant surroundings, providing Mediterranean, vegetarian and *novo andino* cuisine, with newly conceived alpaca and other dishes with French or European influence, and a good selection of wines and piscos. Open Mon–Sat 11am–11pm.

Las Brujas de Cachiche Av Bolognesi 460 ☎4457154 or 4471133. Very trendy and expensive, this interestingly conceived, top-class restaurant and bar serves mainstream Peruvian dishes as well as a range of pre-Columbian and *novo andino* meals such as seafood ceviche and maize-based dishes using only ingredients available more than a thousand years ago.

Caplina Mendiburu 793 ☎4753404. A good cevicheria on the outskirts of Miraflores, close to block 7 of Av El Elejercito, serving tasty, classic ceviches around a square concrete and pebble pond. They also prepare seafood *a la chalca* (Callao local style, often spicy hot, recognised as traditional and one of the best) and *a la Chiclayano* (from northern Peru with a strong coriander sauce), as well as meat and Italian pasta dishes. Open daily 9am–5pm.

Dinnos Pizza Comandante Espinar 408 ☎2190909. This flashy, brightly lit restaurant offers some of the best pizza in Lima, as well as relatively fast service and optional delivery. Open daily, noon–midnight.

La Divina Comida Av Comandante Espinar 300, in the *Hotel Colonial Inn*. A very fine restaurant for a lunchtime set menu ($3–5 with a choice of main course) in terms of quality and value for money; not to be missed if you're in this part of Miraflores.

La Hamaca Av Arequipa 4698 ☎ 242-7978. Another great Lima restaurant where they serve true quality *criollo* meals. Their *ají de gallina* (a chillied chicken dish with ancient roots) is spectacular, but the colonial museum-mansion it's based in is also fantastic.

Madre Natura Chiclayo 815. Located by block 4 of Av Comandante Espinar, this is a cafeteria serving tasty but healthy snacks and meals, located in the Madre Natura complex, with an organic and health products store, "eco" gifts centre and also a wholemeal bakery. Open Mon–Sat 8am–9pm, Sun 9am–2pm.

Mama Lola Diez Canseco 119 ☎42416335. Right in the heart of Miraflores, close to the bottom end of the Park, this welcoming trattoria and pizarra buzzes at night with locals and tour groups alike. Open for lunch and evening meals, Mama Lola serves great Italian dishes such as onion soup and spinach ravioli with ricotta, as well as Peruvian dishes like *tacu tacu*, black beans and seafood.

La Mar Av La Mar 770 ☎4213365. Easily Lima's most trendy and lively cevichería, La Mar is stylish, swanky and very, very busy. Noisy but with great salsa music and strong pisco sours, the restaurant is ultra modern in design, squeezing lots of tables into a relatively small triangle of space. Although Peruvian owned, it's now part of a chain with branches in Costa Rica, Mexico and San Francisco – all flagships for Peru's fantastic ceviche tradition. Here they serve a really wide range of ceviches in all sorts of regional traditions, like *tiraditos* (thin slivers of fish in sweet sauces) with innovative combinations (try the *tiradito poderoso* with sea urchins, and black scallops in a lemon and olive oil vinagrette). Best to get there before 12.30pm to avoid queues.

Patagonia Restaurant Arte y Diseno C Bolívar 164 ☎4468705. A slightly different locale with good service, walls full of photos and paintings, plus a space for theatre and music performances. Food specialities include Italian–Argentine cuisine, and the *pasta fresca* is excellent. Good wines available. Open Mon–Sat 6pm–2am.

Restaurant Huaca Pucllana General Borgoño, block 8 ☎4454042. Tasty, international cuisine with a French flavour and quality Peruvian dishes, including novo andino and excellent traditional *cuy, cabrito* and various fish offerings. The service is outstanding, and the restaurant has an elegant terrace that looks out onto the ancient monument of the Huaca Pucllana (see p.95). Open Mon-Sat 12.30pm–midnight, Sun 12.30–4pm.

Restaurant Naturista El Paraiso Alcanfores 416–453. A great vegetarian restaurant, and a cheerful place to shelter from the hustle and bustle of the Miraflores streets. Open daily 8am–10pm.

Restaurant Tai-i Vegetariano Av Petit Thouars, 5232 ☎2426654. Handily located opposite the artesania markets, this veggie standby offers simple, inexpensive and satisfying food in the shape of set-lunch menu meals plus a range of great Asian dishes, some incorporating cashew nuts and coconut sauces. Open daily 8am–8pm.

La Rosa Nautica Espigon 4, Costa Verde ☎4475450. Located on a pier, this is one of Lima's more expensive seafood restaurants, but has excellent ocean views. The menu provides a wide range of Latin American and European dishes. Jazz performances every Thursday evening. Open daily 12.30pm–12.30am.

Scena Restaurant Bar C San Francisco de Paula Camino 280 ☎2418181. Quite an unusual place, original and spectacular in its own way and ultramodern in design. Food is a fusion of flavours based on the chef's own interpretation of *cocina Peruana* (Peruvian cuisine), with good meats, fish and bar. Open Mon–Fri 12.30–4pm, Sat 7.30pm–12.30am.

El Señor de Sulco Malecon Cisneros 1470 ☎4410183. Specializing in Peruvian cuisine, including *novo andino*, this restaurant uses the finest ingredients in preparing mainly traditional dishes in the traditional way, many cooked only in earthen pots. These type of meals can be found on street stalls all over Peru, only in this case you pay extra because the chef is top quality. Open Mon–Sat noon–midnight.

Barranco and other suburbs

Café Cultural Expreso Virgen de Guadalupe Av Prol San Martin 15-A, Barranco ☎2528907. A unique, atmospheric restaurant and bar situated right beside the Puente de Los Suspiros, serving typical international and Peruvian fare inside an ornate nineteenth-century railway carriage. Live music at weekends.

La Carreta Av Rivera Navarrete 740, San Isidro ☎4422690. One of the best *churrascarias* (Brazilian-style steakhouse) in Lima, based close to San Isidro's Centro Comercial. Designed like an old hacienda, this place serves dishes that are mainly Peruvian or international, and there's a spectacular bar with many quality wines. Open daily noon–midnight.

Centro Turistico Perco's Restaurant C Elias Aguirre 166, San Isidro ☎4456697. Don't be put off by the name, this is Lima's one and only restaurant specialising in jungle region cuisine. They offer venison, wild pig, *paiche* fish and many other excellent and reasonably priced dishes. Open daily 8am–11pm.

Cevichería a George Unión 140, Barranco ☎2475143. A plain and simple no frills cevicher'a that serves some of the tastiest and freshest ceviche in Lima as well as fish and *comida criolla* dishes. Open daily 10am–6pm.

Cevichería El Rey Marino Clara Barton Lte. 10, La calera, Surquillo ☎4488667. Located close to block 43 of Av Avacion this restaurant is another brilliant and unpretentious cevichería; very friendly service, and a good selection of Peruvian music plus plenty of tables. Best at lunchtimes.

Chifa Chun Yion C Unión 126, Barranco ☎4770550. An excellent and very busy Chinese restaurant, quite traditional with some private booths in the back room. Again, not high quality, but very reasonably priced. Open noon–3pm & 7pm–midnight.

Club Suizo Genaro Iglesias 550, Aurora-Miraflores ☎4459230. Located level with block 17 of Avenida Benavides, this fine place offers exquisite Swiss cuisine, including extravagant fondues combining four cheeses, in a very pleasant environment. Open Tues–Sat 11am–11pm, Sun 11am–4pm.

El Italiano Trattoria Pizzeria C Enrique Leon Garcia 376, La Victoria ☎4721281. A local place, not at all touristic, and located in the Urbanizacion Santa Catalina. Unlike most pizzerias or Italian restaurants in Peru, all the pasta, pizzas and other food is freshly prepared on the premises. Open 1–4pm & 6–11pm; closed Mon.

La Fonda de Los Suspiros Av Pedro de Osma 102, Barranco ☎ 2472547 or 998487462. Located right on the square in Barranco, this small but brilliant restaurant delightfully combines quality French and Peruvian cuisine, including traditional Peruvian dishes, such as *pato con arroz* and *ají de gallina*. Open Mon–Sat 12.30–3.30pm & 7.30–11.30pm, Sun 12.30–3.30pm.

Manolo Malecon Pardo, block 1, La Punta, Callao ☎ 4531380. A fine seafood restaurant and bar on the seafront (best sampled when sunny rather than windy). The food is very fresh; try the *chicharones de pulpo* or the *ceviche de pescado*.

Punto Azul Corner of Javier Prado with Av Petit Thouars in San Isidro ☎ 2213747. One of a chain of excellent and unpretentious cevicherías, this one is unusual in that you eat outside at tables right on one of Lima's busiest junctions.

Siam Thai Cuisine Av Caminos del Inca 467, Chacarilla ☎ 720680. Superb Thai food in a delightful, tranquil environment with small indoor gardens and very reasonable service and prices. Best to take a taxi ($4 from Miraflores).

Sushi Ito Av El Polo 740, Monterrico, Surco ☎ 4355817. Located in the Centro Comercial El Polo, this is an excellent, posh sushi restaurant that serves *sashimi* and *maki-temaki*, amongst other dishes. Open Mon–Sat noon–4pm and 7pm–midnight.

Drinking and nightlife

Lima's nightlife is more urban, modern and less traditional than other cities such as Cusco and Arequipa. The suburb of **Barranco** is now the trendiest and liveliest place to hang out.

All forms of **Peruvian music** can be found in Lima, some of them, like **salsa** and **Afro-Peruvian** (see Contexts p.592), are better here than anywhere else in the country. Even Andean folk music can be close to its best here (though Puno, Cusco and Arequipa are all more probable contenders). As far as the **live music scene** goes, the great variety of traditional and hybrid sounds is one of the most enduring reasons for visiting the capital. Obviously, things are at their liveliest on Friday and Saturday nights, equally among the trendy clubs as with folk group *peñas* and the burgeoning *salsadromos* (nightclubs more or less exclusively dedicated to salsa music). Many people may also be surprised to learn that Latin jazz has been evolving in Lima since the late 1960s, with its most famous exponent, Jaime Delgado Aparicio, well-known to European DJs. And with a new generation of young Afro-Peruvians – spearheaded by Gabriel Alegría – now making waves on the international jazz scene, Lima is the perfect place to catch them in situ. Most clubs charge around $5–20 entrance, which often includes a drink and/or a meal. The daily **El Comercio** provides the best **information** about music events, and its Friday edition carries a comprehensive supplement guide to Lima's nightlife, which is easy to understand even if your Spanish is limited.

Bars and clubs

Lima has relatively exciting **clubs**, with the vast majority of its popular **bars** and discos located out in the suburbs of **San Isidro** and **Miraflores**. Most open Thursday to Saturday 10pm–2 or 3am unless otherwise stated. Many clubs have a **members-only policy**, though if you can provide proof of tourist status, such as a passport, you usually have no problem getting in. In summer months (Jan–March) the party sometimes carries on down the coast to the resort of Asia, 110km south, where there are some surprisingly sophisticated nightclubs.

Bars

Brenchley Arms Atahualpa 174, Miraflores ☎ 4459680. Trying to replicate an English pub, *Brenchley Arms* has a pleasant atmosphere and three bars stocked with good beer. Rock music occasionally performed live.

El Dragon Nicolas de Pierola 168, Barranco. Small, dark and fun, *El Dragon* almost always has live music, frequently good Latin rock and jazz.

Habana Café Bar Av Manuel Bonilla 107 ℡4463511, Miraflores. Live music Fri and Sat from 10pm–1am, particularly Cuban, but also great jazz and rock nostalgia alongside a little art gallery.

Juanito's Bar Av Grau 274, Barranco. Probably the most traditional of the neighbourhood's bars; facing onto the Parque Municipal, it is small and basic and offers an excellent taste of Peru as it used to be. The music policy is strictly *criolla* and traditional Peruvian folk, and the front bar is designated for couples only during weekend evenings.

Lion's Head Pub Av Grau 268, Barranco. Located on the second floor, you'll find yet another British-style pub with dartboard, pool table, newspapers, sports TV and, of course, English beers.

Mochileros Bar Av Pedro de Osma 135, Barranco ℡2471225. Located in a fine old Barranco mansion, now converted into an *albergue* and live music bar. It has outside tables and good cocktails (house speciality is *El Beso del Diablo*, consisting of pisco, tequila and grenadilla).

Murphy's Irish Pub C Shell 627, Miraflores ℡2421212. A spacious, modern-looking joint and a good meeting place in the heart of Miraflores. Live music Thurs–Sat, usually rock.

La Posada del Mirador Barranco. Located on the cliff-top point behind the Puente de Suspiros and church, this is a popular evening bar with great views and a lively atmosphere.

Rincon Cervecero Jr de La Unión 1045, Lima Centro ℡4288866. An original Lima bar but in Germanic style with satisfyingly large pitchers of beer and shots, and an excellent atmosphere. The kitchen serves original in-house recipes, and there's a beer festival in October.

The Old Pub San Ramon 295, Miraflores ℡2428155. The most authentic of the English-style pubs in Lima, and easy to find just a block or two from the park in Miraflores, at the far end of Little Italy (San Ramon). It's actually run by an Englishman, and also plays good music and has a dartboard. Sandwiches, salads, chips and roast beef meals available.

Clubs

Aura Larcomar, Miraflores ℡2425516. Well respected for its weekend shows and electronica prowess; now and then presented by international DJs.

Deja-Vu Av Grau 294 Barranco ℡2476989. A heaving dance club from Monday through to Saturday night. Music mainly ranges from trance to techno.

La Esquina del Parque on the corner of Grau and the Boulevard Pazos, Barranco. Right by the plaza in Barranco, this is very popular with the younger Lima set, although it's as much of a music café as a club.

Gotica Larcomar, Miraflores ℡4456343. A fairly exclusive yet popular disco with excellent music, good service and an even better sound system: expect anything from hip-hop and punk to Latin rock, salsa and reggaeton, as well as occasional live bands at weekends.

Karamba Boulevard Los Olivos, Los Olivos, north Lima ⊛www.boulevard-losolivos.com. This is a hectic salsotec based north of Lima Centro in the district of Los Olivos. Split into two levels, walls painted in coconuts, it has a hot tropical feel and plays heavy electronic as well as salsa music. Nearby, also on the Boulevard, there's another popular club, *Kokos*.

Kitsch Av Bolognesi 743, Barranco. A funky and gay-friendly disco-bar with weird decor, known for playing lots of 70s and 80s tunes; it gets hotter late on.

La Noche Av Bolognesi 307, El Boulevard Pazos, Barranco ℡2472186, ⊛www.lanoche.com.pe. Don't let the slightly risque website put you off, this is a top nightclub located at the top end of the Boulevard, this is arguably the top venue in Barranco and one of the best places for meeting people; it.gets really packed at weekends. Musically, it specialises in Latin rock and electronica, with free jazz sessions on Monday evenings. Live music (Mon–Sat 10pm–2am) comes with a small entry fee.

Satchmo Av la Paz 538, Miraflores ℡4428425. A central live venue, best at weekends when performances range from Latin music to jazz, rock and blues. It's reasonably priced and food is available. Open Fri–Sun from 8pm until late.

Peñas and salsadromos

The **peñas** – some of which only open at weekends – are nearly all located in **Barranco** and they are the surest bet for listening to authentic **Andean folk**, although some of them also specialize in Peruvian **criolla,** which brings together a unique and very vigorous blend of Afro-Peruvian, Spanish and, to a lesser extent, Andean music. These days it's not uncommon for some of Lima's best *peñas* to feature a fusion of *criolla* and Latin jazz. Generally speaking, *peñas* don't get going until after 10pm and usually the bands play through to 3 or 4am, if not until first light.

Lima is also an excellent place to experience the Latin American **salsa** scene, and there are **salsadromos** scattered around many of the suburbs. They play a mix of tropical music, salsa, merengue and technocumbia (see Contexts for details on the various musical forms). Most are open Friday and Saturday 10pm–3am.

Las Brisas del Titicaca Jr Wakulski 168, Lima Centro ☎3321901, ✆www.brisasdel-titicaca.com. One of the busiest and most popular venues for tourists in the know and local city people alike; excellent bands and yet one of the cheapest of the city's *peñas*. Open Thurs–Sat 8.30pm–5am (shows from 10.30pm–2.30am).

Del Carajo San Ambrosia 328, Barranco ☎2418904. This is a lively and popular *peña* playing a range of *criolla*, Andean and coastal traditional and modern music. Open Thurs–Sat 10pm–3am.

De Rompe y Raja Restaurant Peña Turística C Manuel Segura 127, Barranco. ☎2473271. Located between blocks 5 and 6 of Avenida Bolognesi, this *peña* presents live music from the three regions of Peru from 10pm. Ideal for groups, with big tables and entertainment into the small hours. Open Thurs–Sat from 9pm.

La Estacion de Barranco Av Pedro de Osma 112, Barranco, ☎2470344. Just across the road from the suburb's main plaza, this established *peña* regularly varies its flavour between folklore, *criolla* and even Latin jazz or rock at times, with a very

good atmosphere most Fridays and Saturdays. Open Tues–Sat 9pm–3am.

Kimbara Av República de Panama 1401, La Victoria ☎2655831. Recently renovated, this is a sprawling, unpretentious choice, with vibrant salsa music, sometimes performed live at weekends.

Manos Morenas Av Pedro de Osma 409, Barranco ☎4670421. A few blocks south of the small plaza, this club usually hosts *criolla* gigs, and has its own permanent dance group. Excellent food and shows, though the atmosphere can be a little constrained.

Peña La Candelaria Av Bolognesi 292, Barranco ☎2471314. An enormous venue presenting live music and dance from the three regions (coast, Andes and Amazon). Open Fri & Sat 10pm–3am.

Peña Don Porfirio C Manuel Segura 115, Barranco ☎4773119. Possibly the only traditional style *peña* left in Lima. Offers dance lessons during the week. Open Fridays after 10pm.

Peña Sachún Av del Ejercito 657, Miraflores ☎4410123. Very lively and popular tourist restaurant with a good reputation for live folkloric music and *criolla* dancing. Open Tues–Sat 8.30pm–3am.

Jazz, rock and Latin jazz

Lima is pretty hot on **jazz** and **rock** music and has several excellent **Latin jazz** acts of its own (see opposite). The clubs are usually packed with a good mix of young people and older bohemian types.

10 Sesenta Los Nardos 1060, San Isidro ☎4410744. Club/pub which serves good food and puts on live Latin jazz and criolla shows.

CC Club Delfus Taberna San Martín 587, Miraflores ☎9431211. Live rock music every Friday and Saturday night, with open jam sessions on Tuesday and Thursday.

Bullfighting

Bullfighting has been a popular pastime among a relatively small, wealthy elite from the Spanish Conquest to the present day, despite some 185 years of independence from Spain. Pizarro himself brought out the first *lidia* bull for fighting in Lima, and there is a great tradition between the controlling families of Peru – the same families who breed bulls on their haciendas – to hold fights in Lima during October and November. They invite some of the world's best bullfighters from Spain, Mexico and Venezuela, offering them significant sums for an afternoon's sport at the prestigious **Plaza de Acho** in Rimac. **Tickets** can be bought in advance from major shops like the Wong and Metro chain of superstores throughout the city. Fights take place most Saturday and Sunday afternoons throughout the year, but the best time to catch a fight is in October or November, when the international bullfighters come to Lima.

El Ekeko Av Grau 266, by the municipal plaza in Barranco ☎2473148. Often has Latin jazz at weekends, though also hosts Peruvian Andean and coastal music, mainly *criolla*. Best to call first to make sure there's live music on when you go.
Jazz Zone Av la Paz 656, Miraflores ☎2418139. Located in the Pasaje El Suche, *Jazz Zone* offers cutting edge live presentations of Latin or Brazilian rock, salsa and jazz as well as fine examples of avant garde Andean folk and occasionally Peruvian ballad singers.

🏃 La Posada del Angel III Av Prol San Martin 157, Barranco ☎2475544. This is the largest of three *Posada del Angel* venues, all within a stone's throw of each other in Barranco. Well-known for its Trova and Latino live music sessions, it has a great bar and also serves snacks and meals. All three locations are richly decorated in kitsch style; the other two are at Pedro de Osma 164 and 218.

Gay and lesbian Lima

Since the **gay and lesbian** scene in Lima is relatively small, there are few gay meeting places, though the main Park and Larcomar centre in Miraflores can be a bit cruisy in the evenings. Lima society has begun to grow more tolerant, but this does depend on which zone you're in. The male culture, however, is still primarily macho, so as a visitor, keeping a relatively low profile makes for an easier time.

Gay bars and clubs

La Cueva Av Aviacion 2514 ☎97888044. A simple disco for gay and lesbian audiences, mostly under 40 years of age; plays 90s music. Great shows on Friday and Saturday, usually peaking around 3am. Open Thurs–Sun from 10.30pm.
Downtown Vale Todo Pasaje Los Pinos 160, Miraflores ☎4446433. Arguably the best gay club in Lima; now and then there are caged go-go dancing boys, occasional striptease acts and a cruise bar as well as dance floors.
Gitano 2050 Berlin 231, Miraflores. Well-known as a Lima gay club, this place is divided into vari-

ous levels with cruising above the dancing. Open Wed–Sun from 9.30pm until late.
Legendaris C Berlin 363, Miraflores ☎4463435. Very fashionable at the moment, Legendaris is a large, comfortable club with personalised service, good drinks and shows, particularly on Saturday night. Open Wed–Sun, 10pm until late.
Sagitario Disco Av Wilson 869, Lima Centro ☎4244383. An indefatigable disco and the longest established gay club in the heart of Lima, its cruising balconies filled with young people, a large number usually gay, dancing through the night, often until 11am the next day.

Arts and entertainment

Going to the **cinema**, **theatre** and **exhibitions** is an important part of life in Lima. Peruvians are a well-cultured people with a distinct passion and intuitive understanding of everything from Latin music and fine arts to ancient textiles and traditional Andean dance forms. Peruvian culture is very much alive and most Peruvians know dozens of songs and several folk dances in common as well as being able to dance salsa with the best of them. Lima being a twenty-first century urban capital, cinema is is an important and vibrant feature of the city's nightlife. The best source of **information** about film, theatre, sporting events and exhibitions is the daily *El Comercio*, especially its Friday supplement.

Cinema

Cinema-going is an especially popular pastime for all Limeños, while the **theatre** attracts a small, select and highly cultured audience. There are clusters of **cinemas** all around the Plaza San Martín, Jirón de la Unión and Avenida Nicolas de Pierola in

Lima Centro, on the fringes of the park in Miraflores and in some of the suburban shopping malls. For any film that might attract relatively large crowds, it's advisable to buy tickets in advance; alternatively, be prepared to purchase them on the black market at inflated prices – queues are often long and large blocks of seats are regularly bought up by touts.

Popular Lima Cinemas

Cinemark Peru Jockey Plaza 12, Av Javier Prado, Surco 4200 ℡4370222.

Cinemark Plaza Lima Sur 7 Av Prol Paseo de la República, Chorrilos ℡4370222

Cineplanet Alcazar 1–8 Santa Cruz 814, Miraflores ℡4527000.

Cineplanet Centro Jr de la Unión, Lima Centro ℡4527000

Cineplante Primavera Av Angamas Este 2684, San Borja ℡4527000

Cinerama El Pacifico Av Pardo 121, Miraflores ℡2430541

Cine Star Benavides Av Benavides 4981, Surco ℡2754323.

Cine Star Aviacion 1-4 Av Aviacion 2423, San Borja ℡2257698.

Cinematografo de Barranco Jr Perez Roca 196, Barranco ℡2474782

Filmoteca PUCP Av Camino Real 1075, San Isidro ℡6161616.

UVK Multicines Larco Mar 1–12 Parque Salazar, Larco Mar, Miraflores ℡4467336.

Cultural centres

As in many cities, Lima's **cultural centres** are often the best place to catch innovative films, music shows and drama. They are often associated with one of the local universities and are open during daytime as well as evenings.

Centro Cultural de la PUCP (Univesidad La Catolica) Av Camino Real 1075, ℡6161616. One of the most active cultural centres in Lima, with innovative theatre, cinema and video, as well as art exhibitions, a library and cafeteria.

Centro Cultural de la UNMSM (Universidad de San Marcos) Avenida Nicolas de Pierola 1222, Parque Universitario, Lima Centro ℡4280052. Often presents folk music and dance, albeit in more of a performance context than participatory. The centre is run by the Universitario de

San Marcos, on the Parque Universitario, and performances are publicized on the noticeboard at the entrance. See p.93 for a fuller description of the venue.

Centro Cultural Ricardo Palma Av Larco 770, Miraflores, ℡4466164 or 4463959. Often hosts excellent concerts of Andean music, but doesn't have the same participatory feel of the *peñas* (see p.108). It does, however, have a library, two exhibition rooms and occasional cinema festivals, plus jazz, dance and theatre performances.

Theatre, ballet and classical music

Lima possesses a prolific and extremely talented **theatre** circuit, with many of its best venues based in Miraflores. In addition to the major theatres, short performances sometimes take place in the bars of the capital's top theatres. The country's major prestige companies, however, are the **National Ballet Company** and the **National Symphony**, both based seasonally at the Teatro Municipal in downtown Lima at block 3 of Jr Ica (℡4282302). There are also the Teatro Larco, at Larco 1036 (℡3300979); Teatro Satchmo at La Paz 526 in Miraflores (℡4444957), Teatro Britianico, Jr Bellavista 527, Miraflores (℡4471135). There are frequent performances, too, by international musicians and companies, often sponsored by foreign cultural organizations, such as the Alianza Francesa, Av Arequipa 4595, Miraflores (℡6108000); the Anglo-Peruvian Cultural Association Theatre, Av Benavides 620, Miraflores (℡4454326); and the Instituto Cultural Peruano Norte Americano, Av Angamos 120, Miraflores.

Art and photographic galleries

Lima's progressive culture of **art** and **photography** is deeply rooted in the Latin American tradition, combining indigenous ethnic realism with a political edge.

The city boasts a few permanent galleries – all free – with temporary exhibitions on display in many of the main museums.

Artco C Rouad y Paz Soldan 325, San Isidro ⑦2213579, ⓦwww.artcogaleria.com. One of the happening painters' galleries in Lima, usually well worth checking out. Open Mon–Fri 11am–8pm, Sat 10.30am–1.30pm & 3.30–7.30pm.

Centro Cultural de la Municipalidad de Miraflores corner of Avenida Larco and Diez Canseco, Miraflores. Hosts a series of innovative photographic exhibitions. Open daily 10am–10pm.

Centro Cultural de la Universidad Católica Av Camino Real 1075, San Isidro. Art gallery hosting visiting exhibitions by foreign artists. Open daily 10am–10pm.

Centro Cultural Ricardo Palma Larco 770, Miraflores. Houses fixed and changing exhibitions

of paintings, photographs and sculpture. Open daily 10am–9pm.

Corriente Alterna Las Dalias 381, Miraflores ⑦2428482. Often presents shows by non-Peruvian painters. Open Mon–Fri 10am–8pm.

Galeria L'Imaginaire Av Arequipa 4595, Miraflores. Usually exhibits Latin American painters and sculptors. Open Mon–Sat 5–9pm.

Sala Cultural del Banco Wiese Av Larco 1101, Miraflores. A contemporary, international art gallery in the Banco Wiese in the heart of downtown Miraflores. Open Mon–Sat 10am–2pm & 5–9pm.

Trapecio Av Larco 743, Miraflores ⑦4440842. Specializes in oils and sculpture. Mon–Sat 5–9pm.

Shopping and supplies

When it comes to **shopping** in Peru's towns and cities, Lima is the most likely to have what you're looking for. It is certainly your best bet for shoes and clothing, particularly if you want a large selection to choose from. The same is true of electronic goods, stationery and recorded music, though bear in mind that most Limeños who can afford it do their main shopping in Miami. Lima also has a good selection of reasonably priced arts and crafts markets and shops, which means you don't have to carry a sack full of souvenirs back from Cusco or Puno. The largest indoor **shopping centre** is the Jockey Plaza at Av Javier Prado Este 4200 in Surco where there are over two hundred shops including two massive department stores (Saga and Ripley), a bowling alley, twelve cinema screens and dozens of restaurant-cafés. Smaller but easier to find, the Centro Comercial Larcomar, at the cliff top end of Larco in Miraflores, has only forty shops but they are complemented by thirty restaurant-cafés, cinema screens, two nightclubs and three bars. For **supermarkets** Metro have the best range at reasonable prices and you'll them find across the city, notably at the San Isidro Comercial Centre, the Ovalo Gutierrez and next to Ripley's on Schell in the centre of Miraflores. For **tobacco products** and pipes, La Casa del Fumador, at Larco 590, Miraflores, is the best place.

The usual **shopping hours** are Monday to Saturday 10am–7pm, though in Miraflores, the main commercial area, many shops and artesania markets stay open until 8pm and sometimes later. Some shops, but by no means all, shut for a two-hour lunch break, usually from 1 to 3pm, and most shops shut on Sundays, though the artesania markets on Avenida La Marina and Petit Thouars tend to stay open all week until 7pm.

Arts and crafts

All types of Peruvian **artesania** are available in Lima, including woollen goods, crafts and gem stones. Some of the best in Peru are on Avenida Petit Thouars between blocks 48 and 54, home to a handful of markets between Av Ricardo Palma and Av Angamos, all well within walking distance of Miraflores centre. Artesania Gran Chimu, Av Petit Thouars 5495, has a wide range of jewellery and carved wooden items, as does Mercado Artesanal, also on Avenida Petit

Thouars, at no. 5321. Another large artesania market area can be visited easily en route to Callao or the Parque de Las Leyendas, located by the roadside blocks 6–8 of the Avenida La Marina, in Pueblo Libre. More places selling artesania are listed below.

Slightly cheaper are the artesania markets on blocks 9 and 10 of Avenida La Marina in Pueblo Libre. A small selection of reasonable quality crafts and antiques are displayed every evening (6–9pm) in the Miraflores Park between Diagonal and Avenida Larco. The **Hatun Raymi Artesania Festival** (late July/early August) is a great gathering of Lima-based artesania producers; it's located on the massive esplanade of the Museo de la Nación and entry is free. In Lima Centro, the Artesania Santo Domingo, at Jr Conde de Superunda 221–223 (a little square pavement area just a stone's throw from the Correo Central), is good for beads, threads and other artesania items.

For **jewellery**, much of Avenida la Paz, in Miraflores, is dedicated to silverwork and other jewellery. In Lima Centro, Casa Wako, Jr de la Unión 841, is probably the best place, specializing in reasonably priced Peruvian designs in gold and silver. Arte y Canela, Centro Comercial Larcomar, stocks fine silver jewellery to suit most tastes, while Nasca, Av La Paz 522, has a nice range of less expensive offerings, much of it in silver. For good-quality **antiques** there's Rafo, Martinez de Pinillos 1055, Barranco (℡ 2470679), who have a good lunchtime restaurant too, and also Collacocha, C Colon 534, parallel to block 11 of Avenida Larco in Miraflores.

Artesania

Agua y Tierra Diez Canseco 298 Miraflores ℡4446980. A wide range of ethnic and traditional healing or *curanderos'* artefacts.

Artesanias Huayruro and Killapura Diez Canseco 392 and 378, Miraflores. These adjacent stores sell crafts and some edible produce from the Andes and Peru's Amazon tribes.

La Casa de Alpaca La Paz 665, Miraflores. Good but expensive alpaca clothing.

Collacocha Colon 534, parallel to block 11 of Avenida Larco, ℡4474422. A small collection of Andean arts and crafts.

Cuy Arts and Crafts Larco 1175 and 874. Handmade crafts of all kinds.

Iskay Av Pedro de Osma 106, Barranco ℡2472102. A crafts and arts gallery and bar conveniently located on the main plaza in Barranco; a reasonable place to begin an evening out in this fascinating artists' quarter.

Las Pallas Cajamarca 212, Barranco ℡4774629. A fascinating, veritable museum of artesania, run by a British woman who has spent most of her life collecting fine works and who may be able to show you the rest of her collection (ring for an appointment).

Santos Alpaca 859 Larco 859, Miraflores. Excellent quality pima cotton and alpaca products at quite reasonable prices.

Books

The best bookshops are in Miraflores, notably the Librería Ibero, with three stores – Larco 199, Av Oscar Benavides 500 (previously Diagonal), and on Comandante Espinar, by the Ovalo Gutierrez – generally have a wide range of books and magazines in English. Also on Comandante Espinar, at 219, in Miraflores there's Zeta Books which has a small selection of new English paperbacks. Lima Centro has a few shops on Avenida Nicolas de Pierola which stock **English-language books** (try the store at no. 689), while The Book Exchange, just around the corner at Ocoña 211, sells or swaps second-hand paperbacks. The ABC Bookstores at Colmena 689, are well supplied with all kinds of works in English. On the Jr de la Unión, the Librería Ayza usually has some interesting publications and maps. Second-hand books (as well as vintage toys) can be found in Lima Centro at Camana 936.

Travel agents and tour operators

For specialist outdoor activities in and around Lima, see p.115. Otherwise, for standard advice, tours, tickets, flights and hotel bookings, the best are: Fertur Peru, Jr Junin 211, Lima Centro (℡4272626, ⓦwww.fertur-travel.com) or in Miraflores at Schell 485 (℡2421900); Lima Tours, Belén 1040, near Plaza San Martín (℡6196900, ⓦwww.limatours.com.pe); Highland Tours, Av Pardo 231, Oficina 401, Miraflores (℡2426292, ⓦwww.highlandperu.com); Lima Vision Jr Chiclayo 444, Miraflores (℡4475323 or 4470482, ⓦwww.limavision.com), who do a variety of city tours, Pachacamac, Nasca and Cusco; Marilí Tours, Diez Canseco 392, Miraflores (℡2410142, ⓦmarilitours.com.pe), who have guides and go to most of Peru, including Cusco, Madre de Dios, Puno and the northern desert region; New Planet Travel (℡4455052900, ⓦwww.newplanettravel.net) have a passion for Lima and offer everything from fast-driving tours to pisco drink packages and horse riding (presumably not simultaneously) and trips to the beach. Overland Expeditions, Jr Emilio Fernandez 640, Santa Beatrice (℡4247762), who specialize in the Lachay Reserve; Paracas Tours, Av Rivera Navarette 723, San Isidro (℡2222621, ⓔparacas@paracastours.com.pe), are a small office albeit with a very professional air ticketing service; Class Adventure Travel, San Martin 800, Miralores (℡4441652, ⓦwww.cat-travel.com) organizes excellent tours and packages including Lima culinary tours, Nazca and desert experiences.

Food

The best place to buy **food** for a picnic is Surquillo Market (daily 6.30am–5.30pm, roughly), a couple of blocks from Miraflores over the Av Angamos road bridge, on the eastern side of the Paseo de la República freeway. This colourful place is fully stocked with a wonderful variety of breads, fruits, cheeses and meats, though it can be a bit dodgy in terms of petty thieving, so keep your wallet and passport close. Alternatively, you could try one of the Metro supermarkets (see Shopping, p.112); all branches accept and change US dollars. Bakeries and delicatessens can be found in most urban districts, including Larco in Miraflores, within a few blocks of Larcomar. The best things to buy for a tasty picnic are the delicious *queso fresco* (white cheese), avocados and pecans. In the centre of Lima you can buy most basic foodstuffs – bread, fruit and so on – either from stalls on Avenida Emancipación or in the central market to the east of Avenida Abancay (see p.90). For **health food**, try Madre Natura, Jirón Chiclayo 815, off the Avenida Comandante Espinar, in Miraflores which stocks a wide range of health foods and ecological products, as well as having its own cafeteria and wholemeal bakery. Other good options are the Natural Co-op on Moquegua, near the corner with Torrico and El Girasol, Camana 327, not far from the Plaza Mayor.

Photographic equipment

Photographic equipment and developing for digital and film are all a little expensive in Lima. Try Kodak Express, Av Larco 1005, or Lab Color Professional, Av Benavides 1171 (℡4467421), both in Miraflores, for films and developing. Agfafoto, Diez Canseco 172, Miraflores, has films and camera accessories, while Renato Service, 28 Julio 442, Miraflores, has excellent camera and video equipment. Foto Digital, Av Larco 1005 (℡4479398) is good for fast developing. For **camera repairs**, try the Camera House, Larco 1150, Oficina 39 (℡9617590) in Miraflores or Miranda's at Jr Cusco 592 (℡4267920) in Lima Centro.

Outdoor activities

Tandem **paragliding** flights of around ten to fifteen minutes can be experienced by jumping off the coastal cliffs in Miraflores with expert guides and teachers, Mike Fernandez, from Aeroextreme (Tripoli 350, Dpto 302, Miraflores ☎2425125 or 99480954) and Marco Mercado of Tandem Flights (Tripoli 340, Dpto 402, Miraflores ☎2417370 or 994092537, ⓦwww.tandemperu.com); no previous experience necessary, from around $45 or so. For **trekking and mountain-climbing** advice and trail maps, visit the Trekking and Backpacking Club, Jirón Huascar 1152, Jesus Maria (☎4232515), the Asociación de Andinismo de la Universidad de Lima, based at the university on Javier Prado Este (☎4376767, meet Wed evenings), or the South American Explorers' Club (see p.118). **Bicycle hire and bike tours** can be arranged with Rentabike, Alcanfores 132, Miraflores (☎6921082).

Of the **trekking companies**, most run trips to the Cordillera Blanca and Colca as well as around the Cusco area and along the Inca Trail; many of the best listed below. For **whitewater rafting** around Cusco and Huaraz, contact Explorandes or Mayuc (see below) or check for other operators in Cusco, Lunahuana or Huaraz (see relevant chapter listings and details). **Diving and scuba** are popular sports in Peru and can be accessed from Lima through Nature Expeditions (☎94104206, ⓦwww.nature-expeditions-peru.com). **Motor Yachts** offer trips from Lima to the nearby islands, Islas Palomino, to see the marine mammals, including a sea lion colony, a nice trip in clear weather; they can be contacted through Ecocruceros, Av Arequipa 4960, of 202, Miraflores (☎2268530, ⓦislaspalomino.com). For **jungle trips**, contact Rainforest Expeditions, Aramburu 166 no. 4b, Miraflores (☎4218183, ⓦwww.perunature.com).

Trekking and biking companies

Bike Tours of Lima C Bolivar 150, Miraflores ☎4453172 ⓦwww.biketoursoflima.com.

Explorandes San Fernando 320, Miraflores ☎4450532, ⓦwww.explorandes.com. Offering itineraries to most areas of Peru, this company tailors trips to individual interests as well as pre-packaged expeditions. Another of Peru's best and longest-established operators.

Incatrek Las Lilas 431, Lima ☎4223671, Ⓔincatrek@hotmail.com. This outfit sometimes runs tours to Tarma, Oxapampa, Pozuzo and Satipo.

Mayuc Portal Confituras, Cusco ☎084/2425824. One of Peru's best and longest-established operators; whilst specializing in rafting, they also operate tours to Nazca, Colca and Titicaca.

Peru Expeditions C Colina 151, Miraflores ☎4472057, ⓦwww.peru-expeditions.com. A professional, helpful company specializing in adventure travel particularly on the coast (Paracas and Ballestas, Nazca), Arequipa and Colca areas. They offer trekking, mountain biking and 4WD tours.

Camping and sports equipment

Alta Montana, Av Julio Bailetti 610, in San Borja (☎3463010) is probably the best place for climbing gear (also serves the mining and forestry industries) whilst Altamira, Arica 800, a block from the Ovalo Gutierrez roundabout, sells a good range of quality **camping equipment**. Best, Av Espinar 320, Miraflores, sells rucksacks, cycling equipment and surfing gear, while Todo Camping, Av Angamos Oeste 350, has a range of tents and other equipment. There's also the Camping Centre, Av Benavides 1620 in Miraflores (☎2421779); Sisperu, at Caminos del Inca 257 in Chacarilla (☎3720428); and the South American Explorers' Club (see p.118) is also worth trying. Metro supermarkets (see Shoppin, p.112) sometimes stock inexpensive tents, sleeping bags and associated camping kit.

For **surfing gear** go to either Klimax, at Jose Gonzalez 488 in Miraflores (☎4421685), Boz, Av Angamos Oeste 1130, between Miraflores and San Isidro

Moving on from Lima

Whilst air travel from Lima is straightforward, apart from connection times between domestic and international flights, the situation for **overland travel by bus** is more complex. Unlike some Peruvian cities, Lima doesn't have a Terrapuerto (single bus terminal), but a mass of individual private bus companies with their own offices and depots.

For buses to **Ica** and the coastal towns en route, the Soyuz/Peru Bus leaves every 15min from Av Carlos Zavala y Loyaza 221 (T4276310 or 2661515) and Av Mexico 333, La Victoria. For **Huaraz**, one of the best options is Movil Tours, Paseo de La Repœblica 749 (T3329000; other depot at Avendia Carlos Izaguirre 535, Los Olivos).

For **Tarapoto** (and **Chachapoyas**), the options are Movil Tours (as above), or Huamanga, located at Jr Montevideo 619 and Luna Pizarro 455 (T3302206), who also depart from the latter address for **Ayacucho**, **Chiclayo**, **Moyobamba**, **Tarapoto** and **Yurimaguas** (you will probably need to change bus at Pedro Ruiz for **Chachapoyas**, see p.432).

Some major bus companies

Among the best **companies**, Cruz del Sur, Ormeño, Tepsa and Oltursur can deliver you to most of the popular destinations up and down the coast, and to Arequipa or Cusco.

Chinchano, a subsidiary of Ormeño, serves the coast as far as Cañete, Chincha and Pisco.

Cruz del Sur is the best choice, if not the cheapest, for most important destinations. Most buses can be caught from Av Javier Prado Este 1109 at the corner with Nicolas Arriola (for reservations call T3115050); tickets can be booked and paid for on W www .cruzdelsur.com.pe.

Oltursa Av Aramburu 1660 (for reservations call T2254499). Covers the coast up as far as Mancora and Tumbes.

Ormeño Av Javier Prado Este 1059 (for reservations call T4721710, W www.grupo -ormeno.com.pe). Good for main national and international services; some buses also pass through the central depot at Carlos Zavala 177, Lima Centro (T4275679).

Most other bus services are detailed in Listings, below.

(T4401033), or Big Head, which has branches in both Larcomar and Jockey Plaza shopping centres. The *Penascal Surf Hotel*, based at Av Las Palmeras 258 in San Bartolo beach an hour south of Lima (T4307436, W www.surfpenascal .com), offer both surfing and Spanish lessons combined and are a good source of advice. **Cycling equipment** is currently available from Bike Mavil, Av Aviación 4011 (T4495234) and Peru Bike, Parque Nueva Castilla, Calle A, d-7, Surco (T4498435).

Listings

Airlines – Domestic Aeroica T4443026, W www .aeroica.net; Aeroparacas, Santa Fe 270, Higuereta, Surco T4494768, W aeroparacas.com; Lan Peru, at Jr de la Union 958, Lima Centro T2138200, also at C las Begonias 780, San Isidro, Tienda 102, Centro Comercial, Jockey Plaza, Surco and Av José Pardo 513, Miraflores T2138200 or 080011234 (free phone), W www.lan.com; Star Peru, Av Comandante Espinar 331, Miraflores T7059000, W www.starperu.com; TACA Peru, T2136060, www.taca.com; TANS, Av Arequipa 5200, Miraflores ☎2418510.

Airlines – International Aerolineas Argentinas, Carnaval y Moreyra 370 ☎080052200 (free), www.aerolineas.com; Air Canada, ☎080052073 (free) www.aircanada.com; Air France, Av Alvarez Calderon 185, 6th floor, San Isidro ☎2130200, www.airfrance.com; American Airlines, Jr Juan de Arona 830, fourteenth floor, San Isidro ☎2117000 or 080040350 (free), www.americanairlines.com; Avianca, Av Paz Soldan 225, Oficina C-5, Los Olivos, San Isidro ☎4440747, 4440748 or 080051936, www.avianca.com; Continental Airlines, Victor Andrés Belaœnde 147, Oficina 101, Edificio Real, San Isidro ☎2214340 or 080070030 (free), www.continentalairlines.com; Delta Airlines ☎2119211, www.delta.com; Iberia, Av Camino Real 390, Office 902, San Isidro ☎4417801 www.iberia.com; KLM, Av Alvarez Calderon 185, sixth floor, San Isidro ☎2130200 www.klm.com; Japan Airlines, ☎2217501 www.jal.com; Lan Chile, Av José Pardo 269, Miraflores ☎2138200 or 0801-1-1234 www.lan.com.

Airport Lima airport applies a flat $30.25 departure tax on international flights, paid on departure at the airport. For domestic flights the departure tax is around $6.05. The airport boasts lots of shops, cafés, internet facilities, locker luggage storage ($8), a post office and a rather expensive left luggage deposit in the international departure area. **American Express** 0800-50629.

Anti-Rabies Centre Centro Antirabico ☎4256313. For vaccinations and emergency treatment.

Banks Banco de la Nación, Av Nicolas de Pierola 1065 and Av Abancay 491; Banco Latino, Paseo de la Repœblica 3505, San Isidro, which has several ATMs; Banco de Credito, Jr Lampa 499, Av Larco 1099, Miraflores (well run and with small queues), and on the corner of Rivera Navarrete and Juan de Arona, San Isidro, both of which offer good rates on travellers' cheques; Banco Continental, Avenida Larco, Miraflores; Interbank, in the Metro Supermarket, corner of Alfonso Ugarte and Venezuela, Lima Centro; and Banco Wiese, Jr Cusco 245, Lima Centro, and Alfonso Ugarte 1292, Diagonal 176, Miraflores.

British-Peruvian Cultural Association Av Areqipa 3495, San Isidro ☎6153434. A good place to meet ex-pats, with occasional events like plays and live music.

Bus companies Always check which terminal your bus is departing from when you buy your ticket; although the most popular and reliable operators are listed in the Moving on from Lima box (p.116), the following companies are also

useful: Chanchamayo, Manco Capac 1052, La Victoria, (☎4701189), for Tarma, La Oroya, San Ramon and La Merced; Cial, Av Abancay 947 and Terminal Paseo de la República (646 ☎3304225), for the North coast including Mancora, Cajamarca and Huaraz; Condor de Chavin, Montevideo 1039 (☎4288122), for Callejón de Huaylas, Huaraz and Chavín; El Condor, Av Carlos Zavala 101, Lima Centro (☎4270286), for Trujillo or Huancayo; Empresa Huaral, 131 Av Abancay, Lima Centro (☎4282254), for Huaral, Ancon and Chancay; Empresa Rosario, Jr Ayacucho 942 (☎5342685), for Huánuco and La Unión; Flores Buses, corner of Paseo de La República and 28 de Julio (☎4243278 or 4310485) for Arequipa and south coast; Leon de Huánuco, Av 28 de Julio, La Victoria 1520 (☎43290880), for Cerro de Pasco, Huánuco, Tarma and La Merced; Libertadores, Av Grau 491, Lima Centro (☎4268067), for Ayacucho, Satipo, and Huanta; Lobato Buses, 28 de Julio 2101–2107, La Victoria (☎4749411), for Tarma, La Merced and Satipo; Mariscal Caceres, Av 28 de Julio 2195, La Victoria (☎4747850) and Morales Moralitos, Av Grau 141 (☎4286252), both of whom whom cover the coast and some other sectors; Linea; Palomino, Av 28 de Julio 1750, La Victoria, for Cusco via Nazca and Abancay; Señor de Luren, Manco Capac 611, for Nazca; Transportes Junin, Av. Nicolás Arriola 240 (at corner with Av Javier Prado), La Victoria (☎3266136), for Tarma, San Ramon, La Merced and the Selva Central; Transportes Rodriguez, Av Roosevelt 354 (☎4280506), for Huaraz, Caraz and Chimbote.

Car rental Alkila, La Paz 745, Miraflores ☎2423939; Avis, Av Javier Prado Este 5235, Camacho, La Molina ☎4341111; Budget, Av Canaval y Moreyra 569, San Isidro (☎4428703 or 4428706, ©reservas@budgetperu.com); Hertz, Cantuarias 160, Miraflores (☎4472129) and at the airport (☎4455716); National, Av España 453, Lima Centro (☎5751390, ©national@terra.com.pe).

Courier services DHL, Centro Comercial Larcomar MG-12, Miraflores (8am–7pm; ☎5172500, www.dhl.com.pe), also at Begonias 514, San Isidro; Federal Express, Pasaje Olaya 260, Miraflores (Mon–Fri 9am–6pm; ☎2422280).

Doctors Dr Bazan works as a "backpackers medic" in Lima ☎97352668, ©backpackersdr @yahoo.com; Dr Aste, Antero Aspillaga 415, Oficina 101, San Isidro ☎4417502, speaks English; Dr Alicia García, Instituto de Ginecología, Av Monterrico 1045, Surco ☎4342650; and Dr Raul Morales, Clínica Padre Luis Tezza, Av del Polo 570, Monterrico ☎4346990, speaks good English.

Embassies and consulates Australia, Av Victor Belaœnde 147, Office 1301, Torre Real 3, San Isidro ☎2228281; Bolivia, Los Castaños 235, San

Isidro ☎4402095 or 4428231; Brazil, Av José Pardo 850, Miraflores ☎4215660; Canada, C Bolognesi 228, Miraflores ☎3193200; Chile, Javier Prado Oeste 790, San Isidro ☎7102211; Ecuador, Las Palmeras 356, San Isidro ☎4217050; Ireland, Paseo de La Republica 5353B, San Antonio, Miraflores ☎2429516; New Zealand, see the UK; South Africa, Victor Andres Belaunde 147 (office 801), Edificio Real Tres, San Isidro ☎4409996; UK, Torre Parque Mar, Av Larco 1301, 22nd floor, Miraflores ☎6173000; US, La Encalada, block 17, Monterrico ☎4343000.

Exchange The easiest way to obtain foreign currency is to use ATMs. In Lima Centro *cambistas* (street moneychangers) gather on the corner of Ocoña, at the back of the *Gran Hotel Bolívar*. Alternatively, you can change cash and travellers' cheques in the smaller hostels and the many *casas de cambio* around Ocoña: Tuscon Express, Ocoña 211a; LAC Dollar, on Camana 779, second floor; and another office in Miraflores at La Paz 211. Also in Miraflores there are several *cambistas* working Larco, particularly on the corners of the first five or six blocks down from the Ovalo. The Metro supermarkets (see Shopping and supplies, p.112) take dollars and will give change in dollars or nuevo soles. You can also change money at the airport, but rates are poorer than in the city centre.

Farmacias Boticas Fasa, Av Benavides 847 ☎6190000, 24hr delivery, accept major credit cards; Inka Farma ☎6198000, delivery service.

Hospitals The following are all well-equipped: Clinica Anglo Americana, Av Salazar, San Isidro ☎2213656; Clinica Internacional, Washington 1475, Lima Centro ☎4288060; Clinica Ricardo Palma, Av Javier Prado Este 1066, San Isidro ☎2248027 or 2222224; and Clinica San Borja, Av Guardia Civil 337, San Borja ☎4753141. All have emergency departments which you can use as an outpatient, or which you can phone for a house call. For an ambulance call ☎4400200 or 3726080, but if you can, take a taxi – it'll be much quicker.

INC – Instituto Nacional de Cultura Av Javier Prado Este 2465, San Borja ☎4769933, for detailed information, particularly on Peru's heritage, or for permission to enter certain archaeological sites.

INRENA C 17, 355 Urb El Palomar, San Isidro, Lima ☎224-3298, ⊛www.inrena.gob.pe. Responsible for Peru's protected areas; you need permission from them to enter some of Peru's Natural Park areas.

Internet services You can find internet cafés virtually anywhere in Lima for about $0.30 an hour: Dragon Fans, C Tarata 230, Miraflores, open 24hr ☎4466814, or at Av Arequipa 2440, Lince ☎4214848; Café Internet, Carabaya 149, Lima Centro ☎2422070, fast, private cabins, coffee; Mondonet, Av Ancash 412; Phantom Internet Café Bar, Av Diagonal 344; Plazanet, Av 28 de Julio 451, Miraflores, which is open 24hr and has a café and TV; Red Cientifica Peruana, Augusto Tamayo 125, San Isidro.

Laundry Many hotels will do this cheaply, but there are numerous *lavanderías* in most areas; the Lavandería Saori, Grimaldi del Solar 175, Miraflores (Mon–Sat 8am–7pm; ☎4443830), is fast; LavaQueen, Av Larco 1158, Miraflores, does washing by the kilo at reasonable prices.

Police Peru's headquarters for the tourist police is in the Museo de La Nación at Javier Prado Este 2465 ☎2258698.

Postal services The main post office is at Pasaje Piura, Jr Lima, block 1 near the Plaza Mayor (Mon–Sat 8am–8pm & Sun 8am–2pm), with other branches in Miraflores, at Petit Thouars 5201, a block from the corner of Angamos (Mon–Fri 8am–8pm). The best bet for sending large parcels is to use KLM (see Airlines, above) who charge about $12 a kilo to Europe. Concas Travel, Alcanfores 345, Oficina 101, Miraflores (☎2417516), can arrange larger shipments. Poste restante letters are kept in the main post office (see above); address mail to Poste Restante, Correo Central, Jirón Conde de Superunda, Lima Centro, Peru.

South American Explorers' Club The clubhouse is at C Piura 135, Miraflores (Mon–Sat 9.30am–5pm; ☎4453306 ⊛www.saexplorers.org); the postal address is Casilla 3714, Lima 100.

Spanish language courses Hispana Spanish School, C San Martin 377, Miraflores (☎4463045, ⊛www.hispanaidiomas.com); Ecela, Gen Recavarres 542, Miraflores (☎4442279); Lima School of Languages, Av Grimaldo del Solar 469, Miraflores (☎2427763, ⊛elsol.idiomasperu.com), where you can start any Monday for small-group or private tuition, full- or part-time.

Taxis and transfers Reliable 24hr taxi companies include: Taxi Seguro ☎22419292 or 2752020; Taxi Amigo ☎3490177; and Taxi Movil ☎4226890.

Telephones Phone kiosks and phone cabin offices (*locutorios*) are found all around the city, many combined with internet facilities (see Basics, p.56).

Tourist Protection Service Basadre 610, San Isidro (☎4211627 or 5748000, 24hr), particularly for help with claims against tourism operators who have failed to fulfil their contracts in one way or another. Their symbol is *i-peru* and they also have an office in Lima airport, Aeropuerto Internacional Jorge Chavez.

Tourist van & driver hire Backpacker Van Express, Av Comandante Espinar 611 ☎4477748; Transporte Manchego Turismo ☎4201289. Translation services Ibanez Traducciones, Miguel Dasso 126, Oficina 301, San Isidro ☎4216526 or 4216511, ☎4414122.

Visas Migraciones, corner of Prolongación Avenida España and Jr Huaraz, near Lima Centro (get there early in the morning to avoid queues). Western Union Main office at Av Petit Thouars 3595, San Isidro ☎4220036 or 4229723.

Around Lima

Stretching out along the coast in both directions, the **Panamerican Highway** runs the entire 2600-kilometre length of Peru, with Lima more or less at its centre. Towns along the sometimes arid coastline immediately north and south of the capital are of minor interest to most travellers, though there are some **glorious beaches** – with next to no restrictions on beach camping – and a very impressive ruin at **Pachacamac**.

The foothills above Lima contain several places of interest, not least the animistic rock outcrops of **Marcahuasi**, a weekend trip from the city. A more ambitious trip would be to the high sierra of the Andes, still only a matter of hours away by comfortable bus or slightly faster colectivo. The attractive mountain towns of **Huancayo**, **Huancavelica** and **Tarma**, all interesting destinations in their own right, are within a day's easy travelling of the capital (see Chapter 5).

The coast

Most of the better **beaches** within easy reach of Lima are to the south, beginning about 30km out at the hulking pre-Inca ruins of **Pachacamac**, a sacred citadel which still dominates this stretch of coastline. The site can easily be combined with a day at one or other of the beaches and it's little problem to get out there from the capital. A good stopover en route to Pisco is the former plantation town and oasis of **Chincha**, a fertile coastal zone in ancient times as exemplified by the substantial number of pre-Inca sites in the region. To the north of Lima, the desert stretches up between the Pacific Ocean and the foothills of the Andes. There's not a huge amount of interest to the visitor here and very little in the way of tourist facilities, but it has a scattering of archaeological sites, all of which are difficult to reach, plus – with easier access – some interesting eco-niches known as *lomas*, shrub-covered hills with their own unique climatic conditions and flora and fauna, of which the **Reserva Nacional Lomas de Lachay** is the best.

Pachacamac

By far the most interesting of the Rimac Valley's ancient sites, **PACHACAMAC** (daily 9am–5pm; $3; ☎4300168) is well worth making time for even if you're about to head out to Cusco and Machu Picchu. The entry fee for the citadel includes admission to the site museum, which merits a quick browse around on the way in; allow a good two hours to wander around the full extent of the ruins. Guides cost $8 for a small group.

Originally one of the most important centres of pilgrimage on the Peruvian coast, Pachacamac functioned from around the time of Christ as a very sacred location which, even in pre-Inca days, housed a miraculous wooden idol, evidently representing, through intricate carvings, a two-faced humanoid, believed to have been the deity, Pachacamac, controller of earthquakes. No one was allowed to look at the idol, not even the high priests. Entering **the ruins**, after passing the restored sectors, which include the **Templo de La Luna** (Temple of the Moon) and the **Convento de las Virgenes del Sol** (Convent of the Sun Virgins, or *Mamaconas*), you can see the later Inca construction of the **Sun Temple** directly ahead. Constructed on the top level of a series of pyramidical platforms, it was built tightly onto the hill with plastered adobe bricks, its walls originally painted in gloriously bright colours. Below this is the **main plaza**, once covered with a thatched roof supported on stilts, and thought to have been the area where pilgrims assembled in adoration. The rest of the ruins, visible though barely distinguishable, were once dwellings, storehouses and palaces. From the very top of the Sun Temple there's a magnificent view west beyond the Panamerican Highway to the **beach** (Playa San Pedro) and across the sea to a sizeable yet uninhabited island, which appears like a huge whale approaching the shore.

Going away from the Pachacamac site via the pueblo of the same name you pick up a hard road heading for the Quebrada Verde area. Within a few kilometres you come across the **Lomas de Lucumo**, a beautiful natural ecosystem at the edge of the desert replete with shrubs and the odd flower thriving on little more than seasonal coastal fog.

A taxi to Pachacamac and back from Miraflores can be found from around $35. **Buses** leave every two hours for Pachacamac from Avenida Abancay and around the Parque Universitario on Calles Montevideo and Inambari in Lima Centro. Alternatively, many of the **tour** agencies in Lima offer half-day tours to the site (see p.114).

▲ Pachacamac

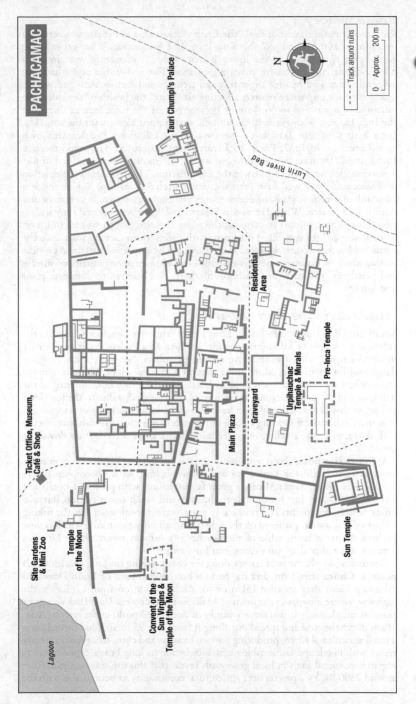

PACHACAMAC

Lurín River Bed

--- Track around ruins

0   Approx.   200 m

N

Ticket Office, Museum, Café & Shop

Tauri Chumpi's Palace

Residential Area

Graveyard

Urpihauchac Temple & Murals

Pre-Inca Temple

Main Plaza

Site Gardens & Mini Zoo

Temple of the Moon

Convent of the Sun Virgins & Temple of the Moon

Sun Temple

Lagoon

Some history

Pachacamac means (more or less) "the Earth's Creator", and the site was certainly occupied by 500 AD and probably for a long time before that. When other *huacas* were being constructed in the lower Rimac Valley, Pachacamac was already a temple-citadel and centre for mass pilgrimages. The god-image of Pachacamac evidently expressed his/her anger through tremors and earthquakes, and was an oracle used for important matters affecting the State: the health of the ruler, the outcome of a war and so on. Later it became one of the most famous shrines in the Inca Empire, with Pachacamac himself worshipped along with the sun. The Incas built their Sun Temple on the crest of the hill above Pachacamac's own sacred precinct. In 1533, Francisco **Pizarro** sent his brother Hernando to seize Pachacamac's treasure, but was disappointed by the spoils, which consisted of just a wooden idol, now shown today in the site museum. This wooden representation of Pachacamac may well have been the oracle itself: it was kept hidden inside a labyrinth and behind guarded doors – only the high priests could communicate with it face to face. When Hernando Pizarro and his troops arrived they had to pass through many doors to arrive at the main idol site, which was raised up on a "snail-shaped" (or spiralling) platform, with the wooden carving stuck into the earth inside a dark room, separated from the world by a jewelled curtain. As well as earthquakes, Pachacamac's powers extended to the absence or presence of disease and pestilence. His wife, or female counterpart, was believed to dominate plant and fish life.

Southern beach towns

South from Pachacamac lie some of Lima's most attractive **beaches**. Closest to the ruins, just a couple of kilometres outside, is **Playa San Pedro**, a vast and usually deserted strip of sand. Constantly pounded by rollers, however, it can be quite dangerous for swimming. Much more sheltered, the bay of **El Silencio**, 6km to the south, was one of the most popular beaches in the 1980s but, suffering at the hands of bad regional planning, it has lost its charming edge due to the low-level pollution that occasionally appears here from new local beachside developments. You may be better off heading to one of the excellent seafood **restaurants** on the cliff above, or to the smaller, more secluded bays a short drive further down the coast.

At **Punta Hermosa**, about ten minutes on the bus beyond El Silencio, you come to an attractive cliff-top settlement and, down below, what's becoming Lima's leading surf resort, **Santa María**, a great family haunt, with plenty of hotels and a reasonable beach. Just south of here the surf and beach resort of **San Bartolo** offers hostels, restaurants and reasonably good waves. South again lies the fishing village of **Pucusana**, gathered on the side of a small hilly peninsula, which is now perhaps the most fashionable of the beaches – a holiday resort where Limeños actually stay rather than just driving out for a swim.

Continuing south, the road cruises along the coast, passing the long beach and salt pools of **Chilca** after 5km, and the curious lion-shaped rock of **León Dormido** (Sleeping Lion) after another 15km or so. About 20km on from Chilca on the highway, where it bypasses the town of Malfa, is the **cafetería** *Dona Paulina*, a great place to sample the best *chicharones* (chunks of deep-fried pork) in the region. **Asia**, 10km down the road and spread out along it from Km 95 to 103, has turned from a small agricultural town, producing cotton, bananas and corn, to a modern trendy resort with hotels and fashionable nightclubs beside its long beach. Some interesting archaeological finds in local graveyards reveal that this site was occupied from around 2500 BC by a pre-ceramic agricultural community associated also with the earliest examples of a trophy-head cult (many of the mummies were decapitated). About 20km on from Asia is the growing surfers' resort of **Cerro Azul**.

Buses to Pachacamac, San Bartolo and Pucusana can be picked up in Lima from one of the bus-stop lay-bys on the Panamericana Sur (south direction); the spot where Avenida Angamos Este crosses the Panamericana is a good bet. Some buses start from the corner of Jirón Montevideo and Jirón Ayacucho in Lima every two hours, passing Pachacamac, El Silencio, Punta Hermosa and Santa Maria on the 65-kilometre journey.

Inland from Lima: into the foothills

There are several destinations in the **foothills of the Andes** which are within relatively easy reach of Lima. The most spectacular is the mystical plateau of **Marcahuasi** (see p.321), but much closer to Lima are the impressive sites of **Puruchuco** and **Cajamarquilla**, which are typical of ruins all over Peru and make a good introduction to the country's archaeology. Both Puruchuco and Cajamarquilla lie near the beginning of the Central Highway, the road that climbs up behind Lima towards Chosica, La Oroya and the Andes. The two sites are only 6km apart and are most easily visited on a half-day guided **tour** from Lima (see p.114). Alternatively, you could take a **colectivo** from Calle Montevideo (daily from 7am; $3) and return by waving passing **buses** on the main Carretera Central, though the Chosica to Lima bus will be the most likely to have spare seats.

Puruchuco

An 800-year-old, pre-Inca settlement, **PURUCHUCO** (daily 9am–5pm; $2; ⊤4942641) comprises a labyrinthine villa close to Km 4.5 of the Carretera Central. Nearby is the small but interesting **Museo de Sito Puruchuco**, containing a complete collection of artefacts and attire found at the site (all of which bears a remarkable similarity to what Amazon Indian communities still use today). The name itself means "feathered hat or helmet" and recent building work in the locality discovered that the Puruchuco site was also a massive graveyard, revealing greater quantities of buried pre-Incas than most other sites in Peru. The villa's original adobe structure was apparently rebuilt and adapted by the Incas shortly before the Spanish arrival: it's a fascinating ruin, superbly restored in a way which vividly captures what life was like before the Conquest. Very close by, in the Parque Fernando Carozi (ask the site guard for directions), two other ruins – **Huaquerones** and **Catalina Huaca** – are being restored, and at **Chivateros** there's a quarry apparently dating back some twelve thousand years.

Cajamarquilla

First occupied in the Huari era (600–1000 AD), **CAJAMARQUILLA** (daily 9am–5pm; $1.50) flourished under the **Cuismancu culture**, a city-building state contemporary with the better-known Chimu in northern Peru. It was an enclosed city containing thousands of small, complex dwellings clustered around a higher section, probably nobles' quarters, and numerous small plazas. The site was apparently abandoned before the Incas arrived in 1470, possibly after being devastated by an earthquake. Pottery found here in the 1960s by a group of Italian archaeologists suggests habitation over 1300 years ago. The **Centro Ecológico Recreacional Huachipa**, a fun theme park and zoo located at Km 9.5 of the Carretera Central (close to the Cajamarquilla turn-off), is somewhere kids may enjoy; there's a large space with walk-on pirate boat, a water world area, an imaginative play area and a zone full of exotic plants and wildlife. A few kilometres east of here, around Km 12.5 of the Carretera Central, there's another archaeological site on the right bank of the Río Rimac: the Inca administrative centre now known as **San Juan de Pariachi**, dating from at least a thousand years ago.

A further 20km into the foothills through sprawling developments, the road comes to the town of **Chosica**, a narrow settlement squeezed in between the steepening dry and rocky foothills and the turbulent river below. Just 35km from Lima itself, Chosica has long been a traditional weekend escape from the city; its unique attraction is as a winter escape from the Lima mist and smog. There's not really that much to visit in Chosica, just some recreation centres, mostly private, in the valley below, but if you want to **stay**, the *Hospedaje Chosica* at Av 28 de Julio 134 (☎3610841; ❷) is very pleasant and exceptionally good value; a family-run place, they have four rooms with baths and six without. For **eating** it's difficult to do better than the *Restaurant Liluzca*, Jr Chiclayo 250, in a small side street off the main road by the plaza; it has outside seating and serves decent food, though it usually closes before 7pm. Above Chosica the road starts to climb fast, winding its way past some impressive-looking hydro power stations into the Andes towards Ticlio and way beyond the beautiful **Mantaro Valley**.

To **get to Cajamarquilla**, the colectivo (see p.124) will drop you off at the refinery turn-off before Km 10 of the Carretera Central, then it's about 4km, or an hour's walk to the **ruins** which are well hidden next to an old hacienda. There are plenty of minibus *colectivos* connecting Lima with Chosica for around $1, but catching a bus on from Chosica to Huancayo, Tarma or Huánuco can be trickier since, although they pass through here, they may well be full already. *Colectivos* or shared taxis may be an easier solution.

North of Lima

There are a couple of shortish trips becoming increasingly popular as long weekend breaks from Lima. One of these is a horseshoe loop connecting the **Chillón and Chancay valleys** via the beautiful town and region of Canta in the foothills of the Andes. Another route, further out from Lima, heads up the Huara Valley from Huacho; although the road can be traced all the way to Huánuco, most people only get as far up into the Andes as **Churin** where their efforts are pleasantly rewarded with a visit to the hot springs. Futher north again, yet still feasible as a day trip from Lima, the recently discovered pyramids of **El Caral** are considered to be the most ancient ruins in the Americas.

The Chillón and Chancay valleys

Leaving Lima and heading north, the Panamerican Highway passes through the **CHILLÓN VALLEY**, dotted with ancient **ruins**, of which the most important are on the south side of the Río Chillón within 3 or 4km of the Ventanilla road. The most impressive is the 2000–3000-year-old **Temple El Paraiso**, which was built by a sedentary farming community of probably no more than 1500 inhabitants and consists of three main pyramids built of rustic stones.

From here, the Panamerican Highway passes the yacht and tennis clubs that make up the fashionable beach resort of **Ancón**, about 30km from Lima, then crosses a high, often foggy, plateau from the Chillón to the **Chancay valley**. This foggy zone, still covered by sparse vegetation, was a relatively fertile *lomas* area (where plants grow from moisture in the air rather than rainwater or irrigation) in pre-Inca days, and evidence of winter camps from five thousand years ago has been found. The highway bypasses the market town of Huaral and runs through **Chancay**, some 65km north of Lima, worth a visit only for its excellent cliff-top seafood **restaurants**, as the sea is too dangerous to swim in at this location. Nearby the unique looking domes of Ecotruly Ashram appear along the beach at Km 63 on the Panamerican Highway, by Chacra y Mar beach (Ⓦwww.ecotrulypark.org, Lima contact Av Javier Prado Este 185 San Isidro, ☏4210016). Set at the foot of desert cliffs and close to the pounding ocean, this ashram offers guided tours of their adobe huts and organic gardens, plus yoga and meditation, hikes and workshops on ecology. Always book visits in advance.

Continuing north from Chancay, the road passes through stark desert for 20km until you reach the **Reserva Nacional Lomas de Lachay**, a protected area of unique *lomas* habitat some 5000 hectares in extent and around 600m above sea-level. Run by the Ministry of Agriculture, the centre maintains the footpaths that thread through the reserve's beautiful scenery. Formed by granite and diorite rocky intrusions some seventy million years ago, the *lomas* – at its best between June and December when it is in full bloom – is home to more than forty types of birds including hummingbirds, parrots, partridges, peregrines and even condors; you may also spot various species of reptile and native deer.

A little further north of the reserve, at Km 133, a track turns off onto a small peninsula and leads to the secluded bay of **El Paraiso** – a magical beach perfect for camping, swimming and scuba-diving. Crossing more bleak sands, the Panamerican Highway next passes through **Huacho**, an unusual place with some interesting colonial architecture and a ruined church in the upper part of town, but mostly made up of recent concrete constructions; being so close to Lima, it's been one of the first to be hit by expanding and migratory populations as well as wealthy Lima families taking on a second home or farmstead.

The easiest way to **get to the reserve** is with an organized tour from Lima (see p.114), but if you are doing it alone continue up the Panamerican Highway for about 6km beyond the turning for Sayan and Churin. The turn-off to the reserve is signposted at the top of a hill, but from the road it's still an hour's walk along a sandy track to the interpretive centre (daily 7am–7pm) at the entrance to the reserve.

Sayan and Churin

Just beyond Huacho a side road turns east into the **Huara Valley** and the foothills of the Andes to reach **SAYAN**, a small farming town where little has changed for decades – the church here has a very attractive colonial interior. **Colectivos** run between Sayan and Huacho every thirty minutes.

Further up the valley lies **CHURIN**, a small thermal spa town, located in the district of Pachangara 210km from Lima, that's very popular with Limeños during holidays. Most of the farmland on the valley floor and the Sayan to Churin road was washed away in the 1998 El Niño, and a new, rough road has been carved out between the boulders littering the valley floor. There are two **spas** in town, both fairly cool, with private and communal baths, but the El Fierro spa, ten minutes by *colectivo* from town, is the hottest and is reputed to be the most curative; all cost about $0.50. Churin is also a good base from which to explore a number of traditional communities as well as archaeological **ruins**, such as Ninash, Kutun, Antasway and Kuray. For climbers, there are also some challenging **peaks** in the

Cordillera Raura (up to 5700m). The main **festival** time here is for San Juan, between June 23rd and 25th annually, which includes a ritual procession to the river for a cleansing bath, to ensure health in the coming year.

There are many **places to stay**, but they all get packed out in the main holiday periods, when prices double. All the hotels are within a couple of blocks of each other in the town centre; try the *Hotel Las Termas* (☎2373094; ④), which has nice rooms and a pool. Churin has many good **restaurants** and cafés, mostly around the main plaza, and local specialities include honey, *alfajores*, *manjar blanca* and cheeses.

An excellent day-trip from Churin can be made to more thermal baths at **Huancahuasi**. **Colectivos** leave from Churin church at around 8am ($4 return), returning mid-afternoon. There are two sets of hot baths at Huancahuasi (both $1), and snacks such as *pachamanca* are prepared outside them. En route to Huancahuasi you'll spot a remarkable early colonial carved facade on the tiny church at Picoy.

There are several **buses** to and from Lima daily (a 6–7hr journey), the best being run by Transportes Estrella Polar; expect to pay around $6.

Caral

Northwards up the coast from Huacho, only the town and port of Supe breaks the monotonous beauty of desert and ocean, until you reach Barranca and the labyrinthine ruins of the **Fortress of Paramonga** (see p.353). Inland from Supe, however, along the desert coast in a landscape which looks more lunar than agricultural, archaeologists have recently uncovered one of the most important archaeological finds of the past century. Thought to be the oldest city in the Americas, the **ancient pyramids of CARAL** have overturned many long-standing assumptions. It's open only to official guided tours as much excavation work is yet to be done, but it is possible to see the site with permission from INRENA (see p.118) on visits organized by some of the better tour companies (Fertur Peru – see p.114 – do a day trip from around $80 per person, including guide, bus and taxi to the site). Difficult to reach without a car, it's connected to the Panamerican Highway by a badly rutted dirt-track road. Transportes Paramonga (Luna Pizarro 251, La Victoria) run buses every day to Supe, usually leaving around 6.20am. From here, if unguided, you'd need to rent a taxi.

This site (☎4312235, ⊛www.caralperu.gob.pe) represents human achievements that took place four thousand years earlier than the Incas: the stone ceremonial structures at Caral were flourishing one hundred years before the Great Pyramid at Giza was even built. The heart of the site covering about 150 acres, with two sunken circular plazas at the base of the largest mound itself measuring 154m by 138m at the bottom, evidently making it the largest pyramid yet found in Peru. Excavations have revealed that this Pirimide Mayor (main pyramid) was terraced with a staircase leading up to an atrium-like platform, culminating in a flattened top housing enclosed rooms and a ceremonial fire pit. Some of the best artefacts discovered here include 32 flutes made from pelican and animal bones and engraved with the figures of birds and even monkeys, demonstrating a connection with the Amazon region.

Travel details

Buses and colectivos

Lima to: Arequipa (12 daily; 14–16hr); Chincha (8 daily; 2–3hr); Cusco (10 daily, some change in Arequipa; 30–40hr); Huacho (12 daily; 2–3hr); Huancayo (12 daily; 6–8hr); Huaraz (10 daily; 9–10hr); Ica (every 15min; 3–4hr); La Merced (8 daily; 7–8hr); Nasca (10 daily; 6hr); Satipo (2 daily; 12–14hr); Pisco (6 daily; 3hr–3hr 30min); Tacna (6 daily; 18–20hr); Tarma (8 daily; 6–7hr); Trujillo (10 daily; 8–9hr).

Flights

Lima to: Arequipa (2 daily; 1hr 20min); Chiclayo (2 daily; 1hr 40min); Cusco (8 daily; 1hr); Iquitos (2 daily; 2hr); Juliaca for Puno (1 daily; 2hr); Piura (2 daily; 1hr 30min); Pucallpa (2 daily; 1hr); Rioja/Moyabamba (2 or 3 weekly; 1hr 30min); Tacna (2 daily; 2hr 30min); Tarapoto (daily; 1hr 30min); Trujillo (2 daily; 50min); Tumbes (1 daily; 2hr 30min).

Nasca and the South Coast

CHAPTER 2 # Highlights

* **Lunahuana** Just a couple of hours' drive from Lima, this beautiful coastal valley is almost always sunny, and a focus for whitewater rafting, mountain biking as well as good local wines and piscos. See p.133

* **Ballestas Islands** Within a morning's boat ride from the town of Pisco, these are guano islands covered in bird and mammalian marine life. See p.141

* **Paracas National Reserve** A beautiful peninsula with stunning desert landscapes touching the Pacific ocean; both beaches and sea are a haven for wildlife, and there is a museum dedicated to the ancient Paracas culture. See p.142

* **Huacachina** A magical oasis surrounded by some of the most arid sand dune desert landscapes in the Americas, Huacachina is both a leisure resort and a healing spa. See p.153

* **Nasca** The world-famous Nasca Lines, including stylised geometric and animal figures, were etched, seemingly impossibly, into a massive desert pampa. See p.154

* **Puerto Inca** An important port for the Incas 500 years ago, this small but secluded resort lies in an area of coast teeming with rare Inca remains as well as offering great access to beaches, coves, fishing and excellent diving. See p.167

▲ Flying over the Nasca Lines

2

Nasca and the South Coast

T he coastal area south of Lima all the way to Chile clings tightly to over 1330km of desert road offering access to enough ancient remains, wildlife and unusual landscapes to tempt any traveller off the Panamerican Highway. The south has been populated as long as anywhere in Peru – for at least nine thousand years in some places – but until last century no one guessed the existence of this arid region's unique cultures, whose enigmatic remains, particularly along the coast, show signs of a particularly sophisticated civilization. With the discovery in 1901 and subsequent study of ancient sites throughout the coastal zone, it soon became apparent that, whilst exhibiting cultural influences similar to nearby highland areas (notably Chavin and Huari), this was home to at least three major pre-Inca cultures: the **Paracas** (500 BC–400 AD), the influential **Nasca** (500–800 AD) and latterly the **Ica** culture, shortly before the Incas took over.

South of Lima, five significant towns dominate the coastal desert region: **Cañete, Chincha, Pisco, Ica** and **Nasca**. All five of these energetic and quite welcoming towns preserve important and intriguing sites from the three cultures, though few visitors stop at the first two, generally more interested in getting to the latter three. Around Pisco, 200km south of Lima, the unspoiled coastline is superb for bird-watching, while the desert plains around Nasca are indelibly marked by gigantic, geometric animal and alien-looking figures that were scratched into the brown earth over a thousand years ago. In the cooler hills above the desert coastal strip you can spot herds of the soft-woolled *vicuña* or see pink flamingoes in their natural Andean habitat at the stunning **Lake Parinacochas**. Just inland from Pisco (the only town in this region actually near the ocean), the adobe Inca remains of **Tambo Colorado** make an interesting diversion, perhaps rounded off by a great seafood dinner at the fisherman's wharf in **San Andres**. Hidden in sand dunes just outside the city of Ica, the oasis resort of **Huacachina** offers the unusual combination of a peaceful desert hang-out alongside sandboarding and dune buggies. A couple of hours drive south many people head daily to the most mysterious and famous of all archaeological sites, the **Nasca Lines**, a perplexing network of perfectly geometric shapes and giant figures etched over almost 500 square kilometres of bleak pampa.

Nasca and Pisco also offer three of the most outstanding wildlife reserves in the country – the rare *vicuña* reserve of **Pampa Galeras** (in the Andes above Nasca),

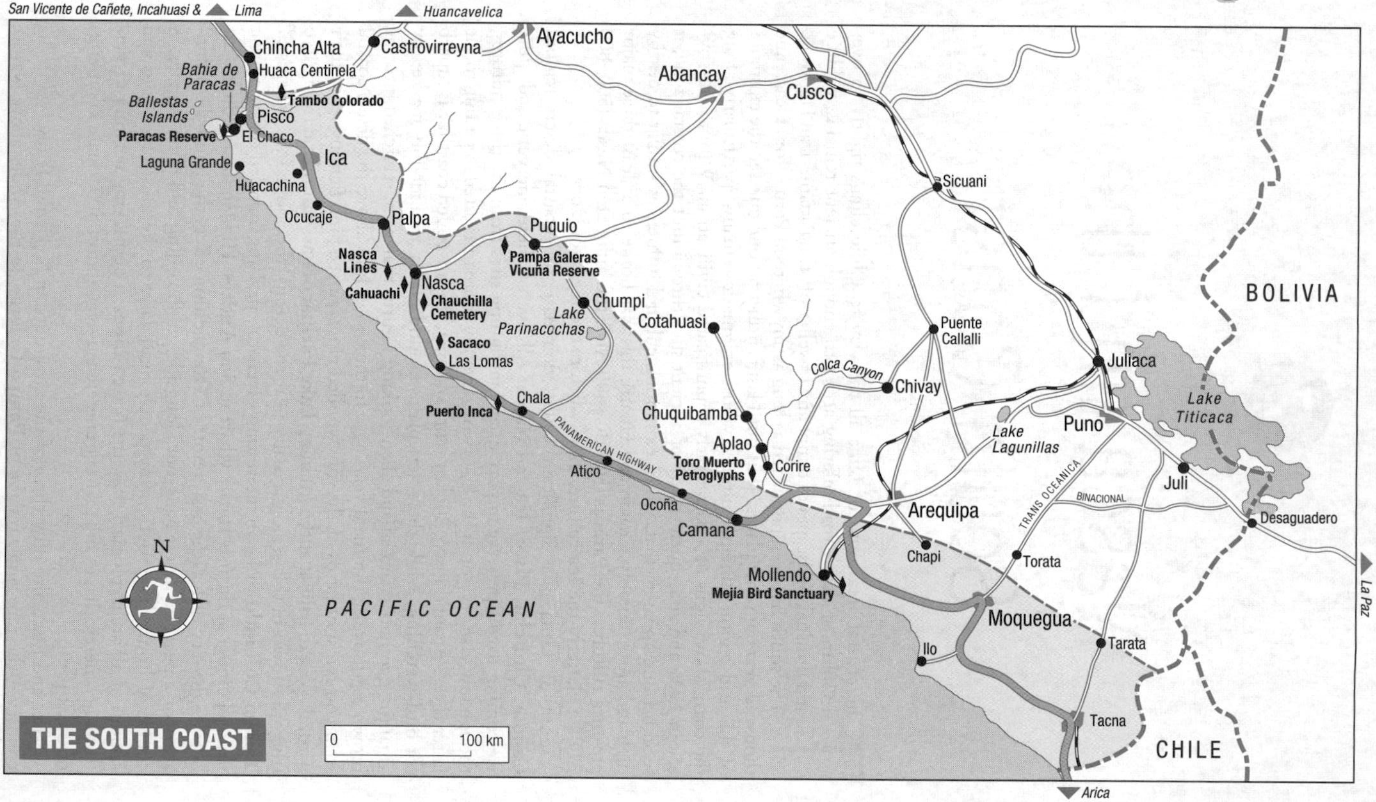

THE SOUTH COAST

La Paz

BOLIVIA

CHILE

Lake Titicaca

Desaguadero

Juliaca

Juli

Puno

Tarata

Tacna

Arica

Lake Lagunillas

Sicuani

Puente Callalli

Chivay

Torata

Moquegua

TRANS OCEÁNICA BINACIONAL

Ilo

Colca Canyon

Arequipa

Chapi

Corire

Mollendo
Mejia Bird Sanctuary

Cusco

Abancay

Cotahuasi

Chuquibamba

Aplao
Toro Muerto Petroglyphs

Camana

Ayacucho

Chumpi

Lake Parinacochas

Ocoña

Atico

PANAMERICAN HIGHWAY

Huancavelica

Castrovirreyna

Puquio

Pampa Galeras Vicuña Reserve

Nasca
Chauchilla Cemetery

Sacaco

Las Lomas

Chala

Puerto Inca

Chinchà Alta
Huaca Centinela
Tambo Colorado

Pisco
El Chaco

Palpa

Nasca Lines
Cahuachi

Ica

Ocucaje

Huacachina

PACIFIC OCEAN

Bahía de Paracas
Ballestas Islands
Paracas Reserve

Laguna Grande

N

0   100 km

San Vicente de Cañete, Incahuasi & ▲ Lima

Travelling south by bus

The south Peruvian coast is served from Lima by several companies, including Cruz del Sur **buses** and Ormeño's Expreson Chinchano service (leaves Lima from Av Javier Prado Este 1059 ☏01/4721710, ⊛www.grupo-ormeno.com.pe), both with depots on Javier Prado Este in San Isidro; most of these services continue on to Pisco, Nasca and Arequipa. A more frequent service from Lima to all towns as far south as Ica, is the Peru Bus Soyuz/Peru Bus, Av Mexico 333, La Victoria (☏4276310, $8–10); these buses leave every ten minutes during the day (every 30min by night) and can also be picked up at stops along the Panamericana Sur in Lima (eg where this highway is crossed by either Av Javier Prado Este or Av Benavides Este). Once in Ica, it can be fun to travel on to Nasca with one of the last Peruvian road routes still connected by large 1970s **colectivo cars**, mainly Dodge Coronets, allowing anyone who fancies doing this segment of the coast a trip – of three hours or so – through glorious desert scenery in relative style and comfort.

and the **Ballestas Islands** and **Paracas National Reserve** (outside Pisco, 20km south or so along the coast). One hour by car south of Nasca, meanwhile, in the middle of the desert, there's an amazing little museum at Sacaco giving background information on a fossilised whale skeleton which still sits in full view in the desert. Further south, just before the town of Chala, **Puerto Inca** is a stunning but still relatively undeveloped beach resort, which was also the key coastal port for the nobles of Inca Cusco.

Once past the town of Camana, south of Chala, the **Panamericana Sur highway** runs inland to within almost 40km of Arequipa (see Chapter 3), where there's a fast road connection into the city. From this junction the highway cuts south across undulating desert to the calm and reasonably attractive colonial town of Moquegua, increasingly visited as a springboard for the region's archaeological heritage, before heading south another 150km to **Tacna**, the last pit stop before the **frontier with Chile**.

Transport is not usually a problem along the South Coast, with local buses connecting all the towns with each other and with Lima, and express buses ploughing along the coastal road between Lima and Arequipa day and night. All the major towns have a decent range of accommodation and restaurants, and **camping** in the wild is possible in many places, though there are formal camp sites only around Nasca and Puerto Inca.

Cañete and Lunahuana

Some 8km south of Cerro Azul, and two hours or so driving from Lima brings you to the busy market town of **CAÑETE**. This is not an obviously attractive town in itself, despite some colonial flavour, but the surrounding marigold and cotton fields and the nearby valley of Lunahuana grant it a certain appeal. In many ways, the Cañete Valley is the nearest place from Lima where you can get a feel for the rural desert coast and there is almost constant sunshine year round. The new roads now extend nearly all the way from Lima, but this particular valley has not yet been over-developed or populated with factories or *pueblos jovenes* (shanties).

With the attractive, inland river-based resort of **LUNAHUANA** just 35km east, few travellers, Peruvian or from overseas, actually stay in Cañete. Several hotels and a wide variety of tour agencies offer trekking, mountain biking, valley tours and, last but certainly not least, whitewater rafting or canoeing. To get to Lunahuana from Cañete you can take either a *colectivo*, the daily 3pm Yauyos bus or a taxi, the latter usually found in the town centre around the bus stops on the main through road. Alternatively, if you're travelling in a group, local minibus owner, Obdulo Sanchez (T996178144), offers reasonable rates. If you wanted to continue on up the valley to Huancayo (see p.322) via Lunahuana, the ETAS buses run once or twice a week from Cañete (T2878831).

As well as eco-adventures, Lunahuana is a great base for exploring the local Inca archaeological complex of **Incahuasi**, established by the Inca Emperor Pachacutec. On the plaza there's a fine colonial church with cool interior and a sky-blue wooden vaulted ceiling. Within easy striking distance there's a horse dressage (*caballos de paso*) centre, a traditional hanging bridge, plus several vineyards and rustic **pisco haciendas**, such as the Bodega Fidelina Candela, Anexo Jita, at Km 37 (Lima T2841030). During the off-season, this is a relatively peaceful spot, a rural area with dry and beautifully sculptured dusty mountainsides surrounding a narrow, irrigated and fertile green valley floor. As well as abundant vineyards, the valley is also dedicated to cultivating maize, cotton, rice, avocados, chillies, limes, papayas and bananas. Further up the valley near the settlement of Taula, there's the Reserva Nacional Paisajita Nor Yauyos, a protected area containing archaeological remains and ancient terracing – evidence of early plant domestication. The forests here, some of the few remaining on the western slopes of the Peruvian Andes, stand in the shadows of the glacial peak, Nevado Pariaca.

Practicalities

Money exchange is possible at the Banco de La Nacion, Jr Grau 398 and **Internet** facilities are close by at Jr Grau 311. **Rafting** usually costs $12–20 an hour – including guide, transport and training – depending on the season (cheapest in low season, May to October). There are several local **tour companies**: *Lunahuana Adventure Tours*, Jr Grau (T96143873), offer tours that are mainly adventure-action based; *Popy Tours*, Jr Grau 380 (T2841162) offer minibus tours to the main valley sites; and *Lunahuana Service Tours*, Jr Grau 284 (T2841111), focus on minibus tours, biking and rafting. **Cicloturismo Peru** (T4337981, Wwww.cicloturismoperu.com), meanwhile, provides opportunities for cycle tours into and around Lunahuana valley, but you need to make arrangements with them in advance.

Accommodation is generally easy to find on the main road, except in high season (particularly December and January). A few kilometres before the main Lunahuana settlement and Plaza de Armas, there's *La Fortaleza del Inca*, Carretera Central Km 31.5 (T99411864, Wwww.fortalezainca.com; ❻), featuring pleasant, well-equipped rooms with private showers based around a courtyard dominated by a swimming pool; breakfast around the pool is included. Much more interesting is the nearby *Refugio de Santiago*, C Real 33, Paullo, Lunahuana 31km (T996394434 or 4362717, Wwww.refugiodesantiago .com, Erefugiodesantiago@yahoo.com; ❺–❻), a beautifully furnished hostel inside a colonial-style house, with an internal courtyard bar and a few acres of gardens with outside tables and one of the finest restaurants (based largely around indigenous and ancient fruits, herbs and vegetables) south of Lima. The hotel also runs walking and minibus tours to interesting sites around the valley. The large, modern resort *Hotel Embassy* (T2841194; ❺–❻) has much less style and comfort, though it does offer a riverside location, reasonably big pool and bar/disco. Close to the Plaza de Armas in town, the *Hostal Casurinas*, Jr Grau 295 (☎2841045; ❸–❹), is cheap, has clean hot showers and is close to much of the action. **Camping** can be found on the grounds of *El Refugio* as well as 2km up the valley at Km 33, overlooking the river at San Jeronimo, or at Km 41.2, Annexo Condoray (☎5318413) where Sra. Carmen Hererra runs Camping El Tambo; prices for both sites are around $5 per person.

For good **food**, apart from the excellent *El Refugio*, there's the traditional *Restaurant Antojitos* on the Plaza de Armas, which serves freshly cooked meals, from breakfast through to late-evening snacks and meals; they also stock some local wines and brandy.

Chincha

At the top of a cliff, **CHINCHA** is a relatively rich oasis that appears after a stretch of almost Saharan landscape – and a mightily impressive sand dune. A busy little coastal centre renowned for its cheap wines and variety of **piscos** (brandies), Chincha is a strong cultural hub for **Afro-Peruvian culture**; the town was developed during the early colonial period when Africans (mainly from Guinea) were brought over as slaves to work on the cotton plantations. Of all the South American countries, racial repression was amongst the harshest in Peru, with prohibitions on people of mixed race (*criollos*) from holding public office. Afro-Peruvians were even banned from playing drums (that's how the Peruvian percussive instrument – the *cajón* – was invented, see Contexts). It wasn't until 1854 that slavery was abolished in Peru and Afro-Peruvians became technically free. Slavery turned into servitude and whilst racial prejudice is not an obvious major social issue in the twenty-first century, there are few, if any, black professionals outside of the entertainment industry, even today.

One of the best places for pisco and local wine (*vino dulce*) is at the 100-year-old **Bodega Naldo Navarro** in Sunampe, 1km north of Chincha, offering free guided tours and samples. Several other local bodegas offer similar tours. For **festivals**, the third Saturday in September is National Pisco Day, when things really get lively along this section of the coast. The area is also well-known for its traditionally rhythmic music and annual, athletic dance festival, Verano Negro, which takes place at the end of February. In November, the Festival de Danzas Negras is an excellent event, a vibrant dance event based on Afro-Peruvian traditions; in both cases the celebrations are liveliest in El Carmen, 10km southeast of Chincha.

Although little-visited, the Chincha area has a number of **ruins**, with numerous *huacas* lying scattered about the oasis. Dominated in pre-Inca days by the Cuismancu (or Chincha) state, activity focused around what were probably ceremonial pyramids. One of these, the majestic **Huaca Centinela**, also known as the little city of Chinchacamac, sits in the valley below the Chincha tableland and the ocean, around thirty minutes' walk from the *Hotel El Sausal* turning (see p.136), some 8km off the Panamericana. Not far from Chincha, 40km up the Castrovireyna road (which leaves the Panamerican Highway at Km 230) is another impressive Cuismancu ruin, Tambo Colorado (see p.146).

Don't miss the **Hacienda San José**, Pueblo San José (daily 9am–6pm; free), 9km southeast of Chincha, in an extensive plantation, where you can see impressive Churrigueresque-domed towers built in the 1680s. Its colourful history includes the tale of an owner murdered on the house's main steps by his slaves. Now a semi-luxurious **hotel** (☎056/221458; ❻), the hacienda is also bookable in Lima through Juan Fanning 328, Oficina 202, Miraflores ☎4445524, ✉hsanjose@terra.com.pe). Note that you don't necessarily have to take a room: non-guests can use the pool and watch local folklore shows, and there are 45-minute **tours** ($3) around the labyrinthine **catacombs**, themselves containing prison cells still clearly showing the poor conditions in which slaves were once shackled.

Practicalities

Most **bus connections from Chincha** can be found at the Terminal Terrestre, Avenida Oscar Benavides. As well as the *Hacienda San José* (see p.135), **accommodation** options include the *Hostal El Condado* (☎056-261424, ✉hostalcondado@terra.com; ⬤), Km 195 on the Panamerican Highway; the rather elegant and upmarket *Hotel El Sausal* (☎056-262451, ☏271262, ✉sausal@exalmar.com.pe; ⬤), Km 197.5, located on the right as you come into town, equipped with its own pool; and the *Hotel El Valle* (☎056-262556; ⬤), on the Panamerican Highway, which offers good rooms at reasonable prices. If these are booked, you can try any one of the several hotels located on the main street. For **eating**, the *Palacio de Mariscos* at the *Hotel El Valle* is excellent and the restaurant *El Fogon* is a reasonable alternative on the main plaza.

Pisco and around

Having suffered severely in the earthquake which devastated this region of Peru early in the evening of August 15th, 2007, and which registered 8 on the Richter Scale, **PISCO** is still reeling from the aftermath. Hundreds of people were killed by the quake and over 15,000 made homeless around Pisco. Many adobe buildings crumbled, and, while modern ones were generally left intact, one hotel collapsed killing some tourists. Worse, around 133 people died when the main church collapsed during a service. The city, which remains one of the most active seismic spots on earth, still looks like it has suffered recent and extensive air bombardment. One year on from the disaster, and with many households still without electricity or water, the townspeople held a demonstration, complaining that little of the promises made for rapid re-development had thus far materialised.

Less than three hours by bus from Lima, Pisco has long been a rewarding stop en route to Nasca, Arequipa or the frontier with Chile. While it's of little interest in itself, the town makes a pleasant enough base; it has several good hotels and hostels, most of which were left intact and provides access to the **Paracas National Reserve**, the wildlife of the **Ballestas Islands** and the well-preserved Inca coastal outpost of **Tambo Colorado**. Just off the Panamerican Highway, the town is also a crossroads for heading up into the Andes: you can take roads from here to Huancavelica and Huancayo, as well as to Ayacucho and Cusco.

El Chaco, some 12km from Pisco, close to the entry to the Paracas National Reserve, has several **hostels**, a half-dozen or so excellent seafront restaurants serving delicious **seafood** and a relatively new scene here based around the jetty catering to the Ballestas Islands boat departures. Money exchange, souvenirs and tour agents for sand buggy rides are also on hand.

Arrival, information and city transport

If you come into Pisco on one of the frequent **buses** run by Ormeño or Cruz del Sur, you'll arrive respectively at San Francisco 259 (☎056/532764) or San Fran-

PISCO

ACCOMMODATION

Hostal El Candelabro	G
Hostal Pisco	E
Hostal La Portada	B
Hostal Residencial San Jorge	A
Hostal San Isidro	F
La Hosteria del Monasterio	C
Posada Hispana Hostal	D

JIRÓN JUAN OSCORES

CALLE MANUEL BARRIANUEVO

CALLE ALIPIO PONCE

CALLE CERRO AZUL

CALLE RAMON ASPILLAGA

CALLE DOS DE MAYO

JIRÓN PROGRESSO

Police Station

Ballestas Travel Service

Cruz del Sur Buses

Ormeño Buses

SAN FRANCISCO

SAN JUAN DE DIOS

BOLOGNESI

Municipal Palace

La Compañia

AVENIDA SAN MARTIN

PLAZA DE ARMAS

Main Church

AYACUCHO

Saki Bus

Soyuz Peru Bus

JIRÓN CALLAO

PEREZ DE FIGUEROLA

Colectivos to Ica

CALLE BEATITA DE HUMAY

CALLE PEDEMONTE

JIRÓN COMERCIO BOULEVARD

INDEPENDENCIA

28 DE JULIO

Pacific Ocean

CALLE AREQUIPA

Buses to San Andres

PLAZUELA BELEN

Seafront & 2

EATING & NIGHTLIFE

Caffe Vecchia Firenze	1
Chifa Ken Chay	3
Restaurant La Viña de Huver	2

0   50 m

CALLE DOCTOR ZUÑIGAN

Market and buses for Paracas   Minimarket

NASCA AND THE SOUTH COAST | Pisco and around

cisco 255, one block east of the Plaza de Armas. The Soyuz (Peru Bus) terminal for Lima and Ica services has a drop-off point 8km east at Repartición, the Pisco turn-off on the Panamericana (the company actually organizes free taxis from here to their offices on the corner of San Juan de Dios and Perez de Figuerola in the Plaza de Armas), and if you arrive from Ica by Saki bus you end up on Calle Dos de Mayo, just one block west of the Plaza.

Tourist information is available from the regional tourism directorate (Mon–Fri 8am–7pm; W www.pisco.info) in the Subprefectura's office next to the police station on the Plaza de Armas; they also have a list of official guides in the area and sometimes maps or photocopied information on the town, islands and local beaches. A somewhat better information service is offered by

137

the staff at the *Posada Hispana Hostal*, Bolognesi 222 (℡056/536363, ⓦwww
.posadahispana.com), who provide informed details about most of the local sites
of interest and worthwhile places to eat. Getting around Pisco is easy – it's a
small enough town to **walk** around the main attractions, and a **taxi** anywhere
in the central area should cost less than $1.

Pretty well all travellers use one of the **tour companies** (see p.140) in town to
get the most out of their time in and around Pisco. Most of the them have competing offices in and around the Plaza de Armas and along Calle San Francisco, and it's
hard to cross the plaza as a traveller without attracting the attention of at least one
tour company sales representative. With most firms offering the same deals at the
same price, however, there really isn't that much to choose between them. Nevertheless, it's advisable to at least check out two or three to see which one offers you
the best and most professional service at the time.

Accommodation

At the time of writing, most of the **accommodation** options below, within two
or three blocks of the Plaza de Armas, were at least partially re-functioning post
quake. Outside of the town centre, the best places to stay are in El Chaco.

In town

Hostal El Candelabro Jr Callao 190–198
℡056/532620. Quite luxurious, with excellent
service; all rooms are equipped with a minibar, TV
and bath. ❺

Hostal Pisco San Francisco 115 ℡056/532018. A
friendly hostel with its own evening music bar – *La
Vela* – in a busy position on Plaza de Armas. Basic
for the price, although most rooms have private
bath. ❷–❸

Hostal La Portada Alipio Ponce 250
℡056/532098. Located a few blocks from the
plaza, this is a great place to stay, good value and
with really comfortable rooms with private bath, hot
water and TV. ❸

Hostal Residencial San Jorge Jr Juan Oscores
267 ℡056/532885, ⓔhotel_san_jorge_residencial
@hotmail.com. A modern hotel, three short blocks
north of the town centre, and with two entrances:
one being on the Barrio Nuevo road, one block
nearer the plaza than Jr Juan Oscores entrance.
Rooms are clean and well-furnished with private
bath, and there's a bit of a garden with ample
parking. ❹–❺

Hostal San Isidro San Clemente 103
℡056/536471, ⓦwww.sanisidrohostal.com. In
a relatively peaceful and safe area of Pisco, this
place is friendly and clean. Tours can be arranged
via staff. ❸

La Hosteria del Monasterio Av Bolognesi 236
℡056/531383. Close to and under same ownership as the *Posada Hispana*, this is well-kept with
reliable hot water and TVs in every room. ❹–❻

Posada Hispana Hostal Av Bolognesi 222
℡056/536363, ⓕ536363, ⓔposadahispana
@terra.com.pe, ⓦwww.posadahispana.com. One
of the best choices in Pisco – very safe and ethni-
cally decorated with a friendly and helpful staff
who are always happy to provide good tourist information. All rooms are clean and equipped with a
TV, telephone, private bath and constant hot water.
Laundry facilities are available, and breakfast is
served on the rooftop patio. ❹–❻

Out of town

Hostal El Mirador El Chaco ℡056/545086,
ⓦwww.elmiradorhotel.com. A popular place close
to the ocean which serves meals and will help
organize tours; best to make advance reservation. ❸

Hostal Los Zarcillos Av Paracas Lote 106, Urb El
Golf ℡ 056/545082, ⓕ545082. Modern and comfortable, this hostel is fairly close to the beach area
for what it's worth. ❹

Hostería Paracas Av Los Libertadores, El Balneario, El Chaco (no phone). A much cheaper alternative to the *Hotel Paracas*, in a good position close
to the entrance to Paracas Reserve. ❺

Hotel Paracas Av 173, Ribera del Mar, El Balneario, El Chaco ℡056/545100. A luxurious option
worth the money, with pool, excellent bar and restaurant (open to non-residents) right on the ocean
and the edge of Paracas Reserve, close to Playa El
Chaco wharf. It's very popular as a weekend retreat
for wealthy *Limeños*, and quite good as a base
for fishing trips and available watersports. ❼

The Town

Perhaps because of its ease of access, the Spanish considered making **Pisco** their coastal capital before eventually deciding on Lima. Today the town's old port has been superseded by the smelly fishmeal factories south along the bay towards Paracas, and even more so by modern Puerto San Martín north of the Paracas Reserve.

Plaza de Armas and around

Pisco's focus of activity is the **Plaza de Armas** and adjoining **Jirón Comercio**; every evening the plaza is crowded with people walking and talking, buying *tejas* (small sweets made from pecan nuts) from street sellers, or chatting in one of several laid-back cafés and bars around the square. Clustered about the plaza, with its statue of liberator San Martín poised in the shade of ancient ficus trees, are a few fine colonial showpieces, including the mansion where San Martín stayed on his arrival in Peru, half a block west of the plaza, and location of the **Club Social de Pisco** until the earthquake in 2007. Unusual in its Moorish style, the **Consejo Provincial** (or Municipal Palace), just to the left if you're facing the church on the Plaza de Armas, is painted in striking blue and white in memory of the liberator San Martín's own colours. One block further away from the plaza down Calle San Francisco, the heavy Baroque **Iglesia de la Compañía**, built in 1689, boasts a superb carved pulpit and gold-leaf altarpiece, plus some crypts with subterranean galleries; however, its state of disrepair means it's presently closed off to the public.

Avenida San Martín and the ACOREMA Centre

If you have an hour or so to spare, it's worth exploring **Avenída San Martín** from the plaza west to the sea, but beware – **tourist muggings** have been happening here in recent years, so go in a group. Here you can see the decaying remains of the old pier, second in size only to the Muelle de Pacasmayo in the north of Peru,

▲ Plaza de Armas

and notice just how much further out the sea edge is today than it clearly was a hundred years or so ago. The Avenida San Martín is also traditional home to many of Pisco's finest mansions, one of which was converted into the **ACOREMA Centre**, Av San Martín 1471 (daily 10am–1pm & 2–6pm; $1; Ⓦwww.acorema .org.pe), a small maritime ecology museum with varied and fascinating collections of shells, interpretative displays, bones of a five-metre humpback whale and the skeleton of a Gray's beaked whale.

Eating and nightlife

You don't have to look far for good food in Pisco, with most restaurants specializing in a wide range of locally caught fish and seafood. Sea turtles are in danger of extinction along the coast here, so it's actually illegal to serve or eat turtle as a food (though it is still on offer in some restaurants). Nightlife is restricted to the lively pubs and bars, on or within a block or two of the main plaza.

Caffe Vecchia Firenze San Francisco 327. A great little snack bar with the best coffee in town.
Chifa Ken Chay C Doctor Zunigan 131. Just two blocks south of the plaza, this Chinese restaurant serves surprisingly good-quality *chifa* dishes for a relatively small town; good food and great value.
Restaurant Acapulco Av Genaro Medrano 620. Located just fifty yards or so from the main fisherman's wharf at San Andres, this is one of the more traditional and popular seafood restaurants in the region, serving massive fish dishes at reasonable prices.
Restaurant El Chorrito ☎056/545045. A pretty tasty seafood restaurant out at El Baleario, en route to Paracas.
Restaurant La Viña de Huver Prolongación Cerro Azul, next to the Parque Zonal. Just a little way from the centre of town, this is easily the busiest lunch spot in Pisco serving excellent, huge and relatively inexpensive ceviche and other seafood dishes in a bustling and appealing environment.

Listings

Banks and exchange Banco de Credito, Perez de Figuerola 162, and Banco Continental, next door on the corner of the Plaza and Independencia will change dollars and travellers' cheques. Most hotels and the tour companies will change dollars cash, but the best rates are from the *cambistas* on the corner of the pedestrian boulevard between Comercio and Progreso and Plaza de Armas.
Bus companies Many local buses leave from the Terminal Terrestre, C San Francisco, block 2, while most of the major companies have their own offices, such as Cruz del Sur, San Francisco 255; Ormeño, on the corner of Ayacucho and San Francisco (☎056/532764); and Oropesa, Calle Commercio. Soyuz Peru Bus has an office on the Plaza de Armas (☎056/535526), corner of San Juan de Dios and Perez de Figuerola (☎056/531014) for passengers from here to the pick-up point at Repartición – the major road intersection where the Pisco turn-off meets the Panamerican Highway – some 8km from the plaza in Pisco. The cheaper Saki buses connecting Pisco and Ica leave from Calle Pedemonte at the corner with Calle Arequipa, just a block and a half from the Plaza.
Hospital C San Juan de Dios 350.
Police Plaza de Armas, C San Francisco ☎034/532165.
Post office Bolognesi 173 (Mon–Sat 8am–7pm).
Telephone office Locutorio Telefónico, C Progreso 123A, Plaza de Armas (daily 7am–11pm).
Tour operators Paracas Overland, C San Francisco 111 ☎056/533855, Ⓦwww.paracasoverland.com .pe; Zarcillos Tours based in the *Hostal Pisco*, Plaza de Armas; Ballestas Travel Service, San Franscisco 249 ☎056/533095; and Ballestas Expeditions, San Francisco 219 ☎056/532373 operate package excursions to the Islas Ballestas and Paracas with good guides and a reliable service. A speedboat takes you out to the Ballestas Islands; after this most people continue on the tour from the Playa El Chaco Wharf to the main sites in the Paracas National Reserve. It's a standard package costing $12 for the islands morning trip and a further $12 for the afternoon tour of the reserve. Most of these companies also organize tours to Tambo Colorado and offer a discount for ten or more people; some of them, such as Reservas Tours Pisco, can arrange for flights over the Nasca Lines for upwards of $80. The Arequipa-based Peru Adventure Tours, Jerusalen 410, Arequipa ☎054/221658, run tours to the Ballestas and Paracas as well as bicycle adventures in the desert.

San Andres, El Chaco and the Ballestas Islands

One of the best trips out from Pisco takes in San Andres, El Chaco and the stunning Ballestas Islands, where the wildlife is more densely populated than almost anywhere in South America, except for the Galapagos. Local tour operators (see Listings, opposite) run combined bus and boat tours leaving Pisco early in the morning and returning towards midday. Tickets start at $12; it's best to buy them the day before. You'll be picked up around 7am from the plaza in front of the *Hostal Pisco*, your hotel or the tour company office.

Both the tour buses and local buses (which leave from Pisco market more or less every 20min in the morning, less frequently after that) run south along the shore past the old port of **San Andres**, where you can watch the fishermen bringing in their catch, usually stopping on the way back. San Andres is still known for its sea turtle dishes, even though it is now illegal to serve them due to the danger of extinction. Warm turtle blood is occasionally drunk in the region, reputedly as a cure for bronchial problems. These days, in order to save these endangered turtles from extinction, it's recommended that visitors avoid turtle dishes and perhaps even consider the merits of reporting any restaurant which offers them it, to a turtle conservation group. The seas around here are traditionally rich in fish life, and dolphins are often spotted; the abundant plankton in the ocean around Pisco and Paracas attracts five species of whales, and in 1988 a new, small species – the *Mesoplodon peruvianus*, which can be up to 4m long – was discovered after being caught accidentally in fishermen's nets.

At the far end of San Andres the road passes the big Pisco Air Force Base before reaching **EL CHACO**, also known as El Balneario, once just a resort for wealthy Limeños, whose expensive resort hotels and large bungalows line the beach close to the entrance to the reserve. In recent years, however, several more reasonably priced hostels and restaurants have opened up, and it's possible to **camp** on the sand, though the nearby Paracas Reserve is a much nicer place to pitch a tent. Most most travellers just pass through, using El Chaco as a jumping-off point to visit the Ballestas Islands. Tour buses will drop you at the wharf, surrounded by pelicans, where you board speedboats, and zip across the sea, circling one or two of the islands and passing close to the famous **Paracas Trident** – a huge cactus-shaped figure drawn in the sandstone cliffs (see p.145).

The **Ballestas Islands** (often called the Guano Islands, as every centimetre is covered in bird droppings), are similar to the Galapagos but on a smaller scale and lie off the coast due west from Pisco. They seem to be alive and moving with a mass of flapping, noisy pelicans, penguins, terns, boobies and Guanay cormorants. The name *Ballesta* is Spanish for crossbow, and may derive from times when marine mammals and larger fish were hunted with mechanical crossbow-style harpoons. There are scores of islands, many of them relatively small and none larger than a couple of football pitches together. The waters are generally rough but modern boats can get close to the rocks and beaches where abundant wildlife sleep, feed and mate. The waters around the islands are equally full of life, sometimes sparkling black with the shiny dark bodies of sea lions and the occasional killer whale. Guides on the boats vary in ability, but most are knowledgeable and informative about marine and bird life.

If you're heading for the much more peaceful **El Chaco,** the **Paracas National Reserve** or the **Ballestas Islands**, the cheapest way is to catch a **bus** from Pisco

market, on the corner of calles Beatita de Humay and Fermin Tanguis. Particularly in the mornings, most of the buses from here only go as far as the waterfront at **San Andres**, which can also be reached for $2–3 in a taxi from town. From San Andres, there are usually at least two buses an hour on to the playa El Chaco wharf in El Balneario, where boats leave for the Ballestas Islands. **Taxis** all the way from Pisco town to El Chaco cost around $4. Cruz del Sur dedicate some buses to covering the south coast between Lima and Nasca, with a ticket office plus drop-off and pick-up point by the *Hotel and Muelle (pier) Zarcillo Paradise*, close to the *Hotel Paracas*.

The Paracas National Reserve

Of greater wildlife interest than the Ballestas Islands, the **Paracas National Reserve**, a few kilometres south of El Chaco, was established in 1975, mainly to protect the marine wildlife – including marine cats and hundreds of sea lions – and amazing birdlife. Its bleak 117,000 hectares of pampa are frequently lashed by strong winds and sandstorms (*paracas* means "raining sand" in Quechua). Home to some of the world's richest seas (a couple of hundred hectares of ocean is included within the reserve's borders), an abundance of marine plankton gives nourishment to a vast array of fish and various marine species including octopuses, squid, whale, shark, dolphin, bass, plaice and marlin. This unique desert is also a staging point for a host of migratory birds and acts as a sanctuary for many endangered species. Schools of dolphins play in the waves offshore; condors scour the peninsula for food; small desert foxes come down to the beaches looking for birds and dead sea lions; and lizards scrabble across the hot sands. People have also been active here – predecessors of the pre-Inca **Paracas** culture arrived here some 9000 years ago, reaching their peak between 2000 and 500 BC.

Plan to stay for a few days, and **take food, water and a sun-hat** – facilities are almost non-existent. The reserve's natural attractions include plenty of superb,

▲ The Ballestas Islands

deserted beaches where you can **camp** for days without seeing anything except the lizards and birdlife, and maybe a couple of fishing boats. **Cycling** is encouraged in the reserve, though there are no rental facilities and, if you do enter on a bike, keep on the main tracks because the tyre marks will damage the surface of the desert. It's a 21km **bus** journey from Pisco (local buses leave Pisco market every 20min; $1 each way), or take an organized **tour** from one of the operators listed on p.140).

On the way from Pisco to the reserve, the road passes some unpleasant-smelling fish-processing factories, which are causing environmental concern due to spillages of fish oil that pollute the bay, endangering bird and sea-mammal life. Just before the entrance to the reserve, you'll pass a bleak but unmistakable concrete obelisk vaguely shaped like a nineteenth-century sailing boat, built in 1970 to commemorate the landing of San Martín here on September 8, 1820, on his mission to liberate Peru from the Spanish stranglehold.

The **entrance** to the reserve is marked by a barrier-gate and guard post (24hr), just off the Panamerican Highway, where you pay the $2 entrance fee, which permits you to stay in the park for up to a week. From here most of the roads are sand tracks, though one surfaced *carretera* continues along the shore line towards the new port and connects with the **park office** (where maps are sometimes available), the **Museo de Sitio Julio Tello** (Tues–Sun 9am–5pm; $1), and the track for Lagunillas and the beaches beyond. Located a little further on from the reserve entrance and park office at Km 27, right between the two major Paracas archaeological sites – Cerro Colorado and Cabeza Largas – the museum depicts human life here over the last 9000 years with interpretative exhibits relating to the National Park and a wide range of Paracas artefacts – mummies, ceramics, funerary cloths and a reconstructed dwelling.

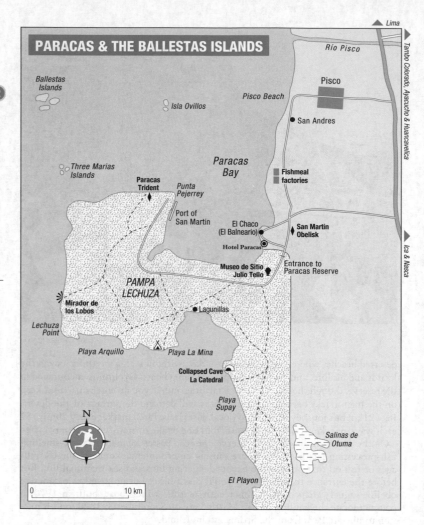

PARACAS & THE BALLESTAS ISLANDS

Lima

Río Pisco

Ballestas
Islands

Isla Ovillos

Pisco

Pisco Beach

San Andres

Three Marias
Islands

Paracas
Bay

Paracas
Trident

Punta
Pejerrey

Fishmeal
factories

Port of
San Martin

El Chaco
(El Balneario)

San Martin
Obelisk

Hotel Paracas

PAMPA
LECHUZA

Museo de Sitio
Julio Tello

Entrance to
Paracas Reserve

Mirador de
los Lobos

Lagunillas

Lechuza
Point

Playa Arquillo

Playa La Mina

Collapsed Cave
La Catedral

Playa
Supay

N

Salinas de
Otuma

El Playon

0   10 km

Tambo Colorado, Ayacucho & Huancavelica

Ica & Nasca

The Necropolis of Cabeza Largas

Right next to the museum is the oldest discovered site in the region, the 5000-year-old **Necropolis of Cabeza Largas**, once containing up to sixty mummies in one grave. Most were wrapped in *vicuña* skins or rush matting, and buried along with personal objects like shell beads, bone necklaces, lances, net bags and cactus-spine needles. A little further on, near the beach where dozens of pink flamingoes hang out between July and November (they return to the high Andean lakes for breeding from December to May), are the remains of a Chavín-related settlement, known as **Disco Verde**, though all there is left to see now are a few adobe walls.

The Paracas Trident (El Candelabro)

Another 2km past the museum you come to a fork in the main road: the paved part continues straight on, parallel to the shore, ending after 20km at **Punta Pejerrey**, which holds the modern port of San Martín, full of fish canneries. There's nothing of interest here, but just before the port a sandy side road leads away from the sea and around the hills on the outer edge of the peninsula.

This trail, which is poorly signposted and barely passable by car, takes you 13km across the hot desert to **the Trident**, a massive 128-metre-high by 74-metre-wide candelabra carved into the hillside. No one knows its function or its creator, though Erich Von Däniken, author of *Chariots of the Gods*, speculated that it was a sign for extraterrestrial spacecraft, pointing the way (inaccurately as it happens) towards the mysterious Nasca Lines that are inland to the southeast (see p.157); others suggest it was constructed as a navigational aid for eighteenth-century pirates. It seems more likely, however, that it was a kind of pre-Inca ritual object, representing a cactus or tree of life, and that high priests during the Paracas or Nasca eras worshipped the setting sun from this spot.

Lagunillas and around

Unless you want to see the Trident figure, instead of heading on toward Punta Pejerrey, it's a better idea to take the dusty sand track that cuts off to the left of the main road, towards the tiny and likeable port of **Lagunillas**, some 6km from the entrance to the park. A fishing hamlet with no accommodation but a few huts serving *conchitas* (scallops) and other seafood, Lagunillas is really the point on Paracas to make for – a strange, very beautiful part of the peninsula, so flat that if the sea rose just another metre the whole place would be submerged. Pelicans and sea lions hang around the bobbing boats waiting for the fisherman to drop a fish, and little trucks regularly arrive to carry the catch back into Pisco. **Taxis** from El Chaco to Lagunillas in the Paracas National Reserve will cost around $8–10, depending on what else is included in the tour.

From Lagunillas the rest of the Paracas Reserve is at your feet. Nearby are the glorious **beaches** of **La Mina** – just 20min walk from Lagunillas and a good place for **camping** – and **Yimaque**, an empty beach where you can stay for days, often without seeing anyone. A track goes off 5km north from Lagunillas to a longer sandy beach, **Arquillo**; on the cliffs a few hundred metres beyond there's a **viewing platform** (Mirador de los Lobos) looking out over a large colony of sea lions (though they were depleted in number by the 1998 El Niño). Another path leads north from here, straight across the peninsula to the Trident and on to Punta Pejerrey. There have been **reports of stingrays** on some of the beaches, so take care, particularly if you're without transport or company; check first with the fishermen at Lagunillas which beaches are the safest.

South around the bay from Lagunillas, drive or walk along the track turning right across the sandy hills and heading away from the museum to what was – prior to the 2007 earthquake – the spectacular cathedral cave **La Catedral**, where you could see, first-hand, high vaulted ceilings lined with bats. A family of sea otters (known in Peru as *gatos marinos*, or "sea cats") lived under the cave's floor of sea-worn boulders and could sometimes been seen sleekly avoiding the huge waves which pound the rocky inner cave walls. The cave collapsed during the quake, but its site is still visible at the end of a vast, curved, gravelly beach whose waves are so strong that local fishermen call it **Playa Supay** (or "Devil's Beach"), so don't be tempted to swim – it's far too dangerous. This track continues to the fishing village of **Laguna Grande**, from where you can track back inland to Ocucaje on the Panamerican Highway between Ica and Nasca. Even in a good 4WD this will take the best part of a day and isn't really recommended without a local guide.

Tambo Colorado

Some 48km northeast of Pisco, and 327km south of Lima, the ruins at **TAMBO COLORADO** were originally a fortified administrative centre, probably built by the Chincha before being adapted and used as an Inca coastal outpost. Its position at the base of steep foothills in the Pisco river valley was perfect for controlling the flow of people and produce along the ancient road down from the Andes. You can still see dwellings, offices, storehouses and row upon row of barracks and outer walls, some of them even retaining traces of coloured paints. The rains have taken their toll, but even so this is considered one of the best-preserved **adobe ruins** in Peru – roofless, but otherwise virtually intact. Though in an odd way reminiscent of a fort from some low-budget Western flick, it is an adobe complex with everything noticeably in its place – autocratic by intention, oppressive in function and rather stiff in style.

The easiest way to get to Tambo Colorado is on a **guided tour** from Pisco (see p.140), which costs less than $20 per person, provided there are at least ten people. You can also travel there independently from Pisco: take the Ormeño **bus** from Jirón San Francisco or the Oropesa bus from Calle Comercio (both leave most mornings, but check first with the bus company as departure times and frequencies vary from day to day; approximately $4 each way). The bus takes the surfaced Ayacucho road, which runs straight through the site, and the ruins are around twenty minutes beyond the village of Humay.

South from Pisco

South from Pisco, the Panamerican Highway sweeps some 70km inland to reach the fertile wine-producing Ica Valley, a virtual oasis in this stretch of bleak desert. **Pozo Santo**, the only real landmark en route, is distinguished by a small, towered and whitewashed chapel, built on the site of an underground well. Legend has it that when Padre Guatemala, the friar Ramon Rojas, died on this spot, water miraculously began to flow from the sands. Now there's a restaurant here where *colectivo* drivers sometimes stop for a snack, but little else.

Beyond Pozo Santo, the Panamerican Highway crosses the Pampa de Villacuri. At the Km 280 marker, there's a track leading north; after about an hour's hike, you'll reach the ruins of an unnamed adobe **fortress** complex, where you can see dwellings, a plaza, a forty-metre-long outer wall and ancient man-made wells, which are still used by local peasants to irrigate their cornfields. Seashells and brightly coloured plumes from the tropical forest which have been found in the graves here suggest that there was an important trade link between the inhabitants of the southern coast and the tribes from the eastern jungles on the other side of the formidable Andean mountain range.

Farther down the Panamerican Highway, the pretty roadside village of **Guadalupe** (at Km 293) signals the beginning of the Ica oasis. To the right there's a large, dark, conical hill, Cerro Prieto, behind which, amongst the shifting sand dunes, there are even more **ruins**, dating from 500 BC. Just a few kilometres on, beyond a string of wine bodegas and shantytown suburbs, you reach Ica itself.

Ica and around

An old but busy city with around 170,000 inhabitants, **ICA** sits in a fecund valley, close to enormous sand dunes some 400m above sea level and around 50km from

The witches of Cachiche

In the down-at-heel suburb of Cachiche, history and mythology have merged into a legend of a local group of **witches**. The story dates back to the seventeenth century, when Spanish witches were persecuted for their pagan beliefs during the Inquisition. Seeking religious refuge, the witches emigrated to Lima, where they were also persecuted for their beliefs before finally settling in the countryside, in particular, in the Ica Valley, in a village called Cachiche. For hundreds of years, the Cachiche witches operated in secret until the 1980s, when there was a renewed interest in alternative health practices and even the Peruvian presidents of the 80s and 90s openly consulted them about health matters. The popularity of Cachiche healing methods grew even more so when a powerful congressman was dramatically cured on TV of a terminal illness by a Cachiche witch. Similar to witchcraft and shamanism throughout the Peruvian coast, Cachiche practices involve the use of San Pedro (see p.583), a psychedelic cactus containing mescaline.

the ocean. The surrounding region is famous throughout Peru for its wine and pisco production. The city's very foundation (1563) went hand in hand with the introduction of grapevines to South America, and for most Peruvian visitors it is the **bodegas**, or wineries, that are the town's biggest draw. The **Museo Regional**'s superb collections of pre-Columbian ceramics and Paracas, Ica and Nasca cultural artefacts would alone make the city worth an excursion, despite some damage by the 2007 quake. Ica's streets and plazas are crowded with hundreds of little *tico* taxis, all beeping their horns to catch potential passengers' attention and making crossing the streets a dangerous affair. Aside from the traffic and the occasional pickpocket – particularly round the market area – Ica is a pleasant place with a friendly and curious population. After a day or less, though, most visitors are ready to head for the relaxing desert oasis resort of **Huacachina**, a few kilometres to the southwest, a much more exotic and restful haven to pass the hot, sunny afternoons. On the edge of town is the rather ramshackle suburb of **Cachiche**, known throughout Peru as a traditional sanctuary for white witches (see box, above).

Arrival, information and city transport

If you arrive in Ica with Ormeño, Jr Lambayeque 180, or Cruz del Sur **buses**, or with Saki bus from Pisco, you'll come in along Prolongación Lambayeque, a few blocks west of Plaza de Armas. Soyuz Peru Bus fast services from Lima arrive close by on Av Matías Manzanilla 130 (T056/224138); Expresso Sudamericano arrive at Av Municipalidad 336; and Flores come in at Salaverry 396, on the corner with Lambayeque. The Plaza de Armas is a good place to get your bearings and the square itself is still relatively quiet, though surrounded by restaurants, the municipal offices, souvenir shops and tour agencies.

To get around the town, most people take **taxis**, mostly small, flimsy and dangerous *tico* cars (try to use one of the rarer, but larger and more solid vehicles), with journeys within town rarely costing more than $2.50. Cheaper still – around $1.50 for anywhere in town and under $4 to Huacachina – are the **mototaxis** (motorcycle rickshaw taxis) which can be hailed anywhere in town. For longer journeys to the outlying parts of town, you can take one of the **microbuses**, which leave from Jr Lima or Prolongación Lambayeque and have their destinations chalked up on their windscreens. **Tourist information** is available from some of the bodegas and tour offices on the Jr Lima side of the Plaza de Armas or at the Automóvil Club at Manzanilla 523.

Accommodation

Finding somewhere to stay in Ica is rarely a problem, though there's very little of particular quality or note in town itself. For style or range of choice, most people go to Huacachina, La Dunas or one of the other out-of-town places.

Hostal La Arboleda C Independencia 165 ☎056/234597. Very cheap yet basic rooms available in this stylish old building. Reasonable service but no hot water. ①

Hostal Aries C Independencia 181 ☎056/235367. The best of Ica's budget hostels, with clean rooms, though bathrooms are communal. There's also a pleasant patio with room for bikes or motorbikes, and service is OK. ①

Hostal Callao Jr Callao 128 ☎056/235976. Very central – just a few metres from the Plaza de Armas – small, simple but clean rooms, some with private shower. ②

Hostal Oasis Jr Tacna 216 ☎056/234767. Hot water and some private bathrooms are available in this rather basic pad. ②–③

Hostal Palace Jr Tacna 185 ☎056/211655. Modern building with its own café next door; it has private bathrooms but no single rooms. ③

Hostal Sol de Ica Jr Lima 265 ☎056/236168, Ⓔsoldeica_hotel@peru.com. Located between the town centre, Huacachina and the Museo Regional, the *Sol de Ica* is quite modern and clean, with a nice swimming pool, though the building has suffered some earthquake damage and no longer looks its best. ⑤

Hotel Arameli Jr Tacna 239 ☎056/239107. A new hotel where all rooms have private bath and hot water; it's clean, central and very friendly. ③–④

Sol y Luna Salaverry 292 ☎ 056/227241. A modern, very clean hotel. Service and facilities such as a laundry, cafeteria and room service are superior to others of a similar price. ❹

The Town

Founded in 1563, and originally called Villa de Valverde de Ica, the settlement was moved (due to regional earthquake activity) after only five years, and renamed **San Jerónimo de Ica**. It was subsequently moved several times until finding itself in its present position in a relatively sheltered river valley protected slightly from the coastal weather (especially the mists) by large sand dunes, but still quite a way from the foothills of the Andes to the east. Ica is one of the first places south of Lima where you can virtually guarantee nice **sunny weather** most of the year. The town is quite a sprawl these days, and although prone to earthquakes, the most recent damage was actually a result of flooding caused by El Niño in 1998, when the Plaza de Armas and most of the main streets were submerged under more than a metre of water.

The Plaza de Armas and around

Ica's colonial heart – the inevitable **Plaza de Armas**, site of the 1820 declaration of independence from Spain – remains its modern centre, smart and friendly, with the inclusion of an obelisk and fountains. The cathedral on the plaza was first constructed in the eighteenth century then remodelled in 1814 with a Neoclassical exterior and a Baroque altar and pulpit. Running east from the plaza, the modern commercial spine is the busy Avenida Grau with the market area parallel, a couple of blocks to the north. Walking alone east of this area is not recommended, as **muggings** are not unheard of.

Most of the other important churches can be found within a few blocks of the plaza. The church of **La Merced**, southwest of the plaza, contains Padre Guatemala's tomb – said to give immense good fortune if touched on New Year's Day. Around the corner on Avenida Municipalidad is the more recent, grander **San Francisco** church, whose stained-glass windows dazzle against the strong sunlight. Quite some stroll south of the plaza, down Jirón Lima, then left along Prolongación Ayabaca, stands a third major church, **El Sanctuario de Luren**. Built on the site of a hermitage founded in 1556, the present construction, Neoclassical in style and with three brick-built *portales*, houses the Imagen del Señor de Lurin, a statue of the patron saint of the town, something of a national shrine and centre for procession and pilgrimage at Easter as well as on the third Sunday every October.

Fiestas in Ica

There are several important **fiestas** in Ica throughout the year. The most enjoyable time to be in town is in **March** after the grape harvest has been brought in, when there are open-air concerts, fairs, handicraft markets, cockfighting and *caballo de paso* (horse dressage – where horses are trained by riders to dance and prance for events or competitions) meetings. Over the **Semana de Ica** (June 12–19), based around the colonial founding of Ica, there are more festivities, including religious processions and fireworks, and again in the last week of September for the **Semana Turística**. On July 25, there's the nationwide **Día Nacional de Pisco**, essentially a big celebration for the national brandy (rather than the town of the same name), mostly held in the bodegas south of Lima, particularly around Ica. As in Lima, **October** is the main month for religious celebrations, with the focus being the ceremony and procession at the church of El Sanctuario de Luren (main processions on the third Sunday and following Monday of October).

There are a few **mansions** of note near the plaza, including the **Casona del Marqués de Torre Hermosa**, block 1 C Libertad. Now belonging to the Banco Continental, it is one of the few examples of colonial architecture to survive in this earthquake-stricken city. In the first block of Calle Dos de Mayo, you can find the **Casona de José de la Torre Ugarte**, once home to the composer of the Peruvian National Anthem. The **Casona Alvorado**, now belonging to the Banco Latino, at Cajamarca 178, is the region's only example of a copy of the Greco-Romana architectural style, while the **Casona Colonial El Porton**, C Loreto 233, conserves some fine colonial architecture and houses a restaurant-*peña* – *Almuerzos Criollos*.

Museo de Piedra

On the Plaza de Armas, the **Museo de Piedra**, Bolívar 178b (guided tours by arrangement; ℡056/213026 or 231933), contains a controversial collection of engraved stones, assembled by the late Dr Javier Cabrera who claimed that the stones are several thousand years old. Few people believe this – some of the stones depict patently modern surgical techniques and, perhaps more critically, you can watch artesans turning out remarkably similar designs over on the pampa at Nasca. Nevertheless, the stones are fine works of art and one enthusiastic local guidebook claims that "dinosaur hunts are portrayed, suggesting that Ica may have supported the first culture on earth". The museum doors are usually closed, so you will probably need to knock on the door or, better, telephone in advance for attention.

El Museo Regional

The **Museo Regional Adolfo Bermudez Jenkins**, block 8 of Av Ayabaca (Mon–Fri 8am–7pm, Sat & fiestas 9am–6pm, Sun 9am–1.30pm; $4, extra if you want to take photos; ℡056/234383), is one of the best archaeological museums in Peru.

While there are exhibits from various ancient cultures, including Paracas, Nasca, Ica, Huari and Inca, the most striking of the museum's collections is its display of **Paracas textiles**, the majority of them discovered at Cerro Colorado on the Paracas Peninsula by Julio Tello in 1927. Enigmatic in their apparent coding of colours and patterns, these funeral cloths consist of blank rectangles alternating with elaborately woven ones – repetitive and identical except in their multidirectional shifts of colour and position. One of the best and most priceless pieces was stolen in October 2004, so security is tight.

The first room to the right off the main foyer contains a fairly gruesome display of **mummies**, **trepanned skulls**, **grave artefacts** and **trophy heads**. It seems very likely that the taking of trophy heads in this region was related to specific religious beliefs – as it was until quite recently among the head-hunting Jivaro of the Amazon Basin. The earliest of these skulls, presumably hunted and collected by the victor in battle, come from the Asia Valley (north of Ica) and date from around 2000 BC.

The museum's main room is almost entirely devoted to pre-Columbian **ceramics and textiles**, possibly the finest collection outside Lima. There are some spectacular Paracas urns – one is particularly outstanding, with an owl and serpent design painted on one side, and a human face with arms, legs and a navel on the other. The room boasts some exquisite Nasca pottery, too, undoubtedly the most colourful and abstractly imaginative designs found on any ancient Peruvian ceramics. The last wall consists mainly of artefacts from the Ica-Chincha culture – note the beautiful **feather cape**, with multicoloured plumes in almost perfect condition. Displayed also in the main room are several **quipus**, ancient calculators using bundles of knotted strings as mnemonic aids that were also used for the recitation of ancient legends, genealogies and ballads. Due to the dryness of the desert climate, they have survived better here on the coast than in the mountains and the Ica collection remains one of the best in the country.

To get to the museum, head west from the Plaza de Armas along Avenida Municipalidad, then turn left onto Calle Elias; continue south for half a kilometre, then turn right onto Calle Ayabaca and the museum is just over the road. Alternatively take bus #17 from the Plaza de Armas. Either way you can't miss the concrete museum building stuck out on its own in the middle of barren desert parkland. Behind the Museo there's an excellent large-scale model of the Nasca Lines.

Bodegas

The best way to escape Ica's hot desert afternoons is to wander around the cool chambers and vaults, and sample the wines at one of the town's **bodegas** or wineries. One of Peru's best is **Vista Allegre** (daily 9am–4.30pm, ☏056/222919), easily reached by taking the orange microbus #8 from Avenida Grau or the market. The bodega itself is an old hacienda still chugging happily along in a forgotten world of its own. There's usually a guide who'll show you around free of charge, then arrange for a wine- and pisco-tasting session at the shop. You don't have to buy anything, but you're expected to tip (around $2–5 a person or small group).

If you follow the road beyond Vista Allegre for another 6km (some of the microbuses carry on this way, or else a taxi should cost $7.50 one way) you'll come to **Bodega Tacama** (☏056/228395, ⓦwww.tacama.com, daily 9am–5pm), a larger, better and more well-known wine producer about 3km from the centre of Ica, which also offers guided tours and tastings. The vineyards here are still irrigated by the Achirana Canal, which was built by the Inca Pachacutec (or his brother Capac Yupanqui) as a gift to Princess Tate, daughter of a local chieftain. According to legend, it took 40,000 men just ten days to complete this astonishing canal, which brings cold, pure water down 4000m from the Andes to transform what was once an arid desert into a startlingly fertile oasis. Clearly a romantic at heart, Pachacutec named it Achirana – "that which flows cleanly towards that which is beautiful". About 35km further south, the oasis of **Bodega Ocucaje** (☏056/408011 Mon–Fri 9am–noon & 2pm–5pm, Sat 9am–noon) is another of Peru's finest vineyards. You can **stay here** at the *Hotel Ocucaje* (ⓢ) and explore the surrounding desert, particularly the Cerro Blanco site where whalebone remains have been found. Any bus or *colectivo* heading south will get to you to within a few kilometres of Bodega Ocucaje (within view), or alternatively a taxi from Ica should cost around $15 one way.

Eating

Most of the **restaurants** in Ica can be found on or within a block or two of the Plaza de Armas. Their quality in terms of food and general ambience varies enormously, but there is ample choice from breakfast to the evening meal. Ica is famous for its sweets, too, and this is reflected in several of the shops around and near to the Plaza de Armas.

Calor Iqueno Av Grau 103. Small and fairly quiet, this snack bar/coffee shop has great hot drinks, yogurts and local *empanadas* (pasties filled with meat, onions and olives).
Cevichería La Candella Block 4 of Jr Lima. Decent food and affordable prices, plus a lively atmosphere and a bar that's open in the evenings. Food served Mon–Fri 11am–5pm.

Chifa Fu Sheng Jr Lima 243. A budget Chinese restaurant, packed with locals in the evenings.
Don Juan Tejas y Chocotejas Jr Lima 171, Plaza de Armas. Some of the best local *dulces* to be tasted in town, including traditional *tejas* sweets made from *manjar blanco* and pecan nuts.
El Eden C Andaguayllas 204. A popular vegetarian restaurant making good use of local ingredients.

El Otro Peñoncito Jr Bolívar 255 ☎056/233921. Less than a block from the plaza, this stylish restaurant has walls tastefully adorned with artwork from Andean cosmology by an Iqueño artist; their speciality is *pollo iqueño* – chicken stuffed with spinach and pecan nuts topped with a pisco sauce. Open daily 7pm–midnight.

Restaurant Galindo Jr Callao 145, just off the Plaza de Armas. A popular locals' dive serving big portions and sometimes the Ica speciality *carapul-* *chra* (pork, chicken and potato casserole). A busy atmosphere with a loud TV.

Restaurant Pasteleria Anita C Libertad 137, Plaza de Armas. This is Ica's slightly upmarket downtown eating and meeting place serving pretty fine traditional cuisine, including excellent *lomo saltado* (see p.53) and lots of sweets and pastries for eating in or out. Has a relatively inexpensive set-lunch menu.

Drinking and nightlife

Not surprisingly, Ica wines are very much a part of the town's life, and locals pop into a **bodega** for a quick glass of pisco at just about any time of the day; most are open 9am–9pm. The best places to do likewise are *La Villa de Ica*, Jr Lima 139, or the *Bodega Matute*, Jr Lima 143, close to each other on the Plaza de Armas with good ranges of piscos, wines, *tejas* and juices which can be sampled over the counter. Another shop for beverages is the *Casa de Artesania* on Calle Cajamarca, just a few metres from the plaza, which serves drinks and sells bottles as well as artesania, including local leather craft.

More of a café-cum-bar, the rather unusual *Quimeras Piano Bar*, Jr Callao 224 (☎056/213186), opens from 8pm until late most evenings, sometimes with live performances by local musicians of *criollo*, Mexican and Cuban material. The only **nightclub** in town is the *Red & Blue Discotheque*, in block 3 of Jr Grau. *Almuerzos Criollos* restaurant-*peña* in the Casona Colonial El Porton, C Loreto 233, often has shows at weekends.

Listings

Airport Carretera Panamericana Sur Km 299.5 (☎056/257210 or 256230).

Banks and exchange Travellers' cheques and cash can be changed at Banco de Credito, Av Grau 109 (Mon–Fri 8am–5pm); Caja Municipa, Av Municipalidad 148 (Mon–Fri 8.30am–6pm); and the Banco de la Nación, Av Matías Manzanilla (Mon–Fri 9am–6pm). For dollars cash try any of the *cambistas* on the corners of the Plaza de Armas.

Bus companies Soyuz Peru Bus, Av Matías Manzanilla 130 ☎056/224138, have a fast and frequent connection for Pisco and Lima; even more frequent are the Flores buses, next door; Condor de Aymaraes, Prolongación Lambayeque 152a; Cruz del Sur, Prolongación Lambayeque 148 ☎056/233333; Expresso Sudamericano, Av Municipalidad 336; Flores, Salaverry 396; Ormeño, Prolongación Lambayeque 180 ☎056/215600.

Internet access Space Net, Huánuco 177, one block from plaza, ☎056/217033, 9am–10pm daily, (slow connection); De Cajon.com, Huánuco 201, ☎056/237396, daily 9am–midnight.

Pharmacy and photography Kodak Express, Jr Lima 252, sells and develops film.

Police The Tourist Police are on block 1 of Prolongación Lambayeque ☎056/233632 or 235421.

Post office San Martín 156, not far from the Plaza de Armas. Mon–Sat 8am–7pm.

Telephones Telefonica Locutorio, Lima 149, Plaza de Armas. Daily 8am–8pm.

Tour operators There are several tour operators in town offering similar excursions such as Ica City Tour (including Huacachina, wine bodegas, the Museo Regional and the barrio of Cachiche), buggy rides in the desert and also trips to the Palpa Valley, various Nasca archaeological attractions, the Ballestas Islands and Paracas; most have shop fronts on the Plaza de Armas and all can arrange for flights over the Nasca Lines: Colibri Tours, Lima 121 ☎056/214406; Huacachina Tours, Av Angostura 355, L-47, close to Hotel Las Dunas entrance ☎056/256582; Las Brujas de Cachiche, C Cajamarca 100 ☎056/211237, ✉las_brujas_de_cachiche_tours@hotmail.com; Desert Travel and Service, Lima 171 (in Tejas Don Juan shop) ☎056/234127; and Diplomatic Travel, Av Municipalidad 132, Of 13 ☎056/237187.

Huacachina

According to myth, the lagoon at **HUACACHINA**, about 5km southwest of Ica, was created when a princess stripped off her clothes to bathe. When she looked into a mirror and saw that a male hunter was watching her she dropped the mirror, which turned into the lagoon. More prosaically, during the late 1940s, the **lagoon** became one of Peru's most elegant and exclusive resorts, surrounded by palm trees, sand dunes and waters famed for their curative powers, and with a delightfully old-world atmosphere. Since then the lagoon's subterranean source has grown erratic and it is supplemented by water that is pumped up from artesian wells, making it less of a red-coloured thick, viscous syrup and more like a green salty swimable lagoon; it retains considerable mystique, making it a quiet, secluded spot to relax. The **curative powers** of the lagoon attract people from all over: mud from the lake is reputed to cure arthritis and rheumatism if you plaster yourself all over with it; and the sand around the lagoon is also supposed to benefit people with chest problems such as asthma or bronchitis, so it's not uncommon to see locals buried up to the neck in the dunes.

Sand dune surfing on the higher slopes is all the rage and you can rent wooden boards or foot-skis for around $2–3 an hour from the cafés along the shoreline. **Dune buggy** adrenaline rides are also traditionally offered from some of the cafe's, hotels and independent kiosks and shops, while boats can also be rented for rowing or peddling on the lagoon. The settlement, still little more than twenty houses or so, is growing very slowly, but one end of the lagoon has been left fairly clear of construction. Climb the dunes at the end of the lake and take in the views from the top early in the morning, before it gets too hot and prior to the noisy dune buggy runs. On the Salvaterra side of the lake there's a great little **library** – Biblioteca Abraham Valdelomar – with a strong ecological focus.

▲ Sand dune surfing, Huacachina

2

Practicalities

To get to Huacachina from Ica, walk down Jirón Lima and take one of the regular orange **buses** (every 20min or so) from outside the Sanctuario de Luren. Alternatively, it's easier and quite cheap to take a taxi ($3–5). On arrival, you'll find a small wooden kiosk, frequently staffed by the local tourist police; they have information sheets and rather poor maps, and will also direct you to accommodation or other services.

The most stylish **accommodation** around is the luxurious and exceptionally elegant *Hotel Mossone* (T056/213630, F213630, Ereservas@derrama.org.pe; ❼), once the haunt of politicians and diplomats, who listened to concerts while sitting on the colonial-style verandah overlooking the lagoon. Outside high season it is sometimes possible to get very reasonable deals, but if you're on a tight budget, the *Hotel Salvatierra*, Malecón de Huacachina (T056/232352, Ejavosalvati@hotmail.com; ❸–❹), is excellent value, and has an enormous amount of character; its splendid dining room holds a number of important murals by the Ica artist Servulo Gutierrez (1914–61), who evidently drank his way through a massive number of pisco bottles in his time here. Most rooms have private bath, there's a good new swimming pool and Internet connections, and the owner's family offers transport to and from Ica whenever possible. The *Hostería Suiza*, Balconario de Huacachina 264 (T056/238762, Ehostesuiza@terra.com.pe; ❼), is very comfortable, cosy, quiet and located at the far end of the lake. There are a couple of hostels with new swimming pools including the *Hospedaje Titanic* (T056/229003; ❸–❹) above the left end of the *malecón*. It's possible to **camp** in the sand dunes around the lagoon – rarely is it cold enough to need more than a blanket.

The **restaurant** *Trattoria Novaro*, close to the *Mossone*, is very popular in the evenings with its wide range of Italian and Peruvian dishes. The *Mossone* itself has a wonderful restaurant, too, but it's very pricey. There are a couple of other decent options: the *Restaurant Moron* for lunches under the bandstand beside the lake, and *La Sirena* serves brilliant fish and other dishes. Desert Adventures (T056/228458, Wwww.desertadventure.net) are one of the Huacachina-based 4WD **desert fun rides** exploring the more remote dune areas ($10 for two hours), although things have toned down a bit since a few tourists were killed in an accident. Several places (hotels included) around the lake rent sand boards and some also offer campers a room for bag storage and a shower.

The Nasca Lines

One of the great mysteries of South America, the **NASCA LINES** are a series of animal figures and geometric shapes, none of them repeated and some up to 200m in length, drawn across some five hundred square kilometres of the bleak, stony **Pampa de San José** or, more simply, the Nasca plain. Approaching from Ica in the North, you first have to cross a wide desert plain and pass through a couple of valleys, including Palpa, before arriving at the Pampa de San José and the Nasca Lines proper. Palpa is famous for its abundant orange groves, but also has ancient lines, geometric and zoomorphic figures of its own, mostly in the vicinity of the Sacramento, Pinchango and Llipata settlements. From Palpa, the road quickly rises up to the level of the Nasca plain where the better known Nasca lines and figures begin to sketch their arcane message across the sand and gravel of the pampa.

Flying over the Nasca Lines

A pricey but spectacular way of seeing the lines – and arguably the only way to fully appreciate them – is to **fly** over them. Flights can be arranged with tour companies in Nasca (see listing below) or directly at the Nasca airstrip (where they depart), about 3km south of Nasca (at Km 447 on the Panamericana highway), and cost from $45–95 a person depending on the season, the size of the group, how long you want to spend buzzing around and how much demand there is on the day; although recent years have seen price increases, this has been matched by an improvement in maintenance standards. Flights can last from ten minutes to a couple of hours, with the duration of the average package being 30–45 minutes. Bear in mind that the planes are small and bounce around in the changeable air currents, which can cause airsickness, and that you'll get a better view on an early morning trip, since the air gets hazier as the day progresses.

Flight operators include Aeroparacas, Jr Lima 169, Nasca (℡01/2716941 or 056/522688, ✉comercial@aeroparacas.com, ℡056/9623915, ⓦwww.aeroparacas .com); and, Alas Peruanas, at the airport (℡/℻056/522444, ✉alas@nzcaperu.com, ⓦwww.alasperuanas.com) who can also fly in from Ica, Pisco or Lima at extra cost.

On the Nasca plain, each of the lines and drawings, even sophisticated motifs like the spider monkey or a hummingbird design, is executed in a single continuous line, most created by clearing away the brush and hard stones of the plain to reveal the fine dust beneath. They were possibly a kind of agricultural calendar to help regulate the planting and harvesting of crops (for more on theories about the Nasca Lines, see box, p.156), while perhaps at the same time some of the straight lines served as ancient sacred paths connecting *huacas*, or power spots. One theory proposes that the Lines were used as running tracks in some sort of sporting competition; whichever theory you favour, they are among the strangest and most unforgettable sights in the country.

The vast majority of people base themselves in Nasca and take a **guided tour** (see p.165) or a flight from there. However, you can visit independently, by taking a **local bus** from Nasca (70¢), a **taxi** from Nasca, which will wait and bring you back again for around $10, or one of the **intercity buses** for Ica and Lima, which leave every couple of hours from the corner of the Panamerican Highway and Jirón Lima on the outskirts of Nasca and let you off at the main *mirador* on the road between Palpa and Nasca. It's usually easy enough to get a lift with a bus or colectivo back to town.

Towards the Lines: Palpa and around

Everyone travels by road to Nasca, either by bus or car. Large 1970s US vehicles act as *colectivos* (see p.43), connecting Ica with Nasca; they can be spotted cruising along in patched-up Dodge Coronets or similar. The road to Nasca from Ica crosses the large strip of desert called the **Pampa de Gamonal.** Winds here frequently achieve speeds of up to 45km per hour, bringing sandstorms in their wake. The name "Gamonal" is a recent invention, a reference to an unfortunate man who, as the local story goes, found a vast amount of treasure here, buried it, and then promptly developed amnesia as to its whereabouts. The Lines themselves begin on the tableland above the small town of **PALPA**, about 90km south of Ica on the Panamerican Highway. Here, amid orange groves, cherry plantations and date farms are a couple of small **hostels**: the basic *Hostal Palpa* (❶) and the simple but clean *Hostal San Francisco* (❷). For great *chupe* or *tortilla de camarones*, meanwhile, there's the **restaurant** *Monterrey*, Av Grau 118 (℡056/404062), next to the Mobil petrol station. The annual Fiesta de la Naranja (Orange Festival) on August 15 sees a few days of processions, dancing, singing and drinking; the main street usually has plenty of stalls selling fruit, nuts and other local produce.

In recent years, a few of Palpa's own archaeological treasures have been opened up to visitors. Just 2km to the north of the town there's a *mirador*, or viewing tower from which geometric lines forming a pattern known locally as a Solar Clock, or **Reloj Solar**, can be seen on the lower valley slopes. It's said that during the equinox seers can tell from the Reloj Solar what kind of harvest there will be. Some 8km by navigable dirt track from Palpa it's possible to see the **petroglyfos de Casa Blanca**, where stone human figures and cubic shapes have been etched on

Theories about the Nasca Lines

The Lines are undoubtedly one of the world's biggest archaeological mysteries and bring many thousands of visitors every year to Peru's South Coast. The greatest expert on and student of these mammoth desert designs was **Maria Reiche,** who escaped from Nazi Germany to Peru in the 1930s and worked at Nasca almost continuously from 1946 until her death in 1998. Standing on the shoulders of US scientist Paul Kosok, a colleague of hers, she believed that the Lines were an astronomical calendar linked to the rising and setting points of celestial bodies on the east and west horizons. The whole complex, according to her theories, was designed to help organize planting and harvesting around seasonal changes rather than the fickle shifts of weather. When certain stars lined up with specific lines, shapes or animals it would signal a time for planting, the coming of the rains, the beginning or end of summer, the growing season or the time for harvesting. It also gave the elite high priests, who possessed this knowledge, a large element of control over the actions of the common populace. In a desert area like Nasca, where the coastal fog never reaches up to obscure the night sky over the pampa, there was a strong emphasis on relating earthly matters to the movements of the heavens and an advanced knowledge of the night skies and how they relate to nature's cycles. Reiche's theories, after 60 years of research, are thought to have established some alignments, many of which were confirmed by the computer analysis (particularly those for the solar solstices) of astronomer Gerald Hawkins (world famous for "decoding" Stonehenge in England), who himself spent much of the 1960s working on the Nasca Lines. Much, however, was left unexplained, and this has allowed more recent theorists to fill out the picture.

Regarding social aspects of the Lines, Toribo Mejí a Xesspe, a Peruvian archaeologist, actually "discovered" the site in 1927 and believed that they were made for walking or dancing along, probably for ritual purposes. The archaeologist Johan Reinhard, meanwhile, has drawn on present-day anthropological studies from the Peruvian Andes to understand the meaning of similar lines today. His research has shown how mountain people still worship mountains and river sources as important gods.

In 2000, Dr Anthony Aveni, one of the world's leading archeo-astronomers, published his thoughts after ten years working on the Lines. He agreed that at least some of the Nasca Lines were pathways meant to be walked in rituals, perhaps consciousness changing like labyrinths, but also relating to the acquisition of water. A statistically significant number of the Lines point towards a section of the horizon where the sun used to rise at the beginning of the rainy season, suggesting to archaeologists, including Aveni, that perhaps they were created to help worship or invoke their gods, particularly those related to rain. Similar explanations have certainly been given by archaeologists about the orientation of the early U-shaped temples in the northern deserts of Peru (see Contexts, p.384). Furthermore, according to Aveni, air and ground surveys revealed that "most of the straight lines on the pampa are one sunken but upright stone. Roughly 4km further on are a series of petroglyphs on the scattered volcanic boulders, known as the **petroglyfos de Chicchictara**. The images depict two-headed snakes, a sunburst, a moon and various animals. There are also a number of other petroglyph sites, including those at Huaraco and Río Grande, and, at the old hacienda Huayuri, in the district of Santa Cruz (accessed by the San Francisco village: turn off Km 384 on the Panamericana Sur Highway), the **lost city of Huayuri**, dating from 1200–1400 AD.

The Nasca Lines
It's still another 30km until you're on the plateau where some of the best Nasca Lines can be seen. At Km 420 of the Panamerican Highway, a tall metal **mirador**

tied to water sources." This certainly fits the anthropological evidence from annual Andean pilgrimages which continue to this day in some parts of Peru.

In 2003, David Johnson from the University of Massachusetts took Dr Aveni's theory further by putting forward evidence that the ancient Nascans mapped the desert to mark the surface where aquifers appeared. His work suggested that large underground rivers run under the pampa and many of the figures are connected to this, in some ways creating a giant map of what's happening under the earth. Zig-zag lines are linked to a lack of underground water; while trapezoids point towards the source of underground water. Archaeological research also suggests that Nasca experienced a serious drought around 550 AD, at the same time as the ancient Nasca's main ceremonial centre – Cahuachi – was abandoned on the plain and more or less contemporaneous with the construction of the trapezoid spaces where evidence of ritual offerings has also been found.

Further ideas about why the lines and figures were drawn by the ancient Nasca include the concept of shamanic flight or out-of-the-body experience, with the symbolic "flight path", as it were, already mapped out across the region. Such an experience is known to be induced by some of the "teacher plants", such as the mescaline cactus San Pedro, which are still used by traditional healers in Peru (see Contexts p.583). Visually, there are clear links and similarities between the animal figures found on the plain and those elaborately painted onto Nasca's fine pre-Inca ceramics. Animal totems or spirit helpers are commonly used, even today, by traditional Peruvian healers to communicate with the "other world".

Most of the above theories are fairly compatible; taken together, they form a matrix of interrelated explanations – agro-astonomical, environmental, spiritual and ritual. However, just how the ancient Nasca people ever constructed the Lines is possibly the biggest mystery of all – not least since they can't even be seen from the ground. In the early 1970s the populist writer Erich Von Däniken claimed that the Lines were built as runways for alien space ships. Less controversially, perhaps, in the 1980s a local school in Nasca tried building its own line and from its efforts calculated that a thousand patient and inspired workers could have made them all in less than a month.

Visual and Multimedia Introductions to the Lines
A follower of Maria Reiche, the Russian expert Veronica Nikitzki, gives absorbing evening lectures in English at Av Espinar 300 (☏056/9699419), near the new Municipal Museum, about all the latest theories on the Lines utilizing a large 3-D model of the Nasca plain for illustrating her points. Her talks are scheduled most days at 5pm, 6pm and 7pm. At the *Nasca Lines Hotel* on Jirón Bolognesi, there's also the Maria Reiche Planetarium with fascinating nightly shows (7pm; $7) explaining the lines and figures as well as covering the southern hemisphere's night sky.

(or viewing tower; 30¢) has been built above the plain. Unless you've got the time to climb up onto one of the hills behind, or take a **flight** over the Lines (see box, p.155), this is the best view you'll get. The rather underdeveloped **Casa Museo y Mausoleo Maria Reiche** (Mon–Sat 9am–5pm; $1), about 1km beyond the *mirador*, consists of three main rooms containing displays of photos, drawings and ceramics relating to the Nasca Lines and the studies of **Maria Reiche**, a premier Nasca Lines researcher (see box, p.156). Housed in her old adobe home in the shadow of the pampa, the museum includes one room dedicated solely to Reiche's personal possessions, showing the spartan reality of her daily life here, right down to her flip-flops.

The Lines are actually a combination of straight lines continuing for many kilometres in some cases across the sandy, stone-strewn plateau; others look like trapezoidal plazas, perfectly created by clearing the stones from the surface for the required pattern. Around seventy other "lines" are actually stylized line drawings of birds and animals (some over sixty yards wide), believed to symbolize both astrological phases and possible ancient Nasca clan divisions, with each figure representing, perhaps, the totem of a particular sub-group of this pre-Inca society and that clan's animal ally in the spirit world.

Nasca and around

Some 20km south of the viewing tower, the colonial town of **NASCA** spreads along the margin of a small coastal valley. Although the river is invariably dry, Nasca's valley remains green and fertile through the continued use of an Inca subterranean aqueduct. It's a small town but an interesting and enjoyable place to stay. Indeed, these days it has become a major attraction, boasting, in addition to the Lines, the excellent **Museo Antonini**, the adobe Inca ruins of **Paredones** only a couple of kilometres to the south, and the **Casa Museo y Mausoleo Maria Reiche** (see above), with access to several of the Nasca desert's animal figures, and two or three important **archaeological sites** within an easy day's range.

The face of Nasca changed after the 1996 earthquake, which necessitated the rebuilding of about half the town. Recently, the Plaza de Armas was reconstructed and work has finally begun on a new municipal museum. Travelling south beyond the airport, you'll see ample evidence of the town's rapid development in the form of new squatter settlements parcelled off into two hundred-square-metre plots. After about six months the squatters receive their legal right to the land, and water and electricity usually follow a few years later.

September is one of the **best times to visit** if you want to participate in one of its fiestas, when the locals venerate the Virgen de Guadalupe (Sept 8) with great enthusiasm. In May, the religious and secular festivities of the Fiesta de las Cruces, go on for days.

Arrival, information and city transport

Roughly halfway between Lima and Arequipa, Nasca is easily reached by bus, *colectivo* or even by small **plane** from Lima; *colectivos* link the airstrip with jirones Bolognesi and Grau in town. Cruz del Sur **buses** drop off close to the *ovalo* (the roundabout on Avenida Los Incas at the entrance to town coming in from north or south) where most other buses stop. Ormeño buses arrive close by at Av de los Incas 112.

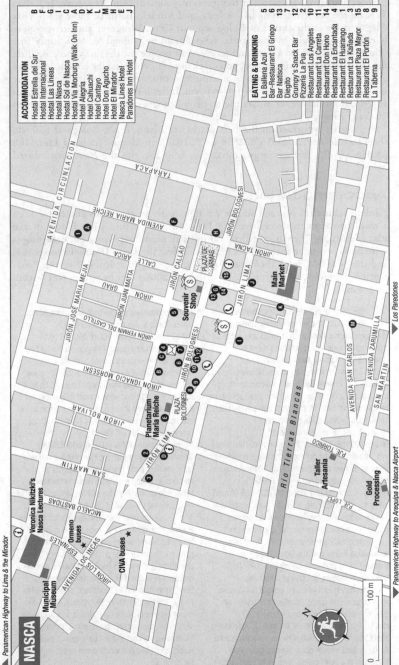

Aqueducts of Cantayoc & **L** ▲

NASCA

Panamerican Highway to Lima & the Mirador ◄

▼ Panamerican Highway to Arequipa & Nasca Airport

▼ Los Paredones

ACCOMMODATION
Hostal Estrella del Sur	B
Hostal Internacional	F
Hostal Las Lineas	G
Hostal Nasca	I
Hostal Sol de Nasca	C
Hostal Via Morburg (Walk On Inn)	A
Hotel Alegria	D
Hotel Cahuachi	K
Hotel Cantayo	L
Hotel Don Agucho	M
Hotel El Mirador	H
Nasca Lines Hotel	E
Paradones Inn Hotel	J

EATING & DRINKING
La Ballena Azul	5
Bar-Restaurant El Griego	6
Bar Natisca	13
Diegito	7
Grumpy's Snack Bar	12
Pizzeria La Pua	2
Restaurant Los Angeles	10
Restaurant La Carreta	11
Restaurant Don Hono	14
Restaurant La Encantada	4
Restaurant El Huarango	1
Restaurant La Kañada	3
Restaurant Plaza Mayor	15
Restaurant El Portón	8
La Taberna	9

Municipal Museum

Veronica Nikitzki's Nasca Lectures

Ormeno buses

CIVA buses

Planetarium Maria Reiche

Souvenir Shop

PLAZA DE ARMAS

Main Market

Rio Tierras Blancas

Taller Artesania

Gold Processing

0 100 m

N

159

Colectivos from Ica arrive at the (presently closed) *Hotel Montecarlo*, Jr Callao 123, on the corner of Avenida Los Incas and Micaelo Bastidas; those from Vista Alegre arrive at the corner of Bolognesi and Grau. Wherever you arrive you're likely to be besieged by tour touts, who should be ignored (or told firmly that you've already booked a hotel and tour). Most people use the noisy, beeping little *tico* **taxis** or **mototaxis (motorcycle–rickshaws)**, which can be hailed anywhere and compete to take you into – or around – town cheaply; you shouldn't pay more than $2.50 for any destination in town. Buses leave every hour for the Nasca airstrip, from the corner of Grau with Jirón Bolognesi, and are normally marked "B-Vista Alegre".

For **tourist information** the best places are Nasca Trails, Bolognesi 550, on the Plaza de Armas (℡056/522858 or 521027) or Alegria Tours, Jr Lima 168 (℡056/523775, ⓦwww.alegriatours.com, who also run the *Hotel Alegria* listed below)

Accommodation

Finding a **hotel** in Nasca is simple enough, with an enormous choice for such a small town; most places are along Jirón Lima or within a few blocks of the Plaza de Armas. There is no official campsite in or around Nasca, but **camping** is sometimes permitted at the *Hostal Alegria* in town, the *Hostal Wasipunko* (see p.161) and the *Nido del Condor*, the closest hotel to the airstrip at Km 447 of the Panamerican Highway, which for $2.50 per person allows you to pitch a tent within its grounds.

Hostal Estrella del Sur Jr Callao 568 ℡056/522764, ⓔestrelladelsurhotel @yahoo.com.mx. Good value, though only some of the compact rooms have windows. ❸–❹

Hostal Internacional Av Maria Reiche 112 ℡056/522744, ⓔhostalinternacional@hotmail.com. In addition to offering the usual hostel accommodation, this place has some quieter and more spacious bungalows out back. Most rooms have private bath, some have TV and all have hot water. ❸

Hostal Las Lineas Jr Arica 299 ℡/ⓕ056/522488, ⓔlineas@terra.com.pe. This modern, affordable hotel overlooks the Plaza de Armas and has its own decent restaurant. All rooms come with private bath and hot water. ❹–❺

Hostal Nasca Jr Lima 438 ℡056/522085 ⓔmarionasca13@hotmail.com. Friendly, basic hostel with shared bathrooms, very clean, airy and popular. It also has a pleasant restaurant and they can exchange dollars and organize taxis, tours and good-value flights over the Lines. ❷–❸

Hostal Sol de Nasca Jr Callao 586 ℡/ⓕ056/522730, ⓔdsalasm@Latinmail.com. Clean, contemporary hostel with TVs, private bath and a rooftop breakfast space. Excellent value with all-day hot water and very friendly service. ❸

Hostal Via Morburg (Walk On Inn) Jr Jose Maria Mejia 108 ℡056/522566, ⓦwww.walkoninn.com. An up to date, secure place offering very good value and in a quiet part of town, with comfortable rooms comprising private bath and constant hot water. There's also a small pool. ❷–❹

Hotel Alegria Jr Lima 166 ℡056/522702, ⓦwww.hotelalegria.net. This popular hostel has rooms with or without private bath set around an attractive garden, as well as a number of newer, plusher, chalet-style rooms with fans and bath. It also runs a café that serves good, affordable set-lunches and their travel agency can arrange tours and bus connections to Lima or Arequipa. Camping is sometimes allowed. ❷–❺

Hotel Cahuachi C Arica 115 ℡056/523786, ⓔcahuachi@terra.com.pe. This spotless modern hotel overlooks the market area near the bridge and has a rooftop patio with views to the mountains. Rooms are available with or without bath. ❸

Hotel Cantayo ℡056/522345 ⓦwww .hotelcantayo.com. Located 15min from the town centre in an old hacienda, this is a stylish luxury spa and hotel resort with pools, gardens, gym, sauna and a yoga programme; lovely if you can afford it. Service is good, and there's also an excellent restaurant serving organic dishes. ❼

Hotel Don Agucho Av Paredones, at corner with Av San Carlos 100 ℡/ⓕ056/522048. One of the nicest options in and around Nasca, this hacienda-style place has comfortable rooms, with bath and TV, entered via cactus-filled passages. There's also a pool and a bar-restaurant; breakfast included in the price. ❺

Hotel El Mirador Jr Tacna 436 ⓣ/ⓕ 056/523741 or 523121. A new, rather non-descript hotel looking straight onto the Plaza de Armas; rooms are mostly rather dark (except those on the top floor) and come with or without bath. There's also a rooftop patio and the price includes breakfast. ❸

🏃 Nazca Lines Hotel Jr Bolognesi ⓣ 056/ 522293, ⓔ reservas@derramajae.org.pe. Luxurious hotel, with its own well-kept pool (which non-residents can use for approximately $5 a day) and an excellent restaurant. ❼

Paradones Inn Hotel Jr Lima 600 ⓣ/ⓕ 056/ 522181, ⓔ paredoneshotel@terra.com.pe. A brand-new hotel in the heart of Nasca's small commercial area, the *Paradones* is smart and clean, with TVs, private bathrooms and hot water. ❹

Out of town

Hostal Wasipunko Km 457, Panamerican Highway, Pajonal ⓣ 056/522330, ⓔ wasipunko @hotmail.com. A delightful, rustic country hostel, with its own small ecological and archaeological

museum. There's no electricity, but it's very clean and rooms (some with private bath) are set around a lovely courtyard, while the restaurant specializes in tasty pre-Inca dishes utilising guinea pigs and local vegetables. It's signposted on the right of the highway some 15km south of Nasca; a taxi from town will cost around $5, or take one of the local buses or colectivos heading south from Nasca's main *ovalo*. ❹–❺

Hotel de la Borda Km 447, Panamerican Highway ⓣ 056/522750. A once luxurious hacienda hotel set in an oasis just 2km off the highway close to the Nasca airstrip, it's certainly not as well kept as it once was, but still has charm and is a comfortable place to stay. The hotel also runs tours, including some to wildlife havens on the nearby coast. ❻–❼

Nido del Condor Km 447, Panamerican Highway ⓣ 056/522424, ⓔ contanas@terra.com.pe. A modern hotel with pools and a camping area, with good deals which sometimes include a flight over the Lines. ❹–❺

The Town

As you come into town, the main street, Jirón Bolognesi, leads straight into the **Plaza de Armas** where there are a few restaurants, bars and a couple of hotels. If you continue straight across the plaza and head along Avenida de la Cultura you soon come to the new town museum – the fascinating **Museo Antonini**, an Italian pre-Columbian archaeological research and study centre, located at Av de la Cultura 600 (daily 9am–7pm; $1.50; ⓣ 056/523444). Opened in 1999, the museum stretches for six long blocks from the Plaza de Armas along Bolognesi and presents excellent interpretative exhibits covering the evolution of Nasca culture, a good audio-visual show and scale model reconstructions of local remains such as the Templo del Escalonado at Cahuachi. The museum complex extends to almost 10,000 square metres and includes an archaeological park that contains the Bisambra aqueduct (fed by the reservoir higher up the valley) and some burial reconstructions.

South along Calle Arica from the Plaza de Armas, the town's **main market**, offering the usual food and electronic goods, is based in a ramshackle collection of huts and stalls on the left just before the river bridge on Calle Arica. The **Taller Artesania**, Pasaje Torrico 240, in Barrio San Carlos, a short walk south of the plaza over the bridge, is worth a visit for its wonderful ceramics produced by the maestro Andres Calle Flores for over twenty years; as long as there are a few customers, they are more than happy to demonstrate the ceramic-making process from moulding to polishing. San Carlos also boasts the **Taller de Cerámica Juan Jose**, at Pasaje Lopez 400, and a **gold processing** operation, both located on the right-hand side about 500m down the Avenida San Carlos from the market bridge. Don't be put off by the fact that they're in someone's back garden – it's fascinating to watch them grind rocks into powder and then extract gold dust from it.

After visiting all that lot in the dusty hot sun of Nasca, cool off with a dip in the enticing **swimming pool** at the *Nasza Lines Hotel* (see above for review; $5 includes a swim, snack and a cold drink).

Los Paredones, the graveyard and the Inca canal

The most impressive archaeological sites around Nasca are some distance out (see p.164), but if you have an afternoon to spare, there are a few interesting spots within easy walking distance. The route covered below will take a leisurely three to four hours on foot.

To **walk to Los Paredones**, an Inca trade centre where wool from the mountains was exchanged for cotton grown along the coast, follow Calle Arica from the Plaza de Armas, cross the bridge, and keep going straight (off the main road which curves to the right). At the end you reach a road which passes below the ruins, following the same route to Puquio as the Inca road from Nasca to Cusco, at the foot of a sandy hillside.

The adobe buildings at Paredones are in a bad state of repair and the site is dotted with *huaqueros'* (grave robbers) pits, but if you follow the path to the prominent central sector you can get a good idea of what the town must have been like. Overlooking the valley and roads, it's in a commanding position – a fact recognized and taken advantage of by local cultures long before the Incas arrived. At the foot of the ruins, you can usually look round a collection of funereal pieces collected and displayed by the Pomez family in their adobe home adjacent to the site.

Another 2km up the Puquio road from Los Paradones (with Nasca in front of you, turn right leaving Paradones) there's a **Nasca graveyard**, its pits open and burial remains spread around. Though much less extensive than the cemetery at Chauchilla (see p.164), it is still of interest – there's an abundance of subterranean galleries, but they're rather hard to find unless you're travelling with a local guide. A half-hour walk up the valley from the graveyard through the cotton fields and along a track will bring you to the former hacienda of **Cantayo** (see p.160), now a converted spa hotel resort with a fabulous restaurant. Just a little further above the hotel, you can make out a series of inverted conical dips, like swallow-holes, in the fields. These are the air vents for a vast underground **canal** system that siphons desperately needed water from the Bisambra reservoir; designed and constructed by the Incas, it is even more essential today. You can get right down into the openings and poke your head or feet into the canals – they usually give off a pleasant warm breeze and you can see small fish swimming in the flowing water.

Eating and drinking

Eating in Nasca offers more variety than you might imagine given the town's small size. Most places are in or around Jirón Bolognesi and Jirón Lima, where, for vegetarians, there are a number of pizza, pasta and snack places worth trying out. What little **nightlife** exists is mainly based around **restaurants** and **bars**, particularly on Lima, Plaza de Armas and Bolognesi.

La Ballena Azul corner of Jr Grau with Jr Callao 698. Considering there's no ocean in sight, this is a surprisingly decent cevichería, serving up very tasty seafood; popular as a lunch venue for local business people.

Bar-Restaurant El Griego Jr Bolognesi 287 ℗056/521480. A friendly local eating-house with fine food and decent drinks at reasonable prices.

Good breakfasts and can be fun in the evening when it functions less as a restaurant and more as a bar.

Bar Natisca Jr Bolognesi 484. A small but lively bar which plays a mix of modern music (reggae, salsa, rock) and serves a variety of snacks and bar food.

Diegito Jr Castillo 375. Aimed at locals rather than tourists, this pleasant restaurant serves mainly criolla dishes, plus pastas and soups, and very reasonable set-lunches.

Grumpy's Snack Bar Jr Bolognesi 282. All earthen floor and bamboo walls, this little establishment serves cool drinks and good breakfasts in a friendly atmosphere.

Pizzeria La Pua Jr Lima 169 ℡056/522990. A very popular trattoria and snack bar, located out of the town centre opposite the *Hostal Alegria*.

Restaurant Los Angeles Bolognesi 266 ℡056/522294. A very nice family-run restaurant with a wide range of freshly cooked foods, from burgers and omelettes to pizza and French fries.

Restaurant La Carreta Bolognesi 270 ℡056/521286. Decent food and reasonable pisco sours. They have live music at fiesta times and often host discos at weekends.

Restaurant Don Hono C Arica 251 ℡056/523066. Opposite the *Restaurant Plaza Mayor*, by the Plaza de Armas, this place is small and relatively inexpensive, with excellent local, national and international cuisine. With the kitchen near the tables, you can have a glimpse of the chef preparing your meal.

Restaurant La Encantada Jr Callao 592 ℡056/522930. Excellent *criolla* food in a nice atmosphere, though pricey.

🏃 **Restaurant El Huarango** C Arica 602 ℡056/521287. The finest restaurant in Nasca, with a rooftop patio and a great ambience. The delicious food, mostly traditional coastal Peruvian dishes such as *aji de gallena*, (chilli chicken) but also including some more international cuisine, is very well-priced.

Restaurant La Kañada Jr Lima 160 ℡056/522917. Nice bamboo style decor and a pleasant atmosphere, often full of gringos eating delicious seafood dishes. Also offers internet access.

Restaurant Plaza Mayor at the corner of C Arica and Jr Bolognesi, on the main plaza ℡056/523548. A large, popular central restaurant on three levels, the *Plaza Mayor* serves plenty of meat dishes, mainly *parrillas*, amid an interesting decor, with Andean godlike figurines on the walls and the feel of a large chunky wooden structure.

🏃 **Restaurant El Portón** Jr Ignacio Moreski 120 ℡056/523490. A lively hang-out at night, especially at weekends with frequent live folk music, a dancefloor and bar. Pastas, meat and seafood dishes are complemented by the colonial mansion-style decor. Best espresso in town.

La Taberna Jr Lima 321. Serves a good selection of local and international dishes, plus a variety of drinks; its walls are covered with graffiti scrawled over the years by passing groups of travellers. There's fun to be had with live folk music playing until around midnight most evenings.

Listings

Banks and exchange Banco de Credito, Jr Lima 495; Interbanc, C Arica 363; and Banco de la Nación, Jr Lima 463. The best rates for dollars cash are with the *cambistas* in the small park outside the *Hotel Nasca*, where Jr Bolognesi and Jr Lima merge, or outside the Banco de Credito.

Bus companies Cruz del Sur, Lima 103, on the corner near the *ovalo* ℡056/522495 and 523713; CIVA, block 1 of Av Guardia Civil ℡056/523019, though note that there's a restaurant out front; Cueva, Av Los Incas 106 ℡056/523061; Ormeño, Av Los Incas 112 ℡056/522058; Señor de Luren, at the roundabout near *Restaurant La Kañada*; Flores, from near the *ovalo*, have Mercedes buses to Arequipa and Cusco; Enlace also has pretty good buses – they only go Lima–Arequipa–Lima – direct, but will pick up passengers when there's space. After 8pm, most buses for Arequipa or Lima stop at the *ovalo* as well as their respective bus depots.

Colectivos Big 1970s US cars operate as *colectivos* between Nasca and Chala (leave from near CIVA bus office) and Nasca and Ica (leave from the main *ovalo* on the Panamericana), daily, around $3–3.50 flat rates. *Colectivos* to Chilla also leave from near the *ovalo*.

Internet facilities Available all over Nasca, but in particular next door to the *Restaurant El Portón*. Also at Fox Internet, Jr Bolognesi block 1; *Mundo Virtual*, Jr Bolognesi 395 and Jr Bolognesi 225; *Restaurant La Kañada* (see above).

Pharmacy Botica Central, Jr Bolognesi 355 at corner with Jr Fermin del Castillo; Botica Alejandra, C Arica 407.

Police Block 5, Jr Lima ℡056/522442 or 522105.

Post office Jr Fermin del Castillo 379. Mon–Sat 8am–8pm.

Shopping For food and drink, try the small market, on Jr Lima, opposite the Banco de La Nacion; the Panificadora La Esperanza bakery at Jr Bolognesi 389; and the Licoria liquor store at C Arica 401. Camera film can be bought at Comercial Charito, C Arica 296, and the unnamed shop at Jr Bolognesi 600, which also develops. Oscar, Jr Bolognesi 465, sells local artesania.

Telephones Jr Lima 525. Daily 7am–11pm.

Archaeological sites around Nasca

Chauchilla Cemetery and **Cahuachi**, after the Lines the most important sites associated with the Nasca culture, are both difficult to reach by public transport, and unless your energy and interest are pretty unlimited you'll want to take an organized tour or at least a local guide/taxi driver (see box, p.165).

Chauchilla Cemetery

Some 27km southeast of Nasca along the Panamerican Highway to Km 464.20, then out along a dirt road beside the Poroma riverbed, **Chauchilla Cemetery** certainly rewards the effort it takes to visit. Once you reach the atmospheric site you realize how considerable a civilization the riverbanks must have maintained in the time of the Nasca culture. The desert landscape rolls gently down towards a small river and copses of Huarango trees on the northern side. To the south are several rain-destroyed adobe pyramids, difficult to discern against the sand. Scattered about the dusty ground are literally thousands of graves, most of which have been opened by grave robbers, leaving the skulls and skeletons exposed to the elements, along with broken pieces of pottery, bits of shroud fabric and lengths of braided hair, as yet unbleached by the desert sun. Further up the track, near Trancas, there's a small ceremonial **temple** – Huaca del Loro – and beyond this at Los Incas you can find Quemazon **petroglyphs**. These last two are not usually included in the standard tour, but if you hire your own guide, you can negotiate with him to take you there – expect to pay $5 extra.

Cahuachi

The ancient centre of Nasca culture, Cahuachi lies to the west of the Nasca Lines, about 30km from Nasca and some 20km from the Pacific. All of the landscape between Nasca town and the distant coastline is a massive, very barren desert-scape – almost always hot, dry and sunny. In many ways it's hard to imagine how ancient peoples managed to sustain such an advanced civilization here; but, as in northern Peru, it had much to do with a close religious and technical relationship with natural water sources, all the more important because of their scarcity. The site consists of a religious citadel split in half by the river, with its main temple (one of a set of six) constructed around a small natural hillock. Adobe platforms step the sides of this twenty-metre mound and although they're badly weathered today, you can still make out the general form. Separate courtyards attached to each of the six pyramids can be distinguished, but their exact use is unknown. The only section of Cahuachi to have been properly excavated so far is the **Templo Escalonado**, a multilevel temple on which you can see wide adobe walls and, on the temple site, some round, sunken chambers. A hundred metres away, from the top of what is known as the main pyramid structure, you can look down over what was once the main ceremonial plaza, though it's difficult to make out these days because of the sands.

Quite close to the main complex is a construction known as **El Estaqueria**, The Place of the Stakes, retaining a dozen rows of *huarango* log pillars. *Huarango* trees (known in the north of Peru as *algarrobo*) are the most common form of desert vegetation. Their wood, baked by the sun, is very hard, though their numbers are much reduced nowadays by locals who use them for fuel. The Estaqueria is estimated to be 2000 years old, but its original function is unclear, though other such constructions are usually found above tombs. The bodies here were buried with ceramics, food, textiles, jewellery and chaquira beads. Italian archaeolo-

Tours around Nasca

Some well-established companies arrange **tours** to the major sites around Nasca, all offering similar trips to Los Paredones, Cantayo, Cahuachi, Chauchilla and the Lines. Tours around Chauchilla Cemetery last two and a half hours and cost about $12–15 a person; a trip to the main mirador (viewing tower) on the Palpa road and the Casa Museo Maria Reiche also takes two and a half hours and also costs from $12. Tours out to the ruined temple complex in the desert at Cahuachi (see p.164) last four hours and cost in the region of $50–75 for a party of four or five; these need to be arranged in advance. There's also the possibility of organising tours to the various petroglyph sites around Palpa (see p.155). One of the latest attractions to be developed is **Cerro Blanco**, an enormous mountain of sand, one of the biggest dunes in the world, providing breathtaking views and a perfect place for sand boarding trips.

The best **tour operators** are Nasca Trails, Bolognesi 550, Plaza de Armas (T/F056/522858 or 523710, Enascatrails@terra.com.pe, Wwww.nascatrails.com.pe); and Alegria Tours, C Lima 168 (T056/523775 or for a 24hr-response call 056/523431, Wwww.alegriatours.com). Alternatively you may want to organize a trip with a guide/driver for your own group; **recommended guides** include Juan Tohalino Vera and Orlando Etchebarne, contactable through Nasca Trails; Jorge Echeandia Canales, C Torrico 340 (T056/521134 or 956714038, Ejorgenasca17@yahoo.com or Ejorgenasca17@gmail.com) an experienced guide who speaks perfect English and is knowledgeable about the region. Local private **minibus hire with driver** can be arranged with Transporte Turistico (T056/522619). For **flights** over the Nasca Lines, see the box on p.155.

---

gist Giuseppe Orefici has worked on Cahuachi for nearly twenty years and has uncovered over three hundred graves, one of which contained a tattooed and dreadlocked warrior. Also around 2000 years old, he's a mere whippersnapper compared with other evidence Orefici has unearthed relating to 4000-year-old pre-ceramic cultures.

Cahuachi is typical of a Nasca ceremonial centre in its use of natural features to form an integral part of the structure. The places where the Nascans lived their everyday lives showed no such architectural aspirations – indeed there are no major towns associated with the Nascans, who tended to live in small clusters of adobe huts, villages at best. One of the largest of these, the walled village of **Tambo de Perro**, can be found in Acari, the next dry valley to the south of modern-day Nasca. Stretching for over a mile, and situated next to an extensive Nasca graveyard, it was apparently one of the Nascans' most important dwelling sites.

East of Nasca

Some 90km inland from Nasca, the Pampa Galeras is one of the best places in Peru to see the **vicuña**, a llama-like animal with very fine wool. The *vicuña* have lived for centuries in the **Pampa Galeras Vicuña Reserve**, which is now maintained as their natural habitat and contains more than five thousand of the creatures. Well signposted at Km 89 of the Nasca to Cusco road, the reserve is easily reached by hopping off one of the many daily Nasca to Cusco **buses** (Tour Huari runs to Puquio at around 4pm; ask the driver to tell you where to get off). The reserve has a shelter, but it's a very basic concrete shack with no beds, and you need written permission from the Ministry of Agriculture and Fauna in Lima; it's best to take an **organized tour** with one of the Nasca companies (see above). However, you can **camp** here without a permit. You can also take a taxi or arrange for a car

Nasca ceramics

In 1901, when Max Uhle "discovered" the Nasca culture, it suddenly became possible to associate a certain batch of beautiful **ceramics** that had previously been unclassifiable in terms of their cultural background: the importance of Nasca pottery in the overall picture of Peru's pre-history asserted itself overnight. Many of the best pieces were found in Cahuachi.

Unlike contemporaneous Mochica ware, Nasca ceramics rarely attempt any realistic imagery. The majority – painted in three or four earthy colours and given a resinous surface glaze – are relatively stylized or even completely abstract. Nevertheless, two main categories of subject matter recur: naturalistic designs of bird, animal and plant life, and motifs of mythological monsters and bizarre deities. In later works it was common to mould effigies to the pots. During Nasca's decline under the Huari-Tiahuanaco cultural influence (see p.559), the workmanship and designs were less inspired. The style and content of the early pottery, however, show remarkable similarities to the symbols depicted in the **Nasca Lines**, and although not enough is known about the Nasca culture to be certain, it seems reasonable to assume that the early Nasca people were also responsible for the drawings on the Pampa de San José. With most of the evidence coming from their graveyards, though, and that so dependent upon conjecture, there is actually little to characterize the Nasca and not much known of them beyond the fact that they collected heads as trophies, that they built a ceremonial complex in the desert at Cahuachi, and that they scraped a living from the Nasca, Ica and Pisco valleys from around 200–600 AD.

and driver through one of the tour companies in Nasca (around $50 for the day for two).

The *vicuña* themselves are not easy to spot. When you do notice a herd, you'll see it move as if it were a single organism. They flock together and move swiftly in a tight wave, bounding gracefully across the hills. The males are strictly territorial, protecting their patches of scrubby grass by day, then returning to the rockier heights as darkness falls.

Puquio, Chumpi and Lago Parinacochas

As soon as you cross over the metal bridge at the entrance to **PUQUIO**, you get a real sense that the desert coast is left behind and the Andean ecology and landscapes abruptly take over. In fact, Puquio was an isolated community until 1926, when the townspeople built their own road link between the coast and the sierra. Located east of the Pampa Galeras Vicuña Reserve along the Cusco road, Puquio is a quiet, relatively uninteresting stop-off, but if you have to break your journey, there's a choice of three hostels, none of them particularly enticing. The road divides here, with the main route continuing over the Andes to Cusco via Abancay.

A side road goes south for about 140km along the mountains to **Lago Parinacochas**; although frequently destroyed by mudslides in the rainy season, the road always seems full of passing trucks, which will usually take passengers there for a small price. Continuing to **Chumpi**, an ideal place to camp, there is some exceptionally stunning sierra scenery. Within a few hours' walk of the town is the beautiful lake, **Lago Parinacochas**, named after the many flamingoes that live there and probably one of the best unofficial nature reserves in Peru. If you're not up to the walk, you could take a day trip from Nasca for about $40; try Alegria Tours (for details, see p.165). From Chumpi you can either backtrack to Puquio, or continue down the road past the lake, before curving another 130km back down to the coast at Chala.

The Panamerican Highway

From Nasca, the **Panamerican Highway** continues for about 1000km to the border with Chile. Apart from Chala and Camana, the road only passes the occasional fishing village or squatter settlement until it reaches the Arequipa turn-off; from there, it's straight south across the northern altiplano desert to Tacna. The desert landscape immediately south of Nasca is stunningly bleak and there's relatively little of specific interest in the 170km of desert between Nasca and Chala. The main exception, however, is the remarkable **Sacaco**, a fossilized whale site with a small museum about 96km south of Nasca. One fossilized whale skeleton is housed within the museum building itself with some interpretative material about the geology and palaeontology of the region on the walls. It can be reached on some tours and also by hopping off one of the Nasca to Chala (or Lima to Arequipa) buses. The site is well hidden to the left of the road going south along the Panamericana Sur, some 11 or 12km after the Las Lomas turn off (which goes to the right). Look out for a small sign on the left and ask the driver where to disembark. From here it's a thirty-minute walk along a sand track for 1 or 2km into the desert, away from the road, coming eventually to a house and cultivated area. Ask at the house for the guardian to open the museum, which is a few hundred metres further. Payment is expected but voluntary (from $2–3 a person should be fine).

Las Lomas is a remote fishing village with a **beach** that's especially good for spotting pelicans, about 90km to the south of Nasca and off the Panamerican Highway. If you're based in Nasca you can take a tour here (see p.165), often taking in Sacaco, or catch the Cueva bus here (a one-hour journey). The **hotel** *Capricho de Verano* (contact through the *Hotel Don Agucho*, see p.160; ●) has a lovely location looking right down onto the beach, and you can also **camp** in the area.

Avoid **Puerto San Juan**, it's the one place of any real size on this stretch of coast, but actually just a modern industrial port for local iron-ore and copper mines. Continue on until you find the first break in the area's starkness, at the olive groves in the Yauca Valley. Just beyond this, at Km 595 of the Panamerican Highway, is a strange-looking and slightly eerie geologically uplifted zone, a natural oasis with its own microclimate stretching for about 20km. Hidden among its *lomas*, misty eco-niches often green with vegetation, are various Inca and pre-Inca ruins. The place is virtually uninhabited today, although it's an unusual but interesting enough place to spend some time **camping** and exploring.

Just 10km before Chala stand the ruins of **Puerto Inca**, the Incas' main port for Cusco, where there's an excellent **beach** and fine diving and fishing to be had. Inca ruins abound close to the hotel and beach. Within a half-day's walk there are caves, grottos, hidden coves, rock formations and plenty of opportunity for getting lost in the desert coastline, birdwatching or even spotting Humbolt penguins if you're patient and lucky enough. There's a **hotel** with restaurant, big parking area, **campsite** ($10) and bungalows right on the beach: the ✳ *Puerto Inka*, Km 610, Panamericana Sur (☎054/778458, or contact in Arequipa at C Arica 406A, Yanahuara ☎054/272663, ✉puertoinka@puertoinka.com.pe, Ⓦwww

.puertoinka.com.pe; **⑤–⑦**); it's worth checking the website for special out-of-season deals. To get to the ruins, take a taxi from Chala (about $10), or catch an Arequipa-bound bus along the Panamerican Highway and ask to be dropped off at Km 610 (it used to be Km 603, but there's a sign for the hotel anyway). It's easy enough to walk the 2–3km from here along a rustic but passable road following a narrow gully to the beach.

A small, quietish town, **Chala** was the main port for Cusco until the construction of the Cusco–Arequipa rail line. Now, it's an agreeable little fishing town, where you can overindulge in fresh seafood. If you want **to stay** in Chala, try the *Hotel de Turistas* (℡054/551111, 501110 or 555111; **④**) for a little comfort and old-fashioned style. There are few less salubrious places along the main drag, or the much more basic *Hotel Grau* (no phone) (**②**), close to the beach.

Camana

About 200km south from Chala, **CAMANA** is a popular Arequipeño beach resort from December to March, when the weather is hot, dry and relatively windless, although ouwith high season it has little to offer. The most popular **beach** is at **La Punta**, around 5km along the Arequipa road. If you do end up there, there try and stay at the *Hotel de Turistas*, Av Lima 138 (℡054/571113 or 571608; **③**) which retains a certain charm and has plenty of comfortable rooms with good showers.

Continuing toward Arequipa (see Chapter 3), the sealed road keeps close to the coast wherever possible, passing through a few small fishing villages and over monotonous arid plains before eventually turning inland for the final uphill stretch into the land of volcanoes and Peru's second largest city. At Km 916 of the Panamerican Highway, a road leads off into the Maches Canyon towards the Toro Muerto petroglyphs, the Valley of the Volcanoes and the increasingly popular destination of **Cotahuasi Canyon** (see p.212). At Rapartición, the road splits: east to Arequipa and south towards Mollendo, Moquegua, Tacna and Chile.

Mollendo, Moquegua and Tacna

There are three major destinations south of Camana: Mollendo, Moquegua and Tacna. **Mollendo** serves as a coastal resort for Arequipa and home of the **Reserva Nacional de Mejía**, a marvellous lagoon-based bird sanctuary. Most people, actually, choose to go on to the old colonial town of **Moquegua**, now an important nodal point on the fast-developing Peruvian road infrastructure, but also an attractive and peaceful place. Going south from Moquegua, the Panamericana continues on through the desert to **Tacna**, whose only attraction is that it's the jumping-off point for **crossing the border into Chile**.

Mollendo and the Mejia bird sanctuary

A pleasant old port with a decent stretch of sand and a laid-back atmosphere, **MOLLENDO** is a relaxed spot to spend a couple of days chilling out on the **beach** and makes a good base from which to visit the nearby nature reserve lagoons at Mejía, also known as the **Reserva Nacional de Mejía bird sanctuary**, just south of town. These can be easily reached by *colectivos* from the top end of Calle Castilla (every 10min).

Several **buses** arrive daily from Arequipa, Moquegua and Tacna, including Empresa Aragon, Calle Comercio, four blocks north of Plaza de Armas; Tepsa,

▲ National Sanctuary and Lakes of Mejía

Alfonso Ugarte 320 (☎054/532872); and Cruz del Sur, on Alfonso Ugarte. Mollendo has a reasonable choice of **accommodation**: *Hostal Cabaña*, Comercio 240 (☎054/534571 and 533833; ❸), with inexpensive rooms, private bath and hot water 24hrs, as well as good service; the *Hostal Brisas del Mar*, Tupac Amaru (☎054/533544; ❹), is a popular place close to the beach; *Hostal El Muelle*, Arica 144 (☎054/533680; ❸), is clean and friendly with pleasant views from some of the rooms; and *Hostal Paraiso*, Arequipa 209 (☎054/533245; ❸), fills up very quickly in January but has nice rooms and some agreeable vistas.

As befits a coastal holiday town, Mollendo has a good selection of **restaurants**. First choice is the superb seafood restaurant *Cevichería Alejo*, Panamerican Highway South, Miramar – it's a little out of town – but worth the twenty-minute walk for its excellent, reasonably priced dishes, in particular their *fuentes de pescado* (literally large serving bowls of freshly cooked fish). At the lower end of the budget, there's a decent pizzeria on the Plaza de Armas, or try the excellent *Chifa Restaurant*, Comercio 412, serving large and tasty Chinese meals for under $4.

If you need to change **money**, you'll get the best rates for dollars cash from the *cambistas* on Plaza Bolognesi; for travellers' cheques, try the Banco de la Nación, Areqipa 243; the Banco de Credito, Comercio 323; or the Banco del Sur, Plaza Bolognesi 131.

The National Sanctuary and Lakes of Mejía

The **National Sanctuary and Lakes of Mejía** ($2), 7km south of Mollendo, is an unusual ecological niche consisting of almost 700 hectares of lakes separated from the Pacific Ocean by just a sand bar, and providing an important habitat for many thousands of migratory birds. Of the 157 species, such as blue-footed boobies, pelicans, penguins and Inca terns, sighted at Mejía, around 72 are permanent residents; the best time for sightings is early in the morning. To **get there**, take an Empresa Aragon **bus** from Arequipa (see p.197); you'll see the lagoons just before you get to Tambo Valley.

Moquegua

Situated on the northern edge of the Atacama Desert, most of which lies over the border in Chile, the **MOQUEGUA** region is traditionally and culturally linked to the Andean region around Lake Titicaca, and many ethnic Colla and Lupaca from the mountains live here. The local economy today is based on copper mining, fruit plantations and wine. More interestingly, for those partial to spirits, Moquegua has a reputation for producing Peru's best **pisco**. Historically, this area is an annex of the altiplano, which was used as a major thoroughfare first by the Tiahuanacu and later the Huari peoples. In the future it may well be the main route for the gas pipeline out of Peru's eastern rainforest regions to the coast. Right now, though, located in a relatively narrow valley, the colonial town of Moquegua has winding streets, an attractive plaza and a lot of adobe houses roofed in thatch and clay.

There's little in town, but the Plaza de Armas is picturesque with its ornate metal fountain designed in 1877 by **Gustave Eiffel**, and the grand ficus trees that fill the space. Close to the plaza, at the corner of calles Tacna and Ayacucho, the **Catedral de Santo Domingo** (Mon–Sat 7am–noon, 4-7pm) was restored after an earthquake in 1868 and now contains a large single nave, two finely worked *retablos*, and, in one of its towers, the first clock to arrive in Moquegua from London in 1798. The cathedral, or *iglesia matriz*, also houses the relics of Santa Fortunata whose remains were excavated from their original resting place in Spain and brought to Peru in the nineteenth century. To the south of the plaza lies the **Museo Regional de Moquegua** (Mon–Fri 8am–4.30pm; $1.50), located in a restored stone building originally constructed in 1778 to house the town prison; it's now home to a modest collection of archaeological and colonial exhibits. On the western side is the **Museo Contisuyo**, C Tacna 294 (Mon–Sun 9am–1pm & 2.30–5.30pm; free), a new archaeological museum that exhibits relics from the region including ceramics, textiles, gold and silver objects and specimens from the Tiahuanuco and Huari cultures as well as the local ancient coastal Chiribaya and Tumilaca cultures.

Arrival and getting around

Moquegua is a busy nodal point for two important roads into the Andes: the Carretera Transoceanica connecting Ilo on the coast to Puno and Juliaca, and the Carretera Binacional to Desaguadero, which shears off from it some distance after Torata. Most people arrive in town by bus, either on Avenida Ejercito or Avenida La Paz, both several long blocks from the heart of town and worth the $1–2 taxi ride. The museums, municipal buildings and post office are nearly all around or within a block or two of the main plaza. **Tourist information** can be found at the Camara de Turismo, Jr Ayacucho 625 (☎053/462008 or 462342), the Regional Tourism Directorate at Jr Ayacucho 1060 (☎053/462236), and from Ledelca Tours, Jr Ayacucho 625 (℡/℻053/462342, 🖂ledelca@viabcp.com); also, some historical information is available from the Museo Contisuyo, in the Plaza de Armas.

Accommodation

If you want to stay over here, there are a few reasonable **hotels** to choose from. Most rooms are in the centre around Jirón Lima, but there are out-of-town options, too.

Alameda Hotel Jr Junin 322 ℡053/462008 or 463971, 🖂alamedahotel@terramail.com.pe. This is friendly, well-run and has a great little café; all rooms have private bathrooms, some with TV. ❹
Hostal Adrianela Miguel Grau 239 ℡053/463469. Rooms all have private baths, colour TVs and hot water, but it's located in the busy and sometimes noisy commercial sector of town close to the market. ❸
Hostal Arequipa C Arequipa 360 ℡053/461338. Basic yet fairly comfortable and good value hostel with private bathrooms. ❸–❹

Hostal Carrera Jr Lima 320 ℡053/462113. A basic but clean hostel, just one block parallel to Plaza de Armas; appeals to backpackers, not least because of its low price. ❷–❸
Hostal Limoñeros Jr Lima 441 ℡053/461649. Just one and a half blocks northwest of the plaza, with constant hot water, cable TV, attractive gardens, semi-rustic atmosphere and a small pool. ❸
Hotel El Mirador in Alto de Villa ℡053/461765, ℻761895, 🖂reservas@derramajae.corg.pe. One of the smartest options in town with swimming pool and all mod cons. ❻

Eating and drinking

Some of the better **restaurants** can be found on the **outskirts of town**, such as the *Restaurante Recreo Turístico Las Glorietas*, in the Calle Antigua de Samegua, serving very good local food in a traditional atmosphere and, on the same street, the equally savoury *Restaurante El Totoral*. **In town** choices include *Restaurant Moraly*, corner of calles Lima and Libertad, for great breakfasts and *Restaurante Palmero*, C Moquegua 644 (6.30am–10pm daily), just half a block from the plaza, which serves mouthwatering *comida criolla* and some local specialities in an open and friendly space. There are two reasonably good Italian restaurants: the *Trattoria La Toscana*, C Tacna 505 (℡053/461043), and the *Pizzeria-Bar Casa Vieja*, C Moquegua 326 (℡053/461647), the former serving the better pizzas and pastas. There's really only one **bar** to speak of and that's the *Bandido Pub*, C Moquegua 333 (℡053/461676, Mon–Sat 6pm–midnight;), where they play good music and serve pizzas cooked in wood-fired earth ovens, as well as reasonably priced drinks.

Around Moquegua

About 24km away, **Torata** is a picturesque district of country homes made with traditional *mojinete* (slanted and gable ended) roofs. There's also an imposing church and old stone mill, both from the colonial period. You can get there by **bus** from the Carretera Binacional ($1, a 30min journey), and there are a few decent restaurants. The **petroglyphs of Torata**, which depict llamas, geometric shapes and what look like maps and water symbols, are within relatively easy reach of Moquegua by following the small *quebrada*, a dry canyon which runs east 200m from the bridge at Km 120.45 of the Carretera Binacional.

For most visitors, it's Moquegua's **bodegas** that are probably the greatest attraction here. Initially established during the colonial era, Moquegua's bodegas have various lines in piscos (including *italia* and *mosto verde*), cognacs, aniseed liqueurs and wines. One of the best for visiting is the Bodega Villegas e Hijos, C Ayacucho 1370 (Mon–Sat 8am–noon & 2–5pm; ℡053/461229), run these days by the welcoming Alberto Villegas Vargas, grandson of the original founder Norberto Villegas Talavera, one of the town's benefactors. The Bodega Zapata, at Km 1142 of the Panamericana Sur (☎053/461164), also produces fine piscos from *quebranta* and *italia* grapes.

Before you hit the bodegas, it may be advisable to check out some of the ancient sites in the region; that way you'll have the opportunity to work up a justifiable thirst. One of the bigger sites around is the archaeological remnant of a Huari (600–1100 AD) citadel that is easily visited by taxi from Moquegua. Sitting atop a truncated hill – **Cerro Baúl**, after which the ruins are named – some 17km northeast of the town, this commanding site once offered its ancient inhabitants a wide view around the Moquegua Valley, allowing them to control the flow of goods and people at this strategic point. Also within striking distance of Moquegua are the majestic Ubinas (5673m, with a 350m crater) and Huaynaputina (4800m) **volcanoes**. Visiting these is an adventurous operation that demands 4WD support from one of the local travel agencies (see opposite). Also in the sierra is the remote town of **Omate**, 130km (3hr) from Moquegua on the back mountain road to Arequipa. Surrounded by unique and impressive terrain formed by rock, volcanic ash and sands, it's also famous for its crayfish. Just 10km from Omate, the natural **thermal baths** of Ulucan (3100m) can be enjoyed.

Into the hills southeast of Moquegua, the town of **Toquepala** and nearby mysterious **caves** of the same name (2500m) can be visited in a day. The caves – occupied by a group of hunter-gatherers from the Archaic era around 9000 years ago – are fascinating but rarely visited. Close to the mine of the same name, these caves contain roughly drawn pictures of cameloid animals, hunting scenes and Andean religious symbols. Again, the best way to find this site is by taking a short tour with a local travel agency. The little-seen **geoglyphs of Chen Chen** can be accessed by car from Moquegua, by taking the track towards Toquepala which leaves the Panamericana Sur between Km 98 and 97; the track passes along the base of some hills where the geoglyphs, mainly large Nasca-like representations of llamas, are scattered around, some hidden from the road.

Listings

Banks and exchange Cash can be changed at the Banco de la Nación, Jr Lima 616; the Banco de Credito on the corner of Moquegua 861 will usually change travellers' cheques; or there are the *cambistas* outside Plaza Bolívar.

Bus companies Bus depots are mainly found on or close to blocks 2 and 3 of Av Ejercito in Moquegua. For buses serving Lima, Tacna, Arequipa and Desaguadero, there's Cruz del Sur, Av La Paz 296 ☎053/462005; Tepsa, at Av del Ejercito 33b ☎053/461171; and also Flores, Avenida del Ejercito, corner with Calle Andres A. Caceres ☎053/462181, ✉florbus@terra.com. pe. For buses to and from Arequipa, Mollendo and Tacna, Empresa Aragon have offices on Calle Balta, four blocks southwest of the Plaza de Armas; and Civa, who go to most destinations in Peru, are at Av del Ejercito 32b. Altiplano, Av Ejercito 444 ☎053/426672, runs direct services to Puno. Transportes Korimayo, Av del Ejercito, also

run buses to Desaguadero and Puno. Similarly, Expreso Turismo San Martín, Av del Ejercito 19, runs buses all the way to Desaguadero, Puno and Juliaca. Generally speaking, most buses arrive and leave from blocks 2 or 3 of Av Ejercito.

Car rental Mili Tour, Av del Ejercito 32 ☎053/464000, from around $35 a day.

Colectivo cars A service to Desaguadero on the Bolivian frontier is offered by Mili Tours, with several cars daily making the four-hour trip; they also run two or three cars a day to Arequipa. There are other *colectivos* for Tacna run by Comite 1, Comite 11 and El Buen Samaritano, each taking four or five passengers daily. El Buen Samaritano, Av del Ejercito, also runs *colectivos* to Desaguadero and offers *expresso* services to take passengers anywhere they like.

Internet access Sybernet, Jr Moquegua 434, half a block from the plaza (daily 8am–11pm); Café Internet, Jr Moquegua 418, which serves drinks (daily 8am–10pm); Niv@net, C Tacna 323, Plaza de Armas (Mon–Fri 8am–10.30pm, Sat 5.30–10.30pm).

Post Office C Ayacucho 560, on the Plaza de Armas (8am–8pm, Mon–Sat).

Telephone office Locutorio Publico, C Moquegua 617 (Mon–Sat 7am–10pm, Sun 7am–1pm & 4–10pm).

Tour operators Ledelca Tours, Jr Ayacucho 625 ☎/℉ 053/462342, sell airline tickets and are the local representatives for DHL and Western Union. They offer city tours (3hr) and the usual countryside tour (3hr) which generally includes a visit to a bodega, or a longer tour to the Chen Chen geoglyphs and the archaeological site of Cerro Baúl (4hr).

Ilo

About 95km southeast of Moquegua, **ILO** is a busy port on the Peruvian Atacama desert coastline, with a population of over 65,000 inhabitants and an economy based around fishing and mining. The most strategically, and economically, important port in Peru, in itself Ilo doesn't offer visitors very much, but it does have one or two interesting **attractions**. As you'd expect, the Plaza de Armas is the civic heart of the city, dominated by the **Templo de San Geronimo** (daily 6am–6pm); built originally in 1871 it contains an antique font created with a sea-shell and brought here from Paris. Built in the form of a single rectangular nave, it has a central tower and one of the three church bells was crafted in 1647. Two blocks away from the Templo there's the *malecón costero* and the seafront developments. The *malecón* boasts *La Glorieta*, an iron bandstand structure built onto a huge boulder overlooking the sea as well as the very modern architecture of the Municipalidad. Nearby, in the *Capitano del Puerto's* offices, there's a small **Museo Naval** (Mon–Fri 8am-3pm; $1.50) with documents and artefacts relating to the maritime past including manuscripts pertaining to Admiral Miguel Grau. Next to the nineteenth-century iron pier, *el Muelle Fiscal*, today you can find a busy wharf utilized by artisan fishermen – fishermen who use small boats and simple nets – and a seafood market.

Ilo is also quite popular for its fifteen or so **beaches** spreading out both north and south of the town. The nearest and most popular is the **Playa Pozo de Lisas**, near the airport; it's extensive and usually empty except weekends in December and January when it's invariably crowded. At the other end of town, to the north, the **Playa Boca del Rio** has fine sand and good views back to the city. About 20km further north, the Playa Pocoma is ideal for camping; the nicer Playa Waikiki is another 4km further north.

Arguably the most interesting local attraction, however, is the **Museo de Sitio El Algarrobal**, about 15km east of town. The museum presents exhibits from the pre-Hispanic cultures of the Ilo region, including textiles from the local Chiribaya culture and mummies, and offers views over the valley of Algarrobal and the old hacienda Chiribaya (1000–1350 AD).

Practicalities

Arriving to Ilo, most buses come in on or close to C Matara. **Buses for Bolivia** also leave from nearby at the corner of Matara and Junin, **buses for Chile** and Arica leave daily with Flores Hnos., on the corner of Jr Ilo with Matara, and there are also **colectivos** leaving for Arica regularly from the same corner. For **buses to Lima and Arequipa** the best company is probably Cruz del Sur, at the corner of Matara with Jr Moquegua (☎053/782206). There are **flights from Ilo** to Cusco, Juliaca, Arequipa and Lima with Aero Continente, TANS Peru and Lan Peru; all leave from the **airport** at Pampa de Palo, 7km south of town (☎053/795021). **Tour agencies** include Mar y Mar Tours, 28 de Julio 605 (☎/℉053/783318,

@marymar@sistemasilo.co.pe) and Romes Tours, Abtao 528 (☎053/781121). If you want to **change money**, head to the Casa de Cambio Dolares Vilca, 28 de Julio 331 ☎053/782728. The **post office** is at Av Mariano Urqueta, block 3 (Mon–Sat 8am–7.30pm).

As far as **accommodation** goes, one of the most comfortable in town is the *Gran Hotel Ilo*, A.A. Caceres (☎053/782411; ⑤); more modest in style and comfort, the *Hostal Torrelio*, Callao 531 (☎053/785349; ❸), is central, clean and friendly. Among the better **restaurants**, *Calienta Negros*, Costanera Sur Km 02 (☎053/782839 or 785184), is popular for most types of Peruvian and standard international dishes and can also cater to vegetarians, while the less expensive *Los Cangrejos*, 28 de Julio 362 (☎053/784324), offers seafood and *comida criolla* in a pleasing environment. The *Chifa Choy Yin*, Jr 2 de Mayo 430 ☎053/782760, is the obvious place to head for Chinese cuisine.

Tacna

Over three hours south of Moquegua and five times larger, **TACNA**, at 552m above sea level, is the last stop in Peru. The only real reason to stay here is if you're coming from or going over the border into **Chile** (see box, opposite) and the border crossing timing demands you stop, or if you feel like a break in your overland journey.

Founded as San Pedro de Tacna in 1535, just three years after the Spanish first arrived in Peru, it was established by Viceroy Toledo as a *reducción de indigenas*, a forced concentration of normally scattered coastal communities, making them easier to tax and use as labour. Almost three hundred years later, in 1811, Francisco Antonio de Zela began the first struggle for independence from Spanish colonialism here. The people of Tacna suffered Chilean occupation from May 1880 until the Treaty of Ancón was signed in August 1929, after a local referendum. Tacna, in fact, has long been noted for its loyalty to Peru and was also highly active in Peruvian emancipation from Spain, though nowadays it's better known as an expensive city that's infamous for both its contraband and pickpockets. The reputation is worse than the reality; the usual precautions (see p.58) are generally adequate and it's not a violent city. Tacna is designated a **Zona Franca** (a tax- or duty-free zone) where visitors can spend up to $1000 in any one trip (with a limit of $3000 in a year) on a range of tax-free electronic, sports and other luxury items. Tacna is also a centre for cyclists, particularly in August when there's usually a bicycle festival attracting competitors and enthusiasts from Bolivia and Chile as well as Peru.

The main focus of activity in this sprawling city is around the **Plaza de Armas** and along the Avenida Bolognesi. At the centre of the plaza, the ornamental *pileta*, designed by Gustave Eiffel, has a Neoclassical base depicting the four seasons while on top of the main fountain are four children holding hands. The nearby Arco Parabólico was erected in honour of the Peruvian dead from the War of the Pacific. Fronting the plaza is the **Catedral**, designed by Eiffel in 1870 (though not completed until 1955) and built from *cantera* stones quarried from the hills of Intiorko and Arunta. Around the corner there's the **Museo Histórico** (Mon–Sat 9am–6pm; free) where, if you have an hour to spare, you can browse around the pre-Conquest artefacts and exhibitions related to the nineteenth-century wars with Chile. The **Alameda Bolognesi**, near the *Hotel de Turistas*, is an attractive, palm-lined avenue constructed in 1840; it's dotted with busts of local dignitaries and also one in fine marble of Christopher Columbus. The **Casa de Zela**, C Zela 542 (Mon–Fri 8am–noon & 3–7pm), houses a small archaeological

Crossing the Chilean border

The **border with Chile** (daily 9am–10pm) is about 40km south of Tacna. Regular **buses and colectivos** to Arica (25km beyond the border) leave from the modern bus terminal, on Hipolito Unanue in Tacna, and three trains a day depart from the station, on Calle Coronel Albarracin (at 7am, 8.30am and 3pm). At around $3.50, the **train** is the cheapest option, but it's slow and you'll have to visit the **Oficina de Migraciones**, Avenida Circunvalación (Mon–Fri 8am–4pm; ☎052/443231; no entry fee), and the Chilean Consulate (Mon–Sat 8am–5.30pm; ☎052/423063 or 721846) on Presbitero Andia, just off Coronel Albarracin, beforehand. You will already have cleared Peruvian customs control on your way into Tacna, along the Panamerican Highway. Tepsa (Leguis 981) and Ormeño (Araguex 698) **buses** leave the bus terminal every couple of hours or so for the one- to two-hour journey to Arica ($4). **Colectivos** (normally around $7) are quicker and slightly more expensive than the bus, but well worth it given the hassle saved, as they'll wait at the border controls while you get your Peruvian exit stamp and Chilean tourist card.

Arica, the first town in Chile, is a fun place to get acquainted with the excellent Chilean wines. Bus and air services from here to the rest of Chile are excellent. The *Hotel Casa Blanca* (②–③), General Lagos 557, is cheap and very pleasant, and the moderately priced *Hostal Muñoz*, C Lynch 565 (③), is excellent value. Good restaurants abound.

Coming back into Peru from Arica is as simple as getting there. *Colectivos* run throughout the day and the train leaves at the same times as the one from Tacna. Night travellers, however, might be required to have a *salvoconducto militar* (safe-conduct card), particularly in times of tension between the two countries; if so, your driver will likely organise it. If you intend to travel at night, check first with the tourist office in Arica, C Prat 305, on the second floor.

museum exhibiting ceramics largely discovered in the region; the building itself has been a recognized historic monument since 1961.

For rail enthusiasts there's the **Museo Ferroviario** (daily 8am–5.30pm; $1), on the corner of Calle Albarracin and Avenida Dos de Mayo, just five minutes' walk from the plaza, containing locomotives, machinery and documents mainly relating to the now defunct Tacna–Arica line, but also a collection of train-related stamps from around the world. There's also a **Parque de la Locomotora**, built on Avenida Grau in 1977, dedicated exclusively to housing the antique Locomotive No. 3, which carried troops to the historic battle of Morro de Arica in 1879. Some 8km north of Tacna, on Cerro Intiorko, the eight steel sculptures of **Campo de Alianza** stand in memory of the war heroes; there's also a small Museo de Sitio which houses some old uniforms, arms and missiles left over from the historic battles.

Practicalities

Arriving by **bus**, you'll most likely alight at one of the Terminal Terrestres (see Listings, p.176). It's easy enough to walk to the centre of town from the Manuel Odria Terminal, but better to take a taxi from the Bolognesi Terminal, where they are easy enough to find. Once in the town centre, you'll find hotels, restaurants and most of the attractions, like the Casa de Zela and the Cathedral, within a few blocks of the Plaza de Armas. The Teatro Municipal and Museo Ferroviario are a little further afield, but within twenty minutes' walk. If you want to take a taxi to these or other sites, the best **taxi** service is offered by Radiotaxi, Gral. Valera 397 (☎052/426532). The **airport**, Aeropuerto Carlos Ciriani Santa Rosa, is out on the Panamericana Sur at Km 5 (☎052/844503). **Tourist information** is sometimes available from the tourist office at Av San

Martín 405 (Mon–Fri 9am–6pm & Sat 9am–1pm; ⊤052/415352), the Plaza de Armas offices at Av Bolognesi 2088 (Mon–Sat 8am–3pm; ⊤052/413501 or 413778), or the Regional Tourism Directorate, Blondell 50 (⊤052/422784). Failing that, try the Dirección Regional de Industria y Turismo, Jr Blondell 506. If you need a **place to stay**, the cheap and reasonable *Hotel Alcazar,* Bolívar 295 (⊤052/424991; ❷–❸), is good value. Alternatively, the *Hotel Las Lido,* Av San Martín 876 (❷–❸), is comfortable and centrally located just off the Plaza de Armas; the *Gran Hotel Central*, Av San Martín 561 (⊤052/412281; ❹), close by the Plaza de Armas, is a modern building and has many rooms with private baths and hot water; and the *Hostal Hogar*, 28 de Julio 146 (⊤052/426811; ❹), is secure and has nice rooms with private baths and TV. The best place for a cheap **meal** is the *Comedor* in the market, but the *Genova*, Av San Martín 649 (⊤052/744809), serves good grills and a wide range of the usual international dishes. *El Caquique*, C Jose Rosa Ara 1903, is the local *picantería* (traditional eating place specialising in spicy comestibles), and probably the best place to try guinea pig. The *Gerolamo Ristorante Di Mare*, Av San Martín 981, has fine seafood, while the popular *La Olla de Barro,* Billinghurst 951, prides itself on Peruvian dishes typical of the region, such as the delicious *choclo con queso* (sweet corn and cheese) or the spicy *picante de Tacnena* (duck in a chili and oregano sauce).

Listings

Airline offices Lan Peru, Apurimac 107 ⊤052/443252; TANS, San Martín 617 ⊤052/447002.

Banks and exchange Cash and travellers' cheques can be changed at the Banco de la Nación, San Martín 320, on the Plaza de Armas; Banco del Sur, Apurimac 245; Banco Continental, San Martín 665; Banco de Wiese, Av San Martín 476; Banco de Credito, San Martín 574; and the Banco Latino, San Martín 507. *Cambistas* hang around in Avenidas Bolognesi and Mendoza. It's a good idea to get rid of your extra nuevo soles before going into Chile (exchange them for US dol-

lars or, if not, Chilean pesos), and the *cambistas* in Tacna usually offer better rates than those in Santiago or Arica anyway.

Buses Buses leave three times a week from outside the train station, on Av 2 de Mayo, or from the Terminal Terrestre, Avenida Manuel Odría. For Desaguadero and La Paz, the company San Martín, Av Circunvalación Norte 1048 (⊤052/840499) run several times a week. Buses for the interior of the region leave from a different Terminal Terrestre Bolognesi on Avenida Circunvalación (⊤052/411786).

Post office Av Bolognesi 361 (Mon–Sat 8am–8pm).

Travel details

Buses and colectivos

Ica to: Arequipa (6 daily; 12hr); Lima (20 daily; 3–4hr); Nasca (8 daily; 2hr).

Moquegua to: Arequipa (10 daily; 2hr); Desaguadero (2 daily; 5hr); Lima (6 daily; 20hr); Puno (3–4 daily; 6hr); Tacna (6 daily; 2hr).

Nasca to: Arequipa (2 nightly, several daily; 12hr); Cusco via Abancay (daily; 20hr); Cusco, via Arequipa (daily; 35hr); Ica (8 daily; 2–3hr); Lima (2–3 daily; 5–6hr).

Pisco to: Ayacucho (1 daily; 12hr); Ica (10 daily; 1hr); Lima (20 daily; 3hr).

Tacna to: Arequipa (5 daily; 6–7hr); Arica (10 daily; 1–2 hr); Cusco (2 daily, 15hr); Desaguadero (2 daily, 6hr); La Paz (2 daily; 12hr); Lima (6 daily; 22hr); Moquegua (6 daily; 2hr); Puno (3 weekly; 8hr).

Flights

Nasca to: Lima, Ica or Pisco (by special arrangement)

Tacna to: Lima (4 weekly; 1hr 30min).

Arequipa, Puno and Lake Titicaca

CHAPTER 3

Highlights

✳ **Santa Catalina** Just exploring the labyrinthine sunlit streets of this Arequipa nunnery is a calming, even spiritual, experience in its own right. See p.187

✳ **Tradición Arequipeña** This massive restaurant, close to downtown Arequipa, bustles with people enjoying delicious *cuy* or *rocoto relleno*. See p.194

✳ **Cruz del Condor** A breathtaking viewing point in Colca Canyon, offering sightings of up to a dozen condors sailing below, around and above. See p.208

✳ **La Calera** Wallow, swim and relax in the fantastic and well renovated hot springs of La Calera, a short distance from Chivay at the head of the Colca Canyon. See p.204

✳ **Cotahuasi Canyon** Not only one of the deepest canyons in the world, this is also one of the most remote places that can be reached relatively easily by bus in Peru. See p.212

✳ **Taquile, Amantani and the Uros Islands** Though very different in character, none of these Lake Titicaca islands have cars or electricity, offering a fascinating glimpse of what life must have been like five hundred years ago. See p.224

✳ **Sillustani** On a little peninsula in Lake Umayo overlooking Titicaca, this is the dramatic site of an ancient temple/cemetery consisting of a ring of tower-like stone *chullpa* tombs. See p.222

▲ Local family on the Uros Islands

3

Arequipa, Puno and Lake Titicaca

While the southern coast of Peru boasts all manner of intriguing cultural sites, the interior of the south is much better known for its geographical features. The Andes take hold again here, punctuated by spectacular lakes, towering volcanoes and deep, stark canyons – a landscape well suited to adventurous outdoor pursuits like trekking, canoeing, climbing or mountain-biking in some extremely beautiful and remote locations, such as the **Colca and Cotahuasi Canyons** or the **Mismi mountain range**, the latter being the official source of the Amazon River. The region has two distinct areas, one centring on Arequipa, not far removed from the coast though high above sea level. The other, the Titicaca Basin, high up east at the northern end of the immense Altiplano which stretches deep into Bolivia. Both are detached from the rest of the country, something reflected as much in political leanings as their landscapes, themselves unique in Peru.

Arequipa, second city of Peru and a day's journey from Lima, sits poised at the edge of the Andes against an extraordinary backdrop of volcanic peaks. Recently designated a UNESCO World Heritage site, the white stone architecture of Arequipa – particularly the **Monasterio de Santa Catalina**, a complex enclosing a complete world within its thick walls – constitutes perhaps the city's main appeal to travellers, but the startlingly varied countryside that is within reach, from the gorges of both the Colca Canyon, massive but dwarfed by the glaciers and volcanoes on either side of the valley, and the more distant Cotahuasi Canyon, to the unsettling isolation of the Valley of the Volcanoes, is worth your time as well. If you're coming from the north, it's one of the last places to really merit a stop before continuing on south to the Chilean border.

Further inland from Arequipa, you'll probably want to spend time in the **Lake Titicaca** area, visiting islands on the world's highest lake, navigable by large boats, getting to know its main town and port – **Puno**, a high, quite austere city with a cold climate and incredibly rarefied air. **Juliaca**, to the north of Puno, makes an alternative, if depressing, base for exploring the lake, or the countryside of this poor, largely peasant area. Alternatively you may fancy some time on one of the huge lake's islands where life has changed little in the last five hundred years. The Titicaca region is renowned for its folk dances and Andean music and, along with Puno, makes an obvious and interesting place to break your journey from Arequipa to Cusco or into Bolivia.

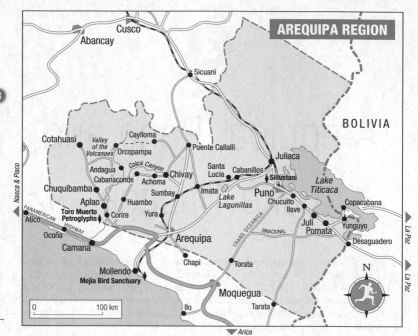

AREQUIPA REGION

Arequipa and around

Arrowheads and rock art prove human occupation around Arequipa for over 10,000 years, beginning with early groups of hunter-gatherers arriving here on a seasonal basis for several millennia from 8000 BC to around 1000 BC when horticulture and ceramic technology began to appear in small settlements along streams and rivers. Initially influenced by the **Paracas** culture and later by the **Tiahuanaco–Huari**, two major local tribes emerged sharing the region: the Churajone living in the far northwest section of the Arequipa region; and the Chuquibamba who thrived higher up in the Andean plateaus above Arequipa until the arrival of the Incas.

The name Arequipa is derived from the Quechua phrase "*ari quepay*", meaning "let's stop here", which, according to local legend, is exactly what the fourth Inca emperor, **Mayta Capac**, said to his generals on the way through the area following one of his conquest trips. Situated well above the coastal fog bank, at the foot of an ice-capped volcano – **El Misti** – and close to four other prominent volcanoes (Chachani, Ampato, Coropuna and Pichupichu), the place has long been renowned for having one of the most beautiful settings and pleasant climates of all Peru's cities. The Ampato volcano is presently active, the source of those wisps of smoke appearing on the horizon. Chachani itself has four main craters: **Coronada** (5400m), **Fatima** (5900m), **Angel** (6005m) and **Chachani** (6075m); while **Pichupichu** – which means "peak to peak" – has thirteen different craters, one known as the Indio Dormido (Sleeping Indian), whose face can be made out if you study the volcano's form carefully from the city.

The Incas were not alone in finding Arequipa to their liking. When Pizarro officially "founded" the city in 1540, he was moved enough to call it Villa Hermosa, or Beautiful Town, and *Don Quixote* author Miguel de Cervantes extolled the city's virtues, saying that it enjoyed an eternal springtime. Today, despite a disastrous earthquake in 1687, it's still endowed with some of the country's finest colonial **churches** and **mansions**, many of which were constructed from white volcanic *sillar*, cut from the surrounding mountains and often flecked with black ash. The worked sillar demonstrates a handsome accommodation of European and native styles expressed by colonial masters working through criollo and indigenous masons. Their art remains permanently set in the city's fine baroque facades, courtyards, city walls, churches, monastery, archways and vaults. In 2000, UNESCO proclaimed Arequipa a World Heritage city and an outstanding example of a colonial settlement. They described the ornamented architecture in the historic centre of Arequipa as "a masterpiece of the creative integration of European and native characteristics, crucial for the cultural expression of the entire region".

The last major **earthquake** to hit the city was on June 23, 2001 when 110 people died, several schools were razed to the ground and one of the Cathedral towers was tumbled. Fortunately, however, the quake happened at 3pm on a Saturday, so many children were spared.

Apart from its splendid colonial city, the Arequipa region possesses some of the finest scenery and pre-Inca terracing in the Andes, as well as the two deepest canyons in the world. Furthermore, the outlying towns and villages, particularly around **Chivay** and the **Colca Canyon**, are relatively accessible yet still surprisingly traditional and stunningly beautiful.

Arequipa

A wealthy city with a population of almost 800,000, **AREQUIPA** maintains a rather aloof attitude towards the rest of Peru. Most Arequipans feel themselves distinct, if not culturally superior, and resent the idea of the nation revolving around Lima. This self-comfortable image arose in the nineteenth century as the city found itself wealthy largely on the back of the wool trade with England. Located 2335m above sea level, and with **El Misti**, the dormant, 5821-metre volcano poised dramatically above, the city enjoys a distinctly poetic appearance. The most traditional of Arequipa's restaurants – *La Tradición Arequipeña* – goes so far as to issue Arequipa passports to its clients, only partly in jest. But besides being the country's second biggest and arguably, after Cusco, most attractive city, Arequipa has some very specific historical connotations for Peruvians. During the eighteenth and nineteenth centuries, this mountainous region converted into an important source of sheep and alpaca wool exports, largely to the UK. Connected to the rest of Peru only by mule track until 1870, Arequipa was slow to become the provincial capital it is today. Money made mainly from exports kept the Arequipa economy growing enough to establish an electric urban tramway in 1913 and then a road up to Puno in 1928. Due in the main to an early wave of rural to urban migration, the city's population doubled in the fifteen years between 1925 and 1940.

Arequipa Festivals

The annual **festival** celebrating Arequipa's foundation with processions, music and poetry, happens in mid-August. There's also a folklore festival in the first week of July. The Cotahuasi region festival is based around May 4 every year (plenty of bullfights, costumed dance groups and drinking). October 8 sees the processions and dances of the **Virgen del Rosario Festival** in Yanahuara and Yura.

Having acquired a reputation as *the* centre of **right-wing political power**, while populist movements have tended to emerge around Trujillo in the north, Arequipa has traditionally represented the solid interests of the oligarchy. Important politicos, like Francisco Javier de Luna Pizarro, who was president of congress on many occasions in the nineteenth century, came from Arequipa. Sanchez Cerro and Odria both began their coups here, in 1930 and 1948 respectively, and Belaunde, one of the most important presidents in pre- and post-military coup years, sprang into politics from one of the wealthy Arequipa families. By 1972 the city's population had reached 350,000. Twenty years later it passed half a million, with many people arriving from the Andean hinterland to escape the violence of Peru's civil war.

The social extremes are quite clear today; despite the tastefully ostentatious architecture and generally well-heeled appearance of most townsfolk, there is much poverty in the region and there's been a huge increase in the number of street beggars in Arequipa. Social polarization came to a head in 2002, when the city's streets were ripped up in political protest against President Toledo's plans to sell off the local electric utility. In 2006, there was a massive protest by people from the communities of the Colca Valley (specifically Collahuas and Cabanas), blocking the only road to the Cruz del Condor, the region's best viewing point for condor spotting and a major tourist attraction, for three weeks. Their argument was that the regional government and bus companies were getting rich from admission tickets to the popular viewing place and that they, the locals, saw no benefits. Since then, they've received the money directly and have built an alternative access road between Corporaque and Madrigal, effectively allowing other views of the canyon and another route to San Juan de Chucchos and the Sangalle Oasis down on the canyon floor.

Despite such differences in wealth, crime is still largely confined to **pickpocketing**, most likely in the Central Market area, the Terrapuerto or on the calles Jerusalen and San Juan de Dios. If you have anything stolen, report it to the **Tourist Police** (see p.198); you can also ask for assistance and advice at the **i-Peru Tourist Office** (see p.183), or contact your consulate.

Arrival, information and city transport

Generally, Arequipa is an almost unavoidable stopping-off point between Lima and the Titicaca, Cusco and Tacna regions, and is a hub for most journeys in the southern half of Peru. From Arequipa you can continue to Cusco, or Titicaca by bus or plane. The train between Arequipa and Puno no longer takes passengers; but it is easy enough to travel to Puno or Juliaca by bus and pick up the train to Cusco. Bolivia is within a day by bus, while Tacna and the Chilean frontier are also highly accessible from Arequipa by road.

Flights land at Arequipa airport (☎054/443464), 7km northwest of town. A red shuttle bus meets most planes and will take you to any hotel in the town centre for $1; alternatively, a taxi will cost $4–5. Most long-distance **buses** arrive at the modern, concrete Terminal Terrestre (☎054/427797) bus station about 4km south from the centre of town or at the newer Terrapuerto (☎054/422277), next door; a taxi to the Plaza de Armas should cost no more than $2–3. It's worth noting, too, that when leaving these terminals by bus, there's a 30¢ charge per head. For full details of operators, contact details and where they connect to, see p.197.

Tourist information is available from the Municipal tourist office at Portal de la Municipalidad 110-i, Plaza de Armas (daily 8.30am–7.30pm; ☎054/221228, ✉iperuarequipa@promperu.gob.pe, ⓦwww.regionarequipa.gob.pe); it's often worth asking here if there are any hotels with current special offers. More general information on Peru is available from the official **i-Peru Promperu Office of Tourist Information and Assistance** in *La Casona de Santa Catalina*, directly opposite the entrance to Monasterio de Santa Catalina, among a few upmarket shops and a cultural café set around the mansion's inner courtyard at C Santa Catalina 210. Information is also available from the **Tourist Police**, C Jerusalen 315 (☎054/201258), who are also particularly helpful with maps, information and safety precautions, plus they have a small exhibition of photos and postcards of major local attractions. The **Terminal Terrestre** also has a kiosk with details of hotels and tour companies, and sometimes maps. For information on **guided tours** of the city and the surrounding area, see the box on p.196. There's also an **i-Peru information office at the airport** (daily 8.30am–7.30pm; ☎054/444564), where they have maps of the city, information on sights and cultural event, and can recommend guides, tour companies and hotels.

A good way to get your bearings and see some major sites on arrival is to take the **Bus Tour**, a daily circular route city tour (office at Av Parra 373 ☎054/258133; ticket costs $10 and you can hop on and off) with a yellow bus which starts at the Plaza de Armas and includes other stops such as Puente Grau, Yanahuara and Carmen Alto. It's easy enough to **walk** around the city centre, but we've detailed available **city tours**, should you want to give your feet a rest (see p.196). If you want a **taxi** it's easy to hail one anywhere in the city; rides within the centre cost about $1.20. For a highly recommended service call Taxi Seguro, Pasaje 7 de Junio 200, Mariano Melgar (☎054/450250) or, second best, Taxi Sur (☎054/465656).

Accommodation

Arequipa has a good selection of **accommodation** in all price ranges, with most of the better options mainly within a few blocks of the Plaza de Armas or along Calle Jerusalen. For ease of reference, they are divided below into three sections: the pleasant area north of Calle Melgar, the central area between Melgar and the main plaza and the area around the plaza and to the south, all within walking distance of the Plaza de Armas.

North of Melgar and Santa Catalina

Bothy Hostal Puente Grau 109 ☎054/282438. Rightly describing itself as the friendliest and arguably funkiest hostal in town, Bothy is comfortable, cheap, central and has a communal area including a DVD/TV room, a kitchen and a great rooftop terrace. Shared rooms, single and double rooms available with shared bath. ❷–❹

La Casa de mi Abuela C Jerusalen 606 ☎054/241206, ⓦwww.lacasademiabuela .com. Innovative family-run hostel, whose name translates as "My Grandma's House", combining elegance, comfort and great value. Rooms are set in a variety of garden environments; there are spacious colonial quarters, chalets, family apartments and a fine swimming pool. It's very secure, has a good library and an excellent cafeteria offering a fantastic buffet breakfast outside under the shady trees. Reserve well in advance during high season. ❻

Casa Andina C Jerusalen 601 ☎054/202070, ⓦwww.casa-andina.com. Fairly luxurious and reasonably good value option, with TVs and minibars in the carpeted rooms, all of which have private bath. Also has a pleasant dining room and bar. ❼

Colonial House Inn Puente Grau 114 ☏054/223533, ⓦ www.colonialhouseinn-arequipa.com. Agreeable place with a pretty covered courtyard, electric heated showers, private bathrooms and access to TV and internet facilities. Well worth it, not least for the nice rooftop breakfast option. ❹

Hostal La Boveda Inn C Jerusalen 402 ☏054/202562. Cheap and rough but conveniently located on the second floor of an old building, with a vegetarian restaurant beneath. Bathrooms are mostly communal albeit with fairly constant hot water. ❷

Hostal Nuñez C Jerusalen 528 ☏054/233268 or 218648, ⓔ hostal_nunez@terra.com.pe. A friendly, family-run place with attractive patios, constant hot water, laundry and telephone service plus secure luggage deposit. A few rooms have private bath, and you can have breakfast (albeit not included in the price) on the terrace. ❷–❸

🏃 **Hostal Posada Santa Catalina** C Santa Catalina 500 ☏054/243705. Genial if elementary, with a spacious, cool café and pleasant courtyard. While only a few rooms have their own toilets and showers, there are great views to El Misti from the roof terrace, where you can also have breakfast while you wash and dry your clothing. ❸

Hotel Libertador Arequipa Plaza Bolívar, Selva Alegre ☏054/282550, ⓦ www.libertador.com.pe. Quite a few blocks from downtown but located in a beautiful setting on the spur above the Barrio San Lazaro, this spacious, luxurious hotel is surrounded by the eucalyptus trees of Selva Alegre Park. The price includes a pool and sports facilities, and they serves excellent breakfasts (not included). ❻

Residencial Yolita Pasaje Velez 204 ☏054/226505. A comfortable lodging, close to *La Casa de mi Abuela*, so a possible alternative if *La Casa* is full. Very friendly, and some upstairs rooms have good views. ❷

Central Arequipa

Hospedaje Caminante Class C Santa Catalina 207a ☏054/203444, ⓔ caminanteaqp@terra .com. Very clean and pleasant, six-room (some with private bath) family-run pad that's also safe and well managed. Extras include a laundry facility and a rooftop terrace with breathtaking views of the city. ❷–❹

Hostal Los Balcones de Moral y Santa Catalina C Moral 217 ☏054/201292, ⓔ losbalconeshotel @hotmail.com. A conveniently located and child-friendly place, where all rooms abut each other on the second floor and have private bath, 24hr hot water (solar by day) and a sun terrace (albeit not

with street views). There's also a cafetería, laundry and luggage deposit, and breakfast is included in the price. ❺

Hostal La Casa del Margott C Jerusalen 304 ☏054/229517, ⓦ www.lacasademargott.com. Based around a colonial courtyard, itself slightly crowded by a massive palm tree, this hostel comprises several rooms (all downstairs) with *sillar* (attractive white volcanic stone from the region) walls and ceilings. All rooms come with good new mattresses and cable TV, as well as optional private bath. Don't miss the tiny bar. ❹–❻

Hostal La Casa de Melgar C Melgar 108-B ☏054/222459, ⓦ www.lacasademelgar.com. An eighteenth-century mansion with stylish tiled floors and exquisite vaulted *sillar* ceilings. Once home to the Bishop of Arequipa, La Casa de Melgar is a nice old place, spacious and stylish, with a friendly atmosphere. The best rooms are those with views over the street, and there's also a small cafetería. ❸

Hostal Le Foyer C Ugarte 114 ☏054/286473, ⓔ hostallefoyer@yahoo.com. The sign outside says "La Villa Real", which is the name of the mansion in which this popular backpackers' hostel is located, just two blocks from the main plaza; you'll need to ring the bell to get in. The hostel itself is clean and friendly, right at the heart of the action, and has a spacious first-floor patio as well as a small, useful book exchange. Rooms are mostly private, some with private bath. ❸

🏃 **La Posada del Monasterio** C Santa Catalina 300 ☏054/206565, ⓔ laposadadelmonasterio@star.com.pe. An early eighteenth-century building where families of the nuns once stayed when visiting them; it has a fine *sillar* courtyard but much of the hotel has been modernized, creating a labyrinthine but plush and pretty environment with a view from many rooms and an inner garden area as well as a bar. ❼

Plaza de Armas and South

Hostal Arequipa Centre C Alvarez Thomas 305 ☏054/496169. Central, simple but spotlessly clean, with a range of rooms from basic to suites with jacuzzis and cable TV. ❷–❹

Hostal Garden San Camilo 116 ☏/ⓕ054/237440. A misleading name but still excellent value, with solar-heated communal showers and lovely, old-fashioned, clean rooms with or without private bath. Located very close to the central market. ❷–❹

Hostal Maison Plaza Portal San Agustín 143 ☏054/218929, ⓔ arequipa@lanet.com.pe. Fairly plush with a lovely *sillar*-domed reception area, and well located on the Plaza de Armas.

Unusually for Peru the price includes a decent breakfast. ❺

Hostal Premier Av Quiroz 100 ☎054/227821, ⓦwww.hostalpremier.com. Associated with Youth Hostelling International, this hostel lacks any architectural merit, but it's clean, safe and friendly. It also runs a travel agency, which you can check out on the website. ❸–❹

🏃 **Point Hostal** Av Lima 515, Vallecito ☎054/286920, ⓦwww.thepointhostels .com. Located in an attractive villa in the suburb of Vallecito, with dormitories and private rooms, a bar,

restaurant, travel centre, book exchange and laundry service. Airport pick-up costs extra. ❹

Sonesta Posada del Inca Portal de Flores 116 ☎054/215530, ⓦwww.sonesta.com/arequipa/. Very well appointed and central, with a top-class restaurant, conference rooms and, more importantly, a rooftop pool and patio with superb views across the city to the southeastern mountains. This is also the only hotel in Arequipa with the dubious advantage of dehumidifiers in all rooms, themselves boasting cable TV, a minibar and an internet connection. ❽

The City

Characterized by white *sillar* stone and arched interior ceilings, Arequipa's architectural beauty comes mainly from the colonial period. In general, the style is stark and almost clinical, except where Baroque and *mestizo* influences combine, as seen on many of the fine sixteenth- to eighteenth-century facades. Of the huge number of religious buildings spread about the old colonial centre, the **Monasterio**

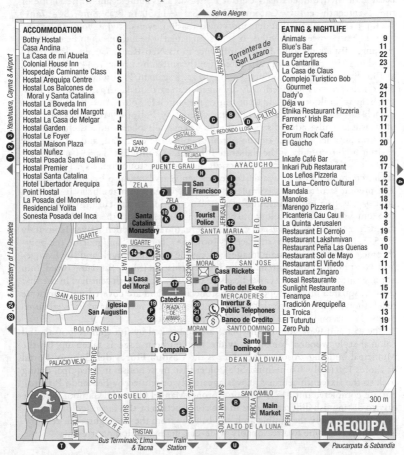

▲ Selva Alegre

ACCOMMODATION
Bothy Hostal — G
Casa Andina — C
La Casa de mi Abuela — B
Colonial House Inn — H
Hospedaje Caminante Class — N
Hostal Arequipa Centre — S
Hostal Los Balcones de Moral y Santa Catalina — O
Hostal La Boveda Inn — I
Hostal La Casa del Margott — M
Hostal La Casa de Melgar — J
Hostal Garden — R
Hostal Le Foyer — L
Hostal Maison Plaza — P
Hostal Nuñez — E
Hostal Posada Santa Calina — N
Hostal Premier — U
Hostal Santa Catalina — F
Hotel Libertador Arequipa — A
Point Hostal — T
La Posada del Monasterio — K
Residencial Yolita — D
Sonesta Posada del Inca — Q

EATING & NIGHTLIFE
Animals — 9
Blue's Bar — 11
Burger Express — 22
La Cantarilla — 23
La Casa de Claus — 7
Complejo Turistico Bob Gourmet — 24
Dady'o — 21
Déja vu — 11
Etnika Restaurant Pizzeria — 11
Farrens' Irish Bar — 17
Fez — 11
Forum Rock Café — 11
El Gaucho — 20
Inkafe Café Bar — 20
Inkari Pub Restaurant — 17
Los Leños Pizzeria — 5
La Luna–Centro Cultural — 12
Mandala — 16
Manolos — 18
Marengo Pizzeria — 14
Picanteria Cau Cau II — 3
La Quinta Jerusalen — 8
Restaurant El Cerrojo — 19
Restaurant Lakshmivan — 6
Restaurant Peña Las Quenas — 10
Restaurant Sol de Mayo — 2
Restaurant El Viñedo — 11
Restaurant Zingaro — 11
Rosal Restaurante — 1
Sunlight Restaurante — 15
Tenampa — 17
Tradición Arequipeña — 4
La Troica — 13
El Tuturutu — 19
Zero Pub — 11

AREQUIPA

0 — 300 m

de Santa Catalina is the most outstanding and beautiful. However, within a few blocks of the colonial **Plaza de Armas** you'll come to half a dozen churches well deserving of a brief visit, and a couple of superb old mansions. Further out, but still within walking distance, you can visit the attractive suburbs of **San Lazaro**, **Cayma** and **Yanahuara**, the latter being particularly renowned for its dramatic views of the valley, with the volcanoes, notably El Misti, patiently watching the city from high above. Another amazing vantage point for views over the city to El Misti is the very impressive black iron viaduct, or **Puente de Fierro**; although spanning half a kilometre, it was well-designed by Gustave Eiffel and built to such high standards by the railway baron Henry May, that it has successfully vaulted the city's bubbling **Río Chili** and withstood the test of Arequipa's severe earthquakes and tremors for over a hundred years.

The Plaza de Armas and around

The **Plaza de Armas**, one of South America's grandest, and the focus of the town's social activity in the early evenings, comprises a particularly striking array of colonial architecture, dotted with palms, flowers and gardens. At its heart sits a newly renovated bronze fountain, topped by an angel fondly known as *turututu* because of the trumpet it carries, but it's the arcades and elegant white facade of the seventeenth-century **Catedral** (Mon–Sat 7–11.30am & 5–8pm, Sun 7am–12.45pm & 5–7.30pm) that demand your attention, even drawing your sight away from El Misti towering behind. It looks particularly beautiful when lit up in the evenings, displaying some French influence in its Neo-Renaissance style. Conse-crated in 1556, the building was subsequently gutted by fire in 1844 and restored in 1868 by Lucas Poblete, before coming to grief again in 2001 when its impressive Neoclassical towers were seriously damaged in an earthquake. Apart from the mas-sive Belgian-built **organ**, said to be one of the largest in South America, a beautiful French-made pulpit and a marble altar created by **Felippo Moratillo**, the vast interior is actually rather disappointing in its generally bland and austere design.

On the southeast corner of the plaza, opposite the cathedral, and rather more exciting architecturally, is the elaborate **Iglesia La Compañía** (daily 10am–1pm & 3.30–7pm; $1), with an extraordinary zigzagging *sillar* stone doorway. The origin-al church, built in 1573, was destroyed eleven years later, also by an earthquake. The present structure was completed in 1660, when the magnificently sculpted doorway, with a locally inspired *mestizo*-Baroque relief, was curiously crafted in two dimensions, using shadow only to outline the figures of the frieze. Inside, by the main altar hangs a *Virgin and Child* by Bernardo Bitto, which arrived from Italy in 1575. In what used to be the sacristy (now the Chapel of San Ignacio), the poly-chrome cupola depicts jungle imagery alongside warriors, angels and the Evange-lists. Next door to the church are the **Jesuit Cloisters** (Mon–Sat 8am–10pm, Sun noon–8pm; 50¢), superbly carved back in the early eighteenth century. In the first cloister, squared pillars support white stone arches and are covered with intricate reliefs showing more angels, local fruits and vegetables, seashells and stylized puma heads. The second cloister is, in contrast, rather austere.

The east and west sides of the plaza are dominated by fine granite portals and colonial-style wooden balconies, while the southern edge is taken up by the Municipal building. Also on the plaza is the **Casona Flores del Campo**, Portal de Flores 136 (daily 10am–5pm; 50¢), older than most houses in Arequipa, dating back to the sixteenth century (it was apparently once used by Fernando Pizarro), but not completed until 1779 by one Coronel Manuel Flores del Campo. It's quite easy to distinguish different stages in the construction of this *casona* (colonial man-sion), most notably the double arch and balcony from the late eighteenth century. These days it's home to a reasonably wide-ranging exhibition of artesania.

Two blocks east of La Compañía and the plaza you'll find the exquisitely restored **Iglesia Santo Domingo** (Mon–Fri 7am–noon & 3–7.30pm, Sat 7–9am & 3–7.30pm, Sun 5.30am–12.30pm), originally built in 1553 by Gaspar Vaez, the first master architect to arrive in Arequipa. Most of what you see today was built between 1650 and 1698, but suffered major damage during the earthquakes of 1958 and 1960. The fine and large main door represents an interesting example of Arequipa's *mestizo* craftsmanship – an Indian face amid a bunch of grapes, leaves and cacti; and the side door is said to be the oldest in the city

Opposite the northeast corner of the cathedral, at C San Francisco 108, stands a particularly impressive colonial mansion, **La Casa de Tristan del Pozo**, also known as La Casa Rickets (Mon–Fri 9am–1pm & 3.45–6pm, Sat 9am–1pm; free; T054/212209). Built in 1737 as a *seminario*, it later became the splendid residence of the Rickets family, who made its fortune from the wool trade in the late nineteenth century, and boasts an extremely attractive traditional facade and courtyard. The stonework above the main door depicts Christ's genealogy, with highly stylized plants supporting five discs, or Jesuit medallions, with JHS (the abbreviation for Jesus) at the centre, Maria and Jose to the side of this, and Joaquin and Ana on the extremes. Now owned and lavishly restored by the Banco Continental, the mansion houses a small museum and art gallery.

North of the plaza, at Santa Catalina 101, the **Casa Arróspide** (also known as the Casa Iriberry) is home to the **Complejo Cultural Chavez de la Rosa** (Mon–Sat 10am–6pm; free). This attractive 1743 colonial house belongs to the law faculty of the University of San Augustin and hosts changing selections of modern works by mostly Peruvian artists. It possesses three main galleries as well as an art store with local art and crafts for sale (Mon–Sat 10am–1pm & 4–8pm). Around the corner is the seventeenth-century **La Casa del Moral**, C Moral 318 (Mon–Fri 9am–5pm, Sun 9am–1pm; $2), restored and refurbished with period pieces. Its most engaging feature is a superb stone gateway, carved with motifs that are similar to those on Nasca ceramics – puma heads with snakes growing from their mouths – surrounding a Spanish coat of arms. The mansion's name – nothing to do with ethics – comes from an ancient *mora* tree, still thriving in the central patio. One block from the Casa del Moral, the elegant 1575 **Iglesia San Agustín** on the corner of Calle Bolívar with Calle San Agustín (Mon–Sun 8am–12.30pm & 5–8pm), has one of the city's finest Baroque facades; added later in the late eighteenth century. Its old convent cloisters are now attached to the university, while inside only the unique octagonal sacristy survived the 1868 earthquake.

Two blocks down from the Plaza de Armas, on the corner of La Merced with Consuelo, is the **Casa Arango**. Built in the late seventeenth century in what was then the city's most important street, it brings together a number of architectural styles, including both *mestizo*-Baroque and nineteenth-century Neoclassical.

Monasterio de Santa Catalina

Just two blocks north of the Plaza de Armas, at C Santa Catalina 301, are the vast protective walls of **Monasterio de Santa Catalina** (daily 9am–4pm; $10, guides are optional at around $3–4), a convent which housed almost two hundred secluded nuns and three hundred servants from the late sixteenth century until it opened some of its outer doors to the public in 1970. The most important and prestigious religious building in Peru, its enormous complex of rooms, cloisters and tiny plazas takes a good hour or two to explore. Some thirty nuns still live here today, but they're restricted to the quarter bordered by calles Bolívar and Zela, worshipping in the main chapel only outside of opening hours.

Originally the concept of Gaspar Vae in 1570, though only granted official licence five years later, the convent was funded by the Viceroy Toledo and the wealthy Maria de Guzmán, who later entered the convent with one of her sisters and donated all her riches to the community. The most striking feature is its predominantly Mudéjar style, adapted by the Spanish from the Moors, but which rarely found its way into their colonial buildings. The quality of the design is emphasized and harmonized by a superb interplay between the strong sunlight, white stone and brilliant colours in the ceilings and the deep-blue sky above the maze of narrow interior streets. You notice this at once as you enter, filing left along the first corridor to a high vaulted room with a ceiling of opaque *huamanga* stone imported from the Ayacucho Valley. Beside here are the **locutorios** – little cells where on holy days the nuns could talk, unseen, to visitors.

The **Novices Cloisters**, beyond, are built in solid *sillar*-block columns, their antique wall paintings depicting the various qualities to which the devotees were expected to aspire and the Litanies of the Rosary. Off to the right, the **Claustro Naranjal** (Orange Tree Cloister), painted a beautiful blue with birds and flowers over the vaulted arches, is surrounded by a series of paintings showing the soul evolving from a state of sin to the achievement of God's grace. In one of the side rooms, dead nuns were mourned, before being interred within the monastic confines.

A new convent, where the nuns now live, is on the right off Calle Cordoba. **Calle Toledo**, a long, very narrow street that's the oldest part of the monastery and connects the main dwelling areas with the **lavandería**, or communal washing sector, is brought to life with permanently flowering geraniums. There are several rooms off here worth exploring, including small chapels, prayer rooms and a kitchen. The *lavandería* itself, perhaps more than any other area, offers a captivating insight into what life must have been like for the closeted nuns; open to the skies and city sounds yet bounded by high walls, there are twenty halved earthenware jars alongside a water channel. It also has a swimming pool with sunken steps and a papaya tree in the lovely garden.

There's a **restaurant**, serving reasonably priced snacks and drinks, just off to the left along the broad Calle Granada, while heading straight on brings you to the **Plaza Socodobe**, a fountain courtyard to the side of which is the **bañera** where the nuns used to bathe. Around the corner, down the next little street, are **Sor Ana's rooms**. By the time of her death in 1686, the 90-year-old Sor Ana was something of a phenomenon, leaving behind her a trail of prophecies and cures. Her own destiny in Santa Catalina, like that of many of her sisters, was to castigate herself in order to offer up her torments for the salvation of other souls – mostly wealthy Arequipan patrons who paid handsomely for the privilege. Sor Ana was beatified by Pope John Paul II in the 1990s.

The **refectory**, immediately before the main cloisters, is deceptively plain – its exceptional star-shaped stained-glass windows shedding dapples of sunlight through the empty space. Nearby, confessional windows look into the **main chapel**, but the best view of its majestic cupola is from the top of the staircase beside the cloisters. A small room underneath these stairs has an intricately painted wall niche with a Sacred Heart centrepiece. The ceiling is also curious, illustrated with three dice, a crown of thorns, and some other less recognizable items. The **cloisters** themselves are covered with murals following the life of Jesus and the Virgin Mary; although they were originally a communal dormitory, their superb acoustics now make them popular venues for classical concerts and weddings.

Close to this area, but not part of the tour these days, there's the **lower choir room** and the **tomb of Sor Ana** within the quite grand and lavishly decorated **main chapel**. Beyond the last sector of the monastery is a rather dark museum full of obscure seventeenth-, eighteenth- and nineteenth-century paintings. The best of these are in the final outer chamber, lined mainly with works from the Cusqueña school. One eye-catching canvas, the first on the left as you enter this

SANTA CATALINA MONASTERY

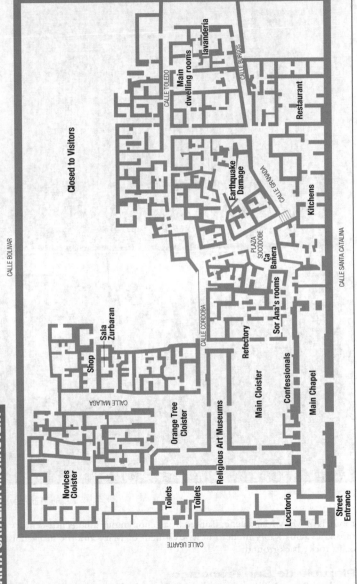

0 — 10 m

CALLE BOLIVAR

Closed to Visitors

CALLE TOLEDO

Main
dwelling rooms

lavandería

CALLE BURGOS

Restaurant

Earthquake
Damage

CALLE GRANADA

Kitchens

PLAZA
SOCODOBE
Ca
Bañera

Sor Ana's rooms

CALLE CORDOBA

Refectory

Sala
Zurbarán

Shop

CALLE MALAGA

Orange Tree
Cloister

Main Cloister

Confessionals

Main Chapel

CALLE SANTA CATALINA

Novices
Cloister

Religious Art Museums

Toilets

Toilets

Locutorio

Street
Entrance

CALLE UGARTE

▲ Santa Catalina Monastery

room, is of Mary Magdalene. Painted by an anonymous nineteenth-century Arequipan, it's remarkably modern in its treatment of Mary and the near-cubist style of its rocky background.

Plazuela de San Francisco

Just above Santa Catalina, the small, leafy **Plazuela de San Francisco**, usually buzzing with students and townspeople, is where you'll find Arequipa's city museum, the Museo Histórico Municipal (Mon–Fri 8am–5pm; $1), which devotes itself principally to local heroes – army chiefs, revolutionary leaders, presidents and poets (including the renowned Mariano Melgar). It's rather a dull collection of memorabilia, though some rooms have interesting photographs of the city there are displays of artefacts from the colonial period and the war with Chile. The university's museums, located on the outskirts of the city, are of greater interest (see below).

Also on the Plazuela de San Francisco, you'll find a striking Franciscan complex, dominated by the Convent and Iglesia de San Francisco (Mon–Sat 9am–noon & 3-5pm; Convent entry $2). Yet another of Gaspar Vaez's projects, this one dating back to 1569, it shows an interesting mix of brick and *sillar* work both inside and on the facade. Original paintings by Baltazar de Prado once covered the central nave, but the earthquake of 1604 destroyed these; however, the nave retains its most impressive feature – a pure-silver altar. Adjoining the church are rather austere convent cloisters and the very simple **Capila del Tercera Orden** (daily 9–11am & 3–5pm; free), its entrance decorated with modest *mestizo* carvings of St Francis and St Clare, founders of the first and second orders. Close to the centre of town, at C Melgar 303, **Monasterio de Santa Teresa** (Mon–Sat 9am–4.30pm, Sun 9am–12.30pm; $1.80; ℡054/242531) is smaller than Santa Catalina but has astonishingly beautiful colonial patios set around a large open courtyard. Internally it posseses some fine religious artwork and murals as well as twelve exhibition spaces and over three hundred works of art.

Monasterio de La Recoleta

While exhibiting fine architecture, it's the archaeology and natural history museums which really draws people to the **Monasterio de La Recoleta** (Mon–Sat 9am–noon & 3–5pm; $1.80; ℡054/270996, ©convento-la-recoleta@terra.com), located on the western side of the Río Chili, which runs its generally torrential course through Arequipa from Selva Alegre directly south, dividing the old heart of the city from what has become a more modern downtown sector including Yanahuara and Cayma. La Recoleta is a large Franciscan monastery standing conspicuously on its own on Callejón de la Recoleta, Ronda Recoleta 117, just ten to fifteen minutes' walk east of the Plaza de Armas. The stunning major and minor cloisters were built in 1651; in 1869 it was converted to an Apostolic Mission school administered by the Barefoot Franciscans. The **museums** here have been open to the public since 1978, housing two rooms of pre-Columbian artefacts including textiles and ceramics, an Amazon room showing artefacts collected over the years from jungle Indian tribes and examples of forest flora and fauna, plus a religious and modern art gallery displaying both Cusqueña and Arequipena classical works, plus a renowned historic library with some 25,000 sixteenth- and seventeenth-century volumes.

The university museums

Arequipa's universities have good academic reputations extending beyond the boundaries of Peru. Of the two main university museums, the Universidad Católica de Santa Maria has one section relatively centrally located in the old quarter of Cercado; the Universidad de San Agustín, on the other hand, is further afield in the suburb of San Lazáro.

Museo Santuarios Andinos (Mon–Sat 9am–6pm, Sun 9am–3pm, $4; ℡054/215013 or 382038, ⓦwww.ucsm.edu.pe/santury/) part of the **Universidad Católica de Santa Maria** and locted at C La Merced 110, is arguably the most important museum in Arequipa today, with displays of some nineteen Inca mummies and a range of archaeological remains; guides are obligatory but their fee, which is additional, is negotiable. The main exhibit is *Juanita*, the sacrificed thirteen-year-old ancient "princess" uncovered in her icy ritual grave on September 8th, 1995, by an expedition from university which included the archaeologist Johan Reinhard along with the well-known *Andinista* Miguel Zarate and Peruvian archae-ologist Jose Chavez. The gravesite, located at the incredible altitude of 6380m on Ampato Volcano, is estimated to be about 500 years old. The girl, or "ice-maiden", Juanita was sacrified to the Apu Ampato and killed, after some time of fasting and herbal sedation, with a blow to the head by a five-pointed granite mace. Tickets include an introduction video and the museum also contains fine examples of associ-ated grave goods like textiles, precious metals and Inca ceramics.

Distinct from Santuarios Andinos, but also a Catholic Uni-affiliate, the **Museo de Arqueología de la Universidad Católica de Santa Maria** (Mon–Sat 9am–5.30pm; ☎054/959636; $2, includes a video and guided tour) is located at C Cruz Verde 303. This museum has seven rooms concentrating on items from pre-Con-quest cultures such as the Huari, Tiahuanuco, Chancay and Inca, and boasts around a thousand different pieces such as stone weapons, ceramics, textiles, grave goods, as well as other worked and ancient stone, wood and metal objects. The largest of Arequipa's museums, meanwhile, the **Museo Arqueológico de la Universidad de San Agustín** (Mon–Fri 8.30am–5pm; $1.80; call for an appointment on ☎054/288881), has good collections of everything from mummies and replicas of Chavín stones to Nasca, Huari and Inca ceramics as well as colonial paintings and furniture. It is stuck out in the university campus along Avenida Independencia (by the corner with Victor Morales), at the intersection between the calles Alvarez Thomas and Palacio Viejo.

The suburbs: San Lázaro, Yanahuara and Cayma

The oldest quarter of Arequipa – the first place the Spaniards settled in this valley – is the barrio **San Lázaro**, an uncharacteristic zone of tiny, curving streets stretching around the hillside at the top end of Calle Jerusalen, all an easy stroll north from the plaza. If you feel like a walk, and some good views of El Misti, you can follow the streambed from here to **Puente Grau** – a superb vantage point. From here, a longer stroll takes you across to the west bank of the Chili, along Avenida Ejercito and out to the suburbs of Yanahuara (1–2km) and Cayma (3–4km), once quite distinct vil-lages until the railway boom of the late nineteenth century, which brought peasant-migrants to Arequipa from as far away as Cusco. Both are built-up now, though they still command stunning views across the valley, above all from their **churches**. There are also one or two fine **restaurants** in these sectors, particularly Yanahuara. Buses and *colectivos* to these areas leave from avenidas Ayacucho and Puente Grau.

The municipal plaza at **Yanahuara** possesses a beautiful **viewing point** (*mira-dor*), which has been made famous by postcards. Buses and *colectivos* to Yanahuara's *mirador* can be caught from the corner of Grau with Santa Catalina (near the *Hostal Posada Santa Catalina*), or it's a fifteen-minute walk from Puente Grau, between blocks 2 and 3 of Av Ejercito. The small **Iglesia Yanahuara** on the tranquil main plaza dates to the middle of the eighteenth century, and its Baroque facade, with a stone relief of the tree of life incorporating angels, flowers, saints, lions and hidden Indian faces, is particularly fine.

Another kilometre or so further out, **Cayma**, once a small suburb with some views over the city, now also reflects the modern commercial, even flashy side of Arequipa with large shops and even one or two nightclubs. Views of the Chachani Volcano can be taken in from here. The **Iglesia de San Miguel** (daily 9am–4pm), built in the early eighteenth century, houses the image of the Virgen de la Candelaria, donated to the city by King Carlos V. It's possible to climb up to the roof of the church which offers great views across Yanahuara and towards the volcanoes to the north.

Eating and drinking

Arequipa **restaurants** serve a wide variety of food, but are particularly famous for a dish called *ocopa*, a cold appetizer made with potatoes, eggs, olives and a fairly spicy yellow chilli sauce. Other delicacies include *rocoto relleno* (a spicy meat-stuffed Andean pepper), *cuy chactado* (the name comes from the round and flat stone – or *chaqueria* – which is placed on top of the guinea pig while frying it), *chupe de camarones* (river shrimp casserole) and *adobo* (pork soaked and cooked in vinegar with maize-beer sediment, onions and chillis). As it's not too far from the Pacific, the town's better restaurants are also renowned for their excellent fresh seafood. **Picanterías** – traditional Peruvian eating houses serving spicy seafood – are particularly well established here. Less traditional but much easier to find there are a number of non-picantería restaurants on both the western – and to a lesser extent the eastern – side of the plaza, many of them having interconnecting first-floor terraces with fine views to the cathedral and square below. Some also offer live music, especially on weekend evenings. Unless otherwise indicated, all the places listed below open daily from 11am to 11pm.

Cafés

Burger Express Portal San Agustín 123. An Italian-style café serving some of the best and strongest coffee in Arequipa, but is otherwise a fairly standard café set-up at street level. The menu includes sandwiches, burgers and other fast foods, as well as full meals.

Fez San Francisco 229. Central, vaguely Middle-Eastern themed place with excellent coffee plus crepes, sandwiches, sweets and probably the best falafel in Peru.

Inkafe Café Bar Portal de Flores, Plaza de Armas. Upstairs to the right of Cinesur and linked to the luxurious *Sonesta Posada del Inca*, it's located on one of only two sunny terraces on the east side of the plaza and serves fine sandwiches, pastas and main dishes. An expensive place to dine, but worth it, not least for the high-quality service.

Inkari Pub Restaurant Pasaje Catedral 113. Half-bar, half-restaurant, this serves good pizzas as well as other food (beef, chicken, pasta) in an often lively environment. There's also a dartboard (dangerously close to the front entrance), tables outside and just about enough room for musicians at weekends.

Los Leños Pizzaria C Jerusalen 407. Just below the corner of Jerusalen and Puente Grau, this café serves a large range of delicious pizzas, pastas and some meat dishes, all very good value. The walls are covered with the graffiti of travellers from every continent.

Manolos C Mercaderes 113. One of Arequipa's longest-established snack bars, offering good service and a delectable selection of meals, cakes and sweets, as well as excellent coffee. Portions are big and prices similar. There's another *Manolos*, newer but almost identical, on the same street at 117.

Restaurant Lakshmivan C Jerusalen 402. A very popular lunchtime vegetarian cafeteria at the back of a small patio, with a background soundtrack of classical music and a tranquil ambience. There's also a range of health-food products, yoghurts and wholemeal bread for sale.

Tenampa Pasaje Catedral 108. A small vegetarian snack bar in the lane behind the cathedral with good set-menus, great yoghurt and scrumptious Mexican tacos. Prices are very reasonable, even if portions aren't overly generous.

Restaurants

La Cantarilla C Tahuaycani 106, Sachaca. A notable, modern *picantería* located in a suburban district to the south of Yanahuara, best at lunchtime where you can enjoy the shaded, spacious patios; everything is cooked over wood fires.

Complejo Turístico Bob Gourmet Alameda Pardo 123 ☏ 054/270528. Combining two of the finest restaurants in the city, this complex is based in the old Club Alemán, overlooking the city from the western banks of the Río Chili, with shady pagodas and a kids' play area. *El Montonero* is its excellent lunchtime restaurant, which is attempting to rescue some traditional regional dishes such as *senca* meatballs and *pesque*, which is made from quinoa with a cheese and steak topping. *Che Carlitos* is a relatively fancy Argentine grill and bar, serving excellent beef and alpaca cuts, but also offering fine salads and some roast vegetables.

El Gaucho Portal de Flores 112. On the plaza but below ground level, this is one of the best meat restaurants in town at quite reasonable prices; try the grills or the *lomo gaucho*.

Govinda C Santa Catalina 120a ☎054/285540. A highly recommended veggie restaurant with a distinctive atmosphere, serving excellent breakfasts, natural yoghurt, juices and mueslis plus very good and inexpensive vegetarian set meals. The restaurant is associated with the Centro Cultural Bhakti Yoga, which offers daily classes (Mon–Sat 6am–8pm).

Mandala C Jerusalen 207 ☎054/229974. A quiet little vegetarian restaurant with a Hindu influence on decor and dishes. There are daily set-lunch menus, mild curries, pizzas and local specialities such as *ocopa* and *rocoto relleno*.

Picantería Cau Cau II C Tronchadero 404, Yanahuara ☎054/254496. One of Arequipa's best value *picantería* restaurants specialising in traditional foods like guinea pigs and *ricotto relleno* and with fine views towards El Misti and the city from its patio garden.

Restaurant El Cerrojo Portal San Augustin 111-A. Serves good food including local dishes such as *cuy*, on an attractive patio overlooking the Plaza de Armas; excellent value and at its best in the evenings.

Restaurant Sol de Mayo C Jerusalen 207 ☎054/254148, ✉reservas@restaurantsoldemayo .com. Located in a different C Jerusalen (in the suburb of Yanahuara) to the one which bisects Arequipa's centre, this place has tables set within and around attractive gardens, live music and superbly prepared, traditional Peruvian dishes, all enjoyed in a convivial atmosphere. It's quite expensive but worth the $2–3 taxi ride out there;

alternatively it's a 15min walk over Puente Grau, then a few blocks up Av Ejercito. Call to reserve a table, since it's a very popular place. Open daily 10am–7pm.

Restaurant El Viñedo San Francisco 319 ☎054/205053. Quite a large, posh place, pricey but worth it for arguably the best Argentine-style steaks and grills in southern Peru, as well as the quality service.

Restaurant Zingaro San Francisco 309 ☎054/217662. A Mediterranean-style menu backed by a modern re-fit of an attractive *sillar* vaulted space, this restaurant offers good food at average prices, with equally good service. Best appreciated in early evening.

Rosal Restaurant Prolongación Av Bolognesi, Yanahuara ☎054/256336. This is an ecological restaurant run by environmentalists and situated in lovely gardens by the river. All the food is delicious and organic, and their avocado stuffed with vegetables is exceptional.

Sunlight Restaurante C Moral 205. A very small but excellent and inexpensive Asian vegetarian restaurant with set lunch menus – including some mild curries – at giveaway prices.

🏃 Tradición Arequipeña Av Dolores 111 ☎054/426467. This is *the* place to try your first *cuy chactado* or *rocoto relleno*. Opened in 1991, several blocks east of the city centre, this is probably the best *picantería* in town. It has a pleasant garden, covered and indoor spaces, and is usually bustling with locals enjoying the extremely fresh and tasty food.

Drinking and nightlife

It's often hard to distinguish between **bars**, restaurants and **nightclubs** (or **discos**, as most are referred to), as many restaurants have a bar and live music while many bars and clubs also serve food. The welcoming **peña** restaurants, for example, concentrated along and in the streets between calles Santa Catalina and Jerusalen, specialise in more traditional music than either the bars or club. Arequipa has a very strong tradition of folk singing and poetry, and folk musicians will wander from *peña* to *peña*, often performing the region's most authentic music: *Yaraví* singing, usually lamenting vocalists accompanied by a guitar. Most *peñas* are open Thursday to Saturday from 8.30pm to midnight, while discos and nightclubs, many just a couple of blocks from the Plaza de Armas, are open nightly until 3 or 4am, and usually charge a small entrance fee (around $2.50). In recent years the youth of Arequipa have developed a preference for Latin and Cuban-style ballads accompanied by electric guitars, drums and sometimes keyboards, so the choice at weekends can be quite extensive.

Arequipa's **cinema** scene is based around the Cinesur, on the plaza at Portal de Flores 112, and the Cine Fenix, General Moran 104. Otherwise the **cultural institutes** put on occasional programmes, especially the Instituto Cultural Peruano-Aleman, C Ugarte 207, which has a cultural events notice board, shows good films in Spanish and German and sometimes has children's theatre. Also worth a try are the Alianza Francesa, at C Santa Catalina 208, where there's also a gallery displaying local artists' work, and the Instituto Cultural Peruano Norte Americano, C Melgar 109.

Bars

Blue's Bar C San Francisco 319-A. Serves food and drink, accompanied most nights by a variety of music, ranging from classical to rock.

La Casa de Claus C Zela 207. A German drinking house, very popular in the evenings and quite stylish with good music and German staples such as sausages and weiner schnitzel.

Déja Vu C San Francisco 319. Small and popular, this place serves seafood, spaghetti and meat dishes, plus, of course, drinks. There's also a big video screen and a nice rooftop patio, which can get crowded at weekends.

Etnika Restaurant Pizzeria C San Francisco 317 ☎ 054/202697. A popular restaurant in the Casona Forum complex, with reasonably tasty pizzas accompanied by good table service; the place usually gets very busy later on in the evenings.

Farrens' Irish Bar Pasaje Catedral 107. Unfortunately, there's rarely any real Irish ale served here, but it's a tidy bar with a wide range of cocktails and whiskies, good rock music and outside tables. Food also served.

Forum Rock Café C San Francisco 317. The liveliest and funkiest scene in the city, with live rock-centric music on Friday and Saturday. Also has a café, a decent bar and serves snacks.

Zero Pub C San Francisco 317. Popular with young locals and calling itself a "temple to rock'n'roll", this bar has a couple of decent pool tables and is decorated with rock iconographic posters.

Clubs and Peñas

Animals C Zela 205, half a block from Iglesia San Francisco ☎ 054/204542. Good drinks with some bar food. Live music occasionally; a good mix of Latin and European dance tunes the rest of the time.

Dady'o Portal de Flores 112, Plaza de Armas. Fairly popular place with disco, karaoke some nights, a Ladies night on Thursdays and sometimes live music.

La Luna – Centro Cultural C Jerusalen 400b ☎ 054/203118. This bar and restaurant gets particularly vibrant when live rock and Latin ballad bands play on the backroom stage, surrounded by New Age-y murals and other paintings. For the most part it's open only at weekends, Thurs–Sat 10pm–3am.

Marengo Pizzeria C Santa Catalina 221 ☎ 054/284883. While primarily a small and cosy place serving really good pizzas and inexpensive pasta dishes, it's actually best known for its good Andean folk music, hosted most Saturday evenings.

La Quinta Jerusalen 522, ☎ 054/200964. Comes to life at night when excellent foods are served up amid live local folklore music. Open most nights, but always with music at weekends.

Restaurant Peña Las Quenas C Santa Catalina 302 ☎ 054/206440. One of the better and larger venues in town, Las Quenas dishes out authentic Andean music, food and good pisco sours; music most weekends and also during the week from June-Sept. Closed on Sun, but open Mon-Sat from 10am for breakfast.

La Troica C Jerusalen 522a. One of the main folklore venues with music almost every night in high season; well frequented by tour groups.

El Tuturutu Portal San Agustín 105. Right on the Plaza de Armas and overlooking the angel fountain of the same name, this restaurant and *peña* has a great atmosphere when busy at weekends.

Shopping

Arequipa's **central market** is one of the biggest and liveliest in Peru, though it's also a prime spot for **pickpockets**. Located a couple of blocks down from Iglesia Santo Domingo, it sells all sorts of food, leather work, musical instruments, inexpensive artesania and even llama and alpaca meat, while offering an excellent range of hats, herbs and even cheap shoe repairs. You can also get a selection of fruit juices, including some combined with eggs and dark, sweet, stout beer. Other places for top-quality **artesania**, **alpaca** goods and **silver** jewellery or wares include Aqlla, Pasaje Catedral 112; El Zanguan, C Santa Catalina 105; Millma's, Pasaje Catedral 117; the stalls and shops around the courtyard at Centro Artesanal Fundo El Fierro, on the second block of Grau; and in the very new and plush Patio del Ekeko, C Mercaderes 141, near the corner with Calle

Tours, trekking and climbing in Arequipa and around

Taking a guided tour is the easiest way to get around this otherwise quite difficult region. It's difficult in a number of ways – the sheer terrain is inhospitable, massive and wild, and the altitude changes between Arequipa city and, say, Chivay, can affect you for a couple of days (mountain sickness with headaches), which makes driving your own rented car tricky until you're properly adjusted. All operators tend to offer similar packages, with **city tours** lasting around three hours, costing $10–20 and usually including the Monasterio de Santa Catalina, La Compañía, the Cathedral, the Church of San Augustín and the Yanahuara Mirador. **Countryside tours** (*tur de campiña*) usually consist of a roughly three-hour trip to the rural churches of Cayma and Sachaca, the old mill at Sabandia, Tingo lagoon and local *miradors*, at a price of $10–30. Most companies offer one- to three-day trips out to the **Colca Canyon** for $20–80 (sometimes with very early morning starts) or to the petroglyphs at **Toro Muerto** for $20–40. Trips to the **Valley of the Volcanoes** and the **Cotahuasi Canyon** are only offered by a few companies from $100 upwards. Specialist adventure activities, such as rafting in the Colca Canyon, mountaineering or serious trekking can cost anything from $55–350 for a three- to six-day outing. Of course, all prices vary according to the season, the quality you demand (in terms of food, transport to start point and whether you have *arrieros* with mules to carry your gear) and the size of the group. Mountain-bike rental ranges from $10–35 a day depending on the type of bike required, size of group, whether or not a guide is needed and which route is selected.

Campamento Base and Colca Trek C Jerusalen 401-b ℡054/206217 or 9600170, ℮colcatrek@gmail.com and ℮colcatrek@gmail.com, ⓦwww.colcatrek .com.pe. An excellent all-round outdoor adventure specialist company run by the well-respected Vlado Soto, specializing in customized tours with a mix of trekking, mountain biking, canoeing and climbing. They operate a well-stocked camping shop and employ excellent guides for the Colca Canyon and more adventurous treks, including Cabana-conde, Tapay and especially Cotahuasi areas. They're also a good source of information on the wider region and will help organize transport.

Giardino Agencia de Viajes C Jerusalen 606a ℡054/221345, ℱ242761, ℮info @giardinotours.com, ⓦwww.giardinotours.com. A well-organized outfit with excellent

Jerusalen. This last place is a shopping mall with a difference: quite upmarket in appearance, the products – silverware, artesania, clothing, quality food – are surprisingly inexpensive. On the second floor there's a very good internet service (not so cheap), cafetería and bar where live shows are presented now and again (every 30min in high season); on the third floor there's a museum of textiles from southern Peru; and on the fourth you'll find an audio-visual exhibition.

For a good selection of colonial and older **antiques**, including some interesting pre-Columbian ceramics, the antiques and art shops at Puente Grau 314b and along blocks 1 to 4 of C Santa Catalina are excellent. Of the latter, the best is Arte Colonial, where there are several jam-packed rooms to explore.

The best baker in town is La Cañasta, C Jerusalen 120, located at the back of a patio, where you can also sit down and eat breakfasts or snacks; it also has a small **delicatessen** counter. The best **bookshops** are the Librería San Francisco, C San Francisco 221, where they stock a wide range of English-language books, including many on the history and wildlife of Peru, and the nearby Librería El Lecto, at C San Francisco 133, which sells a number of books in English, has the best book exchange service in Arequipa and a cultural events notice board.

Camping equipment and maps are best from Campamento Base (or Colca Trek, as it's also known), C Jerusalen 401b, where they stock a good range of tents, two-day tours to Colca Canyon, trekking and climbing trips, plus the usual city and countryside trips as well as a very reliable air and bus ticket buying service.

Hilton Travel and Tours C Santa Catalina 217 ☎054/225948 or 227297. Air tickets, city tours and treks to Colca Canyon, plus a 24-hour trip up El Misti and frequent rides to Toro Muerto. Also offer a five-day adventure tour to Cotahuasi Canyon.

Illary Tour C Santa Catalina 205 ☎054/220844, ✉illarytour@hotmail.com. A friendly and professional outfit with English-speaking guides who take enjoyable trips of two days and more in the Colca Canyon. They provide oxygen, accommodation, transport and even live, private-performance folk music.

Invertur C San Juan de Dios 113 ☎054/213585, 🖷219526. Though they offer both city and countryside tours, their speciality is an all-inclusive two-day trip to Colca. Good English-speaking guides are available.

Naturaleza Activa C Santa Catalina 211 ☎054/695793, ✉naturactiva@yahoo .com. This company specializes in trekking and mountain-bike tours and equipment rental.

Pablo Tour C Jerusalen 400a ☎054/203737, ✉pablotour@hotmail.com, 🌐www .pablotour.com. Specialists in adventure tourism, with great links to hostels and local guides in Cabanaconde and the Oasis *tambo* in the Colca Canyon.

Peru Adventure (and Biking) Tours C Jerusalen 410 ☎054/221658, 🌐www.peru adventurestours.com. A highly professional team, Peru Adventure Tours specialise in offering tours all over Peru, including Colca Canyon and Cotahuasi. They also organise mountain biking tours in the region as well as climbing, trekking and luxury trips.

Zarate Adventuras (or Expediciones) C Santa Catalina 204, Oficina 3 ☎054/202461, 🌐www.zarateadventures.com. A good expedition outfitter as well as a leading trekking and climbing company with over 28 years' experience, and using only professional and qualified guides such as Carlos Zarate, the internationally renowned founder. Treks include rock climbing and canoeing in the usual places such as Colca, El Misti and Cotahuasi, but they also offer more adventurous routes such as from Colca to the Valley of the Volcanoes and another to the Mismi Nevado, official source of the Amazon which overlooks the Colca Canyon from the north.

sleeping bags and all other essentials, plus maps; they're also a good contact for expert guides. Similarly, Zarate Adventures, C Santa Catalina 204, has a significant range of camping and climbing equipment. There are other tour companies that rent out equipment, but not all are of the same quality; some of these are listed in the box below.

Listings

Airlines Lan Peru, C Santa Catalina 118c ☎201224, is the main office, but you can also buy air tickets for Lan Peru flights from Portal San Agustín 135 ☎054/203637; Star Peru, C Santa Catalina 105a ☎054/221896; TACA, Centro Comercial Caima, office 36, Av Cayma 636 ☎054/840510. The Trotomundo office at Portal San Augustin 121 sells tickets for all these airlines. There's a departure tax of about $5 on all flights except those to Colca Canyon.

Banks and exchange Banco de Credito, C San Juan de Dios 125 (ATM); Banco Continental, Block

1 of C San Francisco; and the Banco de la Nación, C Mercaderes 127. It's usually quicker and the rates are generally as good or almost as good in casas de cambio like the one at C San Juan de Dios 120, opposite Banco de Credito, and in the Kodak Express shop at C San Juan de Dios 103.

Bus operators Angelitos Negros, C San Juan de Dios 510 (☎054/213094), for Chapi, Moquegua, Ilo and Tacna; CIVA, Terminal Terrestre or Av Salaverry (☎054/426563), for Cusco, Puno, Lima and Tacna; Cristo Rey, C San Juan de Dios 510 (☎054/213094 or 259848) for Chivay and Cabanaconde; Cromotex,

Terminal Terrestre (☎054/421555), for Chuquibamba, Cotahuasi and Alcha; Cruz del Sur, Terrapuerto (☎054/427728 or 216625, ⊛www.crusdelsur.com.pe) for Lima, Cusco, Tacna or Puno; Del Carpio, Terminal Terrapuerto (☎054/427049 or 430941), for the Majes Valley, Aplao and Pampacolca; Jacantay, Terminal Terrestre, for Juliaca, Puno, Desaguadero and La Paz; Ormeño, Terminal Terrestre (☎054/218885 or 424187), for the coast; San Cristoval, Terminal Terrestre (☎054/422068), for Lima, Cusco, Puno and Juliaca; Sur Express, C San Juan de Dios 537 (☎054/213335), for Chapi, Chivay and Cabanaconde; Tepsa, Terminal Terrestre and Terrapuerto (☎054/212451), for International journeys; Reyna, Terminal Terrestre (☎054/430612), the best for Cotahuasi, Colca, Chivay, Cabanaconde, Andagua in the Valley of the Volcanoes and Cusco; Turismo Alex, Av Olimpico 203 (☎054/202863), for Andaray, Chuquibamba, Cotahuasi (all departing from Terminal Terrestre); TZ Turismo, Terminal Terrestre (☎054/421949), for Corire and Aplao; Ultra Tours, C San Juan de Dios 510, for Chapi; Zeballos, Av Salaverry 107 (☎054/201013), for Lima, Corire, Aplao and Ilo.

Car rental Aerotur and B&G, C Santa Catalina 213 ☎054/219291, 🖷219224, ✉busgom@terra.com.pe, are a reliable company, which rents out 4WD vehicles with or without driver and/or guide, and also rent out satellite phones; Avis, Palacio Viejo 214 ☎054/282519, or at airport ☎653346. Servitours, C Jerusalen 400 ☎054/202856 or 201636, ✉servitours@hotmail.com, also rent 4WD vehicles.

Consulates Bolivia, C Rivera 408, Oficina 06 ☎054/213391; United Kingdom, C Tacna y Arica 156 ☎054/606600; Chile, C Mercaderes 212, Oficina 401 ☎054/233556 or 226787.

DHL and Western Union Their combined offices are at C Santa Catalina 115 ☎054/234288 (Mon–Fri 9am–7pm, Sat 9am–1pm).

Doctor Dr Jaraffe (Mon–Fri 3–7pm; ☎054/215115).

Hospitals Hospital Regional, Av Daniel Alcides Carrion ☎054/231818 (24 hrs) and the Clinica Arequipa, Av Bolognesi ☎054/253416.

Internet facilities La Red, Jerusalen 306B are probably the best in town; C CHIPS Internet, San Francisco 202a are pretty good; ONLINE, C Jerusalen 412a also offer international calling through their server; there's a nameless cybercafé on the plaza at Portal San Agustín 105; and, close to the plaza there's Catedral Internet, Pasaje Catedral 101 (8am–11pm). All stay open seven days a week, some until 8pm or later.

Language courses Rocio Language Classes, C Ayacucho208, Oficina 22 ☎054/224568, ⊛www.spanish-peru.com, offer a range of beginner to technical Spanish courses; the Centro de Idiomas Europeos, José Santos Chocano 249, Umacollo, in front of the Parque Libertad de Expresión ☎054/252619, run courses in Spanish and Portuguese.

Laundry Fairy Laundry, C Jerusalen 528 ☎054/218648; Lavandería Rapida, C Jerusalen 404b; and Magic Laundry, C Jerusalen 404b.

Pharmacies The most central and elegant is the Farmacia Americana on the plaza at Portal San Agustín 103; but there's also the Botica Popular, C Mercaderes 128; and Farmacia Sudamerica, C San Francisco 131.

Photographic film Fotodigital, C Mercaderes 111, has a reasonable stock of Kodak films as well as cameras and binoculars, and also offers a 1hr film-developing service. Foto Peru, C Mercaderes 118, sell and develop most standard Kodak films; Casa Clave, Portal Municipalidad 122, sell Kodak films and develop; Foto Alvis, Portal de Flores, 126, have a wider range of films, including Kodak and Fuji.

Police Tourist Police, C Jerusalen 315 ☎054/201258 or 239888.

Post office C Moral 118 (Mon–Sat 8am–8pm, Sun 9am–2pm).

Telephone Locutorio Publico, C San Juan de Dios 10; and Perusat, C Santa Catalina 105 (Mon–Fri 9am–8pm, Sat 9am–6pm), which offers the best prices and good service especially on international calls.

Trains Although no trains are presently running, it may be worth checking on arrival with Perurail, Av Tacna y Arica 200 ☎054/205540 or 205640, ⊛www.perurail.com.

Visas Migraciones, Urb Quinta Tristan, 2nd park, Distrito José Bustamante y Rivero ☎054/421759.

Volunteering Traveller Not Tourist 118-B, 2nd Floor, C Santa Catalina ☎959856317. ⊛www.travellernottourist.com. Volunteering opportunies with various community projects.

Around Arequipa

The spectacular countryside around Arequipa rewards a few days' exploration, with some exciting and adventurous possibilities for trips from the city. Climbing **El Misti** is a demanding but rewarding trek, while the Inca ruins of **Paucarpata** at the foot of the volcano offer excellent scenery, great views and a fine place for a picnic. The attractive village of **Chapi** makes a good day-trip, while the **Sumbay caves**, just a few hours' drive from Arequipa on the road towards Caylloma, contain hundreds of unique pre-historic paintings.

Yet the greatest attraction is easily the **Colca Canyon**, some 200km to the north of Arequipa, second only to Machu Picchu, and developing fast as a trekking and canoeing destination (best in the dry season, May–Sept). Called the "Valley of Marvels" by the Peruvian novelist Mario Vargas Llosa, it is nearly twice the size of Arizona's Grand Canyon and one of the country's most extraordinary natural sights. Around 120km west of Arequipa, you can see the amazing petroglyphs of **Toro Muerto,** and perhaps go on to hike amid the craters and cones of the **Valley of the Volcanoes**. A little further north is the **Cotahuasi Canyon**, which some people believe could usurp Colca's claim to being the deepest canyon in the world. Most people visit these sites on an **organized trip** with one of the tour companies in Arequipa (see p.196). If you are prepared to put up with the extra hassle, you can visit many of the sites by much cheaper **public transport**. See individual accounts for details.

Paucarpata and around

Set against the backdrop of El Misti, **PAUCARPATA** is a fine place to while away an afternoon with some wine and a picnic lunch. About 7km out of central Arequipa (a good 2hr walk or a quick ride on a local bus, leaving every 30min from the corner of Avenida Salverry and Calle San Juan de Dios in Arequipa), it's a large village surrounded by farmland based on perfectly regular pre-Inca terraces, or *paucarpata* – the Quechua word from which it takes its name. There's a small colonial church on the southwestern edge of the suburb that contains a few Cusqueña school paintings. *Colectivos* travel regularly to Paucarpata from the market area or Calle San Juan de Dios in Arequipa for around 50¢.

Another 2–3km beyond Paucarpata is **Sabandia**, where there's a reconstructed colonial **mill** (daily 9am–5pm; $1) fronted by attractive lawns and a few alpacas and llamas hanging around. The nearby riverbank is another ideal place for a picnic. Built in 1661 to supply the city, along with three others in the region, the mill operated continuously for some three hundred years and was capable of milling 800kg of grain in one eight-hour shift with a single operator. It was only abandoned when industrial milling took root. The surrounding scenery, characterized by Inca terracing and broad vistas of surrounding mountains, is also home to a restored seventeenth-century **windmill**, which makes for an interesting visit. The return trip by **taxi** from Arequipa is about $10, or you can take the Arequipa–Paucarpata *colectivo*, which goes on to Sabandia for the same fare from Arequipa.

If you have your own transport, or take a taxi from Arequipa ($15 return), you can travel the ten kilometres beyond here, through the fertile Socabaya Valley, to the **Casa del Fundador** (daily 10am–5pm), which houses a colonial museum with period furnishings and attractive gardens. Once owned by Garcia Manuel de Carbajal, the original founder of Arequipa, it became the property of the Jesuits, who built a small chapel within the mansion, the latter restored in 1821 by the Archbishop José Sebastian de Goyeneche y Barreda, one of Arequipa's greatest nineteenth-century benefactors. After the Jesuits were expelled from Peru, the

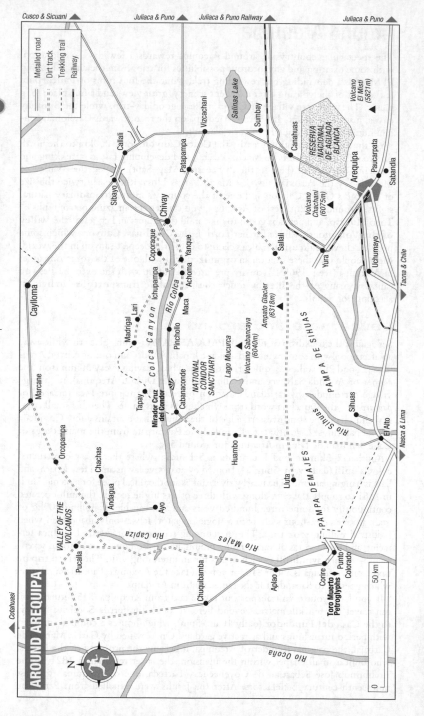

AROUND AREQUIPA

50 km

0

N

Cusco & Sicuani

Juliaca & Puno

Juliaca & Puno Railway

Juliaca & Puno

Metalled road
Dirt track
Trekking trail
Railway

Salinas Lake

Volcano
El Misti
(5821m)

Sumbay

Vizcachani

Canahuas

RESERVA
NACIONAL
DE AGUADA
BLANCA

Arequipa

Paucarpata

Sabandia

Callali

Patapampa

Volcano
Chachani
(6075m)

Uchumayo

Sibayo

Chivay

Coporaque

Sallali

Yura

Tacna & Chile

Caylloma

Yanque

Achoma

Maca

Río Colca

Ichupampa

Ampato Glacier
(6318m)

Marcane

Madrigal

Lari

Pinchollo

Lago Mucurca

PAMPA DE SIHUAS

Volcano Sabancaya
(6040m)

Colca Canyon

NATIONAL
CONDOR
SANCTUARY

Orcopampa

Tapay

Cabanaconde

Mirador Cruz
del Condor

Sihuas

Río Sihuas

El Alto

Nasca & Lima

Chachas

Huambo

VALLEY OF THE
VOLCANOS

Andagua

Ayo

Río Capiza

Lluta

PAMPA DE MAJES

Pucalla

Río Majes

Chuquibamba

Apiao

Corire
Punto
Colorado

Toro Muerto
Petroglyphs

Río Ocoña

Cotahuasi

building was bought at auction, then resold to the Goyeneche family, who kept it until 1947 when the estate was sold off; it was restored in the late 1980s by some local architectural enthusiasts.

Chapi

CHAPI, 45km southeast of Arequipa, is easily manageable as a day's excursion. Though less dramatic than the Colca Canyon, the landscape here is still magnificent, surrounded as it is by mining territory but few peaks much over 5000m. Chapi itself is famous for its white church, the **Santuario de la Virgen de Chapi**, set high above the village at the foot of a valley which itself is the source of a natural spring. Thousands of pilgrims come here annually on May 1 to revere the image of the Virgin, a marvellous burst of processions and fiesta fever. There's no hotel, so if you intend to stay overnight you'll need a **tent**, but there are several basic places to eat. Angelitos Negros **buses** leave from Calle San Juan de Dios in Arequipa, for Chapi at 6 and 7am (3hr; $3.50).

El Misti

If you feel compelled to climb **EL MISTI**, 20km northeast of Arequipa, bear in mind that it's considerably further away and higher (5821m) than it looks from Arequipa. That said, it's a perfectly feasible hike, allowing just two days for the ascent with another day to get back down. Buses (marked "Chiguata"; 1hr; $2.50) leave Avenida Sepulveda and will drop you at the trailhead, from where there's a seven- to eight-hour hike to **base camp**. To spend the night here you'll need at the very least food, drink, warm clothing, boots and a good sleeping bag. Your main enemies will be the altitude and the cold night air, and during the day you'll need to wear some kind of hat or sun block as the sunlight is particularly strong. Note that the climate is changeable and that water is scarce. From the base camp it's another breathless seven hours to the summit, with its excellent panoramic **views** across the whole range of accompanying volcanoes. Any of the tour companies listed on p.196 can drop walkers off at a higher starting point than Chiguata, cutting off a few hours of the first day.

Covering some 300,000 hectares of plateau behind El Misti is the **Reserva Nacional de Aguada Blanca**, the largest protected area in this region, located at 4000m above sea level. A cold and dry *puna* (highland Andes, above the treeline), it's home to *vicuñas*, *guanacos* and *viscachas*, while its reservoirs of El Farile and Aguada Blanca are known for their excellent trout fishing.

The road to Chivay and Colca

The road to Chivay and Colca is itself always a fascinating experience, especially the first hour or so climbing high to the Reserva Nacional de Aguada Blanca, where it's usually possible to spot groups of wild *vicuñas* roaming the pampa. At the crossroads where the trails split between the Chivay or Cusco routes and the old road to Juliaca and Puno, it's possible to make out the unusual volcanic ash strata sandwiched into the impressive cliffs on the northwestern horizon. Heading north you'll soon pass the access track down to the **caves of Sumbay** (around $1). To stay at Sumbay you'll have to **camp**, but if you have a vehicle it's easy enough to stop for an hour or so an hour en route, following the signpost (at Km 103 from Arequipa) down a bad track to the village of Sumbay (4532m), about 1.5km away. At this point you'll need to find the guardian of the cave (often just a small shepherd child) who can open the gate for your car to continue another kilometre to a parking area. From the gate it's a ten-minute walk to the caves, down into a small canyon just before the bridge. The guardian will have to unlock another gate to give you access to the site. Although small, the main Sumbay cave contains a series of 8000-year-old rock paintings representing shamans, llamas, deer, pumas and *vicuñas*. The surrounding countryside is amazing in itself: herds of alpacas roam gracefully around the plain looking for *ichu* grass to munch, and vast sculpted rock strata of varying colours mix smoothly together with crudely hewn gullies.

At Vizcachani where there are a few huts and cafés, the main road splits, left for Chivay and straight on, northeast, for Cusco. The Chivay route continues past circular corrals used as breeding stations for *vicuñas* and alpacas. The next major landmark is the region's highest pass at Patapampa (4800m), marked by a landscape of stone piled cairns set against a high Andean landscape. If you get out of the car or bus here, remember to take it easy; breathlessness is natural until you've been a few days at high altitude. The occasional *viscacha* is often seen around this point, darting between the many rocks and boulders that litter the scene. Another rare species, the yapat plant, can also be spotted at this altitude. Green, semi-spherical and looking like a cross between a brain and a broccoli flower, the yapat plant is traditionally used as a cooking fuel, though it is in danger of extinction and so only local peasants are allowed to utilize them. The road then descends via a winding route towards the Colca Canyon. About forty minutes before arriving at the valley floor, the first of the area's fantastic pre-Inca agricultural terraces can be seen, with the town of Chivay nestled among them.

Chivay and around

Surrounded by some of the most impressive and intensive ancient terracing in South America, **CHIVAY**, 163km north of Arequipa and just four hours by bus from there, lies at the heart of fantastic hiking/mountain biking country. It also makes a good base if you want to go whitewater rafting on the Río Colca.

Arriving at Chivay by road, a new tourism checkpoint issues standard, mandatory **Colca Boleto Turisticos** (general tourist tickets), which cost US$12 and offer "free" entry to the Mirador Cruz del Condor, other main *miradors* and all the major churches in the valley.

Buses to and from Arequipa and Cabanaconde (see p.206) all stop at the new bus terminal in Chivay, a ten-minute stroll from the main plaza, where – if you can't find any info in the terminal itself – bus departure times (usually 5–6am) are sometimes displayed. There are three main companies – Reyna (☎054/531143), Andalucia (☎054/445089) and Turismo Milagros (☎054/708090) all of whom travel two or three times daily to Arequipa ($3; 3–4hr) and Cabanaconde.

Tourist information is available from an office on Av Salaverry 106 (variable hours, but generally 2–8pm) and also from Colca Adventures, on the plaza (☎054/531081, ℮rcordova@terra.com.pe), which specializes in bike rental ($12–18 a day), rafting (from $25 half-day) and kayaking (from $40 a day). For **money changing** in Chivay, the fastest option is the shop next door to Turismo Milagros on the plaza; the Banco de la Nación is, of course, on the plaza. **Telephones** are available in the Turismo Milagros office.

Accommodation

Despite the town's periodic problems with water and electricity, Chivay boasts a surprising choice of reasonably comfortable accommodation, as well as a surfeit of atmospheric, thatched-roof lodgings in the immediate vicinity.

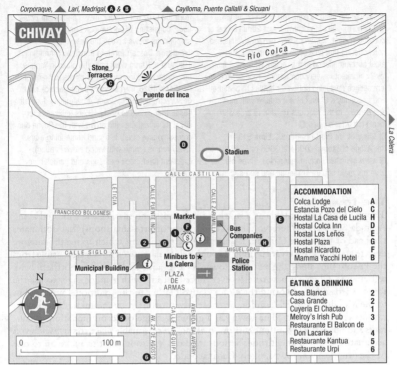

Corporaque, ▲ Lari, Madrigal, Ⓐ & Ⓑ   ▲ Caylloma, Puente Callalli & Sicuani

CHIVAY

Río Colca

Stone Terraces Ⓒ

Puente del Inca

Stadium Ⓓ

CALLE CASTILLA

LETICIA

CALLE PUENTE INCA

CALLE ZARUMILLA

FRANCISCO BOLOGNESI

Market Ⓕ Ⓔ

Bus Companies Ⓗ

CALLE SIGLO XX

MIGUEL GRAU

Minibus to La Calera ★

Municipal Building

Police Station

PLAZA DE ARMAS

N

AV. 22 DE AGOSTO

CALLE AREQUIPA

AVENIDA SALAVERRY

0   100 m

La Calera

ACCOMMODATION

Colca Lodge	A
Estancia Pozo del Cielo	C
Hostal La Casa de Lucila	H
Hostal Colca Inn	D
Hostal Los Leños	E
Hostal Plaza	G
Hostal Ricardito	F
Mamma Yacchi Hotel	B

EATING & DRINKING

Casa Blanca	2
Casa Grande	2
Cuyeria El Chactao	1
Melroy's Irish Pub	3
Restaurante El Balcon de Don Lacarias	4
Restaurante Kantua	5
Restaurante Urpi	6

▼ Arequipa, Yanque & Cabanaconde

In town

Estancia Pozo del Cielo ☎054/531041, ⓦwww .pozodelcielo.com.pe, or in Arequipa ☎054/205838, Ⓕ202606. Sited just over the Puente del Inca from Chivay, next to terraces topped by pre-Inca towers, *Estancia Pozo del Cielo* is the most luxurious option in town. Very nice, if rustic in style with open fire in the reception area, the hotel offers warm, very comfortable rooms, as well as homely service. ⑥–⑧

Hostal la Casa de Lucila C Miguel Grau 131 ☎054/511109, Ⓔviatours@star.com.pe. Reservations can be made in advance in Arequipa at C Jerusalen 302 ☎054/224526. This small but homely house in Chivay within a stone's throw of the plaza. Tastefully decorated rooms – singles to triples – are available, and a continental breakfast is included. The owners also run tours to most of the valley sites. ③–④

Hostal Colca Inn Av Salaverry 307 ☎054/ 531111 or 531088, Ⓔhotelcolcainn@planet .com.pe, ⓦwww.hotelcolcainn.com. Probably the best mid-range hotel in Chivay, clean and modern with private bath, hot water and a decent restaurant. ⑤

Hostal Los Leños C Francisco Bolognesi 906 ☎054/521028 or 286828. Simple, dependably

excellent value and very clean, but no rooms with own shower or toilet. ②–③

Hostal Plaza Plaza de Armas 705. Basic but clean, *Hostal Plaza* is set round a small, attractive and flower-adorned courtyard, itself sometimes used as a – noisy – spillover from the busy restaurant *Casa Blanca*. ②–③

Hostal Ricardito Av Salaverry 121 ☎054/531051, Ⓔricarditos_@hotmail.com. As well as offering decent rooms and fairly permanent hot water, this place also operates a small café – *El Cafeton* – in the same building, with an espresso machine, and there's also the convenience of having Wilfer Internet right next door. ②–③

Outside Chivay

Colca Lodge ☎054/531191, ⓦwww.colca-lodge .com. A few kilometres beyond Corporaque, just before the river bridge back south to the village of Yanque, this luxury lodge has its own thermal-spring swimming pool and offers horseriding as well as mountain biking and short treks or tours to local sites of interest. Part of the big Libertadores hotel chain, it also has great inclusive buffet breakfasts. ⑥–⑧

Mamma Yacchi Hotel Corporaque ☎054/241206, Ⓔreservas@lacasademamayacchi.com, ⓦwww

203

.lacasademamayacchi.com. Out in the countryside on the north side of the canyon, just 20min by car or *combi colectivo*, *Mamma Yacchi* is a lovely thatched hotel offering that little bit extra compared with most accommodation in the region, with great food, lovely architecture, very comfortable rooms, excellent service (including hot-water bottles at bedtime) and frequently a touch of local culture with music and dancing in the spacious restaurant area with local staff after supper. ❻

El Mirador de los Collaguas C Lima 513, in the village of Yanque ☎054/203966 or 521015, ⓦwww.geocities.com/miradorcolca. Three blocks from the main square in Yanque and some 45min

from the Cruz del Condor, this is a pleasant *pousada*, consisting of adobe-look bungalows and with stupendous views across the valley. ❺

Tradición Colca Carretera Principal, C Arentina 108, just a 10min walk from the plaza in Yanque, but contactable in advance by phone in Arequipa ☎054/424926, ⓔreservas@tradicioncolca.com, ⓦwww.tradicioncolca.com. A beautifully decorated hostel that caters to backpackers (discounts for students or visitors who arrive with the Reyna bus company) and offers bike and horseriding tours, lovely rooms (some with wood stove heating), excellent food, book exchange and games room. ❸–❺

The town

Though **Chivay** is notable as a **market** town (with the market itself located along Avenida Salaverry, where you'll also find a slew of artesania shops) that dominates the head of the Colca Canyon, it's not the best place from which to see the canyon, despite an impressive river running through a deep narrow chasm clearly visible from the Puente Inca along the exit road towards Cororaque and the other northern bank settlements. Chivay is nevertheless ever more bustling with gringos eager to use the town as a base for exploring the Colca Canyon either in the traditional way, by bus to the Mirador Cruz del Condor, or, more adventurously, by mountain bike, kayak, raft or serious trekking. The town has a growing range of accommodation, restaurants and bus services for these visitors, making it a reasonable place to stay while you acclimatize to the high altitude. Serious trekkers will soon want to move on to one of the other canyon towns, likely Cabanaconde.

Eating and nightlife

For local **food**, the *Restaurante Kantua* at C Garcilazo de la Vega 510 (☎054/531305), offers the very best of Chivay's Andean cuisine; the *Restaurante El Balcon de Don Lacarias*, at Av 22 de Agosto 102 (☎054/531108), almost fronting the plaza, also offers high-quality dishes, including an Andean buffet, breakfasts and good coffee, and is pleasantly decorated and friendly; the *Casa Blanca*, on the square under *Hostal Plaza*, specializes in local set menus as well as *caldos* and chicken dishes; and the *Casa Grande*, Plaza de Armas 705, dishes up good chicken and chips as well as pizzas, alpaca and vegetarian options; just around the corner at Av Salaverry 107 the *Cuyeria El Chactao* specializes in *cuy*, soups and other local fare. The *Restaurant Urpi*, on Av 22 de Agosta, the main road into Chivay from Arequipa, some three blocks from the plaza, serves great buffets at lunchtimes.

For **nightlife**, just off the plaza on Calle Puente Inca, serves a mean pisco sour; *Restaurante Los Sismos*, by the petrol station on the road in from Arequipa, frequently stages folklore *peñas* as well as serving good alpaca steaks, tasty quinoa and carrot juice, and sometimes even the local cactus drink, *sancayo*; *Melroy's Irish Pub*, opposite the church on the plaza, is popular for its rock music and decent range of cocktails; and *Lobos Pizzeria and Bar* on the plaza (☎054/531081), has a pool table, internet service and a happy hour between 6 and 8pm and is also a contact point for tourist information, though not the official office.

La Calera

Just 5km east of town, slightly further up the Colca Canyon, the road passes mainly through cultivated fields until it reaches the tiny settlement of **LA CALERA**, which boasts one of Chivay's main attractions – a wonderful series of **hot spring pools** (daily 5am–7pm; $4), fed by the bubbling, boiling brooks which emerge from the mountain sides all around at an average natural temperature of 85°C and said to be good for curing arthritis and rheumatism. These thermal baths have been recently renovated, making them the cleanest and best-serviced hot springs in Peru, and a delight not to be missed. There's also a **small museum** (free) on site with models and artefacts demonstrating local customs, such as making an offering to the *pacha mama*, Mother Earth. **Camping** is sometimes permitted by pool 5, but needs to be negotiated with the official at the reception hut on arrival. You can walk there from Chivay in under an hour or take one of the *colectivos* that leave approximately every twenty minutes from the church-side corner of Plaza de Armas in Chivay (50¢).

The Colca Canyon

Claimed to be the deepest canyon in the world at more than 1km from cliff-edge to river bottom, the **COLCA CANYON** may be an impressive sight but is actually some 170m less deep than its more remote rival the Cotahuasi Canyon (see p.212). Colca Canyon was formed by a massive geological fault situated between the two enormous volcanoes of Coropuna (6425m) and Ampato (6318m), with the Río Colca forming part of a gigantic watershed that empties into the Pacific near Camana. Despite being one of Peru's most popular tourist attractions, the Canyon's sharp terraces are still home to more-or-less traditional Indian villages. To the north of Colca, meanwhile sits the majestic Mismi Nevado, a snow-capped peak which belongs to the Chila mountain range, and, according to *National Geographic*, is the official source of the Amazon River.

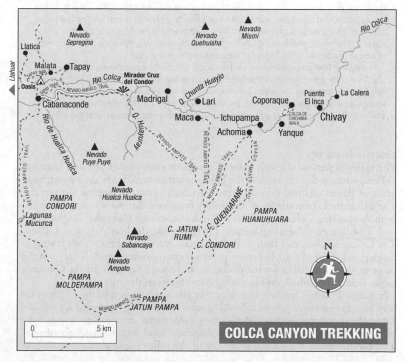

COLCA CANYON TREKKING

There are dozens of **treks** in the Colca Canyon, but if you're planning on descending to the **canyon floor**, even if just for the day, it's best to be fit and prepared for the altitude – it's tough-going and becomes quite dangerous in sections. Guides are recommended, and several tour operators offer this service (see p.196), for which you'll pay from \$40 to over \$100 a day per person. For decent **maps**, contact the South American Explorers' Club in Cusco (see p.266) or Lima (see p.118).

Competition between companies is high, so check out all the options and determine exactly what you're getting – from the quality of your guide (ask to see written reports by travellers who've been with the company and used the same – most tour agents keep a record book of happy customers) to the standard of transport and accommodation, to the quality of equipment used for adventure activities and whether there may be any supplementary charges (for entry to museums and so on). Because of the dangers of mountain sickness, also check whether oxygen is provided – even a bus trip to Chivay can bring on **soroche** if you've only recently arrived from sea level.

Local guides can be found in both Chivay and Cabanaconde (see p.201 and p.208 respectively); enlisting their services directly, rather than going through an agency, can work out significantly less expensive (usually between \$18–35 a day).

Treks from Cabanaconde

A 15-minute walk from the plaza in Cabanaconde takes you past the bullring to the Mirador Achachina, a good spot for seeing condors and viewing the western end of the valley from above. A more classic arrival by foot from Cabanaconde to the top of the Colca Canyon is just ten minutes' walk along a fairly clear track beyond the newly constructed *Casa de Pablo* hostel (❷), itself a five-minute walk from the plaza. The descent from here follows an incredibly steep path, quite dangerous in parts, down to the Oasis (❷), a rustic lodge and camp site right in the bottom of the canyon, below Cabanaconde; it takes one and a half to two hours to descend and four or five to get back up. Many people stay the night, either camping or renting space in one of the huts run by the aforementioned *Casa de Pablo*. Alternatively, there's a growing choice of accommodation in the centre of Cabanaconde (see p.208).

The **Tapay Trail** goes (or returns) via the Oasis. This well-used trekking route connects Cabanaconde with the small settlement of Tapay, a two- to four-day return hike through fine scenery, immense and steep canyons plus tiny hamlets like Cosnirhua (2350m) and Malata as well as various Inca and pre-Inca ruins. Save for the aforementioned camp site – which you'll pass on the first morning – there are no facilities at all in the area.

Some history

The valley is punctuated with some of the finest examples of pre-Inca terracing in Peru, attributed in the main to the Huari cultural era. Massive mountains, huge herds of llamas and traditionally dressed Andean peasants complete the picture. The indigenous communities of this valley form two distinct ethnic groups: the Aymara-speaking **Collaguas**, and the Quechua-speaking **Cabanas**. Traditionally, both groups used different techniques for deforming the heads of their children. The Collaguas elongated them and the Cabanas flattened them – each trying to emulate the shape of their respective principal *apu* (mountain god). Today it is the shape of their hats (taller for the Collaguas and round flat ones for the Cabanas), rather than heads, which mainly distinguishes between the two groups.

Francisco Pizarro's brother, Gonzalo, was given this region in the 1530s as his own private *encomienda* (official colonial Spanish landholding) to exploit for tribute. But in the seventeenth century, the Viceroy Toledo split the area into *corregimientos* that concentrated the previously quite dispersed local populations into villages. This had the effect of a decline in the use of the valley's agricultural terracing, as

An alternative trek is the popular eight-hour hike from Cabanaconde to **Lake Mucurca** (4000m), where the beautiful Ampato volcano is reflected in its crystalline waters. From here, the adventurous, fully acclimatized and well-prepared, can trek along a trail closer to or indeed all the way around (four to six days) the massive and astonishingly beautiful snowcapped mountain peak Ampato. The **Ampato Trail** has one very high pass – around 4850m at the crossing of two trails on Cerro Quenahuane above the Quebrada Condori – and most of the walking is at over 4200m. Local guides are a good idea if you intend to try this trail for the first time; you will need food and camping equipment, and be prepared for snow and ice walking as the weather can change very fast. Starting from Cabanaconde and the Lake Mucurca side, the return down hill can choose to follow trails back to either Achoma, Maca or Cabanaconde.

Colcas de Chichinia

A relatively easy two-hour walk from the village of **Corporaque** takes in the **Colcas de Chichinia**, a semi-intact set of pre-Inca tombs from the Huari. They lie today exposed at the foot of the cliffs on Cerro Yurac Ccacca (also known as Cerro San Antonio).

A path leads out from a block or two just below the plaza, crossing the stream as you leave the settlement behind, and climbing steadily towards a prominent, pink rocky outcrop. The tombs are just below the four-thousand-metre contour line where several overhangs have been partially filled in with stone as permanent thrones for pre-Inca mummies, placed here ceremoniously to spend eternity watching over the valley and gazing east towards several sacred mountain peaks. These days, after the ravages of time and grave-robbers, all that is left of the mummies are skulls and skeletons, some with hair and a few with remnants of the rope and cloth which they were originally wrapped in. To the southwest, the partly tumbled but still impressive **Huari village** can be clearly seen stretching from the tombs down to a major *tambo*-style (Quechua for house or resting-place) building on the bottom corner, which commands views around the valley. Because it's little visited, the path for entry, even to the main, partly fortified **tambo** section, isn't marked and more or less leaves you to find your own route; given this, it's important to take care not to damage the stone walls and agricultural plots you have to find your way through. To get back to Corporaque, you can either drop down to the road and trace this back up to the settlement, or go along the small aqueduct which follows the contour of the hill from the *tambo* back to where you started to climb towards the tombs.

the locals switched to farming the land nearer their new homes. The *corregimientos* created the fourteen main settlements that still exist in the valley today, including Chivay, Yanque, Maca, Cabanaconde, Corporaque, Lari and Madrigal. Most of the towns still boast unusually grand and Baroque-fronted **churches**, underlining the importance of this region's silver mines during the seventeenth and eighteenth centuries. During the Republican era, Colca's importance dwindled substantially and interest in the zone was only rekindled in 1931 when aerial photography revealed the astonishing natural and man-made landscape of this valley – especially its exceptionally elaborate terracing on the northern sides of the mountains which border the Colca Canyon – to the outside world.

The road to the Mirador Cruz del Condor and Cabanaconde

In the mountains to the southwest, dominated by the glaciers of Ampato and Hualca, the volcano Sabancaya can often be seen smoking away in the distance as you travel the 50km or so to the **Mirador Cruz del Condor** and **Caba-**

naconde. From Chivay, the first village the road winds through is **Yanque**, where there's a fine white church, a small archaeology museum, thermal baths down by the river, horseriding facilities, mountain-bike rental and, after **Maca,** some of the area's best-preserved pre-Inca ruins. This town lies right on the fault line and is an extremely high tremor zone whose visible effects can be seen in various land movements, abandoned houses, deep fissures running here and there across fields or through settlements and road re-routings as the route continues on through a very dark tunnel just beyond Maca. Immediately after this tunnel, a number of hanging pre-Inca tombs – *las chullpas colgantes* – are high up in seemingly impossible locations, facing perhaps the best example of agricultural terracing in Peru across the valley.

Mirador Cruz del Condor

As a gateway to **Mirador Cruz del Condor**, the settlement of **Pinchollo** has a **small museum** and a **tourist information** office with photos and a model representing the canyon. Here you can purchase a **tourist ticket** for the Colca area ($12), which covers access to the Mirador Cruz del Condor as well as all the churches in the valley (which don't actually charge). Just a little further down the road, the *mirador* is the most popular point for looking into the depths of the canyon – it's around 1200m deep here – and where you can almost guarantee seeing several condors circling up from the depths against breathtaking scenery (best spotted 7–9am; the earlier you get there the more likely you are to have fewer other spectators around). For safety's sake, however, stand well back from the edge. These days it's a popular spot, and most mornings there will actually be more tourists here than in the Plaza de Armas in Arequipa.

Cabanaconde and around

The bus terminal at the small but growing town of **CABANACONDE** (3300m), 10km on, is a good base from which to descend into the canyon. An impressive high wall and painted gateway mark the town's eighteenth-century cemetery. The town is also home to several semi-destroyed stone buildings and doorways left over from the late colonial (or Viceregal) era. If you can make it for the **Fiesta de la Virgen del Carmen**, usually between 14 and 18 July, you'll see the bullring in full action and the town in the throes of a major religious festival and party. From Cabanaconde the road becomes a little-used dirt track continuing down the valley via Huambo and Sihuas to the coastal Panamerican Highway, where you can catch buses back to Arequipa to complete the circuit. If you're thinking of hitching, be aware that few trucks actually use this route, and it's only recommended in the dry season (June–Sept) for those well prepared with food and camping equipment.

Practicalities

There's a surprising range of **accommodation** in Cabanaconde itself, given that it basically comprises just a few streets. The *Hotel Kuntur Wassi* (T054/812166 or 252989 or for reservations via the Lima office T01/4951639, E kunturwassi @terra.com.pe; ⑤–⑥) is an interesting and very comfortable new place built on the hill, some 80m above the plaza; it has fine views right across the canyon to the Huaro waterfall, and the attractive rooms are laid out in an unusual way, clinging to the hill and incorporating some natural rock features and unusual domed roofs; it also has a restaurant and bar as well as solar-heated water. *Hospedaje Villa Pastor*, (T054/445347 or Lima 01/5672318; ②–③) on the Plaza de Armas, has internet access (rare in Cabanaconde) and comfortable enough rooms. The *Hostal Valle del Fuego* (T054/203737, E hvalledelfuego@hotmail.com; ②–③) is a good backpack-

▲ The Colca Canyon near Cabanaconde

ers' pad and is complemented by the attractive Inca-style restaurant *Rancho del Sol*, while the *Restaurant Rancho del Colca* offers similarly inexpensive lodging for backpackers, mountain bike rental and serves great hot breakfasts.

The **tourist information** office (℡054/280212) is on the main plaza, and although it has very little in the way of printed information to give out, the staff are very friendly and willing to reveal all they know. It's also a good contact point for finding local trekking guides and *arrieros* (men with mules), such as Hugo Barrio Jimenez. Guides for the region generally cost $15–25 a day (one guide for two people) plus $25 for two mules and *arriero*, if required (fifteen to twenty percent more if going over 4000m). The plaza is also where you can find the offices of the four main **bus** companies connecting this settlement with Arequipa and Chivay: Andalucia, Reyna, Turismo Milagros and El Cristo Rey run buses from the Terminal Terrestre in Arequipa daily via Chivay ($3, a 3–4hr trip) and down along the Colca Canyon to Cabanaconde ($4, a 6hr trip); these return from Cabanaconde two or three times a day (morning and night); check the times on or before arrival. Transportes Colca run similar itineraries, as do Turismo Milagros and Andalucia.

Toro Muerto and the Valley of the Volcanoes

It's difficult not to be overwhelmed by the sheer size and isolation of **Toro Muerto** and the **Valley of the Volcanoes**. These two locations, though over 100km apart, are linked by the fact that the rocks on which the Toro Muerto **petroglyphs** are carved were actually spewed out by volcanoes, possibly from as far away as Coropuna or Chachani in the aforementioned valley during the Tertiary period, about fifty million years ago. Both Toro Muerto and the valley can be visited on guided tours from Arequipa (see p.196 for details of tour companies), but many people choose to do one of the most exciting – albeit long and exhausting – trips in southern Peru independently. To combine these two sights by public transport you'll need at least four or five days. Wandering around the petroglyphs takes a day or two; catching the next bus on to the valley will give you another couple of days' camping and hiking. You can return to Arequipa by the same route, or by continuing up the valley and circling back via Caylloma and Chivay, or meeting up with the Arequipa–Cusco/Puno roads high up on the altiplano.

Getting to Toro Muerto

Leaving Arequipa, the bus follows the Lima road to **Sihuas**, a small oasis town where you can see drainage channels cut into the hillside waiting for water to irrigate the desert pampa north of the town. The fertile strip of Sihuas valley is very narrow but recently sprinklers have begun watering the sandy plain above and small sectors are being transformed into farms. This is the first stage of the vast **Majes Project**, which has been working since the early 1980s to irrigate 150,000 acres of the dry pampa, build two hydroelectric power plants and develop a number of new towns.

Just beyond the sprinklers, a few kilometres north of Sihuas, the bus turns off the Panamerican Highway, at a junction marked by an archway over the road and a few restaurants, to head east across stony desert. After around 20km you find yourself driving along the top of a cliff, a sheer drop of almost 1000m separating the road from the Majes Valley below. This striking contortion was created by a fault line running down the earthquake belt that stretches all the way from Ayacucho. Descending along winding asphalt, you can soon see right across the well-irrigated valley floor, the cultivated fields creating a green patchwork against a stark, dusty yellow moonscape. At the bottom, a steel-webbed bridge takes the road across the river to the small village of **Punto Colorado**, dwarfed below a towering and colourful cliff – an ancient river bluff. Stop off at the *Condesuyos* **restaurant** here, on the left just after the bridge, where they serve fresh river crayfish caught locally. It's just 3km from here to the turn-off to the petroglyphs, which is marked by a large sign on the left – "Petroglifos de Torro Muerto", close to the chapel and before the petrol station. From here a track runs almost another 2km to a T-junction by some sandy cliffs; turn right here and continue to the hamlet, keeping left at the electricity pylon. The **entrance to Toro Muerto** is slightly uphill, on the left, where there's a gate-barrier and ticket hut with no fixed hours ($1.50). The petroglyphs are still a stiff kilometre or so uphill along a desert track from here – ask for directions at the entrance.

Toro Muerto practicalities: Corire

The best **place to stay** locally is **CORIRE**, about 2km further down the main road from the signposted turn-off to Toro Muerto – just keep going past past the petrol station. There are a few good **hostels** at Corire and one or two restaurants. The *Hostal El Molino*, Progreso 121 (☎054/472056 or 472002, or in Arequipa 449298; ❷–❸) is an agreeable enough choice as well as a good contact for canoeing or 4WD tours in the valley, or less adventurous visits to the local *pisco*-producing hacienda. The *Hostal Solar*, on the corner of the plaza (❷–❸), features solar-heated hot water and rooms with bath and TV; while *Hostal Willy*, on Avenida Progreso (☎054/472180 or in Arequipa 251711, ⊕257157; ❷), is a very reasonable hostel, most rooms having private bath and a few with TV. There's a *chifa* **restaurant** under *Hostal Willy* and the *Snack-Bar Pollería El Molino* on the plaza is great, with fresh chicken and chips on Sundays. There's also a **Banco de Credito**, at block 1 of 28 de Julio and a **casa de cambio,** on Don Rufo, nearby. There are public **telephones** at Av Progreso 121.

There are fairly regular daily **buses** to Corire from Arequipa. Operating from early morning to early evening, the most regular are with Transportes Zeballos, with others run by TZ Turismo and Del Carpio (see p.196). Returning buses depart from the Plaza de Armas in Corire and, unless full, can be flagged down on the main road at the Toro Muerto turn-off.

The Toro Muerto petroglyphs

The **Toro Muerto petroglyphs** consist of carved boulders strewn over a kilometre or two of hot desert. More than a thousand rocks of all sizes and shapes have been crudely, yet strikingly, engraved with a wide variety of distinct representations. No archaeological remains have been directly associated with these images but it is thought that they date from between 1000 and 1500 years ago; they are largely attributed to the **Wari culture**, though with probable additions during subsequent Chuquibamba and Inca periods of domination in the region. The engravings include images of humans, snakes, llamas, deer, parrots, sun discs and simple geometric motifs. Some of the figures appear to be dancing, others with large round helmets look like spacemen – obvious material for the author Erich Von Däniken's extraterrestrial musings – particularly in view of the high incidence of UFO sightings in this region. Some of the more abstract geometric designs are very similar to those of the Huari culture, which may well have sent an expeditionary force in this direction, across the Andes from their home in the Ayacucho basin, around 800 AD.

There's no very clear route to the **petroglyphs**, which are a good hour's walk from the road, and at least 500m above it. What you're looking for is a vast row of **white rocks**, believed to have been scattered across the sandy desert slopes by a prehistoric volcanic eruption. After crossing through corn, bean and alfalfa fields on the valley floor, you'll see a sandy track running parallel to the road along the foot of the hills. Follow this to the right until you find another track heading up into a large gully towards the mountains. After about 1km – always bearing right on the numerous crisscrossing paths and trying to follow the most well-worn route – you should be able to see the line of white boulders: over three thousand of them in all. The natural setting is almost as magnificent as the petroglyphs themselves, and even if you were to camp here for a couple of weeks it would be difficult to examine every engraved boulder. Unfortunately many have been smashed to make portable souvenirs.

Getting to the Valley of the Volcanoes

Going on to the Valley of the Volcanoes from Toro Muerto, buses and *colectivos* wind uphill for at least another ten hours. After tracing around Mount Coropuna, the second highest Peruvian peak at 6450m, they arrive in the little town of Andagua, at a mere 3450m, which appears at the foot of the valley. Buses continue to Orcopampa, from where you can walk the whole 60km or so down the valley – only for serious hikers wishing to explore the Valley of the Volcanoes and who can stand the heat. Most passengers get off and base themselves at Andagua. The Majes River Lodge (T054/959797731 or 959334957, E jzuniga74@hotmail .com, W www.majesriver.com; 3) offers beds, comfortable rooms with solar hot water, a dining room, outdoor fire, rafting and even shamanic sessions. Local people are also generally very hospitable, often inviting strangers they find camping in the fields to sleep in their houses. Because this is a rarely visited region, where most of the people are pretty well self-sufficient, there are only the most basic of shops – usually set up in homes.

From Andagua, you can get a bus two or three times a week for the six-hour journey to Cotahuasi, or, from Orcopampa, there are infrequent buses and occasional slow trucks that climb up the rough track to **Caylloma**, from where there's a bus service to Chivay and Arequipa; however, it is actually quicker to backtrack to Arequipa via Toro Muerto, on the bus, due to the appalling state of the roads and transport connections. Returning via Caylloma and Chivay, however, rewards with exceptional scenery and the colonial churches of Caylloma.

The Valley of the Volcanoes

Following some 65km of the Río Andagua's course, the Valley skirts along the non-active volcano Coropuna, the highest in Peru (6425m). At first sight just a pleasant Andean valley, the **Valley of the Volcanoes** (Valle de los Volcanoes) is in fact one of the strangest geological formations you're ever likely to see. A stunning lunar landscape, the valley is studded with extinct craters varying in size and height from 200 to 300m. About 200,000 years ago, these small volcanoes erupted when the lava fields were degassed, a result of one of Coropuna's major eruptions.

The main section of the valley is about 65km long; to explore it in any detail you'll need to get **maps** (two adjacent ones are required) from the South American Explorers' Club or the Instituto Geográfico in Lima (see p.118), or from the Instituto de Cultura in Arequipa. As well as a tent – or a sheet of plastic and a good sleeping bag if you're feeling adventurous – you'll need good supplies, especially water and a sunhat; the sun beating down on the black ash can get unbelievably hot at midday.

The best overall view of the valley can be had from Anaro Mountain (4800m), looking southeast towards the Chipchane and Puca Maura cones. The highest of the volcanoes, known as Los Gemelos (The Twins), are about 10km from Andagua. To the south, the Andomarca volcano has a pre-Inca ruined settlement around its base.

Cotahuasi Canyon

First navigated by a Polish expedition in 1981 and declared a Zona de Reserva Turística Nacional in 1988, the magnificent **COTAHUASI CANYON** (Cañon de Cotahuasi), 378km from Arequipa, has since opened up to visits that don't necessarily involve major rafting trips. However, getting to this wild and remote place is even more adventurous and less frequently attempted than the trip to the Valley of the Volcanoes. One of the world's deepest canyons, along with nearby Colca and the Grand Canyon in the US, it runs more or less parallel to the Cordillera de Chila, official source of the Amazon, and boasts some pretty impressive statistics: around 3400m deep and over 100km long.

Arriving from the south along the difficult road from Arequipa (some 375km long) the route passes along the bottom part of the canyon, where the main settlement, **Cotahuasi pueblo**, can be found. It has a variable climate but isn't particularly cold and is rapidly developing a name as an adventure-travel destination. Continuing north to the village of **Alcha** (near to the hot springs of Luicho), the road forks. To the right, it heads into the deeper part of the canyon where you'll find the village of **Pucya** and, further up the valley, heading pretty well northwest you end up at the astonishingly beautiful plateau of Lauripampa, from where you can walk down into the canyon or explore the large natural spread of the massive Puya Raymondi cacti. The left fork continues to the pueblo of **Pampamarca**, where the locals weave lovely woollen blankets. Above the pueblo there is a fabulous trail that leads to the Uscuni waterfalls on one side of the valley and the natural rock formations of the Bosque de Piedras on the other. A little further on you'll find the thermal springs of Josla, an ancient spa that's a joy for tired legs after a long hike.

About 40km from Cotahuasi, the Wari ruins of **Marpa** can be seen straddling both sides of the river, but another hour away is the larger and better-preserved Wari city of **Maucallacta**.

Practicalities

The remote and attractive pueblo of **Cotahuasi** (2684m above sea level), with its quaint narrow streets and a small seventeenth-century church, makes a good base for exploring the canyon, and offers by far the best facilities (try the *Hostal Alcala II*, ☎054/581090; ❷–❸). If you want to stay at Pampamarca, the main alternative, you'll need to take a cooking stove, since there are no cafés or restaurants here, though the six-bedroom *Municipality* (❷) offers very basic **accommodation**. The village of Alcha also has a couple of hotels and a restaurant.

The easiest way to get to Cotahuasi is by taking a **guided tour** from Arequipa (see p.196) who will arrange public or private transportation. Doing it independently, Reyna and Turismo Alex **buses** run the twelve-hour route from Arequipa. Reyna has an office on the plaza in Cotahuasi, at Av Arequipa 201 (☎054/581017).

Puno and Lake Titicaca

An immense region both in terms of its history and the breadth of its magical landscape, the **Titicaca Basin** makes most people feel like they are on top of the world. The skies are vast and the horizons appear to bend away below you. The high altitude (3827m above sea level) means that recent arrivals from the coast have to take it easy for a day or two, though those coming from Cusco will already have acclimatized.

The scattered population of the region is descended from two very ancient Andean ethnic groups or tribes – the **Aymara** and the **Quechua**. The Aymara's Tiahuanaco culture predates the Quechua's Inca civilization by over three hundred years and this region is thought to be the original home for the domestication of a number of very important plants, not least the potato, tomato and the common pepper.

The first Spanish settlement at **Puno** sprang up around a silver mine discovered by the infamous Salcedo brothers in 1657, a camp that forged such a wild and violent reputation that the Lima viceroy moved in with soldiers to crush and finally execute the Salcedos before things got too out of hand. At the same time – in 1668 – the viceroy made Puno the capital of the region, and from then on it became the main port of Lake Titicaca and an important town on the silver trail from **Potosí** in Bolivia. The arrival of the railway, late in the nineteenth century, brought another boost, but today it's a relatively poor, rather grubby sort of town, even by Peruvian standards, and a place that has suffered badly from recent drought and an inability to manage its water resources.

On the edge of the town spreads the vast **Lake Titicaca** – some 8400km of shimmering blue water enclosed by white peaks. Into the lake you find the unusual **Uros floating islands**, basically huge rafts built out of reeds and home to a dwindling and much-abused Indian population. More spectacular by far are two of the populated, fixed islands, **Amantani and Taquile**, where the traditional lifestyle gives visitors a genuine taste of pre-Conquest Andean Peru. Densely populated well before the arrival of the Incas, the lakeside Titicaca region is also home to the curious and ancient tower tombs known locally as **chullpas**: rings of tall, cylindrical stone burial chambers, often standing in battlement-like formations.

The valley down from the **Abra La Raya pass** (4312m), which divides the Titicaca Basin from Cusco, is known as the **Corredor Quechua**, referring to its linguistic predominance, and contains other lesser-visited treasures: around **Ayaveri**, which itself boasts impressive archaeological monuments and thermal baths, there is the **forest of stones at Tinajani**, plus, a further 12km away, a hillside at Tarukani where the **Puyas Raimondi** (see p.373) plants grow up to 12m high. The stepped **pyramid of Pukara**, meanwhile, is one of the region's more ancient stone-built monuments dating from 1000 BC.

The lakeside stretch between Puno and the Bolivian frontier at Desaguaderos is known – also for linguistic reasons – as the **Corredor Aymara**. This sector is full of fascinating but unfortunately slowly decaying colonial relics, particularly the **fine churches** of Chucuito, Acora, Illave, Juli, Pomata and Zepita.

Puno

With a dry, chilly climate – temperatures frequently fall below freezing in the winter nights of July and August – **PUNO** is just a crossroads to most travellers, en route between Cusco and Bolivia or Chile. In some ways this is fair, for it's a breathless place with a burning daytime sun in stark contrast to icy evenings. Yet the town is immensely rich in both living tradition as well as its fascinating pre-Columbian history. The **Pukara culture** emerged here some 3000 years ago leaving behind stone pyramids and carved standing stones, contemporaneous with those of Chavín 1600km further north but still high up in the Andes. The better-known **Tiahuanuco culture** dominated the Titicaca basin between 800 and 1200 AD, leaving in its wake the temple complex of the same name, just over the border in Bolivia, plus widespread cultural and religious influence. The settlement was conquered by the Incas in the fifteenth century and when the Spanish arrived little more than one hundred years later they were soon to discover its wealth – both in terms of tribute-based agriculture and mineral exploitation based on a unique form of slave labour. Even today, Puno's port is a vital staging point for exploring the northern end of Lake Titicaca, with its floating islands and beautiful island communities just a few hours away by boat.

Arrival and information

Buses, **combis** and **cars** arriving from local provincial destinations like Juliaca or along the edge of Lake Titicaca come in at the **Terminal Zonal Terrestre**, Jr Primero de Mayo 703 Simon Bolívar cuadra 9. The main inter-regional and international buses arrive at the **Terminal Departamental e Internacional de Transporte Terrestre**, Av Primero de Mayo at Av Primero de Mayo 703 ⊕051/364733; preferably take a taxi to town from here as its six or seven quite long blocks from Plaza de Armas. At either terminal, ignore anyone who offers you help, unless you have already booked with them (there are thieves operating as touts for hotels or tours). **Colectivos** to and from Juliaca and **Juliaca Airport** (Aeropuerto Manco Capac) tend to leave from Jirón Tacna. If you're coming in from Cusco by train, you'll arrive at the **train station** (⊕051/351041) at Av la Torre 224. Taxis and motorcycle rickshaws leave from immediately outside the

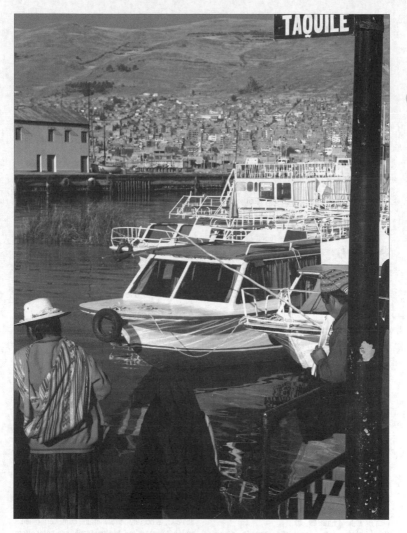

▲ Port, Puno

station and will cost less than $2 to anywhere in the centre of town. The main **port**, used by boats from Bolivia as well as the Uros Islands, Taquile and Amantani, is a fifteen- to twenty-minute walk from the Plaza de Armas, straight up Avenida El Puerto, crossing over Jirón Tacna, then up Jirón Puno.

The Dirección Regional de Industria and Turismo have an office at Jr Ayacucho 682 (Mon–Fri 9am–5pm; ☎051/364976) and can provide leaflets and other information. However, **I-peru Puno** generally offer more useful tourist information from their shopfront on the Plaza de Armas, on the corner of Jirón Lima with Jirón Deustua (daily 8.30am–7.30pm; ☎051/365088, ⓦwww.regionpuno.gob.pe). The **tourist police**, Jr Deustua 538, are very helpful and also give out free maps.

Puno festivals

Famed as the folklore capital of Peru, **Puno** is renowned throughout the Andes for its **music** and **dance**. The best time to experience this wealth of traditional cultural expression is during the first two weeks of February for the **Fiesta de la Candelaria**, a great folklore dance, boasting incredible dancers wearing devilmasks; the festival climaxes on the second Sunday of February; if you're in Puno at this time, it's a good idea to reserve hotels in advance (hotel prices can double). The **Festival de Tinajani,** based around June 27, is set in the bleak altiplano against the backdrop of a huge wind-eroded rock in the Canyon of Tinajani.

Off the beaten trail, it's well worth checking out for its raw Andean music and dance, plus its large sound systems; ask at the tourist offices in Puno or Cusco for details. Just as spectacular, the **Semana Jubilar** (Jubilee Festival) occurs in the first week of November, partly on the Isla Esteves, and celebrates the Spanish founding of the city and the Incas' origins, which legend says are from Lake Titicaca itself. Even if you miss the festivals, you can find a group of musicians playing brilliant and highly evocative music somewhere in the labyrinthine town centre on most nights of the year.

Accommodation

There is no shortage of **accommodation** in Puno for any budget, but most of it is bland compared with Arequipa or Cusco. The town's busy and narrow streets also make places hard to locate, so you may want to make use of a taxi or motorcycle rickshaw.

Central Puno

Hostal Europa Jr Alfonso Ugarte 112 ℡ 051/353026, ℮ hostaleuropa@hotmail.com. Somewhat poorly maintained, but nevertheless offering good rates, this is a very secure hostel with safe luggage store and constant hot water, although few private bathrooms. ③

Hostal Internacional Jr Libertad 161 ℡ 051/352109, ℮ informes@internacionalhostal .com. A modern building with wide corridors and clean, well-kept rooms, themselves carpeted, and with private bath. ④

Hostal Monterrey Jr Lima 441 ℡ 051/351691 or 351632, ℮ monterreytours@hotmail.com. Quiet, central and pretty basic but nevertheless comfortable, this classic backpackers dive offers rooms with or without bath. ④–⑤

Hostal Utama Jr Puno 184 ℡ 051/366418. A new five-storey building just two blocks from the Plaza de Armas, *Utama* is very friendly with good service, while its thirteen rooms each come with private bath. ②–③

Hotel Colon Inn Jr Tacna 290 ℡ 051/351432, ℻ 051/357090, ℮ mail@coloninn .com, ⓦ www.coloninn.com. Converted in *casona* style and very plush, with carpets, private bathrooms and constant hot water. There's also an excellent restaurant/bar and good (albeit non-inclusive) breakfasts; very good value overall. ④–⑤

Hotel Francis Puno Jr Tacna 305 ℡ 051/364228, ⓦ www.francispuno.com. Modern, comfortable and spacious hotel with a restaurant, bar, artesania shop, laundry, safe box, money change, tourist information and luggage deposit. Constant hot water and buffet breakfast included. ⑤–⑥

Hotel Hacienda Jr Deustua 297 ℡/℻ 051/356109 or 365134, ℮ reservas@lahaciendapuno.com, ⓦ www.lahaciendapuno.com. Very stylish, this is the biggest and newest hotel in the city. Hot water, TV, private bath and luggage-storage facilities are among the amenities. ④

West of Jirón Lima

Hostal Vylena Jr Ayacucho 505 ℡/℻ 051/351292, ℮ hostalvylena@hotmail.com. Very clean and quite smart, this friendly family-run hotel offers excellent value, with its own small restaurant and lounge areas. Breakfast included. ③–④

Hotel Balsa Inn Jr Cajamarca 555 ℡ 051/363144 ⓦ www.hotelbalsainn.com. A fine modern hotel conveniently located about one block from the plaza, comprising some twenty well-fitted rooms, most with cable TV, all with private bath and heating. ⑤–⑥

Hotel Helena Jr Ayacucho 609 ℡ 051/352108, ℮ hostelhelenainn@yahoo.es. A very quiet, friendly and clean place that can also help with local tour arrangements. Its best feature would have to be

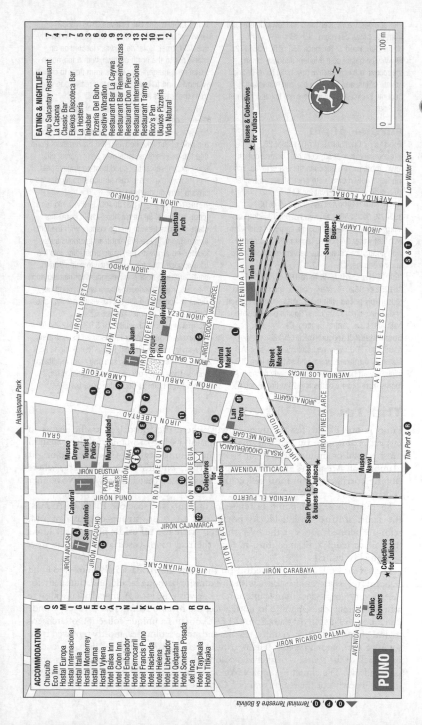

PUNO

ACCOMMODATION
Chucuito	O
Eco Inn	S
Hostal Europa	M
Hostal Internacional	I
Hostal Italia	G
Hostal Monterrey	E
Hostal Utama	H
Hostal Vylena	C
Hotel Balsa Inn	A
Hotel Colon Inn	J
Hotel Embajador	N
Hotel Ferrocarril	L
Hotel Francis Puno	K
Hotel Hacienda	F
Hotel Helena	B
Hotel Libertador	T
Hotel Qelqatani	D
Hotel Sonesta Posada del Inca	R
Hotel Taypikala	Q
Hotel Titikaka	P

EATING & NIGHTLIFE
Apu Salcantay Restauarnt	7
La Casona	4
Classic Bar	1
Ekekos Discoteca Bar	7
La Hostería	5
Inkabar	3
Pizzeria Del Buho	6
Positive Vibration	8
Restaurant Bar La Caywa	9
Restaurant Bar Remembranzas	13
Restaurant Don Piero	3
Restaurant Internacional	13
Restaurant Tamys	12
Rico's Pan	10
Ukukos Pizzeria	11
Vida Natural	2

0   100 m

the fabulous views over town and towards the lake from the breakfast room. **④–⑤**

Hotel Qelqatani Jr Tarapaca 355 ☎051/366172, ⓦwww.qelqatani.com. Modern and very smart, the rooms in this attractive new hotel have TV and private baths, and there's a bar and restaurant. Security is excellent, plus there are fax and internet facilities. **⑦**

Further afield

Eco Inn Av Chulluni 195 ☎051/365525, ⓔecoreservas@speedy.com.pe. Located out of town, more or less opposite the Isla Esteves, Eco Inn has lovely rooms, with great views as well as an astronomical observatory. **⑧**

Hotel Embajador Av Los Incas 289 ☎051/ 352072, ⓕ352562, ⓦwww.hotelembajadorpuno .com. Plenty of modern rooms, carpeted and warm, with hot water 24 hours. There's also a cafeteria with good views over lake, serving excellent *novo andino* cuisine. **④**

Hotel Ferrocarril Av la Torre 185 ☎/ⓕ051/ 351752 or 352011. Very close to the station and reasonably priced with good, old-fashioned service and an excellent restaurant. Rooms have private bath and have central heating. **⑥**

Hostal Italia Jr Teodoro Valcarcel 122 ☎051/367706 ⓦwww.hotelitaliaperu.com. A tastefully furnished, warm and stylish haven, if slightly overpriced and not particularly friendly. All rooms have private baths and 24hr hot water. **⑥**

Hotel Libertador Isla Esteves ☎051/353870, ⓦwww.libertador.com.pe. A renovated and really special former *Hotel de Turistas* located on an island out to the north of town, with a top-notch restaurant, magnificent views from floor to ceiling windows and full spa facilities; a really long way from the fray of Puno's daily life. **⑧**

Hotel Sonesta Posada del Inca Sesqui-centenario 610, Sector Huaje ☎051/36411, ⓦwww.sonesta.com. A very plush hotel bang on the side of the lake between the University of Puno and the Isla Esteves, with over sixty rooms, gift shop, business centre, good heating and carpets. It has its own exclusive train station stop as well as a private jetty on the lake. **⑧**

Hotel Titikaka ☎51/6100400, ⓦwww.inkaterra .com. In typical Inkaterra hotel-chain style, this place does its best to merge visitors with the local environment. There are eighteen luxurious suites located on a private peninsula protruding into the lake opposite the town of Chucuito some 20min south of Puno. Rooms have underfloor heating and the restaurant and lounge have wraparound ter-races to access the site's 270° views across Lake Titicaca. Good internet access. **⑧**

Hotel Taypikala Chucuito ☎051/356042, ⓦwww .taypikala.com. A rather fantastic and stylish New Age-style hotel, built next to the Templo de la Ferti-lidad, with superb rooms, spa and even meditation suites. They also now have the associated *Tay-pikala Lago* hotel at Chucuito, close by. **⑧**

The Town

Puno is one of the few Peruvian towns where the motorized traffic seems to respect pedestrians. Busy as it is, there is less of a sense of manic rush here than in most coastal or mountain cities. It lacks the colonial style of Cusco or the bright glamour of Arequipa's *sillar* stone architecture, but it's a friendly place, where sloping corrugated iron roofs reflect the heavy rains that fall between November and February.

There are three main points of reference in Puno: the spacious **Plaza de Armas**, the **train station** several blocks north, and the vast, strung-out area of old, semi-abandoned docks at the ever-shifting **Titicaca lakeside port**. It all looks impressive from a distance, but, in fact, the real town-based attractions are few and quickly visited.

The seventeenth-century **Catedral** on the Plaza de Armas (daily 7am–noon and 3–6pm; free) is surprisingly large with an exquisite Baroque facade, and, unusually for Peru, a very simple and humble interior, in line with the local Aymara Indians' austere attitude to religion. Opposite its north face, the **Museo Municipal Dreyer**, Conde de Lemos 289 (Mon–Sat 8am–2pm; $1.50), contains a unique collection of archaeo-logical pieces, including ceramics, textiles and stone sculptures, mostly removed from some of the region's *chullpas*. The nearby **Iglesia San Antonio** on Jirón Ayacucho, one block to the south, is smaller and colourfully lit inside by ten stained-glass circu-lar windows. The church's complex iconography, set into six wooden wall niches, is highly evocative of the region's mix of Catholic and Indian beliefs.

Tours around Puno

The streets of Puno are full of touts selling guided tours and trips, but don't be swayed, always go to a respected, established **tour company**, such as one of those listed below. There are four main local tours on offer in Puno, all of which will reward you with views of abundant bird and animal life, immense landscapes and genuine living traditions. The trip to **Sillustani** normally involves a three- or four-hour tour by minibus and costs $5–8 depending on whether or not entrance and guide costs are included. Most other tours involve a combination of visits to the nearby **Uros Floating Islands** (half-day tour; $8–15), **Taquile and the Uros Islands** (full day from $10, or $15 overnight), and **Amantani** (2–5 days from around $10 a day, including transport and food). One company (see Titikayak below) offers kayaking trips on Lake Titicaca itself).

All Ways Travel Jr Tacna 234 ℡/℻051/355552, ✉sales@titicacaperu.com, ⊛www .titicacaperu.com. The most progressive, friendly and helpful of all the tour companies in Puno and the Titicaca region, running most of the usual tours but also offering trips to the wildlife haven of **Anapia**, close to the Bolivian border, where they work with locals on a sustainable tourism project. They have *semi-rapida* ($18) and *rapida* ($42) boats for their full day trips to the Uros and Taquile. This company is involved in social tourism in the Capachica Peninsula and the three islands of Anapia where they help with educational projects in the community (the island of Yuspique can be visited in small sailing boats for its **vicuña** nursery).

Cusi Expeditions Teodoro Valcarcel 164 ℡051/369072 or 051/9590673. A reliable company offering all the usual tours at reasonable prices: Sillustani, Uros, Taquile, Amantani. Also offer trips to Anapia.

Edgar Adventures Jr Lima 328 ℡051/353444, ⊛www.edgaradventures.com. Edgar leads island tours at average prices, but more interestingly they also offer kayaking, horseback trips and visits to Chucuito and the Templo de Fertilidad from about $12 a person, as long as there are four or more in the group.

Leon Tours Jr Libertad 176 ℡051/352771, ✉leontiticaca@terra.com.pe. A highly recommended travel agent representing Transturin in Puno, and specializing in catamaran trips to Bolivia (full day by bus to Copacabana, catamaran to Isla del Sol, then bus to La Paz). They also run tours to Sillustani, Uros, Amantani, Taquile and Tinajani; plus *turismo rustico* with local shaman either on Amantani or near Juli; and offer adventure tourism, mainly in the Cordillera Carabaya (around 5000m), and also down to the rainforest along the Inambari with boats and 4WD vehicles.

Titikayak Jr Bolognesi 334 ℡051/367747, ⊛www.titikayak.com. Kayak tour specialists, with all trips are supported by boats and qualified guides; life-jackets and safety equipment supplied. Most excursions depart from Puno with the options of half- to five-day options.

Zarate Expediciones Aventuras Jr Tacna 246 ℡051/369551 or 354180, ✉zarateexpeditionpuno@hotmail.com. An offshoot of the well-known Zarate family from Arequipa, they offer tours to the Uros, Taquile, Amantani, Sillustani and other lakeside attractions.

High up, overlooking the town and Plaza de Armas, the **Huajsapata Park** sits on a prominent hill, a short but steep climb up Jirón Deustua, turning right into Jirón Llave, left up Jirón Bolognesi, then left again up the Pasaje Contique steps. Often crowded with cuddling couples and young children playing on the natural rockslides, Huajsapata offers stupendous **views** across the bustle of Puno to the serene blue of Titicaca and its unique skyline, while the pointing finger on the large white statue of Manco Capac reaches out towards the lake.

In the northern section of town, at the end of the pedestrianized Jirón Lima, you'll find a busy little plaza called **Parque Pino**, dominated in equal parts by the startlingly blue **Church of San Juan** and the scruffy, insistent shoeshine boys.

Two blocks east from here, towards the lake, you find the **old central market**, which is small and very dirty, with rats and dogs competing for scraps, and beaming Indian women selling an incredible variety of fruits and vegetables. Head from here down Avenida Los Incas, initially between the old rail tracks, to a much more substantial **street market**, whose liveliest day is Saturday.

Moored either down in the port or sometimes out at the Isla Esteves by the *Posada del Inca Hotel*, the nineteenth-century British-built steamship, the **Yavari** (usually Wed–Sun 8am–5pm; for guided tours call ☏051/369329; donation), provides a fascinating insight into maritime life on Lake Titicaca over a hundred years ago and the military and entrepreneurial mindset of Peru in those days. Delivered by boat from England to Arica on the coast, it was designed by James Watt. From Arica it was brought 560km by mule in over 1300 different pieces, having started life as a Peruvian navy gunship complete with bullet-proof windows, but ending up delivering the mail around Lake Titicaca. At times it has used just llama dung as fuel.

Eating, drinking and nightlife

Puno's **restaurant** and **nightlife** scene is fairly busy and revolves mainly around Jirón Lima, but bear in mind that places here shut relatively early – not much happens after 11pm on a weekday. The city's strong tradition as one of the major Andean folklore centres in South America means that you're almost certain to be exposed to at least one live band an evening. Musicians tend to visit the main restaurants in town most evenings from around 9pm, playing a few folk numbers in each, usually featuring music from the altiplano – drums, panpipes, flutes and occasional dancers. The food in Puno is generally nothing to write home about, but the local delicacies of trout and kingfish (*pejerey*) are worth trying and are available in most restaurants. However, the best local fare can be found in small traditional restaurants in the *Huaije* zone, en route to the Isla Esteves; here you'll find various *picanterías*, many with convivial atmospheres and good views.

Nightlife centres around Jirón Lima, a pedestrian precinct where the locals, young and old alike, hang out, parading up and down past the hawkers selling woollen sweaters, craft goods, cigarettes and sweets. Most **bars** are open Monday to Friday 8 to 11pm or midnight, but keep going until 2am at the weekends.

Restaurants and cafés

Apu Salcantay Restauarant Jr Lima 425 ☏051/368295. Offers pizzas and pastas, as well as alpaca and a range of wines, *cuy* and a variety of vegetarian dishes.

La Casona Jr Lima 517. The best restaurant in town, particularly for evening meals, serving excellent *criolla* dishes in an attractive traditional environment. It is also something of a museum, with antique exhibits everywhere, and is very popular with locals.

Inkabar Jr Lima 356 ☏051/368031. A groovy restaurant–bar in the heart of town, serving a wide range of inventive meals, including great alpaca steaks, but catering to all tastes; good value set menus and breakfasts.

Quinta Bolívar Av Simon Bolívar 405, Barrio Bellavista. Quite far from the centre, but worth the trip for its wide range of quality local foods in a traditional setting; the *barrio* is a bit dodgy after dark, so it's advisable to arrive, and depart, with friends and take a taxi.

Restaurant Bar La Caywa Jr Arequipa 410 ☏051/351490. Interestingly decorated eaterie, with photos and artesania from around Peru. The menu itself covers both *novo andino* and international cuisine, and service is good. Open noon to 10pm.

Restaurant Bar Remembranzas Jr Moquegua 200. Open from breakfast until 10pm daily, this place specializes in pizzas, but also serve, alpaca and trout among other delicacies.

Restaurant Don Piero Jr Lima 364. A favourite with travellers and relatively inexpensive, Don Piero has good breakfasts, a fine selection of cakes and a rack of magazines for customer browsing.

Restaurant Internacional Jr Moquegua 201 ☏051/352502 . A classic Puno restaurant, popular with locals for lunch and supper, with a good range of reasonably priced meals; go upstairs for the better atmosphere. Open daily 7am to 10pm.

Restaurant Tamys Jr Moquegua 431 ☏051/363638. Chicken roaster in a well-preserved colonial mansion, where the poet Carlos Oquendo y Amat was born in 1905.

Rico's Pan Jr Moquegua 326. A delightful bakery with fresh goods and coffee. Open daily 5 to 10pm. Closed Sun.

Ukukos Pizzeria Jr Moquegua, block 2. Very nice ambience and varied cuisine, including pizzas, local, *novo andino* and vegetarian. Good service.

Vida Natural Jr Lambayeque 141. Serves probably the best vegetarian food in town including salad, set lunches and yoghurt; although service is sometimes a little slow. Closed Sat.

Bars and nightlife

Classic Bar Jr Tarapaca 330-A ☎051/363596. Well-stocked bar with good service and ambi-

ence, lights and decor, and a variable music policy according to clientele.

Ekekos Discoteca Bar Jr Lima 355, 2nd floor. *Ekekos* offers snacks, drinks, cable TV, books and games; also shows movies and favours a soundtrack of rock, salsa, reggae, trance and techno music. Open daily 5pm–4am.

La Hostería Jr Lima 501. A smart pizzeria and bar, busy in the evenings and a good meeting place.

Pizzeria Del Buho Lima 349 ☎051/363955. A warm, genial environment, crowded with travellers on Puno's cold, dark evenings; serves delicious mulled wines and often has good music.

Positive Vibration Jr Grau 148. A decent bar, trendy and popular with young locals and travellers alike; also serves decent breakfasts and plays rock and reggae music.

Listings

Airlines Lan Peru, Jr Tacna 299 ☎051/367227 in Puno, or Jr San Ramon 125 ☎051/322228, in Juliaca; for Star Peru flights, go to Juliaca office, Jr San Roman 175 ☎051/327478.

Airport Aeropuerto Inca Manco Capac, Juliaca ☎051/328974 or 322905.

Banks and exchange Banco Continental, Jr Lima 400; Banco de la Nación, Ayacucho 215; Banco de Credito, Jr Lima 510 with corner of Grau; and Interbank, Jr Lima 444. *Cambistas* hang out on the corner of Jr Tacna near the central market. There are casas de cambio at Jr Tacna 232 and 255, as well as at Jr Lima 440.

Bus companies From the Terminal Zonal Terrestre, Jr Primero de Mayo 703 Simon Bolívar cuadra 9, buses, *combis* and cars from various companies leave every half an hour at all times of day and night. The companies Copacabana, San Luis, Virgen de Fatima and Porvenir operate cars to llave; for Juli, Empresas Litoral, San Francisco de Borja and Virgen de Fatima also leave from here daily. For Yunguyo, Pomata and Desaguadero there are *combis* hourly. Some *combis* and *couster colectivos* to Juliaca don't leave from the Terminal, but from Jr Tacna (corner with Pasaje Choquehuanca), Av La Torre, near the exit from Puno to Juliaca, Jirón Carabaya, near the Ovalo with Av El Sol. Rossy Tours, Jr Tacna 308 ☎051/366709 and ☎051/9689852, will pick up from hotels for Juliaca airport delivery. The main inter-regional and international buses depart from and arrive at the Terminal Departamental e Internacional de Transporte Terrestre, Av Primero de Mayo at Av Primero de Mayo 703 ☎051/364733. For Cusco, the Inka Express (Empresa de Transportes) Jr Tacna 336 ☎051/365654, ☻www.inkaexpress.com, offers

visits to archaeological attractions en route. Others for Cusco include: CIVA ☎051/365882, Turismo San Luis del Sur ☎051/ 705955; and Cruz del Sur, Av Circunvalacion Este 801 ☎051/322011. For Arequipa/Lima, Alas del Sur ☎051/9660436; Sur-Oriente ☎051/368133; Cruz del Sur ☎051/368524 (tickets delivery ☎363738; Ormeño ☎051/368176; CIAL ☎051/ 367821; and CIVA ☎051/365882. To Desaguadero, Alas del Sur ☎051/9660436; Sagitario ☎051/9676743; CIVA ☎051/365882; and CIAL ☎051/367821. To Tacna direct (many stopping off at Moquegua), Turismo San Martín ☎051/363631; and Expreso Internacional Roel Bus ☎051/369996. To La Paz, Ormeño ☎051/368176 and Panamericano (via Copacabana) ☎051/9676910 or Jr Tacna 245 ☎051/354001. To Puerto Maldonado, only Expreso Sagitario ☎051/9676743 (22hrs) offers a service. Tour Peru, Jr Tacna 282 ☎051/352991 or 368176, run buses to La Paz via Copacabana from outside the Terminal.

Consulate Bolivia, Jr Arequipa 136 ☎051/351251 (Mon–Fri 8.30am–2pm).

Hospital For emergencies call ☎051/352931. Otherwise, try Clinica Los Pinos ☎051/351071, or the Hospital Regional, Av El Sol 1022 ☎051/351020.

Immigration Jr Ayacucho 280 ☎051/357103 or 352801.

Internet facilities *The Café Internet*, Jr Lima 425, offer the best speed and prices; also try TM at corner of Jr Puno with Jr Arequipa, or JM Data, Pasaje Grau 140.

Police The Tourist Police are at Jr Deustua 538 ☎051/353988 and the Policia Nacional's Comisaria can be found at Jr Ramon Castilla 722 ☎051/321591.

Post office Jr Jr Moquegua 269 (Mon–Sat 8am–8pm).

Shopping Mercado Artesanal "Asociación de Artesanos San Jose", C Cahuide, block 3 (daily 8am–7pm); Asociacion de Artesanos "La Cholita", Jr Lima 550, 2nd floor (daily 8am–7pm); Centro de Artesanias "Tucuy Atipac", Jr Lima 339, 2nd floor (daily 8am–7pm); Mercado Artesanal "Asociacion Coriwasi", C Alfonso Ugarte 150 (daily 8am–9pm); Q'orich'aska Artesania, Jr Lima 435 (Sun–Fri 10am–10pm); Ceramica Titikaka (Carlos and Maria), Jr Tarapaca 341 ☎051/363955 for original Andean handmade ceramics (can also see them at work). The unnamed shop at Jr Arbulu 231 sells most traditional Andean musical instruments

(though fairly similar ones can be bought cheaply in the street market, on Av Los Incas).

Taxis ☎051/351616 or 332020.

Telephones and faxes Cabinas Publica de Tele-communicaciones, Jr Lima 439 (daily 7am–10pm).

Theatre The Teatro Municipal, block 1 of Arequipa, has folklore music, dance and other cultural events; for details of what's on, check at the box office.

Train station Peru Rail, Av La Torre, Puno 224 ☎051/351041 or Plaza Bolognesi in Juliaca ☎051/321036, ⊛www.perurail.com. Check at the office or online for special deals plus departure dates and times of the trains for Cusco. It's best to buy your seats at least one or two days in advance.

The Chullpa Tombs of Sillustani

Scattered all around Lake Titicaca you'll find *chullpas*, gargantuan white stone towers up to 10m in height in which the ancient Colla tribe, who dominated the region before the Incas, buried their dead. Some of the most spectacular are at **SILLUSTANI**, set on a little peninsula in Lake Umayo overlooking Titicaca, 30km northwest of Puno. This ancient temple/cemetery consists of a ring of stones more than five hundred years old – some of which have been tumbled by earthquakes or, more recently, by tomb-robbers intent on stealing the rich goods (ceramics, jewellery and a few weapons) buried with important mummies. Two styles predominate at this site: the honeycomb *chullpas* and those whose superb stonework was influenced by the advance of the Inca Empire. The former are set aside from the rest and characterized by large stone slabs around a central core; some of them are carved, but most are simply plastered with white mud and small stones. The later, Inca-type stonework is more complicated and in some cases you can see the elaborate corner jointing typical of Cusco masonry.

The easiest way to get here is on a **guided tour** from Puno (see p.219); alternatively, you can take a **colectivo** from Avenida Tacna most afternoons between 2 and 2.30pm, for under $5. If you want to **camp** overnight at Sillustani (though remember how cold it can be), the site guard will show you where to pitch your tent. It's a magnificent place to wake up, with the morning sun rising over the snowcapped Cordillera Real on the Bolivian side of Titicaca.

Lake Titicaca

An undeniably calming and majestic sight, **LAKE TITICACA** is the world's largest high-altitude body of water, at 284m deep and more than 3200 square miles (or 8300 square kilometres) in area, fifteen times the size of Lake Geneva in Switzerland and higher and slightly bigger than Lake Tahoe in the US. Usually placid and mirror-like, the lake reflects the enormous sky back on itself. All along the horizon, too, the green Andean mountains can be seen raising their ancient backs and heads towards the sun; over on the Bolivian side it's sometimes possible to make out the icecaps of the Cordillera Real mountain chain. A National Reserve since 1978, the lake has over sixty varieties of bird, fourteen species of native fish and eighteen types of amphibian. It's often seen as three separate regions: Lago Mayor, the main, deep part of the lake; Wiñaymarka, the area incorporating various archipelagos that

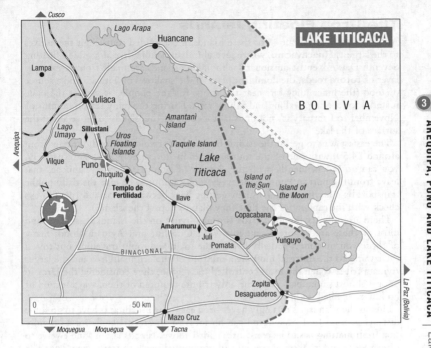

include both Peruvian and Bolivian Titicaca; and the Golfo de Puno, essentially the bay encompassed by the peninsulas of Capachica and Chucuito. The villages that line its shores depend mainly on grazing livestock for their livelihood, since the altitude limits the growth potential of most crops.

Titicaca is where the Quechua Indian language and people merge with the more southerly Aymaras. The curious Inca-built **Chullpa burial tombs of Sillustani** form circles close to the edge of the lake. The man-made **Uros Floating Islands** have been inhabited since their construction centuries ago by Uros Indians retreating from more powerful neighbours like the Incas. Floating platform islands, weird to walk over and even stranger to live on, they are now a major tourist attraction. More powerful and self-determined are the communities who live on the fixed islands of **Taquile** and **Amantani**, often described as the closest one can get to heaven by the few travellers who make it out this far into the lake. There are, in fact, more than seventy islands in the lake, the largest and most sacred being the **Isla del Sol**, an ancient Inca temple site on the Bolivian side of the border which divides the lake's southern shore. Titicaca is an Aymara word meaning "Puma's Rock", which refers to an unusual boulder on the Island of the Sun. The island is best visited from Copacabana in Bolivia, or trips, even arriving by catamaran, can be arranged through one of the tour companies in Puno (see p.219).

Not surprisingly, **fish** are still an important part of the diet of the Titicaca inhabitants, for both the islanders and the ibis and flamingoes which can be seen along the pre-Inca terraced shorelines. The most common fish is a small piranha-like specimen called *carachi*. Trout arrived in the lake, after swimming up the rivers, during the first or second decade of the twentieth century. *Pejerey* (kingfish) established themselves only thirty years ago but have been so successful that there are relatively few trout left. *Pejerey* fishing is an option for tourists.

The Uros Floating Islands

Although there are about 48 of these islands, most guided tours limit themselves to the largest, **Huacavacani**, where several Indian families live alongside a floating Seventh Day Adventist missionary school. The islands are made from layer upon layer of **totora reeds**, the dominant plant in the shallows of Titicaca and a source of food (the inner juicy bits near the roots) for the people, as well as the basic material for roofing, walling and fishing rafts. During the rainy season months of November to February it's not unusual for some of the islands to move about the surface of the lake.

The easiest way to get to the islands is on a short two- to three-hour trip (from around $4.50) with one of the tour agencies in Puno (see p.219). Alternatively, you can go independently with the skipper of one of the many launches that leave from the port in Puno about every thirty minutes, or take the daily public transport boat leaving at 9am, usually getting back between noon and 1pm (always check with the captain for the time they plan to depart the islands).

There are only six hundred **Uros Indians** living on the islands these days, and most of these are a more recent mix with Quechua and Aymara blood; many of those you may meet actually live on the mainland, only travelling out to sell their wares to the tourists; most are a mixture of the original Uros and the larger Aymara tribe. When the Incas controlled the region, they considered the Uros so poor – almost subhuman – that the only tribute required of them was a section of hollow cane filled with lice.

Life on the islands has certainly never been easy: the inhabitants have to go some distance to find fresh water, and the bottoms of the reed islands rot so rapidly that fresh matting has to be constantly added above. Islands last around twelve to fifteen years and it takes two months of communal work to start a new one. The coppery faces of the people literally reflect the relentless strong sunlight bouncing off the surface of the lake almost every day. More than half the islanders have converted to Catholicism, and the largest community is very much dominated by its evangelical school. Thirty years ago the Uros were a proud fishing tribe, in many ways the guardians of Titicaca, but the 1980s, particularly, saw a rapid devastation of their traditional values. Many foreign visitors have been put off by what they experience on landing at the island – sometimes a veritable mobbing by young children speaking a few words of English ("sweets", "money", "what's your name?" and "give it to me"). However, things have improved over recent years and you do still get a glimpse of a very unusual way of life and the opportunity to ride on a *tortora* reed raft.

Taquile and Amantani

Two genuine – non-floating – islands in Titicaca, **Taquile** and **Amantani** are peaceful places that see fewer tourists, both around 25–30km across the water from Puno, just beyond the outer edge of the Gulf of Chucuito. Amantani is the least visited of the two and, consequently, has fewer facilities and costs slightly more to reach by boat.

Daily **boats** for Taquile leave Puno at 8am, returning by around 5.30 or 6pm, while they usually leave for Amantani at 9am, returning between 4 and 4.30pm; as usual, check with the captain for the time they plan to depart the islands. You can go on an organized trip with one of the tour companies listed on p.219, but the agencies use the same boats and charge at least twice the going rate. The sun's rays reflected off the lake can burn even well-tanned skins so it's a good idea to protect your head and shoulders during this voyage. The launches tend to be ageing wooden boats with engines from old North American cars, like the 1962 Dodge which belongs to one of the island captains. Most boats return after lunch the same day, but since this doesn't give you enough time to look around, many visitors prefer to stay a night or two in bed and breakfast **accommodation** (from around $5) in islanders' homes. The only way to guarantee a place to stay is to book in advance through one of Puno's tour agencies (see p.219); if you arrive on spec, you could ask the relevant island authorities or talk to the boat's captain and you may be lucky, but don't bank on it. Sleeping bags and toilet paper are recommended, and fresh fruit and vegetables are appreciated by the host islanders.

Taquile

The island of **TAQUILE** has been inhabited for over ten thousand years, with agriculture being introduced about 4000 BC. Some three thousand years ago it was inhabited by the Pukara culture, who evidently built the first stone terraces here. It was dominated by the Aymara-speaking Tiahuanaco culture until the thirteenth century, when the Incas conquered it and introduced the Quechua language. In 1580, the island was bought by Pedro Gonzalez de Taquile and so came under Spanish influence. During the 1930s it was used as a safe exile/prison for troublesome characters like former president Sanchez Cerro, and it wasn't until 1937 that the residents – the local descendants of the original Indians – regained legal ownership by buying it back.

The **Comunidad Campesina de Taquile** has at least eight operation boats of its own and sells **tickets for rides to the island** directly from the port in Puno (daily, from 7am); although most passengers are locals, tourists are very welcome. Approaching Taquile, perhaps the most attractive of the islands and measuring some 1km by 7km, it looks like a huge ribbed whale, large and bulbous to the east, tapering to its western tail end. The horizontal striations of the island are produced by significant amounts of ancient terracing along Taquile's steep-sided shores. Such terraces are at an even greater premium here in the middle of the lake where soil erosion would otherwise slowly kill the island's largely self-sufficient agricultural economy, of which potatoes, corn, broad beans and the hardy quinoa are the main crops. Without good soil Taquile could become like the main floating islands, depending almost exclusively on tourism for its income.

The island has two main ports: **Puerto Chilcano Doc** (west or Puno side of the island) and **El Otro Puerto** (north side, used mostly by boats of tour agents because it has an easier and equally panoramic access climb). Arriving via Puerto Chilcano Doc, the main heart of the island is reached by some 525 gruelling steps up a steep hill from the small stone harbour; this can easily take an hour of slow walking. When you've recovered your breath, you will eventually appreciate the spectacular view of the southeast of the island where you can see the hilltop ruins of Uray K'ari, built of stone in the Tiahuanaco era around 800 AD; looking to the west you may glimpse the larger, slightly higher ruins of Hanan K'ari. On arrival, before climbing the stairs, you'll be met by a committee of locals who delegate various native families to look after particular travellers – be aware that your family may live in basic conditions and speak no Spanish, let alone English (Quechua being the first language). There are around thirty indigenous Taquileño tourist guides, many who now speak English, so it's not essential to book a visit to Taquile via a travel agent in Puno. The quality can be just as good or even better by **arranging a visit to Taquile directly with the islanders**: first the boat trip from the port and on arrival your accommodation and, if required, guide services. This way you can help keep the economic benefit of tourism in Taquile itself. There is no grid-connected electricity on the island, though there is a solar-powered community loudspeaker and a growing number of individual houses with solar lighting; it's therefore a good idea to take a flashlight, matches and candles.

> ## Taquile culture
>
> Although they grow abundant maize, potatoes, wheat and barley, most of Taquile's population of 1200 people are also weavers and knitters of fine alpaca wool, and are renowned for their excellent cloth. You can still watch the locals drop-spin, a common form of hand-spinning that produces incredibly fine thread for their special cloth. The men sport black woollen trousers fastened with elaborate waistbands woven in pinks, reds and greens, while the women wear beautiful black headscarves, sweaters, dark shawls and up to eight skirts at the same time, trimmed usually with shocking-pink or bright-red tassels and fringes. You can tell if a man is married or single by the colour of his woollen hat, or *chullo*, the former's being all red and the latter's also having white; single men usually weave their own *chullos*. The community authorities or officials wear black sombreros on top off their red *chullos* and they carry a staff of office, a *bastón*.

There are no hotels either, though there are a few small stores that sell artesania, mostly weavings, and a few **places to eat** around the small plaza, notably the *Restaurant San Santiago* (7am–7pm), where fish and chips and honey pancakes are the specialities. The *Restaurant Arenas del Lago* (daily 10am–2.30pm; reservations with Sr Salvador Marca Quispe ☏051/9687624) located two blocks from the plaza, towards the exit for the port, is large, very clean and serves delicious food. Other recommended restaurants, all close to the plaza, include *Flores* and *San Juan*. Elsewhere, there are over twenty restaurants, or eating houses, dotted around the island, most serving the classic local dish of *sopa de quinoa* or *pejerey* fish with French fries.

Amantani

Like nearby Taquile, **AMANTANI**, a basket-weavers' island and the largest on the lake, has managed to retain some degree of cultural isolation and autonomous control over the tourist trade. Of course, tourism has had its effect on the local population, so it's not uncommon to be offered drinks, then charged later, or for the children to sing you songs without being asked, expecting to be paid. The ancient agricultural terraces are excellently maintained, and traditional stone masonry is still practised, as are the old Inca systems of agriculture, labour and ritual trade. The islanders eat mainly vegetables, with meat and fruit being rare commodities, and the women dress in colourful clothes, very distinctly woven. The island is dominated by two small hills: one is the **Temple of Pachamama** (Mother Earth) and the other the **Temple of Pachatata** (Father Earth). Around February 20, the islanders celebrate their main festival with half the 5000-strong population going to one hill, the other half gathering at the other. Following ancient ceremonies, the two halves then gather together to celebrate their origins with traditional and colourful music and dance.

Currently the only available **accommodation** is staying in an islander's house though there are plans to build a hostel. There are no restaurants, but you can buy basic supplies at the artesania trading post in the heart of the island.

Juliaca

There's no particular reason to stop in **JULIACA**, in many ways an uninspiring and geographically very flat settlement, but at the same time it's hard to avoid. This is the first town out of Puno towards Cusco, less than an hour away across a grassy pampa. The wild, flat and relatively barren terrain here makes it easy to imagine a straggling column of Spanish cavalry and foot soldiers followed by a thousand Inca warriors – Almagro's fated expedition to Chile in the 1530s. Today, much as

▲ Locals, Amantani

it always was, the plain is scattered with tiny isolated communities, many of them with conical kilns, self-sufficient even down to kitchenware.

If you come by air to Titicaca, it's Juliaca airport you'll arrive at, even if Puno is your destination. If you're going by road or rail to Cusco from Puno, or anywhere along Lake Titicaca, you have to pass through Juliaca en route. It's less than half an hour by *colectivo* or taxi from Puno, inland from the lakeside, and certainly not an inviting town, looking like a large but down-at-heel, desert-bound work camp. However, there are some good **artesania** stalls and shops on the Plaza Bolognesi, and excellent woollen goods can be purchased extremely cheaply, especially at the **Monday market**. The daily market around the station is worth a browse and sells just about everything – from stuffed iguanas to second-hand bikes.

If you get stranded here and need to sample one of Juliaca's several bland **hotels**, the first choice is the comfortable and safe *Hostal Peru*, San Roman 409 (❷) on

227

the station plaza. If it's full, try the immaculate *Royal Inn Hotel,* San Roman 158 (⊕054/321561; ❺–❼) with heating, carpets, private bathrooms and reasonably good service. Frequent **colectivos** to Puno (45–60min; $2–3) and Lake Titicaca leave from Plaza Bolognesi and from the service station Grifo Los Tres Marias, off Avenida Noriega, two blocks from the plaza. Cruz del Sur **buses** leave from Huancane 443 (⊕054/322011) twice a day for Arequipa and Lima; Empresa San Martin operate from Jr Tumbes 920 to Puno and Moquegua; San Ramon, for Arequipa, are next door at 918 (⊕051/324583). A taxi to Puno will set you back around $12. **Flights** leave daily from the Aeropuerto Manco Capac, 2km north of Juliaca, for Cusco, Arequipa and Lima. Taxis and *colectivos* leave from Plaza Bolognesi for the airport (shouldn't cost more than $5). There's an airport departure tax ($9).

Though rates tend to be better in Puno, you can **change money** with the street dealers on Plaza Bolognesi, with the casa de cambio J.J. Peru on Mariano Nuñez or with the money-changing shops on block 1 of San Martin; alternatively, banks include the Banco de la Nación, Lima 147; Banco Continental, San Ramon 441; and the Banco de Credito, Mariano Nuñez 136.

South to Bolivia

The most popular routes to Bolivia involve overland road travel, crossing the frontier either at **Yunguyo** or at **Desaguadero**. En route to either you'll pass by some of Titicaca's more interesting colonial settlements, each with its own individual style of architecture.

Chucuito to Juli

CHUCUITO, 20km south of Puno, is dwarfed by its intensive hillside terracing and the huge igneous boulders poised behind the brick and adobe houses. Chucuito was once a colonial town and its main plaza retains the **pillory** (*picota*) where the severed heads of executed criminals were displayed. Close to this there's a **sundial**, erected in 1831 to help the local Aymara people regulate to an 8am to 5pm work day. The base is made from stones taken from the Inca **Templo de Fertilidad** – itself located behind the *Hotel Taypikala* (see p.218) – which remains Chucuito's greatest treasure. Inside the temple's main stone walls are around a hundred stone phalluses, row upon row jammed within the temple space, ranged like seats in a theatre. Some of the larger ones may have had particular ritual significance, and locals say that women who have difficulty getting pregnant still come here to pray for help on the giant phalluses. Also on the plaza is the **Iglesia Santo Domingo**, constructed in 1780 and displaying a very poor image of a puma. For **accommo-**

By ferry into Bolivia

Until recently, the best way into Bolivia was undoubtedly on the steamship across Lake Titicaca from Puno to Guaqui. Sadly, the steamer is currently not running, but it's worth checking with the tourist office or at the jetty in Puno's main port for up-to-date information. Expensive, irregular **hydrofoils** from Juli (see p.219) to La Paz (and vice versa) are run along with cultural tours by Crillon Tours in the US (1450 S Bayshore Drive, Suite 85, Miami, FL 33131; ⊕305/358-5353, ⊛www.titicaca.com), also bookable through the tourist office or tour operators in Puno, but you need to book well in advance in all cases. A similarly upmarket **catamaran** service runs on demand; contact Transturin (Av Ayacucho 148 ⊕051/352771, ⊛www.transturin.com) for details.

Crossing the Bolivian border

Yunguyo–Copacabana

The **Yunguyo–Copacabana** crossing is by far the most enjoyable route into Bolivia, though unless you intend staying overnight in Copacabana (or taking the 3hr Puno–Copacabana minibus) you'll need to set out quite early from Puno; the actual **border** (8am–6pm) is a two-kilometre walk from Yunguyo, although there are usually taxis available. The Bolivian passport control, where there's usually a bus for the 10km or so to Copacabana, is a few hundred metres on from the Peruvian border post. The best **hotel** in Yunguyo is *the Hostal Residencial Isabel*, San Francisco 110 (☎014/856084; ❷–❸), which has hot water but only communal bathrooms. You can change money at the Banco de la Nación at Triunfo 219 and 28 de Julio, but there are several **casas de cambio** and street *cambistas* nearby, usually offering better rates and dealing in a greater variety of currencies, though even then you should change only enough to get you to **La Paz**, as the rate is poor. Several **bus companies** run services from Puno over these routes: Empresa Los Angeles has twice-weekly buses to Desaguadero ($2; 3hr); Tour Peru runs daily to Copacabana ($2; also 3hr) and La Paz ($7; 7hr); Altiplano buses also go most days to La Paz ($6); Colectur runs to La Paz via Copacabana daily for around $6; and San Pedro Express runs daily to Yunguyo ($3; 2–3hr), Desaguadero ($3.50; 3hr) and Copacabana ($8; 3hr). From Yunguyo some buses connect with a minibus service to Copacabana, then a Bolivian bus on to La Paz (see Puno Listings, p.221, for addresses and phone numbers of bus companies).

The cheap afternoon **bus** service from Copacabana to La Paz takes you through some of the basin's most exciting scenery. At **Tiquina** you leave the bus briefly to take a passenger **ferry** across the narrowest point of the lake, the bus rejoining you on the other side from its own individual ferry. Once across the lake it's a four- to five-hour haul on to La Paz.

The Desaguadero Crossing

Very little traffic now uses the **Desaguadero Crossing** over the Peru–Bolivia border; it's less interesting than going via Yunguyo, but has the advantage of passing the ruined temple complex of Tiahuanaco in Bolivia. If you do want to travel this route, take one of the early morning **colectivos** (6–9am) from Jr Tacna in Puno to **Desaguadero** ($2; 3–4hr); you'll need to get a stamp in your passport from the Peruvian control by the market and the Bolivian one just across the bridge. If you arrive here by bus, it's a short walk across the border and you can pick up an Ingravi **bus** on to La Paz more or less hourly ($3; 4–5hr), which goes via Tiahuanaco. **Money** can be changed on the bridge approach but the rates are poor, so again buy only as much as you'll need to get you to La Paz. It's not a very friendly town and there's a conspicuous abundance of rubbish on some streets, but there are a few **hotels**, all basic and not particularly clean; the *Hostal San Carlos* is probably the best, with a hot shower option (❷). Similarly, few of the **restaurants** can really be recommended, but the *Pollería El Rico Riko*, close to the border crossing, is not too bad.

From Bolivia to Peru

For anyone **coming into Peru from Bolivia** by either route, the procedure is just as straightforward. One difference worth noting is that when leaving Copacabana, a customs and passport check takes place just before the exit barrier. Now and again Bolivian customs officials take a heavy line and thoroughly search all items of luggage.

dation, try the *Hotel Las Cabañas*, Jr Bolognesi 334 (☎051/351276; ❸), affiliated to Hostelling International where you stay in small huts with constant hot water and a fire for the cool nights. Some 8km beyond Chucuito you pass through the

Aymara settlement of **Plateria**, so named for the coins manufactured here in colonial days, but there's little to stop here for. Similarly, the next village, **Acora**, has a busy Sunday market and is renowned for its fish, but little else. Off the main road, however, about 6km southeast of Acora there are vestiges of the Tiahuanaco culture and the *chullpas* of Molloq'o.

Ilave

About two-thirds of the way between Puno and Juli you pass through the village of **ILAVE**, where a major side road heads off directly down to the coast for Tacna (320km) and Moquegua via (231km). Ilave is quite an important market town and has a large **Sunday market** selling colourful clothing and coca leaves, and also hosts a few shamanic fortune-tellers. The town also has a surprisingly large and modern Terminal Terrestre, where all the **buses** from Puno stop and from where it's possible to catch services to Tacna and Moquegua on the coast. A large Plaza de Armas hosts a statue to Coronel Francisco Bolognesi, hero of the Arica battles between Peru and Chile, while half a block to the south, the ancient and crumbling **Iglesia de San Miguel** has an impressive cupola and belfry. If you want a **place to stay**, the very basic *Hostal Grau*, on the plaza at Jr Dos de Mayo 337 (**❶–❷**), is just about bearable. For **food**, try the *Pollería Ricos Pollo*, Jr Andino 307, towards the market from the plaza.

After crossing the bridge over the Río Ilave, the road cuts 60km across the plain towards Juli, passing by some unusual rock formations scattered across the altiplano of the Titicaca basin, many of which have ritual significance for the local Aymara population. The most important of these is the **Gateway of Amaru Muru**, a doorway-like alcove carved into the rock and said by indigenous mystics to serve as a dimensional link to the ancestors, a belief shared by new agers, who view it as the Andean "star gate", a kind of link to non-Earthly beings and other worlds.

Juli

A few kilometres on from the Amaru Muru rock is the relatively large town of **JULI**, now bypassed by a new road, but nestling attractively between gigantic round-topped and terraced hills. Juli is also known as Pequeña Roma (Little Rome) because of the seven prominent mountains immediately surrounding it, each one of them of spiritual significance to the indigenous inhabitants in terms of earth-magic, healing and fertility. Perhaps because of this, the Jesuits chose Juli as the site for a major mission training centre, which prepared missionaries for trips to the remoter regions of Bolivia and Paraguay. The concept they developed, a form of community evangelization, was at least partly inspired by the Inca organizational system and was extremely influential throughout the seventeenth and eighteenth centuries. The Jesuits' political and religious power is reflected in the almost surreal extravagance of the church architecture.

Fronting the large open plaza is the stone-built parish church of **San Pedro**, marked by its intricately carved Plateresque side altars. Constructed in 1560, it has an impressive cupola, and the cool, serene interior, awash with goldleaf, is home to many superb examples of Cusqueña school artwork. Behind the altar there's a wealth of silver and gold, the woodwork dripping with seashells, fruits and angels. In front of this church you'll often see local shamanic fortune-tellers. Across the plaza from here is the amazing-looking **Casa Zavala** (House of the Inquisition), with its thatched roof and fantastically carved double doors, which is also known as *el carcel* ("the Prison"). Juli's numerous other churches display superb examples of the Indian influence, particularly the huge brick and adobe **Iglesia San Juan**

(Mon–Sat 9am–5pm; $1.50), with its *mestizo* stonework on some of the doors and windows. Cold and musty but with a rather surreal interior, due in part to the play of light through its few high windows, this church was founded in 1775 but is now an excellent **museum of religious art and architecture**, which handsomely rewards the inquisitive visitor. Of the few **hostels** here, try the basic *Hostal Treboles* (❷) on the main plaza, or the *Hostal Municipal* (❷) on the left as you enter the town from the Puno road.

Pomata

Twenty kilometres on lies the historic town of **POMATA**, with its pink granite church of **Santiago Apóstol**, built in 1763. Outside the church, in a prominent location overlooking the lake, is a circular stone construction known as **La Glorieta**; crumbling today, it's still the site where local authorities meet for ceremonial purposes. Pomata's name is derived from the Aymara word for "puma", and you'll see the puma symbol all over the fountain in the Plaza de Armas and outside the church. If you happen to be around the area in October, try to get to Pomata for the **Fiesta de la Virgen de Rosaria** on the first Sunday of the month, a splendid celebration with processions, music and folk dancing, as well the usual drinking and feasting.

Travel details

Buses and colectivos

Arequipa to Cabanaconde (4 daily; 6–8hr); Chivay (8 daily; 4hr); **Cusco** (several daily; 9–12hr); Desaguadero (2 daily; 7–9hr); Lima (10 daily; 14–18hr); Moquegua (4 daily; 3–4hr); Paucarpata (every 30min; 15min); Puno (6 daily; 6hr); Tacna (2–3 daily; 5hr).
Puno to Cusco (8 daily; 6–9hr); Juliaca (3–4 hourly; 30–60min); La Paz via Desaguadero (2 daily; 6–8hr), via Yunguyo (6 daily; 6–8hr); Moquegua (1 daily; 10–12hr); Tacna (3 weekly; 16hr).

Trains

Puno to Cusco (4 weekly; 10–12hr), via Juliaca (1hr 30min) and Sicuani (6hr 30min).

Flights

Arequipa to Cusco (2 daily; 1hr); Juliaca, for Puno (4 weekly; 40min); Lima (3 daily; 1hr).
Juliaca (Puno) to Arequipa (3–5 weekly; 40min); Cusco (5–7 weekly; 40min); Lima (6 weekly; 2hr).

Cusco and around

CHAPTER 4 # Highlights

* **San Blas** Take in the scene of Cusco's vibrant artists' quarter at a table outside the *Muse Bar* overlooking the Plazoleta San Blas. **See p.259**

* **Whitewater rafting** A fast trip down the Vilcanota or Apurimac is one of the most exciting rafting experiences in the world. **See p.263**

* **Pisac** Standing at this Inca citadel offers one of Peru's most amazing panoramas along the Sacred Valley and down onto the beautiful little market town of the same name. **See p.275**

* **Trekking in the footsteps of the Incas** The Inca Trail – a hot spot in danger of being damaged because of its own success – is just one of many breathtaking paths in the Andes around Cusco. **See p.288**

* **Machu Picchu** This most stunning and awe-inspiring of Inca citadels never fails to impress; magically set against spiky, forested mountains and distant glacial summits, it's dwarfed only by the sky. **See p.292**

* **Paucartambo Festival** During the Fiesta de la Virgen del Carmen this quiet town changes into a colourful, haunting display of music and surreal outfits. **See p.309**

▲ Fiesta Virgen del Carmen, Paucartambo

Cusco and around

nown to the Incas as the "navel of the world", **CUSCO** is still an exciting and colourful city, built by the Spanish on the remains of Inca temples and palaces, and as rich in human activity today as it must have been at the height of the empire. Cusco is one of South America's biggest tourist destinations offering a thriving Andean culture, monolithic Inca architecture and treasures from the colonial era, which attract visitors from every corner of the world. In high season between June and September, not just Cusco but all the main attractions in the entire Sacred Valley including, of course, Machu Picchu, literally swarm with visitors from all over the world.

Despite its massive pull, and the sometimes overbearing presence of both tourists and street hawkers, Cusco city and the surrounding sites remain relatively unspoiled. Enclosed between high hills, the heart of the city is the **Plaza de Armas**. From this bustling attractive square, the imposing ceremonial centre and fortress of **Sacsayhuaman** dominates the hillscape. The Inca capital's white-washed streets and red-tiled roofs are home in the 21st century to a rich mix of traditional culture, lively nightlife and a seemingly endless variety of museums, walks and tours. In September 2005, however, Peruvian workers started the second phase of the **Carretera Interoceana**, which by 2011 is planned to connect Cusco and Peru's coastline with Brazil and on to the Atlantic coast. An un-metalled road already covers the route via Puerto Maldonado to the Brazilian frontier, but several major bridges and roadway improvements still need to be completed.

The wider region of Cusco is mainly mountainous, with several peaks over 6000m, and is based around three main cordilleras, or ranges – the **Urubamba** to the north, the **Vilcabamba** to the west and the **Vilcanota** to the east. In the south, equally massive mountains lead to the source of the Amazon at Nevada Mismi, the watershed between Cusco, on the Amazon side, and the Colca Canyon, a major trekking destination close to the city of Arequipa over on the Pacific Ocean side.

Once you've acclimatized – and the altitude here, with the Plaza de Armas in Cusco at 3399m, has to be treated with respect – there are dozens of enticing destinations within easy reach (for more information on acclimatization, see p.242). For most people, the **Sacred Valley** of the Río Urubamba is the obvious first choice, with the citadel of **Machu Picchu** as the ultimate goal. There are also hordes of other Incan ruins – **Pisac** and **Ollantaytambo** in particular – set against glorious Andean panoramas.

The Cusco mountain region boasts some of the country's finest trekking, with the **Inca Trail**, **Salcantay** and **Choquequirao** all within 100km to the

north and **Ausungate** visible on the city's southern horizon. The **Inca Trail** to Machu Picchu is by far the best known and most popular, but alternative trails have been opened or become more popular in recent years because of restrictions placed on the Inca Trail in an effort to conserve it. These new treks all start less than a day's train or bus ride from Cusco. The stunning Inca remains of **Choquequirao**, in the Río Apurimac area, also provide a good alternative archaeological destination with tours leaving from Cusco more or less daily, depending on demand.

Further afield you can explore the lowland **Amazon rainforest** in Madre de Dios, such as the Tambopata and Candamo Reserved Zone, or the slightly nearer Manu Reserved Zone (all covered in Chapter 8), among the most accessible and biodiverse wildernesses on Earth.

Southeast of Cusco lie more Inca and pre-Inca sites at **Tipón** and **Pikillacta**, nearly as spectacular as those in the Sacred Valley yet far less visited, not least because of the lack of local infrastructure for food and travel. Heading south from these, the highly scenic **train journey** to **Puno** and **Lake Titicaca** passes through scenery as dramatic as any in the country. The **best time to visit** Cusco and the surrounding area is during the dry season (May–Sept), when it's warm with clear skies during the day but relatively cold at night. During the wet season (Oct–April) it doesn't rain every day, but when it does, downpours are heavy.

Cusco

Its exclusive access to Machu Picchu makes **CUSCO** one of the most popular destinations in Latin America. Nestling majestically in the belly of a highland valley and fed by two rivers, the city's unique layout was designed by the Incas in the form of a puma. Many of Cusco's finest Inca architectural treasures were so masterfully constructed out of local stone that they are still in great shape today. It may be difficult to get away from other travellers in the old centre yet Cusco's magnificent history and ancient feel – still very much present – will tempt anyone to consider spending much longer here than planned.

Some history

The Cusco Valley and the Incas are synonymous in most people's minds, but the area was populated well before the Incas arrived on the scene and built their empire on the toil and ingenuity of previous peoples. The **Killki**, who dominated the region from around 700–800 AD, while primarily agrarian, also built temple structures from the hard local diorite and andesite stones. Some of these structures still survive, while others were incorporated into later Inca constructions – the sun temple of Koricancha, for example, was built on the foundations of a Killki sun temple.

According to Inca legend, Cusco was founded by **Manco Capac** and his sister Mama Occlo around 1200 AD. Over the next two hundred years the valley was home to the Inca tribe, one of many localized groups then dominating the Peruvian sierra. It wasn't until **Pachacuti** assumed leadership of the Incas in 1438 that Cusco became the centre of an expanding empire and, with the Inca army, took religious and political control of the surrounding valleys and regions. As Pachacuti pushed the frontier of Inca territory outwards, he also masterminded the design of imperial Cusco, canalizing the Saphi and the Tullumayo, two rivers that ran down the valley, and built the centre of the city between them. Cusco's city plan was conceived in the form of a puma, a sacred animal: **Sacsayhuaman**, an important ritual centre and citadel, is the jagged, tooth-packed head; **Pumachupan**, the sacred cat's tail, lies at the junction of the city's two rivers; between these two sites lies **Koricancha**, the **Temple of the Sun**, reproductive centre of the Inca universe, the loins of this sacred beast; the heart of the puma was **Huacapata**, a ceremonial square approximate in both size and position to the present-day **Plaza de Armas,** then going under the slightly different spelling of Aucaypata. Four main roads radiated from the square, one to each corner of the empire.

The overall achievement was remarkable, a planned city without rival, at the centre of a huge empire; and in building their capital the Incas endowed Cusco with some of its finest structures. Stone palaces and houses lined streets which ran straight and narrow, with water channels to drain off the heavy rains. So solidly built, much of ancient Cusco is still visible today, particularly in the stone walls of what were once palaces and temples.

In 1532, when the Spanish arrived in Peru, Cusco was a thriving city, and capital of one of the world's biggest empires. The Spaniards were astonished: the city's beauty surpassed anything they had seen before in the New World; the stonework was better than any in Spain; and precious metals, used in a sacred context across

Fiestas in the Cusco region

As the imperial capital during Inca times, Cusco was the most important place of pilgrimage in South America, a status it retains today. During Easter, June and Christmas, the city centre becomes the focus for relentless **fiestas and carnivals** celebrated by extravagant processions bringing together a vibrant blend of pagan pre-Columbian and Catholic colonial cultures. The throngs of tourists coming and going from Cusco often fill every plane, bus and train in and out of the city, so it's important to book onward tickets a few days in advance.

Around Jan 20 Adoración de los Reyes (Adoration of the Kings). Ornate and elaborate processions leave from San Blas church and parade through Cusco.

Last week of Jan Pera Chapch'y (Festival of the Pear). A harvest festival in San Sebastian, 4km southeast of Cusco, with lively street stalls and processions.

Feb Festividad Carnavales. Folk dancing and traditional food in the streets of Coya, Pisac and Calca; each village celebrates in a different week of the month (check with the tourist office, see p.243).

First week of March Festival de Durasno (Festival of the Peach). Food stalls and folk dancing in Yanahuara and Urubamba.

Easter Week Semana Santa. On Easter Monday there's a particularly splendid procession through Cusco, with a rich and evocative mix of Indian and Catholic iconography. The following Thursday a second procession celebrates the city's patron saint, El Señor de los Temblores (Lord of Earthquakes), and on Easter Friday, street stalls sell many different traditional dishes.

May 2–3 Cruz Velacuy, or Fiesta de las Cruces (Festival of the Cross). All church and sanctuary crosses in Cusco and the provinces are veiled for a day, followed by traditional festivities with dancing and feasting in most communities. Particularly splendid in Ollantaytambo.

Weekend before Corpus Christi Qoyllur Rit'i (Snow Star, or ice festival). Held on the full-moon weekend prior to Corpus Christi in an isolated valley above the road from Cusco via Urcos and Ocungate to the Amazon town of Puerto Maldonado. The festival site lies at the foot of a glacier, Itself considered an *apu*, or mountain god. Close by, and visible during the climb to this festival, is another sacred mountain and snowcapped peak – Ausangate. This is one of the most exciting festivals in the Americas with constant live music that continues for days, several processions and bands and dancers from various communities who make an annual pilgrimage to recharge spiritually at a time when the mountain is said to be blossoming in a metaphysical rather than botanical sense. You'll need to camp, although at around 4600m,

the city, were in abundance throughout Koricancha. They lost no time in plundering its fantastic wealth. **Atahualpa,** the emperor at the time, was captured by Spanish Conquistadors in Cajamarca while en route to Cusco, returning from bloody battles in the northern extremity of the empire. Hearing from the Emperor Atahualpa himself of Cusco's great wealth as the centre of Inca religious and political power, **Francisco Pizarro** reached the native capital on November 15, 1533. The Spanish city was officially founded on March 23, 1534: keeping the same name as it had under the Incas, Cusco was divided up among 88 of Pizarro's men who chose to remain there as settlers. **Manco Inca**, a blood relative of Atahualpa (who was murdered by Pizarro, see p.562), was set up as a puppet ruler, governing from a new palace on the hill just below Sacsayhuaman. After Pizarro's departure, and following twelve months of power struggles, his sons Juan and Gonzalo came out on top and were then free to abuse Manco and his subjects, which eventually provoked the Incas to open resistance. In April 1536 Manco fled to Yucay, in the Sacred Valley, to gather forces for the **Great Rebellion**.

in freezing conditions at the foot of a glacier, it's only for the adventurous; some tour operators do go there, but it's primarily a Quechua Indian festival, with villagers arriving in the thousands in the weeks running up to it.

Corpus Christi (annually, exactly nine weeks after Easter) In this festival, imposed by the Spanish to replace the Inca tradition of parading ancestral mummies, a procession of saints' effigies are carried through the streets of Cusco, even as the local *mayordomos* (ritual community leaders) throw parties and feasts combining elements of religiosity with outright hedonism. The effigies are then left inside the Cathedral for eight days, after which they are taken back to their respective churches, accompanied by musicians, dancers and exploding firecrackers.

Second week of June Cusqueña International Beer and Music Festival. Lively, week-long festival in Cusco, hosting fairly big Latin pop and jazz names, at its best from Thursday to Sunday.

June 16–22 Traditional folk festivals in Raqchi and Sicuani.

June 20–30 Fiesta de Huancaro. An agricultural show packed with locals and good fun, based in the Huancaro sector of Cusco ($1 taxi ride from Plaza de Armas, or go down Avenida Sol and turn right at the roundabout before the airport).

Last week in June Cusco Carnival, or Cusco Week. Daily processions in the Plaza de Armas by army, school and civil defence groups and folk dancers, plus lively music on the streets throughout the day and night, peaking with Inti Raymi.

June 24 Inti Raymi. Popular, commercial fiesta re-enacting the Inca Festival of the Sun in the grounds of Sacsayhuaman.

July 15–17 Virgen del Carmen. Dance and music festival celebrated all over the highlands, but at its best in Paucartambo.

July 28 Peruvian Independence Day. Festivities nationwide, not least in Cusco.

Sept 14–18 Señor de Huanca. Music, dancing, pilgrimages and processions take place all over the region but especially lively in Calca, with a fair in the Sacred Valley.

Sept 25 to early Oct Semana Turistica (Tourist Week). Conferences and street processions in Cusco, but obviously, rather touristy.

First week of Dec Yawar Fiesta. A vibrant, uncommercial *corrida de toros* (bullfight) at the end of the week in Paruro, Cotabambas and Chumbivilcas. A condor, captured by hand, is tied to the back of a bull that battles to the death.

Dec 24 Santuranticuy. Traditional fair of artesania, including handmade, wooden toys in Cusco.

Within days, the two hundred Spanish defenders, with only eighty horses, were surrounded in Cusco by over 100,000 rebel Inca warriors. On May 6, Manco's men laid siege to the city. After a week, a few hundred mounted Spanish soldiers launched a desperate counterattack on the Inca base in Sacsayhuaman and, incredibly, defeated the native stronghold, putting some 1500 warriors to the sword as they took it.

Spanish-controlled Cusco never again came under such serious threat from its indigenous population, but its battles were far from over. By the end of the rains the following year, a rival conquistador, Almagro, had seized Cusco for himself until Francisco Pizarro defeated the rebel Spanish troops a few months later, and had Almagro garroted in the main plaza. Around the same time, a diehard group of rebel Incas held out in Vilcabamba until 1572, when the Spanish colonial viceroy, Toledo, captured the leader **Tupac Aymaru** and had him beheaded in the Plaza de Armas.

From then on the city was left in relative peace, ravaged only by the great earthquake of 1650. After this dramatic tremor, remarkably illustrated on a huge

▲ A & Sacsayhuaman Fortress ruins

CUSCO

0   100 m

B TANDAPATA · C

E
F
G

San Cristobal

CALLE SAPHI

K

N

Museo de Arte Precolombino

Balcon de Cusco

Museo Inka

Catedral

Santa Teresa

Contemporary Art Museum

La Compañia de Jesus

Natural History Museum

Museo Historico Regional

Iglesia y Convento de la Merced

Museo & Convento de San Francisco

Santa Clara

Artesan Market

San Pedro

Central Market

San Pedro Train Station

PLAZA DE ARMAS

PLAZA SAN FRANCISCO

AVENIDA DEL EJERCITO

3 CRUCES DE ORO

ACCOMMODATION

Amaru Hostal	L
Casa de Campo	B
La Casa de la Gringa	D
Casa Real	R
Colonial Palace Hostal	ee
El Dorado	dd
Gran Hostal Machu Picchu	ee
Hacienda Hotel Incatarnbo	A
Hospedaje El Arcano	F
Hospedaje Familiar Casa Grande	X
Hospedaje Turistico San Blas	O
Hostal Caceres	T
Hostal Colonial	gg
Hostal Emperador Plaza	U
Hostal Familiar	M
Hostal El Grial	G
Hostal Huaynapata	J
Hostal Inti Quilla	E
Hostal Mirador de la Nusta	I
Hostal Rojas	Q
Hostal Rumi Punku	H
Hostal Tumi	Y
Hotel Cahuide	K
Hotel Libertador	bb
Hotel Marqueses	cc
Hotel Monasterio	N
Hotel Picoaga	W
Hotel El Rosal – Hogar El San Pedro	hh
Hotel Royal Inca I	aa
Hotel Ruinas	S
Inkaterra la Casona Cusco	P
Loki Hostel	V
Pakcha Real Hostal Familiar	C
Plaza de Armas Hostal	Z
The Point Hostel	ff

canvas in La Catedral de Cusco, **Bishop Mollinedo** was largely responsible for the reconstruction of the city, and his influence is also closely associated with Cusco's most creative years of art. The **Cusqueña school** (see box, p.250), which emerged from his patronage, flourished for the next two hundred years, and much of its finer work, produced by native Quechua and *mestizo* artists such as Diego Quispe Tito, Juan Espinosa de los Monteros, Fabian Ruiz and Antonio Sinchi Roca, is exhibited in museums and churches around the city.

In spite of this cultural heritage, Cusco only received international attention after the discovery of Machu Picchu by **Hiram Bingham's** archaeological expedition of discovery in 1911. With the advent of air travel and global tourism, Cusco has been slowly transformed from a quiet colonial city in the remote Andes into a busy tourist centre with scores of decent hotels, restaurants and shops retailing local peasant craft and also some fine jewellery, much of this replicating Inca style and design.

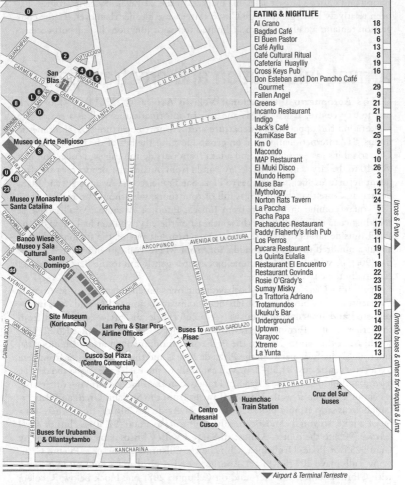

Urcos & Puno ▶

Ormeño buses & others for Arequipa & Lima ▶

EATING & NIGHTLIFE

Al Grano	18
Bagdad Café	13
El Buen Pastor	6
Café Ayllu	13
Café Cultural Ritual	8
Cafetería Huaylliy	19
Cross Keys Pub	16
Don Esteban and Don Pancho Café Gourmet	29
Fallen Angel	9
Greens	21
Incanto Restaurant	21
Indigo	R
Jack's Café	9
KamiKase Bar	25
Km 0	2
Macondo	6
MAP Restaurant	10
El Muki Disco	26
Mundo Hemp	3
Muse Bar	4
Mythology	12
Norton Rats Tavern	24
La Paccha	5
Pacha Papa	7
Pachacutec Restaurant	17
Paddy Flaherty's Irish Pub	16
Los Perros	11
Pucara Restaurant	19
La Quinta Eulalia	1
Restaurant El Encuentro	18
Restaurant Govinda	22
Rosie O'Grady's	23
Sumay Misky	15
La Trattoria Adriano	28
Trotamundos	27
Ukuku's Bar	15
Underground	14
Uptown	20
Varayoc	22
Xtreme	12
La Yunta	13

▼ Airport & Terminal Terrestre

Declared internationally as American Capital of Culture in 2007, Cusco possesses an identity above and beyond its architectural and archaeological legacy. Like its renowned art, Cusco is dark yet vibrant with colour: one minute you're walking down a high, narrow, stone-walled alley listening to the soft moans of a blind old busker, then suddenly you burst onto a plaza full of brightly dressed dancers from the countryside, joining in what, at times, seems like the endless carnival and religious festival celebrations which Cusco is famous for. It's a politically active, left-of-centre city where street demonstrations organized by teachers, lecturers, miners or some other beleaguered profession are commonplace. The leading light of Cusco's left, in the early 1990s, mayor **Daniel Estrada**, with the help of local architect **Guido Gallegos**, contributed to the city's legacy with elegant Inca-like modern fountains and statues, such as the Condor and Pachacutec monuments and the new plaza in San Blas. Since then a huge, largely concrete and circular sundisc monument has been erected on the lower part of Avenida Sol, near Huanchac station and Cusco's largest artesania market. In the 21st century civic progress has been relatively lethargic, though Cusco's streets are cleaner than ever. Traffic congestion remains a daily problem, if limited to major junctions like airport access.

Arrival, information and city transport

Cusco's **Aeropuerto Internacional Velasso Astete** (☏222611) is 4km south of the city centre. It has ATMs and tourist information as well as a reasonable cafeteria on the upper storey departure area. Airport departure tax ($5 domestic flights, $12 international) is paid on ground level to the left of the check-in desks. On arrival it's easy enough to find a taxi from outside the baggage collection hall ($5–10 to the city centre) or a *colectivo* combi from outside the airport car park (frequent departures 90¢), which goes to Plaza San Francisco via Avenida Sol and Plaza de Armas. Note that the airport is full of tour touts, who should be avoided.

If you're coming in by train from Juliaca, Puno or Arequipa, you'll arrive at the Huanchac **train station** in the southeast of the city; you can hail a taxi on the street outside (around $1 to the centre), or turn left out of the station and walk about a hundred metres to Avenida Sol, from where you can either catch a *colectivo* (90¢), or walk the eight or nine blocks up a gentle hill to the Plaza de Armas, essentially the city centre.

Apart from Cruz del Sur, who have their own independent depot at Avenida Pachacutec, a few blocks east of Huanchac railway station and Avenida Sol, **interregional and international buses** (see p.266 for details) arrive and depart from the rather scruffy Terminal Terrestre at Av Vallegos Santoni, block 2 (☏224471) southeast of the centre, close to the Pachacutec monument and roundabout (*ovalo*) and roughly halfway between the Plaza de Armas and the airport. Taxis from here to the city centre cost $1.50–3, or you can walk to the Pachacutec *ovalo* and catch a *colectivo* uphill to either the Plaza San Francisco or the Plaza de Armas – otherwise, it's about a half-hour walk. **Regional buses** from the Sicuani, Urcos and Paucartambo areas stop around blocks 15 and 16 of Av de la Cultura, from where it's a bit of a hike, so you'll almost certainly want to take a taxi ($1.50–3), bus or *combi colectivo* (90¢) to the centre. Almost all **Sacred Valley buses** come and go from Av Grau 525 (for Pisac, Urubamba, Chincheros, Ollantaytambo), near Puente Grau, or Av Tullumayo 207 (for Pisac). Another stop for Urubamba and Calca via Pisac, with Clorinda buses, can be found on C Puputi 208, one block below Recoleta and two blocks up from Avenida La Cultura at the junction with Ejercicios, just beyond the Estadio Univeritario.

Mountain sickness

Soroche, or **mountain sickness**, is a reality for most people arriving in Cusco by plane from sea level and needs to be treated with respect. It's vital to take it easy, not eating or drinking much on arrival, even sleeping a whole day just to assist acclimatization (coca tea is a good local remedy). After three days at this height most people have adjusted sufficiently to tackle moderate hikes at similar or lesser altitudes. Anyone considering tackling the major mountains around Cusco will need time to adjust again to their higher base camps. If you do encounter altitude-related health problems, CIMA at Av Pardo 978 (☏ 255550, ⓦ www.cimaperu.com) specializes in high altitude health. For more information on *soroche* see p.39.

To get up to Sacsayhuaman without the breathtaking experience of walking up there before you've really acclimatized to the altitude, take the **Tranvia Cusco** wooden bus (℡224377 or 740640; $2.50 or less, small children, free) which takes a scenic ride through the historic centre up to Sacsayhuaman and back most days; it's usually found parked outside the *Hostal Familiar* on Calle Saphi, but generally leaves from the Plaza de Armas (Mon–Sat 10am, 11.30am, 2pm, 3.30pm & 5pm).

Information

The main **tourist office**, operated by the Dirección Regional de Industria y Turismo (DRIT) at Portal de Mantas 117–A (Mon–Fri 8am–7pm, Sat 8am–2pm; ℡222032), is a short block from the Plaza de Armas, with information kiosks at the airport (daily 6.30am–4.30pm) and the Terminal Terrestre (Mon–Fri 7am–6.30pm, Sat 7–11am). Another small municipal tourist-information kiosk is sometimes open in the pedestrian area outside San Pedro market.

The main office is well-staffed, spacious and offers a friendly service with sound advice on where to go and how to get there, as well as maps and brochures. Some tourist information is also provided by **i-Peru Tourist Assistance** from their office at Room 203, Av Sol 103 (daily 9am–7pm; ℡252974, 𝔽234498, ℮iperucusco @promperu.gob.pe), as well as from a booth at the airport (daily 6.30am–4.30pm, sometimes later; ℡237364).

Other sources are tour agencies around the Plaza de Armas or along calles Plateros and Procuradores, running uphill from the plaza. They provide leaflets promoting their own tours, but many also offer customized generic plans of the city and simple maps of the Sacred Valley and nearby regions. The Cuscoperu website is a good source of information about Cusco: Ⓦwww.cuscoperu.com.

City transport

Cusco's centre is small enough to **walk** around. **Taxis** can be waved down on any street, particularly on the Plaza de Armas, Avenida Sol and around the market end of Plaza San Francisco; rides within Cusco cost just over $1 and are $2–5 for trips to the suburbs, $10 or more up to Sacsayhuaman and Quenko (some *taxistas* may prefer to do a round-trip, charging double but waiting there for you; in this case give them half in advance and the remainder at the end of the journey). The city **bus** network is incredibly difficult to fathom, though it's cheap, fast and has several networks extending across the entire city. Largely

---

Cusco Tourist Ticket (Boleto Turistico General – Cusco)

The **Cusco Tourist Ticket** ($47 for ten days, students $25) is a vital purchase for most visitors. It's the only way to get into many of the city's and region's main attractions, and covers some sixteen destinations including the archaeological sites of the Sacred Valley (Pisca and Ollantaytambo) as well as Sacsayhuaman, Qenko, Tambo Machay Puca Pucara, Chinchero, Moray and Tipon. The ticket also affords free entry to the Museo de Arte Popular, Museo Historico Regional and the municipal Museo de Arte Contemporaneo, and comes with useful maps and other information, including opening times. It does not, however, give entry to the Cathedral, or Koricancha main temple site.

In theory, it's available from all of the sites included In the ticket, but in practice it's best to buy from the Tourist Information office on Calle Mantas or the i-Peru office at Avenida Sol 103 (Galerias Turisticas, Room 203; ℡227037).

unregulated, the buses are mainly minibuses chalking up their destinations in the front windscreens. Most useful are the **buses and colectivos** that run up and down Avenida Sol every couple of minutes during daylight hours, stopping at street corners if they have any seats left; these charge a flat fare (about 50¢) and can be hailed on virtually any corner along the route.

Accommodation

While there are relatively inexpensive and reasonable mid-range hostels and hotels in most corners of the city, Cusco's **accommodation** is centred in three main zones: east, west and south of the Plaza de Armas. To the **west of the Plaza** along calles Plateros, Procuradores and Saphi (Procuradores and Plateros are particularly noisy at night) there are plenty of busy budget hostels. You can find slightly pricier and more luxurious locations in the area **east of the Plaza** around San Blas and Choquechaca in the artists' quarter.

To the **south of the Plaza**, the San Pedro region around the Central Market and near to the train station for Machu Picchu has improved its facilities in recent years, now offering comfortable and safe accommodation. Closer to the plaza, along Calle Quera and around Avenida Sol, more and varied accommodation can be found.

Architecturally, Cusco also offers a variety of styles to choose from, ranging mainly between Inca- and colonial-style constructions, or combinations of the two.

West of Plaza de Armas

Casa Real Tecsecocha 2 ☎226221, ⓦwww .casarealhoteles.com. Based around a small colonial courtyard, this lovely refurbished hostal is right at the heart of the action. Rooms are small but the beds are really comfortable and the showers hot, and they're available with or without baths and TVs. ❷–❹

Hostal Caceres C Plateros 368 ☎232616. A popular travellers' hangout, half a block from the Plaza de Armas. It has a courtyard and is within a stone's throw of most of Cusco's best bars and cafés. Rooms are simple and unpretentious, many being shared dorms (cheapest dorm bed priced at $5). Some rooms have hot water. ❶–❸

🏃 **Hostal Familiar** C Saphi 661 ☎239353. This quiet and almost homely hostel is one of Cusco's best budget options (it's wise to reserve in advance). Rooms are spartan and can be chilly at night, though the hotel supplies plenty of blankets. There's usually hot water in the mornings and rooms are available with or without private bath (in which case showers are for use by all). Good breakfasts are served in the café, plus there's a free safety deposit box, a cheap left-luggage system and a laundry service. ❷–❹

Hostal Rojas C Tigre 129 ☎228184. Located very centrally in a congenial old mansion with many rooms based around a lovely courtyard. Spaces are large, safe, airy and clean. ❷–❹

Hostal Tumi Siete Cuartones 245 ☎244413. Just off Plateros and a little way up from Iglesia Santa Teresa, this place is popular with young travellers, has a spacious courtyard, plain bedrooms, shared bathrooms, access to a kitchen and a useful notice board. ❷

Hotel Cahuide C Saphi 845 ☎222771, ⓦwww .hotelcahuide-cusco.com. Located a few blocks uphill from the Plaza de Armas, this is a nice place to stay with clean, modern rooms and a useful message board. A bit pricey but better value in low season. ❻–❼

Hotel Marqueses C Garcilaso 256 ☎257819, Ⓕ257819. A splendid and sumptuous hotel now under new management, in an ornate colonial-style building with fine period furnishings. Safe boxes and laundry are available. ❺–❼

Hotel Picoaga Santa Teresa 334 ☎227691, Ⓕ221246, Ⓔreservas@picoagahotel.com.pe; in Lima ☎01/242 8488, Ⓕ444 3181. A first-class hotel in one of Cusco's finest colonial mansions, close to the heart of the city. Service is excellent, and the hotel also has a bar and quality restaurant. ❽

Hotel El Rosal – Hogar El San Pedro C Cascaparo 116, next to the Machu Picchu train station, San Pedro ☎257536, Ⓕ227849. A newish hotel, very clean and with all modern conveniences including private bath, cable TV, heating and a cafeteria. ⑤

Hotel Royal Inca I Plaza Regocijo 299 ☎ 231067 or 222284, ☎ 234221. A fairly up-market hotel (which has a more expensive sister hotel – *Royal Inca II* – next door) with a sauna and massage rooms. Very popular with upmarket package travellers. ⑧

Loki Hostel Cuesta Santa Ana 601, ☎ 243705, ⓦ www.lokihostel.com. Four quite long blocks from the main plaza, Loki offers backpackers a great space to hang out in Cusco; it has dormitories and some private rooms, plus the usual bar and cafeteria. Very popular with younger travellers. ②–④

Plaza de Armas Hostal Portal Mantas y Comercio 114, Plaza de Armas ☎ 231709, ☎ 247130, ⓔ hostal_plaza@terra.com.pe. As central as possible, on the corner of the plaza, this hotel is friendly and has main doors opening onto the square. Rooms facing the plaza obviously have the best views, but they all feature private bath and cable TV. Price includes breakfast. ⑥

East of Plaza de Armas

Amaru Hostal Cuesta San Blas 541 ☎/☎ 225933, ⓔ amaruhostal@speedy.com.pe. There's a rustic colonial feel here, with a lovely garden patio at its centre and another out back with views over town. There are laundry, safety deposit and left-luggage facilities, plus bottled oxygen. Service is very good, some rooms are old and stylish, while those in the back by the patio are newer but less interesting, most with private bath. ④

Casa de Campo Tandapata 296b ☎ 244404, ☎ 243069, ⓔ info@hotelcasadecampo.com. Attractive rooms and cabins (best booked in advance) with great views of the city from a large patio-garden. The quiet, uplifting location on the upper edge of Cusco is dauntingly high for your first couple of days, so take a taxi to avoid exhaustion or altitude sickness. They also offer combined accommodation and language-school courses with the AMAUTA language school, and there's ten percent discount to holders of the *Rough Guide to Peru* and members of the South American Explorers' Club. ⑤

La Casa de La Gringa Tandapata 148 ☎ 241168, ⓦ www.casadelagringa.com. A very pretty place that was once used by monks, its South African owner has lovingly restored the yards and rooms in amazing colours. Funky and enjoyably bohemian, this place has connections for jungle trips, mystical tours and, where appropriate, San Pedro journeys (see p.264). ②–④

Hospedaje El Arcano Carmen Alto 288 ☎ 244037, ☎ 232703. A slightly disorganised but otherwise friendly and amenable hostel on the edge of the attractive San Blas area with a reliable hot-water

system, laundry, family-sized rooms (accommodating 4–5 people) and a comfortable lounge. Rooms come with or without private bath. ③–⑤

Hospedaje Familiar Casa Grande Santa Catalina Ancha 353 ☎ 264156, ☎ 243784. Large, centrally located hotel with an open courtyard, some newly furbished rooms as well as more basic ones, with or without bath. ②–④

Hospedaje Turistico San Blas Cuesta San Blas 326 ☎ 225781, ⓔ sanblascusco@yahoo.com. Located in San Blas, this friendly place features a glass-covered courtyard. Most rooms have private bath and a safe deposit is available. The owners also organize tours to the Inca Trail and do river rafting on the Vilcanota. A good lower mid-range option. ③

Hostal El Grial Carmen Alto 112, San Blas ☎ 223012, ⓔ grial_celta@yahoo.com, ⓦ www.hotelelgrial.com. A relaxed hostal offering a very professional service in a central but quiet corner of San Blas. Nicely furnished, the rooms (one of which – upstairs at the back – has great views over the city) are modernized, spotless and tasteful, all with private bath. Spanish lessons can be arranged here for a reasonable cost through an associated language school and breakfast is served in the main communal space. 24hr internet access. ④–⑥

Hostal Huaynapata Wayna Pata 369 ☎ 228034, ⓔ hostalhuaynapata@terra.com. This modernized hostel is safe and friendly with a 1970s-style decor. It's not that far from the main plaza, and the covered roof terrace has splendid views across the cathedral and down the valley to Ausangate. Price includes breakfast. ⑤

Hostal Inti Quilla Atocsaycuchi 281 ☎ 252659. Small and cheerful hostel, quite a few steps up from the main square, but great value with cosy but relatively spartan rooms, with or without bath. There's also a pretty little courtyard with a massive Andean pine tree, a nice place to read or just relax. ③–④

Hostal Mirador de la Ñusta Tandapata 682 ☎ 248039, ⓔ elmiradordelanusta @hotmail.com. An intimate, cosy and superbly located place directly overlooking the Plazoleta San Blas in the artists' quarter. It has ten nice rooms, a pretty little yard, breakfast, laundry service and reliable hot water. ④

Hostal Rumi Punku Choquechaca 339 ☎ 221102, ⓦ www.rumipunku.com. A welcoming establishment built on an old Inca temple site in one of Cusco's nicest streets. Entered through an ancient stone doorway and based around an inner courtyard, the rooms are really stylish (some lit by resplendent chandeliers) for the price, with private showers and hot water. There's access to a kitchen, a patio, a *comedor* (dining room) and a small sitting room with a fireplace. Best booked in advance during high season. Price includes breakfast. ⑤–⑦

Hotel Monasterio C Palacio 136, Plazoleta Nazarenas ⓣ241777, ⓕ237111, ⓔreservas @peruorientexpress.com.pe, ⓦwww.monasterio .orient-express.com. One of Cusco's newest luxury establishments, this is a fantastic place, set around massive sixteenth-century monastery cloisters; it may cost a mint, but the rooms are top class. There are also tables in the courtyard where you can soak up the atmosphere while sipping drinks and eating delicious food from the plush bar and restaurant. ⑧

Hotel Ruinas Ruinas 472 ⓣ260644 or 245920, ⓕ236291, ⓔruinas@terra.com.pe. A very well-appointed option with superb rooms, many with views from private balconies down to Ausangate. Exceptionally clean, with minibars and safes in each room; there's also a fine lobby, restaurant and bar and email and fax facilities. ⑧

Inkaterra La Casona Cusco Plaza Las Nazarenas 113 ⓣ234010, ⓦwww.inkaterra.com. A newly refurbished, top-notch boutique hotel right in the centre of Cusco. Operated by the Inkaterra group, this is one of the best new places to stay. Although hard to tell from the outside, internally the decor is meticulous in combining style, ethnicity and comfort. They also offer a great range of excursions in Cusco and the Sacred Valley; plus links with Inkaterra Machu Picchu Hotel and the Urubamba Villas. ⑧

Pakcha Real Hostal Familiar Tandapata 300, San Blas ⓣ237484. An excellent family-run hostel in San Blas, this fun, modern home has a shared kitchen, a TV room and patio, constant hot water and reasonable security. Rooms are available with or without bath. The location high above the city centre, however, four steep blocks from Plaza de Armas, is a bit of a hike, and can be testing on arrival from sea level. ③–④

South of Plaza de Armas

Colonial Palace Hostal C Quera 270 ⓣ232151, ⓕ232329, ⓔcuzco@colonialpalace.com. An attractive colonial building with courtyards and clean, comfortable rooms, but still rather pricey given that it's all slightly down-at-heel. Hot water guaranteed 5am–1pm and 5.30–10pm; other facilities include a restaurant, grocery and artesania. All rooms have private bath. ⑤

El Dorado Av Sol 395 ⓣ231235 or 233112, ⓕ240993, ⓔreservasdorado@terra.com.pe. A classic four-star pseudo-colonial, relatively modern hotel. Rooms are spotless and the service is good, but the location – less than two blocks from the Plaza de Armas – can be a bit noisy. ⑥–⑧

Gran Hostal Machu Picchu C Quera 282 ⓣ231111. About two blocks from the Plaza de Armas, this hostel is hard to beat for friendly atmosphere and value in one package. Prices start low since some rooms here are available without private bath; all are set around a colonial courtyard. ③–⑤

Hacienda Hotel Incatambo San Cristobal, 2km along the *carretera* to Sacsayhuaman ⓣ221918 or 222045. A beautiful hacienda converted into a hotel, close to Sacsayhuaman and sharing some of the same magnificent views over the Cusco Valley and down to the city. Rooms are smart and with quality conveniences; many are set around a stunning colonial courtyard. Horseriding is offered on their ample estate. ⑧

Hostal Colonial Matará 288 ⓣ231811 or 247046. Pretty basic, but clean and with hospitable service. Many of its rooms are based around an airy courtyard in an old colonial building, and bathrooms are communal. ①–③

Hostal Emperador Plaza Santa Catalina Ancha 377 ⓣ261733, ⓕ263581, ⓔemperador@terra .com.pe or emperador@nexoperu.com. Comfortable, central option, with a cool, quiet and modern yet rather faceless interior, with 24hr hot water, bath and cable TV in all rooms. Rates include breakfast. ⑥–⑦

🏃 **Hotel Libertador** Plazoleta Santo Domingo 259 ⓣ231961, ⓕ233152, ⓔcusco @libertador.com.pe, ⓦwww.libertador.com.pe. One of the most expensive and exclusive hotels in Peru, set in a thoroughly renovated old mansion close to Koricancha, just a few blocks from the Plaza de Armas. Rooms are stylish and high quality, but it's the spacious lobby with nobbly, genuine Inca stonework that is a real treasure. ⑦

The Point Hostel Meson de la Estrella 172 ⓣ252266 ⓔcusco@thepointhostels.com. Opened in 2006, this fun hostel is just two blocks from the main plaza and close to Plaza San Francisco. It has over seventy beds, laundry, kitchen and book exchange based in a large mansion with its own garden. Dorms ($9) and private rooms both available. ③–⑤

The City

Despite the seemingly complex street structure, it doesn't take long to come to grips with Cusco. The city divides into five distinct areas based around various squares, temples and churches, with the **Plaza de Armas** at the heart of it all. The area **south of the Plaza to Koricancha** starts along the broad **Avenida Sol** running downhill and southeast from the corner of the plaza by the university and Iglesia de la Compañía towards the Inca sun temple at **Koricancha**, Huanchac train station and on to the airport in the south. Running uphill and southwest from the top of Avenida Sol, the area encompassing **Plaza San Francisco** and the Mercado Central follows Calle Mantas past the Plaza and the Iglesia de Santa Clara, and then continues towards the Central Market and San Pedro train station. Just one block west of the central plaza, you'll find the smaller, leafier, neighbouring **Plaza Regocijo**, which has Inca origins and is home to some of the city's finest mansions as well as the modest municipal palace. From the northeast corner of Plaza de Armas, Calle Triunfo leads steeply uphill through a classic Inca stone-walled alley before leading through cobbled streets towards the artesan barrio of **San Blas**. En route it's possible to visit the tiny but elegant **Plaza Nazarenas**, northeast of the centre. Heading northwest along Calle Plateros, uphill from Plaza de Armas, you'll pass through some really charming streets that lead toward the fortress of Sacsayhuaman above the city.

Nearly every site in Cusco is within walking distance of the Plaza de Armas and you can easily cover the main features of each area in half a day, allowing a little extra time for hanging out in the bars and shops en route. It's probably better to split your time into two or three half-day sessions in order to get the best out of the city and allow time for exploring some of the museums and archaeological complexes in depth.

▲ Cusco city centre

The Plaza de Armas and around

Cusco's modern and ancient centre, the **Plaza de Armas** – whose location corresponds roughly to that of the ceremonial *Huacapata*, the Incas' ancient central plaza – is the most obvious place to get your bearings. With the unmistakable ruins of **Sacsayhuaman** towering above, you can always find your way back to the plaza simply by locating the fortress or, at night, the illuminated white figure of Christ that stands beside it on the horizon. The plaza is always busy, its northern and western sides filled with shops and restaurants. Circling the plaza, the **Portal de Panes** is a covered cloister pavement, like those frequently found around Spanish colonial squares, where the buildings tend to have an upper-storey overhang, supported by stone pillars or arches, creating rain-free and sun-shaded walking space virtually all the way around. Usually the *portales* host processions of boys trying their best to sell postcards, and waiters and waitresses attempting to drag passing tourists into their particular dive. Recent restrictions have relegated stalls and shoeshine boys to the hinterland of backstreets emanating from the plaza, particularly the zone facing onto the Plaza Regocijo, behind the Plaza de Armas.

The Portal de Panes used to be part of the palace of Pachacuti, the ancient walls of which can still be seen from inside the *Roma Restaurant* close to the corner of the plaza and Calle Plateros. The plaza's exposed northeastern edge is dominated by the squat **Catedral** while the smaller **Iglesia de la Compañía de Jesus**, with its impressive pair of belfries, sits at the southeastern end. To the north of the Cathedral the relatively new **Balcon de Cusco**, a small square outside the Museo Inka, affords great views over the plaza and is where dances and firework celebrations tend to happen during festivals. There's also a panoramic walkway leading off it, following the rootops up to the cobbled backstreets of upper Cusco, directly beneath the ruins of Sacsayhuaman.

The Catedral

The **Catedral** (Mon–Sun 10am–5pm; entry $5) sits solidly on the foundations of the Inca Viracocha palace, its massive lines looking fortress-like in comparison with the delicate form of the nearby La Compañía. Construction began in 1560; the cathedral was built in the shape of a Latin cross with a three-aisled nave supported by only fourteen pillars. There are two entrances, one via the main central Cathedral doors; the other, more usual, way is through the **Triunfo Chapel**, the first Spanish church to be built in Cusco. Check out its finely carved granite altar and the huge canvas depicting the terrible 1650 earthquake, before moving into the main Cathedral to see the intricately carved pulpit and beautiful cedar-wood seats, as well as a Neoclassical high altar, made entirely of finely beaten embossed silver, and some of the finest paintings of the **Cusqueña school.** In the **Sacristy**, on the right of the nave, there's a large, dark painting of the crucifixion attributed to Van Dyck. Ten smaller chapels surround the nave, including the **Capilla de la Concepíon Imaculada** (Chapel of the Immaculate Conception), and the **Capilla del Señor de los Temblores** (The Lord of Earthquakes), the latter housing a 26-kilogram crucifix made of solid gold and encrusted with precious stones. To the left of the Cathedral is the adjoining eighteenth-century **Iglesia de Jesus Maria**, a relatively small extension to the main church; here you'll find a sombre collection of murals and a lavish main altar.

The Cathedral's appeal lies as much in its folklore and legends, as in its tangible sights. Local myth claims that an Indian chief is still imprisoned in the right-hand tower, awaiting the day when he can restore the glory of the Inca Empire.

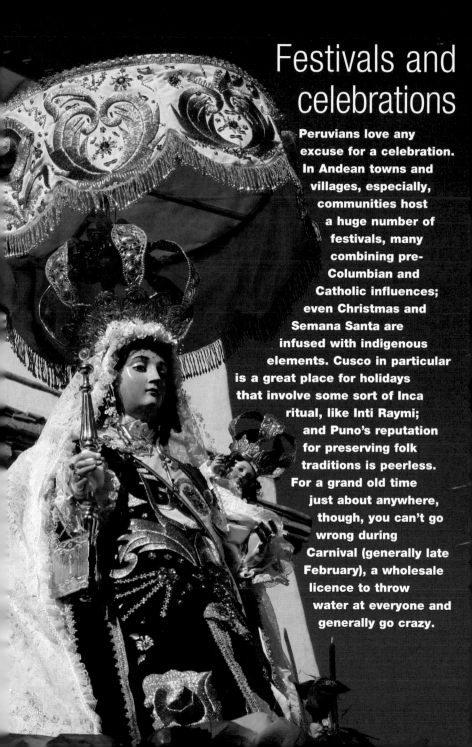

Festivals and celebrations

Peruvians love any excuse for a celebration. In Andean towns and villages, especially, communities host a huge number of festivals, many combining pre-Columbian and Catholic influences; even Christmas and Semana Santa are infused with indigenous elements. Cusco in particular is a great place for holidays that involve some sort of Inca ritual, like Inti Raymi; and Puno's reputation for preserving folk traditions is peerless. For a grand old time just about anywhere, though, you can't go wrong during Carnival (generally late February), a wholesale licence to throw water at everyone and generally go crazy.

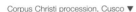

Semana Santa procession, Cusco ▲

Corpus Christi procession, Cusco ▼

Lord of Miracles, Lima ▼

Religious holidays

Though pretty much all festivals in Peru have some link to the religious calendar and come with serious spiritual implications for their participants, the major Christian holidays of Christmas and Easter still provide the basis for the biggest festivities. At **Christmas** time, most families erect **nativities** in front of their homes and churches do likewise, keeping them up until **la Bajada de los Reyes**, or the arrival of the three wise men, on January 6. Christmas celebrations don't see their official end until the fortnight-long **Fiesta de la Candelaria**, or Candlemas, which starts on February 2.

Another important religious holiday, **Semana Santa**, or Holy Week, begins the Friday before Palm Sunday. Mostly celebrated in the Andean region, its traditions vary from town to town, but tend to feature daily pageants and near-constant processions. Major events during the week include **Palm Sunday**, when biblically clad celebrants parade through the streets with mules and palms, and **Virgen Dolores** (Our Lady of Sorrows), a procession that takes place the Friday before Palm Sunday. During this, members of the procession fire pebbles at the crowd (particularly at children and foreigners) so that onlookers can assume the pain of La Madre de Dios, and supposedly reduce her suffering. Ayacucho boasts the most spectacular of the Semana Santa festivities: the townspeople engage in a decadent week of feasting, partying and Carnival-esque raucousness leading up to **Good Friday**.

About two months after Easter Sunday, Peruvians celebrate **Corpus Christi**, honouring the saints. Processions are the most vibrant in Cusco, where church officials carry ornate sacred icons through the streets. Just before Corpus Christi, the **festival of Qoyllur Rit'i** is held on a full moon and blends Catholic and indigenous traditions. Pilgrims trek to the foot of a glacier – considered an *apu*, or mountain god – to recharge their spirits.

Later in the year, in the springtime of mid-October, the streets of Lima are flooded with hundreds of thousands of purple-robed worshippers, praying to the **Lord of Miracles** for the safety of their city from the devastation of another earthquake, and for their own personal miracles. The holiday focuses on a **drawing of Christ**, which according to legend was painted on a clay wall by a slave, and has managed to survive several close encounters with destruction.

Village fiestas and folk traditions

In addition to the major regional and national celebrations, nearly every community has its own saint or patron figure to worship at town or **village fiestas**. These celebrations often mean a great deal to local people, and can be much more fun to visit than the larger countrywide activities. Processions, music, dancing in costumes and eating and drinking form the core activities of these parties. In some cases the villagers, as at the **Fiesta de la Virgen del Carmen**, which takes place in the *pueblo* of **Paucartambo** (usually the second or third weekend in July) near Cusco, will enact symbolic dramas with Indians dressed up as Spanish colonists, wearing hideous blue-eyed masks with long hairy beards. In **Puno** (renowned as the capital of Andean music and folkloric tradition), meanwhile, and in the hills

▲ Fiesta de la Virgen del Carmen, Paucartambo

▼ Fiesta de la Virgen del Carmen, Paucartambo

around towns like **Huaraz** and **Cusco**, it's quite common to stumble into a village fiesta, with its explosion of human energy and noise, bright colours and a mixture of pagan and Catholic symbolism.

The Marinera

Nearly every gathering is an excuse for locals to show off their expressive music – playing the panpipes, cane flutes and charangos prevalent in Andean folk – and dance customs. The national dance, the **Marinera**, is ubiquitous, and combines passionate, snappy drumbeats with slinky coquettish moves, for a steamy and entertaining spectacle. For the month of January, Trujillo's **Festival de Marinera** sees the dance performed with extra passion; this is, after all, the city where the dance originated. The dance mimics the epic courtship between a man and woman, and visitors should be wary of whom they pick as a dance partner; Trujillaños claim that the couple who dares to dance the Marinera are in danger of falling in love for real.

Festival de Marinera, Trujillo ▲

Inti Raymi, Cusco ▼

Inti Raymi

At the end of June, **Inti Raymi** (Quechua for "resurrection of the sun"), one of the largest festivals in South America, draws visitors from all over the world for a lavish and theatrical weeklong presentation of Peru's Inca roots. Based on the Inca ritual of the same name (held on the winter solstice to honour and welcome the sun god and request his return), the festival is celebrated throughout Peru, but most notably in the fortress of **Sacsayhuaman**, where a play about the Incas is performed. Well-known actors take on the main roles in an elaborately staged and costumed production, culminating in a speech given in Quechua by the actor playing the high priest or Inca Queen.

The Cathedral also houses the huge, miraculous gold and bronze **bell of Maria Angola**, named after a freed African slave girl and reputed to be one of the largest church bells in the world. And on the massive main doors of the Cathedral, native craftsmen have left their own pagan adornment – a carved puma's head – representing one of the most important religious motifs and gods found throughout ancient Peru.

The Museo Inka

North of the Cathedral, slightly uphill beside the Balcon de Cusco, you'll find one of the city's most beautiful colonial mansions, **El Palacio del Almirante** (The Admiral's Palace). This palace now houses the **Museo Inka** (Mon–Fri 8am–6pm, Sat and holidays 9am–4pm; $4). The museum, which boasts 10,000 catalogued specimens, features excellent exhibits of mummies, trepanned skulls, Inca textiles, a set of forty green turquoise figurines from the Huari settlement of Pikillacta and a range of Inca wooden *quero* vases (a specific style of slightly tapering drinking vessels). There are also displays of ceramics, early silver metalwork and a few gold figurines, but it's the spacious, organized layout and the imaginative, well-interpreted presentation that make this one of the best museums in Cusco for understanding the development of civilization in the Andes. Constructed on Inca foundations – this time the Waypar stronghold, where the Spanish were besieged by Manco's forces in 1536 – the building itself is noteworthy for its simple but well-executed Plateresque facade, surmounted by two imposing Spanish coats of arms plus the mullioned external balcony.

The Iglesia de la Compañía de Jesus

Looking downhill from the centre of the plaza, the **Iglesia de la Compañía de Jesus** (Mon–Sat 11am–noon & 3–5pm; free) dominates the Cusco skyline. First built over the foundations of Amara Cancha – originally Huayna Capac's Palace of the Serpents – in the late 1570s, it was resurrected over fifteen years after the earthquake of 1650, which largely destroyed the original version, itself constructed in a Latin cross shape with two belfries. The interior is cool and dark, with a grand gold-leaf altarpiece; a fine wooden pulpit displaying a relief of Christ, high vaulting and numerous paintings of the Cusqueña school; and a transept ending in a stylish Baroque cupola. The guilded altarpieces are made of fine cedar wood and the church contains interesting oil paintings of the Peruvian Princess Isabel Ñusta. Its most impressive features, though, are the two majestic towers of the main facade, a superb example of Spanish colonial Baroque design which has often been described in more glowing terms than the Cathedral itself. On the right-hand side of the church, the **Lourdes Chapel**, restored in 1894, is used mostly as an exhibition centre for local crafts.

The Natural History Museum

Alongside La Compañía, an early Jesuit university building houses the **Natural History Museum** (Mon–Fri 9am–noon & 3–6pm; 30¢). The entrance is off an inner courtyard, up a small flight of stairs to the left. The exhibits cover Peru's coast, the Andes and the Amazon jungle, with a particularly good selection of stuffed mammals, reptiles and birds. For a small tip, the doorman outside the university building sometimes allows visitors upstairs to the top of the cupola to admire the view across the plaza.

Around Avenida Sol to Koricancha

Leading away from the Plaza de Armas, Callejón Loreto separates La Compañía Church from the tall, stone walls of the ancient Acclahuasi, or **Temple of the Sun Virgins**, where the Sun Virgins used to make *chicha* beer for the Lord Inca. Today, the Acclahuasi building is occupied by the **Convent of Santa Catalina**, built in 1610, with its small but grand side entrance half a short block down Calla Santa Catalina Angosta; just under thirty sisters still live and worship here.

Inside the convent the **Museo de Arte y Monasterio de Santa Catalina** (Mon–Sat 9am–5pm, Sun and holidays 9am–3.30pm; entry $2) features a splendid collection of paintings from the **Cusqueña school,** as well as an impressive Renaissance altarpiece and several gigantic seventeenth-century tapestries depicting the union of Indian and Spanish cultures. The blending of cultures is a theme that runs throughout much of the museum's fascinating artwork and is particularly evident in the Cusqueña paintings. Another common feature of much of the Cusqueña art here is the disproportionate, downward-looking, blood-covered head, body and limbs of the seventeenth-century depictions of Christ, which represent the suffering and low social position of the Andean Indians and originate from early colonial days when Indians were not permitted to look Spaniards in the eyes.

The Cusqueña school

Colonial Cusco evolved into an exceptional centre for architecture and art. The era's paintings in particular are curious for the way they adorn human and angelic figures in elaborate lacy garments and blend traditional and ancient with colonial and Spanish elements. They are frequently brooding and quite bloody and by the mid seventeenth-century had evolved into a recognizeable school of painting.

The **Cusqueña art movement** dedicated itself to beautifying church and convent walls with fantastic and highly moralistic painting, mainly using oils. The Cusqueña school is best known for portraits or religious scenes with dark backgrounds, serious (even tortured-looking) subjects and a profusion of gold-leaf decoration. Influences came from European émigrés – mainly Spanish and Italian – notably Juan de Illescas, Bernardo Bitti and Mateo Perez de Alessio. At the close of the seventeenth century, the school came under the direction of **Bishop Manuel Mollinedo**. Bringing a number of original paintings (including some by El Greco) with him from his parish in Spain, the Bishop was responsible for commissioning **Basilio Santa Cruz's** fine 1698 reproduction of the *Virgen de la Almudena* which still hangs behind the choir in Cusco's Catedral. He also commissioned the extraordinarily carved cedarwood pulpit in the church at San Blas.

The top Cusqueña artists were **Bernardo Bitti**, a sixteenth-century Italian who is often considered the "father of Cusqueña art" and inventor of the "manierist" style, and **Diego Quispe Tito Inca** (1611–1681) a *mestizo* painter who was influenced by the Spanish Flamenco school and whose paintings were vital tools of communication for priests attempting to convert Indians to Catholicism. Bitti's work is on display in the Museo Historico Regional, while some of Quispe's works can be seen in rooms off the second courtyard in the Religious Art Museum at the Archbishop's Palace in Cusco. The equally renowned **Mauricio Garcia** (eighteenth century) helped to spur the form into a fuller *mestizo* synthesis, mixing Spanish and Indian artistic forms. Many of the eighteenth- and nineteenth-century Cusqueña-*mestizo* works display bold compositions and colours.

By the eighteenth century the style had been disseminated as far afield as Quito in Ecuador, Santiago in Chile and even into Argentina, making it a truly South American art form and one of the most distinctive indigenous arts in the Americas.

Another highlight of the museum, on the first floor at the top of the stairs, is a large fold-up box containing miniature three-dimensional religious and mythological images depicting everything from the Garden of Eden to an image of God with a red flowing cape and dark beard, and a white dove and angels playing drums, Andean flutes and pianos.

On the corner of Maruri and Q'aphchik'ijllu, on the way from Santa Catalina towards Koricancha, there's the **Museo y Sala Cultural** (Mon–Fri 9am–1pm & 4–6pm; free) at the Banco Wiese, where displays include historical documents and archaeological and architectural features; exhibitions vary throughout the year. The focus is often on the restoration work of the Banco Wiese's own premises, an attractive mansion that was once part of the Tupac Inca Yupangui's Pucamarca palace.

The Koricancha complex

The main Inca temple for worship of major deities and a supreme example of Inca stonework underlying colonial buildings can be found just a short walk from the Plaza de Armas, through the Inca walls of Callejón Loreto, then along the busy Pampa del Castillo. The **Koricancha** complex, located at the intersection of Avenida Sol and Calle Santo Domingo (Mon–Sat 8.30am–5pm, Sun 2–5pm; $3), can't be missed, with the Convento de Santo Domingo rising imposingly from its impressive walls, which the conquistadors laid lower to make way for their uninspiring seventeenth-century Baroque church – a poor contrast to the still-imposing Inca masonry evident in the foundations and chambers of the Sun Temple. Prior to the Incas, the Wari culture had already dedicated the site with its own sun temple, known as Inticancha (*inti* meaning "sun" and *cancha* meaning "enclosure"). Before the conquistadors set their gold-hungry eyes on it, Koricancha must have been even more breathtaking, consisting as it did of four small sanctuaries and a larger temple set around a central courtyard. This whole complex was encircled on the inside walls by a cornice of gold, hence the temple's name (Koricancha means "golden enclosure").

Still visible today, there's a large, slightly trapezoidal niche on the inside of the curved section of the retaining wall, close to the chamber identified as the Temple of the Sun, where there once stood a huge, gold disc in the shape of the sun, **Punchau**, which was worshipped by the Incas. Punchau had two companions in the temple: a golden image of **Viracocha**, on the right; and another, representing **Illapa**, god of thunder, to the left. Below the temple was an artificial garden in which everything was made of gold or silver and encrusted with precious jewels, from depictions of llamas and shepherds to the tiniest details of clumps of earth and weeds, including snails and butterflies. Not surprisingly, none of this survived the arrival of the Spanish.

Koricancha's position in the Cusco Valley was carefully planned. Dozens of *ceques* (power lines, in many ways similar to ley lines, though in Cusco they appear to have been related to imperial genealogy) radiate from the temple towards more than 350 sacred *huacas*, special stones, springs, tombs and ancient quarries. In addition, during every summer solstice, the sun's rays shine directly into a niche – the **tabernacle** – in which only the Inca emperor (often referred to as *the* Inca) was permitted to sit. Mummies of dead Inca rulers were seated in niches at eye level along the walls of the actual temple, the principal idols from every conquered province were held "hostage" here, and every emperor married his wives in the temple before assuming the throne. The niches no longer exist, though there are some in the walls of the nearby Temple of the Moon, where mummies of the emperor's concubines were kept in a foetal position.

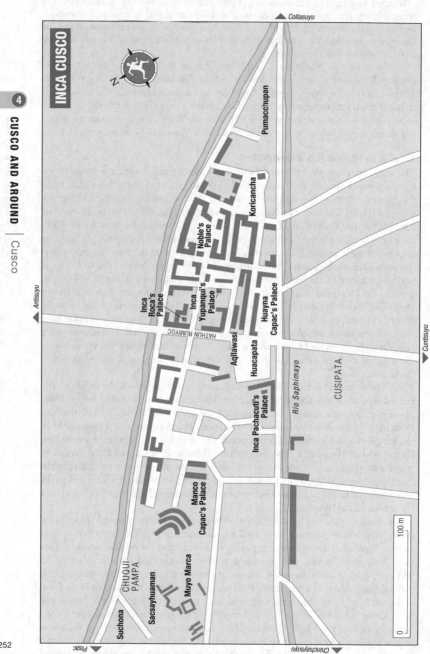

INCA CUSCO

Collasuyu

Pumacchupan

Koricancha

Noble's
Palace

Inca
Roca's
Palace

Inca
Yupanqui's
Palace

HATHUN RUMIYOC

Aqllawasi

Huayna
Capac's Palace

Huacapata

Inca Pachacuti's
Palace

Río Saphimayo

CUSIPATA

Antisuyu

Cuntisuyu

Manco
Capac's Palace

CHUQUI
PAMPA

Muyu Marca

Sacsayhuaman

Suchona

Pisac

Chinchaysuyu

100 m

0

The **Chapel of Santo Domingo** (Mon–Sat 8.30am–6.30pm, Sun 2–5pm) is accessed via the complex reception desk, or by walking past the Temple of the Moon and the Catholic Sacristy to a tiny section of the inner edge of the vast curved wall, which, from the outside, seems to support the chapel. Returning from here via the sacristy, it is possible to see the Catholic priest's vestments, some boasting gold thread and jewels.

To reach the **Koricancha Site Museum** (Mon–Sun 9am–5pm, Tourist Ticket, see p.243), or Museo Arqueológico de Qorikancha, it's a two-minute walk downhill from the Complex reception to the underground museum entrance on block 3 of Avenida Sol. There are only five rooms here, but each contains a number of interesting pieces. The first is pre-Inca, mainly stone and ceramic exhibits; the second Inca, with wooden, ceramic and some metallurgic crafts; in the third, archaeological excavations are illustrated and interpreted; the fourth houses a mummy and some bi-chrome ceramics of the Killki era (around 800 AD), which reflect the art of the pre-Inca Wari culture.

From the museum it is possible to access the **garden**, which, though little more than a green, open, grassy space just outside the main walls of Koricancha, has a particularly beautiful pre-Inca spring and bath that dates to the Wari period, providing evidence of the importance of Koricancha before the Incas arrived on the Andean scene.

Plaza San Francisco and Mercado Central

Ten minutes' walk southwest along Calle Mantas from the Plaza de Armas, then a left turn along Calle San Bernardo, brings you to the **Iglesia y Convento de la Merced** (Mon–Sat 8.30am–noon & 2–5pm; $2), which sits peacefully amid the bustle of one of Cusco's more interesting quarters. First raised with Pizarro's financial assistance on top of the Inca site Limipata in 1536 by Brother Sebastian Castañeda of the Mercedarian order, it was rebuilt some 25 years after the 1650 earthquake in a rich combination of Baroque and Renaissance styles by such native artesans as Alonso Casay and Francisco Monya. The facade is exceptionally ornate and the roof is endowed with an unusual Baroque spire, while inside there's a beautiful star-studded ceiling and a huge silver cross, which is adored and kissed by a shuffling crowd. The monastery's highlight, however, is a breathtaking 1720s monstrance standing a metre high and crafted by Spanish jeweller Juan de Olmos, who used over 600 pearls, more than 1500 diamonds and upwards of 22kg of solid gold. The monastery also possesses a fine collection of Cusqueña paintings, particularly in the cloisters and vestry, and an exceptionally gorgeous white-stone cloister.

Continue another block south and you'll come to the **Plaza San Francisco**, frequently filled with food stalls that couldn't be squeezed into the Central Market or along Calle Santa Clara. The square's southwestern side is dominated by the simply adorned **Museo y Convento de San Francisco** (Mon–Sat 9am–5.30pm; 80¢), built between 1645 and 1652. Inside, two large cloisters boast some of the better colonial paintings by local masters such as Diego Quispe Tito, Marcos Zapata and Juan Espinosa de los Monteros, the latter being responsible for massive works on canvas, one or two of which are on display here.

Passing under a crumbling archway to the left of the church, follow the flow of people along Calle Santa Clara towards the Central Market and you'll come across the small but beautiful **Iglesia de Santa Clara** (daily 6am–6pm; free). Partly restored in 2005 and originally built around a single nave in 1558 by *mestizo* and indigenous craftsmen under the guidance of the architect Brother Manuel Pablo, it contains a gold-laminated altar, small mirrors covering most of the interior, and a few canvasses. The outside walls, however, show more interesting details: finely cut Inca blocks support the upper, cruder stonework, and four andesite columns, much cracked over the centuries, complete the doorway. The belfry is so time-worn that weeds and wildflowers have taken permanent root. Just up the street, in the busy market area next to San Pedro train station, stands another sixteenth-century colonial church, the **Iglesia de San Pedro** (10am–noon & 2–5pm, not Sun; free), whose steps are normally crowded with Quechua market traders. The interior is decorated with paintings, sculptures, gold leaf and some wooden carvings, and an elaborate, carved pulpit. Relatively austere, with only a single nave, the church's main claim to fame is that somewhere among the stones of its twin towers are ancient blocks dragged here from the small Inca fort of Picchu.

The area northwest of the **Mercado Central** (daily 6am–4pm) in front of the Iglesia San Pedro has recently been cleaned up and pedestrianized. There are still street stalls selling every imaginable practical item in the streets below the market building; inside you can find plentiful and exotic foodstuffs plus some herbalist kiosks that stock everything from lucky charms to jungle medicines. The food stalls at the bottom end of the indoor market offer some of the best and cheapest **street meals** in Peru.

Plaza Regocijo and around

The **Plaza Regocijo**, today a pleasant garden square sheltering a statue of Colonel Francisco Bolognesi, a famous Peruvian war martyr, was originally the Inca *cusipata*, an area cleared for dancing and festivities beside the Inca's ancient central plaza. Only a block southwest of the Plaza de Armas, Regocijo is dominated on its northwestern side by an attractively arched municipal building housing the **Museo de Arte Contemporáneo**, (see p.255) with a traditional Inca rainbow flag flying from its roof. Opposite this is the venerable old *Hotel Cusco*, still under refurbishment but formerly the grand, state-run *Hotel de Turistas*, while on the southwest corner of the plaza lies an impressive mansion where more Inca stones mingle with colonial construction, home to the Museo Histórico Regional y Casa Garcilaso. Leading off from the top of Regocijo, Calle Santa Teresa is home to the House of the Pumas and leads to the Iglesia de Santa Teresa.

Museo Histórico Regional y Casa Garcilaso

Once the residence of **Garcilaso de la Vega,** a prolific half-Inca (his mother may have been an Inca princess), half-Spanish poet and author, the mansion now known as the **Museo Histórico Regional y Casa Garcilaso** (see below) is currently home to significant regional archaeological finds and much of Cusco's historic art. Fascinating **pre-Inca** ceramics from all over Peru are displayed, plus a Nasca mummy in a foetal position with typically long (1.5m) hair, embalming herbs and unctures, black ceramics with incised designs from the early Cusco culture (1000–200 BC) and a number of **Inca** artefacts such as *bolas*, maces, architects' plumb-lines and square water-dishes used for finding horizontal levels on buildings. The museum also displays gold bracelets discovered at Machu Picchu in 1995, some gold and silver llama statuettes found in 1996 in the Plaza de Armas when reconstructing the central fountain, and golden pumas and figurines from Sacsay-huaman. From the **colonial** era there are some weavings, wooden *quero* drinking vessels and dancing masks.

The main exhibition rooms upstairs house mainly period furniture and a multitude of Cusqueña paintings, which cross the range from the rather dull (religious adorations) to the more spectacular (like the famous eighteenth-century *Jacob's Ladder*). As you progress through the works you'll notice the rapid intrusion of cannons, gunpowder and proliferation of violence appearing throughout the 1700s, something which was reflected in Cusco art as a microcosm of what happened across the colonial world – emanating from Europe as part of the general march of technological "progress".

Museo de Arte Contemporáneo

The **Museo de Arte Contemporáneo** (Mon–Sat 9.30am–5.30pm; entry by Cusco Tourist Ticket, see p.243) is located in the Municipality building on Plaza Regocijo; it's a welcome and relatively new feature in Cusco, an outlet for the many talented local artists. **Sala 1** shows images of Cusco, mainly paintings but occasional photos of subjects like Inca dancers as well as abstract features, plus some sculpture. **Sala 2** is dedicated to non-Cusco-inspired contemporary art, some of it very abstract but with exhibits changing quite regularly; the sala leads off into a large courtyard with a typically attractive colonial fountain; here you'll find glass cases with dolls in traditional costumes, some regional variations of dance masks (from Paucartambo dance groups, for example) and models of buildings in different Cusco styles. The upstairs **Sala 3** houses more images of Cusco, both ancient and modern.

Calle Santa Teresa

On **Calle Santa Teresa**, the **House of the Pumas** (no. 385) isn't as grand as it sounds yet the six pumas above its entrance were carved during the Spanish rebuilding of Cusco. Turn right at the end of this street and you'll pass the **Iglesia de Santa Teresa** (daily 6am–6pm; free), an attractive but neglected church with stone walls, the upper half of which have paintings featuring St Teresa. Inside, the small brick ceiling has a beautifully crafted dome and there's a gold leaf altar inset with paintings. There's a small **chapel** next door with intricately painted walls (featuring yet more images of St Teresa), usually beautifully candlelit.

Uphill to San Blas

Calle Cordoba del Tucman runs northeast from Plaza de Armas along the northern edge of the Cathedral, past the Museo Inka (see p.249) and up to the small, quiet **Plaza Nazarenas**. The unmistakable **Casa Cabrera** has been transformed into the **Museo de Arte Precolombino** (daily 9am–10.30pm, $1.50; ☎233210) at the top, uphill end of this small square. It boasts many masterpieces dating from 1250 BC to 1532 AD including gold, other precious metals and jewellery well displayed in clear chronological order. Frequent temporary exhibitions are held here, too.

On the northeastern side of Plaza Nazarenas, the ancient, subtly ornate **Capilla de San Antonio Abad** was originally connected to a religious school before becoming part of the university in the seventeenth century. It's not open to the public, but you can usually look around the courtyard of the **Nazarenas Convent**, virtually next door and now home to the plush *Hotel Monasterio* (see p.246); ask permission at the reception desk. Nuns lived here until the 1950 earthquake damaged the building so badly that they had to leave; the central courtyard has since been sensitively rebuilt and has an attractive garden where good (but pricey) meals and drinks are served. Beside the convent, the Inca passage of Siete Culebras (Seven Snakes) leads onto Choquechaca.

San Blas and around

From Choquechaca, turn left into Cuesta de San Blas and after one and a half blocks you'll come to the tiny **Iglesia de San Blas** (Mon–Wed, Fri & Sat 10–11am & 2–5.30pm; $5). The highlight here is an incredibly intricate pulpit, carved from a block of cedar wood in a complicated Churrigueresque style; its detail includes a cherub, a sun disc, faces and bunches of grapes, all believed to have been carved by native craftsman Tomas Tuyro Tupa in the seventeenth century. Outside, along Calle Plazoleta (also called Suytuccato), there are a few art workshops and galleries, the most notable of which is Galería Olave, at no. 651. **The Museo de Cerámica,** Carmen Alto 133, is worth checking out for its pottery, while on the plazoleta is the **Museo Taller Hilario Mendivil,** containing a number of Cusqueña paintings, some interesting murals and religious icons; both operate the standard local shop hours of 10am–6pm. At the barrio's centre, on the southeast side of the Iglesia San Blas, lies the **San Blas Plazoleta**, with 49 gargoyles set on a fountain that's laid out in the form of a *chakana,* or Inca cross, with four corners and a hole at its centre.

Hathun Rumiyoq and the Museo de Arte Religioso del Arzobispado

Backtracking down the Cuesta de San Blas and continuing over the intersection with Choquechaca, head straight on until you come to the narrow alley of **Hathun Rumiyoq.** One of the main streets in ancient Cusco, it provides classic examples of superb Inca stonework, the large cut boulders on the museum side, about halfway along, boast one that has twelve angles in its jointing with the stones around it. Not just earthquake resistant, it is both a highly photographed ruin and a work of art in its own right.

At the end of this passageway, and just one block from the Plaza de Armas, along Calle Triunfo, you'll find the broad doors of the **Museo de Arte Religioso del Arzobispado** (Mon–Sun 9am–5pm; $5), housed in a superb Arabesque-style mansion built on the impressive foundations of Hathun Rumiyoq palace. Once home to Brother Vicente de Valarde and the Marquises of Rocafuert, and later the archbishop's residence, the museum now contains a significant collection of paintings, mostly from the Cusqueña school. There are stunning mosaics in some of the period rooms, and other significant features include the elaborate gateway and the gold-leaf craftsmanship on the chapel's altar.

A short history of San Blas

Originally known as T'oqokachi ("salty hole"), the **San Blas** barrio was the first parish to be established by the Spanish in Cusco and one of twelve administrative sectors in the Inca capital. After the Conquest it became the residence for many defeated Inca leaders. It rapidly grew into one of the more attractive districts in the city, reflecting strong *mestizo* and colonial influences in its architecture and high-quality artesania – even today it's known as the *barrio de los artesanos* (artesans' quarter). Hit hard by the 1950 earthquake, it has been substantially restored, and in 1993 was given a major face-lift that returned it to its former glory.

Eating and drinking

Generally speaking, although **eating out** in Cusco is enjoyable and there are some exceptionally fine restaurants, the food itself is not as varied as in Lima, with all that city's oceanic resources. Cusco prides itself on its traditional dishes, which have evolved this century into a *novo andino* cuisine, combining the best ingredients of the Andes with exquisite Mediterranean and even Argentinian influences. Nevertheless, you'll find it easier to get pizza than roast guinea pig. The more central cafés and restaurants accommodate most tastes, serving anything from a toasted cheese sandwich to authentic Andean or *criolla* dishes. The most popular area for restaurants and bars is around the **Plaza de Armas** and along calles **Plateros** and **Procuradores**, home to several decent, cheap cafés and a few good restaurants, including some excellent eating places along Santa Catalina, both Angosta and Ancha. The trendy **San Blas** barrio has excellent restaurants offering a reasonably priced alternative to the more international cuisine found in most places.

If you're **self-catering**, the Central Market by San Pedro train station sells a wonderful variety of meats, tropical and imported fruits, local vegetables, Andean cheeses and other basics. The market also has a wide range of daytime hot-food stalls where you can get superb freshly squeezed juices and smoothies as well as **takeaway** food (if you have a container to put it in) or meals to eat on the spot.

Cafés and snack bars

Bagdad Café Portal de Carnes 216, Plaza de Armas. Next to and above *La Yunta* (another more easily found café – see below), the Bagdad Café is a popular spot not least because it has tables on a colonial balcony overlooking the plaza. Serves good pizzas, breakfasts, sandwiches, some pasta dishes and cool drinks.

El Buen Pastor Cuesta San Blas 579. One of the best in Cusco, this exceptional bakery has a huge array of sweet and savoury homemade pastries and fine cakes.

Café Ayllu Portal de Carnes 208, Plaza de Armas. Very centrally located with views across the plaza, *Café Ayllu* has been Cusco's most traditional meeting place since the early 1970s. It's busy all day, and service is usually prompt, serving one of the best breakfasts in Peru, including fruit, yoghurt and toasted sandwiches. Rumour has it, though, that it may close soon because its landlord (the Cusco Church) wants to raise the rent.

Café Cultural Ritual Choquechaca 140. This quiet and pleasant little café serves great breakfasts and also has a good vegetarian menu including dishes like *quinoa andina*, a pancake of quinoa with fried manioc. Closed Sun.

Don Esteban and Don Pancho Café Gourmet Av Sol, opposite and a little uphill from the post office. Excellent coffee and cakes served here all day in a pleasant, Euro-deli atmosphere. Also good for breakfasts, sandwiches and quiches.

La Paccha Tandapata 676 ☎262959. A small but very pleasant café serving espresso coffee and great juices inside or out in the small but attractive garden.

Restaurant El Encuentro Santa Catalina Ancha 384 ☎225496. A simple vegetarian café which serves incredibly good value and delicious omelettes, soups, salads as well as the usual health drinks. Open 9am–9pm, closed Sun.

Trotamundos Portal de Comercio 177, Plaza de Armas. An welcoming café warmed by an open log fire which serves a mix of local and international food. The internet section is partitioned off from the café itself, with views over the plaza, a notice board, a stove-fire and games.

Varayoc C Espaderos 142 ☎232404. A welcoming *café literario* with a strong Andean intellectual as well as Swiss atmosphere. It's popular for breakfasts, snacks, cheesecakes or even fondue, and has a magazine rack and several tables where students, tourists and locals mingle, generally sipping hot chocolate, pisco or *mate de coca* (coca-leaf tea – highly recommended for altitude sickness).

La Yunta Portal de Carnes 214, Plaza de Armas. A groovy establishment right on the plaza, specializing in pizza but also offering large salads, soups, omelettes, fish, French fries and excellent juices and jugs of *limonada*. Perfect for lunch or supper and a popular meeting place for adventure tour guides in the early evening. Often plagued by roving Andean folklore bands, entertaining but also hawking their CDs.

Restaurants

Cusco **restaurants** range from the cheap and cheerful to expensive gourmet establishments. Many serve international cuisine but the *quintas*, basic local eating houses, serve mostly traditional **Peruvian food**, full of spice and character. Generally speaking, trout is plentiful, reasonably priced and often excellent, and roast guinea pig (*cuy*) can usually be ordered, but **pizza** seems to lead in the popularity stakes.

This isn't a region particularly noted for its **beef**, but there are a few places serving steaks, and **British** and **Asian** cooking can be found, the latter in some fairly average *chifas*, and one good **curry** house – *Al Grano*. Unless otherwise stated, most restaurants open daily at around 11am and stop serving from 10.30pm through to midnight. There's up-to-date information available on Ⓦwww.cuscorestaurants.com.

Al Grano Santa Catalina Ancha 398 ☎228032. A friendly place serving Asian lunches and suppers, including great curries, in a civilized atmosphere. They have particularly good deals on set-lunch menus (for example, soup and main course for $2.50). Games room downstairs. Closes around 9pm.

Cafetería Huayliiy C Plateros 363. Uninspiring decor but some of the best-value breakfasts in Cusco, plus pizzas, *chifa* meals, trout, lomo saltado (salted beef with chipped potatoes, onions and tomatoes) and a wide range of inexpensive set menus and cakes.

Fallen Angel Plazoleta Nazarenas 221 ☎258184. A gay-friendly restaurant with games suspended on stools from the ceiling and fake leopard-skin trunks. There's also a resident DJ who plays vibrant trip-hop and trance. The decor is an experience in its own right; arty, wicked and inspired, while the garden art is as good as many of Cusco's art museums and much more twenty-first century. The food and cocktails are equally exquisite. Menu wise, try the Andean tenderloin steak with port and balsamic topping, the Andean raviolis stuffed delicately with local sweet potato, the wild mushrooms or the warm salad. Best to book in advance.

Greens Santa Catalina Angosta 135 ☎243379. This brilliantly run restaurant serves superb innovative dishes, both *novo andino* and Mediterranean, using as many organic and green ingredients as possible. Highly recommended and pretty reasonably priced, although reservations are advised.

Jack's Café on corner of Choquechaca and Cuesta San Blas. A popular gringo place, this café serves all-day breakfasts, burgers, pancakes and a whole host of other very tasty plates. Great coffee.

Heladeria Dolce Vita Santa Catalina 370. Easily the best ice cream in Cusco, combining Peruvian fruits with Italian expertise.

Incanto Restaurant Santa Catalina Angosta 135. Based in a large space below *Greens* restaurant, this place nevertheless fills up quickly in the evenings because of its reputation for good service and quality pizza. Also serves fine Peruvian dishes like *aji de gallina*, *lomo saltado* and *locro de zapallo*.

Macondo Cuesta San Blas 571 ☎229415. A cosy and homely gay-friendly restaurant with wacky decor, serving some of the best *novo andino* and Amazonian cuisine you'll find anywhere; try the *yuquitas* (fried slices of manioc) stuffed with *chimbivalcano* (from Chimbivalca) cheese, the vegetarian curry or the *alpaca mignon a la parmesana*. Best in evenings (book in advance), but serves a full menu during the day.

MAP Restaurant Museo de Arte Precolombino, Plaza Nazarenas 231 ☎242476. Set with tables in the fine museum courtyard, this is one of the city's finest restaurants specialising in *novo andino* cuisine, such as guinea pig confit with fork-mashed potatoes.

Mundo Hemp Qanchipata 596, San Blas Ⓦwww.mundohemp.com. Slighty out-on-a-limb up in a quiet part of San Blas, *Mundo Hemp* combines a hemp-based menu with cocktail lounge and a shop full of hemp-based clothing and household artefacts.

Pacha Papa Plaza San Blas 120 ☎241318. A great, inexpensive restaurant set around an attractive courtyard, serving a range of hard-to-find Andean dishes, from a *gulash de alpaca* to the highly nutritious *sopa de quinoa*, and good wines, both Peruvian and Chilean. Reservations recommended.

Pachacutec Restaurant Portal de Panes 105 ☎245041. A grill-based restaurant on a busy corner of Plaza de Armas, with Inca stones from the Inca Pachacuti's palace lining the walls, and both *comida tipica* and *internacional* on the menu. With folklore shows at weekends and evenings from 8pm, it's worth the extra few soles.

Pucara Restaurant C Plateros 309 ☎222027. Popular with tourists, this pleasant restaurant offers inexpensive set menus, fine salads and well-prepared Peruvian cuisine. There's music occasionally in the evenings.

La Quinta Eulalia C Choquechaca 384 ☎241380. One of the very best and most traditional local eating houses, in a backstreet a few blocks above the Plaza de Armas. Plays fine *criolla* music and is good for *cuy chactado* (guinea pig fried with potatoes, tamales and *rocoto*, a round, usually red, pepper-like vegetable which is occasionally spicy hot).

Restaurant Govinda C Espaderos 128. The original vegetarian eating house in Cusco, serving simple healthy food: the fruit-and-yoghurt breakfasts are generally very good and the set lunches excellent value. If you get the chance, eat upstairs where there's more atmosphere and more room. Daily 8.30am–7pm.

Rosie O'Grady's Santa Catalina 360 ☎247935. Find good beer and even better full meals at this swish Irish pub and restaurant. The beefsteak is among the best in Peru.

La Trattoria Adriano C Mantas 105, corner of Av Sol ☎233965. Of all the Italian restaurants in Cusco this serves the best-quality cuisine, especially the pasta dishes, and has a fine selection of good South American and European wines.

Drinking and nightlife

Apart from Lima, no Peruvian town has as varied a **nightlife** as Cusco. The corner of Plaza de Armas, where Calle Plateros begins, is a hive of activity until the early hours, even during the week. Most venues in the city are simply **bars** with a dancefloor and sometimes a stage, but their styles vary enormously, from Andean folk spots with panpipe music to reggae or jazz joints and more conventional **clubs**. Most places are within staggering distance of each other, and sampling them is an important part of any stay in Cusco. Many open around 9pm and keep going until 2 or 3am.

During any of the major **fiestas** (see p.238) you will encounter colourfully costumed dance groups in the streets, but there are few other opportunities to see **folk dancing** beyond the occasional show at a few of the large hotels and more expensive restaurants. Only one group offers regular performances: Dance Performances, at the Centro Qosqo de Arte Nativo, Av Sol 612 (daily 6–10pm; entrance with Cusco Tourist Ticket, ☎227901).

Pubs and bars

Cross Keys Pub C Triunfo 350, second floor ☎229227, ⓦwww.cross-keys-pub-cusco -peru.com. One of the hubs of Cusco's nightlife, this classic drinking dive has the feel of a London pub, with good music, soccer scarves adorning the walls, pool tables and good beers. Food is available and there are often English-language newspapers and magazines, not surprisingly since it's owned by the British Consul.

Indigo Tecsecocha 2 ☎260271. An atmospheric bar justly famous for its Thai cuisine and cocktails. It's best in the evenings when you can warm up by the fireplace, and there are comfortable seats, sofas and swings, games, books and hookahs.

Los Perros Tecsecocha 436. Billing itself as "the original couch bar", *Los Perros* is a trendy hang-out where travellers snack, drink and play board games or read from the wide-ranging library and magazines (books can be exchanged – give two, take one). There's often jazz at weekends.

Km 0 Tandapata 100, San Blas ☎236009. This bar and café is small but nearly always busy and with a very international mix of musicians and drinkers; live music at weekends.

Muse Bar Tandapata 682. A bar and café art gallery, open from 9am until midnight daily, *The Muse* is located on the terrace above the Plazoleta San Blas. It has a cosy atmosphere, good drinks and food all day (8.30am–midnight), with tables outside; also plays live music from roughly 10pm most weekends and sometimes during the week.

Norton Rats Tavern Santa Catalina 116, second floor. Just off the Plaza de Armas, with great views over the square. Best known as a bar with a spacious interior, Norton Rats serves special jungle cocktails and a couple of decent English ales. It plays rock, blues, jazz and Latin music and has a pool table and dartboard, plus satellite TV for sports. There's also a café serving grills and sandwiches.

Paddy Flaherty's Irish Pub C Triunfo 124. Looking much like a British pub, though its wood-panelled walls are garlanded with Irish artefacts and a working model train which circulates the room continuously. The atmosphere is pleasant, if busy, and there's sports TV; it gets particularly lively at weekends, when they often have live Irish music. Serves Guinness.

Rosie O'Grady's Santa Catalina 360 ☎ 247935. A capacious Irish pub and great restaurant (see p.259) with a range of beers, Guinness included. There's great live music on Thursdays and Fridays, plus a popular Friday evening "boat race" drinking competition; satellite TV for sports.

Sumay Misky C Plateros 334. This is actually an interesting restaurant which incorporates the highly popular *Nick's Sports Bar*, the best range of piscos in Cusco and a satellite TV screen. As well as some spectacular and unique main dishes (including tandori guinea pig, *rocoto relleno*, plus quinoa and mushroom risotto) it prepares snacks like potato wedges, cheese toasties as well as alpaca and bacon patties on demand.

Clubs and dance bars

KamiKase Bar Portal Cabildo 274, Plaza Regocijo ☎ 233865. One of Cusco's best-established venues, with modern Andean rock-art decor and basic furnishings. Drinks are quite cheap, though when it hosts live music (most weekends), there's usually a small entrance fee, but it's worthwhile if you're into rock and Andean folk. Happy hour 8–10pm; live music usually starts around 10.45pm, but get there earlier for a good seat.

Mama Africa Portal Harinas 191, second floor, Plaza de Armas. A good, buzzing dance bar with a small entrance fee and happy hour 4–11pm, playing electronic music on Sundays, reggae on Fridays and Saturdays, mixed disco and hip-hop during the week. They also do food, and often show DVDs

(latest Hollywood blockbusters included) in the afternoons and sometimes offers dance classes in salsa and samba. Daily 4pm–6am or later.

El Muki Disco Santa Catalina Angosta 110 ☎ 227797. Near the Plaza de Armas, *El Muki* has been pumping out pop every night for over twenty years. With its atmospheric catacomb-like dance floors, it's a safe space for late-night bopping, charging $2 entrance.

Mythology Portal de Carnes 298, second floor. Comfortable and chilled, but also good for dancing, *Mythology* has two bars, mainly spinning funk, hip-hop and reggae.

Ukuku's Bar C Plateros 316, down the alley and upstairs ☎ 254911. A highly popular venue with one of the best atmospheres in Cusco, teeming with energetic revellers most nights by around 11pm, when the music gets going. There's a small dancefloor and a long bar, with music ranging from live Andean folk with panpipes, drums and *charangos* (small Andean stringed instruments) to DJs or even taped rock. There's often an entrance charge – usually less than $2. Daily 2.30pm–2am, plus large-screen movies most afternoons.

Underground Teqsequocha 429. A smallish yet comfy, homely and relaxing space with one bar and occasional live music, although you can also choose music to play from their wide collection. Sports screen sometimes on.

Uptown Portal Belen 115. On the corner of the plaza, below the cathedral, this is one of the main clubs in town with lots of young people on the street giving out free entry tickets as promotions; it's a busy and fun place to be at weekends with a long barfront, big dancefloor and wall-side stage. Salsa lessons offered between 9–10.30pm most days. Snacks available.

Xtreme Portal de Carnes 298 ☎ 232922. One of Cusco's most popular dance bars, playing a wide range of music, from Latin and Euro pop to reggae. TV and movies during the day. Free drinks 10–11.30pm with the pass handed out on the street outside.

Shopping

Most of the touristy artesania and jewellery **shops** are concentrated in streets like Plateros around the Plaza de Armas and up Triunfo, though Calles Herraje (first right as you head towards San Blas) and San Agustin have slightly cheaper but decent shops with leather and alpaca work. It's worth heading off the beaten track, particularly around San Blas or the upper end of Tullumayo, to find outlets hidden in the backstreets. In the markets and at street stalls you can often get up to twenty percent off, and even in the smarter shops it's quite acceptable to bargain a little.

Cusco **opening hours** are generally Monday to Saturday 10am to 6pm, though some of the central gift stores open on Sundays and don't close until well into the evening. If you're worried about being robbed while making a substantial purchase, it's fine to ask the shopkeeper to bring the goods to your hotel so that the transaction can take place in relative safety.

Camping equipment

Rental or purchase of **camping equipment** is easy in Cusco, but if renting you may be asked to leave your passport as a deposit on more expensive items; always get a proper receipt. For basics such as pots, pans, plates and so on, try the stalls in Monjaspata, less than half a block from the bottom end of San Pedro market, while others such as buckets, bowls and sheets are sold in various shops along Calle Concebidayoq, close to the San Pedro market area.

Andean Life Santa Teresa 381 and Calle Plateros 372, Plaza de Armas ☎261269, ⊛www.andean-life.com. An adventure tour operator with a whole range of camping equipment for rent or sale.
Eric Adventures Urb Velasco Astete B -8-B ☎234764, ⓔcusco@ericadventures.com, ⊛www.ericadventures.com. Has a selection of camping equipment, new and old.
Gregory's Tours C Garcilazo Casa del Abuelo 210, office 111 ☎264199, ⊛www.gregory-adventureperu.com. Tents, sleeping bags, bed mats, stoves and gas to rent. Equipment also for sale and rent at Portal Comercio 121–129.

Inkas Trek C Medio 114. All the gear you'll need, and all available to rent.
Killak Sur C Medio 120. A good choice of equipment, plus they change dollars.
Quechuas Expeditions Procuradores 358 ☎236638. Rents and sells camping equipment and outdoor gear.
Tattoo Outdoors & Travel Plazoleta Las Nazarenas 211. Outdoor pursuits shop with quality – if pircey – clothing and accessories.
X-Treme Tourbulencia Expeditions Plateros 358 ☎224362 ⊛www.x-tremetourbulencia.com. Quite a range of used equipment.

Crafts, artesania and jewellery

Crafts and **artesania** are Cusco's stock in trade, with the best alpaca clothing outside Lima. It's an ideal place to pick up woollen sweaters, ponchos, jackets, weavings or antique cloths, while inexpensive and traditional musical instruments like panpipes, and colourful bags and leather crafts are also common. There's a very central and safe artesania market on the right-hand side going up block 1 of Plateros from the Plaza de Armas, and higher up in Calle Saphi there's an artesania market area more or less opposite the *Hostal Familiar*. Similar rows of artesania stalls can be found on the right-hand side of Triunfo, going uphill.

The new **Centro Artesanal Cusco** at the corner of Huanchac and Tullumayo, close to the huge sun disc fountain on Avenida Sol, has probably the largest and best-value collection of artesania under one roof in Peru; it's a nice, clean and relatively hassle-free shopping environment very close to the train ticket office at Huanchac station. The barrio of San Blas is the traditional quality artisan area of Cusco, home to a number of **jewellers**, art and antique shops. The Cuesta San Blas itself contains some of the finest artesania, new and old oil paintings and craft shops, while Hathun Rumiyoq has more good artesania shops at its bottom end. Around the San Blas plazoleta there are some funky shops and bars, and the main street market day there is Saturday, 10am–6pm. Out of town there are good markets at Pisac and Chinchero, main days being Sunday and Thursday, respectively (see p.275 and p.307).

Agua y Tierra Cuesta San Blas 595. Some excellent jungle textiles, ceramics, jewellery and cushma robes.

Allyu Ecologicos Av Tullumayo 280. Handmade textiles of pure alpaca dyed with local plants and also natural local herbal remedies. Money goes

direct to the craft producers concerned.
Alpaca 3 Plaza Regocijo 202 ⊛ 243233. Good alpaca fabrics, yarns, sweaters and scarves.
Artesanias Yamelin Procuradores 342. A well-stocked bead shop.
Galeria Olave C Plazoleta 651. A superb craft workshop that produces replicas of religious art and traditional Cusco cabinets and furniture.
Joyeria Oropesa Portal de Carrizos, corner of Calle Loreto. Jewellery for the seriously wealthy, specializing in silverwork.
Shaman Shop C Triunfo 393, space 107. A

small but well-stocked mystical store selling everything from candles and incenses to magical talismans and shamanic music. It's also a good place to find contacts for *ayahuasca* and San Pedro ceremonies (see p.264).
Taller de Instrumentos Hathun Rumiyoq 451 (head through the back to the second patio). Rustic workshop producing *charangos*, *quenas* and pan-pipes, often to professional standards.
Werner and Ana Plaza San Francisco 295-A ⊛ 231076. This clothing boutique is owned by some of Peru's top fashion designers.

Food, books and music

Casa Ecologica C Triunfo 393, space 4 off the courtyard, and Portal de Carnes 236 on the Plaza de Armas ⊛ 255427, ⊛ www.casaecologicacusco .com. Good for organic foods, natural medicines and quality ethically sourced textiles.
Central Market San Pedro. The best place for generally excellent and very cheap food – including all the main typical Peruvian dishes like *cau cau* (tripe), rice with meats and veggies and *papas a la huancaina* (see p.618) – provided you feel comfort-able with a street-stall standard of hygiene.
El Chinito Grande Matará 271. A large Chinese-run supermarket with good prices and selection, offering an array of Chinese food, as well as other international foods.
El Croissant Plaza San Francisco 134. Good French bakery – ideal for croissants, French sticks and, best of all, delicious cream pastries.

Gato's Market Santa Catalina Angosta, corner of Plaza de Armas and close to the Cathedral. A good range of typical Peruvian foods.
Heladera Italiana Santa Catalina Ancha 366. Great ice cream selection.
The minimarket shops on C Plateros – numbers 392, 352 and 355 – are small but packed to the rafters with food for trekking expeditions – cheese, biscuits, tins of tuna, nuts, chocolate, raisins and dried bananas.
Libreria Genesis Santa Catalina Ancha at corner with Santa Catalina Angosta. This is probably the best place to find books in English, particularly guides, histories and material on birds or wildlife; it's also a post office agent.
Music Centre Av Sol 230. The best range of Andean and Peruvian cassettes and CDs in Cusco.

Tours in and around Cusco

Tours in and around Cusco range from a half-day city tour to an expedition by light aircraft or a full-on adventure down to the Amazon. **Prices** range from $20 to over $120 a day, and service and facilities vary considerably, so check exactly what's provided, whether insurance is included and whether the guide speaks English. The main agents are strung along three sides of the Plaza de Armas, along Portal de Panes, Portal de Confiturias and Portal Comercio, up Procuradores and along the calles Plateros and Saphi and, although prices vary, many are selling places on the same tours and treks, so always hunt around. Avoid the **tour touts** at the airport or in the plaza at Cusco, and check out the operators in advance at the South American Explorers' Club (see p.266) if you're able to (members also receive a discount with some outfits). If you want to book in advance with reputable companies, there are also a few Lima-based operators in this area (see p.118).

Standard tours around the city, Sacred Valley and to Machu Picchu range from a basic bus service with fixed stops and little in the way of a guide, to luxury pack-ages including guide, food and hotel transfers. The three- to six-day **Inca Trail** is the most popular of the **mountain treks**, with thousands of people hiking it every year. Many agencies offer trips with guides, equipment and fixed itineraries; but it's important to remember that **entry to the Inca Trail** is restricted to only a few hundred people a day and requires tourists to travel with a guide or tour as well as to be registered with the Unidad de Gestión (your tour company does this) before departure. It's best to **book nine to twelve months in advance** and it's a good idea to compare Inca Trail tour options and prices before making your decision; prices vary considerably between $200 and $500 and don't always reflect genuine added value. Check exactly what's provided: train tickets (which class), quality of tent, roll mat, sleeping bag, porter to carry rucksack and sleeping bag, bus down from ruins, exactly which meals are offered and transport to the starting point of the tour.

Adventure tourism

In reality of course, the Inca Trail isn't so popular because it's the most wonderful of all hikes in the Peruvian Andes; it's because of where you end up, the slightly unjust appropriation of a very fine trail name and all the hype that it gets. The mountains to the south and the north of Cusco are full of amazing trekking trails, some of them little touched, most of them still rarely walked (see p.301). Less adventurous **walks** or **horse rides** are possible to Qenko, Tambo Machay, Puca Pucara and Chacan, in the hills above Cusco and in the nearby Sacred Valley (as described above). You can also rent out **mountain bikes** for trips to the Sacred Valley and around, and some outfits arrange guided tours (or contact Renny Gamarra Loaiza, a good biking guide; ☏231300). Many **jungle trip operators** are based in Cusco, and those that also cover the immediate Cusco area are listed below as well as in Chapter Eight, where their jungle-specific trips are detailed. Price wise, jungle tours are usually a minimum of three nights from Cusco and cost from around $45 a night up to hundreds.

Cusco is also a great **whitewater rafting** centre, with easy access to classes 2 to 5 (rivers are generally rated from class 1 – very easy – to class 5 – very difficult/borderline dangerous) around Ollantaytambo on the Río Urubamba and classes 1 to 3 between Huambutio and Pisac, on the Río Vilcanota. From Calca to Urubamba the river runs classes 2 to 3, but this rises to 5 in the rainy season. Calca to Pisac (Huaran) and Ollantaytambo to Chilca are among the most popular routes, while the most dangerous are further afield on the Río Apurimac. The easiest stretch is from Echarate to San Baray, which passes by Quillabamba. Costs range from around $35 to $100 a day, with price usually reflecting quality, but it's always recommendable to use a reputable and well established rafting company. Remember that most travel insurances exclude this kind of adventure activity and always ensure that you are fully equipped with a safety kayak, helmets and lifejackets.

Bungee jumping is the latest craze in Cusco. The tallest **bungee jump facility** in the Americas (122m) is offered by Action Valley Cusco, Santa Teresa 325 (☏240835, ⓦwww.actionvalley.com), just a fifteen-minute walk from the plaza in Poroy (buses here from block 8 of Avenida Sol). Equally breathtaking but slightly less scary is the option of a **hot air balloon** adventure in the Cusco or Sacred Valley areas; contact Globos de los Andes, C Arequipa 271 (☏232352, ⓦwww.globosperu.com).

Psychedelic tourism

Psychedelic tourism is popular in Cusco these days, though not as developed as in Iquitos (see p.549). This doesn't mean that a lot of people take "drugs" and wander around the Andes. Essentially, psychedelic tourism is based on traditional healing techniques that tend to focus on inner consciousness and well-being through often highly ritualized ceremonies. San Pedro or *ayahuasca*, the two principal indigenous **psychedelic plants** that have been used ceremonially in Peru for over 3500 years (see p.583) can be experienced with the assistance of **Another Planet** (Triunfo 120, ⓣ242714 or 241168), who also lead organized spiritual tours. The Shaman Shop, C Triunfo 393, is a good place for contacts; and there's also the Casa de la Serenidad, Tandapata 296a (ⓣ222851), which, besides assisting with altitude problems, offers coca-leaf readings, Reiki, flower and herb baths, and *ayahuasca* or San Pedro ceremonies.

Cusco tour operators

Andean Life Santa Teresa 381 and C Plateros 372, Plaza de Armas ⓣ261269, ⓦwww.andeanlife.com. Strong on the Inca Trail but generally specialists in small-group treks including Salcantay, Lares, Ausangate as well as whitewater rafting and jungle trips. Inca Trail packages from $450.

Andina Travel Plazoleta Santa Catalina 219 ⓣ251892 ⓔandinatravel@terra.com.pe ⓦwww.andinatravel.com. Reputable agents, Andina organize mountain biking as well as alternative treks to the Inca Trail, such as Choquequirao, the Lares Valley, Salcantay and Ausangate. Inca Trail packages from $390.

Apumayo Jr Ricardo Palma 5, Santa Monica, Wanchaq ⓣ 246018 ⓦwww.apumayo.com. Expert operators offering trekking in the Sacred Valley region, mountain biking around Cusco and the Sacred Valley, historic and archaeological tours, tours for disabled people (with wheelchair support for visiting major sites), horseriding, and rafting on the ríos Urubamba and Apurimac. They can customize their trips to suit your agenda, though note that they usually only work with pre-booked groups.

Colibri Tour C Triunfo 392, office 209 ⓣ247849, ⓦwww.colibritrour.com. Specialists on the Inca Trail and will arrange transport and collection from hotel. Also offer treks to Salcantay, Ausangate, Choquequirao and Vilcabamba.

Eric Adventures Urb Velasco Astete B -8-B ⓣ234764, ⓔcusco@ericadventures.com, ⓦwww.ericadventures.com. A good selection of tours, from the Inca Trail to trekking, and with a good reputation for rafting. A day on the Urubamba river can cost as little as $35–40.

Expediciones Vilca C Plateros 359 ⓣ & ⓕ253773 & 244751, ⓔmanuvilca@terra.com.pe, ⓦwww.manuvilcaperu.com. A well-established trekking company with a variety of treks albeit specializing in expeditions to the Manu Biosphere Reserve (see p.521). They can rent you any camping gear you need.

Explorandes Av Garcilaso 316-A, Wanchaq ⓣ238380, ⓕ 233784, ⓔpostmaster@explorandes.com, ⓦwww.explorandes.com; or San Fernando 320, Miraflores, Lima ⓣ 01/4450532 or 2423496, ⓕ 4454686. A long-established company with a range of tours and treks that include the Inca Trail and Cordillera Vilcanota. For their jungle rafting expeditions, see p.519.

Kantu Portal Carrizos 258, Plaza de Armas ⓣ243673. Good for budget rafting, and prices include food and somewhere to sleep overnight (usually a tent).

Manu Expeditions C Humberto Vidal, G-5, Segunda Etapa, Urbanización Magisterio ⓣ226671, ⓕ236706 ⓦwww.manuexpeditions.com, ⓦwww.manuwildlifecenter.com and ⓦwww.birding-in-peru.com. Run, like the *Cross Keys Pub*, by the enigmatic local British Consul and well-known twitcher, Barry Walker, this company specializes in both trips to Manu and birding expeditions, as well as horseriding and mountain adventure tours, including trips to Espiritu Pampa, the Inca site of Choquequirao through the Vilcabamba mountains, to Machu Picchu from Ollantaytambo via Anacachcocha and the Huaynay peaks, and more traditional treks like the Inca Trail.

Manu Nature Tours Av Pardo 1046 ⓣ252721, ⓕ234793, ⓔinfo@manunaturetours.com, ⓦwww.manuperu.com. An award winning, nature-based adventure travel company, they run tours to the jungle (see Chapter 8), plus mountain biking, birdwatching and rafting. They also operate a garden café next to their offices, so you can have a drink and snack if you visit.

MAYUC Portal Confiturias 211, Cusco ⓣ242824, ⓕ232666, ⓔchando@mayuc.com, ⓦwww.mayuc.com. Highly reliable outfit with the experience to organize any tour or trek of your choice, from an extended Inca Trail to visiting the Tambopata-Candamo area. Whitewater rafting is their speciality with standard scheduled 4-day/3-night excursions involving grade 2 to 5 rapids from about $230.

Peru Planet C Suecia 318 ⊤/Ⓕ 251145, Ⓔ info
@peruplanet.net, Ⓦ www.peru-planet.net. A well-
respected local agency offering the usual city tours
as well as the Sacred Valley, Machu Picchu, Inca
Trail, horseriding and rafting.
Peruvian Andean Treks Av Pardo 705, Cusco
⊤ 225701, Ⓕ 238911, Ⓦ www.andeantreks.com.
Expensive, but top-quality options for the Inca Trail,
this 28-year-old company also operates other treks
in the Cusco region and Peruvian Andes. Worth
contacting in advance for their brochure.
SAS Travel C Garcilaso 270, just below Plaza San
Francisco, Cusco ⊤ 249194, Ⓔ info@sastravelperu
.com, Ⓦ www.sastravelperu.com. Reliable and
professional tour and trek operators, specialists in
the Inca Trail but also do Salcantay, Choquequirao,
Ausangate and Vilcabamba as well as the main
jungle destinations. Usually good value.

United Mice C Plateros 351, Cusco
⊤ 221139, Ⓔ reservations@unitedmice
.com, www.unitedmice.com. The top specialists in
guided tours of the Inca Trail and reasonably priced
(4 days, 3 nights for $250 including tax, discounts
for students), with good guides, many of whom
speak English. Food is of a high standard and
their camping equipment is fine. If anything, their
popularity is a drawback, since groups are largish
in high season. Tours which avoid the Inca Trail
tax include: an excellent 5-day trek approaching
Machu Picchu via Mollepata and Salcantay, crossing the river at the hydroelectric station down river
from the ruins for access to Machu Picchu; another
interesting 5-day trek heads for Choquequirao with
a minimum group size of 8 costing around $195 per
person; a 6-day trek to Ausangate which, for around
$205 per person, has a minimum group size of 10.

Listings

Airlines Lan Peru (and Lan Chile), Av Sol 627b
⊤ 255555 or 255553 and at the airport ⊤ 255550,
Ⓦ www.lan.com, for Lima, Puerto Maldonado,
Juliaca, Tacana and Arequipa; TACA Peru, Av Sol
226 ⊤ 249921, Ⓕ 249926, Ⓦ www.taca.com, for
Lima (from about $70 standard, including tax); Star
Peru ⊤ 253791, Ⓦ www.starperu.com; Aerosur
⊤ 254691, Ⓦ www.aerosur.com.
ATMs Global Net ATMs at Portal de Panes 115,
Plaza de Armas; Portal Comercio 117, Plaza de
Armas; in Wanchaq and the San Pedro (for Machu
Picchu) train stations.
Banks and exchange Interbanc, Av Sol 380 (also
has ATM at airport), is good for travellers' cheques,
cash exchange and credit card extraction and has
an ATM; Banco de Credito, Av Sol 189 (has a very
good array of internal ATMs); Banco Continental,
Av Sol 366, changes cash and most travellers'
cheques. For faster service on cash and travellers'
cheque exchange there are hotels or the *casas de
cambio*. There are several *casas de cambio* along
Portal Comercio at the Plaza deArmas; LAC Dollar,
Av El Sol 150, and the Casa de Cambio, Oficina 1,
Av Sol 345, is also OK. Lastly, street *cambistas* can
be found on blocks 2 and 3 of Av Sol, around the
main banks, but as usual take great care here.
Car rental Manu, Av El Sol 520 ⊤ 233382,
Ⓦ www.manurentacar.com; MBB ⊤ 275970,
Ⓦ www.mbbperu.com; AVIS, Garcilasp 210
⊤ 241824.
Consulates Bolivia, Av Pardo, Pasaje Espinar
⊤ 231412; Netherlands, Av El Sol 954 ⊤ 224322;
Ireland, Santa Catalina Ancha 360 ⊤ 243514; UK,

C Humberto Vidal, G-5, Segunda Etapa, Urbaniza-
ción Magisterio ⊤ 226671 or 239974, Ⓕ 236706;
for the USA contact the Instituto de Cultura Peruana
Norte Americana, Av Tullumayo 125 ⊤ 224112.
Courier services DHL, Av Sol 6 ⊤ 244167.
Cultural centre The Alliance Française, Av de la
Cultura 804 (⊤ 223755), runs a full programme of
events including music, films, exhibitions, theatre
and music; phone for details.
Dentists Dr Virginia Valcarcel Velarde, upstairs at
Portal de Panes 123, Plaza de Armas ⊤ 231558;
and Dr Pintur, Centro Comercial Santa Cecilia, by
the Sandy Colour Fotografia, Av Sol ⊤ 233721 or
651211.
Doctors Dr Oscar Tejada ⊤ 233836 (24hr), is
a member of International Assistance for Medical Assistance to Travellers; Dr Dante Valdivia ⊤
231390, 620588 or 252166, speaks English and
German; and Dr Maria Helena ⊤ 650122 or
227385, will visit your hotel.
Hospitals and clinics Hospital Regional, Av de
la Cultura ⊤ 231455, 223030 or 223691; Clinica
Pardo, Av de la Cultura 710, Wanchaq ⊤ 249999;
or the Clinica Laboratorio Louis Pasteur, Tullumayo
768 ⊤ 234727 which has a gynaecologist. For high
altitude health matters contact CIMA Av Pardo 978
⊤ 255550, Ⓦ www.cimaperu.com.
Immigration Migraciones, Av Sol, block 620
⊤ 222741.
Internet facilities Internet access and internet
cafés are very ubiquitous in Cusco: *Ukukos Internet*, first floor, C Plateros 316, is a large space with
good food and bar service; wi-fi access at *Nick's*

Sports Bar and *Sumay Misky* restaurant upstairs at C Plateros 334. Expect to pay around $1–2 an hour for logging on at most places.

Language schools Amigos Spanish School at Zaguan del Cielo B-23 ☎242292, ⓦwww.spanish cusco.com, a not-for-profit institution which funds education and food for local young people through its teaching of Spanish; family stays can also be organized if required. Staff speaks English, Dutch, German, French and Japanese; extracurricular activities include salsa and merengue dance lessons, cooking classes and aerobics at 3400m. The South American Spanish School based at Carmen Alto 112, San Blas ☎223012, ⓦwww.sasschool.org, provides excellent teaching along with hostel or family-home-based accommodation where required. Proyecto Peru, Tecsecocha 429 565, ⓔinfo@proyectoperucentre .org, offer group and individual Spanish lessons, both survival Spanish and technical.

Laundry Ña P'asña, Saphi 578a. Fairly cheap and efficient, with self-service also available; T'Aqsana Wasi, Santa Catalina Ancha 345; Lavandería Louis at Choquechaca 264 is very fast; Lavamachine in both Santa Teresa 383 and Procuradores 50; and Laundry, Teqsecocha 428.

Motorbike hire Peru MotoTours, C Saphi 578 ☎232742, ⓦwww.incamoto.com; and Cusco Motors, C Saphi 592 ☎227025, ⓦwww .cuscomototourperu.com.

Park office, Manu Parque Nacional del Manu, Av Micaela Bastidas 310, Wanchaq, Cusco ☎240898; most travellers are actually unlikely to need to visit this office, since any organised tour to the Manu Biosphere Reserve will have already obtained permission for you.

Post office The main office, at Av Sol 800 ☎225232 (Mon–Sat 7.30am–8pm, Sun 7.30am–2.30pm) operates a quick and reliable poste restante system.

South American Explorers' Club Choquechaca 188 no.4 ☎245484, Apartado 500 ⓦwww.saex-plorers.org. Good information sheets, trip reports and files on virtually everything about Cusco and Peru, including transport, trekking, hotels, internet cafés and tour companies. The excellent clubhouse has a luggage deposit, notice board, library and book exchange. Membership fees would be covered by the discount SE Club members get with some companies on just one tour to the Manu Biosphere Reserve (Mon–Fri 9.30am–5pm, Sat 9.30am–1pm).

Taxis Alo Cusco ☎222222; Llama taxi ☎222000; Central 239 ☎239969.

Telephones Like internet access, and often in the same places, public telephones can be found very cheaply all over the city. Similarly, the right phone card can get you cheap calls in Peru and internationally (see p.55).

Tourist police C Saphi 581 ☎249654 and also Monumento Pachacutec ☎211961.

Tourist protection service Servicio de Protección al Turista, Av Sol 103, Room 203 ☎252974, Ⓕ 234498, ⓔ iperucusco@promperu.gob.pe (daily 9am–7pm).

Train tickets The Estación Huanchac ticket office on Av Pachacutec, Wanchaq ☎238722 or 221992 for reservations, Ⓕ221114, ⓦwww.perurail .com (Mon–Fri 7am–5pm, Sat, Sun and holidays 7am–noon) sells Puno and Machu Picchu tickets. For Machu Picchu it's best to buy in advance from

Bus departures from Cusco

Most inter-regional and international buses depart from the Terminal Terrestre, Av Vallegos Santoni, block 2, Sector Molino Pampa, right side of Río Huatanay, in the district of Santiago ☎224471. Exceptions are Cruz del Sur buses, which depart from Av Pachacutec 510 (5.30am–8pm for tickets; ☎221909) and those of Kamisea (☎246071), for Quillabamba, which depart from the corner of Santiago and Juan Antonio Manya. At the Terminal Terrestre there is an embarcation tax of 30¢, which you pay before alighting; destinations (and bus companies serving them) include:

Abancay - BREDDE (☎243278) and Turismo Ampay (☎227541)

Andahuaylas - Molina Union (☎236144)

Arequipa and Tacna - El Chasqui (☎249961), Pony Express and Turismo Universal (☎243540)

Copacabana and La Paz - Ormeño (☎227501)

Curahuasi, Sahuite and Lima Tambo - Curahuasi (☎227074)

Lima – CIAL (☎249961), CIVA, Flores and Ormeño,

Juliaca, Puno and Desaguadero - CIVA, Cruz del Sur, Libertad (☎432955) and Urkupiña (☎229962)

Quillabamba - Selva Tour (☎ 247975)

The train journey to Machu Picchu

The new improved service offered by **Peru Rail** between Cusco and Machu Picchu – one of the finest mountain train journeys in the world – enhances the thrill of riding tracks through such fantastic scenery even further by offering very good service and comfortable, well-kept carriages. Rumbling out of Cusco around 6am the wagons zigzag their way through the backstreets, where little houses cling to the steep valley slopes. It takes a while to rise out of the teacup-like valley, but once it reaches the high plateau above, the train rolls through fields and past highland villages before eventually dropping rapidly down into the Urubamba Valley utilising several major track switchbacks, which means you get to see some of the same scenery twice. It reaches the Sacred Valley floor just before getting into Ollantaytambo, where from the windows you can already see scores of impressively terraced fields and, in the distance, more Inca temple and storehouse constructions. Ollantaytambo's pretty railway station is right next to the river, and here you can expect to be greeted by a handful of Quechua women selling their mainly woollen craft goods. The train continues down the valley, stopping briefly at Km 88, where the Inca Trail starts, then follows the Urubamba River as the valley gets tighter (that's why there's no road) and the mountain becomes more and more forested as well as steeper and seemingly taller. The end of the line these days is the new station at **Machu Picchu Pueblo** (also known as Aguas Calientes), a busy little town crowded into the valley just a short bus ride from the ruins themselves (see p.298). For information on tickets and schedules, see below.

here, though, if there are any tickets remaining on the morning of departure, these can be actually bought on the day by queuing at San Pedro station (5–7am & 3–4pm, ☎238722). For a full description of the journey see box, above.

Travel agents America Tour, Portal de Harinas 175 ☎ 227208, ⓦwww.americatours.org, mostly book and sell air tickets but also arrange packages within Peru and the Cusco region; and Milla Turismo, Av Pardo 689 ☎231710,

ⓕ231388, ⓦwww.millaturismo.com, will organize travel arrangements, tours, study tours and cultural tourist-related activities.

Vaccinations Cusco Hospital Regional, Av de la Cultura ☎231455 or 223030, offers free yellow fever inoculations every Sat from 11am to 1pm.

Visas Migraciones, Av Sol 620 ☎222741; Mon–Fri 9am–5pm.

Western Union Santa Catalina Ancha 311 ☎ 248028.

Inca sites near Cusco

The megalithic fortress of **Sacsayhuaman**, which looks down onto the red-tiled roofs of Cusco from high above the city, is the closest and most impressive of several historic sites scattered around the Cusco hills. However, there are four other major Inca sites in the area. Not much more than a stone's throw beyond Sacsayhuaman lies the great *huaca* of **Qenko** and the less-visited **Salumpuncu**, thought by some to be a moon temple. A few kilometres further on, at what almost certainly formed the outer limits of the Inca's home estate, you come to the small, fortified hunting lodge of **Puca Pucara** and the stunning imperial baths of **Tambo Machay**.

All these places are an energetic day's **walk** from Cusco, but you'll probably want to devote a whole day to Sacsayhuaman and leave the others until you're more adjusted to the rarefied air. If you'd rather start from the top and work your way downhill, it's possible to take one of the regular buses from Cusco to Pisac and

Map labels:

N

INCA SITES NEAR CUSCO

Tambo Machay

Río Tambomachay

Puca Pucara

— Roads
=== Dirt Tracks
--- Footpaths & Short-cuts

0   500 m

Pisac

Chacan

Salapunco

Río Tica Tica

Quispe Huara

Río Saphi

Qenko

Warden's Hut (west)

Warden's Hut (east)

Río Tullumayo

Rodadero   Calispucyo

Sacsayhuaman

Christ figure

Muya Marca
Temple of the Sun

Cusco

▼ Cusco   ▼ Cusco   ▼ San Blas & Plaza de Armas

Urubamba. One company, Empresa Clorinda, leave from C Puputi 208, one block below Recoleta and two blocks up from Avenida de la Cultura at the junction with Ejercicios, just beyond the Estadio Univeritario. Other regular buses of a similar basic standard depart from Tullumayo 207. Just ask to be dropped off at the highest of the sites, Tambo Machay, from where it's a relatively easy two-hour walk back into the centre of Cusco, or at Qenko, which is closer to Sacsayhuaman and the city. Alternatively, you can take a **horseback tour** ($15–20 for a couple of hours) incorporating most of these sites, but they usually start and finish at Sacsayhuaman or Qenko ($3–5 taxi ride from the centre of Cusco).

Sacsayhuaman

Although it looks relatively close to central Cusco, it's quite a steep forty-minute, two-kilometre climb up to the ruins of Sacsayhuaman from the Plaza de Armas. The simplest route is up Calle Suecia, then right along the narrow cobbled street of Wayna Pata to Pumacurco, which heads steeply up to a small café-bar with a balcony that commands superb views over the city. It's only another ten minutes from the café, following the signposted steps all the way up to the ruins. By now you're beyond the built-up sectors of Cusco and walking in countryside, and there's a well-worn path and crude stairway that takes you right up to the heart of the fortress.

SACSAYHUAMAN (daily 7am–5.30pm; entry by Cusco Tourist Ticket, see p.243) forms the head of Cusco's ethereal puma, whose fierce-looking teeth point away from the city. The name Sacsayhuaman is of disputed origin, with different groups holding that it means either "satiated falcon", "speckled head" or "city of stone". Protected by such a steep approach from the town, the fortress only needed defensive walls on one side. Nevertheless, this "wall" is one of South America's archaeological treasures, actually formed by three massive, parallel stone ramparts zigzagging together for some 600m across the plateau just over the other side of the mountain top from Cusco city and the valley below. These zigzag walls, incorporating the most monumental and megalithic stones used in ancient Peru, form the boundary of what was originally designed as a "spiritual distillation" of the ancient city below, with many sectors named after areas of imperial Cusco. Little of the inner structures remains, yet these enormous ramparts stand 20m high, quite undamaged by past battles, earthquakes and the passage of time. The strength of the mortarless stonework – one block weighs more than 300 tonnes – is matched by the brilliance of its design: the zigzags, casting shadows in the afternoon sun, not only look like jagged cat's teeth, but also seem to have been cleverly designed to expose the flanks of any attacking force. Recently, however, many sacred and ritual objects excavated here have caused archaeologists to consider Sacsayhuaman as more of a ceremonial centre than a fortress, the distinctive, jagged form of these outer walls possibly symbolizing the important deity of lightning.

Originally, the inner "fort" was covered in buildings, a maze of tiny streets dominated by three major towers. The tower of **Muyu Marca**, whose foundations can still be seen clearly, was round, over 30m tall and with three concentric circles of wall, the outer one roughly 24m in diameter. An imperial residence, it apparently had lavish inner chambers and a constant supply of fresh water, carried up through subterranean channels. The other two towers – **Salla Marca** and **Paunca Marca** – had rectangular bases about 20m long and were essentially warriors' barracks, and all three were painted in vivid colours, had thatched roofs and were interconnected by underground passages: in its entirety, the inner fortress could have housed as many as ten thousand people under siege. At the rear of this sector, looking directly down into Cusco and the valley, was a **temple dedicated to the sun**, reckoned by some to be the most important shrine in the entire Inca empire and the most sacred sector of Sacsayhuaman. There is some excavation of these sites going on at the moment, but it's still very difficult to make out anything but the circular tower base.

In front of the main defensive walls, a flat expanse of grassy ground – the esplanade – divides the fortress from a large outcrop of volcanic diorite. Intricately carved in places, and scarred with deep glacial striations, this rock, called the **Rodadero** ("sliding place"), was the site of an Inca throne. Originally there was a stone parapet surrounding this important *huaca*, and it's thought that the emperor would have sat here to oversee ceremonial gatherings at fiesta times, when there would be processions, wrestling matches and running competitions. On the far side of this huge outcrop are larger recreational sliding areas, smoothed by the many centuries of Inca – and now tourists' – backsides. From here you can see another large circular space called Qocha Chincanas, possibly an Inca graveyard, and on its far side the sacred spring of **Calispucyo**, where ceremonies to initiate boys into manhood were held. Excavations here have uncovered crystals and shells (some of the latter all the way from Ecuador), a sign usually associated with water veneration.

Some history

It was the **Emperor Pachacuti** who began work on Sacsayhuaman in the 1440s, although it took nearly a century of creative work to finish it. The chronicler Cieza de León, writing in the 1550s, estimated that some twenty thousand men had been involved in Sacsayhuaman's construction: four thousand cutting blocks from quarries; six thousand dragging them on rollers to the site; and another ten thousand working on finishing and fitting the blocks into position. According to legend, some three thousand lives were lost while dragging just one huge stone. Various types of rock were used, including enormous diorite blocks from nearby for the outer walls, Yucay limestone from more than 15km away for the foundations and dark andesite, some of it from over 30km away at Rumicolca, for the inner buildings and towers. First, boulders were split by boring holes with stone or cane rods and wet sand; next, wooden wedges were inserted into these holes and saturated to crack the rocks into more manageable sizes; finally the blocks were shifted into place with levers. With only natural fibre ropes, stone hammers and bronze chisels, it must have been an enormous task.

During the fateful battle of 1536, Juan Pizarro, Francisco's son, was killed as he charged the main gate in a surprise assault, and a leading Inca nobleman, armed with a Spanish sword and shield, caused havoc by repulsing every enemy who tried to scale Muyu Marca, the last tower left in Inca hands. Having sworn to fight to the death, he leapt from the top when defeat seemed inevitable, rather than accept humiliation and dishonour. After the battle the esplanade was covered in native corpses, food for vultures and inspiration for the Cusco coat of arms, which, since 1540, has been bordered by eight condors "in memory of the fact that when the castle was taken these birds descended to eat the natives who had died in it". The conquistadors wasted little time in dismantling most of the inner structures of the fortress, using the stones to build Spanish Cusco.

Today the most dramatic event to take place at Sacsayhuaman is the colourful – if overly commercial – **Inti Raymi festival** in June (see p.239). However, throughout the year, you may stumble across various **sun ceremonies** being performed here by mystics from the region.

Qenko

An easy twenty-minute walk from Sacsayhuaman, the large limestone outcrop of **QENKO** (daily 7am–5.30pm; entry by Cusco Tourist Ticket, see p.243) was another important Inca *huaca*. Head towards the Cusco–Pisac road along a track from the warden's hut on the northeastern edge of Sacsayhuaman, and Qenko is just over the other side of the main road; the route is straightforward but poorly signposted.

This great stone, carved with a complex pattern of steps, seats, geometric reliefs and puma designs, illustrates the critical role of the Rock Cult in the realm of Inca cosmological beliefs (the surrounding foothills are dotted with carved rocks and elaborate stone terraces). The name of this *huaca* derives from the Quechua word *quenqo*, meaning "labyrinth" or "zigzag", and refers to the patterns laboriously carved into the upper, western edge of the stone. At an annual festival priests would pour sacrificial llama blood into a bowl at the serpent-like top of the main zigzag channel; if it flowed out through the left-hand bifurcation, this was a bad omen for the fertility of the year to come. If, on the other hand, it continued the full length of the channel and poured onto the rocks below, this was a good omen.

The stone may also be associated with solstice and equinox ceremonies, fertility rites and even marriage rituals (there's a twin seat close to the top of Qenko which looks very much like a lovers' kissing bench). Right on top of the stone two prominent round nodules are carved onto a plinth. These appear to be mini versions of *intihuatanas* ("hitching posts" of the sun), found at many Inca sacred sites – local guides claim that on the summer solstice, at around 8am, the nodules' shadow looks like a puma's face and a condor with wings outstretched at the same time. Along with the serpent-like divinatory channels, this would complete the three main layers of the Inca cosmos: sky (condor), earth (puma) and the underworld (snake). Beneath Qenko are several **tunnels and caves**, replete with impressive carved niches and steps, which may have been places for spiritual contemplation and communication with the forces of life and earth. It's been suggested that some of the niches may have been where the mummies of lesser nobles were kept.

At the top end of the *huaca*, behind the channelled section, the Incas constructed an impressive, if relatively small, semicircular **amphitheatre** with nineteen vaulted niches (probably seats for priests or nobles) facing in towards the impressive limestone. At the heart of the amphitheatre rises a natural standing stone, which looks like a frog (representative of the life-giving and cleansing power of rain) from some angles and like a puma from others, both creatures of great importance to pre-Conquest Peru.

Salapunco

A twenty-minute stroll uphill and through the trees above Qenko, to the right of the small hill, along the path (keeping the houses to your right), then emerging onto the fields and turning right, leads to **SALAPUNCO**. Yet another sacred *huaca*, though off the beaten track – also known as the Temple of the Moon and locally called Laqo – this large rock outcrop contains a number of small caves where the rock has been painstakingly carved. At the time of writing an archaeological dig is taking place here. You can see worn relief work with puma and snake motifs on the external rock faces, while in the caves there are altar-like platforms and niches that were probably used to house mummies. The largest of the caves is thought to have been a venue for ceremonies celebrating the full moon, as it sometimes is now, when an eerie silver light filters into the usually dark interior. Close to Salapunco there's another site, called **K'usilluchayoq**, which has some more rock carvings. It's possible to walk down from here to Plaza de Armas via interconnecting trails that initially go through some new barrios above the main Cusco–Pisac road, then down to San Blas.

Chacan and Quispe Huara

An important but little-visited Inca site, **CHACAN** lies about 5km from Sacsayhuaman on the opposite side of the fortress from Qenko and the road to Tambo Machay. It can be safely, though not easily, reached in the dry season (May–Sept) by following the rather indistinct footpaths directly north from the Rodadero at Sacsayhuaman. When you hit the gully coming from the west, follow this up to the site; if you've been walking for ninety minutes or more and haven't found it, the chances are you've already passed it.

Chacan itself was a revered spring, and you can see a fair amount of terracing, some carved rocks and a few buildings in the immediate vicinity; like Tambo Machay, it demonstrates the importance of water as an ever-changing, life-giving force in Inca religion. A pleasant but more difficult walk leads down the Tica Tica stream (keep to the right-hand side of the stream and stay well above it), until you come to **Quispe Huara** ("crystal loincloth"), where a two- to three-metre-high pyramid shape has been cut into the rock. Close by are some Inca stone walls, probably once part of a ritual bathing location. You really need a local map to find your way with any certainty.

Puca Pucara

Although a relatively small ruin, **PUCA PUCARA** (daily 7am–5.30pm; entry by Cusco Tourist Ticket, see p.243), meaning "Red Fort", is around 11km from the city, impressively situated overlooking the Cusco Valley, right beside the main Cusco–Pisac road, and well worth the trip. Between one and two hours' cross-country walk, uphill from Sacsayhuaman and Qenko (longer if you keep to the sinuous main road), this area is dotted with cut rocks. The zone was well populated in Inca days, and many of those people may have been worked to obtain stones for building.

Although in many ways reminiscent of a small European castle, with a commanding esplanade topping its semicircle of protective wall, Puca Pucara is more likely to have been a hunting lodge for the emperor than simply a defensive position. Thought to have been built by the Emperor Pachacutec, it commands views towards glaciers to the south of the Cusco Valley. Easily defended on three sides, it could have contained only a relatively small garrison and may have been a guard post between Cusco and the Sacred Valley, which lies to the northeast; it could also have had a sacred function, as it has excellent views towards the *apu* of Ausangate and is ideally placed to keep tabs on the flow of people and produce from the Sacred Valley to Cusco. In sum, Puca Pucara is a good example of how the Incas combined recreation and spirituality along with social control and military defence.

Tambo Machay

TAMBO MACHAY (daily 7am–5.30pm; entry by Cusco Tourist Ticket, see p.243), less than fifteen minutes' walk along a signposted track that leads off the main road just north of Puca Pucara, is one of the more impressive Inca baths, or Temple of the Waters, evidently a place for ritual as well as physical cleaning and purification. Situated at a spring near the Inca's hunting lodge, its main construction lies in a sheltered gully where some superb Inca masonry again emphasizes their fascination and adoration of water.

The ruins basically consist of three tiered platforms. The top one holds four trapezoidal niches that may have been used as seats; on the next level, underground water emerges directly from a hole at the base of the stonework, and from here cascades down to the bottom platform, creating a cold shower just high enough for an Inca to stand under. On this platform the spring water splits into two channels, both pouring the last metre down to ground level. Clearly a site for ritual bathing, the quality of the stonework suggests that its use was restricted to the higher nobility, who perhaps used the baths only on ceremonial occasions.

About 1km further up the gully, you'll come to a small **grotto** where there's a pool large enough for bathing, even in the dry season. Whilst it shows no sign of Inca stonework, the hills on either side of the stream are dotted with stone terraces and caves, one or two of which still have remnants of walls at their entrance. In Inca, *machay* means "cave", suggesting that these were an important local feature, perhaps as sources of water for Tambo Machay and Puca Pucara.

The Sacred Valley and Machu Picchu

The **SACRED VALLEY**, or Vilcamayo to the Incas, is located about 30km north-west of Cusco, traces its winding, astonishingly beautiful course from here down towards Urubamba, Ollantaytambo and eventually Machu Picchu. It's a steep-sided river valley that opens out into a narrow but very fertile alluvial plain, which was well exploited agriculturally by the Incas. Even within 30km or so of valley, there are several microclimates allowing specializations in different fruits, maizes and other important local plants. The river itself starts in the high Andes south of Cusco and is called the Vilcanota, the same name as the mountain range where it emerges from until the Sacred Valley; from here on down river it's known as the Río Urubamba, a magnificent and energetic river which flows on right down into the jungle to merge with other major headwaters of the Amazon.

Standing guard over the two extremes of the Sacred Valley, the ancient **Inca citadels** of Pisac and Ollantaytambo perch high above the stunning Río Vilcanota-Urubamba and are among the most evocative ruins in Peru. **Pisac** itself is a small, pretty town with one of Peru's best artesania markets, just 30km northeast of Cusco, close to the end of the Río Vilcanota's wild run from Urcos. Further downstream are the ancient villages of **Calca**, **Yucay** and **Urubamba**, the last of which has the most visitors' facilities plus a developing reputation as a spiritual and meditation centre, yet somehow still retains its traditional Andean charm. At the far northern end of the Sacred Valley, even the magnificent ancient town of **Ollantaytambo** is overwhelmed by the astounding temple-fortress clinging to the sheer cliffs beside it. The town is a very pleasant place to spend some time, with several good restaurants and a convenient location in the heart of great trekking country. Unsurprisingly, it's an ideal base from which to take a tent and trek above one of the Urubamba's minor tributaries, or else tackle one of the **Salcantay** trails.

Beyond Ollantaytambo the route becomes too tortuous for any road to follow. Here, the valley closes in around the rail tracks, the Río Urubamba begins to race and twist below **Machu Picchu** itself, the most famous ruin in South America and a place that – no matter how jaded you are or how commercial it seems – is never a disappointment. If you're tempted to explore further afield, the bus journey from Ollantaytambo to Chaullay is exciting, via a precipitous but newly laid road. From Chaullay you can set out for the remote ruins of **Vilcabamba**, the legendary refuge of the last rebel Incas, set in superb hiking country. The main road out of Chaullay, however, continues to descend towards the jungle, following the presently defunct rail line to the tropical town of Quillabamba, springboard to the Amazon rainforest (see p.528).

Getting to the Sacred Valley and Machu Picchu

The classic way to see the Sacred Valley – and Machu Picchu as well – is to take the three- to five-day **hike** along the stirring Inca Trail, which, by booking nine

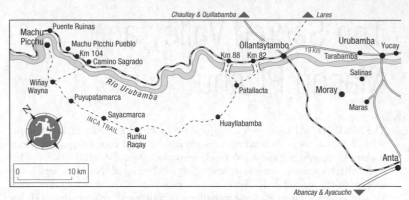

months or more in advance due to the excessive demand, you can do with an official guide or by taking one of the guided treks offered by the many operators in Cusco (see p.264). By road, you can follow the Sacred Valley only as far as Ollantaytambo: the Inca Trail starts just a few kilometres further on.

By bus or taxi from Cusco

Wayra Express, Yanatile, Pitusiray and Richard **buses** for Pisac and Calca leave from the Terminal Terrestre in the mornings, and in the afternoons from a depot at Av Grau 525 at 4pm, 5pm and 5.30pm ($1.80). Near the Puente Grau you'll also find *colectivos* taking people in cars or minibuses to Pisac (40 min; $1.20), Chincheros (50min; $1.50), Urubamba (1hr; $2.40) and Ollantaytambo (1hr 10min; $3.30), from around 6am until mid afternoon. Once in the valley, there are plenty of pickup points in Pisac, Calca and Urubamba. For Urubamba (1hr 20min; $1.20), buses depart Cusco from the aforementioned depot at Av Grau 525 (☎805639), travelling via Chincheros (80¢) – you only pay according to where you're going to – every fifteen minutes from about 5am daily. Additionally, some buses departing from the Avenida Grau depot and marked for Puputi, pass by Tambo Machay and Pisac. Smaller buses leave every thirty minutes for Pisac, Calca (via Tambo Machay) and some for Urubamba, from both Puputi 208 and Tullumayo 207 most mornings, less frequently in afternoons.

Taxis to Pisac from Cusco cost more: about $8–15 one-way. You can also hail one of the many cheap buses or *colectivos* that constantly drive up and down the main road where it passes close to Sacsayhuaman and Qenko.

By train

The **train connecting Cusco with Machu Picchu** has a route almost as spectacular as walking the Inca Trail Itself. To be on the safe side, it's important to buy tickets well in advance online or from either a tour agency or direct at the station ticket office (Av Pachacutec, Wanchaq ☎581414, 238722 or 221992, ⓦwww.perurail.com). Carriages are often fully booked in high season.

There are three classes of railway tickets, and, while itineraries are given below, in high season more trains are often laid on, so timings may vary. The cheapest type of train is the **Backpacker Shuttle** ($48 one way from Cusco, $96 return) leaving 6.50am and arriving at Machu Picchu around 10.50am. The **Vistadome** train ($71 one-way from Cusco, $142 return) has more windows than the Backpacker, plus better service and a free snack, departing Cusco at 6.05am, arriving 9.52am; return journey departs at 3.25pm, arriving in Cusco at 7.41pm. By far the most luxurious – and significantly more costly – tour-

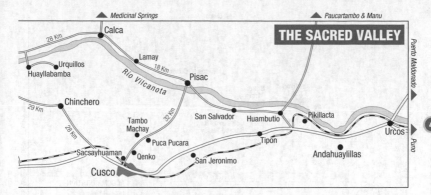

ist train is the **Hiram Bingham** ($588 return) which has classy, old-fashioned style carriages with quality table service, food and guided entry to Machu Picchu all included in the price; departures daily, except Sundays, at 9am from Poroy station, half an hour's drive from Cusco, up above the city on the high plateau dividing the Inca's capital from the Sacred Valley. After a free brunch and coffee, listening to guides explaining the landscape as it passes by, the *Hiram Bingham* pulls into Machu Picchu station around 12.25pm; departs same day at 5.45pm, arriving Cusco around 9.11pm.

It can work out faster and cheaper to catch either train from Ollantaytambo, where there's a scenic little station which can be reached more quickly by bus or car. This option allows you to enjoy a night in Ollantaytambo and, if you want, get up later for the train. There are several trains a day, the first around 5.37am (Backpacker, $31 one-way) and 6.40am (Vistadome, $60 one-way). All Cusco departures for Machu Picchu leave from San Pedro station, the beginning of what is a truly scenic journey. It is sometimes possible to queue from 5am to buy tickets for the same day but it's less stressful if you book in advance from the PeruRail office at Wanchaq station (see opposite). There is a slower local train, but this is meant for locals and people living and working in the valley; it's both difficult and not really on to buy these tickets as a gringo.

Pisac

A vital Inca road once snaked its way up the canyon that enters the Sacred Valley at **PISAC**, and the ruined **citadel**, which sits at the entrance to the gorge, controlled a strategic route connecting the Inca Empire with Paucartambo, on the borders of the eastern jungle. Less than an hour from Cusco by bus, the town is now most commonly visited – apart from a look at the citadel – for its morning **market**, which takes place three times a week.

In addition, the main local **fiesta** – Virgen del Carmen (July 16–18) – is a good alternative to the simultaneous but more remote Paucartambo festival of the same name, with processions, music, dance groups, the usual firecracker celebrations and food stalls around the plaza (see box, p.309).

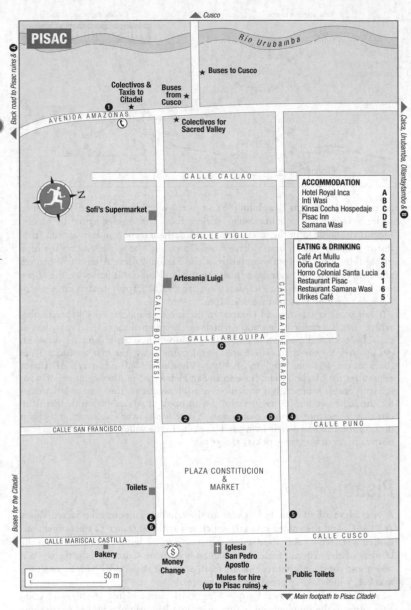

PISAC

Río Urubamba

▲ Cusco

★ Buses to Cusco

Colectivos &
Taxis to
Citadel ★

Buses
from ★
Cusco

AVENIDA AMAZONAS ①

★ Colectivos for
Sacred Valley

CALLE CALLAO

ACCOMMODATION
Hotel Royal Inca   A
Inti Wasi   B
Kinsa Cocha Hospedaje   C
Pisac Inn   D
Samana Wasi   E

Sofi's Supermarket

CALLE VIGIL

EATING & DRINKING
Café Art Mullu   2
Doña Clorinda   3
Horno Colonial Santa Lucia   4
Restaurant Pisac   1
Restaurant Samana Wasi   6
Ulrikes Café   5

Artesania Luigi

CALLE BOLOGNESI

CALLE MANUEL PRADO

CALLE AREQUIPA ©

② ③ Ⓓ ④ CALLE PUNO

CALLE SAN FRANCISCO

PLAZA CONSTITUCION
&
MARKET

Toilets

⑤

Ⓔ
⑥

CALLE CUSCO

CALLE MARISCAL CASTILLA

Bakery

Money
Change $

✝ Iglesia
San Pedro
Apostlo

Public Toilets

Mules for hire
(up to Pisac ruins) ★

0   50 m

▼ Main footpath to Pisac Citadel

Back road to Pisac ruins & Ⓐ

Calca, Urubamba, Ollantaytambo & Ⓑ

Buses for the Citadel

Accommodation

The only time when **accommodation** in Pisac may be hard to find is in September, when the village fills up with pilgrims heading to the nearby sanctuary of Huanca, home of a small shrine which is very sacred to local inhabitants. In Pisac itself there's a surprising selection of places to stay.

Alternatively, you can usually **rent rooms** at low prices from villagers (ask for details at the *Restaurant Samana Wasi*; see p.279), or there is a **campsite** (ask at the *Kinsa Cocha Hospedaje* for details).

see p.279

Hotel Royal Inca ☎ 203064, ℱ 203067, ⓦ www.royalinkahotel.com. The most luxurious place to stay in Pisac, with a pool and all modern conveniences, though it's 2km out of the village on the long road that winds up towards the ruins. ❻

Inti Wasi ☎ 203047, ⓦ www.hotelintiwasi.com. Located about 2.5km down the valley from Pisac on the main road towards Urubamba, this place has a restaurant, swimming pool and bungalow-style accommodation. ❻–❼

Kinsa Cocha Hospedaje Plaza Constitución, C Bolognesi. Small rustic rooms in a house attached to a restaurant on the main square; although the actual accommodation entrance is a block back on Calle Arequipa, reception is via the restaurant. ❷–❸

Pisac Inn Plaza Constitución 333 (for reservations contact via Casilla Postal 1179, Cusco ☎ 203062 ⓔ info@pisacinn.com ⓦ www .pisacinn.com). Very agreeable hotel with lavishly decorated bedrooms (with or without private bath) and a rock-heated sauna, plus good breakfasts and lunches, including vegetarian options (the fabulous restaurant – *Cuchara de Palo* – is open to non-residents). They also change money, rent out mountain bikes and can book tours to nearby ruins. ❹–❺

Samana Wasi Plaza Constitución 509. This is better known as a restaurant; but rooms are simple and clean, arrayed around the upstairs balcony of their courtyard. ❷–❸

The Town and around

Commerce bustles around the **Iglesia San Pedro Apóstol**, an unusually narrow concrete church located in Pisac's central market plaza, which is dominated by an ancient and massive *pisonay* tree. The thriving morning **market** (Tues, Thurs & Sun 8am–3pm), is held in Plaza Constitución, the town's main square, where you can buy hand-painted ceramic beads and pick up the occasional bargain. Even if the market's not on, there are still a number of excellent artesania shops, particularly along Calle Bolognesi, which connects the Sacred Valley road and river bridge with the plaza.

Another out-of-town sight also allows you the chance to buy local goods. About 23km between Cusco and Pisac, just before the road starts steeply down into the Sacred Valley, the relatively new alpaca centre **Awana Kancha** (daily 9am–5.30pm; ☎ 9740797) offers a rare opportunity to see alpacas and llamas close at hand, traditional weaving in practice and to purchase quality alpaca and woollen products.

The citadel

It takes a good ninety minutes to climb directly to the **citadel** (daily 7am–5.30pm; entry by Cusco Tourist Ticket, see p.243), heading up through the agricultural terraces still in use at the back of the Plaza Constitución, but the astounding views and ancient ruins on display are more than worth it. Alternatively, you can catch a bus (20¢) from the end of Calle Mariscal Castilla (the road that runs along the eastern edge of the plaza), or take a taxi, *colectivo* or pick-up (around $3) from the main road, on the corner of Calle Bolognesi and close to the Urubamba bridge; it's usually possible to share the cost on market days, when the town is busier.

Set high above a valley floor patchworked by patterned fields and rimmed by centuries of terracing amid giant landslides, the stonework (water ducts and steps have been cut out of solid rock) and **panoramas** at the citadel are magnificent. From the saddle on the hill, where much of the best Inca architecture sits, you can see over the Sacred Valley to the north, wide and flat at the base, but towering towards the heavens into green and rocky pinnacles. To the south, the valley closes in, but the mountains continue, massive and steepsided, casting shadows on one another. Below the saddle, a semicircle of buildings is gracefully positioned

▲ Inca Citadel, Pisac

on a large natural balcony under row upon row of fine stone terraces thought to represent a partridge's wing (*pisac* meaning "partridge").

In the upper sector of the ruins, the citadel's **Templo del Sol** (Temple of the Sun) is the equal of anything at Machu Picchu and more than repays the exertions of the steep climb. Reached by many of the dozens of paths that crisscross their way up through the citadel, it's poised in a flattish saddle on a great spur protruding north–south into the Sacred Valley. The temple was built around an outcrop of volcanic rock, its peak carved into a "hitching post" for the sun. The hitching post alone is intriguing: the angles of its base suggest that it may have been used for keeping track of important stars, or for calculating the changing seasons with the accuracy so critical to the smooth running of the Inca Empire. Above the temple lie still more ruins, largely unexcavated, and among the higher crevices and rocky overhangs several ancient burial sites are hidden.

Eating

There are a few decent **restaurants** in Pisac, but they can all get busy on market days. There's a good **shop**, Doña Clorinda, at Bolognesi 592, on the corner of the plaza, selling great cakes, and a traditional **bakery** with an adobe oven on a corner of the plaza. Addresses aren't displayed on buildings, but the following restaurants are all pretty much clustered together and relatively easy to find.

Café Art Mullu on the plaza, by the corner with C Bolognesi. This is a fun little place offering meals, snacks – including particularly fine pizzas – and drinks.

Doña Clorinda on the plaza, close to the *Art Mullu* café. Good for cheap lunches, mostly traditional Peruvian dishes. In good weather, you can relax at one of the tables outside.

Horno Colonial Santa Lucia on the corner of the plaza at the corner of C Puno with C Manuel Prado. This is a bakery with arched adobe ovens which also serves good meals of *roccoto relleno* and *cuy* (roast guinea pig) dishes.

Restaurant Pisac Main road 147. A dingy yet friendly place back down on the main road by the taxis, which serves generous portions of standard basic Peruvian fare.

Restaurant Samana Wasi on the corner of Plaza Constitución at no. 509. This has a pleasant little courtyard out the back and very tasty trout, salad and fried potatoes. They also have decent coffee and a post box.

Ulrikes Café C Manuel Prado, along the opposite side of the plaza from the *Restaurant Samana Wasi*. A lovely café serving good coffee, amazing cakes and a range of lovely snacks, pizzas and even vegetarian meals in a large cultural-café space with books, magazines and games.

Listings

Banks and exchange For changing dollars, try the jeweller's shop on the corner of the plaza close to *Restaurant Samana Wasi*. There's an ATM outside *Ulrikes Café*.

Post office On the corner of the plaza where Intihuatana meets Calle Comercio. There's also a post box in the courtyard of *Restaurant Samana Wasi*.

Shops There are several good artesanía stalls – mainly beads and ceramics along Calle Bolognesi; try Walter's or Luigi, just down from Sofi's Supermarket, which itself stocks most of the usual basics and is halfway up Bolognesi, between Av Amazonas by the river bridge and the main plaza where the market takes place.

From Pisac to Urubamba

Known for its medicinal springs, the first significant village between Pisac and Urubamba is **Lamay**, just 3km away. High above this village, on the other side of the Río Vilcanota and just out of sight, are the beautiful Inca terraces of Huchiq'osqo. A little further down the road you come to the larger village of **Calca**, with the popular thermal baths of Machacanca within ninety minutes' walk of the modern settlement, signposted from the town and to which *combi colectivos* (15min; 30¢) run quite frequently, particularly on Sunday. Situated under the hanging glaciers of Mount Sahuasiray, this place was favoured by the Incas for the fertility of its soil, and you can still see plenty of maize cultivation.

Around the end of September and start of October every year there are local **fiestas** and celebrations, which evidently date back at least to early Inca times. The main local ritual theme for the festival is water and there are strong links to a mythic experience high in the hills and tied to the moving shadows of mount Pitusiray. Every year around the beginning of October, the mountain casts shadows over neighbouring peaks and cliffs. Over several days the shadow of Pitusiray, also considered to be a solar clock, moves in a dynamic and very clear representation of a prostrate Inca being leapt upon and transformed by a black puma or jaguar;

it has to be seen to be believed. With this visual effect on the landscape in mind, scores of young people hold a complementary festival focused on the first Sunday in October and based at the **Inca ruins of Urco**, also dedicated to water, which are located just 2km walk above the village of Calca.

Moving down the valley from here the climate improves and you see pears, peaches and cherries growing in abundance, and in July and August vast piles of maize sit beside the road waiting to be used as cattle feed.

Yucay, the next major settlement before you get to Urubamba, had its moment in Peruvian history when, under the Incas, Huayna Capac, father of Huascar and Atahualpa, had his palace here, and you can observe the ruined but finely dressed stone walls of another Inca palace (probably the country home of Sayri Tupac though also associated with an Inca princess) located on the Plaza Manco II. If you fancy a hike, you can also follow the stream up behind the town to the village of San Juan.

There are a few good **places to stay** in Yucay; the *Hostal Yíllary*, Plaza Manco II 107 (T 226607 or 201112; ⑤–⑥), is very friendly, comfortable and excellent value with private bath, a well-tended garden and large rooms in an attractive old building. More upmarket, the *Sonesta Posada del Inca*, Plaza Manco II, 134 (T 201107 or 01/4219667, W www.sonesta.com; ⑧), is based in a beautifully converted eighteenth-century monastery that houses a small museum (open to non-residents) of fine precious metal objects and ceramics. The nearby *Posada del Libertador* (T 201115, F 201116; ⑥–⑦) is another fine colonial mansion noted for accommodating Simon Bolívar when he was in the region with leaders of Peru's patriot army for the public declaration and royal oath of independence sworn in Cusco in 1825. The *Casa Luna* **restaurant**, Plaza Manco II 107, right next to the *Libertador*, offers great pizzas, sandwiches and drinks in a relaxing environment with internet and fax services, bike rental, 4WD tours and also house and bungalow accommodation (④–⑤).

Urubamba and around

URUBAMBA, about 80km from Cusco via Pisac or around 60km via Chinchero, is only a short way down the main road from Yucay's Plaza Manco II, and here the Río Vilcanota becomes the Río Urubamba (though many people still refer to this stretch as the Vilcanota). Although it has little in the way of obvious historic interest, the town is well endowed with facilities and situated in the shadow of the beautiful Chicon and Pumahuanca glaciers.

Regular **buses** connect Cusco with Urubamba and the rest of the Sacred Valley (see p. 274). Buses also connect Urubamba with Cusco, Pisac, Calca and Ollantaytambo. Buses for Ollantaytambo, Cusco and Chinchero leave regularly from Terminal Terrestre, on the main road more or less opposite the *Hotel Incaland*. The *Neuvo Mundo Café* (see p.283) sometimes has some local **tourist information**.

Accommodation

There's a surprisingly wide range of accommodation in Urubamba, considering how small a town it is.

Camping is available at *Camping Los Cedros* ($3 per tent) and *Los Girasoles* ($2.50 per person), which also has private bungalows (③) and shower facilities. Both sites are on the Pumahuanca road, a few blocks beyond Iglesia Torrechayoc, a medium-sized church on the northern edge of town, and are signposted just as the road leaves the built-up area of Urubamba.

Hospedaje El Marquez C Convención 429 ☎201304. A clean, family-run hostel, with a small garden and a couple of rooms with private bath. **①–②**

Hostal Las Jardines C Convención 459 (no phone). *Las Jardines* offers better rooms than most of the other budget places in Urubamba, offering more space and light, and, as the name suggests, also comprises an appealing garden. **②–③**

Hostal Urubamba Jr Bolognesi 665 (no phone). A basic hostel near the police station, one and a half blocks from the Plaza de Armas. **①**

Hotel Incaland on Av Ferrocarril ☎201071 or 201126, ☎201071. A large Best Western hotel with 65 rooms, mainly well appointed bungalows, and a conference centre with internet access, a pool and tennis courts. **③**

Hotel San Augustin Km 69, Panamerican Highway ☎201025. Some twenty minutes' walk down

the main road towards Cusco, just beyond the bridge over the Río Urubamba, *Hotel San Augustin* is a rather plush place to stay, boasting a small pool and a popular restaurant (delicious buffet lunches served Tues, Thurs & Sun). **⑦**

Inkaterra Urubamba Villas Caserio Higuspurco, Km7 from Urubamba ☎01/6100404, ⓦwww .inkaterra.com. Set in attractive gardens where hummingbirds thrive, the accommodation is in distinctive villas, replete with tapestries and open fires. Very special service and high-quality boutique style apart, they also offer great excursions: horse-riding, rafting, trekking, archaeological visits. **⑧**

Posada Las 3 Marias Jr Zavala 307 ☎201006 or in Cusco at ☎225252. A friendly, family-run place offering very clean and intimate accommodation, albeit with a capacity for up to sixteen people over several rooms. **③**

The Town

The Plaza de Armas is laid-back and attractive, with palm trees and a couple of pines surrounded by interesting topiary. At the heart of the plaza is a small fountain topped by a maize plant sculpture, but everything stands in deference to the red sandstone **Iglesia San Pedro**, with its stacked columns below two small belfries. The church's cool interior has a vast, three-tier gold-leaf altar, and at midday light streams through the glass-topped cupola. At weekends there's a large **market** on Jirón Palacio; and at the large **ceramic workshops** set around a lovely garden at Av Berriozabal 111 (☎201002, ☎201177), new and ancient techniques are used to produce colourful, Amerindian-inspired items for sale.

Because of its convenient location and plentiful facilities, Urubamba makes an ideal base from which to **explore** the mountains and lower hills around the Sacred Valley, which are filled with sites of jaw-dropping splendour. The eastern side of the valley is formed by the Cordillera Urubamba, a range of snowcapped peaks dominated by the summits of Chicon and Veronica. Many of the ravines can be hiked, alone or with local guides (found only through the main hotels and hospedajes), and on the trek up from the town you'll have stupendous views of Chicon. **Moray**, a stunning Inca site, part agricultural centre and part ceremonial, lies about 6km north of Maras village on the Chinchero side of the river, within a two- to three-hour walk from Urubamba. The ruins are deep, bowl-like depressions in the earth, the largest comprising seven concentric circular stone terraces, facing inward and diminishing in radius like a multi-layered roulette wheel.

Also within walking distance, the salt pans of **Salinas**, still in use after more than four hundred years, are situated 4kms on from the village of Maras, and a similar distance from Moray. Cross the river by the footbridge in the village, turn right,

▲ Inca terracing, Moray

then after a little over 100m downstream along the riverbank, turn left past the cemetery and up the canyon along the salty creek. After this you cross the stream and follow the path cut into the cliffside to reach the salt pans, which are soon visible if still a considerable uphill hike away. The trail offers spectacular views of the valley and mountains, while the Inca salt pans themselves are set gracefully against an imposing mountain backdrop. A scenic trail (about 1hr walking) leads down through the salt pans and on to the Urubamba river below, where there's a footbridge across to the village of Tarabamba on the road for Urubamba (6km) or Ollantaytambo; *colectivos* pass every twenty minutes or so in both directions.

Eating

Urubamba isn't home to particularly fine **cuisine** but it does offer a wide variety of cafés, bars and quinta (traditional Andean-Peruvian restaurant, usually with tables in a garden and fast service to a limited menu) catering.

La Casa de la Abuela Jr Bolognesi, to the left of the church and one block up on the left. A very friendly restaurant with a beatific courtyard full of flowers and trees, and serving excellent pizzas and very good lasagna.

El Huacatay Jr Arica 620 ☏ 201790, ⓦ www .elhuacatay.com. By a long way the best of Urubamba's top restaurants; this is Andean cuisine in a very appealing environment. Best for lunch; reserve in advance if you can.

The Muse Too at Jr Comercio ☏ 201554. The Muse Too stocks a decent range of drinks, plays good music at weekends and serves delicious pizza. Occasional quiz and/or poker nights.

Nuevo Mundo Café Corner of Av Castilla and Jr Comercio (four blocks up from the Texaco petrol station). Here you'll find wholesome vegetarian meals all day on their patio. They also operate a book exchange and stock trekking food.

Quinta Los Geranios A ten-minute walk along the main Sacred Valley road towards Cusco, on Avenida Conchatupa. A nicer spot and better food than *El Maizal* (see below), Los Geranios serves excellent dishes such as *rocoto relleno (stuffed rocoto, a pepper-like vegetable), chupe de quinoa* (quinoa stew) and *asado a la olla* (pot roast) in a splendid, but usually busy, garden environment. Daily noon–7pm.

Quinta La Mercedes Comercio 445, Plaza de Armas. A rustic place with cheap set-lunch menus.

Quinta Los Pinos Av Castilla 812. Serving excellent food and specializing in local dishes, enjoyed in an atmospheric little courtyard.

Restaurant La Esquina Plaza de Armas at the corner of Jr Comercio and Jr Grau. A great meeting place for travellers, serving alpaca steaks, *ponche de leche* (a hot milk punch), pancakes, pies, juices, drinks and sometimes music at weekends.

Restaurant El Maizal Located close to *Quinta Los Geranios* on the main valley road, this is a popular lunchtime spot with Peruvian tourists, who come for the interesting menu of traditional dishes.

Ollantaytambo and around

On the approach to **OLLANTAYTAMBO** from Urubamba, the river runs smoothly between a series of impressive Inca terraces that gradually diminish in size as the slopes get steeper and rockier. Just before the town, the rail tracks reappear and the road climbs a small hill to an ancient plaza. The backstreets radiating up from the plaza are littered with well-built stone water channels, which still come in very handy during the rainy season, carrying the gushing streams tidily away from the town and down to the Urubamba river. Ollantaytambo was built as an Inca administrative centre rather than a town and is laid out in the form of a maize corn cob: it's one of the few surviving examples of an Inca grid system, with a plan that can be seen from vantage points high above it, especially from the hill opposite the fortress. An incredibly fertile sector of the Urubamba Valley, at 2800m above sea level and with temperatures of 11–23°C (52–73°F), with good alluvial soils and water resources, this area was also the gateway to the Antisuyo (the Amazon corner of the Inca Empire) and a centre for tribute-gathering from the surrounding valleys. Beyond Ollantaytambo, the Sacred Valley becomes a subtropical, raging river course, surrounded by towering mountains and dominated by the snowcapped peak of Salcantay; the town is a popular base for rafting groups.

The valley here is hemmed in by steep and very high mountains, many with snowcapped peaks. As one of the region's main hotspots, and a well-used overnight stop on route to Machu Picchu, it can get very busy here in high season, making it hard to escape being around scores of other travellers. At heart, though, it's a small but very traditional settlement, worth enjoying over a few days, particularly during its highly colourful **fiestas** (the Festival of the Cross, Corpus Christi and Ollantaytambo Raymi fiesta – generally on the Sunday after Cusco's Inti Raymi), or at Christmas, when locals wear flowers and decorative grasses in their hats. On the Fiesta de Reyes, around January 6, there's a solemn procession around town of the three *Niños Reyes* (Child Kings), sacred effigies, one of which is brought down from the sacred site of Marcaquocha, about 10km away in the Patacancha valley, the day before. Many local women still wear traditional clothing and it's common to see them in the main plaza with their intricately woven *manta* shawls, black and red skirts with colourful zigzag patterns and inverted red and black hats.

Some history

The valley here was occupied by a number of pre-Inca cultures, notably the Chanapata (800–300 BC), the Qotacalla (500–900 AD) and the Killki (900–1420 AD), after which the Incas dominated only until the 1530s, when the Spanish arrived. Legend has it that **Ollantay** was a rebel Inca general who took arms against Pachacutec over the affections of the Lord Inca's daughter, the Nusta Cusi Collyu. However, historical evidence shows that a fourteen-kilometre canal, that still feeds the town today, was built to bring water here from the Laguna de Yanacocha, which was probably Pachacutec's private estate. The later Inca Huayna Capac is thought to have been responsible for the trapezoidal Plaza Maynyaraqui and the largely unfinished but impressive and megalithic temples.

As strategic protection for the entrance to the lower Urubamba Valley and an alternative gateway into the Amazon via the Pantiacolla Pass, this was the only Inca stronghold to have successfully resisted persistent Spanish attacks. After the unsuccessful siege of Cusco in 1536–37 (see p.238), the rebel Inca **Manco** and his die-hard force withdrew here, with **Hernando Pizarro** (Francisco's brother), some seventy horsemen, thirty foot-soldiers and a large contingent of native forces in hot pursuit. As they approached, they found that not only had the Incas diverted the Río Patacancha, making the valley below the fortress impassable, but they had also joined forces with neighbouring jungle tribes forming a massive army. After several desperate attempts to storm the stronghold, Pizarro and his men uncharacteristically slunk away under cover of darkness, leaving much of their equipment behind. However, the Spanish came back with reinforcements, and in 1537 Manco retreated further down the valley to Vitcos and Vilcabamba. In 1540, Ollantaytambo was entrusted to Hernando Pizarro, brother of the Conquistador leader.

During the next four hundred years, Ollantaytambo remained a largely agricultural town, little more than a quiet market place and nodal point for a wideranging peasant population. Since the agrarian reform of 1968, Ollantaytambo has been divided into five rural communities, each with an elected president and a committee of *reidores* who represent peasant interests within local government. Outside of bus and train connection times for Machu Picchu, it's still a quiet town today, though the peace was shattered once or twice by terrorist raids on the police station in the plaza during the late 1980s and early 1990s.

Arrival and information

The **train station** is a few hundred metres down Avenida Estacion (also known as Avenida Ferrocarril), on the left after the *Hotel Sauce* as you come down from the plaza towards (but well before) the Cathedral or Templo de Santiago Apóstol. **Tourist information** can be obtained from the CATCCO Museum, one small block from the plaza, or call ☎ 204024 or 204034. There are a few **internet** cafés in town, but the best – like Cyberpath – are down opposite the Cathedral. **Money exchange** is available in the small shop on the corner of the plaza with Calle Ventiderio. The **telephone** and **post office** are on the main plaza. From Ollantaytambo, afternoon taxis ($10–20) and buses ($2.50) return every day to Cusco leave regularly from the small yard just outside the train station, often coinciding with the train timetable. In the mornings the buses depart mainly from Ollantaytambo's main plaza.

Accommodation

There are several **hotels** to choose from, but the better ones are often fully booked weeks ahead.

El Albergue Ollantaytambo Casilla 784 ☎ 204014, Ⓦ www.elalbergue.com. Located right next to the river and the train station at the bottom end of town (the entrance is on the station platform), this

albergue offers discounts to families, although it's advisable to contact them well in advance during the high season. The spacious rooms are stylishly rustic, plus there's a sauna, and they serve tasty breakfasts. For full meals (also available to non-guest) you need to book in advance. ④–⑤

Hospedaje Los Andes C Ventiderio ☏ 204095. A small, cosy hostel in the heart of the town with traditional patio, offering hot water and private bath in some of the simple yet well furnished rooms. ②–③

Hospedaje Las Portadas C Principal ☏ 204008. A small hostel conveniently located on the main road into town, with good views from one or two of the rooms, although baths are shared and the yard is unfortunately concreted. ③

Hostal La Ñusta Carretera Ocobamba ☏ 204035. Very hospitable but basic, this place has simply furnished rooms with shared bath, as well as a patio offering excellent views across to the mountains

and the Wiraccochan face (see p.287). ②

Hostal Ollanta Main Plaza ☏ 204116. Close to the little market and chapel on the main plaza, *Ollanta* is a refurbished and well-run hostel. Very clean but can be noisy at weekends. ②

Hostal Las Orquideas Av Estacion ☏ 204032. Further up the track from the train station to the town, this pleasant place offers small rooms set around a courtyard, with breakfasts available. ③

Hotel Pakaritampu Av Estacion ☏ 204020, ℱ 204105, ℗ www.pakaritampu.com.com. Within a few minutes easy walk of the train station and set in pleasant gardens, this is a safe and plush hotel. It's expensive but worth the money, and inclusive of an excellent buffet breakfast. ⑧

Hostal Sauce C Ventiderio 248 ☏ 204044, ℱ 204048, ℗ www.hostalsauce.com.pe. A modern, safe if not particularly friendly hotel with elegant rooms and fine views. There's also a reasonable restaurant, only open to residents. ⑦

The Town

The main centres of activity are the main **plaza** – the heart of civic life and the scene of traditional folk dancing during festive occasions – the **Inca fortress** and the market below it, and the **train station**.

The useful **Ollantaytambo Heritage Trail** helps you find most of the important sites with a series of blue plaques around town. Close to the central plaza there's the **CATCCO Museo** (Tues–Sun 10am–1pm & 2–4pm; $1.80), which contains interpretative exhibits in Spanish and English about local history, culture, archeology and natural history. It also has a ceramic workshop where you can buy some good pottery.

Downhill from the plaza, just across the Río Patacancha, is the old Inca **Plaza Mañya Raquy**, dominated by the fortress. There are market stalls in the plaza plus a few artesania shops and cafés around, mainly opposite the attractive but smallish church, the Templo de Santiago Apóstol. Built in 1620 it has an almost Inca-style stone belfry containing two great bells supported on an ancient timber. The church's front entrance is surrounded by a simple yet attractive *mestizo* floral relief painted in red and cream.

Climbing up through the **fortress** (daily 7am–5.30pm; entry with **Cusco Tourist Ticket**, see p.243), the solid stone terraces and the natural contours of the cliff remain frighteningly impressive. Above them, huge red granite blocks mark the unfinished sun temple near the top, where, according to legend, the internal organs of mummified Incas were buried. A dangerous path leads from this upper level around the cliff towards a large sector of agricultural terracing which follows the Río Patacancha uphill, while at the bottom you can still make out the shape of a large Inca plaza, through which stone aqueducts carried the water supply. Below the ruins are the **Andenes de Mollequasa terraces** which, when viewed from the other side of the Urubamba Valley (a 20min walk up the track from the train station), look like a pyramid.

High up over the other side of the Río Patacancha, behind the town, are rows of **ruined buildings** originally thought to have been prisons but now considered likely to have been granaries. In front of these, it's quite easy to make out a gigantic, rather grumpy-looking profile of a face carved out of the rock, possibly an **Inca sculpture** of Wiraccochan, the mythical messenger from **Viraccocha**, the major creator god of Peru (see p.581). According to sixteenth- and seventeeth-century histories, such an image was indeed once carved, representing him as a man of great authority; this particular image's frown certainly implies presence, and this part of the mountain was also known as Wiraccochan Orcco ("peak of Viraccocha's messenger"). From here, looking back towards the main Ollantaytambo fortress, it's possible to see the mountain, rocks and terracing forming the image of a mother llama with a young llama, apparently representing the myth of Catachillay, which relates to the water cycle and the Milky Way. *The Sacred Valley of the Incas – Myths and Symbols* (available in most Cusco bookshops), written by Cusco archaeologists Fernando and Edgar Salazar, is a useful companion for identifying and interpreting the sites in this part of the valley.

Eating

For a decent **meal**, it's hard to beat *El Albergue Ollantaytambo* (see p.285), which is only open to residents, except by prior reservation but has a great cook whose food

Trekking and rafting around Ollantaytambo

Ollantaytambo is surrounded by stunning countryside, skyscraping mountain peaks and a number of interesting day-trip options. The Inca **quarries of Cachiqata** can be reached in four hours on horseback with one or other of the tour companies listed in Cusco or Ollantaytambo. It's also possible to camp here and visit the site of an **Inca gateway** or **Intihuatana**. There are the nearer ruins of **Pinkuylluna**, less than an hour away by horse, or the **Pumamarca** Inca ruins about half a day away.

The area around this town is also an excellent spot to begin **trekking** into the hills. One possibility is to head along the main down-valley road to Km 82, where there's a bridge over the Río Urubamba that's becoming an increasingly popular starting point for both the **Inca Trail** and **Salcantay**. There's a hard-going two-day trail to the beautiful and remote lake of **Yanacocha**. Or, alternatively, travelling up the Río Patacancha will take you to the little-visited Inca ruins of **Pumamarca**, on the left of the river where the Río Yuramayu merges with it under the shadows of the Nevada Helancoma. From here the main track carries on along the right bank of the Río Patacancha through various small peasant hamlets – Pullata, Colqueracay, Maracocha and Huilloc – before crossing the pass, with the Nevada Colque Cruz on the right-hand side. It then follows the ríos Huacahuasi and Tropoche down to the valley and community of Lares, just before which are some Inca baths. Beyond the village are several more ruins en route to Ampares, from where you can either walk back to Urubamba, go by road back to Cusco or head down towards Quillabamba. It's at least a two-day walk one way, and you'll need camping equipment and food as there are no facilities at all on the route.

Contact the South American Explorers' Club in Cusco for recent trip reports and good maps to use. It's also possible to do it on horseback via most tour companies here or in Cusco, or you can organize a guided trek with an agency in Cusco (see p.264). The local Museo CATCCO (Ⓣ204024, Ⓔotikary@hotmail.com) also has information on what they are promoting as **Rutas Ancestrales de Ollantaytambo** – Ancestral Routes of Ollantaytambo. This is an entire list of walking circuits that link important points relating to the archaeology or history of the area (a big map of this route can also be found at the entry to the Inca fortress).

Ollantaytambo is something of a centre for **river rafting**, organised largely by KB Tours on the main plaza (Ⓣ204133, Ⓦwww.kbperu.com), who also offer lodging, mountain biking and trekking tours; all activities start from around $45 a day. Alternatively, arrange the rafting with one of the Cusco-based tour companies (see p.264). The river around Ollantaytambo is class 2–3 in the dry season and 3–4 during the rainy period (Nov–March).

betrays a North American influence. There are also several good cafés closer to the centre of town, particularly around the bridge at the top of Avenida Estacion (also known as Ferrocarril) and in the main plaza.

If you want to try the local *chicha* **maize beer**, pop into any of the private houses displaying a red plastic bag on a pole outside the door – the beer is cheap and the hosts usually very friendly and great fun. In the old days, red flowers were used rather than plastic bags to indicate which family in the village had enough *chicha* beer to share with friends and neighbours.

Alcazar C del Medio. A well-used and attractively laid-out space just a stone's throw from the Plaza de Armas, Alcazar serves great breakfasts, snacks, pancakes and good local meat or veggie meals.

Café Restaurant Fortaleza Plaza de Armas. A popular place with gringo travellers, serving good pancakes and tasty but relatively inexpensive pizzas.

Mayupata Restaurant Bar Opposite the Templo de Santiago Apóstol. The plushest big restaurant in town, serving pizzas, other Italian dishes and international cuisine. Not cheap, but has a fine setting by the river bridge.

Restaurant La Ñusta Plaza de Armas. A very friendly café and shop with excellent breakfast, snacks and soups made from fresh vegetables (unusual for this region, despite the fertility of the soil). They also have tables outside facing the plaza.

Restaurant Pukarumi C Ventiderios. Some of the best food in Ollantaytambo, serving up particularly good meat dishes, pizzas and grills. You'll need to arrive before 8pm to be sure of a table.

The Inca Trail

Even though it's just one among a multitude of paths across the Andes, the fabulous treasure of Machu Picchu at the end of its path makes the **INCA TRAIL**, the world's most famous trek. That's not to say you won't see plenty of wonders along the way. The Inca Trail is set in the **Santuario Histórico de Machu Picchu** (National Sanctuary of Machu Picchu), an area of more than 32,000 hectares set apart by the Peruvian state to protect its range of ecological niches from 6271m at the high Andean glacial peak of Nevado Salcantay down to Amazon cloud forest at less than 2000m in Aguas Calientes at the foot of Machu Picchu. Acting as a bio-corridor between the Cusco Andes, the Sacred Valley and the lowland Amazon forest, the sanctuary possesses over 370 species of birds, 47 mammal species and over 700 butterfly species. Some of the more notable residents include the cock-of-the-rock (*Rupicola peruviana*, known as *tunkis* in the Quechua-speaking Andes), spectacled bear (*Tremarctos ornatus*) and condor (*Vultur gryphus*). In addition, there are around 300 different species of orchids hidden up in the trees of the cloud forest.

It's important to choose your **season** for hiking the Inca Trail. May is the best month to venture on a hike here, with clear views, fine weather and verdant surroundings. Between June and September it's usually a pretty cosmopolitan stretch of mountainside, with travellers from all over the globe converging on Machu Picchu the hard way, but from mid-June to early August the trail is simply very busy (and the campsites noisy), especially on the last stretch. From October until April, in the rainy season, it's less crowded but also, naturally, quite a bit wetter. Locals will tell you that the best time to hike the trail is during a full moon, and it certainly adds a more romantic, if not mystical feeling to your journey.

The sanctuary authorities (the Unidad de Gestión del Santuario Histórico de Machu Picchu) have imposed a limit of a maximum of four hundred people a day (this means about two hundred trekkers with two hundred guides and porters per day) on the Inca Trail. In addition, it is mandatory for trekkers to go with a

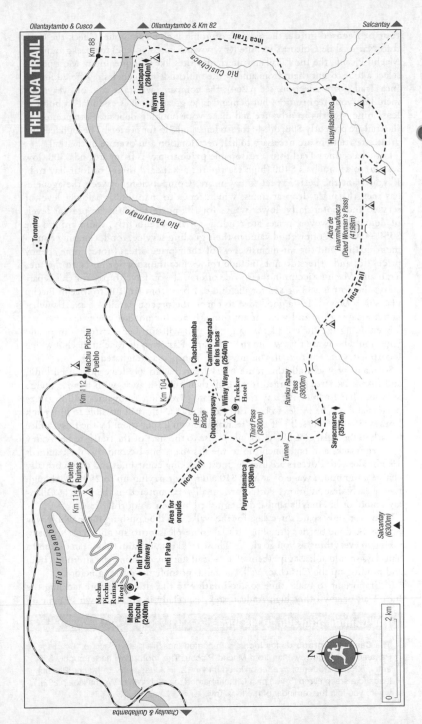

THE INCA TRAIL

Ollantaytambo & Cusco ▲   ▲ Ollantaytambo & Km 82   Salcantay ▲

Km 88

Inca Trail

Liactapata (2640m)

Wayna Quente

Río Cusichaca

Huayllabamba

Torontoy

Río Pacaymayo

Abra de
Huarmihuañusca
(Dead Woman's Pass)
(4198m)

Inca Trail

Machu Picchu
Pueblo

Chachabamba

Camino Sagrada
de los Incas

Km 112

Km 104

HEP
Bridge

Choquesuysuy

Wiñay Wayna (2640m)

Trekker
Hotel

Third Pass
(3600m)

Ruinu Raqay Pass
(3800m)

Sayacmarca
(3575m)

Puente
Ruinas

Km 114

Tunnel

Puyupatamarca
(3580m)

Inca Trail

Area for
orquids

Inti Punku Gateway

Inti Pata

Río Urubamba

Machu
Picchu
Ruinas
Hotel

Machu Picchu
(2400m)

Salcantay
(6300m)

N

Chaullay & Quillabamba ▲

2 km

0

tour or licensed guide, the old days of going it alone are gone. Check the Instituto Nacional de Cultura's website (Ⓦ www.inc-cusco.gob.pe) for background on Machu Picchu, the Inca Trail and alternative sites like Choquequirau. Most people select a tour to suit them from among the multitude of agencies registered for the Inca Trail (for a selection, see p.264); the company will take care of everything including your registration, but demand is so great that it is essential to **book at least nine months in advance** and make your booking deposit. Entrance fees to the trail are presently $88, or $44 for students and $15 for porters. The high fees and greater restrictions are necessary to halt deterioration and overuse of the trail.

For a basic Inca Trail tour a reasonable **price** to pay is from around $300 (low season) to as much as $400 (high season) for a standard three- or four-day trek. If you want the best, expect to pay more. Competition between the agencies has seen the price drop at times, which tends to manifest as a lower level of service and, potentially, lower wages for the porters. With the present levels of demand, however, prices are tending to rise. Frequently, those around the $350–450 mark offer good value in their guiding service, food, camping equipment quality and the all-inclusiveness of their price offers (note: some agency prices do, and others do not, include things like transport or entry to the Inca Trail and Machu Picchu in their price offers). If you have to pay for this separately, the cost is $88 or $55 for the one-day pass from Km104 to Machu Picchu via Wiñay Wayna. It's a good idea to check the precise details of exactly what you are paying for and what, if anything, is not included in the price.

Even doing the Inca Trail with a guide, you will still benefit from a map, and you should be aware that within the Santuario Histórico de Machu Picchu, which incorporates the entire trail, you must only **camp** at a designated site.

So many people walk this route every year that toilets have now been built, and hikers are strongly urged to take all their rubbish away with them – there's no room left for burying any more tin cans. Trekking companies will organize porters and maybe mules to help carry equipment. It is still possible to hire **pack horses** ($8–12) yourself – if they're available you'll spot them by the ticket office (or ask in the village of Huayllabamba) close to the start of the trail – to help carry your rucksacks and equipment up to the first pass, but beyond this pack animals are not allowed. **Porters** are used by most trekking companies and they normally charge a minimum wage of at least $10 a day for carrying up to 25 kilos, though they clearly deserve more. Porters are usually encountered in the plaza at Ollantaytambo, or in Huayllabamba, distinguished by their colourful dress.

If you can only spare three days for the walk, you'll be pushing it the whole way – it *can* be done but it's gruelling. It's far more pleasant to spend five or six days, taking in everything as you go along. Those trekkers who aim to do it in two and a half days should at least give themselves a head start by catching the afternoon train and heading up the Cusichaca Valley as far as possible the evening before.

It's important to make time to **acclimatize** to the altitude before tackling the Inca Trail or any other high Andean trek, especially if you've flown straight up

---

The Camino Sagrado de los Incas

The **Camino Sagrado de los Incas**, a truncated Inca Trail, starts at Km 104 of the Panamerican Highway, 8km from Machu Picchu. The footbridge here (roughly $50 entry, $25 for students, free for children under 12, includes entry to Machu Picchu) leads to a steep climb (3-4hr) past Chachabamba to reach Wiñay Wayna (see p.292), where you join the reminder of the Inca Trail.

from sea level. For more information on acclimatization and mountain sickness, see p.242.

Setting off

Organized tours usually approach the trail by road via Ollantaytambo and then take a dirt track from there to **Chilca**, which adds a few hours to the overall trek but forms the **road trailhead**. Minibuses from Ollantaytambo to Chilca cost $1.20. For groups arriving by train, however, the conventional **rail trailhead** is at Km 88 along the tracks from Cusco, at a barely noticeable stop announced by the train guard. Have your gear ready to throw off the steps, since the train pulls up only for a few brief seconds and you'll have to fight your way past sacks of grain, flapping chickens, men in ponchos and women in voluminous skirts. A **third trail**, known as the Camino Sagrado de los Incas, begins at Km 104 (see box, p.290).

From the station, a footbridge sees you across the Río Urubamba. Once over the bridge the main path leads to the left, through a small eucalyptus wood, then around the base of the Inca ruins of Llactapata (worth a visit for archaeology enthusiasts, though most people save their energy for the trail and other archaeological remains ahead) before crossing and then following the Río Cusichaca upstream along its left bank. It's a good two hours' steep climb to **Huayllabamba**, the only inhabited village on the route and the best place to hire horses or mules for the most difficult climb on the whole trail, the nearby **Dead Woman's Pass**. This section of the valley is rich in Inca terracing, from which rises an occasional ancient stone building. To reach Huayllabamba you have to cross a well-marked bridge onto the right bank of the Cusichaca. Many groups spend their first night at Huayllabamba **campsite**, but if you want to gain distance and time for the second day, there are three commonly used campsites, one at Llulluchayoc, where the trail crosses the Río Huayruro, just half a kilometre above its confluence with the Llullucha stream. This site is also known as **Three White Stones**; another slightly higher site, just below Llulluchpampa, where there are toilets and space for several tents. Or, slightly higher again, actually on the pampa where there's plenty more camping space – a good spot for seeing rabbit-like *viscachas* playing among the rocks. All these campsites are on the trail towards the first and highest pass, but only the top one is within sight of it.

The first and second passes

It takes five hours or so from Huayllabamba to the Abra de Huarmihuañusca, **the first pass** (4200m) and the highest point on the trail. It is the hardest part of the walk – leave this (or at least some of it) for the second day, especially if you're feeling the effects of the altitude. The views from the pass itself are stupendous, but if you're tempted to hang around savouring them, it's a good idea to sit well out of the cutting wind (many a trekker has caught a bad chill here). From here the trail drops steeply down, sticking to the left of the stream into the Pacamayo Valley where, by the river, there's an attractive spot to **camp**, and where you can see playful **spectacled bears** if you're very lucky, or take a break before continuing up a winding, tiring track towards the **second pass** – Abra de Runkuracay – just above the interesting circular ruins of the same name. About an hour beyond the second pass, a flight of stone steps leads up to the Inca ruins of **Sayacmarca**. This is an impressive spot to **camp**, near the remains of a stone aqueduct that supplied water to the ancient settlement (the best spots are by the stream just below the ruins).

The third pass

From Sayacmarca, make your way gently down into increasingly dense cloud forest where delicate orchids and other exotic flora begin to appear among the trees. By the time you get to the **third pass** (which, compared with the previous two, has very little incline) you're following a fine, smoothly worn flagstone path where at one point an astonishing tunnel, carved through solid rock by the Incas, lets you sidetrack an otherwise impossible climb. The trail winds down to the impressive ruin of **Puyupatamarca** – "Town Above the Clouds" – where there are five small stone baths and in the wet season constant fresh running water. There are places to **camp** actually on the pass (ie, above the ruins), commanding stunning views across the Urubamba Valley and, in the other direction, towards the snowcaps of Salcantay (Wild Mountain): this is probably one of the most magical camps on the trail (given good weather), and it's not unusual to see deer feeding here.

It's a very rough, two- or three-hour descent along a non-Inca track to the next ruin, a citadel almost as impressive as Machu Picchu, **Wiñay Wayna** – "Forever Young" – another place with fresh water. These days there's an official *Trekkers Hostal* here (no phone; $10 a bed; $3.50 floor space; $1 for a hot shower) on a first-come, first-served basis; it has a restaurant too – nothing amazing, but with a welcome supply of cool drinks.

Consisting of only two major groups of architectural structures – a lower and an upper sector – Wiñay Wayna's most visible features are stone baths with apparently as many as nineteen springs feeding them, all set amidst several layers of fine Inca terracing. Nearby there's also a small waterfall created by streams coming down from the heights of Puyupatamarca. Much like today, it is believed that Wiñay Wayna was used by Incas as a washing, cleansing and resting point before arriving at the grand Machu Picchu citadel.

This is usually the spot for the **last night of camping**, and, especially in high season, the crowds mean that it's a good idea to pitch your tent soon after lunch, but don't be surprised if someone pitches their tent right across your doorway. To reach Machu Picchu for sunrise the next day you'll have to get up very early with a flashlight to avoid the rush.

A well-marked track from Wiñay Wayna takes a right fork for about two more hours through sumptuous vegetated slopes to **Intipunku**, for your first sight of Machu Picchu – a stupendous moment, however exhausted you might be. Aim to get to Machu Picchu well before 9.30am, when the first hordes arrive off the train from Cusco, if possible making it to the "hitching post" of the sun before dawn, for an unforgettable sunrise that will quickly make you forget the long hike through the pre-dawn gloom – bring a torch if you plan to try it.

Machu Picchu

MACHU PICCHU (daily 6.30am–5pm; standard entry fee is $44; or $22 for students with ID card) is one of the greatest of all South American tourist attractions: beautiful stone architecture enhanced by the Incas' exploitation of local 250-million-year-old rocks of grey-white granite with a high content of quartz, silica and feldspar, set against a vast, scenic backdrop of dark-green forested mountains that spike up from the deep valleys of the Urubamba and its tributaries. The distant glacial summits are dwarfed only by the huge sky.

This most dramatic and enchanting of Inca citadels, suspended on an extravagantly terraced saddle between two prominent peaks, is believed to be in danger

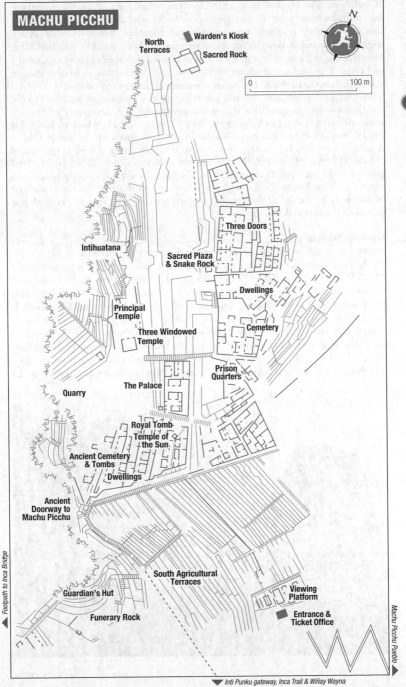

MACHU PICCHU

N

Warden's Kiosk

North
Terraces

Sacred Rock

0 — 100 m

Three Doors

Intihuatana

Sacred Plaza
& Snake Rock

Dwellings

Principal
Temple

Cemetery

Three Windowed
Temple

Prison
Quarters

The Palace

Quarry

Royal Tomb
Temple of
the Sun

Ancient Cemetery
& Tombs

Dwellings

Ancient
Doorway to
Machu Picchu

South Agricultural
Terraces

Guardian's Hut

Viewing
Platform

Funerary Rock

Entrance &
Ticket Office

of **collapse**. The original Inca inhabitants temporarily stabilized the mountain-side, transforming some of the geological faults into drainage channels. They also joined many of the construction stones together, using elaborate multi-angled techniques, making them more resistant to both tremors and landslides. Nevertheless, these spots remain weak and significant damage can be seen on nearby buildings. The National Institute of Culture, which administers Machu Picchu, acknowledges the problems but correcting them is an ongoing process.

With many legends and theories surrounding the position of Machu Picchu, most archaeologists agree that the sacred geography and astronomy of the site were auspicious factors in helping the Inca Pachacuti decide where to build this citadel here at 2492m. The name Machu Picchu apparently means simply Old or Ancient Mountain. It's thought that agricultural influences as well as geo-sacred indicators prevailed and that the site secured a decent supply of sacred coca and maize for the Inca nobles and priests in Cusco. However, it is quite possible to enjoy a visit to Machu Picchu without knowing too much about the history or archaeology of the site or the specifics of each feature; for many it is enough just to absorb the mystical atmosphere.

Some history

Never discovered by the Spanish conquerors, for many centuries the site of Machu Picchu lay forgotten, except by local Indians and settlers, until it was found on July 24, 1911 by the US explorer **Hiram Bingham**. It was a fantastic find, not least because it was still relatively intact, without the usual ravages of either Spanish conquistadors or tomb robbers. Accompanied only by two locals, Bingham left his base camp around 10am and crossed a bridge so dodgy that he crawled over it on his hands and knees before climbing a precipitous slope until they reached the ridge at around midday. After resting at a small hut, he received hospitality from a local peasant who described an extensive system of terraces where they had found good fertile soil for their own crops. Bingham was led to the site by an

▲ Machu Picchu

eleven-year-old local boy, Pablito Alvarez, but it didn't take him long to see that he had come across some important ancient Inca terraces – over a hundred of which had recently been cleared of forest for subsistence crops. After a little more exploration Bingham found the fine white stonework and began to realize that this might be the place he was looking for.

Bingham first theorized that Machu Picchu was the lost city of Vilcabamba, the site of the Incas' last refuge from the Spanish conquistadors. Not until another American expedition surveyed the ruins around Machu Picchu in the 1940s did serious doubts begin to arise over this assertion, and more recently the site of the Incas' final stronghold has been shown to be Espiritu Pampa in the Amazon jungle (see p.306).

Meanwhile, it was speculated that Machu Picchu was perhaps the best-preserved of a series of agricultural centres that served Cusco in its prime. The city was conceived and built in the mid-fifteenth century by **Emperor Pachacuti**, the first to expand the empire beyond the Sacred Valley towards the forested gold-lands. With crop fertility, mountains and nature so sacred to the Incas, an agricultural centre as important as Machu Picchu would easily have merited the site's fine stonework and temple precincts. It was clearly a ritual centre, given the layout and quantity of temples; but for the Incas it was usual not to separate things we consider economic tasks from more conventional religious activities. So, Machu Picchu represents to many archaeologists the most classical and best-preserved remains of a citadel which the Incas used as both a religious temple site and an agricultural (perhaps experimental) growing centre.

The ruins

Though more than 1000m lower than Cusco, Machu Picchu seems much higher, constructed as it is on dizzying slopes overlooking a U-curve in the Río Urubamba. More than a hundred flights of steep stone steps interconnect its palaces, temples, storehouses and terraces, and the outstanding views command not only the valley below in both directions but also extend to the snowy peaks around Salcantay. Wherever you stand in the ruins, spectacular terraces (some of which are once again being cultivated) can be seen slicing across ridiculously steep cliffs, transforming mountains into suspended gardens.

Though it would take a lot to detract from Machu Picchu's incredible beauty and unsurpassed location, it is a zealously supervised place, with the site guards frequently blowing whistles at visitors who have deviated from the main pathways. The best way to enjoy the ruins – while avoiding the guards' ire – is to hire a guide (see p.290), or buy the map and stick to its routes.

The Temple of the Sun and around

The **Temple of the Sun**, also known as the *Torreon*, is a wonderful, semicircular, walled, tower-like temple displaying some of Machu Picchu's finest granite stonework. Constructed to incorporate polyhedrons and trapezoidal window niches, the temple's carved steps and smoothly joined stone blocks also fit neatly into the existing relief of a natural boulder that served as some kind of altar and also marks the entrance to a small cave. A window off this temple provides views of both the June solstice sunrise and the constellation of the Pleiades, which rises from here over the nearby peak of Huayna Picchu. The Pleiades are still a very important astronomical Andean symbol relating to crop fertility: locals use the constellation as a kind of annual signpost in the agricultural calendar, giving information about when to plant crops and when the rains will come. Below the Temple of the Sun is a cave known as the **Royal Tomb**, despite the fact that no graves or human remains have ever been found there. In fact, it probably represented access to the spiritual heart of the mountains, like the cave at the Temple of the Moon (see opposite).

Retracing your steps 20m or so back from the Temple of the Sun and following a flight of stone stairs directly uphill, then left along the track towards Intipunku (see p.297), brings you to a path on the right, which climbs up to the thatched **guardian's hut**. This hut is associated with a modestly carved rock known as the **funerary rock** and a nearby graveyard where Hiram Bingham (see p.294) found evidence of many burials, some of which were obviously royal.

The Sacred Plaza

Arguably the most enthralling sector of the ruins, **El Templo de Tres Ventanas** (Three-Windowed Temple), part of the complex based around the **Plaza Sagrada** (Sacred Plaza) is located back down in the centre of the site, the next major Inca construction after the Temple of the Sun. Dominating the southeastern edge of the plaza, the attractive Three-Windowed Temple has unusually large windows looking east towards the mountains beyond the Urubamba River valley. From here it's a short stroll to the **Templo Principal** (Principal Temple), so called because of the fine stonework of its three high main walls, the most easterly of which looks onto the Sacred Plaza. Unusually (as most ancient temples in the Americas face east), the main opening of this temple faces south, and white sand, often thought to represent the ocean, has been found on the temple floor, suggesting that it may have been allied symbolically to the Río Urubamba: water and the sea.

Intihuatana

A minute or so uphill from here along an elaborately carved stone stairway brings you to one of the jewels of the site, the **Intihuatana**, also known as the "hitching post of the sun". This fascinating carved rock, built on a rise above the Sacred Plaza, is similar to those created by the Incas in all their important ritual centres, but is one of the very few not to have been discovered and destroyed by the conquistadors. This unique and very beautiful survivor, set in a tower-like position, overlooks the Sacred Plaza, the Río Urubamba and the sacred peak of Huayna Picchu. Intihuatana's base is said to have been carved in the shape of a map of the Inca Empire, though few archaeologists agree with this. Its main purpose was as an **astro-agricultural clock** for viewing the complex interrelationships between the movements of the stars and constellations. It is also thought by some to be a symbolic representation of the spirit of the mountain on which Machu Picchu was built – by all accounts a very powerful spot both in terms of sacred geography and its astrological function. The Intihuatana appears to be aligned with four important mountains: the snowcapped mountain range of La Veronica lies directly to the east, with the sun rising behind its main summit during the equinoxes; directly south, though not actually visible from here, sits the father of all mountains in this part of Peru, Salcantay, only a few days' walk away; to the west, the sun sets behind the important peak of Pumasillo during the December solstice; and due north stands the majestic peak of Huayna Picchu. The rock evidently kept track of the annual cycles, with its basic orientation northwest to southeast, plus four vertices pointing to the four directions.

The Sacred Rock

Following the steps down from the Intihuatana and passing through the Sacred Plaza towards the northern terraces brings you in a few minutes to the **Piedra Sagrado** (Sacred Rock), below the access point to Huayna Picchu. A 3m high and

7m wide lozenge of rock sticking out of the earth like a sculptured wall, little is known for sure about the Sacred Rock, but it is thought to have had a ritual function; its outline is strikingly similar to the Incas' sacred mountain of Putukusi, which towers behind it in the east.

Huayna Picchu

The prominent peak of **Huayna Picchu** juts out over the Urubamba Valley at the northern end of the Machu Picchu site, and is easily scaled by any reasonably energetic person. The record for this vigorous and rewarding climb is 22 minutes, but most people take at least an hour. Access to this sacred mountain is restricted to four hundred people a day (the first two hundred are expected to get back down by 10am so that the second two hundred can then go up); there's a guardian with hut just behind the Sacred Rock, where you can register for the climb. From the summit, there's an awe-inspiring **panorama**, and it's a great place from which to get an overview of the ruins suspended between the mountains among stupendous forested Andean scenery.

The Temple of the Moon

Accessed in the same way as Huayna Picchu, but about one-third of the way up, another little track leads to the left and down to the stunning **Templo de La Luna** (Temple of the Moon), hidden in a grotto hanging magically above the Río Urubamba, some 400m beneath the pinnacle of Huayna Picchu. Not many visitors make it this far and it's probably wise to have a guide (and if you've already walked up Huayna Picchu, you might want to save this for another day because it's at least another 45min each way and not that easy-going at times). The guardian by the Sacred Rock will often take people for a small fee (around $1 per person, provided there are two or more). Once you do get there, you'll be rewarded by some of the best stonework in the entire site, the level of craftsmanship hinting at the site's importance to the Inca.

The temple's name comes from the fact that it is often lit up by the moonlight, but some archaeologists believe the temple was most likely dedicated to the spirit of the mountain. The main sector of the temple is in the mouth of a natural cave, where there are five niches set into an elaborate white granite stone wall. There's usually evidence – small piles of maize, coca leaves and tobacco – that people are still making offerings at these niches. In the centre of the cave there's a rock carved like a throne, beside which are five cut steps leading into the darker recesses, where you can see more carved rocks and stone walls, nowadays at least inaccessible to humans. Immediately to the front of the cave is a small plaza with another cut stone throne and an altar. Outside, steps either side of the massive boulder lead above the cave, from where you can see a broad, stone-walled room running along one side of the cave boulder. There are more buildings and beautiful little stone sanctuaries just down a flight of steps from this part of the complex.

If you don't have the time or energy to climb Huayna Picchu or visit the Temple of the Moon, simply head back to the guardian's hut on the other side of the site and take the path below it, which climbs gently for thirty minutes or so, up to **Intipunku**, the main entrance to Machu Picchu from the Inca Trail. This offers an incredible view over the entire site with the unmistakable shape of Huayna Picchu in the background.

Arrival and information

The only ways to get to Machu Picchu are by train or trekking. There has been an occasional helicopter service, too, but there are no roads that connect to this region.

If you arrive **by train**, you'll get off at **Machu Picchu Pueblo station**, at the nearest town to the ruins, which has experienced explosive growth over the last decade or so and is occasionally still referred to by its older name, Aguas Calientes. You walk through a craft market area from the station and over a footbridge; below the bridge you'll see the ticket office and buses. It's from here that you can catch one of the **buses** to the ruins. The first buses leave at 5.20am and continue every 10min or so according to demand until about 4pm, returning continuously until the last bus at 5.30pm; $12 return, $6 one-way, children under 4 half-price. The ticket office is within a few minutes' walk of the railway station; just go through the market stalls and cross the Rio Agua Calientes by a footbridge. Tickets can be bought just below this from a small window, where there's usually a queue to help identify it, and from where buses usually depart. Tickets are stamped with the date, so you have to return the same day. It's possible to walk from Machu Picchu Pueblo to the ruins, but it'll take one and a half to three hours, depending on how fit you are and whether you take the very steep direct path or follow the more roundabout paved road.

Next to the entrance to the ruins there's a **ticket office** (daily 6am–5.30pm; $44, $22 students), where you can also hire a guide ($3.50 per person, for a minimum of 6) and buy a **map**. For **tourist information** and books, there's a municipal information office next to the INC (Instututo Nacional de Cultura) office just off Machu Picchu Pueblo's main square on Avenida Pachacutec. The INC office also sells tickets for Machu Picchu entry which, if you stay overnight here before visiting the site, could save time in the morning. It's easy enough to get into the site before sunrise since the sun rarely rises over the mountains to sheds its rays over Machu Picchu before 7am.

Accommodation

In the main, travellers tend to stay at **Machu Picchu Pueblo** (see below). Despite its exciting buzz, charm and stunning location - enclosed by rocky and forested tall mountains - it's little more than a booming concrete conglomeration of restaurants, shops and hotels.

Near the ruins

The local *consejo*-run **campsite** ($2, collected every morning) is close to the site, just over the Río Urubamba on the railway side of the bridge, from where the buses start their climb up to the ruins of Machu Picchu.

Alternatively, there's the one and only hotel actually up by the entrance to the ruins themselves; this is the very expensive *Machu Picchu Sanctuary Lodge* (℡01/6108300 or 084/984816953, Ⓦwww.sanctuarylodge.net; Ⓞ). The hotel is something of a concrete block, but it's comfortable and has a restaurant, and staying here allows you to explore the site early in the morning or in the afternoons and evenings when most other people have left.

Machu Picchu Pueblo

Although there is an overwhelming choice of **places to stay** in Machu Picchu Pueblo, there can be a lot of competition for lodgings during the high season (June–Sept), when large groups of travellers often turn up and take over entire hotels. Coming to town on an early train will give you some increased choice in where to stay, but for the better places try and book at least a week or two, if not months, in advance.

MACHU PICCHU PUEBLO

0   100 m

N

Parque
Wiñay Wayna   Ⓐ
①
②
③
④
⑤
Ⓑ
Ⓒ
Ⓓ
Ⓕ
Ⓖ

PACHACUTEC
INCA YUPANQUI
WIRACOCHA
WIRACOCHA
YAHUAR HUACA

Hot
Springs

HUANACAURE
COLLASUYO
COLLA RAYMI
CONTISUYO
ANTISUYO
YUPANQUI
SINCHI ROCA
MAYTA CAPAC
CAPAC YUPANQUI
INCA ROCA
PACHACUTEC

Putukusi Trail

Road to Machu Picchu & Campsite

Centro
Cultural
Machu
Picchu
ⓔ
Police
Station
ⓗ
ⓖ
ⓕ
ⓔ
School
PLAZA
Ⓘ
Ⓗ
AVENIDA PACHACUTEC
⑨

ATM
Bus Ticket
Office &
Departure

CRAFT
MARKET
ATM & Bank
(Banco de Credito)
⑩

Rio Aguas Calientes
ALAMEDA HERMANOS AYAR
Ⓙ

Train
Station

AVENIDA IMPERIO DO LOS INCAS
Rio Vilcanota
Rio Alcamayo
Inrena
Office
Ⓚ

EATING

Café Internet Restaurant	7
Chez Maggy's	4
Costandino Restaurant	3
El Gourmet Grill	9
Govinda	1
El Indio Feliz	6
Pizzeria Pachamama	5
Restaurant El Manu	2
Toto's House Restaurant	10
Valle Sagrado Pizzas	8

ACCOMMODATION

Chaska	J
Gringo Bill's	E
Hospedaje Rupa Wasi	B
Hospedaje Samana Wasi	F
Hostal La Cabaña	A
Hostal Los Caminantes	D
Hostal Quilla	C
Inkaterra Machu Picchu	K
Machu Picchu Hostal	H
Machu Picchu Inn	I
Wiracocha Inn	G

Chaska Alameda Hermanos Ayar ☎211045 or 251216 (in Cusco) ℮chaska_machupicchu @hot. Located close to the craft market on the station side of the Rio Aguas Calientes, this is a new hostal with comfortable beds, plain rooms (some with views over the river and town), laundry and cafeteria. ⑤–⑥

Gringo Bill's Colla Raymi 104 ☎211046 or, in Cusco, 223663, ⓦwww.gringobills.com. Also known as the *Hostal Q'oni Unu*, this is one of the most interesting choices in town, with bar, restaurant and rooms, some painted with attractive and rather cosmic murals, forming an appealing complex built into the lower hillside. It offers money changing facilities, a book exchange, laundry, sauna, lunch packs, ample hot water and a relaxed environment. Breakfasts are included, grilled meats are served in the evening and there's also a book exchange. ⑥–⑧

Hospedaje Rupa Wasi C Huanacaure 180 ☎211101, ⓦwww.rupawasi.net. This very homely place is something of an eco-spiritual centre as well as a hostel, built onto the valley side but less than 4min walk left from the plaza and church. Describing itself as an ecolodge, making buildings bricks for the walls with non-degradeable rubbish, it has a range of attractive wooden cabins, with simple but elegantly ethnic décor some with

balconies and the only view to Machu Picchu available from this part of the valley. There's also a gourmet restaurant – the best in town – on the grounds and a massage facility. ⑤–⑦

Hospedaje Samana Wasi Inca Yupanqui, turn right off Pachacutec ☎211170. Also known as Nusta Wasi, this is a reasonably priced place that has hot water and some rooms with private bath, TV and good views across Rio Aguas Calientes. Price includes breakfast. ④–⑤

Hostal La Cabaña Av Pachacutec M20–Lot 3 ☎/℡211048, ⓦwww.lacabanamachupicchu.com. The comfy, stylish rooms come with fresh flowers in this safe and friendly boutique-style hotel, although a deposit is sometimes required to secure bookings. Other features include open lounge areas, a laundry and library, and one of the owners is also a local guide. Price includes a great buffet breakfast. ⑤–⑥

Hostal Los Caminantes Av Imperio de los Incas 138 ☎211007. An older, rambling building, located by the railway at the eastern edge of town, this place has rooms with or without bath and hot water, but not much else. ③

Hostal Quilla Av Pachacutec ☎211009 or, in Cusco, 256568, ℮mariaquilla6@hotmail.com. A very friendly hostel offering breakfasts (included) and good tourist information plus ability to organise guided tours locally. There's a restaurant serving Peruvian dishes and pizzas; rooms have private bath. ⑤

Inkaterra Machu Picchu Km 110 by the rail line on the western edge of the settlement ☎211122 or in Lima 01/6100404, ⓦwww.inkaterra.com. Together with sister hotels in Cusco and the Sacred Valley, this is one of the most elegant and interesting boutique-style hotels in Peru, accessed by an almost hidden entrance on the left, just beyond the edge of town as you walk up the rail track towards Cusco. Both the rooms and communal areas like the bar and restaurant are beautiful, and it has its own swimming pool and extensive and stunningly beautiful gardens replete with an amazing variety of fearless hummingbirds, as well as five hectares of its own protected cloud forest and a range of great excursions, largely archaeology or nature-based. ⑧

Machu Picchu Hostal Av Imperio de los Incas ☎244598. A clean and smart place, located right beside the old station platform on the river side of the tracks; most rooms are based around a small garden, and all have good showers. ⑤

Machu Picchu Inn Av Pachacutec 109 ☎211011, ⓦwww.keyholdingperu.com. A comfortable but plain-looking hotel with a nice geranium garden, pool room and fine restaurant. ⑧

Wiracocha Inn C Wiracocha ☎211088, ⓦwww .wiracochainn.com. A really engaging hotel located in a lane on the right about halfway up Avenida Pachacutec, with a pretty lobby, very colourful and clean bedrooms and a dining room terrace shaded by trees. ⑥–⑦

Machu Picchu Pueblo – The Town

Many people base themselves at the settlement of **MACHU PICCHU PUEBLO** (previously known as Aguas Calientes) in order to visit Machu Picchu ruins at a more leisurely pace or in more depth. The settlement, onnected to the ruins by bus, has decent acccomodation, restaurants and shops. Its warm, humid climate and surrounding landscape of towering mountains covered in cloud forest make it a welcome change to Cusco, but the main attraction (apart from Machu Picchu itself) is the natural **thermal bath** (daily 6am–8.30pm; $3.50), which is particularly enjoyable after a few days on the Inca Trail or a hot afternoon up at Machu Picchu. You can find several communal baths of varying temperatures right at the end of the main drag of Avenida Pachacutec, around 750m uphill from the town's small plaza. The relatively new Machu Picchu Museum (US$2; daily 10am–5pm) in the old station by the road bridge over the river, close to the Municipal Campsite, at the start of the climb and bus route up to the main ruins. The museum now displays some of the exhibits previously on show in Cusco's museums.

There is also a **trail** (90min each way) up the sacred mountain of Putukusi, starting just outside of the town, a couple of hundred yards down on the left if you follow the rail track towards the ruins. The walk offers stupendous views of the town and across to Machu Picchu.

Machu Picchu Pueblo's explosive growth has pretty well reached the limits of the valley here; there's very little flat land that hasn't been built on or covered in concrete. Not surprisingly, this boom town has a lively, bustling feel and enough restaurants and bars to satisfy a small army.

Eating and drinking

There are a lot of pizzerias in Machu Picchu Pueblo, but it's also possible to eat exceptionally well in two or three of the settlement's better restaurants.

Café Internet Restaurant Corner of Contisuyo. Has fast internet access and serves coffee, omelettes, pizzas, trout and spaghetti among other dishes.

Chez Maggy's Av Pachacutec 156, ☎211006. A chain restaurant serving reasonable meals (their speciality being pizzas) and sometimes playing rock music.

Costandino C Huancaure 180, ☎211101. By far the best restaurant in town, *Costandino* started out, in association with the *Hospedaje Rupa Wasi*, in 2008, combining the best of Andean, Italian, Thai and Argentinean cooking. Both main dishes and sweets (try the passion fruit pudding) are exceptional, all made with as much local fresh ingredients as possible, and worth every calorie of the short walk up this street's steps. Good wines and breakfasts, too. Open 5am–3pm and 6–9pm.

El Gourmet Grill Av Pachacutec 138. A rather pretentious name for a pizzeria, though the service is good and they have a range of cocktails plus international dishes.

Govinda Up at the top end of Av Pachacutec, on the left. The Machu Picchu outpost of this well-known chain serves up bona fide veggie meals such as plain salads, squash and quinoa soup.

El Indio Feliz Lloque Yupanqui Lote 4m-12, ☏211090. This place serves exceptional three- or four-course meals of French and local cuisines at remarkably inexpensive prices; try to reserve a table as far in advance as possible.

Pizzeria Pachamama Imperio de los Incas 143 ☏212231. Opposite the small market, and specializing in pizzas, pancakes, breakfasts and *lomo* steak in mushroom sauce.

Restaurant El Manu Av Pachacutec. This place has a nice open dining area (sometimes doubling up as a dance space, quite lively at night), and specializes in trout and pizzas.

Toto's House Restaurant Av Imperio de los Incas ☏211020. A vast restaurant with great views and some tables out front by the rail tracks; they offer an expensive but quite good buffet lunch daily for $10.

Valle Sagrado Pizzas On the plaza. Very popular, with a large space and fine murals; as well as the obvious it serves soups, trout, chicken and juices.

Listings

Banks and exchange ATM by the municipal building, just down from the bus ticket office, and also at the Banco de Credito next to *Toto's House Restaurant*.

INRENA Instituto Nacional de Cultura offices, responsible for management of the national sanctuary of Machu Picchu, are on the rail line, just past the post office, towards the *Inkaterra Machu Picchu* hotel end.

Information i-Peru have an office in the first block of Avenida Pachacutec near the Centro Cultural (☏211104, ✉iperumachupicchu@promperu.gob. pe; 9am-8pm daily).

Internet *Café Internet Restaurant*, corner of Avenida Imperio de los Incas next to the old train station, with decent access ($2 per hour), plus cakes, snacks and drinks (6.30am–10pm); plenty of others along Avenida Pachacutec.

Laundry Most hostals and hotels will offer this, but there are some laundries dotted around, particu-

larly on the station side of Rio Aguas Calientes.

Left luggage Next to the entrance to the ruins (no backpacks or camping equipment are allowed inside; price per item $1.50).

Photography There's a Kodak shop with digital products and some film on Av Imperio de los Incas, on the same block as the *Café Internet Restaurant*.

Police Avenida Imperio de los Incas, just down from the old train station ☏211178.

Post office On the rail tracks, right-hand side, west some 100m or so beyond the Banco de Credito.

Telephones Centro Telefónica, Av Imperio de los Incas 132 ☏ 211091, 🖷211174.

Tour operators Most of the hotels organise tours or have links with operators. See p.264 for a list of companies covering Machu Picchu, Inca Trail etc.

Train tickets From the railway station ticket office, open from around 5am.

Alternative treks to the Inca Trail

There are three main trekking **routes** that have been developed by Cusco-based adventure tour operators in response to the desperate over-demand for the Inca Trail. The most popular of these is **Choquequirau**, and like the Inca Trail, this trek ends at a fabulous ancient citadel. Treks around the sacred glaciated mountain of **Salcantay** are also well-developed and, to some extent, overlap with and link to the Inca Trail itself. Much less walked, but equally breathtaking, is **Ausangate**, another sacred snow-covered peak (with a convenient looping trail) which can be seen on a clear day from Cusco dominating the southern horizon. Cost wise, these treks are similar in price to the Inca Trail, ranging from about $60 to $100 a day.

Choquequirau

An increasingly popular alternative to the Inca Trail, the hike to **CHOQUE-QUIRAU** can be made via trekking tours (3 or 4 days) that leave Cusco on

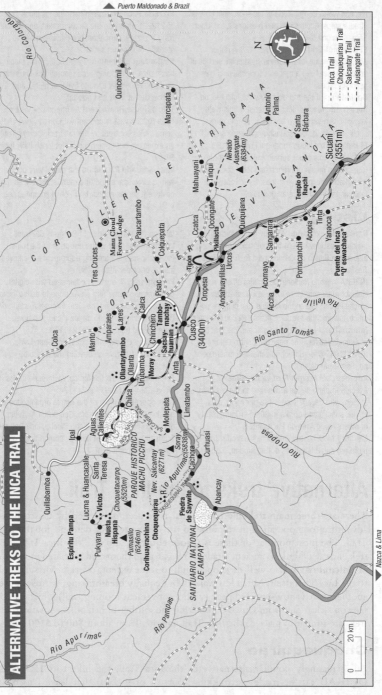

ALTERNATIVE TREKS TO THE INCA TRAIL

Puerto Maldonado & Brazil

Nazca & Lima

N

Inca Trail
Choquequirau Trail
Salcantay Trail
Ausangate Trail

0   20 km

Río Colorado

Quincemil

Marcapata

Antonio Palma

Santa Bárbara

SICUANI
(3551m)

CORDILLERA

Manu Cloud
Forest Lodge

Tres Cruces

Paucartambo

Colquepata

Mahuayani

Tinqui

Nevado
Ausangate
(6384m)

Templo de Raqchi

DE GARABAYA

Ccatca
Ocongate

Quiquijana

Tinta

Acopia

Yanaoca

Puente del Inca
"Q'eswachaca"

CORDILLER

Colca

Manto

Amparaes

Lares

Calca

Pisac

Chinchero

Sacsay-
huaman

Tambo-
machay

Tipón

Pikillacta

Urcos

Oropesa
Andahuayillas

Sangarara

Pomacanchi

Acomayo

Accha

Río Velille

DE VILCANOTA

Ollantaytambo

Ollanta

Moray

Urubamba

Cusco
(3400m)

Anta

Río Santo Tomás

Río Oropesa

Aguas
Calientes

Chilca

Chilca

Mollepata

Limatambo

Soray

Curhuasi

Quillabamba

Ipal

Lucma & Huancacalle

Santa
Teresa

Victos

Choquetacarpo
(5520m)

PARQUÉ HISTORICO
MACHU PICCHU

Nev. Salcantay
(6271m)

Río Apurímac (5830m)

Cachora

SANTUARIO NATIONAL
DE AMPAY

Espíritu Pampa

Pukyara

Ñusta
Hispana

Pumasillo
(6246m)

Corihuayrachina

Choquequirau

Piedra
de Saywite

Abancay

Río Apurímac

Río Pampas

demand and pretty much daily during tourist season. Not quite as spectacular as Machu Picchu, this is still an impressive Inca citadel whose name in Quechua means "Cradle of Gold".

Located 1750m above the Apurimac River and 3104m above sea level in the district of Vilcabamba, Choquequirau is thought to have been a rural retreat for the Inca emperor as well as a ceremonial centre. It was built in the late 15th century and almost certainly had an important political, military and economic role controlling people and produce between the rainforest communities of the Ashaninka (see p.614), who still live further down the Apurimac river, and the Andean towns and villages of the Incas. One can easily imagine coca, macaw feathers, manioc, salt and other Ashaninka products making their way to Cusco via Choquequirau. Sitting among fine terraces under a glaciated peak of the Salcantay range, less than half the original remains have been uncovered from centuries of vegetation, making a visit here similar to what Hiram Bingham may have experienced at Machu Picchu when he discovered the site back in 1911.

Bingham actually came here in 1910 on his search for lost Inca cities. Regardless of the exquisite stonework of the ceremonial complex and the megalithic agricultural terracing, Bingham – as have many archaeologists since – failed to see just how important a citadel Choquequirau actually was. Evidence from digs here suggest that there was a large population which continuously inhabited Choquequirao and nearby settlements even after the Spanish Conquest.

The most direct route up is along the Abancay road from Cusco, about four hours, to Cachora in Apurimac, over 100km from Cusco and some 93km north of Abancay; from here it's a further 30km (15–20hr) of heavy but stunningly beautiful trekking to the remains of the Choquequirau citadel. A longer and even more **scenic route** to Choquequirau involves taking a twelve-day hike from Huancacalle and Pukyura and then over the Pumasillo range, through Yanama, Minas Victoria, Choquequirau and across the Apurimac ending in Cachora.

Taking the direct route, the first two hours are spent hiking to Capuliyo, where, at 2915m, there are fantastic panoramas over the Apurimac Valley. The trail descends almost 1500m from here to Playa Rosalina on the banks of the River Apurimac, where it's possible to camp the first night. The second day has the most gruelling uphill walking – about five hours as far as Raqaypata and a further two or three to Choquequirau itself. You can go in and come out the same way in four to five days. Consisting of nine main sectors, the site was a political and religious centre well-served by a complex system of aqueducts, canals and springs. Most of the buildings are set around the main ceremonial courtyard or plaza and are surrounded by well-preserved and stylish Inca agricultural terracing.

Salcantay

The **SALCANTAY mountain** (6180m) is one of the Cusco region's main *apus*, or gods. Its splendid snowcapped peak dominates the landscape to the northwest of Cusco and it makes for relatively peaceful trekking territory. The main route joins the Machu Picchu railway line and the Urubamba Valley with the lesser-visited village of Mollepata in the Río Apurimac watershed. The trek usually takes from five to seven days and offers greater contact with local people, a wider range of ecological niches to pass through and higher paths than the Inca Trail. This trail is thus recommended for more adventurous trekkers who have already acclimatised.

Most people start on the Urubamba side at Km 82, where the Inca Trail also starts (see p.291). From here you can follow the Inca Trail path up the Cusichaca Valley, continuing straight uphill from the hamlet of Huayllabamba (**mules and muleteers** can be hired here, when available, from around $8 and $12 a day, respectively) ignoring the main Inca Trail that turns west and right here, up towards Deadwoman's Pass – La Abra de Huarmihuañusca. Throughout the trail, the landscape and scenery are very similar to the Inca Trail, though this route brings you much closer to the edge of the glaciers. The trail is steep and hard, up to the high pass at 5000m, which takes you around the southern edge of Salcantay glacier, before descending directly south to the village of Mollepata. The trek is increasingly approached in reverse, with guides and mules hired at Mollepata where there is less competition for them than there is on the Huayllabamba side; this route means you finish up in the Urubamba Valley, between Machu Picchu and Ollantaytambo. There are *colectivos* connecting Mollepata with Cusco daily, taking three to four hours. You can take a ride in a **truck** from Mollepata as far as Soraypampa, cutting out the first eight hours of the usual trek, for around $5. However, the trucks arrive irregularly and this should be considered when budgeting for time.

Ausangate

An important mountain god for the Incas, **AUSANGATE** is still revered daily by local people. You'll see very few people, apart from the occasional animal herder, once you leave the start and end point for this trail – one of the most challenging and exciting treks in Southern Peru – at the village of **Tinqui** at 3800m. Tinqui is reached by a three- to four-hour drive via Urcos. The management at the *Hostal Ausungate* (❶) in Tinque can arrange guides, mules and a muleteer (*arriero*) for trekkers. Some supplies are now available at the trailhead, but it's still safer to bring everything you need with you; there's more choice for everything in Cusco, but some food and cooking utensils could be purchased en route at the town of Urcos.

The **Ausangate Circuit** explores the Cordillera Vilcanota, weaving around many peaks over 6000m. Ausangate, the highest peak at 6372m, remains at the hub of the standard trail. Many of the camps are over 4600m and there are two passes over 5000m to be tackled. A good **map** is essential (the best is the PERU Topographic Survey 1:100,000 – 28-T, available from the South American Explorers' Club, see p.266) and a local guide strongly recommended.

The **first day**'s walking uphill from Tinqui brings you to a natural campsite on a valley floor almost 4500m above sea level close to the hot springs near Upis with tremendous views of Nevada Ausangate. **Day two** requires about six hours of walking, following the valley up and over into the next valley through the high pass of Arapa (4800m) heading for the camping area at the red-coloured lake of Laguna Jatun Pucacocha; from here you can see and hear the Nevada Ausangate's western ice-falls against a backdrop of alpaca herds.

Day three tackles the highest of all the passes – Palomani (5170m) early on. From here there are views over Laguna Ausangatecocha, and the walking continues up and down, passing the Ausangate climb base camp, for another three or four hours but offers some of the best scenery, particularly the Ausungate peak itself.

Day four continues downhill towards the Pitumarca Valley, which you follow left uphill to a campsite beyond Jampa, a remote settlement way beyond the electricity grid, but just this side of the magical Campa Pass (5050m) where centuries worth of stone piles or *cairns* left by locals and travellers adorn the landscape honouring the mountain god. From here there are spectacular views towards the snowcapped peaks of Puka Punta and Tres Picos.

Day five takes you uphill again through the pass and down beside Lake Minaparayoc. From here it's a three- or four-hour descent to the campsite at Pacchanta where there are some welcoming hot springs, traditionally enjoyed by trekkers as they near the end of this trail. After that, it's another three-hour walk back to Tinqui for road transport to Cusco.

Beyond Machu Picchu: into the jungle

The area along the Río Urubamba from Machu Picchu onwards, to the north, is a quiet, relatively accessible corner of the Peruvian wilderness. As you descend by road from Ollantaytambo, over a pass and then down to Chaullay and the jungle beyond, the vegetation along the valley turns gradually into jungle, thickening and getting greener by the kilometre and the air gets steadily warmer and more humid. Most people going down here get as far as the town of Quillabamba, but the road continues deeper into the rainforest where it meets the navigable jungle rivers at Kiteni and Ivochote (see p.529). Some people come to the region to explore the mountains, cloud forest and rainforest areas of this zone, either to check out known Inca ruins or to search out more new ones.

It is relatively easy to visit the hilltop ruins of the palace at **Vitcos**, a site of Inca blood sacrifices, and possible – though an expedition of six days or more – to explore the more remote ruins at **Espiritu Pampa**, now thought to be the site of the legendary lost city of Vilcabamba. The easiest way to see the ruins is on a guided tour with one of the adventure tour companies listed on p.264. If you'd rather travel independently, at least book a local guide through one of the companies in Cusco before setting off.

Major Inca sites are still being discovered in this region. In April 2002 Hugh Thomson (author of *The White Rock*, see p.626) and Gary Zeigler, following rumours of a lost city, led an expedition, which discovered an Inca city in the virtually inaccessible valley bottom at the confluence of the ríos Yanama and Blanco in the Vilcabamba region. Apparently seen briefly by Hiram Bingham nearly a hundred years ago, the coordinates were never recorded and this settlement of forty main buildings set around a central plaza hadn't been spotted since. Although very difficult to access – due to river erosion – there appears to have been an Inca road running through the valley, probably connecting this site to the great Inca citadel of Choquequirao (see p.301). This settlement is believed to have been Manco Inca's hide-out during his rebellion against the conquistadors, which lasted until his execution in Cusco in 1572.

Pukyura and Huancacalle

To visit the ruins at Vitcos or Espiritu Pampa independently, you can get there via the villages of **PUKYURA** and **HUANCACALLE**, in the Vilcabamba River valley. These settlements are reached in six hours by trucks which are usually easily picked up (small fee charged) at Chaullay on the Ollantaytambo–Quillabamba road. Pukyura has a long history of guerrilla fighting and wilful anti-authoritarian independence. Chosen by Manco Inca as the base for his rebel state in the sixteenth century, this area was also the political base in the early 1960s for **Hugo Blanco**, a charismatic *mestizo* from Cusco who had joined a Trotskyist group – the Workers Revolutionary Party. Blanco created nearly 150 syndicates, mainly in the Cusco region, whose peasant members began to work their own individual plots while refusing to work for the hacienda owners. Many landowners went bankrupt or opted to bribe workers back with offers of cash wages. The second phase of

Blanco's "reform" was to take physical control of the haciendas, mostly in areas so isolated that the authorities were powerless to intervene. Blanco was finally arrested in 1963 but the effects of his peasant revolt outlived him: in future, Peruvian governments were to take agrarian reform far more seriously. **Camping** at Pukyura is possible and you can usually arrange independently for an *arriero* here to take you over the two- or three-day trail to Espiritu Pampa. Narcisco Huaman is recommended ($25 per day, including 2 horses), contactable through Genaro, the Instituto Nacional de Cultura representative in Huancacalle. The hour-long walk uphill to Vitcos from Pukyura is easy to do independently, however. If you're seriously interested in exploring this region, you should check on the prevailing political and access rights situation with the Instituto Nacional de Cultura (see p.301) before attempting what is a very ambitious journey.

Vitcos and Espiritu Pampa

In 1911, after discovering Machu Picchu, Hiram Bingham set out down the Urubamba Valley to Chaullay, then up the Vilcabamba Valley to Pukyura, where he expected to find more Inca ruins. What he found – **VITCOS** (known locally as Rosapata) – was a relatively small but clearly palatial ruin, based around a trapezoidal plaza spread across a flat-topped spur. Down below the ruins, Bingham was shown by local guides a spring flowing from beneath a vast, white granite boulder intricately carved in typical Inca style and surrounded by the remains of an impressive Inca temple. This fifteen-metre-long and eight-metre-high sacred white rock – called Chuquipalta by the Incas – was a great oracle where blood sacrifices and other religious rituals took place. According to early historical chronicles, these rituals had so infuriated two Spanish priests who witnessed them, that they exorcized the rock and set its temple sanctuary on fire.

Within two weeks Bingham had followed a path from Pukyura into the jungle as far as the Condevidayoc plantation, where he found some more "undiscovered" ruins at **ESPIRITU PAMPA** – "Plain of the Spirits". After briefly exploring some of the outer ruins at Espiritu Pampa, Bingham decided they must have been built by Manco Inca's followers and deduced that they were post-Conquest Inca constructions since many of the roofs were Spanish-tiled. Believing that, at Machu Picchu, he had already found the lost city of Vilcabamba he was searching for, Bingham paid little attention to these newer discoveries. Consequently, as it was accessible only by mule, Espiritu Pampa remained covered in thick jungle vegetation until 1964, when serious exploration was undertaken by US archaeological explorer Gene Savoy. He found a massive ruined complex with over sixty main buildings and some three hundred houses, along with temples, plazas, wells and a main street. Clearly this was the largest Inca refuge in the Vilcabamba area, and Savoy rapidly became convinced of its identity as the true site of the last Inca stronghold. More conclusive evidence has since been provided by the English geographer and historian John Hemming who, using the chronicles, was able to match descriptions of Vilcabamba, its climate and altitude, precisely with those of Espiritu Pampa.

Getting to these sites really requires expedition-type preparation, the hire of local **guides** (best done through Cusco tour agents) and possibly even mules. You'll need a week or more even to cover the nearer sites. There are no services or facilities as such at any of the sites, none of which is staffed by permanent onsite guardians, so they are free and open as long as you have permission from the Instituto Nacional de Cultura (see, p.301).

The Cusco region

The Cusco region, even forgetting about Cusco city, is one of Peru's most exciting areas. Obviously, the lead attraction is Machu Picchu, but all too many visitors overlook the area's lesser-known attractions. Many people choose to spend at least three days in the immediate vicinity of the city, and nearly everyone takes at least another two or three days to visit Machu Picchu and the other sites in the Sacred Valley, but there's a huge number of other villages and sites to stimulate the energetic traveller with more than a week to spend. The Instituto Nacional de Cultura in Cusco has identified no fewer than 36,000 known archaeological sites in this region.

Chinchero, an old colonial settlement resting on Inca foundations overlooking the Sacred Valley and boasting a spectacular market, is only forty minutes' drive northwest of the city of Cusco. To the northeast, towards the jungle, the attractive village of **Paucartambo**, built in colonial style and famous for its annual festival, nestles among breathtakingly high Andean panoramas close to **Tres Cruces**, a remote mountain spot where locals and globetrotters alike go to experience a uniquely spectacular sun rising from the depths of lowland Amazonia. To the south lie the superb **ruins** of Tipón, Pikillacta, Raqchi and Rumicolca, the rustic and legendary village of **Urcos**, as well as superb trekking country around the sacred **Nevada Ausangate** glaciers (6384m) between the small settlement of **Ocongate** and the larger town of **Sicuani**. And even if you aren't planning to spend time around Lake Titicaca, the rail journey south to Puno (see p.214), which starts off through the Cusco region, is one of the most soul-stirring rides imaginable, though the track is a little bumpy compared with the new road to Puno. One last trip, the highland route between Cusco and Lima, passes through Abancay, Andahuaylas and **Ayacucho**, the latter a beautiful and highly traditional city famous for its churches and artesania.

Chinchero

CHINCHERO ("Village of the Rainbow") lies 3762m above sea level, 28km northwest from Cusco and off the main road, overlooking the Sacred Valley, with the Vilcabamba range and the snowcapped peak of Salcantay dominating the horizon to the west. The bus ride here takes you up to the Pampa de Anta, which used to be a huge lake but is now relatively dry pasture, surrounded by snowcapped *nevadas*. The town itself is a small, rustic place, where the local women, who crowd the main plaza during the market, still wear traditional dress. Largely built of stone and adobe, the town blends perfectly with the magnificent display of Inca architecture, ruins and megalithic carved rocks; relics of the Inca veneration of nature deities. The best time to visit is on September 8 for the lively traditional **fiesta**. Failing that, the market, smaller but less touristy than Pisac's, has good local craftwork.

The **market** (Sunday morning) is in the lower part of town, reached along Calle Manco II. Uphill from here, along the cobbled steps and streets, you'll find a vast **plaza**, which may have been the original Inca marketplace. It's bounded on one side by an impressive wall somewhat reminiscent of Sacsayhuaman's ramparts, though not as massive – it too was constructed on three levels, and some ten classical Inca trapezoidal niches can be seen along its surface. On the western perimeter of the plaza, the raised Inca stonework is dominated by a carved **stone throne**, near which are puma and monkey formations. The plaza is also home to a superb colonial adobe **iglesia** (daily 7am–5.30pm; entry by Cusco Tourist Ticket, available here or in Cusco – see p.243). Dating from the early seventeenth century, it was built on top of an Inca temple or palace, perhaps belonging to the Inca emperor Tupac Yupanqui, who particularly favoured Chinchero as an out-of-town resort – most of the area's aqueducts and terraces, many of which are still in use today, were built at his command. The church itself boasts frescoes, murals and paintings, though decaying, still very beautiful and evocative of its colonial past, and many pertaining to the Cusqueña school and celebrated local artist Mateo Cuihuanito. The most interesting depict the forces led by local chief Pumacahua against the rebel Tupac Amaru II in the late eighteenth century (for more detail see Contexts, p.565).

Practicalities

Buses leave Cusco from Av Grau 525 (☎805639) for Urubamba ($1.20) via Chincheros (80¢) every fifteen minutes from about 5am daily until early afternoon usually; car or minibus *colectivos* can also be found around the Puente Grau for Chincheros, Urubamba and Ollantaytambo. You'll need to keep an eye out for the town or ask the driver to let you know when to get off because the road only passes the outskirts of Chinchero (with a two-hundred-yard walk into the village).

There are just two **places to stay** in town, of which the *Hotel Los Incas* (❷) is the better value, with a typical, rustic restaurant. It's also possible to **camp** below the terraces in the open fields beyond the village, but, as always, ask someone local for permission or advice on this. There are several **restaurants**, all cheap and cheerful, though *Camucha*, Av Mateo Pumacahua 168, at the junction of C Manco Capac II and the main road to Cusco, has a particularly good set lunch.

Northeast of Cusco

The two major places to visit northeast of Cusco are **Paucartambo**, 112km from Cusco, and **Tres Cruces**, another 50km beyond Paucartambo. The road between the two follows the **Kosnipata Valley**, whose name means "Valley of Smoke", then continues through cloudy tropical mountain scenery to the mission of Shintuya on the edge of the Manu National Park (see p.521). Legend has it that the Kosnipata enchants anyone who drinks from its waters at Paucartambo, drawing them to return again and again.

Paucartambo

Eternally spring-like because of the combination of altitude and its proximity to tropical forest, and guarding a major entrance to the jungle zone of Manu, the pretty village of **PAUCARTAMBO** ("The Village of the Flowers") is located some 110km from Cusco in a wild and remote Andean region. A silver-mining colony, run by slave labour during the seventeenth and eighteenth centuries, it's now a popular destination that's at its best in the dry season between May and September, particularly in mid-July when the annual **Fiesta de la Virgen de Carmen** (see box p.309) takes place; visitors arrive in the thousands and the village is transformed from a peaceful habitation into a huge mass of frenzied, costumed dancers.

The Fiesta de la Virgen del Carmen

Paucartambo spends the first six months of every year gearing up for the **Fiesta de la Virgen del Carmen**. It's an essentially female festival: tradition has it that a wealthy young woman, who had been on her way to Paucartambo to trade a silver dish, found a beautiful (if body-less) head that spoke to her once she'd placed it on the dish. Arriving in the town, people gathered around her and witnessed rays of light shining from the head, and henceforth it was honoured with prayer, incense and a wooden body for it to sit on.

The energetic, hypnotic **festival** lasts three or four days (usually July 16–19, but check with the tourist office in Cusco – see p.243), and features throngs of locals in distinctive traditional costumes, as well as dancers and musicians, with market stalls and a small fair springing up near the church. Clamouring down the streets are throngs of intricately costumed and masked dancers and musicians, the best-known of whom are the black-masked Capaq Negro, recalling the African slaves who once worked the nearby silver mines. Note the grotesque blue-eyed masks and outlandish costumes acting out a parody of the white man's powers – malaria, a post-Conquest problem, tends to be a central theme – in which an old man suffers terrible agonies until a Western medic appears on the scene, with the inevitable hypodermic in his hand. If he manages to save the old man (a rare occurrence) it's usually due to a dramatic muddling of prescriptions by his dancing assistants – and thus does Andean fate triumph over science.

On Saturday afternoon there's a **procession of the Virgen del Carmen** itself, with a brass band playing mournful melodies as petals and emotion are showered on the icon of the Virgin – which symbolizes worship of Pachamama as much as devotion to Christianity. The whole event culminates on Sunday afternoon with the dances of the *guerreros* (warriors), during which good triumphs over evil for another year.

The beautiful main **plaza**, with its white buildings and traditional blue balconies, has concrete monuments depicting the characters who perform at the fiesta – demon-masked dancers, malaria victims, lawyers, tourists and just about anything that grabs the imagination of the local communities. Also on the plaza is the rather austere **iglesia**, restored in 1998 and splendid in its own way, simple yet full of large Cusqueña paintings. It's also the residence of the sacred image of the Virgen del Carmen, unusual in its Indian (rather than European) appearance: when the pope visited Peru in the mid-1980s, it was loaded onto a truck and driven to within 30km of Cusco, then paraded on foot to the city centre so that the pope could bless the image. Even if you don't make it to Paucartambo for the festival, you can still see the ruined *chullpa* burial towers at Machu Cruz, an hour's walk from Paucartambo; ask in the village for directions. Travellers rarely make it here outside of festival time, unless en route to the rainforest by road.

Transportes Gallitos de las Rocas **buses** leave from their Cusco office (Av Diagonal Angamos 1952; ℡226895) daily to Paucartambo ($2.50; 4–5hr) and three times a week to Pilcopata. **Trucks**, which leave from the end of Avenida Garcilaso, beyond the Ormeño office, are slightly cheaper but slower and far less comfortable. Buses generally stop off in Paucartambo at the market place, from where you cross the stone bridge into the main part of town up to the plaza, where, during festival times only, there's a **tourist information** office. Whenever you go, it's best to take a **tent**, because **accommodation** is difficult to find: the only options are the *Albergue Municipal* (no phone; ❷) and, by the lower bridge, the *Hotel Quinta Rosa Marina* (no phone; ❸), both central and very basic. When the festival is on, they're fully booked, but it's possible to rent out spaces in some local residents' homes.

Tres Cruces

The natural special effects during **sunrise** at **TRES CRUCES** are in their own way as magnificent a spectacle as the Fiesta de la Virgen de Carmen. At 3739m above sea level, on the last mountain ridge before the eastern edge of the Amazon forest, the view is a marvel at any time: by day a vast view over the start of a massive cloud forest with all its weird vegetation; by night an enormous star-studded jewel. Seen from the highest edge of the Manu Biosphere Reserve, the sunrise is spectacular, particularly around the southern hemisphere's winter solstice in June: multicoloured, with multiple suns, an incredible light show that lasts for hours. **Transport** to Tres Cruces can be a problem, except during the fiesta; however, on Monday, Wednesday and Friday, Transportes Gallinos de las Rocas buses (see above) to Paucartambo continue on to Pilcopata or Salvación; beyond Paucartambo, you can disembark at the Tres Cruces turn-off ($3; about 8hr from Cusco), but be prepared to walk the remaining 14km into Tres Cruces itself, though you may get a lift with a passing vehicle (especially early in the day from late June to mid-July). Cusco tour operators (see p.264) can organize a trip, or you can check the notice boards in the main cafés and backpacker joints in Cusco for people trying to gather together groups to share the cost of a *colectivo* and driver for the two- to three-day trip – usually $30–50 a day, plus food and drink for the driver – or even post a notice yourself. The only **accommodation** in Tres Cruces is an empty house that's used as a visitors' shelter, which fills up very fast at festival times, when **camping** is the only real option, so take a warm sleeping bag, a tent and enough food.

Northwest from Cusco

It takes about thirty hours or so to travel **from Cusco to Lima** via **Abancay** (see p.339), **Andahuaylas** (see p.339) and **Ayacucho** (see p.332), then down to the Pisco Valley on the coast, which is just a few hours from Lima. A more direct route, though only knocking off around four hours from the trip, goes to Abancay, then crosses the Andes to join the coast at Nasca (5–6hr from Lima). If you do take the Nasca route, there are a few opportunities for breaking the journey, for example at *Tampumayu* (056/523490; www.hoteltampumayu.com; ⑤–⑥), a small Andean style hotel-village with individual houses of stone, adobe and pan-tile roofs, a restaurant and bar, located about half way between Puquio and Abancay at Km 361.

Whichever route you choose, you'll pass through the village of **Carahuasi**. Within its district are a couple of diverting sights: by the community of Concacha, and some 3500m above sea level, is the archaeological complex of **Sahuite**, comprising three massive, beautifully worked granite boulders, the best of which graphically depict an Inca village (though the boulders have been partially defaced in recent years). And some 7km from Carahuasi there are the crystal-clear **thermal baths of Conoc**; the healing properties of the water are said to be particularly good for rheumatism, arthritis and muscular pain.

South from Cusco

The first 150km of the road (and rail) south from Cusco towards Lake Titicaca (see p.222) passes through the beautiful valleys of Huatanay and Vilcanota, from where the legendary founders of the Inca Empire are said to have emerged. A region outstanding for its natural beauty and rich in magnificent archaeological sites, it's easily accessible from Cusco and offers endless possibilities for exploration or random wandering. The whole area is ideal for **camping** and **trekking**, and in any case, only the towns of **Urcos** and **Sicuani** are large enough to provide reasonable accommodation (see p.313).

Heading south from Cusco by road, after about 5km you pass through the little pueblo of **San Sebastián**. Originally a small, separate village, it has now become a suburb of the city. Nevertheless, it has a tidy little church, ornamented with Baroque stonework and apparently built on the site of a chapel erected by the Pizarros in memory of their victory over Almagro. The next place of any interest is picturesque **Oropesa**, some 25km on, traditionally a town of bakers, whose adobe church, boasting a uniquely attractive three-tiered belfry with cacti growing out of it, is notable for its intricately carved pulpit and the beautiful, Cusqueña-esque interior murals which look to have been painted between 1580 and 1630. A few kilometres further up the valley, the Inca remains of **Tipón** lie high above the road, little visited but extensive and evocative. Closer to the road, the Huari city of **Pikillacta** is easier to find and worthy of an hour or two. Beyond Urcos but before **Sicuani**, a rather boring transport node of a town, the great **Temple of Raqchi** still stands unusually high as a monument to Inca architectural abilities.

Getting around by train or bus

Perhaps the **best option** is offered by Inka Express, Urb El Ovalo, Av La Paz C-32 (ⓣ247887, ⓔinkaexpress@terra.com, ⓦwww.inkaexpress.com), which has quality buses linking Cusco with Puno but also offering opportunities to stop off at some of the tourist sites, including Tipón and Raqchi (see p.314) en route, with a bilingual tour guide.

Trains (also linking Cusco with Puno) depart at 8am three times a week – on Mondays, Wednesdays and Saturdays during high season – from Huanchac station in Cusco; **buy tickets at least one to three days before travelling**. There's only one class of ticket - the **Andean Explorer train** – at a cost of $143 (one-way, but including lunch and tea) with good waiter service.

As the trains are slow and buses are cheaper, most people travel instead on one of the frequent **buses** or **minibuses**. Many of these bus options are inter-regional carriers listed in the Bus Departure listings in the Cusco box (p.266). As well as these, El Zorro, Sol Andino and Oriental run daily services (from 3.40am every 20min until early afternoon ⓣ240406) from Av de la Cultura 1624 as far as Urcos and Sicuani, passing all the sites covered below except La Raya. Other buses for Sicuani and Urcos leave with Empresa Vilcanota, and others to Urcos ($1), from Av de la Cultura 13230 or the depot behind a Churascaria at the end of block 13 of Avenida de la Cultura (opposite the Hospital Regional).

The Tipón temples and aqueducts

Both in setting and architectural design, **TIPÓN RUINS** (daily 7am–5.30pm; entry by Cusco Tourist Ticket, see p.243) are one of the most impressive Inca sites. From Oropesa, the simplest way to reach the ruins is by backtracking down the main Cusco road some 2km to a signposted track. Follow this up through a small village, once based around the now crumbling and deserted hacienda Quispicanchi, and continue along the gully straight ahead. Once on the path above the village, it's about an hour's climb to the first ruins.

Well hidden in a natural shelf high above the Huatanay Valley, the **lower sector** of the ruins is a stunning sight: a series of neat agricultural terraces, watered by stone-lined channels, all astonishingly preserved and many still in use. The impressive stone terracing reeks of the Incas' domination over an obviously massive and subservient labour pool; yet at the same time it's clearly little more than an elaborate attempt to increase crop yield. At the back of the lower ruins water flows from a stone-faced "mouth" around a spring – probably an aqueduct subterraneously diverted from above. The entire complex is designed around this spring, reached by a path from the last terrace. Another sector of the ruins contains a **reservoir** and **temple block** centred on a large exploded volcanic rock – presumably some kind of *huaca*. Although the stonework in the temple seems cruder than that of the agricultural terracing, its location is still beneficial. By contrast, the construction of the reservoir is sophisticated, as it was originally built to hold nine hundred cubic metres of water which gradually dispersed along stone channels to the Inca "farm" directly below.

Coming off the back of the reservoir, a large tapering stone aqueduct crosses a small gully before continuing uphill, about thirty minutes' walk, to a vast zone of **unexcavated terraces** and dwellings. Beyond these, over the lip of the hill, you come to another level of the upper valley literally covered in Inca terracing, dwellings and large stone storehouses. Equivalent in size to the lower ruins, these are still used by locals who've built their own houses among the ruins. So impressive is the terracing at Tipón that some archaeologists believe it was an Inca experimental agricultural centre, much like Moray (see p.282), as well as a citadel.

With no village or habitation in sight, and fresh running water, it's a breathtaking place to **camp**. There's a splendid stroll back down to the main road – take the path through the locals' huts in the upper sector over to the other side of the stream, and follow it down the hillside opposite Tipón. This route offers an excellent perspective on the ruins, as well as vistas towards Cusco in the north and over the Huatanay/Vilcanota valleys to the south.

Pikillacta and Rumicolca

About 7km south of Oropesa, the neighbouring pre-Inca ruins of Pikillacta and Rumicolca can be seen alongside the road. After passing the Paucartambo turn-off, near the ruins of an ancient storehouse and the small red-roofed pueblo of Huacarpay, the road climbs to a ledge overlooking a wide alluvial plain and Lucre Lake (now a weekend resort for Cusco's workers). At this point the road traces the margin of a stone wall defending the pre-Inca settlement of Pikillacta.

Spread over an area of at least fifty hectares, **PIKILLACTA**, or "The Place of the Flea" (daily 7am–5.30pm; entry by Cusco Tourist Ticket, see p.243), was built by the Huari culture around 800 AD, before the rise of the Incas. Its unique, geometrically designed terraces surround a group of bulky two-storey constructions: apparently these were entered by ladders reaching up to doorways set well off the ground in the first storey – very unusual in ancient Peru. Many of the walls are built of small cut stones joined with mud mortar, and among the most interesting finds here were several round turquoise statuettes. These days the city is in ruins but it seems evident still that much of the site was taken up by barrack-like quarters. When the Incas arrived early in the fifteenth century they modified the site to suit their own purposes, possibly even building the aqueduct that once connected Pikillacta with the ruined gateway of Rumicolca, which straddles a narrow pass by the road, just fifteen minutes' walk further south.

This massive defensive passage, **RUMICOLCA** (open all day; free), was also initially constructed by the Huari people and served as a southern entrance to – and frontier of – their empire. Later it became an Inca checkpoint, regulating the flow of people and goods into the Cusco Valley: no one was permitted to enter or leave the valley via Rumicolca between sunset and sunrise. The Incas improved on the rather crude Huari stonework of the original gateway, using regular blocks of polished andesite from a local quarry. The gateway still stands, rearing up to twelve solid metres above the ground, and is one of the most impressive of all Inca constructions.

Andahuaylillas and Huaro

About halfway between Rumicolca and Urcos, the otherwise insignificant villages of Andahuaylillas and Huaro hide deceptively interesting colonial churches. In the tranquil and well-preserved village of **ANDAHUAYLILLAS**, the adobe-towered church sits above an attractive plaza, fronted by colonial houses, just ten minutes' walk from the roadside restaurant where buses and minibuses drop off and pick up passengers. Built in the early seventeenth century on the site of an Inca temple, the **church** has an exterior balcony from which the priests would deliver sermons. While it's a fairly small church with only one nave, it is nevertheless a magnificent example of provincial colonial art. Huge Cusqueña canvases decorate the upper walls, while below are some unusual murals, slightly faded over the centuries; the ceiling, painted with Spanish flower designs, contrasts strikingly with a great Baroque altar.

To the south, the road leaves the Río Huatanay and enters the Vilcanota Valley. **HUARO**, crouched at the foot of a steep bend in the road 3km from Andahuaylillas, has a much smaller **church** whose interior is completely covered with colourful murals of religious iconography, angels and saints; the massive gold-leaf altarpiece dominates the entire place as you enter. Out in the fields beyond the village, as you climb towards Urcos, you can see boulders which have been gathered together in mounds, to clear the ground for the simple ox-pulled ploughs which are still used here.

Urcos

Climbing over the hill from Huaro, the road descends to cruise past **Lake Urcos** before reaching the town which shares the lake's name. According to legend, the Inca Huascar threw his heavy gold chain into these waters after learning that strange bearded aliens – Pizarro and his crew – had arrived in Peru. Between lake and town, a simple chapel now stands poised at the top of a small hillock: if you find it open, go inside to see several excellent Cusqueña paintings.

The town of **URCOS** rests on the valley floor surrounded by weirdly sculpted hills and is centred on the Plaza de Armas, where a number of huge old trees give shade to Indians selling bread, soup, oranges and vegetables. On one side of the plaza, which is particularly busy during the town's excellent, traditional **Sunday market**, there's a large, crumbling old church; on the other, low adobe buildings.

Practicalities

There's nothing of quality, but you can usually find a **room** around the Plaza de Armas. Try *Hostal Luvic*, Belaunde 196 (no phone; ❶), just to the right of the church; *Alojamiento Municipal*, Jr Vallejo 137 (no phone; ❶), next to the telephones; the *Alojamiento El Amigo*, half a block up from the left of the church (no phone; ❶); or an unnamed place, C Arica 316 (no phone; ❶), on the street coming from Cusco. All are very basic, crumbling old buildings with communal bathrooms.

There are a couple of reasonable **restaurants** on the Plaza de Armas, notably *El Cisne Azul* and the *Comedor Municipal*, both serving the Andean speciality quinoa soup, made of a highly nutritious grain grown at high altitudes and reputed to be good for skin problems. Although Urcos is not really a tourist town, the occasional traveller is made welcome; in the backstreets you can stop off at one of the *tiendas* (advertised by a pole with a blob of red plastic on the end) for a glass of *chicha* beer and some friendly conversation. Note that **electricity** only lasts until midnight, so take some candles or a torch if you plan to be out late. You can get a truck from Urcos all the way to **Puerto Maldonado** in the jungle (see p.508), a journey that takes anything from three days to two weeks depending on how much it rains (at its worst between December and March).

The Temple of Raqchi, the Puente Colgante and Sicuani

Between Urcos and Sicuani the road passes through **San Pedro de Cacha**, the nearest village (4km) to the imposing ruins of the **TEMPLO DE RAQCHI** (daily 9am–5.30pm; $3), built in honour of Viracocha, the Inca creator god. Buses pass within a few hundred metres of the temple entrance. The temple was evidently built to appease the god Viracocha after he had caused the nearby volcano of Quimsa Chata to spew out fiery boulders in a rage of anger, and even now massive volcanic boulders and ancient lava flows scar the landscape in constant reminder. With its adobe walls still standing over 12m high on top of polished stone foundations, and the site scattered with numerous other buildings and plazas, such as barracks, cylindrical warehouses, a palace, baths and aqueducts, Raqchi was clearly an important religious centre. Today the only ritual left is the annual **Raqchi Festival** (usually June 16–22), a dramatic, untouristy fiesta comprising three to four days of folkloric music and dance – performed by groups congregating here from as far away as Bolivia to compete on the central stage. The performances are well stage-managed but the site, in a boggy field, can be mayhem, with hundreds of food stalls, a funfair, Quechua women selling *chicha* maize beer and their drunken customers staggering through the tightly knit crowds.

Also accessed from the Urcos to Sicuani road, there's the **PUENTE COLGANTE**, a hanging or suspension rope bridge that has been rebuilt almost ceremonially every year since before the Spanish conquest. Annually, up to a thousand locals gather on the second Sunday in June to rebuild the bridge using traditional techniques and materials, including *ichu* grasses, to make ropes for the 33-metre span. The building and celebrations generally take three or four days and conclude with ceremony and dancing between the area's principal *ayllus*, or clans. To get to the Puente Colgante you have to get off a **bus or combi** at Combapata, about 30km before Sicuani and 10km further south than Checacupe. From Combapata it's another 31km (45min more by car) to the suspension bridge.

SICUANI, about 20km from Raqchi, is capital of the province of Canchis and quite a thriving agricultural and market town, not entirely typical of the settlements in the Vilcanota Valley. Its busy **Sunday market** is renowned for cheap and excellent woollen artefacts, which you may also be offered on the train if you pass through Sicuani between Puno and Cusco. Although not a particularly exciting place in itself – with too many tin roofs and an austere atmosphere – the people are friendly and it makes an excellent base for trekking into snow-capped mountain terrain, being close to the vast Nevada Vilcanota mountain range which separates the Titicaca Basin from the Cusco Valley. **Camping** is the best way to see this part of Peru, but if you haven't got a tent there are several **hotels** in town, including the reasonably comfortable *Hostal Tairo*, C Mejia 120 (T351297; ❷). The train journey south continues towards Puno and Lake Titicaca (see p.222), with the Vilcanota Valley beginning to close in around the line as the tracks climb **La Raya Pass** (4300m), before dropping down into the desolate *pampa* that covers much of inland southern Peru.

Travel details

Buses

Cusco to: Abancay (6 daily; 6hr); Arequipa (10 daily; 10hr); Argentina (3–4 weekly; 3 days); Ayacucho (3 daily; 18hr); Juliaca (3 daily; 7hr); La Paz (5 weekly; 20hr); Lima via Nasca (2 daily; 25hr), via Pisco and Ayacucho (2 weekly; 35–55hr); Puerto Maldonado (2 daily; 24hr); Puno (3 daily; 8hr); Santiago, Chile (2 weekly; 54hr).

Trains

Cusco to: Juliaca/Puno (3 weekly; 10hr); Machu Picchu Pueblo (4–12 daily; 3–5hr).

Machu Picchu Pueblo (Aguas Calientes) to: Ollantaytambo (6–12 daily; 2–3hr); Cusco (6–12 daily; 4–5hr).

Flights

Cusco to: Arequipa (2 daily; 90min); Ayacucho (2 weekly; 30min); Juliaca (2 daily; 50min); La Paz (2 weekly; 90min); Lima (8–12 daily; 1hr); Puerto Maldonado (2 daily; 40min).

5

The Central Sierra

CHAPTER 5

Highlights

✱ **Marcahuasi** This high plateau covered in unusual rock formations and reports of UFO sightings makes for out-of-this-world weekend camping. See p.321

✱ **Huancayo – Huancavelica train** The last remaining working railroad in the region, this breathtaking high-altitude train journey is one of the finest in the world. See p.331

✱ **Ayacucho** One of the most traditional and architecturally fascinating cities in the Peruvian Andes – renowned for over thirty impressive churches as well as boisterous religious fiestas. See p.334

✱ **Tarma** An attractive little colonial town particularly famous for its fantastic Easter Sunday procession and the associated flower paintings that carpet the roads. See p.340

✱ **San Pedro de Cajas** This scenic and remote village is home to many craftspeople who produce some of Peru's superb modern weavings. See p.341

✱ **Temple of Kotosh** Over 4000 years old, this impressive site's massive stone constructions suggest that complicated stonework began here centuries before anywhere else in the Americas. See p.344

▲ Iglesia Santo Domingo, Ayacucho

The Central Sierra

Once one of the first stops on the itinerary of any visit to Peru, the **CEN-TRAL SIERRA** was hit hard by the rise of terrorism during the 1980s, and the closing of the scenic high mountain railway connecting Lima with Huancayo led to a severe decline in tourism. Happily, though, all this is in the past and this large, green and mountainous region is very much open to visitors. The Central Sierra boasts some of Peru's finest archaeological sites and colonial buildings in the series of traditional towns and cities which punctuate the remote valleys and *cordilleras*. Although significantly fewer travellers make it here, compared with hot spots like Cusco and Machu Picchu, anyone with the time to spare will find this region a worthwhile destination in its own right, as well as somewhere to stop en route to the Central Selva (see p.492).

Huancayo is the obvious place to start exploring, particularly if you're coming from Lima. It's the largest urban centre in the area and is easily reached in a day's travel. If you're approaching from Cusco or the south coast, you are more likely to enter the region via **Ayacucho**, one of the cultural jewels of the Andes replete with colonial churches and some of Peru's finest artesan crafts.

En route up through the Cordillera Occidental – the massive mountain range which separates Huancayo and the beautiful Mantaro Valley from the coast is home to the enigmatic rock formations of **Marcahuasi**, though this is more commonly accessed directly from Lima. The region divides naturally into three sectors pivoting around Huancayo. To the north, pleasant **Huánuco** serves as a good base for exploring some of Peru's most interesting archaeological remains, and **Tingo Maria**, the gateway to the jungle port of Pucallpa. To the northeast you'll find the beautiful and fairly laid-back town of **Tarma**, which has a relatively pleasant climate influenced by the cloud forest to the east, and is a major nodal point for pioneers from the jungle, traders and, to a lesser extent, tourists. South of Huancayo lie the two most traditional of all the Central Sierra's towns: Ayacucho and **Huancavelica**.

Getting to the Central Sierra

After more than a decade of abandonment in terms of passenger service, the world-famous **Lima to Huancayo railway line** (known as "el Tren de la Sierra") has thankfully re-opened, re-launched in 2008 to celebrate the line's centenary. Trains are currently running a few times a month, usually Fridays, for this breathtaking eleven-hour journey; return journeys are mainly nocturnal, though there are exceptions in some months. Itineraries, up-to-date prices and tickets can be obtained online (℡01/2266363, @www.ferrocarrilcentral.com.pe). There are two classes of ticket: Touristic ($90 one adult return; $53 one-way) and Classic ($55 one adult return; $33 one-way).

The Andes Rail Line

The original opening of the Lima to Huancayo railway line into the Andes in the late nineteenth century had a huge impact on the region and was a major feat of engineering. For President Balta of Peru and many of his contemporaries in 1868, the iron fingers of a railway, "if attached to the hand of Lima would instantly squeeze out all the wealth of the Andes, and the whistle of the locomotives would awaken the Indian race from its centuries-old lethargy". Consequently, when the American rail entrepreneur Henry Meiggs (aptly called the "Yankee Pizarro") arrived on the scene, it was decided that coastal guano deposits would be sold off to finance a new rail line, one that faced technical problems (ie, the Andes) never previously encountered by engineers. The man really responsible for the success of this massive project was the Polish engineer, Ernest Malinowski. Utilising timber from Oregon and the labour of thousands of Chinese workers (the basis of Peru's present Chinese communities), Malinowski's skill and determination finished Meiggs' railway over a 30-year period. An extraordinary accomplishment, it nevertheless produced a mountain of debt that bound Peru more closely to the New York and London banking worlds than to its own hinterland and peasant population.

Originally constructed to transport minerals from mines in the Mantaro Valley to the coast, the train still travels up to 4782m above its sea-level starting point, crossing more than fifty bridges and passing through some 69 tunnels. The journey starts at Desamparados railway station, behind the Presidential Palace and the Plaza de Armas in Lima.

Travelling from Lima into the Central Sierra by road is, thanks to the much-improved **Carretera Central**, faster and safer than ever before. Given this, visitors are less likely to suffer from *soroche* (mountain sickness, see p.39), which, when travelling by train, is often produced by the slow climb through the high Ticlio Pass (over 4800m). While cars can generally just whiz through this pass now with passengers hardly noticing the altitude, the road has been frequently blocked in recent times by miners protesting about pay and conditions. To avoid breathlessness and headaches, or the even worse effects of *soroche*, it's still advisable to take the first few days over 3000m pretty easy before doing any hiking or other strenuous activities.

The **road journey** from Lima to Huancayo is almost as spectacular as the "Tren de la Sierra" trip, offering many travellers their first sight of llamas and of Peru's indigenous Indian mountain culture. It usually takes around four to five hours to get to **La Oroya** by road; nearly all of this time is spent high in the Andes as the factories and cloudy skies of Lima are swiftly left behind. **Marcahuasi** and **San Pedro de Casta**, reached via a northern spur road off the Carretera Central en route to La Oroya, are worth spending a couple of days at, if you've got the time to explore a remote and desolate sierra landscape where winds have created unusual rock formations; it's also a great place for weekend camping out of Lima. Beyond Ticlio, you'll find La Oroya, where you can turn north and wind through 130km or so of rather desolate landscape to **Cerro de Pasco**, a bleak mining town and possible approach to Huánuco, Tingo Maria and Pucallpa in the Amazon jungle. Or, you can travel east from La Oroya to Tarma and on to the jungle regions around Chanchamayo, Oxapampa or Satipo. Most visitors to the region, however, choose instead to go 100km or so south to **Huancayo**, through the astonishing **Jauja Valley**, which has beautiful scenery, striped by fabulous coloured furls of mountain.

Tarapoto

CENTRAL SIERRA REGION

0   100 km

N

Río Huallaga

Río Marañón

Tayabamba

Huaraz

Pucallpa

Tantamayo

Llata

Tingo Maria

Puerto Inca

Río Ucayali

Huansala

La Unión

Huallanca

Huánuco

Temple of Kotosh   Ambo

Pozuzo

Puerto Bermudez

Atalaya

Río Urubamba

Cerro de Pasco

Oxapampa

Carhuamayo

Río Perené

Lago de Junín

San Pedro de Cajas

San Ramon

Satipo

Canta

Palcamayo

Acobamba

Marcahuasi

La Oroya

Tarma

San Pedro de Casta

Morococha

Jauja

Río Mantaro

Concepción

Río Ene

LIMA

Chosica

Río Rímac

Huancayo

Huaribamba

Río Mantaro

San Francisco

Santa Rosa de Concepcion

Cotahuasi

Yauyos

Pampas

Lunahuana

Huancavelica

Acobamba

Huanta

Río Apurímac

Quillabamba

Cañete

Abra Chonta

Cave of Pikimachay

Tambo

Quinua

Machu Picchu

Huari   **Ayacucho**

Cusco

Pisco

Abra Apacheta

Vilcasayhuaman

Andahuaylas

Río Pampas

Sahuite

Abancay

Ica

Chalhuanca

PACIFIC OCEAN

Nasca

Marcahuasi and San Pedro de Casta

MARCAHUASI is a high (4100m) plateau that makes a fantastic weekend camping jaunt and is one of the more adventurous but popular excursions from Lima. Its main attractions are the incredible **rock formations** themselves, which, particularly by moonlight, take on weird shapes – llamas, human faces, turtles, even a hippopotamus. Standing at just over 4000m above sea level, it's one of Peru's lesser-known marvels and something of a mystical enigma. Located 90km east of Lima (40km beyond Chosica), the easiest way to visit this amazing site in the difficult-to-access Santa Eulalia Valley is on a day-trip from Lima with either Peru Inka Adventures (Jr Diego de Almagro 535, Jesus Maria, Lima ☏01/995117026,

Ⓦwww.inkasadventures.com), who organize two-day trips for around $170 (minimum of two persons) or, another Lima-based tour company, TEBAC (Trekking and Backpacking Club, Jr Huascar 1152, Jesus Maria, Lima Ⓣ01/997731959, Ⓔtebac@yahoo.com) who also take tours here, including some to the annual **Festival de Aventura** which takes place in Marcahuasi in early November and incorporates live music with outward-bound activities such as mountain biking, marathon running and motocross. Visitors at the end of July may well come across the **annual village festival** involving three days of ceremony, music, dance and festivities. For further Marcahuasi **information** contact the tour companies mentioned above or the Oficina de Información on the main plaza in the village of **SAN PEDRO DE CASTA** where there are also contacts for local guides and *arrieros* with mules (from around $10 a day, plus about $3 per mule).

Unless you're camping, you'll have to stay in the village, located only a few kilometres but two to three hours' hard walking along a mountain path below Marcahuasi. There are no direct buses from Lima to San Pedro, but if you take a *colectivo* from Avenida Grau or Avenida Garcilaso de la Vega in Lima Centro to Chosica, there are buses departing for San Pedro from the town's Parque Echinique. Empresa Santa Maria **buses** usually have signs reading "San Pedro" or "Marcahuasi". If your bus or truck terminates at Las Cruces, you'll have half an hour's walk further to San Pedro.

In San Pedro almost everything is centred around the **Plaza de Armas**. It's a small and simple Andean village, quaint but without much choice in its limited range of facilities. The **tourist office**, Plaza de Armas (Mon–Fri 9am–6pm, Sat 9am–1pm) can help arrange accommodation, though note that you have to register next door to the *albergue municipal* (municipality-run hostel) and pay $3 entrance fee to visit the plateau. For **places to stay**, there's the *albergue municipal* itself with sixteen beds (no phone; ❷), or, much better, the *Hostal Marcahuasi* (no phone; ❷), which is also close to the main square, and has shared bathrooms. There are two **cafés**, but they are not always open, so make sure to bring your own food.

La Oroya

Not a particularly inviting place, **LA OROYA** is a small, desolate mining town that gets fiercely cold at night. Located in a dreary spot above the treeline, some four hours or so by steep uphill road from Lima, La Oroya is some 50km beyond the highest point, the pass or *abra* of Ticlio (4758m). It's also where the road splits: south to Huancayo or northeast to Tarma or Huánuco. On the offchance that you really have to **stay** overnight, try the pretty basic *Hostal Inti*, Arequipa 117 (Ⓣ064/391098; ❶–❷). Many buses stop at large, fast-serving roadside restaurants on the last few kilometres on the way into La Oroya from Lima; but if you're stranded in La Oroya and need **food**, try the *Restaurant Punta Arenas*, Zeballos 323, which is very good for seafood and Chinese dishes, or *Restaurant Los Angeles*, Jr Libertad, block 2 by the Plaza de Armas, with an excellent, inexpensive set-lunch menu. **Buses** to all destinations leave from the terminal five blocks from the Plaza de Armas on Arenales. The central **post office** in La Oroya can be found at Av Horacio Zevallos Gamez 303 (Mon–Sat 8am–1pm & 3–6pm).

Huancayo

A large commercial city with just over 323,000 inhabitants, **HUANCAYO** is the capital of the Junin *departamento*. The city rests at 3244m above sea level and

▲ Feria Dominical market, Huancayo

is only six hours or so by car from Lima and two hours by car from La Oroya. An important market centre thriving on agricultural produce and dealing in vast quantities of wheat, this city makes a good base for exploring the Mantaro Valley and experiencing the region's distinct culture. While the area is rich in pre-Colombian remains, and the cereal and textile potential of the region has long been exploited, the city itself is mostly relatively modern, with very little of architectural or historical interest. It is still a lively enough place with a busy market and even some nightlife at weekends. **Feria Dominical market** on blocks 2–12 of Avenida Huancavelica (best on Sun). Established in 1572 to assist the commerce of the local Indian population, it still sells fruit and vegetables, as well as a good selection of woollen and alpaca clothes and blankets, superb weavings and some silver jewellery. It's also worth trying to coincide a trip with the splendid **Fiesta de las Cruces** each May, when Huancayo erupts into a succession of boisterous processions, parties and festivities.

Some history

The region was dominated by the Huanca tribe from around 1200 AD, and the Huari culture before that, though it wasn't until Pachacuti's forces arrived in the fifteenth century that the Inca Empire took control. Occupied by the Spanish from 1537, Huancayo was formerly founded in 1572 by Jeronimo de Silva, next to the older and these days relatively small town of Jauja. In 1824, the Battle of Junin was fought close to Huancayo, when patriotic revolutionaries overcame royalist and Spanish forces. Apart from the comings and goings of the Catholic Church, Huancayo remained little more than a staging point until the rail line arrived in 1909, transforming it slowly but surely during the twentieth century into a city whose economy was based on the export of agrarian foodstuffs and craft goods. More so than any other Peruvian city – except perhaps Ayacucho – Huancayo was

323

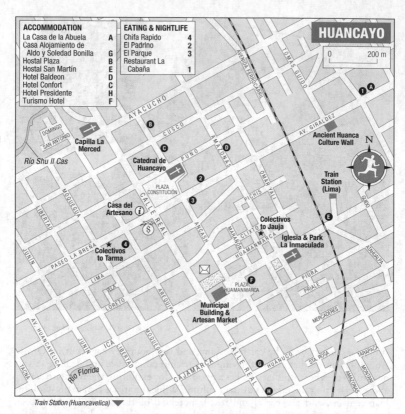

HUANCAYO

0   200 m

ACCOMMODATION

La Casa de la Abuela	A
Casa Alojamiento de Aldo y Soledad Bonilla	G
Hostal Plaza	B
Hostal San Martín	E
Hotel Baldeon	D
Hotel Confort	C
Hotel Presidente	H
Turismo Hotel	F

EATING & NIGHTLIFE

Chifa Rapido	4
El Padrino	2
El Parque	3
Restaurant La Cabaña	1

Train Station (Huancavelica) ▼

paralysed in the years of terror during the 1980s and 1990s. As home to a major army base, it became the heart of operations in what was then a military emergency zone. At times, whole villages and groups of journalists were found murdered, and to this day, some of these incidents remain a mystery as to whether they were acts of terrorism or the handiwork of the army. In 1999, an extensive army operation captured the leader of Sendero Luminoso, Oscar Ramirez Durand, who had taken over from Abimael Guzman in 1992. This essentially cleaned up the area (coincidentally at the start of the presidential electoral campaigns). Consequently, Huancayo is now considered a safe destination (though there are still reports of petty street crime, so the usual precautions should be adhered to) and one where tourists can easily find good accommodation and all the usual facilities offered by large Peruvian towns.

Arrival and information

There are several daily **bus** services arriving direct from Lima to Huancayo via Jauja; the journey costs around $10 and takes six to seven hours. Cruz del Sur (☎064/223367) offers the best and most expensive service, operating in Huancayo from their depot on block 2 of Ayacucho. In the same block, at Jr Ayacucho 274, Turismo Central (☎ 064/223128, ⓦwww.turismocentral.com.pe) run a few comfortable double-decker buses with sofa-bed type seats daily to and from Lima as well as providing regular buses for Huánuco, Tingo Maria, La Merced and Satipo. Other buses similarly tend to arrive at their respective company offices (see p.327), though many will be found on Avenida Mariategui blocks 10–12 in the Tambo district. For a quicker journey between Lima and Huancayo (5–6hr), you can take **colectivos**, which can usually be found on Calle Loreto daily from 7am until 6pm and charge around $15.

Trains to Lima (see p.347) leave from the station (where you can also buy tickets) on Av Ferrocarril 461 (℡064/217724 and 215387), within walking distance of the city centre, while trains for Huancavelica leave from a smaller station in Chilca suburbs (take a taxi; 20min; $2–3). The timings and prices outlined below are subject to frequent changes: the *Tren Expreso* leaves Huancayo for Huancavelica (5hr 30min; $3–5 depending on whether it's the Buffet or the cheaper first class) and vice versa (5hr) at 6.30am Monday to Saturday, and on Sunday departing Huancayo at 2pm and Huancavelica at 6.30am; the cheaper *Tren Ordinario* leaves Monday to Saturday at 1pm. The faster, more expensive and more comfortable *Autovagon* (4hr) only operates on Friday (in both directions), but also runs one-way on Sunday, departing Huancayo at 7pm, before returning from Huancavelica at 6.30am on Monday.

The **tourist office** in Huancayo is in the Casa del Artesano (Mon–Fri 9am–2pm & 4-8pm; ℡064/211799), C Real 481, just on the Plaza de la Constitución where the street meets Paseo La Breña. Information is also available from Dircetur, Av Libertad 204 in Huayucachi district.

Accommodation

The best Huancayo offers in accommodation is its choice between rambling old or modern **traditional city centre hotels** and a more familial setting in smaller out-lying **hostels**. It doesn't offer anything spectacular in terms of rooms with views; for that you need to get out of town.

La Casa de la Abuela Av Giraldez 693 ℡064/234383, ⓦwww.incasdelperu.org. Basic accommodation, with some private rooms available albeit all with shared bath. Otherwise, this hotel has good facilities including table tennis and a dartboard. ❷–❸

Casa Alojamiento de Aldo y Soledad Bonilla Huánuco 332 ℡064/232103. Located some eight blocks from the city centre, this friendly, family-run hostel has constant hot water and some of the staff speak English. ❷–❸

Hostal Plaza Ancash 171 ℡064/210509. Good-value rooms with private bath; go for the rooms at the front as they have most light and best views. ❸

Hostal San Martín Av Ferrocarril 362. A charming little hostel in an old but well-kept building. There's no hot water, but it's conveniently located close to the train station. ❶

Hotel Baldeon Amazonas 543 ℡064/231634. Affordable, family-run accommodation, with hot showers available on request, and use of the kitchen facilities; close to the *colectivos* for Jauja and located only a few blocks from the Plaza de la Constitución. ❶

Hotel Confort Ancash 231 ℡064/233601. Big rooms, most with private bath, although not all have hot showers. There's also a car park. ❷–❸

🏃 **Hotel Presidente** C Real 1138 ℡064/231275. Quite luxurious for Huancayo, with clean rooms and good, friendly service, *Hotel Presidente* is located close to the buses and only a few blocks from the heart of the city. ❺–❻

Turismo Hotel Ancash 729 ℡064/231072, ⓦwww.hoteles-del-centro.com. Another of the town's best hotels, with comfortable rooms and private bath, though its elegance has faded somewhat. The restaurant is generally fine, though its pisco sour drinks aren't what they should be. ❻–❽

The Town

There are two main squares in Huancayo. **Plaza de la Constitución**, named in honour of the 1812 Liberal Constitution of Cadiz, is where you'll find monuments in honour of Mariscal Ramon Castilla (who abolished slavery in Huancayo in 1854), surrounded by ornamental plants of local origin, like *quishuar* and *retama*. This plaza is the site where Huancayo was founded in 1572. Surrounded by the Neoclassical **Catedral de la Ciudad de Huancayo** (daily 7.30–9.30am & 5–7.30pm; free), and some of the town's major public buildings and offices, it was once home to the **Feria Dominical market**, which shifted in the mid-1990s to alleviate traffic problems. **Calle Real** is the main drag running on the western edge of the plaza; it's here you'll find the **Capilla La Merced** (daily 9am–noon & 3–6.30pm; free), a colonial church, once the site for the preparation and signing of the 1839 Peruvian Constitution, and now designated a historic monument. Plaza Huamanmarca is the other main square, fringed by the *Turismo Hotel* and the Municipal Building.

Another significant sight within the city centre is the **Museo del Colegio Salesiano**, at Prolongación Arequipa 10, in the El Tambo district (Mon–Fri 9am–1pm & 3–5pm; $1; ☎064/247763), an excellent natural history museum which has exhibits of local flora and fauna as well a selection of interesting rocks and minerals.

About 1km to the east of Huancayo, only 5min by bus at the end of Avenida Giraldez, the hill **Cerrito de la Libertad** offers great views across the city and partial views over the Mantaro Valley. Another kilometre further on, about fifteen minutes' walk, you'll find the geological formation known as **Torre Torre**, naturally eroded stone towers ranging mostly between 10 and 20m high, offering much better views across the valley. Just 5km from the city centre in the Barrio de San Antonio, the **Parque de la Identidad de Huancayo** covers nearly 6000 hectares, much of it green spaces open for public enjoyment; the main entrance is in the form of a giant gourd, one of the typical regional artesania products, and inside there's a *mirador* (viewing platform), some shady pergolas, cacti and the Laguna de Amalu.

Eating, drinking and nightlife

There are a number of worthwhile **restaurants** dotted around the Plaza de la Constitución: *El Parque*, on the southwest corner of Avenida Giraldez, is especially recommended for its regional dishes, and the excellent *Restaurant La Cabaña* Av Giraldez 652 (064/223303) offers pizzas, grills and trout in a agreeable ambience with occasional live folklore music and dance shows at weekends after 9pm. *El Padrino*, Av Giraldez 133, also serves local dishes, including *papas a la Huancaina*, a delicious local speciality of potatoes in a mildly spicy cheese sauce, topped with sliced egg, a black olive and some green salad. A small, nameless café at Puno 209 serves cheap but tasty sandwiches and breakfasts. The *Rinconcito Oxapampino*, Jr Cuzco 840, serves traditional foods from the central selva region – plenty of salted meats and tropical juices – where the cooking is much influenced by Austro-German immigrants. The best *chifa* (Peruvian-Chinese restaurant) in town, offering some vegetarian options, is the *Chifa Rapido* at Arequipa 511, which serves good-quality and inexpensive noodles, duck and *wantan* dishes, among others.

As well as regular bars – El Tayta, Av Huancavelica 859, plays good music and serves beer as well as cocktails – Huancayo boasts plenty of traditional dance as well as more participatory **nightlife**: local music and dance is performed most Sundays at 3pm in the *Coliseo* on Calle Real, and there are some good *criolla* and folklore *peñas* – *Taka Wasi*, on Calle Huancavelica is good, but only really gets going on Fridays and Saturdays; for Latin and European dance music try *A1A* on the second block of Bolognesi, open most evenings, including Sundays, or *La Noche*, Jr San Antonio 241, in the San Carlos suburb.

Listings

Banks and exchange For travellers' cheques, the Banco de Credito, C Real 1039, is best. To change dollars cash, try your hotel or the street *cambistas* along C Real.

Bicycle rental A good way to explore the local countryside; try Huancayo Tours, C Real 543.

Buses Antezama, Arequipa 1301, for Ayacucho and Andahuaylas; Central, Av Ferrocarril, for Chanchamayo and Tarma; Cruz del Sur, Ayacucho 287, for Lima; Etusca, Puno 220, for Lima; Express Molina, Angaraes 334, for Ayacucho and Andahuaylas; Hidalgo, Loreto 350, for Lima and Huancavelica; Oriental, Ferrocarril 146, for Cerro de Pasco, Huánuco and Pucallpa; Ormeño, Paseo la Breña 218, for Lima; San Juan, Quito 136, for Chanchamayo and Tarma; San Pablo, Ancash 1248, for Huancavelica; Transel, Av Giraldez 247, for Ayacucho and Andahuaylas; Transportes Salazar, Giraldez 245, for Cerro de Pasco, Huánuco and Pucallpa.

Hospital Daniel Carrion 1552 ☎064/222157.

Policia Nacional Av Ferrocarril 555 ☎064/211653.

Policia de Turismo Av Ferrocarril 556 ☎064/219851.

Post office Centro Civico Foco 2 (Mon–Sat 8am–7pm).

Spanish lessons Taught by Katy Cerna ☎064/201959, @katiacerna@hotmail.com. Held in her family home, Spanish lessons are offered at all levels and, if required, can include accommodation; Katy can also arrange for city tours, rural outings and cultural or music events. Prices start at around $200 per week.

Tour operators and guides Sima Tours ☎064/221396 @mpb@simatour.com; Huancayo Tours ☎064/217700; and Adrenalina Tours ☎064/219069 all offer trips throughout the region. Lucho Hurtado, operating out of the *Casa de la Abuela* hostel in Huancayo (☎/₣064/222395, ⓦwww.incasdelperu.org), is a well-recommended local tour guide.

Around Huancayo

Using Huancayo as a base you can make a number of excursions around the stunningly scenic Mantaro Valley. The **Convento de Santa Rosa de Ocopa** (Mon & Wed–Sun 9am–1pm & 3–6pm; $2.50), about 40min or 30km out of town, is easily reached by taking a microbus from outside the Catedral de la Ciudad de Huancayo on Plaza de la Constitución, to the village of **Concepción**. At the centre of the small Plaza de Armas in Concepción you'll find a small seventeenth-century *pileta,* while the square itself fronts both the Neoclassical Iglesia Matriz and the fine colonial Casona Ugarte Leon. From Concepción, another bus covers the last 6km (alternatively, this makes for a comfortable and very pleasant walk to the *convento* (daily except Tues 9am–noon & 3-6pm; $1.25). Founded in 1724, and having taken some twenty years to build, the church was the centre of the Franciscan mission into the Amazon, until their work was halted by the Wars of Independence (see p.566), after which the mission villages in the jungle disintegrated and most of the natives returned to the forest. The cloisters are more interesting than the church, though both are set in a peaceful environment, and there's an excellent library with chronicles from the sixteenth century onwards, plus a **Museum of Natural History and Ethnology** (daily except Tues 9am–noon and 3–6pm; free) containing lots of stuffed animals and native artefacts from the jungle. You can also stay at the convent **guesthouse** (❶).

A trip to the *convento* can be conveniently combined with a visit to the nearby village of **San Jerónimo**, about 12km west, well-known for its Wednesday market of fine silver jewellery.

Another good day-trip from Huancayo (30min by frequent bus from outside the Church of Immaculate Conception) is to the local villages of **Cochas Chicas** and **Cochas Grandes**, whose speciality is crafted, carved gourds. Strangely, Cochas Grandes is the smaller of the two villages, and you have to ask around if you want to buy gourds here. You can buy straight from co-operatives or from individual artisans; expect to pay anything from $3 up to $150 for the finer gourds, and if you are ordering some to be made, you'll have to pay half the money in advance. The etchings and craftsmanship on the more detailed gourds is incredible in its microscopic depth, creativity and artistic skill. On some, whole rural scenes, like the harvest, marriage and shamanic healing are represented in tiny storyboard format. The less expensive, more simple, worked gourds have fairly common geometric designs, or bird, animal and flower forms etched boldly across their curvaceous surfaces.

Some 7km west of Huancayo ($4–5 by taxi) near the present-day pueblo of **Huari**, stand the **Huari-Huilca Archaeological Remains** (800–1200 AD), the sacred complex of the Huanca tribe who dominated this region for over two hundred years before the arrival of the Incas. At the site is a small museum (daily 8am–6pm; $1) showing collections of ceramic fragments, bones and stone weapons.

Further afield, the **Reserva Nacional de Junin** is located 165km northwest of Huancayo, but an excellent trip if you can afford the time and car rental or tour. Located at around 4100m above sea level on the Pampa de Junin, it abounds with aquatic birds around the lakes as well as being home to plenty of *viscachas* in its 5300 hectares. It's possible to **camp** here, but there are no facilities at all.

Jauja

Forty kilometres from Huancayo, on the road to La Oroya, is **Jauja**, a little colonial town that was the capital of Peru before the founding of Lima. Tourist information here is available from Dircetur Junin at Av Grau 528 (Mon–Sat 9am–6pm; ☎064/362897) and also the municipality at Jr Ayacucho 856 (☎064/362017). Surrounded by some gorgeous countryside, Jauja is a likeable place, whose past is reflected in its unspoiled architecture, with many of the colonial-style buildings painted light blue. A much smaller and more languid town than Huancayo, its streets are narrow and picturesque, and the people friendly. Today, Jauja is more renowned for its traditional and well-stocked Sunday and Wednesday markets.

The **Capilla de Cristo Pobre** (daily 7–9am & 3–6pm; $1), located between San Martín and Colina, shares some similarities with Notre Dame de Paris and, perhaps a tenuous claim to fame. Gothic in style, it was also the first concrete religious construction in the Central Sierra. For anyone who wants to experience the outdoor environment around Jauja, it is possible to rent boats ($2 for an hour) on the nearby **Laguna de Paca** (10–15min in *colectivos* from Jauja; 30¢), and row out to the Isla de Amor; according to local legend this lake is said to be the home of a mermaid who lures men to their deaths. The lake is surrounded by *totora* reeds and brimming with birdlife. The shoreline is lined with cafés where decent trout meals can be bought, and, at weekends, *pachamanca* (meat and vegetables placed in a hole in the earth on preheated hot rocks and covered with soil for slow cooking) is served. Just 15km from Jauja there are some Huanca tribe **archaeological remains at Tunanmarca** (30min by taxi; $10 return); the ancient settlement here was occupied between 1200 and 1400 AD and boasts circular constructions as well as aqueducts and other pre-Inca water works.

Practicalities

Buses and **combis** for the 20–30 min ride to Jauja leave every hour from the market in Huancayo or from the corner where Amazonas crosses Avenida Giraldez. For the return journey to Huancayo, both buses and *combis* leave from Jauja's Puente Ricardo Palma, or you can catch a through bus from Lima, which stops two or three times daily in Jauja's Plaza de Armas on its way to Huancayo. Local transport is mostly by **moto taxis**.

If you prefer **staying** in Jauja, the best low-end option is the *Hostal Manco Capac* at Manco Capac 575 (℡064/361620, Ⓔniegemannilse@hotmail.com;❶) with a lovely garden and hot water. Or there's the hotel/restaurant *Ganso de Oro*, at Ricardo Palma 249 (❶). Less value for money options include *Cabezon's Hostal*, Ayacucho 1027 (℡064/362206; ❷), with shared bathrooms; and the *Hostal Francisco Pizarro*, Bolognesi (❶), the cheapest place in town, located opposite the market. Beside the lake there's the recently privatized *Hotel de Turistas* (❻), which is clean and very comfortable. As far as **food** goes, the *Ganso de Oro* restaurant is fine, and the *Marychris*, Jr Bolívar 1166, serves excellent traditional *criolla* lunches, but there aren't many other choices unless you love chicken and chips.

South of Huancayo

The mountainous and remote region south of **Huancayo**, largely out of bounds for much of the 1980s and 1990s, is now attracting visitors by the thousands every year. Not only does this bring in welcome income for many local people but it also ensures that the very Andean towns of Huancavelica and Ayacucho are open to the eyes of the world once again. Both are friendly towns these days, but even more so than Huancayo, they're still waiting for tourism to rebound to what it was before the 1980s. **Ayacucho** is a must for anyone interested in colonial architecture, particularly fine churches, while **Huancavelica** offers a slightly darker history lesson as an area that has suffered both in colonial times as well as more recently in the days of terrorism. The trip out here by train (some 130km from Huancayo), one of the world's highest railway journeys, passes through some stark yet stunning landscapes. Further afield, Ayacucho is some nine hours by bus (see p.332).

Huancavelica

Remote **HUANCAVELICA**, at 3676m, is almost purely Indian in its ethnic makeup, which is surprising considering its long colonial history and a fairly impressive array of Spanish-style architecture.

Originally occupied by hunter-gatherers from about 5000 years ago, the area then turned to sedentary cultivation as the local population was, initially, taken over by the Huari tribe around 1100 AD, a highly organized culture which reached here from the Ayacucho Valley. The Huanca tribe arrived on the scene in the fifteenth century, providing fierce resistance when they were attacked and finally conquered by the Incas. The weight of its colonial past, however, lies more heavily on its shoulders. After mercury deposits were discovered here in 1563, the town began producing **ore** for the silver mines of Peru, replacing expensive imports previously used in the mining process. In just over a hundred years, so many Indian labourers had died of mercury poisoning that the pits could hardly keep going: after the generations of locals bound to serve by the *mitayo* system of virtual slavery had been literally used up and thrown away, the salaries required to attract new workers made many of the mines unprofitable.

Today the mines are working again and the ore is taken by truck to Pisco on the coast. The Mina de la Muerte, as the **Santa Barbara mines** tend to be called around Huancavelica, are also an attraction in their own right, located several kilometres southeast of town (about 1hr 30min by foot); the shield of the Spanish Crown sits unashamedly engraved in stone over the main entrance to this ghostly settlement. There's plenty to explore, but as with all mines, some sections are dangerous and not visitor-friendly, and it's best to ask local advice before setting off.

The Town

Huancavelica's main sights are around the **Plaza de Armas**, where you'll find the two-storey Cabildo buildings, the **Capilla de la Virgen de los Dolores** and, at the heart of the square, a stone *pileta* in octagonal form incorporating two waterspouts, each portraying an Indian face, water gushing from their respective mouths. Also on the plaza, the seventeenth-century **Iglesia Catedral de San Antonio** (Mon–Sat 7am–5.15pm, or for Mass on Sun at 5.30am, 8am, 9.30am and 5.15pm), features a fine altar and pulpit and some excellent paintings. Construction started in 1673, and it took a hundred years to complete. These days it's home to the sacred image of the city's patron – Nuestra Señora de las Mercedes. The elaborate gold-leaf altar was carved from wood, and the silver sheets on display beside it are from the Cusqueña and Huamanguina schools (see p.250). There is a distinct Baroque style in the volcanic stone craftsmanship, and religious paintings decorate the interior representing Heaven, Purgatory, Hell, the Last Supper and the Crucifixion.

There are a handful of other notable churches, two of which – San Francisco and Santo Domingo – are connected to the Cathedral by an underground passage. **San Francisco**, built on the Plaza Bolognesi in 1774 by the Franciscan Order has just about survived several major earthquakes; it has a single nave and some fancy Baroque and Churrigueresque *retablos* of wood and gold leaf. During the nineteenth-century war with Chile, this church was commandeered by the Peruvian army, who sold its fine collection of musical instruments to finance the war effort. Today, the steps of San Francisco are the site, on December 24 and 25, of the awe-inspiring, traditional scissor-dancing performances *(danza tijera)* generally done by men wielding two long machete-like swords apiece.

Santo Domingo is a church and convent complex, founded in 1601, just thirty years after the city was established. The entrance is made from red stone brought from the Pucarumi quarry. Inside there are fine paintings, brought from Rome, of the Virgen del Rosario and the patron St Dominic as well as a fine Baroque altar with some gold-leaf adornment; in the sacristy you can find a painting dating from 1666 representing *El Señor de la Sentencia y Resurrección*. The town is also home to the small **Museo Regional Daniel Hernández Morillo**, in the Instituto Nacional de Cultura building on Plazuela San Juan de Dios, one block from the Plaza de Armas (℡067/753420, Mon–Fri 9am–1pm & 4–6pm; 80¢), containing archaeological exhibits, fossils from the Tertiary period, petrified marine species and displays on pre-Inca Andean cultures. As well as the archaeology and anthropology section, the museum comprises a **Museo de Arte Popular**, showing paintings and objects

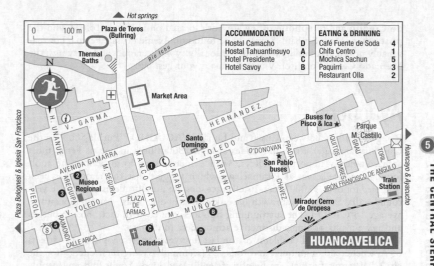

ACCOMMODATION

Hostal Camacho	D
Hostal Tahuantinsuyo	A
Hotel Presidente	C
Hotel Savoy	B

EATING & DRINKING

Café Fuente de Soda	4
Chifa Centro	1
Mochica Sachun	5
Paquirri	3
Restaurant Olla	2

HUANCAVELICA

depicting local culture. These apart, there's little else of interest here, except the Sunday **market**, which sells local food, jungle fruits and carved gourds. A couple of pleasant **walks** from town will bring you to the natural **hot springs** on the hill north of the river, or the **weaving cooperative**, 4km away at Totoral.

Practicalities

The types and schedules for **trains** to and from Huancayo are dealt with on p.325. The route travels through stunningly beautiful countryside, offering a rare opportunity for scenic and smooth rail travel in the Andes. All trains leave Huancavelica from the station at Avenida Augusto Legui (☏067/752898). By far the easiest way to get to Lima is **by bus** via Huancayo. There's also a daily bus to Ayacucho, leaving at 5am with Empresa Ticllas from Av Cáceres 235. For Pisco and Ica (6–10hr depending on condition of road) on the coast, Empresa Oropesa buses leave around 5.30pm from their office on the Plaza Santa Ana. Some **tourist information** can be obtained from Dircetur, V Garma 444 (☏067/452938; ⓦwww.regionhuancavelica.com), and there's one established local tour company – Turismo Andino on block 2 of Barranca (☏067/454190 or 067/967706388, Eturismoandinohvca@yahoo.com). Info on the town is also available at ⓦwww .huancavelicaperu.com.

There's not a wide choice of **accommodation** available in town – the best is the comfortable *Hotel Presidente*, Plaza de Armas (☏067/96752760; ❸–❹), which has both private and communal bathrooms. Otherwise, *Hostal Camacho*, Carabaya 481 (☏067/753298; ❶–❷), is excellent value, with communal bathrooms and hot water most mornings; *Hotel Savoy*, Manchego Muñoz 296 (❶), is basic with small rooms and cold communal showers and toilets; and *Hostal Tahuantinsuyo*, on the corner of Manchego Muñoz and Carabaya (❷), is dingy but at least has hot water most mornings. Snack-style **food** is available from the *Café Fuente de Soda*, on the second block of Manchego Muñoz, which serves juices, sandwiches and other snacks; the restaurant *Chifa Centro*, Jr Virrey Toledo 275, serves reasonable, if not brilliant Chinese food; the *Mochica Sachun, Jr Virrey* Toledo 303, does a great set lunch for around $1 plus a range of meals and stews; *Paquirri,* on Arequipa, serves good local dishes and the *Restaurant Olla,* on Avenida Gamarra, dishes up reasonably priced international and Peruvian meals in a friendly atmosphere. The **Banco** de Credito and telephone office are both located on Jr Virrey Toledo, and the post office (Mon–Sat 8am–8pm) can be found on Avenida Pasaje Ferrua. For reasonably priced **artesania**, including the locally typical ceramics and weavings, the **Mercado Central** on Jirón Victor Garma is your best bet.

Ayacucho

Roughly halfway between Cusco and Lima, **AYACUCHO** ("Purple Soul", in the Quechua language) sits in the Andes around 2800m high in one of Peru's most archaeologically important valleys, with evidence such as ancient stone tools found in nearby caves at Pikimachay, which suggest that the region has been occupied for over 20,000 years. Its **climate**, despite the altitude, is pleasant all year round – dry and temperate with blue skies nearly every day – and temperatures average 16°C (60°F). The surrounding hills are covered with cacti, broom bushes and agave plants, adding a distinctive atmosphere to the city.

Despite the political problems of the last few years, most people on the streets of Ayacucho, although quiet and reserved (seemingly saving their energy for the city's boisterous **fiestas**), are helpful, friendly and kind. You'll find few people speak any English; Quechua is the city's first language, though most of the town's inhabitants can also speak some Spanish.

Some history

Ayacucho was the centre of the **Huari culture**, which emerged in the region around 700 AD and spread its powerful and evocative religious symbolism throughout most of Peru over the next three or four hundred years. After the demise of the Huari, the ancient city later became a major Inca administrative centre. The Spanish originally selected a different nearby site for the city at Huamanguilla; but this was abandoned in 1540 in favour of the present location. Ayacucho's strategic location, vitally important to both the Incas and the Spanish colonials, meant that the city grew very wealthy as miners and administrators decided to put down roots here, eventually sponsoring the exquisite and unique wealth of the city's **churches**, which demonstrate the clearly high level of masonic and woodworking skills of the local craftspeople.

The bloody **Battle of Ayacucho**, which took place near here on the Pampa de Quinoa in 1824, finally released Peru from the shackles of Spain. The armies met early in December, when Viceroy José de la Serna attacked Sucre's Republican force in three columns. The pro-Spanish soldiers were, however, unable to hold off the Republican forces who captured the viceroy with relative ease. Ayacucho was the last part of Peru to be liberated from colonial power.

Though quiet these days, Ayacucho was also a radical university town with a left-wing tradition going back at least fifty years, known around the world for the civil war between terrorists and the Peruvian armed forces during the 1980s (see p.570). Most civilians in the region remember this era as one where they were trapped between two evils – the terrorists on the one hand and the retaliatory military on the other. Because of this, several villages were annihilated by one side or the other. A large proportion of villagers from remote settlements in the region consequently decided to leave the area, which they hoped would offer them relative safety. Despite efforts by Fujimori's government to rehabilitate these communities and entice people back from Lima to their rural homes in the 1990s, many of them remain in the capital today.

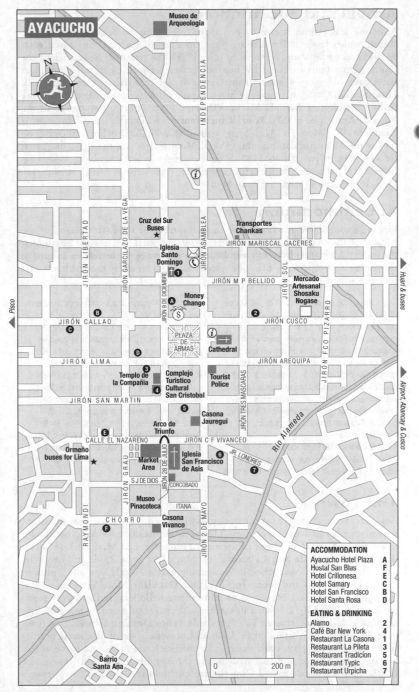

AYACUCHO

Museo de Arqueología

THE CENTRAL SIERRA

Huari & buses

Airport, Abancay & Cusco

Pisco

INDEPENDENCIA

JIRÓN LIBERTAD

JIRÓN GARCILAZO DE LA VEGA

JIRÓN 9 DE DICIEMBRE

JIRÓN ASAMBLEA

Cruz del Sur Buses

Iglesia Santo Domingo

Transportes Chankas

JIRÓN MARISCAL CACERES

JIRÓN M P BELLIDO

JIRÓN SOL

Mercado Artesanal Shosaku Nogase

Money Change

JIRÓN CALLAO

JIRÓN CUSCO

JIRÓN FCO PIZARRO

PLAZA DE ARMAS

Cathedral

JIRÓN LIMA

JIRÓN AREQUIPA

Templo de la Compañia

Complejo Turistico Cultural San Cristobal

Tourist Police

JIRÓN SAN MARTIN

JIRÓN TRES MASCARAS

Arco de Triunfo

Casona Jauregui

Río Alameda

CALLE EL NAZARENO

JIRÓN C F VIVANCEO

Ormeño buses for Lima

JIRÓN GRAU

Market Area

JIRÓN 28 DE JULIO

Iglesia San Francisco de Asis

JR. LONDRES

S J DE DIOS

CORCOBADO

Museo Pinacoteca

RAYMONDI

ITANA

CHORRO

Casona Vivanco

JIRÓN 2 DE MAYO

Barrio Santa Ana

0   200 m

ACCOMMODATION

Ayacucho Hotel Plaza	A
Hostal San Blas	F
Hotel Crillonesa	E
Hotel Samary	C
Hotel San Francisco	B
Hotel Santa Rosa	D

EATING & DRINKING

Alamo	2
Café Bar New York	4
Restaurant La Casona	1
Restaurant La Pileta	3
Restaurant Tradicion	5
Restaurant Typic	6
Restaurant Urpicha	7

5

333

Arrival and information

Most overseas visitors arrive in Ayacucho from Lima on a thirty-five-minute **flight**, which lands at the airport 4km from town – a taxi into town costs $4–5; buses cost 80¢ and leave from just outside the terminal. Nevertheless, the journey from Lima overland by **bus** only takes between eight and nine hours these days, or eighteen hours from Cusco. If you're arriving from Huancayo, Huancavelica, Cusco or Lima, the bus companies mostly have their depots along Jirón 3 Mascaras or Avenida Mariscal Caceres, both within a few blocks of the Plaza de Armas (see p.337). **Tourist information** is available from Direcetur, Jr Asamblea 481 (Mon–Fri 8am–5pm; ☎066/312548, Eayacucho@mincetur.gob .pe) or the Municipalidad building, Portal Municipal 48, on the Plaza de Armas (Mon–Sat 9am–7pm; ☎066/318305, ⓦwww.regionayacucho.gob.pe), which has helpful staff who can arrange trips in the area; there's also a tourist information kiosk at the airport (Mon–Sat 8am–8pm).

Accommodation

Finding a room in Ayacucho is easy enough outside of the Easter period when, because of the colourful religious festivals (see opposite), the town is bursting at the seams with visitors from Lima and elsewhere. Most of the **hotels** are located in interesting old properties – many of which have been tastefully modernized – and service is generally of a high standard.

Ayacucho Hotel Plaza Jr 9 de Diciembre 184 ☎066/312202. Easily the most luxurious hotel in town, set in a fine, stylish colonial mansion, with TVs in every room, private baths and a reasonable restaurant, though service can be slow. Centrally located on the Plaza de Armas. ❼
Hostal San Blas Jr Chorro 167 ☎066/312712. A great budget option with friendly service and pleasant, fairly spacious and comfortable rooms with private bath. There's also the benefit of a laundry, communal cooking facilities and a reliable hot-water system. ❷
Hotel Crillonesa C El Nazareno 165 ☎066/312350. Hostel with great views of the city and valley from its rooftop terrace; there's hot

water and a laundry service, and rooms are clean and very good value. ❶
Hotel Samary Jr Callao 329-335 ☎066/312442. A fine, welcoming place to relax for a few days, just a block east of the Plaza de Armas. ❷–❸
Hotel San Francisco Jr Callao 290 ☎066/312353. Every room in this high-quality hotel has a TV and private shower. There's also nice café on the roof with great views overlooking town. Breakfast is included. ❹–❺
Hotel Santa Rosa Jr Lima 166 ☎066/314614. Only half a block from the Plaza de Armas, based in a stylish old mansion with fine courtyard and a decent restaurant; friendly service, too. ❹

The Town

Ayacucho is an attractive colonial city, with splendid churches and mansions packed together in dense blocks around the central **Plaza de Armas** (also known as the **Plaza Mayor**) at whose centre rests a monument to Mariscal José Sucre. The 1540 **Templo de San Cristóbal**, on block 7 of Jirón 28 de Julio was the first church built in Ayacucho; it has a single nave and only one altar, plus an unusually fine stone and adobe roof. But the **Catedral** (Mon–Sat 11am–3pm; free), just off the Plaza Mayor, is of more interest. Built of red and grey stone between 1612 and 1671, it has a fine, three-aisled nave culminating in a stunning Baroque gold-leaf altarpiece. The **Iglesia de Santo Domingo**, block 2 of Jirón 9 de Diciembre, was founded in 1548 and possesses one of the most beautiful exteriors in the city, with three arches of brick and lime, said to be where heretics were hanged and tortured during the Spanish Inquisition. Inside, the church houses a Baroque and Churrigueresque gold-leaf altar and two images

Festivals and music in Ayacucho

If you can be in Ayacucho for **Semana Santa**, the Holy Week beginning the Friday before Easter, you'll see fabulous daily processions, pageants and nightly candlelit processions centred on the Catedral. But beware of the beautiful procession of the **Virgen Dolores** (Our Lady of Sorrows), which takes place the Friday before Palm Sunday: pebbles are fired at the crowd (particularly at children and foreigners) by expert slingers so that onlookers take on the pain of La Madre de Dios, and so supposedly reduce her suffering. Around May 23, there is the elaborate religious procession of the **Fiesta de las Cruces**, when festivities often involve the local "scissors" folkdance performed by two men, each wielding a rather dangerous pair of cutlasses.

The music of Huancayo is unique and spectacular even within the Peruvian Andes, with each style bearing its own distinct harmonies and melodies, and including Huaynos, Yavari music and Hualilla amongst others. The Ayacucho versions of Huayno and marinera dances are also distinctive.

– El Señor del Santo Sepulcro and the Virgen Dolorosa – only brought out for the Easter processions. In block 1 of Jirón 28 de Julio is the **Jesuit Templo de la Compañía**, built in 1605 and renowned for its distinctive Churrigueresque-style main altar. The **Casona Jauregui**, on block 2 of Jirón Dos de Mayo (Mon–Fri 8.30am–4pm; free), is a lovely seventeenth-century mansion built by Don Cayetano Ruiz de Ochon; it has a superb patio and balcony with two lion statues and a stone shield of Indian influence displaying a two-headed eagle. The **Museo Pinacoteca de San Francisco de Asis** (Mon–Fri 9am–noon & 3–6pm; free), in block 3 of Jirón 28 de Julio, is known for its library of unique historical works, and there are a couple of **art galleries** in town: the Casona Vivanco, Jr 28 de Julio 518 (Mon–Sat 10am–1pm & 3–6pm; 50¢), with a particularly good collection of colonial art, and the Galería de Arte Popular (Popular Art Gallery), Jr Asamblea 138 (Mon–Sat 9am–6.30pm; free), specializing in regional art.

Further out, the **Museo de Arqueología** (Museum of Archeology – also known as Museo Hipolito Unanue), on Av Independencia 502 (Mon–Fri 8am–1pm & 3–5pm, Sat 9am–1pm; 80¢; ☎066/912056), about a thirty-minute walk (taxi, 5min) from the old centre, is located in the University's botanical gardens. This small museum is stuffed full of local archaeological finds, mainly ceramics, dating from several millennia ago, plus exhibits from the Chavín, Huarpa, Nasca and Inca eras.

Arts and crafts

Many visitors come for Ayacucho's thriving **craft industry**, mainly woven rugs and *retablos* (finely worked little wooden boxes containing intricate three-dimensional religious scenes made mainly from papier-mâché). Among the best shops for a wide variety of arts and crafts are artesanias **Helme**, Portal Unión 49, and **Pokra**, Jr Dos de Mayo 128; another good bet is the **Mercado Artesanal Shosaku Nogase**, close to the end of Jirón 9 de Diciembre.

If you've got the time to spare, however, it's more interesting and less expensive to visit some of the actual **craft workshops** and buy from the artesans themselves. Most of these workshops are found in the *barrio* of **Santa Ana**, just uphill from the Plaza de Armas. Locals are always happy to guide visitors in the right direction. Some of the best-quality *retablos* are not all that expensive, but if you want one of their more complicated modern pieces it could cost as much as $300, and take up to three months to complete. For **rugs**, check out Edwin Sulca – probably the most famous weaver here – who lives opposite the church on the Plaza Santa Ana. His work sells from around $100 (almost double in Lima's

▲ Ayacucho

shops), and many of his designs graphically depict the recent political horrors around Ayacucho. Gerado Fernandez Palomino, another excellent weaver, has a store located at his house and workshop located on Jr Paris 600, also in Santa Ana. The best **artesania markets** can be found around the Plazoleta Maria Pardo de Bellido, and at Jirón Libertad, blocks 7–9; the first block of Jirón Paris; second block of Pasaje Bolognesi; and the first two of Jirón Asamblea.

Alabaster carvings – known in Peru as **Huamanga stone carvings** – are another speciality of Ayacucho artesans (Huamanga being the old name for the city). Señor Pizarro, Jr San Cristoval 215, has a reputation as one of the best carvers in town, and the craft cooperative Ahuaccllacta, Huanca Solar 130, is also worth checking out. The tourist office can also make a few recommendations.

Eating and nightlife

Food and nightlife are both surprisingly good in Ayacucho, with the city's distinctive cuisine including *puca picante*, made from pork and potatoes seasoned with yellow chilli peppers and ground toasted peanuts, and the local *chorizo*, which is prepared with ground pork soaked with yellow chilli and vinegar, then fried in butter and served with diced fried potatoes. The courtyard complex of cafés and shops – **Complejo Turistico San Cristobal** – at Jr 28 de Julio 178, offers a popular place for **eating out**; the *Café Bar New York* here is quite popular, serving burgers, pizzas, breakfasts, espresso and cocktails, among other things. Beyond this complex, one of the better restaurants in the city is *Alamo,* Jr Cusco 215, where you can savour the local dishes mentioned above. *Restaurant La Pileta*, Jr Lima 166, is excellent for dinner, preparing typical mountain dishes such as *sopa de quinoa*, while *Restaurant Tradición*, Jr San Martín 406, offers a wide range of Peruvian and international dishes in a sophisticated atmosphere, and *Restaurant La Casona*, Jr M P Bellido, like *Alamo*, serves excellent Andean *criolla* dishes. *Restaurant Typic,* Jr Londres 196, is recommended for set-lunch menus at reasonable prices and the *Restaurant Urpicha*, at Londres 272 (T/F 066/813905), is great for local specialities and *comida criolla* in general, although it gets pretty busy.

If you're after **live music** in the evenings, check out *Los Balcones* on Jirón Asamblea, just one block from the main plaza; it's a disco and *peña* combined. Other Ayacucho *peñas* include: *Arco Blanco*, Jr Asamblea 280, playing Andean folk music most Friday and Saturday nights from 9pm to midnight, while *Machi*, on Jirón Grau, specializes in *criolla* and *huayno*. Club wise, the hippest place these days is *Los Warpas*, on Avenida Mariscal Caceres, Thursday to Saturday nights, while *Los Portales*, Portal Unión 33, has mainly disco music at weekends.

Listings

Airline Star Peru, Jr Lima 261 T 066/816690; LC Busre, Jr Lima 178 T 066/316060.

Banks and ATM There's an ATM at the Banco de Credito on the Plaza Mayor (Mon–Fri 9am–6pm) and Interbanc, also with ATM, at Jr 9 de Diciembre 189, just half a block away from the plaza.

Bus companies The best company is Cruz del Sur, 9 de Diciembre, block 4, for Lima; next up is Ormeño, Jr Libertad 257 T 066/812495, also for Lima. Others include: Empresa Libertadores, Jr 3 Mascaras 496, for Lima, Abancay and Cusco; Empresa Molina, Jr 3 Mascaras 551, for Huancayo; Transmar, Av Mariscal Caceres 896, for Lima, Abancay and Cusco; and Transportes Chankas, 3 blocks north of the Plaza Mayor on Jr Mariscal Caceres, for Andahuaylas. Other bus companies can be found at Pasaje Caceres, block 1, or along blocks 7–17 of Av Mariscal Caceres and blocks 2–4 of Av Manco Capac.

Hospital Hospital Huamanga, Av Venezuela In Canan Alto T 066/312180.

Internet Several internet cafés on Jr Asamblea close to the Plaza de Armas.

Tours around Ayacucho

One of the easiest ways to visit the sites around Ayacucho is to take a **guided tour**, and the tourist information office in Ayacucho can arrange trips in the area. The tourist information offices can advise on guides or companies; and, Carlos Manco, contactable at the Hotel Crillonesa, is another useful source of contacts. Alternatively, all the following companies offer half-day tours to Pikimachay for around $10–15 and half-day tours to Huari for a similar price. Full-day trips to Huari and Quinua will set you back around $20. **Tour companies** to try in Ayacucho include: Urpillay Tours, Portal Union 33 (T 066/315074); Wari Tours, Jr Lima 138 (T 066/311415); and, Willy Tours, Jr 9 de Diciembre 107 (T 066/314075) who offer a range of good value local tours. For adventure tourism, Pierre Verbist (Everbist@terra.com.pe) has a good reputation for organising mountain biking, horseriding and other adventures.

Money change Several shops on the Plaze de
Armas will change dollars and euros.

Post office Jr Asamblea 295, two blocks from the
plaza (Mon–Sat 8am–8pm).

Telephone office Jr Asamblea 293 (daily
8am–8pm).

Tourist police Corner of Dos de Mayo with Jr
Lima, right on the plaza and close to the Cathedral.

Around Ayacucho

Although the city itself is certainly the main pull, there are some quite fascinating places near Ayacucho that are possible to visit. Having said that, it's always a good idea to check with the tourist office beforehand on whether or not it's safe to travel in the rural environs of Ayacucho. At the time of writing, the region had been politically stable for around ten years, but the situation is open to change and some villages are more sensitive than others. The cave of **Pikimachay**, 24km northwest of Ayacucho, on the road to Huanta, where archaeologists have found human (dated to 15,000 BC) and gigantic animal remains, is best visited on a guided tour with one of the tour companies (see box, above). This is also true of the ancient city of **Huari** (sometimes written "Wari"), about 20km north of Ayacucho on the road to Huancayo. Historians claim that this site, which covers about 2000 hectares, used to house some 50,000 people just over a thousand years ago. You can still make out the ancient streets, plazas, some reservoirs, canals and large structures. The small site museum (daily 8am–4.30pm; $1) displays skulls and stone weapons found here in the 1960s.

Located about 37km northeast of Ayacucho, the charming and sleepy village of **Quinua** is almost an hour's bus ride away through acres of tuna cactus, which is abundantly farmed here for both its delicious fruit (prickly pear) and the red dye (cochineal) extracted from the *cochamilla* – larvae that thrive at the base of the cactus leaves. The site of the historic nineteenth-century **Battle of Ayacucho, just outside town on the pampa,** is marked by a striking obelisk, unmistakable at 44m tall. There are still some **artesans** working in Quinua: at San Pedro Ceramics (at the foot of the hill leading to the obelisk) it's often possible to look round the workshops, or try Mamerto Sanchez's workshop on Jirón Sucre. About 120km away, some four hours by road, you can also find **Vilcasayhuaman**, a pre-Conquest construction with a Temple of the Sun, Temple of the Moon and a ceremonial pyramid. Another 25km on from Vilcasayhuaman, at a site called **Intihuatana**, there's another archaeological complex, with a palace, artificial lake and a stone bath. To visit any or all of these sites, it's easiest to go with a local tour company (see box p.337) or hire a taxi.

East to Cusco

With much improved roads – one of Fujimori's better legacies – it now only takes between about 20 and 28 hours to travel **from Ayacucho to Cusco** via **Andahuaylas** and **Abancay**, a distance of almost 600km. From Abancay, the rest of the journey to Cusco is a little less than 200km, usually taking five or six hours and passing through archaeologically interesting terrain en route. Shortly before crossing into the *departamento* of Cusco (see Chapter 4), for instance, the road goes through the village of **Carahuasi** where the community of Concacha (3500m) is home to the archaeological complex of Sahuite, comprising three massive, beautifully worked granite boulders, the best of which graphically depict an Inca village (though they have been partially defaced in recent years). Nearby at Conoc, meanwhile, there are hot medicinal springs.

Andahuaylas and around

It's a long, ten-hour, 270-kilometre haul from Ayacucho across mountain passes and through several valleys to **ANDAHUAYLAS**, a lovely town which serves as airport for the larger Abancay, albeit with little to see or do, despite the backdrop of splendid highland scenery. The main church here, **Catedral de San Pedro**, reflects a plain colonial style and the nearby plaza possesses a *pileta* cut from a solid piece of stone. Another fine example of *sillar* stone construction, the **Puente Colonial El Chumbao** road bridge gives access to the Nasca road and the airport. Some **tourist information** is available online from ⓦ www.regionapurimac.gob.pe.

The **airport** here has flights to Arequipa, Cusco and Lima (Aero Continente, Av Peru 137 ⓣ 751515). The bus terminal is located on the first block of Avenida Lazaro Carillo, and **buses** travel to Lima and Cusco (several daily). Of the **hotels**, El Encanto de Oro, Pedro Casafranca 424 (ⓣ/ⓕ 083/723066, ⓦ www .encantodeoro.4t.com; ❸–❹), is easily the best choice. As for **banks**, the Banco de Credito can be found at Juan Antonio Trelles 255, and the Banco de la Naci"n at Ramon Castilla 545. The **post office** can be found at Av Peru 243 (Mon–Sat 8am–8pm, Sun 8am–3pm).

Only 21km from Andahuaylas the archaeological remains of **Sondor** can be found in the mountains about 2km beyond Laguna Pacucha at 3200m (45min by bus from town). This region, notably in the province of Cotabamba at the village of Ccoyllurqui, is also home to the Yawar Fiesta that takes place every July, usually near the end of the month. The festival involves capturing a live condor and tying it to the back of a bull; the latter represents the conquistadors and the condor indigenous to Peru. Usually the condor kills the bull.

Abancay and around

It's only another 136km to **ABANCAY**, usually covered in five to seven hours, depending on the condition and type of vehicle. Abancay is a larger town, at 2378m above sea level, in the Andean *departamento* of Apurimac. It's a bustling market centre in a beautiful area, again albeit with few sights or tourist facilities (with Cusco so close, the town hosts relatively few tourists), but nevertheless within striking range of a number of stunning sites, not least Choquequirau. For **accommodation**, the most comfortable place is the Hotel de Turistas, Av Diaz Barcenas 500 (ⓣ/ⓕ 083/321017; ❹–❺). For **money exchange**, the Banco de Credito is at Libertad 218 and the Banco de la Nación at Lima 816.

Within the locality, overlooking the Apurimac canyon, are the superb Inca ruins of **Choquequirau**, currently accessible only with a planned expedition through one of the Cusco tour operators (see p.264), but with the potential to become a major attraction. Apart from using it for visiting Choquequirao (see p.301), the Apurimac Canyon – which is formed by the Río Apurimac as it tumbles down into the Amazon – itself repays the trials of a 73km detour northeast (2–3hr in a car) with its magnificent beauty and depth. There is also the Santuario Nacional de Ampay, about 5km north from Abancay (20min by car), where orchids and bromeliads, foxes, deer, spectacled bears, *viscachas*, falcons and owls are often spotted. The forest here is almost 4000 hectares of protected land mostly covered in endangered Intimpa trees. It is open with no entrance fee or staff/guards at the entrance.

North of Huancayo

The area north of Huancayo divides into two main routes. The nearest takes you to **Tarma**, a gentle mountain area, standing at the top of one of Peru's steepest roads down from the Andes into the Central Selva of Chanchamayo and beyond to a large region with two obvious circuitous overland routes: one to the jungle frontier towns of Satipo and Atalaya (see p. 496), and from there on either back up to Huancayo or down into the lowland rainforest area around Pucallpa; another shoot goes to the fascinating Germanic settlements of Oxapampa and Pozuzo (see p.499). Further north, some 280km from Huancayo, lies **Huánuco**, interesting for its nearby archaeological remains, and itself another important gateway to the Pucallpa jungle region (see p.346).

Tarma and around

Tarma is by far the nicest mountain town in this part of Peru, with warmer temperatures and an abundance of wild and farmed flowers, sitting on the edge of the Andes almost within spitting distance of the Amazon forest. Similarly, the region around Tarma, some 60km east of La Oroya (see p.322), is one of Peru's most beautiful Andean regions, with green rather than snow-capped mountains stretching down from high, craggy limestone outcrops into steep canyons forged by Amazon tributaries powering their way down to the Atlantic. It's nevertheless always a good idea to check with your embassy in Lima for up-to-the-minute intelligence on this area since the occasional terrorist column has been known to be active in its remoter sectors. The nearby towns of Palcamayo, San Pedro de Cajas and Acobamba make for pleasant day-trips from Tarma. The well-established settler towns of San Ramon and La Merced (see p.495), meanwhile, are separated by only 10km of road, some 2500m below Tarma on the Río Tulumayo, and are surrounded by exciting hiking country.

The Town

A pretty colonial outpost, **TARMA** makes a good living from its traditional textile and leather industries, and from growing flowers for export as well as for its own use. The town's greatest claim to fame is its connection with **Juan Santos Atahualpa's rebellion** in the 1740s and 1750s: taking refuge in the surrounding mountains, he defied Spanish troops for more than a decade, though peace returned to the region in 1756 when he and his allies mysteriously disappeared. Today Tarma is a quiet place, disturbed only by the flow of trucks climbing up towards the jungle foothills, and the town's famous Easter Sunday procession from the main plaza, when the streets are covered by carpets of dazzling flowers.

Practicalities

Tourist information is available from the Municipal office on the plaza at Jr Dos de Mayo 773 (Mon–Fri 9am–5pm; ☏064/321010); the **post office** is on Callao, within two blocks of the plaza; and the **telephone office** is on the Plaza de Armas. **Money** can be changed and there's an ATM at the Banco de Credito, Lima 407, also on the plaza; money can also be changed in one or two shops on Jirón Moquegua, just by the plaza. Most of the **bus** and **colectivo** offices are clustered on Callao and Castilla near the petrol station, with Transportes Chanchapayo's office, for services to Lima, at Callao 1002 and Transportes Junin, who run the best buses to La Merced and Satipo, stopping briefly at their depot, Amazonas 669, en route to and from Lima. Other buses for Chanchamayo are best caught near the stadium on the exit for San Ramon and La Merced where most buses usually stop. For health matters, the town's hospital is at Av Pacheco 362.

The best **accommodation** in town is at the *Hotel Los Portales,* Av Castilla 512 (T064/321411; ❺); slightly cheaper are the *Hotel Internacional*, Dos de Mayo 307 (T064/321830; ❹), which has hot water between 6pm and 8am, and the *Hotel Galaxia,* Plaza de Armas (❸), with private bathrooms and a car park. The *Hospedaje El Dorado,* Jr Huánuco 488 (T064/321598; ❶), is good value and cleaner than the *Hostal Central*, Huánuco 614 (❷), which nevertheless has its own observatory that non-guests can use on clear Friday nights. There is a food market on Dos de Mayo, just two blocks from the plaza, but one of the best places **to eat** is *Señorial*, Huánuco 138, which serves good standard Peruvian fare. For local fish, try *La Cabaña de Bryan* at Paucartambo 450, or one of the many *chifa* restaurants or *pollerías* located within a couple of blocks' radius of the Plaza de Armas.

Staying out of town there's the lovely *Hacienda Santa Maria,* located just 1.2km from Tarma in the barrio of Sacsamarca (contact in Lima T01/4451214 or locally on T064/321232, Wwww.geocities.com/haciendasantamaria; ❺–❻). A very comfortable old hacienda, owned by the Santa Maria family for two centuries, it offers first-floor rooms with private bath as well as a great restaurant. They also run excellent tours, to the Gruta de Huagapo caves (see below) and the Sanctuary of the Lord of Muruhuay (see below). The *Hospedaje Ecologica - Casa-Hacienda La Florida* (contact in Lima T01/3441358 or locally on T064/321041; ❺–❻), located at Km 39 on the Carretera Central some 20min by car (or taxi from Tarma) further towards La Merced, is another fine out of town option, based on a dairy farm, but with comfortable rooms, home-cooked meals and camp fires, breakfast included, kitchen available and room for camping.

Around Tarma

The rural village of **Palcamayo** makes an interesting day-trip (45 min by *colectivo* from Calle Paucartambo y Otero in Tarma), though its better appreciated if you camp overnight. From here it's an hour's climb to **La Gruta de Huagapo**, which are the country's deepest explored **caves**; if dry they are generally accessible, taking great care, for about 180m without specialized equipment, or up to 1.8km with a guide and full speleological kit. If you've got your own transport, continue 20km along the same road (the only road in the valley) west to the beautiful village of **San Pedro De Cajas**, where craftspeople produce superb-quality weavings. As an example of how landscapes can influence local art forms, the village lies in a valley neatly divided into patchwork field-systems – an exact model of the local textile style.

Also within easy day-tripping distance from Tarma (12km) – just a short *colectivo* ride (about 70¢) – is the small settlement of **Acobamba**, home of the **Sanctuary of the Lord of Muruhuay** (daily 7am–7pm; free), a small church built in 1972 around a rock painting where a vision of Christ on the cross led to this site becoming a major centre of pilgrimage. The chapel has an altar with weavings representing the Resurrection and the Last Supper. Some of the **restaurants** by the church serve excellent *cuy* and *pachamanca*.

There are few local tour companies; the best covering Tarma and around include: Max Adventure, whose main office is in La Merced, at Jr Dos de Mayo 683 (T064/323908, Emaxtraveltarma@hotmail.com); Taruma Tours, Jr Amazonas

1125, Tarma (☎064/321635, ✉taruma_tours@hotmail.com); and Centro Tours, Dos de Mayo 658, Tarma (☎064/321104, ✉turismocentrotours@hotmail.com).

Huánuco and around

The *departamento* of **Huánuco** offers the possibility of several fascinating excursions – notably, the 4000-year-old **Temple of Kotosh** and the impressive ruins at **Tantamayo** – as well as the option of penetrating the wilder parts of the Amazon Basin. Its capital, also called **Huánuco**, is a modern market town and an ideal stopping point on the way to the jungle town of **Tingo María** and the coca-growing slopes at the upper end of the Río Huallaga. The region is usually reached via the Central Highway, which snakes along the spine of the Central Sierra, and La Oroya, then north through Cerro de Pasco. However, for anyone already in or around Huaraz – or those willing to risk possible delays and hardships such as hard terrain, cold nights and the risk of getting stuck overnight if a bus or truck breaks down or you miss a connection, in return for magnificent scenery – there is a direct route over the Cordillera Blanca which takes you to **La Unión** and the preserved Inca ruins of **Huánuco Viejo**, before continuing to the city of Huánuco.

Huánuco

The charming modern city of **HUÁNUCO**, more than 100km east of the deserted Inca town of the same name, and around 400km from Lima, sits nestled in a beautiful Andean valley some 1900m above sea level. It's a relatively peaceful place, located on the left bank of the sparkling Río Huallaga, and depending for its livelihood on forestry, tea and coca, along with a little low-key tourism. Its old, narrow streets ramble across a handful of small plazas, making for a pleasant environment to spend a day or two preparing for a trip down into the jungle beyond Tingo María or exploring some of the nearby archaeological sites, such as the Temple of Kotosh and the ruins at Tantamayo.

The city itself, founded by the Spaniard Gomez de Alvarado in August 1539, contains no real sights, save the usual handful of fine old churches and a small natural history museum. The sixteenth-century **Iglesia de San Francisco** (daily 6am–10pm & 5–8pm) on the Plaza de Armas houses the tomb of the town's founder and shows a strong indigenous influence, its altars featuring richly carved native fruits – avocados, papayas and pomegranates. It also displays a small collection of sixteenth-century paintings. The **Iglesia de la Merced** (daily 6–10am & 5-8pm; free) lies some three blocks south and west from the Plaza de Armas on Calle Hermilio Valdizan, and was built in 1600, in the Romantic style; it's worth a brief look around for its spectacular gold-leaf altarpiece. The **Iglesia de San Cristobal** (daily hours of Mass only; free), three blocks west of the plaza on Calle Damaso Beraun, also has some fine gold-leaf altarpieces, and is said to be built on the site where the chief of the Chupacos tribe once lived and where Portuguese priest Pablo Coimbra celebrated the first Mass in the region. The natural history museum, **Museo de Ciencias**, Jr General Prado 499 (Mon–Fri 8am–noon, Sat 9am–1pm; $1.80), houses regional archaeological finds, mainly pottery, as well as a small display of Andean flora and fauna.

Practicalities

Tourist information is available from the Casa de Aretano, Jr General Prado 718, right by the Plaza de Armas (Mon–Fri 9am–1pm & 4–6pm; also see Ⓔwww .huanucoperu.com for up-to-date information). The **airport** (Ⓣ062/513066) is 6km out of town; there's a **post office** on the plaza (Mon–Sat 8am–7pm), and the **telephone office** is two blocks away along 28 de Julio (daily 8am–9pm). **Internet** cafés can be found in and around the main plaza, and you can change **money** with the *cambistas* on the corner of Dos de Mayo and the Plaza de Armas, or at the Banco de Credito (with ATM), on Dos de Mayo, or the Banco Continental (also has ATM) on the plaza itself. Artesania can be bought in shops along blocks 7 and 8 of Jr General Prado and also blocks 11 of Dos de Mayo and 7 of Jr Huánuco. **Guided tours** to places of interest in the locality, such as Kotosh, are available from Maya Tours, Jr Dos de Mayo 1286.

The best of the budget **accommodation** options is the *Hostal Las Vegas*, 28 de Julio 936 (Ⓣ062/512315; ❷–❸), right on the Plaza de Armas, which has clean rooms, or the well-run but basic *Hostal Residencial Huánuco* on Jirón Huánuco (Ⓣ062/512050; ❸), an attractive colonial building that's also close to the plaza. The best of the pricier options is the very comfortable *Gran Hotel Huánuco*, Jirón Damaso Beraun (Ⓣ062/512410, Ⓦwww.grandhotelhuanuco.com; ❻), right on the Plaza de Armas in the shade of some beautiful old trees. Alternatively, you can **camp** down by the Río Huallaga near the stadium, but watch out for the active insect life.

El Café, on the Plaza de Armas, is the best **restaurant** for international cuisine, as well as a variety of *criolla* dishes, though the *Restaurant Vegetariano,* Dos de Mayo 1044, has nicer (vegetarian, unsurprisingly) food if you're looking for something lighter or simply different. For a better atmosphere in the evenings and the local speciality, *picante de queso* – a spicy sauce made from yellow chillis and onions, poured over cold cheese and potatoes – try *La Casona de Gladys* at General Prado 908 or *La Olla de Barro*, General Prado 852.

Buses to La Unión (5–6hr) with Turismo Union, Jr Tarapaca 449, leave daily at 7.30am, while buses, *colectivos* and trucks to Tingo Maria (2–3hr) and Pucallpa (11 hr; recommended to travel in daylight hours only, due to frequent night robberies in recent years) leave with three different companies daily from block 2 of Hermillo Valdizan, and also with Turismo Central from their office at Tarapaca 552 (usually only a night bus). Buses to Lima (8–10hr), via the Central Highway and La Oroya, leave daily with Cruz del Sur from 28 de Julio 341; Etposa also have a nightly service to Lima leaving 10pm from Hermillo Valdizan 773. Buses for Tantamayo (7–10hr) leave most days at around 7.15am from Jr Tarapaca 449 with Turismo Union; and Transportes Chasqui also run a Tantamayo service from Tarapaca 403 at 7.30am. There are no direct buses from Huánuco to Junin and Huancayo; the best you can do is try to catch one of the Lima buses that passes through La Oroya, where you should disembark and catch a bus or *colectivo* to the Huancayo area.

The Temple of Kotosh

Only 6km from Huánuco along the La Unión road, the fascinating, though poorly maintained, **TEMPLE OF KOTOSH** lies in ruins on the banks of the Río Tingo. At more than 4000 years old, this site predates the Chavín era by more than a thousand years. A more or less permanent settlement existed here throughout the Chavín era (though without the monumental masonry and sculpture of that period) and Inca occupation, right up to the Conquest. The most remarkable feature of the Kotosh complex is the **crossed-hands symbol** carved prominently onto a stone – the gracefully executed insignia of a very early culture about which archeologists know next to nothing – which now lies in the **Museo de Arqueología** (Archeology Museum) in Lima. The site today consists of three sacred stone-built enclosures in generally poor condition; but with a little imagination and/or a good local guide, it is both atmospheric and fascinating to explore one of the most ancient temple sites in Peru .

To get to the site, you can either **walk** along La Unión road, or take the La Unión **bus** (see p.343) from Huánuco and ask the driver to drop you off at the path to Kotosh. Alternatively, a **guided tour** from Huánuco will cost around $8–10 per person, with a **taxi** from the Plaza de Armas costing about the same. It is not recommended for tourists to visit the site alone by night.

Tantamayo

About 150km north of Huánuco, poised in the mountainous region above the higher reaches of the Río Marañón, lies the small village of **TANTAMAYO**, with its extensive ruins nearby. In the village you can hire local **guides** (from $6–10 a day) to take you on a two- to three-hour hike to the scattered sites; Eladio Maticorena is recommended. There are some basic hostels in town.

The ruins of Tantamayo

The precise age of the remote **ruins of Tantamayo** is unknown. Its buildings appear to fit into the Tiahuanaco-Huari phase, which would make them some 1200 years old, but physically they form no part of this widespread cultural movement, and the site is considered to have developed separately, probably originating from tribes migrating to the Andes from the jungle and adapting to a new environment over a long period of time. It is also thought that the ruins might reveal archaeological links to Chavín de Huantar (see p.382) and Kotosh.

At Tantamayo, the architectural development of some four centuries can be clearly seen – growing from the simplest of structures to complex edifices. The thirty separate, massive constructions make an impressive scene, offset by the cloud forest and jungle flourishing along the banks of the Marañón just a little further to the north. Tall buildings dot the entire area – some clearly **watchtowers** looking over the Marañón, one of Peru's most important rivers and a major headwater of the Amazon, others with less obvious functions, built for religious reasons as temple-palaces, perhaps, or as storehouses and fortresses. One of the major constructions, just across the Tantamayo stream on a hill facing the village, was named **Pirira** by the Incas who conquered the area in the fifteenth century. At its heart there are concentric circles of carved stone, while the walls and surrounding houses are all grouped in a circular formation – clearly this was once an important centre for religious ritual. The **main building** rises some 10m on three levels, its bluff facade broken only by large window niches and by centuries of weathering.

West of Huánuco: La Unión to Huánuco Viejo

A small market town high up on a cold and bleak pampa, **LA UNIÓN** is a base for visiting the Inca ruins of Huánuco Viejo, a three- to four-hour hike away. If you do need a **place to stay**, there's the very basic, dirty *Hostal Dos de Mayo* (no phone; ❶), or *Hostal Gran Abilia Alvarado* at Comercio 1196 (no phone; ❷–❸), which is more salubrious but still has mostly shared bathrooms. There are a few **restaurants** around the market area and on Dos de Mayo.

There are buses from Huánuco to **La Unión** but not from here to Huánuco Viejo; the only way to get there is to walk, although given that the route isn't the easiest to follow, it's probably best to take a **taxi** from the Plaza de Armas ($5–7).

Huánuco Viejo

From La Unión a dusty track continues along precipitous and winding mountain roads (sections of which are frequently washed away during the rainy season) to reach the superb Inca stonework of **Huánuco Viejo** (daily 8am–6pm; free); if you do want to walk it, it's best to dedicate at least half a day. The site sits high up on the edge of a desolate pampa, virtually untouched by the Spanish conquistadors. Although abandoned by the Spanish shortly after their arrival in 1539, the city became a centre of native dissent – Illa Tupac, a relative of the rebel Inca Manco and one of the unsung heroes of the Indian resistance, maintained clandestine Inca rule around Huánuco Viejo until at least 1545. As late as 1777 the royal officials were thrown out of the area in a major – albeit short-lived – insurrection.

One of the most complete existing examples of an Inca provincial capital and administrative centre, Huánuco Viejo gives a powerful impression of a once-thriving city – even though it's been a ghost town for four hundred years. The grey stone houses and **platform temples** are set out in a roughly circular pattern radiating from a gigantic *unsu* (Inca throne) in the middle of a plaza. To the north are the **military barracks** and beyond that the remains of suburban dwellings. Directly east of the plaza is the palace and temple known as Incahuasi, and next to this is the Acllahuasi, a separate enclosure devoted to the Chosen Women, or Virgins of the Sun. Behind this, and running straight through the Incahuasi, is a man-made water channel diverted from the small Río Huachac. On the opposite side of the plaza you can make out the extensive administrative quarters.

Poised on the southern hillside above the main complex are over five hundred **storehouses** where all sorts of produce and treasure were kept as tribute for the emperor and sacrifices to the sun. Well away from the damp of the valley floor, and separated from each other by a few metres to minimize the risk of fire, they also command impressive views across the plain.

Arriving here in 1539, the Spanish very soon abandoned the site of Huánuco Viejo to build their own colonial administrative centre at a much lower altitude, more suitable for their unacclimatized lungs and with slightly easier access to Cusco and Lima. The modern city of Huánuco, built along the standard city plans specified by royal decree, grew thoroughly rich, but was still regarded by the colonists as one of those remote outposts (like Chile) where criminals, or anyone unpopular with officialdom, would be sent into lengthy exile.

It's possible to continue overland from La **Unión to Huaraz** by fairly rough dirt roads, mainly used by truckers. The route goes either via Huansala and Huallanca; or, via Conococha and Chiquián (9hr).

From Huánuco to the jungle

The Amazon is the obvious place to move on to from Huánuco unless you're heading back to Lima and the coast. The spiralling descent north is stunning, with views across the jungle, as thrilling as if from a small plane. By the time the bus reaches the town of **Tingo Maria**, a possible stopover en route to Pucallpa, the Río Huallaga has become a broad tropical river, navigable downstream in shallow canoes or by balsa raft. And the tropical atmosphere, in the shadow of the forested ridges and limestone crags of the **Bella Durmiente** mountain, is delightful. From Tingo Maria you can continue the 260km directly northeast on the dirt road through virgin forest, going through the **Pass of Padre Abad**, with its glorious waterfalls, along the way to Pucallpa, jumping-off point for expeditions deep into the seemingly limitless wilderness of tropical jungle (see Chapter 8).

Tingo Maria

Once known as the "Garden City", because of the ease with which gardens, tropical fruit, vegetables and wild flora grow in such abundance, the ramshackle settlement of **Tingo Maria**, 130km north of Huánuco, lies at the foot of the Bella Durmiente (Sleeping Beauty) mountain. According to legend, this is the place where the lovesick Princess Nunash awaits the waking kiss of Kunyaq, the sorcerer. These days the town welcomes more travellers than ever due to the decreased activity in the region's cocaine trade. This is still probably the area's main industry but things aren't quite as wild as they were at times during the 1980s and 1990s; currently the hot spots are deeper into the jungle along the road to Tarapoto. However, that said, even the road on to Pucallpa from Tingo still sees the occasional armed robbery of buses travelling by night.

Despite Tingo Maria's striking setting – 670m above sea level on the forested eastern slopes of the Andes, amid the fecund tropical climate of the *ceja de selva* – today, it is a tatty, ugly town, on which the ravages of Western civilization have left their mark. Dominated by sawmills and plywood factories financed by multinational corporations, with its forest of TV aerials sticking out from the rooftops, the town displays symbols of relative affluence, but the tin roofs and crumbling walls across the township betray the poverty of the majority of its inhabitants. There's little for visitors to see, beyond the rather sorry **zoo and botanical gardens** (Mon–Fri 9am–5pm; free) attached to the university on the edge of town, or – about 14km out of town – the **Cueva de las Lechuzas** (Owls' Cave), the vast, picturesque home to a flock of rare nocturnal parrots (you'll need a torch). Tingo Maria's major **fiesta** period is the last week of July – a lively and fun time to be in town, but on no account leave your baggage unattended.

Practicalities

Accommodation is available at the *Hotel Viena*, Tulumayo 245 (☎062/562194; ②), which is surprisingly comfortable as well as reasonably priced; the simple but excellent-value *Hostal La Cabaña* at Av Raymondi 342 (☎062/562146; ①), where the rooms are small and all bathrooms shared; and the clean and friendly *Hotel Royal* on Av Benavides 206 (☎062/562166; ③). The best option, however is the upmarket *Madera Verde Hotel* (☎062/562047, ℱ561608; ⑤–⑥), 2km south of town, with its own pool (open to non-residents for around $1), and clean, comfortable rooms, most with private bath. The *Villa Jennifer Eco-lodge* (☎062/561611; ⑤–⑥), Carretera Castillo Grande Km 3.4, also has lovely rooms plus a pool, bar and restaurant. For **food** *La Cabaña*, Av Raymondi 644, serves up tasty Peruvian evening meals and lunches. For **tours** to archaeological sites and waterfalls in the region, try Silvia Silva Zamora, Av Raymondi 604 (062/406659, 644@hotmail.com).

Into the jungle

The **bus** from Tingo Maria to Pucallpa (7–8hr; $9) leave at least three times a day from Avenida Raymondi, with journey time dependent on whether it's the dry (May–Oct) or rainy (Nov–April) season. Buses travelling at night are frequently robbed at gunpoint, which is at the very least an unpleasant experience. **Colectivos** leave at all times for both Pucallpa and Huánuco from the corner of Callao with Raymondi, about five blocks from the Plaza de Armas. There are a number of military checkpoints in operation along the way, mainly to counter the drug-trafficking problem (apparently the road is sometimes used as an airstrip by unmarked light aircraft).

Buses and **trucks** also leave from Avenida Raymondi just about every day to Tarapoto (20hr), along the road that follows the Huallaga Valley north via Juanjui (16hr), but this route is not recommended for travellers due to the high level of cocaine smuggling, terrorist activity, armed robbery and army presence in this remote region.

Travel details

Buses, trucks and colectivos

Ayacucho to: Cusco (8 daily; 20–28hr); Huancayo (3 daily; 8–9hr); Lima (6 daily; 9hr); Pisco (6 daily; 6–8hr).
Huancavelica to: Ayacucho (2 daily; 7–9hr); Huancayo (6 daily; 2–3hr); Lima (2 daily; 9hr).
Huancayo to: Ayacucho (3 daily; 8–9hr); Cerro de Pasco (2 daily; 4hr); Huancavelica (6 daily; 2–3hr); Huánuco (2 daily; 5–6hr); Lima (over 10 daily; 6–7hr); Tarma (8–10 daily; 2hr).
Huánuco to: La Unión (2 daily; 5–6hr); Lima (2 daily; 10hr); Pucallpa (4 daily; 11hr); Tantamayo (1 daily; 7–12hr); Tingo Maria (4 daily; 2–3hr).

Trains

Lima to: Huancayo (2 or 3 monthly; 10hr).
Huancavelica to: Huancayo (several weekly; 3–5hr).
Huancayo to: Huancavelica (several weekly; 3–5hr); Lima (2 or 3 monthly; 10hr).

Flights

Ayacucho to: Cusco (1 daily; 1hr 30min); Lima (1 daily; 1hr)
Huancayo to: Lima (1 daily; 35min).
Huánuco to: Lima (1 daily; 1hr 30min).

6

Huaraz and the
Cordillera Blanca

CHAPTER 6

Highlights

* **Sechin** A unique warrior temple site whose outer wall is clad with some of the most gruesome ancient artwork to be found anywhere in South America. See p.354

* **Monterrey and Chancos** Relaxing in either of these two natural thermal baths is both a healthy and a hedonistic experience to remember. See pp.369 & 373

* **Cordillera Blanca** Hiking or climbing in this region is as scenic an adventure as you could hope to find anywhere outside of the Himalayas. See p.372

* **Huascarán** Dividing the Amazon Basin from the Pacific watershed, this mountain is the highest peak in Peru. See p.372

* **Lago Llanganuco** This calm, turquoise-coloured, glacial lake sits 3850m above sea level, dramatically surrounded by Peru's highest peaks. See p.376

* **Caraz** A quaint, attractive town known for its honey and milk products, quietly settled below the enormous Huandoy Glacier and close to the little-visited ruins of Tunshucayco. See p.378

* **Chavín de Huantar** One of the most important ancient temple sites in the Andes – associated with a cult dedicated primarily to a terrifying feline god. See p.382

▲ Cordillera Blanca

6

Huaraz and the Cordillera Blanca

T he **Ancash** region unfurls along an immense desert coastline, where pyramids and ancient fortresses are scattered within easy reach of several small resorts linked by vast, empty beaches. Behind are the barren heights of the dark, dry Cordillera Negra, and beyond that the spectacular backdrop of the snowcapped **Cordillera Blanca**. Sliced north to south by these parallel ranges, the centre of Ancash is focused on the Huaraz Valley, known locally as the **Callejón de Huaylas**. At around 3000m above sea level, it's an ideal base from which to explore some of the best hiking and mountaineering in the Americas.

The *departamento* of Ancash was a rural backwater when created in 1839. These days, the main industries are fishing (mainly restricted to Chimbote, Peru's largest fishing port), tourism (everywhere but Chimbote), mining (gold – over 28,000 kilos between 1997 and 2001, silver, copper and zinc) and agriculture (primarily wheat, potatoes, maize corn and pulses but also cultivation of over forty percent of Peru's commercial marigold flowers). The region has a population of just over one million, with 250,000 of these people living in or around Chimbote. Huaraz, the next biggest urban and market centre, is home to around 150,000 inhabitants. For Peruvian and overseas visitors alike, it offers more in terms of trekking and climbing, beautiful snowcapped scenery, "alpine" flora and fauna and glaciated valleys than anywhere else in the country. It is also extremely rich in history and pre-Colombian remains as well as possessing a truly traditional living culture. Given the severe earthquake damage this area has suffered throughout the twentieth century, it may lack some of the colonial charm seen in Cusco, Arequipa, Cajamarca and Ayacucho, yet more than makes up for it with the majesty and massive scale of its scenery.

Nestling in the valley, the *departamento*'s capital, **Huaraz** – a six- or seven-hour drive north from Lima – makes an ideal base for exploring the region. It's the place to stock up, hire guides and mules and relax after a breathtaking expedition. Besides being close to scores of exhilarating mountain trails, the city is also near the ancient Andean treasure, **Chavín de Huantar**, an impressive stone temple complex which was at the centre of a culturally significant puma-worshipping religious movement just over 2500 years ago.

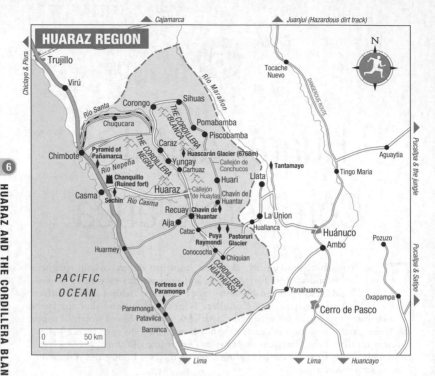

HUARAZ REGION

N

Chiclayo & Piura

Trujillo

Virú

Tocache
Nuevo

Río Marañón

DANGEROUS ROUTE

Corongo

Sihuas

Chuqucara

Pomabamba

Piscobamba

Río Santa

THE CORDILLERA BLANCA

Caraz

Aguaytia

Pucallpa & the jungle

Chimbote

Pyramid of
Pañamarca

Huascarán Glacier (6768m)

THE CORDILLERA NEGRA

Río Nepeña

Yungay

Callejón de
Conchucos

Tantamayo

Tingo Maria

Carhuaz

Chanquillo
(Ruined fort)

Huaraz

Huari

Llata

Casma

Sechin

Río Casma

Callejón
de Huaylas

Chavín de
Huantar

Recuay

Chavín de
Huantar

La Union

Huallanca

Huánuco

Pozuzo

Pucallpa & Satipo

Aija

Catac

Puya
Raymondi

Pastoruri
Glacier

Ambo

Huarmey

Conococha

Chiquian

CORDILLERA HUAYHUASH

Oxapampa

PACIFIC
OCEAN

Fortress of
Paramonga

Yanahuanca

Cerro de Pasco

0   50 km

Paramonga

Patavilca

Barranca

The Ancash Coast

Most people travelling along the **Ancash Coast** from Lima to Huaraz or Trujillo (or vice versa) do the whole trip in a single six-or eight-hour bus ride. For Trujillo this means sticking to the stunning desert scenery of the Panamerican Highway. En route to Huaraz, a well-maintained road climbs furiously from sea level to the breathless heights of the Callejón de Huaylas. Whichever route you take, it's well worth considering a stop at the small beach resort of **Barranca** or the farming and fishing villages of **Casma** and **Chimbote** – all three of which have some intriguing archaeological sites nearby, and offer alternative routes up to Huaraz. Facilities for tourists in these coastal parts are hardly overwhelming, but there are enough services that you won't go wanting. Some **information** on local sites can be found at the municipal website Ⓦ www.muniparamonga.gob.pe/turismo.html.

Barranca and the Fortress of Paramonga

North of Lima, the **Fortress of Paramonga** is the first site of real interest, the best preserved of all Peru's coastal outposts, built originally to guard the southern limit of the powerful Chimu Empire. To explore the ruins, it's best to base yourself at **BARRANCA**, 7km south of the fortress, where there are a few simple **hotels** and two or three places to eat. The *Hotel Jefferson*, at Jr Lima 946 (Ⓣ 01/2352184; ②), is cheap and quite comfortable, or there's the basic *Hostal Colón*, Jr Galvez 407 (❶). The best place to eat is the excellent Chinese **restaurant** on the main street. Nearly all **buses** and **colectivos** on their way between Lima and Trujillo or Huaraz stop at Barranca, and, to get from Barranca to Paramonga, take the efficient local bus service, which leaves from the garage at the northern end of town, every hour or so.

Five kilometres north of Barranca is the smaller town of **Patavilca**, where Bolívar planned his campaign to liberate Peru. The main paved road to Huaraz and the Cordillera Blanca leaves the Panamerican Highway here and heads up into the Andes, but the only facilities in the village are a basic **café**, the *Restaurant Conejo* and a small **museum** (Mon–Sat 9am–5pm; 80¢), which contains local archaeological finds, including some ceramics.

The Fortress of Paramonga

The **FORTRESS OF PARAMONGA** (daily 8am–5.30pm; $2) sits less than 1km from the ocean and looks in many ways like a feudal castle. Constructed entirely from adobe, its walls within walls run around the contours of a natural hillock and are similar in style and situation to the Sun Temple of Pachacamac (see p.121). As you climb up from the road, you'll see the main entrance to the fortress on the right by the site's small **museum** (daily 8am–5pm) and ticket office. Heading into the labyrinthine **ruins**, you'll find the rooms and sections get smaller and narrower the closer you get to the top – where sits the original palace-temple. From here there are commanding views across the desert coast in either direction; across vast sugar-cane fields, formerly belonging to the US-owned Grace Corporation, once owners of nearly a third of Peru's sugar production. In contrast to the verdant verdure of these fields, irrigated by the Río Fortaleza, the fortress stands out in the landscape like a huge, dusty yellow pyramid.

There are differences of opinion as to whether the fort had a military function or was purely a ritual centre, but as most pre-Conquest cultures built their places of worship around the natural personality of the landscape (rocks, water, geomorphic features and so on), it seems likely that the Chimu built it on an older *huaca*, both as a fortified ritual shrine and to mark the southern boundary of their empire. In the late fifteenth century, it was conquered by the Incas, who built a road down from the Callejón de Huaylas. Arriving in 1533 en route from Cajamarca to Pachacamac, Hernando Pizarro, the first Spaniard to see Paramonga, described it as "a strong fort with seven encircling walls painted with many forms both inside and outside, with portals well built like those of Spain and two tigers painted at the principal doorways". There are still red- and yellow-based geometric murals visible on some of the walls in the upper sector, as well as some chessboard-style patterns.

Huarmey and around

North of Paramonga, sand dunes encroach on the main coastal road as it continues the 75km to **HUARMEY**, where you'll find the exhilarating and usually deserted beaches of La Honda, El Balneario and Tuquillo. If you want **accommodation**, there's the basic *Hotel Venus* (❷) and, much better, the *Posada de Huarmey* (☎043/600330; ❹–❺) plus there's a 24-hour **restaurant** geared towards bus and truck drivers. Leaving Huarmey, the road closely follows the shoreline, passing the magnificent Playa Grande, a seemingly endless **beach** with powerful rolling surf – often a luminous green at night owing to phosphorescent plankton being tossed around in the whitewater crests – and a perfect spot for **camping**. Some of the desert you pass through has no plant life at all, beyond the burned-out tumbleweeds that grow around the humps and undulations fringed with curvy lines of rock strata – intrusions of volcanic power from the ancestral age. In places, huge hills crouch like sand-covered jellyfish squatting on some vast beach.

Casma and around

The town of **CASMA**, 70km north of Huarmey, marks the mouth of the well-irrigated Sechin River Valley. Surrounded by corn and cotton fields, this small settlement is peculiar in that most of its buildings are just one storey high and all are modern. Formerly the port for the Callejón de Huaylas, the town was razed by the 1970 earthquake, whose epicentre was just offshore. There's not a lot of interest here and little reason to break your journey, other than to try the local speciality of duck ceviche (flakes of duck meat soaked deliciously in lime and orange juice) or to explore the nearby ruins, such as the temple complex of Sechin, the ancient fort of Chanquillo, as well as the Pañamarca Pyramid, 20km north.

The town boasts several roadside cafés and a small selection of **hotels**: the new *Hostal Celene*, Luis Ormeño 595 (☎043/711065; ❸), has nine relatively large and very clean rooms; the *Hostal Gregori*, close by at C Ormeño 530 (☎043/711073; ❷ & ❸), is also very clean and almost as comfortable with an option of private or shared bath; and the *Hotel El Farol*, Tupac Amaru 450 (☎043/711064, ⓔhostalfarol@yahoo.com; ❹), two blocks from the Plaza de Armas, is friendly and comfortable with private bath, a pool and a decent restaurant which sometimes serves *ceviche de pato*, as described above. The *Hostal Las Aldas*, (☎01/440-3241 or 442-8523; ❸) is pleasant and near the beach at Playa Las Aldas (turn off the Panamericana Norte at Km 345). En route to the Sechin ruins there's the well-run *Hospedaje Las Dunas*, Ormeno 505 (☎043/711057; ❷), which also has a good restaurant and is only ten minutes from town by car or taxi; more central and arguably a better **restaurant**, *Tio Sam*, Huarmey 138, serves *comida criolla*, including seafood, as well as decent *chifa* food. The *Restaurant Lucy*, on Mejia y Mejia has a reputation for excellent north coast-style breakfasts.

Turismo Chimbote **buses**, block 1, Av Luis Ormeño, run at least every hour to Lima (6hr) and Chimbote (40min); for Huaraz, Huandoy buses, Av Luis Ormeño 158 (☎043/712336), take the fastest normal route, finishing at Caraz; while Empresa Moreno buses serve Huaraz three times a week via the scenic but dusty track over the Cordillera Negra via the Callan Pass (6–8hr).

The Sechin ruins

Some 5km, or just over an hour's walk, from Casma – head south along the Panamerican Highway for 3km, then up the signposted side road to Huaraz for about the same distance – lies the ruined temple complex of **SECHIN** (daily 8am–5pm; $2). The site's main section, unusually stuck at the bottom of a hill, consists of an outer wall clad with around ninety monolithic slabs engraved with sometimes monstrous representations of particularly nasty and bellicose warriors along with their mutilated sacrificial victims or prisoners of war. Some of these stones, dating from between 1800 and 800 BC, stand 4m high. Hidden behind the standing stones is an interesting inner sanctuary – a rectangular building consisting of a series of superimposed platforms with a central stairway on either side. The site also contains the small **Museo de Sitio Max Uhle**, which displays photographs of the complex plus some of the artefacts uncovered here, as well as information and exhibits on Moche, Huari, Chimu, Casma and Inca cultures.

Some of the ceremonial centres at Sechin were built before 1400 BC, including the massive, U-shaped **Sechin Alto complex**, at the time the largest construction in the entire Americas. Ancient coastal constructions usually favoured adobe as a building material, making this site rare in its extensive use of granite stone. Around 300m long by 250m wide, the massive stone-faced platform predates the similar ceremonial centre at Chavín de Huantar (see p.382) possibly by as much as four hundred years. This means that Chavín could not have been the original source of temple architectural style, and that much of the iconography and legends associated with what has until recently been called the Chavín cultural phase of Peruvian prehistory actually began 3500 years ago down here on the desert coast.

If you're not up to the walk here, your best option is to take a **motorcycle taxi** from Casma, for $1–2. There are no buses, but some local **colectivos** come here in the mornings from the market area of Casma; alternatively, there are **taxis** from the Plaza de Armas, for around $10–15, including a wait of an hour or so.

Mojeque and Chanquillo

Several other, lesser-known sites dot the Sechin Valley, whose maze of ancient sandy roadways constituted an important pre-Inca junction. The remains of a huge complex of dwellings can be found on the **Pampa de Llamas**, though all you will see nowadays are the walls of adobe huts, deserted more than a thousand years ago. At **Mojeque**, you can see a terraced pyramid with stone stairs and feline and snake designs. Both these sites are best visited from Casma by **taxi**; expect to pay around $10 (return).

Some 12km southeast of Casma lies the ruined, possibly pre-Mochica fort of **Chanquillo**, around which you can wander freely. It's an amazing ruin set in a commanding position on a barren hill, with four walls in concentric rings and watchtowers in the middle, keeping an eye over the desert below. **Trucks** leave for here every morning at around 9am from the Petro Peru filling station in Casma – ask the driver to drop you off at "El Castillo", from where it's a thirty-minute walk uphill to the fort.

The pyramid of Pañamarca

At Km 395 of the Panamerican Highway, a turn-off on the right leads 11km to the ruined adobe pyramid of **Pañamarca**. Three large painted panels can be seen here, and on a nearby wall a long procession of warriors has been painted – but all this artwork has been badly damaged by rain. Although an impressive monument to the Mochica culture, dating from around 500 AD, it's not an easy site to visit; the best way is to get a **taxi** from the Plaza de Armas in Casma for around $6.

Chimbote

Elderly locals say that **CHIMBOTE** – another 25km beyond the turn-off to Pañamarca – was once a beautiful coastal bay, with a rustic fishing port and fine extensive beach. You can still get a sense of this on the southern Panamericana approach, but the smell and industrial sprawl created by the unplanned fishing boom over thirty years ago undeniably dominates the senses. Chimbote has more than thirty fish-packing factories, which explains the rather unbearable stench of stale fish. Despite the crisis in the fishing industry since the early 1970s – overfishing and El Niño have led to bans and strict catch limits for the fishermen – Chimbote accounts for more than 75 percent of Peru's fishing-related activity.

With little of interest to visitors, apart perhaps from some attractive marble sculptures which adorn the central Boulevard Isla Blanca, Chimbote's development constitutes the country's most spectacular urban growth outside Lima. Initially stimulated by the Chimbote–Huallanca rail line (built in 1922), a nearby hydroelectric plant, and government planning for an anticipated rise in the anchovy- and tuna-fishing industry, the population grew rapidly from 5000 in 1940 to 60,000 in 1961 (swollen by squatter settlers from the mountains). Yet even Chimbote was virtually razed to the ground during the 1970 earthquake (see p.375).

Practicalities

The **tourist office**, Bolognesi 421 (Mon–Sat 9am–5.30pm), can advise on transport to nearby sites and sometimes stocks town and regional maps. Limited **information** can also be found at ⓦ www.chimboteonline.com. Most travellers **stay** in Chimbote one night at most. The *Hotel La Casona*, at Av San Pedro 246, in the suburb of Miramar Bajo (Ⓣ 043/322655; ❺), is quite stylish and very comfortable. Located as it is a little way from the noisy town centre, *Hostal El Ruedo*, Lote 15, Urbino Los Pinos (Ⓣ 043/335560; ❷), is relatively free of the smell. The *Gran Chimú*, Jr José Galvez 109, on the Plaza 28 de Julio (Ⓣ 043/321741; ❻), meanwhile, is reasonably priced, offering comfortable rooms and mod cons, and its **restaurant**, though not cheap, serves some of the best food found along this part of the coast; try the ceviche or the *criolla* dishes such as *aji de gallina*. Another option for eating out is the *Restaurant El Rey*, Jr Leoncio Prado 558, or the *Aquarius*, at Haya de La Torre 360, serving excellent vegetarian dishes.

Most important is knowing how to **get out of town**. Most buses call at and leave from the Terminal Terrestre El Chimbador, a few kilometres south of the city centre on Avenida de Los Pescadores on the Carretera Panamericana. All the coastal buses travelling north to Trujillo and south to Lima along the Panamerican Highway stop here; on a busy day, over 100 buses and up to 6000 passengers pass through this depot. While Turismo Huaraz run the only direct Chimbote–Huaraz bus, twice daily (one daytime, one at night) from Av Pardo 1713 (Ⓣ 043/321235), a number of operators – Movil Tours, Turismo Chimbote, Expresso Huandoy and Trans Moreno – all run daily buses to Huaraz via Patavilca and Casma, as well as (mostly nightly) services to Caraz via Huallanca (Cañon del Pato) from Jirón Pardo, between Jirón José Galvez and Manuel Ruiz. Travel **by bus** to Huaraz via the adventurous route up the Cañon del Pato (8–9hr to Caraz) is surprisingly rough, over large tracts where the road appears to follow a stony riverbed. *Colectivos* to Trujillo (2–3hr away) leave regularly from opposite the *Hostal Los Angeles*, while **colectivos** to Lima hang around on Manuel Ruiz, one block towards the sea off Avenida Prado. The airport, where you can get **flights** to (or from) Lima and Trujillo can be found at Km 421 (Ⓣ 043/311844 or 311062).

North to Trujillo: the Santa and Viru valleys

The rarely visited desert area north of Chimbote is littered with archaeological remains, including an enormous defensive wall known as the **Great Wall of Peru**, thought to be over a thousand years old. Twenty kilometres north of Chimbote, the Panamerican Highway crosses a rocky outcrop into the Santa Valley, where the wall – a stone and adobe structure more than 50km long – rises from the sands of the desert. The enormous structure was first noticed in 1931 by the Shippee-

Johnson Aerial Photographic Expedition, and there are many theories about its construction and purpose. Archaeologist Julio Tello thought it was pre-Chimu, since it seems unlikely that the Chimu would have built such a lengthy defensive wall so far inside the limits of their empire. It may also, as the historian Garcilaso de la Vega believed, have been built by the Spaniards as a defence against the threat of Inca invasion from the coast or from the Callejón de Huaylas.

The wall stretches from Tambo Real near the Río Santa estuary in the west up to Chuqucara in the east, where there are scattered remains of pyramids, fortresses, temples and stone houses. To see the wall, take any Trujillo **bus** north from Chimbote (see p.355) along the Panamerican Highway, and get off when you see a bridge over the Río Santa. From here, head upstream for three or four hours and you'll arrive at the best surviving section of the wall, just to the west of the Hacienda Tanguche, where the piled stone is cemented with mud to more than 4m high in places.

Further up the valley – albeit well off the beaten track, with no tourism infrastructure whatsoever – lies a double-walled **construction** with outer turrets, discovered by Gene Savoy's aerial expedition in the late 1950s. Savoy reported finding 42 stone-built strongholds in the higher Santa Valley in only two days' flying, evidence that supports historians' claims that this was the most populated valley on the coast prior to the Spanish conquest. Hard to believe today, it seems more probable if you bear in mind that this desert region, still alive with wildlife such as desert foxes and condors, is fed by the largest and most reliable of the coastal rivers.

The valley's main town is **Viru**, a small place at Km 515 of the Panamerican Highway, with a bridge over the riverbed that, in the dry season, looks as though it has never seen rain. An impressive cultural centre around 300 AD, when it was occupied by the Gallinazo or Viru people, today the town offers very little to the tourist. The most interesting ruin in the area is the **Grupo Gallinazo** near Tomabal, 24km east of Viru up a side road just north of the town's bridge. Here in the valley you can see the dwellings, murals and pyramids of a significant religious and administrative centre, its internal layout derived from kinship networks. The site covers an area of four square kilometres and archaeologists estimate that over ten thousand people sometimes lived here at the same time. You can also make out the adobe walls and ceremonial platform of a Gallinazo temple, on one of the hilltops at Tomabal.

The Huaraz region

Situated in the perfectly steep-sided Callejón de Huaylas valley, **Huaraz** is the focal point of inland Ancash. Only a day's bus ride from either Lima or Trujillo, it's one of the best places in Peru to base yourself if you have any interest in **outdoor adventure** or just sightseeing. As a market town and magnet for hikers, bikers, canoeists and climbers, the city centre has a naturally lively atmosphere, making it the ideal springboard for exploring the surrounding mountainous region. The valley is dominated by the **Cordillera Blanca**, the world's highest tropical range, and **Huascarán**, Peru's highest peak. Weather wise, the region is best experienced between May and September when the skies are nearly always blue and it rains very little. Between October and April, however, it's often cloudy and most afternoons you can expect some rain.

Besides the mountain scenery, the region boasts spectacular ruins such as **Chavín de Huantar**, at the bottom end of the Callejón de Conchucos; the natural thermal baths at **Monterrey** and **Chancos**; and immense glacial lakes, like **Lago Parón**, surrounded by snowcapped peaks, and the beautiful **Llanganuco**. Throughout the whole area, too, you come upon unusual and exotic flora like the enormous, tropical Puya Raymondi plants, and traditional mountain villages where unwritten legends are encapsulated only in ancient carved stones and the memories of the local peasant population.

Huaraz

Occupied since at least 12,000 years ago, the area around Huaraz was responsible for significant cultural development during the Chavín era (particularly 1500–500 BC), although the Incas didn't arrive here until the middle of the fifteenth century. Following the Spanish Conquest of Peru, and up until less than a century ago, **HUARAZ** – 400km from Lima – remained a fairly isolated community, barricaded to the east by the dazzling snowcapped peaks of the Cordillera Blanca and separated from the coast by the dry, dark Cordillera Negra. Between these two mountain chains the powerful Río Santa valley, known as the Callejón de Huaylas, is a region with strong traditions of local independence.

For several months in 1885, the people of the Callejón waged a **guerrilla war** against the Lima authorities, during which the whole valley fell into rebel hands. The revolt was sparked by a native leader, the charismatic **Pedro Pablo Atusparia**, and thirteen other village mayors, who protested against excessive taxation and labour abuses. After they were sent to prison and humiliated by having their braided hair (a traditional sign of status) cut off, the local peasants overran Huaraz, freeing their chieftains, expelling all officials and looting the mansions of wealthy landlords and merchants (many of them expatriate Englishmen who had been here since the Wars of Independence). The rebellion was eventually quashed by an army battalion from the coast, which recaptured the city while the Indians were celebrating their annual fiesta. Even today, Atusparia's memory survives close to local hearts, and inhabitants of the area's remote villages remain unimpressed by the central government's attempts to control the region.

Arrival and information

Most people arrive **by bus** from Lima; you can expect to pay $10–15 for the seven- to eight-hour journey, depending on the level of comfort; Cruz del Sur (Huaraz depot based at corner of jirones José de la Mar and Simón Bolívar) are, as usual, the safest and most comfortable option, closely followed by Movil Tours and Expreso Ancash. All offer day and night buses and a range of services from standard to deluxe, which includes a packed lunch and video. Some cheaper bus companies, as well as Colectivos Comité 14, also run daily services here from

Jirón Leticia in Lima Centro. Companies coming from Trujillo (8–10hr; around $9) include Cruz del Sur, Turismo Chimbote and Colectivos Comité 14. Coming from or going to Chimbote (5–7hr; $8) or Caraz (6–8hr; $8), you'll probably travel with Turismo Chimbote, Rodriguez or Empresa Huandoy; arriving direct from Casma (4–5hr; $7) you'll almost certainly travel on Empresa Moreno. All the above buses come in at and leave from or close to their companies' offices (see p.366 for details).

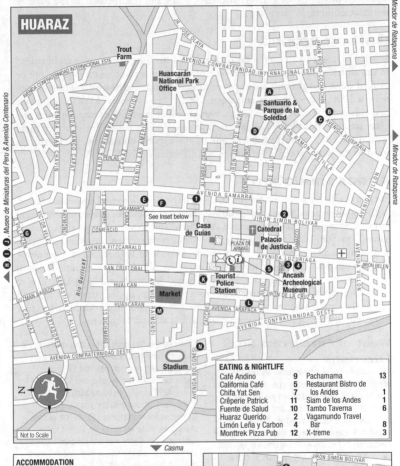

EATING & NIGHTLIFE

Café Andino	9	Pachamama	13
California Café	5	Restaurant Bistro de	
Chifa Yat Sen	7	los Andes	1
Crêperie Patrick	11	Siam de los Andes	1
Fuente de Salud	10	Tambo Taverna	6
Huaraz Querido	2	Vagamundo Travel	
Limón Leña y Carbon	4	Bar	8
Monttrek Pizza Pub	12	X-treme	3

ACCOMMODATION

Albergue Churup	D	Hostal Los	
Alojamiento Alpes Andes		Portales	E
& Casa das Guias	P	Hostal Raymondi	O
Alojamiento		Hostal Schatzi	F
Quintana	K	Hotel Andino	B
B and B Mi Casa	L	Jo's Place	G
Casablanca Hotel	M	Lazy Dog Inn	I
Edward's Inn	N	Llanganuco Lodge	H
Hostal Gyula Inn	Q	Olaza Guest House	A
Hostal Landauro	R	Real Hotel Baños	
Hostal El Patio de		Termales Monterrey	J
Monterrey	J	Steel Guest House	C

359

Few people arrive **by air** since there is no scheduled service, but for those that do, the plane drops off at a small airstrip close to the village of Anta, some 23km north of Huaraz; from here it's thirty minutes into the city by *colectivo* or bus, both of which leave from the main road outside the airstrip.

Tourist information is available from an office on the Plaza de Armas (Mon–Sat 8am–6.30pm, Sun 8am–2pm; ☎043/428812, ⓦwww.regionancash.gob.pe) where the staff are usually helpful and stock photocopies of trekking maps; the **Tourist Police** (☎043/421341) also have maps and information at the back of the same building by the plaza

Getting around

Much of Huaraz town can be easily negotiated **on foot** once you've acclimatized to the altitude (3091m); however, some of the more remote sectors should not be walked alone at night since incidents of mugging and rape have, albeit rarely, been reported here. Using **taxis** in and around the city costs around $1; a long distance taxi ride, say from Huaraz to Caraz, would cost at least $20 during daylight, and taxis are also available by the day from around $35 upwards. For short journeys within the city, the best option is one of the regular **colectivos**, which run on fixed routes along avenidas Luzuriaga and Centenario (70¢).

Accommodation

Even in the high season, around August, it's rarely difficult to find **accommodation** at a reasonable price, though rates do rise during the Semana Turistica in June and in November to January when many Peruvians tend to visit. Within the centre of town, from the Plaza de Armas along Avenida Luzuriaga, there are countless hostels and many smaller places renting out rooms; outside of high season it is definitely worth bargaining. There are really three main areas providing accommodation in the urban area: west of the main streets avenidas Fitzcarrald and Luzuriaga; east of these streets; and another sector, away from the centre, up the Jirón Jose de Sucre hill to the east. There are some peaceful places to choose from out of town, too, some with garden or hot bath, particularly those around Monterrey.

West of Fitzcarrald and Luzuriaga

Alojamiento Quintana Mariscal Caceres 411 ☎043/426060. An increasingly popular backpacker joint, less than three blocks from the Plaza de Armas. It is clean, comfortable and well managed, and most rooms have private bath. ❸–❹

B and B Mi Casa Av Tarapaca (also known as 27 de Noviembre) 773 ☎043/43375, ✉bmark@ddm.com.pe. Just three blocks west of the Plaza de Armas, this place is distinguished by very friendly owners who provide excellent service and have expert cartographical information as well as general tourist info. There's also a dining room serving breakfasts, as well as hot water and private baths. ❷–❹

Casablanca Hotel Av Tarapaca 138 ☎043/422602, ⓦwww.huaraz.com/casablanca. A quite comfortable and upmarket hotel with fine wooden-beamed ceilings, and used by a lot of tour groups; it actually seems quite out of place on this downmarket street. All rooms have private bath and there's has a good restaurant with inclusive breakfast. ❺

Edward's Inn Av Bolognesi 121 ☎043/422692, ⓦwww.edwardsinn.com. One of the most popular trekkers' hostels, located just below the market area and offering all sorts of services, including up-to-the-minute tourist information, in a very convivial atmosphere. Rooms come with or without private bath, and hot water is almost always available. The owner, who speaks English, is a highly experienced trekker, climber and mountain rescuer. ❸

East of Fitzcarrald and Luzuriaga

Alojamiento Alpes Andes and Casa das Guias Parque Ginebra 28-G ☎043/421811, ⓦwww.casadeguias.com.pe. Located on a quiet little plaza in the streets behind Av Luzuriaga, this is a centre for local guides and mountaineers and also has a hostal. It's very clean, with communal rooms and showers at reasonable rates, and you can safely leave baggage here while out of town on trekking expeditions. ❷–❸

Hostal Gyula Inn Parque Ginebra 632 ☎ 043/421567. Located above an internet office, this is relatively plain but excellent value with great views, private bathrooms and access to kitchen facilities; staff are cheerful to boot. ❷

Hostal Landauro Jr José de Sucre 109 ☎ 043/421212, Ewillemml@yahoo.es. A popular place right on the Plaza de Armas, with small but well-decorated rooms (with or without bath) set along narrow balconies boasting views over the town towards the Cordillera Blanca. ❷–❸

Hostal Los Portales Av Raimondi 903 ☎ 043/428184. A spacious, if often dimly lit hotel, well situated for most bus terminals. Rooms are clean with private baths, and large, well-sprung beds and there's also a large, safe luggage store for trekkers, as well as a restaurant. ❺

Hostal Raymondi Av Raimondi 820 ☎ 043/421082. Large, clean and full of character, with a spacious, old-fashioned lobby; rooms themselves are well-appointed if a little dark, with private bath. ❹

Hostal Schatzi Jr Simón Bolívar 419 ☎ 043/423074, ✉ schatzihs@yahoo.com, ⊛ www.schatzihostal.com. A lovely, very friendly little place set around a lush garden patio with small but tidy and nicely furnished rooms; those on the second floor are located on a wraparound wooden balcony with two floors and some views across the garden, town and valley. ❺

Jo's Place Jr Daniel Villarzan 276 ☎ 043/425505, ⊛ www.josplacehuaraz.com. Located 10min from the town centre, over the river bridge, then fourth street on the right, *Jo's Place* is relaxed, with comfortable rooms and a secure atmosphere making for great value, as well as popularity with backpackers. They help organise tours and have a large garden, terrace and views across to the Cordillera Blanca. English newspapers and breakfasts are available. ❸

East of Avenida Gamarra

Albergue Churup Jr Amadeo Figueroa 1257, La Soledad ☎ 043/424200, ⊛ www.churup.com. Just 5min walk from Plaza de Armas, this great-value establishment has a family atmosphere, a garden, lovely wood-burning stove, laundry, kitchen and left-luggage facilities as well as panoramic views. They also have lots of info on local trekking. ❸–❹

Casa Alojamiento La Cabaña Jr José de Sucre 1224 ☎ 043/423428. A popular and very friendly *pensión* with safe, comfortable accommodation, a dining room and hot water all day. Rooms have private bath and TV, while guests also have access to kitchen and laundry facilities, plus a dining room. ❷–❸

Hotel Andino Jr Pedro Cochachín 357 ☎ 043/421662, ⊛ www.hotelandino.com. An uphill hike away from the centre of town, albeit with the reward of beautiful views over the Cordillera Blanca and plush quarters in the best hotel in town. There are a variety of rooms to choose from, with or without terraces and fireplaces, and there's also a gourmet restaurant serving delicious food with a Swiss influence. ❼–❽

Olaza Guest House Jr Julio Arguedas 1242, La Soledad ☎ 043/422529, ⊛ www.olazas.com. Nice large rooms, very clean and newly furbished with private bath as well as access to the kitchen and laundry. This place is also a good source of local information, enjoys a roaring fire in the communal living space and has a roof terrace which is great for its spectacular landscape views as well as being a place to mix and meet with fellow travellers over tea or breakfast. ❺

Steel Guest House C Alejandro Manguina 1467, in front of the *Hotel Andino* ☎ 043/429709, ✉ infor@steelguest.com. A five-storey building with a pleasant communal area on the second floor offering TV, small library and a billiard table. Rooms have private baths, 24hr hot water and there's a laundry available. ❻

Huaraz outskirts and beyond

Lazy Dog Inn ☎ 043/943789330, ⊛ www.thelazydoginn.com. Located some 8km east of Huaraz as the crow flies, they will pick up from the city if contacted in advance, or you can take a taxi ($10); there's a sign for the place at Km 12, a few kilometres beyond Wilkawain ruin, which is the best road route for vehicles. Run by a resident Canadian couple, the hostal itself is beautiful, with a sun image on its outside wall and its accommodation split between a number of very comfortable cabins made from local adobe and utilising eco-fabrics. Service is excellent and the setting is fantastic. ❺–❼

Llanganuco Lodge ☎ 043/943669580, ⊛ www.llanganucolodge.com. A fantastic new lodging catering to everyone from climbers and serious trekkers to educational groups and people simply visiting overnight to stay in comfort by the lake, *Llanganuco Lodge* is located in a magnificent setting right at the entrance to Huandoy

Valley, on the edge of the National Park underneath the Huascaran and Huandoy glaciers (contact in advance for transport or take a taxi). Accommodation is available in suites, rooms and dorms, and there's great food, value and service (the restaurant is excellent) plus a library, games, DVDs and outward bound activities including adventure trails organised on demand. ❹–❺

🏃 **Hostal El Patio de Monterrey** Av Monterrey, Monterrey ☎043/424965, ⓦwww.elpatio .com.pe; reservations ☎01/4480254. Located in the village of Monterrey, just a couple of hundred metres from the thermal baths and only a few kilometres from Huaraz, this luxurious neo-colonial complex of clean, attractive rooms with iron bedsteads and more expensive bungalows, is based around an attractive patio and lovely gardens. ❼–❽

Real Hotel Baños Termales Monterrey Av Monterrey, Monterrey ☎043/727690. An old hotel full of character and style and actually attached to thermal baths (residents have free access). The fine rooms have hot showers, and there's a splendid restaurant overlooking the heated pool. They also have bungalows, which cost a bit more. ❺

The City

Although well over 3000m above sea level, Huaraz has a somewhat cosmopolitan, and very busy, city centre. It has developed rapidly in terms of tourism and commerce since the completion of the highway through the river basin from Paramonga, and the opening of mainly US- and Canadian-owned zinc, silver and gold mines in both the Cordillera Negra and the Callejón de Conchucos. Even so, most tourism activity is geared towards goings-on out of town, like trips to Chavín de Huantar or mountaineering expeditions to the glaciated peaks and trekking country that surround Huaraz.

Avenida Luzuriaga is the town centre's north–south axis, where most of the restaurants, nightlife and tour agencies are based. The Parque Ginebra is set just behind Luzuriaga and the **Plaza de Armas**, a pleasant little plaza but something of an afterthought in terms of city planning and not yet fully integrated into the network of roads.

Virtually the entire city was levelled by the **earthquake of 1970**, and the old houses have been replaced with single-storey modern structures topped with gleaming tin roofs. Surrounded by eucalyptus groves and fields, it's still not quite the vision it once was, but it's a decent enough place in which to recuperate from the rigours of hard travel. There are many easy walks just outside of town, and if you fancy an afternoon's stroll you can simply go out to the eastern edge and follow one of the paths or streams uphill.

The Plaza de Armas and around

The city's major cultural attraction is the **Ancash Museo Arqueológico**, at Av Luzuriaga 762, facing the modern Plaza de Armas (Mon–Sat 9am–5pm, Sun 9am–2pm, ☎043/421551; $1.80). Fronting attractive, landscaped gardens which are full of stones removed from Recuay tombs and temples, this small but interesting place contains a superb collection of Chavín, Chimu, Wari, Mochica and Recuay **ceramics**, as well as some expertly trepanned skulls. It also displays an abundance of the finely chiselled stone monoliths typical of this mountain region, most of them products of the Recuay and Chavín cultures. There's a model of the Guitarrero Cave, a local site showing evidence of human occupation around 10,000 BC. One of its most curious exhibits is a *goniometro*, an early version of the surveyor's theodolite, probably over a thousand years old and used for finding alignments and exact 90-degree angles in building construction. On the other side of the Plaza de Armas from the museum stands the **Catedral** (daily 7am–7pm; free). Completely rebuilt after being destroyed in the 1970 earthquake, it has nothing special to see inside, but its vast blue-tiled roof makes

▲ Garden exhibits, Ancash Museo Arqueológico

a good landmark and, if you look closely, appears to mirror one of the glaciated mountain peaks, the Nevado Huanstán (6395m), behind. Also close to the Plaza de Armas, the Banco Wiese has a **Sala Cultural** where they rotate exhibitions of photos or artwork, mainly relevant to the city or region (Mon–Fri 9am–1pm & 4.30–6.30pm; free).

The only other museum to merit a brief visit is the **Museo de Miniaturas del Peru** (Mon–Fri 9am–5.30pm; $1), in the gardens of the *Gran Hotel Huascarán*, close to the town exit en route down the valley along Fitzcarrald, which contains an interesting collection of pre-Hispanic art from the Huaraz region and a range of local folk art and crafts, including the fine red Callejón de Huaylas ceramics. It also displays a small model of Yungay (see p.375) prior to the entire town being buried under a mudslide, also the result of the 1970 earthquake.

The rest of town

Uphill in the eastern part of town, at the Parque de la Soledad, the **Santuario del Señor de La Soledad** can also be visited; essentially it's another church built since the 1970 earthquake and it houses the powerful sixteenth-century religious image of *El Señor de La Soledad*.

A fifteen-minute walk up Avenida Raimondi from the centre of Huaraz, then across the Río Quillcay bridge and down Avenida Confraternidad Internacional Oeste brings you to the regional trout farm, or **Estación Pesqueria** (daily 8am–5pm; 25¢, includes guided tour), run by the Ministero de Pesqueria. It breeds thousands of rainbow trout every year and you can observe the process from beginning to end (more interesting than you might think); much of the excellent trout available in the restaurants of Huaraz comes from here.

There are one or two vantage points on the hills around the city of Huaraz, but the best and most accessible is the **Mirador de Rataquenua**, about a two-hour walk each way, though not advisable for single tourists since there have been muggings reported on this route. Notwithstanding this, it commands a splendid location, high above the town to the southeast, and looks out over the Callejón de Huaylas. To get there, follow Avenida Villón out beyond the cemetery and up through the woods to the cross. Most taxi drivers will take you there and back for less than $10, which is certainly safer than walking if you're on your own.

Eating, drinking and entertainment

There's no shortage of **restaurants** in Huaraz, though they do vary considerably in value and quality. There's also a lively nightlife scene, with several **peñas** hosting traditional Andean music, as well as a few **clubs** where locals and tourists can relax, keep warm and unwind during the evenings or at weekends. Nightlife joints start to open from 7pm and can go on until 3am. The **folklore centre**, Centro Folklorico Cultural – Waracushun (Jr Bolívar 1101, Belén, Huaraz) helps make local and regional music and dance culture more accessible; open daily 11am–11pm, it generally has live music and dance shows at weekends, and most days serves reasonable meals and snacks.

Restaurants

Café Andino Lucar y Torre 530. A popular upstairs café with library and games, serving breakfasts, good coffee, juices and Mexican food. Another good place to meet other travellers, trekkers and climbers.

California Café 28 de Julio 562. A good place for wi-fi connection and meeting other travellers; the coffee is excellent, there's trekking information and a relaxed atmosphere. Try the all-day American breakfast or waffles, especially if you've worked up an appetite after a few days' hiking.

Chifa Yat Sen Corner of Av Raimondi and Comercio. A pleasant little Chinese restaurant, offering amazing-value three-course set lunches with a Peruvian twist, as well as a range of standard Chinese dishes available most evenings from around 6pm.

Crêperie Patrick Av Luzuriaga 422. Centrally located close to the corner with Av Raimondi,

Crêperie Patrick serves guinea pig, rabbit *al vino* and fondue in addition to excellent crepes, salads and sandwiches.

Fuente de Salud Jr Jose de la Mar 562. A vegetarian restaurant with an excellent reputation; best and cheapest at lunchtimes.

Huaraz Querido Jr Simón Bolívar 981. Easily the best spot in town for fresh fish and seafood; the ceviche is generally delicious. Daily 9am–10pm.

Limón Leña y Carbón Av Luzuriaga 1002. Out on a limb at the southern end of the main drag, this is another really good seafood restaurant that serves fresh fish delivered from Chimbote; the menu also includes local trout, meat dishes and pizzas in the evening.

Monttrek Pizza-pub Av Luzuriaga 646 ☏043/421124. A spacious place, very popular with trekkers and one of the town's top tour and climbing operators (see p.367); it's also

Throughout the year various **fiestas** take place in the city and its surrounding villages and hamlets. They are always bright, energetic occasions, with *chicha* (beer) and *aguardiente* flowing freely, as well as roast pigs, bullfights and vigorous communal dancing with the townfolk dressed in outrageous masks and costumes. The main festival in the city of Huaraz is usually in the first week of February and celebrates **Carnival**. In June (check with the tourist office for exact dates each year because they do vary a lot), Huaraz hosts the **Semana del Andinismo** (the Andean Mountaineering and Skiing Week), which includes trekking, climbing and national and international ski competitions, on the Pastoruri Glacier. Caraz has its own Semana Turistica, usually in the third week of June. Note that during this month prices of hotels in Huaraz and Caraz, as well as restaurants, increase considerably. Other festivals include the **Aniversario de Huaraz**, in July (usually on the 25th), when there are a multitude of civic and cultural events in the city; plus the annual folklore celebrations in the first week of August for Coyllur-Huaraz, as well as the **Virgen de la Asunción** in Huata and Chancas during mid-August. Late September sees the festival of the **Virgen de Las Mercedes**, celebrated in Carhuaz, as well as other rural get-togethers that you'll often come across en route to sites and ruins in the Callejón de Huaylas.

a great meeting place with a useful notice board for contacting like-minded backpackers. The food is delicious and music good, and there's even a climbing wall, as well as maps and aerial photos of the region.

Pachamama Av San José de San Martín 687 ✆043/421834. A fine café-bar, with a spacious and attractive environment, serving good wines and a range of other drinks, fish, chicken, meats and pastas. There's also good music, games and even itinerant exhibitions and silver craft work.

Restaurant Bistro de los Andes Jr Julian de Morales 823 ✆043/426249. A great place for breakfast, with seats outside, good yoghurts, coffee and pancakes; also popular during the evening. Features a book exchange as well. Closed Sun mornings.

Siam de los Andes Corner of Gamarra with Julian de Morales. Excellent Thai stir fries and curries in a welcoming ambience (open 6.30am–10pm).

Pubs and nightlife

Tambo Taverna Jr José de la Mar 776. A restaurant-*peña* serving good drinks, with a great party spirit, a mix of popular sounds and occasional live music (mix of latin, rock and pop) after 10pm.

Vagamundo Travel Bar Jr Julian de Morales 753. Arguably the most trendy and popular bar in Huaraz these days, *Vagamundo* serves great sandwiches as well as a wide range of cocktails.

X-treme Bar Corner of Uribe and Luzuriaga. A popular cocktail lounge and dance floor spinning everything from rock and pop to jazz, blues and Latino – one of Huaraz's best bars.

Shopping

Huaraz is a noted **crafts centre**, producing, in particular, very reasonably priced handmade leather goods (custom-made if you've got a few days to wait around). Other bargains include woollen hats, scarves and jumpers, embroidered blankets, and interesting replicas of the Chavín stone carvings. Most of these items can be bought from the stalls in the small artesanía market in covered walkways set back off Avenida Luzuriaga (daily 2pm–dusk), or, for more choice, in the **Mercado Modelo** two blocks down Raymondi from Luzuriaga. For individual shops, try Tierras Andinas, Parque Ginebra, which has some fine handicrafts and local artwork, or the Centro Artesanal, next to the post office on the plaza, which sells textiles, ceramics, jewellery, stone and leather work.

Huaraz is also renowned for its food, in particular its excellent local cheese, honey and *manjar blanco* (a traditional sweet made out of condensed milk). These can all be bought in the **food market**, in the backstreets around Avenida José de

Most of the **tour agencies** In Huaraz are located along Avenlda Luzurlaga and offer guided city tours, including stopping at all the major panoramic viewpoints (4hr, from around $10). But with a region as exciting as this in terms of outdoor adventure, most people come for something a bit more vigorous, namely trekking, climbing, mountain biking, canoeing or even parapenting.

For the surrounding area the most popular outings are to the **Llanganuco Lakes** (8hr, $10–15 per person), **Chavín de Huantar** (9–11hr, from $10–15 per person), including lunch in Chavín before exploring the ruins, and to the edge of the **Pastoruri Glacier** 70km from Huaraz at 5240m (6–8hr round-trip, from $10 per person), where until recently one could walk on the ice and explore naturally formed ice caverns beneath the glacier's surface. Sadly, the ice is actually retreating these days, so although worth a visit, it's not as spectacular as it used to be. The Pastoruri tour, which usually includes a visit to see the Puya Raymondi plants (see p.373), is rather commercialized and there is often a lot of rubbish lying around the most commonly visited parts of the glacier; it's also worth remembering that Pastoruri is very high and can be bitterly cold, so make sure you're well acclimatized to the altitude, and take warm clothing with you. Most agents can also arrange trips to the **thermal baths** at Chancos (4hr, from $8) and Caraz (6hr, from $10), and some offer adventure activities in the area. Always check if the guide leading your tour speaks English. These are the standard basic tour prices; some companies may charge more if they consider their service superior.

There's greater price variation in the more adventurous tours, treks, biking, mountaineering, canoeing and river-rafting trips, though tariffs generally usually start at around $30 per half day. The Callejón de Huaylas, in particular, offers one of Peru's most scenic **bike rides**, with most routes here going over 3500m. Llanganuco (3800m) from Yungay is popular, as is Carhuaz to the Abra de Punta Olimpica (4800m). The **sun** is very hot here so always use good sunglasses and block. For local biking assistance or to book a bike-based tour, the best option is Mountain Bike Adventures, Lucar y Torre 530 (☏043/424259, ⓦwww.chakinaniperu.com) which offer cross-country, single track and up- or downhill options. For **canoeing**, the most popular section of the Río Santa, which runs along the valley separating the two massive cordilleras, lies between the villages of Jangas and Caraz, navigable between May and October most years with rapids class 2 and 3. Monttrek (see opposite) are among the best canoeing operators, based at Luzuriaga 646, on the second floor

San Martín (daily 6am–6pm). Market Ortiz, Av Luzuriaga 401, is one of the best **supermarkets** in town, while Centro Naturista, Fitzcarrald 356, is good for natural medicines, yoghurt, herbs and cosmetics.

Moving on

Colectivos and **local buses** connect Huaraz with all the main towns and villages north – Carhuaz, Yungay and Caraz – at very reasonable rates (80¢–$3 for up to 2hr); these can be caught from just over the main river bridge from the town centre, on either side of the main road (Avenida Fitzcarrald), beside the Río Quillcay. Just before the same bridge, *colectivos* heading south to Catac ($1) and Olleros ($1.25) can be caught daily every 30min from the end of Jirón Caceres, just below the market area. Buses to Chiquián are run by Chiquián Tours from block 1 of Calle Huascarán, near the market, and leave every hour or so.

Listings

(where they also have a free indoor climbing wall), offer in addition equipment rental, rafting, trekking and rescue expeditions. If you fancy **parapenting**, the Huaraz region is an ideal place (mostly around Caraz and Yungay, particularly around the Pan de Azucar); the local contact is Alberto Sotelo, again contactable through Monttrek. For any of these activities,

If a three-day **trek** with llamas carrying your camping equipment appeals to you, then check out the Peru Llama Trek website ⊛ www.geocities.com/perullamatrek.

Guides and operators in Huaraz
Caillou Aventure Parque Ginebra ☎ 043/421214, ⊛ www.caillouaventure.com. These guys offer rock climbing, trekking, Andinismo (high Andes trekking and climbing) and mountain biking.

High Ascents Pasaje San Juan 250, Independencia ☎ 043/426040. An established company organising climbing and trekking trips around the region.

Monttrek Av Luzuriaga 646 ☎ 043/421124, ⊛ www.monttrek.com. Professional climbing, guides, treks, horse riding, river rafting and snowboarding in the region. They also stock new and used camping and climbing equipment, and the office is a great place to meet other trekkers.

Mountain Bike Adventures Jr Lucre y Torre 530 ☎ 043/424259, ⊛ www.chakinaniperu .com. Offers bike tours with mountain bikes to rent as well as a variety of alternative routes for cyclists with particular interests. English-speaking guides are available and there's the bonus of a book exchange in their office.

Pablo Tours Av Luzuriaga 501 ☎/℻ 043/421145, ⊛ www.pablotours.com. One of the best agencies for standard tours, Pablo Tours is particularly good for organized treks and canoeing, but also offers local cultural and city tours. Note that they get booked up very quickly.

Peruvian Andes Adventures Jr Jose Olaya 532 ☎ 043/421864, ⊛ www.peruvianandes .com. This outfit offer a combination of trekking, climbing and day trips to sites around the region, plus flights and bus tickets.

Pony Expeditions Sucre 1266, in Caraz ☎/℻ 043/391642, ⊛ www.ponyexpeditions .com. A very professional organization that both fits out, and guides, climbing, trekking and mountain biking expeditions in the area. An excellent source of local climbing and trekking information, they also run treks in other regions, such as the Cordillera Huayhuash, the Inca Trail and Ausangate.

Banks and exchange Try Banco Wiese, Jr José de Sucre 766; Interbanc, on Plaza de Armas; Banco de Credito, Av Luzuriaga 691; and Banco de la Nación, Av Luzuriaga. *Cambistas* gather where Morales and Luzuriaga meet, or try the casa de cambio at Luzuriaga 614 for good rates on dollars. All banks open Mon–Fri 9am–6pm.

Buses For local *colectivos* and buses to Anta, Marcara, Carhuaz, Yungay and Caraz, see p.374. Other companies include: Chavín Express, Jr Mariscal Caceres 328 ☎ 043/424652, for Sihuas, Chavín and Huari; CIVA, Morales 650 ☎ 043/429253, for Lima; Colectivos Comité 14, Av Fitzcarrald 216 ☎ 043/421202 or 421739, for Lima and Trujillo; Cruz del Sur, Jr Lucar y Torré 585 ☎ 043/428726, the best for Lima and Trujillo; Empresa Condor de Chavín, Jr Tarapaca 312 ☎ 043/422039, for Chavín and Lima; Empresa Rapido, Caceres 380

☎ 043/422887 for Chiquián, Huallanca and La Union; Empresa Rosario, Jr Caraz 605, for Pomabamba, La Unión and Huánuco; Empresa Sandoval, Tarapaca 582 ☎ 043/426930, for Catac, Chavín, Pomacha, Huari; Expresso Ancash/Ormeño, Av Raimondi 853 ☎ 043/421102, for Lima and Caraz; Movil Tours, Av Raimondi 730 ☎ 043/422555, for Lima, Chimbote and Trujillo; Turismo Huaraz, Jr Caraz 605, for Caraz, Piscobamba, Pomabamba and Chimbote; and Yungay Express, Av Fitzcarrald 261 ☎ 043/727507, for Chimbote and Patavilca.

Doctors and dentists Dr Simon Komori, Jr 28 de Julio 602 (24hr); or try the surgery at Av Luzuriaga 618 (Mon–Fri 9am–5pm).

High Altitude Rescue ☎ 043/493327 and 493291; or, for the Yungay branch ☎ 043/

493333.

Hospital Av Luzuriaga, block 8 ☎043/421861 or 421290; or the San Pedro Clinic, Huaylas 172 ☎043/428811.

Internet facilities Wi-Fi California Café, 28 de Julio 562 (offers local, national and international phone calling at very reasonable prices), plus several others along Avenida Luzuriaga and also Parque Ginebra.

Laundry Lavandería BB, Jr la Mar 674, is the best; otherwise, try Lavandería Huaraz, on Av Fitzcarrald, close to the bridge; and Lavandería El Amigo, on the corner of Jr Simon Bolívar and Jr José de Sucre.

National Institute of Culture Office responsible for ancient monuments, Luzuriaga 766 ☎043/421829.

Police The Tourist Police are on the Plaza de Armas at Jr Larrea y Loredo 716 ☎043/421341 ext 315; National Police are at Jose de Sucre, block 2 ☎043/421330.

Post office Plaza de Armas, Av Luzuriaga 702. Mon–Sat 8am–8pm.

Telephones Locutorio Emtelser, Jr José de Sucre 797 (daily 7am–11pm).

Western Union Av Luzuriaga 556 ☎043/426410.

Around Huaraz

There are a number of worthy sights within easy reach of Huaraz. Only 7km north are the natural thermal baths of **Monterrey**; a similar distance, but higher into the

hills, you can explore the inner labyrinths of the dramatic **Wilkawain temple**. On the other side of the valley, just half an hour by bus, **Punta Callan** offers magnificent views over the Cordillera Blanca, while to the south of the city you can see the intriguing cactus-like Puya Raymondi in the **Huascarán National Park**.

Monterrey

Just fifteen minutes by *colectivo* from the centre of Huaraz (every 10min or so from the corner of avenidas Fitzcarrald and Raimondi; 40¢), the vast **thermal baths** of **MONTERREY** (daily 7am–6pm; $1) include two natural swimming pools and a number of individual and family bathing rooms. Luxuriating in these slightly sulphurous hot springs can be the ideal way to recover from an arduous mountain trekking expedition, but make sure you are fully acclimatized, otherwise the effect on your blood pressure can worsen any altitude sickness. If you're staying at the wonderful old *Real Hotel Baños Termales Monterrey* (p.362), the baths are free. There's also an impressive waterfall just ten minutes' walk behind the hotel and baths.

There's no town here as such, just a street of a few properties, some of which have been converted or purpose-built as hostels or restaurants. At the top end of this street is the hotel and thermal baths, the reason that there's any settlement here at all. As far as **eating** goes, the best restaurant is *El Monte Rey*, opposite Artesania Johao (the ceramic workshop on the main access lane to the baths), which serves great local

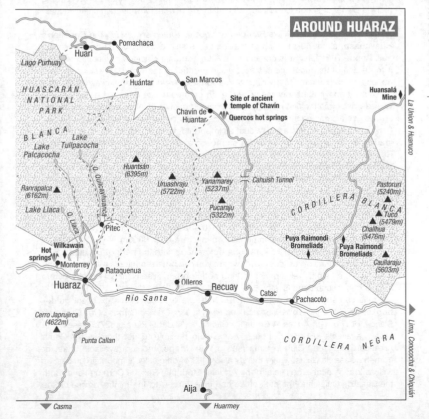

AROUND HUARAZ

food at excellent prices. A close second is the *Hotel Monterrey* itself, which serves very reasonable dishes in some style in their elegant, old-fashioned restaurant.

The temple at Wilkawain

WILKAWAIN, 8km from Huaraz, can be reached from the corner of Avenida Bolívar and 13 de Diciembre; or by following Avenida Centenario downhill from Avenida Fitzcarrald, then turning right up a track (just about suitable for cars) a few hundred metres beyond the **Real Hotel Huascarán**. From here, it's about an hour's stroll, winding slowly up past several small hamlets, to the signposted ruins. If there are four or five of you, a taxi there and back shouldn't come to more than about $2 each.

The temple is an unusual two-storey construction, with a few small houses around it, set against the edge of a great bluff. With a torch you can check out some of its inner chambers, where you'll see ramps, ventilation shafts, and the stone nails that hold it all together. Most of the rooms, however, are still inaccessible, filled with the rubble and debris of at least a thousand years. The temple

Andinismo

In 1932, when a German expedition became the first group to successfully scale Huascarán, the concept of **andinismo** – Andean mountaineering – was born. You don't have to be a mountaineer to enjoy the high Andes of Ancash, however, and there is plenty of scope for trekking as well in the two major mountain chains accessible from Huaraz.

The closest is the **Cordillera Blanca**; for specific routes see p.377. The **Cordillerra Huayhuash**, about 50km south of that range, is still relatively off the beaten tourist trail. About 31km long, it is dominated by the Yerupajá glacier, and *andinistas* claim it to be one of the most spectacular trekking routes in the world. Wherever you end up, be sure to pay heed to the rules of **responsible trekking**: carry away your waste, particularly above the snow line, where even organic waste does not decompose (if you can pack it in the first place, you can pack it back out). Note too that you should always use a camping stove – campfires are strictly prohibited in Huascarán National Park, and wood is scarce anyway. Just as important, though, is to realize that the solar irradiation in this part of the Andes is stronger than that found in the North American Rockies, European Alps or the even the Himalayas. This creates unique glacier conditions, making the ice here less stable and consequently necessitating the addition of an **experienced local guide** essential for the safety of any serious climbing or ice-walking expedition. It's also vital to **be fit**, particularly if you are going it alone.

If you intend to hike at all, it's essential to spend at least a couple of days **acclimatizing** to the altitude beforehand; for high mountain climbing, this should be extended to at least five days. Although Huaraz itself is 3060m above sea level, most of the Cordilleras' more impressive peaks are over 6000m. If you're going to trek in Huascarán National Park, register beforehand with the **park office** (see p.371) and **Casa de Guias office** (see p.371) where you can brush shoulders with experts and there's also a helpful trekkers networking notice board. The National Police operate a mountain rescue team (see p.368).

Ideally you should have detailed maps and one or other of the excellent **guidebooks**, *Trails of the Cordillera Blanca and Huayhuash*, *Classic Climbs of the Cordillera Blanca*, or *The High Andes: A Guide for Climbers* (all detailed on p.627). These aren't always available in Huaraz, though you should be able to get them at the South American Explorers' Club in Lima (see p.118). **Maps**, too, are available there, or from the Casa de Guías, where there's also a list of official local mountain guides, as well as lots of local expertise and the Andean Mountain Rescue Corp on hand. Both the Casa de Guías and the park office can give you up-to-the-minute advice on the base is only about 11m by 16m, sloping up to large slanted roof slabs, long since covered with earth and rocks to form an irregular domed top. The construction is a small replica of the Castillo at Chavín de Huantar (see p.381), with four super-imposed platforms and stairways, and a projecting course of stones near the apex, with a recessed one below it. There was once a row of cats' heads carved beneath this, which is a typical design of the Huari-Tiahuanaco culture that spread up here from the coast sometime between 600 and 1000 AD.

Punta Callan

Some 24km west of Huaraz, **Punta Callan** can be reached in about two hours on the Casma bus from Av Raimondi 336. Ask the driver to drop you off at Callan, shortly before the village of Pira along the road to Casma; from here it's a twenty-minute walk up the path to the promontory. No other spot can quite match the astonishing **views** of the Cordillera Blanca, so save it for a really clear afternoon, when you can best see Huascarán's towering ice cap. The grazing land that sur-

best and safest areas for trekking, since this region is not without its political danger zones. For additional information on trekking in the region, try the tourist information office (see p.360), or one of the tour and travel companies listed on pp.366–367. Also offering very useful assistance to climbers, AOTUM (the Asociación Peruana de Operadores de Turismo de Montaña) is based at the *Hotel Andino* (see p.361). Other Peruvian **mountaineering associations** are all based in Lima (see p.115).

There are three levels of **guides** available: certified mountain guides, who cost upwards of $70 a day; mountain guides undergoing the one-year trial period after training, from $45 a day; and trekking guides, who cost from $35 a day. Note that these costs don't include transport or accommodation. Recommended guides include Alberto Cafferata, a trekking guide contactable through Pony Expeditions (see p.367); David Gonzales Castromonte, Pasaje Coral Vega 354, Huarupampa, Huaraz (☎043/422213); Oscar Ciccomi, who is based in Lima and is contactable through Viajes Vivencial, Los Cerezos 480, Chaclacayo, Lima (☎/☎01/4972394); or Eduardo Figueroa, at *Edward's Inn* (see p.360). All speak English and Spanish. For local **tour operators** offering guided treks, see the box on p.366. High Mountain Guides (members of UIAGM – Unión Internacional de Asociaciones de Guías de Montaña), contactable through the Casa de Guías, include: Selio Billón, with 25 years' experience and one of the founders of La Asociación de Guías and the Casa de Guías; Arista Monasterio, who provides integrated and customised services; Michel Burger (owner of the *Bistro de los Andes* restaurant in Huaraz), who offers trekking and fishing.

Porters cost between $17 and $25 a day, depending on whether they are leaders or assistants, and are not supposed to climb over 6000m, while **mule drivers** (*arrieros*) charge from $10 to $15 a day, plus around $8 a day per animal. Expedition **cooks** usually charge the same as *arrieros*. **Llama-packing** (llamas carry the baggage) is a new initiative designed to promote ecotourism in the region; for Llamatrek, Pasaje Huaullac, Nueva Florida, Huaraz (☎043/425661, ⓦwww .perullamatrek.com) or ask for details in the Casa de Guías, Parque Ginebra 28-G, Huaraz (☎043/421811).

Huascarán National Park Office Jr Federico Sal y Rosas 555, by corner with Belen ☎043/422086.
Mountain Guides Casa de Guias, Parque Ginebra 28-G ☎043/421811.
Mountain Institute Ricardo Palma 100, Pedregal ☎043/423446.
Trekking and Backpacking Club Jr Los Libertadores 134, Independencia, Huaraz ☎01/99784193.

rounds the area is as pleasant as you could find for a picnic, and it's a relatively easy walk of a few hours back down the main road to Huaraz. Passing trucks or buses will usually pick up anyone who waves them down en route. Go early in the day, if you want to be sure you can get a bus back.

Caraz and Cordillera Blanca

The **CORDILLERA BLANCA** extends its icy chain of summits for 140 to 160km north of Huaraz. Under their western shadow lie the Callejón towns, all small, rustic with generally attractive accommodation and busy little markets. No one should come to the **Callejón de Huaylas** without visiting these northern valley towns, and many travellers will want to use them as bases from which to explore one or more of the ten snow-free passes in the Cordillera Blanca. Simply combining any two of these passes makes for a superb week's trekking.

Travelling north along the valley from Huaraz you'll immediately notice the huge number of avocado trees, particularly when their fruit is ripening during the rainy season (Nov–Feb). The name of one of the first villages you pass through after leaving Huaraz, **Paltay**, unsurprisingly, is very close to *"palta"*, the Peruvian word for avocado. Just outside the village, the roadside is lined with a number of ceramics workshops, which sell good pottery. Throughout the valley, you'll notice on the pantiled roofs of the houses an abundance of ornate crosses, which represent Christ's protection against demons, witchcraft and bad spirits, a local tradition that also involves the house being blessed by a priest at a communal party during the final stages of construction.

Further along the valley are the distinct settlements of **Yungay** and **CARAZ**. Physically they have little in common – Yungay is the site of several catastrophic natural disasters, while Caraz has survived the centuries as one of Peru's prettiest little towns – but both are popular bases from which to begin treks into the Cordillera Blanca. The highest range in the tropical world, the Cordillera Blanca consists of around 35 peaks poking their snowy heads over the 6000-metre mark, and until early this century, when the glaciers began to recede, this white crest could be seen from the Pacific. Of the many mountain lakes in the range, **Lake Parón**, above Caraz, is renowned as the most beautiful. Above Yungay, and against the sensational backdrop of Peru's highest peak, **Huascarán** (6768m), are the equally magnificent **Llanganuco Lakes**, whose waters change colour according to the time of year and the sun's daily movements, and are among the most accessible of the Cordillera Blanca's three hundred or so glacial lakes.

Fortunately, most of the Cordillera Blanca falls under the protective auspices of the **Huascarán National Park**, and as such the habitat has been left relatively unspoiled. Among the more exotic **wildlife** that hikers can hope to come across are the *viscacha* (Andean rabbit-like creatures), *vicuña*, grey deer, pumas, foxes, the rare spectacled bear and several species of hummingbirds. All of these animals are shy, so you'll need a good pair of binoculars and a lot of patience to get close to any of them.

The number of possible **hikes** into the Cordillera depends mostly on your own initiative and resourcefulness. There are several common routes, some of which are outlined below; anything more adventurous requires a local guide or a tour with one of the local operators. **Maps** of the area, published by the Instituto Geográfico Militar, are good enough to allow you to plot your own routes, or you can follow one of the standard paths outlined in books such as *Backpacking and Trekking in Peru*

The gigantic and relatively rare **Puya Raymondi** plant, reaching up to 12m in height and with a lifespan of around forty years, is found in the **Huascarán National Park**. Most people assume the Puya Raymondi is a type of cactus, but it is, in fact, the world's largest bromeliad, or member of the pineapple family. Known as *cuncush* or *cunco* to locals (and *Pourretia gigantea* to botanists), it only grows between altitudes of 3700m and 4200m, and is unique to this region; May is the best month to see them, when they are in full bloom and average 8000 flowers and six million seeds per plant. Dotted about the Quebrada Pachacoto slopes (some 50kms south east of Huaraz) like candles on an altar, the plants look rather like upside-down trees, with the bushy part as a base and a phallic flowering stem pointing to the sky. Outside of late April, May and early June, the plants can prove disappointing, often becoming burned-out stumps after dropping their flowers and seeds, but the surrounding scenery remains sensational, boasting grasses, rocks, lakes, llamas and the odd hummingbird.

By far the easiest way to see the Puya Raymondi is on an **organized** tour with one of the companies listed on p.366; most of the Pastoruri Glacier tours include a stop here. Alternatively, you could take a **combi colectivo** to Catac, leaving daily every thirty minutes from the end of Jirón Caceres in Huaraz (roughly $1). From Catac, 45km south of Huaraz, there are a few buses and trucks each day down the La Unión road, which passes right by the plants. Alternatively, it's possible to get off the *combi colectivo* 5km beyond Catac at Pachacoto (where there are a couple of cafés often used as pit stops by truck drivers) and hitch from here along the dirt track that leads off the main road across barren grasslands. This track is well travelled by trucks on their way to the mining settlement of Huansala, and after about 15–20km – roughly an hour's drive – into this isolated region, you'll be surrounded by the giant bromeliads. From here, you can either continue on to La Unión (see p.345), via the Pastoruri Glacier, or return to Huaraz by hitching back to the main road.

and Bolivia by Hilary Bradt or *Trails of the Cordillera Blanca and Huayhuash of Peru* by Jim Bartle (see p.627 for details). The most popular hike is the **Llanganuco to Santa Cruz Loop**, which begins at Yungay and ends at Caraz.

Chancos

Known traditionally as the Fuente de Juventud (Fountain of Youth), the thermal baths (daily 8am–6pm; 75¢–$1.50 depending on treatment) of **CHANCOS**, 30km north of Huaraz, consist of a series of natural saunas inside caves, with great pools gushing hot water in a beautiful stream. It is claimed that the thermal waters are excellent for respiratory problems, but you don't have to be ill to enjoy them, and they make an ideal end to a day's strenuous trekking.

To get there take any of the frequent **buses** or **colectivos** from the first block of Avenida Fitzcarrald or the market area in Huaraz, along the valley towards Yungay or Caraz. Get off at the attractive little village of Marcará and follow the rough road uphill for about 4km, passing several small peasant settlements en route, until you reach the baths. There's no accommodation in Chancos, but the valley bus service is good enough to get you back to Huaraz within an hour or so, or you could camp (ask permission to camp on one of the grassy patches up or down hill from the baths). There are a couple of basic restaurants on hand that are famous for their strong *chicha*, and are particularly popular with locals on Sunday afternoons.

From Chancos a small track leads off to the hamlet of Ullmey, following the contours of the Legiamayo stream to the upper limit of cultivation and beyond into the barren zone directly below the glaciers. Keeping about 500m to the right of the stream, it takes ninety minutes to two hours to reach **Laguna Legia Cocha**, at 4706m above sea level. Hung between two vast glaciers and fed by their icy melted water, the lake is an exhilarating spot, with the added bonus of amazing views across the Santa Valley to Carhuaz in the north, Huaraz in the south and Chancos directly below. If you leave Huaraz early in the morning, you can enjoy a fine day-trip, stopping here for lunch, then heading down to Chancos for a stimulating bath before catching the bus back into town from Marcara.

Carhuaz and around

One of the major towns along the valley, **CARHUAZ**, some 30km from both Huaraz and Yungay, has an attractive, central Plaza de Armas, adorned with palm trees, roses and labyrinths of low-cut hedges and dominated by the solid, concrete Iglesia de San Pedro on its south side. On Sundays the streets to the north and west of the plaza are home to a thriving traditional **market**, where Andean and tropical foodstuffs, herbs and crafts, in particular gourd bowls, can be bought very cheaply. The colourfully dressed women here often sell live guinea pigs from small nets at their feet, and wear a variety of wide-brimmed hats – ones with blue bands indicate that they are married, ones with red bands show that they are single. Many also wear glass beads, on their hats or around their necks, as a sign of wealth.

Practicalities

Combi colectivos to Huaraz (50¢), Chancos (30¢) and Caraz (40¢) arrive at, and depart from, a stop one block west beyond the market side of the plaza, while the **buses** to Lima, Huaraz and Caraz leave from a terminal on block 2 of Avenida La Merced, which is a continuation of the road from the market side of the plaza to the main highway.

There are a few basic **hotels** in Carhuaz: the *Hostal La Merced*, Jr Ucayali 724 (T043/394241; ②–③), has commodious rooms with or without private bath; the centrally based *El Abuelo*, Jr 9 de Diciembre, by the plaza (T043/394456, Wwww .elabuelohostal.com; ⑤–⑥), is comfortable, with hot water. About 1.5km above Carhuaz, a lovely eco-ranch, the *Casa de Pocha* (T043/943613058, Elacasadepocha @yahoo.com; ⑤), at the foot of Hualcan Mountain, offers accommodation in a traditional adobe lodge with eight spacious rooms under red-tiled roofs; hot water is available 24 hours, there's a sauna, twelve-metre swimming pool, horseback riding and the nearby hot springs of La Merced. In addition to Spanish, the owner speaks English, French and Italian. Back in town and right on the plaza, the *Café Heladería El Abuelo* is the best eating place in Carhuaz; it shares the same owner as *El Abuelo Hostal* nearby and serves ice cream, snacks plus full meals (ask for the local delicacy of beanshoots).

Around Carhuaz: Hombre Guitarrera and Mancos

In the 1980s, a cave was discovered a few kilometres north of Carhuaz, on the other side of the Río Santa in the Cordillera Negra. Containing bones of mastodons and llamas and suggesting human occupation dating from as far back as 12,000 BC, it is situated close to a natural rock formation that looks vaguely like a guitar, and the site is now known as the cave of **Hombre Guitarrera** (Guitar Man). It can be accessed in just over an hour's walk, beyond the sports stadium and up the stream past the unusual church, which sits beside the road from Carhuaz to Yungay.

A little further on from Carhuaz, over a river, the road comes to the village of **Mancos**, where there's an unusually attractive plaza, with palm trees and a quaint, modern church with twin belfries sitting under the glistening glacier of Huascarán. On the plaza there's **accommodation** at the *Casa Alojamiento* (❷), which offers clean, comfortable rooms and shared bath. Though there are several restaurants around, none are especially good. The village's main **fiesta**, August 12–16, is in honour of its patron, San Royal de Mancos, and the plaza becomes the focus of highly colourful religious processions, dancing and, later, bullfighting.

Yungay

YUNGAY, 58km up the valley from Huaraz, and just past Mancos, was an attractive, traditional small town until it was obliterated in seconds on May 31, 1970, during a massive earthquake. This was not the first catastrophe to assault the so-called "Pearl of the Huaylas Corridor"; in 1872 it was almost completely wiped out by an avalanche, and on a fiesta day in 1962 another avalanche buried some five thousand people in the neighbouring village of Ranrahirca. The 1970 quake also arrived in the midst of a festival and caused a landslide, and although casualties proved impossible to calculate with any real accuracy, it's thought that over 70,000 people died. Almost the entire population of Yungay, around 26,000, disappeared almost instantaneously, though a few of the town's children survived because they were at a circus located just above the town, which fortunately escaped the landslide. Almost eighty percent of the buildings in neighbouring Huaraz and much of Carhuaz were also razed to the ground by the earthquake.

The new town, an uninviting conglomeration of modern buildings – including some ninety prefabricated cabins sent as relief aid from the former Soviet Union – has been built around a concrete Plaza de Armas a few kilometres from the original site. Yungay still cowers beneath the peak of Huascarán, but it is hoped that it is more sheltered from further dangers than its predecessor. On the way into town from Carhuaz, a car park and memorial monument mark the entrance to the site of the buried **old town of Yungay** (daily 8am–6pm; 75¢), which has developed into one of the region's major tourist attractions. The site, entered through a large, blue concrete archway, is covered with a grey flow of mud and moraine, now dry and solid, with a few stunted palm trees to mark where the old Plaza de Armas once stood. Thousands of rose bushes have been planted over the site – a gift of the Japanese government. Local guidebooks show before and after photos of the scene, but it doesn't take a lot of imagination to reconstruct the horror. You can still see a few things like an upside-down, partially destroyed school bus, stuck in the mud. The graveyard of Campo Santo, above the site, which predates the 1970 quake, gives the best vantage point over the devastation. A tall statue of Christ holds out its arms from the graveyard towards the deadly peak of Huascarán itself, as if pleading for no further horrors.

Practicalities

The best reason for staying here is to make the trip up to the Llanganuco Lakes and Huascarán (trucks leave most mornings from the Plaza de Armas) or simply to use the town as a base for exploring from the heart of the Callejón de Huaylas. Despite its looks, modern Yungay is a reasonable place to stay, and there are a number of acceptable **hostels**. The best place is undoubtedly the new Llanganuco Lodge, at the foot of Huascaran (see p.377). If you're on a budget, though, your best bet is the popular, great value and exceptionally friendly *Hostal Gledel* on Avenida Aries Graziani (☎043/393048; ❶–❷), at the northern end of town; the upstairs rooms are best, and though all rooms share toilet facilities, the hostel is spotlessly clean and a good place to meet trekkers and climbers. For those on an even tighter budget, there's the very basic *Hostal Sol de Oro* (⊤043/393116; **①**), or it's sometimes possible to **camp** in a eucalyptus wood at *Hostal Blanco*, next to the hospital, which also has double rooms (**③**). The *Hostal Yungay*, on the Plaza de Armas (⊤043/393053; **②**), gives out free **maps** and information on the area.

In terms of **restaurants**, on the plaza there's the *Café Pilar*, which is good for breakfast and snacks; for local fish and other decent meals try *Restaurant Alpamayo* located on Avenida Arias Grazziani on the Caraz end of town. The plaza is also the place to catch *combi colectivos* for the road up to Llanganuco ($2, 1hr).

The Llanganuco Lakes

The **Llanganuco Lakes**, at 3850m above sea level, are only 26km northeast of Yungay (83km from Huaraz), but take a good ninety minutes to reach by bus or truck, on a road that crawls up beside a canyon that is the result of thousands of years of Huascarán's meltwater. On the way you get a dramatic view across the valley and can clearly make out the path of the 1970 devastation. The last part of the drive – starkly beautiful but no fun for vertigo sufferers – slices through rocky crevices, and snakes around breathtaking precipices surrounded by small, wind-bent *quenual* trees and orchid bromeliads known locally as *weclla*. Well before reaching the lakes, at Km 19 you pass through the entrance to the **Huascarán National Park** (daily 6am–6pm; $1.50 for day visitors, or $20 for trekkers or mountaineers), located over 600m below the level of the lake; from here it's another thirty minutes or so by bus or truck to the lakes.

The first lake you come to after the park entrance is **Chinan Cocha**, named after a legendary princess. You can rent **rowing boats** by the car park here to venture onto the blue waters (80¢ for 15min), and, if you're hungry, take a picnic from the **food stalls** at the lakeside nearby. The road continues around Chinan Cocha's left bank and for a couple of kilometres on to the second lake, **Orcon Cocha**, named after a prince who fell in love with Chinan. The road ends here and a **loop trail**

▲ Huascarán icecap

begins (see below). A third, much smaller, lake was created between the two big ones, as a result of an avalanche caused by the 1970 earthquake, which also killed a group of hikers who were camped between the two lakes.

Immediately to the south of the lakes is the unmistakable sight of the massive **Huascarán icecap**, whose imposing peak tempts many people to make the difficult climb of 3km to the top. Surrounding Huascarán are scores of lesser, glaciated mountains that stretch for almost 200km and divide the Amazon Basin from the Pacific watershed.

Hiking in and around the Cordillera Blanca

There are many excellent **hikes** in the Cordillera Blanca, almost all of which require acclimatization to the rarefied mountain air, a certain degree of fitness, good camping equipment, plenty of food and good maps. Bear in mind that for some of the hikes you may need guides and mules to help carry the equipment at this altitude (see p.371). One of the most popular routes, the **Llanganuco to Santa Cruz Loop**, is a well-trodden trail offering spectacular scenery, some fine places to camp and a relatively easy walk that can be done in under a week, even by inexperienced hikers. There are shorter walks, such as the trails around the **Pitec Quebrada**, within easy distance of Huaraz, and a number of other loops like the **Llanganuco to Chancos** trek. Experienced hikers could also tackle the circular **Cordillera Huayhuash** route. Detailed information on all these walks is available from the South American Explorers' Club in Lima (see p.118), or, in Huaraz itself, from the Casa de Guías (see p.371), the tourist office (see p.360), or tour companies (see p.366). Below are outlines of two popular treks of differing grades.

The Llanganuco to Santa Cruz Loop

The **Llanganuco to Santa Cruz Loop** starts at the clearly marked track leading off from the end of the road along the left bank of Orcon Cocha. The entire trek

---

Mountain climbing in the Cordillera Blanca

To give a flavour of what you may expect from mountain climbing in the Cordillera Blanca, the **expeditions** below are some of the most popular among serious mountaineers. Remember to take a local guide if you do any of these; they're listed in increasing order of difficulty.

Climbs

Pisco One of the easier climbs, up to 5752m, this is a good way to cut your teeth in the Cordillera Blanca. Little more than a hard trek, really, with access via the Llanganuco Valley (3800m), with a duration of only three days. Rated easy to moderate.

Urus A two-day climb reaching heights of around 5500m; access is via Collon to Quebrada de Ishinca and it takes only two days. Rated easy to moderate for the peaks Ishinca and Urus; or moderate to difficult if you tackle Tocllaraju Mountain (6034m).

Alpamayo A serious and quite technical mountain rising to 5947m, and requiring good acclimatization on an easier climb first. Access is from Cashapampa (accessible by bus from Caraz), and it usually takes around eight or nine days. Rated as difficult.

Huascarán The south summit at 6768m is the classic route and really requires thorough acclimatization. Access is via Mancos (from where it's an hour by bus to the village of Musho), and it normally demands a good week to tackle effectively. Rated, not surprisingly, as difficult.

shouldn't take more than about five days for a healthy (and acclimatized) backpacker, but it's a perfect hike to take at your own pace. It's essential to carry all your food, camping equipment and, ideally, a medical kit and emergency survival bag. Along the route there are hundreds of potential campsites. The best time to attempt this trek is in the dry season, between April and October, unless you enjoy getting stuck in mud and being soaked to the skin.

From Orcon Cocha the main path climbs the Portachuelo de Llanganuco pass (4767m), before dropping to the enchanting beauty of the Quebrada Morococha (a *quebrada* is a river gully) through the tiny settlement of Vaqueria. From here you can go on to Colcabamba and Pomabamba, in the Callejón de Conchucos (though not in the rainy season, when you may well find yourself stranded), or continue on the loop back to the Callejón de Huaylas via Santa Cruz. The loop trail subsequently heads north from Vaqueria up the Quebrada Huaripampa, where you'll probably camp the first night. From here it goes around the icecap of Chacraraju (6000m) – a stupendous rocky canyon with a marshy bottom, snowy mountain peaks to the west and Cerro Mellairca to the east. On the third or fourth day, following the stream uphill, with the lakes of Morococha and Huiscash on your left, you pass down into the Pacific watershed along the Quebrada Santa Cruz, eventually emerging, after perhaps another night's rest, beside the calm waters of Lake Grande. Tracing the left bank and continuing down this perfect glacial valley for about another eight hours, you'll come to the village of **Cashapampa**, which has very basic accommodation. From here it's just a short step (about 2km) to the inviting and very hot (but temperature-controllable) thermal baths of Huancarhuaz (daily 8am–5pm; about $1), and there's a road or a more direct three-hour path across the low hills south to Caraz.

From Hualcayan to Pomabamba

The trek **from Hualcayan to Pomabamba** is one of the longest in the Cordillera Blanca and requires good acclimatization as well as fitness. It takes about a week to cover the route's total distance of around 78km – altitudes vary between 3100 and 4850m. You can get to Hualcayan (3100m) from Caraz by bus (1hr 45min), leaving from the corner of Grau with Santa Cruz, two or three times every morning. Campsites along the way include: Jamacuna (4050m), Osoruri (4550m), Jancanrurish (4200m); Huillca (4000m) and Yanacollpa (3850m). The trail terminates at the village of Pomabamba, where there are thermal baths, a basic hotel and buses back to Yungay.

Caraz and around

The attractive town of **CARAZ**, less than 20km down the Santa Valley from Yungay, sits at an altitude of 2285m, well below the enormous Huandoy Glacier. Mainly visited for the access it gives to a fantastic hiking hinterland, it is also well-known throughout Peru for its honey and milk products. Palm trees and flowers adorn a colonial-looking **Plaza de Armas**, which has survived well the ravages of several major eathquakes. A small daily **market**, three blocks north of the plaza, is usually vibrant with activity, good for fresh food, colourful basketry, traditional gourd bowls, religious candles and hats.

A couple of kilometres northeast of town along 28 de Julio, close to the Laguna Parón turn-off, lie the weathered ruins of **Tumshucaico**, probably the largest ruins in the Callejón de Hualyas. A possible ceremonial centre, dating from the formative period of 1800 BC, replete with galleries and worked stone walls, it may well also have had a defensive function given its dominating position overlooking

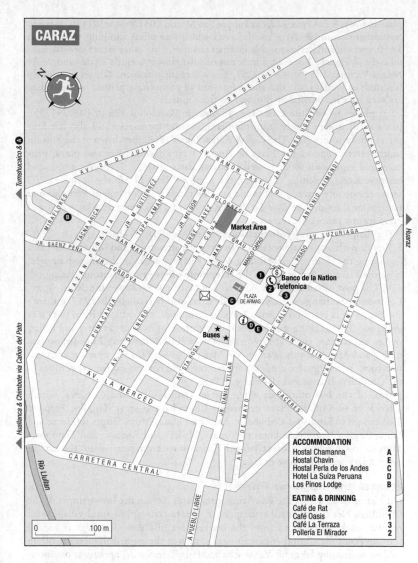

ACCOMMODATION

Hostal Chamanna	A
Hostal Chavin	E
Hostal Perla de los Andes	C
Hotel La Suiza Peruana	D
Los Pinos Lodge	B

EATING & DRINKING

Café de Rat	2
Café Oasis	1
Café La Terraza	3
Pollería El Mirador	2

the valley. These days its edges have been eaten away by the peri-urban growth of Caraz and the extension of local cultivated land.

One of the best **places to stay** is the modern *Hostal Perla de los Andes,* Plaza de Armas (☏043/392007; ❸–❹), with a marbled lobby completely out of character with the laid-back, quite rustic flavour of the rest of Caraz, and comfortable rooms with hot water, private bath and TV; it also has a very nice restaurant. Across the plaza, the attractive old *Hotel La Suiza Peruana,* at Jr San Martín 1133 (☏043/322166; ❸) has shared bathrooms and its own restaurant. Also near the plaza, the better organized and cleaner *Hostal Chavín*, Jr San Martín 1135 (☏043/391171; ❸), is good value and some rooms have private bath. The cheapest

place in town is *Los Pinos Lodge* at Parque San Martín 103 (T043/391130, Wwww
.apuaventura.com; ❶–❸, a youth hostel which also offers camping spaces from
$2.50 a person and has reasonable internet facilities. One other rather unusual hos-
tel is the 🌿 *Hostal Chamanna*, a little out of town down Avenida 28 de Julio, at Av
Nueva Victoria 185 (T043/689257, Wwww.chamanna.com; ❹), set in a lovely
labyrinth of gardens, streams and patios; not all rooms have private bath but they
are very stylish, adorned by distinctive ethnic murals.

For **places to eat**, the *Café Oasis*, Jr Antonio Raimondi 425 (T043/391785),
just a small stone's throw from the plaza, is good for snacks and also has four
pretty cheap rooms (❶). The *Café de Rat*, at Sucre 1266, just down at the bottom
southwestern edge of the Plaza de Armas, serves decent pasta and pizza, pancakes and vegetarian food, as well as having darts, maps, guidebooks, music and
internet access. Fronting the plaza, the nearby *Pollería El Mirador* at Sucre 1202
serves reasonably priced lunches and evening meals from a menu of Peruvian and
international food. The *Café La Terraza*, Jr Sucre 1106, serve snacks, pastas and
pizza from a panoramic terrace.

The helpful **tourist information** office (Mon–Sat 7.45am–1pm & 2.30–
5.30pm), with maps and brochures covering the attractions and some of the hikes
(including the relatively demanding 6–8hr Patapata walk) in the immediate area,
is on the Plaza de Armas, while the **telephone office** is at Jr Antonio Raimondi
410. The **post office** can be found on Jr San Martín 909 (Mon–Sat 8.30am–6pm).
For **money exchange** there's a Banco de Credito at Jr Daniel Villar 217 or there's
the Banco de la Nación on Jirón Antonio Raimondi, half a block from the Plaza
de Armas. For trekking **guides**, local information or help organizing and fitting
out an expedition, there are two excellent local options: Pony Expeditions (see
p.367) and Apu Aventura, Parque San Martin (T043/392159, Wwww.apuaven-
tura.com), who organize guides, porters, cooks and equipment for expeditions in
the Cordillera Blanca and elsewhere in Peru.

Most of the **bus** offices are along jirones Daniel Villar and Cordova, within
a block or two of the Plaza de Armas: Chinachasuyo serve Trujillo; Empresa
Turismo go to Lima and Chimbote; Ancash to Lima; Movil Tours to Huraz and
Lima; Region Norte runs buses to Yungay, Huaraz and Recuay; and Transporte
Moreno to Chimbote. **Colectivos** for Huaraz leave from just behind the market
every thirty minutes, more or less.

Huata and Laguna Parón

Nine kilometres across the Río Santa from Caraz, set on the lower slopes of the
Cordillera Negra, the small settlement of **Huata** is a typical rural village with
regular truck connections from the market area in Caraz. It serves as a good
starting point for a number of easy walks, such as the eight-kilometre stroll up
to the unassuming lakes of Yanacocha and Huaytacocha or, perhaps more interesting, north about 5km along a path up Cerro Muchanacoc to the small Inca
ruins of Cantu. It's possible to camp around Huata if you ask permission from a
local family, but Caraz is pretty close by with facilities for sleeping and eating,
so it's rare anyone will camp here.

Some 30km, more or less, east of Caraz, the deep-blue **Laguna Parón** (4185m)
is sunk resplendently into a gigantic glacial cirque, hemmed in on three sides by
some of the Cordillera Blanca's highest icecaps. There's a mountain refuge (a basic
hut open to anyone to shelter from the night or bad weather) at the lake, run by the
private company that operates the electricity plant at Huallanca; but there are only
basic facilities available (toilet and hot water). It's always open for access, however,

since two guards (one a radio operator) live there. Camping is possible at the refuge or on the east side of the lake, to which there's a clear path on the north bank.

Buses and **colectivos** (4.50am & 1pm; $1.25) travel from Caraz market up to Pueblo Parón, from where it's a hike of 9km (3hr) up to the lake. The last transport back from Pueblo Parón to Caraz is usually at 2.30pm. **Taxis** to the lake (about $12 per person) can be found most days from the Plaza de Armas in Caraz.

The Cañon del Pato

One of Peru's most exciting roads runs north from Caraz to Huallanca, squeezing through the spectacular **Cañon del Pato** (Duck's Canyon). An enormous rocky gorge cut from solid rock, its impressive path curves around the Cordillera Negra for most of the 50km between Caraz and Huallanca. Sheer cliff faces rise thousands of metres on either side while the road passes through some 39 tunnels – an average of one every kilometre. Situated within the canyon is one of Peru's most important hydroelectric power plants; the heart of these works, invisible from the road, is buried 600m deep in the cliff wall. Unfortunately, the road is often closed for a number of reasons – causes include terrorists, bandits, landslides in the rainy season or just the sheer poor quality of the road surface. Much of the first section has been improved in recent years, but from Huallanca to Chimbote it's more like a dry riverbed than a dirt track. Check with the tourist office in Huaraz and local bus companies (see p.367) about the physical and political condition of the road before attempting this journey.

At the end of the canyon the first village you come to is Huallanca, reached by daily **buses** (see p.367) from Huaraz (9am–6.30pm). From here, it's 8km on to Yuramarca where you can either branch off west along an alternative road to Chimbote (another 140km) on the coast, or continue along the valley to Corongo and the Callejón de Conchucos.

The Callejón de Conchucos and Chavín de Huantar

To the east of the Cordillera Blanca, roughly parallel to the Callejón de Huaylas, runs another long natural corridor, the **Callejón de Conchucos**. Virtually inaccessible in the wet season, and off the beaten track even for the most hardened of backpackers, the valley represents quite a challenge, and while it features the town of **Pomabamba** in the north and the spectacular ruins at **Chavín de Huantar** just beyond its southern limit, there's little of interest between the two. The villages of Piscobamba (Valley or Plain of the Birds) and Huari are likely to appeal only as food stops on the long haul (141km) through barren mountains between Pomabamba and Chavín. This is one of the few regions of Peru where bus drivers sometimes allow passengers to lounge around on the roof as they career along precipitous mountain roads, plummeting into each steep drop of the dusty road – an electrifying experience with the added bonus of a 360-degree, ever-changing view.

The Callejón de Conchucos was out of bounds to travellers between 1988 and 1993, when it was under almost complete Sendero Luminoso terrorist control; many of the locals were forced to flee the valley after actual or threatened violence from the terrorists. The region's more distant history was equally turbulent and cut off from the rest of Peru, particularly from the seat of colonial and Republican power on the coast. Until the Conquest, this region was home to one of the fiercest ancient tribes – the Conchucos – who surged down the Santa Valley and besieged the Spanish city of Trujillo in 1536. By the end of the sixteenth century, however, even the fearless Conchuco warriors had been reduced to virtual slavery by the colonial *encomendero* system.

Pomabamba

The small town of **POMABAMBA**, 3000m up in dauntingly hilly countryside, is surrounded by little-known archaeological remains that display common roots with Chavín de Huantar. Today the town makes an excellent trekking base; from here you can connect with the Llanganuco to Santa Cruz Loop (see p.377) by following tracks southwest to either Colcabamba or Punta Unión; alternatively, for a hard day's hike above Pomabamba, you can walk up to the stone remains of Yaino, an immense fortress of megalithic rock. On a clear day you can just about make out this site from the Plaza de Armas in Pomabamba; it appears as a tiny rocky outcrop high on the distant horizon. The climb takes longer than you may imagine, but locals will point out short cuts along the way. The area also abounds in little-explored ruins; try Pony Expeditions in Caraz (see p.367) for further information on these, as well as maps, equipment and advice on trekking in this region.

Practicalities

Direct Empresa Los Andes **buses** leaves from the Plaza de Armas in Yungay at 8.30–9am, while Turismo Huaraz in Huaraz (see p.367) go to Piscobamba and Pomabamba. Alternatively, you can get here from Huaraz via Chavín, on a bus from Lima that comes north up the Callejón de Conchucos more or less every other day. Pomabamba has a few small **places to stay**, the friendliest being the *Hostal Estrada Vidal* (☎043/804615 or 751048; ❷), one block from the plaza at C Huaraz 209; the others are more basic, including the cheaper *Hostal Pomabamba* (☎043/751276; ❶) just off the Plaza de ≠. If **camping** then it's always best to consult with the locals for good spots.

Chavín de Huantar

Only 30km southeast of Huari, or a three- to four-hour journey from Huaraz, the magnificent temple complex of **CHAVÍN DE HUANTAR** is the most important site associated with the Chavín cult (see box, p.385), and although partially destroyed by earthquakes, floods and erosion from the Río Mosna, enough of the ruins survive to make them a fascinating sight and one of *the* most important ones in Peru's pre-history. The religious cult that inspired Chavín's construction also influenced subsequent cultural development throughout Peru, right up until the Spanish Conquest some 2500 years later, and the temple complex of Chavín de Huantar is equal in importance, if not grandeur, to most of the sites around Cusco.

Getting there

The vast majority of people approach the temple complex **from Huaraz**. Empresa Condor de Chavín, Empresa Huascarán, Chavín Express and Empresa Sandoval **buses** leave Huaraz daily around 10am ($4.50; 3–4hr) for Chavín (see p.367 for bus company details), while all the tour companies in Huaraz (see p.366) offer a slightly faster, though more expensive, service ($12–18; 3hr). The buses turn off the main Huaraz to Lima road at the town of Catac, and take a poorly maintained road that crosses over the small Río Yana Yacu (Black Water River). It then starts

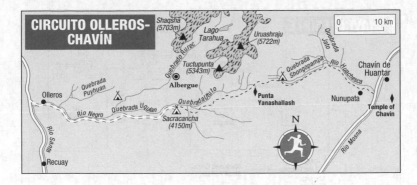

climbing to the beautiful Lake of Querococha (*quero* is Quechua for "teeth", and relates to the teeth-like rock formation visible nearby), which looks towards two prominent mountain peaks – Yanamarey and Pucaraju ("Red Glacier" in Quechua). From here the road, little more than a track now, climbs further before passing through the Tunél de Cahuish, which cuts through the solid rock of a mountain to emerge in the Callejón de Conchucos, to some spectacular but quite terrifying views. A couple of the more dangerous and precipitous curves in the road are known as the Curva del Diablo and Salvate Si Puedes ("Save yourself if you can"), from which you can deduce that this journey isn't for the squeamish or for vertigo sufferers.

An even more adventurous way to reach Chavín is by following the two- to four-day trail over the hills **from Olleros**. **Colectivos** leave daily every thirty minutes from the end of Jirón Caceres in Huaraz, for Olleros ($1.25), from where the hike is fairly simple and clearly marked all the way. It follows the Río Negro up to Punta Yanashallash (4700m), cuts down into the Marañón watershed along the Quebrada Shongopampa, and where this meets the Jato stream coming from the north, the route follows the combined waters (from here known as the Río Huachesca) straight down, southwest to the Chavín ruins another 1500m below. It's quite a **hike**, so take maps and ideally a guide and pack-llamas (see p.371). A good account of this walk is given in Hilary Bradt's *Backpacking and Trekking in Peru and Bolivia* (see p.627), while the South American Explorers' Club in Lima (see p.118) can give advice and information about it.

The temple complex

The magnificent temple complex of **Chavín de Huántar** and its **Sala de Exposición** (daily 9am–5pm; about $4; ☎043/754042) are a must for anyone even vaguely interested in Peruvian archeology. Though the onsite Sala de Exposición features ceramics, textiles and stone relating to the cultural influences of Chavín, Huaras, Recuay and Huari, it is the **Chavín culture** that evolved and elaborated its own brand of religious cultism on and around this magnificent site during the first millennium BC.

Located on a wide valley floor some 100km south east of Huaraz, the original temple was built here around 900 BC, though it was not until around 400 BC that the complex was substantially enlarged and its cultural style fixed. Some archaeologists claim that the specific layout of the temple, a U-shaped ceremonial courtyard facing east and based around a raised stone platform, was directly influenced by what was, in 1200 BC, the largest architectural monument in the New World, at

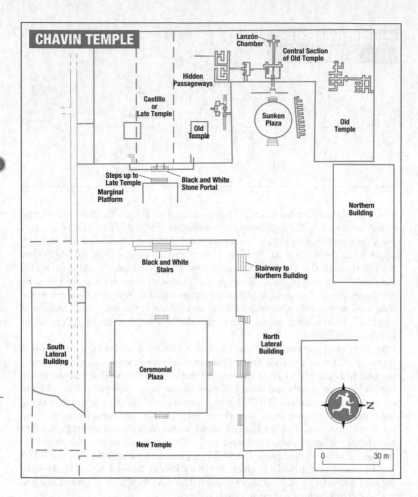

CHAVIN TEMPLE

Lanzón Chamber

Central Section of Old Temple

Hidden Passageways

Castillo or Late Temple

Old Temple

Lanzón Chamber

Sunken Plaza

Old Temple

Steps up to Late Temple

Black and White Stone Portal

Marginal Platform

Northern Building

Black and White Stairs

Stairway to Northern Building

South Lateral Building

Ceremonial Plaza

North Lateral Building

New Temple

N

0   30 m

Sechin Alto (see p.354). By 300 BC, Sechin Alto had been abandoned and Chavín was at the height of its power and one of the world's largest religious centres, with about three thousand resident priests and temple attendants. The U-shaped temples were probably dedicated to powerful mountain spirits or deities, who controlled meteorological phenomena, in particular rainfall, vital to the survival and wealth of the people.

The complex's main building consists of a central rectangular block with two wings projecting out to the east. The large, southern wing, known as the **Castillo**, is the most conspicuous feature of the site: massive, almost pyramid shaped, the platform was built of dressed stone with gargoyles attached, though few remain now.

Some way in front of the Castillo, down three main flights of steps, the **Plaza Hundida**, or sunken plaza, covers about 250 square metres with a rectangular, stepped platform to either side. Here, the thousands of pilgrims thought to have worshipped at Chavín would gather during the appropriate fiestas. And it was here that the famous Tello Obelisk now in the Archaeological and Anthropologi-

The Chavín cult

The **Chavín cult**, whose iconography spread across much of Peru, had a strong impact on the Paracas culture and later on the Nasca and Mochica civilizations. Regional differences suggest it was not a coherent pan-Peruvian religion, but more of a widespread – and unevenly interpreted – cult of the feline god. Theories as to the origin of its inspiration range from extraterrestrial intervention to the more likely infiltration of ideas and individuals or entire tribes from Central America. There is a resemblance between the ceramics found at Chavín and those of a similar date from Tlatilco in Mexico, yet there are no comparable Mexican stone constructions as ancient as these Peruvian wonders. More probable, and the theory expounded by Julio Tello, is that the cult initially came up into the Andes (then down to the coast) from the Amazon Basin via the Marañón Valley. The inspiration for the beliefs themselves, which appear to be in the power of totemic or animistic gods and demons, may well have come from visionary experiences sparked by the ingestion of **hallucinogens**: one of the stone reliefs at Chavín portrays a feline deity or fanged warrior holding a section of the psychotropic mescalin cactus San Pedro (see p.584), still used by *curanderos* today for the invocation of the spirit world. This feline deity was almost certainly associated with the shamanic practice of transformation from human into animal form for magical and healing purposes; the most powerful animal form that could be assumed, of course, was the big cat, whether a puma or a jaguar.

Most theories about the **iconography** of these stone slabs, all of which are very intricate, distinctive in style and highly abstract, agree that the Chavín people worshipped three major gods: the moon (represented by a fish), the sun (depicted as an eagle or a hawk) and an overlord, or creator divinity, normally shown as a fanged cat, possibly a jaguar. It seems very likely that each god was linked with a distinct level of the Chavín cosmos: the fish with the underworld, the eagle with the celestial forces and the cat with earthly power. This is only a calculated guess, and ethnographic evidence from the Amazon Basin suggests that each of these main gods may have also been associated with a different subgroup within the Chavín tribe or priesthood as a whole.

Chavín itself may or may not have been the centre of the movement, but it was obviously at the very least an outstanding ceremonial focus for what was an early agricultural society, thriving on relatively recently domesticated foods as well as cotton, and well-positioned topographically to control the exchange of plants, materials and ideas between communities in the Amazon, Andes and Pacific coast. The name of Chavín comes from the Quechua *chaupin*, meaning navel or focal point, and the complex might have been a sacred shrine to which natives flocked in pilgrimage during festivals, much as they do today, visiting important *huacas* in the sierra at specific times in the annual agricultural cycle. The appearance of the Orion constellation on Chavín carvings fits this theory, since it appears on the skyline just prior to the traditional harvest period in the Peruvian mountains.

cal Museum in Lima (see p.95) was found, next to an altar in the shape of a jaguar and bedecked with seven cavities forming a pattern similar to that of the Orion constellation.

Standing in the Plaza Hundida, facing towards the Castillo, you'll see on your right the **original temple**, now just a palatial ruin dwarfed by the neighbouring Castillo. It was first examined by Julio Tello in 1919 when it was still buried under cultivated fields; during 1945 a vast flood reburied most of it and the place was damaged again by the 1970 earthquake and the rains of 1983. Among the fascinating recent finds from the area are bone snuff tubes, beads, pendants, needles, ceremonial shells (imported from Ecuador) and some quartz crystals associated with ritual sites. One quartz crystal covered in red pigment was found in a grave, placed after death in the mouth of the deceased.

▲ Subterranean sculpture, Chavín de Huantar

Behind the original temple, two entrances lead to **underground passages**. The one on the right leads down to an underground chamber, containing the awe-inspiring Lanzon, a prism-shaped 4.53m block of carved white granite that tapers down from a broad feline head to a point stuck in the ground. The entrance on the left takes you into the labyrinthine inner chambers, which run underneath the Castillo on several levels connected by ramps and steps. In the seven major subterranean rooms, you'll need a torch to get a decent look at the carvings and the granite sculptures (even when the electric lighting is switched on), while all around you can hear the sound of water dripping. Another large stone slab discovered at Chavín in 1873 – the Estela Raymondi, also now in the Archaeological and Anthropological Museum – was the first of all the impressive carved stones to be found. The most vivid of the carvings remaining at the site are the **gargoyles** (known as Cabeza Clavos), guardians of the temple that again display feline and bird-like characteristics.

The pretty village of **Chavín de Huantar**, with its whitewashed walls and traditional tiled roofs, is just a couple of hundred metres from the ruins and has a reasonable supply of basic amenities. The best **accommodation** can be found at the *Hotel Inca Wiracocha* 170 (☎01/5742735 and 043/454021; ❸) which has small well-kept gardens and a very friendly atmosphere; close by, *La Casona,* at Wiracocha 130 (☎043/754048 or 754020; ❷–❸), next door to the town hall on the plaza offers private bathrooms and has a pleasant patio. The *Hostal Chavín* (☎043/454055; ❸) at Inca Roca 141 has comfortable, quiet rooms. Out of town, on the Fundo Cocao some 10km north on the upper banks of the Mosna river, the *Konchukos Tambo Hotel* (☎043/454631; ⓦwww.konchukostambo.com; ❻–❼) offers archaeological and educational tours as well as day hikes; contact in advance to help with transfers. It's also sometimes possible to **camp** by the Baños Quercos thermal springs (ask for update at the Huaraz Tourist Office, tour agencies or in Chavín town), 2km up the valley and a twenty minute-stroll from the village.

For **places to eat** the *Restaurant Chavín Turístico*, C 17 de Enero Sur 439, or the *Restaurant La Ramada*, a few doors further up the same road at no. 577 are both central; but there are others on the same street, like *La Portada*, which are equally as welcoming and serve simple food like soups, meat and rice.

Getting back to Huaraz or Catac, there are **buses** daily from Chavín, more or less on the hour from 3 to 6pm. There's a post and telephone office at C 17 de Enero 365 (6.30am–10pm), plus a small tourist information office on the corner of the Plaza de Armas, next to the market, though it doesn't have regular hours.

North from Chavín

Some 8km north of Chavín is the lovely village of **San Marcos**, a good base for mountain hiking. There are buses every hour from Chavín, or you can walk there in well under two hours. **Accommodation** is available at the *Casa del Señor Luis Alfaro* (❷), though it's a good idea to take a tent just in case all rooms are full. From San Marcos you can climb up another 300m in altitude to the smaller community of Carhuayoc, a 100-year-old village whose population specialize in the production of fine textiles, mainly blankets and rugs (it's a 9hr return jourrney). About 35km from San Marcos, the town of Huari is a good base for a short trek to the scenic Lago Purhuay; it's only 8km from the town and a climb of some 400m, but it usually takes between five and six hours to get there and back. To continue on to Pomabamba from Huari, there are buses every other day, usually leaving at 9pm ($6–7, a 7hr journey).

Cordillera Huayhuash

To the south of Huaraz, the **CORDILLERA HUAYHUASH** offers much less frequented but just as stunning trekking trails as those in the Cordillera Blanca. Most treks start in the small town of **Chiquián**, 2400m above sea level. The most popular trekking route has two options: one for fourteen days, and the second for sixteen days, both of them leaving Chiquián heading for Llamac and the entire cordillera loop (see box p.388).

There are, of course, easier routes, one of which is briefly described below. The mountains here, although slightly lower than the Cordillera Blanca and covering a much smaller area, nevertheless rise breathtakingly to 6634m at the

One of the least-visited and most difficult trails of its kind worldwide, this covers a distance of 164–186km and takes some fourteen days to hike (give or take a couple, depending on your fitness, walking ability and desire), the **Chiquián Loop** lies at altitudes between 2750m and 5000m. Rated as Class 4 (difficult), as the name suggests, the Chiquián Loop starts and finishes in Chiquián; note that maps are essential and local guides with mules advisable.

Route description
Day 1: Chiquián–Llamac
This is an easy first-day walk. The wide and clearly marked path takes hikers to the far end of the valley. After crossing three times from one valley to the other, a short way up will lead walkers to Llamac, a typical highland village.
Day 2: Llamac–Matacancha
A two-hour descent leads hikers to another little Andean village called Pocpa, from where walkers must take the left bank of the river and start climbing to the campsite. The first mountain that appears on the way is the Ninashanca at 5607m (18,391ft). The camping spot is found almost at the far end of this dry and treeless valley.
Day 3: Matacancha–Janca
The first ascent to the Cacananpunta Pass at 4880m (16,006ft) is difficult and must be reached before midday. The first part of this trek culminates with the end of the ascent and the arrival at the highest point, although the descent to the camp does not require a major effort.
Day 4: Janca–Carhuacocha Lake
This day involves significant trekking up and back down, offering views of almost the entire scenery of the Cordillera Huayhuash. Arriving at the lakeside camp, the majestic Cordillera Huayhuash is clearly visible.
Day 5: Carhuacocha Lake–Carnicero
The next pass opens out to Carnicero Valley. A not very steep and beautiful climb takes the hiker to the Rinconada, where the pass forms visually spectacular rocky scenery approximately 300m (984ft) long.

Nevada Yerupajá, some 50km southeast of Chiquián as the crow flies. Yerupajá actually forms the watershed between the Cordillera Huayhuash to the north and the lower-altitude Cordillera Raura to the south. Large and stunning lakes, flocks of alpaca, herds of cattle and some sheep can be seen along the way. High levels of fitness and some experience are required for hiking or climbing in this region and it's always best to tackle it as part of a team, or at least to have a local guide along. The guide will help to avoid the rather irritating dogs that look after the animals in these remote hills and his presence will also provide protection against the possible, but unlikely, threat of robbery. After the town of Chiquián, it's virtually impossible to buy food, so it's a good idea to get most of this in Huaraz or in Lima before arriving, just supplementing with extras such as bread, dry biscuits, dairy products (including good local cheeses), rice and pasta when you arrive here.

One popular Huayhuash trek from Chiquián follows a route to **Llamac-Pampa de Llamac** (a very difficult pass), then on to **Jahuacocha Lake**, where trout fishing is possible. Taking about five days, the scenery on the trek can only be described as breathtaking, the hiking itself as quite hard. The only downside is that you have to walk Chiquián–Llamac twice, and between Rondoy and Llamac a mining company has destroyed much of the beautiful countryside, apparently also polluting the river as well as building a rather ugly road. Most people who come this far, though, prefer

Day 6: Carnicero–Huayhuash–Altuspata
The descent continues to the next valley. One can see several small lakes and rivers along the way.
Day 7: Altuspata–Viconga Lake
The ascent continues towards the pass, which leads the way to Viconga. Walking around the lake through the narrow valley one can reach the next camping spot.
Day 8: Viconga Lake–Huanacpatay
A very long way and one of the toughest hikes on the route, this is where one crosses the Cuyoc Pass at 5100m (16,728ft) next to Mount Cuyoc and close to Puscanturpa at 5442m (17,854ft). Descending from the pass, a small, steep, and difficult corridor leads to the Huanacpatay Valley.
Days 9 and 10: Two days must be set aside for climbing two of the peaks around the Diablo Mudo Pass.
Day 11: Huanacpatay–Huatiac
Another long trekking day. After a deep descent into the endless valley of the Huallapa River one starts seeing trees and plants, with the trail passing close by Huallapa village.
Day 12 : Huatiac–Jahuacocha Lake
The climb continues up to Diablo Mudo Pass at 5000m (16,400ft), an area bereft of plant life. Everything is downhill from the pass until Lake Jahuacocha and past it to the beautiful Cordillera Huayhuash campsite beside this lake.
Day 13: Jahuacocha Lake–Llamac
After almost two weeks the path crosses again into Llamac village. There are two paths from Jahuacocha which lead back to Llamac's campsite, one is direct and very steep and is done in a shorter time, while the second one is longer but with no major or sudden descents.
Day 14: Llamac–Chiquián–Huaraz
A repeat of this stretch, which was the first day's hike: a tough, but marvellous trek through the Cordillera Huayhuash.

to do the Chiquián Loop (see box p.388), which entails a tough couple of weeks, though the really fit might manage it in ten days at a push.

Practicalities

Chiquián is easily reached by **bus** with Empresa Rapido, Mariscal Caceres 312 (☏044/426437) from Huaraz (3hr) who run about six buses daily. There are a few basic **hostels** in Chiquián, one of the best being *San Miguel*, Jr Comercio 233 (☏043/747001; ❶–❷), which has reasonably clean and comfortable beds and a nice little garden. The *Hotel Los Nogales*, Jr Comercio 1301 (☏043/747001, ⒺΗοtel_nogales_chiquian@yahoo.com.pe; ❷–❸) is a reasonable alternative with a choice of rooms with or without private bath and TV.

Only simple food is available in the settlement's two or three **restaurants**, with *El Refugio de Bolognesi*, at Tarapaca 471, offering perhaps the best set-lunch menus. In late August and early September there are some colourful **fiestas** in the town, for the Virgen de Santa Rosa, during the last day of which there is always a **bullfight** with the local football stadium being transformed into an arena. The aim of the game is, as with most rural Peruvian bullfights, just to play with the bull (without hurting him) and this is done not only by the toreador, but by anyone who feels the urge to become a toreador (local youth, drunk men); they can challenge the bull with their poncho, which guarantees a lot of excitement and fun, with the public scattering when the irritated bull comes too close.

Travel details

Buses and colectivos

Barranca to: Casma (6 daily; 2hr); Chimbote (12 daily; 3hr); Huaraz (10–12 daily; 5hr); Lima (16 daily; 3hr).

Caraz to: Chimbote (2 daily; 6–7hr); Huaraz (10 or more daily; 1–2hr).

Chimbote to: Caraz (2 daily; 6–7hr); Huaraz (8–10 daily; 8hr); Lima (12 daily; 6–8hr); Trujillo (12 daily; 3hr).

Huaraz to: Casma (6 daily; 6hr); Chavín (4 daily; 3–4hr); Chimbote (8–10 daily; 7–8hr); Chiquián (4 daily; 3–4hr); Lima (10 daily; 8hr); Trujillo (3 daily; 8–10hr).

Flights

Chimbote to: Lima (1 daily; 1hr); Trujillo (1 daily; 1hr).

Huaraz to: Lima (occasional air taxi service; 35–45min).

Trujillo and the North

CHAPTER 7 # Highlights

✳ **Chan Chan** Located by the ocean near the city of Trujillo, this massive adobe city was built by the Chimu culture in the thirteenth century. See p.409

✳ **Kuelap** Way off the beaten track, this majestic mountaintop citadel rivals Machu Picchu for its setting and archaeological interest. See p.435

✳ **Batán Grande** On the eastern edge of the Americas' largest dry forest, and right next to the beautiful Río de la Leche, twenty-eighth- to eleventh-century pyramids stand as an impressive monument to the ceremonial heart of Sicán culture. See p.451

✳ **Museo de las Tumbas** An excellent museum whose exhibits include precious objects of gold and silver, as well as a replica of the royal tomb of the Lord of Sipán. See p.452

✳ **Valley of the Pyramids** Standing in the hot dry desert of northern Peru is this magnificent collection of adobe pyramids from the Sicán culture, dating around 1100 AD. See p.453

✳ **Máncora beach** Peru's most trendy beach and surf resort, Mˆncora has warm water, strong sunshine and hot nightlife. See p.471

▲ Adobe relief detail, Chan Chan

Trujillo and the North

hough very remote and little visited, the northern reaches of Peru possess unique treasures in culture, archaeology and natural environment; this fascinating region definitely rewards anyone who has the time to explore it. At least part of this region's appeal is that it is visited by fewer tourists than Southern Peru, but, additionally, it has a real wealth of archaeological heritage and better coastal weather than Lima or the South, particularly during the high season (May to September). It's an immensely varied corner of the country, ranging from welcoming city oases along the desert coast to secluded villages in the Andes where you may well be the first foreigner to pass through for years. On top of this, the entire area is brimming with imposing and important pre-Inca sites, some of them only discovered in the last decade or two.

Trujillo is one of the country's little-visited jewels, located on the seaward edge of the vast desert plain at the mouth of the Moche Valley. Its attraction lies mainly in its nearby ruins – notably **Chan Chan** and the huge, sacred pyramids of the **Huaca del Sol** and **Huaca de la Luna** – but also partly in the city itself, and excellent outlying beach communities. **Huanchaco**, only 12km from Trujillo, is a good case in point, essentially a fishing village and a likeable resort within walking distance of sandy beaches and massive ancient ruins.

The northern desert coast beyond Trujillo offers a wide variety of other towns and equally amazing sites. Known as the **Circuito Nororiental** (North-Eastern Circuit), this whole region, including Trujillo, the archaeological sites around Chiclayo, the beaches between Piura and Tumbes, plus the big loop east to Chachapoyas, Kuelap and also Cajamarca high up in the Andes, is almost a country in its own right and is a great alternative to the usual Nasca–Arequipa–Cusco route.

There are established bus **touring routes** through the Andean region above Trujillo, all of which present the option of winding through the beautifully situated mountain town of **Cajamarca** as a nodal focus. It was here that Pizarro first encountered and captured the Inca Emperor Atahualpa, beginning the Spanish conquest of Peru. Around the modern city are a number of fascinating Inca ruins, many of which are linked together through a system of canals that were used for sacred as well as practical purposes. Cajamarca is also one of the springboards for visiting the smaller town of **Chachapoyas** and the ruined citadel complex of **Kuelap**, arguably the single most overwhelming pre-Columbian site in Peru. Beyond, there are possible routes down to Amazon headwaters and the jungle towns of **Tarapoto** and even **Iquitos** – long and arduous journeys, but well worth it if you have the time, enthusiasm and necessary equipment. Another more adventurous bus route back to Trujillo from Cajamarca (or vice versa) goes via the old colonial outpost of **Huamachuco**; and, with INRENA permission (see p.67), the right equipment and a local guide, you can even make an expedition to the remote

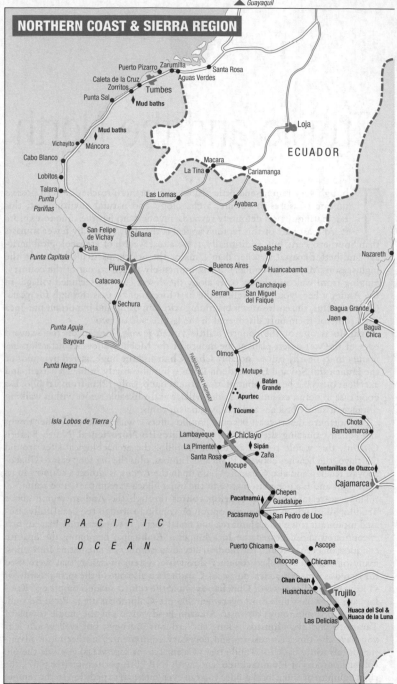

NORTHERN COAST & SIERRA REGION

Guayaquil

Puerto Pizarro
Zarumilla
Santa Rosa
Caleta de la Cruz
Aguas Verdes
Zorritos
Tumbes
Punta Sal
Mud baths

Mud baths

Loja

ECUADOR

Vichayito
Máncora
Cabo Blanco
Lobitos
Macara
Talara
La Tina
Cariamanga
Punta Pariñas

Las Lomas
Ayabaca

Nazareth

San Felipe de Vichay
Sullana
Punta Capitala
Paita
Piura
Sapalache
Catacaos
Buenos Aires
Huancabamba
Serran
Canchaque
Sechura
San Miguel del Faique

Bagua Grande
Jaen
Bagua Chica

Punta Aguja
Bayovar

Olmos

Punta Negra

Motupe

Batán Grande

Apurtec

Túcume

Chota
Bambamarca

Isla Lobos de Tierra

Lambayeque
Chiclayo
La Pimentel
Sipán
Santa Rosa
Zaña
Mocupe

Ventanillas de Otuzco

Cajamarca

PACIFIC

Chepen
Guadalupe
Pacatnamú
Pacasmayo
San Pedro de Lloc

OCEAN

Puerto Chicama
Ascope
Chocope
Chicama

Chan Chan
Huanchaco
Trujillo
Moche
Huaca del Sol & Huaca de la Luna
Las Delicias

PANAMERICAN HIGHWAY

Lima

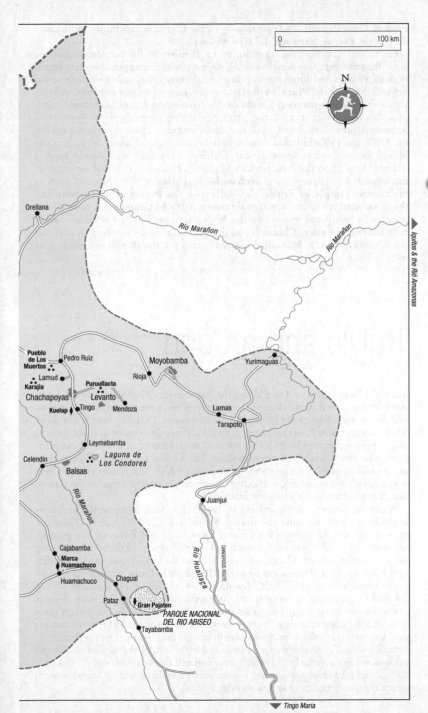

ruins of **Gran Pajaten**, a site pertaining to the Chachapoyas culture and located deep in the **Parque Nacional del Río Abiseo**.

The coastal strip north of Trujillo, up to **Tumbes** by the Ecuadorian border, is for the most part a seemingly endless desert plain, interrupted by a few small, isolated villages and some new squatter settlements, but only two substantial towns, **Chiclayo** and **Piura**. In the last twenty years or so, just outside Chiclayo, archaeologists have uncovered some of the coast's most important temple ruins, pyramids and nobles' tombs, the latter containing a wealth of precious metal ceremonial items associated with the Sicán culture. These discoveries during the 1980s and 1990s initiated some excellent new regional museums such as the Museo de las Tumbas, located near Chiclayo. You may well decide to pass straight through on the Panamerican Highway, but you'd miss out on some of the most vivid and important **archaeological sites** in the Americas, such as the ancient **Temple of Sipán**, the **Valley of the Pyramids** at **Túcume** and the ceremonial centre and ecological reserve at **Batán Grande**. There are also a couple of adventurous routes into the Andes, and, perhaps best of all, a number of beach resorts, such as **Chicama** and the warm seas of the hottest new surf and beach scene in Peru at **Máncora**, located between Cabo Blanco and the border with Ecuador.

Trujillo and around

Just eight hours north of Lima along the Panamerican Highway, **Trujillo** looks every bit the oasis it is, standing in a relatively green, irrigated valley bounded by arid desert at the foot of the brown Andes mountains. Despite a long tradition of leftist politics, today Peru's northern capital only sees the occasional street protest, and is more recognized by its lavish colonial architecture and colourful old mansions. The city is lively and cosmopolitan, but known for its friendly citizenry and is small enough to get to know in a couple of days. The coastal **climate** here is ideal, as it's warm and dry without the fog you get around Lima, or the intense heat characteristic of the northern deserts.

One of the main reasons for coming to Trujillo is to visit the numerous **archaeological sites** dotted around the nearby Moche and Chicama valleys. There are three main areas of interest within easy reach, first and foremost the gigantic adobe city of **Chan Chan** on the northern edge of town. To the south, standing alone beneath the Cerro Blanco hill, you can find the largest mud-brick pyramids in the Americas, the **Huaca del Sol** and **Huaca de la Luna**, while further away to the north of Trujillo, in the **Chicama Valley**, the incredible remnants of vast pre-Inca irrigation canals, temples and early settlement sites stand in stark contrast to the massive, green sugar-cane plantations of the haciendas. In many ways these sites are more impressive than the ruins around Cusco – and most are more ancient too. Vast urban as well as religious architectural complexes define pre-Inca construction here. The pyramids, courtyards and high walls of the various sites are all constructed from adobe bricks which have suffered from the occasional rains over the last eight hundred years or so, consequently requiring a little imagination to mentally reconstruct them as you wander around.

Trujillo

The heart of **TRUJILLO** comprises some twenty blocks of colonial-style architecture all focused around a wide main plaza. Radiating from here, the buildings get steadily more modern and less attractive. In the heat of summer, between December and March, the populace are most busy in the mornings, with the central market, offices and banks acting as the hives of activity. In the evenings, when things cool down, the restaurants and clubs take their turn to come alive. Trujillo is famous for its traditional dances, like the *marinera*, but the younger folk are equally into Latin pop, salsa and rap music.

It may not have the international flavour of Lima or the diversity of culture or race, but its citizens are very proud of their history, and the local university is well respected, especially when it comes to archaeology. One or two of the surrounding communities, which make their living from fishing or agriculture, are also renowned across Peru for their traditional healing arts, usually based on *curanderos* who use the coastal hallucinogenic cactus, San Pedro, for diagnosing and sometimes curing their patients.

Some history

On his second voyage to Peru in 1528, **Pizarro** sailed by the site of ancient Chan Chan, at that point still a major city and an important regional centre of Inca rule. He returned to establish a Spanish colony in the same valley, naming it Trujillo in December 1534 after his birthplace in Extremadura. In 1536, the town was besieged by the Inca Manco's forces during the second rebellion against the conquistadors. Many thousands of Conchuco Indian warriors, allied with the Incas, swarmed down to Trujillo, killing Spaniards and collaborators on the way and offering their victims to Catequil, the tribal deity. After surviving this attack, Trujillo grew to become the main port of call for the Spanish treasure fleets, sailors wining and dining here on their way between Lima and Panama. By the seventeenth century it was a walled city of some three thousand houses covering three square miles. The only sections of those walls that remain are the **Herrera rampart** and a small piece of the facade on Avenida España.

Trujillo continued to be a centre of popular rebellion, declaring its independence from Spain in the Plaza de Armas in 1820, long before the Liberators arrived. The enigmatic APRA (American Popular Revolutionary Alliance, see p.568) leader, **Haya de la Torre**, was born here in 1895, and ran for president, after years of struggle, in the elections of 1931. The dictator, Sanchez Cerro, however, counted the votes, (unfairly, some believe), and declared himself the winner. APRA was outlawed and Haya de la Torre imprisoned, provoking Trujillo's middle classes to stage an uprising. Over one thousand deaths resulted, many of them APRA supporters, who were taken out to the fields of Chan Chan by the truckload and shot. Even now, the 1932 massacre resonates amongst the people of Trujillo, particularly the old APRA members and the army, and you can still see each neighbourhood declaring its allegiance in graffiti to one side or the other.

APRA failed to attain political power in Peru for another 54 years, when Alan Garcia was President for the first time; but it was the revolutionary military government in 1969 that truly unshackled this region from the tight grip of a few **sugar barons**, who owned the enormous haciendas in the Chicama Valley. The haciendas were then divided up among the worker co-operatives – the Casa Grande, a showcase example, is now one of the most profitable and well-organized agricultural ventures in Peru. APRA and Garcia are back in Peru's political driving seat again some twenty years after the first rather unsuccessful attempt at assuming power.

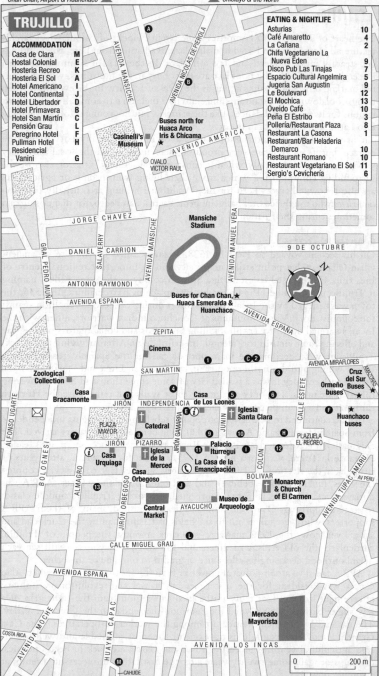

TRUJILLO

ACCOMMODATION

Casa de Clara	M
Hostal Colonial	E
Hosteria Recreo	K
Hosteria El Sol	A
Hotel Americano	I
Hotel Continental	J
Hotel Libertador	D
Hotel Primavera	B
Hotel San Martín	C
Pensión Grau	L
Peregrino Hotel	F
Pullman Hotel	H
Residencial Vanini	G

EATING & NIGHTLIFE

Asturias	10
Café Amaretto	4
La Cañana	2
Chifa Vegetariano La Nueva Eden	9
Disco Pub Las Tinajas	7
Espacio Cultural Angelmira	5
Jugeria San Augustin	9
Le Boulevard	12
El Mochica	13
Oveido Café	10
Peña El Estribo	3
Pollería/Restaurant Plaza	8
Restaurant La Casona	1
Restaurant/Bar Heladeria Demarco	10
Restaurant Romano	10
Restaurant Vegetariano El Sol	11
Sergio's Cevichería	6

AVENIDA MANSICHE

AVENIDA NICOLAS DE PIEROLA

Casinelli's Museum

Buses north for Huaca Arco Iris & Chicama ★

AVENIDA AMERICA

OVALO VICTOR RAUL

JORGE CHAVEZ

Mansiche Stadium

DANIEL CARRION

ANTONIO RAYMONDI

AVENIDA ESPAÑA

Buses for Chan Chan, Huaca Esmeralda & Huanchaco ★

AVENIDA ESPAÑA

ZEPITA

Cinema

AVENIDA MIRAFLORES

Cruz del Sur Buses ★

Ormeño buses

SAN MARTIN

Zoological Collection

Casa Bracamonte

INDEPENDENCIA

Casa de Los Leones

Iglesia Santa Clara

Huanchaco buses ★

PLAZA MAYOR

Catedral

PIZARRO

Palacio Iturregui

PLAZUELA EL RECREO

Casa Urquiaga

Iglesia de la Merced

La Casa de la Emancipación

Casa Orbegoso

BOLIVAR

Monastery & Church of El Carmen

Central Market

Museo de Arqueología

AYACUCHO

CALLE MIGUEL GRAU

AVENIDA ESPAÑA

Mercado Mayorista

AVENIDA LOS INCAS

COSTA RICA

0   200 m

CAHUIDE

Lima & the South ▼

Arrival, information and city transport

You're most likely to arrive in the city by bus or *colectivo* from Lima. Most of the **buses** have terminals close to the centre of town near the Mansiche Stadium, on avenidas Daniel Carrion or España to the southwest, or east of it along avenidas America Norte or Ejercito (see p.405, for details). **Colectivos** also mostly leave from and end up on Avenida España. If you're arriving by day it's fine to walk to the city centre, though at night it's best to take a taxi ($2–3).

If you **fly** into the city, you'll arrive at the airport, about 10km away, near Huanchaco. Taxis into the city will cost around $7, or you can get a bus, which leaves every twenty minutes between approximately 6am and 7pm daily from the roundabout just outside the airport gates (50¢).

For **tourist information** and photocopied city maps, go to the very helpful i-Peru office at Jr Pizarro 412 (Mon–Sat 8am–7pm, Sun 8am–2pm; ☎044/294561, ✉iperutrujillo@promperu.gob.pe) upstairs on the Plaza Mayor. The **Tourist Police**, at POLTUR, Jr Independencia 630 (Mon–Fri 8am–7pm; ☎044/291705), are very helpful, too. The official **Camara Regional de Turismo** (☎044/203718; Mon–Fri 9am–1pm & 4–8pm, Sat 9am–1pm), is next door to the Tourist Police at Independencia 628, where further information and maps are available.

City transport

The colonial heart of the city is encircled by the Avenida España. More or less at the centre of the circle is the ubiquitous main plaza, known as the **Plaza Mayor** or the Plaza de Armas. The main streets of Pizarro and Independencia originate at the plaza; the only other streets you really need to know are San Martín and Bolívar, parallel to Pizarro and Independencia, and Gamarra, where many of the banks are to be found.

Getting around the city and its environs is cheap and easy, using the numerous **local buses**, **colectivos** (flat rates around 50¢) and **minibuses**. **Taxis** cost less than $1.50 for rides within Trujillo and can be hailed anywhere, but if you need to call one, Taxi Seguro (☎044/253473) is best. **Car rental** is available (see p.405). **Colectivos** are abundant for journeys in and around the city; going north towards Huanchaco and Chan Chan, the best places to catch *colectivos* are beside the stalls near the Mansiche Stadium (see p.413). Going south, towards the Huaca de la Luna and the Huaca del Sol, *colectivos* can be picked up at the big service station at the junction where the Panamerican Highway heads towards Moche and Chimbote (see p.413).

Accommodation

The majority of Trujillo's **hotels** are within a few blocks of the central Plaza Mayor: most of them are to the south, but a number of reasonable ones are to be found along Jirón Pizarro, Independencia and San Martín. However, many people prefer to stay out of the city centre, at the nearby beach resort of Huanchaco (see p.407).

Central Trujillo

Hostal Colonial Jr Independencia 618 ☎044/268261, ☎223410, ✉hostalcolonialtruji @hotmail.com. An attractive, centrally located place with some English-speaking staff members. Rooms are fine but for guaranteed peace and quiet get a room at the back; all have TVs, plus there's a patio, small library and cafeteria. ❹–❺

Hotel Americano Jr Pizarro 764 ☎044/241361. Plenty of character but a bit shabby; the rooms, like everything else in this grand old hotel, are spacious but not spotless, and only some come with private bath. It's nevertheless a favourite with budget travellers, not least for the friendly service and great prices. ❷–❹

Hotel Continental Jr Gamarra 663 ☎044/241607, ☎249881. Plain but centrally located and popular with Peruvian business types. Rooms are clean with private bath, TV and reliable hot water. Breakfast is included. ⑤–⑥

Hotel Libertador Jr Independencia 485 ☎044/232741, ℻235641, or for reservations 01/5186500, Ⓦ www.libertador.com.pe. Formerly the *Hotel de Turistas*, this place is particularly grand, with excellent service and a superb restaurant renowned for its *criolla* dishes. The large, plush rooms have all modern conveniences. ⑦–⑧

Hotel San Martín San Martín 743–749 ☎044/235700 and 252311. Lots of decent rooms in a large, rather tired-looking concrete building. Good service, and all rooms have private bath and TV. Often busy with conference goers. ④–⑤

Peregrino Hotel Av Independencia 978, ☎044/203989, Ⓦ www.peregrinohotel.com. While primarily a place that specialises in events and weddings, both the service and the rooms are of quite a high standard, but not cheap. There's a good bar plus restaurant and internet access available. ⑦–⑧

Pullman Hotel Jr Pizarro 879 ☎/℻044/223589 or 471645, Ⓔ ivrest@hotmail.com. One of the city centre's newest and nicest hotels, the *Pullman* is cool and plush with solar water heating, good restaurant and bar plus all modern conveniences. ⑥

Pensión Grau C Miguel Grau 631. Good central location and a bit noisy, if nevertheless clean. Only some rooms with private bath. ②

Residencial Vanini Larco 237 ☎044/200878, Ⓔ enriqueva@hotmail.com. A little outside the

downtown area, but a very good value, family-run hostal. There's a choice of private bath, while the cheapest rooms are actually small rooms on the roof terrace. ②–④

Further afield

🏃 **Casa de Clara** Cahuide 495, Santa Maria, Trujillo ☎044/ 299997/243347, cell 044/949662710, Ⓔ casadeclara@yahoo.com, Ⓦ www.xanga.com/CasaDeClara. Located near Huayna Capac 542, this is very nice bargain accommodation, with private bath, breakfast and internet available. They also organize reliable and affordable tours in the region. ②–③

Hostería Recreo C Estete 647 ☎044/246991. Away from the centre but still within easy walking distance of the Plaza Mayor, this is a very comfortable hotel with friendly service and its own restaurant. ④

Hostería El Sol Los Brillantes 224, off block 12 of Av Mansiche in Santa Ines ☎044/231933. Built in the shape of a Bavarian castle, *El Sol* is slightly out of the way, with dark but comfortable rooms, all with private bath. ②–③

Hotel Primavera Av Nicolas de Pierola 872, Primavera district ☎044/231915. Located close to the Panamerican Highway, this concrete building lacks style but offers large, clean rooms with a/c comfort and private bath. There's also a small swimming pool, and the service is good. ③

The City

From the graceful colonial mansions and Baroque churches at its heart, Trujillo's grid system gives way to commercial buildings, light industry and shantytown suburbs, before thinning out into rich sugar-cane fields that stretch far into the neighbouring Chicama Valley. At the city's centre is its dominating force – the university **La Libertad**. Founded by Bolívar in 1824, the picturesque school is surrounded by elegant, Spanish-style streets, lined with ancient green ficus trees and overhung by long, wooden-railed balconies. **Gamarra** is the main commercial street, dominated by ugly, modern, brick and glass buildings, shops, hotels and restaurants. The other main avenue, older and more attractive, is **Jirón Pizarro**, where much of the city's nightlife is centred and which has been pedestrianized from block 8 to the pleasant **Plazuela El Recreo**. Life for most Trujillanos still revolves around the old town, centred on **Plaza Mayor** and bounded roughly by San Martín, Ayacucho, Almagro and Colón.

In addition to the city's many **churches**, Trujillo is renowned for its **colonial houses**, most of which are in good repair and are still in use today. These should generally be visited in the mornings (Mon–Fri), since many of them have other uses at other times of day; some are commercial banks and some are simply closed in the afternoons.

Fiestas in Trujillo

Trujillo's main **fiestas** turn the town into even more of a relaxed playground than it is normally, with the **marinera** dance featuring prominently in most celebrations. This regional dance originated in Trujillo and is accompanied by a combination of Andalucian, African and Aboriginal music played on the *cajón* (rhythm box) and guitar. Energetic and very sexual – this traditional dance represents the seduction of an elegant, upper-class woman by a male servant – the *marinera* involves dancers holding handkerchiefs above their heads and skillfully prancing around each other. You'll see it performed in peñas all over the country but rarely with the same spirit and conviction as here in Trujillo. The last week in January, sometimes running into February (check with the tourist information office in Trujillo, or on their website, for any particular year), is the main **Festival de la Marinera**. During this time there's a National Marinera Competition – *el Concurso Nacional de Marinera* – taking place in the city over several weeks, with dance academies from all over Peru.

The main **religious fiestas** are in October and December, with October 17 seeing the procession of El Señor de los Milagros, and the first two weeks of December being devoted to the patron saint of Huanchaco – another good excuse for wild parties in this beach resort. February, as everywhere, is **Carnival** time, with even more *marinera* dancing evenings taking place throughout Trujillo.

Plaza Mayor and around

Trujillo's **Plaza Mayor** (also known as the **Plaza de Armas**) is packed with sharp-witted shoeshine boys around the central statue – the *Heroes of the Wars of Independence*, a Baroque marble work created by German Edmundo Muller. The two colonial mansions that front it have both been tastefully restored: **Casa Bracamonte**, Jr Independencia 441, is closed to visitors but has some interesting cast ironwork around its patio windows, while the Banco de la Nación-owned **Casa Urquiaga** (Mon–Fri 9am–3pm, Sat 10am–1pm; free, with 30min guided tours often available), Jr Pizarro 446 (also known as Casa Calonge), is said to be the house where Bolívar stayed when visiting Trujillo; it's also home to some first-class Rococo-style furniture and a fine collection of ancient ceramics.

Plaza Mayor is also home to the city's **Catedral** (daily 7–11.45am & 4–9pm; free), built in the mid-seventeenth century, then rebuilt the following century after earthquake damage. Known locally as the Basilica Menor, it's plain by Peruvian standards but houses some colourful Baroque sculptures and a handful of paintings by the Quiteña school (a deeply religious style of painting that originated in eighteenth-century Quito). Inside the cathedral, the **Museo de Catedral** (daily 8am–2pm; $2) exhibits a range of mainly eighteenth- and nineteenth-century religious paintings and sculptures.

Just behind the plaza at San Martín 368, is a **zoological collection** (Mon–Fri 8am–7pm, Sat 8am–1pm; $1.50), full of dozens of bizarre stuffed animals from the coastal desert and Andean regions, as well as a large bird display and lots of amazing sea creatures (including a now extinct crab some 70cm across) and a number of reptiles.

From Plaza Mayor to the Central Market

Just off the plaza, the **Iglesia de La Merced**, Jr Pizarro 550 (daily 8am–noon and 4–8pm; free), first built in 1536, destroyed by a major earthquake in 1619, then rebuilt in 1634, is worth a look for its unique, priceless Rococo **organ**, plus its attractive gardens. Around the corner from here, between the Plaza de Armas and the Central Market, stands the most impressive of Trujillo's colonial houses – the **Casa Orbegoso**, at Jr Orbegoso 553 (Mon–Sun 9.30am–7pm; free). This

▲ Cathedral in the Plaza Mayor, Trujillo

old mansion was the home of **Luís José Orbegoso**, former president of Peru, and houses displays of period furniture, glass and silverware amid very refined decor. Born into one of Trujillo's wealthiest founding families, Orbegoso fought for independence and became president of the republic in 1833 with the support of the liberal faction. However, he proved to be the most ineffective of all Peruvian leaders, resented for his aristocratic bearing by the *mestizo* generals, and from 1833 to 1839, although still officially president, he lost control of the country – first in civil war, then to the Bolivian army, and finally to a combined rebel and Chilean force. Today, even his family home has been invaded – although it's still in perfect condition and maintains the outstanding colonial elegance, there are temporary art exhibition spaces, and the main rooms around the courtyard have been converted into offices.

Trujillo's main market, the **Central Market** (known locally as the Mercado de los Brujos: the Witches' Market) is only 100m from here, on the corner of Ayacucho and Gamarra. As well as selling most essentials, such as juices, food and clothing, it has an interesting line in **herbal stalls** and healing or magical items, not to mention unionized shoe-cleaners. There's a second, much busier market, the Mercado Mayorista, further out, on Avenida Costa Rica in the southeast corner of town.

From the market, head east along Ayacucho until you reach the corner of Junin, where you'll find the University's **Museo de Arqueología y Antropología**, Jr Junin 682 (Mon 9.30am–2pm, Tues–Fri 9.15am–1pm & 3–7pm, Sat & Sun 9.30am–4pm; $1.50, including optional 30min guided tour in Spanish; ☎044/249322), which specializes in ceramics, early metallurgy, textiles and feather work.

East of Plaza Mayor

East of the plaza, on the corner of Jirón Pizarro and Gamarra, stands another of Trujillo's impressive mansions, **La Casa de la Emancipación**, at Jr Pizarro 610 (Mon–Sat 9.15am–12.30pm and 4–6.30pm; free). The building was remodelled in the mid-nineteenth century by the priest Pedro Madalengoitia (the reason it's also sometimes known as the Casa Madalengoitia), and is now head office of the Banco Continental. The main courtyard and entrance demonstrate a symmetrical and austere design, while the wide gallery has some impressive marble flooring. Inside are a couple of interesting late eighteenth-century murals depicting peasant life, and paintings or historical photographs are usually exhibited in at least one of its rooms.

Further down the same road, two blocks east of the Plaza Mayor, is the **Palacio Iturregui**, Jr Pizarro 688 (Mon–Sun 11am–6pm; $1.50), a striking mid-nineteenth-century mansion. Built by the army general Don Juan Manuel de Iturregui y Aguilarte, the house is used today by the city's Central Club, who allow visitors to look round some of the rooms. The highlight of the building is its pseudo-classical courtyard, encircled by superb galleries, with tall columns and an open roof, which provides a wonderful view of the blue desert sky. The courtyard can be seen at any time of the day, by just popping your head inside.

At the eastern end of Jirón Pizarro, five blocks from the Plaza Mayor, there's a small, attractive square known as the restored **Plazuela El Recreo** where, under the shade of some vast 130-year-old ficus trees, a number of **bars** and food stalls act like a magnet for young couples in the evenings. This little plaza was, and still is, an *estanque de agua* – a water distribution point – built during colonial days, but tapping into even more ancient irrigation works.

A couple of minutes' walk south from the Plazuela, on the corner of Colón and Bolívar, stands the most stunning of the city's religious buildings, the **Monasterio El Carmen** (Mon–Sat 9am–1pm; $1 ☎044/241823). Built in 1759 but damaged by an earthquake in the same year, its two brick towers were then rebuilt using bamboo for safety in case they toppled again. The church was also built above ground level to save it from El Niño's periodic flooding. Inside you can see the single domed nave, with exquisite altars and a fine gold-leaf pulpit. The processional and recreational cloisters, both boasting fine vaulted arches and painted wooden columns, give access to the **Pinacoteca** (picture gallery), where you can see Flemish works including *Last Supper* (1625) by Otto van Veen, one of Rubens' teachers. There are also some interesting figures carved from *huamanga* stone and a room showing the process of restoring oil paintings.

Northeast of Plaza Mayor

Jirón Independencia runs northeast from the Plaza Mayor and has a couple of minor attractions. Just one block from the plaza, at Independencia 628, stands the **Casa de los Leones** (Mon–Fri 9am–6pm; free), a colonial mansion that's larger and more labyrinthine than it looks from the outside and which holds exhibitions of photos, art, culture, crafts and wildlife, mostly of local historical or environmental interest. A few minutes further along Jirón Independencia, on the corner of Junin, you'll find the **Iglesia Santa Clara** (Sun only 8am–6pm; free), which contains fine religious paintings and examples of Baroque architecture. If you go in, be sure to check inside its chapel to see the altar covered with gold leaf and the pulpit with high-relief carvings.

Casinelli's Museum

The most curious museum in Trujillo is set in the middle of the road, in the basement of the Mobil filling station at Nicolas de Pierola 601, on the Ovalo Victor Raul, just north of the large Mansiche Stadium. **Museo Casinelli** (daily 9.30am–1pm & 3–7pm; $2) is simply stuffed with pottery and artefacts spanning thousands of years, collected from local *huaqueros*. The Salinar, Viru, Mochica, Chimu, Nasca, Huari, Recuay and Inca cultures are all represented, with highlights including **Mochica pots** with graphic images of daily life, people, animals and anthropomorphic deities. Señor Casinelli sometimes shows his visitors around personally and will point out his exquisite range of **Chimu silver artefacts**, including a tiny set of panpipes.

Eating and drinking

There's no shortage of **bars** or **restaurants** in Trujillo. Some of the liveliest are along Jirón Independencia, Pizarro, Bolívar and Ayacucho, to the east of Plaza Mayor. A speciality of the city is good, reasonably priced **seafood**, particularly ceviche, which is probably best appreciated on the beach at the nearby resorts of Buenos Aires or Huanchaco (see p.407). Goat and beans are a local speciality, too; if you get the chance try *cabrito con frijoles*, a truly traditional dish of goat marinated in *chicha* beer and vinegar and served with beans cooked with onions and garlic.

Asturias Jr Pizarro 739. Tasty fruit juices plus alcoholic drinks, lunchtime meals and snacks at this busy coffee bar.

Café Amaretto Jr Gamarra 368. Great coffee and cakes, breakfast and snacks; smallish space but fast and friendly service.

Chifa Vegetariano "La Nueva Eden" Jr Pizarro 687. Chinese health food and vegetarian restaurant serving dishes with yoghurt, quinoa and *maca* (a medicinal root believed to be useful for regulating menstruation and also male virility); it has cheap set-lunch menus.

Espacio Cultural Angelmira On the corner of Independencia with Junin ☎044/297200. A plush, fascinating little café and bar with the associated Museo del Juguette (Toy Museum) in the same building as well as an art gallery and library.

Jugeria San Augustin Jr Pizarro 691 ☎044/259591. An excellent juice bar, very popular with Trujillo's youth, and offering an enormous choice of tropical drinks, beers, sandwiches and snacks in a friendly environment. Will take phone orders and deliver to your door.

Le Boulevard Jr Pizarro 844. A pleasant lunchtime spot in the pedestrian section of Pizarro, with a nice little patio and very good, inexpensive, set lunches.

El Mochica Bol'var 462. A superb, smart restaurant serving exquisite *criolla* dishes and local cuisine (if you're in luck they'll have *cabrito con frijoles*).

Oveido Café Jr Pizarro 737. Stuck between *Restaurant Romano* and *Restaurant/Bar Heladeria*

Demarco, this is a quality café serving very nice – if a bit pricey – breakfasts. Service is excellent and the clientele mostly Trujillo's well-to-do or businessmen.

Pollería/Restaurant Plaza Jr Pizarro 501. A very popular roast chicken joint on the corner of the Plaza Mayor; the fried potatoes aren't bad either.

Restaurant La Casona San Martín 677. A modest, quiet restaurant serving local dishes such as *cabrito* (goat and rice); excellent lunches at fantastically cheap prices.

Restaurant Romano Jr Pizarro 747 ☎044/252251. Small, friendly restaurant specializing in good Peruvian and Italian dishes. Good-sized portions, and exceptional value with its *económico familia* or *turístico* set menus, although it gets very crowded in the evenings, and reservations are advised.

Restaurant Vegetariano El Sol Jr Pizarro 660. Open for lunches and evening meals, *El Sol* serves simple, reasonably priced vegetarian fare (the best in town), mostly based on rice, alfalfa, soya, maize and fresh vegetables. It's particularly popular with locals at lunchtime.

Restaurant/Bar Heladeria Demarco Jr Pizarro 725 ☎044/234251. A relatively posh, Italian-style ice cream parlour-cum-bar and restaurant serving international and Peruvian dishes.

Sergio's Cevichería Independencia 925. A small and surprisingly cheap seafood restaurant that serves very fresh food, cooked fish and squid as well as ceviche; excellent value for lunch.

Nightlife and entertainment

Trujillo boasts a fairly active **nightlife**, with several **peñas** and **nightclubs** celebrating local culture, dance and music, as well as Latin rhythms and the latest global popular sounds. One feature of Trujillo nightlife is **drive-in disco**, mostly associated with motels, pick-up joints or other places for illicit affairs. They tend to be located around the outskirts of the city; try *Pussy Cat*, Av Nicolas de Pierola 716, or *La Herradura*, Av Teodoro Valcarcel 1268, both in Urbino Primavera. On a more cultural level, the city is famous for its January *marinera* **dance fiesta** and occasional international dance jamborees.

Clubs and peñas

🏃 **La Cañana** San Martín 791 ☎044/232503. A highly popular restaurant-peña (as well as a discotheque), serving excellent meals; has a great atmosphere and good danceable shows that generally start after 10pm and carry on into the early hours.

Disco Pub Las Tinajas corner of Pizarro and Almagro. Very central and lively at weekends; plays rock and pop.

Peña El Estribo San Martín 810. A large, newly restored and very popular dance and music venue with great weekend shows of coastal folklore and *musica negra*.

Listings

Airlines Lan Peru, Jr Pizarro 342 ☎044/221469 and Star Peru, Almagro 539 ☎044/293392. All flights out of Trujillo airport are liable to $4 airport tax.

Airport Aeropuerto Carlos Martinez de Pinillos, on the road to Huanchaco ☎044/464013 (7am–9pm daily).

Artesania markets Liga de Artesanos, Jr Colón 423 (Mon–Sat 9am–noon & 3–7pm); and the Asociación de Pequeños Industriales y Artesanatos de Trujillo, located at Av Espana, block 18 (Mon–Sat 9am–8pm, Sun 9am–4pm); or there's Los Tallanes, San Martín 455.

Banks and exchange Banco de Credito, Jr Gamarra 562; Banco Wiese, Jr Pizarro 314; Banco Latino, Jr Gamarra 574; Banco de la Nación, Jr Almagro 297. The Casa de Cambios Martelli, Jr Bolívar 665, give the best rates in town for dollars cash, or try the *cambistas* (though be very careful, especially after dark) on the corner of Jr Pizarro and Gamarra, or on the Plaza Mayor. A safer bet are the numerous casas de cambio found on block 6 of Pizarro.

Buses Arguably the best coastal bus services are operated by Cruz del Sur, Amazonas 437 ☎044/261801, and Ormeño, Av Ejercito 233 ☎044/259782, but there are a host of others, including: Alto Chicama, José Sabogal 305, Urbino Palermo ☎044/203659, for Chicama; Linea, Av America Sur 2857 for Cajamarca and Huaraz; Palacios, Av España 1005 ☎044/233902, for Huamachuco; San Pedro Express, Av Mansiche 375, for Chepen; Tepsa, Diego de Almagro 849 ☎044/205017, and Transportes Chiclayo, Av America Norte 2404 ☎044/243341, both for the North coast; Transportes Guadalupe, Av Mansiche 331 ☎044/246019, for Tarapoto, Yurimaguas and Juanjui; Turismo Chimbote, Jr Nicaragua 194–198 ☎044/245546, for Chimbote, Casma, Huaraz and Caraz.

Car rental Jr Ayacucho 414, Oficina 11 (☎/ ☎044/234985).

Consulates UK, Av Jr Nazareth 312 ☎044/235548, ☎255818 (Mon–Fri 9am–5pm).

Hospital Hospital Belen de Trujillo, Bolívar 350 ☎044/245281 (24 hours); Hospital Regional Docente de Trujillo, Av Manseriche 795 ☎044/231581 (24 hours).

Immigration Av Larco 1220, Urbanización Los Pinos for visa renewals.

Internet facilities There are several internet cafés along Pizarro (Macrochips at 183a, Masterdata at 197, Megatel at 510, Net@House at 551) between the Plaza Mayor and Gamarra. A 24hr service is available at Interc@ll, Zepita 728.

Laundry Two of the best places in town are Luxor, Jr Grau 637, and Lavandería El Carmen, Jr Pizarro 759.

Photography Foto Express, Jr Pizarro 582, is centrally located and has a reasonably good range of film, plus offering developing. For films and photographic equipment, try Foto Para Ti, Jr Pizarro 645 or Foto Expres Trujillo, Pizarro 582.

Post office Serpost (Mon–Sat 8am–7pm) is based at Jr Independencia 286, a block and a half southwest of the plaza.

Shopping For traditional musical instruments, try the shop at Jr Pizarro 721. There's a good supermarket for general provisions at Junin 372.

Telephones Telefónica del Peru, Bolívar 658 (daily 7am–11pm). There's also a telephone and fax office at Bolívar 611.

Tour operators and guides Most companies offer 3hr tours to Chan Chan and Huanchaco from around $10–12 per person (including the site museum, Huaca Arco Iris and Huaca Esmeralda), and to *huacas* del Sol and Luna from $8–10. For Chicama sites, expect to pay $20 plus. Recommended operators include: America Tours, Jr Pizarro 476 ☎044/235182; Clara Brava's Tours (see *Casa de Clara* in Accommodation, p.400); Guía Tours, Independencia 580 ☎044/25170 (operators since 1975), ☻www.guiatours.com.pe; and Trujillo Tours, Diego de Almagro 301 ☎044/233091, ☻ttours@terra.com.pe (mainly offering half-day options in and around the city).

Chicama, Chiclayo, Piura & Tumbes ▲

AROUND TRUJILLO

▼ Panamerican Highway to Lima

Around Trujillo

The closest of the coastal resorts to Trujillo is the beachfront *barrio* of **Buenos
Aires**, a five-kilometre stretch of sand southwest of Trujillo – very popular with
locals and constantly pounded by surf. Like other coastal resorts, its seafood restaurants are an attraction, though it doesn't have as much style or life as **Huanchaco**.
For those in search of sand and seafood out the city, the villages of **Moche** and **Las
Delicias** are within easy reach.

Moche and Las Delicias

After crossing the Río Moche's estuary, two kilometres south of Trujillo, you'll
come across the settlements of **MOCHE** and **LAS DELICIAS**, both within an

easy bus ride of the Huaca del Sol and Huaca de la Luna (see p.414). Moche is a small village some 4km south of the city, slightly inland from the ocean, blessed with several **restaurants** serving freshly prepared seafood, including one of the best in the whole Trujillo region, the *Restaurant Mochica*, serving *shamba*, a very substantial soup. Close by, Las Delicias, 5km south of Trujillo, boasts a beautiful, long **beach** and a handful of reasonable restaurants. To reach Las Delicias from Trujillo, catch the direct **bus** (hourly service) marked "Delicias" from the corner of avenidas Moche and Los Incas. For **accommodation**, the clean and agreeable *Hostal Janita*, C Montero 340 (℡044/485286; ❸), overlooking the sea in Las Delicias, is the only choice at present. Las Delicias' main claim to fame is that the *curandero* El Tuno once lived at Lambayeque 18, right on the beach. By arrangement with his family there you can sometimes witness the fascinating diagnostic healing sessions that are now practised by El Tuno's apprentices, often involving rubbing a live guinea pig over the patient's body, then splitting the animal open and removing its innards for inspection while the heart is still pumping. It is believed to reveal the patient's problems – one of which may be nausea after viewing the event – after which he or she is sent away with a mix of healing herbs.

Huanchaco

Although no longer exactly a tropical paradise, **HUANCHACO**, 12km west, or twenty minutes by bus, from Trujillo, is still a beautiful and relatively peaceful resort, though there is a thriving scene geared toward surfers and young travellers. Until the 1970s, Huanchaco was a tiny fishing village, quiet and little known to tourists. Today it consists of half-finished adobe houses, concrete hotels and streets slowly spreading back towards Trujillo, and makes an excellent base for visiting many of the sites around the region, in particular the nearby ruins of **Chan Chan**. While development is on the rise, its intrinsic fishing village appeal hasn't entirely diminished.

The best time to visit Huanchaco is during its June **fiesta** week, at the end of the month, when a large *totora* raft comes ashore accompanied by a smaller flotilla of *caballitos* (literally meaning "little horses"; on the Peruvian coast it usually refers to small shapely reed boats used by the local fishermen for millenia). But even out of season the town is always lively, with people on the beach, others fishing, and a few travellers hanging around the restaurants.

Arrival and information

To get to Huanchaco from Trujillo, **taxis** cost around $4–5, or it's easy enough to take the frequent orange and yellow **microbus** from block 13 of Avenida España (on the far side of the road from the town centre), by the corner with Independencia, or pick up a bus or one of the white **colectivos** marked Empresa Caballitos de Tortora (50¢) from the Mobil or Shell petrol stations at Ovalo Victor Raul. On the way out to Huanchaco the bus travels the whole length of Calle Estete (returning via Colón); to get back into the city there's normally a line of microbuses picking up passengers from the waterfront. On the way back, it's best to check with the driver that the *colectivos* are going all the way back into Trujillo, because some of them turn left at the Ovalo Victor Raul and head towards Esperanza instead. Be aware that due to the quite rapid growth of the pueblo, street and block numbers are in a state of transition, so it's quite easy to get confused by Huanchaco addresses.

Internet access can be found at Beach Internet, Los Pinos 533 where they also offer fax and copying facilities. Both the *Hotel Bracamonte* and the *Hospedaje Familiar La Casa Suiza* (see p.408) also offer internet access.

Accommodation

The town is well served by the kind of accommodation range you'd normally expect at a popular beach resort. Many families also put people up in **private rooms**, such as the *Hospedaje Las Gaviotas*, Los Pinos 535 (☎044/461858; ❷) or the *Hospedaje Jimenez*, Colón 378 (☎044/461844; ❷). To locate others, just look out for the signs reading "Alquila Cuarto" on houses, particularly in the summer (Dec–Feb). It's also possible to **camp** here, in the grounds of *Hotel Bracamonte*.

🏄 **Hospedaje Familiar La Casa Suiza** Los Pinos 451 ☎044/461285, Ⓦwww .casasuiza.com. One of the best, most friendly budget places in Huanchaco, with a range of different rooms (some with bath), a lovely rooftop terrace and a book exchange. There are laundry and internet facilities, they rent out body boards and surfboards, and the staff speak English. ❷–❸

Hospedaje Nirvana Av Ricardo Palma 425 ☎044/462502, Ⓦwww.nirvanahospedaje.com. Located next door to the *Big Ben* restaurant and just half a block from the sea, and offering rooms that are small but comfortable enough, all with cable TV and hot water. Internet access available. ❸–❹

Hospedaje Sunset Ribera 600 ☎044/461863. Where many of the visiting surfers hang out; there's no hot water, but great views of the sea and hammocks on the balcony, plus a small restaurant. ❶

Hostal Ancla La Rivera 198 ☎044/461030. Overlooking the beach, this well-established lodging has an interesting collection of old photos and memorabilia in its bar and cafeteria. Rooms at the front can be noisy, though. ❸

Hostal Caballito de Totora La Ribera 219 ☎/Ⓕ044/461154, Ⓦwww.caballitodetotora.com. Right on the seafront, this place offers rooms with ocean views plus cheaper, less panoramic options. There's also a small pool, garden, cafeteria and sun terraces; some members of staff speak English. Price includes breakfast, and rates are quite a lot cheaper in low season. ❺

Hostal Los Esteros Larco 618 ☎044/461300 Ⓦwww.losesteroshuanchaco.com. An attractive option with sea views, where the tidy rooms all come with private bath and hot water. ❺

Hostal Solange Los Ficus 258 ☎044/461410. This is a small, very comfortable, easy-going and friendly family-run hostel situated just two blocks from the beach, where you can do your own cooking if you wish. ❷–❸

🏄 **Hotel Bracamonte** Los Olivos 503 ☎044/461162, Ⓕ461266, Ⓦwww .hotelbracamonte.com.pe. A lovely complex of different-sized chalets with solar-heated showers. Very welcoming for children, it has a pool, a games room, internet access, laundry facilities, a good restaurant and terraces with views over the ocean. You can camp in the grounds for from $3 per person or $12 including tent rental. ❻

Huanchaco Hostal Larco 287 ☎044/461272, Ⓕ461688. Good-value, comfortable hostel with pleasant gardens, a cafeteria and a small pool. The service is excellent and most rooms have TV and private bath. There's also a dorm, pool room and parking. One of the entrances faces the sea, and the other opens onto the tiny but attractive Plaza de Armas. ❹–❻

The Town

The town's only historical sight is the old, square **Iglesia Soroco**, perched high on the coastal cliffs – a fifteen-minute walk uphill from the seafront. The second church in Peru to be built by the Spanish, it sprang up in 1540 on top of a pre-Inca temple dedicated to the idol of the Golden Fish, and was rebuilt after its destruction during the earthquakes of 1619–1670.

Huanchaco hasn't entirely lost its intrinsic fishing village appeal. There is a long jetty (30¢), which has recently been renovated, and where you can jostle with fishermen for the best **fishing** positions; just at the entry to the pier is a small artesania **market**. Stacked along the beach, the rows of *caballitos del mar* – the ancient seagoing rafts designed by the Mochicas – are still used by locals today. They are constructed out of four cigar-shaped bundles of *totora* reeds, tied together into an arc tapering at each end. The fishermen kneel or sit at the stern and paddle, using the surf for occasional bursts of motion. The local boat-builders here are the last who know the craft of making *caballitos* to the original design of the Mochicas. Some of the fishermen offer ten- to fifteen-minute trips ($2) on the back of their *caballitos*.

Eating and nightlife

There are seafood **restaurants** all along the front in Huanchaco, one or two of them with verandas extending to the beach. Not surprisingly, seafood is the local speciality, including excellent crab, and you can often see women and children up to their waists in the sea collecting shellfish. The fishermen can also usually be seen returning around 3–4pm on their *caballitos*. A kilo of fresh fish can be bought for under $2, but the catches these days aren't huge.

Anyone looking for **nightlife** should check out the small bars on La Ribera, just a few blocks south from the pier. More cultured, the café-bar *El Tribu*, at Los Pinos 540, is more laid-back and associated with a sculptor's workshop.

Club Colonial Grau 272 ☎044/461015. A beautifully restored colonial house adorned with paintings, old photos and fine stained-glass work. The food is sumptuous, with an extensive menu of traditional dishes, but it's not cheap. The garden is the residence of some penguins and a couple of rare Tumbes crocodiles.

Huanchaco Beach Restaurant Malecón Larco 602. Very tasty fish dishes, and excellent views across the ocean and up to the clifftop Iglesia Soroco.

Restaurant El Caribe Atahualpa 100. Just around the corner from the seafront to the north of the pier, this restaurant has great ceviche and is very popular with locals.

Restaurant Don Pepe Malecón Larco 502 ℮ donpepe@huanchaco.zzn.com. Among the best-positioned seafront restaurants, with a balcony overlooking the *caballitos del mar* and the fishermen mending their nets; it's not cheap, but the food, especially their selection of seafood dishes, is quite good.

Restaurant Big Ben Av Larco 836. Serves probably the best and certainly the most expensive seafood dishes in Huanchaco, including excellent crab and sea urchin if you're lucky.

Restaurant Marimar Av Victor Larco 525. Just north of the pier, this is another good spot for seafood and great views of the pier and ocean; try the *sudado de pescado* or the *langostino al ajo* for full-flavour dishes.

Wave Av Larco 640. South of the pier, this is a tiny Mexican restaurant and bar upstairs from a surf school; it has a great atmosphere day and night with a bit of a beach scene.

The Chan Chan complex

The ruined city of **CHAN CHAN** stretches across a large sector of the Moche Valley, beginning almost as soon as you leave Trujillo on the Huanchaco road, and ending just a couple of kilometres from Huanchaco. A huge complex even today, its main focus and museum site is the Tschudi sector (see p.410), which needs only a little imagination to raise its weathered mud walls to their original grandeur, and picture the surprisingly complex, rule-bound society, where slaves carried produce back and forth while artisans and courtiers walked the streets slowly, stopping only to give orders or chat with people of similar status.

Some history

Chan Chan was the capital city of the **Chimu Empire**, an urban civilization that appeared on the Peruvian coast around 1100 AD. The Chimu cities and towns throughout the region stretch from Tumbes in the north to as far south as Paramonga. Their cities were always elaborately planned, with large, flat-topped buildings for the nobility and intricately decorated adobe pyramids serving as temples. Chimu artwork, particularly ceramics, was mass-produced. Recognized as fine goldsmiths by the Incas, the Chimu panelled their temples with gold and cultivated palace gardens where even the plants and animals were made from precious metals. The city walls were brightly painted, and the style of architecture and relief decoration is sometimes ascribed to the fact that the Mochica (who predated the Chimu in this valley by several centuries) migrated from Central America into this area, bringing with them knowledge and ideas from a more advanced civilization, like the Maya. The Chimu inherited ideas and techniques from a host of previous cultures along the coast, including the Mochica, and, most importantly, adapted the techniques from many generations of trial and error in irrigating the Moche Valley. In the desert, access to a regular water supply was critical in the development of an urban civilization like that of Chan Chan, whose very existence depended on extracting water not only from the Río Moche but also, via a complicated system of canals and aqueducts, from the neighbouring Chicama Valley.

With no written records, the **origins of Chan Chan** are mere conjecture, but there are two local legends. According to one, the city was founded by **Taycanamu**, who arrived by boat with his royal fleet; after establishing an empire, he left his son, Si-Um, in command and then disappeared over the western horizon. The other legend has it that Chan Chan's construction was inspired by an original creator deity of the same name, a dragon who made the sun and the moon and whose earthly manifestation is a rainbow. Whatever the impulse behind Chan Chan, it remains one of the world's marvels and, in its heyday, was one of the largest pre-Columbian cities in the Americas. By 1450, when the Chimu Empire stretched from the Río Zarumilla in the north to the Río Chancay in the south and covered around 40,000 square kilometres, Chan Chan was the centre of a chain of provincial capitals. These were gradually incorporated into the Inca Empire between 1460 and 1480.

The events leading to the city's demise are better documented than those of its birth: in the 1470s **Tupac Yupanqui** led the Inca armies down from the mountains in the east and cut off the aqueducts supplying Chan Chan with its vital water supply. After lengthy discussions, the Chimu council managed to persuade its leader against going out to fight the Incas, knowing full well that resistance would be met with brutality, and surrender with peaceful takeover. The Chimu were quickly deprived of their chieftains, many of them taken to Cusco (along with the highly skilled metallurgists) to be indoctrinated into Inca ways. Sixty years later when the first Spaniards rode through Chan Chan they found only a ghost town full of dust and legend, as the Incas had left to fight their civil war and the remaining Chimu were too dispirited to organize any significant urban life.

The ruins

Of the three main sectors specifically opened up for exploration, the **Tschudi temple-citadel** is the largest and most frequently visited. Not far from Tschudi, **Huaca La Esmeralda** displays different features, being a ceremonial or ritual pyramid rather than a citadel. The third sector, the **Huaca Arco Iris** (or **El Dragon**), on the other side of this enormous ruined city, was similar in function to Esmeralda but has a unique design which has been restored with relish, if not historical perfection. Entrance to these three archaeological sites of the wider Chan Chan complex and the **Museo de Sitio** (daily 9am–4pm, closed Christmas week; $3.50, or $1.75 for students with ID cards) is included on the same **ticket**, called the *Talon Visitante*, which is valid for only two days (but you can try asking for an extension if you need more time). Although you can visit each sector separately, there are only two **ticket offices**, at the entrance to the Museo de Sitio, located a few hundred metres before the entrance to the Tschudi temple-citadel, and at the entrance to the Tschudi temple-citadel. There's a small interpretive centre at the Tschudi complex entrance, as well as toilets, a cafeteria and souvenirs, plus a full-size model of a Chimu warrior in full regalia. **Guided tours** are easily arranged (around $3 for the museum); guides for the Tschudi complex ($6 an hour) usually hang around at the Tschudi entrance, and, if you want, will also take you round the *huacas*. The Museo de Sitio, has an interesting eight-minute multimedia show

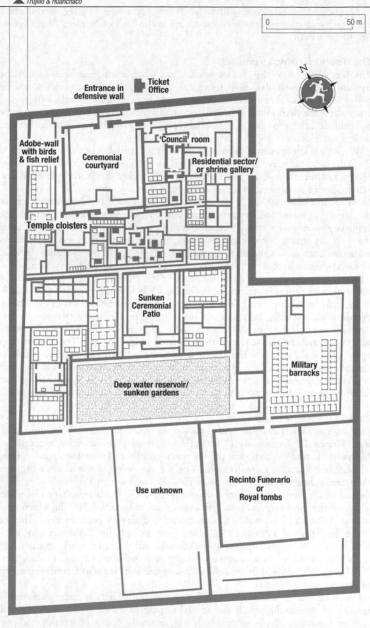

0   50 m

N

Entrance in
defensive wall

Ticket
Office

Adobe-wall
with birds
& fish relief

Ceremonial
courtyard

'Council' room

Residential sector/
or shrine gallery

Temple cloisters

Sunken
Ceremonial
Patio

Military
barracks

Deep water reservoir/
sunken gardens

Use unknown

Recinto Funerario
or
Royal tombs

CHAN CHAN TSCHUDI TEMPLE-CITADEL

in Spanish, but not much else of note. The museum uses models, ceramics and other archaeological finds to reconstruct life in the hot but irrigated desert before Trujillo was built.

The Tschudi temple-citadel

The best place to get an idea of what Chan Chan must have been like, is the **Tschudi temple-citadel**, even though it's now stuck out in the desert among high ruined walls, dusty streets, gateways, decrepit dwellings and open graves. Only a few hundred metres from the ocean at Buenos Aires beach, and bordered by cornfields, this was once the imperial capital from which the Chimu elite ruled their massive domain.

Very little is known about the history or even the daily life of those who lived in Tschudi; unfortunately, the Chimu didn't leave as much of a record as the earlier Mochica culture, whose temples were built on the other side of the Moche Valley. But following the marked route around the citadel through a maze of corridors, chamber, and amazingly large plazas, you will begin to form your own picture of this highly organized ancient civilization. For example, in a courtyard just past the entrance gateway, some twenty-five seats are set into niches at regular intervals along the walls. By sitting in one niche and whispering to someone in another, you can witness an unusual acoustic effect: how this simply designed **council room** amplifies all sounds, making the niches seem like they're connected by adobe intercoms.

Fishing net motifs are repeated throughout the citadel's design, particularly in the **sunken ceremonial patio** (an antechamber before the entrance to the *audiencias*, or little temples area), and show how important the sea was to the Chimu people, both mythologically and as a major resource. Dedicated to divinities and designed to hold offerings and tributes, the **audiencias** lead to the **main ceremonial courtyard** and also to the corridor of fish and bird designs. The westernmost open point of the site is the burial area, known as the **Recinto Funerario**, and was the most sacred part of Tschudi, where the tomb of El Señor Chimo and his wives was located. Beyond the citadel extend acres of untended ruins that are dangerous for foreigners – some, certainly, have been robbed after wandering off alone.

Huaca La Esmeralda

One of the most beautiful, and possibly the most venerated of Chimu temples, **Huaca La Esmeralda** (The Emerald Temple) lies in ruins a couple of kilometres before Tschudi, just off the main Trujillo to Huanchaco road. Unlike Tschudi, the *huaca*, or sacred temple, is on the very edge of town, stuck between the outer suburbs and the first cornfields. It was built in the twelfth or early thirteenth century – at about the same time as the Tschudi temple-citadel – and is one of the most important of the *huacas* scattered around Trujillo. Uncovered only in 1923, its adobe walls and decorations had already been severely damaged in the freak rains of 1925 and 1983. Now you can only just make out what must have been an impressive multicoloured **facade**. All the relief work on the adobe walls is original, and shows marine-related motifs including friezes of fishing nets containing fish, waves, a flying pelican, a sea otter and frequent repetitive patterns of geometrical arabesques.

The *huaca* has an unusually complex structure, with two main platforms, a number of surrounding walls and several sloping pathways giving access to each section. From the top platform, which was obviously a place of worship and possibly the cover to a royal tomb, you can see west across the valley to the graveyards of Chan Chan, out to sea, over the cultivated fields around the site and into the primitive brick factory next door. Only some shells and *chaquiras* (stone and coral necklaces) were found when the *huaca* was officially dug out some years ago, long after centuries of *huaqueros* (treasure hunters) had exhausted its more valuable goods. These grave robbers nearly always precede the archaeologists. In fact, archaeologists are often drawn to the sites they eventually excavate by the trail of treasures that flow from the grave robbers through dealers' hands into the market in Lima and beyond.

La Huaca Arco Iris

La Huaca Arco Iris (the Rainbow Temple) is the most fully restored ruin of the Chan Chan complex and one of the oldest sectors at 1100 years old, located just to the left of the Panamerican Highway, about 4km north of Trujillo in the middle of the urban district of La Esperanza. The *huaca* consists of two tiers: the **first tier** is made up of fourteen rectangular chambers, possibly used for storing corn and precious metals for ritual purposes, while a path slopes up to the **second tier**, a flat-topped platform used as a ceremonial area where sacrifices were held and the gods apparently spoke. From here, there is a wide view over the valley, towards the ocean, Trujillo, and the city of Chan Chan.

Several interpretations have been made of the **central motif**, which is repeated throughout the *huaca* – some consider it a dragon, some a centipede and some a rainbow. Most of the main **temple inner walls** have been restored, and they are covered with the re-created central motif. The outer walls are decorated in the same way, with identical friezes cut into the adobe, in a design that looks like a multi-legged serpent arching over two lizard-type beings.

Getting there

Taxis are cheap and reliable enough to use for visiting sites around Trujillo; a half day with one taxi can cost as little as $20. To get to the Chan Chan museum by public transport take the orange and yellow Huanchaco-bound **microbus** from Avenida España in the city (see p.407) and make sure you get off well before the junction where the road divides (one way leads to Huanchaco and the other to the airport); the museum is easy to spot, but it's best to play it safe by asking the driver to drop you at the Museo de Sitio when you jump on board. Take the same orange and yellow Huanchaco-bound microbus from Avenida España and get off at the concrete Tschudi/Chan Chan signpost about 2km beyond the outer suburbs. From here, just follow the track to the left of the road for ten to fifteen minutes until you see the ticket office (on the left), next to the high defensive walls around the inner temple-citadel. To get to Huaca La Esmeralda, catch a **colectivo** (see p.407) or the orange and yellow Huanchaco-bound microbus from Trujillo and get off at the colonial church of San Salvador de Mansiche, at blocks 14 and 15 of Avenida Mansiche, then follow the path along the right-hand side of the church for three blocks (through the modern barrio of Mansiche), until you reach the *huaca*. To get to the Huaca Arco Iris, take the regular Comité 19 red and blue **microbus** from the centre of Trujillo, or any of the other *colectivos* heading north from Trujillo to Esperanza (they are usually clearly marked in the windscreens). Get off the bus at the blue concrete sign on the side of the main road; the *huaca* is to the west of the highway, surrounded by a tall wall and set back a hundred metres or so, but largely hidden by urban sprawl.

Huacas del Moche

Five kilometres south of Trujillo, in a barren desert landscape beside the Río Moche, two temples really bring ancient Peru to life. Collectively known as the **Huacas del Moche**, these sites make a fine day's outing and shouldn't be missed even if you only have a passing interest in archaeology or the ancient civilizations of Peru. The stunning **Huaca del Sol** (Temple of the Sun) is the largest adobe structure in the Americas, and easily the most impressive of the many pyramids on the Peruvian coast. Its twin, the **Huaca de la Luna** (Temple of the Moon), is smaller, but more complex and brilliantly frescoed. This complex is believed to have been the capital, or most important ceremonial and urban centre, for the Moche culture, at its peak between 400 and 600 AD.

Although very much associated with the Moche culture and nation (100–600 AD), there is evidence of earlier occupation at these sites, dating back two thousand years to the Salinar and Gallinazo cultures, indicated by constructions underlying the *huacas*. The area continued to be held in high regard after the collapse of the Moche culture, with signs of Wari, Chimu and Inca offerings here demonstrating a continued importance. The latest theory suggests that these *huacas* were mainly ceremonial centres, separated physically by a large graveyard and an associated urban settlement. Finds in this intermediate zone have so far revealed some fine structures, plus pottery workshops and storehouses.

To **get there** from Trujillo take one of the golden-coloured **colectivos**, marked "Campina de Moche", which run every thirty minutes from the corner of Suarez with Los Incas, near the Mercado Mayorista, to the base of Huaca del Sol (50¢); or, pick up one of the blue *colectivos* with a gold stripe that leave from the south side of Ovalo Grau (every 10–15 min). Some *colectivos* go all the way to the Huaca de la Luna, but many prefer to drop you off on the road, within sight, but still a ten- to fifteen-minute walk away.

Huaca del Sol

The **Huaca del Sol** itself is presently off limits to visitors, but it's an amazing sight from the grounds below or even in the distance from the Huaca de la Luna, which is very much open to the public. Built by the Mochica around 500 AD, and extremely weathered, its pyramid edges still slope at a sharp 77 degrees to the horizon. Although still an enormous structure, what you see today is about thirty percent of the original construction. On top of the base platform is the demolished stump of a four-sided, stepped pyramid, surmounted about 50m above the desert by a ceremonial platform. From the top of this platform you can clearly see how the Río Moche was diverted by the Spanish in 1602, in order to erode the *huaca* and find treasure. They were quite successful at washing away a large section of the site but found precious little except adobe bricks.

Estimates of the pyramid's brickwork vary, but it is reckoned to contain somewhere between 50 million and 140 million adobe blocks, each of which was marked in any one of a hundred different ways – probably with the maker's distinguishing signs. It must have required a massively well-organized labour supply to put together – Calancha, a Spanish historian, wrote that 200,000 Indian workers were required. How the Mochica priests and architects decided on the shape of the *huaca* is unknown, but if you look from the main road at its form against the silhouette of Cerro Blanco, there is a remarkable similarity between the two, and if you look at the *huaca* sideways from the vantage point of the Huaca de la Luna, it has the same general outline as the hills behind.

Huaca de la Luna

Clinging to the bottom of Cerro Blanco, just 500m from Huaca del Sol, is another Mochica edifice, the **Huaca de la Luna** (8.30am–4pm; $3.50, includes a 45min guided tour; ☎044/291894 for information from the university museum in town), a ritual and ceremonial centre that was built around the same time as the Huaca del Sol. What you see today is only part of an older complex of interior rooms built over

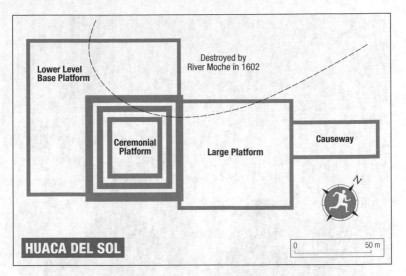

six centuries that included a maze of interconnected patios, some covered and lavishly adorned with painted friezes. The **friezes** are still the most striking feature of the site, rhomboid in shape and dominated by an anthropomorphic face surrounded by symbols representing nature spirits, such as the ray fish (symbol of water), pelicans (symbol of air) and serpent (symbol of earth). Its feline fangs and boggle-eyes are stylizations dating back to the early Chavín cult and it's similar to an image known to the Moche as **Ai-Apaec**, master of life and death. The god that kept the human world in order, he has been frequently linked with human sacrifice, and in 1995, archaeologists found 42 skeletons of sacrificial victims here. Sediment found in their graves indicates that these sacrifices took place during an El Niño weather phenomenon, something that would have threatened the economic and political stability of the nation. Ceramics dug up from the vast graveyard that extends between the two *huacas* and around the base of Cerro Blanco suggest that this might have also been a site for a cult of the dead, while the fact that it is built at the foot of the sacred Cerro Blanco and incorporates some rocky outcrops into one of the patios suggests that this may also have been somewhere honouring *apus*, or mountain spirits.

Behind the *huaca* are some frescoed rooms, discovered by a grave robber in the early 1990s, displaying multicoloured murals (mostly reds and blues). The most famous of these paintings has been called *The Rebellion of the Artefacts* because, as is fairly common on Mochica ceramics, all sorts of objects are depicted attacking human beings, getting their revenge, or rebelling. All in all, some 6000 square metres of polychrome reliefs have been uncovered. Oddly enough, the excavation work here is being well financed by the company that now owns virtually all the country's beer brands.

The Chicama Valley

Like Moche, the Chicama Valley is full of **huacas** and ancient sites, the most famous being the **Huaca El Brujo**. Locals have a long tradition as *huaqueros*, or grave robbers. Also, rumours abound about vile deaths from asphyxiation, a slow process sometimes lasting days, for anyone who ventures into a tomb: "Le llamó la huaca", they say – "the *huaca* called him".

▲ Archaeologists at work, Huaca de la Luna

The **Chicama Valley**, north of the Río Moche and about 35km from Trujillo, is home to the remains of fortresses and an irrigation system that dates back nearly 6000 years when the Río Chicama was once connected to the fields of Chan Chan by a vast system of canals and aqueducts over 90km long. Today, however, the region looks like a single enormous sugar-cane field, although in fact, it's divided among a number of large sugar-producing co-operatives, originally family-owned **haciendas** that were redistributed during the military government's agrarian reforms in 1969.

The **sugar cane** was first brought to Peru from India by the Spaniards in the seventeenth century and quickly took root as the region's main crop. Until early in the twentieth century, the haciendas were connected with Trujillo by a British-operated rail line, whose lumbering old wagons used to rumble down to Trujillo full of molasses and return loaded with crude oil; they were, incidentally, never washed between loads. Although the region still produces nearly half of Peru's sugar, it has diversified as well. These days, Chicama is also well-known for the fine Cascas semi-*seco* **wine** it produces. The haciendas are also renowned for the breeding of *caballos de paso* – **horses** reared to compete in dressage and trotting contests – a long-established sport that's still popular with Peruvian high society. For more laid-back recreation, the isolated seaside village of Puerto Chicama, 65km north of Trujillo, offers excellent surfing opportunities.

To get to sites in the Chicama Valley, there are **buses** and *colectivos* available, but it is a good day-trip from Trujillo and many people prefer to go on a **guided tour** from there (see p.405), or to hire a taxi with driver and guide for the day ($25–35). The whole valley is also well served by **local colectivos**, and although they have no fixed timetables, it's quite easy to get from one village or site to another. If you want to go by public transport from Trujillo, catch one of the **buses** marked "Puerto Chicama", "Paijan" or "Chicama", which leave every thirty minutes from opposite Casinelli's Museum, or alternatively either earlier on the route from either the Mercado Mayorista (where most of the buses start), the Ovalo Larco (at the western end of Pizarro, which becomes Avenida Larco as it leaves the town centre), or the Ovalo del Papa a few hundred metres further north. To get to El Brujo from Trujillo, take a bus to Chocope from the Chicago bus terminal on Avenida America Sur, then pick up a *colectivo* from Chocope. For El Brujo, you need a *colectivo* to Magdalena de Cao. Cars run every thirty minutes to Magdalena (50¢) from Chocope. You can usually find **taxis** in Chicama or Chocope who'll take you to the sites for a few dollars per person.

Huaca El Brujo

Fifty kilometres north of Trujillo, the **HUACA EL BRUJO** (Mon–Sat 9am–5.30pm; $3.50), whose name means "Temple of the Wizard", is a Mochica-built complex of associated adobe temple ruins incorporating the Huaca Cao Viejo to the south, plus the Huacas Cortada and Prieto, slightly to the north. Most of the recent discoveries have been made in Huaca Cao Viejo, some 60km from Trujillo, and investigations at the site mean that much of it is off limits to visitors. It's best to go with a tour operator from Trujillo (there's a good exhibition about the site at the Museo de la Nación in Lima, see p.102).

To **get to** the *huaca*, you have to pass through the nearby village of **Magdalena de Cao**, about 5km from the site and the nearest place that local **colectivos** actually pass through; Magdalena de Cao is the ideal place to sample *chicha del año*, an extra-strong form of **maize beer** brewed in the valley.

Large adobe temple constructions dominate the actual site which itself is made up of three main ceremonial *huacas*: Cortada, Cao Viejo and Prieta. Some of the walls on these *huacas* are adorned with figures in high relief and painted murals, discovered here as recently as 1990. On the top, third layer of the **Huaca Cortada**, there's a painted character with startled eyes, a sacrificial knife in one hand and a decapitated head in the other (decapitation apparently being common practice amongst the Mochica). The **Huaca Cao Viejo** is a larger pyramid, topped by a ceremonial platform some 30m high, and clearly of great significance to the Mochica ceremonial world and religious hierarchy.

Quite literally a heap of rubbish, **La Huaca Prieta** sits right next to the Playa El Brujo at the edge of the ocean, ten minutes' walk west of the main Huaca El Brujo site. It may be a garbage dump, but it is one that has been accumulating rubbish for some 6500 years, and is crowded with evidence and clues about the evolution of culture and human activity on this coast. This small, dark hill is about 12m high and owes its discolouration to thousands of years of decomposing organic remains. On the top, there are signs of subterranean dwellings, long since excavated by archaeologists Larco Hoyle and Junius Bird.

Puerto Chicama

PUERTO CHICAMA, known also as **Puerto Malabrigo**, 13km northwest of the roadside town of Paijan, and 74km north of Trujillo, is a small fishing village that once served as a port for the sugar haciendas, but is now much better known as a surfers' centre, offering some of the best surfing waves on Peru's Pacific coast. If you want a **place to stay**, try the *Hostal El Hombre* (❷), the traditional surfers' place, or *Hostal Chicama* (❷), both with a nice sea view. The place has a real lack of facilities, though, and there are seldom any boards to hire locally – which won't affect serious surfers, who generally bring their own. More of interest to seasoned surfers, the surf here is said to have "the longest lefthand breaking surf in the world" often reaching heights of over 2m and running for over 2km at times. Novice surfers may want to check out the gentler waters of Máncora (see p.471). To get here, you can catch one of the **buses** from Trujillo marked "Puerto Chicama", "Paijan", "Chicama" or "Ascope", which leave every 30min from opposite Casinelli's Museum.

Cajamarca and around

Whether or not you are planning to venture to the nearby sites or the rainforests of Amazonas, **Cajamarca** is worth a visit. A sierra town, it is second only to Cusco in the grace of its architecture and the soft drama of its mountain scenery. Above all, though, it's the friendliness of the people that distinguish Cajamarca. There are two main routes into this mountain valley from Trujillo, each exciting and spectacular. The speediest way is to head up the coast via **Pacasmayo**, then turn inland along a relatively new paved road which follows the wide Río Jequetepeque Valley, passing small settlements and terraced fields as well as the large dam, *la represa Gallito Ciego*, an impressive structure at Km 35. Regular buses and *colectivos* from Trujillo do this route, completing the journey in about eight hours. A slower route (usually two days) is by bus along the old road, currently in a poor state of repair, from Trujillo through **Huamachuco** and **Cajabamba**.

The proud and historic city of Cajamarca remains relatively unaffected by the tourist trade, despite its intrinsic appeal as the place where Pizarro captured and eventually killed the Inca Emperor, Atahualpa. It also makes a very dramatic starting point for visiting the ruins of **Chachapoyas** and the jungle regions around **Tarapoto** and **Yurimaguas**, although most people choose the faster and more frequented route from Chiclayo via Olmos and Jaen to access this region.

Cajamarca

An attractive city that's almost Mediterranean in appearance, **CAJAMARCA**, at 2720m above sea level, squats below high mountains in a neat valley. Despite the altitude, the climate is surprisingly pleasant, with daytime temperatures ranging from 6 to 23°C (43–75°F); the rainy season is between the months of December and March. The city's stone-based architecture reflects the cold nights up here – charming as it all is, with elaborate stone filigree mansions, churches and old Baroque facades. In contrast, the interiors of most buildings are actually quite austere in appearance with plain walls and roofs. Cajamarca is never overcrowded with tourists; in fact, it's unusual to see any foreign travellers outside of the main season, June to September. The narrow streets throng with locals going to and from the market or busy at their daily toil. Things have changed, though, in recent years following the discovery of Peru's largest **gold mine** at nearby Yanacocha, in the hills to the west of the city. Despite local concern that gold extraction and refining processes are polluting the groundwater, the mines have provided an economic boost to the town, creating more jobs. The look and feel of the city has changed little, though it has smartened up and there is a larger expatriate presence than before.

Some history

The fertile Cajamarca Basin was domesticated long before cows arrived to graze its pastures, or fences were erected to parcel up the flat valley floor. As far back as 1000 BC it was occupied by well-organized tribal cultures, the earliest sign of the Chavín culture's influence on the northern mountains. The existing sites, scattered all about this region, are evidence of advanced civilizations capable of producing elaborate stone constructions without hard metal tools, and reveal permanent settlement from the **Chavín** era right through until the arrival of the conquering **Inca** army in the 1460s. Over the next seventy years, Cajamarca developed into an important provincial garrison town, evidently much favoured by Inca emperors as a stopover on their way along the Royal Highway between Cusco and Quito. With its hot springs, it proved a convenient spot for rest and recuperation after the frequent Inca battles with "barbarians" in the eastern forests. The city was endowed with sun temples and sumptuous palaces, and their presence must have been felt even when the supreme Inca was over 1000km away to the south in the capital of his empire.

Atahualpa, the last Inca lord, was in Cajamarca in late 1532, relaxing at the hot springs, when news came of **Pizarro** dragging his 62 horsemen and 106 foot soldiers high up into the mountains. Atahualpa's spies and runners kept him well-informed of the Spaniards' movements, and he could quite easily have destroyed the small band of weary aliens in one of the rocky passes to the west of Cajamarca. Instead he waited patiently until Friday, November 15, when a dishevelled group entered the silent streets of the deserted Inca city. For the first time, Pizarro saw Atahualpa's camp, with its sea of cotton tents, and an army of men and long spears. Estimates varied, but there were between 30,000 and 80,000 Inca warriors, out-numbering the Spaniards by at least two hundred to one.

Pizarro was planning his coup along the same lines that had been so successful for Cortés in Mexico: he would capture Atahualpa and use him to control the realm. The plaza in Cajamarca was perfect, as it was surrounded by long, low buildings on three sides, so Pizarro stationed his men there. The next morning, nothing happened and Pizarro became anxious. In the afternoon, however, Atahualpa's army began to move in a ceremonial procession, slowly making their way across the plain towards the city of Cajamarca. Tension mounted in the Spanish camp.

Leaving most of his troops outside on the plain, Atahualpa entered with some five thousand men, unarmed except for small battle-axes, slings and pebble pouches. He was carried into the city by eighty noblemen in an ornate carriage – its wooden poles covered in silver, the floor and walls with gold and brilliantly coloured parrot feathers. The emperor himself was poised on a small stool, richly dressed with a crown placed upon his head and a thick string of magnificent emeralds around his aristocratic neck. Understandably bewildered to see no bearded men and not one horse in sight he shouted, "Where are they?"

A moment later, the Dominican friar, **Vicente de Valverde**, came out into the plaza; with the minimum of reverence to one he considered a heathen in league

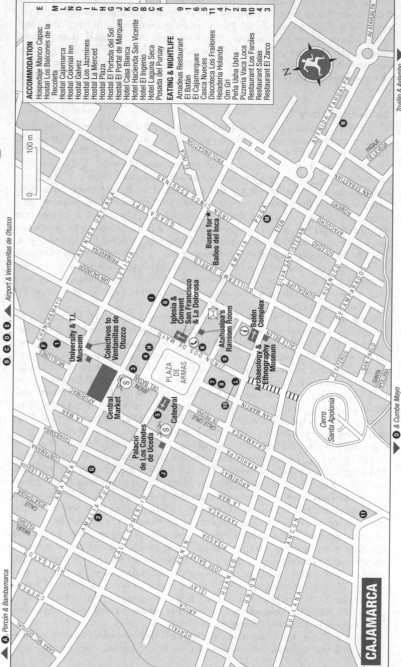

with the devil, he invited Atahualpa to dine at Pizarro's table. The Lord Inca declined the offer, saying that he wouldn't move until the Spanish returned all the objects they had already stolen from his people. The friar handed Atahualpa his Bible and began preaching unintelligibly to the Inca. After examining this strange object Atahualpa threw it angrily to the floor. As Vicente de Valverde moved away, screaming – "Come out, Christians! Come at these enemy dogs who reject the things of God." – two cannons signalled the start of what quickly became a **massacre**. The Spanish horsemen flew at the five thousand Indians, hacking their way through flesh to overturn the litter and capture the emperor. Knocking down a two-metre-thick wall, many of the Inca troops fled onto the surrounding plain with the cavalry at their heels. Spanish foot soldiers set about killing those left in the square with such speed and ferocity that in a short time most of them were dead. Not one Indian raised a weapon against the Spaniards. Atahualpa, apparently an experienced warrior-leader, had badly underestimated his opponents' crazy ambitions and technological superiority – steel swords, muskets, cannons, and horsepower.

Arrival and information

Most people arrive in Cajamarca by **bus**, at one of the main bus company offices, many of which are on the third block of Avenida Atahualpa (see p.426, for details), a major arterial route running almost directly east out of the city. If you **fly** into Cajamarca it'll probably be with the daily flight from Lima with ATSA ($60), or with Aero Condor on one of its connections with Trujillo and Chimbote; you'll arrive at the airport (☎076/822523), 3km out of town along Avenida Arequipa. Buses leave from just outside the airport every twenty minutes or so for the market area, a couple of blocks below the Plaza de Armas in the city (60¢). Alternatively, a **motorcycle taxi** there costs less than $1, or a **taxi** will be around $1.50. A taxi to the Inca Baths costs $2.50–3.

Free maps and **tourist information** are available from the ITINCI office in the Belén Complex, on block 6 of Calle Belén (Mon–Fri 7.30am–1pm & 2.15–5.30pm; ☎076/822903, ⓦwww.inccajamarca.gob.pe). Alternatively, the University Museum, Arequipa 269 (Mon–Fri 7am–2.45pm), has some leaflets and maps, as do many of the tour companies listed on p.426, which can give advice and information; Sierra Verde Tours and Cumbe Mayo Tours on the plaza and the nearby Cajamarca Tours (see p.426) are among the most helpful. Free tourist information is also sometimes available from the university office at Batán 289, next door to the museum.

Accommodation

Most of Cajamarca's **accommodation** is in the centre of the city, around the Plaza de Armas, although there are also some interesting options, such as the *Hostal Galvez* with its natural hot spring baths, a few kilometres away at Baños del Inca, approximately 2–3km directly east of the city centre.

In Cajamarca

Hostal Los Balcones de la Recoleta Amalia Puga 1050 ☎/℉076/363302, ⓔhscajama@correo.dnet.com.pe. A beautifully restored late nineteenth-century building wrapped around a courtyard full of flowers. All rooms have private bath and some have period furniture. ❹

Hostal Cajamarca Jr Dos de Mayo 311 ☎076/362532. A lovely colonial building set around an attractive courtyard with an excellent restaurant, *Los Faroles*. Rooms are comfortable and make for reasonable value. ❺

Hostal Colonial Inn Los Heroes 350 ☎/℉076/313551. Halfway between the town centre and the bus offices, in an old, brightly painted building. Rooms are without or with bath, plus it has its own good Chinese restaurant. ❷–❸

Hostal Los Jazmines Amazonas 775 ☎076/361812, ✉ahospedajelosjamines@yahoo .com. A comfortable new hostel in a converted colonial house plus a courtyard with cafeteria serving great snacks. Some rooms have private bath. ❷

Hostal La Merced Chanchamayo 140 ☎076/362171. A small, friendly hostel which offers good value. Rooms are clean, with private bath, although hot water can sometimes be a problem. While there's access to laundry facilities, towels, soap and toilet paper are not generally provided. ❷

Hostal Plaza Amalia Puga 669 ☎076/362058. Situated in a once-lovely building on the Plaza de Armas, this is a rambling old place with creaky wooden floors. It's still good value, though, and rooms come with or without private bath. ❸

Hostal El Portada del Sol Pisagua 731 ☎076/363395 or 01/2254306, ⓦwww .hostalportadadelsol.com. A charming colonial house with well-kept wooden floors, ceiling beams and an attractive covered patio where visitors can enjoy breakfast. All rooms have private bath, and there's also good internet access. ❹

Hostal El Portal de Marques C Comercio 644 ☎/℗076/828464, ⓦwww.portal-delmarques.com. An attractive colonial house on two floors with a large courtyard, quite grand and spacious restaurant, plus very clean and tidy rooms with carpets, private baths and TVs. Extras include a good restaurant, bar and internet access. ❺–❼

Hotel Casa Blanca Jr Dos de Mayo 446 ☎076/822141. A fine old mansion tastefully modernized to produce a comfortable hotel and a couple of shared patios; the floors, however, are still rickety, wooden and full of character, and there's hot water and private baths and TVs in every room. ❹

Hotel El Ingenio Av Via de Evitamiento 1611–1709 ☎076/367121, ⓦwww.elingenio.com. A rather plush hotel located in a wonderful, converted old mansion with a patio, gardens and stylish bar; it's target market is mainly mine engineers, who likewise frequent the fine bar and restaurant. ❻–❼

Out of town

Albergue Baños del Inca located behind the thermal bath complex ☎076/348385 ⓦwww .cajamarca.net. This place has a number of chalets, all very comfortable and with their own built-in thermal bathrooms, TV, minibar, bedroom and living room. Many of the chalets afford stunning views of, and direct access to, the complex of atmospheric steaming baths. Highly recommended and excellent value for what you get. Dormitories are also available for more budget-minded travellers. ❶–❹; chalets ❼

Hacienda San Antonio at Km 5 on the Baños del Inca road, then 1 or 2km down its signposted driveway ☎076/360905, ✉hsanantonio@terra .com.pe. An old hacienda with about 150 beds, its own chapel, dairy and very attractive gardens, close to the Río Chonta. There are open fireplaces and all rooms have private bath and are finely decorated. Breakfast and a ride on their *caballos de paso* (horses) are included. ❻

Hospedaje Manco Capac Manco Capac 712. A very basic, inexpensive hostel run by the local parish, with shared bathrooms and minimal amenities. Located right in front of the entrance to the thermal baths, this place is really aimed at poorer Peruvians who need access to the baths, but is also a good budget option for travellers. ❶–❷

Hostal Galvez Manco Capac 552 ☎076/348396. Right beside the Baños del Inca, some 6km from the city centre, this comfortable hotel has thermally heated water pumped straight to your room. ❺

Hotel Hacienda San Vicente 2km west of the city centre towards Cumbe Mayo ☎076/362644, ✉hacienda-san-vicente@yahoo.com. A luxuriously renovated hacienda with the full range of facilities. Room designs have been strongly influenced by Gaudi's works. ❻

Hotel Laguna Seca Manco Capac 10988 ☎076/584311. Very close to the Inca Baths, this is a good place to rest up; there is thermal spring water in the rooms and also private access to some of the hot springs. Service is good. ❽

Posada del Puruay 5km north of the city ☎076/367928, ✉informes@posadapuruay.com .pe. A country mansion converted into a luxury hotel-museum. All rooms have colonial furniture as well as all the modern conveniences, but the place is especially notable for its ecological approach and has an organic garden. ❼–❽

The City

Often considered the Cusco of the Northern Peruvian sierra, **Cajamarca** is nevertheless smaller and doesn't have near the wealth of Inca stone ruins or post-conquest churches that its southern sister city possesses. There are, however, several important colonial churches and, of course, the famous Inca Emperor's Ransom Room, all of which draws visitors up here from the coast.

One **ticket** allows entrance to three of Cajamarca's main attractions, **Atahualpa's Ransom Room**, the **Iglesia Belén** and the **Archaeology and Ethnography Museum** (all Mon–Fri 9am–1pm & 3–6pm), the latter two of which form part of the **Belén Complex**. The ticket costs $5, and can be bought at either the Ransom Room or the complex.

Plaza de Armas

The city is laid out in a grid system centred around the **Plaza de Armas**, which was built on the site of the original triangular courtyard where Pizarro captured the Inca leader Atahualpa in 1532. Today the plaza is distinguished by its lovely low trees, fine grass and a wealth of topiary: trimmed bushes adorn the square, most cut into the shapes of Peruvian animals, such as llamas. On the northwest side of the plaza is the late seventeenth-century **Catedral** (daily 8–11am & 6–9pm; free), its walls incorporating various pieces of Inca masonry, and its interior distinguished only by a splendid Churrigueresque altar created by Spanish craftsmen. On the other side of the plaza is the strange-looking **Iglesia San Francisco** (Mon–Fri 9am–noon & 4–6pm; free), in whose sanctuary the bones of Atahualpa are thought to lie, though they were originally buried in the church's cemetery. Attached to the church, the **Convento de San Francisco** houses a **museum** (Mon–Fri 9am–noon & 4–6pm; 50¢) devoted to religious art – not as good as the one in Cusco (see p.253), but still offering an interesting insight into the colonial mind.

One of Cajamarca's unique features was that, until relatively recently, none of the churches had towers, in order to avoid the colonial tax rigidly imposed on "completed" religious buildings. The eighteenth-century chapel of **La Dolorosa** (Mon–Fri 10am–5pm; free), next to San Francisco, followed this pattern; it does, however, display some of Cajamarca's finest examples of stone filigree, both outside and in.

Around the Plaza de Armas

The most famous sight in town, the so-called **Atahualpa's Ransom Room** or El Cuarto del Rescate (Mon–Sat 9am–1pm & 3–5pm, Sun 9am–noon, closed Wed; $5) at Amalia Puga 722, is the only Inca construction still standing in Cajamarca. Lying just off the Plaza de Armas, across the road from the Iglesia San Francisco, the Ransom Room can, however, be a little disappointing, especially if you've been waiting a long time, as it is simply a small rectangular room with Inca stonework in the back yard of a colonial building. It has long been claimed that this is the room which Atahualpa, as Pizarro's prisoner, promised to fill with gold in return for his freedom, but historians are still in disagreement about whether this was just Atahualpa's prison cell, rather than the actual Ransom Room. There is, however, a line drawn on the wall at the height to which it was supposed to be filled with treasure, and you can also see the stone on which Atahualpa is thought to have been executed. The room's bare Inca masonry is notably poorer than that which you find around Cusco, and the trapezoidal doorway is a post-Conquest construction – probably Spanish rather than native. A far better example of colonial stone craft can be seen at the **Palacio de los Condes de Uceda** (9am–4pm; free), Apurimac 719, on the other side of the plaza, one block beyond the cathedral. This splendid colonial mansion has been taken over and conserved by the Banco de Credito, but you are free to wander in and have a look around.

A block north of the Plaza de Armas, in the streets around Apurimac, Amazonas, Arequipa and Leticia, you'll find Cajamarca's **Central Market** (daily 6am–5pm).

Because Cajamarca is the regional centre for a vast area, its street market is one of the largest and most intriguing in Peru – you can find almost anything here from slingshots, herbs and jungle medicines to exotic fruit and vegetables, as well as the usual cheap plastic imports. It is generally a busy, friendly place, but beware of **pickpockets**.

Slightly farther north of the market along Arequipa is the **University Museum**, at no. 269 (Mon–Fri 8am–2pm; 50¢; note that entry is not includeed in the Cajamaraca ticket mentioned in the box above). As well as having a good range of informative tourism leaflets and brochures, it has fascinating collections of ceramics, textiles and other objects spanning some three thousand years of culture in the Cajamarca Basin; the museum also includes mummies, carved stones, drawings of the Cumbe Mayo petroglyphs and some erotic pots. Look out for the work of Andres Zevallos, whose representations of local people are reminiscent of Ribera and whose landscapes are in the style of Matisse.

The Belén Complex

The **Belén Complex** (Mon–Fri 8.30am–noon & 4–6pm, Sat & Sun 8.30am–noon; $5 for the whole complex plus El Cuarto del Rescate) of buildings known as the **Conjunto Monumental de Belén**, on Calle Belén just southeast of the plaza, houses a variety of institutions, including two hospitals (in the lower part, the Hospital de Hombres has an exceptionally attractive stone-faced patio with fountains), a small medical museum (part of the university administration, the Instituto Nacional de Cultura) and the **Iglesia Belén**, whose lavish interior boasts a tall cupola replete with oversized angels.

However, the most interesting part of the complex is the **Archaeology and Ethnography Museum**. Located in what used to be the Hospital de Mujeres, over the road from the main complex, the museum displays ceramics and weavings from the region, as well as one or two objects that have been brought here from the jungle tribes to the east. Look out for the elaborate stone carvings on the archway at the entrance to the museum, which depict a mythic woman with four breasts, symbolizing fertility, and date back to when the building was a women's hospital.

Eating and drinking

You can eat very well in Cajamarca. There are some sophisticated **restaurants** – like *El Cajamarques* – specializing in the local, meat-based cuisine, but there are also lots of smaller speciality shops worth visiting to try out their pastries or fresh fruit ice creams. The Panaderia Campos, Comercio 661, serves great pastries and cakes, as well as local cheeses and postcards mostly taken by Sr Campos himself.

Amadeus Restaurant Jr Dos de Mayo 930, just above the plaza ☎076/829815. A rather elegant restaurant serving pastas and pizzas as well as quality *comida criolla* and other dishes such as pasta, burgers and steak.

El Batán Jr del Batán 369. Set in a converted colonial building, there's an art gallery on the first floor and other paintings adorn the dining room walls. The food's good, and includes local dishes that don't appear on the tourist menus; be sure to ask for *comida Cajamarqueña*. There's also live music on Fridays and Saturdays.

El Cajamarques Amazonas 770 ☎076/362128. An upmarket, traditional Cajamarca cuisine restaurant decorated with colonial paintings, weapons and other artefacts. The cooking is excellent, and portions emphasize quality rather than quantity.

Casca Nueces Amalia Puga 554. Very popular with locals for its delicious *humitas* (sweet maize-meal pasties) and large slices of cream cake.

Heladeria Holanda Amalia Puga 657, on the plaza. There's a real artisan at work here preparing some excellent ice cream using local milk and fresh fruit. Try the unique coca flavour: it may even be good for the altitude.

Om Gri San Martín 360. Not far from the plaza, this is an excellent spaghetti house serving a wide range of Italian dishes in a highly atmospheric ambience.

Pizzeria Vaca Loca San Martín 330. If you can set aside any associations the name (Mad Cow) may bring up, you'll enjoy the town's best pizzas at this busy spot.

Restaurant Los Faroles *Hostal Cajamarca*, Jr Dos de Mayo 311. One of the best restaurants in town for *criolla* dishes, served in a quiet, plush atmosphere; if you like well-flavoured potatoes ask for the dish *caldo verde*, a potato soup made with local green herbs; otherwise, for a starter, you could try the *humitas*, made from maize meal.

Restaurant Salas Jr Amalia Puga 637, Plaza de Armas. A small restaurant with an old-fashioned atmosphere and good service. The menu's similar to *El Zarco's* (see below), if slightly more upmarket with better food, particularly the breakfasts, though the portions are smaller.

Restaurant El Zarco Jr del Batán 170. One of the few local cafés to stand out in Cajamarca, *El Zarco* is always packed with locals. It plays a wide range of mostly Latin music and offers an enormous variety of tasty, large-portioned tasty dishes, including excellent trout. It's by no means upmarket, even if a plethora of friendly red-coated waiters lend a refined, 1920s atmosphere.

Nightlife and entertainment

Nightlife isn't really Cajamarca's strong point, with the odd bar or café playing host to occasional local music, often incorporating violins as well as the more usual Andean instruments and guitars. During fiesta times at least, you should have no trouble finding traditional music and dancing. At weekends, many of the **peñas** host good live music, and the clubbier **video pub** or **disco** scene is at its liveliest.

Peña Usha Usha, Amalia Puga 320, is the best venue in town for live Peruvian, especially *criolla* music, as well as Cuban troubador-style performances. A small space particularly busy at weekends but also entertaining during the week when owner Jaime Valera inspires locals and tourists alike with his incredibly talented and versatile guitar playing and singing. Often lit only by candle, this bar has a cosy, inviting atmosphere that will appeal to everyone. There are one or two discos, including: *Mamba*, Av Atahualpa 493, which also serves meals, and *Discoteca Los Frailones*, at the corner of Peru with Cruz de la Piedra, six blocks up Santa Apolonia from the plaza, which plays all kinds of music and has fantastic views over the city from the dance floor

Listings

Airlines LC Busre (daily flights to Lima) Jr Comercio 1024 ☎076/361098.

Banks and exchange Banco Continental, Jr Tarapaca 725; Banco de Credito, C Comercio 679; Banco de la Nación, Jr Tarapaca 647; and Inter-banc, Plaza de Armas. *Cambistas* hang out along Jr del Batán, between *Restaurant El Zarco* and the Plaza de Armas. There's a good casa de cambio at Jr Arequipa 724 (Mon–Fri 9am–1.45pm & 3.30–7pm) opposite the Banco de Credito.

Fiestas in Cajamarca

The best time to visit Cajamarca is during May or June for the **Festival of Corpus Christi**. Until the early twentieth century this was the country's premier festival, before it was superseded by the traditional Inca sun festival, Inti Raymi, held at Sacsayhuaman in Cusco. Corpus Christi nevertheless actually coincided with the sun festival and is traditionally led by the elders of the Canachin family, who, in the Cajamarca area, were directly descended from local pre-Inca chieftains. The procession here still attracts Indians from all around, but increasing commercialism is eating away at its traditional roots. Nevertheless it's fun, and visited by relatively few non-Peruvian tourists, with plenty of parties, bullfights, *caballos de paso* meetings and an interesting trade fair. The city's other main fiesta is **Dia de Cajamarca** (Cajamarca Day), usually around February 11, which is celebrated with music, dancing, processions and fireworks.

Buses Cruz del Sur, Av Atahualpa 600
☎076/361737 for coastal destinations like Trujillo
and Lima; Empresa Arberia, Av Atahualpa 315
☎076/366812; Expreso Cajamarca and Transportes
Arberia, Atahualpa 290 ☎076/363337; Transportes
Atahualpa, Atahualpa 299 ☎076/363060; Palacios,
Atahualpa 312 for Huamachuco and Celendin
and Chachapoyas; and Emtrafesa, Atahualpa 281
☎076/369663, for Trujillo, Chiclayo or Lima.
Car rental Cajamarca Tours, Jr Dos de Mayo 323
☎076/362813, and Promotora Turística, Manco
Capac 1098, Baños del Inca ☎076/363149.
Hospital Mario Urteaga 500 ☎076/362414.
Internet Cybernet, Jr del Comercio 924, on the
plaza.
Photography Centro Plaza, Jr Dos de Mayo 484,
has films, cameras and does developing; Video
Plaza Filmaciones, Amalia Puga 681; or Foto
Andina, Amalia Puga 663.
Police Plaza Amalia Puga 807 ☎076/365572.
Post office Amalia Puga 778 (Mon–Sat 8am–9pm).
Shopping For leathercraft, ceramics, woollens,
jewellery and local hats (*sombreros de paja*)

famous throughout Peru for their quality, try the
inexpensive artesania stalls lining the steps up to
the sanctuary on Cerro Santa Apolonia and also in
block 7 of Calle Belén; one of the best artesania
shops in town is without a doubt; Quinde, Jr Dos
de Mayo 264 (☎076/361031), which shouldn't be
missed; there's also the Casa Luna, Jr 2 de Mayo
334, which not only sells good artesania and exhibits and sells a range of local artwork and crafts, but
also has a cafeteria and sometimes does storytell-
ing for children.
Taxis Taxi Seguro, Av Independencia 373
☎076/365103, are the best.
Telephone office Cabinas Publicas (daily 7am–
11pm) can be found on the plaza at Jr Dos de
Mayo 460, just below the *Hotel Casa Blanca*.
Tour and travel agents Cajamarca Tours, Jr Dos
de Mayo 323 ☎076/365674, is one of the better
travel agencies in town for sorting out flights and
buying air tickets; Cumbe Mayo Tours, Amalia Puga
635 ☎076/362938, is one of the best for city tours
and tours to sites in the region.

Around Cajamarca

Within a short distance of Cajamarca are several attractions that can easily be visited on a day-trip from the city. The closest is the **Cerro Santa
Apolonia**, with its pre-Inca carved rocks, though these are not nearly as
spectacular as the impressive aqueduct at **Cumbe Mayo**, or the ancient temple
at **Kuntur Huasi**. However, the most popular trip from Cajamarca is to the
steaming-hot thermal baths of **Baños del Inca**, just 5km from the city centre. A
four-kilometre walk from Cajamarca lies the small village of **Aylambo**, known
for its ceramics workshops, where you can even try your hand at making your
own pots.

Cerro Santa Apolonia

A short stroll southeast from Cajamarca's Plaza de Armas, two blocks
along Jirón Dos de Mayo, brings you to a path up the **CERRO SANTA APO-
LONIA**, a hill that overlooks the city and offers great views across the valley.
At the top of the hill are the sensitively landscaped and terraced gardens known
as the **Parque Ecología** (daily 7am–6pm; 50¢), whose entrance is beside the
Iglesia Santisima Virgen de Fatima, a small chapel at the top of the steps as
you walk up from town. At the highest point in the park, you'll find what is
thought to have been a sacrificial stone dating from around 1000 BC. It is popularly known as the Inca's Throne, and offers a great overview of the valley.

Just 2km southwest of the hill, along the road to Cumbe Mayo, is a further group of
ruins – prominent among them an old pyramid, known to the Spanish as a temple
of the sun, but now called by the locals Agua Tapada (Covered Water). Quite possibly, there is a subterranean well below the site – they're not uncommon around here
and it might initially have been a temple related to some form of water cult.

AROUND CAJAMARCA

0   4 km

▼ *Trujillo & Chiclayo*

Baños del Inca and the Ventanillas de Otuzco

Many of the ruins around Cajamarca are related to water, in a way that seems to both honour it in a religious sense and use it in a practical way. A prime example of this is the **BAÑOS DEL INCA** (daily 6am–6.30pm; $1–2), just 5km east of the city. The actual price depends on the type and grade of bath – the quality ranges from the Imperial, which is the best, through the Turistas, followed by the standard Pavilions A, B and C. There is also an excellent new sauna (women only 8–10.45am & 2–4.45pm and mixed sessions 5–7.45am, 11am–1.45pm & 5–7.45pm; $2.80). The hot-water outdoor pool is open 6am–6.45pm with sessions of up to 1hr 45min. It's a fifteen-minute bus ride from block 10 of Amazonas; local **buses** and **colectivos** leave when full, usually every ten minutes or so (35¢). As you approach you can see the steam rising from a low-lying set of buildings and hot pools. The baths, which date from pre-Inca times, have long been popular with locals, though the whole place could do with a bit of a face-lift. Having said that, wallowing in the thermal waters is a glorious way to spend an afternoon. There's a restored Inca bath within the complex, but the stonework, though very good, is not original. It was from here that the Inca army marched to their doom against Pizarro and co.

An enjoyable two-hour (one way) walk can be enjoyed by following the road southeast from outside the baths to the pleasant pueblo of **Llacanora**; there are frequent **colectivos** to take you back to Cajamarca, but this service tends to fizzle out after 6pm. For those with more time, it's possible to **walk** from here (3–4hr one way), following the Río Chonta gently uphill to its source, to another important site, the **Ventanillas de Otuzco** (daily 9am–5pm; $1), 8km from Cajamarca. The Ventanillas (Windows) are a huge pre-Inca necropolis where the dead chieftains of the Cajamarca culture were buried in niches, sometimes metres deep, cut by hand into the volcanic rock. If you don't fancy the walk, you can take one of the **colectivos** direct from Cajamarca to the Ventanillas (50¢), which leave every twenty minutes or so from Del Batan, just below the Central Market.

Aylambo

A four-kilometre walk along Avenida R. Castilla to the south of Cajamarca brings you to the small village of **AYLAMBO**, known for its ceramics workshops. You can buy a wide range of locally made earthenware products or even try your hand at making your own pottery. Special workshops are also laid on for children; ask at one of the tour agents in Cajamarca for details (see p.426). There are plenty of **buses** here from Avenida Independencia in Cajamarca (15min; 50¢), if you want to save your legs for the many trails that wind around the village through attractive, forested land.

Cumbe Mayo

Southwest of Cajamarca stands the ancient aqueduct and canal of **CUMBE MAYO**, stretching for over 1km in an isolated highland dale. Coming from Cajamarca, there's an odd natural **rock formation**, the Bosque de Piedras (Forest of Stones), where clumps of eroded limestone taper into thin, human figure-like shapes – known locally as *los frailones* (the friars) because of their resemblance to robed monks. A little further on, you'll see the well-preserved and skillfully constructed **canal**, built almost 1200 years before the Incas arrived here. Dotted along the canal there are some interesting **petroglyphs** attributed to the early Cajamarca culture. The amount of meticulous effort which must have gone into crafting the aqueduct, cut as it is from solid rock with perfect right angles and precise geometric lines, suggests that it served a more ritual or religious function rather than being simply for irrigation purposes. In some places along the canal, the rocks have been cut into rectangular shapes. According to archaeologists, these are remains left by the quarrying of stones for the construction of the canal. Cumbe Mayo originally carried water from the Atlantic to the Pacific watershed (from the eastern to the western slopes of the Andes) via a complex system of canals and tunnels, many of which are still visible and in some cases operational. To the right-hand side of the aqueduct (with your back to Cajamarca) there is a large face-like rock on the hillside, with a man-made **cave** cut into it. This contains some 3000-year-old petroglyphs etched in typical Chavín style (you'll need a torch to see them) and dominated by the ever-present feline features. There's a small but interesting site **museum** ($1.50) with toilets at the entrance and, further on, past the first small hill, the guardian has a hut; if he doesn't catch visitors for payment at the museum he usually finds them here.

There are no **buses** from Cajamarca, and only infrequent **combi colectivos**, so it's best to take an organised tour (from about $10 per person). You can **walk** the 20km here in maybe five or six hours, starting from the back of the Cerro Santa Apolonia, though with an altitude of 3600m, it's not an easy stroll. Most people take a **tour** (9am–2pm; $8–10 per person) with one of the companies (see p.426). For **places to stay**, the *Parador Turístico* (no phone; ❷), by the museum in Cumbe Mayo, has basic, pleasant rooms, but is rarely open. Similarly, the small **cafeteria** here is usually closed; so if you want to stay in this area it's best to bring a **tent**, though you'll need to get **permission** first from the Instituto Nacional de Cultura, located in the Belén complex by the tourist office.

Kuntur Huasi

Largely destroyed by the ravages of time and weather, **KUNTUR HUASI** was clearly once a magnificent temple. You can still make out a variation on Chavín designs carved onto its four stone monoliths. Apart from Chavín itself, this is the most important site in the northern Andes relating to the feline cult; golden ornaments and turquoise were found in graves here, but so far not enough work has been done to give a precise date to the site. The anthropomorphic carvings indicate differences in time, suggesting Kuntur Huasi was built during the late Chavín era, around 400 BC. Whatever its age, the pyramid is an imposing ruin amid quite exhilarating countryside.

It's possible to **walk** the 90km from Cumbe Mayo to Kuntur Huasi, in the upper part of the Jequetepeque Valley, to the east of the Cajamarca Basin. This trek, however, takes three or four days, so you'll need a **tent** and **food**. Alternatively, you can get on the Trujillo **bus** from Avenida Atahualpa in Cajamarca to Chilete, a small mining town about 50km along the paved road to Pacasmayo. Here, you need to change to a local bus (leaving every hour or so) to the village of San Pablo (with two small, basic **hotels**), from where it's just a short downhill walk to the ruins. The journey can take from two to five hours by public transport, so most people choose the easiest option – an organized **tour** from Cajamarca for around $30 per person (see p.426).

South from Cajamarca: Huamachuco and Gran Pajaten

It's a long, rough, but rewarding journey south from Cajamarca to the small town of **Huamachuco**, jumping-off point for visiting the archaeological site of **Marca Huamachuco** as well as the fabulous, rarely visited and very remote ruins of **Gran Pajaten**. The whole journey from Cajamarca to the ruins takes at least five days, and involves a combination of bus and hiking. To get to Huamachuco, take the Palacios **bus**, which leaves three times a week from Avenida Atahualpa in Cajamarca, for the five- or six-hour ride to Cajabamba, where you need to change to a more local bus for the three-hour journey on to Huamachuco. Travelling by day you'll be rewarded with spectacular views coming down from the green pastures of Cajamarca and across the almost tropical Condebamba Valley before ascending to Cajabamba.

If you need to stay over in **Cajabamba**, just about the only reasonable **accommodation** can be found at the *Hostal Flores*, L.Pradon 137 (℡076/851086; ❶), on the plaza, where the simple rooms have private bath and are set around a pleasant courtyard. For **eating**, try the *Restaurant Cajabambino II*, at Grau 1193, next to the market, which serves up tasty plates of local trout and chicken dishes. The *Café Grau*, on Grau just before the plaza, offers excellent fruit salads. All the **bus companies** are located within a block of the market.

Huamachuco

Infamous in Peru as the site of the Peruvian army's last-ditch stand against the Chilean conquerors back in 1879, **HUAMACHUCO**, at 3180m, is a fairly typical Andean market town, surrounded by partly forested hills and a patchwork of fields on steep slopes. The site of the battle is now largely covered by the small airport, while the large Plaza de Armas in the centre of town possesses an interesting colonial archway in one corner, which the Liberator Símon Bolívar once rode through. Now, however, it's flanked by the modern, and less visually appealing, cathedral.

Take a three-hour walk for about 6km from the plaza to the dramatic circular pre-Inca fort of **Marca Huamachuco** (daily 6am–6pm; free), the main reason most travellers end up in this neck of the woods. What with the fort being located on top of one of several mountains dominating the town, it's hard to get a **taxi** to take you there, although Alosio Rebaza, at D. Nicolau 100 (T076/441488) will transport people in his 4WD vehicle ($12 for up to four, or $25 if you want him to wait for you). Some 3km long, the **ruins** date back to around 300 BC, when they probably began life as an important ceremonial centre, with additions dating from between 600 and 800 AD. The fort was adopted possibly as an administrative outpost during the Huari-Tiahuanaco era (600–1100 AD), although it evidently maintained its independence from the powerful Chachapoyas nation, who lived in the high forested regions to the north and east of here (see p.431). An impressive, commanding and easily defended position, Marca Huamachuco is also protected by a massive eight-metre-high wall surrounding its more vulnerable approaches. The *convento* complex, which consists of five circular buildings of varying sizes towards the northern end of the hill, is a later construction and was possibly home to a pre-Inca elite ruler and his selected concubines; the largest building has been partially reconstructed. A guardian controls entry to the *convento* buildings and should be offered a small tip ($1 per person), while an information sheet providing a **plan** of the site and some brief details is available from the Municipalidad in Huamachuco.

Practicalities

Of the **bus** companies, Gran Turismo pull in at Balta 790; Anita at San Martín 700; Palacios at Castilla 167; Negreiros at Suarez 721 (off Balta); Agreda at block 7 of Balta; and Sanchez Lopez at Balta 1030 (though their booking office is on the plaza).

For **accommodation**, try the *Hostal Huamachuco*, at Castilla 354 (T076/441393; ②), near the Plaza de Armas, for rooms with or without bath in their old building. There's also the *Noche Buena* (③), on the plaza adjoining the cathedral, which is modern, clean and has private bath and TV. Slightly cheaper, the *Casa de Hospedaje Las Hortencias*, Castilla 130 (T076/441049; ②), has fairly basic rooms with bath in a friendly house and a nice courtyard where you can lounge around. All get full during festival times when you should try to book in advance.

The best bets for **food** are the restaurants *El Karibe*, on the Plaza de Armas, which serves *cuy* (guinea pig) and goat, and the restaurant in *Casa de Hospedaje Las Hortencias* hotel, which does a delicious *caldo de gallina* (a very fine hen stew) and a limited choice of other dishes. The *Café Venezia*, at San Martín 780, rustles up great desserts and has excellent coffee made from beans fresh from the Marañón Valley, while *Bar Michi Wasi*, at San Ramon 461 on the plaza, is small but trendy, with a nice atmosphere, and definitely the place to press locals for information about nearby attractions.

On the first weekend in August the **Fiesta de Waman Raymi** is held at nearby Wiracochapampa, bringing many people from the town and countryside to the Inti Raymi-style celebrations. Other festivals in the region include the **Fiesta de Huamachuco** (celebrating the founding of the city) on August 13–20, a week of festivities including a superb firework display on August 14 and aggressive male *turcos* dancers during the procession.

Money can be changed at the Caja Municipal or the Caja Rural, both on the plaza, or in several of the shops along the first few blocks of San Martín. The colourful rural **market** is on block 9 of Balta.

The ruins of Gran Pajaten

Agreda **buses** connect Huamachuco twice weekly (Wed & Sat) with the village of **Chagual** (around twelve very bumpy hours) where you can hire mules and guides (from $8 a day per mule) for the four- or five-day trek via the settlements of Pataz (20km, a 6hr walk from Chagual) and Los Alisos (another 8km or 3hr walk) to the true trailhead for the extremely remote ruins of **GRAN PAJATEN** – a further three or four days' walk. Occasional mining vehicles also go from Chagual to Pataz. If you're interested in seeing these highly regarded ruins of a sacred city, **permission** must first be obtained from the Instituto Nacional de Cultura (see p.67); and this is generally only given to those who can demonstrate a serious and specific interest and reason for visiting this special site.

The main archaeological site at Gran Pajaten is known as **Ruinas de la Playa**. Discovered in 1973, they cover some four hectares, with around 25 buildings, both round and square, built mainly of a slate-type stone (sometimes called *piedra pizarra*). One of the round structures is thought to have been a temple, another living quarters. Many of the walls have typical Chachapoyan (similar to those found around Kuelap, see p.435) geometric and anthropomorphic figures that have been created by the way in which these frequently thin stones are placed in the walls.

Chachapoyas, Kuelap and around

There are two routes up to Chachapoyas, the best, and by far the fastest, is the road leaving the coast from Chiclayo and Piura via Olmos, Jaen and Bagua; this route has fewer and lower passes. But a fascinating **alternative route to Chachapoyas**, though much more arduous (at least until the road is paved all the way) and significantly longer, winds its way up and down several massive valleys and passes. On the map it looks deceptively nearer and more direct, yet it meanders along on a bumpy dirt track, often very narrow, all the way from Cajamarca across stunning and steep Andean terrain, via the pleasant town of Celendin, and stopping in Tingo, the entry point for the fabulous remains of the **citadel of Kuelap**, some way before Chachapoyas.

If you have the time, explore some of the other amazing archaeological sites of unique pre-Inca **Chachapoyas culture**, many of which – such as Balsas, Leymebamba and Jalca – are en route to Kuelap, itself the most famous of Chachapoyan archaeological remains; several other major sites lie beyond. Highly civilized, the Chachapoyans left their mark in numerous tombs and impressively sophisticated fortifications. To a large extent the ancient culture lives on in some of the remote communities like **La Jalca**, whose seventeenth-century stone-built village **church** has the Chachapoyan zigzag built into its design. The houses in the village are lovely, conical, thatched-roof constructions with walls of *tapial*-type mudwork.

The route winds through green mountain scenery, past dairy herds and small houses in a variety of earthy colours, and crosses into the Marañón Valley beyond Leymebamba, reaching heights of almost 4000m before descending to the town of Chachapoyas. The whole trip takes at least twenty hours, and involves changing buses at **Celendin**.

The **bus companies** Inca Atahualpa (the better of the two) and Palacios both run daily services along the 112-kilometre route from Avenida Atahualpa in Cajamarca to Celendin ($4–5; 4–5hr), where you can get twice-weekly (Thurs & Sun) Transportes Virgen del Carmen and Empresa Jauro buses from Jr Caceres 108 (seven blocks from the Plaza de Armas) for the fourteen-hour journey to Chachapoyas ($6–7). The seats are often sold out the day before, so buy tickets **in advance** if possible. If you have to break the journey overnight at Celendin, and need **accommodation**, try the *Hotel Loyers* (**❷**), on Jirón Galvez, or the good value and fairly friendly *Hostal Celendin,* Jr Unión 305 (**☎**076/555239; **❷**), set in a colonial-style building, with private baths and its own restaurant. The *Restaurant Jalisco*, on the plaza, serves good breakfasts and other **food** (but watch out for overcharging). If you happen to be here on a Sunday, check out the great **market**, just a block north of the plaza, which has bargains in leather goods.

Chachapoyas and around

Even in the early twenty-first century, Chachapoyas remains well off the beaten track, though it has become a firm favourite for those who have made it to this remote and beautiful destination. An unlikely capital of the *departmento de Amazonas* because of its small size and location 2334m up in the Andes quite distant from lowland Amazonia, **CHACHAPOYAS**, is poised on an exposed plateau between two river gorges. In Aymara, Chachapoyas means "the cloud people", perhaps a description of the fair-skinned tribes who used to dominate this region, living in one of at least seven major cities (like Kuelap, Magdalena and Purunllacta), each one located high up above the Utcubamba Valley or a tributary of this, on prominent, dramatic peaks and ridges. Many of the local inhabitants still have light-coloured hair and remarkably pale faces. The town today, although friendly and attractively surrounded by wooded hills, is of no particular interest to the traveller except as a base from which to explore the area's numerous archaeological remains – above all the ruins of **Kuelap**.

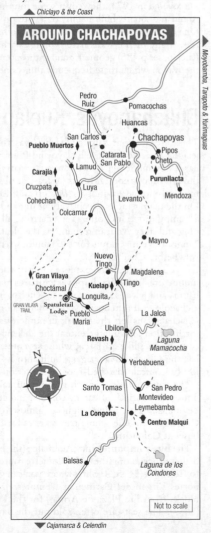

▲ *Chiclayo & the Coast*

AROUND CHACHAPOYAS

Moyobamba, Tarapoto & Yurimaguas

Pedro Ruiz · Pomacochas

Huancas

San Carlos · Chachapoyas
Pueblo Muertos ◆ · Pipos
Catarata · Cheto
San Pablo
Lamud · **Purunllacta**
Carajía ◆
Cruzpata · Luya · Levanto · Mendoza
Cohechan
Colcamar

Mayno

Nuevo
Tingo · Magdalena
Gran Vilaya ◆ · Tingo
Choctámal · **Kuelap**
GRAN VILAYA · Longuita
TRAIL · **Spatuletail**
Lodge · Pueblo · La Jalca
Maria
Ubilon
Revash · Laguna
Mamacocha
N
Yerbabuena

Santo Tomas · San Pedro
Montevideo
Leymebamba
La Congona ◆ · **Centro Malqui**

Balsas · Laguna de los
Condores

Not to scale

Arrival, information and getting around

The fastest route to Chachapoyas is by **bus** from Chiclayo, taking about ten hours. The best company is Civa (**☎**041/478048), whose buses arrive at their Chachapoyas depot at San Juan de La Libertad 464; Trans Servis Kuelap, Bolognesi 536 (**☎**041/478128) also has daily buses connecting Chachapoyas town with Chiclayo. There are also buses coming up from the coast (from both Chiclayo and Piura) that pass the Chachapoyas turn-off at the small settlement and army camp of Pedro Ruiz (*Hotel Casa Blanca;* **❷**) en

▼ *Cajamarca & Celendin*

route to Moyobamba and Tarapoto. Many people hop off the bus here and take a local **colectivo** (usually waiting outside the corner by the *Hotel Casa Blanca*) or bus on to Chachapoyas. The other, much harder going alternative is the long, rough route via Cajamarca (see p.431).

Other **buses and colectivos** arrive within a couple of blocks of the Plaza de Armas on block 3 of Grau (for Kuelap), along blocks 3/4 of Jirón Ortiz Arrieta, or around the corner on Jirón Salamanca, blocks 7/8. **Transport around town** tends to be by motorcycle rickshaw, with a flat rate cost of 50¢. For general **tourist information** the best place is i-Peru's office at Jr Ortiz Arrieta 588 (Mon–Sat 8am–1pm & 3–7pm; ☎041/477292, ✉iperuchachapoyas@promperu .gob.pe); you can also ask at the Dirección Subregional de Industria y Turismo ITINCI, C Chincha Alta 445 (Mon–Fri 9am–5.30pm; ☎041/457047), just a block from the plaza. For in-depth **advice** on local archaeological sites, try the Instituto Nacional de Cultura, Jr Junin 817 (Mon–Fri 9am–6pm). The Camayoc Foundation, established to protect and promote this region, also has a highly informative website ⓦwww.camayocperu.com.

Accommodation

There aren't many **hotels** to choose from here and certainly nothing particularly plush. Most of those listed, however, are friendly and do their best to keep you warm and comfortable. Most provide hot water and private bathrooms, but are rather stark and offer little in the way of luxury.

Gran Hotel Vilaya Jr Ayacucho 755 ☎041/477664. Located on the Plaza de Armas, this is a relatively comfortable, quality hotel, with its own restaurant. All rooms have private bath and hot water. ❺

Hostal Danubio Plazuela Belén ☎041/477337. Very clean and peaceful, this hostel is popular with travellers on a budget. The rooms are quite small and are available with or without private bathroom. There's also a restaurant, although breakfast is not included. ❷–❸

Hostal Kuelap Jr Amazonas 1057 ☎041/457136. Clean and friendly, although most rooms have shared bath and no hot water. ❷

Hotel Amazonas Jr Grau 565 ☎041/477199. A popular budget place on the Plaza de Armas, with an attractive, traditional patio. Rooms are available with or without private bath. ❷–❸

🏃 **Hotel Revash** on the Plaza de Armas, Grau 517 ☎041/477391. Almost stylish rooms, mostly with private bath, and some with good views over the plaza. There's hot water, laundry facilities and the management (as Andes Tours) also run tours to Kuelap, Levanto, the Revash Circuit, among other sites. ❷

Hotel El Tejado Jr Grau 534 ☎041/477654. Based on the Plaza de Armas and operating its own tours, it also has a pleasant, if rather dark, restaurant for breakfast (with traditional *tamales* or *juanes*, rice and chicken cooked and served in a leaf) overlooking the square. Most rooms have private bathrooms. ❸–❹

The Town

Chachapoyas was once a colonial possession rich with gold and silver mines as well as extremely fertile alluvial soil, before falling into decline during the Republican era. Recently, however, with the opening up of the road networks in these parts, it has developed into a thriving little market town (with a wide range of fruits and veggies, some craft goods, and some smaller woollen accessories such as straps and belts), supporting a mostly Indian population of around ten thousand, themselves with a reputation for being among the most friendly and hospitable people in Peru. As well as the cathedral and the municipal buildings, the tranquil **Plaza de Armas** contains a colonial bronze fountain, a monument to Toribio Rodriguez de Mendoza. Born here in 1750, he is considered the main source of Peru's own ideological inspiration behind independence from the mother country Spain. There's a small **museum** (Mon–Fri 9am–4pm, Sat 9am–1pm) on the plaza, featuring ceramics, some mummies, stone axes and ancient bone needles used for

Tour operators in Chachapoyas

There are several **local tour operators** in Chachapoyos. Andes Tours, (☎041/477391) run from the *Hotel Revash* (see p.433) are well-organized and well-equipped operators able to take visitors to all the main sites and also off the beaten track, including Gran Vilaya on request. Vilaya Tours, Jr Grau 624 (☎041/477506, ⓦwww.vilayatours .com) have a good reputation, and offer a variety of tours including one to the fabulous Gocta waterfalls, Peru's highest. Chachapoyas Tours, Grau 534 (☎041/478078, ⓦwww.chachapoyastours.com) are experienced, competent and have links with accommodation lodges in the Choctamal and Levanto areas, and also offer tours to Kuelap and Karajia. One well-known local **guide** is Martín Chumbe, Jr Piura 909, also contactable through the *Gran Hotel Vilaya* (see p.433), who speaks some English and charges around $30 a day for tours of sites in the region, including Kuelap. Other recommended guides include Julio Soto Valle, Jr Libertad 812 (☎041/477498) and Oscar Arce Caceres, from the *Hostal Estancia Chillo*, some 4 or 5km south of Tingo at the base of Kuelap ruins.

sewing, among other ancient objects. The town also possesses a couple of churches of some interest, notably the **Iglesia del Señor de Burgos**, known for its attractive colonial imagery, and the **Iglesia de Santa Ana**, the first church built here by the Spanish. The tourism infrastructure in Chachapoyas or the surrounding region is very limited, but, if you are prepared to camp, you can explore a wealth of interesting sites in little-charted territory.

Eating and nightlife

While **wining and dining** isn't Chachapoyas' forte, there are nevertheless some surprising culinary delights. Places tend to close early (around 10pm), except for nightclubs, which are open much later. Nevertheless, there are several reasonable places for breakfast, lunch or evening meals; none of them are expensive.

Cuyería, Pollería y Panadería Virgen Asunta Jr Puno 401. *The* place to go for roast *cuy*, though you have to order it a couple of hours in advance.
Licoria Kuelap Ayacucho 826. A fairly traditional drinking bar, popular with locals at weekends, and playing a varied selection of Latin and rock music, as well as some reggae and rap.
Restaurant Chacha Jr Grau 545, located next to the *Hotel Amazonas*. An excellent restaurant serving well-priced and well-prepared Peruvian fare; very popular at lunchtime.
Restaurant Vegetariano El Eden Jr Grau, half a block down from the plaza towards the market. This is a superb and very accommodating vegetarian restaurant serving brilliant breakfasts, snacks, lunches and juices; try the mixed juice with *maca* herb.

Rittual Nightclub Jr Ayacucho 113. Just a couple of blocks from the plaza, and the liveliest club in town, playing a mix of Latin, reggae and rock, and serving a reasonable selection of beer and spirits.
Las Rocas Jr Ayacucho 932. A friendly little café where typical local food is served, including staple mountain meals such as rice and potato dishes and soups, which are usually made with chicken, quinoa and potato. A popular lunchtime place.
Silvia Snack Bar Ayacucho 828. Probably best for the locally made fruit-based wines and spirits (they make a good blackberry drink – ask for the *copa mora*).
La Tushpa Jr Ortiz Arrieta 753 ☎041/777198. A great restaurant for meat dishes, particularly *cuy*, *chicharonnes* (deep fried pork pieces) and burgers; also serves pizzas and *tamales*.

Listings

Banks and exchange The Banco de Credito, on the Plaza de Armas, will change dollars and cash travellers' cheques, and can sometimes advance cash against Visa cards.

Film and photography Foto Castaneda on Jr Ayacucho 948.
Post office Grau 561, on the plaza (Mon–Sat 8am–7pm).
Telephone The Telefónica office is at Jr Triunfo 851.

Kuelap and Gran Vilaya

The main attraction for most travellers in the Chachapoyas region is the unrestored ruin of **Kuelap**, one of the most overwhelming pre-Inca sites in Peru. Just 40km south of Chachapoyas (along the Cajamarca road), the ruins were discovered in 1843, above the tiny village of Tingo in the remote and verdant Utcubamba Valley. In 1993, Tingo was partly destroyed by flash floods, when more than a hundred homes were washed away, yet the village is still inhabited and remains an important point of access for visiting the ruins. These days, however, a new village, Nuevo Tingo, has been built higher up above the valley. Cars and colectivo mini-buses from Chachapoyas pass through Nuevo Tingo and continue their winding, precipitous route on a circular anti-clockwise route via Choctamal to Pueblo Maria, where there is a range of rustic accommodation (see p.436) within two to three hours hike of Kuelap itself.

Also best reached from this road, but far less accessible – at least two days' walk – is the collection of ruins known as **Gran Vilaya**. If you intend to venture beyond Kuelap to Gran Vilaya, you must first obtain **permission** from the Instituto Nacional de Cultura in Chachapoyas (see p.433). The entry point for Gran Vilaya is the village of Choctámal, about half an hour before you get to Pueblo Maria, but on the same road, where there also just happens to be a great lodge, Spatuletail Lodge (☎041/478838, Ⓦwww.marvelousspatuletail.com; $40 or Ⓖ), with seven bedrooms, toilets and even a hot tub. An impressive, quite ornate building, it's also well located within a day's walk (or horse ride) of both Kuelap and Gran Vilaya, and in fact this is the start of the great Gran Vilaya trail which follows ancient Inca stone roads.

Among the other places possible to visit are the ruined city of **Purunllacta**, one of the likely capitals of the Chachapoyas people, and also **Carajía** and the **Pueblo de los Muertos**, two impressive cliff-face burial centres for the elite of this quite sophisticated culture. The land here is full of ravines and very steep-sided valleys. All land over 3500m is considered *jalca*, or wild, and should be approached only with a guide. Spectacled bears, puma, and white-tailed deer roam while hummingbirds abound on these remote highland plains.

Getting there

If you're coming **from Cajamarca** and **Celendin**, the **bus** passes right through Tingo. From **Chachapoyas**, it's possible to visit the ruins independently by taking a **colectivo** from the corner of Grau and Salamanca (usually leaving between 6am to 11am) **to Pueblo Maria or to Tingo**.

The easiest approach – particularly, if you plan to sleep locally and walk, which is the best way to appreciate this site – is via Pueblo Maria, some three hours from Chachapoyas by a sometimes precipitous track. From **Pueblo Maria to Kuelap** it's a two to three hour hike, but it's a fairly level and easy-going walk along dirt roads and tracks. En route, you'll pass through Cuchapampa, Quisango and Malcapampa hamlets. It's possible to hire a **horse** for you and/or your bags from Pueblo Maria (just ask the *hospedaje* owner, see p.436). Unlike the Tingo route, there's very little climbing involved and you'll arrive at Kuelap with more energy to enjoy this archaeological marvel.

If you're approaching **Kuelap** via **Tingo** it's a hard but hugely rewarding 1500-metre climb (around 4hr up and about 2hr back down) from the west bank of the Río Utcubamba. Leave early to avoid the mid-morning sun, and remember to carry all the water you'll need with you. **Mules or horses** are usually available for hire from the hostel ($5–10 per day) in Tingo (see p.436), or at El Chillo ($8–12 per day), on the road to Tingo. Alternatively, **colectivos** go from Tingo to the Kuelap car park (3hr). And of course, you can always go on an organized day tour from Chachapoyas with a **guide** (from $20 per person; see p.434).

Accommodation

Apart from the obvious choice of the Spatuletail Lodge (see p.435), there are also a few **hostels** in the area. **Pueblo Maria** boasts several **hospedajes** (community phone line: ℡041/813088) and a women's textile cooperative with shop in the village, all very reasonably priced. The *Casa Hospedaje Changali* on the left as you arrive in the village, after the school (❷) is particularly good value. **Tingo**, too, has a very basic, unnamed hostel (no phone; ❶). There are also two recently furbished rooms with enough space for twelve people with sleeping bags and a shared toilet facility, managed by the Guardian at the entrance to **Kuelap** site (no phone; ❶); snacks are also available here during the day. If this mini lodge is full, then the Guardian can usually advise of space within households of neighbouring hamlets. Camping is usually free, just ask the INC Guardian.

The Kuelap ruins

The ruined citadel of **KUELAP** (daily 8am–2pm; $4) built by the Chachapoyas tribe high on a ridge, about 3000m above sea level, commands terrific views of the surrounding landscape, but it is the structure itself which immediately arrests your attention.

It has been calculated that some forty million cubic feet of building material was used at Kuelap, three times the volume needed to construct the Great Pyramid of Egypt. An estimated three thousand people would have lived here at its height, working mainly as farmers, builders and artisans and living in little round stone houses. Its enormous **walls** tower up to 20m high, and are constructed from gigantic limestone slabs arranged in geometric patterns, with some sections faced with rectangular granite blocks over forty layers high. The average wall thickness is around 80cm and the largest stone 2m thick. Inside the ruins lie the remains of some two hundred round stone houses, many still decorated with a distinctive zigzag pattern (like the modern ceramics produced by the locals), small, carved animal heads, condor designs, deer eye symbols and intricate serpent figures. These are similar in style to the better known Kogi Indian villages of today's northern Colombia; and, indeed, there are thought to be linguistic connections between the Kogi and the Chachapoyas peoples, and possible links to a Carribean or even Mayan influence. There are a few rectangular buildings, too, which are associated with the later Inca occupation of Kuelap. Some of the structures in the central area have been recognized as kitchens because of their hearths, and there are a few that still have ancient pestles. The higher part of the site was restricted to the most privileged ranks in Chachapoyas society, and one of the buildings there, with fine curved outerwalls, is believed to have been a temple, or at least to have had a ceremonial function.

The site is overgrown to some extent with old trees laden with epiphytes. Even though it's high, this is still considered to be cloud forest. There are also various enclosures and huge crumbling watchtowers partly covered in wild subtropical vegetation, shrubs and even trees. One of these towers is an inverted, truncated cone containing a large, bottle-shaped cavity (known as the *tintero* or ink well), possibly a place of sacrifice, since archaeologists have found human bones there, though these could date from after the original inhabitants of Kuelap had abandoned the citadel.

Occupied from about 600 AD, Kuelap was the strongest, most easily defended of all Peruvian fortress cities, something that can be seen in the narrowing defensive form of the main entry passageways. This is thought to be the site which the rebel Inca Manco considered using for his last-ditch stand against the conquistadors in the late 1530s. He never made it here, ending up instead in the equally breathtaking Vilcabamba, northeast of Cusco. While Kuelap was in fact conquered by the

Incas in the late fifteenth century but vacated before the arrival of the Spanish, some commentators believe that if the Incas had in fact decided to make their stand against the Spanish here, the history of Peru and maybe Western South America may well have taken a very different course.

The guardian at the site can also give information about the other, smaller ruins in the immediate vicinity such as **Revash**, a thirteenth-century burial site, built by the Revash culture (contemporaneous with the Chachapoyas people), where mummies and rock paintings are on view. The remains here consist mainly of limestone-built tombs and are within three to four hours' hike from the village of Santo Tomas. Revash can be accessed via trails from the village of **Choctámal** (see below).

The Gran Vilaya ruins and around

The name **GRAN VILAYA** refers to a superb complex of almost entirely unexcavated ruins scattered over a wide area. Explorer Gene Savoy claimed to have "discovered" them in 1985, though travellers have been hiking into this area for years and there were several sketch maps of the ruins in existence years before he arrived. Despite Savoy's claim to have found thousands of buildings, a more conservative estimate puts the record at some 150 sites divided into three main political sections. About thirty of these sites are of note, and about fifteen of these are of real archaeological importance.

Colectivos can drop you off at **Choctámal** (before Pueblo Maria, but along the same road), from where you can walk to *Spatuletail Lodge* (see p.435) or the full five or six hours from Choctámal to Gran Vilaya's remote, largely unexplored and hard-to-find sites. The best way to reach them is with a decent **guide** and some mules (see p.435) who could also take you to see the impressive network of Chachapoyan ruins spread out across an area about thirty miles (east to west) and fifteen miles (south to north), all requiring demanding hiking through stunning cloud forest. **Camping equipment and food** are essential items to carry. Also, note that once you get beyond Choctámal and Pueblo Maria, it's often hard to use money, and it can prove handy to have some **trade goods** with you – pencils, fruit, chocolate, bread, canned fish or biscuits – and, of course, camping gear, unless you want to be completely dependent on the local hospitality.

Purunllacta

Among other charted ruins in the Utcubamba Valley are those of the archaic metropolis of **PURUNLLACTA**. These can be reached fairly easily by taking the daily **bus** from (the street) Grau in Chachapoyas to Pipos on the Mendoza road. Get off here and **walk** to the village of **Cheto**, from where it's a short climb to the ruined city itself. The return trip can be done in the same day, though it's more enjoyable to **camp** at the site.

Purunllacta was one of the seven major cities of the Chachapoyas culture – and probably the capital – before they were all conquered by the Inca Tupac Yupanqui in the 1470s. The **site** consists of numerous groups of buildings scattered around the hilltops, all interconnected by ancient roads and each one surrounded by elegant agricultural terraces. At the centre of the ruined city you can clearly make out rectangular stone buildings, plazas, stairways and platforms. The most striking are two storeys high, and made of carved limestone blocks.

Carajía

A characteristic of the Chachapoyas region is its **sarcophagi**, elaborately moulded, earthenware coffins, often stuck inaccessibly into horizontal crevices high up along cliff faces and painted in vivid colours. These were built by the Chachapoyas people in the twelfth and thirteenth centuries. A fine example – and a rewarding excursion, 46km southwest from Chachapoyas – are the sarcophagi at **Carajía**. To get here catch one of the early morning **colectivos** or pick-ups headed for **Luya** from Grau and Salamanca in Chachapoyas. At Luya ask a local for directions to **Shipata**, where the path to the sarcophagi begins. From Shipata, walk down one side of the valley, over a bridge and then up the other side for about five minutes before taking a less clearly marked path to your right. The entire, spectacular **walk** from Luya takes about four hours.

Pueblo de los Muertos

The **PUEBLO DE LOS MUERTOS** (City of the Dead), located some 30km to the north of Chachapoyas and about 10kms from Luya, where you'll find over-grown roundhouse foundations plus some more examples of **sarcophagi**, some up to 2m high and carved with human faces. Six were originally found here and three have been put back in their original sites to stare blankly across the valley from a natural fault in the rock face. Each one has been carefully moulded into an elongated egg-like shape from a mixture of mud and vegetable fibres, then painted purple and white with geometric zigzags and other superimposed designs.

The Pueblo de los Muertos can be reached by taking the daily Chiclayo **bus** from the market in Chachapoyas, getting off at the bridge Puente Tingobamba on the main road. From here there's a track to the settlement of Lamud, close to the site. In total, it's of walk of some three or four hours; ask for directions as you go.

La Jalca

Almost three hours south by road from Chachapoyas, the traditional village of **La Jalca** is within walking distance of a number of ruins. The folklore capital of the region, La Jalca also lays claim to some amazing fourteenth-century stone walls and a seventeenth-century stone-built **church,** with characteristic Chachapoyan zigzag built into it. There's a good little **hostel** in town – the *Hospedaje Comunitario*, just beyond the church, and within walking distance of the plaza (no phone; ❷). The houses in the village, built in typical Chachapoyas fashion along the ridge, are lovely, conical thatched-roofed constructions with walls of *tapial*-type mudwork.

Leymebamba and Laguna de los Condores

About two-thirds of the way along the road from Chachapoyas to Cajamarca, in the section between Tingo and Celendin, you'll find the town of **Leymebamba**, some 80km (3–4hr) by road from Chachapoyas and another eight to ten hours from Cajamarca. This is the location for the superb **Museo de Leymebamba** (Mon–Sat 8.30am–4.30pm; $1), which houses around 150 mummies from the Chachapoyas culture's mausoleum of the not-too-distant **Laguna de los Condores**. The museum itself is the product of local labour and skills, using traditional materials and construction techniques including stonework, timber and *tapial*. There are only a couple of **hostels**, the best being the *Didogre*, 16 de Julio 320 (❷), which is nevertheless very basic.

Into the jungle: Tarapoto and downriver to Iquitos

It's possible just to visit the **jungle** for a day or two from Chachapoyas, Piura or Chiclayo by reaching over the Andes in a **bus** or flying to **Tarapoto**. For the very adventurous and those with lots of time, though, a **journey by land and river** could take you all the way from Chachapoyas via Tarapoto and Yurimaguas to the Peruvian jungle capital of **Iquitos** (see p.531) on the Amazon, not far from the Brazilian border. It's difficult to estimate the duration of this trip – there are always long waits for connections and embarkations – but it's unlikely to take much less than a week's hard travelling. This town acts as something of a centre for trips exploring the wildlife and flora of this region, and it is the gateway to Juanjui and the backroad along the edge of the rainforest to Tingo Maria – a route not presently recommended for travel because of its reputation for lawlessness and cocaine production. Tarapoto is also the start point for one of Peru's best Amazon river trips; by road to Yurimaguas, then by river boat following the Río Huallaga further into the jungle, along the edge of one of Peru's best and least-visited protected lowland forests, the remote rainforest haven of **Reserva Nacional de Pacaya Samiria** (see p.543).

Tarapoto and around

About 18hrs by road from Chiclayo, **TARAPOTO**, known as the "City of Palms", is a well-developed jungle settlement, with surfaced roads, fairly good hotels, a large market and an unexpectedly high proportion of young professionals and business people. This is due to the wealth of agriculture, and ultimately the soil, in the Rio Mayo valley around here. Evidence of this can be found at the town centre tropical plant nursery, Vivero Jardin Calleys, opposite the *Hotel Nilas* at Jr Moyobamba 171. Tarapoto is also a good base from which to explore this part of Peru, visit the folkloric locus of Lamas (see p.440), prepare for a jungle trip, or do some **whitewater rafting** on the Río Mayo (ask the tour companies for details).

The town, founded in 1772, lies just 420m above sea level and has an agreeable temperature range of 29–37°C (85–99°F). The Río Huallaga flows on from here, via the Amazon, until it finally empties into the Atlantic Ocean many thousands of kilometres away. A strange sort of place, Tarapoto has a large **prison** and a big drug-smuggling problem, with people flying coca paste from here to Colombia, where it is processed into cocaine for the US market (see box below). Nevertheless, the locals tend to be friendly and pleased to see tourists, themselves still few and far between.

Practicalities

The daily **buses** from Chiclayo to Tarapoto ($16, a 16–20hr trip) mostly arrive at, and leave from, blocks 6 to 8 of Avenida Salaverry. Probably the best bus for Chiclayo, Trujillo or Lima is Movil Tours, Avenida Salaverry 858. Paredes Estrellas, next door, is the next best bus for the coastal destinations. Tarapoto has its own **airport**, too, 5km from the centre of town (see "Travel details", on p.475, for information about flights). If you need a reliable **taxi service**, call Taxi Expreso (☏042/524962).

The main **post office** is at Jr San Martín 482 (Mon–Sat, 8am–7pm). The **tourist information** office is at Oficina Zonal de Industria y Turismo (☏042/522567, ✉ itatpto@viaexpresa.com.pe, ⓦ www.regionsanmartin.gob.pe), Jr Angel Delgado, block 1; there's also a good tourist information office in Lamas, just twenty

The road south from Tarapoto: a travellers' warning

The route **south from Tarapoto** via Juanjui (150km) and Tingo Maria (a further 350km) through wild frontier jungle territory is not currently recommended for travellers. It passes through one of the most dangerous areas in Peru, dominated by the illegal **coca-growing industry**, and the army have been present in the region for years. Now and again there are confrontations and shoot-outs, and the region remains pretty well beyond the control of law and order. On some parts of the road from here to Tingo Maria, buses suffer regular armed **robberies**, some involving fatalities. It's simply not worth the risk of travelling here at the moment.

minutes by car from downtown Tarapoto. For **internet**, the best is probably Mundonet, one block from the Plaza Mayor at Jr San Martín 205 (℡042/528531).

The best **accommodation** in Tarapoto, with a rooftop pool, large rooms, cable TV and private baths is the *Hotel Nilas*, Jr Moyobamba 173 (℡042/527321 ☻nilas -tpto@terra.com.pe; ❺–❻); there's also the mid-range options like the clean *La Mansion*, on Jr Maynas 280 (℡042/530471 ☻info@altamirahotel.com.pe; ❹–❺), which is very comfortable, has a swimming pool, garden, private baths and TVs; or the more basic *Hostal Pasquelandia*, at Pimental 341 (℡042/52290; ❷), the *Hostal Melendez*, C Ursua block 4 (❶–❷), and the *Hostal Central,* on Jr San Martín (℡042/522234; ❶).

The **restaurants** here are surprisingly good, especially the *Rea Grill,* Jr Moyobamba 331, which serves superb evening meals including a mix of standard Peruvian dishes augmented with jungle produce such as yucca and plantains. The *El Manguare,* Jr Moyobamba 161, on the main plaza offers a good, cheap lunch menu, while *El Camarón,* on Jirón San Pablo de la Cruz, is renowned for its delicious Amazon River shrimp. Further afield – 45min by *colectivo* (a bit longer by *mototaxi)* – the pleasant restaurant *El Mono y El Gato*, near the Cataratas de Ahuashiyacu (see below), serves interesting local dishes with very fine views. For ice creams, there's *Cachete*, on the plaza.

Cataratas de Ahuashiyacu

Half an hour by taxi from Tarapoto, along the road east towards Yurimaguas you'll find the entrance to the **Cataratas de Ahuashiyacu** (40¢), a popular and scenic local **swimming** spot, with small but very pretty waterfalls. These falls are one of several ecotourist destinations around Tarapoto. Other contenders, all within easy taxi reach, include the **waterfalls** of Huacamaillo and also those of Shapaja (21km), the village of Chazuta with its fine ceramic tradition, the stunning Laguna Azul (50km from town) and the wild rainforest of the valley of Shilcayo. The reality is that this newly opened up jungle region is full of quite astonishing natural treasures, many yet to be revealed to the travelling public.

Lamas

An obvious and pleasant day-trip from Tarapoto is **LAMAS**, a nearby Indian village and folklore capital of the *departamento* of San Martín, about 20km up into the forested hills and surrounded by large pineapple plantations at around 800m above sea level. The village is based around three interconnected levels or plateaux; the lower level is mainly living spaces, whilst most commerce is on the second level. Not surprisingly, the best views are from the third. **Colectivos** to Lamas leave every hour or so from the Plaza de Armas in Tarapoto ($1; 30min; taxis $15 return, 20min). The inhabitants of Barrio Huayco are reputed to be direct descendants of the Chanca tribe that escaped from the Andes to this region in the

Peru's mythic wildlife

In wildlife terms, Peru can justifiably be dubbed mega-biodiverse: a wealth of ecological niches make it a unique haven for over 1800 bird species, an enormous variety of reptiles, mammals and primates and a record-breaking diversity of ants. The country is perhaps the last great bastion for wild jaguars and giant otters, and you'll also find tapirs, anacondas, caiman, condors and spectacled bears in abundance. While the twenty-first-century threat from both human population growth and climate change remains a burning issue, less well-known is the fact that many of these creatures were considered sacred to ancient Peruvians.

Hummingbird ▲

Etching of a hummingbird, Nasca Lines ▼

Sacred aspects of birds and animals

The art of ancient Peru clearly describes a **cosmovision** with at least three principal domains, each associated with an appropriate and powerful animal: the **condor** frequently represents the sky domain and acts as a link between heaven and earth; **jaguars** are kings of the earthly plane; while serpents, specifically the **boa constrictor**, are linked with the earthly plane's underbelly and possibly the underworld. In many jungle areas, **pink dolphins** are considered dangerous spirit beings, while **insect** spirits play an important role in the daily lives of some Amazon Indian tribes even today; when an **Ashaninka** falls sick, for instance, it's not uncommon for a shaman to assign the cause of the illness to one or other of the ant species.

Birds

Condors, depicted on ancient ceramics, are still the iconic symbol of the Peruvian Andes, their large, partly bald heads often represented on the magical staffs of many coastal shaman. **Hummingbirds**, of which there are 127 different species in Peru, have been depicted on ceramics here for over three thousand years and one was etched onto the desert plane at Nasca over 1300 years ago. Ancient **owl**-shaped ceramics are regularly found in tombs on the coast; even today, this fearsome night hunter is closely associated with shamanic traditions and healing powers.

Jaguars

Scary feline imagery, often based on the **jaguar** (*Panthera onca*), has been used on

Peruvian ritual ceramics and metalware for over three thousand years in Peru and is believed to have represented one of the major ancient universal Peruvian deities. Still king of the **Amazon** today, the jaguar often weighs 150kg or more, living mainly in rainforests, savannas and swamps, and regularly stalking large game such as tapirs, caiman and occasionally people.

Ants

Both **bullet** and **leaf-cutter ants** are commonly encountered in the Peruvian rainforest and are well integrated into the mythology of the tribes; some believe that leaf-cutters – which routinely strip whole trees of their foliage, systematically exploiting a radius around their nest – can magically harm people who break specific **social taboos**. Some Amazon tribes even use bullet ant stings during **male initiation rituals**, to see which of the young men are truly brave.

Boa Constrictors

The **boa constrictor** is thought of as an important spirit being in most Peruvian Amazon tribes, and to see one in an **ayahuasca** vision (see p.585) is associated with seeing the spirit of the *ayahuasca* vine itself. There are ten boa contrictor subspecies, measuring an average of ten feet in length. They kill their prey through slow constriction, squeezing out the victim's breath before finally crushing its bones and swallowing.

Pink Dolphins

Smartest out of the five freshwater dolphin species, the **pink Amazonian dolphin** (*Inia geoffrensis*) is known as *bufeo* in Peru. Mythologically speaking, it's an apparently

▲ Jaguar

▼ Bullet ant

▼ Boa constrictor

Pink river dolphin ▲

Blue and gold macaws ▼

Cock-of-the-rock ▼

friendly creature believed to wickedly impersonate an attractive young man who seduces girls with a view to breeding with them, usually stealing the newborn away into the deep underworld of the river. Despite their intelligence and ability to work in teams herding and harvesting fish, pink dolphins are still hunted by humans today.

Wildlife hotspots

▶▶ **Around Iquitos** The rivers and jungle around Iquitos are great for spotting wildlife, and the **Pacaya Samiria National Reserve** is one of the most pristine areas: jaguars, boa constrictors and pink dolphins abound. As an aid to understanding the sacred aspects of wildlife, some lodges also offer **ayahuasca** sessions.

▶▶ **Colca Canyon** With sharp eyes and good binoculars, you can find condors in most parts of Peru's coast and highlands. The real hot spot, though, is the **Cruz del Condor** in the Colca Canyon, itself easily accessible from Arequipa or Chivay.

▶▶ **Manu National Park and Tambopata-Candamo Reserve** Closer to the Andes, and, in the case of Manu, with a greater variety of altitude and eco-niches, these are fantastic rainforest regions where **ant species** are common and **jaguars** are occasionally spotted, along with owls and hundreds of bird species (particularly macaws).

▶▶ **Pampa Hermosa Lodge** Though generally difficult to spot, Peru's national bird, the **Cock-of-the-Rock**, can be more or less guaranteed within a short walk of this lodge in the central jungle region, accessible from San Ramon and La Merced.

▶▶ **Sacred Valley** More common and easier to spot than condors, Peru's varied species of **hummingbirds** can be found anywhere in the country, particularly in the Sacred Valley of the Incas, near Cusco, and usually in the mornings, hovering mesmerically around flowering shrubs.

fifteenth century, fleeing the conquering Inca army. The people keep very much to themselves, carrying on a highly distinctive lifestyle which combines jungle and mountain Indian cultures – the women wear long blue skirts and colourfully embroidered blouses, and the men adorn themselves on ceremonial occasions with strings of brightly plumed, stuffed macaws. Everyone speaks a curious mixture of Quechua and Cahuapana (a forest Indian tongue) and the town is traditionally renowned for its *brujos* (wizards). The best month to visit is August when the village **festival** is in full swing. The days are spent dancing and drinking, and most of the tribe's weddings occur at this time. The Lamas people today have a large hinterland of forested hills, dotted with their relatively small gardens where they grow maize, bananas, coffee and very sweet pineapples.

An excellent **tourist information** office can be found on the small plaza in Lamas (T042/543013; Mon–Sat 7am–2.30pm) and there are at least two good **artesania** shops: Amachay, a museum-cum-shop which sells inexpensive Lamas artesania, from gourds and baskets to fossils as well as the local Lamas organic coffee (Oro Verde); and Artesania Tropical, Jr San Martín 1203. Down on the lower level of the village, the Cachique family sell eco-artesania. There are a few **restaurants**, the best being on the main street at the second level, close to the **Lamas Museo Etnográfico**, which has some displays about local crafts and culture as well as information on flora and fauna There are also a couple of basic **hotels** here, but the place with the best view is the *Albergue Los Girasoles* (T042/543439, Estegmaiert @yahoo.de; ❹), opposite the Mirador Los Chancas, a smart new hostel at the very top level of the Lamas hills and interestingly built along ecological lines; the operators also run a café and serve pizzas here, as well as organize interesting **eco-adventure treks** through local communities of the remote Lamas controlled hills. Alternatively, you can easily make it here and back from Tarapoto in a day.

Yurimaguas

From Tarapoto it's another 140km north along pretty but rough jungle tracks to the frontier town of **YURIMAGUAS**. In the dry season (Jun–Sept) you can do this journey by one of the frequent **colectivos** ($10) or **buses** from the Shilcayo *barrio* market area in Tarapoto; it takes about five or six hours. But from November to March it's more likely to take between eight and ten hours. Try and travel

Down river to Iquitos

From Yurimaguas, you can travel all the way to **Iquitos** by river (roughly $20 on deck or $35 for cabins, a three- to five-day trip). As soon as you arrive in Yurimaguas, head straight to La Boca port to look for boats, since they get booked up in advance. Boats leave regularly though not at any set times; it's simply a matter of finding a reliable captain (preferably the one with the biggest, newest or fastest-looking boat) and arranging details with him. The price isn't bad and includes food, but you should bring your own hammock if you're sleeping on deck, and bring clean bottled water, as well as any extra treats, like canned fish, and a line and hooks (sold in the town's *ferreterías*) if you want to try fishing.

The scenery en route is electric: the river gets steadily wider and slower, and the vegetation on the riverbanks more and more dense. Remember, though, that during the day the sun beats down intensely and a sunhat is essential to avoid **river fever** – cold sweats (and diarrhoea) caused by exposure to the constant strong light reflected off the water. On this journey the boats pass through many interesting settlements, including Santa Cruz and Lagunas, starting point for trips into the huge Pacaya-Samiria National Reserve (see Chapter 8).

this route by day if possible, because there's less risk of being robbed or encountering trouble on the road. There's photos and interesting if sparse information on Yurimaguas at www.yurimaguasperu.com and www.yurimaguas.net, but the bustling market town of Yurimaguas has little to recommend it, other than its **three ports**, giving access to the Río Huallaga. The most important is the downriver port of **La Boca**, where all the larger boats leave from, including those to Iquitos. The port is located some fifteen to twenty minutes' walk from the town centre, or a $1 ride in a motorcycle rickshaw. The second, middle port, known as **Puerto Garcilaso**, is closer to the heart of Yurimaguas and mainly used by farmers bringing their produce into town from the nearby farms in smaller boats. Fishermen primarily use the third, upper port, called **Puerto Malecón Shanus**.

Accommodation options in Yurimaguas include the *Hostal Cesar Gustavo* (❷), the most comfortable and friendly of the basic hostels, and the good-value *Hostal La Estrella* (❷). Slightly pricier, but better quality and with a good restaurant, is the *Hostal el Naranjo* (☎065/352650; ❸), while the *Hostal de Paz* (☎065/352123; ❸) is clean and friendly. For **food**, try the *Restaurant Copacabana*, which serves a range of Peruvian and standard international dishes, or the *Pollería Posada*, for chicken and chips. The *Café La Prosperidad* specializes in delicious fruit juices, and there's an excellent cevichería, *El Dorado*, by the Puerto Malecón Shanuse in Barrio La Loma.

The Northern Desert

The **Northern Desert** remains one of the least-visited areas of Peru, mainly because of its distance from Lima and Cusco, the traditional hubs of Peru's tourist trail, but it is still an invaluable destination for its distinctive landscape, wildlife, archaeology and history. Before Pizarro and the conquistadors first dropped anchor here in 1532, some argue that Northern Peru had the greatest density of citadels and urban settlements, previous and contemporaneous, anywhere in the Americas. When Pizarro set foot on these Northern beaches, this region was part of the Inca and previously Chimu empires. The area of desert around Chiclayo, such as the **Lambayeque Valley**, has yielded fantastic quantities of tomb gold, silver and precious stones such as emeralds in recent decades, and, as recently as December 2008, yielded one of the most significant Peruvian archaeological finds for some time, a ruined city originally built by the Huari (Wari) culture.

Northern Peru now has some excellent new museums besides the breathtaking coastal beauty of its desert environment, which itself contains the largest dry forest in the Americas, almost entirely consisting of *algarrobo* (carob) trees. The main cities of **Chiclayo** and **Piura** (the first Spanish settlement in Peru) are lively commercial centres, serving not only the desert coast but large areas of the Andes as well. If, like a lot of travellers, you decide to bus straight through from Trujillo to the Ecuadorian border beyond **Tumbes** (or vice versa) in a single journey, you'll be missing out on some unique attractions.

The coastal resorts, such as the very trendy **Máncora** and **Punta Sal**, but also **Cabo Blanco** and, further south **La Pimentel**, the beach serving Chiclayo's population, are among the best reasons for stopping: though small, they usually have at least basic facilities for travellers, and, most importantly, the ocean is warmer here than anywhere else in the country. The real jewels of the region, however, are the archaeological remains, particularly the **Valley of the Pyramids** at **Túcume** and the older pyramid complex of **Batán Grande**, two immense pre-Inca ceremonial centres within easy reach of Chiclayo. Equally alluring is the **Temple of Sipán**, where some of Peru's finest gold and silver grave goods were found within the last fifteen years.

The Panamerican Highway from Trujillo to Chiclayo

The **Panamerican Highway**, mainstay of the north's transport system, offers the fastest route north from Trujillo, passing through an impressively stark and barren landscape with few towns of any significance – though the valleys here have yielded notable archaeological finds dating from Peru's Early Formative Period (see Contexts).

San Pedro de Lloc, the first settlement of any real size, stands out for miles around with its tall, whitewashed buildings and old town walls that contain one mansion of note, the Casa de Raymondi (ask in the Biblioteca for the key-holder). There are a few reasonable restaurants here, including the *Bar-Recreo Los Espinos*, Jr Dos de Mayo 720. Some 3km from the town (ask for directions at the Biblioteca or one of the restaurants), at Cerro Chilco, it's still possible to visit the ruins of the ancient Indian settlement of **Loc**. Generally, though, San Pedro is a quiet little village with little to see, whose only claim to fame is its local culinary delicacy of stuffed lizards.

Some 10km north of here, the Panamerican Highway passes by the growing port town of **Pacasmayo**; many buses pull in here to pick up passengers and it is a possible stop off en route between Trujillo and Chiclayo. If you have your own car, it's a good place to stop for a meal or a drink and take twenty minutes to explore the seafront promenade. However, there are few **hotels** here (see p.444), if you decide to spend the night. Despite the town's grim initial appearance, the area around the old jetty, thought to be the largest and most attractive surviving pier on the coast of Peru, possesses some dilapidated colonial mansions.

The one historical site along this stretch of the Panamerican Highway is a few kilometres north of Pacasmayo, just before the village of **Guadalupe**, where a track leads off left to the well-preserved ruins of **Pakatnamu** (The City of Sanctuaries), overlooking the mouth of the Río Jequetepeque. Being off the main road and far from any major towns, the ruins of this abandoned city have survived relatively untouched by treasure hunters or curious browsers. The remains include pyramids, palaces, storehouses and dwellings. The place was first occupied during the Gallinazo period (around 350 AD), then was subsequently conquered by the Mochica and Chimu cultures. You can get here by **colectivo** or **bus** from Pacasmayo, but you'll still have to walk the 6km from the main highway to the site unless you take a taxi (also from Pacasmayo). It gets very hot around midday, and there's little shade and **no food** or drink available at the site, so bring your own.

Buses pick up and drop off passengers around the avenue at the centre of Pacasmayo, just a couple of blocks from the ocean. Expresso Cajamarca, Roggero, Transportes Atahualpa, Linea and Vulkano all stop in the main street, Leoncio Prado; Emtrafesa's depot is at Av 28 de Julio 104, just around the corner; while Cruz del Sur are at Jr Espinar C-7/90. Several buses a day go inland from here to

Cajamarca ($5; 6–7hr) or up the coast to Chiclayo ($1.70; 2hr), Trujillo ($2; 2–3hr) and Lima ($10; 10–12hr). The seafront at Pacasmayo has one or two good seaside **hotels**, such as the *Hotel Pakatnamu*, Malecón Grau 103 (T044/521051; ❺), and *Hotel La Estacion*, Malecón Grau 69 (T044/521718, F521888, Eelhotel@terra .com.pe; ❹–❺), which has rooms with TV and a weekend disco in the summer. *Hostal Cesar's Palace*, Leoncio Prado 1a (T044/521945; ❸), is also decent enough, with fairly comfortable rooms with TV. The seafront has a good **restaurant**, *El Encuentro de Ignacio*; you may also try *Chifa Tip Top*, at Leoncio Prado C/18, which is cheap and very popular with locals. The **Banco de Credito** is on the small Plaza de Armas, near the seafront.

Chiclayo and around

Some 770km north of Lima, **Chiclayo** is a large commercial centre thanks more to its strategic position for the export of produce like coffee and rice from the other side of the Andes than to any industrial development. Nearby **Lambayeque**, boasts two excellent and important **archeology museums**.

Despite being the northern base of several successive ancient cultures, the Chiclayo region's most interesting period was during the first millennium AD in the Lambayeque Valley. First came the Mochica-dominated settlements, which produced such magnificent treasures as were recently encountered at the **Temple of Sipán**. Then followed the Sicán culture, equally rich in iconographic imagery and fine ritual objects and garments, and responsible for the enormous desert temple complex of **Batán Grande** and the city of pyramids at **Túcume**, which compare in importance to the Moche and Chimu complexes around Trujillo. More recent and far less inscrutable ruins are to be found in the colonial ghost town of **Zaña**.

The Chiclayo area and Lambayeque Valley contains such a wealth of intriguing and appealing archaeological sites that it's best to start off by learning a bit more about the history and culture of the region by taking in the four main museums. Two of these, the **Museo Brüning** (one of Peru's best ceramic museums) and the **Museo de**

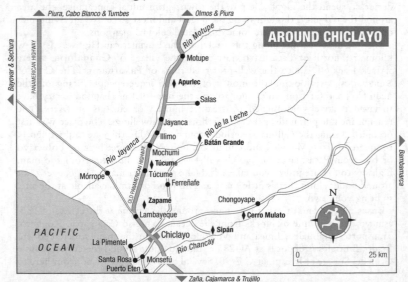

las **Tumbas Reales de Sipán** (Museum of the Royal Tombs of Sipán), are located in Lambayeque itself, just 12km or so from Chiclayo. The other principal museums, **Museo del Sitio Túcume** and **Museo Sicán** (devoted to the Sicán culture originally based at Batán Grande), are further out, one in the Valley of the Pyramids, the other en route to Batán Grande in the town of Ferreñafe.

Most places can be reached independently by taking a **colectivo** from the market area of Chiclayo, but you'll find it much easier to see all the archaeological sites if you've got your own transport. You'll probably get the most out of these, however, by going with a knowledgeable local **guide** on an organized tour from Chiclayo. **Taxi** drivers can also be hired by the day or half-day (usually around $15–30).

Chiclayo

The commercial centre of northern Peru, **CHICLAYO** is better famed for its banks than its heritage. Nevertheless it has its own attractions, even if most of the city is an urban sprawl modernizing and growing rapidly. The city has an incredibly busy feel to it, with people and traffic moving fast and noisily everywhere during daylight hours. Tourists tend to attract attention in the main streets, not least because they aren't seen very often.

Arrival, information and city transport

The José Abelado Quiñones González **airport** is 2km east of town, and easily reached by taxi for $3–5. **Buses** connecting Chiclayo with La Pimentel and Lambayeque use the Terminal Terrestre Oeste, on the first block of Angamos, just off block 1 of San José. Services for all the southern cities – Trujillo, Lima and so on – use the Terminal Terrestre La Victoria on Calle Mochica, where it meets the Panamericana Sur, which has a waiting area, a left-luggage deposit and a hostel.

For **tourist information** there are kiosks in the Parque Principal and nearby just a block down Balta Sur. Better still, the main **Regional Tourist Office** is just a couple of blocks from the Parque Principal on Av Sáenz Peña 839 (Mon–Fri 9am–5.30pm, Sat 9am–1pm; ☏074/233132 or 238112, ⓦwww.regionlambayeque.gob.pe). You can also try the information desk at the *Garza Hotel* (see below). Alternatively, you can contact the Tourist Police (see p.448). Although not essential, tickets to most sites and museums can still be bought independently, it's possible to buy a general Lambayeque **Tourist Ticket** ($5), available from the Instituto Nacional de Cultura, Av Gonzalez 375 (☏074/237261) in Chiclayo, and sometimes also available from the main local archaeological museums; the ticket covers the main museums and sites in the region, including those at Túcume, Sipán, Lambayeque, Ferreñafe and Batán Grande.

The centre of town is fine to **walk** around, but if you need a **taxi** try Chiclayo Rent-a-Car, Av Grau 520, Santa Victoria (☏074/229390, ⓕ237512), which also has offices at the *Gran Hotel Chiclayo* (see below) and the airport (☏074/244291).

Accommodation

Finding **a place to stay** is relatively simple in Chiclayo; but if you want peace and quiet, or to camp, you may prefer one of the out-of-town options like the beautiful *Hospedaje Rural Los Horcones* (see p.456), right by the Museo de Sitio at Túcume, in the Valley of the Pyramids; with a car or taxi, this is also a terrific base from which to explore all the other sites in the region. In Chiclayo itself, most of the reasonably priced hotels are clustered around the Plaza de Armas.

Garza Hotel Bolognesi 756 ☏074/228172, ⓦwww.garzahotel.com. Very central and pretty comfortable, with a pool and sauna, good food and staff that provide useful tourist information. They also rent out cars and jeeps. ❼

Gran Hotel Chiclayo Av Federico Villareal 115 ☏074/234911, ⓕ223961, ⓦwww.granhotelchiclayo.com.pe. The best, most luxurious hotel in town, even if it is a little way from the centre. For that trifling inconvenience, you get spacious, very comfortable rooms, excellent showers, a fine restaurant, decent swimming pool and even a hot little casino-bar. ❽

Hostal Sicán Av Maria Izaga 356 ☏074/237618. Nicely decorated, central, friendly and has TVs in rooms. The quietest beds are at the top, and the price includes breakfast. ❹

Hotel Europa on El'as Aguirre ☏074/237919, ⓔhoteleuropachiclayo@terra.com.pe. A very clean hotel with extremely friendly service and a small cafeteria. All rooms have private bath. ❸

Hotel Las Musas Los Faiques 101, Urb Santa Victoria ☏074/239884 or 239885, ⓦwww.lasmusashotel.com.pe. Upmarket lodgings that are a little less expensive than you'd expect, with excellent service, nice rooms, a cool lobby and casino. ❼

Hotel Royal San José 787 ☏074/233421. A brilliant budget option offering large, quite elegant rooms at affordable prices, some overlooking the Parque Principal (watch out for the Sunday morning parades). Rooms are available with or without private bath. ❷

The City

At the heart of this hectic but friendly city is its central plaza, known as the **Parque Principal**, where there's a futuristic fountain that's elegantly lit at night. You'll also find the Neoclassical **catedral** here, built in 1869 and with its main doorway supported by Doric columns, and the **Palacio Municipal**, a Republican edifice built in 1919. Along Calle San José, you'll find the **Convento Franciscano Santa Maria**, built in the early seventeenth century but destroyed, apart from the second cloister, by El Niño rains in 1961. But the main focus of activity is along **Avenida José Balta**, between the plaza and the town's fascinating **market area**, including the indoor **Central Market** and massive semi-covered market lanes, part of which is called the **Feria Balta**. Nearby, the biggest market of all, the **Mercado Modelo**, is packed daily with food vendors at the centre, and other stalls around the outside, this is one of the best markets in the north – and a revelation if you've just arrived in the country. The market has a whole section of live animals, including wild fox cubs, canaries and even the occasional condor chick, and you can't miss the ray fish, known as *la guitarra*, hanging up to dry in the sun before being made into a local speciality – *pescado seco*. But the most compelling displays are the herbalists' shops, or mercado de brujos (witches market), selling everything from herbs and charms to whale bones and hallucinogenic cacti. Further out on the eastern edge of town there's an even bigger, cheaper, wholesale market – **Mercado Mochoqueque** – which is a fascinating window into life in this part of the world; it's best to come early on Tuesday or Friday, but if you stray here, beware there are a lot of **pickpockets**.

Elsewhere in town there's the small, attractive chapel of **La Véronica** on Calle Torres Paz. Built at the end of the nineteenth century, its most notable feature is the altarpiece of silver- and gold leaf. In the **Plazuela Elías Aguirre**, just around the corner there's a statue in honour of the *comandante* of this name, who was a local hero serving the Republicans in the Battle of Angamos during the War of the Pacific.

Eating and nightlife

Eating out in or near Chiclayo offers quite a lot of variety. Being close to the ocean, seafood is the most common local dish, but the city also enjoys *criolla* meat dishes, such as *lomo saltado,* and Italian food – particularly pizzas. One local speciality is rehydrated dried fish (*pescado seco*), often prepared from flat ray fish with potatoes.

The best of Chiclayo's **restaurants** with top *criolla* cooking, is the excellent *Pueblo Viejo*, Maria Izaga 900, though it's better still when there's live music on Fridays. If you can't get in here, try the *Restaurant Mi Tia*, Elías Aguirre 698, for snacks, pasta and goat dishes at very reasonable prices. Specializing in typical Chiclayano cooking, there's the good-value *Restaurant Romana*, Av José Balta Sur 512, open all day; or, right on the Plaza de Armas at Elías Aguirre 824, the *Restaurant Las Americas*, which offers decent international dishes and good, basic *criolla* fare. Slightly more upmarket is *El Huaralino*, La Libertad 155, Urbino Santa Victoria, which does Chiclayano dishes, including *tortilla de raya*. For good set breakfasts, the *Snack Bar 775*, at Ugarte 775, offers the best value and is close to the *Hotel Europa*. Of the two good pizzerias on Av Jose Balta Sur, just a few blocks down from the Parque Principal, *Pizzeria Nueva Venecia*, Av Balta 365, is the better choice.

For a little **nightlife**, try the *Discotek Pub Las Leathers*, San José 604, lively and close to the main plaza; *Centro Turístico El Señorío*, Maria Izaga 654, which has food and live *criolla* music on Friday and Saturday after 10.30pm. For more up-tempo music, try the trendy but friendly *Yomiuri*, Sáenz Peña 997, which serves drinks and Japanese food in the evenings but doesn't warm up until quite late. The **disco** *Excess*, on Virgilio D'Allors, is lively, while *La Gaviota*, another disco, at Alfonso Ugarte 401 in La Pimentel, can be fun at weekends.

Listings

Airlines Almost daily flights with both Lan Peru and Star Peru: Lan Peru, Av Sáenz Peña 637 ☏074/236475; Star Peru, Av Bolognesi 316 ☏074/271173.
Airport Aeropuerto Internacional Jose Abelardo Quiñones Gonzales, Av Bolognesi ☏074/233192 (24hrs).
Banks and exchange The main banks are concentrated around the Parque Principal. *Cambistas* can be found on the corners of the Parque Principal, particularly Av José Balta, or there's the casa de cambio Hugo Barandiaran at Av Balta 641A (Mon–Fri 9.30am–5pm) next to the Banco Continental. The best bank for changing travellers' cheques is the Banco de Credito, Av José Balta Sur 888.
Buses Civa, Bolognesi 714 (☏074/223434), for Chachapoyas and Lima; Cruz del Sur, Bolognesi 888 (☏074/225508), for Trujillo, Lima and Tumbes or Mancora; Empresa El Cumbe, Quiñones 425 (☏074/231454), for Cajamarca; Dias, Bolognesi 536, for Cajamarca and Cajabamba or Celendin; Empresa Huancabamba, Bolognesi 536, for Huancabamba; Ejetur, Bolognesi 536, for Rioja, Moyobamba, Tarapoto and Yurimaguas; Movil, Bolognesi 195 (☏074/271940), for Chachapoyas, Tarapoto or Lima; and Turismo Kuelap, Bolognesi 536, for daily buses to Chachapoyas. The town's Terminal Terrestre has smaller, slower buses serving the locality and up and down the coast.

Car rental Mines Rent a Car inside the *Gran Hotel Chiclayo* ☏074/234911 or 9682532.
Hospital C Hipolito Unanue 180 ☏074/237776 (24hr).
Internet Click-Click, close to the plaza at San José 604, upstairs; and at San José 104.
Post office Elías Aguirre 140, seven blocks west of the plaza (Mon–Sat 8am–8pm, Sun 8am–2pm).
Taxi Robert Huima Suloeta, C Leticia 566 ☏074/498439.
Telephones Telefónica del Peru, Av José Balta 815; there's also a Locutorio Publico at both Av José Balta 827 and Elías Aguirre 631, the latter within a stone's throw of the plaza.
Tour operators Tours around the area include trips to Túcume, Batán Grande and the Museo Brüning (plus occasional shamanic tours) last 4–8hr and cost $15–30. The best are offered by Sipán Tours, 7 de Enero 772 (☏/☏074/229053, ☏www.sipantours.com) and InkaNatura Travel, in the lobby of the *Gran Hotel Chiclayo* (☏074/209948, ☏opcix@inkanatura.com), or in Lima (☏01/4402022). Other companies include Indiana Tours, Colon 556 (☏074/222991) and Lizu Tours, Elías Aguirre 418, second floor (☏074/228871, ☏lizu_tours@latinmail.com).
Tourist police Sáenz Peña 830 ☏074/236700 ext 311 (Mon–Sat 8am–6pm); also on call 24hr.

Along Chiclayo's coast

An attractive beach resort just 14km southwest of Chiclayo, **La Pimentel** is a pleasant settlement with an attractive colonial-style centre around the **Plaza Diego Ferre**. More importantly, though, it offers a decent **beach** for swimming and **surfing** (competitions take place in Dec and Jan). The town is known for its small-scale fishing industry, much of it using the traditional *caballitos del mar* (made of totora reeds). For a small fee (25¢) you can access the long pier that divides the seafront *malecón* in two, where you can watch the fishermen. There are plenty of seafood **restaurants** at the south end near to where the *caballitos del mar* are stacked; upstairs at *Restaurant Las Gaviotas* (☏074/452808) is as good as any.

More picturesque is the small fishing village of **La Caleta Santa Rosa,** about 5km south of La Pimentel. Here the beach is crowded with colourful boats and fishermen mending nets; the best and freshest **ceviche** in the Chiclayo area can be found in the restaurants on the seafront here (try the *Restaurant Puerto Magnolia*). The area known as **El Faro** (the lighthouse), slightly to the south of Santa Rosa, is the best location for surfing. Continuing from here along the road inland for about 5km, you come to the small town of **Monsefú**, known as the "city of flowers" because of the local cottage industry that supplies blooms to the area. It's also known for its fine straw hats, straw-rolled cigarettes and the quality of its cotton, all of which you can buy at the daily **market**. Another 4km south from here you come to the colonial village of **Etén** and its nearby ruined church, the Capilla del Milagro, built after of a local's vision of the Christ child in 1649. Southwest, towards the sea, lie the wide avenues of largely derelict Puerto Etén, just another 4km away, where there are abandoned nineteenth-century train carriages.

La Pimentel is easily reached by **bus** every thirty minutes from block 5 of Vicente da la Vega in Chiclayo (50¢). Regular **colectivos** from Avenida Ugarte connect Chiclayo with La Pimentel, Santa Rosa, Monsefú and Puerto Etén (50¢). There's also reasonable, relatively inexpensive accommodation at the *Garnola Hostal*, Jr Quiñones 109 (T 074/452964; ❷-❸), offering a selection of rooms, some with fine sea views, a laundry area on the roof and parking next door.

Zaña

The ruined colonial settlement of **ZAÑA** sits in the desert about 12km away from the modern town of Mocupe, itself 38km south of Chiclayo along the Panamerican Highway. Elaborate arches, columns and sections of old churches, such as the once elegant **Convento de San Agustín**, stand partly overgrown by shrubs, giving evidence of what was once an opulent city. Founded in 1553, it became a centre for meting out justice to thieves, witches and errant slaves, but its wealth actually originated from the nearby port of Cherrepe, from where it controlled the passage of vessels along the coast between Lima and Panama. Zaña rapidly grew rich, and its subsequent excesses were soon notorious, attracting the attention of **pirates**, including a band led by one **Edward Davis**, who sacked the place in 1668. The city subsequently lost much of its prestige and most of the important families moved out, the rest following a few years later when news arrived of another English pirate off the Peruvian coast – Francis Drake. The final blow came in 1720, when the waters of the Río Zaña swept through the streets, causing such damage that the settlement was abandoned. Today, all you can see are some ruined buildings.

Buses to Mocupe and Zaña can be caught hourly from 7 de Enero 1349 in Chiclayo (50¢, a 45–60min trip). It is possible to get one of the Chiclayo **tour** companies to include this sector on a local itinerary, but there are none specifically arranged on a regular basis.

The Temple of Sipán

The **TEMPLE OF SIPÁN** (Tues–Sun 9am–6pm; $2), 33km southeast of Chiclayo, discovered in 1987 by archaeologist Walter Alva has proved to be one of the richest **tombs** in the entire Americas. Every important individual buried here, mostly Mochica nobles from around 200–600 AD, was interred prostrate with his or her own precious-metal grave objects, such as gold and silver goblets, headdresses, breastplates and jewellery including turquoise and lapis lazuli, themselves now on show in the Museo de las Tumbas Reales de Sipán (see p.452). The most important grave uncovered was that of a noble known today as **El Señor de Sipán**, the Lord of Sipán. He was buried along with a great many fine golden and silver decorative objects adorned with semi-precious stones and shells from the Ecuadorian coast.

There are two large adobe **pyramids**, including the Huaca Rajada, in front of which there was once a royal tomb; the place certainly gives you a feel for the people who lived here almost two millennia ago, and it's one of the few sites in Peru whose treasures were not entirely plundered by either the conquistadors or more recent grave robbers. There's also a **site museum**, displaying photos and illustrations of the excavation work plus replicas of some of the discoveries.

To get here take one of the **combi colectivos** ($1; 45min) which leave Chiclayo every morning from Jr 7 de Enero 1552, or alternatively from Avenida Arica, six blocks east of the Mercado Modelo. If you want to stay overnight near the site, there are a couple of **rooms** available at the *Parador Turística* (❷), or you can **camp** ($1) in the grounds.

Pampagrande and around

Pampagrande is, amazingly, a rarely visited site even though it was one of the largest and most active Mochica administrative and ceremonial centres in the region and was populated by thousands. Located in the desert some 20km more or less west of the Temple of Sipán, it can be reached along dusty tracks, but you'll need a local driver to find it. Also worth a visit is the site of **Cerro Mulato**, near the hill town of **Chongoyape**, some 80km out of Chiclayo along the attractive Chancay Valley. From Chongoyape, another dirt road traces an alternative route through the desert to Cerro Mulato. Here you can see some impressive Chavín **petroglyphs**, and in the surrounding region, a number of Chavín graves dating from the fifth century BC. There's also a conservation area at Chaparri (turn left at the entrance to Chongoyape for the Cruz de Mira Costa). **Buses** to Chongoyape leave every hour or so from Avenida Saenz Peña in Chiclayo ($1.50; 90min). But to see all these sites at the same time in one day you really need to **hire** a local man with a car, preferably but not essentially, a 4WD. Tour companies and taxi drivers in Chiclayo can help with this (see p.448).

The Sicán culture

First coming to the attention of the modern world in the early 1990s, the **Sicán culture** is associated with the Naymlap dynasty, based on a wide-reaching political confederacy emanating from the Lambayeque Valley between around 800 and 1100 AD. Legend has it that a leader called **Naymlap** arrived by sea with a fleet of balsa boats, his own royal retinue and a green female stone idol. Having been sent to establish a new civilization, Naymlap set about building temples and palaces near the sea in the Lambayeque Valley. On his death, he was entombed and his spirit was said to fly away to another dimension. The region was then successfully governed by Naymlap's twelve grandsons, until one of them was tempted by a witch to move the green stone idol. Legend has it that this provoked a month of heavy rains and flash floods, rather like the effects of El Niño today, bringing great disease and death in its wake. Indeed, glacial ice cores analysed in the Andes above here have indicated the likelihood of a powerful El Niño current around 1100 AD.

The Sicán civilization, like that of Mochica culture in the Moche Valley around Trujillo, depended on a high level of **irrigation technology** combined with a tight political coherence, not least concerning the difficult problems surrounding rights of access to water supplies in such a vast and dry desert region. The civilization also had its own copper money and sophisticated ceramics, many of which featured an image of the flying **Lord of Sicán**. The main thrust of the Lord of Sicán designs is a well-dressed man, possibly Naymlap himself, with small wings, a nose like a bird's beak and, sometimes, talons rather than feet. The Sicán culture showed a marked change in its burial practices from that of the Mochicas, almost certainly signifying a change in the prevalent belief in an afterlife. Whilst the Mochica people were buried in a lying position – like the Mochica warrior in his splendid tomb at Sipán (see p.449) – the new Sicán style was to inter its dead in a sitting position.

The Sicán monetary system, the flying Lord of Sicán image and much of the culture's religious and political infrastructures were all abandoned after the dramatic environmental disasters caused by El Niño in 1100 AD. **Batán Grande,** the culture's largest and most impressive city, was partly washed away and a fabulous new centre, a massive city of over twenty adobe pyramids at **Túcume** (see p.453), was constructed in the Leche Valley. This relatively short-lived culture was taken over by Chimu warriors from the south around 1370 AD, who absorbed the Lambayeque Valley, some of the Piura Valley area and about two-thirds of the Peruvian desert coast into their empire.

Ferreñafe

Founded in 1550 by Captain Alfonso de Osorio, **FERREÑAFE**, just 18km northeast of Chiclayo, was once known as the "land of two faiths" because of the local tradition of believing first in the power of spirits and second in the Catholic Church. These days the town is best known for its excellent new **Museo Nacional de Sicán** (Tues–Sun 9am–5pm; $3; ☎074/286469), which has an audiovisual introduction and a large collection of exhibits, mostly models depicting daily life and burials of the Sicán people, a great way to gen up and get a visual concept before or after visiting the local archaeological sites themselves. One central room is full of genuine treasures, including the famous ceremonial headdresses and masks. Curiously, Ferreñafe is home to more Miss Peru winners than any other town in the country.

Buses to Ferreñafe leave Chiclayo every hour from Jose Bsalta Norte at the corner with Andres Rasuri, and, if you want to stay over, there are several **restaurants** and two basic **hostels**, including one run by the municipalidad, named, prosaically enough, the *Hotel Municipalidad* (❸). You can follow the new road, which leaves Ferreñafe from the northern end of town, to Batán Grande (see below). It's about a fifteen- to twenty-minute drive on this road.

Batán Grande and around

The site at **BATÁN GRANDE**, 57km northeast of Chiclayo, incorporates over twenty pre-Inca temple pyramids, and over ninety percent of Peru's ancient gold artefacts are estimated to have come from here – you'll notice there are over 100,000 holes, dug over the centuries by treasure hunters. Batán Grande is also known to have developed its own copper-smelting works, which produced large quantities of flat copper plates between 5 and 10cm long. These artefacts, called *naipes,* are believed to have been used and exported to Ecuador as a kind of monetary system.

The **Sicán culture** arose to fill the void left by the demise of the Mochica culture around 700 AD (see box, opposite), and were the driving force in the region from 800 to 1100 AD, based here at Batán Grande. Known to archaeologists as the Initial Lambayeque Period, judging by the beauty and extent of the pyramids here, this era was clearly a flourishing one. Nevertheless, Batán Grande was abandoned in the twelfth century and the Sicán moved across the valley to Túcume (see p.453), probably following a deluge of rains (El Niño) causing devastation, epidemics and a lack of faith in the power of the ruling elite. This fits neatly with the legend of the Sicán leader *Naymlap*'s descendants, who evidently brought this on themselves by sacrilegious behaviour. There is also some evidence that the pyramids were deliberately burnt, supporting the latter theory.

The main part of the **site** that you visit today was mostly built between 750 and 1250 AD, comprising the Huaca del Oro, Huaca Rodillona, Huaca Corte and the Huaca Las Ventanas, where the famous **Tumi de Oro** was uncovered in 1936. The tomb of **El Señor de Sicán** (not to be confused with the tomb of El Señor de Sipán, see p.449), on the north side of the Huaca El Loro, contained a noble with two women, two children and five golden crowns; these finds are exhibited in the excellent **museum** in Ferreñafe. From the top of these pyramids you can just about make out the form of the ancient ceremonial plaza on the ground below.

Part of the beauty of this site comes from its sitting at the heart of an ancient forest, dominated by *algarrobo* trees, spreading out over some 13,400 hectares, a veritable oasis in the middle of the desert landscape. This **National Sanctuary of the Pomac Forest** is the largest dry forest in western South America. The site's interpretative centre (074/974632390), at the main entrance, has a **cafeteria**, hostel **accommodation** (no phone and rarely available; ❷), a **camping** area, a small, archaeological museum with a scale model of the site, and sometimes, guides with motorbikes or *mototaxis*. Entry, guide and ride can cost between $4 and $8 per person, and **horseriding** from here to the main temple complex is sometimes available for a dollar or two more.

A kilometre or so in from the interpretative centre you'll find the oldest *algarrobo* tree in the forest, the **árbol milenario**; over a thousand years old, its spreading, gnarled mass is still the site for pagan rituals, judging from the offerings hanging from its twisted boughs, but it's also the focus of the **Fiesta de las Cruces** on May 3. In the heart of the reserve lies the Bosque de Poma, where over forty species of birds such as mockingbirds, cardinals, burrowing owls and hummingbirds have been identified, and most visitors at least see some iguanas and lizards scuttling into the undergrowth. Rarer, but still hanging around, are wild foxes, deer and anteaters. There's also a **mirador** (viewing platform) in the heart of the forest, from where it's possible to make out many of the larger *huacas*.

To visit the site in just one day, it's best to take a **guided tour** or **taxi** from Chiclayo or Ferreñafe, though you could take public transport: **colectivos** to Batán Grande pueblo (10km beyond the site) leave each morning from block 16 of 7 de Enero in Chiclayo – go as early as possible and ask to be dropped at the interpretative centre ($1.50, a 2hr trip; check with the driver for return journey times).

Another road in and out of the forest, which is hard to trace but passes by the Huaca El Loro, comes from the nearby village of **Illimo**, the next settlement north of Túcume. You'll need a decent car, preferably but not essentially 4WD, and a local driver or good map. If you take this route you'll be rewarded by close contact with small, scattered desert communities, mainly goat herders and peasant farmers, many of whose houses are still built out of adobe and lath.

Lambayeque

The old colonial town of **LAMBAYEQUE**, just 12kms from Chiclayo city, must have been a grand place before it fell into decay last century; fortunately, it seems on the road to recovery, helped by its popular museums and vibrant Sunday **markets**. The buildings here worth seeing include the early eighteenth-century **Iglesia de San Pedro**, parallel to the main square between Dos de Mayo and 8 de Octubre, which is still holding up and is the most impressive edifice in the town, with two attractive front towers and fourteen balconies. But the dusty streets of Lambayeque are better known for their handful of colonial *casonas*, such as **La Casa Cúneo** (8 de Octubre 328), and a few doors down **La Casa Descalzi**, which has a fine *algarrobo* doorway in typical Lambayeque Baroque style. **La Casa de la Logia Masónica** (Masonic Lodge), at the corner of calles Dos de Mayo and San Martín, is also worth checking out for its superb balcony, which has lasted for about four hundred years and, at 67m, is thought to be the longest in Peru.

Lambayeque's main draw, however, are its two fantastic museums. The oldest, though quite new itself, is the modern **Museo Arqueológico Nacional Brüning** on block 7 of Avenida Huamachuco (daily 9am–5pm; $3; ☎074/282110). Named after its founder Hans Heinrich Brüning, an expert in the Mochica language and culture, the museum possesses superb collections of early ceramics, much of which has only recently resurfaced and been put on display. The museum has actually only just reopened, bringing from its vaults some of the fine ceramics found over the last hundred years or so in the region, and having lost its most recent main collection to Lambayeque's new jewel, the **Museo de las Tumbas Reales de Sipán** or

Museum of the Royal Tombs of Sipán (Tues–Sun 9am–5pm; $3; ☏074/283978). This museum is an imposing concrete construction in the form of a semi-sunken or truncated pyramid, reflecting the form and style of the treasures it holds inside. This mix of modernity and indigenous pre-Columbian influence is a fantastic starting point for exploring the archaeology of the valley. You'll need a good hour or two to see and experience all the exhibits, which include a large collection of gold, silver and copper objects from the tomb of **El Señor de Sipán** (see p.449), including his main emblem, a staff known as **El Cetro Cuchillo**, found stuck to the bones of his right hand in his tomb. The tomb itself is also reproduced as one of the museum's centrepieces down on the bottom of the three floors. The top floor mainly exhibits ceramics, while the second floor is dedicated to El Señor de Sipán's ornaments and treasures. Background music accompanies the visitor around the museum circuit using instruments and sounds associated with pre-Hispanic cultures of the region. A musical finale can usually be caught on the ground floor.

The Lambayeque Valley has long been renowned for turning up pre-Columbian metallurgy – particularly gold pieces from the neighbouring hill graveyard of **Zacamé** – and local treasure hunters have sometimes gone so far as to use bulldozers to dig them out, but it's the addition of the Sipán treasures that's given the biggest boost to Lambayeque's reputation, and the museum is now one of the finest in South America.

Practicalities

On a rather more prosaic note, Lambayeque is also known for its sweet pastry **cakes** – filled with *manjar blanca* (a condensed milk product, very popular in Peru) and touted under the unlikely name of *King-Kongs*. In any of the town's streets, you'll be bombarded by street vendors pushing out piles of the cake, shouting "King-Kong! King-Kong!" For a really good **meal**, however, visit *El Cantaro* at lunchtime; located at C Dos de Mayo 180 (☏074/282196) and known by most taxi drivers, it is one of the most traditional restaurants in the region, serving ceviche, duck, goat and other local specialities. For **accommodation**, the *Hostal Brüning*, Av S Bolívar 578 (☏074/283549; ❸), is fine, with private baths and comfortable rooms. To get to Lambayeque take the short **colectivo** ride north from the street Pedro Ruiz close to the main Chiclayo market areas.

Túcume and around

The site of **TÚCUME** (daily 8am–4.30pm; $2.80 for students; guides sometimes available from $2), also known as the **Valley of the Pyramids**, contains 26 adobe pyramids, many clustered around the hill of **El Purgatorio** (197m), also known as Cerro La Raya (after a ray fish that lives within it, according to legend), and is located some 33km north from Chiclayo. Although the ticket office closes at 4.30pm and the museum shortly after this, the site is accessible after these hours (being part of the local landscape and dissected by small paths connecting villages and homesteads), with the main sectors clearly marked by good interpretive signs.

Covering more than two hundred hectares, Túcume was occupied initially by the **Sicán culture**, which began building here around 1100 AD after abandoning **Batán Grande**. During this time, known as the Second Lambayeque Period, the focus of construction moved to Túcume where an elite controlled a complex administrative system and cleared large areas of *algarrobo* forest (as is still the case today in the immediate vicinity of the Valley of the Pyramids and Cerro El Purgatorio at Túcume). Reed seafaring vessels were also essential for the development of this new powerful elite. The Sicán people were clearly expert seamen and traded along the coast as far as Ecuador, Colombia and quite

▲ Túcume

probably Central America. To the east, they also traded with the sierra and the jungle regions beyond. They were also expert metallurgists working with gold, silver, copper and precious stones, and their elaborate funerary masks are astonishingly vivid and beautiful.

At Túcume's peak, in the thirteenth and early fourteenth centuries, it was probably a focus of annual pilgrimage for a large section of the coastal population, whose Sicán leaders were high priests with great agro-astrological understanding, adept administrators, a warrior elite, and expert artisans. It wasn't long, however, before things changed, and around 1375 AD the **Chimu** invaded from the south. Within another hundred years the **Incas** had arrived, though they took some twenty years to conquer the Chimu, during which time it appears that Túcume played an important role in the ensuing military, magical and diplomatic intrigues. Afterwards, the Incas transported many Chimu warriors to remote outposts in the Andes, in order to maximize the Incas' political control and minimize the chances of rebellion. By the time the **Spanish** arrived, just over half a century later, Túcume's time had already passed. When the Spanish chronicler, Pedro Cieza de León, passed by here in 1547, it was already in ruins and abandoned.

Today, Túcume remains an extensive site with the labyrinthine ruins of walls and courtyards still quite visible, if slightly rain-washed by the impact of recent heavy El Niño weather cycles, and you can easily spend two or three hours exploring. The site has two clearly defined sectors: North is characterized by the large monumental structures; while the South has predominantly simpler structures and common graveyards. The adobe bricks utilized were loaf-shaped, each with their maker's mark, indicating control and accounting for labour and tribute to the elite. Some of the pyramids have up to seven phases of construction, showing that building went on more or less continuously.

There's a **viewing point**, reached by a twisting path that leads up El Purgatorio hill, from where you can get a good view of the whole city. This hill, circular and cone-shaped, at the very centre of the occupied area, was and still is considered by locals to be a sacred mountain. Access to it was restricted originally, though there is evidence of later Inca constructions, for example an altar site. It is still visited these days by the local *curanderos*, healing wizards who utilize shamanic techniques and the psychoactive San Pedro cactus in their weekly rituals, which researchers believe are similar to those of their ancestors and which could be one possible explanation for the name El Purgatorio (the place of the purge).

The architecturally distinctive **Museo de Sitio** (daily 9am–5pm, though site is generally accessible 24hr) at the entrance to the site, has exhibits relating to the work of **Thor Heyerdahl**, who found in Túcume the inspiration for his *Kon Tiki* expedition in 1946 when he sailed a raft built in the style of ancient Peruvian boats from Callao, near Lima, right across the Pacific Ocean to Polynesia, as he tried to prove a link between civilizations on either side of the Pacific. The museum also covers the work of archaeologist Wendell Bennett, who in the late 1930s was the first person to scientifically excavate at the site. More esoterically,

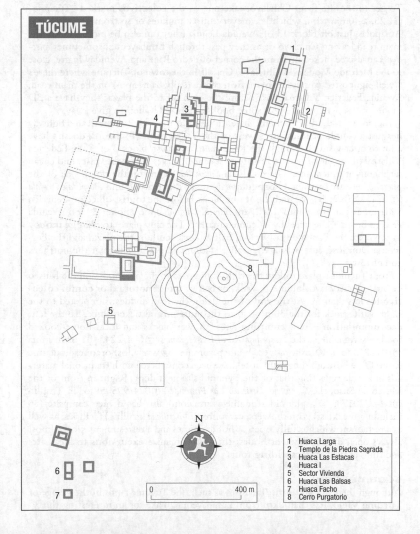

TÚCUME

1 Huaca Larga
2 Templo de la Piedra Sagrada
3 Huaca Las Estacas
4 Huaca I
5 Sector Vivienda
6 Huaca Las Balsas
7 Huaca Facho
8 Cerro Purgatorio

N

0 — 400 m

Túcume has a local reputation for **magical power**, and a section of the museum has been devoted to a display of local *curanderismo*. There's also an attractive picnic area, and a ceramic workshop where they use 2500-year-old techniques. Completed in 1991, the museum was constructed to reflect the style – known as *la ramada* – of colonial chapels in this region, built by local indigenous craftsmen centuries ago and using much the same materials.

Shamanic healing is a strong local tradition and one renowned healer, Don Victor Bravo, who helped to design the shamanic section of the museum's exhibits, lives very close to the ruins of Túcume; anyone seriously interested in participating in one of his *mesa* ceremonies (see p.583) might try asking for an introduction through the *Hospedaje Rural Los Horcones* (see p.456).

Practicalities

To get to the site from Chiclayo, take one of the **colectivos** marked "Túcume" ($1.25, a 40min trip), which leave every thirty minutes or so from a yard on Las Amapolas, just off block 13 of Avenida Leguia (they can also be picked up on the main road leaving Chiclayo or as they pass through Lambayeque; sometimes *colectivos* can also be picked up from the corner of Pedro Ruiz and Avenida Ugarte, close to the Mercado Modelo in Chiclayo. Get off in the town of Túcume where there's a well-signposted **tourist information** centre (daily 8am–5pm) on the main road, Avenida Federico Villareal, just before the turn off to the plaza; they have a 3D model of the pyramid site plus some books, maps and leaflets to give away.

Túcume's modern settlement, based alongside the old Panamerican Highway lies just a couple of kilometres west of the Valley of the Pyramids and doesn't have a lot to offer visitors, though the *Restaurant La Sabrosa*, block 3 of Calle Federico Villareal (three blocks beyond the tourist office), serves reasonably tasty and cheap set menus at lunchtime. There's also a *Snack Bar Jugeria* on the north side of the plaza. There are two small **hospedajes** in town: the tricky to find *Hospedaje Acafala* (T074/422029; ❷), located about one block before the tourist office on Federico Villareal as you come into town, and *Hostal Las Balsas* (no phone; ❷), on Avenida Agosto Belguia, the street by Túcume's market. The only places to **change money** in town are the Banco de la Nación, half a block south of the plaza, and the Ferretería Don José, just before the police station and petrol garage at the northern end of town.

From Túcume's plaza follow the right-hand road to the pyramids and the Museo de Sitio, a dusty two-kilometre walk, or better, take a **mototaxi** or **combi colectivo** for less than $1. At the end of the fields, the road divides: signposted to the right, is the track for the 30m or so to the museum and ticket office. To the left, **accommodation** – plus **camping** sites, shower blocks and local home-cooked food – is available at the *Hospedaje Rural Los Horcones* (T074/2243401 or in Lima T01/2243367, E loshorcones@viabcp.com.pe, W www.loshorconesdetucume.com; ❹), whose buildings and hotel have been constructed with traditional materials in a style reflecting that of the pyramid site next door. Right in front of the Museo de Sitio, the *Complejo Turistico Las Piramides* (T074/995959 or in Trujillo T044/370178, E laspiramidestucume@terra.com) also has a nice campsite ($6 including breakfast) with showers, campfire and *parillada* (grilling) facilities, as well as a restaurant which is fully open at holiday times and a refreshment kiosk almost always open during daylight hours; they also organize **excursions** to local sites and ruins as well as **horseriding** tours.

Túcume Viejo

Although there are no tourist facilities as such, the Túcume ruins in the village of **Túcume Viejo**, less than 2km from Lambayeque, make for an interesting thirty-

> ### Healing session in Salas
>
> About twenty minutes by car from Túcume, taking a back road for 17km off the old Panamerican Highway at Km 47 (27km north of Túcume) brings you to the **Pueblo of Salas**, known locally as the capital of folklore medicine on the coast of Peru. Here the ancient traditions of **curanderismo** are so strong that it's the major source of income for the village. Most nights of the week, but especially Tuesdays and Fridays, there'll be healing sessions going on in at least one of the houses in the village, generally starting around 10pm and ending at roughly 4am. The sessions, or *mesas*, are based on the ingestion of the hallucinogenic **San Pedro cactus** and other natural plants or herbs, and they do cost money (anything up to $200 a night, though the amount is usually fixed and can be divided between as many as five to ten participants). Combining healing with divination, the *curanderos* utilize techniques and traditions handed down from generation to generation from the ancient Sicán culture. To contact a *curandero* about participating in a session, the best bet is to ask a local tour operator, or a trustworthy taxi driver from Túcume, to take you to the village one afternoon to see what can be arranged.

minute walk. To **get there**, turn left along the sand track at the fork in the road just before you get to the site museum. Although an ancient site, check out the crumbling colonial adobe walls and a once-painted adobe brick gateway as well as the church, all of which have an elegant and rather grandiose feel, suggesting perhaps that the early colonists were trying to compete for attention with the Valley of the Pyramids. There's also the **Museo Santos Vera**, a local *curandero*'s museum full of magical paraphernalia, less than a kilometre beyond the entrance to the village. En route to Túcume Viejo, some 500m beyond the *Hospedaje Rural Los Horcones*, a right-hand track takes you to the **Huaca Sagrada**, part of the pyramid complex which is difficult to find, located as it is on the northern side of the Huaca Larga and effectively closed off from the main site. There's not that much to see there at the moment as the remaining small temple is closed off and the stone can just be glimpsed through gaps in the wall; at present the archaeologists' priority is to protect the *huaca* from the encroaching growth of the pueblo's current inhabitants.

North to Piura: through the Sechura Desert

Buses and colectivos between Chiclayo and Piura tend to use a fast new section of the Panamerican Highway, which cuts straight across the **SECHURA DESERT** and bypasses the small town of Olmos in the east and the town of Sechura in the west. Chiclayo bus companies (see p.448) do the journey in three hours ($3.50), while plenty of slightly faster *colectivos* ($6; 3hr) leave daily from Pedro Ruiz and Luis Gonzalez. Sechura, 52km south of Piura, is nevertheless still on the route of a few *colectivos* that take the old **coastal road** to Piura, via the oil refinery of **Bayovar**, a journey of around six hours. There's a quaint seventeenth-century **church** on the main square, whose tall twin towers lend the town an air of culture. Local legend has it that the church was built over an ancient temple, from where an underground tunnel containing hidden treasure led out to the ocean.

Piura and around

The city of **PIURA** feels very distinct from the rest of the country, cut off to the south by the formidable Sechura Desert, and to the east by the Huancabamba mountains. **Francisco Pizarro** spent ten days in Piura in 1532 en route to his fateful meeting with the Inca overlord, Atahualpa, at Cajamarca. By 1534 the city, then known as **San Miguel de Piura**, had well over two hundred Spanish inhabitants, including the first Spanish women to arrive in Peru. As early as the 1560s, there was a flourishing trade in the excellent indigenous **Tanguis cotton**, and Piura today still produces a third of the nation's cotton.

Despite this precarious existence, Piura is the oldest colonial city in Peru and people here see themselves primarily as Piuranos rather than Peruvians, and the city has a strong oasis atmosphere, entirely dependent on the vagaries of the **Río Piura** – known colloquially since Pizarro's time as the Río Loco, or Crazy River. During the twentieth century Piura grew into a *departamento* of well over 1.5 million people, around a quarter of whom actually live in the city. With temperatures of up to 38°C (100°F) from January to March, the region is known for its particularly wide-brimmed straw sombreros, worn by everyone from the mayor to local goat-herders. You'll have plenty of opportunities to see these in **Semana de Piura** (first two weeks of Oct), when the town is in high spirits. Beds are a little scarce during the holiday, so it's best to **book** in advance at that time.

Arrival, information and city transport

El Dorado **buses** from Trujillo and Tumbes, Dorado Express buses from Tumbes, Sullana and Aguas Verdes, buses from Chiclayo, and EPPO buses from Talara and Máncora all arrive around blocks 11 and 12 of Avenida Sanchez Cerro. All other buses arrive at their companies' offices (see p.461). **Colectivos**, mainly from Tumbes and Talara, also arrive and depart from the middle of the road at block 11 of Avenida Sanchez Cerro, ten minutes' stroll from the centre of town. If you arrive by one of the daily **planes** from Lima, Trujillo or Tumbes, you'll land at Piura airport (for flight information call ☎073/344503), 2km east of the city; a **taxi** into the centre costs $2–3.

The official **tourist office** in Piura offers friendly and useful advice from the Municipal building at Ayacucho 337, on the Plaza de Armas (Mon–Fri 9am–1pm & 4–8pm, Sat 9am–1pm, ☎073/310772), or you can also get information from the Ministry of Tourism, Jr Lima 775 (Mon–Fri 9am–1pm & 4–6pm; ☎073/327013 ⓦ www.regionpiura .gob.pe). Failing these, your best bet is one of the tour companies listed on p.461. The quickest way of getting around the city is by the ubiquitous **motorcycle rickshaw**, which you can hail just about anywhere for 50¢. In-town **taxi** rides are set at around $1.

Accommodation

A wide range of **hotels** and **hostels** are spread throughout the town, with most of the cheaper ones on or around Avenida Loreto or within a few blocks of Avenida Grau and the Plaza de Armas.

Hospedaje California Junin 835 ☎073/328789. A family-run establishment, brightly painted and decorated with plastic flowers, giving it a somewhat kitschy feel. It's good value and popular with backpackers, and while there are no private baths, rooms are usually equipped with fans. ❶–❷

Hospedaje Terraza Av Loreto 530. Cleaner and a much more pleasant option than some of the affordable lodgings in this area, but still pretty basic; rooms have fans, but baths are shared. ❷
Hostal La Capullana Junin 925 ☎073/321239. Cleanish place with a welcoming atmosphere. All

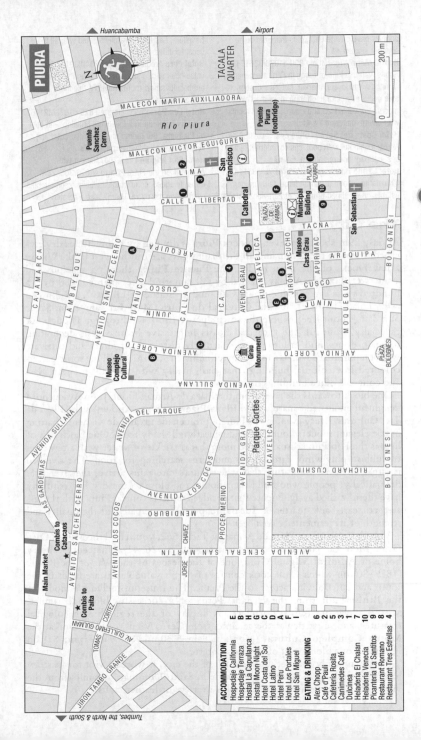

PIURA

Huancabamba

Airport

TACALA QUARTER

MALECON MARIA AUXILIADORA

Río Piura

Puente Sanchez Cerro

Puente Piura (footbridge)

MALECON VICTOR EGUIGUREN

LIMA

San Francisco

PLAZA PIZARRO

CALLE LA LIBERTAD

Catedral

PLAZA DE ARMAS

Municipal Building

San Sebastian

TACNA

AREQUIPA

CAJAMARCA

LAMBAYEQUE

AVENIDA SANCHEZ CERRO

HUANUCO

CUSCO

CALLAO

ICA

AVENIDA GRAU

HUANCAVELICA

Museo Casa Grau

APURIMAC

AREQUIPA

BOLOGNESI

JIRON AYACUCHO

CUSCO

JUNIN

MOQUEGUA

JUNIN

AVENIDA LORETO

Museo Complejo Cultural

AVENIDA LORETO

Grau Monument

PLAZA BOLOGNESI

AVENIDA SULLANA

AVENIDA DEL PARQUE

AVENIDA SANCHEZ CERRO

Parque Cortés

AVENIDA GRAU

HUANCAVELICA

AVENIDA SULLANA

LAS GARDENIAS

AVENIDA LOS COCOS

AVENIDA LOS COCOS

RICHARD CUSHING

BOLOGNESI

MENDIBURO

PROCER MERINO

AVENIDA LOS COCOS

Main Market

Combis to Catacaos

Combis to Paita

AV GUILLERMO GULMAN

TOMAS

CORTEZ

JORGE

CHAVEZ

AVENIDA GENERAL SAN MARTIN

JIRON TAMBO GRANDE

Tumbes, the North & South

200 m

N

ACCOMMODATION
Hospedaje California	E
Hospedaje Terraza	B
Hostal La Capullanca	H
Hostal Moon Night	G
Hotel Costa del Sol	C
Hotel Latino	D
Hotel Peru	A
Hotel Los Portales	F
Hotel San Miguel	I

EATING & DRINKING
Alex Chopp	6
Café d'Pauli	2
Cafetería Rosita	5
Canimedes Café	3
Dulcinea	1
Heladeria El Chalan	7
Heladeria Venecia	10
Picantería La Santitos	9
Restaurant Romano	8
Restaurant Tres Estrellas	4

doubles have private bath, plus there are some cheaper singles. **②**

Hostal Moon Night Junin 899 ⊕073/336174. Hotels with this kind of name in Peru are generally aiming for the lovers' market, but it's still comfortable and pretty central, offering more than average modern conveniences and clean, spacious rooms with private bath and TV. **②**

Hotel Costa del Sol Av Loreto 649 ⊕073/302864. A luxurious hotel with pool, casino, internet facilities, car park and restaurant. **⑦–⑧**

Hotel Latino Huancavelica 720 ⊕073/335114, ⓔhoslatino@hotmail.com. A large, fairly modern establishment aimed primarily at Peruvian business

travellers, *Latino* is centrally located with all the usual facilities. **④**

Hotel Peru Arequipa 476 ⊕073/333919. Good-value hotel with a spacious lobby and good restaurant/bar; its smart rooms have TV, telephone, fan and private bath. **④**

Hotel Los Portales C Libertad 875 ⊕073/321161. A luxury hotel set in a lovely old building with pool on the plaza; the rooms are full of character and very clean, if slightly overpriced. **⑧**

Hotel San Miguel Lima 1007, corner with Apurimac on the Plaza Pizarro ⊕073/305122. A decently priced, comfortable hotel with some rooms overlooking the plaza. There's also a cafeteria. **④**

The City

At only 29m above sea level, modern **Piura** is divided by a sometimes dry riverbed. Most of the action and all the main sights are on the west bank. Within a few blocks of the main bridge, the **Puente Piura**, there's a spacious and attractive **Plaza de Armas**, shaded by tall tamarind trees planted well over a hundred years ago. On the plaza you'll find a "Statue of Liberty", also known as La Pola (The Pole), and the **Catedral de Piura** (Mon–Fri 7am–8pm, Sat & Sun 8am–noon; free), where the town's poorest folk tend to beg. Though not especially beautiful, the cathedral boasts impressive bronze nails decorating its main doors, and inside, the spectacularly tasteless gilt altars and intricate wooden pulpit are worth a look. Surrounding the plaza, you'll see some pastel-coloured low colonial buildings that clash madly with the tall, modern glass and concrete office buildings nearby.

One block towards the river from the Plaza de Armas, along Jirón Ayacucho, a delightful elongated square, called **Plaza Pizarro**, is also known as the Plaza de Tres Culturas. Every evening the Piurans promenade up and down here, chatting beside elegant modern fountains and beneath tall shady trees. One block east of here is the Río Piura, usually little more than a trickle of water with a few piles of rubbish plus white egrets, gulls and terns searching for food. The riverbed is large, however, indicating that when Piura's rare rains arrive, the river rises dramatically; people who build their homes too close to the dry bed regularly have them washed away. Puente Piura bridge connects central Piura with the less aesthetic east-bank quarter of **Tacala**, renowned principally for the quality and strength of its fermented *chicha* beer.

A block south of the Plaza de Armas, at Tacna 662, you'll find the **Museo Casa Grau** (Mon–Sat 9am–1pm & 3–6pm; free; ⊕073/326541), nineteenth-century home of **Admiral Miguel Grau**, one of the heroes of the War of the Pacific (1879–80), in which Chile took control of Peru's valuable nitrate fields in the south and cut Bolivia's access to the Pacific. The museum includes a model of the British-built ship, the *Huascar*, Peru's only successful blockade runner, as well as various military artefacts. A display of the region's archaeological treasures, and in particular the ceramics from Cerro Vicus, can be found at the **Museo Complejo Cultural** (Mon–Fri 9am–5.30pm, Sat 9am–1pm; $1) on Huánuco, one block west of Avenida Loreto.

The town's daily **market**, in the north of the city, is worth a visit for its straw hats (invaluable in the desert), well-made in Santo Domingo, ceramics from the villages of Chulucanas and Simbila, plus a variety of leather crafts.

Eating, drinking and nightlife

Most of Piura's **restaurants** and **cafés** are centred around the Plaza de Armas area, with many of the cafés specializing in delicious **ice cream**. Piura's speciality is a very sweet toffee-like delicacy, called **natilla**, which can be bought at street stalls around the city. In the evenings, you'll find most Piurans strolling around the main streets, mingling in the plazas, and drinking in the cheap **bars** along the roads around Junín. For a spot of late-night **drinking and dancing**, there's *Blue Moon*, Ayacucho 552 (☏073/335013), popular with locals and starting around 10pm; *JL Disco Bar*, upstairs at Av Grau 495, loud and hectic at weekends; *La Nueva Calesa*, Jr Ayacucho 565; *Studio 1*, in the Centro Comercial; and *Tony's*, Avenida Guardia Civil de Castilla in Miraflores on the other side of town.

Alex Chopp Huancavelica 538. A popular venue with a friendly atmosphere, serving good draught beers and fine seafood in the evenings.

Café d'Pauli Lima 541. A smart new café serving pricey but delicious ice creams, cakes, teas and coffee.

Cafetería Rosita Av Grau 223. Serves heavenly sandwiches and green *tamales*, and has a few veggie options as well as great breakfasts.

Canimedes Cafe Lima 440. Open in daytime only, serves healthy foods including good breakfasts, yoghurt and fig breads.

Dulcinea C La Libertad 597. A small bar and mini-supermarket, very central and well stocked with breads, pies, pasties and sweet pastries.

Heladería El Chalan Plaza de Armas. Excellent service in a bright and busy atmosphere, serves sandwiches, juices, cakes and wonderful ice creams. They also have a newer place behind the cathedral.

Heladería Venecia C La Libertad 1007. Choose your ice cream from a wide variety of flavours and enjoy it on the cool and elegant patio.

Picantería La Santitos C La Libertad 1014. Only open for lunch, this place serves a good choice of traditional *criolla* dishes such as *majado de yuca* (mashed *yuca* with pieces of pork) and *seco de chavelo* (mashed plantain with pieces of beef), in a renovated colonial house.

Restaurant Romano Jr Ayacucho 580. A popular and quite large local backstreet eating-house serving a host of reasonably priced dishes, from burgers and sandwiches to the usual Peruvian cuisine such as *lomo saltado*.

Restaurant Tres Estrellas Arequipa 702. The best restaurant in town for serious *criolla* dishes – try the goat (*cabrito*) with rice and *tamales*.

Listings

Airlines Lan Peru, Grau 140 ☏073/302145.

Banks and exchange The Banco Continental is on the Plaza de Armas, at the corner of Ayacucho and Tacna. *Cambistas* are at block 7 of Av Arequipa, near the corner of Av Grau; but by far the safest and quickest casa de cambio is Piura Dolar by block 6 of Av Arequipa.

Buses CIAL, Bolognesi 817 (☏073/304250), for Huaraz, Lima and Tumbes; Cruz del Sur, Circunvalación block 1, with an office at corner of Bolognesi with Lima (bus passes both on way through town), just a few blocks south of the Plaza de Armas in the centre (☏073/337094), for Lima and the coast; Coop de El Dorado, Av Sanchez Cerro 1119 (☏073/325875), for Trujillo, Chiclayo and north; Transporte Loja, Av Sanchez Cerro 1480 (☏073/309407), for the alternative Ecuadorian crossing via Loja; Emtrafesa, Los Naranjos 255,

Urb Club Grau (☏073/337093), for Chiclayo, Trujillo and Tumbes; Linea, Av Sanchez Cerro 1215 (☏073/327821), for Chiclayo and Tumbes; Tepsa, Av Loreto 1195 (☏073/323721), for Trujillo and Tumbes; and Trans-EPPO, Sanchez Cerro 1141 (☏073/331160), for Talara and Máncora.

Internet There's a large, busy internet café at Sanchez Cerro 265, large and busy (daily 9am–11pm).

Post office Plaza de Armas, on the corner of C Libertad and Ayacucho (Mon–Sat 8am–4pm).

Shopping There's a supermarket, good for general provisions, by the Grau monument; and for local sweets, nuts and fruit, the shop at Sanchez Cerro 285 is hard to beat.

Tour operators Piura Tours, Ayacucho 585 ☏073/328873; Tallan Tours, Tacna 258 ☏073/334647.

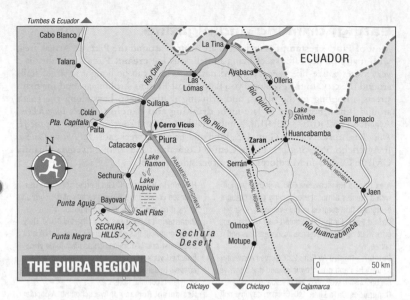

THE PIURA REGION

0   50 km

Catacaos

Just 12km south of Piura is the friendly, dusty little town of **CATACAOS**, worth a visit principally for its excellent, vast **market** (there's something here most days, but it's best at weekends 10am–4pm). Just off the main plaza, the market sells everything from food to crafts, even filigree gold and silver work, with the colourful hammocks hanging about the square being a particularly good buy. The town is renowned locally for its **picanterías** (spicy food restaurants), which serve all sorts of local delicacies, such as *tamalitos verdes* (little green-corn pancakes), fish-balls, *chifles* (fresh banana or sweet potato chips), goat (*seco de cabrito*) and the local *chicha* beer. One of the better **restaurants** *La Chayo*, San Francisco 493 (☎073/370121), serves huge portions while you sample the *chicha*. While you're here you could also try the sweet medicinal drink *algarrobina*, made from the berries of a desert tree, and available from bars and street stalls.

From Piura, regular **combi colectivos** for Catacaos leave when full, usually every twenty minutes or so (35¢; 20min), from block 12 of Sanchez Cerro, or from the far side of Puente Piura.

North of Piura: Talara and Cabo Blanco

Going north from Piura, the towns of **Sullana** and Talara and the coastal resort of **Cabo Blanco** are significant landmarks on route towards Ecuador. **TALARA**, however, is best known as an oil-exporting centre and has little to offer the visitor, taking its name and function from the country's most important coastal oilfield. Cabo Blanco – where the cold Humboldt current meets the warm, equatorial El Niño, a stroke of providence that creates an extraordinary abundance of marine life – has nice beaches and is renowned the world over for its fishing.

How Pizarro found Atahualpa

It was at Serran, then a small Inca administrative centre in the hills above Piura, that Francisco **Pizarro** waited in 1532 for the return of a small troop of soldiers he had sent up the Inca Royal Highway on a discovery mission. It took the soldiers, led by **Hernando de Soto**, just two days and a night to reach the town of Cajas, now lost in the region around Huancabamba and Lake Shimbe.

At Cajas, the Spaniards gained their first insight into the grandeur and power of the Inca Empire, although, under orders from Atahualpa, the town's 2000-warrior Inca garrison had slunk away into the mountains. The Spaniards were not slow to discover the most impressive Inca buildings – a sacred convent of over five hundred virgins who had been chosen at an early age to dedicate their lives to the Inca religion. The soldiers raped at will, provoking the Inca diplomat who was accompanying De Soto to threaten the troops with death for such sacrilege, telling them they were only 300km from Atahualpa's camp at Cajamarca. This information about Atahualpa's whereabouts was exactly what De Soto had been seeking. After a brief visit to the adjacent, even more impressive, Inca town of Huancabamba – where a tollgate collected duties along the Royal Highway – he returned with the Inca diplomat to rejoin Pizarro. Realizing that he had provided the Spanish with vital information, the Inca diplomat agreed to take them to Atahualpa's camp – a disastrous decision resulting in the massacre at Cajamarca (see p.419).

Sullana

Leaving Piura, the Panamerican Highway heads directly north, passing through the large town of **SULLANA** after 40km. This major transport junction has little of interest to travellers, except perhaps as a rest before or after taking the inland route to Ecuador. If you do stop, take a quick look at the **Plaza de Armas**, which boasts fine views over the Río Chira, and is the location for the old church of La Santisima Trinidad. Most **bus companies** have their offices on or just off Avenida Lama; EPPO have buses twice daily to Máncora, while Emtrafesa serves Tumbes and Chiclayo. There are regular **combis** from Avenida Lama to Piura and Paita, each one hour away (90¢), while the faster **colectivos** cost slightly more. *Combis* for the inland border crossing with Ecuador at La Tina or close by at Ayabaca, leave in the morning from Avenida Buenos Aires, close to the main market.

Talara

TALARA, some 70km further north, would be more attractive if it wasn't for the entrance to the city being strewn with plastic rubbish. Until 1940, it was no more than a small fishing hamlet, though its deep-water harbour and tar pits had been used since Pizarro's time for caulking wooden ships – Pizarro had chosen the site for the first Spanish settlement in Peru, but it proved too unhealthy and he was forced to look elsewhere, eventually hitting on Piura. Today the town is highly industrialized, with several fertilizer plants as well as the oil business (although you can find an unpolluted **beach** at La Pena, 2km away). Talara's **oil reserves** were actually directly responsible for Peru's last military coup in 1968. President Belaunde, then in his first term of office, had given subsoil concessions to the multinational company IPC, declaring that "if this is foreign imperialism what we need is more, not less of it". A curious logic, it led to the accusation that he had signed an agreement "unacceptable to true Peruvians". Within two months of the affair, and as a direct consequence, he was deposed and exiled. One of the initial acts of the new revolutionary government was to nationalize IPC and declare the Act of Talara null and void.

Cabo Blanco

Thirty kilometres or so north of Talara, there's a turning off the highway to the old fishing hot spot of **CABO BLANCO**. Thomas Stokes, a British resident and fanatical fisherman, discovered the place in 1935, and it was a very popular resort in the post-war years. **Hemingway** stayed for some months in 1951, while two years later the largest fish ever caught with a rod was landed here – a 710-kilo black marlin. International fishing competitions still take place, and the area is much reputed for swordfish. The fishing club where Hemingway is supposed to have written *The Old Man and the Sea* offers **accommodation** (**6**), which includes access to a nice pool, an excellent seafood **restaurant** and **fishing** and water-sports facilities. It also has one of the few free and official **campsites** in Peru.

From here to Tumbes the Panamerican Highway cuts across a further stretch of desert, for the most part keeping tightly to the Pacific coastline. It's a straight road, except for the occasional detour around bridges destroyed by the 1998 El Niño. To the right of the road looms a long hill, the **Cerros de Amotape**, named after a local chief whom Pizarro had killed in 1532 as an example to potential rebels.

Tumbes and the northern beaches

About 30km from the Ecuadorian border and 287km north of Piura, **TUMBES** is usually considered a mere pit stop for overland travellers. However, the city has a significant history and, unlike most border settlements, is a surprisingly warm and friendly place. On top of that, it's close to many of Peru's finest **beaches** and the country's only serious mangrove swamp, **Los Bosques de Manglares**. In the rural areas around the city, nearly half of Peru's commercial tobacco leaf is produced but the extensive paddy fields and banana plantations are more obvious.

It can get very hot and humid between December and March, while the rest of the year it offers a pleasant heat, compared with much of Peru's southern coast. The sea is warm and whilst mosquitoes can be bothersome between September and January, they rarely make their presence felt on the beaches. Locals tend to be rather laid-back and spontaneous, a trait reflected in the local oral traditions such as **las cumananas**, an expression in popular verse, often by song with a guitar. The verse is expected to be sparky, romantic, comical and even sad, but most importantly it is spur-of-the-moment and rap-like.

Border relations with Ecuador

Tumbes was the first town to be "conquered" by the Spanish and has maintained its importance ever since – originally as the gateway to the Inca Empire and more recently through its strategic position on the controversial **frontier with Ecuador**. Despite three regional wars – in 1859, 1941–42 and 1997–98 – the exact line of the border remains a source of controversy. Maps of the frontier vary depending on which country you buy them in, with the two countries claiming a disparity of up to 150km in some places along the border. The traditional enmity between Peru and Ecuador and the continuing dispute over the border mean that Tumbes has a strong Peruvian army presence and a consequent strict **ban on photography** anywhere near military or frontier installations. Most of the city's hundred thousand people are engaged in either transport or petty trading across the frontier – huge numbers of Peruvians cross the border everyday to buy cheaper Ecuadorian products – and are quite cut off from mainstream Peru, being much nearer to Quito than Lima, 1268km to the south.

Tumbes itself may not have much to offer the traveller beyond decent hotels, restaurants, some okay bars and better money-changing options than at the Ecuadorian frontier, but the region around it is rich in ocean and mangrove **wildlife**. In fact, the area may well be the most attractive for beach life in the whole of Peru. These days the beach resort of **Máncora** is where people come from as far away as Lima for holidays, making it a very busy place in December and January, and some holiday weekends. But there are plenty of other beautiful beaches and, inevitably, plans for development in store – though these won't become reality for quite some time.

Some history

Pizarro didn't actually set foot in Tumbes when it was first discovered by the Spanish in 1527. He preferred to cast his eyes along the Inca city's adobe walls, its carefully irrigated fields and its shining temple, from the comfort and safety of his ship. However, with the help of translators he set about learning as much as he could about Peru and the Incas during this initial contact. An Inca noble visited him aboard ship and even dined at his table. The noble was said to be especially pleased with his first taste of Spanish wine and the present of an iron hatchet.

The Spaniards who did go ashore made reports of such grandeur that Pizarro at first refused to believe them, sending instead the more reliable Greek cavalier, **Pedro de Candia**. Dubious descriptions of the temple, lined with gold and silver sheets, were confirmed by Candia, who also gave the people of Tumbes their first taste of European technological might – firing his musket to smash a wooden board to pieces. Pizarro had all the evidence he needed; he returned to Spain to obtain royal consent and support for his projected conquest.

The Tumbes people hadn't always been controlled by the Incas. The area was originally inhabited by the **Tallanes**, related to coastal tribes from Ecuador who are still known for their unusual lip and nose ornaments. In 1450 they were conquered for the first time – by the **Chimu**. Thirteen years later came the **Incas**, organized by Tupac Inca, who bulldozed the locals into religious, economic and even architectural conformity in order to create their most northerly coastal terminus. A fortress, temple and sun convent were built, and the town was colonized with loyal subjects from other regions – a typical Inca ploy, which they called the *mitimaes* system. The valley had an efficient irrigation programme, allowing them to grow, among other things, bananas, corn and squash.

Pizarro longed to add his name to the list of Tumbes' conquerors yet after landing on the coast of Ecuador in 1532, with a royal warrant to conquer and convert, and despite the previous friendly contact, some of the Spanish were killed by Indians as they tried to beach. Moreover, when they reached the city it was completely deserted with many buildings destroyed and, more painfully for Pizarro, no sign of gold. It seems likely that Tumbes' destruction prior to Pizarro's arrival was the result of inter-tribal warfare directly related to the **Inca Civil War**. This, a war of succession between Atahualpa and his half-brother, the legitimate heir, Huascar, was to make Pizarro's role as conqueror a great deal easier, and he took the town of Tumbes without a struggle.

Arrival, information and city transport

Most **buses** coming to Tumbes arrive at offices along Avenida Tumbes Norte (also known as Avenida Teniente Vasquez), or along Piura, although a new Terminal Terrestre is planned for the near future. Ormeño and Continental

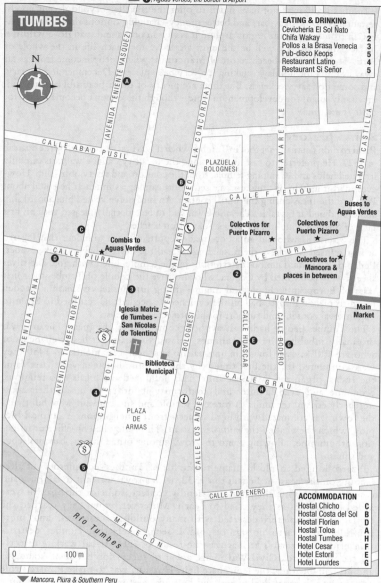

TUMBES

Mancora, Piura & Southern Peru ▼

EATING & DRINKING

Cevichería El Sol Ñato	1
Chifa Wakay	2
Pollos a la Brasa Venecia	3
Pub-disco Keops	5
Restaurant Latino	4
Restaurant Si Señor	5

ACCOMMODATION

Hostal Chicho	C
Hostal Costa del Sol	B
Hostal Florian	D
Hostal Toloa	A
Hostal Tumbes	H
Hotel Cesar	F
Hotel Estoril	E
Hotel Lourdes	G

Within the map labels:

CALLE ABAD PUSIL
AVENIDA TENIENTE VASQUEZ
PLAZUELA BOLOGNESI
NAVARETTE
RAMON CASTILLA
PASEO DE LA CONCORDIA
CALLE F FEIJOU
Buses to Aguas Verdes ★
Combis to Aguas Verdes
Colectivos for Puerto Pizarro ★
Colectivos for Puerto Pizarro ★
CALLE PIURA
AVENIDA SAN MARTIN
Colectivos for Mancora & places in between ★
CALLE PIURA
AVENIDA TACNA
AVENIDA TUMBES NORTE
CALLE A UGARTE
Main Market
Iglesia Matriz de Tumbes - San Nicolas de Tolentino
BOLOGNESI
CALLE HUASCAR
CALLE BODERO
Biblioteca Municipal
CALLE BOLIVAR
CALLE GRAU
PLAZA DE ARMAS
CALLE LOS ANDES
CALLE 7 DE ENERO
Río Tumbes
MALECON

0   100 m

buses from Ecuador stop at Av Tumbes Norte 216. See Listings, p.468, for full details of bus company offices. Comite *colectivos* also pull in at Tumbes Norte 308 (☎072/525977). If you're **flying** in from Lima, Tumbes airport just north of the city limits is quite a contrast, just a small low building and very laid-back; Lan Peru, *Hotel Rizzo*, Jr Bolognesi 216 (☎072/521228) presently fly here from Lima and Piura. A **taxi** into town should cost around $5, about a ten-minute journey.

Taxis will happily take passengers directly from the town centre or airport to the main beaches. A car to Punta Sal, for instance, costs around $25 and takes about an hour.

Tourist information is available from Jr Bolognesi 194, the first floor of the Centro Cívico, on the Plaza de Armas (8am–1pm & 2–6pm, ☎072/524940, ⓦwww.regiontumbes.gob.pe). Tumbes is quite pleasant and easy to get around **on foot**, or you can hail one of the many **motorcycle rickshaws**, which will take you anywhere in the city for around 50¢.

Accommodation

Central Tumbes is well endowed with **places to stay**. Some of the better budget options are strung out from the Plaza de Armas along Calle Grau.

Arrecife Hotel Fausino Piaggio 158, Zorritos ☎072/544462, ⓦwww.arrecifehotel.com. Located over 30km south of the city in Zorritos, almost all the way to Punta Sal, this place is right on the beach and among pretty gardens and patios; rooms are clean and simple with attractive bare stone walls. Great service. ❹

La Casa del Grillo Av Los Pinos 563, Zorritos ☎072/544222, ⓔcasagrillo@yahoo.es. Another fine choice if you're after cheap and cheerful hostel accommodation outside the city; on the main road in Zorritos (30km south of Tumbes) very close to the beach.

Hostal Chicho Av Tumbes Norte 327 ☎074/523696. New and good value; some rooms come with private bath and TV, and the ones at the back are quieter with individual mosquito netting. ❸

Hostal Costa del Sol Av San Martín 275 ☎072/523991, ⓦwww.costadelsolperu.com. Located close to the Plaza de Armas, the *Costa del Sol* offers very comfortable rooms with air-condi-

tioning and private baths and cable TV, as well as a nice pool. ❼–❽

Hostal Florian C Piura 400 ☎072/522464. A large hotel, slightly down-at-heel, but with comfortable beds at reasonable rates. Most rooms have a private bath. ❸–❹

Hostal Tumbes C Grau 614 ☎072/522203. Very pleasant rooms all with their own showers, the best value of which are upstairs, affording better light. ❷

🏃 **Hotel Cesar** C Huascar 313 ☎072/522883. Small, very friendly and good value, offering plain but nicely decorated spaces, all with private bath and fans (rather than air conditioning) and most with TVs. ❸

Hotel Estoril C Huascar 317 ☎072/521360 or 524906. Small, comfortable and exceptionally good value, if undistinguished. All rooms with private bath. ❷

Hotel Lourdes C Bodero 118 ☎072/522126. Located in a quiet side street, *Lourdes* is notably clean and well looked after, with private bathrooms and very helpful staff. ❸

The City

Although it has very few real sights, Tumbes is a surprisingly elegant city, at least around the broad **Plaza de Armas**, which is bounded by large trees, and beyond which sit the **Biblioteca Municipal** and the rather plain **Iglesia Matriz de Tumbes – San Nicolas de Tolentino**, built in the seventeenth century but restored in 1995, making it now one of the most modernized churches in Northern Peru. It has an understated Baroque facade and both cupolas are covered in mosaics. Located in the amphitheatre or stage at the southern end on the main plaza, the **municipal mural** entitled *Encuentro de Dos Mundos* (Encounter of Two Worlds) depicts a bold and vivid jungle, conquistador- and Inca-inspired scene symbolizing the influence of Spain on ancient Peru and in particular the Battle of the Mangroves.

An attractive pedestrian precinct, the **Paseo de la Concordia**, decorated with colourful tiles and several large sculptures and statues, leads off the plaza between the cathedral and the *biblioteca* to the Plazuela Bolognesi. Older and slightly grubby is the long **Malecón** promenade that runs along the high riverbanks of the Río Tumbes, a block beyond the southern end of the Plaza de Armas. At the western end of the Malecón, you can see a massive Modernist **sculpture**, *Tumbes Paraiso del Amor y el Eterno Verano* (Tumbes Paradise of Love and Eternal Summer), depicting a pair of lovers kissing. Leading off eastwards from the northern edge of the plaza, is Calle Grau, an attractive old-fashioned hodgepodge of a street, lined with wooden colonial buildings.

Eating and drinking

Tumbes has some excellent **restaurants** and is the best place in Peru to try *conchas negras* – the **black clams** found only in these coastal waters, where they grow on the roots of mangroves. The *Pub-disco Keops*, C Bolívar 121, on the plaza, has a rustic-style **bar** at the front with a music scene going on behind it; at weekends they sometimes have live music.

Cevicheria Meche C Lobitos 160 ☏072/858412. The best place in town for seafood; try a ceviche with *conchas negras* or a huge steaming dish of *sudado de pescado* (usually a whole fish steamed and served with a mildly sweet sauce).

Cevichería El Sol Ñato C Bolívar 608. The second best place in town for a wide range of seafood, but only open for lunches.

Chifa Wakay C Huascar 417. Dishes up well-priced, tasty Chinese food.

Pollos a la Brasa Venecia C Bolívar 237. Does exactly what it says in its name – a great place for chicken.

Restaurant Latino C Bolívar 163. Right on the Plaza de Armas, this old-fashioned eatery specializes in excellent Continental and American breakfasts.

Restaurant Si Señor C Bolívar 119. Serves mostly beer and seafood, right on the Plaza de Armas.

Listings

Airport Aeropuerto Pedro Canga Rodriguez, Av Panamericana Norte 1276 ☏072/525102.

Banks and exchange Banco de Credito, C Bolívar 135, and Banco de la Nación, on the corner of C Grau and C Bolívar, by the Plaza de Armas; Banco Continental is at Bolívar 129. *Cambistas* are at the corner of Bolívar with Piura.

Bus companies CIAL, Av Tumbes Norte 556 (☏072/526350), for Lima; CIVA, Av Tumbes Norte 518 (☏072/525120) for south down the coast; Cruz del Sur, Av Tumbes Norte 319 (☏072/522350 or 896163), for Lima and the coast; El Dorado, Piura 459 (☏072/523480), for Máncora; Emtrafesa, Av Tumbes Norte 596 (☏072/522894), for Chiclayo and Trujillo; Nor Pacífico, Av Tumbes Norte, for Piura, Chiclayo and Máncora; Oltursa, Av Tumbes Norte 946 (☏072/526524) for Lima; Ormeño and Continental, Av Tumbes (one block beyond CIAL depot and over the road; ☏072/522228), for Trujillo.

Ecuadorian Consulate C Bolívar 155, Plaza de Armas ☏072/523022 (Mon–Fri 9am–4pm).

Internet Vernet, Jr Bolognesi 242.

Mountain biking Panaca Tours ☏072/972658-5426 (from $60 for a very full day).

Police Corner of Av Mayor Novoa and C Zarumilla ☏072/522525.

Post office Av San Martín 208. Mon–Sat 8am–8pm.

Telephones The Telefónica del Peru office is on Avenida San Martín in the same block as the post office.

Tour operators Tumbes Tours, Av Tumbes Norte 351 (☏072/524837, ⓦwww.tumbestours.com) run a number of tours including a 4-day/3-night trip exploring the nearby Puerto Pizarro mangrove swamp, as well as local beaches from $20 per person per day, depending on size of group. Preference Tours, Grau 427 ☏072/525518, are good for general tourist information and tickets, and organize most standard local tour packages.

Around Tumbes

Along the coast around Tumbes you'll find some of the best **beaches** in the country, with a pleasantly warm sea for swimming. Among them are **Caleta de la Cruz**, 23km southwest (45min), reputed to be the bay where Pizarro first landed, **Punta Sal**, 50km southwest (1–2hr), Zorritos, 34km southwest (1hr) and **Máncora**, about 100km to the south (2hr). **Buses and colectivos** to all four resorts leave daily from the main market in Tumbes, on Ramon Castillo, but return buses aren't that frequent, so check return times with the driver before you leave Tumbes. Nor Pacífico and Santa Rosa buses (see opposite) also go to Máncora from their offices in Tumbes. It's also fairly easy to get south as far as Máncora in two *colectivo* rides; the first from block 1 of Avenida Tumbes Norte as far as Los Organos (70min; $1.25); change here for another car to Máncora (30min; $70c).

Puerto Pizarro and the Isla de Amor

If you've never seen a mangrove swamp, **PUERTO PIZARRO**, 13km northeast of Tumbes, is perhaps worth a visit, though it has no specific link with the conquistador it's named after, and the waterfront today is full of rubbish; better to plough on to Los Bosques de Manglares de Tumbes (see box, pp.470–471). **Taxis** and **colectivos** leave regularly for Puerto Pizarro from calles Piura and Navarette in Tumbes.

An ancient fishing port, Puerto Pizarro was a commercial harbour until swamps grew out to sea over the last few centuries, making it inaccessible for large boats and permanently disconnecting Tumbes from the Pacific. Overlooking Puerto Pizarro port are the brightly painted bungalows of the **hotel** *Puerto Pizarro* (❸), which occupies the nicest bit of waterfront; the hotel has a pool, private bathrooms, palm trees and a restaurant-café. There are a few other, basic hostels in town should this be full.

An **information** and ticket booth is situated on the sea front, near to some stalls selling shells and other items. From here you can take slow, basic but pleasant **boat trips** ($15 each person) out to the **ISLA DE AMOR**, where there's a bathing beach and a café. The boat operators will inform you of the history of the area and the mangroves themselves, as well as point out wildlife like the magnificent frigate bird (also called scissor-tail) and the occasional white iguana languishing amongst the mangroves. The tour will also take you through **mangrove creeks** where you'll see the *rhizopora* tree's dense root system. Perhaps the highlight of the boat trip is a tour around the centre for the protection of Peru's only indigenous, and **endangered crocodile** (*Crocodylus acutus americano*) run by FONDERES, funded by the Peruvian government. There are only forty of these crocodiles left in the wild (where they can live for a hundred years), having been hunted in the past for their skin, and the centre has bred around 225 in captivity. It's possible to see the crocodiles at most life stages, with the largest growing to around 3m.

The Mud Baths of Hervidore

Located 40km south of Tumbes (40–50min by car), these amazing mud baths are little visited yet apparently very good for your skin; they're certainly fun. Set about 3km from the Panamericana Highway (turn off at Bocapan, Km 1214, signpost reads "Parque Nacional Cerros de Amotape"), they're surrounded by hills and *algarrobo* trees, a really peaceful and relaxing spot. These *pozos de barro* (mud baths) were discovered by the archaeologist Raymondi in 1882, though were almost certainly used for centuries before that. There are several mud baths, with a lower pool for washing down. Temperatures and health effects vary pool by pool; some of this is noted on small wooden signs, with analysis of the mud detecting iron oxides, calcium chloride, sodium chloride, aluminium chloride and magnesium chloride among other chemical components.

Punta Sal

Located some 2km along a track from Km 1187 of the Panamerican Highway, also known in the north as the Panamericana Norte, **PUNTA SAL**, considered by many to be the best **beach** in Peru, has extensive sands and attractive rocky

The Tumbes region is well endowed with natural resources, not least the three major **protected areas** of the Sanctuario Nacional Los Manglares de Tumbes, the Parque Nacional Cerros Amotape and the Zona Reservada de Tumbes. These, plus the El Angulo Hunting Reserve, encompass many habitats only found in this small corner of the country. If you're short of time, it is just about possible to travel between these in just a day, but contact the local conservation organization – Pronaturaleza, Av Tarapaca 4–16, Urbino Fonavi (℡072/523412), on the outskirts of Tumbes – beforehand for impartial, expert advice. **Permission** from INRENA, opposite Pronaturaleza's office, is needed to enter all of these areas, though this is a formality for which no fees are payable.

The Sanctuario Nacional Los Manglares de Tumbes

The **Sanctuario Nacional Los Manglares de Tumbes** comprises most of the remaining **mangrove swamps** left in Peru, which are under serious threat from fishing and farming (shrimp farming in particular). The best way to visit the sanctuary is via the Pronaturaleza centre near Zarumilla, here called **CECODEM** (Centro de Conservación para el Desarrollo de los Manglares); *combis* run from Tumbes market to Zarumilla regularly (70¢; 20min), from where it's only 7km down a track to CECODEM; a motorcycle taxi will cost $1.50, and you can arrange for the driver to return to pick you up. If arranged in advance with Pronaturaleza in Tumbes (at least one day before), CECODEM offer a walking **tour** (2–3hr) following a raised walkway through the mangroves and a **canoe trip** with a guide ($15 for up to six people). The centre also presents a lot of interpretive material about the mangroves, of which there are five species here. Red mangrove is the most common and this is where the *conchas negras* thrive, although the 1998 El Nino weather introduced large amounts of fresh water into the shell beds here, causing significant damage. The mangroves also

outcrops, swarming with crabs at low tide. It's a safe place to swim and a heavenly spot for diving in warm, clear waters.

Several **hotels** here were destroyed by the 1998 El Niño, but the best place to stay is still the plush but friendly *Hotel Caballito del Mar* (℡072/540058 or from Lima 01/2414455, ⓦwww.hotelcaballitodemar.com; ⑥), overlooking the sea at the southern end of the beach, with its own swimming pool right by the exquisite ocean (very peaceful in low season), a restaurant, sun terraces and really comfortable rooms; a quality place, they offer massage and inclusive breakfast, although local tours and fishing trips cost extra. Less expensive is the *Hospedaje Hua Punta Sal* (℡072/540023, ⓔhuapuntasal@yahoo.com; ④ ⑤), towards the middle of the beach, an older and more rustic wooden building, where some rooms have ocean views; service is very good, plus there's a restaurant (camping only for pre-arranged tour groups).

There are a couple of small bodega shops in Punta Sal, so drinks and general groceries can be bought without leaving the beach area and travelling to one of the towns up or down the Panamericana. In the low season you'll probably have a beautiful beach pretty much to yourself; in high season it's a good idea to book your accommodation in advance. At the northern end of the point, there's also the secluded, rather exclusive Punta Sal Club Hotel (contact in Lima at Miguel Dasso 126, Of 210 ℡072/540088 or in Lima at 01/4425961, ⓦwww.puntasal .com.pe; 8), with comfortable cabin-style accommodation right on the beach, a pool, great bar and restaurant facilities; it also offers fishing, horseriding and snorkelling. Fishing trips from here, famous for the high concentration of striped and black marlin, cost from around $230 for a half-day (you can take up to six people contain over two hundred bird species, including eight endemic species, notably the rather splendid mangrove eagle.

Zona Reservada de Tumbes

This reserve extends right up to the Ecuadorian border and covers over 75,000 hectares of mainly tropical forest. The best route is inland, due south from Tumbes via Pampas de Hospital and El Caucho to El Narranjo and Figueroa on the border, but transport from Tumbes is only regular as far as Pampas de Hospital, and only occasionally further on to El Caucho, which is where the best forest is. Potential sightings include monkeys, many bird species, small cats and snakes, though the **Río Tumbes crocodile** is a highly endangered species, found only at two sites along this river. There is some small hope for this unique creature in the form of a local breeding programme, but the whole area is under threat from gold-mining, mainly from across the border in Ecuador at the headwaters of the river. Pollution, too, from Tumbes is generating further disturbance.

Parque Nacional Cerros de Amotape

Home to the best-preserved region of dry forest anywhere along the Pacific coast of South America, the **Parque Nacional Cerros de Amotape** contains six other distinct habitats that cover over 90,000 hectares. Access is via Corrales, 5km south of Máncora, or via Chillo, just north of Sullana; you'll need permission from INRENA to visit (see above, or if coming via Chillo you can visit them en route at Encuentro de los Pilares). Animals that you just may see here include the black parrot, desert foxes, deer, white-backed squirrels, *tigrillos* (ocelots), puma and white-winged turkeys. Remember to take all your drinking and other **water** needs with you when entering this zone.

for this, double the price for a full day). See Tumbes section (p.467) for accommodation options in nearby Zorritos.

Máncora

The most fashionable beach in Peru with the young at heart, even attracting the **surf** crowd from Ecuador and Brazil, **Máncora** (ⓦ www.vivamancora.com) is also a highly welcome and very enjoyable stopover when travelling along the north coast. Well served by public transport and spread out along the Panamerican Highway, parallel to a beautiful sandy beach, swimming is safe and the surfing can be pretty good.

Máncora enjoys warm waters and its position is blessed as the place where northern tropical currents meet with the much, much cooler southern one. At Lobitos, the next beach down the coast from Cabo Blanco (30km south of Máncora) the sea is cold. This geographical position gives Máncora near perfect surf conditions at times, with barrel waves achieving up to 4m in height. You can hire gear from several places, including the Soledad Surf Company, Av Piura 316 (ⓣ 01/99830425 in Lima), which sells and rents equipment as well as offering surf and Spanish lessons, or from the *Godwanaland* restaurant. Surf lessons are also available from *Del Wawa* (see p.472) at around $15 an hour (board rentals $5hr). The popular Máncora **half-pipe** (daily 3–6.30pm) offers skateboarding facilities and lessons; you can find it on the hill, by taking the road up behind *Restaurant Ramjosy* (road to the lighthouse); it's behind the *Hospedaje Salvalito*.

At the north end of the main drag, there's a plaza and just beyond this there's sometimes a street market, though only the usual clothing, shoes and food.

▲ Fishermen, Máncora

Between here and the south end you'll find most of the town's hotels and restaurants, and a promenade with hippie **artesania** stalls, selling sea-inspired crafts and jewellery.

Mud baths

If the beach isn't relaxing enough, you can always head to Poza de Barro, or the local **mud baths** (\$1). Set 11km from the main road and surrounded by hills and *algarobba* trees, the warm natural bath appeared in the shaft following oil extraction in the 1980s. It's now visited for its cleansing subterranean waters (no sign of oil today). It has basic toilets and a changing hut. To **get here** you can a take a taxi or ride a horse (the latter through a local tour company, will take a good day). The entry road to the mud baths is off the Panamericana, just north of Máncora next to the "Comunidad Máncora Campesino" sign by the bridge.

Practicalities

All the main **hotels** are located between the bridge at the south entrance to town and the plaza towards the north end, though there are several cheaper basic hostels strung out along the southern end of the Panamerican Highway and some more remote and upmarket options on Vichayito beach, beyond the southern entrance to Máncora.

The local surf scene focuses around *Del Wawa*, Avenida Piura, Frente al Point (℡073/258427, Ⓦwww.delwawa.com; ❹), a small beachside hotel with brilliant architecture, cool rooms, hammocks and a great restaurant. The *Hostal Sol y Mar* (℡073/258106, Ⓔhsolymar@hotmail.com; ❷) is probably the best value and also very popular with the surfing crowd; it is right on the beach, has a good swimming pool and games courts, plus a decent restaurant and bar, private baths and its own little shop and internet café; The *Hostal El Mar* (❺), meanwhile, overlooks the sea, has smart, cabin-like rooms, private baths and hammocks, and meals are included. The *Hotel Las Garzas*, Av Piura 262 (℡074/258110; ❸–❹), has thirteen rooms, a restaurant and parking facilities plus a nice garden with hammocks; quite quiet and peaceful for this town. The *Point Hostel*, Playa El Amor, 01/994042418, Ⓦwww

.thepointhostels.com; ❸–❹), is pretty central, right on the beach, offers surf gear plus other rentals, has a games room and runs one of the town's best bars. *Hotel Sunset*, Avenida Antigua Panamericana Norte 196 073/258111, ⓌWww.hotelsunset .com.pe; ❻), is a stylish boutique hotel on a secluded beach with a good cliff-top restaurant and fine service.

There's a notice board advertising rooms and bungalows for **rent**, as well as surfing lessons, in the Locutorio Publico **telephone office** and shop, on block 5 of Avenida Piura opposite the small church and close to the Banco de la Nación. Nearby you'll find the Cabinas **Internet** Máncora at Av Piura 605.

For **eating**, there's a surplus of restaurants in the centre of town, mainly along the Panamerican Highway. On the beach, the relatively new tourist-orientated complex *The Bird House*, close to the *Hostal Sol y Mar*, is the in place to be. Divided into shops, bars and cafés, mostly franchised out, it has a wide range of international (including burgers, ham and eggs) and local cuisine available, surf shop, cocktails, ice creams and a pleasant beachside, shaded lounge area. At Panamericana Norte 233 there's the colourful Italian-Peruvian restaurant, *El Tuno*. The *Restaurant Arplan*, and opposite this the *Espada*, at Av Piura 655, are both reasonably good, offering a range of fish dishes, including surprisingly affordable lobster; generally speaking, though, their prices are not that cheap. The *Cevicheria Meche*, C Lobitos 160, and *Jugeria Mi Janet* opposite, have excellent and very fresh seafood, while both the *Restaurant Jugeria Regina's*, in the centre, is good for fruit salads and breakfasts. For **shopping**, Comercial Marlon II, next to the ATM and Municipal building, has a superb range of groceries, including wholemeal bread, local honey and wines. There's a hectic **nightlife** scene based in the bars, beachside hotels and on the beach itself, especially during Peruvian holiday times. It's easy to find - just follow the sounds after dark, even if the only club as such is *Las Terrazas*, on the main drag, backing onto the beach.

The **bus companies** are all in the main street, Avenida Piura, where you can buy tickets for their selection of daily and nightly services up or down the coast, connecting Tumbes with Lima and the major cities in between. Transportes EPPO run five buses between here and Piura ($3, 3hr) from their office just north of the plaza, towards the northern end of Máncora at Grau 470. Other bus companies, including the quality service of Cruz del Sur, Av Piur 656 (☏074/858107) is almost as good Civa, Av Piura 656 (☏074/858026), and a close third, Ormeño, Av Piura 499 (☏074/858334), go daily to Piura and Chiclayo, and also have connections for Cajamarca (as well as buses from Ecuador). El Dorado, Av Grau 111 (an extension of Piura), run south to Piura, Chiclayo and Trujillo daily and nightly. Nor Pacífico and Santa Rosa buses stop at the plaza en route between Tumbes and Piura. CIVA and Cial buses stop opposite the Comisaria. *Colectivos* depart from near the EPPO office for Los Oreganos (50¢, 30min), from where there are other *combis* to Talara ($1, 1hr). *Colectivos* and *combis* also patrol up and down the Panamerican Highway looking for passengers for Tumbes ($2.50, 1hr 30min–2h).

Vichayito

VICHAYITO, a stupendous and largely empty beach, is the continuation south from Máncora's less extensive (but closer to the road) strip of sand. It makes for a relaxing alternative, with good swimming, some surf and lovely coastal scenery – though the village is developing rather quickly. To **get here**, take the rough (old Panamerican) highway on the right just as you leave Máncora; it's a fifteen minute, bumpy journey by *mototaxi*. You could also walk from Máncora along the coast (about 1hr), but make sure you take **water** with you.

It has very comfortable, spacious **rooms/apartments** with balconies and facilities including hammocks, a swimming pool and a children's play area, although electricity is not always guaranteed. Further back off the beach, virtually in the dunes 7km south of Máncora and 4km north of Los Organos (another wide beach), the *Sol de Vichayito* (contact in Lima on ℡01/996376090 or 2612321, Ⓔsoldevichayito@ terra.com.pe; ❺) offers **cabin-style accommodation**, with private bathrooms and terraces; some rooms also have kitchenettes. One of the best places to **eat**, *El Mirador* (℡073/973767098 or Lima 01/271-6751, Ⓦwww.elmiradordevichayito. com; ❺ ❻), is at the southern end of the main development at Km 1155 and is accessed by wooden steps from the beach (and runs a café on the beach itself). The main restaurant at the top of the hill offers northern-style ceviches and other meals as well as a breezy bar with good views.

Crossing the border at Aguas Verdes

Crossing the Peru–Ecuador border is relatively simple in either direction. Three kilometres before the busy frontier settlement of **Aguas Verdes**, you'll find the **Peruvian immigration office** (daily 24hr), where you get an exit or entry stamp and tourist card for your passport. Once past these buildings, it's a twenty-minute walk or a short drive to Aguas Verdes. **Combis** for the border leave Tumbes from block 3 of Tumbes Norte. A **taxi** from Tumbes costs $5–6. From Aguas Verdes, you just walk over the bridge into the Ecuadorian border town of **Huaquillas**, and the **Ecuadorian immigration office** (daily 24hr), where you'll get entry or exit stamps and tourist card. If coming from Ecuador to Peru, Tumbes is the nicer **place to stay** close to the border; it has a greater choice of hotels and restaurants and it's much easier to make southerly connections from here, though another option is to take a bus direct from the frontier to Sullana ($6; 2–3hr), from where there are buses and *colectivos* regularly to Piura (50¢; 45min). Formalities wise, it's simply a reversal of the above procedure.

If going north, frequent buses depart to all the major destinations in Ecuador from Huaquillas. The best bet is to go on to Cuenca (5hr), an attractive, small Ecuadorian city and a major cultural centre, although Machala is nearer (75km) and has some accommodation and other facilities.

In both directions the authorities occasionally require that you show an **onward ticket** out of their respective countries. Unless you intend to recross the border inside a week or two, it's not worth taking out any local currency: changing Peruvian nuevo soles in Ecuador or Ecuadorian sucres in Peru usually involves a substantial loss, and inflation is such that even two weeks can make quite a difference. The area of **no-man's-land** between the two countries' posts is basically a street market where everyone gets hassled to change money – grab a **taxi** to ease the passage. The best policy is to change as little money as possible (because of the **poor exchange rates** mentioned above) and, if you take a taxi, be firm on the price in advance.

The **Peruvian customs** point, a concrete complex in the middle of the desert between the villages of Cancas and Máncora and more than 50km south of the border, was inactive following the 1999 agreements between Ecuador and Peru. When it is operating, however, most buses are pulled over and passengers have to get out and often have to show documents to the customs police, while the bus and selected items of luggage are searched for contraband goods. This rarely takes more than twenty minutes, as they are quite efficient.

Crossing the border via La Tina and Loja

The alternative frontier crossing between **La Tina** and **Macará** is a very pleasant alternative, its main advantage being the scenery en route to Loja. The crossing is most conveniently approached by *combi* from Sullana, leaving in the mornings from Avenida Buenos Aires, near the main market ($3, 3hr). Hours for the **Peruvian immigration office** (daily 9am–noon & 2–5pm) are much the same as those for the **Ecuadorian immigration office** (daily 8am–1pm & 2–6pm).

There's nowhere to stay in La Tina, but a couple of basic **hostels** are to be found in Macará in Ecuador. Buses on to **Loja** (5hr) depart from Macará and it may be possible to connect on arrival and travel from Sullana to Macará in one day. Macará itself is located some 3km from the border; **motorcycle taxis** (70¢; 10min) take people into town. Alternatively, there are also **buses** direct to Loja from Piura (see below). The journey between the border and Macará is extremely hot – it's only a few kilometres, but if the sun's out, take water to drink. You can change **money** (dollars, sucres or soles) in Macará, and in La Tina or at the bank (Mon–Fri) on the Ecuadorian side of the international bridge.

Travel details

Buses and colectivos

Cajamarca to: Cajabamba (6 daily; 5hr); Celendin (4 daily; 4–5hr); Chachapoyas (2 weekly via Celendin; 16–19hr); Chiclayo (10 daily; 7–9hr); Lima (several daily; 15hr).

Chachapoyas to: Cajamarca (2 weekly via Celendin; 15hr); Chiclayo (several daily; 10–12hr); Kuelap (several daily; 3hr); Rioja/Moyobamba (3 daily; 9–12hr).

Chiclayo to: Cajamarca (10 daily; 7–9hr); Chachapoyas (several daily; 10–12hr); Huancabamba (2 weekly; 15hr); Lima (8–10 daily; 14hr); Piura (12 daily; 4hr); Trujillo (12 daily; 3hr); Tumbes (8 daily; 10hr).

Piura to: Chiclayo (12 daily; 2–3hr); Huancabamba (2–3 daily; 12hr); La Tina and Loja (4 daily; 10–12hr); Lima (8 daily; 13–15hr); Tumbes (8 daily; 4–6hr).

Sullana to: La Tina, Ecuador (3 daily; 2hr).

Trujillo to: Cajamarca (several daily; 8hr); Chiclayo (12 daily; 3hr); Lima (12 daily; 9hr); Piura, via Chiclayo (8 daily; 7hr); Yurimaguas (2–3 daily; 12–15hr).

Tumbes to Máncora (several daily; 1–2 hrs); Aguas Verdes (hourly; 20min); Chiclayo (8 daily; 10hr); Lima (8 daily; 23hr); Puerto Pizarro (hourly; 25min).

Flights

Cajamarca to: Lima (several weekly; 2hr).

Chiclayo to: Iquitos (3 weekly; 2hr); Lima (2 daily; 2hr); Piura (1 daily; 30min); Tarapoto (2 weekly; 90min); Trujillo (1 daily; 45min).

Piura to: Lima, via Chiclayo (2 daily; 2hr); Trujillo (1 daily; 1hr).

Tarapoto to: Iquitos (6 weekly; 1hr 30min); Lima (1 or 2 daily; 1hr 30min); Yurimaguas (1–2 weekly; 25min).

Trujillo to: Chiclayo (1 daily; 45min); Iquitos (4 weekly; 2hr); Lima (2 daily; 2hr 30min); Piura (1 daily; 1hr).

Tumbes to: Lima (4 weekly; 2hr 30min).

8

The Jungle

CHAPTER 8

Highlights

✱ **Pampa Hermosa Lodge**
Just eight hours' drive from
Lima, this sumptuous cloud
forest lodge, one of the
jewels of Peru, offers access
to a Cock-of-the Rock
refuge, where Peru's national
birds dance every evening;
in an adjacent reserved
woodland, South America's
oldest and largest cedar
trees sway quietly in the
breeze. See p.494

✱ **Iquitos** A fun, vivacious city,
ridiculously hot during the
day, with an equally sizzling
bar and club scene when the
sun goes down. See p.531

✱ **Dolphin watching** Quite
common in the rivers around
Iquitos, pink river dolphins
and blue dolphins are a
fantastic sight as they leap
around your canoe. See p.547

✱ **Ayahuascero healing** A
hallucinatory experience,
usually in a jungle settlement,
as the shaman's ancient
chants waft over the silver
moonlit leafy canopy above
the clearing. See p.549

✱ **Tambopata-Candamo
Reserve** You'll be hard-
pushed to find anywhere as
rich in flora and fauna as
this, the most biodiverse area
of rainforest in the Amazon.
See p.516

✱ **Manu Biosphere Reserve**
Another excellent place to
experience a truly pristine
rainforest and see plenty of
jungle wildlife – from giant
otters in secluded lakes to
motionless caiman littering
the river banks. See p.521

▲ Manu Biosphere Reserve

8

The Jungle

The Amazon, the rainforest, the selva, the jungle, the green hell (*el infierno verde*) – all attempt to name this huge, vibrant area of Peru. Few people think of Peru in terms of jungle, yet well over half the country is covered by dense tropical rainforest, with its eastern regions offering unrivalled access to the world's largest and most famous river, the **AMAZON**. These days, as a global centre for biodiversity, the Peruvian jungle is a conservation priority. The forested Andean slopes along the western edge of the Amazon hold world records for many species, including 365 ants discovered on a ten-hectare study plot. In 2002, meanwhile, over 40 ant species were discovered in one single tree canopy. Some areas of forest, like the Manu Biosphere Reserve (see p.521) possess between 150 and 200 different tree species per hectare, and Manu is also home to over 200 mammal species and over 13 different primates (not including tourists).

Whether you look at it up close, from the ground or a boat, or fly over it in a plane, the Peruvian **jungle** seems endless. In fact, it is disappearing at an alarming rate. Campaigns raising awareness of its importance as a unique ecosystem and as a vital component of the global environment (not to mention the wealth of wildlife and sheer beauty of the vegetation) have brought the matter into the international spotlight. Across the planet, deforestation is responsible for some twenty percent of carbon emissions, themselves one of the main causes of global warming. The tropical rainforest is also both a massive store of carbon and a natural soak for additional carbon, as the trees are continuously growing.

Of the Amazon's original area, around seventy percent remains largely intact, with at least twelve percent of this remaining area located in Peru, a region that receives over 2000mm of rainfall a year and experiences average temperatures of 25–35°C (77–95°F). Sharing the western edge of the Amazon with Colombia, Ecuador and Brazil, Peru's jungle forms part of what is probably the most biodiverse region on Earth. Until the last few years, much that lies beyond the main waterways was relatively untouched and often unexplored. Jaguars, anteaters and tapirs still roam the forests, huge anaconda snakes live in the swamps, toothy caimans (of the South American *alligatoridae* family) sunbathe along riverbanks and trees like the enormous shihuahuaco, strong enough to break an axe head, rise like giants from the forest floor. Over fifty indigenous tribes still live scattered throughout the Peruvian section of the Amazon, many surviving primarily by hunting, fishing and gathering, as they have done for thousands of years.

The Peruvian rainforest cover is not uniform tropical woodland; mainly due to the influence of the Andes at the jungle's western edge, Peru's selva possesses a wide a range of ecological niches, each with distinct protected areas and offering different possibilities to the visitor. In the north, the main access point is the city of **Iquitos** in the heart of Peru's largest chunk of lowland jungle where the trees

THE JUNGLE REGION

0   200 km

ECUADOR   COLOMBIA

Río Putumayo

Río Pastaza

Río Napo

Río Santiago

Río Morona

Río Tigre

Iquitos

Río Amazonas   Pevas

Caballococha

Leticia

Tábatinga

Borja

Puerto América

Barranca

Río Marañon

Nauta

Santa Rosa

Santa Cruz

Lagunas

Requena

PACAYA SAMIRIA NATIONAL PARK

Yurimaguas

Moyombamba

Chachapoyas

Tarapoto

Contamana

BRAZIL

N

Río Huallaga

DANGEROUS ROUTE

Pucallpa

Huaraz

Tingo Maria

Río Ucayali

Huánuco

Pozuzo

Oxapampa

Cerro de Pasco

Atalaya

Río Urubamba

Sepahua

Río Purús

La Merced

Río Tambo

Río Ene

Kiteni

Quillabamba

Río de las Piedras

Iñapari

Iberia

BOLIVIA

Tarma

Satipo

LIMA

Huancayo

MANU BIOSPHERE RESERVE

Boca Manu

Río Madre de Dios

Puerto Maldonado

Huancavelica

Shintuya

Ayacucho

Pillcopata

Pt Heath

Abancay

Cusco

TAMBOPATA-CANDAMO RESERVED ZONE & BAHUAJA-SONENE NATIONAL PARK

Río Tambopata

Pisco

Nasca

Manaus, Belém & the Atlantic

are tall, the Amazon River already enormous and the flat land along the river banks regularly flooded. Further up the Río Amazonas, closer to the Andes but still swathed in lowland forest you find the immense **Pacaya Samiria Reserva Nacional** (National Reserve), a little visited wildlife haven; and south of here, in the central selva, the high jungle starts in the stunning **Chanchamayo Valley**, blessed with crystalline rivers, numerous protected areas for bird-watching and exploration, plus reasonably good road links and routes on to the frontier town of **Satipo**. Also in the central selva, the fast growing city and river port of **Pucallpa** offers lowland forest although unlike Iquitos, is accessible by bus from Lima via Tingo Maria, or, with numerous connections on poor roads, via the Chanchamayo

Valley. At the southeastern limit of Peru's territory, close to and accessible from Cusco and the road-connected jungle city of **Puerto Maldonado**, you'll find the greatest biodiversity in three globally important protected areas: the **Parque Nacional de Manu**, which runs from cloudforest on the slopes of the Andes down to relative lowland forest; the **Reserva Nacional de Tambopata**, located at the foot of the Andes but in a predominantly lowland eco-niche; and, neighbouring this, the relatively newly formed protected area of the **Parque Nacional Bahuaja-Sonene**, still rarely visited but home to an exceptional variety of wildlife.

At about six times the size of England, or approximately the size of California, it's not surprising that the Peruvian Amazon possesses a variety of ecotypes. Since it's easier to access than many other South American jungle regions, increasing numbers of travellers are choosing to spend time here, and the tangled, sweltering **Amazon Basin** rarely fails to capture the imagination of anyone who ventures beneath its dense canopy. In the **lowland areas**, away from the seasonally flooded riverbanks, the landscape is dominated by red, loamy soil, which can reach depths of 50m. Reaching upwards from this, the primary forest – mostly comprising a huge array of tropical palms, with scatterings of larger, emergent tree species – regularly achieves evergreen canopy heights of 50m. At ground level the vegetation is relatively open (mostly saplings, herbs and woody shrubs), since the trees tend to branch high up, restricting the amount of light available. At marginally higher altitudes, a large belt of **cloud forest** (*ceja de selva*) sweeps along the eastern edges of the Andes. Stunningly beautiful and the most biodiverse of all these rainforest zones, this has nevertheless been the focus of significant oil and gas prospecting and exploitation during the last decade or so, homing in on some of the world's largest remaining fossil-fuel reserves. Ironically, one of the major threats to the rainforest in 2009 appears to be large-scale plans to grow biofuels there, including soya bean and palm-tree plantations.

The **Río Amazonas** itself, which can lay claim to being the biggest river in the world bar none, originally flowed east to west, before becoming an inland sea when the Andes began to rise along the Pacific edge of the continent around 100 million years ago. Another 40 million years of geological and climatic action later saw this "sea" break through into the Atlantic, which reversed the flow of water and gave birth to the mighty 6500-kilometre river. Starting in Peru as an insignificant glacial trickle on the Nevada Misma, northeast of the Colca Canyon, the waters swell as they move down through the Andes, passing Cusco before gaining the name **Río Tambo** and cascading down through the cloud forest, passing through the Toto, Santiago, Apurimac, Ene and Tambo valleys until they reach the Ashaninka tribal territories in the Gran Pajonal. At this point, the Río Tambo meets the **Río Urubamba**, the major sacred river of the Incas that rushes past Machu Picchu down through rocky canyons. When these two already massive headwaters meet, in the rainforest more or less directly east of Lima in the heart of Peru, they form the much larger **Río Ucayali**, which is already less than 200m above the level of the Atlantic Ocean, still many thousands of miles away. After their merge point, at the small jungle town of **Atalaya**, the river and its tributaries – still the basis of jungle transport – are characterized by slow, wandering courses. In the last couple of years, a logger's road has connected Atalaya with Lima and the coast. Erosion and deposits continue to shift water courses along the slow, low Amazon, and oxbow lakes are constantly appearing and disappearing, adding enormous quantities of time and fuel to any river journey in the lowlands. In Northern Peru, the Amazon river languidly meanders past **Iquitos**, an isolated but vibrant city, on its way towards Brazil and eventually the Atlantic; but it's still at least a two-week journey by boat to the mouth of the Earth's biggest river which, at any one moment, carries around twenty percent of the planet's fresh water.

Some history

Many archaeologists think that the initial spark for the evolution of Peru's high cultures came from the jungle. Archaeological evidence from **Chavín**, **Chachapoyas** and **Tantamayo** cultures seems to back up such a theory – ancient Andean people certainly had continuous contact with the jungle areas – and the **Incas** were unable to dominate the tribes, their main contact being peaceful trade in treasured items such as plumes, gold, medicinal plants and the sacred coca leaf. At the time of the **Spanish Conquest**, fairly permanent settlements existed along all the major jungle rivers, with the people living in large groups to farm the rich alluvial soils. The arrival of the Europeans began an apparently irreversible process of breaking these up into smaller and scattered groups (a process exacerbated by the nineteenth-century rubber boom, see p.482).

For centuries, however, the Peruvian jungle resisted major colonization. Although **Alonso de Alvarado** had led the first Spanish expedition, cutting a trail through from Chachapoyas to Moyobamba in 1537, most incursions ended in utter disaster, defeated by disease, the ferocity of the tribes, the danger of the rivers, climate and wild animals – and perhaps by the inherently alien character of the forest. Ultimately, apart from white man's epidemics (which spread much faster than the men themselves), the early conquistadors had relatively little impact on the populations of the Peruvian Amazon. Only **Orellana**, one of the first Spaniards to lead exploratory expeditions into the Peruvian Amazon, managed to glimpse the reality of the rainforest, though even he seemed to misunderstand it when he was attacked by a tribe of blond women, one of whom managed to hit him in the eye with a blow-gun dart. These "women" are nowadays considered to be men of the Yagua tribe (from near Iquitos), who wear straw-coloured, grass-like skirts and headdresses.

By the early eighteenth century the **Catholic Church** had made deep but vulnerable inroads into the rainforest regions. Resistance to this culminated in 1742 with an indigenous uprising in the **central selva** led by an enigmatic character from the Andes calling himself **Juan Santos Atahualpa**. Missions were destroyed, missionaries and colonists killed, and Spanish military expeditions defeated. The result was that the central rainforest remained under the control of the indigenous population for the next ninety years or so. Similarly, in 1919 the Ashaninka tribe blockaded rivers, ejecting missionaries and foreigners from their ancestral lands, and – during the 1990s – went on to defeat Shining Path terrorists in hand-to-hand combat. Even today, the Ashaninka still occasionally close their land and rivers to outsiders when major disputes arise (for example over territory and resources).

The rubber boom

As "white-man's" technology advanced, so too did the possibilities of conquering Amazonia. The 1830s saw the beginning of a century of massive and painful exploitation of the forest and its population by **rubber barons**. Many of these wealthy men were European, eager to gain control of the raw material desperately needed following the discovery of the vulcanization process. Moreover, during this era the jungle regions of Peru were better connected to Brazil, Bolivia, the Atlantic, and ultimately Europe, than they were to Lima or the Pacific coast. The peak of the boom, from the 1880s to just before World War I, had a prolonged effect. Treating the natives as little more than slaves, men like the notorious **Fitzcarrald** (see box, p.509) made overnight fortunes, and large sections of the forests were explored and subdued. In 1891, for example, the British-owned Peruvian Corporation was granted the 500,000-hectare "Perene Colony" in the central rainforest in payment of debts owed by the Peruvian state. That the granted land was indigenous territory was ignored – the Ashaninka who lived in the area were considered a captive labour force that was part of the concession. The process only fell into decline when the British explorer Clements Markham brought Peruvian rubber plants to Malaysia, where the plants grew equally well but were far easier to harvest.

Agricultural expansion and the colonos

Nineteenth-century colonialism also saw the progression of the **extractive frontier** along the navigable rivers, which involved short-term economic exploitation based on the extraction of other natural materials, such as timber

Indigenous jungle tribes

Outside the few main towns of the Peruvian jungle, there are few sizeable settlements, and the population remains dominated by between 35 and 62 **indigenous tribes** – the exact number depends on how you classify tribal identity – each with its own distinct language, customs and dress. For most tribes, the jungle offers a **semi-nomadic** existence, and in terms of material possessions, they have, need and want very little. Communities are scattered, with groups of between ten and two hundred people, and their sites shift every few years. For subsistence they depend on small, cultivated plots, fish from the rivers and game from the forest, including wild pigs, deer, monkeys and a great range of edible birds. The main species of edible jungle fish are *sabalo* or doncella (types of oversized catfish), *carachama* (an armoured walking catfish), the feisty piranha (generally not quite as dangerous as Hollywood depicts) and the giant *zungaro* and *paiche* – the latter, at up to 200kg, being the world's largest freshwater fish. In fact, food is so abundant that jungle dwellers generally spend no more than three to four days a week engaged in subsistence activities, which, as some anthropologists like to point out, makes them "relatively affluent". Not many of us can satisfy all our needs so easily.

After centuries of external influence (missionaries, gold seekers, rubber barons, cash-crop colonists, cocaine smugglers, soldiers, oil companies, illegal loggers, documentary makers, anthropologists and now tourists), many jungle Indians speak Spanish and live pretty conventional, westernized lives, preferring jeans, football shirts and fizzy bottled drinks to their more traditional clothing and *manioc* beer (the tasty, filling and nutritious *masato*). While many are being sucked into the money-based labour market, however, others, increasingly under threat, have struggled for cultural integrity and territorial rights; some have retreated as far as they are able beyond the enclosing frontier of our world. In 1996, for instance, oil workers encountered some previously uncontacted groups while clearing tracts of forest for seismic testing in the upper Río de las Piedras area of Madre de Dios, northwest of Puerto Maldonado. In this region, some of the last uncontacted tribal communities in the Amazon – Nahua, Mashco and other groups – have been keeping their distance from outside influences.

In 2002 these same remote groups came out of the forest en masse to prevent further intrusion by aggressive **illegal loggers** in their last remaining territory at the headwaters of the Río de las Piedras. In August of that year some four hundred Indians appeared on the riverbanks as a flotilla of illegal logging launches made its way upstream from Puerto Maldonado. Shaking and rattling their bows and arrows, the Indians raised long vines as a barrier across the river and then attacked the boats, badly injuring several loggers (for more on the story of these natives' fight for independence, see p.613). In 2008, reports from Brazilian authorities and Survival International showed how "uncontacted" Indian groups were trying to escape attacks by armed loggers by fleeing across the Brazilian border in search of uninhabited rainforest areas to make their home. In reality, however, this isolated region is already inhabited by Brazilian tribes and inter-tribal fighting may well ensue.

and animal skins; coupled to this was the advance of the **agricultural frontier** down from the Andes. Both kinds of expansion assumed that Amazonia was a limitless source of natural reserves and an empty wilderness – misapprehensions that still exist today. The agricultural colonization tended to be by poor, landless peasants from the Andes and was concentrated in the Selva Alta, on the eastern slopes of that range. From the 1950s, these *colonos* became a massive threat to the area's ecosystem when, supported by successive government land grants, credit and road building, subsistence farmers and cattle ranchers inflicted large-scale deforestation.

In the 1960s, President Fernando Belaunde made the colonization of Amazonia central to his political agenda – believing it to be a verdant, limitless and "unpopulated" frontier that was ripe for development, offering land to the landless masses. New waves of *colonos* arrived and, once again, indigenous inhabitants were dispossessed and yet more rainforest cleared. Things quietened down between 1968 and 1980, during the military regime, but when Belaunde returned to power in 1980, peasant colonization continued, by and large along tenuous penetration roads built by the government, but also with further state sponsorship and funding by international banks.

Over the last few decades, the intrusion of **oil and timber companies** has seen repeated exploitation of the rainforest. Even worse, vast tracts of forest have disappeared as successive waves of *colonos* have cleared trees to grow cash crops (especially coca); this large-scale, haphazard **slash-and-burn agriculture** has been shown by conservationists to be unsustainable.

Coca barons and narco-terrorists

When the Peruvian economy began to suffer in the mid-1980s, foreign credit ended, and those with substantial private capital fled, mainly to the US. The government, then led by the young Alan García, was forced to abandon the jungle region, and both its colonist and indigenous inhabitants were left to survive by themselves. This effectively opened the doors for the **coca barons**, who had already established themselves during the 1970s in the Huallaga Valley, and who moved into the gap left by government aid in the other valleys of the *ceja de selva* – notably the Pichis-Palcazu and the Apurimac-Ene. Over the subsequent decade, illicit coca production was responsible for some ten percent of the deforestation that occurred in the Peruvian Amazon during the entire twentieth century; furthermore, trade of this lucrative crop led to significant corruption and, more importantly, supported the rise of **terrorism**. Strategic alliances between coca growers (the colonists), smugglers (Peruvians and Colombians) and the terrorists (mainly, but not exclusively, Sendero Luminoso) led to a large area of the Peruvian Amazon becoming utterly lawless. Each party to this alliance gained strength and resources whilst the indigenous peoples of the region suffered, stuck seemingly powerless in the middle.

Over the last fifteen years or so, the Peruvian authorities have persecuted the *colonos* for their illegal crops, and their greatest successes in this area have come largely from among the indigenous groups themselves, like the Ashaninka tribe. Armed by the authorities, these tribespeople were among the vanguard of resistance to the **narco-terrorists**, whose movement, once rooted in politics and agriculture, had become bloodthirsty, power-hungry and highly unpopular. In the aftermath of the civil war, which began to fizzle out with the capture of Sendero's leader in 1992, the international financial institutions, whose earlier loans had helped fund the disastrous colonization, started to partly determine development policy in the Peruvian Amazon so that those same loans could be repaid; resources such as fossil fuels, lumber and land were privatized and sold to the highest bidder.

The Amazon today

The neo-liberal agenda led by the ex-President Fujimori opened the Amazon to new investment. It also created a huge increase in **informal mining**. Hordes of landless peasants from the Cusco region flocked into the Madre de Dios to make their fortune from **gold mining**. In itself this was neither illegal nor an environmental threat, but the introduction of front-loader machines and trucks – which supplanted child labour in the mines in the early 1990s – increased the environmental damage and rate of territorial consumption by this unregulated industry. By 1999, a massive desert had appeared around Huaypetue, previously a small-time, frontier mining town, and the neighbouring communities of Amarakeiri Indians (who have been panning for gold in a small-scale, sustainable fashion for some thirty years) are in serious danger of losing their land and natural resources. Attempts by NGOs and pro-Indian lawyers to maintain the boundaries of Indian reserves and communities are constantly thwarted by colonists who are supported by local government.

As the danger from terrorism faded in the mid-1990s, **oil and gas exploration** by multinational companies began in earnest. Initially the Peruvian government appeared to be bending over backwards to assist them, and the reserves discovered – initially in the Madre de Dios and Camisea regions – have left only Amazonian indigenous organizations and environmental conservationists active in opposition. In 2006, a Chinese company, SAPET, exploring for fossil fuel reserves in the southeast Peruvian Amazon, announced it would not enter territory inhabited by some six hundred isolated members of the Piro tribe. In the same year, in northern Peru, the Achuar Indians won a landmark victory against Argentine oil company, PlusPetrol, after a blockade of Peru's largest oil installation by eight hundred natives lasting almost two weeks, and protesting against environmental damage caused by oil production. An agreement was eventually reached, including promises of improved environmental performance, oil production royalties for the Indians and acknowledgement that they oppose oil production on their land.

While mining and petroleum and gas exploitation continue apace, improvements to the jungle road infrastructure and the recent diverting of the global timber market focus from Southeast Asia back to the Amazon, mean that unsustainable **logging** now appears to be the major contemporary threat to Indian cultures and their lush tropical rainforest environment. The way things are going it's hard to see how much longer the indigenous peoples can maintain their traditional territories. Without their forest habitat intact, future generations of jungle Indians will be unable to survive. The recent Peruvian governments of Toledo and, now, Alan Garcia, have continued Fujimori's approach of privatization and engagement with multinational companies for the exploitation of Peru's resources, particularly those hidden beneath the rainforest canopy. At the same time, high level officials – even Congressmen – stand accused of illegal logging to satisfy, in particular, Asian markets. In 2008, when the Peruvian government tried to change the laws around community land ownership, to make it easier for foreign investors to actually buy areas of rainforest for lumber, palm oil plantations and other forms of agro-industrial development, many of the tribes united in protest, once again blocking access to oil and gas installations in some parts of the jungle. Interestingly, this attempted liberalisation of the Peruvian community land sale law was a requirement of the country's new trade agreement with the US.

Cocaine has been a leading jungle export for several decades, and while the late 1990s witnessed the price of coca drop in Peru as production shifted to Colombia (during which time peasants and jungle Indians alike began looking in earnest for **alternative cash crops**, like chocolate and coffee products, or newer options like *uña de gato*, a newly rediscovered medicinal herb, and *barbasco*, a natural pesticide) production has rapidly expanded since the start of the twenty-first century. With Colombia now largely cut out of the equation by a combination of USA anti-drugs policy and the rise of the Tijuana Cartel on the Mexican border with the USA, Peruvian cocaine mainly leaves the country overland en route to Mexico or Brazil. Squeezed out of one spot, the problem has simply re-emerged closer to home.

Getting into the jungle

Given the breadth and quality of options, it's never easy to decide which bit of the jungle to head for. Your three main criteria will probably be budget, ease of access and the depth and nature of jungle experience you're after. **Flying** to any of the main jungle towns is surprisingly cheap and can save an arduous few days' journey overland. Once you've arrived, a number of **excursions** can be made easily and cheaply, though the best experience comprises a few nights at one of the better **jungle lodges**. For a more intimate (but often tougher) experience, it's easy enough to arrange a **camping expedition** and a guide, travelling in canoes or speedboats into the deeper parts of the wilderness.

Jungle hazards

Going even a little off the beaten track in the jungle involves arduous travelling, through an intense mesh of plant, insect and animal life. It's an environment that's not to be taken lightly: apart from the real chance of getting lost (see p.491), the popular image of poisonous snakes, jaguars and mosquitoes is based on fact, though these dangers don't actually come hunting for you. Always consult your doctor on how to prevent diseases before departing for Peru if you are planning to spend *any* time in the rainforest regions.

DENGUE FEVER There is no inoculation against **dengue fever**, a mosquito-transmitted viral infection that occurs mainly in urban Amazonia. The best prevention is by avoiding bites (see "Malaria" below, though note that the dengue mosquito is primarily diurnal). Symptoms include high fevers, headache, severe pains in muscles and joints, vomiting and a red skin rash after the first few days. The illness usually lasts around ten days and can be treated with paracetamol. If haemorrhaging occurs (in this, as well as in any other case, of course), see a doctor immediately. Recovery is usually at least partially complete within a few weeks .

JIGGERS Small insects that live in cut grass, **jiggers** can also be a very irritating problem; they stick to and bury their heads in your ankles before slowly making their way up your legs to the groin, causing you to itch furiously. You can either pick them out one by one as the natives do, or apply sulphur cream (ask for the best ointment from a *farmacia* in any jungle town).

LEISHMANIASIS Endemic to certain zones, **leishmaniasis** (known in Peru as *uta*) is transmitted by sandfly bites and is rarely contracted by short-term visitors to the jungle. Symptoms start with skin sores that begin to ulcerate, followed by fever and swelling of the spleen. There is no prophylactic and if untreated it can lead to severe degeneration of skin and facial tissue, usually around the upper lip and lower nose areas. There is treatment available, but many untreated cases among relatively malnourished Peruvian peasants and Indians have resulted in permanent and quite horrific disfigurement.

MALARIA The most significant disease in the Amazon, **malaria** has two common forms in South America: *Plasmodium vivax* and *Plasmodium falciparum*. The latter is the most common, but both are found in the Peruvian Amazon and thought to be fast adapting to modern medicines. Of the **prophylactics**, many have side-effects (some psychological, others physiological), so do some independent research as well as consulting your doctor. Mosquitoes are mainly, but not exclusively nocturnal, coming out at dusk and disappearing at sunrise; the best **protection** is to use roll-on

A costlier option is to take a **river cruise** on a larger boat, with one of a few operators based in Iquitos. This offers two significant advantages: firstly, the boats are comfortable, with good service and food; and secondly, the programmes take you to remote areas in style, and can then penetrate the deeper forest (such as the rarely visited Pacaya Samiria National Reserve) in well-equipped speedboats. Unlike lodge-based operations, both canoe expeditions and cruises aren't fixed to specific locations, so they can customize programmes and routes. Whichever option you choose, bear in mind that both accommodation and tours tend to work out cheaper during periods of lower demand according to the annual cycle of US and European holiday seasons, though growing trends in **ecological tourism** and psychedelic, or jungle **mystic experiences**, are now bringing groups throughout the year.

Most easily accessed by air from Lima or by boat from Brazil, the **northern selva** can also be reached from the northern Peruvian coast via an increasingly popular but still adventurous route that takes the Río Huallaga from Yurimaguas (see p.441), a four- to five-day boat journey that can be broken by a visit

DEET (diethyltoluamide) repellents, to wear clothing that's treated with diluted DEET repellent and covers exposed skin and to sleep under mosquito nets. Note that DEET harms plastics. Even with the best effort possible, you can't be sure of avoiding bites, especially when camping in the rainforest or on night walks, so always take what your GP prescribes. Malaria starts three or four weeks after contact, usually with a *combination* of severe nausea, high fevers, delirium and chills; get medical help as soon as possible if you have these symptoms – it's easier to treat in the early stages.

PARASITES Parasites are quite common, so it's best to **boil drinking water** and use sterilizing tablets or crystals. Around human settlements, including the muddier parts of larger towns, you can pick up parasites through the soles of your feet; the best precaution is to wear shoes rather than flip-flops or sandals. Also, get a medical check-up at a centre that specializes in tropical diseases when you return home.

RIVER SICKNESS The most likely hazard you'll encounter is **river sickness**, a general term for the effect of the sun's strong rays reflected off the water. After several hours on the river, particularly at midday and without a hat, you may get the first symptom – the runs – sometimes followed by nausea or shaking fever; in extreme cases these can last for a day or two. Antidiarrhoea medicine should help (Lomotil, Imodium or something similar); otherwise drink plenty of fluids and take rehydration salts dissolved in water.

SNAKES It's unlikely that you will encounter any **snakes**. If you do, nearly all of them will disappear as quickly as they can – only the poisonous *shushupe* (a bushmaster) is fearless. The fer-de-lance, or *jergon*, is also quite common; it's smaller and packs less venom than the bushmaster, but can still be deadly. Most bites occur by stepping on a sleeping snake or picking it up with a handful of vegetation; be constantly aware of this possibility. If anyone does get bitten, the first thing to remember is to keep calm – most deaths result from shock, not venom. Try to kill the snake for identification, but, more importantly, apply a temporary tourniquet above the bite and find medical help *immediately*. Some natives have remedies even for a potentially deadly *shushupe* bite.

YELLOW FEVER Yellow fever is simple to prevent by a shot that covers you for ten years. Consult your doctor to find the nearest inoculation centre, and remember to obtain a **certificate of inoculation**, which you are sometimes required to show on entry into many of Peru's jungle regions. If you can't, you run the risk of being subject to on-the-spot inoculation, wherever you may be.

to the immense **Pacaya Samiria National Reserve** at the heart of the upper Amazon. The area's biggest centre of population, **Iquitos**, capital of the remote and massive frontier region of Loreto, is one of Peru's most welcoming cities, despite the presence of oil wells, cocaine traffickers and the US Drug Enforcement Agency. It's also the most organized and established of the Peruvian Amazon's tourist destinations, and has many reputable companies offering a range of jungle visits, from luxury lodges and cruises (see pp.546–548) to rugged survival expeditions. From Iquitos you can catch a **ferry** upstream, south to the growing town of **Requena**, similar to how Iquitos was around fifty years ago. Further upriver lies **Pucallpa**, much larger and more modern, with a good direct road link to Lima and routes by bus or boat deeper into Peru's central jungle region.

Pucallpa is the largest port and a rapidly growing industrialized jungle town in the **Central Selva**, best reached by scheduled air flights or the largely paved road from Lima. Nearby is **Lago Yarinacocha**, a laid-back lake resort with limited amenities that has declined in popularity as a major destination over the past few decades, mainly due to a combination of terrorist infiltration, over-industrialization and the improvement of facilities in other competing jungle regions. However, it remains a good introduction to the rainforest and is reached by a relatively easy overland trip from Lima. Another sector of this central jungle region – **Chanchamayo** – can be reached by road in eight to twelve hours from Lima. Winding fast but precariously down from the Andean heights of Tarma, the Carretera Central is now paved all the way to **Satipo**, a jungle frontier town, relatively close to the **Río Ene**, the name given to the Amazon's major headwater after the Río Apurimac merges with a major tributary, the Río Mantaro, as it pours down from the Huancayo area of the sierra. En route to Satipo the road passes through the cloud forest via La Merced, from where there are bus connections to the quasi-European settlemet of **Oxampampa** and, a little further into the forest, the fascinating Tirolean settlement of **Pozuzo**.

The jungles of southeastern Peru, bursting with biodiversity, are now excellently supplied in terms of lodges, guides, boats and flights to enable budget travellers and those with more money and less time to get deep into the jungle for the full experience. Cusco is arguably the best base for trips into the **southern selva**, with air and road access to the frontier town of **Puerto Maldonado**, itself a great base for visitng the nearby forests of **Madre de Dios** which boast the **Tambopata-Candamo Reserved Zone** and the **Bahuaja-Sonene National Park**, an enormous tract of virgin rainforest close to the Bolivian border. Many naturalists argue that this region is the most biodiverse on Earth, and thus the best place to head for wildlife. Rather alarmingly, though, one hydrocarbon concession has been given for exploration on the edge of Bahuaja-Sonene National Park. An expedition into the **Manu Reserved Zone** (part of the larger **Manu National Biosphere Reserve**) will also bring you into one of the more exciting wildlife regions in South America. For a quicker and cheaper taste of the jungle, you can go by bus from Cusco via Ollantaytambo to **Quillabamba**, on the **Río Urubamba**, which flows north along the foot of the Andes, through the dangerous and unforgettable whitewater rapids of the **Pongo de Mainique**.

Getting around the jungle

The three most common forms of **river transport** are canoes (*canoas*), speedboats (*deslizadoras*) and larger riverboats (*lanchas*). Whichever you choose, it's a good idea to make sure you can get along with the boatman (*piloto*) or captain and that he

Jungle essentials

For all visits
- certificate of inoculation against yellow fever (check with your embassy for prevailing health requirements)
- malaria pills (start course in advance as directed by prescribing doctor)
- roll-on insect repellent containing DEET
- suitable clothing (wear socks, trousers and long sleeves in the evenings)
- toilet paper
- waterproof poncho, cagoule (hooded nylon pack-away raincoat) or overclothes

3–5 days at a lodge or basic facility
Above plus . . .
- antidiarrhoea medicine (eg, Lomotil or Imodium)
- blanket or thick cotton sheet for sleeping
- mosquito net for sleeping under
- multipurpose knife (with can and bottle opener)
- plastic bags for packing and lining your bags (a watertight box is best for camera equipment and other delicate valuables). Note that cardboard boxes dissolve on contact with the Río Amazonas or rain shower
- sunhat (especially for river travel)
- torch and spare batteries
- waterproof matches and a back-up gas lighter

5 days or more away from facilities
Above plus . . .
- candles
- compass and a whistle (in case you get lost)
- cooking pots, stove (or the ability to cook over a fire and a supply of dry wood) and eating utensils
- filled water container (allow for a gallon a day)
- first-aid box or medical kit (including tweezers, needles, scissors, plasters, bandages, adhesive tape, sterile dressings, antiseptic cream, antibiotics and painkillers)
- fishing line and hooks (unsalted meat makes good bait)
- food supplies (mainly rice, beans, cans of fish, crackers, noodles and fruit; chocolate is impractical, as it melts)
- gifts for people you might encounter (batteries, knives, fish-hooks and line, camera film, and so on)
- a hammock or mat, plus a couple of blankets
- insect-bite ointment (antihistamines, tiger balm or *mentol china*; toothpaste as a last resort)
- a good knife and machete
- quick-dry clothing
- petrol for boats, useful for bargaining for rides
- rope
- running shoes, sandals (ideally plastic or rubber); rubber boots or strong walking boots if you're going hiking
- water sterilizers (good tablets, crystals or a decent filter)

really does know the rivers. **Canoes** can be anything from a small dugout with a paddle, useful for moving along small creeks and rivers, to a large eighteen-metre canoe with panelled sides and a *peque-peque* (on-board engine) or a more powerful outboard motor. **Speedboats** tend to have lightweight metal hulls and are obviously faster and more manoeuvrable, but also more expensive. **Riverboats**

To enter protected areas, such as the Pacaya Samiria National Reserve, or the Manu and Tambopata-Candamo reserved zones, official permission is essential from, and a small daily fee ($6) payable to, the **Instituto Nacional de Recursos Naturales (INRENA).** As a tourist, this will usually be handled for you locally by your tour company. Independent travel within these areas is discouraged, but for scientific research one may need to do this directly. For all Peruvian jungle protected areas contact INRENA at C Ricardo Palma 113, 4th floor, Iquitos (℡065/232980). In Lima, INRENA can be contacted at: C 17, 355 Urb El Palomar, San Isidro, Lima ℡01/225-2803 or 224-3298, @comunicaciones@inrena.gob.pe, Ⓦwww.inrena.gob.pe. The increase in illegal logging and the vulnerability and consequent jumpiness of remote Indian communities still trying to eek a living in these areas makes it all the more important to get permission.

come in a range of sizes and vary considerably in their river-worthiness, and you should always have a good look at the boat before buying a ticket or embarking on a journey; note that the smaller one- or two-deck riverboats are frequently in worse condition (and noisier) than larger ones. The best are the Iquitos-based tour boats, with cabins for up to thirty passengers, dining rooms, bars, sun lounges and even jacuzzis on board. Next best are the larger vessels with up to three decks that can carry two hundred passengers, with hammock spaces and a few cabins (for which you pay two to three times as much); if you're over 1.8m tall, it's best to take a hammock as the bunks may be too small. Always try to get a berth as close as possible to the front of the boat, away from the noise of the motor. On the larger riverboats (especially between Pucallpa and Iquitos, or Tabatinga and Iquitos) you can save money on hotels prior to departure by hanging around in your hammock, as most captains allow passengers to sling one up and sleep on board for a few days before departure. Riverboats travelling upstream tend to stay close to the bank, away from the fast central flow, and while this means longer journeys, they're much more visually interesting than travelling up the middle of the river, particularly on the larger ones where it can be hard to make out even huts on the banks.

Anyone who intends **hitching** along the river system should remember that the further you are away from a town, the harder it is to lay your hands on **fuel** (even if you should come across a multinational company drilling in the middle of the forest) as well as clean water and food to buy. You'll usually be expected to contribute financially, but however much you offer, no one will take you upriver if they're short on fuel. Taking your own supply (a 55-gallon container, for example) is a little difficult but isn't a bad idea if you're going somewhere remote. As a last resort it's possible to get hold of a **canoe** or **balsa raft** and paddle (downstream) from village to village, but this has obvious dangers and is certainly not an option if there are any rapids to negotiate; mortal danger awaits anyone who would be foolish enough to attempt to go through the Pongo de Mainique on the Río Urubamba by raft. In addition to the obvious dangers of rapids, travelling alone by river exposes you to severe risk of getting lost, robbed or simply stuck on an unpopulated riverbank for the night (or even a week or more in many remote areas) before finding a passing boat or local settlement. It isn't advisable to travel these rivers without the help of reliable local expertise; this inevitably means a good tour company with professional guides, or reliable local Indian guides.

Guides don't need to have official status but they should be experienced in the region and willing to help out (remember that natives are often the best guides).

▲ The Amazon

There are several ways of enlisting this kind of help: by paying significant sums for a commercially operated jungle tour; by going to the port of a jungle town and hiring someone and his boat; or by hopping along the rivers from one village to the next with someone who is going that way anyway and who will be able to introduce you to the villagers at the next stage. This last and most adventurous option will normally involve long waits in remote settlements; with the jungle being an essentially laid-back place, there's one thing certain to get a *selvatico* (jungle dweller) mad, and that's a gringo with a loud voice and pushy manner. If you choose to travel this way, remember that you are imposing yourself on the hospitality of the locals and that you are dependent on them: be sensitive to their needs, their privacy and their possessions. Always offer **goods or cash** in return for any genuine help. Fishing hooks, nylon fishing line, tins of fish, trade cloth, clothes, fresh batteries and even shotgun cartridges are appreciated.

Bear in mind also that **getting lost** is a real danger, even for local people. By straying less than a hundred metres from camp, the river or your guide, you can find yourself completely surrounded by a seemingly impenetrable tangle of undergrowth. If there are any, one trail looks very much like the next to the unaccustomed eye. If you're with a group who will look for you when they realise you are lost, a sensible strategy is to shout, blow a whistle (always carry one!) or bang the base of big buttress-root trees as Indians do when they get lost on hunting forages. If there's no-one likely to come looking for you, a better option is to **find moving water** and follow it downstream to the main river, where there's more probability of finding a settlement or passing boat. If you get caught out overnight, the best places to sleep are: beside a fire on the river bank; in a nest you could make for yourself in between the buttress roots of a large tree; higher up in a tree that isn't crawling with biting ants; or in a hammock.

The Central Selva

Directly east of Lima and easily accessible by road, the Central Selva region is endowed with a variety of rainforest eco-niches. Its close proximity to the highlands allows a unique appreciation of the changing scenery, from high Andean to high and then low jungle. Three main circuits or routes can be followed by crossing the Andes at Tarma (see p.340) or Tingo Maria (see p.346). From either of these crossings, largely asphalted roads lead on to the modern jungle city of **Pucallpa**, one of Peru's fastest-growing settlements with a population of over 300,000. Capital of the independent *departamento* of Ucayali, its main attraction is as a lowland rainforest experience and in particular the **Lago Yarinacocha** – a huge, beautiful, oxbow lake where you can swim, rest up and watch schools of dolphin. Wildlife expeditions and visits to nearby native Shipibo tribe communities can be arranged with local tour companies, although indigenous Indian life here is increasingly westernized. If you want to avoid the more conventional tours, it's really a matter of taking your chances travelling by river to a more remote area and looking for a local guide. Pucallpa is also a main point of departure for trips downstream to the larger destination of Iquitos (see p.531), a thousand kilometre, week-long journey.

Closer to Lima yet less explored by tourists, the **Chanchamayo** region – famous for its fantastic coffee – offers the usual attractions of the cloud forest. A stupendous and very steep road descends from Tarma down to the jungle gateway towns of **San Ramon** and **La Merced**, separated by a fifteen-minute drive. From here it's possible to travel north, visiting the unique Austro-German settlements of **Pozuzo** and **Oxapampa**, both rich agricultural centres located within a mosaic of little-visited protected areas, including the stunningly beautiful **Parque Nacional Yanachaga Chemillen**. From these towns, rough roads now connect overland to Pucallpa via Ciudad Constitución and Puerto Inca.

An easier paved road heads east from Chanchamayo and the twin towns of San Ramon and La Merced towards the lower forest region focused around the frontier town of **Satipo**, where **Ashaninka tribespeople** often come to town in traditional robes and barefeet to sell produce and buy basic foodstuffs, machetes and other tools. From Satipo it's possible to visit native communities and some of South America's finest **waterfalls**. From the end of the sealed road from Lima, an old dirt road connects Satipo with the mountain city of Huancayo, making possible a circular route either back towards Lima or on to other parts of the Central Sierra (see Chapter 5). Depending on the weather and conditions, a new dirt track, built mainly by loggers in the last few years, now connects Satipo with Atalaya (7hr), a frontier town at the confluence of the Tambo and Urubamba rivers. From Atalaya, light aircraft fly to Lima (Saturdays only) or you can take a river boat north towards Pucallpa.

The Chanchamayo Valley

The **Chanchamayo Valley**, only 300km from Lima and 750m above sea level, marks the real beginning of the central selva directly east of the capital. Originally settled in 1635 by Franciscan monks on mules, the region was repeatedly reclaimed by the native tribes. These days access is easy and relatively safe, with much of the produce from the area's rich tropical fruit plantations (oranges and pineapples) and productive *chacras* (gardens), transported over the Andes by road to Lima. Several buses depart daily from Lima to the valley towns of **San Ramon** and **La Merced**. Separated by only 10km of road, some 2500m below the attractive Andean town of Tarma, they are surrounded by rapidly disappearing cloud forest, coffee plantations, orange groves and brilliant hiking country. Getting there, the road winds down in ridiculously precipitous curves, keeping tight to the sides of the **Río Tarma** canyon, at present used for generating hydroelectric power.

At San Ramon this river merges with the Tulumayo to form the Río Chanchamayo; beyond La Merced, it forges the stunningly beautiful **Perene Valley**, weaving a whitewater route down towards Satipo and relatively low selva. Once a cloud-forest zone inhabited only by Ashaninka and Yanesha Indians, the last hundred and fifty years saw much of the best land cleared by invading colonists, missionaries and companies in search of timber or rubber. In the last few decades, waves of settlers from the Huancayo region of the Andes have entered the region, particularly since the paving of the Lima road during the mid-1990s. The asphalt presently ends in **Satipo**, a small but busy frontier town. Beyond here, there's really little tourism infrastructure, yet it's a reasonable base from which to visit some of Peru's least explored and tamed jungle region. Another road runs from La Merced on to the fascinating Austro-German settlements of **Oxapampa**, **Pozuzo** and even the massive jungle city of **Pucallpa** (though the latter is much more easily reached from Lima via Tingo Maria on a significantly better road) on the Rio Ucayali.

San Ramon

The smaller twin settler town, **SAN RAMON**, is a nicer place than La Merced (see p.495) to break your journey, though the latter is the communications hub and is better for road connections deeper into the selva. Founded originally as a fort in 1849, to assist the colonisation of the region in the face of fierce indigenous resistance, the town now enjoys several good restaurants, decent accommodation and a leafy Plaza Mayor, as well as at least a couple of worthwhile attractions within easy reach.

Practicalities

Tourist information is sometimes available from the municipal office at Jr Pardo 110 (☎064/331265). Among the best **hostels** and close to the Empresa Junin bus stop, there's the *Hotel Conquistador*, at Progreso 298 (☎064/331157 or 331771 ⓔconquistador@viabcp.com; ❹), which has great hot showers, lots of once well-appointed rooms and a good breakfast option. Opposite there's *Hotel Chanchamay* at Progreso 292 (☎064/331312, ⓔHotel-chanchamay_7@hotmail.com, ❷–❸), offering rooms with or without private baths. *El Refugio*, Av El Ejercito 490 (☎064/331082 ⓦwww.hotelelrefugio.com.pe; ❺), is a three-star hotel with private bath and fan provided. *El Rancho*, on Calle Tulumayo s/n Playa Hermosa (☎064/331511, ⓔbungalowselrancho@yahoo.es; ❸–❹), offer a number of well looked after bungalows at very reasonable prices in the shade of avocado and mandarin trees beside the river Tulumayo.

Foodwise, the *Restaurant Chanchamayo's*, Av San Ramon s/n, serves some of the best-quality regional and international food, including steak and fries; or, for Italian fare, there's *Chanchamayo-Italia Ristorante*, by the Plaza Mayor at Tarma 380, excellent for mainly homemade pastas and pizzas as well as good coffee. Superb Chinese food – in fact unbeatable in the region – can be found at *Chifa Siu*, C Progreso 440. Next door, a small dark café, *Las Delicias*, serves great sandwiches, juices and coffee, but often closes by midday. The chicken from *Broaster Chanchamayo*, C Progreso 380, is delicious and worth stopping for, while *El Tiroles*, near the Mercado Modelo at C las Orchideas 128, serves excellent sandwiches, juices and full meals, mostly based on locally smoked meats. **Drinks** are best enjoyed in the *Licoria Roma II*, Jr Progreso 185, on the main street, where there's a wide range of wines, beer, coffee-based liqueurs and *pisco*. Local **craft goods** and souvenirs can be found in San Ramon's main street, at *Arestania Chanchamayo*, Jr Progreso 480.

Around San Ramon

About 5km from San Ramon, the **Catarata El Tirol** waterfalls enjoy a 35-metre drop into an attractive plunge pool and is accessed by a pleasant 45-minute (2km) country walk from the riverside village of Playa Hermosa (itself five minutes from San Ramon in a *mototaxi* or car), along a dirt tack surrounded by orchids and lianas. Alternatively, for less than a dollar you can get there in *mototaxi*, then walk back. Further afield, there's the stunningly beautiful lodge and similarly breathtaking reserved forest area of **Pampa Hermosa.** Covering some 11,000 hectares, this reserve is blessed with a fabulous jungle-style lodge (℡01/225-1776, ⓔsignori@ terra.com.pe, ⓦwww.pampahermosalodge.com; ❼–❽), offering an exceptionally comfortable stay in verdant virgin cloudforest; advanced bookings only. Accessible by 4x4 vehicles (the lodge managers can arrange transport), it takes around two hours to reach from San Ramon, crossing the Puente Victoria bridge and following first the Oxabamba river, then climbing up beside the bubbling Ulcumayo gorge. Local *combi-colectivos* only go to Pampa Hermosa (also known as Nueva Italia) on Thursday and Saturday mornings, leaving the Parque de los Enamorados in San Ramon around 5am (4–5hr).

Transport around Chanchamayo and beyond

San Ramon, La Merced and Satipo are all accessible direct by bus from Lima (Empresas Junin, ℡064/323494, and Turismo Central both offer bus-camas – buses with comfortable reclining seats). Other bus companies, like Expreso San Ramon and Empresa Los Angelitos (first two blocks of Progreso, San Ramon) link the valley with Tarma and Huancayo in the sierra. Although San Ramon and, more so La Merced, offer a pleasant climate and somewhere to stay east of the Andes and within easy striking distance of Lima, the main reason for travellers to stop off here is for a taste of the *ceja de selva*, the **cloud forest zone** along the western edge of the Amazon. *Colectivo* cars link the twin towns of San Ramon and La Merced 24hr a day, leaving from within one block of each town's main plaza. Tour agencies in La Merced offer day trips and longer tours with 4x4 travel where required, though buses and *colectivo* cars and slower *combis* also reach most regional destinations. You can head deeper into the lower Amazon Basin by bus or *colectivo* from the bus depot (Terminal Terrestre) in La Merced to the jungle town of Satipo. Other buses link La Merced with Oxapampa and Pozuzo; and dirt roads also link with Pucallpa via Puerto Inca (the final 298km from La Merced), along the corridor formed by the rivers Pichis and Pachitea. For speed and comfort, however, the best way to Pucallpa is direct from Lima on the sealed road via Huánuco and Tingo Maria. The only other way into the forest is by river. Motorized **canoes** leave for the Tambo and Ene rivers from the end of the road at Puerto Ocopa, about two dusty hours by *colectivo* or taxi from Satipo. Once you go beyond Satipo, though, you are well beyond the tourist trail, with minimal if any facilities available. The lowland jungle town of Atalaya, located where the Río Tambo meets the Urubamba river, can now be reached by dirt track and *colectivo* from Satipo; it also has an airport and weekly flights to Lima and Pucallpa, though the latter is also accessible by river canoe from here.

Within twenty minutes' walk of the lodge, Peru's national bird – the vermillion cock-of-the rock (Rupicola Peruvian, or *gallito de la roca*, as its known in Peru) can be seen every afternoon between 4.30pm and dusk. Several impressive waterfalls dissect the reserve's unusually rich vegetation, including orchids, royal palms, lianas and giant ferns, and the reserve also boasts what is considered to be the oldest cedar tree in South America, fondly known as *el abuelo* (the grandfather); totally breathtaking, it's so wide at its base that it takes sixteen people to circle its circumference hand in hand. Various treks using local hill paths can also be planned to start or finish at *Pampa Hermosa*, which is only a few hours' walk from the end of forest cover and the start of mountain scenery; the Andean community of Ninabamba is less than six hours' trek. Slightly nearer, a trek to the tiny settlement of Alto Peru offers possible glimpses of spectacled bears and access to pre-Columbian remains dating back at least 5000 years.

La Merced

The market town of **LA MERCED**, some 10km further down the attractive valley, is larger and busier than San Ramon, with more than twelve thousand inhabitants, a thriving Saturday market and several hectic restaurants and bars crowded around the Plaza de Armas.

Close to La Merced, the **Jardín Botánico El Perezoso**, 15km from town, boasts 10,000 species of plants, including the tall, red *bastones del emperador*; it requires about two hours for a thorough visit. Other local attractions include native communities such as **Pampa Michi**, on the banks of the Perene river, less than an hour by road en route to Satipo; not to everyone's taste, this Ashaninka village has opened its doors to tourists for a number of years now and routinely performs dances and music to order while selling handicrafts.

Accommodation is plentiful in and around town. Central and pretty good in terms of quality and service is *Hostal Rey*, Jr Junin 103 (☏064/531185; ❹) with cable TV, private bath, restaurant and laundry. Other offerings include the *Hostal El Eden*, Jr Ancash 342, on the main plaza (☏064/531183; ❹), which has clean bedrooms and friendly service, most with private bath; and, the *Hostal Los Victor*, Jr Tarma 373 (☏064/531026; ❸), on the Plaza de Armas, has rooms with or without private bath and is one of the better budget options. At the entrance to town, coming from San Ramon, the upmarket *Fundo San José* (☏064/531816, ⓦ www.fundosanjose.com.pe; ❻), offers quality bungalow accommodation with great views across the valley and a nice swimming pool.

For **food**, the Restaurant *Shambari Campa*, Jr Tarma 383, serves some good local dishes, including venison and *zamaño* (agouti). For chicken you'll find it hard locally to beat the *Broaster Chanchamayo*, Jr Junin 580; while for meat cuts in general, the *Restaurant El Gaucho*, Av Ancash s/n, is better. **Nightlife** in La Merced revolves around the disco and bar *Kametsa Café Rock*, located just out of town at Puente Herreria; it has a large and lively dance floor, best between 10pm and 1am (Thurs–Fri). **Buses** leave more or less constantly from the **Terminal Terrestre** in La Merced, where it's just a matter of checking out which bus, *combi* or car is going where, and when. For **local tour companies**, the sensible option is Max Adventures, Jr 2 de Mayo 682 (☏064/323908, ⓔmaxadventureperu@gmail.com), with over seven year's experience and offering all inclusive packages or tours to Oxapampa, Villa Rica, Pozuzo, Tarma, the Huagapo cave and Satipo; excursions include visits to waterfalls, botanical and oquid gardens, native villages, coffee-processing plants and river rafting (by prior arrangement).

Satipo

A real jungle frontier town where the indigenous Ashaninka Indians come to buy supplies and trade, **SATIPO** is an ideal town in which to get kitted out for a jungle expedition, or merely to sample the delights of the selva for a day or two. Boasting a couple of small **airstrips** and also accessible by a three- to four-hour bus ride east from La Merced, the settlement was first developed around the rubber extraction industry some eighty years ago, and now serves as an economic and social centre for a widely scattered population of over forty thousand colonists, offering them tools, food supplies, medical facilities and banks; the bustling daily **market** is best sampled at weekends.

In the 1940s, the first dirt road extended here from Huancayo, but it wasn't until the 1970s that a road was opened here from Lima via La Merced; prior to this there were only mule trails from this direction. With the surfacing of the Carretera Marginal road all the way from Lima in the late 1990s – a veritable carpet unfurling through the jungle valleys – many more recent settlers have moved into the region, but the rate of development is putting significant pressure on the last surviving groups of traditional forest dwellers, mainly the **Ashaninka tribe**, who have mostly taken up plots of land and either begun to compete with the relative newcomer farmers or moved into one of the ever-shrinking zones out of contact with the rest of Peru. You often see the tribespeople in town, unmistakable in their reddish-brown or cream *cushma* robes.

Practicalities

Tourist information and local crafts are available from kiosks in Satipo's main plaza. The town's best **accommodation** includes the *Hotel Majestic*, Jr Colonos Fundadores 408 (☏064/545762; ❸–❹), with wonderfully cool rooms but no hot water. The *Hospedaje Fernadez*, Jr Francisco Irazola 691 (☏064/545741; ❸–❹), is small but very clean with good new beds and great showers. There's also the *Hostal Palmero*, C Manuel Prado 228 (☏064/545020; ❸–❹), which has over forty beds and is noisy but bearable. Other basic accommodation is available around the market area and along the road to the airstrip.

For **eating**, the *Café Yoli*, Jr Manuel Prado 234, between the plaza and the market, is great for coffee, juices, snacks and breakfasts, while the *Recreo Turístico El Jaguar*, fifth block of Jirón Rubén Callegari (☏064/509948), has a range of tasty jungle cuisine available. Another good restaurant, the *Laguna Blanca*, located in the *Club Centro Social* on the Avenida Marginal towards Río Negro (entrance opposite the Medina petrol and service station), serves *zamaño* (agouti) forest meat as well as venison and excellent river fish such as *doncella*, a large tasty catfish. For **money changing** or ATM, the Banco de Credito is opposite *Café Yoli* on Jirón Manuel Prado.

Around Satipo

While Satipo sits in the middle of a beautiful valley, today the landscape around the town is more orange plantation than virgin forest; the best way to get a feel for the valley is by following a **footpath** from the other side of the suspension bridge, which leads over the river from behind the market area, to some of the plantations beyond town. Here you can see the local agriculture at closer quarters, as you pass some rustic dwellings. Further afield, local *colectivos* go to the end of the Carretera Marginal into relatively new settled areas such as that around **San Martín de Pangoa** – a frontier settlement that is growing fast on lumber, citrus and coca plantations. Instead of retracing your steps from Satipo via La Merced and San Ramon, you can follow a breathtaking direct road to **Huancayo** – Los

Andes buses do the six to eight hour journey daily (May–Oct); the rough road passes Todopampa at 4200m, where there's an even rougher route, for those with 4x4s, which goes from the pueblo of Manzanilla to Concepción (4hr) via lake Llangunchuco and the village of Comas.

Satipo is also the southernmost large town on the jungle-bound Carretera Marginal, and a dirt road continues to **Puerto Ocopa** (a small river port originally founded by Franciscan missionaries in 1918), connected daily to Satipo by *colectivo* cars and a strategic location for travelling deeper into the forest along the rivers Tambo and Ene. For the adventurous, a river boat down the Río Tambo, a flight or even a loggers' road (not always passable) to **Atalaya**, deeper into the central selva, is an exciting excursion, though this is way off the tourist trail and any potential visitors should be warned that facilities are few and it's real jungle frontier stuff. One air-taxi company fly on demand if you can pay the $400 per hour air-taxi rate, to either Sepahua (on the Rio Urubamba) and Atalaya (at the confluence of the rios Urubamba and Tambo, which together continue north as the Rio Ucayali). Note that these are remote areas, largely beyond the arm of the law, and should only be visited with local guides who know the current political situation.

There aren't many **tour operators** working in this part of the Peruvian jungle, but one reliable independent operator is Raul Dionicio (ⓔsatipoadventure @hotmail.com), who runs tours on the Tambo river visiting Ashaninka communities such as Betania and Koriteni Tarso. The mountain ranges south and east of the Tambo and Ene rivers, respectively, have recently been made into the **Parque Nacional de Otishi**. On the Río Ene side of this new national park, the highest single drop waterfall in Peru – *las Cataratas de Parijaro* – is a veritable jewel even among Peru's vast collection of impressive natural assets. The remote nature of this site and the total lack of infrastructure makes it very difficult to reach as an independent traveller, but the UK-based *Ecotribal* (Lima ☎01 99576 4287, or, in the UK ☎0044/07968-731247, ⓦwww.ecotribal.com) operates eco-adventure tours in the region, including treks and river rafting to the Parijaro waterfall, on the edge of the Parque Nacional de Otishi in collaboration with the local Ashaninka communities (**bookings** should be made six months or more in advance of the departures which are usually in July or August).

Oxapampa

Slightly off the beaten track, some 78km by road (2hr) north of La Merced, and nearly 400km east of Lima, lies the small settlement of **OXAPAMPA**, a a pleasant and well-organized frontier town strongly influenced culturally and architecturally by the nearby Tyrolean settlement of Pozuzo. It is also a conspicuously clean town, situated on the banks of the Río Chontabamba, some 1800m above sea level; the Mercado Municipal, one block from the main square, is probably the cleanest and most relaxed in Peru. The main local **fiesta**, meanwhile, takes place at the end of August; on the thirtieth, Oxapampa celebrates its founding, while on the thirty-first the traditional Torneo de Cintas takes place, when local young men compete on horse back to collect ribbons from a post.

Practicalities

For **tourist information** on Oxapampa and around, there are two active websites: ⓦwww.oxapampa.pe and ⓦwww.oxapampaonline.com. Tourism infrastructure is incipient in Oxapampa, but there is one tour agency and some independent local guides already operational: *Ecotours Oxapampa* (☎063/462659, ⓔecotours _oxapampa@yahoo.com or ⓔtoursoxa@hotmail.com) and Jose Luis Zevallos Baldeom (☎963697695, ⓔjoseoxa@hotmail.com), who has his own inflatable raft for river running and exploring some of the region's scenic areas. **Souvenirs** from the region can be found on the plaza at *Pecky's* shop, Jr Bolognesi 212.

Accommodation

Although Oxampampa is a small town, there's a surprising range of fine **places to stay**, mostly around the same price in the mid-range bracket. Budget accomodation is more disappointing.

Albergue Bottger Av Mariscal Castilla, block 6 ☏063/762377, ✉bottger_d@yahoo.com. Just five blocks' walk from the plaza, this *albergue* is based in a luxurious modern mansion built and panelled largely from cedar and *diablo fuerte* wood; they serve brilliant breakfasts, rooms are spacious and super-clean, and there's a splendid matrimonial suite above the bar. ❹–❺

Albergue Familiar Carolina Egg Av San Martin 1085 ☏063/462331 or 963-9691436, ✉fraucarolinaegg_oxa@hotmail.com, ⓦwww.bungalowsfraucarolinaegg.com. A lovely complex of independent rooms and bungalows, very close to the Terminal Terrestre, on the corner of Av Mullenbruc with C Loeckle, where the *colectivos* stop and start. This is an exceptionally friendly and well run (by a family descended from the original nineteenth-century colonists) place, and the breakfasts are amazing. ❹–❺

Eco-albergue Yanachaga Near Huancabamba some 24km along the road to Pozuzo ☏063/462506, ✉isab58@yahoo.es. A rural retreat with stone-built rooms comprising private baths with hot water, as well as a restaurant serving great homegrown food (breakfast included in price). ❸–❹

Edelweiss Near the the entrance to town ☏063/762567, ✉posadaedelweiss@hotmail

.com, ⓦwww.posadaedelweiss.com. A hundred-year-old cedar wood house with forty beds based in chalets around a garden, with hammocks and a barbecue available for use; there are no TVs but there is a shared kitchen and spacious, stylish dining room. ❹–❺

Loeckle Sinty Av San Martin, block 12, Pasaje San Alberto ☏063/462180 or 462615, ✉sikels @yahoo.es. A wooden house built seventy years ago to a similar specification as the large wooden church on Oxapampa's main plaza. Rooms are independent cabins opening out onto a pleasant garden, and there's also wi-fi internet access and cable TV. ❹–❺

Rocio Av San Martin. Located just off the plaza, this is one of the town's few cheaper options, offering TVs and hot water in less than salubrious surroundings. ❷–❸

El Trapiche Jr Mullembruck, first block ☏063/462551, ✉emiliohassinger@hotmail.com, ⓦwww.oxapampabungalows.com. Located in countryside just on the far edge of town, *El Trapiche* has developed over the last seven years with a fine restaurant and several two-storey cypress-wood cabins for accommodation; the management also have good contacts with local tour guides and frequently organise typical Austro-German dances and fiestas. ❹–❺

Eating and drinking

Good **food** is a speciality of the region, with two great restaurants on the main plaza: the *Restaurante Tipico Oxapampino*, first block of Mariscal Castillo, is older with more traditional meat dishes and superb breakfasts at very reasonable prices; while, the *Oasis*, Jr Bolognesi 363, is plastic and modern but with superb set-menu lunches as well as smoked pork and trout a la carte dishes (upstairs it specialises in roast chicken). *Casa del Baco*, in the Miraflores suburb on way into town at Km 2.5, comprises a good restaurant serving typical local beef and ham dishes (and also offers camping; ❹–❺). For **drinks** and snacks in the evening, *El Sanguchon*, on Prolongacion Bolognesi less than 2 blocks from the plaza, serves great *aguardiente* (sugar-cane alcohol) based cocktails, burgers in a friendly and enjoyable ambience.

Around Oxapampa

As a result of its economic dependence on timber, rocoto peppers, livestock and coffee, most of the forest immediately around the town has been cleared for cattle grazing, plantations and timber. There are nevertheless several sites of interest close to Oxapampa, including a small bat cave, Tinicueva; a trout farm, El Wharapu; a sugar cane alcohol ranch and a suspension footbridge and old wooden church, the Iglesia Santa Rosa, around the nearby settlement of Chontabamba. Some forty minutes by car from Oxapampa, the **waterfalls Catarata Anana** offer a pleasant half-day excursion, ideal for a picnic.

Meanwhile, 30km or so from Oxapampa, lies the **Parque Nacional Yanachoja Chemillen**, a 122,000-hectare reserve dominated by dark mountains and vivid landscapes, where grasslands and cloud forest merge and separate. Established as a protected area in 1986, it's accessed via the Cañon de Huancabamba (for which *colectivos* depart most mornings from Oxapampa bus station). Best visited in the dry season (May–Sept), there are vast quantities of bromeliads, orchids, cedars, dwarf brocket deer, giant rats and even the odd spectacled bear, some jaguar and around 427 bird species here, including a significant variety of hummingbirds. It's also home to around sixty Yanesha Indian communities. For access to Yanachaga Chemillen permission is needed from INRENA, along with advance payment of $2 a day (INRENA has a Park office in Oxapampa, on third block of Jirón Pozuzo, ☏063/462544, ✉pnych1@yahoo.es, ⊛www.pnyanaqchegachemillen.com; or, see INRENA's Lima contacts on p.118).

The town of **Vila Rica**, some 72km from Oxapampa, lying at 1480m in the *ceja de selva*, offers overland access to the Pichis and Palcazu valleys, the region's principal producers of coffee, pineapple and coca. Only 12km from town you'll find the **Catarata El Encanto** (The Spell or Enchantment Waterfalls), which has three sets of falls; rainbows frequently appear and there are deep, dangerous plunge pools.

Pozuzo

Some 80km further down into the rainforest, at 823m above sea level, **POZUZO** is significantly smaller than Oxapampa. Reached via a very rough road that crosses over two dozen rivers and streams, the vista of wooden chalets with sloping Tyrolean roofs has endured ever since the first **Austrian and German colonists** arrived here under the auspices of the aptly named Baron Schutz von Holzhausren and the then President of Peru General Ramon Castilla in the 1850s, as part of a grand plan to establish settlements deep in the jungle. The original deal between Germany and Peru included the building of roads, schools and churches; but, the Austro-Germans needed to be of Catholic religion, have some kind of office and impeccable reputation.

The first group of three hundred, mainly Tirolean, immigrants left Europe in 1857 on the British ship *Norton*, arriving Lima on July 28. During the overland journey, cutting their way through jungle, almost half the colonists died of disease, accident or exhaustion. The town of Pozuzo was founded in 1859 when the area was ripe with virgin forest and crystalline rivers owned by the Yanesha tribe. Nine years later, a second group of immigrants arrived to reinforce the original population, which had been left, more or less abandoned, by the Peruvian authorities. The colonists began to expand their population and territory; first, Oxapampa was founded in 1891, by the Bottger family, then others went on to found Villa Rica in 1928.

Today the economy of Pozuzo is economy based on beef cattle; but lederhosen are worn for fiestas and **Tirolean dances** are still performed, creating a peculiar combination of European rusticism (the local dance and music is still strongly influenced by the German colonial heritage) and native Peruvian culture. Moreoever, many of this unusual town's present inhabitants still speak German, eat *schitellsuppe*, waltz very well and dance the polka. Pozuzo still receives relatively few tourist visitors, but is aware of its peculiar interest; places to check out include the fine **Iglesia San Jose**, built in stone and wood during 1875, the **Museo Schaffere** (displaying photos and curios of the indigenous tribes), the very Germanic Casa Budweiser with its stylish chimney and the more recently built Casa de Cultura de Pozuzo (2004). Among the most noteworthy of the colonists houses, perhaps the Casa Tipica Palmatambo and the Casa Tipica Egg Vogt are among the most interesting, the latter with its own small family museum; on the edge of town, the **Casa de Zacarias Schuler** still operates a water-powered mill for crushing sugar cane to make the non-alcoholic drink *huarapo*.

Practicalities

For fairly impartial local information, call ☎063/287546 or check out ⊛www .pozuzo.org, or call Prusia Tours in Lima (☎01/242-9876, ⊛www.prusiatours .com). **Colectivos** leave for Pozuzo leave every couple of days from the *Terminal Terrestre* in Oxapampa or the bus depot in La Merced. Arguably the best **places to stay** are *El Mango*, C Pacificación 185 (☎063/287528, ✉elmango_pozuzo@hotmail .com; ❹), offering excellent rooms and great smoked sausages; *Hospedaje Maldonado* (☎063/287507; ❸–❹) with private and shared baths; and *Frau Maria Egg Albergue Familiar* (☎01/444-9927 or 063/287559, ⊛www.pozuzo.com; ❸–❹). The nearby settlement of Prusia also offers good accommodation, including the *Hostal Prusia* on Avenida Cristobal Johann (☎01/963-9710896, ✉Tibaro9@hotmail .com; ❸–❹), which has a reasonable cafeteria. Most of the hostals in Pozuzo provide great **traditional local food**. Also, out at Guacamayo, a regionally based tour company offers comfortable rooms for trekkers and river rafters (✉eduardo @pozuzoaventura.com; ❸–❹).

Around Pozuzo

En route to Pozuzo from La Merced, the road passes through the small town of **Huancabamba**, starting point for a four- or five-day trek up into the high Andes on an old Inca road crossing the Cordillera Huagurucho via the Abra Anilcocha pass (4500m) towards Lago Chinchaycocha and Cerro de Pasco. Out of town, the main attraction is the **Catarata Delfin**, which has an 80m drop and is an hour's walk from the Delfin hydroelectric plant by the Cañon de Huancabamba. At **Guacamayo**, beyond the Puente Prusia bridge and accessible only by 4x4 vehicles, it's possible to visit a natural habitat for the cock-of-the rock bird which can be seen most afternoons following a thirty-minute stroll beyond the road. The area, which abounds in orchids, ancient ferns and palm trees, is also great for canoeing, trekking and mountain biking.

Pucallpa

Long an impenetrable refuge for **Cashibo** Indians, **PUCALLPA** was developed as a camp for rubber gatherers at the beginning of the twentieth century. In 1930 it was connected to Lima by road (850km of it), and since then its expansion has been intense and unstoppable. Sawmills surround the city and spread up the main highway towards Tingo María and the mountains, and there's an impressive floating harbour at the nearby port of **La Hoyada**, where larger commercial vessels land. Until 1980 this area was a province in the vast Loreto *departamento*, controlled from Iquitos, but months of industrial action eventually led to the creation of a separate *departamento* – Ucayali. The end of financial restrictions from Iquitos, which exports down the Amazon to the Atlantic, and the turn of traffic towards the Pacific, were both significant and generally positive changes. The floating dock can service cargo boats of up to 3000 tons, and in 1996, the selling off of contracts for oil exploitation to foreign companies by Fujimori's government gave Pucallpa a further burst of energy and finance. In the twenty-first century, the city has so far been one of the main routes for lumber coming from the Peruvian Amazon to Lima and the Pacific coast for export markets. Cattle ranching is also big around here, putting increasing pressure on the rainforest's ecosystems and biodiversity.

A sprawling, hot and dusty city with over 400,000 inhabitants, there is little in the urban area of great interest to travellers, most of whom get straight in a *moto-taxi* or a local bus for **Lago Yarinacocha**. If you stay a while, though, it's difficult not to appreciate Pucallpa's relaxed feel – or the entrepreneurial optimism in a city whose red-mud-splattered streets are fast giving way to concrete and asphalt. The annual festival for visitors – the **Semana Turistica de la Region Ucayali** – is usually held in the last week of September, and comprised mostly of artesania and forest produce markets plus folklore music and dance.

Arrival, information and city transport

From Lima, Pucallpa is served by several **bus companies**, all of which go via Huánuco (roughly the halfway point); the full journey is supposed to take approximately 24 hours but can take longer; note that it's often difficult to get seats on the buses if you pick them up outside of Lima. If you arrive with Tepsa from Lima (see p.116), you'll get off outside their offices at Jr Raymondi 649; Ucayali Express offices are by the corner of 7 de Junio with San Martín; while if you travel with León de Huánuco, you disembark close to the Parque San Martín, at the corner of Jirón 9 de Diciembre and Jirón Vargas. Boats arrive either at the **floating port** of La Hoyada on the eastern side of town, about 2km from the Plaza de Armas ($1.50 by *motokar*, $3 by taxi) or, much nearer to town, at the Malecón Grau (see below p.505). Pucallpa **airport** (℡061/572767) is only 5km west of town and is served by buses (20min; 50¢), *mototaxis* (15min; $1.75) and taxis (10min; $5). Lan Peru, at the corner of Jirón San Martín with Tarapaca, (℡061/594347), operate flights between Pucallpa, Lima and Iquitos, and Star Peru, Jr 7 de Junio 865 (℡061/590586) fly here from Tarapoto, Lima and Iquitos once a week. There are also irregular services run by Air Taxis (℡061/570059 and 575221), based at the airport, from Cruzeiro do Sul just over the Brazilian border.

Tourist information is available at the regional office on Jr Dos de Mayo 111 (℡061/575110, ⓦwww.regionucayali.gob.pe) or from the municipal office at Jr Raimondi 220. Laser Viajes y Turismo, Jr Raimondi 399 (℡061/571120, ⓦwww .laserviajesyturismo.com) at the corner with Jirón Tarapaca, offer some of the best local tours, packages and travel tickets. For **money exchange** there's Banco de Credito, Calle Tarapaca, two blocks from the Plaza de Armas towards the main market by Parque San Martín, though for good rates on dollars cash try the *cambistas* on Calle Tarapaca, where it meets the Plaza de Armas. **Payphones** are available at Telefónica del Peru, Ucayali 357, or on Jirón Independencia; **internet** services can be found all over the centre of the city. **Artesanía shops** can be found at Jr Mariscal Cáceres block 5, Jiron Tarapaca block 8 and Jirón Tanca block 6. The **post office** is at San Martin 418 (8am–7pm Mon–Sat).

One of the best ways of **getting around** Pucallpa is as the locals do, by **motorbike**; these can be rented by the hour (about $2) from the workshop at Jr Raimondi 654. Otherwise, **colectivos** leave from near the food market on

Avenida 7 de Junio, while **mototaxis** and **taxis** can be picked up almost anywhere in town.

The Town and around

If you have an hour or so to while away in the town itself, both the downtown **food market** on Jirón Independencia and the older central **market** on Dos de Mayo are worth checking out; the latter in particular comprises varied stalls full of jungle produce. The port of **La Hoyada** and the older nearby **Puerto Italia** are also bustling with activity by day. Among the few other attractions in town is the **Usko-Ayar Amazonia School of Painting**, at Jr Sanchez Cerro 467 (Mon–Fri 8am–5pm; free), also the home of the school's founding father, the self-taught artist **Pablo Amaringo**. Once a *vegetalista-curandero*, Dom Amaringo used to use the hallucinogenic *ayahuasca*, as do most Peruvian jungle healers, as an aid to divination and curing; his students' works, many of which are displayed at his house, display the same *ayahuasca*-inspired visions of the forest wilderness as his own paintings do.

On Calle Inmaculada, the **Museo Regional de História Natural**, or the Regional Natural History Museum (Mon–Sat 9am–6pm; $1.50), exhibits dried and stuffed Amazon insects, fish and animals, and has good displays of local crafts, including ceramics produced by the Shipibo Indians, plus other material objects such as clothing and jewellery from local Indian tribes. There are also works by the Pucallpa-born wood sculptor **Augustin Rivas,** who once ran an artists' haven at Lago Yarinacocha, but now runs ayahuasca sessions in the Iquitos region; more of Rivas's work can be seen and bought at his house on Jr Tarapaca 861 (Mon–Sat 10am–noon & 3–5pm).

Some 6km out of town, along the highway towards Lima, there's a small lakeside settlement and zoological park at Barboncocha. Known as the **Parque Natural y Museo Regional de Pucallpa** (daily 8am–5pm; $1), it consists of almost two hundred hectares of lakeside reserve with plenty of alligators, birds (particularly parrots and macaws), boa constrictors and the usual caged monkeys and black jaguars. *Colectivos* to Barboncocha can be caught from near the food market on Avenida 7 de Junio; or hail a motorcycle taxi (20min; $3–4) from anywhere in town.

Accommodation and Eating

The best **places to stay** are found out at Yarinacocha, but in the city the better options include the *Grand Hotel Mercedes*, Jr Raimondi 610 (℡061/571191; ❺), which has a great swimming pool, lovely gardens, a reasonable restaurant and comfortable rooms. For those on a budget, the *Hostal Sun,* Ucayali 380 (℡061/598142; ❷–❸) which has friendly service and small but clean rooms, with or without baths. Like all jungle cities, Pucallpa has developed a cuisine of its own; one of the unique dishes you can find in some of these restaurants is *inchicapi* – a chicken soup made with peanuts, manioc and coriander leaves. **Restaurants** are fairly plentiful and include the *Chifa Han Muy*, Jr Inmaculada 247, which does a wonderful blend of Peruvian Chinese and tropical jungle cuisine. For steak or chicken dishes, it's hard to beat the restaurant in the *Hotel Inambu*, Av Centenario 271. Slightly cheaper and with excellent fish dishes, there's the *Restaurant El Golf*, at Jr Huascar 545, or the *Restaurant El Alamo*, on block 26 of Carretera Yarinacocha. Try the local speciality *patarashca* (fresh fish cooked in *bijao* leaves), or the delicious *sarapatera* (soup in a turtle shell).

Lago Yarinacocha and Puerto Callao

Some 9km from Pucallpa, and easily reached by bus or *colectivo* (20min; 30–50¢) from the food market on the corner of Jirón Independencia and Ucayali, **LAGO YARINACOCHA** is without doubt the most beautiful place to stay near Pucallpa. The lake is gigantic and, apart from the tiny main port where the buses drop off, is edged with secondary forest growth around most of its perimeter. Dolphins can usually be seen surfacing and diving into water; but this is best witnessed by renting one of the rowing boats (about $1.50 an hour) available daily from the lakeside. Around the port itself, and to a lesser extent, hidden behind the vegetation elsewhere, there is considerable settlement, but most of it is rustic and wooden. River channels lead off towards small villages of **Shipibo Indians** and the limited range of tourist lodges.

The port, which is where most travellers stay, is **PUERTO CALLAO**, a small town known locally (and slightly ironically) as the "Shangri-la de la Selva". Here, the bars and wooden shacks are animated by an almost continuous blast of *chicha* music. The settlement boasts one of the best jungle Indian craft workshops in the Amazon, the **Moroti-Shobo Crafts Co-operative** – a project originally organized by Oxfam but now operated by the local Shipibo and Conibo Indians. Located on the main plaza, it sells some beautifully moulded ceramics, carved wood and dyed textiles, most of them very reasonably priced. Various **excursions** to see wildlife, visit Indian villages or just to cross the lake, are all touted along the waterfront. The standard day-trip goes to the Shipibo village of **San Francisco** ($10), sometimes continuing to the slightly remoter settlements of **Nuevo Destino** and **Santa Clara** (around $15). San Francisco is now almost completely geared towards tourism, so for a more adventurous trip you'll do better to hire a *peque-peque* canoe and boatman on your own (from around $30 a day); these canoes can take up to six or seven people and you can share costs, though if you want to go further afield (say on a three-day excursion) expect prices to rise to $150 a day.

There's also a pristine botanical garden, the **Jardín Botánico Chullachaqui** (daily 9am–5pm; free) on the far right-hand side of the lake. To reach it you have to take a *peque-peque* canoe, a 45-minute ride ($2) from Callao Puerto, then walk for a little over half an hour down a clearly marked jungle trail. On arrival, you'll find the garden in a beautiful and exotic location with over 2300 medicinal plants, mostly native to the region.

Practicalities

Towards the waterfront, known as the Malecón Yarinacocha, are most of the liveliest **bars** (try *Peña La Catahua*); the best place **to eat** for atmosphere and local fish dishes in Yarinacocha is *La Maloca,* also on the Malecón. If you fancy something quieter, the lodges around the lake (see below) make a good spot for an evening drink. As for **hotels**, *El Pescador* (no phone; ❷–❸) offers good if basic accommodation, as does *Hostal Los Delfines* (☏061/571129; ❸–❹); both offer off-season deals in the ❶–❷ range. You can also **camp** anywhere along the lake (though bear in mind that you'll need to keep a lookout for thieves).

If you fancy something more luxurious, try the **tourist lodges** that surround the lake: they're far more expensive than a basic hotel, but are wonderfully positioned with individual chalets, mosquito-proof restaurants and organized trips onto the lake and into the forest. The well-established *La Cabaña* (❺) – possibly the first jungle lodge built in Peru – is an excellent place to stay, though the management requests **bookings** in advance, not least so that they can send their boat to Puerto Callao to meet visitors; they have an office in Pucallpa at Jr 7 de Junio 1043 (☏061/616679, 🖷579242). Another comfortable lodge, *La Perla* (☏061/961600, 🌐www.alojamientolaperla.com; ❹–❺) is family-run with a highly recommended

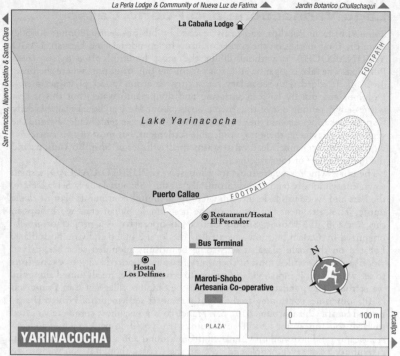

La Cabaña Lodge

San Francisco, Nuevo Destino & Santa Clara ◄

Lake Yarinacocha

FOOTPATH

Puerto Callao   FOOTPATH

Restaurant/Hostal
El Pescador

Bus Terminal

Hostal
Los Delfines

Maroti-Shobo
Artesania Co-operative

N

0   100 m

PLAZA

YARINACOCHA

Pucallpa ►

restaurant (patrons only unless booked in advance); it is located more or less next door to *La Cabaña* and has room for up to twelve visitors, with accommodation in bungalows. Like *La Cabaña*, it can be reached only by boat. A third lodge, *Albergue Amazónico Jana Shobo* (☎061/596943, ⓌWwww.janashobo.tk; ⑥), has a restaurant, library, comfortable rooms, organises bonfires and drum-dancing, and, more prosaically, will pick up from Pucallpa airport.

Not a lodge at all, it is sometimes possible to stay in the Medical Centre (❶–❷) at the village of **Nueva Luz de Fatima**, a small settlement a little further down the same bank of Yarinacocha, beyond *La Perla* lodge. Gilber Reategui, an English-speaking neighbour of the Medical Centre, can arrange for meals if required; he is also a jungle guide and has a *peque-peque* called *Mi Normita*, which is usually beached at Puerto Callao on the lake when not touring. Write to Sr Gilber Reategui, c/o Ruperto Perez, Maynas 350, Yarinacocha, Pucallpa, Ucayali, Peru for advance bookings. José Silva Nube, Jirón Aguaytia 145 (opposite the *Hostal Los Delfines*, ☎061/597143) offers his services as a local guide in the area and has his own boats.

A new Lima-based operator, *Runcato* (☎01/4653018, ⓌWwww.runcato.com) runs culturally authentic and **responsible tours** from Pucallpa to a more distant Shipibo-Conibo Indian community and lodge at **Puerto Nuevo**, including options for *ayahuasca* ceremonies, natural herbal baths and wildlife spotting (eg pink dolphins); only one or two expeditions are run every year, so it's important to contact this company several months in advance.

Downriver to Iquitos

Travelling **from Pucallpa to Iquitos** on a boat sounds more agreeable than it actually is. Very few Peruvians, except boatmen, would ever dream of it – over 1000km of water separates the two towns, with very little in between but the endless undulations of the river and verdant forest hemming you in on either side. However, if you are going that way, you may want to relax in a hammock for a few days and arrive in the style the rubber barons were accustomed to.

Riverboats generally leave Pucallpa from Malecon Grau at the corner with Jirón 9 de Diciembre between the streets Ucayali, Tacna and Tarapaca. The cheapest and most effective way of finding a boat is to go down to the port and ask around. Try to fix a price and a departure date with a reputable-looking outfit; it should cost around $40 per person, including food, but if you want a cabin this can rise to about $70. Few boats on this stretch of water actually have cabins, though, and while they're useful for storing your gear, you'll probably be more comfortable (and certainly cooler) sleeping in a hammock, strung under some mosquito netting. It's quite usual for passengers to string them up on the deck several days before departure – which can mean great savings on hotel costs and less risk of the boat leaving without you. If the captain asks for money upfront, don't give the whole bundle to him; you may never see him or his boat again. Additionally, even when everything looks ready for departure, don't be surprised if there is a delay of a day or two – boats leave frequently but unpredictably. **Food** on board can be very unappetizing, so it's worth taking some extra luxuries, like a few cans of fish, a packet or two of biscuits, and several bottles of water. Depending on how big the boat is and how many stops it makes, the journey to Iquitos normally takes five to seven days. Before you leave there's a certain amount of **paperwork** to go through, since this is a commercial port and one of the main illicit cocaine trails; you'll have to show your documents to the port police and get permission from the naval office (your captain should help with all of this).

En route to Iquitos, boats often stop at the settlements of Contamana (10hr; $10) and Requena (a further 4–5 days; $30). In theory it's possible to use these as pit stops – hopping off one boat for a couple of days while waiting for another – but you may end up stuck here for longer than you bargained. There isn't much at **Contamana**, on the right bank of the Ucayali, but it's okay to **camp**, and **food** can be bought without any problem. A better stopping point is the larger and more pleasant **Requena**, developed during the rubber boom on an isolated stretch of the Río Ucayali, a genuine jungle town that is in many ways like Iquitos was just fifty years ago. There are a couple of basic **hostels** here and one quite good one; contact Amazon Tours and Cruises with Green Tracks, Requena 336 (T065/23161), in Iquitos, see p.548). Alternatively, you can **camp** on the outskirts of town. For those going downstream, it's about a day's journey from Iquitos, with **boats** leaving regularly. You can also access Pacaya Samiria National Reserve (see p.488) by boat from here, though most people reach it from Iquitos or Lagunas. A few hours to the north, just a few huge bends away, the Río Marañón merges with the Ucayali to form the mighty Amazon.

The southern selva: Madre de Dios and the Río Urubamba

A large, forested region, with a manic climate (usually searingly hot and humid, but with sudden cold spells – *friajes* – between June and August, due to icy winds coming down from the Andean glaciers), the **southern selva** regions of Peru have only been systematically explored since the 1950s and were largely unknown until the twentieth century, when rubber began to leave Peru through Bolivia and Brazil, eastwards along the rivers.

Named after the broad river that flows through the heart of the southern jungle, the still relatively wild *departamento* of **MADRE DE DIOS**, like so many remote areas of Peru, is changing rapidly. Living in one of the last places affected by the rubber boom at the turn of the twentieth century, the natives here – many of whom struggle to maintain their traditional ways of life, despite the continuing efforts of *colonos* and some of the less enlightened Christian missionaries – were left pretty much alone until the push for oil in the 1960s and 1970s brought roads and planes, making this now the most accessible part of the Peruvian rainforest. As the oil companies moved out, so prospectors took their place, panning for gold dust along the river banks, while agribusiness moved

in to clear mahogany trees or harvest the bountiful Brazil nuts. Today the main problems facing the Indians, here as elsewhere, are loss of territory, the merciless pollution of their rivers, devastating environmental destruction (caused mainly by large-scale gold-mining) and new waves of oil exploration by multinationals.

Madre de Dios is centred on the fast-growing river town of **Puerto Maldonado**, near the Bolivian border and just 180m above sea level, supposedly founded by legendary explorer and rubber baron **Fitzcarrald**. The town, which extends a tenuous political and economic hold over the vast *departamento*, has a fast-growing population of over 40,000 (100,000 total in the region of Madre de Dios). Yet, while the *departamento*'s scattered towns and villages are interesting for their

---

Madre de Dios indigenous groups

Off the main Madre de Dios waterways, within the system of smaller tributaries and streams, live a variety of different **indigenous groups**. All are depleted in numbers due to contact with Western influences and diseases, but while some have been completely wiped out over the last twenty years, several have maintained their isolation. Many tribes were acculturated as late as the 1950s and 1960s, and occasionally "uncontacted" groups turned up during the 1980s and 1990s. These are, however, usually segments of a larger tribe that split or dispersed with the arrival of the rubber barons, and they are fast being secured in controllable mission villages. Most of the native tribes that remain in, or have returned to, their traditional territories now find themselves forced to take on seasonal work for the *colonos* who have staked claims around the major rivers. In the dry season (May–Nov), this usually means panning for gold – the region's most lucrative commodity. In the rainy season, Brazil nut collection takes over. The timber industry, too, is well established, and most of the accessible large cedars are already gone.

If you go anywhere in the jungle, especially on an organized tour, you're likely to stop off at a **tribal village** for at least half an hour or so, and the more you know about the people, the more you'll get out of the visit. Downstream from Puerto Maldonado, the most populous indigenous group are the **Ese Eja** tribe (often wrongly, and derogatorily, called 'Huarayos' by *colonos*). Originally semi-nomadic hunters and gatherers, the Ese Eja were well-known warriors who fought the Incas and, later on, the Spanish expedition of Alvarez Maldonado – eventually establishing fairly friendly and respectful relationships with both. Under Fitzcarrald's reign, they suffered greatly through the **engaño system**, which tricked them into slave labour through credit offers on knives, machetes, pots and pans, which then took years, or in some cases a lifetime to work off. Today they live in fairly large communities and have more or less abandoned their original bark-cloth robes in favour of shorts and T-shirts.

Upstream from Puerto Maldonado live several native tribes, known collectively (again, wrongly and derogatorily) as the Mashcos but actually comprising at least five separate linguistic groups – the **Huachipaeri**, **Amarakaeri**, **Sapitoyeri**, **Arasayri** and **Toyeri**. All typically use long bows – over 1.5m – and lengthy arrows, and most settlements will also have a shotgun or two these days, since less time can be dedicated to hunting when they are panning for gold or working timber for *colonos*. Traditionally, they wore long bark-cloth robes and had long hair, and the men often stuck eight feathers into the skin around their lips, making them look distinctively fierce and cat-like. Having developed a terrifying hatred of white people during the rubber era, they were eventually conquered and settled by missionaries and the army about forty years ago. Many Huachipaeri and Amarakaeri groups are now actively engaging with the outside world on their own terms, without interference from organizations with their own agendas. These days some of their young men and women have gone through university education and subsequently returned to their native villages.

Wild West energy and spirit, most visitors come for the wildlife, especially in the strictly protected **Manu Biosphere Reserve** – still essentially an expedition zone – and the cheaper, less well-known **Tambopata-Candamo Reserved Zone**, chiefly visited by groups staying at lodges; between them these areas encompass some of the most exciting jungle and richest flora and fauna in the world.

The newest protected area is **Bahuaja–Sonene National Park**; created in 2000 and surrounded largely by a massive rainforest area formed by the Tambopata river, it is intended to show the Peruvian government's support for this region as an ecological treasure. Taken together, these two zones comprise some 1.5 million hectares, much the same size as Manu.

As in all jungle regions, human activity here is closely linked to the river system, and Manu and Tambopata are actually among the most easily reached parts of the Amazon: from Cusco, Manu is either a day's journey by bus then a couple days more by canoe, or a thirty-minute flight in a light aircraft; Tambopata, is reached by a forty-minute scheduled flight to Puerto Maldonado (or an 18–20hr bus journey), plus a few hours in a motorized canoe to get to lodges upriver.

Slightly less accessible than the protected zones, but nevertheless offering travellers staying in Puerto Maldonado a taste of the rainforest, are **Lago Sandoval** and the huge expanse of **Lago Valencia**, both great wildlife locales east along the Río Madre de Dios and close to the Bolivian border. At the least, you're likely to spot a few caimans and the strange hoatzin birds, and if you're lucky, larger mammals such as capybara, tapir, or, less likely, a jaguar – and at Valencia, you can fish for piranha. A little further southeast of here, less than a couple of hours in a decent motorized launch, lies **Las Pampas del Heath**, the only tropical grassland within Peru. It now lies within the Bahuaja-Sonene National Park, so special permission is needed from the INRENA office (see p.513) to visit it. The grasslands extend eastward across northern Bolivia to the Pantanal region of Brazil, one of the wildlife gems of the Americas.

The **Río Madre de Dios** itself is fed by two main tributaries, the **Río Manu** and the **Río Alto Madre de Dios**, which roll off the Paucartambo Ridge (just north of Cusco), which divides the tributaries from the **Río Urubamba** watershed and delineates Manu Biosphere Reserve. At Puerto Maldonado, the Madre de Dios meets with the **Río Tambopata** and the **Río de las Piedras**, then flows on to Puerto Heath, a day's boat ride away on the Bolivian frontier. From here it continues through the Bolivian forest into Brazil to join the great Río Madeira, which eventually meets the Amazon near Manaus.

West of Puerto Maldonado, on the other side of Cusco from the Río Madre de Dios, the **Río Urubamba** flows on past Machu Picchu and down to the jungle area around the town of **Quillabamba**, before gushing beyond the end of the road at the frontier settlement of **Kiteni** and then falling through the rapids at the **Pongo de Mainique** and into the lowland rainforest, where it continues north to Iquitos, then east to the Atlantic Ocean many thousands of kilometres away.

Puerto Maldonado

A remote settlement even for Peru, **PUERTO MALDONADO** is a frontier colonist town with strong links to the Cusco region and a great fervour for bubbly jungle *chicha* music. With an economy based on unsustainable lumber and gold extraction, and highly sustainable Brazil-nut gathering from the rivers and forests of Madre de Dios, it has grown enormously over the last twenty years from a small, laid-back outpost of civilization to a busy market town. Today it's the thriving, safe (and fairly expensive) capital of a region that feels very much on the threshold of major upheavals, with a rapidly developing tourist industry. The town is changing shape fast, with the population rising from 10,000 to 60,000 (mostly colonists from the mountains) in the last seven years and with concrete roads spreading from the old centre, all of them busy and lined with occupied shops and properties. The feel you get here is of a rapidly growing, but still intimate and small city, whose young people spend endless evenings sitting row upon row in front of the web-connected glare of computer monitors, in hopes of procuring lucrative careers in the future.

Some history

Whilst gold mining and logging – both mostly illegal frontier businesses – keep the town buzzing today, it was rubber that established Puerto Maldonado at the beginning of the twentieth century. During the 1920s came the game hunters, who dominated the economy of the region, and after them, mainly in the 1960s, the exploiters of mahogany and cedar trees arrived – leading to the construction of Boca Manu airstrip, just before the oil companies moved in during the 1970s. Most of the townspeople, riding coolly around on Honda motorbikes, are second-generation *colonos*, but there's a constant stream of new and hopeful arrivals – rich and poor from all parts of South America, and even the occasional gang from the US.

The lure, inevitably, is **gold**. Every rainy season the swollen rivers deposit a heavy layer of gold dust along their banks and those who have been quick enough to stake claims on the best stretches have made substantial fortunes. In such areas there are thousands of unregulated miners, using large front-loader earth-moving machines, destroying a large section of the forest, and doing so very quickly. Gold lust is not a new phenomenon here – the gold-rich rivers have brought Andean Indians and occasional European explorers to the region for centuries. Even the Incas may well have utilized a little of the precious

The saga of Fitzcarrald

While the infamous rubber baron, **Fitzcarrald** (often mistakenly called Fitzcarraldo), is associated with the founding of Puerto Maldonado, he actually died some twelve years before the event; his story is, however, relevant to the development of this region. While working rubber on the Río Urubamba, Fitzcarrald evidently caught the gold bug after hearing rumours from local Ashaninka and Machiguenga Indians of an Inca fort protecting vast treasures, possibly around the Río Purus. Setting out along the Mishagua, a tributary of the Río Urubamba, he managed to reach its source, and from there walked over the ridge to a new watershed which he took to be the Purus, though it was in fact the Río Cashpajali, a tributary of the Río Manu. Leaving men to clear a path, he returned to Iquitos, and in 1884 came back to the region on a boat called *La Contamana*. He took the boat apart, and, with the aid of over a thousand Ashaninka and other Indians, carried it across the "Purus". But, as he cruised down, attacked by tribes at several points, Fitzcarrald slowly began to realize that the river was not the Purus – a fact confirmed when he eventually bumped into a Bolivian rubber collector.

Though he'd ended up on the wrong river, Fitzcarrald had discovered a link connecting the two great Amazonian watersheds. In Europe, the discovery was heralded as a great step forward in the exploration of South America, but for Peru it meant more rubber, a quicker route for its export and the beginning of the end for Madre de Dios' indigenous tribes. Puerto Maldonado was founded in 1902, and as exploitation of the region's rubber peaked, so too was there an increase in population of workers and merchants, with Madre de Dios ultimately becoming a *departamento* of Peru in 1912. German director **Werner Herzog** thought this historical episode a fitting subject for celluloid, and in 1982 directed the epic *Fitzcarraldo*.

PUERTO MALDONADO

Río Madre de Dios

National Police

Port area (Madre de Dios)

BILLINGHURST

LORETO

CARRION

Viewing Platform over river

PLAZA GRAU

Municipal Building

Captain of the Port

CUSCO

Teatro Municipal

Cinema

PLAZA DE ARMAS

2 DE MAYO

Banco de la Nación

Banco de Credito

N

G PRADA

ERNESTO RIVERO

J TRONCOSO

Old Market

LEON DE VELARDE

MOQUEGUA

TACNA

Money Change

Market

ICA

AV FITZCARRALD

LAMBAYEQUE

PIURA

EATING & NIGHTLIFE
Bar Isaica	5
La Casa Nostra	16
Cevicheria El Catamaran	10
Chifa Wa Seng	14
Heladeria Gusitos del Cura	6
Karambola Restaurant & Disco-Pub	4
Natur	17
Peña la Choza	12
Pizzeria Trattoria El Horno	11
Pizzerria Leños Y Carbon	9
Plaza Bar	2
Pollos a la Brasa la Estrella	13
Refrigerios Rossy	8
Te Dulce Espera	15
Teocas Disco	1
La Vaca Loca	7
Witite	3

ACCOMMODATION
Cabaña Quinta	C
Don Carlos	H
Hospedaje Amarumayo	D
Hospedaje Moderno	A
Hospedaje Peru Amazonico	G
Hospedaje Rey Port	F
Hospedaje Tres Fronteras	E
Wasai	B

0   200 m

& Port Area (Tambopata)

stuff – the Inca Emperor Tupac Yupanqui is known to have discovered the Río Madre de Dios, naming it the Amarymayo ("serpent river"). Perhaps, too, it's more than coincidental that one suggested location for the legendary city of "**El Dorado**"(known in southern Peru as **Paititi**), where the Incas hid their most valuable golden objects from the Spanish conquerors, is in the high forests close to the Río Alto Madre de Dios.

Arrival, information and getting around

If you arrive by plane, the blast of hot, humid air you get the moment you step out onto the runway of the city's small but modern and air-conditioned **airport** (082/571533), is an instant reminder that this is the Amazon Basin. Lan Peru operate daily jets from Lima via Cusco. Unless you're being picked up as part of an organized tour, **airport transfer** is simplest and coolest by *mototaxi*, costing around $2.75 for the otherwise impossibly hot eight-kilometre walk.

Most **buses** from Cusco (principally with the companies CIVA and Huareño) arrive at Puerto Maldonado's Avenida Tambopata; buses to and from Juliaca finish and start from the main market area. These days, with surfacing and bridges over the rivers being improved all the time, the bus journey between Cusco and Puerto Maldonado can be done in 18–24 hours. The **road to the Brazilian frontier** is also now ninety percent asphalt and construction has begun on a massive bridge over the Rio Madre de Dios which, by 2011, will arrive straight onto the present Plaza de Armas in downtown Puerto Maldonado.

Puerto Maldonado has two main **river ports**, one on the Río Tambopata, at the southern end of León de Velarde, the main street; the other on the Río Madre de Dios, at the northern end of León de Velarde; from the former, there's a very cheap **ferry** service across the river to the Transoceanica to Brazil which will be there until the new river bridge is completed.

On occasions, visitors arriving here (by road or air) have to go through a yellow fever **vaccination checkpoint**. The airport has a **tourist information** kiosk (ⓦ www.regionmadredededios.gob.pe), which is rarely staffed plus some **artesania** shops. The quickest way of **getting around town** and its immediate environs is to hail a *mototaxi* (85¢ in-town flat rate, but check before getting in) or passenger-carrying motorbikes (35¢, also a flat rate).

Accommodation

Puerto Maldonado has a reasonable range of **hotels**, most of them either on or within a couple of blocks of León de Velarde. All the better hotels offer protection against mosquitoes and some sort of air-conditioning.

Cabaña Quinta Cusco 535 ☎082/571045, ⓦ www.hotelcabanaquinta.net. This is close to the port and town centre and is one of the more popular hotels in town. Rooms are comfortable, some have fans, more expensive ones air-conditioning, and all complemented by a small attractive garden. There's also an excellent bar-restaurant, wi-fi internet and a small pool. ❺–❼
Don Carlos León de Velarde 1271 ☎082/571029, ⓦ www.hotelesdoncarlos.com. This well-run place overlooks the Río Tambopata in a relatively pretty spot, within walking distance of the centre, but just beyond the heart of town. It has a swimming pool, good restaurant and a generous array of rooms, most with fans and TVs, some with a/c; all have private bath. ❻–❼
Hospedaje Amarumayo Libertad 433 ☎082/573860 ⓔ residenciaamarumayo@hotmail .com. Located some 6km northwest from the town centre but only five minutes from the airport, this is a good deal, not least because it has a small pool and friendly staff; rooms have fans and private baths. ❹
Hospedaje Peru Amazonico Jr Ica 269 ☎082/571799, ⓔ peruamazonico@hotmail.com. Bright and clean, this small place has ample sized rooms around a little courtyard, all with cable TV and wi-fi access. The spacious lobby area is always quite cool. ❹

Hospedaje Rey Port León de Velarde 457 ☎082/572685. Friendly but sometimes noisy; the beds are basic, rooms are small. ❸
Hospedaje Tres Fronteras Jr Arequipa 357 ☎082/300011. Less than a block from the main plaza, *Tres Fronteras* is housed in a modern concrete building with a cool, tiled interior, and plain but comfortable small rooms, each with TV, fan and good bathrooms. Unusually, the beds have orthopaedic mattresses. ❹
Hospedaje Moderno Jr Billinghurst 359 ☎082/300043, ⓔ hospedaje_moderno@hotmail .com. A brightly painted, very friendly and well-kept hotel, with something of a frontier-town character, not least by the nature of its clientele who are mainly river traders. The rooms here are small, with shared bath but do have TVs. ❷
Wasai Parque Grau on Billingshurst ☎/ⓕ 082/572290, ⓔ info@wasai.com, ⓦ www.wasai.com; or in Cusco ☎082/221826; or Lima ☎01/436-8792. The best of the more expensive options, offering fine views over the Río Madre de Dios, and a swimming pool with a waterfall and bar set among trees, overlooking a canoe-builder's yard. All rooms are cabin-style with TV and shower, and staff here also organize local tours and run the *Wasai Lodge* (see p.520). ❻

The Town

Puerto Maldonado's streets are laid out in a rigid grid pattern, not emanating from a central plaza as in most Peruvian cities, but stretching out from the port and Tambopata riverfront, towards the airport and forest edge. The main street, **León de Velarde**, nevertheless ends at the **Plaza de Armas**, where there's a bizarre, Chinese pagoda-style clock tower at its centre. In a few years, the Transoceanic road-bridge will come straight onto this square, where, only thirty years ago, the town's only TV was sometimes set up outside the unremarkable Municipal building for the people to watch an all-important event like Peru playing football. These days there are satellite TV dishes all over town and the youth of Puerto Maldonado are more familiar with computer software than they are with jungle mythology.

The streets, earthen except for the main drags, show few signs of wealth, despite the gold dust that lures peasants here from the Andes. While the busy city centre combines the usual bars and restaurants with pool halls, hammock shops and offices, buzzing all the while with motorbikes and *chicha* music, there really isn't much in the way of specific attractions, and most visitors come here primarily to enter the forest and stay in a lodge. It's nevertheless interesting to follow Jirón Billingshurst from the main plaza, descending the steep steps down to the **main port** area, situated on the Río Madre de Dios, and offering an otherwise rare glimpse of the river, which is largely shielded from view by the ever-growing rows of wooden houses and lumber yards; here you can see boat-builders, loggers and even take a ferry over to the other side of the river and see the town from a different perspective. The main market, at block 4 of Jirón Ica, just eight short blocks from the Plaza de Armas, is quite large, busy and brimming over with jungle produce, including brazil nuts; it also has a couple of rainforest medicine practioners.

Eating, drinking and nightlife

You should have no problem finding a good **restaurant** in Puerto Maldonado. Delicious river fish are always available, even in ceviche form, and there's usually venison or wild pig fresh from the forest (try *estofado de venado*). One of the best (though also priciest) eateries is the one in *Wasai* (see p.511), where you can enjoy an enormous plate of food while watching life pass by along the river. Similarly, the restaurant at the *Cabaña Quinta* is hard to beat for its excellent three-course set lunches, often including fresh river **fish** and fried manioc, while just around the corner, the *Cevicheria El Catamaran*, one block away from the plaza at 26 de Diciembre 241 serves fantastic fish dishes from a panoramic viewing point hanging over the lower port suburbs and looking down the Madre de Dios river towards Bolivia and Brazil.

Back on the plaza, the café *Heladería Gusitos del Cura* is great for ice creams and snacks. Close by, the swish restaurant and bar *La Vaca Loca*, which serves tasty steaks and great salads, has the kind of trendy internal decor which brings to mind cultured Brazilian-style places. On the other side of the plaza, the cosy *Pizzeria Trattoria El Horno*, is very popular with travellers and locals alike, and at weekends you may have to wait a while for a table. One the west side of the plaza near the Municipal building, there's *Refrigerios Rossy*, a small café, good for sandwiches and morning coffee; around the corner on Carrion the *Pizzerria Leños y Carbon* serves up great chicken and chips. And if you like grilled **chicken**, you're spoiled for choices: for the best, try *Pollos a la Brasa La Estrella*, Velarde 474 (☎082/573107). On Dos de Mayo, at no. 253, *Chifa Wa Seng* successfully combines traditional **Chinese** meals with an abundance of jungle foodstuffs. For **vegetarian food** there's *Natur*, at León de Velarde 928, but their dishes are a little uninspiring.

Along León de Velarde are a number of **cafés and bars**, one or two of which have walls covered in typical *selvatico*-style paintings, developed to represent and romanticize the dreamlike features of the jungle – looming jaguars, brightly plumed macaws in the treetops and deer drinking water from a still lake. Locals are very keen on sweet and savoury **snacks**, and if you fancy trying some yourself pop into *Tu Dulce Espera* or *La Casa Nostra*, all on the fifth block of Velarde. The first sells typical sweets, while the latter two offer delicious, traditionally prepared tropical fruit **juices** (including mango, passionfruit, pineapple and *carambola* – a local favourite), for less than 75¢ a glass, as well as tamales, *papas rellenas* (stuffed potatoes) and a range of exotic-looking cakes. Delicious (but hard to eat) *aguaje* palm fruits are sold at several street corners along León de Velarde.

There's a surprisingly busy **nightlife** in this laid-back town, especially at weekends. In the early evenings, most people just stroll around, stopping occasionally to sit and chat in the Plaza de Armas or in bars along the main street. At weekends and fiesta times, however, it's possible to sample rock, reggae, *chicha*, *cumbia* or Latin pop music music at one of the town's venues. Places get packed by 10pm on Friday and Saturday nights, with people moving from one club to another. The best **club** in town, with Shipibo designs adorning the walls, is *Witite*, at León de Velarde 151 (Fri & Sat; usually free entry), which has a surprisingly advanced sound system playing the whole range of Latino music. Also close to the plaza, there's the *Teocas Disco*, with a large dance floor, plus a couple of decent bars on Calle Loreto: *Bar Isaica* and *Plaza Bar* opposite. Just off the other side of the plaza, *Karambola Restaurant and Disco-Pub*, at Jr Arequipa 162, offers decent grub and live music shows, sometimes with Brazilian-style dancing girls, at weekends. A couple of kilometres out of town, back on the airport road, the *Peña La Choza* (take a *mototaxi*; $2) provides a massive heaving dance area plus cheap food and beer every Saturday night.

Listings

Airlines Lan Peru, corner of León de Velarde with 2 de Mayo ☎082/573677.

Banks and exchange There are two banks on the plaza: Banco Credito, Arequipa 334; and Banco de la Nación, Jr Daniel Carrion 233 (both Mon–Fri 9am–1pm & 5–7pm). *Cambistas* usually hang out on the corner of Prada and Puno. Your hotel may also change dollars.

Captain's office León de Velarde, between Av Gonzalez Prada and Dos de Mayo. For permits to travel by river into the jungle (Mon–Sat 8am–6pm)

Consulates Bolivia, Jr Loreto, on the Plaza de Armas (Mon–Fri 8am–3.30pm).

Immigration Jr Ica 727, second floor ☎082/571069.

INRENA Instituto Nacional de Recursos Naturales is where you have to go for permission to enter the National Parks of the region: Dirección Sub-regional Agraria Madre de Dios, Av 28 de Julio 482, Puerto Maldonado; or, in Lima: C 17, 335 Urb El Palomar, San Isidro ☎01/224-3298, ⓔcomunicaciones @inrena.gob.pe.

Policia Nacional (National Police) One block from the Plaza on Billingshurst, more or less opposite the Hospedaje Moderno.

Post office León de Velarde 675, opposite the corner of Jr Jaime Troncoso (Mon–Sat 8am–8pm, Sun 8am–3pm).

Telephones There are public phones in most parts of town, many located outside of shops and bars.

Moving On From Puerto Maldonado

There are two main roads out of Puerto Maldonado: Avenida Fitzcarraldo brings you out at the cattle ranches on the far side of the airstrip; while if you turn off on 28 de Julio, you can take the road – now known as the Transoceanica – as far as you like in the direction of Cusco. A third road, which will become perhaps the most important overland route by 2011, is the other end of the Transoceanica which connects Puerto Maldonado, Cusco and Peru with Brazil by road all the way to the Atlantic. A regular bus and *colectivo* ($5) service now connects Puerto Maldonado with **Laberinto** (leaving from the main market on Ernesto Rivero), some ninety minutes away. Formerly a gold-mining frontier settlement, since the early 1990s it has been surpassed in importance by the settlement of **Masuko**, deeper into the forest, and is now important mainly for its role as an upriver port for Puerto Maldonado; most boats going upstream begin their journeys from Laberinto, though if you're planning to visit Manu Biosphere Reserve, you should set out from Cusco (see p.264).

Into Brazil

The route **into Brazil** was first opened for use by trucks in the late 1980s and whilst still not commonly used by independent travellers, the route is now pretty easy to follow. The road is now almost completely sealed to and beyond the border with Brazil, and only the last big bridge, over the Rio Madre de Dios, remains to be completed. It's therefore now possible to cross with relative ease via Iñapari, where the Peruvian police and Immigration offices are based on the border within only four hours of Puerto Maldonado. There is almost no forest along the road now, which, culturally, is an Andean corridor penetrating the jungle, leaving in its wake just secondary growth, cattle ranches, *chacra* farms and Brazil-nut gathering communities like Mavila and Iberia.

There are currently no regular flights to Brazil from Puerto Maldonado, but details about ad hoc services can be obtained from officials at the airport. Several *colectivo* cars (4hrs; $15) leave Puerto Maldonado daily, from 4am onwards, to Iñapari and the frontier; it's best to book at least one day in advance and they will pick you up from your hotel: Nuevo Peru, Jr Piura 790 (082/574235); or, Iñapari Tours, Jr Piura 768 (082/793574).

After crossing the Rio Madre de Dios on a ferry to Triunfo, *colectivos* take about four hours to reach the frontier. Just beyond a small river bridge, Puente Yaverija, the road enters the small and final Peruvian settlement of **Iñapari** where there are a couple of basic hostels, notably *Hostal Milagros* (no phone; ❷–❸). Make sure to get your exit or entry stamp from Peruvian border post here (Mon–Fri 8.30am–noon & 2.30–7pm; Sat and Sun 9am–noon & 2.30–6pm). It's only a kilometre or so from here to the Brazilian settlement of **Assis Brasil**, which has more to offer in terms of cafés and hostals than Iñapari, but is still a bit of a dump. The best option is to take a car with Brazilian drivers ($10 a person or $40 a whole car) from here a further 112km to **Brasileia**, a much larger town which also connects via a walkable bridge with the Bolivian free-trade zone town of **Cobija**. Brazilian Federal Police and customs now have their offices just a couple of kilometres into Brazil on their side of the Rio Acre bridge. From Brasileia, *colectivos* and buses for Rio Branco leave regularly from close to the Ponte Augusto do Araujó.

Around Puerto Maldonado

Madre de Dios boasts spectacular virgin lowland rainforest and exceptional wild-life. Brazil-nut tree trails, a range of lodges, some excellent local guides and ecologists, plus indigenous and colonist cultures are all within a few hours of Puerto Maldonado. Serious jungle trips can be made here with relative ease and without too much expense, and this part of the Amazon offers easy and uniquely rewarding access to rainforest that is much less disturbed than that around Iquitos, or Manaus in the heart of the Brazilian Amazon, for example.

Less than one hour downriver from Puerto Maldonado (90min on the return upriver) is **Lago Sandoval**, a large lake where the Ministry of Agriculture have introduced the large *paiche* fish. At its best on weekday mornings (it gets quite crowded at other times), there are decent opportunities for spotting wildlife, in particular **birds** similar to those at Lago Valencia. You may even spot a **giant otter** (*Pteronura brasilensis*); for more information about these endangered creatures, see p.605. It's also possible to walk to the lake (about 1hr), and once here boatmen and canoes can usually be obtained by your guide for a couple of hours, as can food and drink. Incidentally, if you're travelling to the lake by river, most guides will show you the ruined hulk of an old boat lying close to the riverbank. If they claim it had anything to do with Fitzcarrald, don't believe them; it may be similar in style to Fitzcarrald's, but in fact it's smaller and is a far more recent arrival – it's a hospital boat that was in use until two or three decades ago.

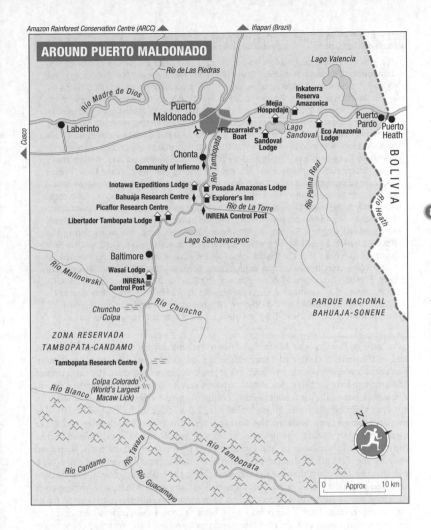

AROUND PUERTO MALDONADO

Amazon Rainforest Conservation Centre (ARCC)　　　　Iñapari (Brazil)

Lago Valencia

Río de Las Piedras

Río Madre de Dios

Puerto Maldonado

Inkaterra Reserva Amazonica

Mejia Hospedaje

Puerto Pardo　Puerto Heath

Cusco

Laberinto

"Fitzcarrald's" Boat

Sandoval Lodge

Lago Sandoval

Eco Amazonia Lodge

B O L I V I A

Chonta

Community of Infierno

Río Tambopata

Río Palma Real

Río Heath

Inotawa Expeditions Lodge

Posada Amazonas Lodge

Bahuaja Research Centre

Explorer's Inn

Picaflor Research Centre

Río de La Torre

Libertador Tambopata Lodge

INRENA Control Post

Lago Sachavacayoc

Baltimore

Wasai Lodge

INRENA Control Post

Río Malinowski

PARQUE NACIONAL BAHUAJA-SONENE

Chuncho Colpa

Río Chuncho

ZONA RESERVADA TAMBOPATA-CANDAMO

Tambopata Research Centre

Colpa Colorado (World's Largest Macaw Lick)

Río Blanco

Río Tavara

Río Tambopata

Río Candamo

Río Guacamayo

N

0　Approx　10 km

From Puerto Maldonado, it takes the best part of a day by canoe with a *peque-peque*, or around two hours in a *lancha* with an outboard, to reach the huge lake of **Lago Valencia**. On the way you can stop off to watch some gold-panners on the Madre de Dios and visit a small settlement of **Ese Eja Indians**; about thirty minutes beyond, you turn off the main river into a narrow channel that connects with the lake. Easing onto the lake itself, the sounds of the canoe engine are totally silenced by the weight and expanse of water. Towards sunset it's quite common to see caimans basking on the muddy banks, an occasional **puma** or the largest rodent in the world, a **capybara**, scuttling away into the forest. Up in the trees around the channel lie hundreds of hoatzin birds, or *gallos* as they are called locally – large, ungainly creatures with orange and brown plumage, long wings and distinctive spiky crests. The strangest feature of the hoatzin is the claws at the end of their wings, which they use to help them climb up into overhanging branches beside rivers and lakes; they have almost lost the power of flight.

The Tambopata-Candamo Reserved Zone

Arguably containing some of the world's finest and most biodiverse rainforest, the **Tambopata-Candamo Reserved Zone** ($30 entry fee) is accessible from many of the lodges in the Puerto Maldonado region. Initially an area of less than 6000 hectares, it was transformed into a Reserved Zone mainly due to the scientific work of the adjacent *Explorer's Inn* lodge (see p.519). In 1990, after further studies had proved the value of the forest in terms of biodiversity conservation, the reserved sector was expanded to almost 1.5 million hectares. In 2000 the **Bahuaja-Sonene National Park** was enlarged, and incorporated almost 250,000 hectares of the original Tambopata-Candamo Reserved Zone. Described by National Geographic as one of the planet's seven "iconic natural sanctuaries", it's not possible to visit the National Park, except for licensed operators coming down from the Alto Tambopata on rafting expeditions or on tours to one of the major macaw **colpas** (salt-licks) in the region. Like most licks, they attract wild birds and animals because they offer the salts, minerals and clay required for their nutrition and also function as digestive aids for these creatures. Although reducing the Tambopata-Candamo Reserved Zone, the expansion of the National Park is something of a major success for conservation in Peru; yet, despite this there are fears that the Peruvian government has plans to open up the park at some future point to gas and oil exploitation. For more details, contact **TReeS** (c/o John Forrest, Tambopata Reserve Society, PO Box 33153, London NW3 4DR, UK), a UK organization maintaining strong links with the Tambopata area; they should be able to offer you detailed and up-to-date information on the situation and the environmental work going on there. They can also advise you about many of the lodges.

An easy walk from the Madre de Dios riverbank brings you to the lake's one real **settlement**, a cluster of thatched huts around a slightly larger schoolhouse. Fewer than seventy people live here – a schoolteacher, a lay priest, the shop owner and a few fishing families. Some tour groups stay in a small **camp** further down, a seasonal nut-collectors' *campamento*, comprising just one cooking hut with an adjacent sleeping platform, though there is also a lodge and a hospedaje. By day most people go for a **walk in the forest** – something that's both safer and more interesting with a guide, though whichever way you do it you'll immediately sense the energy and abundance of life. Quinine trees tower above all the trails, surpassed only by the Tahuari hardwoods. Around their trunks you'll often see *pega-pega*, a parasitic ivy-like plant that the shamans mix with the hallucinogenic *ayahuasca* into an intense aphrodisiac. Perhaps more useful are the liana vines; one thin species dangling above the paths can be used to take away the pain from a *shushupe* snake bite. Another, the *maravilla* or *palo de agua*, issues a cool stream of fresh water if you chop a section, about half a metre long, and put it to your lips. You may come upon another vine, too – the sinister *matapalo* (or *renaco*), which sometimes extends over dozens of trees, sucking the sap from up to a square kilometre of jungle.

You can also take a **canoe up the lake** for a bit of fishing, passing beaches studded with groups of lazy-looking turtles sunning themselves in line along the top of fallen tree trunks – when they notice the canoe, each one topples off, slowly splashing into the water one after another. It takes a bit more to frighten the **white caimans** away; many can be seen soaking in the sun's strong rays along the margin of the lake. Sometimes over 2m in length, they're a daunting sight, although they won't bite unless you happen to step on one. At night, it's possible to glide along the water, keeping close to the bank, looking for the amber glint reflected from a pair of caiman eyes as the beam from your torch catches them. This is how the locals hunt them, fixing the crocs with a beam of light, then moving closer before blasting them with a shotgun; as a tourist, though, it's enough just to look into their gleaming eyes in the pitch darkness and, in some cases, your guide may catch a small one to show you it close up before letting it go again. The only sound on the lake will be the grunting of corvina fish vibrating up through the bottom of the canoe.

Both Lago Valencia and Lago Sandoval are superbly endowed with **birdlife**. In addition to the hoatzin there are kingfishers, cormorants, herons, egrets, pink flamingoes, skimmers, macaws, toucans, parrots and gavilans. And behind the wall of trees along the banks hide deer, wild pigs and **tapir**. If you're lucky enough to catch a glimpse of a tapir you'll be seeing one of South America's strangest creatures – almost the size of a cow, with an elongated rubbery nose and spiky mane. In fact, the tapir is known in the jungle as a *sachavaca* ("forest cow" – *sacha* is Quechua for "forest" and *vaca* is Spanish for "cow"). The easiest fish to catch are **piranha** – all you need is some line, a hook, and a chunk of unsalted meat; throw this into the lake and you've got yourself a piranha.

Another good trip, if you've got at least three days to spare (two nights minimum), is up to the **Río Heath**, a national rainforest sanctuary, though while the **Pampas del Heath** are excellent for watching macaws they don't have the primary forest necessary for a great variety of wildlife. A shorter trip – five hours up and about two hours down the Río Tambopata – is to **Tres Chimbales**, where there are a few houses belonging to the Infierno community on the Río Tambopata; it's possible to spend two or three days watching for wildlife, walking in the forest and fishing. From here you can visit **Infierno** village itself, spread out along the river, peppered with thatched and tin-roofed huts.

One other possibility, though something not commonly done by gringos, is to **travel into Bolivia** on one of the cargo boats that leave more or less every week from Puerto Maldonado. Before embarking on this, however, you'll have to clear your **passport and visa** with the Puerto Maldonado police and Migraciones offices (see p.513). Puerto Pardo is the last Peruvian frontier settlement (Bolivian formalities can usually be dealt with at the frontier post of Puerto Heath, from where you continue by river to Riberalta). Be aware that the journey from Puerto Maldonado to Riberalta is rough and usually takes ten to fourteen days; always make sure that the boat is going all the way or you might get stuck at the border, which, by all accounts, is not much fun, and you might have to wait days for another boat. From Riberalta there are land and air connections to the rest of Bolivia, as well as river or road access into Brazil via the Río Madeira or Guajará-Mirim.

Organized tours around Puerto Maldonado, Tambopata-Candamo Reserved Zone and Parque Nacional Bahuaja Sonene

Compared with independent travel, an **organized excursion** saves time and adds varying degrees of comfort. It also ensures that you go with someone who knows the area, probably speaks English, and, if you choose well, can introduce you to the flora, fauna and culture of the region. It's also worth noting that you are less likely to get ripped off with a registered company with a fixed office and contact details, especially if you should need redress afterwards.

Most people **book** a trip in Cusco before travelling to Puerto Maldonado, though it is possible to contact most of the operators in Puerto itself, either at the airport or through one of the offices (see p.518), or through the cafés on León de Velarde. **Flying from Cusco or direct from Lima** is the quickest way to reach Puerto Maldonado, and most tour agencies will organize plane tickets ($40–60 each way) for you if you take their tours. It's possible to buy a jungle package that does not include the airfare; this can work to your advantage, especially if you're able to secure one of the discounted air tickets (to as low as $35 each way) from Cusco to Puerto Maldonado. The cheapest option is a two-day and one-night tour of the Puerto area, but on these you can expect to spend most of your time travelling and sleeping. Frankly, the Amazon deserves a longer visit, and you're only looking at $25–50 more for an extra day.

Of the ever-increasing number of **lodges** and **tour operators** around Puerto Maldonado, mainly on the ríos Madre de Dios and Tambopata, all offer a good taste of the jungle, but the quality of the experience varies from area to area and lodge to lodge – all lodges tend to offer full board and include transfers, though always check the level of service and ask to see photos at the lodges' offices in Cusco or Lima. It's also worth checking out what costs will be once you're there; complaints are common about the price of drinks, although given the distance they've travelled, the mark-up is hardly surprising. Remember, too, that even the most luxurious place is far removed from normal conveniences, and conditions tend to be rustic and relatively open to the elements. Varying in capacity (the largest can accommodate up to a hundred, the smaller no more than a dozen or so), most lodges have huts, cabins or bungalows built from wood and palm fronds gathered from the forest. Toilets can be anything from standard WC, covered in mosquito netting to earth privies, while sleeping arrangements can range from bunk rooms to pretty comfy twin doubles with doors and mosquito-net windows. Food is generally good, though you may want to take supplements or treats. Note that most lodges require guests to get up very early in the morning on the day of departure in order to arrive at Puerto Maldonado airport in good time – generally speaking, the nearer the lodge to the town, the longer you can sleep in.

It's a good idea to shop around before arriving: that way you can spend time getting a feel of what's available. Otherwise, you can just walk up Plateros, Saphi and Procuradores, or around the Plaza de Armas, in Cusco and you'll find most of their offices (see p.264). Many of the longer, more established companies have their offices out of the centre.

Lodges and operators

Amazon Rainforest Conservation Centre (ARCC) ☎082/572961, ⊛www .laspiedrasamazontour.com. The only operator with a lodge on the little-explored Río de las Piedras, this outfit offers well-organized and adventurous tours on that self-same river. This is actually a relatively new project protecting the area around Lake Soledad, some seven hours (175kms) by boat from Puerto Maldonado, and claims to have doubled the wildlife count of the Tambopata river area, including several monkey species, giant otters and black caiman, as well as macaw licks close by. Their well-built new lodge boasts eight comfortable hexagonal bungalows built from polished hardwood with palm roofs, all set in a clearing surrounded by giant rainforest trees and illuminated by soft electric lighting (re-charging point available). The same company also owns a camp at Tipishca, closer to Puerto Maldonado and en route to the ARCC lodge. Prices start at around $200 for three nights, but they suggest you call or email to discuss costs.

Bahuaja Research Centre ☎/℻082/573348. A small lodge on the Río Tambopata, roughly a couple of hours by boat from Puerto Maldonado, and aimed at the less well-heeled travel-

ler, this is fairly basic – toilets and showers are shared – but enjoys a pleasant setting. Visits go to Tres Chimbales and Lago Sachavacayoc, with guided tours in English and Spanish, plus there are extensive trails in the surrounding forest. The research side of the operation is associated with the UK organization Greenforce. From $165 per person for four days and three nights.

Eco Amazonia Lodge Portal de Panes 109, Oficina 6, Cusco ☎084/236159, ℻225068, ℮ecolodge@chasqui.unsaac.edu.pe; Av Larco 1083, Oficina 408, Miraflores, Lima ☎/℻01/2422708. Less than 2hr downriver of Puerto Maldonado, this large establishment offers basic bungalows and dormitories. While the area abounds in stunning oxbow lakes, it can't claim the variety of flora and fauna of the Tambopata-Candamo Reserved Zone, yet it is recommended for birdwatching, plus it has swamp-forest platforms and is the only lodge in the area with tree-canopy access. Packages usually include visits to Lago Sandoval, about 30min upriver, plus organized visits can be made to the Palma Real community (though this is often anticlimactic and of dubious value to both tribe and tourist) and a monkey island. From $40–60 per person per night according to length of stay.

Explorandes San Fernando 320, Miraflores, Lima ☎01/4450532 or in Cusco ☎084/238380, ⓦwww.explorandes.com. A veteran company operating whitewater rafting expeditions, including a twelve-day trip starting out from Puno by road, then travelling down through cloud forest, and finally rafting through class 3 to 5 rapids along the Río Tambopata to Puerto Maldonado, where the last night is spent in a lodge (note they don't operate a lodge themselves, but select one according to the needs and interests of their cleints). From $1500 per person, for a minimum of four people.

Explorer's Inn Plateros 365, Cusco ☎084/235342; or in the Peruvian Safaris Lima office, Alcanfores 459, Miraflores ☎01/447888 or 4474761, ⒻＰ2418427, ⓦwww.peruviansafaris.com; office in Puerto Maldonado at Av Fitzcarrald 136 ☎082/572078. In the Tambopata-Candamo Reserved Zone, 58km (about 3hr) in a motorized *canoa* upriver from Puerto Maldonado, this is a large, well-organized lodge where research has contributed towards building a world-record list of species (580 birds and 1230 butterflies). Spanish- or English-speaking guides are available (boots are provided for jungle walks), and there are excellent displays, mostly in English, about rainforest ecology, plus there are radio links to the outside world. Food is good, and accommodation is generally in twin rooms with private bath. The price includes full board as well as airport transfers, with inclusive expeditions to a nearby macaw salt-lick (*colpa*) – generally requiring one night camping out – plus there's a superb network of well-marked jungle trails. From $180 per person for three days and nights; enquire about rates for special-interest visitors (eg ornithologists).

Inkaterra Reserva Amazonica Andalucia 174, Lima ☎01/6100404, ⓦwww.inkaterra.com; or, in Cusco at Plazoleta Las Nazarenas 113 ☎084/245315. One of the Peruvian jungle's most luxurious and stylish lodges, located an hour and a half downstream from Puerto Maldonado on the Rio Madre de Dios, this is a great place for a gentle introduction to the wild. The main lodge building is truly palatial and also contains the restaurant, bar and lounge areas. Accommodation is in exceptionally comfortable, native-style bungalows on stilts off the ground, with fantastic showers and an atmosphere conducive to a quiet appreciation of the rainforest environment. Inkaterra offer a varied menu of half- or full-day excursions including walking the trails of the reserve with competent guides; exploring the rainforest by night; visits to Lago Sandoval, a jungle farm and

a native community; fishing and bird-watching in the nearby Tambopata Reserve; and, in Puerto Maldonado itself, a visit to their impressive Butterfly House. The lodge is surrounded by its own protected rainforest area and boasts this part of Peru's only canopy walkway. The food and service is top class and there are plenty of nice touches, such as natural soaps, sandals and provision of ample towels. A swimming pool is planned for 2009. Costs range from $285 to almost $500 for three days and two nights.

Inotawa Expeditions Fonavi J9, Puerto Maldonado (daily 9–11am & 4–5pm) ☎082/572511; or Lima 01/4674560, ⓦwww.inotawaexpeditions.com. Located on the Río Tambopata quite close to the start of the Bahuaja-Sonene National Park, Inotawa operate a nice lodge in a good location, offer expeditions to Colpa Colorado, a macaw and animal salt-lick a further 8hr into the forest from their lodge. Prices start at around $150 for three days/two nights and $400 for five nights, but the minimum group required is six.

Libertador Tambopata Lodge C Nueva Baja 432, Cusco ☎084/245695, ⓦwww.tambopata-lodge.com. Located in the Tambopata-Candamo Reserved Zone, 12km up the Río Tambopata from the *Explorer's Inn* (and nearly 4hr from Puerto Maldonado), the lodge has comfortable, individual cabin-style accommodation and offers excellent tours of the forest, in Spanish and English. It's located quite close to a community of *colonos*, some of whom farm while others pan for gold. Trips include a visit to Lago Condenado and sometimes Lago Sandoval, plus the Chuncho *colpa* by arrangement. From $170 per person for three days/two nights.

Mejia Hospedaje ☎082/571428. On the shores of the popular Lago Sandoval, this is a rustic-style hostal rather than a lodge, but perfect for canoe exploration of the lake. It's rarely full, so it's fine to just turn up here by canoe from Puerto Maldonado without prior arrangement (get the boatman to drop you off on the trail from the Tambopata riverbank). One of two accommodation options on the lake, this is an expanded family home with ten doubles and basic, shared toilet facilities. Prices come in at $18.20 per person per day (dependent on season and open to negotiation), including food.

Picaflor Research Centre ⒺＰpicaflor_rc@yahoo.com. Located on the Tambopata River some 78km from Puerto Maldonado, this place is run by Britsh woman Laurel Hanna and her family. *Picaflor* is relatively new and has its own volunteer programme as well as offering research and tourism stays. Prices are in the region of $45–55 per person per day.

Posada Amazonas Lodge, Refugio Amazonas and Tambopata Research Centre contact through Rainforest Expeditions, Aramburu 166, 4B, Lima 18 ☏01/4218347, ⊛www.perunature.com. This company is hard to better anywhere in the world for the quality of its facilities and guides; these are arguably the region's best selection of lodges, with the three located at different stages along the Rio Tambopata. They also maintain excellent relationships with local communities. The nearest of these lodges to Puerto Maldonado, the *Posada Amazonas*, is part-owned by the Ese Eja indigenous community of Infierno. It's possible to organise trips combining this comfortable lodge with the more remote *Refugio Amazonas* and the most remote of all the region's lodges - the TRC (*Tambopata Research Centre*). As an organisaton very hot on wildlife research and conservation across all its lodges, Rainforest Expeditions have combined, in TRC, a very comfortable new lodge, built in 2005, in an area of great bird diversity (including good populations of primates and large mammals), with serious and long-term research at the world's biggest macaw *colpa*, the Colpa Colorado. A minimum of six days is recommended for complete tours. The intermediate newer lodge, *Refugio Amazonas*, is a truly splendid mix of traditional hut design and extravagant architectural beauty, with 24 spacious rooms with large comfortable beds under mosquito nets opening out onto the forest, plus a great dining room and busy bar. The lodge is close to two lakes where otters are sometimes spotted, and also has an engaging educational trail for kids. Activities wise, it offers kayaking on the Tambopata river (no previous experience required), canopy climbing up emergent trees (training offered), forest mountain-biking trails (start just 10min from the lodge). It's also possible to arrange a bike ride back from the community of Infierno, where the company's river port is based, back to Puerto Maldonado along the dirt track road (2 hr). From $90 per day per person.

Sandoval Lodge InkaNatura, Manuel Bañon 461, San Isidro, Lima ☏01/4402022, ⊛www.inkanatura

.com, or C Ricardo Palma, J1 Urb Santa Monica, Cusco ☏084/255255. On the shores of Lago Sandoval, and usually accessed by canoe, this is the only lodge offering regular trips to this zone. It's medium-sized and features one large communal building as a bar and dining room, plus it boasts electricity and hot water. Most groups spend time on the lake or explore the small, well-trodden surrounding trail system. Guides speak several languages, including English. From $70 per person per day, depending on size of group, nature of visit and length of stay.

Tambopata Tours León de Velarde 171, Puerto Maldonado ☏082/571320, ⊛www.tambopata-tours.com. This company do not own a lodge but customise trips, selecting lodges and guides to suit client's pockets and interests. They will help organise jungle camping, lodge stays, birdwatching, fishing trips and visits to communities, the local canopy walkway or even *ayahuasca* ceremonies.

Tierra Peru ☏01/992912703, ℮indra396 @hotmail.com, ⊛www.tierraperu.8m.com. This operator, based in Lima, is not a lodge as such, but offers excellent and customised services for wildlife watching, photo-safaris, birdwatching and trekking with a specialist guide: stunning trips (with regular sightings of jaguar, harpy eagles, hummingbirds, penguins and dolphins) in the Amazon region, including Madre de Dios, the cloud forest, highlands, Pacific Ocean and elsewhere, are led by Sandra Llontop, an experienced naturalist guide. Private and fixed departures.

Wasai Lodge owned by the *Wasai* hotel in Puerto Maldonado (see p.511 for contact details). Four hours upriver from Puerto Maldonado, this relatively new and smallish lodge is set in the forest, with a pleasant jungle bar and dining area. Spanish- and English-speaking guides are available, with 15km of trails in the vicinity plus trips to the Chuncho *colpa* on request. Usually from $360 per person for four days and three nights, but sometimes offered with promotional discounts at around $175, including a visit to Lago Sandoval plus the last night at the *Wasai* (avoiding the early morning start); $500 plus for seven days/six nights, including a visit to the *colpa*.

Independent travel

Travelling independently can be rewarding, though note that most of the major river trips (including Lago Valencia) require visitors to obtain **permission** from the Captain's Office in Puerto Maldonado (see p.513) – though boatmen and guides generally do this and also organize payment of entry fees for you at the **INRENA office** (Dirección Sub-regional Agraria Madre de Dios, Av 28 de Julio 482, Puerto Maldonado; or, in Lima: Calle 17, 335 Urb El Palomar, San Isidro, Lima ☏01/224-3298, ℮comunicaciones@inrena.gob.pe).

The Manu Biosphere Reserve

Encompassing almost two million hectares of virgin cloud- and rainforest on the foothills of the eastern Andes, the Manu area was created in 1973 as a national park, and then elevated to the status of Biosphere Reserve by UNESCO in 1977. In 1987 it became a World Natural Heritage Site. About half the size of Switzerland, the **Manu Biosphere Reserve** covers a total of 1,881,200 hectares of relatively pristine rainforest, from crystalline cloudforest streams and waterfalls down to slow-moving, chocolate-brown rivers in the dense lowland jungle – a uniquely varied environment. The only permanent residents within this vast area are the teeming forest wildlife; a few virtually uncontacted native groups who have split off from their major tribal units (Yaminahuas, Amahuacas and Machiguenga); the park guards; and the scientists at a biological research station situated just inside the park on the beautiful Lago Cocha Cashu, where flocks of macaws pass the time cracking open Brazil nuts with their powerful, highly adapted beaks.

For **flora and fauna**, the Manu is pretty much unbeatable in South America, home to 20,000 vascular plant types (one five-square-kilometre area was found to contain 1147 species of vascular plants, almost as many as in the whole of Great Britain), with over 5000 flowering plants, 1200 species of butterfly, 1000 types of bird, 200 kinds of mammal and an unknown quantity of reptiles and insects. Rich in macaw salt-licks, otter lagoons and prowling jaguars, there are thirteen species of monkey and seven species of macaw in Manu, and it still contains other species in serious danger of extinction, such as the giant otter and the black caiman (*Melanosuchus niger*).

The reserve is divided into three zones. By far the largest, **Zone A** is the core zone, the **National Park**, which is strictly preserved in its natural state. **Zone B** is a Buffer Zone, generally known as the **Reserved Zone** and set aside mainly for controlled research and tourism. **Zone C** is the Transitional or **Cultural Zone**, an area of human settlement for controlled traditional use. Accessible only by boat, any expedition to Manu is very much in the hands of the gods, because of the temperamental jungle environment; the region experiences a rainy season from December to March, and is best visited between May and August when it's much drier, although at that time the temperatures often exceed 30°C (86°F).

The highlight of most organized visits to Manu is the trail network and lakes of **Cocha Salvador** (the largest of Manu's oxbows, at 3.5km long) and **Cocha Otorongo**, both bountiful jungle areas rich in animal, water and birdlife. The latter is best known for the **giant otters** (see box, p.521) that live there; because of this,

Otorongo otters

The **giant otters** of Lago Otorongo in Manu National Park are one of the world's most endangered species, and contact with people has to be minimized for their safety and long-term conservation. They are also bio-indicators of the environment, since they only live where there is clean, healthy water and a wide choice of fish, and so conservation of their rainforest environment is of primary importance. Only the oldest female of the group is mated with, so reproduction is very slow – the "queen" otters only have two or three cubs a year, usually around October, which can be expected to live for around thirty years. The top-ranking male otters are responsible for defending the group and do very little fishing, taking the catch from younger males instead.

Although they appear friendly as they play in their large family groups, they can be very aggressive, able to keep jaguars at bay and kill caimans who approach their lakeside nesting holes, which they mark by mixing male urine with clay at the entrance.

▲ White caiman, Manu National Park

canoeing is not permitted, but there is a floating platform which can be manoeuvred to observe the otters fishing and playing from a safe distance (though your guide has to book a time for this): 30–50m is good enough to observe and photograph them, though as this is Manu's most popular tourist area, you're likely to meet other groups and there can be severe competition for access to the platform. Other wildlife to look out for includes the plentiful **caimans**, including the two- to three-metre white alligators and the rarer three- to five-metre black ones, and you can usually see several species of **monkey** (including dusky titis, woolly monkeys, red howlers, brown capuchins and the larger spider monkeys – known locally as *maquisapas*). Sometimes big mammals such as **capybara** or **white-lipped peccaries** (called *sajinos* in Peru) also lurk in the undergrowth.

The flora of Manu is as outstanding as its fauna. Huge **cedar trees** can be seen along the trails, covered in hand-like vines climbing up their vast trunks (most of the cedars were taken out of here between 1930 and 1963, before it became a protected area). The giant **catahua trees**, many over 150 years old, are traditionally the preferred choice for making dugout canoes – and some are large enough to make three or four – though second choice is the **lagarto tree**.

Just east of Zone B, but often visited in combination with it or with Zone C, is the **Manu Wildlife Centre**, a comfortable lodge some 90min downriver from Boca Manu (see p.526) by motorized dugout. Owned by Manu Expeditions (see p.527) and the non-profit Selva Sur Conservation Group, it's located on privately owned rainforest and is built of the same sustainable local materials that the native Machiguenga Indians use – bamboo, wood, and palm-frond roofing – and all rooms are screened with mosquito nets. It operates close to a superb salt-lick where small parrots and larger, more colourful macaws can be seen, and claims to be strategically located in an area of forest that has the highest diversity of microhabitats in the Manu; *tierra-firme* (lowland forest that doesn't get flooded), transitional flood plain, *varzea* and bamboo forest are all found close by, and an astounding 530 bird species have been recorded in one year alone. The Blanquillo macaw-and-parrot salt-lick is only thirty minutes away by river, with floating blinds to access the wildlife attracted here. About an hour's walk through the forest there's also a large *colpa* where tapirs and Brocket deer regularly come. The centre also features mobile canopy towers, making it possible to see more birds and even monkeys; access to these is by rope and harness, but there's also a static canopy platform with a spiral stairway.

The only viable way of **visiting Manu** is by joining an organized **tour** through one of the main Cusco agents, which is safer and generally cheaper than doing it yourself. However, you can travel independently as far as Boca Manu, but unless you've secured a highly exclusive special **permit** (see box above), you then have to head away from the reserve on one of the canoes that go most weeks (cargo and river permitting) to Puerto Maldonado. For this you'll need to be well stocked and prepared for a rough voyage of several days – plus a few more if you have to hitch along the way. The only significant settlement en route is **Boca Colorado** at the confluence of the Ríos Colorado and Madre de Dios, a small gold-miner's service town full of vermin, human and animal. Remember, this region is well off the beaten tourist trail and is relatively wild territory, populated by *colonos*, indigenous Indians and even **smugglers and terrorists**.

Approaching the reserve

Manu Biosphere Reserve is more easily reached from **Cusco** than it is from Puerto Maldonado. Flying direct to Boca Manu (see p.526) from Cusco will dramatically affect the price and the amount of time you get in the reserve (it's only a 30–45min flight but costs from $400), and twin-engined planes can be chartered from the airport in Cusco. Most people, however, travel there on transport organized by their tour operators; otherwise, **buses** operated by Gallito de las Rocas (Av Manco Capac 105, Cusco; ☏084/277255) go to Pilcopata and usually beyond to Salvación at about 10am most Mondays and Fridays ($7; a 10–14hr journey depending on road conditions). **Trucks**, generally loaded to the brim with beer, fuel and passengers, leave Cusco from Avenida Huascar, and some from the Coliseo, every Monday, Wednesday, Friday and Sunday for Shintuya ($7.50; an 18–25hr journey in good conditions). All of the necessary **provisions and equipment** (see box on p.489) should be bought in Cusco. Don't forget to bring a sturdy pair of binoculars for getting the best out of the wildlife you will inevitably see.

The first four- to six-hour stage is by road to the attractive town of **Paucartambo** (see p.308), over stupendous narrow roads with fine panoramas of the region's largest glaciated **mountain** of Ausungate, a major *apu* – or god – for the Incas and also the locals today. From Paucartambo onwards, the precipitous and gravelly

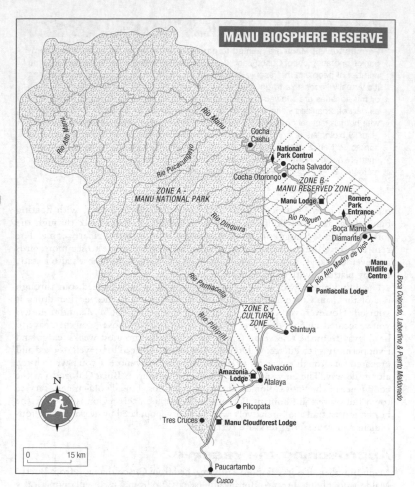

MANU BIOSPHERE RESERVE

Río Alto Manu

Río Manu

Cocha
Cashu

Río Pucacungayo

National
Park Control

Cocha Salvador

Cocha Otorongo

ZONE A -
MANU NATIONAL PARK

ZONE B -
MANU RESERVED ZONE

Manú Lodge

Romero
Park
Entrance

Río Dinguira

Río Pinguen

Boca Manu
Diamante

Río Alto Madre de Dios

Manu
Wildlife
Centre

Río Pantiacolla

Pantiacolla Lodge

Río Piñipiñi

ZONE C -
CULTURAL
ZONE

Shintuya

N

Amazonia
Lodge

Salvación

Atalaya

Pilcopata

Tres Cruces

Manu Cloudforest Lodge

0   15 km

Paucartambo

Cusco

Boca Colorado, Labertino & Puerto Maldonado

nature of the road down through the cloud forest to the navigable sections of the Río Alto Madre de Dios means that access is supposedly limited to one direction per day, except Sunday, when it's a free-for-all. You can travel down on Monday, Wednesday and Friday, and back up on Tuesday, Thursday and Saturday.

It's another 30km to the turn off to **Tres Cruces** (see p.310), at the reserve's southern tip; from here the road winds down, at times along narrow stretches of quite bad track with drops of well over 300m only a few feet away. Somehow the beauty overrides the scariness for most people, and a surprising amount of **wildlife** can usually be spotted as the track continues downhill – Andean guans, mountain motmots, woodcreepers, oropendulas and the brilliant-red *gallo de las rocas* (the national bird of Peru) can all be seen. Of course, you're more likely to get a glimpse of these if you're travelling with a good guide who has a well-trained eye.

Exploring the reserve

The first settlement you come to in the high jungle is **Chontachaca**, which is Quechua for "Chonta Bridge" (*chonta* being the common hardwood palm whose wood is used throughout the Peruvian Amazon for Indian bows and arrow points). Vehicles rarely stop here, and shortly beyond you pass through the slightly larger **Patria**, another frontier-type village, where coca is grown in some quantities. Turkeys, pigs and children play beside the road and the town's grassed-over, neglected concrete fountain says a lot about this place, which is more noted for its cockfighting fiestas than anything else. Around here the jungle is being cleared for cash crops and so much vegetation is being burned that planes are occasionally unable to land in Cusco because of the rising smoke.

At the next town, **PILCOPATA**, the road crosses a river over a new steel bridge; to the right, a rickety old wooden one is left to decay in memory of a truck that destroyed it and fell into the water in the mid-1990s. Most buses and trucks stop here for the night, and there's a basic **hotel** (❶), a few small shops and a simple market. The road then skirts the Río Alto Madre de Dios, which eventually merges with the Río Manu to form the great Río Madre de Dios. The forest around here hides some fascinating **petroglyphs**, etched onto boulders by Indians before the Spanish arrived. However, these are along the Río Pishiyura, hidden in the restricted area of Manu and reported to be protected by a still largely unacculturated group of Mashco-Piro Indians, who shoot arrows at intruders. This is also one of the areas where the legendary Inca city of gold – **El Dorado**, or **Paititi** – is reputed to lie.

The following day takes you on to the small riverside settlement of **Atalaya** (10–12hr from Cusco); some tours cross the river to spend the night at an old hacienda which has been converted into an attractive tourist **lodge** – *Amazonia Lodge* (❺, half board), 600m above sea level on the edge of the cloud forest. The food here is excellent and it's one of the few Peruvian jungle lodges to have solar-heated showers; the owners can be contacted in Cusco (Ramiro Yabar Calderon, C Matara 334 ☎084/231370, ✉amazonia@correo.dnet.com.pe). They also offer full board and excursions in the region at a higher price, and frequently work with Manu Expeditions (see p.527). There are also a few **restaurants** in town.

Twenty minutes down the road from Atalaya, at the pueblo of **Salvación**, 28km before Shintuya, the Manu Biosphere Reserve has an office where your guide will usually be expected to show his permits. There are also a couple of rough **hostels** and one or two places to get some **food** – a bowl of jungle soup or, if you're lucky, fish with manioc. Trucks, mostly carrying timber, go from here to Cusco every Tuesday, Thursday and Saturday. Two hours beyond Atalaya, at **Shintuya**, the road finishes. The **Dominican Mission** here has been in existence for forty years, though recently many of the indigenous members have left after making good money with their chainsaws – some of them now own trucks to facilitate the supply of timber out to Cusco and beyond. There's no hotel, but there's no problem about **camping** if you ask permission – the best spot is beside the small stream that enters the main river (the water is cleaner here). Keep a watchful eye on your baggage, as Shintuya also has a sizeable transient population, passing to and from the gold-mining areas downriver. If you're travelling independently, all that remains to do is to seek out a canoe and a reliable boatman/guide, and if you've brought some of your own fuel to bargain with, it should be relatively easy to find a decent deal at the mission; the Moscosa family (especially Cesar, Pepe and Darwin) are reliable guides. Boats from Shintuya cost from around $500 for a week (though it can be double this if it's a busy season); if it's big enough, and most are, the boat can be shared between as many as seven or eight, and the price of an extra week isn't that much more. Remember that things happen on a different timescale in the Peruvian jungle, so get the boat organized as soon as you arrive, and try to make an early start the next day. If it can be arranged, it's a good idea to take a surplus, small dugout canoe for entering smaller channels and lagoons. Alternatively, you may be able to catch one of the cargo boats prepared to take passengers direct to Boca Colorado for around $30.

Downriver, in a *lancha* with outboard motor, it's half a day down the Alto Madre de Dios to **Boca Manu**, a mere 300m above sea level and little more than a small settlement of a few families living near the airstrip. There are no hostels here (people do **camp** on the other side of the river, but these are mostly visiting Indians or tour groups) and while there is a small shop here (prices double those in Cusco, with no guarantee of supply), the population mainly serves the gold-mining settlements downstream towards Puerto Maldonado. Close by is the native Piro community of **Diamante**, responsible for managing the **airstrip**, a major link to Cusco. In 1983, when it was controlled by cocaine smugglers, this was the scene of Hollywood-style drama, when an unmarked Colombian plane overloaded with cocaine crashed into the vegetation at the end of the airstrip. The gang leader had his men torch the plane after the crash; its remains are still there in the undergrowth. The Peruvian army later regained control of the strip, but now the Piro make a little money from each flight that uses it and sell good, cheap artesania at the small hut that serves as the airport terminal.

Organized tours of the Manu Biosphere

There are quite a few **organized tours** competing for travellers who want to visit Manu. Many are keen to keep the impact of tourism to a minimum, which means limiting the number of visits per year (it's already running well into the thousands). However, they do vary quite a bit in quality of guiding, level of comfort and price range. If you go with one of the companies listed below, you can generally be confident that they have a good reputation both for the way they treat their tourists and the delicate ecology of the rainforest itself.

Caiman Plateros 359, Cusco ☎084/254041, ℱ254042, ℮explorcaiman@terra.com.pe. A relatively new company, but with some experienced and professional guides, Caiman specialize in Manu, basically offering four days and three nights from around $300. Their six- to nine-day tours are better, since they do include exploring within the Manu reserve itself, including Lago Otorongo, with a chance of spotting the giant river otter family that lives there (more in the region of $500–600).

Casa Machiguenga Contactable through Manu Expeditions (see opposite), this is a lodge rather than a tour operator. Owned by the Machiguenga Indian communities of Tayakome and Yombebato (but established by a German NGO as the Machiguenga are still undergoing a capacity-building programme), it's pretty rustic, with accommodation in huts, albeit with modern conveniences such as hot water and showers available; $35–45 per night per person.

Ecological Adventures Manu Plateros 356, Cusco ☎084/261640, ℱ225562, ℮manuadventures@terra.com.pe, ℗www.manuadventures.com. Jungle-trip specialists and one of the first operators running trips into Manu, with their own vehicles, boats and multilingual guides. Their camping-based tours are cheaper than most, with the eight-day option going in and

out by bus, but they also offer shorter options which go in by bus and out by plane. Tour-only price for five-night trip from $580.

Expediciones Vilca Plateros 359, Cusco ☎/ℱ084/253773, ℗www.manuvilcaperu.com. Manu specialists, *Vilca* have a good reputation and their guides are well informed, taking eco-tourism seriously. Their eight-day tour includes camping in Zone B, plus a visit to the macaw lick at Blanquillo as well as three nights in *albergues*, from around $600–790, depending on whether you take a bus or plane in. They also offer five- and six-day trips, including flights to and/or from Boca Manu from around $720.

InkaNatura Travel C Ricardo Palma, J1 Urb. Santa Monica, Cusco ☎084/255255, ℗www.inkanatura.com; or in Lima via InkaNatura Travel, Manuel Bañon 461, San Isidro, Lima ☎01/4402022. InkaNatura (the in-house travel agency of Selva Sur, a Cusco-based non-profit conservation group) offer customized travel, from four to five days, operating from the Manu Wildlife Centre, where one of the nearby highlights is the world's largest tapir salt-lick. They also accommodate people at the *Cock of the Rock Lodge* (owned and operated principally), located 6hr by road from Cusco, in one of the best cloud-forest locations for birdwatching.

Prices are in the range $1050–1150, and discounts available to groups of six or more.

Manu Expeditions C Humberto Vidal Unda G-5, Segunda Etapa, Urb. Magisterial, Cusco ☎084/226671, ⊛www.ManuExpeditions.com. One of the best and the most responsible companies, run by a British ornithologist. They offer three- to nine-day camping expeditions into Zone B and to the Manu Wildlife Centre, with solar-powered radio communications and av interpretation, as well as top-quality service and English-speaking guides. They also offer air and overland transfers to Boca Manu (they have their own overland transport), and food, beds (or riverside campsite) and bird-blinds are all included. Prices range from $700–2000,

with discounts available to South American Explorers' Club members.

Pantiacolla Tours C Sapphi 554, Cusco ☎084/238323, ⊛www.pantiacolla.com. A company with a growing reputation for serious eco-adventure tours. Their cheapest option is also the longest, a nine-day tour that takes groups in and out by bus and boat, while the more expensive five- to seven-day trips go in by road and out by plane from Boca Manu. They have an excellent lodge on the Río Alto Madre de Dios at Itahuania, and their tours into Zone B are based in tents at prepared campsites. Prices start at around $700, with discounts available to South American Explorers' Club members.

Onward travel to Puerto Maldonado

It is possible, if you are adventurous, to follow an unregulated downriver route with few facilities from Boca Manu to Puerto Maldonado. Although you're more likely to have already found a boat going downriver from Shintuya, many will also pick up at Boca Manu for the one-day journey downstream ($10) to the sleazy gold-mining frontier town of **Boca Colorado** (also known as **Banco Minero**), at the mouth of the Río Colorado. Boca Colorado has a number of very basic **hotels**, but all have rats running around – they can be heard scampering across wooden-planked floorboards when the town generator goes off and the settlement's televisions fade into silence at 11pm every night. There are also a few simple **restaurants** serving surprisingly tasty food. It's possible to **camp** but, again, don't let your gear out of your sight. From here it's at least one more day ($15 as a passenger in boats going in the same direction, depending on the speed of the boat) on to **Labernito** – from where it's a two-hour bus ride to Puerto Maldonado.

Río Urubamba and around

Traditionally the home of the Matsiguenga and Piro Indians, the **Río Urubamba** rolls down from the Inca's Sacred Valley to the humid lower Andean slopes around the town of **Quillabamba**. The river remains unnavigable for another 80km or so, with regular buses following a dirt road that continues deeper down into the jungle via the settlement of **Kiteni**, where the Urubamba river becomes navigable, to the even smaller frontier settlement of **Ivochote**. From here on, the river becomes the main means of transport, through the Amazon Basin right to the Atlantic, interrupted only by the impressive **Pongo de Mainique** – whitewater rapids, just a few hours downstream from Ivochote. These rapids are generally too dangerous to pass between November and March.

Unlike the Manu Biosphere Reserve, most of the Urubamba has been colonized as far as the *pongo*, and much of it beyond has suffered more or less permanent exploitation of one sort or another for over a hundred years (rubber, cattle, oil and, more recently, gas). Consequently, this isn't really the river for experiencing pristine virgin forest, but it is nevertheless an exciting and remote challenge and a genuine example of what's going on in the Amazon today. Far fewer tour companies operate in the Río Urubamba region than do in Manu or Madre de Dios, but as the political situation continues to improve, and entrepreneurial optimism revives further around Cusco, it seems likely that more adventure tours will become available in the lower Urubamba and that the area will open up further to organized river-rafting and forest-trekking.

Quillabamba

A rapidly expanding market town, growing fat on profits from coffee, tropical fruits, chocolate and, to a certain extent perhaps, the proceeds of cocaine production, **QUILLABAMBA** is the only Peruvian jungle town that's easily accessible by road from Cusco, and the main attraction here for tourists is a quick look at the selva. Coming from Cusco, the initial section of road is a narrow gravel track along precipitous cliffs, notoriously dangerous in the rainy season, but after a few hours, having travelled over the magical Abra Malaga – the main pass on this road – the slow descent towards Chaullay starts. From here on, you'll see jungle vegetation beginning to cover the valley sides; the weather gets steadily warmer and the plant life thickens as you gradually descend into the Urubamba Valley.

Your first sight of the town, which tops a high cliff, is of old tin roofs, adobe outskirts and coca leaves drying in the gardens. It's a pleasant enough place to relax, and you can get all the gear you need for going deeper into the jungle; the **market** sells all the necessities like machetes, fish-hooks, food and hats. Just ten minutes' walk from here, the **Plaza de Armas**, with its shady fountain statue of the town's little-known benefactor, Don Martín Pio Concha, is the other major landmark. Other than that, though about 4km away, the once attractive river beach at Sambaray is a bit of a dump these days; much nicer and quite a popular resort is the nearby waterfall area of **Siete Tinjas**.

Practicalities

The main town is a stiff climb above the river, though **buses** from Calle Huascar in Cusco terminate by the market on the Plaza Grau side of town; **colectivos** from Calle General Buendio, by the San Pedro railway station in Cusco, or the plaza in Ollantaytambo, also finish their journeys near the market in Quillabamba, as do trucks and *colectivos* (best picked up from the plaza in Ollantaytambo). Buses back to Cusco leave Quillabamba from the market or block 5 of San Martin several times a day.

For **accommodation**, the *Hostal Quillabamba*, Av Prolongación Miguel Grau 590 (℡084/281369; ❸–❹), very close to the market, offers modern, comfortable rooms and also has a car park, swimming pool, hot water and a good restaurant. Just around the corner, the *Hostal Señor de Torrechayoc*, Av Grau 548 (℡084/281553; ❸), has modern, clean rooms with or without bath. The *Hotel Don Carlos*, Jr Libertad 546 (℡084/281371; ❸), just up from the Plaza de Armas, is cosy, friendly and popular with Peruvians. Rooms are smart and the place has a garden courtyard; it's also a good place to make connections for organized (though relatively costly) overland trips to Kiteni, and river trips onwards from there. Along the first block of Jirón Cusco are some very inexpensive little **restaurants**, such as the *Restaurant Los Amantes* and the *Restaurant La Estrella*, both of which serve decent set meals including the usual *estofado de res*, *caldo de gallina* (hen soup) or chicken and chips dishes. *Don Cebas*, Jr Espinar 235, on the Plaza de Armas, serves snacks and drinks.

The Banco de Credito, on Libertad, is your best bet for **changing dollars** and travellers' cheques; failing that, try the Banco Continental, on the first block of Jirón España. Sometimes *cambistas* will change dollars cash on the street outside these banks, or in the better hotels. **Telephone** calls can be made from Telefónica del Peru, Bolognesi 237–249, or there's a smaller company at Jr Cusco 242.

Kiteni and the Pongo de Mainique

By the time you reach **KITENI**, five to eight hours deeper into the jungle, the Río Urubamba is quite wide and, with the forest all around, the valley is hotter, more exotic and much greener than before. Still a small *poblado*, until over twenty-five years ago Kiteni was a small Matsiguenga Indian village.

To get to Kiteni and Ivochote from Quillabamba, **buses** and **colectivos** ($10–15 per person) leave from Ricardo Palma, close to the Plaza Grau, every day from 8 to 10am. With the importance of the massive gas fields being exploited just below the Pongo, there is more river and road traffic these days and the end of the road, or jungle frontier, is constantly moving, if still keeping more or less to the course of the Urubamba river.

Pongo de Mainique

Kiteni's main draw – beyond its small jungle-settlement atmosphere – is as a staging point for the awe-inspiring **Pongo de Mainique**, possibly the most dangerous 2km of (barely) navigable river in the entire Amazonian system, made famous by Michael Palin in his TV travel documentary. The road from Quillabamba towards the Pongo passes through Kiteni but ends a few hours further on at the village of Ivochote. Travelling down the river, just before you reach the *pongo* there's a community at **San Idriato**. The people here, known as the Israelites, founded their village around a biblical sect; the men leave their hair long and, like Rastas, they twist it up under expandable peaked caps. Across the Urubamba from San Idriato the small community of **Shinguriato**, upstream from the Río Yuyato mouth, is the official entrance to the *pongo* itself.

Tours to the Pongo

There are boats going down river through the **Pongo** most days between May and October, and it's often possible to pay for a ride on one. Other people may approach you in Quillabamba or Kiteni for a trip to the *pongo* and perhaps a little camping and fishing; the merits of these are entirely dependent upon the price you have to pay and the confidence you have in the guide. **Tours** down the Urubamba to the *pongo* can sometimes be arranged with one of the Cusco adventure tour operators detailed below. If there are enough of you, though, it might be more economical to **rent a canoe and boatman** (preferably with a powerful outboard motor) for a couple of days; this will cost from around $100 a day, including fuel. To arrange any of these options you'll do best hanging around the port at Kiteni, on the beach behind the *guardia*'s huts, or asking in one of the few bars and cafés.

If you want to take an organised tour or whitewater raft trip down through the Pongo, it's best to organize this in Cusco with one of the rafting companies (see p.264). To go downriver **without renting a boat** or taking an organized trip requires a great leap of faith and confidence in the universe as well as being at the dock early every morning and asking every boat that leaves if it's going to the *pongo*. Boats do take goods and people to the lower Urubamba communities, and are often more than willing to take extra passengers for a relatively small fee. Have all your baggage with you in case one is going, but check whether it's coming back up. This way a return trip shouldn't cost more than about $40–50; if you want to go all the way to Sepahua (where there's an airstrip with weekly airtaxi connections to Satipo and the Central Selva), expect to pay from around $60 one-way. You may have to wait a few days until there's one going all the way, but this is much easier than going hungry on a desolate beach somewhere below the *pongo*. Boats tend to arrive from downstream in the afternoon and it's often worth checking with them when they intend to go back.

The rapids are **dangerous** at any time of year, and virtually impossible to pass during the rainy season (Nov–March). As you get nearer, you can see a forested mountain range directly in front of you; the river speeds up, and as you get closer, it's possible to make out the great cut made through the range over the millennia by the powerful Urubamba. Then, before you realize, the craft is whisked into a long canyon with soaring rocky cliffs on either side: gigantic volcanic boulders look like wet monsters of molten steel; imaginary stone faces can be seen shimmering under cascades; and the danger of the *pongo* slips by almost unnoticed as the walls of the **canyon** will absorb all your attention. The main hazard is actually a drop of about 2m, which is seen and then crossed in a split second. Now and then boats are overturned at this dangerous drop, usually those that try the run in the rainy season – although even then natives somehow manage to come upstream in small, non-motorized dugouts.

The northern selva: Iquitos and Río Amazonas

At the "island" city of **Iquitos**, by far the largest and most exciting of Peru's jungle towns, there are few sights as magnificent as the **Río Amazonas**. Its tributaries start well up in the Andes, and when they join together several hours upstream from the town, the river is already several kilometres wide, though a mere 116m above sea level. The town's actual location, only 104m above sea level yet thousands of miles from the ocean and surrounded in all directions by brilliant green forest and hemmed in by the maze of rivers, streams and lagoons, makes for a stunning entry to the northern jungle.

Most people visit Iquitos briefly, before moving on into the **rainforest**, but wisely, few travellers actually avoid the place entirely. It's a buzzing, cosmopolitan tourist town, connected to the rest of the world by river and air only. Iquitos is the kind of place that lives up to all your expectations of a jungle town, from its elegant reminders of the rubber-boom years to the atmospheric shantytown suburb of **Puerto Belén**, one of Werner Herzog's main locations for his film *Fitzcarraldo*, where you can buy almost anything, from fuel to *ayahuasca*.

Tourist facilities here have developed gradually over the last thirty years – the town has a friendly **café- and club-scene**, interesting **museums** and beautiful turn-of-the-century buildings, and the surrounding region has some great island and lagoon **beaches**, a range of easy excursions into the rainforest and the possibility of continuing down the Amazon into Colombia or Brazil. The area has also become something of a **spiritual focus**, particularly for gringos seeking a visionary experience with one of the many local shamans who utilize the sacred and powerful hallucinogenic *ayahuasca* vine in their religious psycho-healing sessions (see p.549).

The carnival known as **Omagua** (local dialect for "lowland swamp") has grown vigourously over recent years and now involves not only townspeople, but hundreds of Indians as well, with plenty of chanting and dancing. The main thrust of activities (as always) is on the Friday, Saturday and Sunday before Ash Wednesday, and on Monday the town celebrates with the traditional Umisha dance around a sacred tree selected for the purpose. It's similar to maypole dancing in Britain, though in Iquitos the dancers strike the tree with machetes; when it eventually falls, children dive in to grab their share of the many gifts previously suspended from it.

Perhaps the best time to visit Iquitos, however, is at the end of June (supposedly June 23–24, but actually spread over three or four days), when the main **Fiesta de San Juan** takes place. Focused around the small artesania market of San Juan (San Juan being the patron saint of Iquitos), some 4km from the city and quite close to the airport, it's the traditional time for partying and for eating *juanes*, delicious little balls of rice and chicken wrapped in jungle leaves; the best place for these is in San Juan itself. June is also the time for **Iquitos Week**, bascially seven days of partying centred around the Fiesta de San Juan, though tending to spread right across the month. In October the municipality's tourism directorate organizes an **international rafting competition**, which draws enthusiasts from every continent for a short five hour, nineteen-kilometre river race, plus a longer six-day race. Jet ski racing is being planned, though the environmental concerns may well outweigh the tourism benefits of this. At the end of the month there's the **Espiritos de La Selva** (Spirits of the Jungle) festival, which coincides with Halloween and All Souls. For more on this, contact the Iquitos tourist information office (p.534).

Unlike most of the Peruvian selva, the **climate** here is little affected by the Andean topography, so there is no rainy season as such; instead, the year is divided into "high water" (Dec–May) and "low water" (June–Nov) seasons. The upshot is that the weather is always hot and humid, with temperatures averaging 23–30°C (74–86°F) and with an annual rainfall of about 2600mm. Most visitors come between May and August, but the high-water months are perhaps the best time for seeing **wildlife**, because the animals are crowded into smaller areas of dry land.

Iquitos and around

Self-confident and likeable, **IQUITOS** is for the most part, a modern city, built on a wide, flat river plain. Only the heart around the main plaza contains any older, architecturally interesting buildings, but the river port and market area of **Belén** boasts rustic wooden huts on stilts – a classic image of Iquitos. If it weren't for the abundant stalls and shops selling jungle Indian craft goods it would be hard to know that this place was once dominated by hunter-gatherer **tribes** like the Iquito, Yaguar, Bora and Witito who initially defended their territory against the early Spanish missionaries and explorers. The townsfolk today, however, are warm and welcoming, wear as little clothing as possible and are out in numbers during the relative cool of the evening.

Though founded in 1757 under the name of San Pablo de los Napeanos, the present centre of Iquitos was established in 1864. By the end of the nineteenth century Iquitos was, along with Manaus in Brazil, one of *the* great rubber towns. From that era of grandeur a number of structures survive, but during the last century the town veered between prosperity (as far back as 1938 when the area was explored for oil) and the depths of economic depression. However, its strategic position on the Amazon, which makes it accessible to large ocean-going ships from the distant Atlantic, has ensured its continued importance. At present, still buoyed by the export of timber, petroleum, tobacco and Brazil nuts, and dabbling heavily in the trade of wild animals, tropical fish and birds, as well as an insecticide called *barbasco*, long used by natives as a fish poison, Iquitos is in a period of quite wealthy expansion.

The river has receded significantly from the main **riverfront**, which has necessitated moving the town's downriver port away from its centre. Some locals blame downstream canalization for this shift, others point to a drop in rainfall along the Amazon's headwaters in other parts; or it may be that increasing deforestation of the *ceja de selva* higher up means that, during the rainy season, rainwater simply runs off the surface, leaving none to gradually filter down during the dry season. Whatever the reason, the riverfront now stretches all the way from the old port and market of Belén, which the Amazon waters hardly reach any more, to the newer (literally) floating port of **Puerto Masusa**, 3km downriver.

Expeditions around Iquitos are the most developed in the Peruvian jungle, offering a wide and often surprising range of attractions. As usual, anything involving overnight stays is going to cost a fair bit, though there are also cheap day-trips. With all organized visits to Indian villages in this area, expect the inhabitants to put on a quick show, with a few traditional dances and some singing, before they try to sell you their handicraft (occasionally overenthusiastically). Prices range from $1 to $5 for necklaces, feathered items (mostly illegal to take out of the country), bark-cloth drawings, string bags (often excellent value) and blowguns; most people buy something, since the Indians don't actually charge for the visit. While the experience may leave you feeling somewhat ambivalent – the men, and particularly the women, only discard Western clothes for the performances – it's a preferable situation to the times when visits were imposed on communities by unscrupulous tour companies. Visitors are now these Indians' major source of income, and it seems that the Bora and Yaguar alike have found a niche they can easily exploit within the local tourist industry. There are some good independent contacts who can help you find or organize the right trip. The Iquitos tourist office (see p.534) has a list of registered **freelance guides** and is usually helpful in providing up-to-date contacts for them.

Arrival, information and city transport

If you've come by boat from Yurimaguas (5 days), Pucallpa (6–7 days), Leticia or Tabatinga (both 3 days), you'll arrive at **Puerto Masusa**, some eleven blocks northeast of the Plaza de Armas. Flights land at Iquitos **airport**, Aeropuerto Internacional de Francisco Secada Vignetta (℡065/260147), 6km southwest of town and connected by taxis ($4–5) and cheaper *mototaxis* ($2). Once you're off the plane, you're likely to be surrounded by a horde of desperate **touts**, all trying to persuade you to take their jungle tours or stay in their lodges; at this stage, the best thing to do is to avoid conversation with any of them, apart perhaps from saying you'll meet them in a couple of hours – which will give you time to get settled in and think about where you want to go and how much you are prepared to pay (see above for info on freelance guide contacts). **Buses** from Nauta pull in on the Plaza de Armas and on calles Huallaga and La Condamine. The first things you'll notice when getting to central Iquitos are the vast quantities of motorbikes; the next thing is probably the high visability of **street kids**.

The local *consejo* run a helpful **tourist information** kiosk at the airport (daily 8am–9pm; ℡065/260251), and the very helpful and friendly main i-Peru

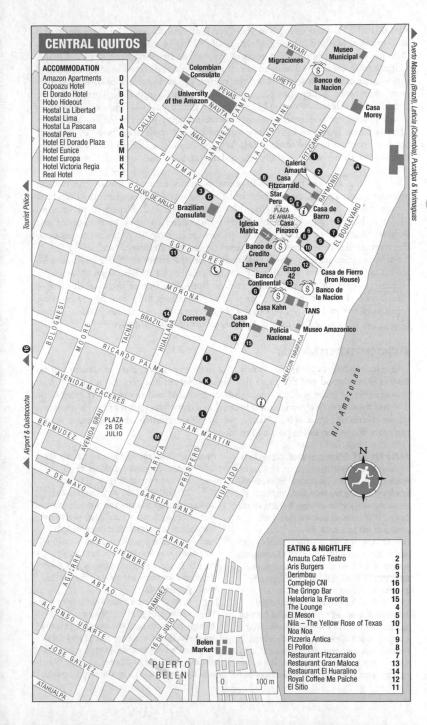

CENTRAL IQUITOS

ACCOMMODATION

Amazon Apartments	D
Copoazu Hotel	L
El Dorado Hotel	B
Hobo Hideout	C
Hostal La Libertad	I
Hostal Lima	J
Hostal La Pascana	A
Hostal Peru	G
Hotel El Dorado Plaza	E
Hotel Eunice	M
Hotel Europa	H
Hotel Victoria Regia	K
Real Hotel	F

EATING & NIGHTLIFE

Amauta Café Teatro	2
Aris Burgers	6
Derimbau	3
Complejo CNI	16
The Gringo Bar	10
Heladeria la Favorita	15
The Lounge	4
El Meson	5
Nila – The Yellow Rose of Texas	10
Noa Noa	1
Pizzeria Antica	9
El Pollon	8
Restaurant Fitzcarraldo	7
Restaurant Gran Maloca	13
Restaurant El Huaralino	14
Royal Coffee Me Paiche	12
El Sitio	11

Puerto Masusa (Brazil), Leticia (Colombia), Pucallpa & Yurimaguas

Tourist Police

Airport & Quistococha

533

PROMPERU tourist office is in the City Hall building on the Plaza de Armas at Napo 232 (daily 8.30am–7.30pm, ☎065/236144 Ⓔiperuiquitos@promperu .gob.pe, ⓌWww.regionloreto.gob.pe). As well as stocking brochures and maps, helping with accommodation and keeping a list of registered tour operators and guides, the office also sells CDs of the region's music and videos of local attractions. For more in-depth inquiries, the Direccion Regional de Turismo can be found at Av Ricardo Palma 113, 5th floor. There's also an online English language newspaper for Iquitos (www.iquitostimes.com), run by Mike Collis who "retired" here from the UK. **City tours** of Iquitos itself are offered by many of the tour companies and some hotels (try the *Hostal La Pascana* for tickets); they take about three hours, usually leave daily at 9am and again at 2pm, costing around $12.

For getting around town you'll probably want to make use of the rattling *mototaxis*; alternatively, motorbikes can be rented – try the shop near the Ferretería Union (block 2 of Raymondi), or the one at Yavari 702. Expect to pay around $2.50 an hour or $15 for twelve hours (you'll need to show your passport and licence). Remember to check the brakes before leaving. If you want to get onto the river itself, canoes can be rented from the port at Bellavista (see p.540).

For money exchange it's best not to do it on the street with the *cambistas* who have a bit of a reputation (particularly at the corner of Prospero with Morona) for ripping tourists off, especially after around 8pm. Use one of the casas de cambio on Sargento Lores or the banks (see p.539). The street kids, too, have a growing reputation for picking pockets, but they're certainly not all bad, and a Transit House has been built for them in Iquitos, so things may improve.

Accommodation

Like every other jungle town, Iquitos is a little expensive, but the standard of its **hotels** is very good and the range allows for different budgets. Even a room in an average sort of place will include a shower and fan, and many others offer cable TV and minibars. Accommodation located **north of the plaza** offers closer access to the riverboat port and Río Nanay, while the area **south of the plaza** is nearer the main shops and Belén port and market.

North of Plaza de Armas

Amazon Apartments Napo 274, on the Plaza de Armas ☎065/243088. Somewhere between an apartment building and hotel room, these suites are aimed mostly at the business traveller, although they do offer rooms as well, and there's also a small pool and jacuzzi. ⑤–⑦

El Dorado Hotel Napo 362 ☎065/232574. Located less than a block from the Plaza de Armas, this is a reasonably good, if less than spacious, hotel with cable TV, restaurant and a small pool (also available to restaurant patrons). ⑦

Hobo Hideout Putumayo 437 ☎065/234099, Ⓔmail@safarisrus.net. A ramshackle but charming backpacker hostel in the heart of Iquitos offering a range of rooms, some with private bathrooms. There's a restaurant here with superb meals, but it's a good idea to book your evening meal in the morning if you want to taste the wild game offered on the

menu, since they may need to buy it specially. The owner leads some jungle expeditions. ②–③

Hostal La Pascana Pevas 133 ☎065/ 231418, Ⓕ233466, Ⓔhs_pascana@tsi .com.pe, ⓌWww.pascana.com. Popular with travellers, *La Pascana* offers a ventilated, quiet haven from Iquitos' sometimes hectic street life, with appealing doubles based around a small courtyard close to the river, less than two blocks from the Plaza de Armas. It's clean and friendly, and there's also a book exchange and travel service. Best to book in advance. ③

Hotel El Dorado Plaza Napo 258, Plaza de Armas ☎065/222555, ⓌWww .eldoradoplazahotel.com. As well as being the first five-star in Iquitos, this is the best quality hotel in the entire Peruvian Amazon. Rooms are large and spacious with excellent showers, a/c, cable TV and large beds, and there's a very large and superbly cool and tastefully decorated lobby with a glass lift rising to all six floors. In addition to the expected, fine service, *El Dorado* boasts a nice pool, a *maloca*-style bar, quality restaurant and some fantastic rainforest-inspired paintings by the local artist Francisco Grippa (see p.537). ❽

South of Plaza de Armas

La Casa Fitzcarraldo Av La Marina 2153, ☏065601138 or 601139, ⓦwww .lacasafitzcarraldo.com. Located in a large house on Av La Marina towards the port area of Bellavista, this family run b&b offers tastefully decorated and spacious accommodation with a naturally cooled and very clean swimming pool (less than $2 entry for non-resident visitors), plus great food, drinks, lovely orchid-rich gardens and a three-level treehouse with panoramic views. ❹–❻

Copoazu Hotel Prospero 644 ☏065/232373, ⓔhotel_copoazu@yahoo.com. A modern hotel with comfortable rooms and a fairly central location offering airport transfer, 24hr room service, money change and a safe if required. ❹

Hostal La Libertad Arica 361 ☏/ⓕ065/235763. A fine backpackers' place; rooms have private bath, hot water and cable TV, plus there's a restaurant and it's also home to a good tour company. ❸

Hostal Lima Prospero 549 ☏065/221409. The place doesn't look like much from the outside but is surprisingly pleasant, possessing a certain jungle flavour, with parrots on the patio. Rooms have private bath and fans. ❷–❸

Hostal Peru Prospero 318 ☏065/231531. Rather down-at-heel, though quite popular with locals and travellers alike, perhaps because of its old-fashioned architecture and fittings. It has shared bathrooms, fans in all rooms and some have cable TV. ❷–❸

Hotel Eunice Arica 780 ☏065/233405, ⓕ243607. Very friendly and good value hotel with some amazingly large rooms, some of which include stereos, TV and minibar. ❺

Hotel Europa Prospero 494 ☏065/231123, ⓔheuropa@meganet.com.pe. Central located with a pleasant ambience, small restaurant and bar. All rooms have cable TV, a/c, minibar and private bath. ❺–❼

Hotel Victoria Regia Ricardo Palma 252 ☏065/231983, ⓦwww.victoriaregiahotel .com. Quite luxurious for Iquitos with a small pool, good security and sterling service. ❽

Real Hotel Malecón Tarapaca ☏065/231011. The former *Gran Hotel Iquitos*, this really doesn't look so grand today, despite its location right between El Boulevard and the Malecón Tarapaca. Nevertheless some of its rooms are very spacious with fine bathrooms and superb views over the waterfront. There's also a decent restaurant. ❻

The Town

Much of Iquitos' appeal derives from its being the starting point for excursions into the **rainforest** (see pp.542–548), but the town is an interesting place in its own right, if only for the lively local people and magnificent rubber boom architecture. Like Manaus, Iquitos evolved into an almost European city during the rubber boom. Many of the late eighteenth- and early nineteenth-century buildings are decorated with Portuguese tiles (*azulejos*), some of which are brilliantly extravagant in their Moorish inspiration, and the **Casa Kahn**, on block 1 of Sargento Lores, is a particularly fine example.

Plaza de Armas and around

The central **Plaza de Armas** is still weirdly dominated by the towering presence of an abandoned and dilapidated high-rise hotel, built during the boom of the early 1980s (and initiated by the then President Belaunde's drive to open up the Amazon in economic terms), before the economy slumped and terrorism temporarily slowed tourism in the region. These days, it has little function other than as a foundation for antennas. The plaza's modern fountain attracts strolling townsfolk when illuminated at night, though its sound is generally drowned out by the *mototaxis* and cars whizzing around the square. On the southwest side of the plaza the **Iglesia Matriz**, the main Catholic church, houses paintings by the Loretano (Loreto is the *departmento* Iquitos is located in) artists Americo Pinasco and Cesar Calvo de Araujo depicting biblical scenes. The **Museo Municipal** (Mon–Fri 8am–noon & 3pm–5pm; free), by the tourist office on the plaza, has an interesting, albeit a little half-baked, collection of exhibits featuring *manguare* drums, stuffed animals, information on some tree and plant products from the forest, a large preserved *paiche* fish and some animal skulls.

On the southeast corner of the plaza, you'll find the unusual, majestic **Casa de Fierro** (Iron House), which was restored just a few years ago and is hard to miss with its silvery sides glinting in the afternoon sunshine. Designed by Gustave Eiffel for the 1889 Paris exhibition and later shipped in pieces to Iquitos and reconstructed here in the 1890s by one of the local rubber barons, these days it's home to a quality restaurant located on the upper storey.

One block southeast of Plaza de Armas are the two best sections of the **old riverfront**, El Boulevard and Malecón Tarapaca, both of which have been

▲ Plaza de Armas, Iquitos

recently restored to some of its former glory. **El Boulevard** is the busiest of the two areas, especially at night, full of bars and restaurants and with a small **amphitheatre** where some kind of entertainment occurs most nights, from mini-circuses to mime, comedy and music. The **Malecón Tarapaca** boasts some fine old mansions, one of which, at no. 262, with lovely nineteenth-century *azulejo* work, is presently one of the town's better bakeries. On the corner with Putumayo there's the military-occupied building (no photos allowed), which was once the Art Nouveau **Hotel Palace**, no longer open to the public but nevertheless one of the city's historical icons. Also on Malecón Tarapaca is the Municipal museum, **Museo Amazónico** (Mon–Fri 8am–1pm & 3–7pm, Sat 9–1pm; $1.50, 80¢ for students), devoted to the region's natural history and tribal culture. Its collection includes some unusual life-sized human figures in traditional dress from different Amazon tribes; each fibreglass sculpture was made from a cast that had encapsulated the live subject for an hour or so. There's also a gallery devoted to previous *prefectos* of Loreto, some oil paintings, a few stuffed animals and a small military museum.

Just around the corner you'll find the quaint one storey **Casa Cohen**, on the corner of Prospero with Morona, still a working shop, built in 1905 and beautifully adorned with iron work, colourful *azulejos* and *pilastras* – all reflecting the past days of rubber boom commerce and glory. In a similar vein of interest, the **Casa Fitzcarrald**, at Napo 200–212, was once home to the legendary rubber baron of the same name but unfortunately is not open to the public; it was built of *adobe* and *quincha* and has a central patio with arches, plus ceilings of roughly sawn wood.

Amazon Art Gallery

In the Punchana sector of Iquitos, the **Galería de Arte Amazonica** (Amazon Art Gallery), Trujillo 438 (call for an appointment ☎065/253120), exhibits the work of the Peruvian painter **Francisco Grippa** and a few other national and local artists. Grippa, who lives and works mainly in Pevas (see p.543), arrived in the Amazon in the late 1970s after being educated in Europe and the US, and his work, described variously as figurative and expressionist, displays an obsession with light and colour, focusing on subjects such as Shipibo Indians, jungle birds and rainforest landscapes. There's more art to be found at **Galería Amauta**, Nauta 248, where there are exhibitions of oil paintings, caricatures and photographs, mostly by local artists.

Puerto Belén

The most memorable part of town and best visited around 7am when it's most active, **Puerto Belén** looms out of the main town at a point where the Amazon, until recently, joined the Río Itaya inlet. Consisting almost entirely of wooden huts raised on stilts and, until a few years ago, also floating on rafts, the district has earned fame among travellers as the "Venice of the Peruvian Jungle". Actually more Far Eastern than European in appearance, with obvious poverty and little glamour, it has changed little over its hundred or so years, remaining a poor shanty settlement trading in basics like bananas, manioc, fish, turtle and crocodile meat. Whilst filming *Fitzcarraldo* here, Herzog merely had to make sure that no motorized canoes appeared on screen: virtually everything else, including the style of the *barriada* dwellings, looks exactly the way it did during the nineteenth century.

Ask for directions to **Pasaje Paquito**, the busy herbalist alley in the heart of this frenetic Río Amazonas economic community, synthesizing the rich flavour of the place. Here you'll find scores of competing stalls selling an enormous variety of natural jungle medicines as well as some of the town's cheapest artesania.

Eating and drinking

Food in Iquitos is exceptionally good for a jungle town, specializing in fish dishes but catering pretty well to any taste. Unfortunately, many of the local delicacies are now in danger of disappearing entirely from the rivers around Iquitos – notably, river turtle, alligator and the enormous and very tasty *paiche* fish. Eating out is something of a popular pastime in the lively, even energetic evenings, which usually stretch out well into the early hours of the morning, particularly at weekends (we've given telephone numbers where reservations are advised). There are some good **bars and pubs** on the Boulevard, some serving excellent grub, and the first block of Putumayo, very close to the plaza, is known as "Little England" because of a legion of British or US-run pubs and restaurants. This is always a busy spot at night and one of Iquitos' best areas for drinking.

Al Carbon Condamina 115. This is the most traditional of all restaurants in Iquitos, only open in the evenings and serving mostly meat dishes – try *cechina* (smoked pork) or *tacacho* (mashed bananas fried with bacon) – most of which are largely cooked over charcoals. Excellent salads are available, too.

Aris Burgers Prospero 127 ☎065/231479. Actually serving more than burgers (though these are quite delicious), including plates with a variety of river fish and even *caiman* meat, plus the best French fries in town. It's the most popular meeting spot in Iquitos and a bit of a landmark for taxi and *motokar* drivers.

Heladeria La Favorita Prospero 413. A roomy café specializing in juices and delicious jungle-fruit-flavoured ice creams.

Jungle Jim's Putumayo 168 ☎065/235294. If you're still in the mood for alligator after your jungle trip, this is the place to get it. The newest English pub in town, *Jungle Jim's* serves a superb range of drinks as well as great regional cuisine. There are tables inside as well as on the street, and the place stays open as late as customers want. Accepts most major credit cards.

El Meson El Boulevard ☎065/231857. A popular restaurant serving a wide range of local dishes – try the *tacacho* (plantains and pork), or *pescado a la Loretano* (fish). It's not cheap, though a good meal can be had for well under $10, and the location is perfect, right at the heart of El Boulevard and with tables out front.

Nila – The Yellow Rose of Texas Putumayo 180 ☎065/241010. *Nila's* serves tasty local dishes from a reasonably priced menu and the location is handy, near the plaza, with tables outside on the street. There's great coffee, friendly service and late hours (usually until 1 or 2am).

Pizzeria Antica on Napo, between the plaza and the Malecon ☎065/241988.

A new Italian with an extensive and delicious menu, including good vegetarian options. Meals are served in a large space with ceiling fans and driftwood decor, and there's a nice bar on the second level.

El Pollon Prospero 151. A spacious restaurant and café fronting the Plaza de Armas. Popular with locals, especially at lunchtime, and serving a wide range of tasty meals, cool juices and ice creams.

Restaurant Fitzcarraldo Napo 100 ☎065/243434. A great place, close to the nightly action and located on the corner of the Malecón in the old headquarters of the once very successful Orton Bolivian Rubber Company; it was bought from them by Fitzcarrald in 1897, just two months before he drowned on a trip into the jungle. It isn't cheap but serves some of the best salads in town plus good pastas, fish and *comida criolla*.

Restaurant Gran Maloca Sargento Lores 170 ☎065/233126 ℮maloca@tvs.com.pe. One of Iquitos' finest restaurants, lavishly decorated, with jungle paintings adorning the walls and a high-ceilinged, cool interior. Food is excellent, with nice jungle ice creams.

Restaurant El Huaralino Huallaga 490 ☎065/223300. Some of the best *comida criolla* in town with great set-lunch menus; so popular with locals that it's often hard to get a table. Large and airy in a fairly central, ventilated location.

Royal Coffee "Me Paiche" Putumayo 133 ☎065/231304. Reasonably priced and usually fairly quiet, with decent pizzas, pastas and sandwiches, plus a range of other meals, snacks and drinks. If you phone in an order, they can also deliver to your hotel.

El Sitio Block 4 of Sargento Lores. A very creative snack bar/restaurant, inexpensive and with delicious *anticuchos*, *tamales*, *juanes* and fruit juices; best to get there before 9pm, or you'll miss out on the tastiest treats.

Nightlife

Whilst mainly an extension of eating out and meeting friends in the main streets, the **nightlife** in Iquitos is vibrant, and there are a number of highly charged discos, clubs and bars worth knowing about. They're quite easy to locate, especially if you are up and about after 11pm when things generally get going in the downtown areas, particularly around the Plaza de Armas and nearby Malecón Tarapacá.

Iquitos has an unusually active **gay scene** for a Peruvian jungle town, mainly due to many gays fleeing here during the terrorist years (the mid-1980s to the early 1990s), when they suffered persecution, and there are now four or five dedicated **gay clubs**.

Bars and clubs

Agricobank Pablo Rosel 300 ☎065/236113. A smaller version of Complejo CNI and perhaps less vibrant, this is nonetheless a great and much more centrally located place to enjoy the local live music scene. Open Fri and Sat 10pm–late; $1 entrance.

Amauta Café Teatro Nauta 250 ☎065/233109. Different music – from jazzy jungle creole to folklore and female singers performing romantic ballads – programmed from day to day, and there are tables outside and snacks available. Open Mon–Sat 10pm–2am.

Berimbau Putumayo 467. Very central and pretty hectic, *Berimbau* is one of the newest and flashiest nightclubs in Iquitos, spinning good rock and Latin dance music most nights, and serving cool drinks at several bars on different levels by various dance floors. There's also good a/c, which is pretty important here.

Complejo CNI Mariscal Caceres, block 13. More of a covered outdoor arena, this gives a flavour of what the Iquitos youth get up to at weekends, with over 1000 people dancing all night to mostly live salsa, *chicha* and cumbia bands, but with significant Brazilian influence creeping in.

The Lounge Putumayo 341. A very popular Australian-run lounge bar with great cocktails and up-to-the-minute rock, dance and trance

sounds; some good inexpensive food too, including curries.

Noa Noa Fitzcarrald 298 ☎065/222993. Easily identified after 11.30pm by the huge number of flashy motorbikes lined up outside, this is the liveliest Iquitos club, attracting young and old, gringo and *Iquiteño* alike. It has three bars and plays lots of Latino music, including the latest technocumbia. Mon–Sat 10pm–late; $6 entrance.

Gay clubs

Bar La 4.40 Opposite the Hospital Regional, in Punchana. Good music and a reasonable bar.

Calipso Block 10 of Putumayo. Another fun gay – though not exclusively – bar, located in an old house and playing ambient and tropical music. Thurs–Sat midnight–5am; 50¢.

Las Castañitas In front of the electricity power plant in the suburb of Punchana. A glitzy little joint with a good range of cocktails and a music policy combining rock and Latin music. Best to take a taxi as it's a little hard to find.

Discoteca 2003 Block 25 of Putumayo. Located a little way out of the centre of town, but a lively and pleasant spot playing pop and dance music, usually getting going after 11pm. Thurs–Sat.

Tragoteca La Jarra Av Quinones, near the *Pamachicha* restaurant. Small but popular, this music bar kicks off from around 10pm Thurs–Sun.

Listings

Airlines Lan Peru, Prospero block 2 (next to Banco de Credito) ☎065/232421; TANS, Arica block 2; Star Peru, Napo 298 ☎065/236208; Grupo 42, Prospero 215 ☎065/221071 or 233224, for reasonably priced flights to Requena, Angamos and Santa Rosa.

Airport Aeropuerto Internacional Francisco Secada Vignetta, 6km southwest of town ☎065/260147.

Banks and exchange Banco de Credito, Putumayo 201; Banco Wiese, Prospero 282, for MasterCard; Banco de la Nación, block 4 Condamine; Banco Continental, Prospero Block 3, with a 24hr ATM, and also on Sargento Lores, block 1; and the

Banco del Trabajo, block 1 of Prospero, has an ATM taking Visa. Casa de cambio, corner of Sargento Lores with Prospero. The only place said to be reasonably safe for changing with *cambistas* on the street is at the corner of Morona with Arica, by the post office (daytime only for safety).

Bike rental Jungle Bike ☎065/266631.

Consulates Brazil, Morona 238 ☎065/232081; Colombia, corner of Nauta with Callao ☎094/231461; UK, Putumayo 182 ☎065/222732.

Hospital Regional de Loreto, Av 28 de Julio, Punchana ☎065/252004.

Internet Soho Internet, Putumayo 382 has fast computers and snacks; El Cyber, Arica 122 on the Plaza de Armas, is a large and popular internet facility (no drinks or food).

Jungle supplies Mad Mick's Trading Post, Putumayo 184b. Very centrally located, this shop has been specifically established to provide the basic essentials for a jungle trip, including rubber boots, rainproof ponchos, sunhats, fishing tackle, etc. They will rent out rubber boots with a deposit returned in exchange for boots after jungle trip.

Laundry LavaCenter, Prospero 459 ☏065/242136; Lavandería Imperial, Putumayo 150; Lavandería Popular, C Loreto 640.

Migraciones Av Mariscal Cáceres, block 18 %T065/235371. This is the immigration office where you need to go to extend or renew your Peruvian tourist card or visa.

Pacaya Samiria National Reserve Office Ricardo Palma 113, third floor ☏065/233980, ⊜rnps-zrg@aeci.org.pe. Good for maps, information on the National Reserve and permission to enter it.

Pharmacies Botica Amazonicas, Prospero 699 ☏065/231832; Botica Virgen de Chapi, Prospero 461.

Police Tourist police, Sargento Lores 834 ☏065/242801; also, for Guardia Nacional, the Comisaría at Morona, Calle Morona 120 ☏065/231123.

Post office SERPOST, Arica 402 (Mon–Sat 7am–7.30pm).

Shopping Artesanias La Jungla, Prospero 483 (baskets, mats, hammocks, gourds, postcards and souvenirs); Artesanias Sudamerica, Casa de Fierro, Plaza de Armas, Prospero 175 (hammocks and alpaca goods); Artesanias, Prospero 572 and Artesanias Todo Peru, Prospero 685 (hammocks, hats, jewellery, musical instruments and souvenirs); Bazar Daniela, 9 de Diciembre 234 (useful trade items for visiting local villages, such as cloth, beads and coloured threads); Comercial Cardinal, Prospero 300 (fishing tackle, compasses, knives); Taller de Arte, Prospero 593/595 (carved wooden sculptures and household artefacts). Other centres for artesania include: Anaconda, Malecon Tarapaca (8am–9pm daily) and Mercado Artesanal San Juan, Av Quiñones Km 4.5 (8am–9pm).

Telephones Sargento Flores 321 (daily 7am–11pm); international phone calls at Napo 349, next to Western Union office.

Short trips and tours from Iquitos

Hiring a **bike** (see Listings, p.539) can be an intriguing way to explore in and around Iquitos, but it's certainly quicker to use *mototaxis* with so many of them around. The closest place you can escape to without a guide or long river trip is **Padre Isla**, an island opposite town in the midst of the Amazon, over 14km long and with beautiful beaches during the dry season. It's easily reached by canoe from Belén or the main waterfront.

Alternatively, some 4km northeast of the centre of Iquitos, just 15min by bus, the suburb of **Bellavista** on the Río Nanay, is the main access point for smaller boats to all the rivers. There's a rather small (and smelly) **market** selling jungle products, plus some bars and shops clustered around a port, where you can rent canoes for short trips at around $5 an hour. Like Iquitos, Bellavista has recently been experiencing its highest and lowest recorded water levels, with all of the associated flooding and drying up; the bars sit on their stilts high above dried mud during the dry season, and the boats are moored some forty metres further out than they used to be. From Bellavista you can set out by canoe ferry for **Playa Nanay**, the best beach around Iquitos, where bars and cafés are springing up to cater to the weekend crowds. Be aware that currents here are pretty strong, and although there are lifeguards, drownings have occurred.

About twenty minutes by boat from Bellavista, involving a fifteen-minute walk from the beach village in the dry season, but accessible the entire way when the river is high, the fascinating **Amazon Animal Orphanage and Pilpintu-wasi Butterfly Farm** (Tues–Sun 9am–5pm; $5, $3 for students; ☏065/232665, ⊜pilpintuwasi@hotmail.com) is located near the village of Padre Cocha. Here you can explore a fantastic array of butterflies in a natural environment, plus a number of jungle animals, all rescued from certain death (rather than being bought for display). The animal orphanage is a new addition adding signicant variety to the experience.

Speedboats go downstream to Santa Rosa, Tabatinga and Leticia (all on the three-way frontier, see p.548) several times a week, taking up to ten hours there and twelve hours back, for around $50–70. The main companies have their offices on Raymondi, just a few blocks from the Plaza de Armas: Expreso Loreto, Raymondi 384 (☎065/238021); Transtur, Raymondi 328 (☎065/242367); and Transportes Rapido, Raymondi 346 (☎065/222147). There is also Brastours, Jr Condamine 384 (☎065/223232), who specialize in boats and flights to Tabatinga, Brazil.

Larger **riverboats** go upstream from Puerto Masusa to Lagunas (three days), Yurimaguas (five days), Pucallpa (six–seven days), or downstream to Pevas (about one day), Leticia and Tabatinga (both three days). Check with the commercial river transporters for a rough idea of departure dates and times, and keep an eye out for the *Juliana* (used by Herzog in his film) and the *Oro Negro*, which costs $50 to the border, including food but not drink. Take along a good book, plenty of extra food and drink, a hammock, a sweater and one or two blankets; it's usually possible to sling your hammock up and sleep free of charge on the larger boats in the days leading up to the unpredictable departure. It's also advisable to secure your baggage with a chain to a permanent fixture on the deck and also keep bags locked, as **theft** is not uncommon.

The **IMET Botanical Gardens** (Mon–Fri 9am–3pm, Sat 9am–noon; free), located in Pasaje San Lorenzo, Calle Quinonez (take a *mototaxi* and ask to drop you before Orvisa), lures visitors to see its well-kept jungle gardens with labeled medicinal plants such as *uña de gato* (cat's claw), a great tonic for the immune system.

From the corner of Bermudez and Moore, behind the church on the Plaza 28 de Julio, **microbuses** go to the lagoon at **Quistococha** (a 20–30min journey; $1 entry). Taxis and *mototaxis* can be picked up anywhere in town, but from the Plaza de Armas should cost around $6 or $3, respectively. One kilometre long, and up to 8m deep, the waters have been taken over by the Ministry of Fishing for the breeding of giant *paiche*, and there's a **zoo** of sorts with small site **museum** of jungle natural history, as well as a small lakeside beach, restaurant and bar and an aviary.

On the western edge of Iquitos, an affluent of the Nanay forms a long lake called **Moronacocha**, a popular resort for swimming and water-skiing; some 5km further out (just before the airport), another lake, **Rumococha**, has facilities on the Río Nanay for fishing and hunting; again, these are easily accessible by *mototaxi*. Beyond this, still on the Nanay, are the popular weekend beach and white sands of **Santa Clara**. The village of **Santo Tomas** is only 16km from here; a worthwhile trip and well connected by local buses, this agricultural and fishing village, located on the banks of the Río Nanay, is renowned for its jungle artesania, and has another beach, on the **Lago Mapacocha**, where you can swim and canoe. There's also one really good fish restaurant here, on the riverfront, run by the Chrichigno family, best during the day, before the mosquitoes come out. If you get the chance, try to make your visit coincide with **Santo Tomas' fiesta** (Sept 23–25), a huge party with dancing and *chicha* music.

Short tours in the area (which can be arranged with most of the main hotels or lodge operators) include a boat trip that sets out from Bellavista and travels up the Río Momón to visit a community of Yaguar or Bora Indians at **San Andres**, just beyond *Amazon Camp* (see p.546), then goes downriver to **Serpentario Las Boas**, an anaconda farm near the mouth of the Momón. Here you can see and touch anacondas and more (boas, sloth and monkeys, to name a few), slithering around in what is essentially someone's backyard. The whole trip lasts around two hours and costs about $10 per person. A longer tour, lasting around four hours and costing

$15–20, includes the above but also takes you onto the Río Amazonas to visit an alligator farm at **Barrio Florida** and to watch dolphins playing in the river.

Around Iquitos

The massive river system around Iquitos offers some of the best access to Indian villages, lodges and primary rainforest in the entire Amazon. If you want to go it alone, **colectivo boats** run up and down the **Río Amazonas** more or less daily, and although you won't get deep into the forest without a guide or the facilities offered by the lodge and tour companies, you can visit some of the larger riverine settlements on your own.

One of the first major settlements on the banks of the Amazon is the small river town of **Tamshiyacu**, en route to Nauta upstream; a couple of hostels, including the *Hospedaje Mercedes* (①), just beyond the plaza, and the *Hospedaje Dianita* (①) a little beyond, accompanied by a few bars and stores, make it a useful stopping point, if you need one. A long day's ride (130km) further upstream from Iquitos lies **Nauta**, at the mouth of the Río Marañón. South from Nauta, **Bagazan** is another couple of hours (40km) further up the Río Ucayali, after which it's another 50km to **Requena**, at the mouth of the Río Tapiche. A new road from Iquitos to Nauta has considerably shortened the journey and has begun to open up tourism to the west of Nauta on the ríos Marañón and Tigre and into the Pacaya Samiria National Reserve (only a short boat ride from

AROUND IQUITOS

Río Napo

ExplorNapo Lodge,
Amazon Explorama ACTS Field Station
& Sucusari Reserve

Sinchicuy
Lodge · Mazán · Indiana · Amazon Explorama Lodge

Amazon Rainforest Lodge

Río Momón

Amazon Explorama
CEIBA TOPS

Río Amazonas

Río Nanay

Amazon Camp

Heliconia Amazon
River Lodge

Iquitos

Zungarococha
Resort · Quisto
Cocha

Cumaceba
Lodge

Amazon
Retreat Centre

Santa
Maria

Río Tamshiyacu

N

Río Itaya

Río Tahuayo

Río Yanayacu

Refugio Altiplano

Río Tigre

Río Marañón

Muyuna Lodge

Blue Morpho
Nauta · Libertad

Amazon Refuge

Cocoma Lodge

Río Yanayacu

Río Pucate · Clavero
Bagazan

Genaro
Herrera

Mayo Creek

Río Curahuaba

Cumaceba
Creek

Lago
Cumaceba

Río Samiria

Requena

PACAYA SAMIRIA
NATIONAL RESERVE

Río Ucayali

Río Tapiche

Angamos

BRAZIL

//// Best areas for spotting
wildlife & adventure
expeditions

0 ———— 50 km

Pucallpa

Nauta), though the best sectors of the reserve are arguably easier to get to from Lagunas. The upper Río Tigre is also excellent for its access to wildlife, but it's at least three days away by boat.

Lagunas

There are excellent organized tours available from **LAGUNAS**, close to the Pacaya Samiria National Reserve. To get there, you can take a bus (faster than a boat) as far as Nauta, near the "start" of the Río Amazonas, where the Ucayali and the Marañón rivers merge. From here it's some three days upstream by boat to Lagunas ($10–25 depending on whether you take hammock space or a shared cabin) along the Rio Marañon. The settlement is located some twelve hours downstream from Yurimaguas and also accessible from there by *colectivo* boat (from $8). There are a couple of **hostels** in Lagunas: the *Hostal Montalban* (❷), on the Plaza de Armas, is basic and small but suffices, as does the slightly cheaper *Hostal La Sombra* (❶) at Jr Vasquez 1121.

Lagunas is a starting point for trips into the huge **Pacaya Samiria National Reserve** ($30 fee for a five-day entry pass from INRENA, see p.118), comprising around two million hectares of virgin rainforest (about 1.5 percent of the total landmass of Peru) leading up to the confluence between the Marañón and the Huallaga rivers, two of the largest Amazon headwaters and possessing between them the largest protected area of seasonally flooded jungle in the Peruvian Amazon. The reserve is a swampland during the rainy season (Dec–March), when the streams and rivers all rise, comparable to the Tambopata-Candamo Reserved Zone in southeastern Peru or the Pantanal swamps of southwestern Brazil in its astonishing density of visible wildlife. This region is home to the **Cocoma tribe** whose main settlement is Tipishca, where the native community are now directly involved in ecotourism. They can be hired as guides and will provide rustic accommodation, but can only be contacted by asking on arrival. It's possible to arrange **guides** here (from around $20 a day, which can be shared between a few fellow travellers) to explore the reserve. Visitors should be aware that around 100,000 people, mostly **indigenous communities**, still live in the reserve's forest; they are the local residents and their territory as well as customs should be respected. These tribal communities are also a source for detailed information on the sustainable management of river turtles, since, in recent years some of the communities have been collaborating on ecological conservation projects. There's a public **ferryboat** or *lancha* you can catch that travels up to Pacaya Samiria, but it's advisable not to give yourself too tight a schedule for the outing as a whole, as public transport services can be fairly unreliable. You should of course be well prepared with mosquito nets, hammocks, insect repellent and all the necessary food and medicines (see p.489). The reserve office (see p.540) provides **maps** and information on the region, when available.

From Lagunas, it's also possible to explore the **Tibilo** area, one of the best jungle regions in South America, not least because of its massive extent and the seasonal flooding which significantly increases the wildlife safari options. As well as being richly populated with monkeys, the lower Pacaya River area, at least in the dry season, is excellent for **birdwatching** (see *Peru's mythic wildlife* colour insert), around the temporary ponds and lakesides, where you can expect to find macaws, toucans, tiger herons, several varieties of kingfishers, among numerous other tropical species.

Pevas

Downstream from Iquitos lies **PEVAS**, some 190km to the east and reached in a day by **colectivo riverboat** or in a few hours by speedboat. The oldest town in the

Peruvian Amazon, it's an attractive, largely palm-thatched town and still a frontier place. The economy here is based primarily on fishing (visit the market where produce is brought in by boat every day), and dugout canoes are the main form of transport, propelled by characteristically ovoid-bladed and beautifully carved paddles, which are often sold as souvenirs, sometimes painted with designs. The **Witoto and Bora Indians**, largely concentrated around Pevas, actually arrived here in the 1930s after being relocated from the Colombian Amazon. They are now virtually in everyday contact with the riverine society of Pevas, producing quality artefacts for sale to passers-by and yet retaining much of their traditional knowledge of songs, dances and legends, plus significant ethno-pharmacological practice in rainforest medicine. The nearby Bora village of Puca Urquillo is a good example, a large settlement based around a Baptist church and school, whose founders moved here from the Colombian side of the Río Putumayo during the hardships of the rubber era rather than be enslaved. A number of local Indian groups can be visited, including the Bora, the Witoto and the less-visited Ocainas. Costs are from $60 per person per day, with extra for speedboat transport from Iquitos.

▲ Bora Indian, Pevas

Artist Francisco Grippa also lives in Pevas, though his work is actually exhibited in Iquitos at the **Amazon Art Gallery** (see p.537), while the surrounding flood forest is home to hundreds of caimans and significant **birdlife**, including several types of parrots, eagles and kingfishers. As well as birds, the area is good for **butterfly watching**, and November, in particular, is a great time to study orchids and bromeliads in bloom; it's also noted for its **fishing** – piranha being one of the easiest kinds to catch. For a good **place to stay**, try the *Casa de la Loma* (write to GreenTracks, PO Box 555, Iquitos; ☎/℗ 065/221184, ✉ info@greentracks.com; ➋), run by an American nurse. Set on a small hill close to Pevas, the lodge was set up by two nurses from Oregon who operate a separate (free) clinic here for the two thousand or so local inhabitants. They have five large bedrooms with shared bathrooms, and there's electricity, a refrigerator and a kitchen. Visits can be customized to suit individual requirements and interests.

Lodges, cruises and guides

If you're planning on an expedition beyond the limited network of roads around Iquitos, you'll have to take an organized trip with a **lodge operator**, a **river cruise** or hire a **freelance guide**. The larger local entrepreneurs have quite a grip on the market, and even the few guides who remain more or less independent are hard to bargain with since so much of their work comes through the larger agents. That said, they mostly have well worked-out itineraries, though you should always deal with an established company or agent – check out which outfits are **registered** at the tourist office in Iquitos – and insist on a written contract and receipt. Be aware that there's no shortage of **con artists** among the many **touts** around town, some of whom brandish quality brochures which belong to companies they are not actually affiliated with. Under no circumstances should you hand money over until you are 100% certain who you are dealing with.

A general rule of thumb is that any expedition of fewer than five days is unlikely to offer more wildlife than a few birds, some monkeys and maybe a crocodile if you're lucky; any serious attempt to visit virgin forest and see wildlife in its natural habitat requires a week or more. That said, if Iquitos is your main contact with the Amazon and you're unlikely to return here, you can rent a boat for an overnight trip from upwards of $40–50 per person. A group in low season may well be able to negotiate a three-day trip for as little as $30 per person per day, though there will be little guarantee of quality at this price. One or two of the smaller camps sometimes offer deals from as little as $30, but make sure they provide all the facilities you require. There's an almost infinite amount of jungle to be rewardingly explored in any direction from Iquitos, and one of the less-visited but nevertheless interesting areas – at least in terms of being relatively accessible yet still quite untouched and wild – lies **east between Iquitos and the Brazilian border**. It's nevertheless difficult to access this region without the help of a local guide and/or tour company; public boats plying this stretch of the Río Amazonas rarely stop and certainly don't give any time for passengers to explore. If you do want to stop off and spend some time here, Pevas (see p.543) is a good base for making river trips more or less independently, at least without going through an Iquitos tour company, though it's always a good idea to make use of local guides.

Tourist Protection Service

If your jungle trip really doesn't match what the agency led you to believe when selling you the tickets, it would help future visitors if you report this to the local tourist office and/or the 24-hour hotline of the **Tourist Protection Service** in Iquitos (☎ 065/233409, ✉ postmaster@indecopi.gob.pe).

Lodges

Guided tours require some kind of camp set-up or tourist **lodge** facilities. There are two main types of jungle experiences available from Iquitos – what Peruvian tour operators describe as **"conventional"** (focusing on lodge stays) and what they describe as **"adventure trips"** (going deeper into the jungle). Prices given are per person.

Amazon Camp Contact through Amazon Tours and Cruises (see p.548). A pleasant, conventional lodge on the Río Momón between the Yaguar and Bora Indian villages. This place can be visited in a day-trip, though it's more fun and a better deal if you stay longer. Around $100 per night.

Amazon Explorama ACTS Field Station (Amazon Conservatory for Tropical Studies) Contact Explorama (see below). An hour's walk from the company's *ExplorNapo Lodge* (see p.547), this particular establishment owns some 750 hectares of primary forest and was used for research though it's available for short visits and is quite comfortable, with separate rooms and shared dining and bathroom facilities. There's a medicinal plant trail with an information booklet corresponding to the numbered (marked/tagged) plant species on the path, but the really special feature is the well-maintained canopy walkway (the Amazon's longest), whose top-most platform is 35m high. Can be visited in conjunction with other Explorama lodges; $100–400 per day, depending on size of group, length of trip and the number of lodges visited.

Amazon Explorama CEIBA TOPS Contact Explorama, Av La Marina 340, Iquitos ☎065/ 253301, ✆252533, ✉amazon@explorama.com, 🌐www .explorama.com, or Box 445, Iquitos; toll-free in the US ☎1-800/707-5275. Explorama are the top operator in the region, with over 35 years' experience and over five hundred beds across their various lodges and locations; they aren't cheap, but do offer great quality. Explorama also now have their own very well-equipped river ferryboat – the *Amazon Queen*. Some 40km from Iquitos, this is the most luxurious lodge in the Peruvian Amazon, with a fantastic jungle swimming pool with a water slide, proper bar and dining areas, surrounded by 40 hectares of primary forest and 160 hectares of *chacra* and secondary growth. Accommodation is in smart conventional bungalows with a/c and flushing toilets, or in simpler bungalow-huts. Phone and internet ($3 for 10 minutes) connection available. Very popular in high season, so be sure to book well in advance. Can be visited in conjunction with other Explorama lodges; $100–400 per day, depending on size of group, length of trip and the number of lodges visited.

Amazon Explorama Lodge contact Explorama (see above). In a 195-hectare reserve and 90km

from Iquitos, this was Explorama's first lodge. Well equipped, it retains its rustic charm and acts as base camp for long-range programmes. Bora Indian talking drums (*manguare*) announce meal times in the dining room and guides often play Peruvian music in the bar during the evenings. Bedrooms have no locks and are simple but attractive, with individual mosquito nets; toilets are latrine-style but well maintained, and showers are cold. A few animals – including a tapir, an otter and several macaws – come and go around the place, and you can swim with dolphins in the Amazon, plus there are night walks and visits to the nearby Yaguar Indians. Can be visited in conjunction with other Explorama lodges; $100–400 per day, depending on size of group, length of trip and the number of lodges visited.

Amazon Rainforest Lodge Putumayo 159, Iquitos ☎065/233100 or 241628, ✉info@amazon-lodge.com, 🌐www.amazon-lodge.com; in Lima ☎01/2663388. Up the Río Momón (1–3hr, depending on water levels), the heart of this large lodge, run by an English resident, is a stunning restaurant and bar with a large viewing tower above. Accommodation is in very comfortable new bungalows with bathrooms, private toilets, internet access, cable TV and hammocks out front for relaxing. There is a great swimming pool which uses filtered well water, with the longest (34m) water slide in the Peruvian jungle. There's also a trampoline, pool table and games. There are conventional trips to local Indian villages that include fishing, jungle walks, birdwatching, plus *ayahuasca* sessions ($20) with local healers, one of whom has built a temple space at the back of the lodge. This is one of the best value lodges in terms of the swish accommodation offered. Prices range from $90 a day for adults (all inclusive apart from drinks and internet), kids half-price.

Amazon Refuge Nauta 242, ☎065/965685002, ✉info@amazonrefuge.com, 🌐www.amazonrefuge .com; international sales office: World Class Travel 808 NW 13th Street, Gainesville, Florida 32601, USA. ☎1-352-371-3100, or Toll Free 1-800-771-3100. A great lodge owned in collaboration with the San Juan de YanaYacu Indian Community, the *Amazon Refuge* is located one and a half hours by boat up the relatively remote Rio Yanayacu. Based in 200 acres of primary rainforest and surrounded by a 2000-acre Indian community nature reserve, the lodges buildings are constructed using naturally felled trees and thatched palm roofs. Accommodations is in private bungalows each with modern bath facilities. The service and English-speaking guides are top rate and, not least because of the lodge's proximity to Pacaya Samiria National Park, this outfit also specializes in wildlife and cultural treks into the National Park.

Amazon Retreat Centre ☎065/231127, ✉cloud @ec-red.com, ⊛www.shamanism.co.uk. Based near the charming village of Mishana on the Río Nanay, they have strong UK links and specialize in plant diets and *ayahuasca* ceremonies, sometimes lasting for up to two or three weeks, as well as artistic retreats, particularly painting. The surrounding Reserva Nacional Allpahuayo Mishana (58,000 hectares) is unique for its white sands (known as *varillales*) and inundated forest (*igapo*) that hosts endemic bird species and, during the rainy season, offers opportunities for exploring its black-water creeks where there are surprisingly few mosquitoes due to the acidity of the creeks and rivers. Accommodation is in *tambos* (traditional bungalow-huts on stilts) with good privacy and excellent river views. Fresh fish, vegetables and fruits available.

Blue Morpho C Moore 144, Iquitos ☎/℻065/ 231168, ⊛www.bluemorphotours.com. Blue Morpho have two lodges: one, more of a camp, deep in the jungle on the Río Galvez, a tributary of the Río Aucayacu (accesses from the riverside town of Genaro Herrera); and a newer 180-acre site much nearer at Km 53 of the Iquitos to Nauta road. They offer mid-price-range ($50–80) adventure rather than luxury and really demand a minimum of five or six days' commitment; they can sometimes organize *ayahuasca* shamanic ceremonies

Cumaceba Lodge Putumayo 184 ☎/℻065/ 232229, ⊛www.cumaceba.com. A highly recommended budget option with a lodge on the Amazon and also a camp on the more distant Río Yarapa. The lodge has accommodation in private rustic bungalows with individual bathrooms, as well as the usual communal dining area and hammock lounge, while lighting is by kerosene lamps. They take visitors to the local Yaguar village and on jungle walks; bird- and dolphin-watching also form part of their programmes. Optional extras include trips to the Pacaya Samiria National Reserve, water-skiing (June–Nov) and *ayahuasca* sessions. Around $120 for three days.

🏊 **ExplorNapo Lodge** contact Explorama (see p.546). Over ninety miles from Iquitos, on the Río Sucusari (Orejon Indian for "way in and out"). This lodge controls 3000 hectares of surrounding forest, the ExplorNapo Reserve, and its palm-roofed

buildings, hammock areas and dining room/bar are linked by thatch-covered walkways; during full moons you can sometimes hear tropical screech owls and the common potoos. From here there's easy access (less than an hour's walk) to the canopy walkway (see Amazon Explorama CTS Field Station, p.546); and further into the forest there is a jungle camp – *ExplorTambos* – where visitors can experience a night out in the middle of the forest away from any lodge, lights or people. Two hours' walk from *ExplorNapo Lodge* deep into primary forest, this is in many ways the ultimate jungle experience; a small collection of open-sided *tambo*-style huts, offering a night close to the earth, the elements and, of course, the animals. Can be visited in conjunction with other Explorama lodges; $100–400 per day, depending on size of group, length of trip, the level of quality and number of lodges visited.

Heliconia Amazon River Lodge Ricardo Palma 242, Iquitos ☎065/31959, or contact via the *Hotel Victoria Regia* (see p.535) ⊛www.amazonriverexpeditions.com. A pleasant lodge, 80km downriver from Iquitos, with accommodation in twin rooms with private bathrooms. They offer a basic three-day programme at around $100 per day.

🏊 **Muyuna** Putumayo 163 ☎065/242858 (Lima 01/445-9441), ⊛www.muyana.com. Based 120km upriver from Iquitos, up a tributary called Yanayacu, this lodge is fairly close to the Reserva Nacional de Pacaya Samiria. Accommodation is in attractive cabins, with private mosquito-proof rooms, en suite bathrooms and white-tiled showers; they offer jungle walking, river safari trips in canoes and other traditional excursions like piranha fishing, searching out *Vittoria regia* (renamed *Vittoria amazonica*) plants and alligator spotting. The Río Yanayacu is also pretty good for wildlife (see the photos in their ground-floor office) with lots of lakes, and most of the locals make their living from fishing rather than agriculture, as the soil here is relatively poor. They use their own dedicated guides, many of whom have a university background. Their jungle tours and lodge work hard to distinguish themselves from competitors as protectors of wild animals' right to remain free rather than be kept in zoos or cages, and they see their role as providing a service to enable people to see the animals, with respect, in the forest. It's a stance which ensures their reputation as one of the greenest eco-tour companies in the region, and needless to say they're reliable, with all their tours are sold directly by them to their clients; the standard charges are around $80–90 a day.

Refugio Altiplano Raymondi 171 ☎065/ 222001 ✉refugioaltiplano@lycos.com ⊛www .refugioaltiplano.org. A jungle lodge noted mainly for its *ayahuasca* ceremonies, groups visit a lodge on the Río Tamshiyacu some 50km upriver from Iquitos. **Sinchicuy Lodge** Pevas 246, Iquitos ☎065/231618. Reasonably priced, though a little too near a native village for there to be much wildlife in the immediate vicinity. Nevertheless, it does offer a relatively cheap rural setting and an agreeable out-of-town option. From $40 per day.

Zungarococha Resort Ricardo Palma 242, Iquitos ☎065/231959. A lodge offering the kind of comfortable rooms and bar associated with good middle-range conventional lodges, yet located only 14km from Iquitos on the Río Nanay. It offers jungle treks, nightwalks and the usual canoe exploration. From $60 to $75 a day.

Riverboat and cruise operators

Amazon Explorama – Amazon Queen Ferryboat Av La Marina 340, Iquitos ☎065/252530 or 252526 or 253301, ☎252533, ⓦwww .explorama.com; or Box 445, Iquitos; toll-free in the US ☎1-800/707-5275. A superbly converted ferryboat now operating with up to 180 passengers and nine crew members, mainly connecting Iquitos with Exporama's busiest lodge, CEIBA TOPS, and sometimes travelling down the Amazon and up the Río Napo. With its 365-horsepower engine it makes CEIBA TOPS in about 90min, while a large, comfortable lounge, card deck and carpeted bar on the second deck makes for a comfortable journey.

Amazon Tours and Cruises with Green Tracks Requena 336, Iquitos ☎065/231611, ⓦwww .amazontours.net; in the US 10 Town Plaza, PMB, 231, Durango, CO 81301, ☎970-884-6107. Offers luxury boats, running up the Río Amazonas to Requena, Pacaya Samiria National Reserve and down to Pevas, Leticia and Manaus, and will also organise airport transfers, city tours and a range of jungle trips, mostly around Iquitos.

Junglex Av Quinones 1980, Iquitos ☎065/261583; in Lima ☎01/2262640, ⓦwww.junglex.com. With several luxurious river boats of varying sizes, possibly the fanciest on the Amazon, *Junglex* offer three to six nights visiting the Río Ucayali and Rio Marañon for nature and fishing trips. They also go to the Pacaya Samiria National Reserve.

The three-way frontier

Leaving or entering Peru via the Río Amazonas inevitably means crossing the **three-way frontier**, nearly 300km from Iquitos. The cheapest and most common route is by river from Iquitos, some twelve hours in a *lancha rapida*, a big speedboat with two outboard motors, or three to four days downriver in a standard *lancha* riverboat which will usually have two or three decks, the middle one being for swinging your own hammock. Some services go all the way to **Leticia (Colombia)** or **Tabatinga (Brazil)**, but many stop at one of the two small Peruvian frontier settlements of Santa Rosa or Islandia; at Chimbote, a few hours before you get to Santa Rosa and on the right as you head towards the frontier, is a small police post, the main **customs checkpoint** (*guarda costa*) for river traffic. The region is interesting in its own right as the home of the **Tikuna Indians**, once numerous but today down to a population of around ten thousand. It's possible to arrange visits to some native communities from Leticia, and you can buy some of their excellent craftwork – mainly string bags and hammocks – from stores in that town.

Santa Rosa is your last chance to complete formalities with *migraciones* if you haven't already done so at the Iquitos office (see p.540) – essentially obtaining an **exit stamp** from Peru, if you're leaving, or getting an **entry stamp and tourist card** if arriving, which can take up to an hour. On larger boats, you often don't have to disembark here, as the Migraciones official may board the vessel and do the paperwork there and then. There are several cafés and a few **hostels**; the small *La Brisa del Amazonas* (❸) is a **restaurant** whose owner is also a useful contact for local **information**, including contacts for local guides. Ferryboats connect the town with Tabatinga and Leticia; most boats prefer to use Tabat-

Shamans and ayahuasca sessions

Ayahuasca sessions, or psychedelic tourism, have become a booming business in Iquitos. A new facility has opened near the city, operated by an NGO – the Centro Medico ONG Shapinguito (Iquitos–Nauta road Km 45.5 ℡065/231566, with an Iquitos office at Tacna 327); open to all interested parties, this clinic offers healing and working with *ayahuasca* usually in association with the female **shaman** Norma Panduro Navarro. Costs start at as little as $300 a month, including room and board as well as *ayahuasca* ceremonies. A well-known local *ayahuasca* guide, Francisco Montes (Sachamama, 18km from Iquitos on the road to Nauta; try asking around for him in hotels or tourist office) offers very traditional ceremonies with all the comforts of a lodge. Another popular shaman is Augustin Rivas, a famous sculptor who has dedicated over thirty years to working with *ayahuasca*; his sessions are run through *Yushintayta Lodge*, contactable via the *Hostal La Pascana*, Pevas 133 (℡065/231418); the lodge is located on the Río Tamshiyacu. In addition, many if not most of the jungle lodges around Iquitos regularly organize *ayahuasca* sessions for their clients. Similarly, many of the independent guides will organize sessions with shamans at their jungle camps. This sacred business is not regulated at all right now and, given the extremely sensitive states of mind achieved by ingesting *ayahuasca* (which can be much more powerful than LSD), it's important not only to feel comfortable with the scene and setting, but also with the person leading it. For information on ayahuasca and other teacher plants, see p.583.

inga, especially in low-water season – it's a long, muddy hike from the quay to the surfaced streets of Leticia, whereas at Tabatinga's two ports, the road goes right to the water's edge.

The only other way of crossing these three borders is by **flying** – a much less interesting approach, but not necessarily a more expensive one (though there's an airport departure tax of $2). Flights from Iquitos to Santa Rosa are operated by TANS, and both Varig and Rico fly to Manaus via Tabatinga at least three times a week. From Leticia, Avianca fly to a few major Colombian cities, including Bogotá, several times a week. If you're flying the other way, from Santa Rosa to Iquitos, TANS **tickets** can be bought from Señor Teddy, who operates out of one of the restaurants in this tiny town – just ask anywhere for him.

Into Colombia: Leticia

Having grown rich on tourism and contraband (mostly cocaine), **LETICIA** has more than a touch of the Wild West about it, but is still relatively safe. There's no physical border at the port or between Leticia and Tabatinga, though disembarking passengers sometimes have to go through a **customs check**, so carry your passport at all times. If you want to go on **into Colombia**, the cheapest way is to take a canoe to Puerto Asis, where you can latch on to the bus transport system, but to do this, or to stay overnight, you'll need to get a Colombian **tourist card** from the DAS office (Departmento Administrativo de Seguridad, C 9, 9–62, ℡098/5927189 or 5924878; open 24hr) just a few blocks from the port.

If you do stay, be warned that it's a lively town, with cumbia and salsa music blasting out all over the place, and establishments remaining open until the wee hours of the morning. The best of the basic **hotels** are *Residencial Monserrate* (❹) and *Residencial Leticia* (❷–❸), but much nicer are the *Colonial*, located near the port square at Carrera 10 (℡098/0057919; ❻), which has air-conditioning and private baths, and the swish *Anaconda* at Carrera 11 (℡098/5927891 or 5927119; ❽), which has a pool and an attractive *maloca*-style bar. The cheapest **place to eat**, and

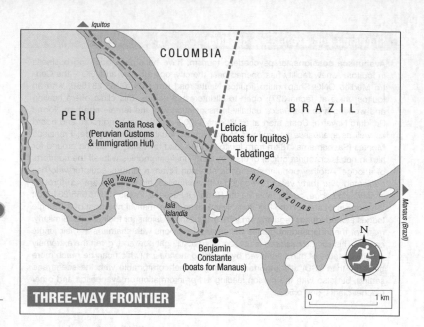

THREE-WAY FRONTIER

with the greatest variety of food, is at the riverside market, though the *Bucaneer* and *La Taguara* **cafés**, both at Carrera 10, are much better.

Into Brazil: Tabatinga

Smaller than Leticia, **TABATINGA** is hardly the most exciting place in South America, and many people stuck here waiting for a boat or plane to Manaus or Iquitos prefer to hop over the border to Leticia for the duration of their stay, even if they don't plan on going any further into Colombia. There are two docks here: at the smaller of the two, where smaller boats and canoes come and go with local produce and passengers, you'll encounter **customs checks**; Port Bras, the larger dock, is where you find the big *recreo* boats heading for Manaus. Brazilian **entry and exit formalities** are processed at the Policia Federal office (☎097/34122180; 10am–8pm, though 24hr for emergencies); if you're entering Brazil you'll usually be asked to show an exit ticket or prove that you have $500. There are a few **places to stay**. Try the *Hotel Paje*, Rue Pedro Teixeira 367 (☎097/34122774; ❸), or the much nicer and friendlier *Hotel Te Contei*, Av da Amizade 1813 (☎097/34122377 or 34132566; ❺), which is entered via the rickety spiral stairway over a pizzeria of the same name. There are a handful of other **restaurants** dotted about, mainly by the smaller dock.

Continuing on downstream **into Brazil** on boats to Manaus, a four- to seven-day journey that is often very crowded, costs $40–80 depending on their size, condition and whether or not you require a cabin. They leave from both Tabatinga and **Benjamin Constante**, on the other side of the Amazon, usually starting from the former in the early afternoons (frequently on Wednesdays, but also less regularly on most other days of the week) and calling at the latter an hour or so later. If there are no boats in Tabatinga, however, it may be worth taking a speedboat ferry ($8; a 30min trip) to Benjamin Constante to see if there are any departing just from there. If you've arrived from Iquitos on a boat that's continuing all the way to Manaus, it's important to let the captain know whether or not you need to go into Tabatinga to quickly sort your visa business (use a taxi) and then meet the boat at Benjamin Constante. Bear in mind that it's virtually impossible to get from Islandia to the federal police in Tabatinga and then back to Benjamin Constante in less than an hour and a half.

Pirarucu Turismo, Rua Santos Dumont 2 (☎097/91515936) in Tabatinga, specialize in **cheap flights and boat trips** from here downriver to Brazil or back up into Peru.

Travel details

Buses and trucks

Cusco to: Puerto Maldonado (several daily; 18–24hr); Quillabamba via Ollantaytambo (2–3 most days; 12hr), or via Calca Lares (2–3 weekly; 18hr); Shintuya (1–2 every Mon, Wed, Fri & Sat; 16–20hr).
Iquitos to: Nauta (daily; 4hr).
Lima to: Pucallpa (daily; 16–24hr via Huánuco); La Merced (several daily; 7hr).
La Merced to: Lima (several daily; 7hr); Pucallpa, via Puerto Bermudez (weekly; 24hr); Satipo (several daily; 2–3hr).
Puerto Maldonado to: Cusco (several daily; 18–24hr); Iñapari and Brazilian frontier (several daily; 4hr).

Boats

Boca Manu to: Shintuya (irregular, 1 daily on average; 6hr); Puerto Maldonado (irregular; 2–4 days).

Iquitos to: Leticia and Tabatinga (several weekly; 9–12hr or 3–4 days, depending on boat); Pucallpa (several weekly; 5–7 days); Nauta (1 or 2 daily; 8–10hr).
Pucallpa to: Iquitos (several weekly; 5–7 days); Nauta (several weekly; 5–6 days).
Shintuya to: Boca Manu (irregular, 1 daily on average; 6hr); Puerto Maldonado (irregular; 2–4 days).

Flights

Iquitos to: Lima (several daily; 2hr); Pucallpa (daily; 1hr 30min); Santa Rosa (irregular; 1hr 30min); Tarapoto (daily; 1hr).
Pucallpa to: Lima (5 weekly; 1hr 30min); Tarapoto (several weekly; 1hr).
Puerto Maldonado to: Cusco (2–3 daily; 35min); Lima (2–3 daily; 2hr).

Contexts

Contexts

History

The first Peruvians were descendants of the nomadic tribes which had crossed into the Americas during the last Ice Age (40,000–15,000 BC), when a combination of ice packs and low sea levels exposed a neck of solid "land" that spanned what's now the Bering Strait. Following herds of game animals from Siberia into what must have been a relative paradise of fertile coast, wild forest, mountain and savannah, successive generations continued south through Central America. Some made their way down along the Andes, into the Amazon, and out onto the more fertile areas of the Peruvian and Ecuadorian coast, while others found their niches en route.

In a number of tribes there seem to be cultural memories of these long migrations, encapsulated in their traditional mythologies – though these aren't really transcribable into written histories. There is, however, archaeological evidence of human occupation in Peru dating back to around 15,000–20,000 BC, concentrated in the **Ayacucho Valley**, where these early Peruvians lived in caves or out in the open. Around 12,000 BC, slightly to the north in the **Chillon Valley** (just above modern Lima), comes the first evidence of significant craft skills – stone blades and knives for hunting. At this time there were probably similar groups of hunter tribes in the mountains and jungle too, but the climatic conditions of these zones make it unlikely that any significant remains will ever be found.

The difficulties of traversing the rugged terrain between the highlands and coast evidently proved little problem for the early Peruvians. From 8000 to 2000 BC, **migratory bands** of hunters and gatherers alternated between camps in the lowlands during the harsh mountain winters, and highland summer "resorts", their actual movements well synchronized with those of wild animal herds. One important mountain encampment from this **Incipient Era** has been discovered at **Lauricocha**, near Huánuco, at an altitude of over 4000m. Here the art of working stone – eventually producing very fine blades and arrow points – seems to have been sophisticated, while at the same time a growing cultural imagination found expression in cave paintings depicting animals, hunting scenes and even dances. Down on the coast at this time other groups were living on the greener *lomas* belts of the desert in places like **Chilca** to the south, and in the mangrove swamps around **Tumbes** to the north.

An awareness of the potential uses of plants began to emerge around **5000 BC** with the **cultivation** of seeds and tubers (the potato being one of the most important "discoveries" later taken to Europe), to be followed over the next two millennia by the introduction, presumably from the Amazon, of gourds, Lima beans, then squashes, peanuts and eventually cotton. Towards the end of this period a climatic shift turned the coast into a much more arid belt and forced those living there to try their hand at **agriculture** in the fertile riverbeds, a process to some extent paralleled in the mountains.

With a stable agricultural base, permanent settlements sprang up all along the coast, notably at **Chicama**, **Asia** and **Paracas**, and in the sierra at **Kotosh**. The population began to mushroom, and with it came a new consciousness, perhaps influenced by cultural developments within the Amazon Basin to the east: **cultism** – the burial of the dead in mummy form, the capturing of trophy heads and the building of grand religious structures – made its first appearance. At the same time there were also overwhelming technological advances in the spheres of weaving, tool-making and ornamental design.

The pyramids of Caral

Located in a relatively remote spot in the desert coast in a landscape which looks more lunar than agricultural, archaeologists have recently uncovered one of the most important archaeological finds in a hundred years or more. Thought to be the oldest city in the Americas, the archaeological remains of **Caral** have overturned many assumptions made by archaeologists in recent decades. Possibly the most important discovery since Machu Picchu was rediscovered in 1911, this site represents human achievements which occurred four thousand years earlier than the Incas. The stone-built ceremonial structures at Caral were flourishing a hundred years before the Great Pyramid at Giza was built.

Just one of around a dozen sites in the Supe Valley 120km north of Lima, just 22km inland from the ocean, radiocarbon dating proves that the site was fully functioning for around five hundred years, from around 2600 BC, complete with six stone platform mounds, with ceremonial plazas below and irrigation channels serving the surrounding fields. First discovered in 1905, Caral was then largely ignored by archaeologists because, though large, no gold or even ceramics had ever been unearthed. It was, in fact, a pre-ceramic site whose importance resided in another technology, that of early domestication of plants including cotton, squashes, beans and guava.

Some of the best artefacts discovered here, in a ceremonial fire pit by the circular amphitheatre, include 32 flutes made from pelican and animal bones, and engraved with the figures of birds and even monkeys, demonstrating a connection with the Amazon region even this long ago.

The six mounds, or pyramids, are arranged together around a large plaza. Archaeologists believe that the pyramids were constructed in a maximum of two phases, which tends to suggest the need for particularly complex social structures for planning, decision-making and the mobilization of a large sector of the population to provide sufficient labour as and when it was required. Around the pyramids there is evidence that there were many residential structures. Inside one of the houses, archaeologists have discovered the remains of one body which was buried in the wall and appears to have been a natural death rather than the sign of a sacrifice.

Before the advent of urban living and stone ceremonial pyramids at Caral, the region was only populated by a few coastal villages, each with around a hundred inhabitants. Around 2700 BC it appears that a number of larger villages emerged, principally, it seems, based around the successful domestication and early cultivation of the cotton bush plant. To date, however, it is unclear whether cotton was first domesticated here on the Peruvian coast or over the Andes on the edges of the Amazon basin where it is still one of the most prized crops for many of the indigenous tribes, many of which, like the Ashaninka, were almost certainly thriving at the time of Caral. Back in Caral, the early use of cotton was nothing short of a bio-technological revolution, not only providing cloth for garments but more importantly permitting the fabrication of nets for fishing in the rich coastal waters, as well as net or woven bags for carrying produce and fish back home to their settlements. The introduction of cotton fishing nets would have transformed the lives of coastal communities, giving them sufficient and relatively easy protein, more spare time to evolve social and religious practices and surplus food to trade with neighbouring communities. The emergence of barter- and tribute-based market centres, perhaps closely aligned with sacred centres of pilgrimage, would have begun to take on greater significance as the emerging society depended more and more on the fruit of farming and coastal communities. There would have been a strong interdependence between coastal fishing communities and agricultural communities irrigating the foothills just a half a day's walk inland from the ocean.

At its heyday it's thought that at least three thousand people were living in Caral. If the other seventeen yet unexcavated sites in the area had held similar-sized populations, then the total population living, working and worshipping in the Supe Valley around 4600 years ago might have been as high as 20,000 or even more. It appears to have been abandoned quite rapidly after about five hundred years of booming inhabitance; theories as to why include the possibility of drought, which would have forced them to move to another valley in search of available water and even more fertile soils.

The Chavín Cult

From around 1200 BC to 200 AD – the **Formative Era** – agriculture and village life became established. Ceramics were invented, and a slow disintegration of regional isolation began. This last factor was due mainly to the widespread dispersal of a religious movement, the **Chavín Cult**. Remarkable in that it seems to have spread without the use of military force, the cult was based on the worship of nature spirits, and an all-powerful feline creator god. This widespread feline image rapidly exerted its influence over the northern half of Peru and initiated a period of inter-relations between people in fertile basins in the Andes and some of the coastal valleys. How and where the cult originated is uncertain, though it seems probable that it began in the eastern jungles, possibly spreading to the Andes (and eventually the coast) along the upper Río Marañón. There may well have been a significant movement of people and trade goods between these areas and the rainforest regions, too, as evidenced by the many jungle-bird feathers incorporated into capes and headdresses found on the coast. More recent theories, however, suggest that the flow may have been in the opposite direction, starting on the coast. The stone and adobe temples, for instance, in the Sechin area, pre-date the Chavín era, yet seem to be culturally linked.

The Chavín Cult was responsible for excellent progress in **stone carving** and **metallurgy** (copper, gold and silver) and, significantly, a ubiquity of temples and pyramids emerged as religious and cultural centres. The most important known centre was the temple complex at **Chavín de Huantar** in Ancash, though a similar one was built at **Kotosh** near Huánuco; its influence seems to have spread over the northern highlands and coast from Chiclayo down as far as the Paracas Peninsula (where it had a particularly strong impact). There were immense local variations in the expressions of the Chavín Cult: elaborate metallurgy in the far north; adobe buildings on stone platforms in the river valleys; excellent ceramics from **Chicama**; and the extravagant stone engravings from Chavín itself. In the mountains life must have been very hard, based on subsistence agriculture and pilgrimages to the sacred shrines – most of which probably originated around ideas formulated by an emergent caste of powerful priest-chiefs. On the coast there was an extra resource – seafood – to augment the meagre agricultural yields.

Towards the **end of the Chavín phase**, an experimental period saw new centres attempting to establish themselves as independent powers with their own distinct cultures. This gave birth to **Gallinazo** settlements in the Viru Valley; the **Paracas culture** on the south coast (with its beautiful and highly advanced textile technology based around a cult of the dead); and the early years of **Tiahuanaco** development in the Lake Titicaca region. These three cultural upsurges laid the necessary foundations for the flourishing civilizations of the subsequent Classical Era.

The Classical Era

A diverse period – and one marked by intense development in almost every field – the **Classical Era** (200–1100 AD) saw the emergence of numerous distinct cultures, both on the coast and in the sierra. The best-documented, though not necessarily the most powerful, are the **Mochica** and **Nasca** cultures (both probably descendants of the coastal Paracas culture) and the **Tiahuanaco**, all forebears of the better-known Incas. In recent years, though, archaeological discoveries in the Lambayeque Valley on the north coast have revealed important ceremonial centres – particularly the **Sicán** culture's massive sacred complex of truncated pyramids at **Batán Grande**. Contemporaneous with the Mochica, to the south, there is also strong evidence that the Sicán revered the same demonic spirit or god, named **Ai-Apaec** in the Mochica language, the "Winged Decapitator", who kept the world of human life and death in order. Ai-Apaec is also associated with the veritable treasure-trove found in the royal tombs at **Sipán**, just south of Lambayeque, and those of the Vicus culture, to the north, near Piura.

The **Mochica culture** has left the fullest evidence of its social and domestic life, all aspects of which, including its work and religion, are vividly represented in highly realistic pottery. The first real urban culture in Peru, its members maintained a firm hierarchy, an elite group combining both secular and sacred power. Ordinary people cultivated land around clusters of dwelling sites, dominated by sacred pyramids – man-made *huacas* dedicated to the gods. The key to the elite's position was probably their organization of large irrigation projects, essential to the survival of these relatively large population centres in the arid desert of the north coast. In the Mochica region, nature and the world of the ancestors seem the dominant cultural elements; occasional human sacrifices were offered and trophy heads were captured in battle. The peak of their influence came around 500 to 600 AD, when they had cultural and military control of the coast from Piura in the north to the Nepena Valley in the south.

More or less contemporaneous with the Mochica, the **Nasca culture** bloomed for several hundred years on the south coast. The Nasca are thought to be responsible for the astonishing lines and drawings etched into the Pampa de San José, though little is known for certain about their society or general way of life. The Nasca did, however, build an impressive temple complex in the desert at **Cahuachi**, and their burial sites have turned up thousands of beautiful ceramics whose abstract designs can be compared only to the quality and content of earlier Paracas textiles.

Named after its sacred centre on the shore of Lake Titicaca, the **Tiahuanaco culture** developed at much the same time as the Mochica – with which, initially at least, it peacefully coexisted. Tiahuanaco textiles and pottery spread along the desert, modifying both Mochica and Nasca styles and bending them into more sophisticated shapes and abstract patterns. The main emphasis in Tiahuanaco pottery and stonework was on symbolic elements featuring condors, pumas and snakes – more than likely the culture's main gods, representing their respective spheres of the sky, earth and underworld. In this there seem obvious echoes of the deified natural phenomena of the earlier Chavín cult.

Although initially peaceable, the Tiahuanaco influence is associated in its decadent phase with **militarism**. Originating either at Huari, in the sierra near Ayacucho, or on the central coast, this forceful tendency extended from 650 to

1100 AD and was dominated by what today is called the **Huari–Tiahuanaco culture**. The ruins at Huari cover some eight square kilometres and include high-walled enclosures of field stones laid and plastered with mud, decorated by only a few stone statues along Tiahuanaco lines. Whether or not this was the actual inspirational centre, by around 1000 AD Huari-Tiahuanaco features were dominant in the art forms over virtually all of Peru.

In the north the Valley of the Pyramids, or **Túcume**, was another major ceremonial centre, covering more than two hundred hectares. Initially begun by the Sicán culture, who started building here around 1100 AD after abandoning their earlier centre at Batán Grande, it reached its peak in the thirteenth and early fourteenth centuries, during the power vacuum in the Mochica Valley, between the decline of the Mochica and the rise of the Chimu. Archeologists believe that this must have been a time of abundance and population growth in this desert region, with optimum weather conditions for agriculture, the improvement of irrigation techniques and plentiful seafood.

An increasing prevalence of **intertribal warfare** characterized the era's later period, culminating in the erection of defensive forts, a multiplication of ceremonial sites, including over sixty large pyramids in the Lima area. The **Huaca Pucllana** is one of these pyramids, a vast pre-Inca adobe mound which can be visited in the suburb of Miraflores, in Lima. It has a hollow core running through its cross section and is thought to have been constructed in the shape of an enormous frog, a symbol of the rain god, who spoke to priests through a tube connected to the cavern.

Eventually Huari-Tiahuanaco influence on the coast was uprooted and overturned by the emergence of three youthful mini-empires – the **Chimu**, the **Cuismancu** and the **Chincha**. In the mountains its influence mysteriously disappeared to pave the way for the separate growth of relatively large tribal units such as the **Colla** (around Titicaca), the **Inca** (around Cusco) and the **Chanca** (near Ayacucho).

Partly for defensive reasons, this period of isolated development sparked off a city-building urge which became almost compulsive by the Imperial Period in the thirteenth century. The most spectacular urban complex was **Chan Chan** (near modern Trujillo), built by the **Chimu** on the side of the river opposite to earlier Mochica temples but indicating a much greater sophistication in social control, the internal structure of the culture's clan-based society reflected in the complex's intricate layout. By now, with a working knowledge of bronze manufacture, the Chimu spread their domain from Chan Chan to Tumbes in the north and Paramonga in the south – dominating nearly half the Peruvian coastline. To the south they were bounded by the **Cuismancu**, less powerful, though capable of building similar citadels (such as Cajamarquilla near Lima) and of comparable attainment in craft industries. Further down the coastline, the **Chincha** – known also as the **Ica culture** – also produced fine monuments and administrative centres in the Chincha and Pisco valleys. The lower rainfall on the southern coast, however, didn't permit the Chincha state – or (to an extent) the Cuismancu – to create urban complexes anything near the size of Chan Chan.

The Incas

With the **Inca Empire** (1200–1532 AD) came the culmination of the city-building phase and the beginnings of a kind of Peruvian unity, as the Incas, although originally a tribe of no more than around 40,000, gradually took over each of the separate coastal empires. One of the last to go – almost bloodlessly, and just sixty

Manco Capac (cultural hero c.1200 AD)	Viracocha Inca
Sinchi Roca	Pachacuti (1438–71)
Lloque Yupanqui	Topac Yupanqui (1471–93)
Mayta Capac	Huayna Capac (1493–1525)
Capac Yupanqui	Huascar (1525–32)
Inca Roca	Atahualpa (1532–33)
Yahuar Huaca	

years before the Spanish conquest – was the Chimu, who for much of this **Imperial Period** were a powerful rival.

Based in the valleys around Cusco, the Incas were for the first two centuries of their existence much like any other of the larger mountain tribes. Fiercely protective of their independence, they maintained a somewhat feudal society, tightly controlled by rigid religious tenets, though often disrupted by inter-tribal conflict. The founder of the dynasty – around 1200 AD – was **Manco Capac**, who passed into Inca mythology as a cultural hero. Historically, however, little is known about Inca developments or achievements until the accession in 1438 AD of Pachacuti, and the onset of their great era of expansion.

Pachacuti, most innovative of all the Inca emperors, was the first to expand their traditional tribal territory. The beginnings of this expansion were in fact not of his making but the response to a threatened invasion by the powerful, neighbouring Chanca Indians during the reign of his father, **Viracocha**. Viracocha, feeling the odds to be overwhelming, left Cusco in Pachacuti's control, withdrawing to the refuge of Calca along the Río Urubamba. Pachacuti, however, won a legendary victory – Inca chronicles record that the very stones of the battlefield rose up in his defence – and, having vanquished the most powerful force in the region, shortly took the Inca crown for himself.

Within three decades Pachacuti had consolidated his power over the entire sierra region from Cajamarca to Titicaca, defeating in the process all main imperial rivals except for the Chimu. At the same time the capital at **Cusco** was spectacularly developed, with the evacuation and destruction of all villages within a ten-kilometre radius, a massive programme of agricultural terracing (watched over by a skyline of agro-calendrical towers), and the construction of unrivalled palaces and temples. Shrewdly, Pachacuti turned his forcible evacuation of the Cusco villages into a positive plan, relocating the Incas in newly colonized areas. He also extended this practice towards his subjugated allies, conscripting them into the Inca armies while their chiefs remained as hostages and honoured guests at Cusco.

Inca territory expanded north into Ecuador, almost reaching Quito, under the next emperor – **Tupac Yupanqui** – who also took his troops down the coast, overwhelming the Chimu and capturing the holy shrine of Pachacamac. Not surprisingly the coastal cultures influenced the Incas perhaps as much as the Incas influenced them, particularly in the sphere of craft industries. Even compared to Pachacuti, Topac Yupanqui was nevertheless an outstandingly imaginative and able ruler. During the 22 years of his reign (1471–93) he pushed Inca control southwards as far as the Río Maule in Chile; instigated the first proper census of the empire and set up the decimal-based administrative system; introduced the division of labour and land between the state, the gods and the local *allyus*; invented the concept of Chosen Women (Mamaconas); and inaugurated a new class of respected individuals (the Yanaconas). An empire had been unified not just physically but also administratively and ideologically.

At the end of the fifteenth century the Inca Empire was thriving, as vital as any civilization before or since. Its politico-religious authority was finely tuned, extracting what it needed from its millions of subjects and giving what was necessary to maintain the status quo – be it brute force, protection or food. The only obvious problem inherent in the Inca system of unification and domination was one of over-extension. When **Huayna Capac** continued Topac Yupanqui's expansion to the north he created a new Inca city at **Quito**, one which he personally preferred to Cusco and which laid the seed for a division of loyalties within Inca society. At this point in history, the Inca Empire was probably the largest in the world even though it had neither horse nor wheel technology. The empire was over 5500km long, stretching from southern Colombia right down to northern Chile, with Inca highways covering distances of around 30,000km in all.

Almost as a natural progression from over-extending the empire in this way, the divisions in Inca society came to a head even before Huayna Capac's death. Ruling the empire from Quito, along with his favourite son **Atahualpa**, Huayna Capac installed another son, **Huascar**, at Cusco. In the last year of his life he tried to formalize the division – ensuring an inheritance at Quito for Atahualpa – but this was fiercely resisted by Huascar, legitimate heir to the title of Lord Inca and the empire, and by many of the influential Cusco priests and nobles. In 1527, when Huayna Capac died of the white man's disease, smallpox, which had swept down overland from Mexico in the previous seven years, killing over thirty percent of the indigenous population, civil war broke out. Atahualpa, backed by his father's army, was by far the stronger and immediately won a major victory at the Río Bamba – a battle that, it was said, left the plain littered with human bones for over a hundred years. A still bloodier battle, however, took place along the Río Apurimac at Cotabamba in 1532. This was the decisive victory for Atahualpa, and with his army he retired to relax at the hot baths near Cajamarca. Here, informed of a strange-looking, alien band, successors of the bearded adventurers whose presence had been noted during the reign of Huayna Capac, they waited.

The Spanish conquest

Francisco Pizarro, along with two dozen soldiers, stumbled upon and named the Pacific Ocean in 1513 while on an exploratory expedition in Panama. From that moment his determination, fired by native tales of a fabulously rich land to the south, was set. Within eleven years he had found himself financial sponsors and set sail down the Pacific coast with the priest Hernando de Luque and Diego Almagro.

With remarkable determination, having survived several disastrous attempts, the three explorers eventually landed at **Tumbes** in 1532. A few months later a small, Pizarro-led band of Spaniards, less than two hundred men, arrived at the Inca city of **Cajamarca** to meet the leader of what they were rapidly realizing was a mighty empire. En route to Cajamarca, Pizarro had learned of the Inca civil wars and of Atahualpa's recent victory over his brother Huascar. This rift within the empire provided the key to success that Pizarro was looking for.

The day after their arrival, in what at first appeared to be a lunatic endeavour, Pizarro and his men massacred thousands of Inca warriors and captured Atahualpa. Although ridiculously outnumbered, the Spaniards had the advantages of surprise, steel, cannons, and, above all, mounted cavalry. The **decisive battle** was over in a matter of hours: with Atahualpa prisoner, Pizarro was effectively in control of the Inca Empire. Atahualpa was promised his freedom if he could fill the famous Ransom Room at Cajamarca with gold. Caravans overladen with the precious metal arrived from all over the land and within six months the room was filled: a treasure worth over 1.5 million pesos, which was already enough to make each of the conquerors extremely wealthy. Pizarro, however, chose to keep the Inca leader as a hostage in case of Indian revolt, amid growing suspicions that Atahualpa was inciting his generals to attack the Spanish. Atahualpa almost certainly did send messages to his chiefs in Cusco, including orders to execute his brother Huascar who was already in captivity there. Under pressure from his worried captains, Pizarro brought Atahualpa to trial in July 1533, a mockery of justice in which he was given a free choice: to be burned alive as a pagan or strangled as a Christian. They baptized him and then killed him.

With nothing left to keep him in Cajamarca, Pizarro made his way through the Andes to Cusco where he crowned a puppet emperor, **Manco Inca**, of royal Indian blood. After all the practice that the Spaniards had had in imposing their culture on the Aztecs in Mexico, it took them only a few years to replace the Inca Empire with a working colonial mechanism. Now that the Inca civil wars were over, the natives seemed happy to retire quietly into the hills and get back to the land. However, more than wars, **disease** was responsible for the almost total lack of initial reaction to the new conquerors. The native population of Peru had dropped from some 32 million in 1520 to only five million by 1548 – a decline due mainly to new European ailments such as smallpox, measles, bubonic plague, whooping cough and influenza.

Colonial Peru

Peru's vast wealth, of resources as well as treasure, was recognised early on. Between the sixteenth and seventeenth centuries Spain established only two Viceroyalties in the Americas: first in Mexico, then shortly afterwards in Peru. Queen Isabella indirectly laid the original foundations for the political administration of Peru in 1503 when she authorized the initiation of an **encomienda system**, which meant that successful Spanish conquerors could extract tribute for the Crown and personal service in return for converting the natives to Christianity. They were not, however, given title to the land itself. As governor of Peru, Pizarro used the *encomienda* system to grant large groups of Indians to his favourite soldier-companions. In this way, the basic colonial land-tenure structure was created in everything but name. "Personal service" rapidly came to mean subservient serfdom for the native population, many of whom were now expected to raise animals introduced from the Old World (cattle, hens, etc) on behalf of their new overlords. Many Inca cities were rebuilt as Spanish towns, although some, like Cusco, retained native masonry for their foundations and even walls. Other Inca sites, like Huánuco Viejo, were abandoned in favour of cities in more hospitable lower altitudes. The Spanish were drawn to the coast for strategic as well as climatic reasons – above all to maintain constant oceanic links with the homeland via Panama.

The **foundation of Lima** in 1535 began a multilayered process of satellite dependency which continues even today. The fat of the land (originally mostly gold and other treasures) was sucked in from regions all over Peru, processed in Lima, and sent on from there to Spain. Lima survived on the backs of Peru's municipal capitals which, in turn, extracted tribute from the scattered *encomenderos*. The *encomenderos* depended on local chieftains (*curacas*) to rake in service and goods from even the most remote villages and hamlets. At the lowest level there was little difference between Inca imperial exploitation and the economic network of Spanish colonialism. Where they really varied was that under the Incas the surplus produce circulated among the elite within the country, while the Spaniards sent much of it to a monarch on the other side of the world.

In 1541 Pizarro was assassinated by a disgruntled faction among the conquistadors who looked to Diego Almagro as their leader, and for the next seven years the nascent colonial society was rent by civil war. In response, the first **viceroy** – Blasco Nuñez de Vela – was sent from Spain in 1544. His task was to act as royal commissioner and to secure the colony's loyalty to Spain; his fate was to be killed by Gonzalo Pizarro, brother of Francisco. But Royalist forces, now under Pedro de la Gasca, eventually prevailed – Gonzalo was captured and executed, and Crown control firmly re-established.

Colonial society

During this time, **Peruvian society** was being transformed by the growth of new generations: creoles, descendants of Spaniards born in Peru, and *mestizos*, of mixed Spanish and native blood, created a new class structure. In the coastal valleys where populations had been ravaged by European diseases, slaves were imported from Africa. There were over 1500 black slaves in Lima alone by 1554. At the same time, as a result of the civil wars and periodic Indian revolts, over a third of the original conquerors had lost their lives by 1550. Nevertheless effective power remained in the hands of the independent *encomenderos*.

In an attempt to dilute the influence of the *encomienda* system, the Royalists divided the existing twenty or so municipalities into **corregimentos**, smaller units headed by a *corregidor*, or royal administrator. They were given the power to control the activities of the *encomenderos* and exact tribute for the Crown – soon becoming the vital links in provincial government. The pattern of constant friction between *encomenderos* and *corregidores* was to continue for centuries, with only the priests to act as local mediators.

Despite the evangelistic zeal of the Spanish, **religion** changed little for the majority of the native population. Although Inca ceremonies, pilgrimages and public rituals were outlawed, their mystical and magical base endured. Each region quickly reverted to the pre-Inca cults deep-rooted in their culture and cosmology. Over the centuries the people learned to absorb symbolic elements of the Catholic faith into their beliefs and rituals – allowing them, once again, to worship relatively freely. Magic, herbalism and divination have continued strongly at the village level and have successfully pervaded modern Peruvian thought, language and practice (the Peruvian World Cup football squad in 1982 enlisted – in vain – the magical aid of a *curandero*.). At the elite level, the Spanish continued their fervent attempts to convert the entire population to their own ritualistic religion. They were, however, more successful with the rapidly growing *mestizo* population, who shared the same cultural aspirations.

Miraculous occurrences became a conspicuous feature in the popular Peruvian Catholic Church, the greatest example being Our Lord of Miracles, a cult which originated among the black population of colonial Lima. In the devastating earthquake of 1665, an anonymous mural of the Crucifixion on the wall of a chapel in the poorest quarter was supposedly the only structure left standing. The belief that this was a direct sign from God took hold among the local population, and Our Lord of Miracles remains the most revered image in Peru. Thousands of devotees process through the streets of Lima and other Peruvian towns every October, and even today many women dress in purple throughout the month to honour Our Lord of Miracles.

In return for the salvation of their souls the native population were expected to surrender their bodies to the Spanish. Some forms of service (*mita*) were simply continuations of Inca tradition – from keeping the streets clean to working in textile mills. But the most feared was a new introduction, the *mita de minas* – **forced work in the mines**. With the discovery of the "mountain of silver" at Potosí (now Bolivia) in 1545, and of mercury deposits at Huancavelica in 1563, it reached new heights. Forced off their smallholdings, few Indians who left to work in the mines ever returned. Indeed, the mercury mines at Huancavelica were so dangerous that the quality of their toxic ore could be measured by the number of weekly deaths. Those who were taken to Potosí had to be chained together to stop them from escaping: if they were injured, their bodies were cut from the shackles by sword to save precious time. Around three million Indians worked in Potosí and Huancavelica alone; some had to walk over 1000km from Cusco to Potosí for the privilege of working themselves to death.

In 1569, **Francisco Toledo** arrived in Peru to become viceroy. His aim was to reform the colonial system so as to increase royal revenue while at the same time improving the lot of the native population. Before he could get on with that, however, he had to quash a rapidly developing threat to the colony – the appearance of a **neo-Inca state**. After an unsuccessful uprising in 1536, Manco Inca, Pizarro's puppet emperor, had disappeared with a few thousand loyal subjects into the remote mountainous regions of **Vilcabamba**, northwest of Cusco. With the full regalia of high priests, virgins of the sun and the golden idol of Punchau (the sun god), he maintained a rebel Inca state and built himself impressive new palaces and fortresses between Vitcos and Espiritu Pampa – well beyond the reach of colonial power. Although not a substantial threat to the colony, Manco's forces repeatedly raided nearby settlements and robbed travellers on the roads between Cusco and Lima.

Manco himself died at the hands of a Spanish outlaw, a guest at Vilcabamba who hoped to win himself a pardon from the Crown. But the neo-Inca state continued under the leadership of Manco's son, Sairi Tupac, who assumed the imperial fringe at the age of ten. Tempted out of Vilcabamba in 1557, Sairi Tupac was offered a palace and a wealthy life by the Spanish in return for giving up his refuge and subversive aims. He died a young man, only three years after turning to Christianity and laying aside his father's cause. Meanwhile Titu Cusi, one of Manco's illegitimate sons, declared himself emperor and took control in Vilcabamba.

Eventually, Titu Cusi began to open his doors. First he allowed two Spanish friars to enter his camp, and then, in 1571, negotiations were opened for a return to Cusco when an emissary arrived from Viceroy Toledo. The talks broke down before the year was out and Toledo decided to send an army into Vilcabamba to rout the Incas. They arrived to find that Titu Cusi was already dead and his brother, **Tupac Amaru**, was the new emperor. After fierce fighting and a near-escape, Tupac Amaru was captured and brought to trial in Cusco. Accused of plotting to overthrow the Spanish and of inciting his followers to raid towns, Tupac Amaru was beheaded as soon as possible – an act by Toledo that was disavowed by the Spanish Crown and which caused much distress in Peru.

Toledo's next task was to firmly establish the viceregal position – something that outlasted him by some two centuries. He toured highland Peru seeking ways to improve Crown control, starting with an attempt to curb the excesses of the *encomenderos* and their tax-collecting *curacas* (hereditary native leaders) by implementing a programme of **reducciones** – the physical resettlement of Indians in new towns and villages. Hundreds of thousands of peasants, perhaps millions, were forced to move from remote hamlets into large conglomerations, or *reducciones,* in convenient locations. Priests, or *corregidores*, were placed in charge of them, undercutting the power of the *encomenderos*. Toledo also established a new elected position – the local mayor (or *varayoc*) – in an attempt to displace the *curacas*. The *varayoc*, however, was not necessarily a good colonial tool in that, even more than the *curacas*, his interests were rooted firmly in the *allyu* and in his own neighbours, rather than in the wealth of some distant kingdom.

Rebellion

When the Hapsburg monarchy gave way to the Bourbon kings in Spain at the beginning of the eighteenth century, shivers of protest seemed to reverberate deep in the Peruvian hinterland. There were a number of serious **native rebellions** against colonial rule during the next hundred years. One of the most important, though least known, was that led by **Juan Santos Atahualpa**, a *mestizo* from Cusco. Juan Santos had travelled to Spain, Africa and, some say, to England as a young man in the service of a wealthy Jesuit priest. Returning to Peru in 1740 he was imbued with revolutionary fervour and moved into the high jungle region between Tarma and the Río Ucayali where he roused the forest Indians to rebellion. Throwing out the whites, he established a millenarian cult and, with an Indian army recruited from several tribes, successfully repelled all attacks by the authorities. Although never extending his powers beyond Tarma, he lived a free man until his death in 1756.

Twenty years later there were further violent native protests throughout the country against the enforcement of *repartimiento*. Under this new system the peasants were obliged to buy most of their essential goods from the *corregidor*, who, as monopoly supplier, sold poor-quality produce at grossly inflated prices.

In 1780, another *mestizo*, José Gabriel Condorcanqui, led a rebellion, calling himself **Tupac Amaru II**. Whipping up the already inflamed peasant opinion around Cusco into a revolutionary frenzy, he imprisoned a local *corregidor* before going on to massacre a troop of nearly six hundred royalist soldiers. Within a year Tupac Amaru II had been captured and executed but his rebellion had demonstrated both a definite weakness in colonial control and a high degree of popular unrest. Over the next decade several administrative reforms were to alter the situation, at least superficially: the *repartimiento* and the *corregimento* systems were abolished. In 1784, Charles III appointed a French nobleman – Teodoro de Croix – as the new viceroy to Peru and divided the country into seven *intendencias* containing 52 provinces. This created tighter direct royal control, but also unwittingly provided the pattern for the republican state of federated *departmentos*.

The end of the eighteenth century saw profound changes throughout the world. The North American colonies had gained their independence from Britain; France had been rocked by a people's revolution; and liberal ideas were spreading everywhere. Inflammatory newspapers and periodicals began to appear on the streets of Lima, and discontent was expressed at all levels of society. A strong sense of **Peruvian nationalism** emerged in the pages of *Mercurio Peruano* (first printed in the 1790s), a concept that was vital to the coming changes. Even the architecture of Lima had changed in the mid-eighteenth century, as if to welcome the new era. Wide avenues suddenly appeared, public parks were opened, and palatial salons became the focus for the discourse of gentlemen. The philosophy of the Enlightenment was slowly but surely pervading attitudes even in remote Peru.

When, in 1808, Napoleon took control of Spain, the authorities and elites in all the Spanish colonies found themselves in a new and unprecedented position. Was their loyalty to Spain or to its rightful king? And just who was the rightful king now?

Initially, there were a few unsuccessful, locally based protests in response both to this ambiguous situation and to the age-old agrarian problem, but it was only with the intervention of outside forces that independence was to become a serious concern in Peru. The American War of Independence, the French Revolution and Napoleon's invasion of Spain all pointed towards the opportunity of throwing off the shackles of colonialism, and by the time Ferdinand returned to the Spanish throne in 1814, royalist troops were struggling to maintain order throughout South America. Venezuela and Argentina had already declared their independence, and in 1817 San Martín liberated Chile by force. It was only a matter of time before one of the great liberators – **San Martín** in the south or **Bolívar** in the north – reached Peru.

San Martín was the first to do so. Having already liberated Argentina and Chile, he contracted an English naval officer, Lord Cochrane, to attack Lima. By September 1819 the first rebel invaders had landed at Paracas. Ica, Huánuco and then the north of Peru soon opted for independence, and the royalists, cut off in Lima, retreated into the mountains. Entering the capital without a struggle, San Martín proclaimed Peruvian **independence** on July 28, 1821.

The Republic

San Martín immediately assumed political control of the fledgeling nation. Under the title "Protector of Peru" he set about devising a workable **constitution** for the new nation – at one point even considering importing European royalty to establish a new monarchy. A libertarian as well as a liberator, San Martín declared freedom for slaves' children, abolished Indian service and even outlawed the term "Indian". But in practice, with royalist troops still controlling large sectors of the sierra, his approach did more to frighten the establishment than it did to help the slaves and peasants whose problems remain, even now, deeply rooted in their social and territorial inheritance.

The development of a relatively stable political system took virtually the rest of the nineteenth century, although Spanish resistance to independence was finally extinguished at the battles of Junin and Ayacucho in 1824. By this time, San Martín had given up the political power game, handing it over to **Simón Bolívar**, a man of enormous force with definite tendencies towards megalomania. Between them, Bolívar and his right-hand man, Sucre, divided Peru in half, with Sucre first president of the upper sector, renamed Bolivia. Bolívar himself remained dictator of a vast Andean Confederation – encompassing Colombia, Venezuela, Ecuador, Peru and Bolivia – until 1826. Within a year of his withdrawal, however, the Peruvians had torn up his controversial constitution and voted for the liberal **General La Mar** as president.

On La Mar's heels raced a generation of *caudillos*, military men, often *mestizos* of middle-class origins who had achieved recognition (on either side) in the battles for independence. The history of the early republic consists almost entirely of internal disputes between the creole aristocracy and dictatorial *caudillos*. Peru plunged deep into a period of domestic and foreign plot and counterplot, while the economy and some of the nation's finest natural resources withered away.

Generals **Santa Cruz** and **Gamarra** stand out as two of the most ruthless players in this high-stakes power game: overthrowing La Mar in 1829, Santa Cruz became president of Bolivia and Gamarra of Peru. Four years later the liberal creoles fought back with the election of General Orbegoso to the presidency. Gamarra, attempting to oust Orbegoso in a quiet palace coup, was overwhelmed and exiled. But the liberal constitution of 1834, despite its severe limitations on presidential power, still proved too much for the army – Orbegoso was overthrown within six months.

Unable to sit on the sidelines and watch the increasing pandemonium of Peruvian politics, Santa Cruz invaded Peru from Bolivia and installed himself as "Protector" in 1837. Very few South Americans were happy with this situation, least of all Gamarra, who joined with other exiles in Chile to plot revenge. After fierce fighting, Gamarra defeated Santa Cruz at Yungay, restored himself as president of Peru for two years, then died in 1841. During the next four years Peru had six more presidents, none of notable ability.

Ramon Castilla was the first president to bring any real strength to his office. On his assumption of power in 1845 the country began to develop more positively on the rising wave of a booming export in guano (bird droppings) fertilizer. In 1856, a new moderate constitution was approved and Castilla began his second term of office in an atmosphere of growth and hope – there were rail lines to be built and the Amazon waterways to be opened up. Sugar and cotton became important exports from coastal plantations and the guano deposits alone yielded a revenue of $15 million in 1860. Castilla abolished Indian tribute and managed to emancipate slaves without social-economic disruption by buying them from their "owners"; guano income proved useful for this compensation.

His successors fared less happily. **President Balta** (1868–72) oversaw the construction of most of the rail lines, but overspent so freely on these and a variety of other public and engineering works that it left the country on the brink of economic collapse. In the 1872 elections an attempted military coup was spontaneously crushed by a civilian mob, and Peru's first civilian president – the laissez faire capitalist **Manuel Pardo** – assumed power.

The War of the Pacific

By the late nineteenth century Peru's foreign debt, particularly to England, had grown enormously. Even though interest could be paid in guano, there simply wasn't enough. To make matters considerably worse, Peru went to war with Chile in 1879.

Lasting over four years, this **"War of the Pacific"** was basically a battle for the rich nitrate deposits located in Bolivian territory. Peru had pressured its ally Bolivia into imposing an export tax on nitrates mined by the Chilean-British Corporation. Chile's answer was to occupy the area and declare war on Peru and Bolivia. Victorious on land and at sea, Chilean forces had occupied Lima by the beginning of 1881 and the Peruvian president had fled to Europe. By 1883 Peru "lay helpless under the boots of its conquerors", and only a diplomatic rescue seemed possible. The **Treaty of Ancón**, possibly Peru's greatest national humiliation, brought the war to a close in October 1883.

Peru was forced to accept the cloistering of an independent Bolivia high up in the Andes, with no land link to the Pacific, and the even harder loss of the nitrate fields to Chile. The country seemed in ruins: the guano virtually exhausted and the nitrates lost to Chile, the nation's coffers were empty and a new generation of *caudillos* prepared to resume the power struggle all over again.

The twentieth century

Modern Peru is generally considered to have been born in 1895 with the forced resignation of General Caceres. However, the seeds of industrial development had been laid under his rule, albeit by foreigners. In 1890 an international plan was formulated to bail Peru out of its bankruptcy. The **Peruvian Corporation** was formed in London and assumed the $50 million national debt in return for "control of the national economy". Foreign companies took over the rail lines, navigation of Lake Titicaca, vast quantities of guano and were given free use of seven Peruvian ports for 66 years as well as the opportunity to start exploiting the rubber resources of the Amazon Basin. Under Nicolás de Piérola (president 1879–81 and 1895–99), some sort of stability had begun to return by the end of the nineteenth century.

In the early years of the twentieth century, Peru was run by an oligarchical clan of big businessmen and great landowners. Fortunes were made in a wide range of exploitative enterprises, above all sugar along the coast, minerals from the mountains, and rubber from the jungle. Meanwhile, the lot of the ordinary peasant worsened dramatically.

One of the most powerful oligarchs, **Augusto Leguía** rose to power through his possession of franchises for the New York Insurance Company and the British Sugar Company. He became a prominent figure, representing the rising bourgeoisie in the early 1900s, and in 1908 he was the first of their kind to be elected president. Under his rule the influence of foreign investment increased rapidly, with North American money taking ascendancy over British. It was with this capital that Lima was modernized – parks, plazas, the Avenida Arequipa and the Presidential Palace all date from this period. But for the majority of Peruvians, Leguía did nothing. The lives of the mountain peasants became more difficult, and the jungle Indians lived like slaves on the rubber plantations. Not surprisingly, Leguía's time in power coincided with a large number of Indian rebellions, general discontent and the rise of the first labour movement in Peru. Elected for a second term, Leguía became still more dictatorial, changing the constitution so that he could be re-elected on another two occasions. A year after the beginning of his fourth term, in 1930, he was ousted by a military coup – more as a result of the stock market crash and Peru's close links with US finance than as a consequence of his other political failings.

During Leguía's long dictatorship, the **labour movement** began to flex its muscles. A general strike in 1919 had established an eight-hour day, and ten years later the unions formed the first National Labour Centre. The worldwide Depression of the early 1930s hit Peru particularly badly; demand for its main exports (oil, silver, sugar, cotton and coffee) fell off drastically. Finally, in 1932, the Trujillo middle class led a violent uprising against the sugar barons and the primitive working conditions on the plantations. Suppressed by the army, nearly five thousand lives are thought to have been lost in the uprising, many of the rebels being taken out in trucks and shot among the ruins of Chan Chan.

The rise of the **APRA** – the American Popular Revolutionary Alliance – which had instigated the Trujillo uprising, and the growing popularity of its leader, **Haya de la Torre**, kept the nation occupied during World War II. Allowed to participate for the first time in the 1945 elections, APRA chose a neutral candidate – **Dr Bustamante** – in place of Haya de la Torre, whose fervent radicalism was considered a vote loser. Bustamante won the elections, with APRA controlling 18 out of 29 seats in the Senate and 53 out of 84 in the Chamber of Deputies.

Post-war euphoria was short-lived, however. Inflation was totally out of hand and apparently unaffected by Bustamante's exchange controls; during the 1940s the cost of living in Peru rose by 262 percent. With anti-APRA feeling on the rise, the president leaned more and more heavily on support from the army, until General Odría led a coup d'état from Arequipa in 1948 and formed a military junta. By the time Odría left office, in 1956, a new political element threatened oligarchical control – the young **Fernando Belaunde** and his **National Youth Front** (later Acción Popular), demanding "radical" reform. Even with the support of APRA and the army, Manuel Prado barely defeated Belaunde in the next elections: the unholy alliance between the moneyed establishment and APRA has been known as the "marriage of convenience" ever since.

The economy remained in dire straits. Domestic prices continued to soar and in 1952 alone there were some two hundred strikes and several serious riots. Meanwhile much more radical feeling was aroused in the provinces by **Hugo Blanco**, a charismatic *mestizo* from Cusco who had joined a Trotskyist group – the Workers Revolutionary Party – which was later to merge with the FIR – the Revolutionary Left's Front. In La Convención, within the *departamento* of Cusco, Blanco and his followers created nearly 150 syndicates, whose peasant members began to work their own individual plots while refusing to work for the hacienda owners. Many landowners went bankrupt or opted to bribe workers back with offers of cash wages. The second phase of Blanco's "reform" was to take physical control of the haciendas, mostly in areas so isolated that the authorities were powerless to intervene. Blanco was finally arrested in 1963 but the effects of his peasant revolt outlived him: in future, Peruvian governments were to take agrarian reform far more seriously.

Back in Lima, the elections of 1962 had resulted in an interesting deadlock, with Haya de la Torre getting 33 percent of the votes, Belaunde 32 percent and Odría 28.5 percent. Almost inevitably, the army took control, annulled the elections and denied Haya de la Torre and Belaunde the opportunity of power for another year. By 1963, though, neither Acción Popular nor APRA was sufficiently radical to pose a serious threat to the establishment. Elected president for the first time, Belaunde quickly got to work on a severely diluted programme of agrarian reform, a compromise never forgiven by his left-wing supporters. More successfully, though, he began to draw in quantities of foreign capital. President de Gaulle of France visited Peru in 1964 and the first British foreign secretary ever to set foot in South America arrived in Lima two years later. Foreign investors were clamouring to get in on Belaunde's ambitious development plans and obtain a rake-off from Peru's oil fields. But by 1965 domestic inflation had so severely damaged the balance of payments that confidence was beginning to slip away from Belaunde's international stance.

Land reform and the military regime

By the mid-1960s, many intellectuals and government officials saw the agrarian situation as an urgent economic problem as well as a matter of social justice. Even the army believed that **land reform** was a prerequisite for the development of a larger market, without which any genuine industrial development would prove impossible. On October 3, 1968, tanks smashed through the gates into the courtyard of the Presidential Palace. General Velasco and the army seized power, deporting Belaunde and ensuring that Haya de la Torre could not even participate in the forthcoming elections.

The new government, revolutionary for a **military regime**, gave the land back to the workers in 1969. The great plantations were turned virtually overnight into cooperatives, in an attempt to create a genuinely self-determining peasant class. At the same time guerrilla leaders were brought to trial, political activity was banned in the universities, indigenous banks were controlled, foreign banks nationalized and diplomatic relations established with East European countries. By the end of military rule, in 1980, the land-reform programme had done much to abolish the large capitalist landholding system.

Even now, though, a shortage of good land in the sierra and the lack of decent irrigation on the coast mean that less than twenty percent of the landless workers have been integrated into the cooperative system – the majority remain in seasonal work and/or the small-farm sector. One of the major problems for the military regime, and one which still plagues the economy, was the **fishing crisis** in the 1970s. An overestimation of the fishing potential led to the build-up of a highly capital-intensive fish-canning and fish-meal industry, in its time one of the world's most modern. Unfortunately, the fish began to disappear because of a combination of ecological changes and over-fishing – leaving vast quantities of capital equipment inactive and thousands of people unemployed.

Although undeniably an important step forward, the 1968 military coup was always an essentially bourgeois revolution, imposed from above to speed up the transformation from a land-based oligarchy to a capitalist society. Paternalistic, even dictatorial, it did little to satisfy the demands of the more extreme peasant reformers, and the military leaders eventually handed back power voluntarily in democratic elections.

The 1970s and 1980s

After twelve years of military government the 1980 elections resulted in a centre-right alliance between Acción Popular and the Popular Christian Party. **Belaunde** resumed the presidency having become an established celebrity during his years of exile and having built up, too, an impressive array of international contacts. The policy of his government was to increase the pace of development still further, and in particular to emulate the Brazilian success in opening up the Amazon – building new roads and exploiting the untold wealth in oil, minerals, timber and agriculture. But inflation continued as an apparently insuperable problem, and Belaunde fared little better in coming to terms with either the parliamentary Marxists of the United Left or the escalating guerrilla movement led by Sendero Luminoso.

Sendero Luminoso (the Shining Path), founded in 1970, persistently discounted the possibility of change through the ballot box. In 1976 it adopted armed struggle as the only means to achieve its "anti-feudal, anti-imperial" revolution in Peru. Following the line of the Chinese Gang of Four, Sendero was led by **Abimael Guzman** (alias **Comrade Gonzalo**), whose ideas it claimed to be in the direct lineage of Marx, Lenin and Chairman Mao. Originally a brilliant philosophy lecturer from Ayacucho (specializing in the Kantian theory of space), before his capture by the authorities in the early 1990s Gonzalo lived mainly underground, rarely seen even by Senderistas themselves.

Sendero was very active during the late 1980s and early 1990s, when it had some 10,000–15,000 secret members. Rejecting Belaunde's style of technological development as imperialist and the United Left as "parliamentary cretins", they carried out attacks on business interests, local officials, police posts and anything regarded as outside interference with the self-determination of the peasantry. On the whole, members were recruited from the poorest areas of the country and from the Quechua-speaking population, coming together only for their paramilitary operations and melting back afterwards into the obscurity of their communities.

Although strategic points in Lima were frequently attacked – police stations, petrochemical plants and power lines – Sendero's main centre of activity was in the sierra around **Ayacucho** and **Huanta**, subsequently spreading into the remote regions around the central selva and a little further south in **Vilcabamba** – site of the last Inca resistance, a traditional hide-out for rebels, and the centre of Hugo Blanco's activities in the 1960s. By remaining small and unpredictable, Sendero managed to wage its war on the Peruvian establishment with the minimum of risk of major confrontations with government forces.

Belaunde's response was to tie up enormous amounts of manpower in counter-insurgency operations whose main effect was to increase popular sympathy for the guerrillas. In 1984 more than six thousand troops, marines and anti-terrorist police were deployed against Sendero, and at least three thousand people, mostly peasants, are said to have been killed. "Disappearances", especially around Ayacucho, still occur and most people blame the security forces for the bulk of them. In August 1984 even the chief of command of the counter-insurgency forces joined the criticism of the government's failure to provide promised development aid to Ayacucho. He was promptly dismissed for his claims that the problems were "the harvest of 160 years of neglect" and that the solution was "not a military one".

By 1985, new urban-based terrorist groups like the Movimiento Revolucionario Tupac Amaru (**MRTA**) began to make their presence felt in the shantytowns around Lima. Belaunde lost the **1985 elections**, with APRA taking power for the first time and the United Left also getting a large percentage of the votes.

Led by a young, highly popular new president, **Alan García**, the APRA government took office riding a massive wave of hope. Sendero Luminoso, however, continued to step up its tactics of anti-democratic terrorism, and the isolation of Lima and the coast from much of the sierra and jungle regions became a very real threat. With Sendero proclaiming their revolution by "teaching" and terrorizing peasant communities on the one hand, and the military evidently liquidating the inhabitants of villages suspected of "collaboration" on the other, these years were a sad and bloody time for a large number of Peruvians.

Sendero's usual tactics were for an armed group to arrive at a peasant community and call a meeting. During the meeting it was not uncommon for them publicly to execute an "appropriate" local functionary – like a Ministry of Agriculture official or, in some cases, foreign aid workers – as a statement of persuasive terror. In May 1989 a British traveller found himself caught in the middle of this conflict and was shot in the head after a mock trial by Senderistas in the plaza of Olleros, a community near Huaraz in Ancash, which had offered him a bed for the night in its municipal building. Before leaving a village, Sendero always selected and left "intelligence officers", to liaise with the terrorists, and "production officers", to ensure that there was no trade between the village and the outside world – particularly with Lima and the international market economy.

Guzman's success had lain partly with his use of Inca millennial mythology and partly in the power vacuum left after the implementation of the agrarian reform and the resulting unrest and instability, and Sendero's power, and even its popular appeal, advanced throughout the 1980s. In terms of territorial influence, it had spread its wings over most of central Peru, much of the jungle and to a certain extent into many of the northern and southern provincial towns.

Much of Sendero's funding came from the **cocaine trade**. Vast quantities of coca leaves are grown and partially processed all along the margins of the Peruvian jungle. Much of this is flown clandestinely into Colombia where the processing is completed and the finished product exported to North America and Europe for consumption. The thousands of peasants who came down from the Andes to make a new life in the tropical forest throughout the 1980s found that coca was by far the most lucrative cash crop. The cocaine barons paid peasants more than they could earn elsewhere and at the same time bought protection from Sendero (some say at a rate of up to $10,000 per clandestine plane-load).

The 1980s, then, saw the growth of two major attacks on the political and moral backbone of the nation – one through terrorism, the other through cocaine. With these two forces working hand in hand the problems facing García proved insurmountable. To make things worse, a right-wing death squad – the **Rodrigo Franco Commando** (RFC) – appeared on the scene in 1988, evidently made up of disaffected police officers, army personnel and even one or two Apristas (APRA members).

The appointment of **Agustin Mantilla** as Minister of the Interior in May 1989 suggested knowledge and approval of the RFC at the very highest level. Mantilla was widely condemned as the man behind the emergence of the death squads and their supply of arms. He was known to want to take back by force large areas of the central Andes simply by supplying anti-Senderista peasants with machine guns. Opposition to the arming of the peasantry was one topic on which the military and human rights organizations seemed to agree. Many of the arms would probably have gone straight to Sendero, and such action could easily have set in motion a spiral of bloody civil war beyond anyone's control.

The **MRTA** had less success than the Senderistas, losing several of their leaders to Lima's prison cells. Their military confidence and capacity were also devastated when a contingent of some 62 MRTA militants was caught in an army ambush in April 1988; only eight survived from among two truckloads.

Meanwhile, the once young and popular President Alan García got himself into a financial mess and went into exile, having been accused by the Peruvian judiciary of high-level corruption and possibly even stealing millions of dollars from the people of Peru.

The 1990s

The year **1990** proved to be a turning point for Peru. In the run-up to that year's elections, there were four main candidates: the popular and internationally renowned author Mario Vargas Llosa, with his new right-wing coalition, Fredemo; Luís Alvacastro, general secretary of APRA (and minister in charge of the economy under Garcia); Alfonso Barrantes in control of a new left-wing grouping, Acuerdo Socialista; and Henry Peace of the United Left.

Vargas Llosa was the clear favourite as the poll approached, although he had blotted his copybook somewhat during 1989, when he had briefly bowed out of the electoral process, accusing his fellow leaders within Fredemo (which is essentially an alliance between Acción Popular and the Popular Christian Party) of making it impossible for him to carry on as a candidate. Still, by the time of the election he was back, and firmly in charge. APRA, having had five pretty disastrous years in power, were given virtually no chance of getting Alvacastro elected, and the left were severely split. Barrantes was by far the most popular candidate on that side. However, in creating Acuerdo Socialista, and thereby taking away half of the United Left's vote, he effectively spoilt both their chances.

In the event, the real surprise came with lightning speed from a totally unexpected quarter in the guise of an entirely new party – Cambio 90 (Change 90), formed only months before the election – led by a young college professor of Japanese descent, **Alberto Fujimori**. Fujimori came a very close second to Vargas Llosa in the March election, with 31 percent of the total against Llosa's 35 percent. Since a successful candidate must gain half the votes to become president, a second round was scheduled for June.

Once the initial shock of the result had been absorbed, Fujimori rapidly became favourite to win the **second poll**, on the grounds that electors who had voted for left-wing parties would switch their allegiance to him. While Vargas Llosa offered a Thatcherite, monetarist economic shock for Peru, Fujimori recommended protecting all public industries of strategic importance – the oil industry being one of the most important. Llosa was for selling such companies off to the private sector and exposing them to the full power of world market forces. However, ordinary Peruvians were clearly worried that such policies would bring them the kind of hardships that had beset Brazilians or Argentinians, and Fujimori swept into power in the second round of voting, almost immediately adopting many of Vargas Llosa's policies – the price of many basics such as flour and fuel trebled overnight. Fujimori did, however, manage to turn the nation around and gain an international confidence in Peru, reflected in the country's stock exchange – one of the fastest-growing and most active in the Americas.

However, the real turning point, economically and politically, was the capture of Sendero's leader **Abimael Guzman** in September 1992. Captured at his Lima hideout (a dance school) by General Vidal's secret anti-terrorist police, DINCOTE, even Fujimori had not known about the raid until it had been successfully completed. With Guzman in jail, and presented very publicly on TV as the defeated man, the political tide shifted. The international press no longer described Peru as a country where terrorists looked poised to take over, and Fujimori went from strength to strength, while Sendero's activities were reduced to little more than the occasional car bomb in Lima as they were hounded by the military in their remote hide-outs along the eastern edges of the Peruvian Andes. A massive boost to Fujimori's popularity, in the elections of 1995 he gained over sixty percent of the vote. Perhaps it was also a recognition that his strong policies had paid off as far as the economy was concerned – inflation dipped from a record rate of 2777 percent in 1989 to ten percent in 1996.

The mid-1990s was also the time when the **MRTA** terrorists battled with Fujimori and his government. On December 17, 1996, the MRTA really hit the headlines when they infiltrated the Japanese Ambassador's residence, which they held under siege for 126 days, with over three hundred hostages. Some of these were released after negotiation, but Fujimori refused to give in to MRTA demands for the freedom of hundreds of their jailed comrades. Peruvian forces stormed the building in March 1997 as the terrorists were playing football inside the residence, massacring them all, with only one hostage perishing in the skirmish. Fujimori's reputation as a hard man and a successful leader shot to new heights.

He continued to grow in popularity, despite Peru going to **war with Ecuador** briefly in January 1995, May 1997, and more seriously in 1998. The Ecuadorian army, which was accused of starting the fighting, imposed significant losses on the Peruvian forces. This dispute was inflamed by the presence of large oilfields in the region, currently on what the Peruvians claim is their side of the border, a claim the Ecuadorians bitterly dispute: Ecuadorian maps continue to show the border much further south than Peruvian maps. The two countries signed a formal peace treaty in 1998, although the dispute remains fresh in most people's minds.

In economic terms, Fujimori also seemed to be holding his own. Despite many aid organizations confirming widespread poverty and unemployment in Peru, and the nation being hit hard by El Niño in 1998, the economy stayed buoyant. Politically, too, Fujimori gained substantially in July 1999, when he appeared on TV, live from Huancayo, to announce the imminent capture of **Oscar Ramirez Durand**, alias Comrade Feliciano, Guzman's number two and the leader of Sendero Luminoso. An army battalion had already been sent to the Huancayo region in 1997 to destroy Sendero's stronghold; it took them two years, but they managed to achieve a result just in time for the start of the 2000 electoral campaign. At the end of the twentieth century, Sendero were left with only a few scattered remnants in one or two parts of the sierra and *ceja de selva*, and just one active cell in the cocaine-producing region of the Huallaga Valley.

The twenty-first century

The scars of the civil war period remain strongly etched in the Peruvian consciousness. An estimated 69,000 people died in the violence between 1980 and 2000. Nevertheless, it is political intrigue, corruption and protest which continue to dominate the scene.

The run-up to the **elections** of April 9, 2000, was marked by Fujimori's controversial decision to stand for a third term of office, despite constitutional term limits. He reasoned that the constitution was introduced during his second term, thus he was entitled to stand for one more. Even with his firm control of the media (especially TV), he encountered strong opposition in the person of **Alejandro Toledo**, a *serrano* Perú Posible candidate representing the interests of Andean cities and communities. Toledo had worked his way up from humble beginnings to become a UN and World Bank economist before standing for president; such was the worry over his popularity that a smear campaign surfaced a few weeks before the voting, accusing him of shunning an illegitimate daughter and organizing a disastrous financial pyramid scheme in the early 1990s.

Fujimori polled 49.87 percent of the vote, missing outright victory by just 14,000 votes; Toledo followed behind with just over 40 percent. There were unproven allegations of fraud and vote rigging, and Toledo eventually withdrew from the contest. However, Fujimori was forced to resign in November 2000 following revelations that his head of intelligence, Vladimiro Montesinos, had been video-taped bribing politicians before the last election and had also secreted away hundreds of millions of dollars (believed to be drug money) into Swiss and other bank accounts around the world. It quickly became clear that Montesinos had exerted almost complete control of the president, the army, the intelligence service and the cocaine mafia during the preceding few years. Soon after, Fujimori fled to Japan.

New elections were held in April 2001, which Toledo won easily, inheriting a cynical populace and a troubled domestic situation, with slow economic growth and deteriorating social conditions. His term of office, which ended in November 2006, was certainly a rocky one: in June 2002, riots broke out in Arequipa over Toledo's government's attempts to privatize the city's electric utility, followed a month later by paralyzing transportation strikes and then furious demonstrations in the northern *ceja de selva* region. Despite lack of popular support and with little or no backing from Peru's powerful elite business classes, Toledo clung onto his office until 2006, when in a general election he was replaced, amazingly, by an older, plumper and hopefully wiser, Alan García – the very same man and ex-President who left Peru and his first term of office in disgrace back in 1988. Despite his bad governance, Garcia, a charismatic political speaker, managed to persuade the nation to give him a second chance when he won the election against Ollanta Humala, an ex-military commander with both socialist and nationalistic tendencies. Many of Peru's voters are too young to remember his mistakes, so APRA and García, once again, have political control of Peru.

Meanwhile, Fujimori returned to South America via Chile in late 2005, and was arrested on arrival. Charged with human rights abuses and corruption (including payments to members of Congress and illegal wiretapping), he was extradited to Peru in 2007; his trial is still ongoing and running parallel to similar accusations and legal actions against his once right-hand man, Montesinos, who also remains locked up in relative luxury somewhere in Lima (for up to date info on the trial, see ⓦwwwfujimoriontrial.org).

In his first two years in office, Garcia has had some significant successes, though his popularity, particularly outside of Lima, has dropped significantly. The success has mostly come in the form of a rapid rise in foreign investments in mineral exploitation alongside big leaps in the price of primary resources, in particular copper. To enable this process, the President has dropped most of APRA's socialist stances in favour of strong alliances with big business interests and by taking further the neo-liberal policies followed by Fujimori in the 1990s. In 2007 and 2008, public protest from the left, from exploited indigenous communities and also from environmental NGOs has increased sharply, with much of the discontent provoked by a new and controversial Fair Trade Agreement between Peru and the USA. In September 2008, only nineteen percent of the country liked what he was doing despite an official economic growth rate of around nine percent per annum. Even right wing leaders were critical of Garcia for pretending to represent a populist party while pursuing policies that actually only benefit the already wealthy.

Cultural chronology of Peru

20,000–10,000 BC ▶ First evidence of human settlement in Peru. Cave dwellings in the Ayacucho Valley; stone artefacts in the Chillon Valley.

8000–5000 BC ▶ Nomadic tribes, and more permanent settlement in fertile coastal areas. Cave paintings and fine stone tools.

5000–2000 BC ▶ The domestication of plants, like cotton, and the consequent introduction of cultivation and establishment of stable settlements are characteristic. Early agricultural sites include notably the pyramid-based culture of Caral, and also the older Huaca Prieta in the Chicama Valley, and Kotosh.

1200 BC–200 AD ▶ Formative Era and emergence of the Chavín Cult, with great progress in ceramics and metallurgy. Temple complex at Chavín de Huantar, and important sites at Kotosh and Sechin.

300 AD ▶ Technological advance marked above all in the Viru Valley – the Gallinazo culture – and at Paracas.

Sites in the Viru Valley, at Paracas, and the growth of Tiahuanaco culture around Lake Titicaca.

200–1100 AD ▶ Classical cultures emergent throughout the land. Mochica culture and Temples of the Sun and Moon near Trujillo; further Tiahuanaco development; Nasca Lines and Cahuachi complex on the coast; Wilkawain temple; Huari complex; and Tantamayo ruins.

1200 ▶ The age of the great city-builders. Well-preserved adobe settlements survive at Chan Chan (near Trujillo) and Cajamarquilla (Lima).

1438–1532 ▶ Expansion of the Inca Empire from its bases around Cusco, north into Ecuador and south into Chile. Inca sites survive throughout Peru, but the greatest are still around Cusco – Sacsayhuaman and Machu Picchu above all. Inca Highway constructed from Colombia to Chile, parts of which are still in existence.

1535 ▶ Foundation of Lima. Colonial architecture draws heavily on Spanish influences, though native craftsmen also leave their mark. Church building, above all at Arequipa (Santa Catalina Convent) and around Cusco. The Spanish city of Cusco incorporates much Inca stonework. Meanwhile, the rebel Incas build new cities around Vilcabamba. Throughout, colonial rule building follows European fashions, especially Baroque, including churches, mansions and a few public buildings.

1569 ▶ **Francisco Toledo** arrived in Peru as viceroy with a view to reforming the colonial system so as to increase royal revenue, while at the same time improving the lot of the native population. Before he could get on with that, however, he had to quash a rapidly developing threat to the colony – the appearance of a **neo-Inca state.**

1572 ▶ After fierce fighting and a near-escape, Tupac Amaru was captured and brought to trial in Cusco. Accused of plotting to overthrow the Spanish and of inciting his followers to raid towns, he was subsequently beheaded – an act by Toledo that was disavowed by the Spanish Crown and which caused much distress in Peru.

1742 ▶ **Juan Santos Atahualpa**, a *mestizo* from Cusco who had travelled to Spain, Africa and, some say, to England as a young man, returned to Peru imbued with revolutionary fervour and moved into the high jungle region between Tarma and the Río Ucayali where he roused the forest Indians to rebellion.

1821 ▶ The great liberators – **San Martín** in the south or **Bolívar** in the north – reached Peru in 1819, entering the capital without a struggle, San Martín proclaimed Peruvian **independence** on July 28, 1821.

1870s ▶ Construction of the high-altitude rail lines and other engineering projects. First exploitation of Amazonian rubber.

1890–1930 ▶ Much modernization in Lima (Presidential Palace, etc), grandiose public buildings elsewhere. Massive urban growth in Lima from the 1930s onwards.

1963 ▶ Organized shantytowns begin to grow around Lima.

1990s ▶ Road improvements under Fujimori; and a firm hand to deal with Sendero Luminoso and MRTA.

2000–2003 ▶ Fujimori flees to Japan, economic instability, protests over coca eradication programme and attempt to privatize utility in Arequipa.

2006 ▶ Political elections are held with Ollanta Humala, an ex-military commander, and Alan Garcia, the once shamed ex-president, as the main candidates.

Inca life and achievement

I n less than a century, the Incas developed and knitted together a vast empire peopled by something like twenty million Indians. They established an imperial religion in relative harmony with those of their subject tribes; erected monolithic fortresses, salubrious palaces and temples; and, astonishingly, evolved a viable economy – strong enough to maintain a top-heavy elite in almost godlike grandeur. To understand these achievements and get some idea of what they must have meant in Peru five or six hundred years ago, you really have to see for yourself their surviving heritage: the stones of Inca ruins and roads; the cultural objects in the museums of Lima and Cusco; and their living descendants who still work the soil and speak Quechua – the language used by the Incas to unify their empire. What follows is but the briefest of introductions to their history, society and achievements.

Inca society

The Inca Empire rapidly developed a **hierarchical structure**. At the highest level it was governed by the **Sapa Inca**, son of the sun and direct descendant of the god Viracocha. Under him were the priest-nobles – the royal **allyu** or kin-group who filled most of the important administrative and religious posts – and, working for them, regional *allyu* chiefs, **curacas** or *orejones*, responsible for controlling tribute from the peasant base. One-third of the land belonged to the emperor and the state; another to the high priests, gods, and the sun; the last third was for the *allyu* themselves. Work on the land, then, was devoted to maintaining the empire rather than mere subsistence, though in times of famine storehouses were evidently opened to feed the commoners.

Life for **the elite** wasn't, perhaps, quite as easy as it may appear; their fringe benefits were matched by the strain and worry of governing an empire, sending armies everywhere and keeping the gods happy. The Inca nobles were nevertheless fond of relaxing in thermal baths, of hunting holidays and of conspicuous eating and drinking whenever the religious calendar permitted. *Allyu* chiefs were often unrelated to the royal Inca lineage, but their position was normally hereditary. As lesser nobles (*curacas*) they were allowed to wear earplugs and special ornate headbands; their task was to both protect and exploit the commoners, and they themselves were free of labour service.

The hierarchical network swept down the ranks from the important chiefs in a decimalized system. One of the *curacas* might be responsible for 10,000 men; under him two lower chiefs were each responsible for 5000, and so on until in the smallest hamlets there was one man responsible for ten others. Women weren't counted in the census. For the Incas, a household was represented by the man and only he was obliged to fulfil tribute duties on behalf of the *allyu*. Within the family the woman's role was dependent on her relationship with the dominant man – be he father, brother, husband or eldest son.

In their conquests the Incas absorbed **craftsmen** from every corner of the empire: goldsmiths, potters, carpenters, sculptors, masons and *quipumayocs* (accountants) were frequently removed from their homes to work directly for the emperor in Cusco. These skilled men lost no time in developing into a new and entirely separate class of citizen. The work of even the lowest servant in the palace was highly regulated by a rigid division of labour. If a man was employed to be a woodcutter he wouldn't be expected to gather wood from the forests; that was the task of another employee.

Throughout the empire young girls, usually about nine or ten years old, were constantly selected for their beauty and serene intelligence. Those deemed perfect enough were taken to an *acclahuasi* – a special sanctuary for the "**chosen women**" – where they were trained in specific tasks, including the spinning and weaving of fine cloth, and the higher culinary arts. Most chosen women were destined ultimately to become *mamaconas* (Virgins of the Sun) or the concubines of either nobles or the Sapa Inca himself. Occasionally some of them were sacrificed by strangulation in order to appease the gods.

For most Inca **women** the allotted role was simply that of peasant/domestic work and rearing children. After giving birth a mother would wash her baby in a nearby stream to cleanse and purify it and return virtually immediately to normal daily activities, carrying the child in a cradle tied on her back with a shawl. As they still are today, most babies were breast-fed for years before leaving their mothers to take their place in the domestic life cycle. As adults their particular role in society was dependent first on sex, then on hierarchical status.

Special regulations affected both the **old** and **disabled**. Around the age of fifty, a man was likely to pass into the category of "old". He was no longer capable of undertaking a normal workload, he wasn't expected to pay taxes, and he could always depend on support from the official storehouses. Nevertheless, the community still made small demands by using him to collect firewood and other such tasks; in much the same way the kids were expected to help out around the house and in the fields. In fact, children and old people often worked together, the young learning directly from the old. Disabled people were obliged to work within their potential – the blind, for instance, might de-husk maize or clean cotton. Inca law also bound the deformed or disabled to marry people with similar disadvantages: dwarfs to dwarfs, blind to blind, legless to legless.

The **Inca diet** was essentially vegetarian, based on the staple potato but encompassing a range of other foods like quinoa, beans, squash, sweet potatoes, avocados, tomatoes and manioc. In the highlands, emphasis was on root crops like potatoes, which have been known to survive in temperatures as low as 15°C (59°F) at over 5000m. On the valley floors and lower slopes of the Andes maize cultivation predominated.

The importance of **maize** both as a food crop and for making *chicha* increased dramatically under the Incas; previously it had been grown for ceremony and ritual exchange, as a status rather than a staple crop. The use of **coca** was restricted to the priests and Inca elite. Coca is a mild narcotic stimulant which effectively dulls the body against cold, hunger and tiredness when the leaves are chewed in the mouth with a catalyst such as lime or calcium. The Incas believed its leaves possessed magical properties; they could be cast to divine future events, offered as a gift to the wind, the earth or the mountain *apu*, and they could be used in witchcraft. Today it's difficult to envisage the Incas' success in restricting coca-growing and use; even with helicopters and machine guns the present-day authorities are unable to control its production.

Expansion and control

In Inca eyes the known world was their empire, and **expansion** therefore limitless. They divided their territories into four basic regions, or **suyos**, each radiating from the central plaza in Cusco: Chincha Suyo (northwest), Anti Suyo (northeast),

Cunti Suyo (southwest) and Colla Suyo (southeast). Each *suyo* naturally had its own particular problems and characteristics but all were approached in the same way – initially being demoralized or forced into submission by the Inca army, later absorbed as allies for further conquests. In this way the Incas never seemed to over-extend their lines to the fighting front.

The most impressive feature of an **Inca army** must in fact have been its sheer numbers – a relatively minor force would have included 5000 men. Their armour usually consisted of quilted cotton shirts and a small shield painted with designs or decorated with magnificent plumes. The common warriors – using slingshots, spears, axes and maces – were often supported by archers drafted from the "savages" living in the eastern forests. When the Spanish arrived on horseback the Incas were quick to invent new weapons: large two-handed hardwood swords and *bolas* (wooden balls connected by a string), good for tangling up the horses' legs. The only prisoners of war traditionally taken by a conquering Inca army were chieftains, who lived comfortably in Cusco as hostages against the good behaviour of their respective tribes. Along with the chiefs, the most important portable idols and *huacas* of conquered peoples were held in Cusco as sacred hostages. Often the children of the ruling chieftains were also taken to Cusco to be indoctrinated in Inca ways.

This pragmatic approach towards their subjects is exemplified again in the Inca policy of **forced resettlement**. Whole villages were sometimes sent into entirely new regions, ostensibly to increase the crop yield of plants like coca or corn and to vary their diet by importing manioc and chillis – though it was often criminals and rebellious citizens who ended up in the hottest, most humid regions. Large groups of people might also be sent from relatively suspect tribes into areas where mostly loyal subjects lived, or into the newly colonized outer fringes of the empire; many trustworthy subjects were also moved into zones where restlessness might have been expected. It seems likely that the whole colonization project was as much a political manoeuvre as a device to diversify the Inca economic or dietary base. As new regions came under imperial influence, the threat from rebellious elements was minimized by their geographical dispersion.

Economy, agriculture and building

The main **resources** available to the Inca Empire were agricultural land and labour, mines (producing precious and prestigious metals such as gold, silver or copper) and fresh water, abundant everywhere except along the desert coast. With careful manipulation of these resources, the Incas managed to keep things moving the way they wanted. Tribute in the form of **service** (*mita*) played a crucial role in maintaining the empire and pressurizing its subjects into ambitious building and irrigation projects. Some of these projects were so grand that they would have been impossible without the demanding whip of a totalitarian state.

Although a certain degree of local barter was allowed, the state regulated the distribution of every important product. The astonishing Inca **highways** were one key to this economic success. Some of the tracks were nearly 8m wide and at the time of the Spanish Conquest the main Royal Highway ran some 5000km, from the Río Ancasmayo in Colombia down the backbone of the Andes to the coast at a point south of the present-day Santiago in Chile. The Incas never used the wheel, but gigantic llama caravans were a common sight tramping along the roads, each animal carrying up to 50kg of cargo.

Every corner of the Inca domain was easily accessible via branch roads, all designed or taken over and unified with one intention – to dominate and administer an enormous empire. **Runners** were posted at *chasqui* stations and *tambo* rest-houses which punctuated the road at intervals of between 2km and 15km. Fresh fish was relayed on foot from the coast and messages were sent with runners from Quito to Cusco (2000km) in less than six days. The more difficult mountain canyons were crossed on bridges suspended from cables braided out of jungle lianas (creeping vines) and high passes were – and still are – frequently reached by incredible stairways cut into solid rock cliffs.

The primary sector in the economy was inevitably **agriculture** and in this the Incas made two major advances: large terracing projects created the opportunity for agricultural specialists to experiment with new crops and methods of cultivation, and the transportation system allowed a revolution in distribution. Massive agricultural **terracing projects** were going on continuously in Inca-dominated mountain regions. The best examples of these are in the Cusco area at Tipón, Moray, Ollantaytambo, Pisac and Cusichaca. Beyond the aesthetic beauty of Inca stone terraces, they have distinct practical advantages. Terraced hillsides minimize erosion from landslides, and using well-engineered stone channels gives complete control over irrigation. Natural springs emerging on the hillsides became the focus of an intricate network of canals and aqueducts extending over the surrounding slopes which had themselves been converted into elegant stone terraces. An extra incentive to the Inca mind must surely have been their reverence of water, one of the major earthly spirits; the Inca terraces are often so elaborately designed around springs that they seem to be worshipping water as much as utilizing it.

Today, however, it is Inca construction which forms their lasting heritage: vast **building projects** masterminded by high-ranking nobles and architects, and supervised by expert masons with an almost limitless pool of peasant labour. Without paper, the architects resorted to imposing their imagination onto clay or stone, making miniature models of the more important constructions – good examples of these can be seen in Cusco museums. More importantly, Inca masonry survives throughout Peru, most spectacularly at the fortress of Sacsayhuaman above Cusco, and on the coast in the Achirana aqueduct, which even today still brings water down to the Ica Valley from high up in the Andes. In the mountains, Inca stonework gave a permanence to edifices which would otherwise have needed constant renovation. The damp climate and mould quickly destroy anything but solid rock; Spanish and modern buildings have often collapsed around well-built Inca walls.

Arts and crafts

Surprisingly, Inca masonry was rarely carved or adorned in any way. Smaller stone items, however, were frequently ornate and beautiful. High technical standards were achieved, too, in **pottery**. Around Cusco especially, the art of creating and glazing ceramics was highly developed. They were not so advanced artistically, however; Inca designs generally lack imagination and variety, tending to have been mass-produced from models evolved by previous cultures. The most common pottery object was the *aryballus*, a large jar with a conical base and a wide neck, thought to have been used chiefly for storing *chicha*. Its decoration was usually geometric, often associated with the backbone of a fish: the central spine of the pattern was adorned with rows of spikes radiating from either side.

Fine plates were made with anthropomorphic handles, and large numbers of cylindrically tapering goblets – *keros* – were manufactured, though these were often of cedar wood rather than pottery.

The refinements in **metallurgy**, like the ceramics industry, were mostly developed by craftsmen absorbed from different corners of the empire. The Chimu were particularly respected by the Incas for their superb metalwork. Within the empire, bronze and copper were used for axe-blades and tumi knives; gold and silver were restricted to ritual use and for nobles. The Incas smelted their metal ores in cylindrical terracotta and adobe furnaces, which made good use of prevailing breezes to fire large lumps of charcoal. Molten ores were pulled out from the base of the furnace. Although the majority of surviving metal artefacts – those you see in museums – have been made from beaten sheets, there were plenty of cast or cut solid gold and silver pieces, too. Most of these were melted down by the conquistadors, who weren't especially interested in precious objects for their artistic merit.

Religion

The Inca **religion** was easily capable of incorporating the religious features of most subjugated regions. The setting for beliefs, idols and oracles, more or less throughout the entire empire, had been preordained over the previous two thousand years: a general recognition of certain creator deities and a whole pantheon of nature-related spirits, minor deities and demons. The customary form of worship varied a little according to the locality, but everywhere they went the Incas (and later the Spanish) found the creator god among other animistic spirits and concepts of power related to lightning, thunder and rainbows. The Incas merely superimposed their variety of mystical, yet inherently practical, elements onto those that they came across.

The main religious novelty introduced with Inca domination was their demand to be recognized as direct descendants of the creator-god **Viracocha**. A claim to divine ancestry was, to the Incas, a valid excuse for military and cultural expansion. They felt no need to destroy the *huacas* and oracles of subjugated peoples; on the contrary, certain sacred sites were recognized as intrinsically holy, as powerful places for communication with the spirit world. When ancient shrines like Pachacamac, near Lima, were absorbed into the empire they were simply turned over to worship on imperial terms.

The sun is the most obvious symbol of Inca belief, a chief deity and the visible head of the state religion (Viracocha was a less direct, more ethereal, force). The sun's role was overt, as life-giver to an agriculturally based empire, and its cycle was intricately related to agrarian practice and annual ritual patterns. To think of the Inca religion as essentially sun worship, though, would be far too simplistic. There were distinct layers in **Inca cosmology**: the level of creation, the astral level and the earthly dimension.

The first, highest level corresponds to Viracocha as the creator-god who brought life to the world and society to mankind. Below this, on the astral level, are the celestial gods: the sun itself, the moon and certain stars (particularly the Pleiades, patrons of fertility). The earthly dimension, although that of man, was no less magical, endowed with important *huacas* and shrines which might take the form of unusual rocks or peaks, caves, tombs, mummies and natural springs.

The astral level and earthly dimension were widespread bases of worship in Peru before the Incas rose to power. The favour of the creator was the critical factor in their claims to divine right of imperial government, and the hierarchical structure of religious ranking also reflects the division of the religious spheres into those that were around before, during, and after the empire and those that only stayed as long as Inca domination lasted. At the very top of this **religio-social hierarchy** was the Villac Uma, the high priest of Cusco, usually a brother of the Sapa Inca himself. Under him were perhaps hundreds of high priests, all nobles of royal blood who were responsible for ceremony, temples, shrines, divination, curing and sacrifice within the realm, and below them were the ordinary priests and chosen women. At the base of the hierarchy, and probably the most numerous of all religious personalities, were the **curanderos**, local curers practising herbal medicine and magic, and making sacrifices to small regional *huacas*.

Most **religious festivals** were calendrically based and marked by processions, sacrifices and dances. The Incas were aware of lunar time and the solar year, although they generally used the blooming of a special cactus and the stars to gauge the correct time to begin planting. Sacrifices to the gods normally consisted of llamas, *cuys* or *chicha* – only occasionally were chosen women and other adults killed. Once every year, however, young children were apparently sacrificed in the most important sacred centres.

Divination was a vital role played by priests and *curanderos* at all levels of the religious hierarchy. Soothsayers were expected to talk with the spirits and often used a hallucinogenic snuff from the vilca plant to achieve a trance-like state and communion with the other world. Everything from a crackling fire to the glance of a lizard was seen as a potential omen, and treated as such by making a little offering of coca leaves, coca spittle or *chicha*. There were specific problems which divination was considered particularly accurate in solving: retrieving lost things; predicting the outcome of certain events (the oracles were always consulted prior to important military escapades); receiving a vision of contemporaneous yet distant happenings; and the diagnosis of illness.

Ancient wizardry in modern Peru

B earing in mind the country's poverty and the fact that almost half the population is still pure Amerindian, it isn't altogether surprising to discover that the ancient shamanic healing arts are still flourishing in Peru. Evidence for this type of magical health therapy stretches back over three thousand years on the Peruvian coast. Today, healing wizards, or *curanderos* (Spanish for "healers"), can be found in every large community, practising healing based on knowledge, which has been passed down from master to apprentice over millennia. *Curanderos* offer an alternative to the expensive, sporadic and often unreliable service provided by scientific medics in a developing country like Peru. But as well as being a cheaper, more widely available option, *curanderismo* is also closer to the hearts and understanding of the average Peruvian.

With the resurgence of herbalism, aromatherapy, exotic healing massages and other aspects of New Age "holistic" health, it should be easier for us in the developed world to understand *curanderismo* than it might have been a decade or so ago. Combine "holistic" health with psychotherapy, and add an underlying cultural vision of spiritual and magical influences, and you are some way towards getting a clearer picture of how healing wizards operate.

There are two other important characteristics of modern-day Peruvian *curanderismo*. Firstly, the last four hundred years of Spanish domination have added a veneer of Catholic imagery and nomenclature to Peruvian beliefs. Nature spirits and denizens have become saints or demons, while ancient mountain spirits and their associated annual festivals continue disguised as Christian ceremonies. Equally important for any real understanding of Peruvian shamanism is the fact that most, if not all, *curanderos* use hallucinogens. The tribal peoples in the Peruvian Amazon who have managed, to a large extent, to hang on to their culture in the face of the oncoming industrial civilization, have also maintained their spiritual traditions. In almost every Peruvian Amazon tribe these traditions include the regular use of hallucinogenic brews to give a visionary ecstatic experience. Sometimes just the shaman partakes, but more often the shaman and his patients, or entire communities, will indulge together, singing traditional spirit-songs that help control the visions. The hallucinogenic experience, like the world of dreams, is the Peruvian forest Indian's way of getting in touch with the **ancestral world** or the world of spirit matter.

Psychedelic tourism

The best way of engaging the Amerindian plant medicine cosmos is through several of the **tourist lodges** in and around Iquitos (see p.546). For a little over $1100 it's possible to get a two-week package deal including pick-up from Lima, a flight to Iquitos, a boat to a jungle lodge, food, accommodation and at least two *ayahuasca* sessions with a local shaman. Shorter and cheaper sessions are available if you just want to suss out the situation once you arrive in Iquitos. More possibilities are available in and around Cusco (see p.263). If you want to do some research before coming out, which is definitely advised, take a look at: Ⓦwww.ayahuasca -shamanism.co.uk and Ⓦwww.shamanism.co.uk.

The origins of shamanism

The history of healing wizards in Peru matches that of the ritual use of hallucinogens and appears to have emerged alongside the first major temple-building culture – **Chavín** (1200 BC–200 AD). Agriculture, ceramics and other technical processes, including some metallurgy, had already been developed by 1200 BC, but Chavín demonstrates the first unified and widespread cultural movement in terms of sacred architectural style, and the forms and symbolic imagery used in pottery throughout much of Andean and coastal Peru during this era. Chavín was a religious cult which seems to have spread from the central mountains, quite possibly from the large temple complex at Chavín de Huantar near Huaraz. Taking hold along the coast, the image of the central Chavín deity was woven, moulded and carved onto the finest funerary cloths, ceramics and stones. Generally represented as a complex and demonic-looking feline deity, the Chavín god always has fangs and a stern face. Many of the idols also show serpents radiating from the deity's head.

As far as the central temple at Chavín de Huantar is concerned, it was almost certainly a centre of sacred pilgrimage, built-up over a period of centuries into a large ceremonial complex used at appropriate calendrical intervals to focus the spiritual, political and economic energies of a vast area (at least large enough to include a range of produce for local consumption from tropical forest, high Andean and desert coast regions). The magnificent stone temple kept growing in size until, by around 300 BC, it would have been one of the largest religious centres anywhere in the world, with some three thousand local attendants. Among the fascinating finds at Chavín there have been bone snuff-tubes, beads, pendants, needles, ceremonial spondylus shells (imported from Ecuador) and some **quartz crystals** associated with ritual sites. One quartz crystal, covered in red pigment, was found in a grave, placed after death in the mouth of the deceased. Contemporary anthropological evidence shows us that quartz crystals still play an important role in shamanic ceremonies in Peru, the Americas, Australia and Asia. The well-documented Desana Indians of Colombia still see crystals as a "means of communication between the visible and invisible worlds, a crystallization of solar energy, or the Sun Father's semen which can be used in esoteric undertakings".

In one stone relief on the main temple at Chavín the feline deity is depicted holding a large **San Pedro cactus** in his hand. A Chavín ceramic bottle has been discovered with a San Pedro cactus "growing" on it; and, on another pot, a feline sits surrounded by several San Pedros. Similar motifs and designs appear on the later Paracas and Mochica craft work, but there is no real evidence for the ritual use of hallucinogens prior to Chavín. One impressive ceramic from the Mochica culture (500 AD) depicts an owl-woman – still symbolic of the female shaman in contemporary Peru – with a slice of San Pedro cactus in her hand. Another ceramic from the later Chimu culture (around 1100 AD) also shows a woman healer holding a San Pedro.

As well as coca, their "divine plant", the **Incas** had their own special hallucinogen: vilca (meaning "sacred" in Quechua). The vilca tree (probably *Anadenanthera colubrina*) grows in the cloud-forest zones on the eastern slopes of the Peruvian Andes. The Incas used a snuff made from the seeds, which was generally blown up the nostrils of the participant by a helper. Evidently the Inca priests used vilca to bring on visions and make contact with the gods and spirit world.

Shamanism today

Still commonly used by *curanderos* on the coast and in the mountains of Peru, the San Pedro cactus (*Trichocereus panchanoi*) is a potent hallucinogen based on active mescaline. The *curandero* administers the hallucinogenic brew to his or her clients to bring about a period of revelation when questions are asked of the intoxicated person, who might also be asked to choose some object from among a range of magical curios which all have different meanings to the healer. Sometimes a *curandero* might imbibe San Pedro (or one of the many other indigenous hallucinogens) to see into the future, retrieve lost souls, divine causes of illness or discover the whereabouts of lost objects.

On **the coast**, healing wizards usually live near the sea on the fringes of a settlement. Most have their own San Pedro plant that is said to protect or guard their homes against unwanted intruders by letting out a high-pitched whistle if somebody approaches. The most famous *curandero* of all used to live just outside Trujillo on the north coast of Peru. Eduardo Calderon – better known in Peru as **El Tuno** – was a shaman and a healer. His work consisted of treating sick and worried people who came to him from hundreds of miles around by utilizing a combination of herbalism, magical divination and a kind of psychic shock therapy involving the use of San Pedro.

Many coastal wizards get their most potent magic and powerful plants from a small zone in the northern Andes. The mountain area around Las Huaringas and Huancabamba, to the north of Chiclayo and east of Piura, is where a large number of the "great masters" are believed to live and work. But it is in the Amazon Basin of Peru that shamanism continues in its least-changed form.

Even on the edges of most jungle towns there are *curanderos* healing local people by using a mixture of jungle Indian shamanism and the more Catholicized coastal form. These wizards generally use the most common tropical forest hallucinogen, **ayahuasca** (from the liana *Banisteriopsis caapi*). Away from the towns, among the more remote tribal people, *ayahuasca* is the key to understanding the native consciousness and perception of the world – which for them is the natural world of the elements and the forest plus their own social, economic and political setup within that dominant environment.

The Shipibo tribe from the central Peruvian Amazon are famous for their excellent ceramic and weaving designs: extremely complex geometric patterns usually in black on white or beige, though sometimes reds or yellows too. These designs were traditionally inspired by visions received while the shaman was under the influence of *ayahuasca*, whose effect is described as "the spirits coming down".

It is clearly hard to generalize with any accuracy across the spectrum of healing wizards still found in modern Peru, yet there are definite threads connecting them all. On a practical level even the most isolated jungle shaman may well have trading links with several coastal *curanderos* – there are many magical cures imported via a web of ongoing trans-Andean trading partners to be found on the *curanderos'* street market stalls in Lima, Trujillo, Arequipa and Chimbote. It has been argued by some of the most eminent Peruvianists that the initial ideas and spark for the Chavín culture came up the Marañón Valley from the Amazon. If this is so, then these ideas could well have brought with them – some three thousand years ago – the first shamanic teachings to the rest of ancient Peru, possibly even the use of power plants and other tropical forest hallucinogens, since these are so critical to understanding even modern-day Peruvian Amazon Indian religion. One thing that can certainly be said about ancient healing wizards in modern Peru is that they question the very foundations of our rational scientific perception of the world.

Peruvian music

Latin America's oldest musical traditions are those of the Amerindians of the Andes. Their music is best known outside these countries through the characteristic panpipes of poncho-clad folklore groups. However, there's a multitude of rhythms and popular musics found here that deserve a lot more recognition, including *huayno* and *chicha*, until recently relatively unknown abroad, as well as the distinct coastal tradition of Afro-Peruvian music, rooted in black slaves brought to work in the mines.

For most people outside Latin America the sound of the Andes is that of bamboo panpipes and *quena* flutes. What is most remarkable is that these instruments have been used to create music in various parts of this large area of mountains – which stretch 7200km from Venezuela down to southernmost Chile – since before the time of the Incas. Pre-Conquest Andean instruments – conch-shell trumpets, shakers which used nuts for rattles, ocarinas, wind instruments and drums – are ever-present in museum collections. And the influence of the Inca Empire means that the Andean region and its music spreads far beyond the mountains themselves. It can be defined partly through ethnicity, partly through language – **Quechua** (currently spoken by over six million people) and **Aymara**, both of which are spoken alongside Spanish and other Amerindian languages.

The dominant areas of Andean culture are **Peru**, Ecuador and Bolivia, the countries with the largest indigenous Amerindian populations in South America. Here, in rural areas, highly traditional Andean music, probably little different from pre-Inca times, still thrives today at every kind of celebration and ritual. But beyond this is a huge diversity of music, differing widely not only between countries but between individual communities. Andean people tend to identify themselves by the specific place they come from: in music, the villages have different ways of making and tuning instruments and composing tunes, in the same way as they have distinctive weaving designs, ways of dressing or wearing their hats. Use of different scales involving four, five, six and seven notes and different singing styles are also found from place to place, tied to specific ritual occasions and the music which goes with them.

Andean music can be divided roughly into three types: firstly, that which is of **indigenous origin**, found mostly amongst rural Amerindian peoples still living very much by the seasons with root Amerindian beliefs; secondly, music of **European origin**; and thirdly, **mestizo music**, which continues to fuse the indigenous with European in a whole host of ways. In general, Quechua people have more vocal music than the Aymara.

Traditional music

Panpipes, known by the Aymara as *siku*, by the Quechua as *antara* and by the Spanish as *zampoña*, are ancient instruments, and archaeologists have unearthed panpipes tuned to a variety of scales. While modern panpipes – played in the city or in groups with other instruments – may offer a complete scale, allowing solo performance, traditional models are played in pairs, as described by sixteenth-century chroniclers. The pipes share the melody, each with alternate notes of a whole scale, so that two or more players are needed to pick out a single tune using a hocket technique. Usually one player leads and the other follows. While symbolically this demonstrates reciprocity within the community, practically it enables players to play for a long time without getting too "high" from dizziness caused by over-breathing.

Played by blowing (or breathing out hard) across the top of a tube, panpipes come in various sizes, those with a deep bass having very long tubes. Several tubes made of bamboo reed of different length are bound together to produce a sound that can be jaunty, but also has a melancholic edge depending on tune and playing style. Many tunes have a minor, descending shape to them. Playing is often described as "breathy" as over-blowing is popular to produce harmonics. In general those who play panpipes love dense overlapping textures and often syncopated rhythms.

Simple **notched-end flutes**, or **quenas**, are another independent innovation of the Andean highlands found in both rural and urban areas. The most important pre-Hispanic instrument, they were traditionally made of fragile bamboo (though often these days from plumbers' PVC water pipes) and played in the dry season, with **tarkas** (vertical flutes – like a shrill recorder) taking over in the wet. *Quenas* are played solo or in ritual groups and remain tremendously popular today, with many virtuoso techniques.

Large **marching bands of drums and panpipes**, playing in the co-operative "back and forth" leader/follower style that captivated the Spanish in the 1500s, can still be seen and heard today. The drums are deep-sounding, double-headed instruments known as *bombos* or *wankaras*. These bands exist for parades at life-cycle fiestas, weddings and dances in the regions surrounding the Peruvian–Bolivian frontier and around Lake Titicaca. Apart from their use at fiestas, panpipes are played mainly in the dry season, from April to October.

There is something quite amazing about the sound of a fifty-man panpipe band approaching, especially after they've been playing for a few hours and have had a few well-earned drinks. It is perfectly normal for a whole village to come together to play as an orchestra for important events and fiestas. Andean villages are usually composed of *ayllus* (extended families) whose land is often divided up so that everyone gets a share of various pastures, but with everyone working together at important times such as harvest and when caring for communal areas. Music is an integral part of all communal celebrations and symbolically represents that sharing and interdependence: drinks are drunk from communal glasses which everyone will empty in turn. The organization and values of each community are reflected in the very instrument an individual plays, down to the position of players within circles and groups.

Folk music festivals to attract and entertain the tourist trade are a quite different experience to music in the village context. While positively disseminating the music, they have introduced the notion of judging and the concept of "best" musicianship – ideas totally at odds with rural community values of diversity in musical repertoire, style and dress.

Charangos and mermaids

The **charango** is another major Andean instrument whose bright, zingy sounds are familiar worldwide. This small guitar – with five pairs of strings – was created in imitation of early guitars and lutes brought by the Spanish colonizers, which Amerindian musicians were taught to play in the churches. Its small size is due to its traditional manufacture from armadillo shells, while its sound quality comes from the indigenous aesthetic which has favoured high pitches from the pre-Columbian period through to the present.

In rural areas in southern Peru, particularly in the Titicaca region and province of Canas, the *charango* is the main instrument – used by young, single men to woo and court the female of main choice. In this area, the tradition often involves the figure of a **mermaid**, *la sirena*, who offers supernatural aid to the young men embarking on a musical pursuit of their chosen one. The ethno-musicologist Tom Turino records that most towns and villages around Titicaca claim a *sirena* lives in a nearby spring, river, lake or waterfall, and notes that new *charangos* are often left overnight in such places – wrapped in a piece of woven cloth, along with gifts – to be tuned and played overnight by the *sirena*. Some villagers construct the sound box in the shape of a mermaid, including her head and fish tail, to invest their *charango* with supernatural power.

When young men go courting at the weekly markets in larger villages they will not only dress in their finest clothes, but get up their *charangos* in elaborately coloured ribbons. These represent the number of women their *charango* has sup-posedly conquered, thus demonstrating their manliness and the power of their instrument. At times a group of young people will get together for the ancient **circle dance** called the *Punchay Kashwa,* where the men form a half-circle play-ing their *charangos*, facing a half-circle of young women. Both groups dance and sing in bantering "song duelling" fashion, participants using a set syllabic and rhyming pattern so that they can quickly improvise. "Let's go walking" one might call, with a riposte such as "A devil like you makes me suspicious", or an insult like "In the back of your house there are three rotten eggs".

In Peru, the *charango* was regarded until the 1960s as an "Indian" instrument of the rural, lower classes. Brought to towns and cities by rural migrants, it crossed over when Spanish-speaking middle-class musicians – who until then had only played European instruments such as guitars and mandolins – began to play it, and also as a result of the cultural evaluation following the 1969 Revolution. The Peruvian ideological movement known as **Indigenismo**, active between 1910 and 1940, was also influential in the *charango*'s reappraisal. *Indigenismo* was a regionalistic and nationalistic movement that lauded indigenous culture as the true Peruvian culture, rejecting *criolla* and Hispanic values. The movement was particularly strong in Cusco, where *charango* performance by *mestizos* became part of its identity.

Charango styles

Charangos were originally made from the shell of an armadillo but as the animal has become rare and protected, today's instruments are made of wood. There are many sizes and varieties: from those capable of deeper, richer, bass sounds, with large round backs, to flat-backed instruments with more strident metal strings.

Tunings vary from place to place and from musician to musician, with some preferring metal strings, others nylon, to suit a variety of strumming and pluck-ing techniques. Nylon strings are often thought to produce "deeper", "clearer", "sweeter" sounds. In certain areas of Peru, for instance at the time of potato planting, a *charango* may play potato-planting songs and dances strictly in strum-ming style with a single-line melody vibrating amongst open sounding strings. In contrast, **mestizo styles** – used when playing creole musical forms such as *waynos*, *marineras*, *yaravís* and *vals criollo* – may favour plucked melodic playing styles which can be very complex.

Song and brass

Most **singing** in the Andes is done by women, and the preferred style is very high-pitched – almost falsetto to Western ears. There are songs for potato-grow-ing, reaping barley, threshing wheat, marking cattle, sheep and goats, for build-ing houses, for traditional dances and funerals and many other ceremonies.

The astonishing diversity of music, ensembles and occasions can be heard clearly on the superb *Smithsonian Folkways Traditional Music of Peru* series, documented and compiled by music ethnologist Raúl Romero. These recordings are mainly from the Mantaro Valley, an area known for its saxophone and clarinet ensembles, and include women singing accompanied by the ancient *tinya* drum and violin, and also the harp as well as clarinets and brass bands. There are so many festivities with music that the music profession is considered profitable, and there are a great number of **brass bands** (first introduced in the 1920s as part of mandatory military service) as well as **orchestras** (*típicas*) composed of saxophones, clarinets, violins and diatonic harp.

Romero notes that urbanization, modernization and migration, rather than undermining the need for traditional music, has led to its successful adaptation of new forms and revival. He also notes the importance of *mestizo* and bilingual Spanish-Quechua culture in this process.

The context of the musical performance is still the determining factor in its style. Music that continues pre-Hispanic models is to be found within the context of closed community and ritual. Music that is *mestizo*, recreating regional traditions, is dynamically driven by the fiesta system. New musical styles have evolved through migration to the capital Lima, with radio, vinyl and CD as their main vehicles of communication.

Music in Cusco

Music explodes from every direction in the once Inca lands, but nowhere more so than in **Cusco**, a good first base for getting to grips with Andean music. Stay a week or two and you will hear just about every variety of Andean folk music that is still performed.

The Andean harp: Don Antonio Sulca

Blind musician **Don Antonio Sulca**, of Ayacucho, is one of the great masters of the Andean harp – one of the mountains' most characteristic instruments. This huge harp has a sound box built like a boat and a mermaid's head decoration (like many *charangos*). Its form is thought to have evolved from the harp brought from Spain in the sixteenth century and the Celtic harp brought by the Jesuits to the missions. It has 36 strings spanning five octaves and including resonant bass notes. In processions in the Andes, harpists often sling their instruments upside down across their shoulders, plucking with a remarkable backhanded technique.

Sulca plays solo or, more often, with his group **Ayllu Sulca**, composed of members of his *ayllu* (his extended family), on fiddles and mandolins. Their songs are mostly *huaynos* sung in Quechua. The most familiar of them, *Huerfano pajarillo* (*Little Orphan Bird*), about a bird that has strayed too far from home, is an allegory of the plight of the Amerindians forced to migrate to earn a living. His stately style of playing *yaravís* – slow sad tunes – is unmatched. A pre-Hispanic form, they probably acquired their doleful, introspective character during the early colonial period, when at least eighty percent of the Amerindian population perished. The *yaraví* composed at the death of the last member of the Inca royal family, Tupac Amaru, in 1781, became the best-known of all Peruvian tunes – **El Condor Pasa (Flight of the Condor)**.

Don Antonio Sulca also plays **dance music** from the early twentieth century, when forms like the foxtrot, waltz and tango were given the Inca touch to produce hybrid forms like the sublime waltz **incaico** *Nube Gris* (*Grey Cloud*). His version of his city's unofficial hymn, *Adiós pueblo Ayacucho* (*Farewell, People of Ayacucho*), celebrates emotional ties to the place where the Amerindians beat back the Spanish at the time of the Conquest.

The streets are the best place to start. Most street musicians are highly talented performers and will play for hours on end. Around noon, you might see **Leandro Apaza** making his way down the great hill of Avenida Tullumayo. Carrying an Andean harp on his shoulder, he is led down the street by a small boy because, like many accomplished regional musicians, he is blind. He will turn right onto Hatun Rumiyoq, the narrow alley that every visitor to Cusco visits at some time to see the large stone perfectly fitted into place in the side wall of Inca Roca's palace. Leandro sets up his harp directly across from the great stone. **Benjamin Clara**, who sometimes accompanies him on mandolin, may already be there waiting. Benjamin cannot always meet Leandro downtown as he is lame as well as sightless and needs to be carried (see Discography, *Blind Street Musicians of Cusco*, p.594).

The two are there to earn their living by playing the traditional music of the Quechua people. Their repertoire includes a host of styles, the most recognizable being the *huayno*, an unmistakable dance rhythm reminiscent of a hopped-up waltz, which once heard is not easily forgotten. It is musically cheerful, though the lyrics can be sorrowful, and sometimes full of double meaning, occasionally sexually explicit – a fact often not realized by those who cannot understand Quechua.

Very few such musicians achieve any kind of media fame. If they do, it usually means the chance to perform in small clubs or restaurants for a meagre guaranteed wage plus whatever they receive in tips. One such individual is **Gabriel Aragón**. Another blind musician, he is a huge man, obviously *mestizo*, and possessed of a gentle voice and a soft touch on his harp. His fame means that he will often travel for an engagement, which may be a club date, a wedding or a traditional festival. At his restaurant gigs, he serves up some of the finest traditional folk melodies, ballads and dance tunes – a nostalgic repertoire greatly appreciated by older members of the community.

Conjuntos and concerts

Cusco's tavern scene, like that of any urban region, also plays host to young *cholo* and *mestizo* groups. They are constantly on the move throughout the evening, playing one set in each of the available venues in town during the tourist season. You can pick the club with your favourite ambience and settle in – most of the groups will pass through in the course of an evening, so you are almost bound to hear each of them at some point as the entertainment goes on all night long.

This kind of "one-night tour" is limited only by the size of a city. In Lima, for example, a group of this type might confine itself to a specific area of town. The smaller mountain villages, by contrast, might have only one venue – and if they are lucky a local band. In regions of heavy tourism, such as Cusco or Ollantaytambo, there is usually a proliferation of groups. If you end up at one of these mini-fiestas, you may be egged on to dance, especially if you are a woman, and definitely be forced to join in a drink. Go along with it, do your best, and don't mind being the butt of the odd joke. It will be worth it.

The ensembles typically consist of five to seven members. Their **instrumentation** includes one or two guitars, a *charango*, *quenas*, other flutes, panpipes and simple percussion. Harps, considered something of a dying art due to their size, weight, fragility and cost, are rarer these days. Most of the musicians are adept at more than one instrument and are likely to switch roles during their set. Their performing is a social event, and their tour a rolling party as they are usually accompanied on their rounds by friends (you are welcome to join them).

As these musicians grow older many of them end up in the backup band of a veteran professional, rather than in a group of traditional musicians. This type of **conjunto** is most likely to be made up of urban middle-class musicians, usually serious students of music since early in life. They often have some type of classical training, may be able to compose and arrange, and, although emotionally tied to ancestral heritage, the bulk of their repertoire is newly composed using traditional idioms played on both modern and traditional instruments. They will also be able to play a variety of standards – classic pieces of traditional highland folk. These ensembles are usually quite well paid and do not normally move about throughout the evening. They play at the more elite nightclubs, hotel lounges and arts centres and sometimes, if lucky, tour abroad.

Although by the very nature of their own background and that of their audience, these bands are not staunch traditionalists, they are promoted as such by those in charge of international cultural exchange. On tour abroad, they usually play well-known traditional pieces, and often accompany **folkloric dance groups**, while another part of their repertoire may be what is marketed as **Andean New Age** music, a blend of traditionalism with modern sounds. The vocal presentation of these groups is generally more accessible to foreign ears than the piercing falsetto tones of a traditional vocalist.

Huaynos and orquestas típicas

Europeans may know the Andes through the sound of bamboo panpipes and *quenas*, but visit the Peruvian central sierra and you find a music as lively and energetic as the busy market towns it comes from – a music largely unknown outside the country. These songs and dances are **huaynos**, one of the few musical forms that reaches back to pre-Conquest times, although the **orquestas típicas** that play them, from sierra towns like Huancayo, Ayacucho and Pucará, include saxophones, clarinets and trumpets alongside traditional instruments like violins, *charangos* and the large Amerindian harp.

The music is spirited and infectious, the focus gradually shifting from Inca past and a pan-Andean image to the contemporary cultures of regional departments. Because of the larger size of the *provinciano* colonies from Ancash, Junin and Ayacucho in Lima, the urban-country style primarily grew up around performers from these departments, including Pastorita Huancarina (Ancash), Hermanos Zevallos (Junin), Flor de Huancayo (Junin), Princesita de Yungay (Ancash) and Paisanita Ancashina (Ancash). Names such as Paisanita Ancashina (Little Fellow Country-woman from Ancash) clearly evoke nostalgia of place and *paisano* loyalty, helping to ensure commercial success and bolster regional group unity and pride.

While some voices maintain the high-pitched dense quality of Andean singing, many major stars incorporate Western vibrato (absent in traditional Andean singing) and a clear – from the diaphragm – vocal style. As musicians have become more professional, specializing in certain styles, technical performance on instruments has become cleaner and instrumental breaks hotter. Arrangements too have become tighter and follow other urban popular forms with vocal verses and instrumental solos.

The names of the singers express the passion of the people for the flora and fauna of their homeland – **Flor Pucarina** (The Flower of Pucará) and **Picaflor de los Andes** (Hummingbird of the Andes) are two of those singing in the 1960s represented on GlobeStyle's *huayno* compilation. Another CD of this music, on the Arhoolie label, features the most celebrated *huayno* singer of all time – **El Jilguero de Huascarán**. When he died in 1988, thousands of people packed the streets of Lima to attend his funeral, and recordings he made over thirty years ago are still sold on the streets today.

The buoyant, swinging rhythms of *huayno* songs are deceptive, for the lyrics fuse joy and sorrow. The musical style is regionally marked with typical *mestizo* instrumental ensembles of the region represented and musical features, such as specific guitar runs, identifying musicians with, for example, Ayacucho or Ancash. Sung in a mixture of Spanish and Quechua, they tell of unhappy love and betrayal, celebrate passion and often deliver homespun philosophy. As Picaflor sings in *Un pasajero en tu camino*: "On the road of romance, I'm only a passenger without a destination". At the same time, texts often allude to region of origin or specific towns, important hooks for local audiences.

As well as in their sierra home, *huaynos* can be heard in Lima and other coastal towns, where they were brought by Andean migrants in the 1950s. Before then the music of the coastal towns and cities was **música criolla**, heavily influenced by music from other parts of Latin America, Spain and Europe – a bourgeois music including everything from foxtrot to tango, which filtered down to the working class, often as hybrids called, for example, Inca-Fox. In the 1950s and 1960s, migrants who often found themselves living in desperate poverty in the shantytowns, scraping a living as maids, labourers or street-traders, would meet up at a Lima *coliseo* (a form of stadium) on a Sunday to dance to their music and assert identity and pride.

Between 1946 and 1949 there were thirty such centres for *espectaculos folkloricos* in Lima, but only two remained by the mid-1970s and there are none left today. A blend of resources from the two worlds, this music served as an aid to *provincianos* in the process of forging a new identity for themselves. But the *coliseos* began to lose their public as people began to demand more traditional performances of highland music and dance. In the 1960s and 1970s regional-migrant clubs began to take control over the commercial entrepreneurs who had failed to reward the musicians well. Sunday performances switched to these new clubs which gave a share of the fee to the musicians and featured traditions specifically from their home regions.

Urban *huaynos* are performed and recorded by **orquestas típicas** and enjoy enormous popularity. In the rural areas the style is more rustic. Andean highland settlements are isolated by deep river valleys, which made communication difficult in the past. Because of this, students of Quechua are tormented by the extreme variation in language sometimes found between two relatively close villages. One would expect a similar variation between song styles; this is sometimes the case, but the *huayno* beat is pan-Andean. Each district does add its own peculiar flavour, but as the saying goes, a *huayno* is a *huayno*, at least until you listen closely. During daylight hours, some forty Lima radio stations broadcast nothing but *huaynos*. Shortwave-radio fans, or visitors to Peru, can tune in for a quick education.

Afro-Peruvian music

Afro-Peruvian music has its roots in the communities of black slaves brought to work in the mines along the Peruvian coast. As such, it's a fair way from the Andes, culturally and geographically. However, as it developed, particularly in the twentieth century, it drew on Andean and Spanish, as well as African, traditions, while its modern exponents also have affinities with Andean *nueva canción*. The music was little known even in Peru until the 1950s, when it was popularized by the seminal performer Nicomedes Santa Cruz, whose body of work was taken a step further in the 1970s by the group Peru Negro. Internationally, it has had a recent airing through David Byrne's Luaka Bop label, issuing the compilation, *Peru-Negro*, and solo albums by the now world-renowned **Susana Baca**.

Susana Baca, who grew up in the black coastal neighbourhood of Chorrillos, near Lima, has brought international acclaim to Afro-Peruvian music. Interviewed at WOMAD 1998, she recalled family traditions of getting together for a Sunday meal, and then making music, with her father playing guitar, her mother, aunts, uncles and friends singing and dancing. By the time she was a teenager and first heard the recordings of Nicomedes Santa Cruz, she realized she had absorbed quite a repertoire of the traditional songs black people had carried with them to Peru as slaves.

Susana Baca runs her own Instituto Negrocontinuo, with her husband Ricardo Pereira; its aim is to promote and increase the diffusion of Afro-Peruvian music, and to link together old and young musicians through a series of workshops on all aspects of the music and its culture. Her passion for Afro-Peruvian culture and music first emerged at school and has increased steadily over the years. "We studied the culture of the Spanish and of the Incas which made the Andean girls proud, but we black girls didn't find our people in the history of Peru at all", recalls Baca. "Blacks came to Peru as servants of Spanish and Portuguese, as slaves to be bought and sold. As a child I was aware that we had our way of cooking, our music, dances, even our own traditional medicines – but it was only in the 1960s that this was first really asserted in public. A lot of people until then had been silenced, some ashamed of the whole history of slavery, of the sufferings of their great grandparents, rejecting their past. But then it began to take on a positive hue and people began to understand what it meant to be black."

One of the essential instruments of Afro-Peruvian music is the *cajón* – a box which the percussionist sits astride, leaning down to play. This is the same *cajón* that eventually made its way into Spanish flamenco – through Paco de Lucía who, according to an apocryphal story, played in Lima in 1978 and first heard the *cajón* played at a party. Susana remembers, "It's true, I was there, I even sang and there was a great group of Peruvian musicians playing and of *cajoneros*, and Paco de Lucía liked it all so much they gave him a *cajón*. The instrument is so important because it carries the rhythm and the voice sings within that dialogue between guitar and *cajón*. My mother always said that it was the box of the people who carried fruit and worked in the ports. When they had a free moment they used them to play and sing and dance. Later they had a more special construction, different woods with a hole in one side that gives a more sophisticated sound, more reverberation. Cuba and Brazil also have similar traditions which also emerged amongst black musicians in ports."

Baca's own performing style is intimate and rooted in close contact with her band "Nothing is written down, the musicians improvise and invent, so we need to be able to see each other's eyes to make a good performance, to share and enjoy and release the power of the music. You can hear it in *La Canción para el Señor de los Milagros* (*The Song for the Lord of Miracles*). It's a song of adoration for a Christ who is celebrated for two days in October in Lima. It's now one of the most important popular festivals – people follow the Christ figure in such numbers through the streets the city comes to a halt. It's wonderful. They asked me to sing that sacred song and I do."

Nicomedes Santa Cruz is the towering figure in the development of Afro-Peruvian music. A poet, musician and journalist, he was the first true musicologist to assert an Afro-Peruvian cultural identity through black music and dance, producing books and recordings of contemporary black music and culture in Peru. In 1959, with his group **Conjunto Cumanana**, he recorded the album *Kumanana*, followed in 1960 by *Ingá* and *Décimas y poemas Afroperuanos*. In 1964 he recorded a four-album set *Cumanana*, now regarded as the bible of Afro-Peruvian music. Santa Cruz himself followed in the footsteps of **Porfirio Vasquez**,

Compilations

Afro-Peruvian Classics: The Soul of Black Peru (Luaka Bop, US). A unique blend of Spanish, Andean and African traditions, this is different to Caribbean and other Latin black cultures. The compilation includes the definitive dance song *Toro Mata*, the first Afro-Peruvian success outside Peru, covered by the Queen of Salsa, Celia Cruz. A fine collection intended to introduce the music to a wider audience outside Peru, it does a great job.

The Blind Street Musicians of Cusco: Peruvian Harp and Mandolin (Music of the World, US). Stirringly played *marineras*, *huaynos*, traditional tunes and instrumental solos exactly as heard on the streets of Cusco in 1984–85 from Leandro Apaza on a 33-stringed harp; Benjamin Clara Quispé and Carmen Apaza Roca on armadillo-shelled mandolins (not *charangos*); Fidel Villacorte Tejada on *quena*. Excellent ambience recorded in musicians' homes and *chichería* bars.

Flutes and Strings of the Andes (Music of the World, US). The superbly atmospheric recordings of amateur musicians from Peru – harpists, *charanguistas*, fiddlers, flautists and percussionists, recorded in 1983–84 on the streets and at festivals – bring you as close to being there as you can get without strapping on your pack and striding uphill.

From the Mountains to the Sea: Music of Peru, The 1960s (Arhoolie, US). Brilliant window into the mix of indigenous, *criolla*, *mestizo*, Latin, tropical and European styles to be found in the capital, including Peruvian rock, *cumbias*, *valses*, *boleros*, *sanjuanitos*, *huaynos* and tangos. Captures the spirit of many different groups, combinations of instruments and atmospheres.

Huayno Music of Peru Vols 1 and 2 (Arhoolie, US). These excellent collections of *huayno* music from the 1950s to the 1980s focus on a slightly more local style than the GlobeStyle disc. Vol 1 includes songs from the master, Jilguero del Huascarán, while Vol 2 is drawn from the recordings of Discos Smith, a small label that released *huayno* and *criolla* music in the late 1950s and 1960s.

Huaynos and Huaylas: The Real Music of Peru (GlobeStyle, UK). A tremendous selection of urban *orquestas típicas*, who replace traditional instruments with saxophones, clarinets and violins, this is a real eye- and ear-opener. The performers include the late Picaflor de los Andes, and Flor Pucarina, with a host of songs expressing loss and love rooted in the Peruvian countryside.

Kingdom of the Sun (Nonesuch Explorer, US). An atmospheric mix of Peru's Inca heritage and religious festivals recorded in Ayacucho, Chuschi and Paucartambo.

Mountain Music of Peru (Smithsonian Folkways, US). John Cohen's selection, including a song that went up in the *Voyager* spacecraft, brings together music from remote corners of the mountains where music is integral to daily life, and urban songs telling of tragedies at football matches. Good sleeve notes, too.

Peru and Bolivia. The Sounds of Evolving Traditions. Central Andean Music and Festivals (Multicultural Media, US). Lively, accessible introduction to today's sounds from both Peru and Bolivia, from Japanese aficionado Norio Yamamoto's brilliant and diverse selection of recordings. Each piece in its natural context from people's homes to clubs to fiestas to streets with live local audiences. Harps, violins, drums, panpipes and much more. Moving from Cusco to Ayacucho, La Paz to Lima, Lake Titicaca and back to Marcapata village near Cusco. Good notes.

The Rough Guide to Music of the Andes (World Music Network). A vigorous and broad range of Andean music from contemporary urban-based groups – including major 1960s musicians Los Kjarkas and Ernesto Cavou, and their 1980s European travelling brethren Awatinas and Rumillajta; soloists Emma Junaro, Jenny Cardenas and Susana Baca; seminal Chilean group Inti Illimani and new song, or Nueva Canción, singer Victor Jara. Plus saxes and clarinets from Picaflor de los Andes.

Traditional Music of Peru: Vol 1 Festivals of Cusco; Vol 2 The Mantaro Valley; Vol 3 Cajamarca and the Colca Valley; Vol 4 Lambayeque (Smithsonian Folkways, US). A definitive series of field recordings from the 1980s and 1990s of music from specific areas. Includes the whole spectrum of music to be heard if you travelled around the whole of Peru. Excellent CD booklets, too.

Artists and albums

Ayllu Sulca

Blind harpist Don Antonio Sulca encapsulates everything that is *mestizo* music – the emergence of a hybrid blend between Amerindian and Spanish cultures. A virtuoso since early childhood, he plays as a soloist but mostly as part of his band – his *ayllu* – which includes three of his sons.

Music of the Incas (Lyrichord, US). Accompanied by violin, mandolin and *quenas*, Sulca plays ancient Inca melodies and more recent waltzes with pace and swing, including rustic versions of salon music.

Susana Baca

One of the few Afro-Peruvian artists touring worldwide, Susana Baca grew up in the coastal *barrio* of Chorrillos and learned traditional Afro-Peruvian songs from her family (see box, p.593). Dedicated to reviving and strengthening this past and making it relevant to the present, she runs the Instituto Negrocontinuo (Black Continuum) in Lima and is as involved with the integral dance and other aspects of Afro-Peruvian culture as the music.

Susana Baca (Luaka Bop/Warner Bros, US). Taking up the mantle of Chabuca Granda and Nicomedes Santa Cruz, these are fine versions of Afro-Peruvian and criolla classics sung with conscious emotion and passion.

Belem

Belem are one of the bands which have made *chicha* a force to be reckoned with in urban Peru.

Chicha (Tumi, UK). A pioneering release of Peru's hot fusion music. Belem's mix of *huayno*, salsa, *cumbia* and a touch of rock, deserves a listening. Andean pipe music, it ain't.

Arturo "Zambo" Cavero and Oscar Aviles

Arturo "Zambo" Cavero is one of the great male voices of black Peruvian music, as well as being an accomplished *cajón* player. During the 1980s he teamed up with Oscar Aviles to become a celebrated partnership, their music seen as reflecting the suffering, patriotism and passion of the black people of Peru. As a key member of the group Los Morochucos, Oscar Aviles gained the reputation of being "*La Primera Guitarra del Peru*" – Peru's leading Creole guitarist.

Y siguen festejando juntos (IEMPSA, Peru). Classic Afro-Peruvian music with the most representative voice and guitar musicians on the scene.

On the Wings of the Condor (Tumi, UK). One of the most popular Andean albums ever, but none the worse for that: the engaging sound of the panpipes and *charangos*, smoothly and beautifully arranged.

Hermanos Santa Cruz

Hermanos Santa Cruz are family members of Nicomedes Santa Cruz.

Afro Peru (Discos Hispanos, Peru). Carrying on the tradition and heritage laid down by their forefathers, the Santa Cruz brothers present a 1990s version of Afro-Peruvian traditions.

Nicomedes Santa Cruz

The first true musicologist to assert Afro-Peruvian cultural identity through black music and dance.

Kumanana (Philips, Peru), *Socabon* (Virrey, Peru). Two albums showcasing Santa Cruz's majestic musicological studies of Afro-Peruvian music and culture.

who came to Lima in 1920 and was an early pioneer of the movement to regain the lost cultural identity of Afro-Peruvians. A composer of *décimas*, singer, guitarist, *cajonero* (box player) and *zapateador* (dancer), he founded the Academia Folklórica in Lima in 1949. Through Santa Cruz's work and that of the group **Peru Negro** and the singer and composer **Chabuca Granda**, Latin America came to know Afro-Peruvian dances, the names of which were given to their songs such as *Toro Mata*, *Samba-malató*, *El Alcatraz* and *Festejo*.

Chicha

Chicha, the fermented maize beer, has given its name to a hugely popular brew of Andean tropical music, one which has recently spread to wider Anglophone world music circles. The music's origins lies in the rapidly urbanizing Amazon of the late 1960s, in places like Iquitos and Pucallpa, where bands such as **Los Mirlos** and **Juaneco y Su Combo** fused *cumbia* (local versions of the original Colombian dance), traditional highland *huayno* and Western rock and psychedelia. In the 1970s, mass migration carried *chicha* to Lima, and by the mid-1980s, it had become the most widespread urban music in Peru. Most bands have lead and rhythm guitars, electric bass, electric organ, a *timbales* and conga player, one or more vocalists (who may play percussion) and, if they can, a synthesizer.

The first *chicha* hit, and the song from which the movement has taken its name, was *La Chichera* (*The Chicha Seller*) by **Los Demonios de Mantaro** (The Devils of Mantaro), who hailed from the central highlands of Junin. Another famous band are **Los Shapis**, another provincial group established by their 1981 hit *El Aguajal* (*The Swamp*), a version of a traditional *huayno*. **Pastorita Huaracina** is one of the more well-known female singers. Another good band – and the first to get a Western CD release – are **Belem**, based in Lima.

While most lyrics are about love in all its aspects, nearly all songs actually reveal an aspect of the harshness of the Amerindian experience – displacement, hardship, loneliness and exploitation. Many songs relate to the great majority of people who have to make a living selling their labour and goods in the unofficial "informal economy", ever threatened by the police. Los Shapis' *El Ambulante* (*The Street Seller*) opens with a reference to the rainbow colours of the Inca flag and the colour of the ponchos the people use to keep warm and transport their wares. "My flag is of the colours and the stamp of the rainbow/ For Peru and America/Watch out or the police will take your bundle off you!/ Ay, ay, ay, how sad it is to live/How sad it is to dream/I'm a street seller, I'm a proletarian/Selling shoes, selling food, selling jackets/I support my home".

Chicha has effectively become a youth movement, an expression of social frustration for the mass of people suffering racial discrimination in Peruvian society.

In the last few years, *chicha* has even made it to the pages of the Western rock and world music press, largely through the efforts of New York-based label, Barbès. Their 2007 anthology, *The Roots of Chicha*, met with almost universal critical acclaim, the first time many of the originators of the genre had been heard outside of Peru. In Peru itself, this belated international recognition has witnessed a resurgence in interest in seminal artists like Juaneco y Su Combo, currently feted by the Lima cognoscenti and the subject of their own recent Barbès retrospective, *Juaneco y Su Combo: Masters of Chicha Volume 1*. The label even have their own in-house band, Chicha Libre, whose excellent debut, *¡Sonido Amazonico!*, was released in early 2008.

Peru's performers

Many performers have achieved mass appeal and recording contracts in Peru and can support themselves solely by their work as musicians. Nationally celebrated performers include **Florcita de Pisaq** (a *huayno* vocalist), **Pastorita Huaracina** (a singer of both *cholo* and *mestizo* varieties) and **Jaime Guardía** (a virtuoso of the *charango*).

These performers take pride in being bearers of tradition, play at most traditional festivals and hire themselves out to wealthier villages to provide music for those festive events that require it. Although they may hold little attraction for the wealthy urban population (who tend to deny their roots), they often appear at large venues in major urban areas. They appeal to the displaced campesinos and city migrants who live in the *pueblos jóvenes*, or squatter settlements, which have sprung up on the outskirts of the large coastal cities.

Recordings of these artists are generally only available locally, but they can sometimes be found in shops catering for Latin American immigrants. Occasionally, an artist of this type will end up on an album collection.

Front rooms and festivals

There is a large contingent of non-professional musicians, and, in Peruvian cities, the middle class often perform in impromptu ensembles **at home** in their living rooms. They tend to play *huaynos* or *chicha*, styles accompanied by falsetto singing in Spanish or Quechua, and often a mixture of both.

The only way to hear a performance in someone's living room is, of course, to get yourself invited. Fortunately, this isn't difficult to do in the Andes, where only a committed sociopath could avoid making friends. To speed the process, bring alcohol with you, accept every drink offered, be sure to encourage others to drink from your bottle, eat everything served to you and ask to learn the words and sing along. You'll quickly pick up the dance steps.

For the less gregarious, **festivals** are an equally rewarding source of traditional music. One of the best takes place in January on the **Isla Amantani** in Lake Titicaca, its exact date, as is often the case in the Andean highlands, determined by astronomical events. This particular festival occurs during a period often called the "time of protection", when the rainy season has finally begun. It is related to the cleansing of the pasturage and water sources; stone fences are repaired, walking paths repaved, and the stone effigies and crosses that guard the planting fields replaced or repaired. A single-file "parade" of individuals covers the entire island, stopping to appease the deities and provide necessary maintenance at each site. At the front are local non-professional musicians, all male, playing drums and flutes of various types.

There are, too, festivals that are celebrated on a larger scale. On the day of the June solstice (midwinter in the Andes) the Inca would ceremonially tie the sun to a stone and coax it to return south, bringing warmer weather and the new planting season. **Inti Raymi**, the Festival of the Sun, is still observed in every nook and cranny in the Andean republics, from the capital city to the most isolated hamlet. The celebration, following a solemn ritual that may include a llama sacrifice, is more of a carnival than anything else. Parades of musicians, both professional bands and thrown-together collages of amateurs, fill the streets. You will be expected to drink and dance until you drop, or hide in your room. This kind of party can run for several days, so be prepared. Anyone spending more than two weeks in the Andes is almost bound to witness a festival of some sort.

Written by Jan Fairley, with thanks to Thomas Turino and Raúl Romero, Gilka Wara Céspedes, Martin Morales and Margaret Bullen. Adapted from the *Rough Guide to World Music, Vol 2*. Additional contribution by Brendon Griffin

Wildlife and ecology

Peru boasts what is probably the most diverse array of **wildlife** of any country on earth; its varied ecological niches span an incredible range of climate and terrain. The Amazon region covers 60 percent of Peru's land surface, yet has only 12 percent of its population; the highlands cover 28 percent of the land but are home to only 36 percent of the country's people. The desert coast, where 52 percent of Peruvians live, comprises a mere 12 percent of it's land area. Between these three major zones, the ecological reality is continuous inter-gradation, encompassing literally dozens of unique habitats, moving gradually through a whole series of environments in which many of the species detailed below overlap. Mankind has occupied Peru for perhaps twenty thousand years, but there has been less disturbance there, until relatively recently, than in most other parts of our planet, which makes it a top class ecotourist and wildlife photo-safari destination.

The coast

The coastal desert is characterized by an abundant sea life and by the contrasting scarcity of terrestrial plants and animals. The Humboldt current runs virtually the length of Peru, bringing cold water up from the depths of the Pacific Ocean and causing any moisture to condense out over the sea, depriving the mainland coastal strip and lower western mountain slopes of rainfall. Along with this cold water, large quantities of nutrients are carried up to the surface, helping to sustain a rich planktonic community able to support vast numbers of fish, preyed upon in their turn by a variety of coastal birds: gulls, terns, pelicans, boobies, cormorants and wading birds are always present along the beaches. One beautiful specimen, the Inca tern, although usually well camouflaged as it sits high up on inaccessible sea cliffs, is nevertheless very common in the Lima area. The Humboldt penguin, with grey rather than black features, is a rarer sight – shyer than its more southernly cousins, it is normally found in isolated rocky coves or on offshore islands. Competing with the birds for fish are schools of dolphins, sea lion colonies and the occasional coastal otter. Dolphins and sea lions are often spotted off even the most crowded of beaches or scavenging around the fishermen's jetty at Chorrillos, near Lima.

One of the most fascinating features of Peruvian birdlife is the vast, high-density colonies: although the number of species is quite small, their total population is enormous. Many thousands of birds can be seen nesting on islands like the Ballestas, off the **Paracas Peninsula**, or simply covering the ocean with a flapping, diving carpet of energetic feathers. This huge bird population, and the **Guanay cormorant** in particular, is responsible for depositing mountains of guano (bird droppings), which form a traditional and potent source of natural fertilizer.

In contrast to the rich coastal waters the **desert** lies stark and barren. Here you find only a few trees and shrubs; you'll need endless patience to find wild animals other than birds. The most common animals are feral **goats**, once domesticated but now living wild, and **burros** (or donkeys) introduced by the Spanish. A more exciting sight is the attractively coloured **coral snake** – shy but deadly and covered with black and orange hoops. Most animals are more active after sunset; when out in the desert you can hear the eerily plaintive call of the *huerequeque* (or **Peruvian thick-knee** bird), and the barking of the little **desert fox** – alarmingly similar to the sound of car tyres screeching to a halt. By day you might see several species of small birds, a favourite being the vermilion-headed **Peruvian flycatcher**. Near water – rivers, estuaries and lagoons – desert wildlife is at its most populous. In addition to residents such as **flamingoes**, **herons** and **egrets**, many migrant birds pause in these havens between October and March on their journeys south and then back north.

In order to understand the coastal desert you have to bear in mind the phenomenon of **El Niño**, a periodic climatic shift caused by the displacement of the cold Humboldt current by warmer equatorial waters; it last occurred in 1998. This causes the plankton and fish communities either to disperse to other locations or to collapse entirely. At such a period the shore rapidly becomes littered with carrion since many of the sea mammals and birds are unable to survive in the much tighter environment. Scavenging condors and vultures, on the other hand, thrive, as does the desert where rain falls in deluges along the coast, with a consequent bloom of vegetation and rapid growth in animal populations. When the Humboldt current returns, the desert dries up, its animal populations decline to normal sizes (another temporary feast for the scavengers). While it used to be at least ten years before this cycle was repeated, global warming over the last two decades has witnessed the pattern becoming much more erratic. Generally considered a freak phenomenon, El Niño is probably better understood as an integral part of coastal ecology; without it the desert would be a far more barren and static environment, virtually incapable of supporting life.

The mountains

In the **Peruvian Andes** there is an incredible variety of habitats. That this is a mountain area of true extremes becomes immediately obvious if you fly across, or along, the Andes towards Lima – the land below shifting from high *puna* to cloud forest to riparian valleys and eucalyptus tracts (introduced from Australia in the 1880s). The complexity of the whole makes it incredibly difficult to formulate any overall description that isn't essentially misleading: climate and vegetation vary according to altitude, latitude and local characteristics.

The Andes divides vertically into three main regions, identified by the Incas from top to bottom as the Puna, the Qeswa and the Yunka. The **Puna,** roughly 3800–4300m above sea level, has an average temperature of 3–6°C (37–43°F), and annual rainfall of 500–1000mm. Typical animals here include the main Peruvian cameloids – llamas, alpacas, guanacos and *vicuñas* – while crops that grow well here include the potato and quinoa grain. At 2500–3500m, the **Qeswa** has average temperatures of around 13°C (55°F), and a similar level of rainfall at 500–1200mm. The traditional forest here, including Andean pines, is not abundant and has been largely displaced by the imported Australian eucalyptus trees; the main cultivated crops include maize, potatoes and the nutritious *kiwicha* grain. The *ceja de selva* (cloud forest) to high forest on the eastern side of the Andes in the relatively low-lying **Yunka**, at 1200–2500m, has at least twice as much rain as the other two regions and abundant wildlife, including Peru's national bird, the red-crested *gallito de las rocas* (cock-of-the-rocks). Plant life, too, is prolific, not least the orchids. On the western side of the Andes there is much less rainfall and it's not technically known as the Yunka, but it does share some characteristics: both sides have wild river canes (*caña brava*), and both are suitable for cultivating bananas, pineapples, *yuca* and coca.

Much of the Andes has been settled for over two thousand years – and hunter tribes go back another eight thousand years before this – so larger predators are rare, though still present in small numbers in the more remote regions. Among the most exciting you might actually see are the **mountain cats**, especially the **puma**, which lives at most altitudes and in a surprising number of habitats. Other more remote predators include the shaggy-looking **maned wolf** and the likeable **spectacled bear**, which inhabits the moister forested areas of the Andes and actually prefers eating vegetation to people.

The most visible animals in the mountains, besides sheep and cattle, are the cameloids – the wild **vicuña** and **guanaco**, and the domesticated **llama** and **alpaca**. Although these species are clearly related, zoologists disagree on whether or not the alpaca and llama are domesticated forms of their wild relatives. Domesticated they are, however, and have been so for thousands of years; studies reveal that cameloids appeared in North America some forty to fifty million years ago, crossing the Bering Straits long before any humans did. From these early forms the present species have evolved in Peru, Bolivia, Chile, Argentina and Ecuador, and there are now over three million llamas – 33 percent in Peru and a further 63 percent over the border in Bolivia. The alpaca population is just under four million, with 87 percent in Peru and only 11 percent in Bolivia.

Of the two wild cameloids, the *vicuña* is the smaller and rarer, living only at the highest altitudes (up to 4500m) and with a population of just over 100,000, although it is greater in numbers in Peru than the guanaco, of which there are around 4000 here (there are over 500,000 in Argentina alone).

Andean deer are quite common in the higher valley and with luck you may even come across the rare **mountain tapir**. Smaller animals tend to be confined to particular habitats – rabbit-like **viscachas**, for example, to rocky outcrops; **squirrels** to wooded valleys; and **chinchillas** (Peruvian chipmunks) to higher altitudes.

Most birds also tend to restrict themselves to specific habitats. The **Andean goose** and **duck** are quite common in marshy areas, along with many species of waders and migratory waterfowl. A particular favourite is the elegant, very pink, **Andean flamingo**, which can usually be spotted from the road between Arequipa and Puno where they turn Lake Salinas into one great red mass. In addition, many species of passerines can be found alongside small streams. Perhaps the most striking of them is the **dipper**, which hunts underwater for larval insects along the stream bed, popping up to a rock every so often for air and a rest. At lower elevations, especially in and around cultivated areas, the **ovenbird** (or horneo) constructs its nest from mud and grasses in the shape of an old-fashioned oven; while in open spaces many birds of prey can be spotted, the comical **caracaras**, **buzzard-eagles** and the magical **red-backed hawks** among them. The **Andean condor** (see p.606) is actually quite difficult to see up close as, although not especially rare, they tend to soar at tremendous heights for most of the day, landing only on high, inaccessible cliffs, or at carcasses after making sure that no one is around to disturb them. A glimpse of this magnificent bird soaring overhead will come only through frequent searching with binoculars, perhaps in relatively unpopulated areas, or at one of the better-known sites such as the Cruz del Condor viewing platform in the Colca Canyon (see p.205).

Tropical rainforest

Descending the eastern edge of the Andes, you pass through the distinct habitats of the Puna, Qeswa and Yunka before reaching the lowland jungle or rainforest. In spite of its rich and luxuriant appearance, the **rainforest** is in fact extremely fragile. Almost all the nutrients are recycled by rapid decomposition, with the aid of the damp climate and a prodigious supply of insect labour, back into the vegetation – thereby creating a nutrient-poor soil that is highly susceptible to large-scale disturbance. When the forest is cleared, for example, usually in an attempt to colonize the area and turn it into viable farmland, there is not only heavy soil erosion to contend with but also a limited amount of nutrients in the earth, only enough for five years of good harvests and twenty years' poorer farming at the most. Natives of the rainforest have evolved cultural mechanisms by which, on the whole, these problems are avoided: they tend to live in small, dispersed groups, move their gardens every few years and obey sophisticated social controls to limit the chances of overhunting any one zone or any particular species.

Around eighty percent of the Amazon rainforest was still intact at the start of the twenty-first century, but for every hardwood logged in this forest, an average of 120 other trees are destroyed and left unused or simply burnt. Over an acre per second of this magnificent forest is burned or bulldozed, equating to an area the size of Great Britain, every year, even though this doesn't make economic sense. According to the late rainforest specialist Dr Alwyn Gentry, just one hectare of primary rainforest could yield up to $9000 a year from sustainable harvesting of wild fruits, saps, resins and timber – yet the average income per hecatre from ranching or plantations in the Amazon is a meagre $30 a year.

Amazon flora and fauna

The most distinctive attribute of the Amazon Basin is its overwhelming abundance of plant and animal species. Over six thousand species of plants have been reported from one small 250-acre tract of forest, and there are at least a thousand species of birds and dozens of types of monkeys and bats spread about the Peruvian Amazon. There are several reasons for this marvellous natural diversity of flora and fauna. Most obviously, it is warm, there is abundant sunlight and large quantities of mineral nutrients are washed down from the Andes – all of which help to produce the ideal conditions for forest growth. Secondly, the rainforest has enormous structural diversity, with layers of vegetation from the forest floor to the canopy 30m above providing a vast number of niches to fill. Thirdly, since there is such a variety of habitat as you descend the Andes, the changes in altitude mean a great diversity of localized eco-systems.

The great diversity of flora has assisted the evolution of equally varied fauna in the Amazon. With the rainforest being stable over longer periods of time than temperate areas (there was no Ice Age here, nor any prolonged period of drought), the fauna has had freedom to evolve, and to adapt to often very specialized local conditions. But if the Amazon Basin is where most of the plant and animal species are in Peru, it is not easy to see them. Movement through the vegetation is limited to narrow trails and along the rivers in a boat. The river banks and flood plains are richly diverse areas: here you are likely to see **caimans, macaws, toucans, oropendulas, terns, horned screamers** and the primitive **hoatzins** – birds whose young are born with claws at the wrist to enable them to climb up from the water into the branches of overhanging trees. You should catch sight, too, of one of a variety of **hawks** and at least two or three species of **monkeys** (perhaps the **spider monkey**, the **howler** or the **capuchin**). And with a lot of luck and more determined observation you may spot a rare **giant river otter**, **river dolphin**, **capybara**, or maybe even one of the **jungle cats**.

In the jungle proper you're more likely to find mammals such as the **pecary** (wild pig), **tapir**, **tamandua tree sloth** and the second largest cat in the world, the incredibly powerful **spotted jaguar**. Characteristic of the deeper forest zones, too, are many species of birds, including **hummingbirds** (more common in the forested Andean foothills), **manakins** and **trogons**, though the effects of widespread hunting make it difficult to see these around any of the larger settlements. Logging is proving to be another major problem for the forest fauna since with the valuable trees dispersed among vast areas of other species in the rainforest, a very large area must be disturbed to yield a relatively small amount of timber. Deeper into the forest, however, and the further you are from human habitation, a glimpse of any of these animals is quite possible. Most of the bird activity occurs in the canopy, 30–40m above the ground, but with such platforms as the ACEER Canopy Walkway (ⓦwww .explorama.com) and another, newer one at Inkaterra's Reserva Amazonica (ⓦwww.inkaterra.com) on the Rio Madre de Dios, things are a little easier.

Amazon flora

Aguaje palm (*Mauritia flexuosa*) A tropical swamp plant, commonly growing up to 15m tall, with fan-shaped leaves that can be be over 2m long, and barrel-shaped fruit (6–7cm long) with a purple, plastic-like skin. The thin layer of yellow pulp beneath the skin is consumed raw, made into a drink or used to flavour ice cream. The leaves can be used for roof-thatch or, more commonly, floor-matting. Younger leaves are utilized to make ropes, hammocks, net bags and sometimes baskets.

Ayahuasca (*Banisteriopsis caapi*) Interpreted from Quechna as "Vine of the Soul" or "Vine of the Dead", this is found exclusively in northwest Amazonia and is also called *yage* and *caap*. These names also refer to the hallucinogenic brew, in which *ayahuasca* is the main ingredient, used widely in the Peruvian Amazon and by *curanderos*.

Brazil nut tree (*Bertholletia excelsa*) Up to 30m tall, these take over ten years to reach nut-bearing maturity, when a single specimen can produce over 450kg every year during the rainy season.

Breadfruit (*Artocarpus altilis*) The tree known locally as *pan del arbol*, related to the rubber tree, is cut open and dried so that the large brown beans can be taken and boiled for eating. Only in Central America are the whole fruits eaten and even in Peru, people only bother with these when they are out of bananas and *yuca* (manioc). The sap is a good medicine for hernias.

Caimetillo Some spots in the primary forest are devoid of ground growth apart from this one species of small tree. Many Indians see these glades as *supay chacras* ("demons' gardens") and they keep away from them at night. The scientific explanation is that the azteca ant that lives on them has such acidic faeces that nothing else can grow where they live.

Capirona Related to the eucalyptus, this tree protects itself from insects by shedding its bark every two to three months. A fast grower, achieving 12m in just five years, it burns long and well and is consequently sold as firewood. Its sap can be applied to the throat for laryngitis, or mixed with lime and used as a gargle.

Catahua (*Eurocrypitan*) A large, hardwood emergent tree reaching nearly 50m, this tree depends on the Saki monkey for reproduction and seed dispersal. Its fruits are poisonous to most other animals.

Charapilla A gigantic tree, characterized by its six-metre base and a trunk over 1m in diameter. One of the hardest trees in the Iquitos region, it is rarely cut for timber because of its light yellowy colour. Young Conibo warriors were once tested for their strength and ability by how long they took to cut through the wood of ones that had already fallen. The fruit is eaten roasted, although the Achual of the Río Tigre prefer to eat them raw. The leaves are small and used for birth control by the Conibo.

Coca Cocaine is just one of the alkaloids in coca leaves, which are traditionally sacred to Andeans. A vital aid in coping with the altitude, climate and rigours of the region, they help withstand low temperatures and act as a hunger depressant. Research also shows that they have a nutritional value, containing more calcium than any other edible plant, which is important in the Andes, an area with few dairy foods.

Epiphytes Often shrub-like plants, epiphytes live in the crowns or branching elbows of trees but are functionally independent of them. In the higher jungle areas, they are extremely common and diverse, encompassing various species of orchids, cacti, bromeliads and aroids. There are over five-hundred varieties of orchids recorded in the Amazon, many of them to be found in the *ceja de selva*.

Genipap (*Genipa americana*) Also called *huito*, this is related to coffee but is quite different. Growing up to 20m, it has small creamy flowers and fruit that's eaten ripe or used to make an alcoholic drink that alleviates arthritic pains and bronchial ailments. Unripe juice is taken for stomach ulcers. The sap turns from transparent to blue-black after exposure to the air and is used as a dye, or body and face paint.

Inga (*Inga edulis*) Belonging to the mimosa family and growing to over 35m, there are over 350 species in the *Inga* genus. Its most distinctive feature is its long bean pods containing sweet white pulp and large seeds, which some Indian groups use to treat dysentry.

Manioc The most important of cultivated plants in the Peruvian Amazon, and known in Peru as *yuca*, its most useful parts are the large, phallic-shaped tuber roots, the brunt of many indigenous jokes. High in carbohydrates and enzymes, which assist digestion of other foods, it is roasted (to get rid of the cyanide it contains) or brewed to make *masato* beer. It is also the basis of tapioca. As far as its medicinal functions go, the juice from the tubers is applied as a head wash for scabies or can be mixed with water to ease diarrhoea.

Monkey-ladder vine (*Leguminosae casalpinioideae*) Also known as the turtle-ladder vine, this unusual-looking vine spirals high up to blossom in the canopy of primary forests.

Peach palm Also known as the *pihuayao*, and common in most areas of the Peruvian rainforest, its new shoots are the source for the Yaguar and Witoto Indians' "grass" skirts and headdresses. The bark of the stems is used for interior wall partitions in native houses. The cork-like insides of the stems are made into sleeping mats, a particularly important symbol of marriage among the Achual tribe along the Río Tigre. From its fallen trunks, the larvae of beetles are gathered as a delicacy by many indigenous groups.

Quinilla This yellow flowering tree is easy to spot, not so much by its tall, straight forty-metre trunk, but by the sweetly scented carpet of flowers beneath it, or the yellow, cauliform patterns of its canopy, seen when flying over the forest.

Rubber tree (*Hevea brasiliensis*) Known as *jebe* in Peru and *seringuera* closer to the Brazilian border, as a valuable export these trees were the key to the Amazon's initial exploitation.

Sabre pentana (*Lupuna*) A softwood tree, mainly used as ply and now in danger of extinction, this is still one of the most impressive plants in the Peruvian Amazon, at nearly 50m tall and home to harpy eagles, which nest in the same tree for life (if the tree is felled, the bird dies with it by refusing to eat again). The trees are scattered across the forest and are sometimes used by Indians as landmarks when travelling along the rivers.

Stilt palm (*Socratea exorrhiza*) Also abundant in the jungle, reaching heights of up to 15m, with a thin trunk and very thorny stilt roots that grow like a tepee above the ground. Its long thin leaves are used by some indigenous groups as a treatment for hepatitis. The most utilized part is the hard bark, which can be taken off in one piece for use as flooring or wall slats.

Thatch palm (*Lepidocaryum tenue*) A relatively thin plant growing to around 4m and with a noticeably ringed trunk. Its leaves are used as roof-thatch throughout the Peruvian Amazon.

Ungurahui palm (*Oenocarpus bataua*) The rotting trunks of this palm are home to the suri larvae of the rhinoceros beetle, a favoured food of local Indians. Its green fruits can also be squeezed for their oil, which is used to treat vomiting, diarrhoea and even malaria. The trunk and leaves are often used in house construction.

Walking palm (*Socratea exercisia*) The wood is often used for parquet flooring. Tradition has it that it developed spikes to protect itself against the now extinct giant sloth, which used to push it over.

Wild mango (*Grias neuberthii*) The wild mango tree is frequently seen as an ornamental plant around rainforest lodges. A member of the Brazil nut family, it's actually unrelated to the true mango (*Mangifera indica*), but can grow up to 20m, with thin, spindly trunks and branches. Their delicate yellow flowers are odorous, but the fruit can be eaten raw, boiled or roasted and has a medicinal function as a purgative; the seed is grated to treat venereal tumours and associated fevers, as well as being used as an enema to cure dysentery. The bark can be used to induce vomiting.

Amazon fauna

Anteaters There are four main types of anteaters in Peru; all have powerful curved front claws but no teeth, using instead their long tongues to catch insects in holes and rotting vegetation, and share long, tube-like snouts. They have only one baby at a time, which clings to the mother's back when they move through the forest. Giant anteaters (*Myrmecophaga tridactyla*), which can be 2m long with hairy non-prehensile tails, are black, orange-brown and whiteish, with a a diagonal black and white shoulder stripe. Solitary creatures, they can be seen day or night, and, while normally passive, can defend themselves easily with their powerful front legs. Collared anteaters, or southern tamandua (*Tamandua tetradactlya*), are smaller, at less than 1m long. Arboreal and terrestrial, they too are nocturnal and diurnal, though they move slowly as they have poor eyesight. Northern tamandua (*Tamandua mexicana*) are restricted to the northern jungles in Peru. The silky or pygmy anteater (*Cyclopes didactylus*) is quite small, rarely exceeding 25cm in length. It's a smoky-grey to golden colour on the upper parts, sometimes with dark-brown stripes from its shoulders to its rear. It's also distinguished by the soft whistling noise it makes.

Armadillos Of the giant armadillos and nine-banded long-nosed armadillos, the former are up to 1m long, the latter usually half this. Both are covered in bony armour and have small heads with wide-set ears and grey to yellow colouring. Mostly nocturnal, they tend to feed on ants and termites, some fruit and even small prey. Giant armadillos are good diggers and live in burrows.

Bats Bat species comprise almost forty percent of all mammals in the Amazon, and all North, Central and South American bats belong to the suborder *Microchiroptera*. Vampire bats, which feed on the blood of mammals, are known to transmit rabies and are commonest in cattle-ranching areas rather than remote forest zones.

Brazilian tapir (*Tapirus terrestris*) Known as *sachavaca* ("forest cow" in Quechua) in Peru, this is the largest forest land mammal at around 2m long, brown to dark grey in colour and with a large upper lip. Their tails are stumpy, their feet three-toed and their backs noticeably convex. Largely nocturnal, they browse swampy forests for fruit and grasses.

Capybara (*Hydrochaeris hydrochaeris*) The world's largest (but friendly) rodent, the tan or grey capybara can be over 1m and will give warning yelps to its family when scared. They eat aquatic vegetation and grasses, but are also known to fish and eat lizards when they come across them.

Dolphins The pink river dolphin (*Inia geoffrensis*) is about 2m long and has a noticeable dorsal fin. They feed exclusively on fish and will swim with or within a few metres of people. The smaller grey dolphin or tucuxi (*Sotalia fluviatilis*) achieves a maximum length of 1.5m and has a more prominent dorsal fin, and usually jumps further and is more acrobatic than the pink dolphin.

Giant otter (*Pteronura brasiliensis*) Just over 1m long, ending in a thickish tail with a flattened tip. Their alarm call is a snort and they are very aggressive when in danger. They eat fish and move in extended family groups, with the males doing the least fishing but the most eating.

Manatee (*Trichechus inunguis*) Almost 3m in length, with a large tubular body, a flat tail, short front flippers and a whiskery face, this aquatic mammal is relatively common in the Iquitos area. They feed on water hyacinths and other aquatic vegetation, taking advantage of the high-water season to graze on the flooded riverside floor.

Paca (*Agouti paca*) Chestnut-brown and white-striped, this large, fat rat- and pig-like creature has plenty of flesh but a tiny tail, hardly visible beneath the rump hair. It's primarily nocturnal and feeds on roots and fallen fruit.

Peccaries (*Tayassuidae*) Peccaries, or wild boar, are stocky with relatively spindly legs and biggish heads. The white-lipped peccary (*Tayassu pecari*) is up to 1m long and moves quickly in dangerous herds of fifty to a few hundred. Their diet is fruit and palm nuts, which they scour vast tracts of forest to find. The collared peccary (*Tayassu tajacu*) is smaller and moves in groups of five to twenty.

Red brocket deer (*Mazama americana*) Rarely much over 1m in length, these are mostly brown to grey, with large eyes, and the males have unbranched antlers which slope back. They are found in the forest or at waterholes, feeding on fruit and fungi.

Sloths The most common sloth in Peru is the brown-throated three-toed sloth (*Bradypus variegatus*). Up to 1m in length, they have small, round heads and whitish or brown faces with a short tail and long limbs. Their claws help them cling to branches, where they spend most of their time sleeping, but their slow movement makes them hard to spot (though you may see them around jungle lodges, where they are often kept as pets).

Cats

Large cats in Peru include the black, elongated **Jaguarundi** (*Felis yagouaroundi*) and the slender, spotty **Margay** (*Felis wieldii*). But better known are the **Ocelots** (*Felis pardalis*), smallish with black spots and thin stripes on their torso, with short tails and long slender legs. Operating by day and night, they hunt rodents, lizards and birds, mostly in the rainforest.

Jaguar (*Pantera onca*) Powerfully built, jaguars are almost 2m long, with black spots on silvery to tan fur; they hunt large mammals, though they fish too. Mainly rainforest dwellers, they are most frequently spotted sunning themselves on fallen trees. If you meet one, the best way to react is to make lots of noise.

Puma (*Felis concolor*) Brown to tan in colour, pumas hunt by day and night, preferring large mammals, but stooping to snakes, lizards and rats. They're most likely to be encountered in the Andes, and although wary of humans, can be dangerous. Guides advise waving one's arms around and shouting in these situations.

Primates

All South American primates are monkeys, which form a group of their own – **Platyrrhini** – subdividing into three main families: marmosets and tamarins (*Callitrichidae*); monkeys (*Cebidae*); and the Goeldi's monkey (*Callimiconidae*). Each of these has many types within it.

Capuchin monkey (*Cebus apella*) Reddish-brown, with a black cap and paler shoulders, this noisy creature moves in groups of up to twenty while searching for fruit, palm nuts, birds' eggs and small lizards.

Dusky titi monkey (*Callicebus moloch*) The necks of these reddish-brown creatures are hidden by thick fur, giving them a stocky appearance belied by their hairless faces. Eating leaves and fruit, they are found in dense forest near swamps, or bamboo thickets beside rivers.

Pygmy marmoset (*Cebuella pygmaea*) These rarely achieve more than 15cm in length, and are distinguished by their tawny to golden-grey head and forequarters and mane of hair, plus slender tails. Found in the lower understorey of the trees in flood forests, they feed on tree sap, insects and fruit.

Saddle-backed tamarin (*Saguinus fuscicollis*) The most widespread species of tamarin in the forests of Manu and around Iquitos, though there are a further thirteen subspecies of these. Black to reddish-brown, they are diurnal and arboreal, living under the tree canopy and eating nectar, fruit and insects.

Spider monkey (*Ateles paniscus*) These are entirely black, with a small head and long arms, legs and tail, and can be seen swinging through the primary forest in groups of up to twenty. Highly sociable, intelligent and noisy, they feed on fruit, flowers and leaves.

Woolly monkey (*Lagothrix lagothricha*) Mostly brown, they have a strong tail, which helps them travel through the upper and middle storeys of the forest in groups of up to sixty. They eat fruit, palm nuts, seeds and leaves and are found in primary forest, including wooded flood plains.

Birds

Andean condor (*Vultur gryphus*) Up to 1.3m long, with a wingspan of 3.5m and mostly black with a white neck ruff and white wing feathers, these are rarely seen in groups of more than two or three. Their habitat is mainly at 2000–5000m, but they are also seen on the coast of Peru, feeding off carrion.

Black-headed cotingas (*Cotingidae*) Related to flycatchers, they have a symbiotic relationship with a number of fruiting trees. The scaled fruiteater (*Ampliodeon tschudii*) is frequently seen in the upper canopy, usually alone but sometimes in pairs or, less frequently, in large mixed flocks.

Curassow (*Crax mitu*) Their well-developed crests are mainly black, with a shiny blue mantle; both the bill and legs are red. Their booming song can be heard as they move in small flocks of two to five birds.

Fasciated tiger-heron (*Tigrisoma fasciatum*) Graceful river birds with short, dusky bills and a black crown, named for the stripy appearance of their rufous and white underparts.

Hawk (*Buteo magnirostris*) Grey to brown in colour, these are not great flyers or hunters, depending mainly on insects, vertebrates and small birds.

Hoatzin (*Opisthocomus hoazin*) Their most distinctive features are long mohican crests, and the hooks which the young have on their shoulders. Also, they haven't evolved full stomachs and their chromosomes are close to those of chickens. Usually spotted in sizeable and gregarious gangs, they are poor flyers and hide in swampy areas. Indians use hoatzins' feathers for arrow flights.

Hummingbirds (*Trochilidae*) Distinguished by the fastest metabolisms and wing beats of any bird (up to eighty per second) and the ability to rotate their wings through 180 degrees, some varieties are the smallest birds in the world. Many tribes have a special place for hummingbirds in their religious beliefs.

Macaws (*Psittacidae*) Noisy, talkative creatures with strong bills, macaws mate for life (which can be as long as a hundred years), and pairs fly among larger flocks. Common macaws in Peru include the blue and yellow macaw (*Ara ararauna*) which grows to almost 1m and has a very long pointed tail, the scarlet macaw (*Ara macao*) and the red and green macaw (*Ara cloroptera*).

Nunbirds With slender red bills and mostly black plumage, black-fronted nunbirds (*Monasa nigrifrons*) are found in ones or twos at all levels of the rainforest

Update on Conservation and Environmental Politics in Peru

Considering Peru's vital importance as a reservoir for planetary biodiversity, it was somewhat alarming to see Peru lead the blocking of a 140-country initiative in a recent global forum for biodiversity held in Bonn, Germany. The aim of this meeting was to provide a regulatory framework to protect against the potential damage by genetically modified or trans-genetic cultivars. The Peruvian lobby was led by Alexander Grobman, who also happens to represent the Monsanto group (the world's largest producer of genetically modified seeds) in Peru; but worse than this, Grobman was aided in Bonn by the Peruvian Minister for Agriculture and the Peruvian Chancellor.

Climate change is already showing serious impacts on Peru's priceless environment and the country has been identified as a region which has the most to lose from global warming. The glaciers are retreating fast. South America possesses more than 99 percent of the world's tropical glaciers, with over seventy percent of these located in Peru, where they act as a reservoir of meltwater which provides water and hydro-electricity for urban areas, industry and agriculture in the Andes and the desert coast, even during the dry season. The Peruvian glaciers, essential stores of the planet's most basic resource, have been described by Lonnie Thompson (an Ohio State University glaciologist) as the "water towers of the world". Nevertheless, Peru's most visited glacier - Pastoruri (see p.366), near the city of Huaraz - and previously the country's main ski resort, has finally split itself into two halves; retreating at an incredible 20m every year, it has lost more than half of its surface area since 1995 and will almost certainly vanish completely before 2020. CONAM, Peru's National Environment Agency estimates that by 2025, Peru will be the first country in South America to experience "permanent water stress", principally, of course, along the urbanised coastal belt.

Ground and water pollution, amongst the worst in the world, has also become a concern around some of Peru's Andean mining towns. La Oroya, just four hours by road from Lima, has been a major mining centre since 1922 when the US Cerro de Paso Corporation established its first smelter here. The three plants now operating around La Oroya, presently owned by Doe Run Co, also based in the US, are said, by the Ministry of Energy and Mines, to produce around 1.5 tonnes of lead and over 800 tonnes of sulphur dioxide every day. These levels of pollution are significantly greater than permitted under Peruvian law and blood samples from newborn babies in the town of La Oroya found over 8.8 micrograms of lead per decilitre, very close to the maximum a baby can cope with without damaging its cognitive abilities. Despite this, in 2007, Doe Run Co talked the Peruvian government into postponing a deadline for clean-up operations until 2012.

Perhaps the only good news for Peru's environment and indigenous communities was Perupetro's (the state body responsible for oil and gas exploration rights) decision in, May 2008, not to auction concessions in some of the areas where isolated and uncontacted Indians are known to be living. Their landmark decision marked a successful campaign for Survival International (see p.614) and the Peruvian indigenous people's federations.

and are noted for their noisy performance in the early evenings. White-fronted nunbirds (*Monasa morphoeus*) are slightly smaller and with a white forehead but are similar in behaviour.

Oropendulas (*Icteridae*) Related to the blackbird family, these like living near human habitations, their vibrant croaking making them unmistakable. One of the commonest varieties is the large black oropendula (*Gymnostinaps guatimoziuus*), which has with a long brilliant lemon-yellow tail, with two black central tail feathers.

Swainson's thrush (*Catharus ustulatus*) Small in stature but magnificent in voice, this timid, solitary bird lives mainly in lower primary forest. The Lawrence thrush is able to imitate other bird calls (over a hundred have been noted from one bird alone).

Tinamous (*Tinamidae*) Rather like chickens with long beaks, the many varieties include the rare black tinamou (*Tinamus osgoodi*), the great tinamou (*Tinamus major*), noted for its tremulous whistling noises and the grey tinamou (*Tinamus tao*), similar in behaviour to the great tinamou.

Toucans (*Ramphastidae*) Unmistakable for their colourful plumage and large bill, there are many varieties. One of the more common is the white-throated toucan (*Ramphastos tucanus*), also one of the largest, mainly black but with bursts of orange and red and a white throat and chest. Rarer and smaller is the yellow-ridged toucan (*Ramphastos culminatus*), with a distinctive yellow ridge across the top and a yellow and blue band close to the eyes.

Trumpeters (*Psophiidae*) Common, largely terrestrial birds that eat vegetation, small lizards and shiny objects (gold, silver and sometimes diamonds), they are often kept as pets in Indian and colonist settlements. The grey-winged trumpeter (*Psophia crepitans*) tends to be recognized by its nocturnal guttural sounds, which sound like the loud purring of a cat. Grey in the wild, its wings turn white in captivity.

Vultures (*Cathartidae*) Carrion-eaters, this family includes the Andean condor (see p.606) and the stunning king vulture (*Sarcoramphus papa*), which has mainly white plumage with black rump, tail and flight feathers. It's mostly spotted in solitary flight and sometimes in pairs. Other vultures include the turkey vulture (*Cathartes aura*), the greater yellow-headed vulture (*Cathartes melambrotus*), the lesser yellow-headed vulture (*Cathartes burrovianus*) and the black vulture (*Coragyps atratus*) seen around every rubbish dump throughout Peru.

Reptiles and amphibians

Amphibians Frogs grow to surprising sizes in Peru. Most are nocturnal and their chorus is heard along every Amazonian river after sunset. The most commonly spotted is the cane toad (*Bufo marinus*), which secretes toxins that protect it. More common still is the leaf-litter dweller (*Bufo typhonius*), but it's harder to spot as it imitates the colour and form of dead leaves.

Caimans (*Alligatoridae*) There are four types of caiman in Peru: the black caiman (*Melanosuchus niger*) is increasingly rare due to hunting; while the spectacled caiman (*Caiman crocodilus*) is usually found sunbathing along river beaches; rhe smaller musky caiman and smooth-fronted caiman are found in small tributaries and lakes.

Iguanas Often reaching up to a metre long and marked by a spiky crest along their backs, these are wholly vegetarian leaf-eaters which can be seen sleeping on high branches soaking up the sun. Less often they can be seen swimming in rivers, mainly to get away from predators, such as hawks.

Snakes Peru has the world's widest variety of snakes, but it's rare to meet the anacondas, rainbow boas (*Epicrates cenchria*), fer-de-lances (*Bothrops atrox*) or bushmasters (*Lachesis muta*) in the Amazon. Anacondas kill mainly by twisting their tails around tree roots in lakes or riverbanks, then floating out from this before attacking. They also stun fish by violently expelling air from their coiled bodies. Smaller snakes tend to be scared of people and you're more likely to see them in retreat than heading for you.

Yellow-footed tortoise (*Geochelone denticulata*) The only land tortoise in the Amazon, it can grow up to around 1m long but is generally half this size. In pre-historic times, however, they reached the proportions of a Volkswagen Beetle.

Indigenous rights and the destruction of the rainforest

Within the next generation, Peru's jungle tribes may cease to exist as independent cultural and racial entities in the face of persistent and increasing pressure from external colonization. The indigenous people of the Peruvian jungles are being pushed off their land by an endless combination of slash-and-burn colonization, big oil companies, gold-miners, timber extractors and coca-growing farmers organized by drug-trafficking barons and, at times, "revolutionary" political groups.

All along the main rivers and jungle roads, settlers are flooding into the area. In their wake, forcing land-title agreements to which they have no right, are the main timber companies and multinational oil corporations. In large tracts of the jungle the fragile selva ecology has already been destroyed; in others the tribes have been more subtly disrupted by becoming dependent on outside consumer goods and trade or by the imposition of evangelical proselytizing groups, and the Indian way of life is being destroyed.

The first **Law of Native Communities**, introduced in 1974, recognized the legal right of indigenous peoples to own lands that were held collectively and registered as such with the Ministry of Agriculture. Despite this recognition, however, the military government of the time wasn't trying to stop colonization. Such land titling as did occur was a two-edged sword – whilst it guaranteed a secure land base to some communities, it implied that land not so titled was unavailable to them, effectively making it available for colonization.

However, as the most significant legal tool they had in the 1970s, the indigenous communities adopted **land rights legislation** to help protect their territory, even if the creation of native communities as legal entities represented the imposition of a non-indigenous socio-political structure. New self-determination groups sprang up throughout the 1970s and 1980s, such as AIDESEP (Inter-ethnic Association for the Development of the Peruvian Amazon) and CONAP (Coalition of Indigenous Nationalities of the Peruvian Amazon). Since then more regional political structures have been established, usually based on natural geographical boundaries such as rivers. These function as intermediaries between the community and the national levels of Amazonian political organization.

In May 2008, Alan Garcia's government very publicly created Peru's first Ministry of the Environment during the Lima-based European Union- Latin America and the Caribbean Summit whose main focus was climate change. Cynics saw this as a direct attempt for Peru to access new and future global funds for conservation, rather than a serious effort to protect the country's rainforests and mega-biodiversity. Within weeks of the new Ministry's creation, the government also announced plans to open up community-owned lands for commercial investment by making fundamental changes to the law of land ownership in the Andes and Amazon regions; a move which was integral to the new free trade agreement between Peru and the USA. The concept is straightforward: without long-term ownership of large areas of land, big corporations are simply unlikely to invest in massive agri-business schemes such as soya production and the cultivation of crops for biofuels. The only good news is that Antonio Brack, the new Peruvian Minister for the

Environment, was in Europe during December 2008, seeking finance for avoided deforestation schemes, the first of which was begun by a partnership between two UK organisations (Cool Earth, ⊛www.coolearth.org, and Ecotribal, ⊛www.ecotribal.com) in collaboration with indigenous communities in the Peruvian Amazon in February of the same year.

Notwithstanding Peru's vested interest in mitigating climate change, logging of the Amazon region also continues apace, up to eighty percent of it possibly illegal but whitewashed with official documents by the time it reaches Lima and the port of Callao for export. Since deforestation is responsible for nineteen percent of present global CO_2 emissions, this in itself is an obvious travesty; but considered side-by-side with the concomitant destruction of forest habitats and biodiversity, it is also bio-genocide. Mafia-led and apparently with tacit support from some sec-

An Amarakaeri Indian of Madre de Dios speaks for himself

Below is an account by a local Amarakaeri Indian from the southeast province of Madre de Dios, a witness to the way of life that colonists and corporations are destroying. Originally given as testimony to a human rights movement in Lima, it is reprinted by permission of Survival International.

"We Indians were born, work, live, and die in the basin of the Madre de Dios River of Peru. It's our land – the only thing we have, with its plants, animals, and small farms: an environment we understand and use well. We are not like those from outside who want to clear everything away, destroying the richness and leaving the forest ruined forever. We respect the forest; we make it produce for us.

Many people ask why we want so much land. They think we do not work all of it. But we work it differently from them, conserving it so that it will continue to produce for our children and grandchildren. Although some people want to take it from us, they then destroy and abandon it, moving on elsewhere. But we can't do that; we were born in our woodlands. Without them we will die.

In contrast to other parts of the Peruvian jungle, Madre de Dios is still relatively sparsely populated. The woodlands are extensive, the soil's poor, so we work differently from those in other areas with greater population, less woodland, and more fertile soils. Our systems do not work without large expanses of land. The people who come from outside do not know how to make the best of natural resources here. Instead they devote themselves to taking away what nature gives and leave little or nothing behind. They take wood, nuts, and above all gold.

The man from the highlands works all day doing the same thing whether it is washing gold, cutting down trees, or something else. Bored, he chews his coca, eats badly, then gets ill and leaves. The engineers just drink their coffee and watch others working.

We also work these things but so as to allow the woodland to replenish itself. We cultivate our farms, hunt, fish and gather woodland fruits, so we do not have to bring in supplies from outside. We also make houses, canoes, educate our children, and enjoy ourselves. In short we satisfy almost all our needs with our own work, and without destroying the environment.

In the upper Madre de Dios River wood is more important than gold, and the sawmill of Shintuya is one of the most productive in the region. Wood is also worked in other areas to make canoes and boats to sell, and for building houses for the outsiders. In the lower region of the river we gather nuts – another important part of our economy. Much is said about Madre de Dios being the forgotten Department of Peru. Yet we are not forgotten by people from outside nor by some national and foreign companies who try to seize our land and resources. Because of this we have formed the Federation of Indian Peoples of Madre de Dios to fight for the defence of our lands and resources."

tors of the Ministry of Agriculture, combating these excesses may well be the biggest challenge for the new Minister of Agriculture, who plans to establish, as fast as he can, a forestry police-force of three to four thousand individuals. However, with the forest six times the size of England, this may well be too little, too late.

Poison gold

Peru's worst example of **illegal gold-mining** is found in the southeastern jungles of Madre de Dios, home to the Amarakaeri Indians, where monster-sized machinery is transforming one of the Amazon's most biodiverse regions into a huge muddy scar. A number of gold-miners have already moved into the unique Tambopata Reserved Zone, a protected jungle area where giant otters, howler monkeys, king vultures, anacondas and jaguars are regularly spotted.

All plant life around each mine is turned into gravel, known in Peru as *cancha*, for just a few ounces of gold a day. Front-loading machines move up to about 30m depth of soil, which is then washed on a wooden sluice where high-pressure hoses separate the silt and gold from mud and gravel. Mercury, added at this stage to facilitate gold extraction, is later burnt off, causing river and air pollution. The mines are totally unregulated, and the richer, more established mining families tend to run the show, having the money to import large machines upriver from Brazil or by air from Chile.

The indigenous tribes are losing control of their territory to an ever-increasing stream of these miners and settlers coming down from the high Andes. As the mercury pollution and suspended mud from the mines upstream kill the life-giving rivers, they have to go deeper and deeper into the forest for fish, traditionally their main source of protein. Beatings and death threats from the miners and police are not uncommon.

There is a hope that **improved gold-mining technology** can stem the tide of destruction in these areas. Mercury levels in Amazon rivers and their associated food chains are rising at an alarming rate. However, with raw mercury available for only $13 a kilo there is little obvious economic incentive to find ways of using less hazardous materials. Cleaner gold-mining techniques have, however, been developed in Brazil. Astonishingly simple, the new method utilizes a wooden sluice with a gentler slope (instead of a steeper, ridged slope) to extract the gold from the washed river sediment and gravel. Trials have shown that this increases gold yields by up to forty percent, and the addition of a simple sluice box at the base of the slope has also led to the recovery of some 95 percent of the mercury used in the process. The same project has also developed a procedure of test boring to estimate quantities of gold in potential gravel deposits, which minimizes unnecessary and uneconomic earth-moving in search of gold. If taken on board by gold-miners in the Amazon and elsewhere, these techniques should reduce environmental damage. However, the fact remains that pressure by **international environmental groups**, and the publicity that they generate, continues to make a difference.

Biopiracy

Foreign corporations have staked their claim to patents protecting corporations' intellectual property rights on traditional Andean and Amazon plants. This "**biopiracy**" reduces options for developing countries to reap any benefits that their wealth of plant resources and ethnobotanical knowledge may generate. Any "equitable sharing of the benefits" as required by the Biodiversity Convention is a difficult goal if the bioprospector can slash intellectual property rights over whatever he/she finds.

Bioprospecting is said by its proponents to be an important tool for sustainable development and the conservation of resources through sustainable and fair sharing of benefits. Some argue that it is legalized "biopiracy". It is also quite a boom industry as well as being seen as a "green" investment.

Theoretically, corporations and research institutions gain from exploitation of genetic gems, while communities providing raw materials and knowledge share in the profits. At the same time, biodiversity conservation is promoted. But many communities and NGOs working with them claim that the "biopirates" have not lived up to their promises. Furthermore, they say that money is not enough; they also demand scientific and intellectual credit.

Earlier this decade, the US company Pure World took out a patent on **maca**, a traditional Andean crop used for centuries as a sexual stimulant, though they steered clear of patenting any particular variety. Instead, they identified and patented the active ingredients present in the roots. Although maca exports have risen rapidly, its price has fallen as production has increased, thus reducing the returns to the Peruvian farmers who feel they have lost control of their crop. Indigenous peoples' and farmers' organizations from the Andes and the Amazon responded by calling for the patent to be abandoned and on the government to act.

They got some apparent support in April 2003, when the Biological Diversity Convention was ratified, giving countries the ability to make money from genes, drugs and other products developed from their native plants and other wildlife. In an ideal world, therefore, companies developing products such as yellow beans or "natural Viagra" from traditional crop varieties should be paying royalties to the originators of the product – the farmers of the Andes and other regions of the world whose "prior art" is currently being exploited and "pirated". Still, the overarching matter remains unresolved.

For further information check out the Erosion, Technology and Concentration Action Group website: ⓦwww.etcgroup.org.

Indian resistance

Even now, in the twenty-first century, the largest of Peru's indigenous tribes or nations, like the **Ashaninka** and **Achuar**, have been standing firm against exploitation and invasion from outside influences. More amazing still, in 2002, hundreds of previously **uncontacted Indians** defended their land with bows and arrows against illegal loggers. Suvival International estimate that there are some fifteen uncontacted tribes living in the Peruvian Amazon today.

Uncontacted Indians confront illegal loggers

Four hundred naked jungle Indians tried to protect their ancestral forests in the Peruvian Amazon in July 2002 by running vines across the murky, slow-moving Río de las Piedras in what is arguably the remotest corner of our planet. The vines were used to stop several motorized canoes full of chainsaw-equipped loggers who were heading upriver in search of mahogany trees for the lucrative international markets. Once they had them trapped, the Indians fired five-foot-long arrows made from river cane, with feather flights and hardwood tips, at the terrified loggers.

The biggest jungle Indian attack on the outside world in Peru for over thirty years, the incident brought to public attention one of the last significant groups of uncontacted rainforest Indians and, further, the fact that they are prepared to act together to defend their forests. This 400-strong group are believed to represent a total population of around 1500 semi-nomadic uncontacted peoples who have been systematically retreating from the frontier of Western civilization for at least 130 years, ever since the peak of the rubber boom in the late nineteenth century. This area of forest represents their last-ditch stand – from here there is nowhere for them to go. These uncontacted Amazon Indians, possibly from the Mashco-Piro or Nahua groups, represent some of the last uncontacted tribal peoples on the planet.

Illegal logging is now the major threat to the rainforest in this corner of the Peruvian Amazon, which contains the largest remaining store of virgin mahogany trees in Peru. Not only do the loggers destroy great swathes of forest to take out just one highly valuable mahogany tree, but they also bring with them flu and other viruses which are frequently deadly to previously uncontacted peoples. In the last six years at least some of Peru's uncontacted tribes have been on the move, fleeing from the loggers. Survival International have been monitoring the situation and helped to generate worldwide media attention in early 2008.

The Ashaninka situation

More worldly-wise, perhaps, than the uncontacted Indians, Ashaninka tribal representatives, sometimes working in conjunction with indigenous political umbrella organizations, have gone increasingly regularly to Lima to get publicity and assert their claims to land. For the Ashaninka, this territorial struggle has been and continues to be for titles on the **Ene** and **Tambo**, the only regions left to them after four centuries of "civilizing" influence. In publicity terms they have met with some success. The exploitation of the forests has become a political issue, fuelled in the early 1980s within Peru (and outside) by the bizarre events surrounding Werner Herzog's filming of *Fitzcarraldo*, a film *about* exploitation of Indians, yet whose director so angered local communities that at one stage they burned down a whole production camp.

With the rise of Sendero Luminoso things got much worse for some indigenous Peruvian Amazon groups. Again, the Ashaninka suffered greatly because of their close proximity to the Sendero heartlands. Sendero are now virtually extinct, due in part to the fierce stand taken by the Ashaninka themselves, and in the last few years, the Ashaninka have regained control of much of the territory they had lost to the terrorists.

The biggest problems they face include a vast increase in illegal logging since 2004, the imminent arrival of petrol companies to start seismic testing, plus a constant threat of organized land invasions by settlers from the mountain regions, who frequently ally themselves with the loggers, cocaine growers and smugglers, and often also have the support of regional authorities. Although terrorism and allegiance to the Shining Path has never been entirely eradicated from what was once simply Ashaninka territory, in terms of ideology, the political revolutionary fervour of the late 1980s and early 1990s has been replaced by a spreading religious evangelicalism.

While the Indians have certainly undergone a radical growth in political awareness, in real terms they have made little progress. Former President Belaunde, whose promises of human rights in the late 1970s led to many thousands of Ashaninka making their way down to polling stations by raft to vote for him, has merely speeded up the process of colonization, and in the Ene region alone, the Indians face multinational claims to millions of acres of their territory. To make matters worse, President Fujimori changed the law in 1995 to allow colonization of Indian lands if they had been "unoccupied" for two years or more. Obviously, with many of the traditional rainforest Indians having a semi-nomadic existence, depending on hunting and gathering for survival, colonists can take over an area of forest claiming it as uninhabited, even though it's part of traditional territory. This law change particularly affected the Ashaninka, who had already been forced to leave their usual scattered settlements for self-protection against the terrorists. At the close of the twentieth century, they had largely moved back into their original settlements and territories, though closely followed by more waves of colonists. The civil war against Sendero, in which the Ashaninka played a significant role, did much to unite the traditionally scattered Ashaninka nation, but whether or not it has prepared them sufficiently well to hold things together remains to be seen.

Peru's white gold

In recent decades, not only have poverty and the promise of a better life led thousands of Peruvian peasants down the road of guerrilla warfare and bloody terror, but also many of them, sometimes the same individuals, have transformed the most sacred plant of the Incas into one of the world's most commercial cash crops. Seen by many peasants as a road to fortune and freedom, for others cocaine is a scourge, bringing violence, the mobsters and deforestation in its wake.

The only peasants who make decent money engage in "cooking" **cocaine**. Illegal "kitchens", makeshift coke refineries, have become the main means of livelihood for many ordinary families, as the equipment is simple – oil drums, a few chemicals, paraffin and a fire. Bushels of coca leaves are dissolved in paraffin and hydrochloric acid, heated, and stirred, eventually producing the pasta, which is then washed in ether or acetone to yield powdery white cocaine.

Peru's coca industry netted an estimated $3 billion in 1984 – twenty percent of the country's gross national product. By the end of the 1980s this figure was much higher and the problem had become one of global dimensions. However, a combination of market saturation and political pressure from the US, backed up by anti-cocaine money and hardware like police helicopters, seems to have changed the situation substantially. In 1996 the Peruvian price of cocaine had dropped by over fifty percent on the street, down to almost $4 a gram. Colombian drug cartels were buying less from Peru, having been hit hardest by US anti-cocaine policies, and the protection once afforded by Sendero Luminoso terrorists had turned into more of a liability than anything else. By the end of the twentieth century there was also increasing US intervention, including aerial patrols over the northern jungle border between Peru and Colombia firing on unmarked planes that refuse to identify themselves. Production of cocaine in Peru has dropped further while it has started to rise in Colombia, and these lower levels of supply have brought Peru's internal price for cocaine back up to a street level of $10 a gram. It seems unlikely that cocaine production will be reduced much further, since there are always new export opportunities and a steady home market; but the basic crop – coca plants – no longer offers quite the relatively stable, safe and so much more remunerative option to small-time cash-croppers that it did just a couple of years ago.

Coca, the plant from which cocaine is derived, has travelled a long way since the Incas distributed this "divine plant" across fourteenth-century Andean Peru. Presented as a gift from the gods, coca was used to exploit slave labour under the Spanish rule: without it the Indians would never have worked in the gruelling conditions of colonial mines such as Potosi.

The isolation of the active ingredient in coca, **cocaine**, in 1859, began an era of intense medical experimentation. Its numbing effects have been appreciated by dental patients around the world, and even Pope Leo XIII enjoyed a bottle of the coca wine produced by an Italian physician, who amassed a great fortune from its sale in the nineteenth century. The literary world, too, was soon stimulated by this white powder: in 1885 Robert Louis Stevenson wrote *Dr Jekyll and Mr Hyde* during six speedy days and nights while taking this "wonder drug" as a remedy for his tuberculosis, and Sir Arthur Conan Doyle, writing in the 1890s, used the character of Sherlock Holmes to defend the use of cocaine. On a more popular level, coca was one of the essential ingredients in Coca-Cola until 1906. Today, cocaine is one of the most fashionable – and expensive – illegal drugs.

From its humble origins cocaine has become very big business. Unofficially, it may well be the biggest export for countries like Peru and Bolivia, where coca grows best in the Andes and along the edge of the jungle. While most mountain peasants always cultivated a little for personal use, many have now become dependent on it for obvious economic reasons: coca is still the most profitable cash crop and is readily bought by middlemen operating for extremely wealthy cocaine barons. A constant flow of semi-refined coca – pasta, the basic paste – leaves Peru aboard Amazon riverboats or unmarked light aircraft heading for laboratories in Colombia. From here the pure stuff is shipped or flown out, mostly to the US via Miami or Los Angeles. Much of the rest is refined in Peruvian cocaine "kitchens" in the *ceja de selva* or Lima, before finding its way into the nostrils of wealthy Limeños, or going over the border into Brazil and further afield.

Few people care to look beyond the wall of illicit intrigue that surrounds this highly saleable contraband. In the same vein as coffee or chocolate, the demand for this product has become another means through which the privileged world controls the lives of those in the developing world, at the same time endangering the delicate environmental balance of the western edge of Amazonia. As Peruvian Indians follow world-market trends by turning their hands to the growing and "cooking" of coca, more staple crops like cereals, tubers and beans are cultivated less and less.

It's a change brought about partly by circumstance. Agricultural prices are state-controlled, but manufactured goods and transport costs rise almost weekly, preventing the peasants from earning a decent living from their crops. Moreover, the soil is poor and crops grow unwillingly. Coca, on the other hand, grows readily and needs little attention.

Peruvian recipes

P eruvian cooking – even in small restaurants well away from the big cities – is appealing stuff. The nine recipes below are among the classics, fairly simple to prepare and (with a couple of coastal exceptions) found throughout the country. If you're travelling and camping you'll find all the ingredients listed readily available in local markets; we've suggested alternatives if you want to try them when you get home. All quantities given are sufficient for four people.

Ceviche

A cool, spicy dish, eaten on the Peruvian coast for at least the past thousand years.

1kg soft white fish (lemon sole and halibut are good, or you can mix half fish, half shellfish)
2 large onions, sliced
1 or 2 chillis, chopped
6 limes (or lemons, but these aren't so good)
1 tbsp olive oil
1 tbsp fresh coriander or cilantro leaves
salt and pepper to taste

Wash and cut the fish into bite-sized pieces. Place in a dish with the sliced onions. Add the chopped chilli and coriander. Make a marinade using the lime juice, olive oil, salt and pepper. Pour over the fish and place in a cool spot until the fish is "soft cooked" (from 10 to 60min). Serve with boiled potatoes (preferably sweet) and corn on the cob.

Papas a la Huancaina

An excellent and ubiquitous snack – cold potatoes covered in a mildly *picante* cheese sauce.

1 kg potatoes, boiled
1 or 2 chillis, chopped
2 cloves of garlic, chopped
200g soft goat's cheese (feta is ideal, or cottage cheese will do)
6 saltines or crackers
1 hardboiled egg
1 small can of evaporated milk

Chop very finely or liquidize all the above ingredients except for the potatoes. The mixture should be fairly thin but not too runny. Pour sauce over the thickly sliced potatoes. Arrange on a dish and serve garnished with lettuce and black olives. Best served chilled.

Palta Rellena

Stuffed avocados – another very popular snack.

2 avocados, soft but not ripe
1 onion, chopped
2 tomatoes, chopped

2 hardboiled eggs, chopped
200g cooked chicken or tuna fish, cold and flaked
2 tbsp mayonnaise

Cut the avocados in half and remove the stones. Scoop out a little of the flesh around the hole. Gently combine all the other ingredients before piling into the centre of each avocado half.

Causa

About the easiest Peruvian dish to reproduce outside the country, though there are no real substitutes for Peruvian tuna and creamy Andean potatoes.

1kg potatoes
200g tuna fish
2 avocados, the riper the better
4 tomatoes
salt and black pepper
1 lemon

Boil the potatoes and mash to a firm, smooth consistency. Flake the tuna fish and add a little lemon juice. Mash the avocados to a pulp, add the rest of the lemon juice, some salt and black pepper. Slice the tomatoes. Press one quarter of the tuna fish over this, then a quarter of the avocado mixture on top. Add a layer of sliced tomato. Continue the same layering process until you have four layers of each. Cut into rough slices. Serve (ideally chilled) with salad, or on its own as a starter.

Locro de Zapallo

A vegetarian standard found on most set menus in the cheaper, working-class restaurants.

1kg pumpkin
1 large potato
2 cloves of garlic
1 tbsp oregano
1 cup of milk
2 corn on the cobs
1 onion
1 chilli, chopped
salt and pepper
200g cheese (mozarella works well)

Fry the onion, chilli, garlic and oregano. Add half a cup of water. Mix in the pumpkin as large-cut lumps, slices of corn on the cob and finely chopped potato. Add the milk and cheese. Simmer until a soft, smooth consistency, and add a little more water if necessary. Serve with rice or over fish.

Pescado a la Chorillana

Probably the most popular way of cooking fish on the coast.

4 pieces of fish (cod or any other white fish will do)
2 large onions, chopped
4 large tomatoes, chopped
1 or 2 chillis, chopped into fairly large pieces

1 tbsp oil
half a cup of water

Grill or fry each portion of fish until done. Keep hot. Fry separately the onions, tomatoes and chilli. Add the water to form a sauce. Pile the hot sauce over each portion of fish and serve with rice.

Asado

A roast. An expensive meal for Peruvians, though a big favourite for family gatherings. Only available in fancier restaurants.

1kg or less of lean beef
2 cloves of garlic
200g butter
1 tin of tomato puree
salt and pepper
1 tbsp soy sauce
2 tomatoes
1 chilli, chopped

Cover the beef with the premixed garlic and butter. Mix the tomato puree with salt, pepper and soy sauce. Liquidize the tomatoes with the chopped chilli. Spread both mixtures on the beef and cook slowly in a covered casserole dish for four or five hours. Traditionally the *asado* is served with *pure de papas*, which is simply a runny form of mashed potatoes whipped up with some butter and a lot of garlic. A very tasty combination.

Quinoa Vegetable Soup

Quinoa – known as "mother grain" in the Andes – is "a natural whole grain with remarkable nutritional properties", quite possibly a "supergrain" of the future. It's simple and tasty to add to any soups or stews.

4 cups of water
quarter of a cup of quinoa
half a cup of diced carrots
quarter of a cup of diced celery
2 tbsp finely chopped onions
quarter of a green pepper
2 mashed cloves of garlic
1 tbsp vegetable oil
half a cup of chopped tomatoes
half a cup of finely chopped cabbage
1 tbsp salt
some chopped parsley

Gently fry the quinoa and all the vegetables (except the cabbage and tomatoes) in oil and garlic until browned. Then add the water, cabbage and tomatoes before bringing to the boil. Season with salt and garnish with parsley.

Aji de Gallina

Literally translated as "Chillied Chicken", this is not as spicy as it sounds, but utilizes a delicious cheesy yellow sauce.

1 chicken breast
1 cup of breadcrumbs
2 soupspoons of powdered yellow chilli
50g Parmesan cheese
50g ground nuts
1 cup of evaporated milk (more if the sauce seems too dry)
1 sliced onion (red or white)

Boil the chicken breast, then strain and fry it for a bit. Mix the hot chicken water with the breadcrumbs. Meanwhile, in a pot, heat two tablespoons full of olive oil and brown the onions. Mix in the yellow chilli powder. Mix in the breadcrumbs as liquidized as possible. After a few minutes still on the heat, add in the Parmesan cheese, the chicken, salt to taste and finally the ground nuts. Boil for another ten minutes. Add the evaporated milk just before serving and stir in well. Decorate the plate with boiled potatoes, preferably of the Peruvian yellow variety (if not white will do), cut into cross-sectional slices about a centimetre or so thick. Add a sliced egg and black olives on top.

Thanks to Señora Delia Arvi Tarazona for this recipe.

Books

T here are few books published exclusively about Peru and very few Peruvian writers ever make it into English. Many of the classic works on Peruvian and Inca history are now out of date (o/p), though frequently one comes across them in libraries around the world or bookshops in Lima and Cusco. Travel books, coffee-table editions and country guides are also generally available in Lima bookshops. Others can be obtained through the South American Explorers' Club (see p.41).

Inca and ancient history

Anthony Aveni *Nasca: Eighth Wonder of the World*. One of the more recent works on the amazing Nasca Lines and sites, by a leading scholar who has spent twenty years excavating here. Contains much on the history of the Nasca people and explores the complex relationships between water, worship, social order and the environment.

Kathleen Berrin *The Spirit of Ancient Peru: Treasures from the Museo Arqueol—gico Rafael Larco Herrera* (o/p). Essentially a detailed exhibition catalogue with essays by reputable Andeanists and plenty of quality illustrations and photographs representing one of Peru's finest collections of mainly pre-Inca artefacts.

Hiram Bingham *Lost City of the Incas*. The classic introduction to Machu Picchu: the exploration accounts are interesting but many of the theories should be taken with a pinch of salt. Widely available in Peru.

Peter T. Bradley *The Lure of Peru: Maritime Intrusion into the South Sea 1598–1701* (o/p). A historical account of how the worldwide fame of the country's Inca treasures attracted Dutch, French and English would-be settlers, explorers, merchants and even pirates to the seas and shores of Peru. It includes descriptions of naval blockades of Lima and various waves of buccaneers and their adventures in search of Peru.

Richard Burger *Chavín and the Origins of Andean Civilisation*. A collection of erudite essays, essential reading for anyone seriously interested in Peruvian prehistory.

Geoffrey Hext Sutherland Bushnell *Peru* (o/p). A classic, concise introduction to the main social and technological developments in Peru from 2500 BC to 1500 AD; well illustrated, if dated in some aspects.

Pedro De Cieza De Leon *The Discovery and Conquest of Peru (Latin America in Transition)*. A new paperback version of the classic post-Conquest chronicler account.

Evan Hadingham *Lines to the Mountain Gods: Nasca and the Mysteries of Peru*. One of the more down-to-earth books on the Nasca Lines, including maps and illustrations – also available through the South American Explorers' Club in Lima.

John Hemming *The Conquest of the Incas*. The authoritative narrative tale of the Spanish Conquest, very readably brought to life from a mass of original sources.

Thor Heyerdahl, Daniel Sandweiss and Alfredo Navárez *Pyramids of Túcume*. A recently published description of the archeological site at Túcume plus the life and society of the civilization which created this important ceremonial and political centre around 1000 years ago. Widely available in Peruvian bookshops.

Richard Keatinge (ed) *Peruvian Prehistory*. One of the most up-to-date and reputable books on the ancient civilizations of Peru – a collection of serious academic essays on various cultures and cultural concepts through the millennia prior to the Inca era.

Ann Kendall *Everyday Life of the Incas* (o/p). Accessible, very general description of Peru under Inca domination.

Alfred L. Kroeber and Donald Collier *The Archeology and Pottery of Nasca, Peru: Alfred Kroeber's 1926 Expedition*. A historical perspective on the archeology of Peru.

Kim MacQuarrie *The Last days of the Incas*. Available in both hardback and paperback, this is a thoroughly researched and highly dramatic account of Francisco Pizarro's conquest, depicting well the Inca rebellion and subsequent guerrilla war; the book also covers the modern search for lost Inca cities and archaeological discoveries right up to 2007.

J. Alden Mason *Ancient Civilisations of Peru*. Reprinted in 1991, an excellent summary of the country's history from the Stone Age through to the Inca Empire.

Michael E. Moseley *The Incas and their Ancestors*. A fine overview of Peru before the Spanish Conquest, which makes full use of good maps, diagrams, sketches, motifs and photos.

Keith Muscutt *Warriors of the Clouds: A Lost Civilization in the Upper Amazon of Peru*. Some superb photos of the ruins and environment left behind by the amazing Chachapoyas culture of northern Peru.

William Hickling Prescott *History of the Conquest of Peru*. Hemming's main predecessor – a nineteenth-century classic that remains a good read, if you can find a copy.

Johan Reinhard *Nasca Lines: A New Perspective on their Origin and Meaning*. Original theories about the Lines and ancient mountain gods – available through the South American Explorers' Club and the better bookshops in Lima. The same author also wrote *The Sacred Centre: Machu Picchu* (Nuevas Imagenes, Lima), a fascinating book, drawing on anthropology, archaeology, geography and astronomy to reach highly probable conclusions about the sacred geology and topography of the Cusco region, and how this appears to have been related to Inca architecture, in particular Machu Picchu.

Gene Savoy *Antisuyo: The Search for the Lost Cities of the Amazon* (o/p). Exciting account of Savoy's important explorations, plus loads of historical detail.

Garcilasco de la Vega *The Royal Commentaries of the Incas* (2 vols, o/p). Many good libraries have a copy of this, the most readable and fascinating of contemporary historical sources. Written shortly after the Conquest, by a "Spaniard" of essentially Inca blood, this work is the best eyewitness account of life and beliefs among the Incas.

Oscar Medina Zevallos *The Enigma of Machu Picchu* available from ⓦwww .cuscobooks.com. Written by a Peruvian explorer and historical writer, this book tries to answer some of the difficult questions posed by Machu Picchu.

Modern history and society

Americas Watch *Peru under Fire: Human Rights since the Return to Democracy*. A good summary of Peruvian politics of the 1980s.

Susan E. Benner and Kathy S. Leonard *Fire from the Andes: Short Fiction by Women from Bolivia, Ecuador, and Peru*. A fascinating read of unique and passionate writing.

Sally Bowen and Jane Holligan *The Imperfect Spy: the many lives of Vladimiro Montesinos*. Tracing the emergence of Montesinos who virtually ran Peru throughout the 1990s, as head of SIN (Servicio de Inteligencia Nacional), this well-researched book covers his upbringing and career in a highly engaging and accessible style. It provides a fascinating insight into the corruption and power in the CIA and the mafia, as manifested in Peru.

Eduardo Calderon *Eduardo El Curandero: The Words of a Peruvian Healer*. Peru's most famous shaman – El Tuno – outlines his teachings and beliefs in his own words.

Carlos Cumes and Romulo Lizarraga Valencia *Pachamamas Children: Mother Earth and her Children of the Andes in Peru*. A New Age look at the culture, roots and shamanistic aspects of modern Peru.

James Higgins *Lima: a cultural and literary history*. A scholarly book showing great affection for Lima, carefully weaving together both its culture and social history. It guides the reader through Lima's historical sites; with particular emphasis on the colonial era, it covers museums as well as literature and art, culminating with a section on modern-day culture.

🏃 **F. Bruce Lamb and Manuel Cordova-Rios** *The Wizard of the Upper Amazon*. Masterful reconstruction of the true story of Manuel Cordoba Rios – "Ino Moxo" – a famous herbal healer and *ayahuascero* from Iquitos who was kidnapped as a young boy and brought up by Indians in the early twentieth century. Offers significant insight into indigenous psychedelic healing traditions.

Holligan de Diaz-Limaco *Peru in Focus*. A good (if small) general reader on Peru's history, politics, culture and environment.

E. Luis Martin *The Kingdom of the Sun: A Short History of Peru* (o/p). The best general history, concentrating on the post-Conquest period and bringing events up to the 1980s.

Nicole Maxwell *Witch-Doctor's Apprentice* (o/p). A very personal and detailed account of the author's research into the healing plants used by Amazonian Peruvian tribes; a highly informative book on plant lore.

Sewell H. Menzel *Fire in the Andes: U.S. Foreign Policy and Cocaine Politics in Bolivia and Peru*. A good summary of US anti-cocaine activities in these two countries, written by credible academics.

David Scott Palmer (ed) *Shining Path of Peru*. A modern history compilation of meticulously detailed essays and articles by Latin American academics and journalists on the early and middle phases of Sendero Luminoso's civil war in Peru.

Michael Reid *Peru: Paths to Poverty* (o/p). A succinct analysis tracing Peru's economic and security crisis of the early 1980s back to the military government of General Velasco.

Orin Starn, Carlos Degregori and Robin Kirk (eds) *The Peru Reader: History, Culture, Politics*. One of the best overviews yet of Peruvian history and politics, with writing by characters as diverse as Mario Vargas Llosa and Abimael Guzman (imprisoned ex-leader of Sendero Luminoso).

Flora and fauna

Allen Altman and B. Swift *Checklist of the Birds of Peru*. A useful summary with photos of different habitats.

J.L. Castner, S.L. Timme and J.A. Duke *A Field Guide to Medicinal and Useful Plants of the Upper Amazon*. A guide to the most common and useful plants of the Upper Amazon, of interest to enthusiasts and scientists alike. Contains handy colour plates.

L.H. Emmons *Neotropical Rainforest Mammals: A Field Guide*. An excellent paperback with over 250 pages of authoritative text, 29 colour plates and other illustrations covering 260 species.

🏃 **Steven L. Hilty and William L. Brown** *A Guide to the Birds of Colombia*. One of the few classic ornithology guides covering the fascinating and rich birdlife of Peru and its surrounding countries. It contains 69 colour and black and white plates, is 836 pages long and has a useful index.

M. Koepke *The Birds of the Department of Lima*. A small but classic guide, for many years the only one available that covered many of Peru's species, and still good for its excellent illustrations.

Richard E. Schultes and Robert F. Raffauf *The Healing Forest*. An excellent and erudite large-format paperback on many of the Amazon's most interesting plants. It's well illustrated with exquisite photographs and is a relatively easy read.

Richard E. Schultes and Robert F. Raffauf *Vine of the Soul*. One of the best large-format books about the indigenous use and chemical basis of the hallucinogenic plant *ayahuasca*, so commonly used by tribal peoples in Peruvian Amazonia.

Thomas Valqui *Where to Watch Birds in Peru*. Divided into seven sections or regions of Peru, it covers 151 of the most important birding sites, featuring details on how to reach the locations as well as where to stay nearby. Naturally, it also gives plenty of information on what books to look for, plus over 60 maps and thorough descriptions of birds and their habitats. Incorporates an up-to-date Peru bird checklist.

Walter Wust *Manu: el ultimo refugio*. This is an excellent coffee-table book on the wildlife and flora of Manu National Park by one of Peru's foremost wildlife photographers. Available in most good bookshops in Lima and Cusco.

Travel

Timothy E. Albright and Jeff Tenlow *Dancing Bears and the Pilgrims Progress in the Andes: Transformation on the Road to Quolloriti*. A slightly dry report on the Snow Star annual festival of Quoyllur Rit'i, which is attended by tens of thousands of Andean peasants at the start of every dry season.

Patrick Leigh Fermor *Three Letters from the Andes*. Three long letters written from Peru in 1971 describing the experiences of a rather upper crust mountaineering expedition.

Christopher Isherwood *The Condor and the Cows* (o/p). A diary of Isherwood's South American trip after World War II, most of which took place in Peru. Like Paul Theroux, Isherwood eventually arrives in Buenos Aires, to meet Jorge Luis Borges.

John Lane *A Very Peruvian Practice*. This comical and well-written autobiographical travel book about Lane's work as advisor to a new ladies' health clinic in Lima, paints a colourful picture of life in Peru – from bullfights to funerals, and the rainforest to Andean mountaintops.

Dervla Murphy *Eight Feet in the Andes*. An enjoyable account of a rather adventurous journey Dervla Murphy made across the Andes with her young daughter and a mule. It can't compare with her Indian books, though.

Matthew Parris *Inca Kola, A Traveller's Tale of Peru*. Very amusing description of travelling in Peru, with a perspicacious look at Peruvian culture, past and present.

Tom Pow *In the Palace of Serpents: An Experience of Peru*. A well-written insight into travelling in Peru, spoilt only by the fact that Tom Pow was ripped off in Cusco and lost his original notes. Consequently he didn't have as wonderful a time as he might have and seemed to miss the beauty of the Peruvian landscapes and the wealth of its history and culture.

Paul Theroux *The Old Patagonian Express*. Theroux didn't much like Peru, nor Peruvians, but for all the self-obsessed pique and disgust for most of humanity, at his best – being sick in trains – he is highly entertaining.

Hugh Thomson *The White Rock.* One of the best travelogue books on Peru for some time, focusing mainly on the archaeological explorations and theories of an English Peruvianist.

George Woodcock *Incas and Other Men* (o/p). An enjoyable, light-hearted tour, mixing modern and ancient history and travel anecdotes, that is still

a good introduction to Peru over fifty years after the event.

Ronald Wright *Cut Stones and Crossroads: A Journey in the Two Worlds of Peru.* An enlightened travel book and probably the best general travelogue writing on Peru over the last few decades, largely due to the author's depth of knowledge of his subject.

Peruvian writers

Martín Adán *The Cardboard House.* A poetic novel based in Lima and written by one of South America's best living poets.

Ciro Alegria *Broad and Alien is the World.* Another good book to travel with, this is a distinguished 1970s novel offering persuasive insight into life in the Peruvian highlands.

Jose Maria Arguedas *Deep Rivers, Yawar Fiesta.* Arguedas is an *indigenista* – writing for and about the native peoples. *Yawar Fiesta* focuses on one of the most impressive Andean peasant ceremonial cycles involving the annual rite of pitching a live condor against a bull, the condor representing the indigenous Indians and the bull the Spanish Conquistadors.

Mario Vargas Llosa *Death in the Andes, A Fish in the Water, Aunt Julia and the Scriptwriter, The Time of the Hero, Captain Pantoja and the Special Service, The Green House, The Real Life of Alejandro Mayta, The War of the End of the World, Who Killed Palomino Molero?.* The best-known and the most brilliant of contemporary Peruvian writers, Vargas Llosa is essentially a novelist but has also written on Peruvian society, run his own TV current affairs programme in Lima and even

made a (rather average) feature film. *Death in the Andes* deals with Sendero Luminoso and Peruvian politics in a style which goes quite a long way towards illuminating popular Peruvian thinking in the late 1980s and early 1990s. His ebullient memoir, *A Fish in the Water*, describes, among other things, Vargas Llosa's experience in his unsuccessful running for the Peruvian presidency. *Aunt Julia*, the best-known of his novels to be translated into English, is a fabulous book, a grand and comic novel spiralling out from the stories and exploits of a Bolivian scriptwriter who arrives in Lima to work on Peruvian radio soap operas. In part, too, it is autobiographical, full of insights and goings-on in Miraflores society. Essential reading – and perfect for long Peruvian journeys. His latest novel – *The Way to Paradise* (*El Paraiso en la Otra Esquina*) – is a fictional recreation of the life and times of Flora Tristan and Paul Gauguin.

Cesar Vallejo *Collected Poems of Cesar Vallejo.* Peru's one internationally renowned poet – and deservedly so. Romantic but highly innovative in style, it translates beautifully.

Novels set in Peru

Peter Mathiessen *At Play in the Fields of the Lord.* A celebrated American novel, which catches the energy and magic of the Peruvian selva.

James Redfield *The Celestine Prophecy.* A best-selling novel that uses Peru as a backdrop. Despite not having much to say about Peru, it's a popular topic of conversation among travellers in the 1990s; some were actually inspired to visit Peru from having read this intriguing book, which expresses with some clarity many New Age concepts and beliefs.

Unfortunately the book's descriptions of the Peruvian people, landscapes, forests and culture bear so little relationship to the Peruvian reality that it feels like the author has never been anywhere near Peru.

Specialist guides

John Biggar *The High Andes: A Guide for Climbers* (Andes, 93 Queen St, Castle Douglas, Kirkcudbrightshire, Scotland DG7 1EH). The first comprehensive climbing guide to the main peaks of the Andes, with a main focus on Peru but also covering Bolivia, Ecuador, Chile, Argentina, Colombia and Venezuela.

Ben Box *Cusco and the Inca Trail*. A good general guide to Peru's most popular destination.

Bradley C. Johnson *Classic Climbs of the Cordillera Blanca (2004)*. Available in paperback only, this is a must for anyone seriously wanting to climb in Peru's most popular mountaineering destination.

Hilary and George Bradt *Backpacking and Trekking in Peru and Bolivia*. Detailed and excellent coverage of some of Peru's most rewarding hikes – worth taking if you're remotely interested in the idea, and good anyway for background on wildlife and flora.

Charles Brod *Apus and Incas: A Cultural Walking and Trekking Guide to Cusco*. An interesting selection of walks in the Cusco area. Available locally.

Richard Danbury *The Inca Trail: Cuzco and Machu Picchu*. Good, highly informative and smoothly written guide to this trekking destination, with fine contextual pieces. Also includes practical information for Lima.

Peter Frost *Exploring Cusco*. A very practical and stimulating site-by-site guide to the whole Cusco area (where it is widely available in bookstores). Unreservedly recommended if you're spending more than a few days in the region, and also for armchair archaeologists back home.

Peter Frost and Jim Bartle *Machu Picchu Historic Sanctuary*. A well-written and beautifully photographed coffee-table book on South America's most alluring archaeological site.

Latin Works *Machu Picchu Guide*. A small booklet with accurate detail on the various compounds within the archaeological site.

Copeland Marks *Exotic Kitchens of Peru*. Released in 2001, this is the latest book on Peruvian food, cooking and the culture and variety of the country's types of kitchens.

David Mazel *Pure and Perpetual Snow: Two Climbs in the Andes*. Climbing reports on Ausangate and Alpamayo peaks. Available locally or from the South American Explorers' Club.

Lynn Meisch *A Traveller's Guide to El Dorado and the Incan Empire*. Huge paperback full of fascinating detail – well worth reading before visiting Peru.

Barry Walker and Jon Fjeldsa *Birds of Machu Picchu*. A splendid full colour booklet focusing on the birdlife found in Peru's best known National Sanctuary and the area within which the Inca Trail is located.

Language

Language

Language

Although Peru is officially a Spanish-speaking nation, a large proportion of its population, possibly more than half, regard Spanish as their second language. When the conquistadors arrived, Quechua, the official language of the Inca Empire, was widely spoken everywhere but the jungle. Originally known as Runasimi (from *runa*, "person", and *simis*, "mouth"), it was given the name Quechua – which means "high Andean valleys" – by the Spanish.

Quechua was not, however, the only pre-Columbian tongue. There were, and still are, well over **thirty Indian languages** within the jungle area and, up until the late nineteenth century, **Mochica** had been widely spoken on the north coast for at least 1500 years.

With such a rich linguistic history it is not surprising to find non-European words intruding constantly into any Peruvian conversation. **Cancha**, for instance, the Inca word for "courtyard", is still commonly used to refer to most sporting areas – *la cancha de basketball*, for example. Other linguistic survivors have even reached the English language: **llama**, **condor**, **puma** and **pampa** among them. Perhaps more interesting is the great wealth of traditional **Creole slang** – utilized with equal vigour at all levels of society. This complex speech, much like Cockney rhyming slang, is difficult to catch without almost complete fluency in Spanish, though one phrase you may find useful for directing a taxi driver is *de fresa alfonso* – literally translatable as "of strawberry, Alfonso" but actually meaning "straight on" (*de frente al fondo*).

Once you get into it, **Spanish** is the easiest language there is – and in Peru people are eager to understand even the most faltering attempt. You'll be further helped by the fact that South Americans speak relatively slowly (at least compared with Spaniards in Spain) and that there's no need to get your tongue round the lisping pronunciation.

Among **dictionaries,** you could try the *Dictionary of Latin American Spanish* (University of Chicago Press).

Pronunciation

The rules of **pronunciation** are pretty straightforward and, once you get to know them, strictly observed. Unless there's an accent, words ending in d, l, r, and z are **stressed** on the last syllable, all others on the second last. All **vowels** are pure and short.

A somewhere between the "A" sound of back and that of father

E as in get

I as in police

O as in hot

U as in rule

C is soft before E and I, hard otherwise: **cerca** is pronounced "serka"

G works the same way, a guttural "H" sound (like the ch in loch) before E or I, a hard G elsewhere – **gigante** becomes "higante"

H is always silent

J is the same sound as a guttural G: jamón is pronounced "hamon"

LL sounds like an English Y: tortilla is pronounced "torteeya"

N is as in English unless it has a tilde (accent) over it, when it becomes NY: mañana sounds like "manyana"

QU is pronounced like an English K

R is rolled, RR doubly so

V sounds more like B, vino becoming "beano"

X is slightly softer than in English – sometimes almost SH – except between vowels in place names where it has an "H" sound – for example México (Meh-Hee-Ko) or Oaxaca

Z is the same as a soft C, so cerveza becomes "servesa"

Below is a list of a few essential words and phrases, though if you're travelling for any length of time a dictionary or phrase book is obviously a worthwhile investment – some specifically Latin American ones are available (see p.631). If you're using a **dictionary**, bear in mind that in Spanish CH, LL, and Ñ count as separate letters and are listed after the Cs, Ls, and Ns respectively.

Words and phrases

Basics

Yes, No	Sí, No	Now, Later	Ahora, Más tarde
Please, Thank you	Por favor, Gracias	Open, Closed	Abierto/a, Cerrado/a
Where...?, When...?	¿Dónde...?, ¿Cuándo...?	With, Without	Con, Sin
What...?, How much...?	¿Qué...?, ¿Cuánto...?	Good, Bad	Buen(o)/a, Mal(o)/a
		Big, Small	Gran(de), Pequeño/a
		More, Less	Más, Menos
Here, There	Aquí, Allí	Today, Tomorrow	Hoy, Mañana
This, That	Este, Eso	Yesterday	Ayer

Greetings and responses

Hello, Goodbye	Hola, Adiós	I don't speak Spanish	No hablo español
Good morning	Buenos días	My name is . . .	Me llamo . . .
Good afternoon/night	Buenas tardes/noches	What's your name?	¿Como se llama usted?
See you later	Hasta luego		
Sorry	Lo siento/discúlpeme	I am English	Soy inglés(a)
Excuse me	Con permiso/perdón	. . . American	americano/a
How are you?	¿Como está (usted)?	. . . Australian	australiano/a
I (don't) understand	(No) Entiendo	. . . Canadian	canadiense
Not at all/ You're welcome	De nada	. . . Irish	irlandés(a)
		. . . New Zealander	neozelandés(a)
Do you speak English?	¿Habla (usted) inglés?	. . . Scottish	escocés(a)
		. . . Welsh	galés(a)

Hotel and transport needs

I want	Quiero	Is there a hotel nearby?	¿Hay un hotel aquí cerca?
I'd like	Querría	How do I get to...?	Por dónde se va a. . .?
Do you know. . .?	¿Sabe. . .?	Left, right, straight on	Izquierda, derecha, derecho
I don't know	No sé		
There is (is there)?	(¿)Hay(?)	Where is. . .?	¿Dónde está. . .?
Give me. . .	Deme. . .	. . .the bus station	. . .la estación de autobuses
(one like that)	(uno así)		
Do you have. . .?	Tiene . . .?	. . .the train station	. . .la estación de ferrocarriles
. . .the time	. . .la hora		
. . .a room	. . .un cuarto	. . .the nearest bank	. . .el banco más cercano
. . .with two beds/ double bed . . .	. . .con dos camas/ cama matrimonial	. . .the post office	. . .el correo
It's for one person (two people)	es para una persona (dos personas)	. . .the toilet	. . .el baño/sanitario
		Where does the bus to. . . leave from?	¿De dónde sale el camión para. . .?
. . .for one night (one week)	. . .para una noche (una semana)	Is this the train for Lima?	¿Es éste el tren para Lima?
It's fine, how much is it?	¿Está bien, cuánto es?	I'd like a (return) ticket to. . .	Querría un boleto (de ida y vuelta) para. . .
It's too expensive	Es demasiado caro	What time does it leave (arrive in...)?	¿A qué hora sale (llega en. . .)?
Don't you have anything cheaper?	¿No tiene algo más barato?	What is there to eat?	¿Qué hay para comer?
Can one. . . ?	¿Se puede. . .?	What's that?	¿Qué es eso?
. . .camp (near) here?	¿. . .acampar aquí (cerca)?	What's this called in Spanish?	¿Como se llama este en Castillano?

Some useful accommodation terms

Ventilador	Desk fan or ceiling fan	Cama matrimonial	Double bed
Aire-acondicionado	Air-conditioned	Sencillo	Single bed
Baño colectivo /compartido	Shared bath	Cuarto simple	Single room
		Impuestos	Taxes
Agua caliente	Hot water	Hora de salida	Check-out time
Agua fría	Cold water		

Eating and drinking

Basics

Arroz	Rice	duros	hard-boiled
Avena	Oats (porridge)	pasados	lightly boiled
Galletas	Biscuits	revueltos	scrambled
Harina	Flour	Mermelada	Jam
Huevos	Eggs	Miel	Honey
fritos	fried	Mostaza	Mustard

| Pan (integral) | Bread (brown) | Queso | Cheese |
| Picante de... | spicy dish of ... | | |

Soup (sopas) and starters

Caldo	Broth		peanuts, manioc
Caldo de gallina	Chicken broth		(*yuca*) and fresh
Causa	Mashed potatoes and		coriander herb
	shrimp	Palta	Avocado
Conchas a la	Scallops with	Palta rellena	Stuffed avocado
parmesana	Parmesan	Papa rellena	Stuffed fried potato
Huevos a la rusa	Egg salad	Sopa a la criolla	Noodles, vegetables
Inchicapi	Appetizing jungle soup		and meat
	made from chicken,		

Seafood (mariscos) and fish (pescado)

Calamares	Squid	Langosta	Lobster
Camarones	Shrimp	Langostino a	Crayfish in spicy
Cangrejo	Crab	lo macho	shellfish sauce
Ceviche	Marinated seafood	Lenguado	Sole
Chaufa de mariscos	Chinese rice with	Paiche	Large jungle river fish
cojinova	seafood	Tiradito	Ceviche without onion
Corvina	Sea bass		or sweet potato
Erizo	Sea urchin	Tollo	Small shark
Jalea	Large dish of fish with	Zungarro	Large jungle fish
	onion		

Meat (carnes)

Adobo	Meat/fish in mild chilli	Estofado	Stewed meat (usually
	sauce		served with rice)
Ají de gallina	Chicken in chilli sauce	Higado	Liver
Anticuchos	Skewered heart	Jamón	Ham
	(usually lamb)	Lechón	Pork
Bifstek (bistek)	Steak	Lomo asado	Roast beef
Cabrito	Goat	Lomo saltado	Sautéed beef
Carapulcra	Pork, chicken and	Mollejitos	Gizzard
	potato casserole	Pachamanca	Meat and vegetables,
Carne a lo pobre	Steak, fries, egg and		cooked over hot
	banana		buried stones
Carne de res	Beef	Parillada	Grilled meat
Chicharrones	Deep-fried pork skins	Pato	Duck
Conejo	Rabbit	Pavo	Turkey
Cordero	Lamb	Pollo (a la brasa)	Chicken (spit-roasted)
Cuy	Guinea pig (a	Tocino	Bacon
	traditional dish)	Venado	Venison

Vegetables (legumbres) and side dishes

Ají	Chilli	Papa rellena	Fried potato balls,
Camote	Sweet potato		stuffed with olives,
Cebolla	Onion		egg and mincemeat
Choclo	Corn on the cob	Tallarines	Spaghetti noodles
Fideos	Noodles	Tomates	Tomatoes
Frijoles	Beans	Yuca a la Huancaina	Manioc (like a yam) in
Hongos	Mushrooms		spicy cheese sauce
Lechuga	Lettuce		

Fruit

Chirimoya	Custard apple (green and fleshy outside, tastes like strawberries and cream)	Maracuya	Passion fruit
		Palta	Avocado
		Piña	Pineapple
		Tuna	Pear-like cactus fruit (refreshing but full of hard little seeds)
Lucuma	Small nutty fruit (used in ice creams and cakes)		

Sweets (dulces)

Barquillo	Ice cream cone	Manjar blanco	Sweetened condensed milk
Flan	Crème caramel		
Helado	Ice cream	Mazamorra morada	Fruit/maize jelly
Keke	Cake	Panqueques	Pancakes
		Picarones	Doughnuts with syrup

Snacks (bocadillos)

Castañas	Brazil nuts	Sandwich de lechón	Pork salad sandwich
Chifles	Fried banana slices	Tamale	Maize-flour roll stuffed with olives, egg, meat and vegetables
Empanada	Meat or cheese pie		
Hamburguesa	Hamburger		
Salchipapas	Potatoes, sliced frankfurter sausage and condiments	Tortilla	Omelette-cum-pancake
Sandwich de butifara	Ham and onion sandwich	Tostadas	Toast

Fruit juices (jugos)

Especial	Fruit, milk, sometimes beer	Papaya	Papaya
		Piña	Pineapple
Fresa	Strawberry	Platano	Banana
Higo	Fig	Surtido	Mixed
Manzana	Apple	Toronja	Grapefruit
Melón	Melon	Zanahoria	Carrot
Naranja	Orange		

Beverages (bebidas)

Agua	Water	Limonada	Real lemonade
Agua mineral	Mineral water	Masato	Fermented manioc beer
Algarrobina	Algarroba-fruit drink		
Café	Coffee	Pisco	White-grape brandy
Cerveza	Beer	Ponche	Punch
Chicha de jora	Fermented maize beer	Ron	Rum
Chicha morada	Maize soft drink	Té	Tea
Chilcano de pisco	Pisco with lemonade	....con leche	....with milk
Chopp	Draught beer	....de anis	....aniseed tea
Cuba libre	Rum and coke	....de limón	....lemon tea
Gaseosa	Soft carbonated drink	....hierba luisa	....lemon-grass tea
Leche	Milk	....manzanilla	....camomile tea

Numbers and days

1	un/uno, una	60	sesenta
2	dos	70	setenta
3	tres	80	ochenta
4	cuatro	90	noventa
5	cinco	100	cien(to)
6	seis	101	ciento uno
7	siete	200	doscientos
8	ocho	201	doscientos uno
9	nueve	500	quinientos
10	diez	1000	mil
11	once	2000	dos mil
12	doce	first	primero/a
13	trece	second	segundo/a
14	catorce	third	tercero/a
15	quince	Monday	lunes
16	dieciséis	Tuesday	martes
20	veinte	Wednesday	miércoles
21	veintiuno	Thursday	jueves
30	treinta	Friday	viernes
40	cuarenta	Saturday	sábado
50	cincuenta	Sunday	domingo

Glossary of Peruvian terms

Aguajina Refreshing palm-fruit drink

Ayllu Kinship group, or clan

Apu Mountain god

Arriero Muleteer

Barrio Suburb, or sometimes shantytown

Bauda Curve in the river

Burro Donkey

Cacique Headman

Callejón Corridor, or narrow street

Campesino Peasant, country dweller, someone who works in the fields

Ceja de la selva Edge of the jungle

Chacra Cultivated garden or plot

Chaquiras Pre-Columbian stone or coral beads

Chicha Maize beer, or a form of Peruvian music

Chifa Peruvian-Chinese restaurant

Colectivo Collective taxi

Cordillera Mountain range

Curaca Chief

Curandero Healer

Empresa Company

Encomienda Colonial grant of land and native labour

Extranjero Foreigner

Farmacia Chemist

Flaco/a Skinny (common nickname)

Gordo/a Fat (common nickname)

Gringo A European or North American

Hacienda Estate

Huaca Sacred spot or object

Huaco Pre-Columbian artefact

Huaquero Someone who digs or looks for huacos

Jirón Road

Lomas Place where vegetation grows with moisture from the air rather than from rainfall or irrigation

Mamacona Inca Sun Virgin

Masato Manioc beer

El monte The forest

Paiche The world's largest freshwater fish, often found on jungle menus

Pakucho Jungle variant of "gringo"

Peña Nightclub with live music

Peque-peque Onomatopoeic word used for small boat motor engines (usually a four or nine horsepower with the propeller on a long shaft which helps to steer the canoe and can be lifted easily out of the water in shallows)

Plata Silver; slang for "cash"

Poblado Settlement

Pongo Whitewater rapids

Pueblos Jóvenes Shantytowns

Puna Barren Andean heights

Quebrada Stream

Remolino Whirlpool

Restinga Area of forest that lies above the river flood level on a permanent basis

Selva Jungle

Selvático Jungle dweller

Serrano Mountain dweller

Shushupero "Drunk" or inebriated individual, from the deadly *shushupe* snake

Sierra Mountains

Siete raices Strong medicinal drink, mixed from seven jungle plants and *aguardiente*

Soroche Altitude sickness

Tambo Inca Highway rest-house

Tienda Shop

Tipishca Oxbow lake

Tramites Red tape, bureaucracy

Unsu Throne, or platform

Varzea Forest which gets regularly flooded

Travel
store

UK & Ireland

Britain
Devon & Cornwall
Dublin **D**
Edinburgh **D**
England
Ireland
The Lake District
London
London **D**
London Mini Guide
Scotland
Scottish Highlands
& Islands
Wales

Europe

Algarve **D**
Amsterdam
Amsterdam **D**
Andalucía
Athens **D**
Austria
Baltic States
Barcelona
Barcelona **D**
Belgium &
Luxembourg
Berlin
Brittany & Normandy
Bruges **D**
Brussels
Budapest
Bulgaria
Copenhagen
Corsica
Crete
Croatia
Cyprus
Czech & Slovak
Republics
Denmark
Dodecanese & East
Aegean Islands
Dordogne & The Lot
Europe on a Budget
Florence & Siena
Florence **D**
France
Germany
Gran Canaria **D**
Greece
Greek Islands
Hungary

Ibiza & Formentera **D**
Iceland
Ionian Islands
Italy
The Italian Lakes
Languedoc &
Roussillon
Lanzarote &
Fuerteventura **D**
Lisbon **D**
The Loire Valley
Madeira **D**
Madrid **D**
Mallorca **D**
Mallorca & Menorca
Malta & Gozo **D**
Moscow
The Netherlands
Norway
Paris
Paris **D**
Paris Mini Guide
Poland
Portugal
Prague
Prague **D**
Provence
& the Côte D'Azur
Pyrenees
Romania
Rome
Rome **D**
Sardinia
Scandinavia
Sicily
Slovenia
Spain
St Petersburg
Sweden
Switzerland
Tenerife &
La Gomera **D**
Turkey
Tuscany & Umbria
Venice & The Veneto
Venice **D**
Vienna

Asia

Bali & Lombok
Bangkok
Beijing
Cambodia
China

Goa
Hong Kong & Macau
Hong Kong
& Macau **D**
India
Indonesia
Japan
Kerala
Korea
Laos
Malaysia, Singapore
& Brunei
Nepal
The Philippines
Rajasthan, Dehli
& Agra
Shanghai
Singapore
Singapore **D**
South India
Southeast Asia on a
Budget
Sri Lanka
Taiwan
Thailand
Thailand's Beaches
& Islands
Tokyo
Vietnam

Australasia

Australia
East Coast Australia
Fiji
Melbourne
New Zealand
Sydney
Tasmania

North America

Alaska
Baja California
Boston
California
Canada
Chicago
Colorado
Florida
The Grand Canyon
Hawaii
Honolulu **D**
Las Vegas **D**
Los Angeles &
Southern California
Maui **D**

Miami & South Florida
Montréal
New England
New York City
New York City **D**
New York City Mini
Orlando & Walt
Disney World® **D**
Oregon &
Washington
San Francisco
San Francisco **D**
Seattle
Southwest USA
Toronto
USA
Vancouver
Washington DC
Yellowstone & The
Grand Tetons
Yosemite

Caribbean
& Latin America

Antigua & Barbuda **D**
Argentina
Bahamas
Barbados **D**
Belize
Bolivia
Brazil
Buenos Aires
Cancún & Cozumel **D**
Caribbean
Central America on a
Budget
Chile
Costa Rica
Cuba
Dominican Republic
Ecuador
Guatemala
Jamaica
Mexico
Peru
Puerto Rico
St Lucia **D**
South America on a
Budget
Trinidad & Tobago
Yucatán

D: Rough Guide
DIRECTIONS for
short breaks

Available from all good bookstores

Visit us online

www.roughguides.com

Information on over 25,000 destinations around the world

- **Read** Rough Guides' trusted travel info
- **Access** exclusive articles from Rough Guides authors
- **Update** yourself on new books, maps, CDs and other products
- **Enter** our competitions and win travel prizes
- **Share** ideas, journals, photos & travel advice with other users
- **Earn** points every time you contribute to the Rough Guide community and get rewards

BROADEN YOUR HORIZONS

Avoid Guilt Trips

Buy fair trade coffee + bananas ✓

Save energy – use low energy bulbs ✓
 – don't leave tv on standby ✓

Offset carbon emissions from flight to Madrid ✓

Send goat to Africa ✓

Join Tourism Concern today ✓

Slowly, the world is changing.
Together we can, and will, make a difference.

Tourism Concern is the only UK registered charity fighting exploitation in one of the largest industries on earth: people forced from their homes in order that holiday resorts can be built, sweatshop labour conditions in hotels and destruction of the environment are just some of the issues that we tackle.

Sending people on a guilt trip is not something we do. We know as well as anyone that holidays are precious. But you can help us to ensure that tourism always benefits the local communities involved.

Call 020 7133 3330
or visit **tourismconcern.org.uk** to find out how.

A year's membership of Tourism Concern costs just £20 (£12 unwaged) – that's 38 pence a week, less than the cost of a pint of milk, organic of course.

Fighting Exploitation in Tourism

TourismConcern

Small print and
Index

A Rough Guide to Rough Guides

Published in 1982, the first Rough Guide – to Greece – was a student scheme that became a publishing phenomenon. Mark Ellingham, a recent graduate in English from Bristol University, had been travelling in Greece the previous summer and couldn't find the right guidebook. With a small group of friends he wrote his own guide, combining a highly contemporary, journalistic style with a thoroughly practical approach to travellers' needs.

The immediate success of the book spawned a series that rapidly covered dozens of destinations. And, in addition to impecunious backpackers, Rough Guides soon acquired a much broader and older readership that relished the guides' wit and inquisitiveness as much as their enthusiastic, critical approach and value-for-money ethos.

These days, Rough Guides include recommendations from shoestring to luxury and cover more than 200 destinations around the globe, including almost every country in the Americas and Europe, more than half of Africa and most of Asia and Australasia. Our ever-growing team of authors and photographers is spread all over the world, particularly in Europe, the USA and Australia.

In the early 1990s, Rough Guides branched out of travel, with the publication of Rough Guides to World Music, Classical Music and the Internet. All three have become benchmark titles in their fields, spearheading the publication of a wide range of books under the Rough Guide name.

Including the travel series, Rough Guides now number more than 350 titles, covering: phrasebooks, waterproof maps, music guides from Opera to Heavy Metal, reference works as diverse as Conspiracy Theories and Shakespeare, and popular culture books from iPods to Poker. Rough Guides also produce a series of more than 120 World Music CDs in partnership with World Music Network.

Visit www.roughguides.com to see our latest publications.

Rough Guide travel images are available for commercial licensing at www.roughguidespictures.com

Rough Guide credits

Text editor: Brendon Griffin
Layout: Dan May
Cartography: Animesh Pathak
Picture editor: Nicole Newman
Production: Rebecca Short
Proofreader: Andrew McCulloch
Cover design: Chloë Roberts
Photographer: Tim Draper, Susan Porter
Editorial: Ruth Blackmore, Andy Turner, Keith
Drew, Edward Aves, Alice Park, Lucy White,
Jo Kirby, James Smart, Natasha Foges, Róisín
Cameron, Emma Traynor, Emma Gibbs, Kathryn
Lane, Christina Valhouli, Monica Woods, Mani
Ramaswamy, Harry Wilson, Lucy Cowie, Helen
Ochyra, Amanda Howard, Alison Roberts, Joe
Staines, Peter Buckley, Matthew Milton, Tracy
Hopkins, Ruth Tidball; **Delhi** Madhavi Singh,
Karen D'Souza, Lubna Shaheen
Design & Pictures: London Scott Stickland, Dan
May, Diana Jarvis, Mark Thomas, Chloë Roberts,
Nicole Newman, Sarah Cummins, Emily Taylor;
Delhi Umesh Aggarwal, Ajay Verma, Jessica
Subramanian, Ankur Guha, Pradeep Thapliyal,
Sachin Tanwar, Anita Singh, Nikhil Agarwal
Production: Rebecca Short, Vicky Baldwin

Cartography: London Maxine Repath, Ed
Wright, Katie Lloyd-Jones; **Delhi** Rajesh
Chhibber, Ashutosh Bharti, Rajesh Mishra,
Animesh Pathak, Jasbir Sandhu, Karobi Gogoi,
Alakananda Bhattacharya, Swati Handoo,
Deshpal Dabas
Online: London George Atwell, Faye Hellon,
Jeanette Angell, Fergus Day, Justine Bright, Clare
Bryson, Aine Fearon, Adrian Low, Ezgi Celebi,
Amber Bloomfield; **Delhi** Amit Verma, Rahul Kumar,
Narender Kumar, Ravi Yadav, Debojit Borah,
Rakesh Kumar, Ganesh Sharma, Shisir Basumatari
Marketing & Publicity: London Liz Statham,
Niki Hanmer, Louise Maher, Jess Carter, Vanessa
Godden, Vivienne Watton, Anna Paynton, Rachel
Sprackett, Libby Jellie, Laura Vipond, Vanessa
McDonald; **New York** Katy Ball, Judi Powers,
Nancy Lambert; **Delhi** Ragini Govind
Manager India: Punita Singh
Reference Director: Andrew Lockett
Operations Manager: Helen Phillips
PA to Publishing Director: Nicola Henderson
Publishing Director: Martin Dunford
Commercial Manager: Gino Magnotta
Managing Director: John Duhigg

Publishing information

This seventh edition published July 2009 by
Rough Guides Ltd,
80 Strand, London WC2R 0RL
14 Local Shopping Centre, Panchsheel Park,
New Delhi 110017, India
Distributed by the Penguin Group
Penguin Books Ltd,
80 Strand, London WC2R 0RL
Penguin Group (USA)
375 Hudson Street, NY 10014, USA
Penguin Group (Australia)
250 Camberwell Road, Camberwell,
Victoria 3124, Australia
Penguin Group (Canada)
195 Harry Walker Parkway N, Newmarket, ON,
L3Y 7B3 Canada
Penguin Group (NZ)
67 Apollo Drive, Mairangi Bay, Auckland 1310,
New Zealand
Cover concept by Peter Dyer.

Typeset in Bembo and Helvetica to an original
design by Henry Iles.
Printed and bound in Singapore by SNP Security
Printing Pte Ltd
© Dilwyn Jenkins 2009
No part of this book may be reproduced in any
form without permission from the publisher except
for the quotation of brief passages in reviews.
656pp includes index
A catalogue record for this book is available from
the British Library
ISBN: 978-1-84836-053-2

Help us update

We've gone to a lot of effort to ensure that the
seventh edition of **The Rough Guide to Peru** is
accurate and up-to-date. However, things change
– places get "discovered", opening hours are
notoriously fickle, restaurants and rooms raise
prices or lower standards. If you feel we've got it
wrong or left something out, we'd like to know,
and if you can remember the address, the price,
the hours, the phone number, so much the better.

Please send your comments with the subject
line "**Rough Guide Peru Update**" to
© mail@roughguides.com. We'll credit all
contributions and send a copy of the next edition
(or any other Rough Guide if you prefer) for the
very best emails.
Have your questions answered and tell others
about your trip at
® community.roughguides.com

SMALL PRINT

Acknowledgements

The author would like to thank Carlos, Jorge and Ignacio Montenegro, Maritza, Herman, Carmen, Davarian, Jhin, Rainforest Expeditions, Inkaterra and to all those who held the fort at home, particularly Tess, Bethan, Max, Teilo, Claire, Danny and Jenny.

The editor would like to thank Dilwyn for all his help, humour and hard travelling, and Mani Ramaswamy for her wit and counsel. Thanks also to Nicole Newman, Dan May, Katie Lloyd-Jones, Alison Roberts, Andrew McCulloch, Animesh Pathak and Chloë Roberts.

Readers' letters

SMALL PRINT

Thanks to all the readers who have taken the time to write in with comments and suggestions (and apologies if we've inadvertently omitted or misspelt anyone's name):

Delicia Andrés, Elizabeth Ballon, Clara Bravo, Daniel Brown, Carlos Burga, Erin Burger, Ivette Cabrera, Edwin Junco Cabrera, Christian Caceres, Karlos Caceres, Julio Campero, Florinda Canali, Gemma Cartwright, Anna Coleman, Istvan Czinke, Kirk Dearden, Hanna Dorve, Emma Dunmore, Becky Ellis, Ingrid Espinoza, Verónica Estève, Michael Falk, Mike Freeman, Arturo Alfredo Henriquez Garino, Kevin Geary, Sebastina Gerschefski, Martin Godinez, Jan Goldstein, Alejandro Gonzales, Romina Verme Gómez-Sánchez, Yarda Gruss, Michael Gynn, Sharon Herkes, Grace Huang, Miguel Hundskopf, Vanda Ingham, Mauricio Chacon Jimenez, Aud Kennedy, Sarah Lane, Morgan Lloyd, Charles Mango, Karhen Marquez, Cristina Mazur, Denise Fernandez Mendez, James Mill, Jamie Miller, Vicky Ale Burgos Moore, Alberto Morán, Katrina Munir, Jill Neff, Ilse Niegemann, Louise Obermayer, Jim O'Sullivan, Yunus Emre Ozigci, Roberto Arias Pacco, Amy Page, Celeste Peraza, Rodrigo Antonio Petrel, Stephanie Quinn, David Quintana, Karen Ramakers, Ingrid Regout, Mark Riley, Edwin Anarcaya Roca, Domingos Sávio Rodrigues, Jhim Rodriguez, Xavier Ruchti, Veronica Saez, Veronica Janssen Samanez, Raúl E. Sánchez Scaglioni, Marta Schlemayer, Abby Seiff, Joan Bericat Serra, Susan Sharp, Eldivia Sidenta, AJ Stick, Charlie Strader, Timm Stütz, Rachel Thomas, Henry Pederse Tor, Charo Torres, Adolfo Urrutia, Ricardo Sanchez Uychoco, Marco Verme, Michael White, Oscar Willener, Carlo Fabrizzio Garmendia Wilson, Paul Yule.

Photo credits

All photos © Rough Guides except the following:

Introduction

Aerial view of the rainforest near Iquitos © Paul Harris photolibrary

Two Alpacas in valley in Andes © Kevin Schafer/Getty Images

Machu Picchu © Ritterbach Ritterbach photolibrary

Things not to miss

05 Trujillo © Andrew Watson photolibrary

14 The Floating village of Belén, Iquitos © Paul Harris photolibrary

15 Shipibo Indian woman selling crafts outside her home near Pucallpa © Tony Morrison/South American Pictures

18 Machu Picchu trek – Inca Trail, Urubamba © Peru Images/Alamy

19 Roundhouse, Kuelap, Chachapoyas © James Brunker/Magical Andes Photography

20 Andean Shaman (witch doctor) © Marco Garro/AFP/Getty Images

22 Rainforest canopy walkway, Amazon © Michael Doolittle/Alamy

23 Vicuña in the Andean Cordillera © Emmanuel Lattes/Alamy

26 Ruins of Inca city, Machu Picchu © Gavin Hellier/Robert Harding

Black and whites

p.478 Manu National Park © Juan Carlos photolibrary

p.491 Pacaya-Samiria National Preserve © Andoni Canela photolibrary

p.522 Madre de Dios, Manu National Park, White Caiman © Max Milligan photolibrary

p.536 Traffic passing through the City Square in Iquitos © Paul Harris photolibrary

p.544 Bora Indian, Headman of village © James Sparshatt/Axiom

Festivals and celebrations colour section

Procession in Semana Santa © Kazuyoshi Nomachi/Corbis

Religious parade during Corpus Christi, Cusco © Nacho Calonge photolibrary

Worshippers march during procession of Black Christ © Walter Hupi/Corbis

Traditional dance, "La Marinera", in the northern city of Trujillo © Reuters

Inti Raymi, Peru, Cusco Festivals © Jtb Photo photolibrary

Peru's Mythic Wildlife colour section

Andean condor, Colca Canyon © Tui De Roy photolibrary

Violet fronted brilliant hummingbird, Manu National Park © Pete Oxford/Nature Picture Library

Jaguar © Chris Sharp/South American Picture Library

Bullet ant © Premaphotos/naturepl.com/NPL

Boa constrictor © Gerry Ellis/Minden Pictures/FLPA

Pink river dolphin © Andre Seale photolibrary

Blue and Gold Macaw © Morales Morales photolibrary

Andean Cock-of-the-Rock © Kevin Schafer/Corbis

SMALL PRINT

Index

Map entries are in colour.

INDEX

651

INDEX

INDEX

Map symbols

maps are listed in the full index using coloured text

-------	International boundary	⌂	Hut
-----	Chapter boundary	⌂	Lodge
▬▬▬▬	Panamerican Highway	Å	Campsite
══════	Major road	↯	Viewpoint
══════	Minor road	∩	Arch
▬▬▬▬	Pedestrianized street	♦	Ancient site/point of interest
······	Dirt track	♥	Museum
······	4 wheel drive	▮	Fort
··········	Under construction	⏛	Monument
⊞⊞⊞⊞⊞	Steps	▣	Restaurant
------	Path	◉	Hotel
══╋══	Railway	★	Public transport stop
– – –	Ferry route	⊞	Hospital
───────	Waterway	ℂ	Telephone office
峰	Mountain range	ⓘ	Information office
▲	Mountain peak	⊠	Post office
⌗	Cliffs	@	Internet
◓	Cave	⑀	Bank
⩓	Hot spring	▬	Building
⬭	Saltpan	✚	Church
⌇	Pass	⬭	Stadium
∴	Ruins	▨	Park
✈	Airport	▭	Market